Successful
College Writing

SKILLS | STRATEGIES | LEARNING STYLES

KATHLEEN T. McWHORTER
Niagara County Community College

BEDFORD/ST. MARTIN'S
Boston • New York

For Bedford/St. Martin's

Executive Editor: Leasa Burton
Senior Developmental Editor: Jane Carter
Senior Production Editor: Bill Imbornoni
Senior Production Supervisor: Dennis J. Conroy
Senior Marketing Manager: Molly Parke
Editorial Assistant: Karrin Varucene
Copy Editor: Rosemary Winfield
Indexer: Melanie Belkin
Photo Researcher: Julie Tesser
Permissions Manager: Kalina K. Ingham
Art Director: Lucy Krikorian
Text Design: Brian Salisbury
Cover Design: Donna Lee Dennison
Cover Art: Skyfire, 2007 (oil on board), Marta Martonfi-Benke, © Marta Martonfi-Benke/Bridgeman.
Composition: Graphic World Inc.
Printing and Binding: RR Donnelley and Sons

President: Joan E. Feinberg
Editorial Director: Denise B. Wydra
Editor in Chief: Karen S. Henry
Director of Development: Erica T. Appel
Director of Marketing: Karen R. Soeltz
Director of Production: Susan W. Brown
Associate Director, Editorial Production: Elise S. Kaiser
Managing Editor: Shuli Traub

Library of Congress Control Number: 2011936171 (with Handbook)
2011936158 (without Handbook)

Manufactured in the United States of America.

6 5 4 3 2
f e d c b

For information, write: Bedford/St. Martin's, 75 Arlington Street, Boston, MA 02116
(617-399-4000)

ISBN: 978-0-312-67608-7 (Student Edition with Handbook)
ISBN: 978-0-312-67609-4 (Student Edition without Handbook)
ISBN: 978-0-312-67610-0 (Instructor's Annotated Edition)

Acknowledgments

Other texts assume that first-year composition students already possess the basic skills they will need to succeed in college, but my own experience tells me that this is not true. That is why I wrote *Successful College Writing*. It uses a unique, highly visual, student-centered approach to teach students the classroom and study skills they need while guiding them through the writing strategies and activities that form the core of composition instruction. The overwhelmingly positive response to the first four editions demonstrates that *Successful College Writing* fulfills an important need.

The fifth edition continues to meet students where they are and get them where they need to go by building on the strengths of earlier editions while bringing the coverage into the digital age. This new edition adds coverage of skills needed for successful online learning, strengthens instruction in essential critical reading and thinking skills, and introduces students to visual literacy, business writing, and online presentations.

PROVEN FEATURES OF *SUCCESSFUL COLLEGE WRITING*

True to its goal of offering more coverage of essential skills, *Successful College Writing* provides abundant guidance and support for inexperienced writers along with thorough help with reading and study skills. Every chapter of *Successful College Writing* provides practical, student-oriented instruction, along with extra help for those students who need it.

Practical, step-by-step writing assignments. *Successful College Writing* provides the tools to approach writing as a flexible, multifaceted process, alleviating some of the frustration students often feel. Part 1 begins this process by emphasizing the importance of writing to students' success in college and career, and it alerts students to the expectations their instructors will have for them as writers. Part 2 provides detailed coverage of the writing process—from choosing and narrowing a topic and generating ideas to developing and supporting a thesis, drafting essays and paragraphs, and revising and editing. Each chapter in Part 2 includes the following:

- plenty of skill-building exercises, many of them collaborative
- a running example showing different stages of a student essay
- Essay in Progress activities that lead students through each step in writing an essay

Parts 3 and 4 cover the patterns of development that students encounter most frequently in college and on the job. Guided Writing Assignments in each chapter lead students step by step through the process of writing a particular type of essay, giving student writers the support they need, whether they are working in class or on their own. Instructors will also find these assignments easy to teach, as they provide lots of tips for generating and evaluating ideas, developing a thesis, organizing and drafting the essay, and revising and editing.

Part 5 provides instruction for writing the research project, including information about finding useful and reliable sources and incorporating and documenting material borrowed from sources. Part 6 covers writing in academic and business settings, from writing about literature, taking essay exams, and creating a portfolio to making presentations and writing résumés, job application letters, memoranda, and business emails.

Appealing, helpful visuals. Because inexperienced writers are often more comfortable with images than with text, *Successful College Writing* employs a visual approach to writing instruction. Look for the following visual aids throughout the book:

- Writing Quick Starts at the beginning of each chapter provide engaging images for students to respond to.
- Graphic Organizers—charts that display relationships among ideas—are tools both for analyzing readings and for planning and revising essays, and they present students with an alternative to traditional outlines.
- Revision Flowcharts help students systematically read and revise their own essays as well as review those of their peers.
- Visualizing the Reading activities following one of the readings in each chapter in Parts 2 and 3 give students a simple way to chart key features of the reading, with the first part of each chart done for them to provide guidance.
- Figures and boxes throughout the text reinforce key points and summarize information.

A unique emphasis on learning styles. Students learn in different ways, yet most writing texts do not take these differences in learning style into account. In this text, I focus on four learning styles that are relevant for writing:

- verbal versus spatial learning
- creative versus pragmatic learning
- concrete versus abstract learning
- social versus independent learning

A brief questionnaire in Chapter 2 (and on the Web site) enables students to assess their learning styles. Recognizing that no one strategy works for every student, the text includes a variety of methods for generating ideas and revising an essay. Alternative strategies are identified by the "Learning Style Options" icon *Learning Style Options* found in the margins throughout the text.

Attention to study skills. Students need practical survival strategies that they can use not only in their writing course but in all their college courses. Chapter 1 includes advice on such critical topics as the following:

- time management
- assessing and managing stress
- academic integrity
- working with classmates

Chapter 25 includes practical advice on preparing for and taking essay examinations, and Chapter 26 offers practical advice on crafting and delivering an oral presentation.

Integrated coverage of reading. Because reading is essential to successful writing, *Successful College Writing* provides detailed coverage of active reading and reading text and visuals critically:

- The Guide to Active Reading in Chapter 3 helps students improve their comprehension and build skills that they can apply to the readings within this text as well as to those that they encounter in their other college classes.
- The Guide to Responding to Text in Chapter 4 provides thorough coverage of critical reading and interpreting visuals.

Over the years, my work with students has convinced me that skills taught in isolation are seldom learned well or applied. So each of the chapters on the patterns of development in Part 3 reinforces the reading skills taught in Chapters 3 and 4. As students develop their writing skills by writing a particular type of essay, they simultaneously learn practical strategies for reading that type of essay.

High-interest readings. In addition to guidelines for reading different types of texts, *Successful College Writing* includes reading selections from the diverse array of texts students are likely to encounter in their personal, academic, and professional lives. Since students who enjoy what they read become more proficient readers, the selections in this text were carefully chosen not only to function as strong rhetorical models but also to interest students. The professional readings include selections from such well-known writers as Bill Bryson, Annie Dillard, Barbara Ehrenreich, Susan Orlean, William Safire, and Brent Staples, and topics range from the boomerang generation to Internet addiction to war pornography.

Comprehensive coverage of research and documentation. Because the Internet has made source-based writing increasingly challenging, *Successful College Writing* provides three full chapters on writing with sources, covering both electronic and print sources. Students learn to do all of the following:

- locate sources and take effective notes
- evaluate a source's relevance and reliability
- synthesize and integrate sources
- avoid plagiarism
- document sources using MLA and APA documentation formats

Thorough reference handbook. The handbook in Part 7 covers basic grammar, sentence problems, punctuation, mechanics, spelling, and ESL troublespots and includes the following:

- hand-corrected examples to make needed revisions easy to understand
- key grammatical terms defined in the margin

- helpful revision flowcharts and summary boxes
- sentence and paragraph exercises

It also reinforces students' learning with plenty of opportunities for practice, with exercises in the text and cross-references to additional grammar exercises online at *Exercise Central*.

Attention to outcomes. *Successful College Writing* helps students build proficiency in the four categories of learning that writing programs across the country use to assess student work:

- rhetorical knowledge
- critical thinking, reading, and writing
- writing processes
- knowledge of conventions

For a table that correlates the Council of Writing Program Administrators (WPA) outcomes to features of *Successful College Writing*, see pages xv to xxi.

NEW TO THE FIFTH EDITION

The main goals of the revision — based on feedback from instructors and students who used the text — were to strengthen the coverage of critical reading and thinking, including coverage of visual literacy, so crucial in today's online world; to increase coverage of APA documentation style, which is used widely in psychology, nursing, and other social science disciplines; to add coverage of new classroom skills, such as using electronic tools and taking online classes; and to include coverage of online presentations and business writing for the many students who work while taking classes. As always, I also wanted to update the book with current and engaging professional reading and student writing.

New! More on critical reading and thinking. A new Chapter 4 helps students learn to approach texts of all kinds with a critical eye, providing strategies to use in each of the following areas:

- evaluating the reliability of sources
- understanding the nuances of words
- differentiating between fact and opinion
- analyzing tone
- looking for purposeful omissions

A new critical thinking component has also been added to the apparatus following the professional readings to guide students in applying these strategies, both in response to the reading selection and in relation to the chapter's rhetorical pattern.

New! Enhanced coverage of visual literacy. Chapter 4 also guides students in interpreting and responding to visual texts, including advertisements, photographs, and graphics. Exercises are included to provide needed practice, and one reading per chapter now includes a visual that students are asked to analyze.

New! More coverage of APA documentation style. Coverage is strengthened by the addition of a student essay demonstrating APA in-text citations and references. And both MLA and APA coverage are now made easier to reference by the addition of a list of the citation and documentation models included in the text.

New! Updated coverage of electronic classroom success skills. Electronic tools, like texting and email, have never been more commonplace, so learning to use these tools appropriately in the classroom has never been more important. *Successful College Writing* now includes coverage of the following:

- emailing and texting when your audience is your instructor
- participating in online discussions
- taking notes effectively on a laptop
- managing online courses effectively

New! Added coverage of online presentations and business writing. A new Chapter 26 offers guidance for giving an oral presentation, including creating PowerPoint and Web-based presentations, and it includes two annotated PowerPoint slides as models. The chapter also presents guidelines for writing effective business documents and provides annotated models of common business documents such as résumés, job application letters, memos, and business emails.

New! Updated professional and student readings. The book includes twenty-two new professional reading selections and six new essays by student writers. Many of the new readings deal with important contemporary issues, such as the following:

- the benefits and risks of multitasking
- war pornography: graphic images from war zones
- freegans: dumpster diving for a cause

The six new student essays discuss topics such as the discovery of a friend's eating disorder, a definition of guerrilla art, and arguments in support of organ donation and of restrictions on explicit song lyrics. A number of the new essays demonstrate effective use of sources, as well.

DIGITAL OPTIONS FOR *SUCCESSFUL COLLEGE WRITING*, FIFTH EDITION

Successful College Writing, Fifth Edition, is more than just the printed book. Online, you will find both free and affordable premium resources to help your students get even more out of your course. You will also find convenient instructor resources, such as the Instructor's Resource Manual, which includes sample syllabi, resources for teaching, and an updated bibliography of the latest in learning style research. To learn more about or to order any of the products below, contact your Bedford/St. Martin's sales representative, email sales support at **sales_support@bfwpub.com**, or visit **bedfordstmartins .com/successfulwriting/catalog**.

Companion Web Site for *Successful College Writing*

Send students to the companion Web site—**bedfordstmartins.com/successfulcollege**— for free and open resources. Choose flexible premium resources to supplement the book, or upgrade to an expanding collection of helpful digital content.

Free and open resources for *Successful College Writing* on the companion site allow students to do the following:

- take online reading quizzes to test their understanding of the reading selections
- take the online learning styles inventory
- complete the interactive graphic organizers
- link to thousands of additional exercises at *Exercise Central*
- access tutorials on avoiding plagiarism and evaluating online sources, guides to preparing effective graphs, charts, and presentation slides, and an annotated collection of links to credible Web sites

VideoCentral: English is a growing collection of videos for the writing class that captures real-world, academic, and student writers talking about how and why they write. *VideoCentral* can be packaged with *Successful College Writing* for free. An activation code is required.

Re:Writing Plus gathers all of Bedford/St. Martin's premium digital content for composition into one online collection. It includes hundreds of model documents, the first-ever peer review game, and *VideoCentral: English. Re:Writing Plus* can be purchased separately or packaged with the print book at a significant discount. An activation code is required.

E-book Options

Assign an interactive e-book. With extra multimedia content and tools for writers, the ***Successful College Writing e-Book*** lets students search, annotate, and share notes easily. Instructors can customize and rearrange chapters, add and share notes, and link to quizzes and activities. The *Successful College Writing e-Book* can be purchased stand-alone or packaged with a print book.

Other e-book formats. Students can purchase *Successful College Writing* in popular e-book formats for computers, tablets, and e-readers. For details, visit **bedfordstmartins .com/ebooks**.

CompClass for Successful College Writing, **Fifth Edition**, is an easy-to-use online course space designed for composition students and instructors. It comes preloaded with the *Successful College Writing e-Book*, as well as other Bedford/St. Martin's premium digital content, including *VideoCentral*. Powerful assignment and assessment tools make it easier to customize content and to keep track of your students' progress. *CompClass for Successful College Writing*, Fifth Edition, can be purchased separately at **yourcompclass .com** or packaged with the print book at a significant discount. An activation code is required.

MORE OPTIONS FOR STUDENTS

Add more value to your text by choosing one of the following resources, free when packaged with *Successful College Writing*. To learn more about package options or any of the products below, contact your Bedford/St. Martin's sales representative or visit **bedfordstmartins.com/successfulwriting/catalog**.

Additional Exercises for Successful College Writing, by Carolyn Lengel and Jess Carroll, are available with the text. These exercises are keyed specifically to the handbook available in the full version of the book.

The Bedford/St. Martin's ESL Workbook, **Second Edition,** by Sapna Gandhi-Rao, Maria McCormack, and Elizabeth Trelenberg, covers grammar issues for multilingual students with varying English-language skills and cultural backgrounds. To reinforce each lesson, instructional introductions are followed by illustrative examples and exercises. Answers are provided at the back.

From Practice to Mastery, by Barbara D. Sussman, Maria Villar-Smith, and Carolyn Lengel, gives students all the resources they need to practice for—and pass—the Florida Basic Skills Exit Tests in reading and writing. It includes pre- and post-tests, abundant practices, and clear instruction on all the skills covered on the exams.

Taking the CUNY Assessment Test in Writing, by Laurence Berkley, provides strategies and models students need to pass the City University of New York's writing exam. It includes step-by-step guidance for crafting an effective response, tips for editing and proofreading, and lots of opportunities for practice.

i-series presents multimedia tutorials in a flexible format—because there are things you can't do in a book. To learn more about package options or any of the products below, contact your Bedford/St. Martin's sales representative or visit **bedfordstmartins.com**.

- *ix visualizing composition 2.0* (available online) helps students put into practice key rhetorical and visual concepts.
- *i-claim: visualizing argument* (available on CD-ROM) offers a new way to see argument—with 6 tutorials, an illustrated glossary, and over 70 multimedia arguments.
- *i-cite: visualizing sources* (available online as part of *Re:Writing Plus*) brings research to life through an animated introduction, four tutorials, and hands-on source practice.

Portfolio Keeping, Second Edition, by Nedra Reynolds and Rich Rice, provides all the information students need to use the portfolio method successfully in a writing course.

Oral Presentations in the Composition Course: A Brief Guide, by Matthew Duncan and Gustave W. Friedrich, offers students the advice they need to plan, prepare, and present their work effectively. With sections on analyzing audiences, choosing effective language, using visual aids, collaborating on group presentations, and dealing with the fear of public speaking, this booklet helps students develop strong oral presentations.

INSTRUCTOR RESOURCES

Bedford/St. Martin's wants to make it easy for you to find the support you need—and to get it quickly.

Instructor's Annotated Edition of *Successful College Writing* puts information right where busy instructors need it: on the pages of the book itself. The marginal annotations offer teaching tips, analysis tips with readings, last-minute in-class activities, vocabulary glosses, additional assignments, and potential answers to exercises.

Instructor's Resource Manual, Fifth Edition, by Kathleen T. McWhorter, Michael Hricik, Mary Applegate, and Rebecca J. Fraser (see **bedfordstmartins.com /successfulwriting/catalog**), helps instructors plan and teach their composition course. This text is available in print or in a PDF format that can be downloaded from the Bedford/St. Martin's online catalog or the companion Web site. The Instructor's Manual includes practical advice on designing an effective course, using learning styles in the teaching of writing, and finding resources for teaching composition. It also contains sample syllabi, tips for assessing student writing and using the writing center, and special help for those teaching as adjunct instructors.

Teaching Composition: Background Readings, Third Edition, edited by T. R. Johnson of Tulane University, addresses the concerns of both first-year and veteran writing instructors. This collection includes 30 professional readings on composition and rhetoric written by leaders in the field. The selections are accompanied by helpful introductions, useful activities, and practical insights for inside and outside the classroom. The new edition offers up-to-date advice on avoiding plagiarism, classroom blogging, and more.

TeachingCentral offers the entire list of Bedford/St. Martin's print and online professional resources in one place. You will find landmark reference works, sourcebooks on pedagogical issues, award-winning collections, and practical advice for the classroom — all free for instructors at **bedfordstmartins.com/teachingcentral**.

Bits collects creative ideas for teaching a range of composition topics in an easily searchable blog format at **bedfordbits.com**. A community of teachers — leading scholars, authors, and editors — discuss revision, research, grammar and style, technology, peer review, and much more. Take, use, adapt, and pass the ideas around. Then come back to the site to comment or share your own suggestions.

Portfolio Teaching, a companion guide for instructors, provides the practical information instructors and writing program administrators need to use the portfolio method successfully in a writing course.

Bedford Coursepacks allow you to integrate our most popular content into your own course management systems quickly and easily. For details, visit **bedfordstmartins .com/**.

Ordering Information

To order any of the ancillaries, please contact your Bedford/St. Martin's sales representative, email sales support at **sales_support@bfwpub.com**, or visit our Web site at **bedfordstmartins.com**. Note that activation codes are required for *VideoCentral: English, Re:Writing Plus,* and *CompClass.* Codes can be purchased separately or packaged with the print book at a significant discount.

To order *VideoCentral: English* packaged for free with the print book, use these ISBNs:

- With handbook: 978-1-4576-1087-5
- Without handbook: 978-1-4576-1138-4

To order *Re:Writing Plus* (which includes *VideoCentral: English* and *i-cite: visualizing sources*) packaged with the print book, use these ISBNs:

- With handbook: 978-1-4576-1083-7
- Without handbook: 978-1-4576-1141-4

To order the online, interactive e-book packaged with the print book, use these ISBNs:

- With handbook: 978-1-4576-1062-2
- Without handbook: 978-1-4576-1158-2

For information about other e-book formats including the CourseSmart e-book, go to **bedfordstmartins.com/ebooks**.

To order *CompClass for Successful College Writing*, Fifth Edition, packaged with the print book, use these ISBNs:

- With handbook: 978-1-4576-1069-1
- Without handbook: 978-1-4576-1159-9

To order *ix visualizing composition 2.0* packaged with the print book, use these ISBNs:

- With handbook: 978-1-4576-1249-7
- Without handbook: 978-1-4576-1248-0

To order *i-claim: visualizing argument* packaged with the print book, use these ISBNs:

- With handbook: 978-1-4576-1085-1
- Without handbook: 978-1-4576-1177-3

ACKNOWLEDGMENTS

A number of instructors and students from across the country have helped me to develop and revise *Successful College Writing*. I would like to express my gratitude to the following instructors, who served as members of the advisory board for the first edition. They provided detailed, valuable comments and suggestions about the manuscript as well as student essays and additional help and advice during its development: Marvin Austin, Columbia State Community College; Sarah H. Harrison, Tyler Junior College; Dan Holt, Lansing Community College; Michael Mackey, Community College of Denver; Lucille M. Schultz, University of Cincinnati; Sue Serrano, Sierra College; Linda R. Spain, Linn-Benton Community College; and Jacqueline Zimmerman, Lewis and Clark Community College. I would also like to thank the following instructors and their students, who class-tested chapters from *Successful College Writing* and provided valuable feedback about how its features and organization worked in the classroom: Mary Applegate, D'Youville College; Michael Hricik, Westmoreland County Community College; Lee Brewer Jones, DeKalb College; Edwina Jordan, Illinois Central College; Susan H. Lassiter, Mississippi College; Mildred C. Melendez, Sinclair Community College; Steve Rayshich, Westmoreland County Community College; Barbara J. Robedeau, San Antonio College; and Deanna White, University of Texas at San Antonio.

I am indebted to the valuable research conducted by George Jensen, John DiTiberio, and Robert Sternberg on learning-style theory that informs the pedagogy of this book. For their comments on the coverage of learning styles in this text, I would like to thank John DiTiberio, Saint Louis University; Ronald A. Sudol, Oakland University; and Thomas C. Thompson, The Citadel. My thanks go to Mary Jane Feldman, Niagara County Community College, for designing the field test of the Learning Styles Inventory and conducting the statistical analysis of the results. I would also like to thank the instructors and students who participated in a field test of the Learning Styles Inventory: Laurie Warshal Cohen, Seattle Central Community College; Lee Brewer Jones, DeKalb College; Edwina Jordan, Illinois Central College; Jennifer Manning, John Jay College; Mildred Melendez, Sinclair Community College; Paul Resnick, Illinois Central College; and Deanna M. White, University of Texas at San Antonio.

I benefited from the experience of those instructors who reviewed the fourth edition, and I am grateful for their thoughtful comments and helpful advice: Andrew S. Andermatt, Clinton Community College; Jonathan Barker, Richmond Community College; Manuel B. Blanco, Laredo Community College; Joy Bodenmiller, Jamestown Community College; Nandan Choksi, Broward Community College; Susan Muaddi Darraj, Harford Community College; Anissa Graham, University of North Alabama; Joseph D. Haske, South Texas College; Candace Henry, Westmoreland County Community College; Michael J. Hricik, Westmoreland County Community College; Elizabeth Jones, Wor-Wic Community College; Greg Kemble, Yuba College; Dorothy Miller, Harford Community College; Lisa G. Minor, University of North Alabama; Randall Mueller, Gateway Technical College; Kyle Page, Clinton Community College; Bryan Peters, Jefferson College; Karen Petit, Community College of Rhode Island; Karyn Riedell, Arizona State; Patricia Stockman Sansbury, Florida State College at Jacksonville; Lillian N. Simpson, Community College of Rhode Island; Amanda Skjeveland, Hagerstown Community College; Michelle Springer, Gateway Technical College; Michael Urso, Community College of Rhode Island; Victor Uszerowicz, Miami Dade College; Stephanie R. Voss, Pratt Community College; Sareca Wilson, Oklahoma State University Institute of Technology.

I am grateful to the following students whose work appears in this text: Kate Atkinson, Kaitlyn Botano, Andrew Decker, Sunny Desai, Nicholas Destino, Rajat Dmeeni, Robin Ferguson, Heather Gianakos, Sonia Gomez, Blake Huan, Micah Jackson, Christine Lee, Eric Michalski, Mina Raine, Nick Ruggia, Ted Sawchuck, Quinne Sember, James Sturm, Harley Tong, and Karen Vaccaro.

I also want to thank Elizabeth Gruchala-Gilbert for her research assistance, Lucy MacDonald and Mark Gallaher for their thoughtful updating of the Instructor's Resource Manual, and Kathleen McCoy for her insightful and creative revision of the Teaching Tips that appear in the Instructor's Annotated Edition of the book.

Many people at Bedford/St. Martin's have contributed to the creation and development of *Successful College Writing*. Each person with whom I have worked is a true professional: Each demonstrates high standards and expertise; each is committed to producing a book focused on student needs.

To Chuck Christensen, former president of Bedford/St. Martin's, I attribute much of my success in writing college textbooks. Twenty-seven years ago, I signed a contract for my first textbook with Chuck. Under his guidance, it became a best-seller. From Chuck I learned how to translate what I teach to the printed page. Joan Feinberg, current president, has become another trusted adviser. I value her editorial experience and appreciate the creative energy she brings to each issue and to each conversation. I also must thank Erica Appel, director of development in Bedford's New York office, for her forthright advice and for valuable assistance in making some of the more difficult decisions about the book. Special thanks to Kimberly Hampton, new media editor, for her careful and talented work on the new e-book version.

I also appreciate the advice and guidance that Karen R. Soeltz, Molly Parke, and their colleagues in the marketing department at Bedford/St. Martin's have provided at various junctures in the revision of this text. Karrin Varucene, editorial assistant, has helped prepare the manuscript in innumerable ways. William Imbornoni, senior project editor, deserves special recognition for guiding this revision through the production process.

I owe the largest debt of gratitude to John Elliott and Jane Carter, my developmental editors, for their valuable guidance and assistance in preparing this revision. Their careful editing and attention to detail have strengthened the fifth edition significantly. They helped me to reinforce the book's strengths and to retain its focus on providing extra help to the student. Finally, I must thank the many students who inspired me to write this book. From them I have learned how to teach, and they have shown me how they think and learn. My students, then, have made the largest contribution to this book, for without them I would have little to say and no reason to write.

Kathleen T. McWhorter

Features of *Successful College Writing,* Fifth Edition, Correlated to the Writing Program Administrators (WPA) Outcomes Statement

Desired Student Outcomes	Relevant Features of *Successful College Writing*
Rhetorical Knowledge	
Focus on a purpose	• Chapter 2, personal and impersonal writing (p. 24) • Chapter 3, interpreting visuals (p. 47), adapting reading skills to different materials (p. 47), and avoiding misconceptions (pp. 47–48) • Chapter 4, responding critically to text and images (pp. 67, 77–83) • Chapter 5, purpose (pp. 106–7) • Chapters in Parts 3 and 4, extensive discussion of the purpose(s) of the rhetorical pattern of development covered in that chapter • *VideoCentral,** videos on rhetorical purpose
Respond to the needs of different audiences	• Chapter 2, students' learning styles (p. 43) • Chapter 4, analyzing readings (p. 90) • Chapter 5, audience (pp. 107–9) • Chapter 10, tone and diction (pp. 215–17) • Chapters in Parts 3 and 4, considering one's audience for the rhetorical pattern of development covered in that chapter • Chapters 19 and 20, anticipate opposing viewpoints (pp. 519–20, 530–31, 533, 552, 561–562), analyze the audience's existing views about the claim (pp. 530, 533, 548–49, 559–60), and adjust one's argument accordingly (pp. 518–19, 530, 552, 561–62)
Respond appropriately to different kinds of rhetorical situations	• Chapter 1 (pp. 3–21), academic expectations • Chapter 2 (p. 23), the range of settings in which college students will be expected to write, the types of writing college students are likely to encounter (pp. 24–26), the kinds of writing employees are likely to be expected to produce (p. 26), and strategies for succeeding in a range of writing situations, especially writing in college (pp. 27–33) • Chapters in Parts 3 and 4, "Scenes from College and the Workplace" boxes (for example, on p. 228) • Part 5, advice for writing using sources • Part 6, advice about writing in specific academic contexts (Chapter 24, "Reading and Writing about Literature"; Chapter 25, "Essay Examinations and Portfolios") and about writing in the workplace (Chapter 26, "Oral Presentations and Business Writing")

* This resource is available packaged with the print book. See the preface for details.

Use conventions of format and structure appropriate to the rhetorical situation	• Chapter 22, appropriate formats for writing a paper using sources (pp. 637, 640–62, 663–81) • Chapter 26, appropriate business writing formats, including résumés, job application letters, memoranda, and business emails (pp. 744–51); and appropriate design and formatting of slides in presentation software, such as PowerPoint (pp. 741–42) • Companion Web site: Tutorials on designing documents, preparing presentation slides, and preparing charts and graphs; a model documents gallery
Adopt appropriate voice, tone, and level of formality	• Chapter 5 (pp. 107–9), voice, tone, and level of formality • Chapter 10, voice, tone, and level of formality (pp. 215–17) • Chapters 11 ("Narration"), 12 ("Description"), 14 ("Process Analysis"), and 20 ("Writing Arguments"), advice about tone appropriate to the mode
Understand how genres shape reading and writing	• Chapters 19–20, reading arguments (pp. 511–41) and writing arguments (pp. 542–72) • Chapter 22 (594–619), research project • Chapter 24 (pp. 685–715), literary analysis • Chapter 25 (pp. 719–28) essay examinations • Chapter 26, PowerPoint presentations (pp. 741–42), résumés and job application letters (pp. 745–46, 748–49), memoranda (pp. 746, 750), and business email and other electronic media for business (pp. 747, 751)
Write in several genres	• Chapter 20 (pp. 542–72), argument • Chapter 23 (pp. 620–82), research • Chapter 24 (pp. 683–715), literary analysis • Chapter 25 (pp. 719–28), essay examinations • Chapter 26, PowerPoint presentations (pp. 741–42), résumés and job application letters (pp. 745–46, 748–49), memoranda (pp. 746, 750), and business email and other electronic media for business (pp. 747, 751) • Companion Web site: Tutorials on preparing presentation slides and charts and graphs

Critical Thinking, Reading, and Writing	
Use writing and reading for inquiry, learning, thinking, and communicating	• The entire book is informed by an emphasis on the connection between reading and writing • Chapter 2 (pp. 22–43), the importance of reading and writing for college success and the distinctive qualities and demands of academic reading and writing • Chapter 3 (pp. 44–65), reading actively • Chapter 4 (pp. 66–98), thinking critically about text and images • Parts 3 and 4, thinking critically about the features of the genre, including thinking critically about characteristic flaws in the chapter's pattern (for example, pp. 231–33, the Making Connections box on pp. 237, 251, 253, 256–57)
Understand a writing assignment as a series of tasks, including finding, evaluating, analyzing, and synthesizing appropriate primary and secondary sources	• Guided Writing Assignments in the chapters in Parts 3 and 4, writing assignments broken down into doable, focused thinking and writing activities, including recursive processes of invention and research, analysis and synthesis of information and ideas (for example, pp. 240–48) • Part 5 (pp. 573–682), detailed coverage of finding, evaluating, using, and acknowledging primary and secondary sources • *VideoCentral**: videos on integrating sources
Integrate their own ideas with those of others	• Chapter 22 and 23, integrating information from sources with the students' own ideas (pp. 610–12, 630–36); introducing quotations, paraphrases, and summaries (pp. 630–36), and avoiding plagiarism (pp. 613–14, 630) • Companion Web site: *Re:Writing,* "The Bedford Research Room": checklist for integrating sources • *i-cite: visualizing sources**: Tutorials and practice on citing all kinds of sources • *VideoCentral**: Videos on integrating sources
Understand the relationships among language, knowledge, and power	• Chapters in Parts 3 and 4: thinking critically about possible flaws in the pattern of development (for example, p. 253)

* This resource is available packaged with the print book. See the preface for details.

Processes	
Be aware that it usually takes multiple drafts to create and complete a successful text	• Chapters 7 (pp. 140–63) and 9 (pp. 180–201), reading and revising a draft critically • Guided Writing Assignments in the chapters in Parts 3 and 4, pattern-specific coverage of revision (for example, pp. 245–47) • Chapter 25, portfolio keeping as an opportunity for reflection on the writing process (pp. 728–35) • *Portfolio Keeping,* Second Edition, portfolio keeping as a reflection of the writing processes (additional resource)
Develop flexible strategies for generating ideas, revising, editing, and proofreading	• Chapter 5, discovering ideas to write about through freewriting, mapping, brainstorming, and other techniques for generating ideas (pp. 99–121) • Chapter 9, "Revising Content and Organization" (pp. 180–201) • Chapter 10, "Editing Sentences and Words" (pp. 202–24) • Guided Writing Assignments in Parts 3 and 4, pattern- and genre-specific coverage of generating ideas, revising, editing, and proofreading (for example, pp. 240–48) • Companion Web site: *Exercise Central,* grammar exercises
Understand writing as an open process that permits writers to use later invention and rethinking to revise their work	• Chapter 9, "Revising Content and Organization" (pp. 180–201) • Guided Writing Assignments in Parts 3 and 4, pattern- and genre-specific advice on revising (for example, pp. 245–47) • Chapter 25, portfolio keeping as an opportunity for reflection on the writing process (pp. 728–35) • *Portfolio Keeping,* Second Edition, discusses portfolio keeping as a reflection of writing processes (additional resource) • *Teaching Composition,* Chapter 2, "Thinking about the Writing Process" (additional resource for instructors)

Understand the collaborative and social aspects of writing processes	• Opportunities to work collaboratively in exercises throughout the book • Instructor's Annotated Edition, options for having students work collaboratively • *Re:Writing Plus**: "Peer Factor," an online game to instill best practices for peer review • *Instructor's Resource Manual for Successful College Writing,* Chapter 5 on peer review (for instructors) • *Oral Presentations in the Composition Course: A Brief Guide,* Chapter 9, "Presenting as a Group" (additional resource)
Learn to critique their own and others' works	• Chapter 9, "Revising Content and Organization" (pp. 188–92) • Guided Writing Assignments in Parts 3 and 4, pattern- and genre-specific advice on peer review and revision (for example, pp. 245–48) • Revision Flowcharts in Parts 3 and 4, pattern-specific guidance for critical review and revision (for example, pp. 246–47) • *Re:Writing Plus**: "Peer Factor," an online game to instill best practices for peer review
Learn to balance the advantages of relying on others with the responsibility of doing their part	• Opportunities to practice balancing the advantages of relying on others with the responsibility of doing their part in exercises throughout the book • Chapter 1, "Work with Classmates" (pp. 17–18), advice about working collaboratively
Use a variety of technologies to address a range of audiences	• Chapter 1, using electronic tools effectively (p. 14), taking notes on a laptop (pp. 20–21) • Chapter 2, writing and researching online (pp. 25–26), using online dictionaries (pp. 30–31) • Chapter 22, using the Web (pp. 603–5), email (p. 606), and online communities for research (p. 606); finding sources using the library online catalog and periodical databases (pp. 597–603). • Chapter 26, using visual aids (objects and PowerPoint slides) in making oral presentations (pp. 740–42), designing effective PowerPoint slides (pp. 741–42) • Companion Web site: Online graphic organizers in each of the modes • *ix visualizing composition 2.0,** interactive assignments and guided analysis for multimedia texts

* This resource is available packaged with the print book. See the preface for details.

Knowledge of Conventions	
Learn common formats for different kinds of texts	• Chapter 23, formats for writing a paper using sources (pp. 637, 640–62, 666–81) • Chapter 26, formatting of slides in presentation software, such as PowerPoint (pp. 741–42); business writing formats, including those for writing résumés, job application letters, memoranda, and business emails (pp. 744–51) • Companion Web site: Tutorials on designing documents, preparing presentation slides, and preparing charts and graphs; a model documents gallery
Develop knowledge of genre conventions ranging from structure and paragraphing to tone and mechanics	• Chapter 7, structure of essays, organizing supporting details, creating graphic organizers (pp. 140–63) • Chapter 8, structure of paragraphs (pp. 166–67) • Chapter 9, revising for organization (p. 187) • Chapter 10, writing concisely, varying sentences, editing to create an appropriate tone and level of diction, choosing appropriate words, and editing to avoid errors of grammar, punctuation, and mechanics (pp. 202–24) • Guided Writing Assignments in Parts 3 and 4, mode-specific organizational strategies (for example, pp. 244–45) • Handbook (full edition), correcting errors of grammar, punctuation, mechanics, and spelling. • *Re:Writing Plus**: "Make-a-Paragraph Kit," animated tutorials on grammar issues
Practice appropriate means of documenting their work	• Chapter 23, documenting sources in MLA style (pp. 640–62) • Chapter 23, documenting sources in APA style (pp. 640–62) • Companion Web site: *Re:Writing*: "Bedford Bibliographer" • *ix visualizing composition 2.0,** tutorials and practice on citing all kinds of sources
Control such surface features as syntax, grammar, punctuation, and spelling	• Chapter 10, writing concisely, varying sentences, editing to create an appropriate tone and level of diction, choosing appropriate words, editing to avoid errors of grammar, punctuation, and mechanics (pp. 202–24) • Guided Writing Assignment in Parts 3 and 4, pattern- and genre-specific advice about editing and proofreading (for example, p. 248) • Handbook (pp. 753–73), instruction in correcting errors of grammar, punctuation, mechanics, and spelling • Companion Web site: *Re:Writing: Exercise Central*, diagnostic test and exercises to practice editing for errors in grammar, punctuation, and spelling

* This resource is available packaged with the print book. See the preface for details.

Composing in Electronic Environments	
Use electronic environments for drafting, reviewing, revising editing, and sharing texts	• Chapter 1, using electronic tools effectively (p. 14), taking notes on a laptop (pp. 20–21) • Chapter 2, writing and researching online (pp. 25–26), using online dictionaries (pp. 30–31) • *Re:Writing Plus**: "Peer Factor," an online game to instill best practices for peer review • Instructor's Annotated Edition, tips for incorporating online drafting and revising throughout the text • Companion Web site: Online, mode-specific graphic organizers • *Instructor's Resource Manual for Successful College Writing,* Fifth Edition, "Teaching and Learning Online" (p. 127) (for instructors) • *Teaching Composition: Background Readings*, "Teaching Writing with Computers" (pp. 305–37) (for instructors)
Locate, evaluate, organize, and use research material collected from electronic sources	• Chapter 23, using the Web, email, and online communities for research (pp. 603–6), finding sources using a library's online catalog and periodicals databases (pp. 597–603) • Companion Web site: "Research and Documentation Online," "Evaluating Online Sources Tutorial," "The Bedford Research Room" with research guides, a variety of checklists, and other resources on locating and evaluating online sources • *Instructor's Resource Manual for Successful College Writing,* Fifth Edition, "Teaching and Learning Online" (p. 127) (for instructors) • *Teaching Composition: Background Readings*, "Teaching Writing with Computers" (pp. 305–37) (for instructors)
Understand and exploit the differences in the rhetorical strategies and in the affordances available for both print and electronic composing processes and texts	• Chapter 2, writing and researching online (pp. 25–26), using online dictionaries (pp. 30–31) • Chapter 26, using visual aids (objects and PowerPoint slides) in oral presentations, designing effective PowerPoint slides (pp. 740–42) • Companion Web site: Online, mode-specific graphic organizers • *ix visualizing composition 2.0** interactive assignments and guided analysis, practice with multimedia texts • *Instructor's Resource Manual for Successful College Writing,* Fifth Edition, "Teaching and Learning Online" (p. 127) (for instructors) • *Teaching Composition: Background Readings,* "Teaching Writing with Computers" (pp. 305–37) (for instructors)

* This resource is available packaged with the print book. See the preface for details.

8 Writing Effective Paragraphs   165

9 Revising Content and Organization   181

10 Editing Sentences and Words 203

PART 3 Patterns of Development 225

11 Narration: Recounting Events 227

23 Writing a Paper Using Sources   **621**

LANGUAGE AND LITERATURE

POPULAR CULTURE

TECHNOLOGY

As a college student, you probably have many responsibilities. You may need to balance the demands of college with the needs of your family and the requirements of your job. In addition, you are probably attending college to make a change in your life—to better your prospects. You may not have chosen a specific career path yet, but you eventually want a rewarding, secure future. Consequently, you are ready to pursue a course of study that will lead you there.

I have written this book to help you achieve your goals by becoming a successful college writer. In writing the book, I have taken into account your busy lifestyle and made this book practical and easy to read. As simply and directly as possible, the text explains what you need to know to sharpen your writing skills. You will also find it easy to locate the information you need within the text. You can use the brief contents on the inside front cover, the detailed contents, or the comprehensive index at the end of the book to locate information. In addition, numerous flowcharts, boxes, and other visual aids appear throughout to help you quickly find the information or writing assistance you need. I also show how the writing strategies you are learning apply to other college courses and to the workplace. Throughout the book you will find tips for completing reading and writing assignments in your other college courses, and Chapters 1–4 contain useful study-skills advice, as well.

HOW THIS BOOK CAN HELP YOU SUCCEED

There are no secrets to success in writing, no tricks or miracle shortcuts. Rather, becoming a successful student writer requires hard work, guidance and feedback, and skills and strategies. You must provide the hard work; your instructor and classmates will provide you with the guidance and feedback. This book introduces you to the skills and strategies that successful writers need to know. Specifically, this book will help you succeed in your writing course in the following ways:

- **By emphasizing the connection between reading and writing.** You have been reading nearly your entire life. You could probably read sentences and paragraphs before you could write them. This book shows you how reading and writing are connected and how to use your critical reading and thinking skills to improve your writing.
- **By including readings on topics and issues of interest and concern to college students.** The readings in this book have been selected from a wide range of sources—including newspapers, popular magazines, special-interest magazines, blogs, and other Web sites—that represent some of the many texts you will encounter in both your personal life and your academic life.
- **By offering you both professional and student models of good writing.** As you work with the essays in this book, you will discover that both professional writers and student writers follow the same principles in organizing and presenting their ideas. You

will also have opportunities to examine, react to, and discuss the ideas presented in these essays and to relate those ideas to your own life.

- **By helping you discover the writing strategies that work best for you.** You may have noticed that you don't learn in the same way as your best friend or the person who sits next to you in class. For example, some students learn better by listening, while others learn better by reading. Because not all students learn in the same way, Chapter 2 includes a Learning Style Inventory that will help you discover how you learn. As you work through the writing assignments throughout the book, you will find lists of Learning Style Options that suggest different ways that you can approach a given writing task. Feel free to experiment with these options; try one and then another. You will probably discover some techniques that work better or take less time than those you are currently using.

- **By helping you identify and eliminate frequently occurring problems with sentence structure, grammar, punctuation, and mechanics.** Sections in Chapter 7, "Drafting an Essay," and in Chapter 10, "Editing Sentences and Words," provide strategies for fixing errors that students commonly make. In addition, Chapters 11–18 and 20 all provide editing and proofreading tips particular to the type of essays you will be writing in each chapter. Part 7, "Handbook: Writing Problems and How to Correct Them," covers important grammar rules and provides exercises that allow you to practice applying those rules. For more help, a student workbook, *Additional Exercises for Successful College Writing*, is available, and *Exercise Central*, available on the companion Web site, offers online grammar practice.

HOW TO USE THIS BOOK

In writing this book, I have included many features that I use when I am actually teaching a class. Each is described below along with suggestions for how the feature can help you become a successful writer.

A Guide to Active Reading

Chapter 3, "Reading in College," includes specific, practical strategies that will help you get the most out of the selections in this book as well as the reading assignments in your other courses. The Guide to Active Reading, starting on page 48, explains, step by step, how to improve your comprehension and build your critical reading skills.

A Guide to Reading and Thinking Critically

Chapter 4, "Responding Critically to Text and Images," offers valuable strategies for evaluating and reacting to what you read. You will learn how to evaluate sources of information, understand shades of meaning, and differentiate fact from opinion, for example. You will also learn how to interpret and respond to visuals, including photographs and a variety of graphics.

Detailed Coverage of Each Stage of the Writing Process

Part 2 of the text, "Strategies for Writing Essays," includes six chapters (Chapters 5–10) that cover each stage of the writing process in detail. Each step in the process is illustrated by the example of a student, Christine Lee, as she generates ideas for, drafts, and revises an essay. Chapter 9, "Revising Content and Organization," includes an important section on working with classmates to revise an essay (p. 188), with plenty of practical suggestions for you to use both as a writer seeking advice and as a peer reviewer.

Annotated Student Essays

Throughout the text, student essays illustrate different types of writing or different writing strategies. These student examples are usually found in sections titled "Students Write," and most of them have been annotated to call your attention to particular writing features. Within the annotations and the text that they refer to, color-coded highlighting is used for features like the thesis statement, topic sentences, and source citations as well as features distinctive to the particular kind of writing, such as sensory details in description. A portion of a sample annotated student essay appears below.

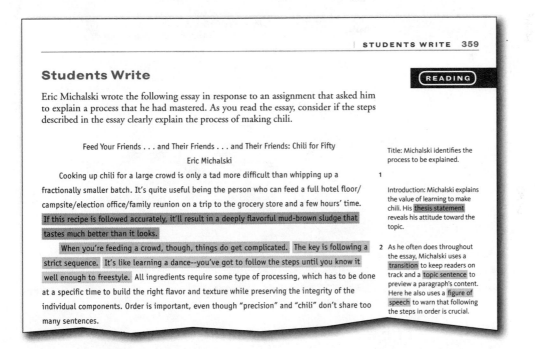

| STUDENTS WRITE 359

Students Write

READING

Eric Michalski wrote the following essay in response to an assignment that asked him to explain a process that he had mastered. As you read the essay, consider if the steps described in the essay clearly explain the process of making chili.

Feed Your Friends . . . and Their Friends . . . and Their Friends: Chili for Fifty

Eric Michalski

Cooking up chili for a large crowd is only a tad more difficult than whipping up a fractionally smaller batch. It's quite useful being the person who can feed a full hotel floor/campsite/election office/family reunion on a trip to the grocery store and a few hours' time. If this recipe is followed accurately, it'll result in a deeply flavorful mud-brown sludge that tastes much better than it looks.

When you're feeding a crowd, though, things do get complicated. The key is following a strict sequence. It's like learning a dance--you've got to follow the steps until you know it well enough to freestyle. All ingredients require some type of processing, which has to be done at a specific time to build the right flavor and texture while preserving the integrity of the individual components. Order is important, even though "precision" and "chili" don't share too many sentences.

Title: Michalski identifies the process to be explained.

Introduction: Michalski explains the value of learning to make chili. His thesis statement reveals his attitude toward the topic.

As he often does throughout the essay, Michalski uses a transition to keep readers on track and a topic sentence to preview a paragraph's content. Here he also uses a figure of speech to warn that following the steps in order is crucial.

A section in Chapter 4, "How to Approach the Student Essays in This Book" (p. 96), explains how to read and examine student essays and apply what you learn to improve your writing. In addition, use the questions following these student essays to help you discover how other students apply the techniques you are learning to their writing.

Graphic Organizers

Throughout the text you will find Graphic Organizers—diagrams that offer a visual approach to organizing and revising essays. A sample Graphic Organizer appears below. As you draft and revise, refer frequently to the graphic organizer for the particular type of essay you are writing. The text also demonstrates how to draw your own organizers to help you analyze a reading, structure your ideas, and write and revise drafts, and interactive graphic organizers appear on the book's Web site (bedfordstmartins.com/successfulcollege).

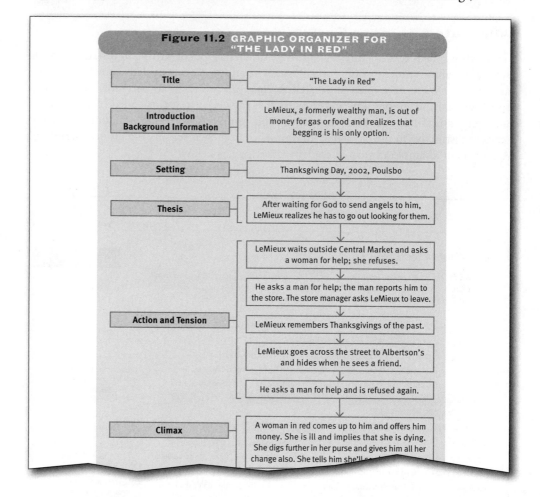

Figure 11.2 GRAPHIC ORGANIZER FOR "THE LADY IN RED"

Title — "The Lady in Red"

Introduction Background Information — LeMieux, a formerly wealthy man, is out of money for gas or food and realizes that begging is his only option.

Setting — Thanksgiving Day, 2002, Poulsbo

Thesis — After waiting for God to send angels to him, LeMieux realizes he has to go out looking for them.

Action and Tension —
LeMieux waits outside Central Market and asks a woman for help; she refuses.

He asks a man for help; the man reports him to the store. The store manager asks LeMieux to leave.

LeMieux remembers Thanksgivings of the past.

LeMieux goes across the street to Albertson's and hides when he sees a friend.

He asks a man for help and is refused again.

Climax — A woman in red comes up to him and offers him money. She is ill and implies that she is dying. She digs further in her purse and gives him all her change also. She tells him she'll...

Guided Writing Assignments

Chapters 11–18 and 20 contain writing guides that "walk you through" a writing assignment step by step. The Guided Writing Assignments are shaded, as in the sample on the next page. You can refer to this guide as often as you need to while you complete the assignment in the chapter or other similar assignments. Think of it as a tutorial to which you can always turn for tips, examples, and advice.

A GUIDED WRITING ASSIGNMENT

The following guide will help you write a process analysis essay. It may be either a how-to or a how-it-works essay. Although you will focus on process analysis, you may need to integrate one or more other patterns of development in your essay.

The Assignment

Write a process analysis essay on one of the topics below or one of your own choosing. Be sure the process you choose is one that you know enough about to explain to others or can learn about through observation or research. Your audience consists of readers who are unfamiliar with the process, including your classmates.

How-To Essay Topics

1. How to improve _____ (your study habits, your wardrobe, your batting average)
2. How to be a successful _____ (diver, parent, gardener)
3. How to make or buy _____ (an object for personal use or enjoyment)
4. How to prepare for _____ (a test, a job interview, an oral presentation)

How-It-Works Essay Topics

1. How your college _____ (spends tuition revenues, hires professors, raises money)
2. How _____ works (an answering machine, a generator, email, a cell phone)
3. How a decision is made to _____ (accept a student at a college, add or eliminate a local or state agency)
4. How _____ is put together (a quilt, a news broadcast, a football team, a Web site)

As you develop your process analysis essay, you will probably use narrative strategies, description (for example, to describe equipment or objects), or illustration (such as to show an example of part of the process).

For more on narration, description, and illustration, see Chapters 11–13.

Generating Ideas

The following guidelines will help you select a process to write about and choose details to include. You may want to use one of the prewriting techniques discussed in Chapter 5. Consider your learning style when you select a prewriting technique. You might try questioning, group brainstorming, or sketching a diagram of a process.

Revision Flowcharts

Many chapters include flowcharts that will help you identify what you need to revise in a first draft. Each flowchart lists key questions to ask about a draft and offers suggestions for how to revise to correct any weaknesses you uncover. (See the sample below.) You can also use the questions in the appropriate revision flowchart to guide classmates who are reviewing your essay.

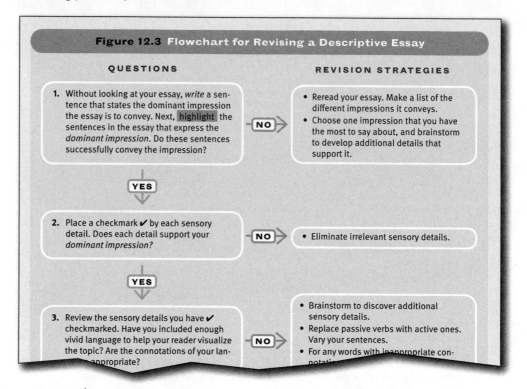

Figure 12.3 Flowchart for Revising a Descriptive Essay

QUESTIONS

REVISION STRATEGIES

1. Without looking at your essay, *write* a sentence that states the dominant impression the essay is to convey. Next, highlight the sentences in the essay that express the *dominant impression*. Do these sentences successfully convey the impression?

   NO →
   - Reread your essay. Make a list of the different impressions it conveys.
   - Choose one impression that you have the most to say about, and brainstorm to develop additional details that support it.

   YES

2. Place a checkmark ✔ by each sensory detail. Does each detail support your *dominant impression*?

   NO →
   - Eliminate irrelevant sensory details.

   YES

3. Review the sensory details you have ✔ checkmarked. Have you included enough vivid language to help your reader visualize the topic? Are the connotations of your language appropriate?

   NO →
   - Brainstorm to discover additional sensory details.
   - Replace passive verbs with active ones. Vary your sentences.
   - For any words with inappropriate connotations

Writing Using Sources

Often, as you write and revise an essay you will find that you need facts, statistics, or the viewpoint of an expert to strengthen your own ideas. Chapter 21, "Planning a Paper with Sources," shows you where to start and gives helpful advice for evaluating different types of sources. Chapter 22, "Finding Sources and Taking Notes," explains how to locate sources in the library and on the Internet and how to extract the information you need. Chapter 23, "Writing a Paper Using Sources," demonstrates how to use, integrate, and document information from sources within an essay. For your convenience, this book includes guidelines for using two widely recommended styles for documenting sources: MLA (green-bordered pages) and APA (orange-bordered pages). In addition, color-coded visuals provide clear models for documenting books, articles, and Web sites.

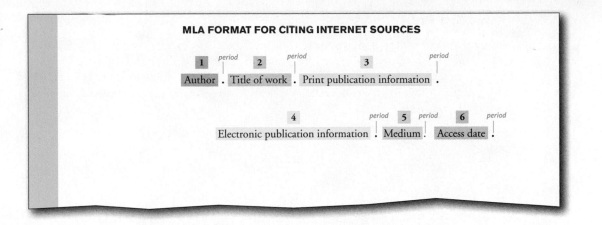

Handbook

Part 7, "Handbook: Writing Problems and How to Correct Them," is a user-friendly reference that you can consult to review problem areas or to check rules about grammar, punctuation, or mechanics. Refer to this section often to help make your papers error free. Your instructor may also refer you to this part of the book by writing either revision symbols (such as *"cs"* for "comma splice") or the numbers and letters of specific sections (such as *7a* for a pronoun reference problem) on your papers. You can refer to the list of revision symbols or to the complete contents for the handbook, both included at the back of the book, to find the information you need. You can also look up grammar concepts, punctuation marks, or problem areas in the index.

A Final Word

In my high school and early college years, I was an okay writer but never a skilled writer. I certainly never imagined myself writing a textbook, and yet *Successful College Writing* is my tenth college textbook. How did I learn to write well? I learned from my college writing courses and from my instructors, both in English classes and in other disciplines as well. I learned from my husband, who used to read and comment on my papers while we were in college. I learned from friends and classmates; I continue to learn from colleagues, editors, and most importantly from my own students, who deserve clear and concise expression. Never stop learning: I know I will not. I wish you success.

Kathleen T. McWhorter

PART 1

Academic Quick Start

CHAPTER 1

Succeeding in College

The photographs on the opposite page show two first-year college students. One is a successful student, and the other is a very frustrated one. Why is one student successful and the other not?

Write a paragraph, based on your experiences with education up to this point, that explains what factors you think contribute to academic success and/or frustration. Be specific; discuss tasks that students need to know how to perform to be successful. You might offer tips or identify pitfalls or trouble spots, as well. You might also consider nonacademic factors, such as jobs and family responsibilities, that play crucial roles in student success.

What skills did you identify as contributing to college success? You may have mentioned being motivated and organized, performing well in class, knowing how to read and study, or knowing how to write papers and exams. All these skills, and many others, contribute to academic success. This chapter presents numerous strategies for success to help you develop the skills you need for a successful college career.

Strategies for Success

You can start preparing for college success even before you enter the classroom. To begin, make sure you

- focus on success,
- manage your time effectively,
- organize a writing and study area,
- develop effective study strategies, and
- learn to manage stress.

Focus on Success

No doubt you are enthusiastic about jumping into your college studies, but you may be concerned about how you will juggle a job, your family life, and school. You also may be wondering whether you have the skills and abilities necessary to get the grades you want. Having doubts and concerns is normal, but it is important to think positively and to focus on success. Here are a few success strategies.

- **Define success.** *Success* means different things to different people, and you need to decide what it means to you. Is a rewarding career your highest priority? Are relationships with family and friends important? What about helping others? Define what *success* means to you, and decide how college fits into your definition of success.
- **Develop long-term goals that will lead to success.** Once you have defined *success*, you need to determine the long-term goals that will get you there. What do you intend to accomplish this term? This year? In the next four years? Complete Exercise 1.1 to help you define your goals. List where you would like to be and what you would like to be doing at each of the times listed. You may have multiple goals, so list as many as apply.
- **Take responsibility for achieving those goals.** Only you are in charge of your own learning and reaching your goals. You can do as little or as much as you want to achieve your goals, but you take the responsibility either way.
- **Visualize success.** To keep your goals in mind, close your eyes and imagine yourself achieving your goals. For example, picture yourself finishing your first year of college with high marks or walking across the stage at graduation. Never visualize failure.
- **Develop essential skills that will help you achieve success.** Success is not a matter of luck. It is a matter of specific skills, such as communicating effectively and visualizing success, that will help you achieve success.

Exercise 1.1

List what you expect to accomplish in the next two weeks.	1. 2.
List what you expect to have accomplished by the end of this semester.	1. 2. 3.
List what you will accomplish within the next year.	1. 2. 3.
List what you will have accomplished by graduation.	1. 2. 3.
Where do you see yourself five years after you graduate?	1. 2. 3.

Exercise 1.2

Write a paragraph describing your academic and professional goals. Include the specific steps you need to take to achieve those goals.

Manage Your Time

Examine the two student schedules shown in Figures 1.1 (below) and 1.2 (on the next page). Which student is more likely to meet his or her deadlines? Why?

FIGURE 1.1 Planner with Due Dates

NOVEMBER	NOVEMBER
10 Monday	Thursday 13 *10 am Essay 3 due*
11 Tuesday *3 pm History exam*	Friday 14 *1 pm Anthro quiz*
12 Wednesday	Saturday 15
	Sunday 16

FIGURE 1.2 Planner with Detailed Schedule

November	November
10 Monday	Thursday 13
am—outline English Essay 3	10 am Essay 3 due
6 pm History study group	5–8 pm Work
	9–10 pm Study Anthro chapters
11 Tuesday	Friday 14
am—Draft Essay 3	am—Review Anthro notes and
3 pm History exam	chapter highlighting
6–8 pm Work	
Read Anthro Ch. 20	1 pm Anthro quiz
12 Wednesday	Saturday 15
10 am Writing Center—review Essay 3	9–4 Work
Read Anthro Chs. 21–22	
	Sunday 16
	Read Bio Ch. 17
	Review Bio lab
	Read History Ch. 15

The student planner in Figure 1.1 shows only test dates and assignment deadlines. Figure 1.2 shows a planner that details how and when the student will meet those deadlines. The student who uses the planner in Figure 1.2 is likely to complete his or her work with less stress and worry.

The biggest challenge for most first-year college students is managing time. The most successful students spend two hours outside of the classroom for every hour spent in the classroom (more for reading- or writing-intensive courses). College students are required to spend only twelve to eighteen hours per week in class or lab. For many students, the remainder of their time is unstructured, and as a result, they never seem to get organized. Others are overwhelmed by the workload and the challenge of integrating college study into already busy lives. Still others tend to study nonstop: by never finding free time for relaxation, they set themselves up for burnout.

To avoid these traps and manage your time effectively, you need to establish goals and plan your activities.

Establish Positive, Realistic, Short-Term Goals

The first step in managing your time is establishing goals that are positive and realistic. Keep in mind a broad, long-term goal—like earning a bachelor's degree in elementary education in four years—before setting short-term goals that you can achieve more quickly. A short-term goal could be finishing an assigned paper by next Friday. Setting a time frame is a critical step toward accomplishing each of your goals.

Plan Your Activities

If you let days "just happen," you're not likely to accomplish much. You need to plan your activities. You may prefer a tightly structured or loosely structured plan—or something in between. Consider both the term and weekly plans, and choose the one that works best for you. If you are not sure, experiment by trying out both.

The term plan. Once you have a sense of the work that you will need to complete for each of your courses, block out four to six hours per week for each course. Remember, the rule of thumb is that for every hour spent in class you should plan to work two hours outside of class. Study for each course during the same time period each week. For instance, you might reserve Monday, Wednesday, and Thursday evenings between 8:00 and 10:00 p.m. for your writing course. This plan establishes a routine for study. The tasks you work on each week will vary, but you will always be certain you have enough time to get everything done. If you have trouble starting on assignments, this plan may be the best one for you.

The weekly plan. Take ten minutes at the beginning of each week to specify when you'll work on each course, taking into account upcoming assignments. Figure 1.2 is a good example of how to organize a weekly plan.

Regardless of which plan you choose, you need to purchase a student planner or pocket calendar—or use an electronic calendar—for recording assignments, due dates for papers, and upcoming exams. You'll also want to schedule time to work on your coursework, whether you schedule this time daily, weekly, or across the term. Keep this planner or calendar with you at all times and check it daily. It will help you get and stay organized.

Each time you begin studying, assess what needs to be done and determine the order in which you will do these tasks. Although you may be tempted to tackle short or easy tasks first, it is usually best to work on the most challenging assignments first, when your concentration is at its peak.

Avoid Procrastination

Procrastination is putting off things that need to be done; you know you should work on an assignment, but you do something else instead. To avoid procrastination, divide the task into manageable parts. Don't attempt to do the whole task, but do plan to complete one part. Avoid making excuses. It is easy to say you don't have enough time to get everything done, but often that is not true. Also avoid escaping into routine tasks such as shopping, cleaning, or washing your car rather than completing the task.

Organize a Writing and Study Area

You don't need a lot of room to create an appropriate space for studying and writing. Use the following suggestions to organize an efficient work area:

- **Choose a setting that is conducive to writing and studying.** Your work area should be relatively free of distractions, well lit, comfortable, and equipped with all the tools you need—a clock, a computer, a calculator, pens, pencils, paper, a pencil sharpener.

- **Find a quiet area.** If you live on campus, your dormitory room probably includes a desk or work area. If your dorm is noisy, consider studying in the library or another quiet place. Libraries offer free carrel space where you can work without distractions. Many also offer study rooms for group work or secluded areas with comfortable chairs if you do not need a desk.

    If you live off campus, find a place where you won't be disturbed by family or roommates. Your work area need not be a separate room, but it should be a place where you can spread out your materials and find them undisturbed when you return. Otherwise, you may waste a great deal of time setting up your work, figuring out where you left off, and getting started again. In addition, you should find a quiet place on campus where you can study between classes.

Exercise 1.3

Using the suggestions listed above and those you learned through discussion with your classmates, write a paragraph describing what you can do to organize an area that is conducive to writing and studying.

"Study Smarter"

Does either of these situations sound familiar?

"I just read a whole page, and I can't remember anything I read!"
"Every time I start working on this assignment, my mind wanders."

If so, you may need to improve your concentration. No matter how intelligent you are or what skills or talents you possess, if you cannot keep your mind on your work, your classes, including your writing class, will be unnecessarily difficult. Try the following concentration skills to help you "study smarter," not harder:

- **Work at peak periods of attention.** Find out the time of day or night that you are most efficient and least likely to lose concentration. Do not try to work when you are tired, hungry, or distracted by others.
- **Work on difficult assignments first.** Your mind is freshest as you begin to work. Putting off difficult tasks until last may be tempting, but you need your fullest concentration when you begin challenging assignments.
- **Vary your activities.** Do not complete three reading assignments consecutively. Instead, alternate assignments: for example, read, then write, then work on math problems, then read another assignment, and so on.
- **Use writing to keep you mentally and physically active.** Highlight and annotate as you read. These processes will keep you mentally alert.
- **Avoid electronic distractions.** Turn off the TV and your iPod. Silence your cell phone so you are not interrupted by phone calls or text messages. Ignore incoming email.

- **Approach assignments critically.** Ask questions as you read. Make connections with what you have already learned and with what you already know about the subject.
- **Challenge yourself with deadlines.** Before beginning an assignment, estimate how long it should take and work toward completing it within that time limit.
- **Keep a list of distractions.** When you are working on an assignment, stray thoughts about other pressing things are bound to zip through your mind. You might remember that your car has to be inspected tomorrow or that you have to buy your mother's birthday present next week. When these thoughts occur to you, jot them down so that you can unclutter your mind and focus on your work.
- **Reward yourself.** Use fun activities, such as emailing a friend or getting a snack, as a reward when you have completed an assignment.

Exercise 1.4

Not all students study the same way, and most students study differently for different courses. List below the courses you are taking this semester. For each, identify a study strategy that works for that course. Compare your list with those of other students and add useful techniques you have discovered.

Course	Study Strategies to Try
1.	
2.	
3.	
4.	
5.	

Manage Stress

The pressures and obligations of school lead many students to feel overwhelmed and overstressed. As a successful student, you need to monitor your stress. Take the quiz on page 10 to assess your stress level.

Stress is a natural reaction to the challenges of daily living, but if you are expected to accomplish more or perform better than you think you can, stress can become overwhelming. You can respond to stress either positively or negatively. For example, you can use stress to motivate yourself and start a project or assignment, or you can let it interfere with your ability to function mentally and physically. Here are some effective ways to change your thinking and habits and reduce stress.

- **Establish your priorities.** Decide what is more and less important in your life. Let's say you decide college is more important than your part-time job, for example. Once you have decided this, you won't worry about requesting a work schedule to accommodate your study schedule because studying is your priority.

Exercise 1.5

Complete the following Stress Mini Quiz. If you answered "Always" or "Sometimes" to more than two or three items, identify at least two ways you can begin to reduce your stress level.

	Always	*Sometimes*	*Never*
1. I worry that I do not have enough time to get everything done.	❏	❏	❏
2. I regret that I have no time to do fun things each week.	❏	❏	❏
3. I find myself losing track of details and forgetting due dates, promises, and appointments.	❏	❏	❏
4. I worry about what I am doing.	❏	❏	❏
5. I have conflicts or disagreements with friends or family.	❏	❏	❏
6. I lose patience with small annoyances.	❏	❏	❏
7. I seem to be late, no matter how hard I try to arrive on time.	❏	❏	❏
8. I have difficulty sleeping.	❏	❏	❏
9. My eating habits have changed.	❏	❏	❏
10. I find myself needing a cigarette, drink, or prescription drug.	❏	❏	❏

- **Be selfish and learn to say no.** Many people feel stress because they are trying to do too many things for too many people—family, friends, classmates, and coworkers. Allow your priorities to guide you in accepting new responsibilities.
- **Simplify your life by making fewer choices.** Avoid simple daily decisions that needlessly consume time and energy. For example, instead of having to decide what time to set your alarm clock each morning, get up at the same time each weekday morning. Choose fixed study times and adhere to them without fail.
- **Focus on the positive.** Do not say, "I'll never be able to finish this assignment on time." Instead ask yourself, "What do I have to do to finish this assignment on time?"
- **Separate work, school, and social problems.** Create mental compartments for your worries. Don't spend time in class thinking about a problem at work. Leave work problems at work. Don't think about a conflict with a friend while attempting to write a paper. Deal with problems at the appropriate time.
- **Keep a personal journal.** Writing is not just for school. Taking a few minutes to write down details about your worries and your emotions can go a long way toward relieving stress. Be sure to include your goals and how you plan to achieve them.

> **Exercise 1.6**
>
> *Using the guidelines on pages 9–10, write a brief paragraph listing ways you successfully manage stress or ways you could improve how you manage stress.*

Classroom Skills

What you do within the classroom largely determines your success in college. Make sure that you

- polish your academic image,
- demonstrate academic integrity,
- communicate effectively with your instructors,
- use electronic tools effectively,
- listen carefully and critically,
- ask and answer questions appropriately,
- work with classmates,
- take effective notes in class, and
- manage online courses effectively.

Polish Your Academic Image

Your academic image is the way you are seen and thought of as a student by your instructors and other students. How you act and respond in class plays a large part in determining this image.

> *Do ...*
>
> Make thoughtful contributions to class discussions.
>
> Maintain eye contact with instructors.
>
> Ask questions if information is unclear to you.
>
> Refer to assigned readings in class.
>
> Be courteous to classmates when you speak.
>
> *Don't ...*
>
> Read or send text messages during class.
>
> Work on homework during class.
>
> Sleep or daydream in class.
>
> Remain silent during class discussion.
>
> Interrupt others or criticize their contributions.

When you see yourself as a serious student, you project that positive academic image to your instructors and classmates. Don't underestimate the value of communicating daily—through your words and actions—that you are a hardworking student who takes your college experience seriously. A student who takes his or her studies seriously is more likely to be taken seriously and to find the assistance he or she needs.

Exercise 1.7

Rate your academic image by checking "Always," "Sometimes," or "Never" for each of the following statements.

	Always	Sometimes	Never
I arrive at classes promptly.	❏	❏	❏
I sit near the front of the room.	❏	❏	❏
I look and act alert and interested in the class.	❏	❏	❏
I make eye contact with instructors.	❏	❏	❏
I complete reading assignments before class.	❏	❏	❏
I ask thoughtful questions.	❏	❏	❏
I participate in class discussions.	❏	❏	❏
I complete all assignments on time.	❏	❏	❏
I turn in neat, complete, well-organized papers.	❏	❏	❏
I refrain from carrying on conversations with other students while the instructor is addressing the class.	❏	❏	❏
I say "hello" when I meet my instructors on campus.	❏	❏	❏

To project a positive image, you must actively participate in class at every opportunity. Keep in mind the following suggestions:

- **Prepare to participate.** As you read an assignment, make notes and jot down questions to use as a starting point for class participation.
- **Organize your remarks.** Plan in advance what you will say or ask in class. Work on stating your ideas clearly.
- **Say something early in a discussion.** The longer you wait, the more difficult it will be to say something that has not already been said.
- **Keep your comments brief.** You will lose your classmates' attention if you ramble. Your instructor may ask you to explain your ideas further.
- **Be sensitive to the feelings of others.** Make sure that what you say does not offend or embarrass other class members.

Participation in class involves more than just speaking out. It also involves making a serious effort to focus on the discussion and to record important ideas that others may have. Be sure to take notes on class discussions, record whatever the instructor writes on the chalkboard, keep handouts from PowerPoint presentations, and jot down ideas for future writing assignments.

Exercise 1.8

Write a brief statement about how you think others perceive you as a student. Refer to the list of tips about building a positive academic image on page 12. What tips do you normally follow? Which do you most need to work on?

Demonstrate Academic Integrity

Academic integrity—conducting yourself in an honest and ethical manner—is important in the college classroom. It involves avoiding the obvious forms of dishonesty such as copying homework, buying a paper on the Internet, and cheating on exams or helping others do so.

But it also involves avoiding intellectual dishonesty, either deliberate or unintentional, in which you use the ideas or language of others without giving credit to the author. This form of academic dishonesty is known as plagiarism. An example of intentional plagiarism is cutting and pasting information into your paper from the Internet without indicating that it is borrowed. Unintentional plagiarism occurs when you use language too similar to that of the original source or forget to place quotation marks around a quotation. To learn how to avoid these various forms of plagiarism, refer to Chapter 22, pp. 613–15.

Communicate Effectively with Your Instructors

Meeting regularly with your instructor will help you understand and meet the course objectives. Take advantage of your instructor's office hours, or speak to him or her after class. Use the following tips to communicate with your instructors:

- **Don't be afraid to approach your instructors.** At first, some of them may seem distant or unapproachable. In fact, they enjoy teaching and working with students. They may not become your best friends, but they can answer questions you have about a reading, help you with problems you may experience with an assignment, and suggest directions to take with a topic for a paper or research project. You will find that most instructors are happy to help you and to serve as valuable sources of information on research, academic decisions, and careers in their respective fields.
- **Learn your instructors' contact information.** Most instructors keep office hours—times during which they are available and ready to talk with you and answer your questions. Some instructors also give out their email addresses. In either case, though, you have to take the initiative to contact them.
- **Prepare for meetings with your instructor.** Write out specific questions in advance. If you need help with a paper, be sure to bring along all the work (drafts, outlines, research sources) you have done so far.
- **Stay in touch with your instructor.** If you absolutely cannot attend class for a particular reason, be sure to notify your instructor and explain. Unexcused absences generally lower your grade and suggest that you are not taking your studies seriously. In addition, if personal problems interfere with your schoolwork, let your instructors know. They can refer you to the counseling services on campus and may grant you an extension for work missed for an emergency.

Use Electronic Tools Effectively

Email, texting, and instant messaging (IM) are now widely used for academic purposes on college campuses. Some colleges have a system that allows students to text questions to a reference librarian, for example. Many instructors have course management systems that enable students and professors to communicate electronically.

Not all instructors, however, encourage students to communicate with them using email, texts, and IMs. Use the following guidelines to send appropriate messages:

- **Text only if invited.** Do not text your instructor unless he or she has invited you to do so—and even then text only when you are certain that it's appropriate to do so. (For example, your instructor might allow you to text him or her if you're going to be unavoidably late for a major classroom event or if you're participating in an off-campus learning experience and texting is the only way to report to the classroom.)
- **Do not take advantage of access to your instructor.** It would not be appropriate, for instance, to try to get your instructor to respond to IMs the night before a paper is due.
- **Use appropriate language.** The abbreviations made necessary by texting and instant messaging are not appropriate for formal writing, such as course assignments. Even emails to instructors should use formal language unless the instructor has set a less formal tone in his or her own emails to you.

Computers are increasingly being used as a participatory classroom tool, and they are also used for collaborating on writing assignments. For example, an instructor might hold virtual office hours. Others may schedule a time for an IM chat about an assignment or a reading. Use the following suggestions for participating in online discussions and collaboration:

- **Become familiar with the software or course management system before you attempt to post messages.** If you need help, try to find print instructions or a model or demo. You can also get help from your campus computer center or classmates.
- **Be sure to read all previous posts before posting your comments.** You want to be sure someone else has not already said what you plan to say.
- **Plan ahead.** Unlike in-class discussions, you have the luxury of thinking through what you want to say before you say it.
- **Show respect and consideration.** Make it easy for classmates and your instructor to read your postings. Use correct spelling and grammar, and format your comment using spacing, boldface, numbered lists, and so on where appropriate.
- **Place your comments within a context.** Make it clear whether you are responding to another posting (if so, give the date and poster's name), a reading assignment (give the chapter or page), or a lecture (give the date).

Exercise 1.9

In the chart on page 15 is a list of options for communicating electronically with classmates and instructors. Fill in the chart with the possible benefits and drawbacks of each method. When would it be effective to use each option? In what circumstances should you not use that option? When is it best to have a face-to-face meeting? Compare your completed chart with those of classmates.

Options	Communicating with Classmates		Communicating with Instructors	
	Benefits	Drawbacks	Benefits	Drawbacks
Email				
Phone				
Instant messages (IMs) or text messages				
Social networks (examples: Facebook and MySpace)				
Message board in electronic course materials (such as WebCT or Blackboard)				

Listen Carefully and Critically

Of the most common ways people communicate—reading, writing, speaking, and listening—listening is the skill that you perform most frequently in a classroom. Think about the classes you attended this week; you probably spent far more time listening than reading, writing, or speaking. Because you spend so much time doing it, you need to listen carefully and critically—grasping what is said and questioning and reacting to what you hear.

Becoming a Careful Listener

Did you know that you can process information faster than speakers can speak? As a result, your mind has time to wander while listening. Try using the following suggestions to maintain your attention in the classroom:

- **If you are easily distracted by sights and sounds, sit in the front of the room** so you can focus more easily on the speaker.
- **Take notes.** Writing will help focus and maintain your attention.
- **Try to anticipate the ideas the speaker will address next.** This activity keeps your mind active.
- **Sit comfortably but do not sprawl.** A serious posture puts your mind in gear for serious work.

- **Maintain eye contact with the speaker.** You will feel more personally involved and will be less likely to drift off mentally.
- **Avoid sitting among groups of friends.** You will be tempted to talk to or think about them, and you risk missing information that the speaker is presenting.

Listening Critically

In many classes, you are expected both to understand what the speaker is saying and also to respond to it. Here are a few suggestions for developing your critical-listening skills:

Maintain an open mind. It is easy to shut out ideas and opinions that do not conform to your values and beliefs. Try to avoid evaluating a message either positively or negatively until it is complete and understandable.

Avoid selective listening. Some listeners hear what they want to hear; they do not remember ideas with which they disagree. This is dangerous, since you may miss important points in a discussion. Make a deliberate attempt to understand the speaker's viewpoint, and distract yourself from disagreeing by taking notes or creating an informal outline of the speaker's main points.

Avoid oversimplification. When listening to difficult, unpleasant, emotional, or complex messages, it is tempting to simplify them by eliminating their details, reasons, and supporting evidence. For example, if you are listening to a speaker describe his or her wartime experiences in Iraq, the speaker's details may be unpleasant but are important to understanding his or her experience.

Focus on the message, not the speaker. Try not to be distracted by the speaker's clothing, mannerisms, speech patterns, or annoying quirks.

Exercise 1.10

Working with a classmate, identify at least five topics that you would need to listen to critically to avoid the pitfalls listed above.

Ask and Answer Questions

You can learn more from your classes if you develop or polish your questioning skills. This means asking questions when you need information and clarification, and answering questions posed by the instructor to demonstrate and evaluate your knowledge and express interest in the class. Use the following tips to strengthen your questioning and answering skills:

- **Conquer your fear of speaking in class.** Stop worrying what your friends and classmates will think: Speak out.
- **While reading an assignment, jot down questions as they occur to you.** Bring your list to class, and use it when your instructor invites questions.
- **Form your questions concisely.** Don't apologize for asking, and don't ramble.

- **Don't worry if your questions seem unimportant or silly.** Other students probably have the same questions but are reluctant to ask them.
- **Focus on critical questions.** Instead of asking factual questions, think about questions that focus on how the information can be used, how ideas fit together, how things work, what might be relevant problems and solutions, or what the long-term value and significance of the information are.
- **Think before responding.** When answering questions, try to compose your response before volunteering to answer.

Exercise 1.11

Working with a classmate, brainstorm a list of questions you could ask about the content presented in this chapter.

Work with Classmates

Many college assignments and class activities involve working with other students. For example, in this book, many chapters contain a box titled "Trying Out Your Ideas on Others" that asks you to work with other students. Group projects vary, and therefore your approach may vary depending on the discipline, the course, and the instructor. Some groups may be assembled to discuss problems; others may carry out an activity, such as examining a piece of writing; others may research a topic and present their findings.

Understanding the Purpose

Many students expect to learn from their instructors but do not realize they can learn from one another as well. Group projects enable students to share experiences, understand classmates' thinking, and evaluate new ideas and approaches to completing a task. For example, if you are working with several classmates to prepare a panel discussion, you may observe that different classmates approach the task differently. Some may begin by brainstorming about the topic; others may begin by asking questions; still others may start by reading about or researching the topic. To benefit most from group projects, be sure you understand the task and then analyze it. Ask yourself, "What can I learn from this?" You will get more out of an assignment if you are focused on outcomes.

Keeping Groups Functioning Effectively

Some students complain that group projects are time-consuming and often unproductive. If you feel that way about a project, take a leadership role and make it work. On the following page are some suggestions for making groups work more effectively.

Despite your best efforts and those of other group members, not all groups function effectively. Conflicts may arise; members may complain; a group member may not do his or her share. Since your grade on the project may depend on every other member's work, your best interests require you to address these problems quickly and effectively if they occur. Use the following suggestions to do so:

- If members miss meetings, offer to remind everyone of the time and place.
- Establish a more detailed timetable if the work is not getting done.

Do . . .	Don't . . .
Set a good example as a committed and productive group member.	Take a passive role by allowing others in the group to do the bulk of the planning and work.
Work with serious, energetic, and creative classmates, if you have a choice.	Work with people who will be easily distracted and less likely to get their work done.
As a group, decide on an action plan, distribute responsibilities, and establish a firm schedule.	Work haphazardly, so that some tasks do not get done and others are duplicated.
Stay focused on the project during group meetings.	Waste time by allowing group discussions to wander off topic or turn into a social situation.
Do the best work you can, and get it done on time, since each member's work affects the grade for the project.	Complain about your workload or hold up the group by completing your part late or insufficiently.
Assign tasks wisely and equitably in a way that best uses members' strengths.	Assign important preliminary tasks to a member who works slowly or is disorganized.
Address potential problems quickly.	Allow interpersonal problems or other conflicts to get in the way of productivity

- Offer to take on a greater share of the work if it will help get the assignment done.
- Ask questions that may stimulate unproductive members' ideas and interest.
- Suggest that uncommunicative members share their ideas in written form.
- Encourage the students who are causing the problem to propose solutions.

   If you are unable to resolve problems or conflicts, discuss them with your instructor.

Take Effective Notes in Class

To become a successful student, you also need to take careful notes on your classes and review those notes. Plan on reviewing notes at least once each week. Researchers have shown that most people retain far more information when they interact with it using more than one sense. For instance, if a student only listens to a lecture or discussion, he or she will probably forget most of it within a couple of weeks, well before the next exam. However, if a student takes accurate notes and reviews them regularly, then he or she is likely to retain the main points and supporting details needed to understand the concepts discussed in the class. Following are some useful note-taking tips:

- **Read assignments before the lecture.** Whenever possible, read any textbook material to which the lecture corresponds *before* the lecture. Familiarity with the topic will make note-taking easier.
- **Don't attempt to record everything.** Record only main ideas and key details. Avoid writing in complete sentences; instead use words and phrases. Develop a system of abbreviations, signs, and symbols, as well.
- **Pay attention to your instructor's cues to what is important.** These cues include repetition of points, changes in voice or rate of speech, listing or numbering of points, and the use of the chalkboard or visuals.
- **Avoid tape-recording the class.** Tapes takes too long to play back and encourage you to not pay full attention during class.
- **Don't plan to recopy hand-written notes.** Your time is valuable; recopying is time-consuming. You can better use the time reviewing and studying your notes.
- **Leave plenty of blank space in hand-written notes.** Use this space to fill in information you missed during the lecture or to add examples.
- **When you must miss a class, borrow notes from a classmate who you know is a good student.**
- **Review and study your notes immediately after the lecture.** While the class is still fresh in your mind, you can fill in missed information, clarify relationships, and add examples. If you wait a day or more, your memory of the class will fade. See below for a system that facilitates study of your notes.

Here are two of the most popular and efficient methods of taking notes on class lectures, discussions, and readings.

Two-Column Method

This note-taking method is valuable for all learners. Draw a vertical line from the top of a piece of paper to the bottom. The left-hand column should be about half as wide as the right-hand column.

In the wider, right-hand column, record ideas and facts as they are presented in a lecture or a discussion. In the narrower, left-hand column, note your own questions as they arise during the class. When you go home and review your notes, add summaries of major concepts and sections to the left-hand margin. This method allows you to quickly review an outline or overview of a lecture by reading the left-hand column and to study specific information and examples in the right-hand column. See the figure on the next page.

Modified Outline Method

The modified branch or outline method uses bullets for main ideas and dashes for detailed information within a section. The more detailed the information gets, the farther to the right you indent your outline entries.

Good note-taking is a hallmark of a successful student. It gets easier with practice, and developing your own symbols over time will help make note-taking quicker and more consistent for you. When you take good notes and review them regularly, you are replacing the inefficient and exhausting strategy of cramming for exams—a strategy that loads information into your memory only temporarily—with a system of learning that allows deeper, longer-term retention of information.

THE TWO-COLUMN METHOD OF NOTE-TAKING

Writing process	*Prewriting—taking notes, writing ideas, drawing a cluster diagram, researching, writing questions, noting what you already know, outlining, etc.*
	Writing—drafting
(How many drafts does the average writer complete?)	*Rewriting—revision = "to see again"*
	2 types: global = major rehaul (reconsidering, reorganizing)
	local = rewording, correcting grammar (editing for correctness & style)
NOT linear	*Writing is not a linear process. May go back to prewriting after writing, etc.*

THE MODIFIED OUTLINE METHOD OF NOTE-TAKING

Writing is a process.
- *Prewriting*
  - *Taking notes*
  - *Writing ideas*
  - *Drawing a cluster diagram*
  - *Researching*
  - *Writing questions*
  - *Noting what you already know*
  - *Outlining*
- *Writing*
  - *First drafts*
    - *On paper*
    - *On cards*
    - *On computer*
  - *Later drafts*
- *Rewriting, or revision (means "to see again")*
  - *Global*
    - *Major revision*
    - *Reconsidering ideas*
    - *Reorganizing*
  - *Local*
    - *Rewording for style*
    - *Rewriting for correct grammar, spelling, punctuation*

Note-Taking on Your Laptop

Some students use their laptops to take notes during class. The advantages of using a computer are that your notes are easy to read and can easily be edited, reorganized, and integrated with notes taken on reading assignments. However, carrying a laptop can be cumbersome, and you have to worry about its security. Also, because you can see only one screen of content at a time, you may not be able to see connections and logical progressions of ideas unless you print out your notes. If you do decide to take notes electronically, use the tips in the box below to make the process work for you.

Do . . .	**Don't . . .**
Make sure you can plug in your laptop or that you have sufficient battery power.	Allow distracting programs such as email and instant messaging to compete for your attention.
Set up a folder for each course. Create a separate file for each day's notes, and include the date of the lecture in naming the file.	Risk interrupting the class with annoying beeps and buzzes. Turn off the sound.
Save your document frequently so you don't lose anything.	
Keep a pen and paper handy to record diagrams, drawings, and other nonverbal material.	

Manage Online Courses Effectively

Online courses are growing in popularity. Although convenient, they require more self-direction and ability to work alone than traditional classes do. They also require a great deal of online writing, reading, and research. Here are some tips for succeeding in online courses:

- **Try to avoid taking online courses during your first term in college**. First learn what is expected in college courses by attending traditional classes. When you are familiar with college expectations, you will be better prepared to take an online course.
- **Set regular hours to devote to your online course.** Even if a class does not meet at a specified time, many students find it effective to build blocks of time into their weekly schedule for their online course. Otherwise, it becomes easy to put off classwork.
- **Keep up with the work.** Most students who fail online courses do so because they fall hopelessly behind on reading and assignments. Work on your online course several times each week, regardless of whether you have an assignment due.
- **Plan on doing a lot of reading.** You will read your textbooks, and you also will read communications from your professor and other students.
- **Maintain your concentration.** Turn off cell phone, music, IM, and email while working on your computer.
- **Make sure your online postings are serious and do not waste classmates' time.** Avoid complaining about the work.

CHAPTER 2

Writing in College

WRITING QUICK START

The photographs on the opposite page show several situations in which college students use writing. Brainstorm a list of other situations in which you use writing, such as on-the-job writing and personal writing. What did your list reveal about the importance of writing?

Most, if not all, college classes require some form of writing—exams, essays, journals, reports, and so forth. Strong writing skills are essential to college success, so the time and effort you spend in improving your writing skills are certainly worthwhile.

The main purpose of this chapter—and of this entire book—is to help you succeed in your writing class as well as in other classes that involve writing. In this chapter, you will learn what is expected of you as a college writer. You will learn about the importance of improving your writing skills and discover useful strategies for doing well in your writing class. This chapter will also help you learn and write more effectively by analyzing your learning style.

Academic Writing: What to Expect

In college you will probably do more writing than you did at previous educational levels. You will be expected to write in your writing class and in most other classes as well. Instructors consider writing a means of learning—not just a means of testing and evaluating what students have already learned. The following section explains what you can expect about writing in college.

Expect Your Writing to Move from More Personal to Less Personal

Much of your writing up to now may have been about yourself and your experiences. In college you can expect to write less about yourself and more about ideas. You will still often be asked to share your personal perspective when expressing ideas. For example, in a communications class you might write a film review. In other cases you will be writing to inform—to present information about a subject in an objective, nonpersonal way. For example, in a sociology class you might write an essay explaining what the 1.5 generation is. Or you may be writing to persuade—to convince your readers to think or act a certain way. For example, you might write an essay for your criminal justice class arguing that the penalties for drunk driving should be increased or a proposal to convince college officials that more security is needed on campus. In doing so, you might draw on your personal knowledge or experience, but you would need to depend mostly on objective evidence to persuade your readers. In general, therefore, you will find that in college much less writing is done in the first person (*I, me*) and much more is done in the third person (*it, they, he, she*). When given a writing assignment, make sure it is clear how much of your personal experience and personal opinion, if any, is appropriate for the assignment.

Expect Your Writing to Take Different Forms

In college you will write much more than essays and exam answers. Depending on your field of study, you may also be required to write in a variety of specialized *genres,* such as logs, case reports, abstracts, patient observation charts, and diagnostic evaluations. Each genre has its own set of conventions and expectations. A lab report is a good example. It has a specific purpose (to report the results of a laboratory experiment), follows a specific format (Introduction, Materials and Methods, Observation), has an expected style of writing (brief, factual, and concise), and uses technical and specialized language (names of instruments, names of chemicals, names of procedures).

As you encounter new genres, it is helpful to read samples written in that form. Be sure to ask questions so you understand exactly what your instructor expects.

Expect to Use the Language of the Discipline

Each academic discipline has its own language—words and phrases that are used only or primarily in that discipline. The words *photosynthesis* and *homeostasis,* for example, are used primarily in biology-related fields, and the words *allegory, symbolism,* and *mythology* are used in literary fields. When you write in a particular discipline, you are expected to use the language of that discipline. In doing so, the first step is to learn the language. See Chapter 3 for suggestions on learning vocabulary. When you write a paper, concentrate first on expressing your ideas, but as you revise, check to be sure you have used the appropriate language of the discipline.

Expect to Use Standard American English

Although nonstandard English (slang, incorrect grammar, misspellings) may be appropriate in some settings (such as informal conversation or text messages and emails to friends), you are expected to use standard, correct American English for academic writing. As you revise and proofread your writing, concentrate on correctness. Refer to a grammar handbook or consult an online writing resource that offers help with particular problems. You can also refer to Chapter 10 of this book (for help with sentence-level problems) and—unless you are using the Brief Edition—the handbook at the back of the book.

Expect to Use and Document Scholarly Sources

Although you have probably written research papers in high school, more college writing assignments will require you to use library or Internet sources to acquire needed information or to support your own ideas. Depending on the assignment, you will need to summarize, paraphrase (express in your own words), and quote the sources you use.

In college, writers are often required to use scholarly sources rather than popular sources such as newsstand magazines and personal Web sites. Scholarly sources are those written by experts in the field and published by professional organizations in the field. In many cases popular sources may not be appropriate because they may not offer expert, trustworthy opinion. In other cases they may not be sufficient: They may not offer enough detail or provide enough background information, for example. Chapters 21 and 22 of this book offer help in locating and using scholarly sources. Be sure to consult your reference librarian if you need additional help.

It is important in college writing to give credit to all sources that you use in your writing. This includes language that you quote and information that you borrow and express in your own words. Chapter 23 of this book will show you how to correctly document the sources you use.

Expect to Write and Research Online

Many college writing assignments involve online skills. Most instructors expect you to write your assignments, essays, and research papers on a computer. (If you are new to using a computer for writing, your college writing lab or computer lab may offer resources and advice to help you get started.) Some instructors may ask you to work online with a classmate on a piece of writing. You may also be asked to write about articles and essays that you find online, and some research paper or class discussion topics may require online research.

Expect to Collaborate with Classmates

More often than in high school, college instructors expect student writers to collaborate, or work together, on a piece of writing. Collaboration is a form of learning about a subject as well as a means of improving your writing by learning from others. In an environmental studies class, for example, you may be asked to work with classmates on a report on a local air-quality problem. Because collaboration on writing projects is expected in a wide variety of career fields, many instructors consciously build collaborative activities into their courses. To learn to collaborate successfully, refer to Chapter 9, p. 188.

Why Strive to Improve Your Writing Skills?

Most college students ask themselves the following two questions:

- How can I improve my grades?
- How can I improve my chances of getting a good job?

The answer to both questions is the same: Improve your writing, reading, and thinking skills. The following sections explain how these skills, especially writing, are essential to your success in college and on the job.

Writing Skills Help You Succeed in College and Career

College courses such as psychology, biology, and political science demand that you read articles, essays, reports, and textbooks and then react to and write about what you have read. In many courses, you demonstrate what you have learned by writing exams, reports, and papers.

Writing is important on the job, as well. In most jobs, workers need to communicate effectively with supervisors, coworkers, patients, clients, and customers. You can expect to write plenty of letters, email messages, memos, and reports. A study performed by the Collegiate Employment Research Institute found that employers consistently want the "total package" in recent college graduates. Employers want job candidates who have not only the technical knowledge to work but also strong oral and written communication skills.[*]

Because your writing course offers both immediate and long-range benefits, it is one of the most important college courses you will ever take. You will learn how to express your ideas clearly, structure convincing arguments, prepare research papers, and write essay exams. Your writing course will also help you improve your reading and thinking skills. As you read, respond to, and write about the readings, you will learn how to analyze, synthesize, and evaluate ideas.

---

[*] Betsy Stevens, "What Communication Skills Do Employers Want? Silicon Valley Recruiters Respond," *Journal of Employment Counseling* 42 (March 2005): 2–9.

Writing Helps You Learn and Remember Things

Taking notes, outlining, summarizing, or annotating focuses your attention on the course material and gets you thinking about the subject matter as you connect and define ideas. In addition, writing facilitates learning by engaging two senses at once. Whereas you take in information visually by reading or aurally by listening, writing engages your sense of touch as you put your pen to paper or your fingers on a keyboard. In general, the more senses you use in a learning task, the more easily learning occurs and the more you remember about the task later on. You can often remember something more easily if you write it down.

Writing Helps You Think More Clearly

Writing forces you to think through a task. Getting your ideas down on paper or on a computer screen helps you evaluate them. Writing, then, is a means of sorting ideas, exploring relationships, weighing alternatives, and clarifying values.

Writing Helps You Solve Problems

When you solve problems, you identify possible actions that may change undesirable situations (your car won't start) to desirable ones (your car starts). Writing makes problem solving easier by helping you define the problem. By describing the problem in writing, you can often see new aspects of it.

One student, for example, had a father-in-law who seemed hostile and uncooperative. The student described her problem in a letter to a friend: "He looks at me as if I'm going to take his son to the end of the earth and never bring him back." When she reread this statement, the student realized that her father-in-law might resent her because he was afraid of losing contact with his son. She began to think of ways to reassure her father-in-law and strengthen their relationship. Writing about the problem helped the student define it and discover ways to solve it. Similarly, writing can help you think through confusing situations and make difficult decisions.

Developing Strategies for Writing

Establishing a study area, planning your time, and using academic services such as the writing center are all strategies that will help you succeed in your courses. Other strategies will also make a big difference in your writing—starting with a positive attitude, keeping a journal, and planning to get the most out of conferences with your writing instructor.

Start with a Positive Attitude

You have the potential and ability to be a successful writer. To approach your writing course positively and to get the most out of it, use the following suggestions:

1. **Think of writing as a process.** Writing is not a single act of getting words down on paper. Instead, it is a series of steps—planning, organizing, drafting, revising, and editing and proofreading. In addition, most writers go back and forth among these steps. Chapters 5 to 10 cover these steps of the writing process.

2. **Be patient.** Writing is a skill that improves gradually. Don't expect to see dramatic differences in your writing immediately. As you draft and revise your essays, your writing will improve in small ways that build on one another.

3. **Expect writing to take time, often more time than you planned.** Realize, too, that on some days writing will be easier than on other days.

4. **Focus on learning.** When you are given a writing assignment, ask, "What can I learn from this?" As you learn more about your own writing process, write down your observations (see the section on journal writing on p. 32).

5. **Use the support and guidance available to you.** Your instructor, your classmates, and this book can all help you become a better writer. In Parts 3 and 4 of the text, Guided Writing Assignments will lead you, step by step, through each chapter assignment. You will find tips, advice, and alternative ways of approaching the assignment.

6. **Look for ideas in the readings.** The essays in this book have been chosen to spark your interest and to touch on current issues. Think of every assigned reading as an opportunity to learn about a topic that you might not otherwise have the time to read or think about. Chapter 3 provides instructions on active reading, and Chapter 4 provides strategies for reading critically and responding to text and visuals. Together, they will help you get the most out of your reading assignments.

7. **Attend all classes.** Writing is a skill, not a set of facts you can read about in a book; it is best learned through interactions with your instructor and classmates.

FIGURE 2.1 Excerpted Sample Syllabus for a College Writing Course

I. General Information

Course Title:	English Composition I
Prerequisite:	English 070 or placement test
Instructor:	John Gillam
Email:	gillam@indiana.edu

A good way to contact your instructor

Course Number:	ENG 161
Semester:	Fall
Phone:	(724) 555-7890
Office Hours	
& Location:	MWF 3–5
	English Department offices in Ryan Hall

Important: Be sure to use them.

II. Text

McWhorter, Kathleen T. *Successful College Writing*, 5th Edition. New York: Bedford, 2012.

III. General Course Objectives

1. The student will learn to organize his or her thoughts into a meaningful written work.

   Planning and organizing are expected.

Grammar is important.

2. The student will easily recognize grammar mistakes.
3. The student will be familiar with different types of writing.
4. The student will be able to use several different writing styles.

What you will be graded on

IV. Specific Course Objectives

1. The student will write papers using the following strategies: description, illustration, process analysis, comparison and contrast, classification and division, and cause and effect.

   Learn these strategies.

Correctness counts: Allow time for proofreading.

2. The student will edit and proofread for errors in grammar, punctuation, mechanics, and spelling.

Read assign- ·············· 3. The student will be tested on reading comprehension.
ments carefully.   4. The student will write a research paper using appropriate documentation.
                    5. The student will critically analyze readings that use specific writing strategies.
Learn about   6. The student will use the Internet as a tool for research.
documentation.

V. Classroom Procedures

Attendance is ··········· *Absences*: The student is responsible for attendance. Attendance affects perfor-
essential.   mance, and all students are expected to take part in class discussions and peer-
                        review editing sessions. Each student is expected to be present and is responsible
                        for class notes and assignments. If absent, the student is responsible for arranging
                        an appointment with the instructor to discuss the notes and assignments missed.

                        Format for papers: Papers must be typed double-spaced using a 12-point font.   Keep a copy of
                        Be sure to keep a copy of each assignment for yourself.   assignments.

VI. Disability Statement

If you need to have special arrangements made due to a physical or learning   Don't hesitate to
disability, please notify the instructor as soon as possible. (Disclosure of the   ask for needed
type of disability is not required.)   services.

VII. Grading

All papers must be turned in on the due date. Late papers will be lowered   Meeting deadlines
one letter grade. No papers will be accepted after the last day of class. If you   is essential.
do not understand the grade assigned to a paper, <u>see me immediately</u>. You are
encouraged to save all papers in a folder to enable you to keep track of progress   The instructor
and compute your own grade.   encourages
                                                                                     questions.

VIII. Tentative Schedule

Week of Sept. 5:   Course Introduction   Read these
                    Ch. 1 (Succeeding in College)   chapters the
                    Ch. 2 (Writing in College)   first week. Your
                                                                                     instructor may
Week of Sept. 12:   Writing Assessments   not remind you of
                    Ch. 3 (Reading in College)   reading assign-
                    Ch. 4 (Responding Critically to Text and Images)   ments, so check
                    Ch. 5 (Prewriting)   the syllabus
                                                                                     weekly.
Week of Sept. 19:   Ch. 7 (Drafting an Essay)
                    Ch. 11 (Narration)
                    Draft of Essay #1 due

Week of Sept. 26:   Ch. 13 (Illustration)   Assignment
                    Draft of Essay #2 due   due dates

Use Your Course Syllabus

The syllabus is the most important document you will receive in your first week of class. Some instructors place the syllabus on the course's Web site as well. A syllabus usually describes how the course operates. It includes information on the required texts, attendance policy, grading system, course objectives, weekly assignments or readings, due dates of papers, and dates of exams. Think of a syllabus as a course guide or course planner that directs you through your writing class. Examine the accompanying excerpt from a sample syllabus illustrating how an instructor might organize a writing course.

A course syllabus can be prepared in various styles. Some instructors prefer to use a weekly format for a syllabus and then give specific assignments in class. The sample syllabus in Figure 2.1 is formatted this way. Some instructors avoid dates by using a general outline of assignments and requirements and then craft the assignment schedule as the class masters each topic. Still other instructors prefer a highly structured syllabus that lists daily assignments as well as required readings, long-term writing assignments, and group work. Whatever format the syllabus takes, read it carefully at the beginning of the course, and check it regularly so that you are prepared for class. Mark all deadlines on your calendar. Ask your instructor any questions you may have about the syllabus, course structure, deadlines, and his or her expectations about course objectives. Note his or her answers on your syllabus or in your course notebook.

Pay particular attention to the course objectives section of the syllabus, where your instructor states what he or she expects you to learn in the course. Objectives also provide clues about what the instructor feels is important and how he or she views the subject matter. Since the course objectives state what you are expected to learn, papers and exams will measure how well you have met these objectives.

Make a copy of each course syllabus. Keep one syllabus in the front of your notebook for easy reference during class or while you are studying. Keep another syllabus in a file folder at home in case you lose your notebook on campus.

Exercise 2.1   Getting the Most from Your Syllabus

Review the syllabus that your writing class instructor distributed. Write a paragraph describing your expectations and concerns about your writing course based on the syllabus. Be sure to include information on the questions listed below. If the syllabus does not contain the information, consult your college catalog for general policies and your instructor for specific questions.

1. What are you expected to learn in the course?
2. What kinds of essays will you write?
3. What are the grading and attendance policies?
4. Is class participation expected and required? Is it part of your grade?
5. Is research required? Is Internet use required or expected?

Use the Right Writing Tools

How often do you need to look up a word in a dictionary? Have you ever used an online dictionary? (If not, visit www.m-w.com.) Do you prefer using a hard-bound or an online dictionary? Each has its advantages, and which dictionary you use depends on your purpose and your personal preferences.

To be successful in college, you will need the right learning tools. Your textbooks are essential, but you will also need quick access to other sources of information. Be sure you have each of the following handy in your writing and study area:

- The URL of an online dictionary (such as www.merriam-webster.com for the Merriam-Webster Dictionary, shown on the next page)
- A reliable hard-bound collegiate dictionary, such as *Merriam-Webster's Collegiate Dictionary* or *Webster's New World Dictionary*
- A paper-bound pocket dictionary to carry to class or to the library
- A thesaurus (dictionary of synonyms), such as *Roget's Thesaurus.* You may have a thesaurus as part of your word-processing program.

- The URLs of Internet search engines. See Chapter 22, pages 604–5, for suggestions.
- The URL of an online reference desk, such as www.refdesk.com, for factual information
- CDs or USBs for saving and transporting your work
- Classmates' and instructors' email addresses
- Specialized accessories your classes may require, such as a graphing calculator or a foreign language dictionary

Exercise 2.2

Record below the online reference sources that you have found useful or helpful. Compare your list with lists of other students, and add any sources that seem useful to your list.

Online Reference Sources

1.

2.

3.

4.

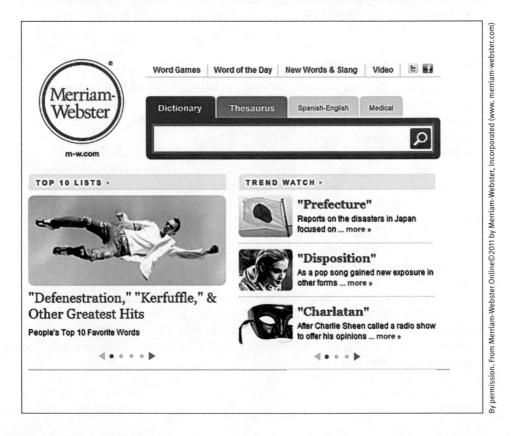

Use the College Writing Center

Many colleges have a writing center that offers individualized help with any college writing assignment—not just assignments for your writing class. The center uses student tutors as well as professional staff to help you; some centers offer online tutorial services as well. Some function on a walk-in basis; others require an appointment. Computers may be available for your use as well.

You can expect the writing center staff to help you with an assignment, but do not expect them to write your paper for you or to correct all of its errors. The staff can help you understand an assignment, come up with ideas, organize your ideas, revise, use appropriate format and documentation, and understand errors on a graded paper.

When you visit the writing center, be sure to bring your assignment, all drafts of your essay, and any articles or essays to which the assignment refers. Also bring paper and pen or pencil.

Keep a Writing Journal

Use a **writing journal** in either a notebook or a computer file to record daily impressions, reflect on events or on reading assignments, comment on experiences and observations, explore relationships among people or ideas, ask questions, and test ideas. You should write in your journal frequently—every day if possible.

Benefits of Journal Writing

- **A journal is a place to practice.** Writing can best be improved through practice. Record conversations, summarize or react to experiences, or release frustrations. Remember, regardless of what you write about, you are writing and thereby improving your skills.
- **A journal is a place to experiment.** Try out new ideas and express things that you are learning about yourself—your beliefs and values. Experiment with different voices, different topics, and different approaches to a topic.
- **A journal is a place to warm up.** Like an athlete, a writer benefits from warming up. Use a journal to activate your thought processes, loosen up, and stretch your mind before you tackle your writing assignments.
- **A journal is a place to reflect on your writing.** Record problems, strategies you have learned, and ways to start assignments. You might also find it helpful to keep an error log and a misspelled word log.
- **A journal is a source of ideas.** If you are asked to choose your own topic for an essay, leaf through your journal. You'll find plenty of possibilities.
- **A journal is a place to respond to readings.** Use it to collect your thoughts about a reading before writing an assigned essay. (You will learn more about response journals in Chapter 3.)

How to Get Started

Your first journal entry is often the most difficult one to write. Once you've written a few entries, you'll begin to feel more comfortable. Here's how to get started.

1. **Write in a spiral-bound notebook or create a computer file.** Be sure to date each entry.
2. **Set aside five to ten minutes each day for journal writing.** "Waiting times" at the bus stop, at the laundromat, or in long lines provide opportunities for journal writing, as do "down times," such as the ten minutes before a class begins or the few minutes between finishing dinner and studying.
3. **Concentrate on capturing your ideas—not on being grammatically correct.** Try to write correct sentences, but do not focus on grammar and punctuation.
4. **If you are not sure what to write about, consult Figure 2.2 (p. 34).** Coding your entries as shown in the figure will make you more aware of your thought processes and help you distinguish different types of entries.
5. **Reread your journal entries on a regular basis.** By doing so, you will discover that rereading entries is similar to looking at old photographs: They bring back vivid snippets of the past for reflection and appreciation.

> **Writing Activity 1**
> Write a journal entry describing your reaction to one or more of your classes this semester. For example, you might write about which classes you expect to be most or least difficult, most or least enjoyable, and most or least time-consuming.

Get the Most out of Writing Conferences

Many writing instructors schedule periodic writing conferences with individual students. These conferences are designed to give you and your instructor an opportunity to discuss your work and your progress in the course. Such conferences are opportunities for you to get help with your writing skills. If the conferences are optional, be sure to schedule one.

The following tips will help you get the most out of a writing conference:

1. **Arrive on time or a few minutes early.**
2. **Bring copies of the draft essay you are currently working on as well as previously returned papers.** Have them in hand, not buried in your backpack, when your conference begins.
3. **Reread recently returned papers ahead of time,** so that your instructor's comments are fresh in your mind. Review your notes from any previous conferences.
4. **Allow your instructor to set the agenda,** but come prepared with a list of questions you need answered.
5. **Take notes, either during or immediately after the conference.** Include the comments and suggestions offered by your instructor. You might also consider writing a journal entry that summarizes the conference.
6. **Revise the draft essay you and your instructor discussed as soon as possible,** while the suggestions for revision you received are still fresh in your mind.

FIGURE 2.2 Starting Points for Journal Writing

Codes for Your Journal Entries	Type of Writing	Ideas for Subjects
〈 〉	Describing	a daily event a sporting event an object a cartoon or photograph an overheard conversation
!!	Reacting to	a person a world, national, local, or campus event a passage from a book a magazine or newspaper article a film, song, or concert a television program a radio personality a fashion or fad
←	Recollecting	an important event a childhood experience an impression or a dream a favorite relative or friend
?	Questioning	a policy a trend a position on an issue
↔	Comparing or contrasting	two people two events or actions two issues
ex	Thinking of examples of	a personality type a type of teacher, supervisor, or doctor
+ −	Judging (evaluating)	a rule or law a decision a musician or another performer an assignment a radio or television personality a political candidate

Assessing Your Learning Style

Each person learns and writes in a unique way, depending in part on his or her experiences, personality, and prior learning. Discovering your learning style will give you an important advantage in your writing course and in your other courses. In this section and the following one, you will assess how you learn by using a Learning Style Inventory. You will learn specific strategies to learn more effectively, capitalizing on your strengths and overcoming your weaknesses.

What Is Your Learning Style?

Have you noticed that you do better with some types of academic assignments than with others? Hands-on assignments may be easier than conducting research, for example. Have you discovered that it is easier to learn from some instructors than from others? You may prefer instructors who give plenty of real-life examples or those who show relationships by drawing diagrams. Have you noticed differences in how you and your friends study, solve problems, and approach assignments? You may be methodical and analytical, whereas a friend may get flashes of insight. You may be able to read printed information and recall it easily, but a friend may find it easier to learn from class lectures or a videotape. Have you noticed that some students prefer to work alone on a project, while others enjoy working as part of a group?

These differences can be explained by what is known as **learning style**, or the set of preferences that describes how you learn. The Learning Style Inventory in the box below is intended to help you assess your learning style. After you have completed the Learning Style Inventory, you'll find directions for scoring on page 38.

LEARNING STYLE INVENTORY

Directions: Each numbered item presents two choices. Select the one alternative that best describes you. There are no right or wrong answers. In cases in which neither choice suits you, select the one that is closer to your preference. Check the letter of your choice next to the question number on the answer sheet on page 38.

1. In a class, I usually
   a. make friends with just a few students.
   b. get to know many of my classmates.
2. If I were required to act in a play, I would prefer to
   a. have the director tell me how to say my lines.
   b. read my lines the way I think they should be read.
3. Which would I find more helpful in studying the processes by which the U.S. Constitution can be amended?
   a. a one-paragraph summary
   b. a diagram

4. In making decisions, I am more concerned with
   a. whether I have all the available facts.
   b. how my decision will affect others.

5. When I have a difficult time understanding how something works, it helps most if I can
   a. see how it works several times.
   b. take time to think the process through and analyze it.

6. At a social event, I usually
   a. wait for people to speak to me.
   b. initiate conversation with others.

7. I prefer courses that have
   a. a traditional structure (lectures, assigned readings, periodic exams, and assignments with deadlines).
   b. an informal structure (class discussions, flexible assignments, and student-selected projects).

8. If I were studying one of the laws of motion in a physics course, I would prefer to have my instructor begin the class by
   a. stating the law and discussing examples.
   b. giving a demonstration of how the law works.

9. Which set of terms best describes me?
   a. fair and objective
   b. sympathetic and understanding

10. When I learn something new, I am more interested in
    a. the facts about it.
    b. the principles behind it.

11. As a volunteer for a community organization that is raising funds for a hospice, I prefer the following tasks.
    a. stuffing envelopes for a mail campaign
    b. making phone calls asking for contributions

12. I would begin an ideal day by
    a. planning what I want to do during each hour of the day.
    b. doing whatever comes to mind.

13. If I wanted to learn the proper way to prune a rosebush, I would prefer to
    a. have someone explain it to me.
    b. watch someone do it.

14. It is more important for me to be
    a. consistent in thought and action.
    b. responsive to the feelings of others.

15. If I kept a journal or diary, it would most likely contain entries about
    a. what happens to me each day.
    b. the insights and ideas that occur to me each day.

16. If I decided to learn a musical instrument, I would prefer to take
    a. one-on-one lessons.
    b. group lessons.

17. If I worked in a factory, I would prefer to be a
    a. machine operator.
    b. troubleshooter.
18. I learn best when I
    a. write down the information.
    b. form a mental picture of the information.
19. If I gave a wrong answer in class, my main concern would be
    a. finding out the correct answer.
    b. what others in class thought of me.
20. I prefer television news programs that
    a. summarize events through film footage and factual description.
    b. deal with the issues behind the events.
21. Whenever possible, I choose to
    a. study alone.
    b. study with a group.
22. In selecting a topic for a research paper, my more important concern is
    a. choosing a topic for which there is adequate information.
    b. choosing a topic I find interesting.
23. To help me reassemble a complicated toy or machine I took apart to repair, I would
    a. write a list of the steps I followed when taking the toy or machine apart.
    b. draw a diagram of the toy or machine.
24. As a member of a jury for a criminal trial, I would be primarily concerned with
    a. determining how witness testimony fits with the other evidence.
    b. judging the believability of witnesses.
25. If I were an author, I would most likely write
    a. biographies or how-to books.
    b. novels or poetry.
26. A career in which my work depends on that of others is
    a. less appealing than working alone.
    b. more appealing than working alone.
27. When I am able to solve a problem, it is usually because I
    a. worked through the solution step by step.
    b. brainstormed until I arrived at a solution.
28. I prefer to keep up with the news by
    a. reading a newspaper.
    b. watching television news programs.
29. If I witnessed a serious auto accident, my first impulse would be to
    a. assess the situation.
    b. comfort any injured people.
30. I pride myself on my ability to
    a. remember numbers and facts.
    b. see how ideas are related.
31. To solve a personal problem, I prefer to
    a. think about it myself.
    b. talk it through with friends.

32. If I had one last elective course to take before graduation, I would choose one that presents
    a. practical information that I can use immediately.
    b. ideas that make me think and stimulate my imagination.

33. For recreation, I would rather do a
    a. crossword puzzle.
    b. jigsaw puzzle.

34. I can best be described as
    a. reasonable and levelheaded.
    b. sensitive and caring.

35. When I read a story or watch a film, I prefer one with a plot that is
    a. clear and direct.
    b. intricate and complex.

Answer Sheet

Directions: Check either *a* or *b* in the boxes next to each question number.

Column One			Column Two			Column Three			Column Four			Column Five		
	a	*b*		*a*	*b*		*a*	*b*		*a*	*b*		*a*	*b*
1			2			3			4			5		
6			7			8			9			10		
11			12			13			14			15		
16			17			18			19			20		
21			22			23			24			25		
26			27			28			29			30		
31			32			33			34			35		
Total														

Directions for Scoring

1. On your answer sheet, add the checkmarks in each *a* and *b* column, counting first the number of *a*s checked and then the number of *b*s.

2. Enter the number of *a*s and *b*s you checked in the boxes at the bottom of each column.

3. Transfer these numbers to the Scoring Grid on page 39. Enter the number of *a* choices in column one in the blank labeled "Independent," the number of *b* choices in column one in the blank labeled "Social," and so on.

4. Circle your higher score in each row. For example, if you scored 2 for Independent and 5 for Social, circle "5" and "Social."

5. Your higher score in each row indicates a characteristic of your learning style. If the scores in a particular row are close to one another, such as 3 and 4, this suggests that you do not have a strong preference for either approach to learning. Scores that are far apart, such as 1 and 6, suggest that you favor one way of learning over the other.

Interpreting Your Scores

The Learning Style Inventory is divided into five parts; each question in the inventory assesses one of five aspects of your learning style. Here is how to interpret the five aspects of your learning style.

Scoring Grid

Column	Number of Checkmarks	
	Choice *a*	Choice *b*
One	_____ Independent	_____ Social
Two	_____ Pragmatic	_____ Creative
Three	_____ Verbal	_____ Spatial
Four	_____ Rational	_____ Emotional
Five	_____ Concrete	_____ Abstract

1. Independent or Social

These scores indicate the level of interaction with others that you prefer. *Independent* learners prefer to work and study alone. They focus on the task at hand rather than on the people around them and are often goal oriented and self-motivated. *Social* learners are more people oriented and prefer to learn and study with classmates. They often focus their attention on those around them and see a task as an opportunity for social interaction.

2. Pragmatic or Creative

These scores suggest how you prefer to approach learning tasks. *Pragmatic* learners are practical and systematic. They approach tasks in an orderly, sequential manner. They like rules and learn step by step. *Creative* learners, in contrast, approach tasks imaginatively. They prefer to learn through discovery or experiment. They enjoy flexible, open-ended tasks and tend to dislike following rules.

3. Verbal or Spatial

These scores indicate the way you prefer to take in and process information. *Verbal* learners rely on language, usually written text, to acquire information. They are skilled in the use of language and can work with other symbol systems as well. *Spatial* learners prefer to take in information by studying graphics such as drawings, diagrams, films, or videos. They can visualize in their minds how things work or how things are positioned in space.

4. Rational or Emotional

These scores suggest your preferred approach to decision making and problem solving. *Rational* learners are objective and impersonal; they rely on facts and information when making decisions or solving problems. Rational learners are logical, often challenging or questioning a task. They enjoy prioritizing, analyzing, and arguing. In contrast, *emotional* learners are subjective; they focus on feelings and values. Emotional decision makers are socially conscious and often concerned with what others think. In making a decision, they seek harmony and may base a decision in part on its effect on others. Emotional decision makers are often skilled at persuasion.

5. Concrete or Abstract

These scores indicate how you prefer to perceive information. *Concrete* learners pay attention to what is concrete and observable. They focus on details and tend to perceive tasks in parts or steps. Concrete learners prefer actual, tangible tasks and usually take a no-nonsense approach to learning. *Abstract* learners look at a task from a broader perspective. They tend to focus on the "big picture" or an overview of a task. Abstract learners focus on large ideas, meanings, and relationships.

A Word about Your Findings

The results of the Learning Style Inventory probably confirmed some things you already knew about yourself as a learner and provided you with some new insights as well. Keep in mind, though, that there are other ways to measure learning style.

- The inventory you completed is an informal measure of your learning style. Other, more formal measures—including Kolb's *Learning Style Inventory,* the *Canfield Instructional Styles Inventory,* and the *Myers-Briggs Type Indicator*—may be available at your college's counseling or academic skills center.
- The inventory you completed measures the five aspects of learning style that are most relevant to the writing process. However, many other aspects of learning style exist.
- You are the best judge of the accuracy of the results of this inventory and how they apply to you. If you think that one or more of the aspects of your learning style indicated by the inventory do not describe you, trust your instincts.

How to Use Your Findings

Now that you have identified important characteristics of your learning style, you are ready to use the findings to your advantage—to make learning easier and improve your writing skills. As you do so, keep the following suggestions in mind:

1. **If you have a strength in one area, you can still act in the opposite way.** For example, if you scored highly on the pragmatic scale, you are still capable of creative thinking.

2. **Learning style tendencies are not fixed, unchangeable characteristics.** Although you may have a higher score on the independent scale, for example, you can learn to function effectively in groups.

3. **Experiment with approaches that are not necessarily suited to your learning style.** Some students find that when they try a new approach, it works better than they expected. A verbal learner, for example, may discover that drawing a diagram of how a process works is an effective learning strategy.

4. **Learning style is not an excuse to avoid learning.** Don't make the mistake of saying, "I can't write poetry because I'm not a creative learner." Instead, use what you know about your learning style to guide your approach to each task. If you are a pragmatic learner, try writing a poem about a tangible object or place or a real event.

Applying Your Learning Style to Your Writing

Writing is a process that involves planning, organizing, drafting, revising, editing, and proofreading. You'll learn more about each of these steps in Chapters 5 to 10. Each step in the writing process can be approached in more than one way. For example, one of the first steps is to select a topic to write about. A social learner may prefer to brainstorm about possible topics with a friend. A verbal learner may find that flipping through a news magazine brings topics to mind. A spatial learner may see a photograph that generates ideas for topics. Someone who is a social as well as a spatial learner may prefer to discuss photographs with a classmate.

Let's consider an example involving two hypothetical students. Yolanda and Andrea, classmates in a first-year writing course, are assigned to write an essay describing an event that has influenced their lives. Yolanda writes a list of possible events and arranges them in order of importance in her life. After selecting one of these events, she draws a diagram showing the circumstances that led up to the event and the effects that the event had on her. Before she begins writing, Yolanda decides on the best way to organize her ideas and creates an outline.

Andrea lets her mind roam freely over various events in her life while she is out jogging. All of a sudden an idea comes to mind, and she knows what she wants to write about. She jots down everything she can recall about the event, in the haphazard order that each remembered detail comes to her. From these notes, she selects ideas and writes her first draft. Andrea writes numerous drafts, experimenting with different organizations. Finally, she produces an essay with which she is satisfied.

Although Yolanda and Andrea approach the same assignment in different ways, they both write effective essays. Yolanda prefers a deliberate and systematic approach because she is a pragmatic learner. Andrea, a creative learner, prefers a less structured approach. Yolanda spends a great deal of time planning before writing, while Andrea prefers to experiment with various versions of her paper.

Because students' learning styles differ, this book presents alternative strategies for generating ideas and for revising your writing. These choices are indicated by the marginal note "Learning Style Options" (see p. 78 for an example). The following advice will help you take advantage of these learning style alternatives:

1. **Select an alternative that fits with how you learn.** If you are writing an essay on insurance fraud and are given the choice of interviewing an expert on insurance fraud or finding several articles in the library on the topic, choose the option that best suits the way you prefer to acquire information.
2. **Experiment with options.** To sustain your interest and broaden your skills, you should sometimes choose an option that does not match your preferred learning style. For example, if you are an independent learner, interviewing the insurance fraud expert may help you strengthen your interpersonal skills.
3. **Don't expect the option that is consistent with your learning style to require less attention or effort.** Even if you are a social learner, an interview must still be carefully planned and well executed.
4. **Keep logs of the skills and approaches that work for you and the ones you need to work on.** The logs may be part of your writing journal (see p. 32). Be specific: Record the assignment, the topic you chose, and the skills you applied. Analyze your log, looking for patterns. Over time, you will discover more about the writing strategies and approaches that work best for you.

Your learning style profile also indicates your strengths as a writer. As with any skill, you should try to build on your strengths, using them as a foundation. Work with Figure 2.3 (p. 43) to identify your strengths. First circle or highlight the characteristics that you scored higher on in the five areas of learning style. Then refer to the right-hand column to see your strengths as a writer in each area.

Writing Activity 2
Write a two-page essay describing your reactions to the results of the Learning Style Inventory. Explain how you expect to use the results in your writing course or other courses.

Writing Activity 3
Using your responses to the Writing Quick Start on page 23 and the results of the Learning Style Inventory, write a two-page profile of yourself as a student or as a writer.

FIGURE 2.3 Your Strengths as a Writer

Learning Style Characteristic	Strengths as a Writer
Independent	You are willing to spend time thinking about a topic and are able to pull ideas together easily.
Social	You usually find it easy to write from experience. Writing realistic dialogue may be one of your strengths. You tend to have a good sense of whom you are writing for (your audience) and what you hope to accomplish (your purpose).
Pragmatic	You can meet deadlines easily. You recognize the need for organization in an essay. You tend to approach writing systematically and work through the steps in the writing process.
Creative	You tend to enjoy exploring a topic and often do so thoroughly and completely. Your writing is not usually hindered or restricted by rules or requirements.
Verbal	You may have a talent for generating ideas to write about and expressing them clearly.
Spatial	You can visualize or draw a map of the organization of your paper. Descriptions of physical objects, places, and people come easily.
Rational	You tend to write logically developed, well-organized essays. You usually analyze ideas objectively.
Emotional	Expressive and descriptive writing usually go well for you. You have a strong awareness of your audience.
Concrete	You find it easy to supply details to support an idea. You are able to write accurate, detailed descriptions and observations. You can organize facts effectively and present them clearly.
Abstract	You can develop unique approaches to a topic; you can grasp the point to which supporting ideas lead.

CHAPTER 3

Reading in College

Your Mass Communication instructor has asked your class to study the photograph on the opposite page and discuss its meaning.

Write a paragraph explaining what the photograph suggests to you about mass communication and why the instructor might have asked you to study it. Be detailed and specific. Study the photograph's content, and then try to discover what statement it makes about communication.

To explain the meaning of the photograph, you had to think beyond the obvious action it portrays. You had to interpret and evaluate the photograph to arrive at its possible meaning. To complete this evaluation, you did two things. First, you grasped what the photograph showed; then you analyzed what it meant.

Reading involves a similar process of comprehension and evaluation. First, you must know what the author *says;* then you must interpret and respond to what the author *means.* Both parts of the process are essential. This chapter will help you succeed with both parts of the reading process.

In this chapter, you will learn to be a more active reader, a reader who becomes engaged and involved with a reading assignment by analyzing, challenging, and evaluating ideas. The chapter contains a Guide to Active Reading (p. 48) in which you will learn what to do before, during, and after reading to strengthen your comprehension and increase your recall. You will also learn how to approach difficult assignments and how to draw a diagram, called a *graphic organizer,* that will help you grasp both the content and the organization of an assignment. In the next chapter, you will find guidelines for thinking and reading critically, interpreting visuals, and responding to text. As you improve your ability to read and respond thoroughly and carefully, you'll learn more about what you read. You'll also do better on exams and quizzes that ask you to apply, connect, and evaluate ideas.

Getting Started

Becoming an active reader involves developing new skills, as well as changing any misconceptions you may have about reading in college.

Reading for Success

Reading skill is essential for college success. In some ways, it is a hidden skill, because when you think of college success, what probably comes to mind is attending classes, writing papers, and studying for and taking exams. A closer look at each of these activities reveals, however, that reading is involved in each task. It is the primary means through which you acquire ideas and gather information. To use reading as a tool for success, use the following suggestions:

- **Assume responsibility for reading assignments.** In college, you can expect instructors to offer you less help with your reading assignments. They won't remind you to do them, and they often won't check to see if you are keeping up with them. It is tempting to let them go undone, especially when you are pressured to complete other work. Use the time-management suggestions in Chapter 1 (pp. 5–7) to build in time each week to complete all assignments. Instructors will assume that you are keeping up with reading assignments and that you are learning the material as you do. Most instructors won't tell you *how* to learn it, either. Consequently, you will have to learn how best to learn each subject. Experiment with different methods—taking notes on assignments, preparing study sheets that summarize important information, highlighting (see pp. 55–56), outlining (see Chapter 7), and annotating (see p. 56).
- **Think and read critically.** Most students expect to learn and memorize information, but in college, reading and understanding the literal content of reading assignments is often not enough. You must go beyond what an article or essay *says* and focus on what

it *means*. You also need to think about how true, useful, and important the information is. Instructors expect you to interpret, evaluate, and respond to the ideas you have read about. They expect you to read and think critically, questioning and challenging ideas as you encounter them. To develop your critical-thinking skills, pay particular attention to the Strategies for Critical Thinking and Reading in Chapter 4 (pp. 68–77) and to the section in Chapters 11–19 titled "Thinking Critically About . . . ."

- **Pay attention to visuals.** Much of what you read will be accompanied by visuals, including drawings, photographs, charts, graphs, and so forth. Writers use these to clarify or emphasize ideas, condense information, explain a complicated process, or illustrate a particular viewpoint. Get used to thinking about the purpose of a visual and the way that it relates to the text that accompanies it. For more on visuals, see Interpreting Visuals in Chapter 4 (pp. 77–86).

- **Adapt your reading skills to different materials.** In college, you will encounter a wide range of materials, and you will be expected to read each skillfully. In addition to reading textbooks, you may read articles, essays, critiques, field reports, scientific studies, and Internet sources. You will need to use different strategies for reading each type of material. For each type, begin by noticing how it is organized and what its purpose might be. Then, devise a strategy for identifying what is important to learn and remember about it.

- **Polish your vocabulary skills.** An extensive vocabulary is a powerful tool and is essential to effective written and oral communication. Don't be satisfied with your current repertoire of words. Notice words; keep track of new ones you encounter by creating a vocabulary log or computer file. Look for new ways in which familiar words are used. Use these new words and new meanings as soon as possible, so they become part of your active vocabulary.

- **Use reading to help you write.** By studying the writing of others, you can improve your own writing. As you read an article, essay, or textbook assignment, take note of the writer's techniques. For example, notice how the writer organizes paragraphs, how he or she uses language to express ideas, and how ideas are developed throughout the work.

Avoiding Misconceptions

Much misinformation exists about how to read effectively and efficiently. This section dispels some popular misconceptions about reading.

- **Not everything on a page or a screen is equally important.** Whether you are reading an article in an online sports magazine, a biography of a president, or an essay in this book, each text contains a mixture of important and not-so-important ideas and information. Your task as a reader is to sort through the material and evaluate what you need to know.

- **You should not read everything the same way.** Your purpose affects what you read, how rapidly and how carefully you read, what you pay attention to, and what (if anything) you skip. For instance, if your psychology instructor assigns an article from *Psychology Today* as a basis for class discussion, you would read it differently than if you were preparing for a quiz based on the article. Your familiarity with a

For more on how to read selectively by scanning and skimming, see Working with Text: Reading Sources in Chapter 21 (pp. 592–93).

topic also affects how you read. Effective readers vary their reading techniques to suit what they are reading and why they are reading it.

- **Reading material once is often not sufficient.** In many academic situations, you will need to read chapters, articles, or essays more than once to discover the author's position, summarize the author's key ideas, and analyze the strength of the supporting evidence that he or she provides.
- **Not everything in print or online is true.** Just as you don't believe everything you hear, neither should you believe everything you read. Be sure to read with a critical, questioning eye and, at times, with a raised eyebrow. To evaluate a text, consider the authority of the author and the author's purpose for writing. As you read, try to distinguish facts from opinions, value judgments, and generalizations. If you were to read an article titled "Woman Loses Thirty Pounds in One Week," for example, your critical, questioning eye would probably be wide open. Be sure to keep that eye open when you read scholarly essays as well.

A GUIDE TO ACTIVE READING

When you attend a ball game or watch a soap opera, do you get actively involved? Baseball fans cheer some players and criticize others, evaluate plays and calls, offer advice, and so forth. Similarly, soap-opera fans get actively involved in their favorite programs—reacting to sudden turns of events, sympathizing with some characters, and despising others. By contrast, if you are not a fan of a baseball team or soap opera, you might watch the game or show passively, letting it take its course with little or no personal involvement or reaction. Like fans of a sports team or soap opera, active readers get involved with the material they read. They question, think about, and react to ideas using the process outlined in Figure 3.1.

The chart on page 50 shows how active and passive readers approach a reading assignment in different ways. As you can see, active readers get involved by using a step-by-step approach. The sections that follow explain each of these active reading steps in more detail.

Before Reading

Never start reading an essay or other reading assignment without preparation. Your mind isn't ready. Instead, use previewing and guide questions to discover what the reading is about and focus your mind on the topic.

Preview

Previewing is a quick way to familiarize yourself with an essay's content and organization. Previewing enables you to decide what you need to know from the material, and it has a number of other benefits as well:

- It helps you get interested in the material.
- It enables you to concentrate more easily on the material because you have a mental outline of it before you read and know what to expect.
- It helps you remember more of what you read.

FIGURE 3.1 The Active Reading Process

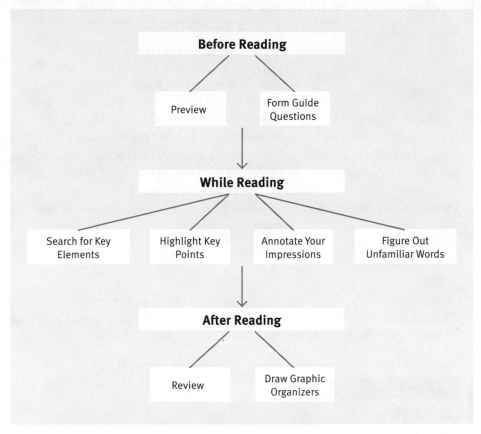

To preview a reading assignment, use the guidelines in the following list. Remember to read *only* the parts of an essay that are listed.

1. **Read the title, subtitle, and author.** The title and subtitle may tell you what the reading is about. Check the author's name to see if it is one you recognize.
2. **Read the introduction or the first paragraph.** These sections often provide an overview of the essay.
3. **Read any headings and the first sentence following each one.** Headings, taken together, often form a mini-outline of the essay. The first sentence following a heading often explains the heading further.
4. **For an essay without headings, read the first sentence in a few of the paragraphs on each page.**
5. **Look at any photographs, tables, charts, and drawings.**
6. **Read the conclusion or summary.** A conclusion will draw the reading to a close. If the reading concludes with a summary, it will give you a condensed view of the reading.
7. **Read any end-of-assignment questions.** These questions will help focus your attention on what is important in the reading and on what you might be expected to know after you have read it.

APPROACHES TO READING: ACTIVE VERSUS PASSIVE

Passive Reading	**Active Reading**
Passive readers begin reading.	Active readers begin by reading the title, evaluating the author, and thinking about what they already know about the subject. Then they decide what they need to know before they begin reading.
Passive readers read the essay only because it is assigned.	Active readers read the essay while looking for answers to questions and key elements.
Passive readers read but do not write.	Active readers read with a pen in hand. They highlight or underline, annotate, and write notes as they read.
Passive readers close the book when finished.	Active readers review, analyze, and evaluate the essay.

The following essay has been highlighted to illustrate the parts you should read while previewing. Preview it now.

READING

American Jerk
Be Civil, or I'll Beat You to a Pulp
Todd Schwartz

Todd Schwartz is a writer based in Portland, Oregon. A longer version of this essay originally appeared in the *Oregon Humanities Review* in 2008 under the title "The Great Civility War." The version below was published in 2009 in the *Utne Reader*.

It was the most civil of times, it was the least civil of times, it was the age of politeness, it was the age of boorishness, it was the epoch of concern, it was the epoch of who cares, it was the season of hybrid, it was the season of Hummer, it was the spring of Obama, it was the winter of hate speech . . . 1

With apologies to Mr. Dickens (or not: screw him), we have arrived at simultaneously the most and least civil moment in U.S. history. A moment when a roomful of even relatively evolved people will react with discomfort to an off-color joke about people of color—and when those same people have no compunction whatsoever about loudly ignoring one another as they blather into their cell phones. 2

We have never been more concerned about the feelings of minority groups, the disabled, and the disadvantaged. Yet we have never been less concerned about the feelings of anyone with whom we share the road, the Internet, or the movie theater. 3

   Political correctness holds such sway that holidays go unnamed for fear of   4
insulting or excluding someone. Schools won't let teachers use red pens to correct papers, because little Ethan's or Emily's self-esteem might be bruised. No one is "poor,"
but many are "socioeconomically disadvantaged." Civility and thoughtfulness in
speech have never been so complete or so codified.

   All of which is well intentioned and mostly a wonderful thing. I'm all for being   5
polite and caring and Golden Rule-ish. Sadly, like a lovely field of wildflowers—which
in reality is filled with bloodsucking ticks and noxious pollen—we live oh-so-politely
in what must certainly be the rudest era in recorded history. Maybe even prehistory.

   Neanderthals were probably nicer to each other than we are.   6

   Pick your poison: reality television, slasher movies, video games, online porn,   7
cell phones, automated answering systems, giant assault vehicles for trips to the
grocery store, car stereos played at volumes easily heard on Jupiter, web-powered
copyright infringement, people who will not shut their inane traps in movie theaters, and, lord help us, now even people who won't shut their inane traps during
live theater.

We're all talking to someone all the time, but it's ever more rarely to the people we are 8
actually with. Our cell phones blare ringtones that no one else wants to hear. We love
to watch TV shows about the stunningly predictable results of hand-feeding a grizzly
bear or lighting a stick of dynamite with a cigarette. We also love shows where people
lie to others for money and programs where snarky, slightly talented folks say vicious
things to hopeful, and usually more talented, contestants.

Civility rules, friends.   9

Civility is dead, jerks.   10

Why? I have a few theories.   11

The first is that America is in the same position as Rome found itself in about 420 CE, 12
meaning that we've reached the peak of our civilization and now everything is going
to Tartarus in a chariot. We're too far from our food and energy sources, and fewer and
fewer of the Druids and Visigoths like us anymore. So we desperately cling to a patina of
civility while we grab a snack and watch large, toothy predators devour people.

The second is that sunlight contains tiny spores that lodge in the cerebellum, mak- 13
ing the infected believe they are the center of the universe.

My final and somewhat less cutting edge theory is that a large percentage of 14
people are just clueless, distracted, and self-absorbed, unable to process concepts
such as spatial awareness (for example: when you are walking in the same direction
with several hundred people in, say, an airport terminal, DON'T JUST STOP IN THE MID-
DLE OF THE FLOW!).

But I digress.   15

I am not here to judge whether being civil and considerate is somehow better than 16
being a mindless dillweed. You must make that choice for yourself. We inhabit the
most civil of times and the least—and I completely honor and respect your freedom to
choose your side in the Great Civility War.

Just don't get in my way. I'm on my cell in the Escalade, and I can't be bothered. 17

Exercise 3.1

*Based only on your preview of the essay "American Jerk," answer the following questions
as either true or false. If most of your answers are correct, you will know that previewing
helped you gain a sense of the essay's context and organization. (For the answers to this
exercise, see p. 65.)*

_____ **1.** The reading is primarily about civility and the lack of it.

_____ **2.** The author blames the Internet for our society's lack of civility.

_____ **3.** The author suggests that political correctness does not go far enough.

_____ **4.** People are often not intentionally rude but simply are distracted or unaware.

_____ **5.** Society is unconcerned about minorities.

Form Questions to Guide Your Reading

Before you begin reading, you will want to improve your intent to remember. Look
again at the guidelines for previewing on pages 49–50. You can use these parts of
an essay to form questions. Then, as you read, you can answer those questions and

thereby strengthen your comprehension and memory of the material. The following suggestions will help you start devising your questions:

- **Use the title of an essay to devise questions.** Then read to find the answers. Here are a few examples of titles and relevant questions.

Essay Title	*Question*
"Part-time Employment Undermines Students' Commitment to School"	Why does part-time employment undermine commitment to school?
"Human Cloning: Don't Just Say 'No'"	What are good reasons to clone humans?

- **Use headings to devise questions.** For example, in an essay titled "Territoriality," headings include "Types of Territoriality" and "Territorial Encroachment." Each of these headings can easily be turned into a question that becomes a guide as you read: What are the types of territoriality? and What is territorial encroachment and how does it occur?

Not all essays lend themselves to these techniques. For some essays, you may need to dig deeper into the introductory and final paragraphs to form questions. Or you may discover that the subtitle is more useful than the title. Look again at your preview of "American Jerk." Using the introductory paragraphs of that essay, you might decide to look for answers to this question: Why is Schwartz negative toward Americans?

While Reading

As an active reader, you should use a variety of techniques as you read to focus your attention, improve your comprehension, and engage and record your thoughts. While you are reading, your goal is to determine which ideas are important and which are less so. Also look for key organizational elements of the material, and record your reactions and thoughts to ideas as you encounter them. Because some readings will be difficult, be sure to pay attention to unfamiliar vocabulary and take action when you have trouble understanding the text.

Search for Key Elements

When you know what to look for as you read, you will read more easily and do less rereading. When you read assigned articles, essays, or chapters, search for the following key elements:

1. **The meaning of the title and subtitle.** In some cases, the title announces the topic and reveals the author's point of view. In others, the meaning or the significance of the title becomes clear only as you read the text.
2. **The introduction.** The opening paragraph or paragraphs should provide background information, announce the topic, and get the reader's attention.
3. **The author's main point.** Usually, a **thesis statement** directly expresses the one big idea that the piece of writing explains, explores, or supports. The thesis is often placed in the first or second paragraph to let the reader know what lies ahead. But

For more about thesis statements, see Chapter 6, p. 125.

it may at times appear at the end instead. Occasionally, a thesis will be implied or suggested rather than stated directly.

4. **The support and explanation.** The body of the piece of writing should support or give reasons for the author's main point. Each paragraph in the body has a topic sentence, which states what the paragraph is about. Each topic sentence should in some way explain or support the essay's thesis statement.

5. **The conclusion.** The final paragraph or paragraphs should restate the author's main point or offer ideas for further thought.

You'll learn much more about each part of an essay in Chapters 6 to 8.

Now read the "American Jerk" again, paying attention to the marginal notes that identify and explain the various parts of it.

American Jerk
Be Civil, or I'll Beat You to a Pulp
Todd Schwartz

Todd Schwartz is a writer based in Portland, Oregon. A longer version of this essay origi- nally appeared in the *Oregon Humanities Review* in 2008 under the title "The Great Civility War." The version below was published in 2009 in the *Utne Reader*.

Title and subtitle suggest idea of conflict over behavior

It was the most civil of times, it was the least civil of times, it was the age of politeness, 1 it was the age of boorishness, it was the epoch of concern, it was the epoch of who cares, it was the season of hybrid, it was the season of Hummer, it was the spring of Obama, it was the winter of hate speech . . .

Introductory paragraph and illustration suggest contradictory attitudes

With apologies to Mr. Dickens (or not: screw him), we have arrived at simultaneously 2 the most and least civil moment in U.S. history. A moment when a roomful of even rela- tively evolved people will react with discomfort to an off-color joke about people of color—and when those same people have no compunction whatsoever about loudly ignoring one another as they blather into their cell phones.

Thesis statement

We have never been more concerned about the feelings of minority groups, the dis- 3 abled, and the disadvantaged. Yet we have never been less concerned about the feel- ings of anyone with whom we share the road, the Internet, or the movie theater.

Support: contradictory attitudes toward groups

Political correctness holds such sway that holidays go unnamed for fear of insult- 4 ing or excluding someone. Schools won't let teachers use red pens to correct papers, because little Ethan's or Emily's self-esteem might be bruised. No one is "poor," but many are "socioeconomically disadvantaged." Civility and thoughtfulness in speech have never been so complete or so codified.

All of which is well intentioned and mostly a wonderful thing. I'm all for being polite 5 and caring and Golden Rule-ish. Sadly, like a lovely field of wildflowers—which in real- ity is filled with bloodsucking ticks and noxious pollen—we live oh-so-politely in what must certainly be the rudest era in recorded history. Maybe even prehistory.

Neanderthals were probably nicer to each other than we are. 6

Pick your poison: reality television, slasher movies, video games, online porn, cell 7 phones, automated answering systems, giant assault vehicles for trips to the grocery

Support: examples of rudeness

store, car stereos played at volumes easily heard on Jupiter, web-powered copyright infringement, people who will not shut their inane traps in movie theaters, and, lord help us, now even people who won't shut their inane traps during live theater.

We're all talking to someone all the time, but it's ever more rarely to the people we are actually with. Our cell phones blare ringtones that no one else wants to hear. We love to watch TV shows about the stunningly predictable results of hand-feeding a grizzly bear or lighting a stick of dynamite with a cigarette. We also love shows where people lie to others for money and programs where snarky, slightly talented folks say vicious things to hopeful, and usually more talented, contestants.

8   Support: more examples

Civility rules, friends.

Civility is dead, jerks.

Why? I have a few theories.

9
10   Contradictions introduce reasons to follow
11

The first is that America is in the same position as Rome found itself in about 420 CE, meaning that we've reached the peak of our civilization and now everything is going to Tartarus in a chariot. We're too far from our food and energy sources, and fewer and fewer of the Druids and Visigoths like us anymore. So we desperately cling to a patina of civility while we grab a snack and watch large, toothy predators devour people.

12   Support: first reason

The second is that sunlight contains tiny spores that lodge in the cerebellum, making the infected believe they are the center of the universe.

13   Support: second reason

My final and somewhat less cutting edge theory is that a large percentage of people are just clueless, distracted, and self-absorbed, unable to process concepts such as spatial awareness (for example: when you are walking in the same direction with several hundred people in say, an airport terminal, DON'T JUST STOP IN THE MIDDLE OF THE FLOW!).

14   Support: third reason

But I digress.

15

I am not here to judge whether being civil and considerate is somehow better than being a mindless dillweed. You must make that choice for yourself. We inhabit the most civil of times and the least—and I completely honor and respect your freedom to choose your side in the Great Civility War.

16   Conclusion: affirms thesis statement

Just don't get in my way. I'm on my cell in the Escalade, and I can't be bothered.

17   Final humorous word

Highlight Key Points

As you read, you will encounter many new ideas. You will find some ideas more important than others. You will agree with some and disagree with others. Later, as you write about what you have read, you will want to return to the main points to refresh your memory. To locate and remember these points easily, it is a good idea to read with a highlighter or pen in hand. Highlighting is an active reading strategy because it forces you to sort and sift important ideas from less important ideas.

Develop a system of highlighting that you can use as you read to identify ideas you plan to reread or review later on. Use the following guidelines to make your highlighting as useful as possible:

1. **Decide what kinds of information to highlight before you begin.** What types of tasks will you be doing as a result of your reading? Will you write a paper, participate in a class discussion, or take an exam? Think about what you need to know, and tailor your highlighting to the particular needs of the task.

2. **Be selective.** If you highlight every idea, none will stand out.
3. **Read first; then highlight.** First read a paragraph or section; then go back and mark what is important within it. This approach will help you control the tendency to highlight too much.
4. **Highlight key elements, words, and phrases.** Mark the thesis statement, the topic sentence in each paragraph, important terms and definitions, and key words and phrases that relate to the thesis.

Annotate to Record Your Impressions

When you annotate, you jot down your ideas about what you are reading in the margins of the essay. Think of your annotations as a personal response to the author's ideas. Your annotations can take several forms, including questions that come to mind, personal reactions (such as disagreement or surprise), or brief phrases that summarize important points. Later on, when you are ready to write about or discuss the reading, your annotations will help you focus on major issues and questions. Following is a partial list of what you might annotate:

- Important points (such as the thesis) to which you react emotionally
- Places where you need further information
- Places where the author reveals his or her reasons for writing
- Ideas you disagree or agree with
- Inconsistencies

Sample annotations for a portion of "American Jerk" are shown below.

Exercise 3.2

Reread "American Jerk" on page 54. Highlight and annotate the essay as you read.

SAMPLE ANNOTATIONS

What examples are there other than political correctness?

Civility rules, friends.
Civility is dead, jerks.
Why? I have a few theories.

Need more information

The first is that America is in the same position as Rome found itself in about 420 CE, meaning that we've reached the peak of our civilization and now everything is going to Tartarus in a chariot. We're too far from our food and energy sources, and fewer and fewer of the Druids and Visigoths like us anymore. So we desperately cling to a patina of civility while we grab a snack and watch large, toothy predators devour people.

The second is that sunlight contains tiny spores that lodge in the cerebellum, making the infected believe they are the center of the universe.

Does distractedness and lack of awareness excuse poor behavior?

My final and somewhat less cutting edge theory is that a large percentage of people are just clueless, distracted, and self-absorbed, unable to process concepts such as spatial awareness (for example: when you are walking in the same direction with several hundred people in, say, an airport terminal, DON'T JUST STOP IN THE MIDDLE OF THE FLOW!).

Figure Out Unfamiliar Words

If you were to look up in a dictionary every unfamiliar word that you ever came across in a reading, you would not have enough time to complete all your assignments. You can often figure out the meaning of a word by using one of the following strategies:

- **Look for clues in surrounding text.** You can often figure out a word from the way it is used in its sentence or in surrounding sentences. Sometimes the author may provide a brief definition or synonym; other times a less obvious context clue reveals meaning.

BRIEF DEFINITION	Janice *prefaced,* or introduced, her poetry reading with a personal story. [*Prefaced* means "introduced."]
CONTEXT CLUE	In certain societies young children are always on the *periphery,* and never in the center, of family life. [*Periphery* means "the edges or the fringe," which is far away from the center.]

- **Try pronouncing the word aloud.** Hearing the word will sometimes help you grasp its meaning. By pronouncing the word *magnific,* you may hear part of the word *magnify* and know that it has something to do with enlargement. *Magnific* means "large or imposing in size" and "impressive in appearance."
- **Look at parts of the word.** If you break down the parts of a word, you may be able to figure out its meaning. For example, in the word *nonresponsive* you can see the verb *respond,* which means "act or react." *Non* means "not," so you can figure out that *nonresponsive* means "not acting or reacting."

After Reading

One of the biggest mistakes you can make when you finish reading an assignment is to close the book, periodical, or browser window and move immediately to another task. If you do, you will likely forget most of what you read because your brain will not have had time to process and digest the material. Instead, take a few minutes to review the material by drawing a graphic organizer. The time you spend drawing will increase your comprehension and recall.

Understanding Difficult Readings

At one time or another, all students experience difficulty with a reading assignment. Perhaps you just can't "connect" with the author, the topic, or the writing style. Regardless of the problem, however, you know you must complete the assignment.

The Troubleshooting Guide shown in Table 3.1 lists some typical problems that students experience with difficult reading material and identifies strategies for solving them.

Review

Do you simply close a book or put away an article after you have read it? If so, you are missing an opportunity to reinforce your learning. If you are willing to spend a few minutes reviewing and evaluating what you read, you can dramatically increase the amount of information you remember.

To review material after reading, use the same steps you used to preview a reading (see p. 49). You should do your review immediately after you have finished reading. Reviewing does not take much time. Your goal is to touch on each main point one more time, not to embark on a long and thorough study. Pay particular attention to the following elements:

- **The headings**
- **Your highlighting**
- **Your annotations**
- **The conclusion**

As part of your review, it is also helpful to write a brief summary of the essay. See the section on summarizing in Chapter 4 for detailed suggestions on how to write a summary (pp. 88–89).

Draw a Graphic Organizer

If you are having difficulty following a long or complicated essay, try drawing a graphic organizer—a diagram of the structure of an essay's main points. Even if you are not a spatial learner, you will probably find a graphic organizer helpful. Think of a graphic organizer as a means of tracking the author's flow of ideas.

To draw detailed graphic organizers using a computer, visit www.bedfordstmartins.com/ successfulcollege.

The graphic organizer format is shown in Figure 3.2. When you draw a graphic organizer, be sure it includes all the key elements of an essay listed on pages 53–54. An example of a graphic organizer for "American Jerk" appears in Figure 3.3 (p. 61). Work through the organizer, and reread the essay (pp. 54–55), paragraph by paragraph, at the same time.

TABLE 3.1 Difficult Readings: A Troubleshooting Guide

Problems	Strategies for Solving Them
The sentences are long and confusing.	1. Read aloud. 2. Divide each sentence into parts, and analyze the function of each part. 3. Express each sentence in your own words.
The ideas are complicated and hard to understand.	1. Reread the material several times. 2. Rephrase or explain each idea in your own words. 3. Make outline notes. 4. Study with a classmate; discuss difficult ideas. 5. Look up the meanings of unfamiliar words in a dictionary.
The material seems disorganized or poorly organized.	1. Study the introduction for clues to organization. 2. Pay more attention to headings. 3. Read the summary or conclusion. 4. Try to discover the organization by writing an outline or drawing a graphic organizer (see pp. 60 and 61).
The material contains many unfamiliar words.	1. Look for clues to meaning in the surrounding text. 2. Try pronouncing words aloud to see if they remind you of related words. 3. Break words into parts whose meaning you know. 4. Use a dictionary when necessary.
You cannot get interested in the material.	1. Think about something you've experienced that is related to the topic. 2. Work with a classmate, discussing each section as you go.
You cannot relate to the writer's ideas or experiences.	1. Find out some background information about the writer. 2. Imagine yourself having the writer's experiences. How would you react differently?
The subject is unfamiliar; you lack background information on the subject.	1. Obtain a more basic text or other source that moves slower, offers more explanation, and reviews fundamental principles and concepts. 2. For unfamiliar terminology, consult a specialized dictionary within the field of study. 3. Ask your instructor to recommend useful references.

Figure 3.2 GRAPHIC ORGANIZER: KEY ELEMENTS
TO INCLUDE

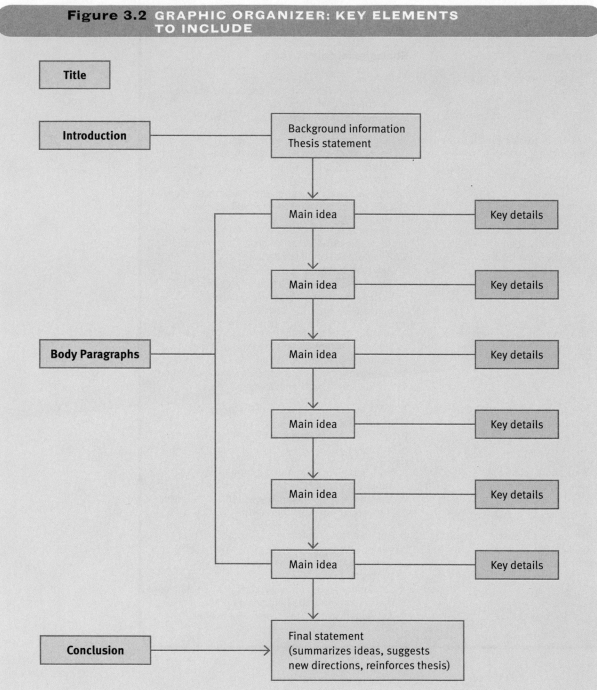

Figure 3.3 GRAPHIC ORGANIZER FOR "AMERICAN JERK"

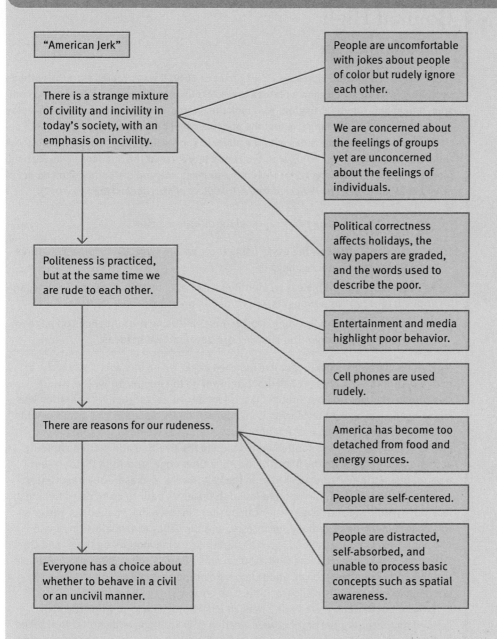

"American Jerk"

There is a strange mixture of civility and incivility in today's society, with an emphasis on incivility.

People are uncomfortable with jokes about people of color but rudely ignore each other.

We are concerned about the feelings of groups yet are unconcerned about the feelings of individuals.

Politeness is practiced, but at the same time we are rude to each other.

Political correctness affects holidays, the way papers are graded, and the words used to describe the poor.

Entertainment and media highlight poor behavior.

Cell phones are used rudely.

There are reasons for our rudeness.

America has become too detached from food and energy sources.

People are self-centered.

Everyone has a choice about whether to behave in a civil or an uncivil manner.

People are distracted, self-absorbed, and unable to process basic concepts such as spatial awareness.

Working with Text

READING

Combat High

Sebastian Junger

This essay first appeared in *Newsweek* magazine in 2010. It was adapted from the author's book *War*, which describes how a platoon of soldiers lived in the Korengal Valley of Afghanistan. Junger and Tim Hetherington, who took the photographs that appear with the essay and wrote his own book, *Infidel*, about the platoon, spent portions of a fourteen-month period in 2007 and 2008 embedded with the platoon. The documentary film they made about the experience, *Restrepo* (2010), won the Grand Jury Prize at the Sundance Film Festival. Junger is also a contributing editor to *Vanity Fair* magazine and the author of a number of other books, including *The Perfect Storm: A True Story of Men against the Sea* (1997).

Before you begin reading this essay, read the directions below.

1. Before you read, preview the essay using the steps on page 49. Write at least three questions to guide your reading.

2. As you read, highlight the essay, identifying its key elements. At the same time, annotate it to record your thoughts, ideas, and impressions.

3. When you have finished reading, review the essay using the guidelines on page 59. Then draw a graphic organizer showing the development of ideas.

Most of the fighting was at four or five hundred yards, so no one ever got to see—or had to deal with—the effects of all that firepower on the human body. There were exceptions, though. One day Prophet (as the American eavesdropping operation was known) called in saying they'd overheard enemy fighters discussing how they wouldn't shoot at the Americans unless a patrol crossed to the east side of the valley. Soon afterward, Afghan soldiers spotted armed men in the riverbed and started shooting at them. The men fled up the flanks of the Abas Ghar ridge, and Third Platoon sent a patrol out of the KOP (the main base in the valley) to give chase. They took contact as soon as they crossed the river and found themselves badly pinned down behind a rock wall. Within seconds every American position in the valley opened up. The enemy was caught in the open without much cover, and the valley essentially turned into one enormous shooting gallery. The KOP started dropping mortars on them, and Observation Post 3 engaged them with a .50 cal and a Barrett sniper rifle, and the trucks opened up from above Babiyal, and Outpost Restrepo swung its 240s around and poured gunfire across the valley for almost an hour. 1

It was a hot day and there hadn't been much fighting lately, so when the men jumped on the guns most of them were wearing only flip-flops and shorts. They joked and laughed and called for cigarettes between bursts. Once in a while a round would crack past us, but mostly it was just a turkey shoot at a wide-open mountainside where the enemy had nowhere to hide. Hot brass was filling up the fighting positions, and more was cascading down out of the weapons every second. At one point I watched a shell drop into Pemble's untied shoe, and he slipped it off, wiggled the shell out, and then slipped his shoe back on without ever stopping firing. The lieutenant was shirt- 2 less on the ammo hooch, calling coordinates into the KOP, and some of the Afghans were firing from the hip even though they didn't stand a chance of hitting anything that way, and Jackson was up on the guard position unloading one of the machine guns. Restrepo alone had to be putting out a thousand rounds a minute, and the Abas Ghar was sparkling with bullet-strikes even though it was broad daylight. Finally Hog showed up—Hog was the radio call-sign for the A-10s—and dropped a couple of bombs on the mountain for good measure.

At some point a call came in over the radio that the Scouts were watching a guy   3
crawl around on the mountainside without a leg. They watched until he stopped mov-ing, and then they called in that he'd died. Everyone at Restrepo cheered. That night I couldn't sleep, and I crept out of my bunk and went and sat on the roof of the ammo hooch. It was a nice place to watch the heat lightning out along the Pech river or to lie back on the sandbags and look up at the stars. I couldn't stop thinking about that cheer; in some ways it was more troubling than all the killing that was going on. Stripped of all politics, the fact of the matter was that the man had died alone on a mountainside trying to find his leg. He must have been crazed with thirst and bewil-dered by the sheer amount of gunfire stitching back and forth across the ground look-ing for him. At one point or another every man in the platoon had been pinned down long enough to think they were going to die—bullets hitting around them, bodies braced for impact—and that's with just one or two guns. Imagine a whole company's worth of firepower directed at you. I got the necessity for that kind of overkill, but I didn't get the joy. It seemed like I either had to radically re-understand the men on this hilltop, or I had to acknowledge the power of a place like this to change them.

"You're thinking that this guy could have murdered my friend," Steiner explained   4
to me later. "The cheering comes from knowing that that's someone we'll never have

Messages on a grenade bandolier

A soldier shows the hole in his helmet from a shot to the head during a firefight. He survived and later had two bullets with wings tattooed onto his chest
to portray the "angels" that were watching over him at the time.

to fight again. Fighting another human being is not as hard as you think when they're
trying to kill you. People think we were cheering because we just shot someone, but we
were cheering because we just stopped someone from killing us. That person will no
longer shoot at us anymore. That's where the fiesta comes in."

Combat was a game that the United States had asked Second Platoon to become   5
very good at, and once they had, the United States had put them on a hilltop without
women, hot food, running water, communication with the outside world or any kind of
entertainment for more than a year. Not that the men were complaining, but that sort
of thing has consequences. Society can give its young men almost any job, and they'll
figure how to do it. They'll suffer for it and die for it and watch their friends die for it,
but in the end it will get done. That means only that society should be careful about
what it asks for. In a very crude sense the job of young men is to undertake the work
that their fathers are too old for, and the current generation of American fathers has
decided that a certain six-mile-long valley in Kunar province needs to be brought under
military control. Nearly 50 American soldiers have died carrying out those orders. I'm
not saying that's a lot or a little, but the cost does need to be acknowledged. Soldiers
themselves are reluctant to evaluate the costs of war (for some reason, the closer you
are to combat the less inclined you are to question it), but someone must. That evalua-

tion, ongoing and unadulterated by politics, may be the one thing a country absolutely owes the soldiers who defend its borders.

There are other costs to war as well—vaguer ones that don't lend themselves to conventional math. One American soldier has died for every hundred yards of forward progress in the valley, but what about the survivors? Is that territory worth the psychological cost of learning to cheer someone's death? It's an impossible question to answer but one that should keep getting asked. Ultimately, the problem is that they're normal young men with normal emotional needs that have to be met within the very narrow options available on that hilltop. Young men need mentors, and mentors are usually a generation or so older. That isn't possible at Restrepo, so a 22-year-old team leader effectively becomes a father figure for a 19-year-old private. Up at Restrepo a 27-year-old is considered an old man, an effeminate Afghan soldier is seen as a woman, and new privates are called "cherries" and thought of as children. Men form friendships that are not at all sexual but contain much of the devotion and intensity of a romance. Almost every relationship that occurs in open society exists in some compressed form at Restrepo, and almost every human need from back home gets fulfilled in some truncated, jury-rigged way. The men are good at constructing what they need from what they have. They are experts at making do.   6

As for a sense of purpose, combat is it—the only game in town. Almost none of the things that make life feel worth living back home are present at Restrepo, so the entire range of a young man's self-worth has to be found within the ragged choreography of a firefight. The men talk about it and dream about it and rehearse for it and analyze it afterward but never plumb its depths enough to lose interest. It's the ultimate test, and some of the men worry they'll never again be satisfied with a "normal life"—whatever that is— after the amount of combat they've been in. They worry that they may have been ruined for anything else.   7

War is a lot of things, and it's useless to pretend that exciting isn't one of them. It's insanely exciting. The machinery of war and the sound it makes and the urgency of its use and the consequences of almost everything about it are the most exciting things anyone engaged in war will ever know. Soldiers discuss that fact with each other and eventually with their chaplains and their shrinks and maybe even their spouses, but the public will never hear about it. It's just not something that many people want acknowledged. War is supposed to feel bad because undeniably bad things happen in it, but for a 19-year-old at the working end of a .50 cal during a firefight that everyone comes out of OK, war is life multiplied by some number that no one has ever heard of. In some ways 20 minutes of combat is more life than you could scrape together in a lifetime of doing something else. Combat isn't where you might die—though that does happen—it's where you find out whether you get to keep on living. Don't underestimate the power of that revelation. Don't underestimate the things young men will wager in order to play that game one more time.   8

"I like the firefights," O'Byrne admitted to me once. We'd been talking about going home and whether he was going to get bored. "I know," he added, probably realizing how that sounded. "Saddest thing in the world."   9

Answers to Exercise 3.1

1. True   **2.** False   **3.** False   **4.** True   **5.** False

CHAPTER 4

Responding Critically to Text and Images

The photograph on the opposite page shows examples of popular newsstand journalism. Suppose you are taking a sociology class and are studying popular culture. Your instructor asks you to examine publications such as these, read and evaluate a few articles, and be prepared to discuss in class what they reveal about Americans' needs and values.

Write a list of questions about the articles whose titles are shown in the photograph. Include questions that would help you evaluate the articles' purpose and identify to whom they appeal. Then study the photographs on the front covers. Write a few sentences explaining why they may have been included and what they accomplish.

As you analyzed the titles of the articles featured on the covers, you had to think and react critically; you had to question and evaluate. This process is known as *critical thinking*.

In this chapter you will learn strategies for both thinking critically and reading critically. You will learn to interpret visuals, including photographs and graphics. This chapter also includes a Guide to Responding to Text that offers strategies to help you organize your ideas about what you have read.

SCENES FROM COLLEGE AND THE WORKPLACE

- In an *art history* class, your instructor assigns a critical review of a museum exhibit that your class recently visited. She asks you to read the review and write an essay agreeing or disagreeing with the critic's viewpoint and expressing your own views.

- For a *zoology* course, your instructor distributes an excerpt from the book *When Elephants Weep: The Emotional Lives of Animals* that displays several photographs of elephants interacting and asks you to write a paper summarizing, analyzing, and evaluating evidence presented about animal emotions.

- You are working as an *inspector* for the Occupational Safety and Health Administration (OSHA). Part of your job is to read, interpret, and evaluate corporate plans to comply with OSHA safety standards.

Strategies for Critical Thinking and Reading

In elementary and high school, students memorize facts to develop a basic foundation of knowledge in reading, writing, science, and mathematics. In college, you will learn and memorize new information, but you are also expected to analyze what you learn, develop your own opinions, and conduct your own research. In other words, your college instructors expect you to *think critically*—to interpret and evaluate what you hear and read—and not simply accept something as "the truth" because an instructor says it or you read it somewhere. (Thinking critically also means not rejecting something just because it contradicts what you currently believe or previously learned.) In this context, the term *critically* does not mean "negatively." Rather, it means "thoughtfully and analytically"—that is, thinking deeply about the information you encounter.

In your college courses and your daily life, it is important to think critically about written and visual materials that you encounter. Whether you are looking at a textbook chapter, an essay or article, or an online reference source, you will need to analyze and evaluate the ideas presented. *Critical reading*, then, is a form of critical thinking that you use to analyze written text and visuals.

Developing your critical-thinking and -reading skills will enable you to distinguish good information from incomplete, inaccurate information. You will become a savvy consumer who can compare options and avoid scams, frauds, and misleading advertising. You will become an informed citizen who can evaluate issues, examine politicians' campaign platforms and promises, and analyze people's political and economic motives. In the workplace, you will become a valued employee who can evaluate and solve problems, recognize trends, and analyze causes and effects. In college, you will become a careful reader who can evaluate research sources to determine if they are reliable or unreliable. In particular, you will be able to conduct Internet research more effectively by identifying accurate and trustworthy sites. Critical reading will also enable you to recognize relationships between ideas and disciplines. For example, understanding basic human psychology will help you in other courses, such as economics, because critical thinking about consumer spending patterns will help you recognize psychological concepts that help to explain them. The strategies in the remainder of this section will help you become a critical thinker who is ready to handle the demands of your daily life, your college classes, and your job.

Evaluate Information Sources

We live in a world of sensory overload. We are surrounded by news, opinions, advertisements, and other kinds of information everywhere we look (or listen). Developing your critical-thinking skills will help you to evaluate this avalanche of information. Begin by thinking about your various information sources—how factually accurate they try to be, whether they are written by people with experience in the field, whether they have been reviewed by editors or experts in the field, and whether they show bias toward a particular view of a situation and, therefore, might misrepresent it.

Newspapers

Newspapers vary in how skilled their reporters are in obtaining accurate and complete information and in how rigorously they check facts before publishing a news story. As the word *news* suggests, they tend to focus on what is new—unexpected events and recent trends—and to give less attention to more familiar and predictable patterns that may be equally important or even more so. Most newspapers have an editorial page or opinion section in which the paper's editors and contributors offer their views on current issues and other topics. These pieces are likely to reflect the writers' personal views on controversial questions, political or otherwise, so be aware of this as you read. Also keep in mind that some newspapers tend to be liberal in their views, while others are conservative. These tendencies often show up not just on the editorial page but also in the way news stories are presented, such as where a story appears or what kind of language is used to describe an issue.

Television News

TV news broadcasts also require close scrutiny. Because networks are interested in attracting and keeping viewers, they sometimes focus on events that their staff members think will achieve this goal rather than on developments that are more important. News programs may focus on stories that have high visual appeal at the expense of those with less compelling images. Finally, some networks have a particular political bias or slant, and their news coverage is aimed at furthering this agenda. For the same reasons, radio news deserves scrutiny.

Magazines

Literally thousands of magazines are published every year. Some are devoted to specific interests, such as home schooling, organic food, or Latin American politics. Others report, analyze, and comment on national, state, or local news; still others focus on particular issues, such as finance, art, or literature. Although such magazines can be excellent sources of information, their content, like that of newspapers and television, is influenced by the perspectives and biases of their editors and writers. Magazines also vary in their fact-checking and in the skill of their journalists. Magazines that focus on gossip and celebrities are viewed as less reliable than news magazines.

The Internet

For many people, the Internet is the first place they turn for news and research because it is free and easy to access. However, anyone can create a Web site and post on it anything he or she wants, regardless of its accuracy. Be particularly cautious when using blogs (online diaries), which contain personal opinions that are not reviewed by editors. For more information on evaluating Internet sources, read Chapter 21 (pp. 585–87).

Scholarly Journals

Scholarly journals report research and developments in a particular academic or professional field. Examples include the *Journal of Psychology* and the *Journal of the American Medical Association.* They tend to be highly trustworthy sources because they are peer-reviewed. That is, the journals' editors accept only articles that have been evaluated and approved by other authorities in the field. In scientific fields, journal articles must be based on research that follows strict standardized procedures and must make connections to related research on the topic. Articles in scholarly journals can use specialized vocabulary, so you need to read them slowly and carefully. Fortunately, most articles begin or end with an *abstract*, a one- or two-paragraph summary of the findings of the research study.

Exercise 4.1

On your own or as part of a class discussion, evaluate the reliability of each of the information sources in the list below. Do some research if necessary to learn more about them. How seriously should you take each source? Which exist solely for entertainment? Which are likely to be highly biased? Which would be acceptable as references in an academic research paper? Rate the reliability of each on a scale of 1 to 5, with 1 being completely unreliable and 5 being very trustworthy.

1. an opinion column in the *Washington Post* (newspaper)
2. a feature story in the *National Enquirer* (newspaper/magazine)
3. an editorial in the *Wall Street Journal* (newspaper)
4. *Meet the Press* (a TV news program)
5. www.thesmokinggun.com
6. www.census.gov (Web site of the U.S. Census Bureau)
7. www.tmz.com
8. *The Journal of Economic Research*

9. Wikipedia (www.wikipedia.org)

10. a feature article in *InStyle Magazine* (a women's fashion magazine)

Understand the Nuances of Words

Words are powerful, and their power can be used in many ways. On the positive side, words can inspire, comfort, educate, and calm. At the other end of the spectrum, words can inflame, annoy, and deceive. Professional writers understand that word choices influence readers and listeners, and they choose words that will help them achieve their objective. To think critically, consider the following aspects of word choice.

Denotation

A **denotation** is the literal meaning of a word. For example, the denotation of the word *obese* is "very fat."

Connotation

A **connotation** is the set of additional meanings or associations that a word has taken on. Often, a word's connotation has a much stronger effect on readers or listeners than its denotation does. A politician who weighs much more than the average or recommended amount for his height might be described as "pleasingly plump" (which carries an almost pleasant connotation), as "quite a bit overweight" (which is an objective-sounding, statistical statement of fact), or as "morbidly obese" or "grossly fat" (which gives readers a negative impression of the politician). Always pay attention to the connotations that words carry and consider why the writer made his or her particular word choices.

Exercise 4.2

For each of the following words, think of one word with a similar denotation but a positive connotation and then another word with a similar denotation but a negative connotation.

■ **Group (of people): positive connotation, <u>audience</u>; negative connotation, <u>mob</u>**

1. choosy
2. cheap
3. girl
4. bold
5. walk

Euphemism

A **euphemism** is a word or phrase that is used to avoid a word that is unpleasant, embarrassing, or otherwise objectionable. For example, a company may say that it is *downsizing* its workforce when it fires people. That same company may say it is *moving into international sourcing* when it eliminates jobs in the United States and sends them overseas. Euphemisms seek to sugar-coat an unpleasant reality, and as a critical thinker you should always be alert for them, particularly when reading about politics and business.

> ### Exercise 4.3
>
> 1. The media often report about people from other countries who come to the United States without permission from the U.S. government or who stay here after their permission to visit has expired. Two terms are used to refer to these people—*illegal aliens* and *undocumented immigrants*. Discuss which term seems to have a more negative connotation and which seems more neutral. Why does each term carry the connotations it does? Is the more neutral term a euphemism? Why, or why not?
>
> 2. Brainstorm a list of euphemisms currently in use in the media.

Distinguish Fact from Opinion

College textbooks present factual information that has been checked and rechecked over many years (often, over hundreds or even thousands of years) and is therefore highly reliable. In addition, when textbook authors write about topics that are matters of opinion and controversy (rather than topics that most scholars in the field agree on), they usually identify the different schools of thought. Many other reading materials—newspapers, magazines, advertisements, Web sites, and so forth—present a mixture of fact and opinion without distinguishing between the two. For example, an advertisement may state that an American-made car offers the best warranty coverage of all American cars, then describe the features of the warranty, but make no attempt to compare the warranty to another car's warranty. (For a more detailed discussion of fact and opinion, refer to Chapter 21, pp. 588–89.)

Facts

Facts are objective statements of information that can be verified—that is, their truth can be established with evidence. The following are facts:

- Most people who use marijuana do not go on to use more dangerous drugs.
- Texting while driving has caused many accidents.

How do you know a fact when you see it? Facts can be checked in trustworthy sources such as online dictionaries and Web reference sources like refdesk.com. (Note that for the purposes of academic writing, Wikipedia is *not* considered a trustworthy reference source for checking facts.)

Opinions

Opinions are subjective—that is, they differ by individual. They express attitudes, feelings, or beliefs that cannot be definitely established as either true or false, at least at the present time. Often, they put forth a particular position or agenda. Even scholarly journals put forth some ideas that are the authors' opinions based on their own research and that of earlier researchers. Only time and further research will tell if these opinions become facts. The following are opinions:

- It is likely that marijuana use will be legalized in all fifty states by 2020.
- People who text while driving should be fined and have their driver's licenses revoked.
- To prevent permanent hearing loss in musicians and audience menbers, performers should be required to meet decibel noise exposure limits.

Exercise 4.4

For two of the following topics, write one statement of fact and one statement of opinion:

1. voter turnout rates in presidential elections
2. cell-phone use in classrooms
3. alternative energy solutions
4. the Super Bowl

Evaluate Whether Information Is Reliable

You may have heard the term *spin doctor*. This phrase describes a public relations specialist who puts a positive spin on bad news. Reading and thinking critically require you to understand when information is presented fairly and when it is spun for some purpose—to influence public opinion, to sell something, to win votes, and so forth.

In general, the most reliable information is based on solid *evidence*. Just as police look for evidence to discover who committed a crime, you must look for evidence that supports any assertion made by a writer. If the writer offers little or no evidence, you should question the assertion. The following types of evidence are often considered relevant and valid.

Personal Experience or Examples

Personal experience can be powerful evidence. For example, no one understands cancer like a person who has suffered with the disease and survived. Different people can experience the same event very differently, however, so be careful about generalizing from the experiences of any single person. Furthermore, even though several people may report similar experiences, their reports may not be sufficient evidence to make a sweeping generalization.

Statistical Data

Statistics are often collected and made public by academic researchers or professional research organizations, and these statistics tend to be reliable because the people reporting them try to be as objective and accurate as possible. However, be wary of people who use data in ways that try to hide the truth rather than clarify it. For example, a soda company may claim that "90% of the people in a taste test preferred our cola to our competitor's cola." This statement may be true, but what if the taste test were conducted at the company's headquarters? Would that create a different result than a taste test run in a neutral location, such as a mall? In thinking critically about how reliable a statistical survey is, also consider factors such as how many people were surveyed, how they were selected, when the survey was done, and how the questions were worded.

Eyewitness Reports

Eyewitness reports are often considered powerful evidence, but studies suggest that eyewitness testimony in criminal cases is often inaccurate. Also, different people can interpret the same situation in different ways. Suppose that a building bursts into flames and a man is seen running out of the building. One person may think, "What a lucky man! He escaped from the burning building." Another person may think, "That man started the fire to burn this building down and collect the insurance money."

Experimental Evidence

The results of scientific experiments and studies are usually considered highly reliable because they are based on the *scientific method*, which is a set of procedures that researchers follow to investigate their theories. The conclusions that can be drawn from the results of a single study may be fairly narrow, though. Moreover, experiments are not always designed or conducted as carefully as they should be. Even when they are, uncontrollable factors can influence the results. For example, scientific research studies on the safety of a drug can be contradictory. In addition, although most scientists try to be objective and neutral, you need to consider who is conducting the research and whether the researchers have an interest in its outcomes (such as an economic motive or a political agenda) that might influence how they design and conduct it. In rare cases, researchers have even falsified results and misrepresented the data to produce the outcomes they wanted.

Exercise 4.5

Consider each of the following statements and the context in which it is made. List what sorts of information are missing that would help you weigh the evidence and evaluate the claim being made. What further types of evidence would you need to accept or reject the claim?

1. On the label of a bag of cookies: "CONTAINS 45% LESS FAT and 0 grams of TRANS FAT!"

2. In a printed campaign flyer for mayoral candidate Mary Johnson: "My opponent, Joe Smith, has been accused of serious conflicts of interest in the awarding of city contracts during his term as mayor."

3. In large print on the cover of a novel you see at the supermarket checkout: "'This novel is a . . . wild and exciting . . . ride through the rough-and-tumble days of the Gold Rush . . . full of . . . adventure and excitement. . . . Memorable.' – *The New York Times*."

Analyze the Author's Tone

Have you ever noticed that people can use the same words to mean different things in different situations? The tone of the words in each situation can convey a very different meaning. Consider a police officer who pulls you over for speeding, approaches the car, and says to you, "Could you please step out of the car?" A police officer would say these words very differently than an employee at a car wash who says the same words so that he can vacuum the interior of your vehicle.

Tone refers to how a writer sounds to readers, and it is influenced by how the writer feels about the readers and his or her topic. Recognizing an author's tone will help you interpret and evaluate the message and its effect on you.

Tone is revealed primarily through word choice and stylistic features such as sentence patterns and length. A writer can communicate surprise, disapproval, disgust, admiration, gratitude, or amusement, for example. Table 4.1 lists some words commonly used to describe tone.

Many writers and speakers feel passionately about their beliefs, and sometimes they have a personal charisma or physical attractiveness that makes people more open to hearing their message. Be sure not to get carried away by a writer or speaker's tone or commitment. As a critical thinker, your job is to analyze words, facts, and tone to determine how they affect you and whether you are being told the complete story. It is even more important to watch for subtle tones that may be hidden within a message. For example, a writer may use an apparently sympathetic tone in describing a political candidate's recent questionable financial deals: "Poor Mayor Jones must not have realized that taking money for political favors is illegal." This writer is using a mocking or sarcastic tone as a way of criticizing the candidate.

Exercise 4.6

Read each of the following statements, and describe its tone. Refer to Table 4.1 to locate terms that describe the tone. Which words in the statement are clues to the tone?

1. When you are backpacking, you can reduce the risk of back injury by adjusting your pack so that most of its weight is on your hip belt rather than your shoulder straps.

2. Do you eat canned tuna? Then you are at least partially responsible for the deaths of thousands of innocent dolphins, who are mercilessly slaughtered by fishermen in their quest for tuna.

TABLE 4.1 Words Commonly Used to Describe Tone

angry	disapproving	informative	persuasive
apathetic	earnest	instructive	pessimistic
arrogant	flippant	ironic	playful
assertive	forgiving	irreverent	reverent
bitter	formal	joyful	righteous
caustic	frustrated	loving	sarcastic
cheerful	hateful	malicious	satiric
compassionate	humorous	mocking	serious
condemning	impassioned	nostalgic	sympathetic
condescending	incredulous	objective	vindictive
cynical	indignant	optimistic	worried
detached			

3. The penalty for creating and launching a computer virus should include a personal apology to every person who was affected by the virus, and each apology should be typed—without errors!—on a manual typewriter.

4. Piles of solid waste threaten to ruin our environment, pointing to the urgent need for better disposal methods and strategies for lowering the rate of waste generation.

5. All poets seek to convey emotion and the complete range of human feeling, but the only poet who fully accomplished this goal was William Shakespeare.

Exercise 4.7

Consider the following situation: A developer has received permission to bulldoze an entire city block filled with burned-out tenement buildings and abandoned factories. In their place, the developer is going to build a community of three hundred upscale condominiums for people who work in the city and want to live close to their jobs.

Write three different sentences (or paragraphs) that react to this news. Make the tone of your first sentence outraged. *Make the tone of your second sentence* joyful. *Make the tone of your third sentence* nostalgic.

Look for Purposeful Omissions

Writers and speakers sometimes mislead by omission—that is, by what they do not say. They may leave out essential background or context, include only details that favor their own position, or ignore contradictory evidence. They may also use the passive voice (to avoid taking or assigning responsibility for an action) or use vague nouns and pronouns (to avoid specifying exactly what or whom they are referring to).

Consider an article written by a woman who has home-schooled her children. As an advocate of home schooling, she is likely to emphasize her children's educational progress and her own sense of personal fulfillment achieved by teaching her children. However, she may not address arguments made by opponents of home schooling—that home-schooled children sometimes feel lonely or isolated from their peers, for example. She also may refer to home schooling as "better" for children without specifying exactly what it is better than (her local public school, public schools in general, any kind of school) or in what way it is better.

The same writer may also describe a research study that concludes that home-schooled children excel academically. Other studies, however, have found that home-schooled children do not differ in academic achievement from traditionally educated students. If the writer does not mention these findings, she has chosen to ignore contradictory evidence, reporting only evidence that she wants the reader to know. In any case, the writer needs to identify the study she cites rather than simply say something like, "A research study on home schooling concluded that . . ." or "It has been found that. . . ."

Regardless of what you are reading, ask yourself the following questions to be sure you are getting full and complete information:

- Is any important information omitted? What, if anything, am I not being told?
- Is any evidence that contradicts the writer's or speaker's position not being reported?
- Has the writer or speaker selectively reported details to further his or her cause?

• On the basis of my own experiences, how do I evaluate this material? Is there another side to this argument or aspect to this topic that I should consider?

To answer these questions, you may need to do some additional reading or research. That is what the college experience is all about—learning from as many sources as possible, taking in many points of view, and using your critical-thinking skills to formulate your own opinions.

Exercise 4.8

Read the following scenarios, which you are likely to encounter in your everyday life. In each situation, what information is being withheld from you? In other words, what other information do you need to evaluate the situation?

1. You see a TV ad for a fast-food restaurant that shows a huge hamburger topped with pickles, onions, and tomatoes. The announcer says, "For a limited time, get your favorite burger for only 99 cents!"

2. You open your mailbox and find a letter from a credit-card company. The letter invites you to open a charge card with no annual fee and offers you instant credit if you return the attached card in a postage-paid envelope.

3. You get an offer from a DVD club that appears to be a good deal. As part of your introductory package, you can buy five DVDs for only ninety-nine cents, plus shipping and handling.

Exercise 4.9

The reading "Combat High" appeared in Chapter 3 (p. 62). Use the Guide to Responding to Text in this chapter (p. 86) to answer the questions below.

1. Using the information you find in the introduction to the reading and in the reading itself, evaluate Sebastian Junger's qualifications to write about combat experiences. Is he a trustworthy and reliable source?

2. Describe the author's tone. What effect does the tone have on you as a reader? How effective do you find it?

3. Identify at least five words with positive or negative connotations.

4. Does the author use euphemisms? If so, give several examples.

5. What information may have been omitted?

6. Is the author fair or biased? Justify your answer.

Interpreting Visuals

Many articles, essays, books, and other materials you will read in college rely on visual images to express important parts of their meaning. Visual messages appear everywhere in your daily life as well—on television, on the Internet, in print magazines and newspapers, and on signs, flyers, and billboards. In the workplace, visuals are used to present information, sell products, report trends, show corporate organization, and demonstrate processes.

Visuals include photographs, cartoons, advertisements, illustrations, drawings, PowerPoint slides, and graphics (charts, diagrams, maps, graphs, tables, and flowcharts). These powerful tools can help you share information, convey impressions, provoke thought, raise questions, and trigger emotions. In your writing in college and in the workplace, you will probably find opportunities to use visuals for all these purposes. As an active and critical reader, you should study the visuals you encounter as carefully as you read, analyze, and evaluate written text.

On page 79, for example, is a public service advertisement from the World Wildlife Fund. What do you notice first? Your eye probably goes to the tiger in a lush jungle setting in the small framed snapshot, and you recognize this as a common kind of nature photograph demonstrating the magnificence and beauty of jungle animals. Then you realize that the photograph is surrounded by a larger one showing a natural habitat destroyed by deforestation. When you then consider the captions, you realize the purpose of the ad—to warn against the human destruction of natural habitats and the animals that live there. This ad makes a dramatic and compelling statement that nature is worth protecting and is at risk of being destroyed.

The visuals make the ad much more noticeable and engaging than one with only written text that simply states the problem and explains why jungle habitats are in danger. The twin images with their corresponding text deliver a strong and effective message.

Following are some suggestions for analyzing photographs and some common kinds of graphics.

Interpreting Photographs

A photograph can appear by itself, but it is usually accompanied by a caption or text that discusses or refers to the photograph. Use the following suggestions when analyzing photographs and any words that accompany them. Refer to the following photograph as you read these guidelines.

1. **Preview the photograph.** Look at it quickly. Your goal is to form a first impression—to notice its general subject. What did you notice first, and how did that affect you?

    Look at the photograph in Figure 4.1 (p. 80). What was your first reaction? You probably noticed the young man first and then noticed that he was sitting on a soccer ball.

2. **Study the photo as a whole, and then examine its parts.** Identify the focal point of the photograph. Then look closely at the details, examining both the foreground and the background. Details can provide important clues. If you are a verbal learner, it may be helpful to translate the photo into words; you will be able to remember it more easily, and its purpose may become more obvious.

    As you look at Figure 4.1, you first see the young man sitting on the ball in the foreground. In the background you notice the graffiti on the wall behind him. An important detail in this photograph is that the young man is holding a book and is reading.

Learning Style Options

There are as few as 3,200 tigers left in the wild.
Don't wait until they're gone.

Protect the future of nature.

WWF
worldwildlife.org/tigers

3. **Read the caption, if there is one.** The caption, appearing above, beside, or below the photograph, usually gives background about it and may offer clues about what the author (or his or her editor) wants to emphasize.

   The caption in Figure 4.1 indicates that the person who chose the photo wanted to emphasize the book and the act of reading.

4. **Read the accompanying text, if any.** Although a photograph should be analyzed and evaluated on its own merit, look for connections between the photo and any written text that accompanies it (whether or not the text refers to the photo). Ask yourself how the photo relates to the ideas presented in the text and what, if anything, it adds to these ideas.

FIGURE 4.1 Reading Happens Anytime, Anywhere

Figure 4.1 appeared in a college textbook about secondary education in a chapter on building literacy skills. What connection does this photograph have to that topic? The photograph depicts the central literacy skill—reading—and presents it as a universal skill that is useful in unusual contexts.

5. **Determine the purpose and message of the image.** Why was it created and used? Photos can be powerful, and they are often chosen to elicit a strong reaction. As with print text, the purpose may be to inform, to amuse, to shock, to persuade, or some combination of these or other motives. Analyze your response to the photo; it can help you discover why someone chose to include it. Ask yourself what point the person might be trying to make.

In Figure 4.1 the photo puts the intellectual act of reading in a surprising physical context—a soccer-ball seat and the background of a wall filled with distracting graffiti. The author seems to be making a point about the act of reading, suggesting that it can take place in unexpected, even uncomfortable circumstances. The larger message seems to be that reading can be an important and pleasurable task, regardless of when and where it occurs.

6. **Think critically about the photograph.** Consider whether it is representative or typical of the situation or subject. Also consider the emotional effect of the photograph. How does it make you feel? What emotions do you think it might produce in others? Would you feel as strongly about the topic without the photo? How

effective is it in achieving its purpose? What other kind of illustration might the writer or editor have used?

Figure 4.1 shows someone reading in an unusual place and posture. Because people read in a wide variety of situations and contexts, the photograph seems intended to make the college students using the textbook appreciate the universal nature of reading. At the same time, it also suggests an idea related to building literacy skills in secondary education—the challenges that many high school students face in finding time and space in which to read. Finally, because it is slightly amusing, it engages the attention of the textbook users in a way that a photo of someone reading in a more ordinary setting, such as indoors in a chair, might not.

Exercise 4.10

Study the photograph below, using the guidelines listed on pages 78–79. Then answer the following questions:

1. Describe your first impression of the photo.
2. Summarize what is happening in the photo.
3. What does the caption contribute to your understanding of the photo?
4. This photograph appeared in a sociology textbook titled *Deviance and Conformity* in a section titled "Norms and a Range of Tolerance." Why did the author include the photo in a chapter that discusses *deviance* (behaving in ways different from the usual or traditionally acceptable ones) and in a section of the chapter that focuses on *norms* (standards of behavior)?
5. What other kinds of photos or images might the writer have used to make the same point?

A nontraditional marriage ceremony

Exercise 4.11

Examine one of the photographs that accompanies the reading "Combat High" in Chapter 3 (pp. 62–65), and write a paragraph explaining what it contributes to the reading.

Exercise 4.12

Discuss what types of photographs might be useful to include in each of the following writing tasks:

1. An essay opposing the whaling industry
2. An essay describing problems faced by cyberbullying victims
3. A research paper on teen slang
4. An argumentative essay opposing casino gambling
5. A report about unhealthy fast-food menu items

Interpreting Graphics

Graphics are commonly used to organize and condense information, making lengthy or complicated data easier to understand. Writers use a wide range of types of graphics; the purpose of each of the common types is summarized on the next page (p. 83).

Use the following suggestions when reading and interpreting graphics. Refer to the multiple bar graphs shown in Figure 4.2 as you apply suggestions 2 to 7 below.

1. **Read any reference to the graphic in the main text.** Many authors refer to the graphics they include, providing a context for the graphic, offering a reason it was included, or giving a summary of what it is intended to show. When you locate the reference in the text, finish reading it before you examine the graphic. Even if the text does not mention the graphic, look for connections between the two. To understand complicated graphics, you may need to go back and forth several times between the text and the graphic.

    This graphic appeared in a report published by *CQ Researcher,* a print and on-line periodical that publishes a weekly in-depth report on a current social or political issue. The text of this report, "Caring for Veterans: Does the VA Adequately Serve Wounded Vets?" does not directly mention the graphic, although it discusses many of the issues addressed in the graph.

2. **Read the title and the caption, if there is one.** The title identifies the subject of the graphic, and the caption provides important information about what it shows. In some cases, the caption will specify the key point for the graphic.

    The title of Figure 4.2 identifies the subject—brain injuries of veterans—and states the main point that these injuries are costly to the Veterans Administration. The caption provides background and suggests that the graphic is considering both brain damage and post-traumatic stress disorder to be forms of brain injury.

3. **Examine how the graphic is organized.** Read the column headings, labels, or other text used to indicate the organizational method. Find out what variables are involved.

    In Figure 4.2, the top graph displays number of casualties by their type and by the war in which they were suffered. How is the bottom graph organized?

4. **Look at the legend, if there is one.** The legend is the guide to the colors, symbols, terms, and other important information in the graphic. In maps, the legend usually contains a scale explaining how measurements should be read. (For example, a map may be scaled so that one inch on the map represents one mile.)

    In Figure 4.2, the legend for the top graph explains the color scheme used to distinguish the two wars that the graph represents.

5. **Analyze the graphic's purpose.** Based on what you see, determine the key purpose. Is it to show change over time, to represent a process or a structure, or to compare statistics from different countries?

    The purpose of Figure 4.2 is clear. It displays the number of casualties and emphasizes the large numbers of brain injuries and psychological traumas suffered by veterans.

Type of Graphic	Purpose	Example
Pie (circle) chart	To show the relationships among parts of a whole; to show how given parts of a unit are divided or classified	A chart showing the proportions of different racial and ethnic groups in the U.S. population
Bar graphs	To make comparisons between quantities or amounts	A graph comparing the percentage of the U.S. population living in cities for each decade from 1770 to 2010
Line graphs	To show changes in a variable over time or to compare relationships between two or more variables	A graph comparing spending on advertising from 2009 to 2011 in different media, such as TV networks, the Internet, and print newspapers and magazines
Tables	To organize and condense data; to compare and classify information	A table showing how many calories men and women need daily for various age groups with either an active or a sedentary lifestyle
Diagrams and flowcharts	To explain processes or procedures or show how things work	A diagram showing the process by which the U.S. Constitution can be amended

6. **Study the data to try to identify trends or patterns.** Also note unexpected changes (such as sudden increases or decreases in amounts), surprising statistics, or unexplained variations.

In Figure 4.2, note that there is a consistently higher number of casualties in Iraq than in Afghanistan.

7. **Make a brief summary note about any trends or patterns you find.** Writing will crystallize the idea in your mind, and your note will be useful for review.

A summary note of Figure 4.2 might read, "The wars in Iraq and Afghanistan have produced a large number of casualties among soldiers, including those who have been killed (dead and wounded, and those evacuated for reasons besides

FIGURE 4.2

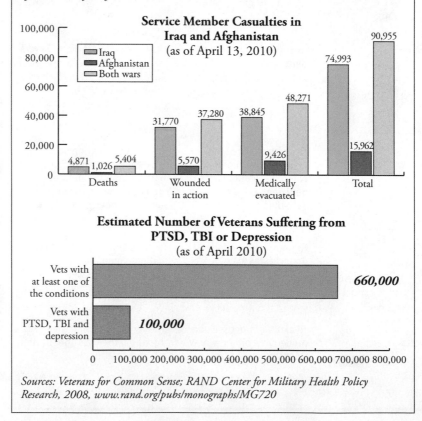

Brain Injuries Put Strain on VA Benefits

Nearly 91,000 U.S. soldiers have either died, been wounded or medically evacuated for noncombat-related reasons thus far in the Iraq and Afghanistan wars (top). The 760,000 veterans who suffer from either post-traumatic stress disorder (PTSD) or traumatic brain injury (TBI), or both, have put the Veterans Benefits Administration under increasing pressure to meet the needs of the country's injured veterans.

Service Member Casualties in Iraq and Afghanistan
(as of April 13, 2010)

- Iraq
- Afghanistan
- Both wars

	Deaths	Wounded in action	Medically evacuated	Total
Iraq	4,871	31,770	38,845	74,993
Afghanistan	1,026	5,570	9,426	15,962
Both wars	5,404	37,280	48,271	90,955

Estimated Number of Veterans Suffering from PTSD, TBI or Depression
(as of April 2010)

Vets with at least one of the conditions — **660,000**

Vets with PTSD, TBI and depression — **100,000**

0 100,000 200,000 300,000 400,000 500,000 600,000 700,000 800,000

Sources: Veterans for Common Sense; RAND Center for Military Health Policy Research, 2008, www.rand.org/pubs/monographs/MG720

battlefield injuries). Large numbers of veterans also suffer from one or more of the following conditions—PTSD, TBI, or depression."

8. **Think critically about the graphic.** Consider questions like these: Are the data from a reputable source? Is the information current and accurate? How objective is the graphic? Are the data presented fairly? Is the meaning of the data clear, or is anything vague or confusing? Are the scale or units of measurement misleading in any way? Could the information be presented differently to show a different trend or outcome?

In Figure 4.2, the data are from two different sources. The first source listed, Veterans for Common Sense, is a nonprofit organization that was formed, according to a statement on its Web site, "to raise the unique and powerful voices of veterans so that our military, veterans, freedom, and national security are protected and enhanced, for ourselves and for future generations." The second source is a part of the RAND Center, a well-known nonprofit institution dedicated to research and analysis to improve policy and decision making. Its Web site says that its "core values" are quality and objectivity. The second source seems more reliable than the first because it is less likely to be biased in favor of a certain policy agenda. It is unclear, however, which sources were used for each graphic.

Notice, too, that the first graph presents actual numbers, and the second offers estimates. The accuracy of the first graph can be questioned since the figures given for each category of casualty (deaths, wounded in action, and medically evacuated) for Iraq and Afghanistan do not quite add up to the figures given as the total casualties for each war. In the second graph, the labels to the left of the two bars are confusing in relation to each other and to the caption that introduces the two graphs. Apparently the bottom label means "Vets with all three conditions," so that the 100,000 figure in that bar would be included in the 660,000 figure in the first bar. But the caption gives a total of 760,000 for veterans with either PTSD, TBI, or both—with no mention of depression. The significance of the information in the graphic would be clearer if the caption and labels were clearer about the role that depression plays.

Exercise 4.13

Study the table on the following page using the guidelines presented above, and answer the following questions:

1. How is the table organized?
2. What is the purpose of the table?
3. What trends and patterns are evident for bachelor's degrees? For master's degrees? For both degrees? What differences in trends and patterns are there between the two degrees?
4. Write a brief summary note.
5. Do you consider the source of the data to be reliable?
6. Note that the table reports data in ten-year intervals from 1968 to 1988 and then in five-, four-, and seven-year intervals. Consider possible reasons for this variation. Does an increased frequency of reporting make the increases seem less dramatic?

TABLE Academic Degrees Conferred by Sex

	Bachelor's Degree					Master's Degree				
Year	Total	Men	%	Women	%	Total	Men	%	Women	%
1968	632,289	357,682	57	274,607	43	176,749	113,552	64	63,197	36
1978	921,204	487,347	53	433,857	47	311,620	161,212	52	150,408	48
1988	994,829	477,203	48	517,626	52	299,317	145,163	48	154,154	52
1998	1,172,000	523,000	45	649,000	55	406,000	183,000	45	223,000	55
2003	1,312,503	537,079	41	775,424	59	512,645	211,381	41	301,264	59
2007	1,524,092	649,264	43	874,828	57	604,607	238,216	39	366,391	61
2014*	1,582,000	633,000	40	949,000	60	693,000	275,000	40	418,000	60

*Projected

Source: Unpublished tabulations, Bureau of Labor Statistics, Current Population Survey. 2003 and 2014 (projected) data, Tables 27 & 28, "Projections of Education Statistics to 2014," National Center for Education Statistics, U.S. Department of Education; 2007 update. U.S. Department of Education, National Center for Education Statistics (2009). Condition of Education 2009.

Exercise 4.14

For each of the following, discuss what type of graphic might be used to advance the writer's purpose and help the reader grasp the material more easily:

1. To show the religious affiliations of Americans in 2011
2. To show percentages of registered voters who participated in each presidential election from 1988 to 2008 for five age groups, four racial or ethnic groups, four levels of education, five categories of marital status, and eight categories of income
3. To compare percentages of African Americans, whites, Latinos, and Asian Americans who divorced in each decade from 1970 to 2010
4. To show the process by which a legal immigrant can become a citizen
5. To show where divorce in the United States occurs at an average rate, at a below-average rate, and at an above-average rate

A GUIDE TO RESPONDING TO TEXT

Active reading is the first step in understanding a text, but equally important is responding. Once you respond to material, you understand it better.

When an instructor assigns a reading, some form of response is always expected. You might be expected to participate in a class discussion, summarize the information as part of an essay exam, or research the topic further and report your findings. One type of response that instructors assign is a **response paper,** which requires you to read an essay, analyze it, and write about some aspect of it. For some assignments, your instructor may suggest a particular direction for the paper. At other times, you decide how to respond to the essay.

Before beginning any response paper, make sure you understand the assignment. If you are uncertain of what your instructor expects, be sure to ask. You may also want to check with other students to find out how they are approaching the assignment. If your instructor does not mention length requirements, ask how long the paper should be.

In a response paper, you may include a brief summary as part of your introduction (see the next section); but you should concentrate on interpreting and evaluating what you have read. Do not attempt to discuss all of your reactions, however. Instead, choose one key idea, one question the essay raises, or one issue it explores.

For example, suppose your instructor asks you to read an article titled "Advertising: A Form of Institutional Lying" that tries to show that advertisements deceive consumers by presenting half-truths, distortions, and misinformation. Your instructor asks you to write a two-page paper about the essay but gives you no other directions. In writing this response paper, you might take one of the following approaches:

- Discuss how you were once deceived by an advertisement, as a means of confirming the author's main points.
- Evaluate the evidence and examples the author provides to support his claim; determine whether the evidence is relevant and sufficient.
- Discuss the causes or effects of deception in advertising that the author overlooks (you might need to consult other sources to take this approach).
- Evaluate the assumptions the author makes about advertising or consumers.

For an assignment like this one or for any response paper, how do you decide on an issue to write about? How do you come up with ideas about a reading? This guide will help you. It presents a step-by-step process for discovering ideas for response papers, as shown in Figure 4.3. Notice that it begins with summary writing to check and clarify

FIGURE 4.3 Active Response to a Reading

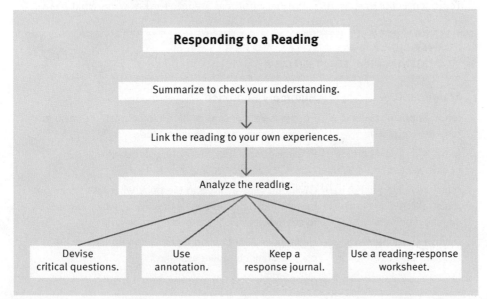

your understanding, moves to connecting the ideas to your own experiences, and then offers numerous strategies for analyzing the reading. Each of these steps is discussed below within the context of a reading assignment.

Summarize to Check Your Understanding

A **summary** is a brief statement of major points, and summarizing is something that we all practice every day. When a friend asks, "What was the movie about?" we reply with a summary of the plot. A summary presents only the main ideas, not details. Your summary of a movie would not include specific scenes or dialogue, for example. When summarizing print text, a summary is less than one-fifth of the original.

Summarizing is an excellent way to check whether you have understood what you have read. If you have difficulty writing a summary, you probably do not understand what is important in the reading. Summarizing is an excellent way to improve your retention of the material and makes it easier for you to keep track of a writer's important ideas. Summaries can be reviewed easily and quickly in preparation for a class discussion or exam.

For more on journal writing, see Chapter 2, p. 32.

Many students keep a journal in which they write summaries of essays as well as other responses to what they read. Journal writing is a good way to generate and record ideas about an essay, and your journal entries can serve as useful sources of ideas for writing papers.

To write an effective and useful summary, use the following seven guidelines:

1. **Read the entire essay before attempting to write anything.**
2. **Highlight or annotate as you read.** These markings will help you pick out what is important to include in your summary.
3. **Write your summary as you reread the essay.**
4. **Write an opening sentence that states in your own words the author's thesis—the most important idea the entire essay explains.**
5. **Include the author's most important supporting ideas.** Use either highlighted topic sentences or marginal summary notes as a guide for knowing what to in-

---

CONVERTING MARGINAL NOTES TO SUMMARY SENTENCES

Marginal Note	Summary Sentence
(para. 2) politeness and rudeness together	People make conscious efforts to be polite but also are unconsciously thoughtless and rude.
(para. 4) political correctness in excess	Political correctness has gone overboard.
(para. 12) being out of touch with real survival causes rudeness	Civilization has evolved to the point where we no longer have to focus on the basics of survival, which causes us to act selfishly while pretending to be civil.
(para. 14) people have stopped paying attention	Unintentional distraction and self-absorption are the causes of much rudeness.

clude. Marginal summary notes briefly state the content of each paragraph. If you write notes similar to those on pages 54–55, you can easily convert them into sentences for your summary. Following is a list of the marginal notes written for the essay "American Jerk," which appeared in Chapter 3 (p. 54). Also shown are sentences that have been generated from the notes, which then become part of the sample summary paragraph below.

6. **Present the ideas in the order in which they appear in the original source.** Be sure to use transitions (connecting words) as you move from one supporting idea to another.

7. **Reread your summary to determine if it contains sufficient information.** Would your summary be understandable and meaningful to someone who has not read the essay? If not, revise it to include additional information.

Here is a sample summary for the essay "American Jerk." It was written by a student using the preceding seven steps.

> Although people believe they are acting politely, rudeness and incivility are on the rise. We overdo political correctness, yet we behave rudely to everyone around us. Media, entertainment, and cell-phone usage illustrate improper behavior and support our rudeness. The author believes that because our civilization has evolved to the point that we are no longer concerned with basic survival, we can act selfishly while pretending to be civil. The author also contends that people are simply distracted and self-absorbed but not intentionally rude. The bottom line is that people must choose their own behavior and decide how they will act.

The writer expresses Schwartz's thesis in her own words.

The order of ideas parallels the order in Schwartz's essay.

The writer continues to use her own words—not those of Schwartz.

Exercise 4.15

Write a summary of the section "Avoiding Misconceptions" in Chapter 3 (pp. 47–48).

Link the Reading to Your Own Experiences

One way to start ideas flowing for a response paper is to think about how the reading relates to your own experiences. This builds a bridge between you and the author and between your ideas and the author's.

- **Begin by looking for useful information in the essay that you could apply or relate to other real-life situations.** Think of familiar situations or examples that illustrate the subject. For example, for "American Jerk," which considers incivility in society in general, you might write a journal entry about incivility among college students.
- **Try to think beyond the reading itself.** Recall other material you have read and events you have experienced that are related to the reading. In thinking about "American Jerk," for example, you might recall an article about cell-phone use for texting.

- **Use the key-word response method for generating ideas.** Choose one or more key words that describe your initial response, such as *angered, amused, surprised, confused, annoyed, curious,* or *shocked.* For example, fill in the following blank with key words describing your response to "American Jerk."

"After reading the essay, I felt _____."

The key-word response you just wrote will serve as a point of departure for further thinking. Start by explaining your response; then write down ideas as they come to you, trying to approach the reading from many different perspectives. Here is the result of one student's key-word response to "American Jerk."

For more on freewriting, see Chapter 5, pp. 110–11.

Possible Topic #1: how generations create their own values

Possible Topic #2: how behavior changes with changes in technology

> After reading "American Jerk," I felt annoyed and insulted. I agree that the world has changed because of cell phones, but I don't think that these changes have made people ruder. Each generation creates its own rules and values, and the cell-phone generation is doing that. If media and entertainment were horrible and insulting, then people wouldn't watch them. Humans are evolving, and our expectations have to evolve with technology. Some people do act like they are polite when they actually do rude things all the time. Behavior comes from people. People have to change it.

Exercise 4.16

Review the three preceding techniques for linking a reading to your own experiences. Choose one of those techniques, and use it on the topic of rudeness in public life.

Analyze the Reading

Analyzing, like summarizing, is a skill we use every day. After you see a movie, you ask a friend, "So what did you think of it?" Your friend may praise the plot, criticize the photography, or comment on the believability of the characters. When you analyze a reading, then, you comment on any aspect of the essay—such as the author's fairness or accuracy, his or her method of presentation, the quality of the supporting evidence provided, or the intended audience. To discover ideas for analysis, you could devise critical questions, use annotation, keep a response journal, and use a reading-response worksheet.

Devise Critical Questions

Asking critical questions and then answering them is a useful method for analysis and for discovering ideas for a response paper. Here are three sample questions and the answers that one student wrote in response to them after reading the essay "American Jerk."

Possible topic: how to teach politeness and effective methods

Can we turn the tide and find a way to return to a polite society?

I think that adults emphasize politeness less than in the past. Parents and teachers hardly try to instill it in children. People no longer have to learn etiquette. To improve manners would require us to rethink how we raise and educate children.

Is technology causing people to be less civil, or is it just an excuse?

Technology has changed the way that people communicate with each other. Technology makes it easier to have less personal contact with others, but it does not encourage rudeness. It's possible to use technology and still be civil to other people.

Possible topic: the effect of technology on human behavior

Why are people more distracted and thoughtless now than they used to be?

People have probably always been distracted and thoughtless, but today so many things clamor for our attention that it is easier than ever to be distracted. We are focused less on the people around us and more on the electronics we use throughout the day.

Possible topic: the effect of distractions on the ways that people interact with each other

> **Essay in Progress 1**
> Write a list of critical questions about the reading "American Jerk" on page 50 or another essay assigned by your instructor. Use *why, how,* and *what* questions to generate ideas about the reading.

Use Annotation

In the Guide to Active Reading in Chapter 3 (p. 48), you learned to annotate as you read. Annotation can also be used to analyze and respond to a reading when you read it for the second time and are preparing to write about it. As you read an essay for the second time, record additional reactions that occur to you. Some students prefer to use a different color of ink to record their second set of annotations. Refer to the sample student annotation shown on p. 56.

> **Essay in Progress 2**
> Reread "American Jerk" or the other assigned essay, this time adding annotations that record your reactions to and questions about the essay as you read.

Keep a Response Journal

A response journal is a section of your writing journal (see Chapter 2, p. 32) in which you record your reactions to and questions about readings. Experiment with these two ways to organize a response journal until you discover the one that works best for you.

The Open-Page Format

On a blank page, write, outline, draw, or create a diagram to express your reactions to an essay. Because the open-page format encourages you to let your ideas flow freely, it may work well for creative and spatial learners. Figure 4.4 shows one student's open-page response journal entry for "American Jerk." This entry suggests several possible topics to write about—identifying generational differences in defining civility, determinating standards for civility, and recognizing subjectivity in evaluating behavior.

FIGURE 4.4 Sample Open-Page Journal Format

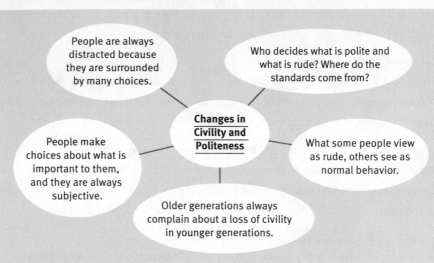

The Two-Column Format

Divide several pages of your journal into two vertical columns. If you journal on a computer, you can insert a table with two columns. Label the left side "Quotations" and the right side "Responses." Under "Quotations," jot down five to ten quotations from the text. Choose remarks that seem important—that state an opinion, summarize a viewpoint, and so forth. In the right column, next to each quotation, write your response to the quotation. You might explain it, disagree with or question it, relate it to other information in the reading or in another reading, or tie it to your own experiences. The two-column format forces you to think actively about an essay while you question what you have read and draw connections. Because it provides more structure than the open-page format, students who tend to be pragmatic or concrete learners may find it effective.

Figure 4.5 follows the two-column format. In this entry, the writer has uncovered several possible topics—types or degrees of rudeness, the meaning of "socio-economically disadvantaged," and self-centered behavior.

For more on paraphrasing, see Chapter 21, pp. 611–12.

You may find it useful to paraphrase the quotation before writing your response. Paraphrasing forces you to think about the meaning of the quotation, and ideas for writing may come to mind as a result. To use paraphrasing, add a "Paraphrases" column to your journal between the "Quotations" column and the "Responses" column.

> **Essay in Progress 3**
>
> For "American Jerk" or another essay, write a response in your journal using the open-page format or the two-column format.

Use a Reading-Response Worksheet

An easy way to record all of your ideas about a reading in one place is to use a reading-response worksheet. The worksheet guides your response while directing your thinking. A blank worksheet is shown in Figure 4.6 on page 94. Notice that it includes space for

FIGURE 4.5 Sample Two-Column Journal Format

Quotations	Responses
"A moment when a roomful of even relatively evolved people will react with discomfort to an off-color joke about people of color—and when those same people have no compunction whatsoever about loudly ignoring one another as they blather into their cell phones."	This statement implies that racial jokes and talking on your cell phone are somehow on the same level of rudeness.
"No one is 'poor,' but many are 'socioeconomically disadvantaged.'"	There is a distinction between "poor" and "socio-economically disadvantaged," and it's an important one. The first term has to do with money, but the second one also has to do with culture and opportunities.
"The second is that sunlight contains tiny spores that lodge in the cerebellum, making the infected believe they are the center of the universe."	This is a joke, but the author is saying that everyone sees themselves as important; this is a bad thing; and schools, churches, and parents teach this message to children to build self-esteem.

recording your first impressions, a summary, connections to your own experiences, ideas for analysis, and additional sources.

Using Your Learning Style

If you are a *verbal* or *social* learner, you probably find reading a comfortable and convenient way to obtain information. If you are a *spatial* learner, though, you may prefer graphic images (like those in videos and films) to printed text. Regardless of your learning style, most of your assignments will be in print form. Therefore, you need to use your learning style in a way that enhances your reading and writing. The following guidelines for active reading and response are tailored to the various learning styles:

Learning Style Options

- If you are a *spatial* learner, create mental pictures of people and places. For example, while reading the essay "American Jerk," on p. 54, you might create a mental image of a person behaving rudely. In addition, use graphic organizers and diagrams to organize the ideas in an essay. As you annotate, use symbols to connect the ideas within and between paragraphs (for example, see the symbols listed for the reading-response journal on p. 34).
- If you are a *social* learner, discuss a reading assignment with a classmate both before and after reading. Preview the essay together, sharing ideas about the topic. After reading the essay, discuss your reactions to it. In both instances, use the Guide to Active Reading in Chapter 3 (p. 48) and the Guide to Responding to Text in this chapter (p. 86) to get started.
- If you are an *abstract* learner, a *creative* learner, or both, you may overlook details and instead focus on the "big ideas" and overall message of a reading. Be sure to highlight important points and to concentrate on facts and supporting details.

FIGURE 4.6 Sample Reading-Response Worksheet

READING-RESPONSE WORKSHEET

TITLE: _____

AUTHOR: _____

FIRST IMPRESSIONS: _____

_____

_____

SUMMARY: _____

_____

_____

_____

_____

CONNECTIONS TO YOUR OWN EXPERIENCES: _____

_____

_____

_____

ANALYSIS (issue, aspect, feature, problem)

1. _____

_____

_____

2. _____

_____

_____

_____

ADDITIONAL SOURCES OR VISUALS (if needed)

1. _____

_____

2. _____

_____

3. _____

_____

- If you are a *concrete* learner, a *pragmatic* learner, or both, you may like to focus on details instead of seeing how ideas fit together and contribute to an author's overall message. Use graphic organizers to help you create a larger picture. Try to make the essay as "real" as possible; visualize events occurring or the author writing. You might visualize yourself interviewing the author, alone or with a panel of classmates.

- If you are an *emotional* learner, you may focus on your feelings about people or events in the essay and overlook the way an author uses them to convey an overall message. Keep this question in mind: How does the author use these people or events to get his or her message across?

- If you are a *rational* learner, you may see how logical or clear the presentation of ideas is and overlook more subtle shades of meaning. Be sure to annotate, which will draw out your personal reactions to a piece of writing.

Essay in Progress 4

Discuss "American Jerk" with a classmate. Make notes as you discuss. If you chose another essay, pair up with a classmate who also chose that essay, or ask your classmate to read the essay you have chosen.

Essay in Progress 5

Write a two- to four-page paper in response to "American Jerk" or the essay you have chosen. Use the following steps to shape the ideas you generated in Essays in Progress 1 to 4:

1. Reread the writing you did in response to the reading. Look for ideas that seem worthwhile and important enough to become the basis of your essay.

2. Look for related ideas. Try to find ideas that fit together to produce a viewpoint or position toward the reading.

3. Do not attempt to cover all your ideas. Your essay should not analyze every aspect of the essay. Instead, you should focus on one feature or aspect.

4. Write a sentence that states your central point. This sentence will become your thesis statement. It should state what your essay will assert or explain.

5. Collect ideas and evidence from the reading to support your thesis. Your thesis should be backed up by specifics in the reading.

6. Organize your ideas into essay form. Your paper should have a title, introduction, body, and conclusion.

7. Revise your essay. Be sure that you have explained your ideas clearly and have provided support from the reading for each one.

8. Proofread for accuracy and correctness. Use the Suggestions for Proofreading in Chapter 10 (pp. 221–22).

For more on thesis statements, see Chapter 6. For more on organizing your ideas, see Chapter 7. To help you revise your essay, see Chapter 9. For more on editing and proofreading, see Chapter 10.

How to Approach the Student Essays in This Book

Use the following suggestions when reading student essays:

- **Read an essay several times.** During your first reading, concentrate on the writer's message. Then read the essay again as many times as necessary to analyze its writing features. For example, first notice how the writer supported the thesis statement, and then look at the language used to create a particular impression.
- **Read with a pen or marker in hand.** As you discover writing techniques that are emphasized in the chapter, mark or annotate them.
- **Focus on characteristics.** Each chapter in Part 3 presents the characteristics of a particular method of organization. Consider how the student essay demonstrates some or all of that method's characteristics.
- **Focus on techniques.** Each chapter in Part 3 offers specific techniques and suggestions for writing a particular type of essay. Review these techniques and observe how the writer applied them.
- **Focus on what is new and different.** Ask yourself the following questions as you read: What is the writer doing that you haven't seen before? What catches your attention? What works particularly well? What techniques might be fun to try? What techniques would be challenging to try? For example, if a writer begins his or her essay with a striking statistic, consider whether you could use a striking statistic to begin your essay.
- **Use student essays to train your critical eye.** Although student essays are reasonably good models, they are not perfect. Look for ways the essays can be improved. Once you can see ways to improve someone else's essay, you will be better equipped to analyze and improve your own writing.
- **Use graphic organizers to grasp the essay's structure.** In Part 3, a graphic organizer is presented for each method of organization. Compare the essay to the graphic organizer, noticing how the essay contains each element.

Students Write

Karen Vaccaro wrote the following essay in response to "American Jerk." As you read, notice how Vaccaro analyzes Schwartz's points about civility and the lack of it in our society.

READING

Introduction: Identifies the article Vaccaro is responding to

In her thesis statement Vaccaro states how her ideas differ from those of Schwartz.

Vaccaro agrees with Schwartz.

"American Jerk"? How Rude! (but True)

In his article "American Jerk," Todd Schwartz claims that Americans today are both the most   1
and the least civil we have ever been. Although the painful truth in these observations is a bit hard
to take, Schwartz eases the reality by providing a great deal of humorous relief. Schwartz's claim
is an apt one, and most of his observations about our current culture are accurate, but some of his
observations and accusations are broad generalizations that don't always hold true.

"We have never been more concerned about the feelings of minority groups, the disabled,   2
and the disadvantaged," Schwartz writes in paragraph 3, and he is right. We have become a
culture obsessed with being PC (politically correct). I often carefully choose and often second-
guess the words I use to describe anyone of a different race or physical or mental ability, for

fear of offending anyone. And yet many people I encounter seem hardly concerned about offending me. Schwartz is right that "we have never been less concerned about the feelings of anyone with whom we share the road, the Internet, or the movie theater" (para. 3). Cyclists seem to have taken over city streets and even shout insults at me when I am walking in a crosswalk (and they are breaking the law by ignoring a red light). Despite many methods used to discourage theater goers from using their cell phones, cell phones ring during films, concerts, and plays. In fact, last week I was at a live theater performance, and in the middle of an important scene, a cell phone rang in the audience — twice.

Vaccaro offers examples of lack of concern.

In another example of how (overly) civil we've become, Schwartz writes, "Schools won't let **3** teachers use red pens to correct papers because . . . self-esteem might be bruised" (para. 4). This reminded me of the teaching internship I did while studying abroad in China one semester. I taught an English writing course to Chinese high school students. One day I was marking up the students' papers with a red pen (as I thought teachers were supposed to do). Another American teacher said, "I thought teachers weren't supposed to mark students' papers with red pens anymore." I asked if red was offensive to Chinese students. "No," she answered. "Some of my teachers back home in America said it's because red is a harsh color that really stands out from the black and white." "Well, yes, I thought that was the point," I said. "But it can make some students feel bad," she responded. "That's the silliest thing I've ever heard," I said as I went back to marking my students' papers with the red pen. Have we become so "civil" that we're afraid to teach students? Don't young men and women come to class expecting to learn something, knowing that at some point they will need to be corrected to see their mistakes so that they can truly learn?

Vaccaro connects Schwartz's ideas to her own experience and affirms his ideas.

Then there are the less civil aspects of our culture, as Schwartz so accurately points out. We **4** Americans have become obsessed with reality television shows that often take advantage of the misfortune and embarrassment of others. In addition, "giant assault vehicles" (para. 7) dwarf other cars on the road, guzzle gas, often take up more than one parking space, and seem unnecessary on city streets in a time of environmental awareness and concern. Furthermore, we are so interested in our technological gadgets that we ignore real human-to-human interactions. "We're all talking to someone all the time," Schwartz writes, "but it's ever more rarely to the people we are actually with" (para. 8). I have noticed that my boyfriend often whips out his new iPhone. Even when we're walking and talking, catching up after days of not seeing one another, he's playing a new game, downloading a new app, or chatting with his friends. I myself can be guilty of this rude behavior. Sometimes I am spending time with one friend but will be texting another friend. I know it's rude, but I do it anyway (usually because the friend I'm with is doing the same thing and therefore it seems okay). We no longer realize how rude it is to divide our attention between two sources instead of giving our friend or loved one our full, undivided attention.

Vaccaro identifies another of Schwartz's points that she agrees with and admits that she is guilty of it as well.

Where I must disagree with Schwartz, though, is his sweeping, unfounded statement that we **5** are now living in "what must certainly be the rudest era in history" (para. 5). Really? Are we ruder

Vaccaro moves to points with which she disagrees.

than people who enslaved others and denied them any and all rights, including the right to be treated like human beings and not animals? Are people who refuse to "shut their inane traps" (para. 7) ruder than people in the time of segregation? It might be easy to convince ourselves that the present must be the rudest time in our history, since it is freshest in our minds, and we know it very well. But if Schwartz took time to flesh out his observations and accusations with concrete examples, he might rethink such a generalization.

Conclusion: Vaccaro points out the value of Schwartz's article.

Even if it doesn't fix the problems it calls attention to, Schwartz's entertaining and witty article forces us to stop and think about how contemporary American culture straddles the line between civility and rudeness. Many of his examples illustrate the hypocrisy of our behaviors and ways of thinking. Ultimately, Schwartz is correct in his claim that "we have arrived at simultaneously the most and least civil moment in U.S. history" (para. 2). I doubt, though, that Neanderthals—with their barbaric weapons and primitive hunting instincts—"were probably nicer to each other than we are" (para. 6).

Analyzing the Writer's Technique

1. Express Vaccaro's thesis (central point) in your own words.
2. What kinds of information does Vaccaro include to support her thesis?
3. Where would additional examples help Vaccaro support her thesis?

Reacting to the Reading

1. Vaccaro admits to texting one friend while visiting with another. Are you also guilty of acts of incivility? If so, describe one.
2. What steps or actions could be taken to build Americans' awareness of their lack of civility?
3. Do you agree or disagree that our culture is obsessed with political correctness? Give examples to support your answer.
4. Write a journal entry describing an act of incivility that you have observed or experienced that particularly disturbed or annoyed you.

PART 2

Strategies for Writing Essays

CHAPTER 5

Prewriting: How to Find and Focus Ideas

Study the photo on the opposite page. What is happening in the photo? What do you think the man could be reacting to?

Take out a sheet of paper or open a new computer file, and write whatever comes to mind about the photo and what you think might be happening in it. You might write about times when you've felt the same emotions you think the man is expressing, or you might write about times when you've seen others express strong emotions in a public place. Try to write nonstop for at least five minutes, jotting down or typing whatever ideas cross your mind. Don't stop to evaluate your writing or to phrase your ideas in complete sentences or correct grammatical form. Just record your thinking.

You have just used *freewriting,* a method of discovering ideas about a topic. Read over what you wrote. Suppose you were asked to write an essay about joy or exuberance. Do you see some starting points and usable ideas in your freewriting? In this chapter, you will learn more about freewriting as well as a number of other methods, in addition to those described in Chapter 4, that will help you find ideas to write about. You will also learn how to focus an essay by considering why you are writing (your purpose), whom you are writing for (your audience), and what perspective you are using to approach your topic (point of view). These steps are all part of the beginning of the process of writing an essay, as illustrated in Figure 5.1 (p. 103).

Choosing and Narrowing a Topic

When you begin an essay assignment, it's a good idea to allow time for choosing a broad topic and then narrowing it to be manageable within the assigned length of your paper. Skipping this step is one of the biggest mistakes you can make in beginning a writing assignment. You can waste a great deal of time working on an essay only to discover that the topic is too large or that you don't have enough to say about it.

Choosing a Topic

In some writing situations, your instructor will assign the topic. In others, your instructor will allow you to write on a topic of your choice. Or you may be given a number of possible topics to choose from, as in the Guided Writing Assignments in Chapters 11–18, 20, and 24 of this text. In the latter cases, use the following guidelines to choose a successful topic:

1. **Invest time in making your choice.** It may be tempting to grab the first topic that comes to mind, but you will produce a better essay if you work with a topic that interests you and that you know something about.
2. **Focus on questions and ideas rather than topics.** For example, the question, Do television commercials really sell products? may come to mind more easily than the broad topic of advertising or commercials.
3. **Use your journal as a source of ideas.** Chapter 2 describes how to keep a writing journal, and Chapter 4 explains how to use a response journal. If you have not begun keeping a journal, start one now; try writing in it for a few weeks to see if it is helpful.
4. **Discuss possible topics with a friend.** Conversations with friends may help you discover worthwhile topics and give you feedback on topics you have already thought of.
5. **Consult Table 5.1 (p. 104) or Table 5.3 (p. 119).** A number of specific sources of ideas for essay topics are listed in Table 5.1. Table 5.3 groups topics from this chapter's exercises into broad categories.

FIGURE 5.1 An Overview of the Writing Process

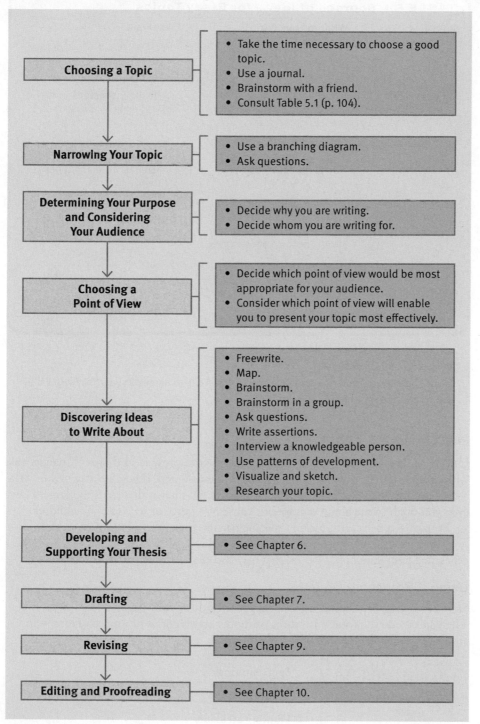

TABLE 5.1 Sources of Ideas for Essay Topics

Source	What to Look For	Example
Your classes	Listen for issues, controversies, and new ideas that might be worth exploring.	A discussion in your education class leads you to the topic of standardized testing.
Daily activities	Take note of incidents at work and at sporting or social events.	A health inspector's visit at work suggests an essay on restaurant food safety.
Newspapers and magazines	Flip through recent issues; look for articles that might lead to promising topics.	You find an interesting article on a hip-hop musician and decide to write about her career.
Radio, television, and the Internet	Listen to your favorite radio station for a thought-provoking song, or look for ideas in television programs and commercials or on the Web.	Commercials for diet soda suggest an essay on the diet-food industry.
The world around you	Look within your household or outside of it. Notice people, objects, and interactions.	You notice family members reading books or newspapers and decide to write about the value of leisure time.

Essay in Progress 1
Using the suggestions on page 102 and in Table 5.1 to stimulate your thinking, list at least three broad topics.

Narrowing a Topic

Once you have chosen a topic, the next step is to narrow it so that it is manageable within the length of the essay your instructor has assigned. If you are assigned to write a two- to four-page essay, for example, a broad topic such as divorce is too large. However, you might write about one specific cause of divorce or its effects on children.

To narrow a topic, limit it to a specific part or aspect. The following techniques—branching and questioning—will help you do so. Later in the chapter, you will learn idea-generating techniques (pp. 110–17) that may also be used to narrow a broad topic.

Using a Branching Diagram

Start by writing your broad topic at the far left side of your paper or computer screen. Then subdivide the topic into three or more subcategories or aspects. Here is an example for the broad topic of wild-game hunting.

■ **Wild-game hunting**
- Sport hunting
- As source of food
- Hunting accidents

Then choose one subcategory and subdivide it further, as shown here.

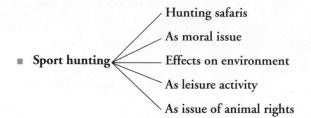

■ **Sport hunting**
- Hunting safaris
- As moral issue
- Effects on environment
- As leisure activity
- As issue of animal rights

Continue narrowing the topic in this way until you feel you have found one that is both interesting and manageable.

Keep in mind that once you begin planning, researching, and drafting the essay, you may need to narrow your topic even further. The following example shows additional narrowing of the topic "effects on environment."

■ **Effects on environment**
- **Prized species may become endangered.**
- **Hunters may spoil pristine wilderness areas.**
- **Regulated hunting helps control animal populations.**

Any one of these narrowed topics would be workable for a two- to four-page essay. Did you notice that as the narrowing progressed, the topics changed from words and phrases to statements of ideas?

Exercise 5.1

Use branching diagrams to narrow three of the following broad topics to more manageable topics for a two- to four-page essay:

1. Divorce

2. Manned space travel

3. School lunches

4. Air travel safety measures

5. Campaign finance rules

6. Alternative energy sources

Essay in Progress 2
Narrow one of the broad topics you chose in Essay in Progress 1 to a topic manageable for a two- to four-page essay:

Asking Questions to Narrow a Broad Topic

Use questions that begin with *who, what, where, when, why,* and *how* to narrow your topic. Questioning will lead you to consider and focus your attention on specific aspects of the topic. Here is an example of questioning for the broad topic of divorce.

Questions	*Narrowed Topics*
Why does divorce occur?	• Lifestyle differences as a cause of divorce • Infidelity as a cause of divorce
How do couples divide their property?	• Division of assets during a divorce
Who can help couples work through a divorce?	• Role of friends and family • Marital counselor's or attorney's role in divorce
What are the effects of divorce on children?	• Emotional effects of divorce on children • Financial effects of divorce on children
When might it be advisable for a couple considering divorce to remain married?	• Couples who stay together for the sake of their children • Financial benefit of remaining married

As you can see, the questions about divorce produced several workable topics. At times, however, you may need to ask additional questions to get to a topic that is sufficiently limited. The topic "emotional effects of divorce on children," for example, is still too broad for an essay. Asking questions such as "What are the most typical emotional effects?" and "How do divorcing parents prevent emotional problems?" would lead to more specific topics.

Exercise 5.2

Use questioning to narrow three of the following subjects to topics that would be manageable within a two- to four-page essay:

1. Senior citizens
2. Mental illness
3. Environmental protection

4. Cyber bullying
5. Television programming

Thinking about Your Purpose, Audience, and Point of View

Once you have decided on a manageable topic, you are ready to determine your purpose and consider your audience.

Determining Your Purpose

A well-written essay should have a specific purpose or goal. There are three main purposes for writing—to *express* yourself, to *inform* your reader, and to *persuade* your reader. For example, an essay might express the writer's feelings about an incident of road rage that he or she observed. Another essay may inform readers about the primary causes of road rage. Still another essay might attempt to persuade readers to vote for funding to investigate the problem of road rage in the local community.

As you plan your draft essay, ask yourself two critical questions.

- Why am I writing this essay?
- What do I want this essay to accomplish?

Some essays can have more than one purpose. An essay on snowboarding, for example, could be both informative and persuasive: It could explain the benefits of snowboarding and then urge readers to take up the sport because it is good aerobic exercise.

Considering Your Audience

Considering your **audience**—the people who read your essay—is an important part of the writing process. Many aspects of your writing—how you express yourself (the type of sentence structure you use, for example), which words you choose, what details and examples you include, and what attitude you take toward your topic—all depend on the audience. Your **tone**—how you sound to your audience—is especially important. If you want your audience to feel comfortable with your writing, be sure to write in a manner that appeals to them.

If you were describing a student orientation session to a friend, you would use a different tone and select different details than you would if you were describing the orientation in an article for the student newspaper. Consider the following examples and notice how they differ.

TELLING A FRIEND

Remember I told you how nervous I am about attending college in the fall? Well, guess what? I went to my student orientation over the weekend, and it was much better than I had expected! I even met one of my psych teachers—they call them "instructors" here—and he was so nice and down-to-earth that now I'm starting to get excited about going to college.

Language: casual
Sentence Structure: shorter sentences
Tone: familiar, friendly

WRITING FOR THE STUDENT NEWSPAPER

College student orientations are often thought to be stuffy affairs where prospective students attempt to mix with aloof professors. For this reason, I am pleased to report that the college orientation held on campus last weekend was a major success and not a pointless endeavor after all. Along with my fellow incoming first-year students, I was impressed with the friendliness of instructors and the camaraderie that developed between students and faculty.

Language: more formal
Sentence Structure: longer sentences
Tone: serious, formal

How to Consider Your Audience

As you consider your audience, keep the following points in mind:

- **Your readers are not present and cannot observe or participate in what you are writing about.** If you are writing about your apartment, for example, they cannot visualize it unless you describe it in detail.

- **Your readers do not know everything you do.** They may not have the same knowledge about and experience with the topic that you do, and they may not know what specialized terms mean.
- **Your readers may not necessarily share your opinions and values.** If you are writing about raising children and assume that strict discipline is undesirable, for example, some readers may not agree with you.
- **Your readers may not respond in the same way you do to situations or issues.** Some readers may not see any humor in a situation that you find funny. An issue that you consider only mildly disturbing may make some readers upset or very angry.

The following box lists questions you can ask to analyze your audience:

- **What does your audience know or not know about your topic?** If you are proposing a community garden project to an audience of city residents who know little about gardening, you would need to describe the pleasures and benefits of gardening to capture their interest.
- **What is the education, background, and experience of your audience?** If you are writing your garden-project proposal for an audience of low-income residents, you might emphasize how much money they could save by growing vegetables, but if you are proposing the project to middle-income residents, you might stress instead how relaxing gardening can be and how a garden can beautify a neighborhood.
- **What attitudes, beliefs, opinions, or biases is your audience likely to hold?** If, for example, your audience believes that most development is harmful to the environment and you are writing an essay urging your audience to agree to a new community garden, consider emphasizing how the garden will benefit the environment and decrease development.
- **What tone do your readers expect you to take?** Suppose you are writing to your local city council urging council members to approve the community garden. Although the council has been stalling on the issue, your tone should be serious and not accusatory. As community leaders, the council members expect to be treated with respect.

When Your Audience Is Your Instructor

Instructors occasionally direct students to write for a particular audience, such as readers of a certain magazine or newspaper, but you can usually assume that your audience is your instructor. You should not, however, automatically assume that he or she is an expert on your topic. In most cases, it is best to write as if your instructor were unfamiliar with your topic. He or she wants to see if you understand the topic and can write and think clearly about it. For academic papers, then, you should provide enough information to demonstrate your knowledge of the subject. Include background information, definitions of technical terms, and relevant details to make your essay clear and understandable.

1. Write a one-paragraph description of a current television commercial for a particular product. Your audience is another college student.

2. Write a description of the same commercial for one of the following writing situations:

   a. An assignment in a business marketing class: Analyze the factors that make the advertisement interesting and appealing. Your audience is a marketing instructor.

   b. A letter to the company that produces the product: Describe your response to the advertisement. Your audience is the consumer relations director of the company.

   c. A letter to your local television station: Comment favorably on or complain about the advertisement. Your audience is the station director.

Choosing a Point of View

Point of view is the perspective from which you write an essay. There are three types—*first, second,* and *third person.* In choosing a point of view, consider your topic, your purpose, and your audience.

Think of point of view as the "person" you become as you write. For some essays, you may find first-person pronouns (*I, me, mine, we, ours*) effective and appropriate, such as in an essay narrating an event in which you participated. For other types of essays, second-person pronouns (*you, your, yours*) are appropriate, as in an essay explaining how to build a fence: "First, *you* should measure . . ." At times, the word *you* may be understood but not directly stated, as in "First, measure . . ." Many textbooks, including this one, use the second person to address student readers.

In academic writing, the third-person point of view is prevalent. The third-person point of view is less personal and more formal than both the first person and the second person. The writer uses people's names and third-person pronouns (*he, she, they*). Think of the third person as public rather than private or personal. The writer reports what he or she sees.

Working with a classmate, discuss which point of view (first, second, or third person) would be most appropriate in each of the following writing situations:

1. An essay urging students on your campus to participate in a march against hunger to support a local food drive

2. A description of a car accident on a form that your insurance company requires you to submit in order to collect benefits

3. A paper for an ecology course on the effects of air pollution caused by a local industry

Discovering Ideas to Write About

Many students report that one of the most difficult parts of writing an essay is finding enough to say about a narrowed topic. In the following sections, you will learn a number of useful strategies for discovering ideas to write about. Experiment with each before deciding which will work for you. Depending on your learning style, you will probably discover that some strategies work better than others. You may also find that the technique you choose for a given essay may depend in part on your topic.

Freewriting

When you use **freewriting**, you write nonstop for a specific period of time, usually five to ten minutes. As you learned in the activity that opens this chapter, freewriting involves writing whatever comes to mind, regardless of its relevance to your topic. If nothing comes to mind, just write the topic, your name, or "I can't think of anything to write." Then let your mind run free: Explore ideas, make associations, jump from one idea to another. The following tips will help you:

- **Be sure to write nonstop.** Writing often forces thought.
- **Don't be concerned with grammar, punctuation, or spelling.**
- **Write fast!** Try to keep up with your thinking. (Most people can think faster than they can write.)
- **Record ideas as they come to you** and in whatever form they appear—words, phrases, questions, or sentences.
- **If you are freewriting on a computer, darken the screen** so that you are not distracted by errors, formatting issues, and the words you have already written.

Next, reread your freewriting, and highlight or underline ideas that seem useful. Look for patterns and connections. Do several ideas together make a point; reflect a sequence; or suggest a larger, unifying idea? Here is an excerpt from one student's freewriting on the broad topic of violence in the media.

> There seems to be a lot of violence in the media these days, particularly on TV. For example, last night when I watched the news, the camera man showed people getting shot in the street. What kind of people watch this stuff? I'd rather watch a movie. It really bothered me because people get so turned off by such an ugly, gruesome scene that they won't want to watch the news anymore. Then we'll have a lot of uninformed citizens. There are too many already. Some people do not even know who the vice president of the U.S. is. A negative thing--that is the media has a negative impact on anyone or group who want to do something about violence in the inner city. And they create negative impressions of minority and ethnic groups, too. If the media shows one Latino man committing a crime, viewers falsely assume all Latinos are criminals. It's difficult to think of something positive that can be done when you're surrounded by so much violence. It's all so overwhelming. What we need in the inner city is not more coverage of violence but viable solutions to the violence we have. The media coverage

of violent acts only serves to make people think that this <u>violence is a normal state of</u> <u>affairs and nothing can be done</u> about it.

A number of different subtopics surfaced from this student's freewriting:

The media's graphic portrayal of violence

The negative effect of media violence on viewers

The media's portrayal of minority and ethnic groups

Any one of these topics could be narrowed into a manageable topic for an essay.

If you are a creative learner or feel restricted by organization and structure, freewriting may appeal to you because it allows you to give your imagination free rein.

Learning Style Options

Exercise 5.5

Set a clock or timer for five minutes and freewrite on one of the following broad topics. Then review and highlight your freewriting, identifying usable ideas with a common theme that might serve as a topic for an essay. Starting with this potential topic, freewrite for another five minutes to narrow your topic further and develop your ideas.

1. Rap music
2. Blogs
3. How to be self-sufficient
4. Pressures on college students
5. Job interviews

Mapping

Mapping, or **clustering**, is a visual way to discover ideas and relationships. It is also a powerful tool for some writers. Here is how it works.

1. Write your topic in the middle of a blank sheet of paper, and draw a box or circle around it.
2. Think of ideas that are related to or suggested by your topic. As you think of them, write them down in clusters around the topic, connecting them to the topic with lines (see Figure 5.2, p. 112). Think of your topic as a tree trunk and the related ideas as branches.
3. Draw arrows and lines or use highlighting to show relationships and connect groups of related ideas.
4. Think of still more ideas, clustering them around the ideas already on your map.
5. If possible, experiment with mapping on a computer, using a graphics program such as the draw function available in Microsoft Word. You can then cut and paste items from your map into an outline or draft of your essay.

The sample map in Figure 5.2 was done by a student working on the topic of the costs of higher education. In this map, the student compared attending a local community college and attending an out-of-town four-year college. A number of different subtopics evolved, including the following:

- Transportation costs
- Social life
- Availability of degree programs
- Room and board costs

FIGURE 5.2 Sample Map

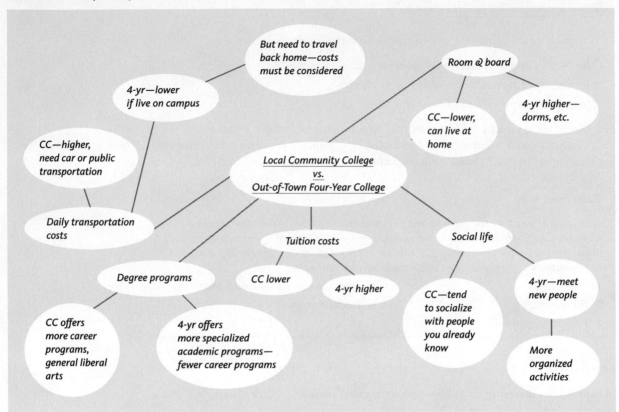

Learning Style Options   Mapping may appeal to you if you prefer a spatial method of dealing with information and ideas. It also appeals to creative learners who like to devise their own structure or framework within which to work.

Exercise 5.6

Narrow one of the following topics. Then select one of your narrowed topics, and draw a map of related ideas as they come to mind.

1. Presidential politics
2. Daydreaming
3. Tattoos
4. Cable TV
5. Year-round schooling

Brainstorming

When you do **brainstorming**, you list everything that comes to mind when you think about your topic—impressions, emotions, and reactions, as well as facts. Record words or phrases rather than sentences, and give yourself a time limit; it will force ideas to come faster. If you use a computer, you might use bullets or the indent function to brainstorm.

The following example shows a student's brainstorming on the narrowed topic of the disadvantages of home schooling.

Topic: Disadvantages of Home Schooling

- Parent may not be an expert in each subject
- Libraries not easily accessible
- Wide range of equipment, resources not available
- Child may be confused by parent playing the role of teacher
- Child does not learn to interact with other children
- Child does not learn to compete against others
- Parents may not enforce standards
- Parents may not be objective about child's strengths and weaknesses
- Child may learn only parent's viewpoint--not exposed to wide range of opinions
- Special programs (art, music) may be omitted
- Services of school nurse, counselors, reading specialists not available

Three clusters of topics are evident—unavailable services and resources (highlighted in purple), limits of parents, and problems of social development (highlighted in green). Once the student selected a cluster of topics, he did further brainstorming to generate ideas about his narrowed topic.

Learning Style Options

Brainstorming is somewhat more structured than freewriting because the writer focuses only on the topic at hand instead of writing whatever comes to mind. If you are a pragmatic learner, brainstorming may help you release your creative potential.

Brainstorming can also work well when it is done in groups of two or three classmates. Use a chalkboard in an empty classroom, share a large sheet of paper, sit together in front of a computer screen, or use networked computers. Say your ideas aloud as you write. You'll find that your classmates' ideas will trigger more of your own. Group brainstorming often appeals to students who are social learners and who find it stimulating and enjoyable to exchange ideas with other students.

Exercise 5.7

Choose one of the following subjects and narrow it to a manageable topic for a two- to four-page paper. Then brainstorm, either alone or with one or two classmates, to generate ideas to write about.

1. Value of music
2. National parks
3. Credit-card fraud
4. Texting
5. Web advertising

Questioning

Questioning is another way to discover ideas about a narrowed topic. Working either alone or with a classmate, write down every question you can think of about your topic. As with other prewriting strategies, focus on ideas, not correctness. Don't judge or evaluate ideas as you write. It may help to imagine that you are asking an expert on your topic anything that comes to mind.

Here is a partial list of questions one student generated on the narrow topic of the financial problems faced by single parents.

Possible Topics:
income disparity

financial planning

Why do many female single parents earn less than male single parents?

How can single parents afford to pay for day care?

Is there a support group for single parents that offers financial advice and planning?

How do single parents find time to attend college to improve their employability?

child support

establishment of credit

employability

How can women force their former husbands to keep up with child support payments?

How can single female parents who don't work outside the home still establish credit?

Are employers reluctant to hire women who are single parents?

Is it more difficult for a working single parent to get a mortgage than for a couple in

which only one spouse works?

Beginning a question with "What if . . ." is a particularly good way to extend your thinking and look at a topic from a fresh perspective. Here are a few challenging "What if . . ." questions about the financial situation of single parents:

What if the government provided national day care or paid for day care?

What if single parents were not allowed to deduct more than one child on their

income tax?

What if there were financial support groups for single parents?

Learning Style Options

You may find questioning effective if you are an analytical, inquisitive person, and social learners will enjoy using this technique with classmates. Since questions often tend to focus on specifics and details, questioning is also an appealing strategy for concrete learners.

Exercise 5.8

Working either alone or with a classmate, choose one of the following topics, narrow it, and write a series of questions to discover ideas about it.

1. The campus newspaper
2. Learning a foreign language
3. Financial aid regulations
4. Late-night talk radio shows
5. Government aid to developing countries

Writing Assertions

The technique of **writing assertions** forces you to look at your topic from a number of different perspectives. Abstract learners who prefer to deal with wholes rather than parts or who tend to focus on larger ideas rather than details often find this technique appealing. Begin by writing five to ten statements that take a position on or make an assertion about your topic. Here are a few possible assertions for the topic of the growing popularity of health food.

Learning Style Options

> Supermarkets have increased their marketing of health foods.
>
> Health food is popular because buying it makes people think they are hip.
>
> Health food is popular because it is chemical-free.
>
> Health food tricks people into thinking they have a healthy lifestyle.

Review your list of assertions, choose one statement, and try brainstorming, freewriting, or mapping to generate more ideas about it.

Exercise 5.9

Working either alone or with one or two classmates, write assertions about one of the following topics:

1. Advertising directed toward children
2. Buying a used car from a private individual
3. Needed improvements in public education
4. Characteristics of a good teacher
5. Attempts to encourage healthier eating on campus

Using the Patterns of Development

In Parts 3 and 4 of this book, you will learn nine ways to develop an essay—narration, description, illustration, process analysis, comparison and contrast, classification and division, definition, cause and effect, and argument. These methods are often called *patterns of development.* In addition to providing ways to develop an essay, the patterns of development may be used to generate ideas about a topic. Think of the patterns as doors through which you can gain access to your topic. Just as a building or room looks different depending on which door you enter, so you will see your topic in various ways by approaching it through different patterns of development.

The list of questions in Table 5.2 (p. 116) will help you approach your topic through these different "doors." For any given topic, some questions will work better than others. If your topic is voter registration, for example, the questions listed for definition and process analysis would be more helpful than those listed for description. The strategy may appeal to you if you are a pragmatic learner who enjoys structured tasks or a creative learner who likes to analyze ideas from different viewpoints.

Learning Style Options

As you write your answers to the questions, also record any related ideas that come to mind. If you are working on a computer, create a table listing the patterns

TABLE 5.2 Using the Patterns of Development to Explore a Topic

Pattern of Development	Questions to Ask
Narration (Chapter 11)	What stories or events does this topic remind you of?
Description (Chapter 12)	What does the topic look, smell, taste, feel, or sound like?
Illustration (Chapter 13)	What examples of this topic are particularly helpful in explaining it?
Process Analysis (Chapter 14)	How does this topic work? How do you do this topic?
Comparison and Contrast (Chapter 15)	To what is the topic similar? In what ways? Is the topic more or less desirable than those things to which it is similar?
Classification and Division (Chapter 16)	Of what larger group of things is this topic a member? What are its parts? How can the topic be subdivided? Are there certain types or kinds of the topic?
Definition (Chapter 17)	How do you define the topic? How does the dictionary define it? What is the history of the term? Does everyone agree on its definition? Why or why not? If not, what points are in dispute?
Cause and Effect (Chapter 18)	What causes the topic? How often does it happen? What might prevent it from happening? What are its effects? What may happen because of it in the short term? What may happen as a result of it over time?
Argument (Chapters 19 and 20)	What issues surround this topic?

Learning Style Options

in one column and your questions in another. This way, you can brainstorm ideas about various rhetorical approaches. Pragmatic and creative learners will find this technique helpful.

One student who was investigating the topic of extrasensory perception (ESP) decided to use the questions for definition and cause and effect. Here are the answers she wrote:

Definition (How can my topic be defined?)

- ESP, or extrasensory perception, is the ability to perceive information not through the ordinary senses but as a result of a "sixth sense" (as yet undeveloped in most people).

- Scientists disagree on whether ESP exists and how it should be tested.

Cause and Effect (Why does my topic happen? What does it lead to?)

- Scientists do not know the cause of ESP and have not confirmed its existence, just the possibility of its existence.
- The effects of ESP are that some people know information that they would (seemingly) have no other way of knowing.
- Some people with ESP claim to have avoided disasters such as airplane crashes.

Using the patterns of development helps to direct or focus your mind on specific issues related to a topic.

Exercise 5.10

Use the patterns of development to generate ideas on one of the following topics. Refer to Table 5.2 (p. 116) to form questions based on the patterns.

1. Buying only American-made products
2. Effects of email spam
3. Community gardens in urban areas
4. How high-speed trains would change travel
5. Cell-phone usage

Visualizing or Sketching

Especially if you enjoy working with graphics, **visualizing** or actually **sketching** your topic may be an effective way to discover ideas. If you are writing a description of a person, for example, close your eyes and visualize that person in your mind. Imagine what he or she is wearing; study facial expressions and gestures.

Here is what one student "saw" when visualizing a shopping mall. Possible subtopics are annotated.

As I walked through the local mall, I crossed the walkway to get to Sears and noticed a large group of excited women all dressed in jogging suits; they were part of a shopping tour, I think. I saw a tour bus parked outside. Across the walkway was a bunch of teenagers, shouting and laughing and commenting on each other's hairstyles. They all wore T-shirts and jeans; some had body adornments--pierced noses and lips. They seemed to have no interest in shopping. Their focus was on one another. Along the walkway came an obvious mother-daughter pair. They seemed to be on an outing, escaping from their day-to-day routine for some shopping, joking, and laughing. Then I noticed a tired-looking elderly couple sitting on one of the benches. They seemed to enjoy just sitting there and watching the people walk by, every now and then commenting on the fashions they observed people wearing.

Possible Subtopics:

tour-group shopping

body piercing

teenage behavior

Visualization is a technique particularly well suited to spatial and creative learners.

Learning Style Options

Exercise 5.11

Visualize one of the following situations. Make notes on or sketch what you "see." Include as many details as possible.

1. A traffic jam
2. A couple obviously "in love"
3. A class you recently attended
4. The campus snack bar
5. A sporting event

Researching Your Topic

For more information on locating, using, and crediting sources, refer to Chapters 21 and 23.

Do some preliminary research on your topic in the library or on the Internet. Reading what others have written about your topic may suggest new approaches, reveal issues or controversies, and help you determine what you do and do not already know about the topic. This method is especially useful for an assigned essay with an unfamiliar topic or for a topic you want to learn more about.

Learning Style Options

Take notes while reading sources. In addition, be sure to record the publication data you will need to cite each source (author, title, publisher, page numbers, and so on). If you use ideas or information from sources in your essay, you must give credit to the sources of the borrowed material. While research may be particularly appealing to concrete or rational learners, all students may need to use it at one time or another depending on their topic.

Exercise 5.12

Do library or Internet research to generate ideas on one of the narrowed topics listed here.

1. A recent local disaster (hurricane, flood)
2. Buying clothing on e-Bay
3. Preventing terrorism in public buildings
4. Controlling children's access to television programs
5. Reducing the federal deficit

Exercise 5.13

Choose two prewriting techniques discussed in this chapter that appeal to you. Experiment with each method by generating ideas about one of the topics from the previous exercises in the chapter. These topics are listed in Table 5.3. Use a different topic for each prewriting technique you choose.

Essay in Progress 3

Keeping your audience and purpose in mind, use one of the prewriting strategies discussed in this chapter to generate details about the topic you narrowed in Essay in Progress 2.

TABLE 5.3	Broad Topics from Chapter 5 Exercises
Family Matters	Divorce Senior citizens Mental illness Year-round schooling Controlling children's access to television programs
College Life	Pressures on college students The campus newspaper Learning a foreign language Financial aid regulations Characteristics of a good teacher Attempts to encourage healthier eating on campus A class you recently attended The campus snack bar
Community Concerns	Cyberbullying Car accidents Needed improvements in public education Community gardens in urban areas A traffic jam A recent local disaster (hurricane, flood)
National Government	Manned space travel Air-travel safety measures Campaign finance rules Environmental protection Presidential politics National parks Government aid to developing countries Preventing terrorism in public buildings Reducing the deficit
World Issues	Alternative energy sources
Consumer Culture	Television advertising Credit-card fraud Web advertising Advertising directed toward children Buying a used car from a private individual Buying only American-made products Buying clothes on e-Bay Effects of email spam Cell-phone usage
Entertainment Culture	Television programming Rap music Cable TV Value of music Late-night talk radio shows A sporting event

(continued on next page)

TABLE 5.3 *(continued)*

Technology Issues	Blogs
	Texting
	Cell-phone usage
Everyday Life	School lunches
	How to be self-sufficient
	Job interviews
	Daydreaming
	Tattoos
	How high-speed trains would change travel
	A couple obviously "in love"

Students Write

In this and the remaining five chapters of Part 2, we will follow the work of Christine Lee, a student in a first-year writing course who was assigned to write about a recent trend or fad in popular culture.

Lee decided to use questioning to narrow her topic and freewriting to generate ideas about the topic. Here is an example of her questioning.

SAMPLE QUESTIONING

What are some recent fads or trends?

  Freak dancing

  Political blogging

  Extreme sports

  Tattooing and body piercing

  Reality TV

Lee decided to explore two of these experiences further: tattooing and body piercing and reality TV. She did so by asking another question.

Why are these trends popular?

1. Tattooing and body piercing

  They are forms of self-expression.

  They can be considered an art form--body art.

  They can be used to commemorate a particular person or event, such as the loss of a
    loved one.

  They can make a fashion statement and identify people as part of a group.

2. Reality TV

> People are more likely to identify with real people, not actors.
>
> The shows are usually contests, which keep viewers watching until the last episode.
>
> They are unscripted and often unpredictable.
>
> Survivor was popular because money was involved.

After looking over the answers to her questions, Lee chose reality TV as her topic, and she decided to focus on its evolution and popularity. The following excerpt from her freewriting shows how she started to develop her topic.

SAMPLE FREEWRITING

When *Survivor* was first on TV everyone was watching and talking about it at school and work. It was new and different, and it was interesting to watch how people started to act when a million dollars was at stake. Everybody had a favorite and someone else they loved to hate. After that season it seemed like every network had two or three competition reality shows they were trying out. They get more and more ridiculous and less tasteful with every new show. And now they are coming up with shows based on talent and beauty contests, like *American Idol*. Now I'm getting tired of all these "real" people as they defend their pettiness by saying "It's just a game." In the end I'll go back to watching *Modern Family* because it's funny (which *Big Brother* never is), and *Brothers and Sisters* because they talk about serious issues that real people deal with. Maybe we'd all like to think that we wouldn't be as petty and mean as all of these contestants, but with all of these "real" people on TV these days, I can't relate to a single one of them.

As you work through the remaining chapters of Part 2, you will see how Lee develops her tentative thesis statement in Chapter 6, her first draft in Chapter 7, a specific paragraph in Chapter 8, and her final draft in Chapter 9. In addition, in Chapter 10, you will also see a portion of her final draft, edited and proofread to correct sentence-level errors.

Developing and Supporting a Thesis

Study the cartoon on the opposite page; it humorously depicts a serious situation. Working alone or with one or two classmates, write a statement that expresses the main point of the cartoon. Your statement should not just describe what is happening in the cartoon but also state the idea that the cartoonist is trying to communicate to his audience.

The statement you have just written is an assertion around which you could build an essay. Such an assertion is called a *thesis statement*. In this chapter, you will learn how to write effective thesis statements and how to support them with evidence. Developing a thesis is an important part of the writing process shown in Figure 6.1, which lists the skills presented in this chapter while placing them within the context of the writing process.

FIGURE 6.1 An Overview of the Writing Process

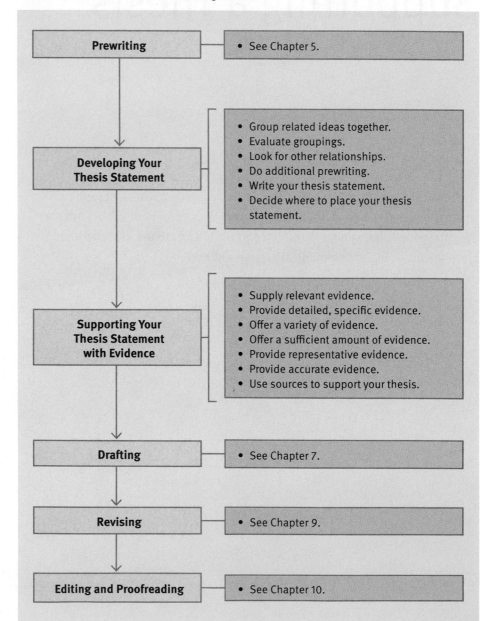

Prewriting
- See Chapter 5.

Developing Your Thesis Statement
- Group related ideas together.
- Evaluate groupings.
- Look for other relationships.
- Do additional prewriting.
- Write your thesis statement.
- Decide where to place your thesis statement.

Supporting Your Thesis Statement with Evidence
- Supply relevant evidence.
- Provide detailed, specific evidence.
- Offer a variety of evidence.
- Offer a sufficient amount of evidence.
- Provide representative evidence.
- Provide accurate evidence.
- Use sources to support your thesis.

Drafting
- See Chapter 7.

Revising
- See Chapter 9.

Editing and Proofreading
- See Chapter 10.

What Is a Thesis Statement?

A **thesis statement** is the main point of an essay. It explains what the essay will be about and expresses the writer's position on the subject. It may also give clues about how the essay will develop or how it will be organized. Usually a thesis statement is expressed in a single sentence. When you write, think of a thesis statement as a promise to your reader. The rest of your essay delivers on your promise.

Here is a sample thesis statement.

Playing team sports, especially football and baseball, develops skills and qualities that can make you successful in life because these sports demand communication, teamwork, and responsibility.

In this thesis, the writer identifies the topic—team sports—and states the position that team sports, especially football and baseball, equip players with important skills and qualities. After reaching the end of this statement, the reader expects to discover what skills and qualities football and baseball players learn and how these contribute to success in life.

Developing Your Thesis Statement

A thesis statement usually evolves or develops as you explore your topic during prewriting: Do not expect to be able to sit down and simply write one. As you prewrite, you may discover a new focus or a more interesting way to approach your topic. Expect to write several versions of a thesis statement before you find one that works. For some topics, you may need to do some reading or research to get more information about your topic or tentative thesis. Your thesis may change, too, as you organize supporting evidence and draft and revise your essay.

For more on prewriting, see Chapter 5.

For more on library and Internet research, see Chapter 22.

Your learning style can influence how you develop a thesis statement. Some students find it helpful to generate facts and details about a narrow topic and then write a thesis statement that reveals a large idea that is demonstrated by the details (pragmatic and concrete learners). Other students find it easier to begin with a broad idea, focus it in a thesis statement, and then generate details to support the thesis (creative and abstract learners).

Learning Style Options

Coming Up with a Working Thesis Statement

To come up with a preliminary or working thesis for your paper, reread your prewriting, and highlight details that have to do with the same subtopic. Write a word or phrase that describes each group of related ideas.

For example, a student working on the topic of intelligence in dogs noticed in her brainstormed list that the details she highlighted could be grouped into two general categories—details about learning and details about instinct. Here is how she arranged her ideas.

Learning

follow commands

perform new tricks

read master's emotions

adapt to new owners

get housebroken

serve as guide dogs for blind people

roll up clothing to carry it more easily

carry empty water dish to owner

Instinct

females deliver and care for puppies

avoid danger and predators

seek shelter

automatically raise hair on back in response to aggression

When you've grouped similar details together, the next step is to decide which group or groups of ideas best represent the focus your paper should take. In some instances, one group of details will be enough to develop a working thesis for your paper. At other times, you'll need to use the details in two or three groups. The student working on a thesis for the topic of intelligence in dogs evaluated her groups of details and decided that instinct was unrelated to her topic. Consequently, she decided to write about learning.

If you are not satisfied with how you have grouped or arranged your details, you probably don't have enough details to come up with a good working thesis. If you need more details, use prewriting to generate more ideas. Be sure to try a different prewriting strategy than the one you used previously. A new strategy may help you see your narrowed topic from a different perspective. If your second prewriting does not produce better results, consider refocusing or changing your topic.

For more on prewriting, see Chapter 5.

Essay in Progress 1

If you used a prewriting strategy to generate details about your topic in response to Essay in Progress 3 in Chapter 5 (p. 119), review your prewriting, highlight useful ideas, and identify several sets of related details among those you have highlighted.

Writing an Effective Thesis Statement

A thesis statement should introduce your narrowed topic, revealing what your essay is about, and state the point you will make about that topic. Use the following guidelines to write an effective thesis statement or to evaluate and revise your working thesis:

1. **Make an assertion.** An **assertion**, unlike a fact, takes a position, expresses a viewpoint, or suggests your approach toward the topic.

LACKS AN ASSERTION	Hollywood movies, like *127 Hours* and *The King's Speech*, are frequently based on true stories.
REVISED	Hollywood movies, like *127 Hours* and *The King's Speech*, manipulate true stories to cater to the tastes of the audience.

2. **Be specific.** Try to provide as much information as possible about your main point.

TOO GENERAL	I learned a great deal from my experiences as a teenage parent.
REVISED	From my experiences as a teenage parent, I learned to accept responsibility for my own life and for that of my son.

3. **Focus on one central point.** Limit your essay to one major idea.

FOCUSES ON SEVERAL POINTS	This college should improve its tutoring services, sponsor more activities of interest to Latino students, and speed up the registration process for students.
REVISED	To better represent the student population it serves, this college should sponsor more activities of interest to Latino students.

4. **Offer an original perspective on your topic.** If your thesis seems dull or ordinary, it probably needs more work. Search your prewriting for an interesting angle on your topic.

TOO ORDINARY	Many traffic accidents are a result of carelessness.
REVISED	When a driver has an accident, it can change his or her entire approach to driving.

5. **Avoid making an announcement.** Don't use phrases such as "This essay will discuss" or "The subject of my paper is." Instead, state your main point directly.

MAKES AN ANNOUNCEMENT	The point I am trying to make is that people should not be allowed to smoke on campus.
REVISED	The college should prohibit smoking on campus.

6. **Use your thesis to preview the organization of the essay.** Consider using your thesis to mention the two or three key concepts on which your essay will focus, in the order in which you will discuss them.

Exercise 6.1

Working in a group of two or three students, discuss what is wrong with each of the following thesis statements. Then revise each thesis to make it more effective.

1. In this paper, I will discuss the causes of asthma, which include exposure to smoke, chemicals, and allergic reactions.

2. Jogging is an enjoyable aerobic sport.

3. The crime rate is decreasing in American cities.

4. Living in an apartment has many advantages.

5. Children's toys can be dangerous, instructional, or creative.

Essay in Progress 2

Keeping your audience in mind, select one or more of the groups of ideas you identified in Essay in Progress 1, and write a working thesis statement based on these ideas.

Placing the Thesis Statement

Your thesis statement can appear anywhere in your essay, but it is usually best to place it in the first paragraph as part of your introduction. When your thesis appears at the beginning of the essay, your readers will know what to pay attention to and what to expect in the rest of the essay. When your thesis is placed later in the essay, you need to build up to the thesis gradually in order to prepare readers for it.

Using an Implied Thesis

In some professional writing, especially in narrative or descriptive essays, the writer may not state the thesis directly. Instead, the thesis may be strongly implied by the details the writer chooses and the way those details are organized. Although professional writers may use an implied thesis, academic writers—including professors and students—generally state their thesis. You should always include a clear statement of your thesis for your college papers.

Supporting Your Thesis Statement with Evidence

After you have written a working thesis statement, the next step is to develop evidence that supports your thesis. **Evidence** is any type of information, such as examples, statistics, or expert opinion, that will convince your reader that your thesis is reasonable or correct. This evidence, organized into well-developed paragraphs, makes up the body of your essay. To visualize the basic structure of an essay, look ahead to Figure 7.2 on page 143.

Choosing Types of Evidence

Although there are many types of evidence, it is usually best not to use them all. Analyze your purpose, audience, and thesis to determine which types of evidence will be most effective. If your audience is unfamiliar with your topic, provide definitions, historical background, an explanation of a process, and factual and descriptive details. If your purpose is to persuade, use comparison and contrast, advantages and disadvantages, examples, problems, statistics, and quotations to make your argument. Table 6.1 lists various types of evidence and gives examples of how each type could be used to support a working thesis on acupuncture. Note that many of the types of evidence correspond to the patterns of development discussed in Parts 3 and 4 of this text.

Exercise 6.2

1. Working in a group of two to three students, discuss and list the types of evidence that could be used to support the following thesis statement for an informative essay:

   The pressure to become financially independent is a challenge for many young adults and often causes them to develop social and emotional problems.

2. For each audience listed here, discuss and record the types of evidence that would offer the best support for the preceding thesis.

   a. Young adults

   b. Parents of young adults

   c. Counselors of young adults

TABLE 6.1 Types of Evidence Used to Support a Thesis

Working Thesis Acupuncture, a form of alternative medicine, is becoming more widely accepted in the United States.

Types of Evidence	Example
Definitions	Explain that in acupuncture, needles are inserted into specific points of the body to control pain or relieve symptoms.
Historical background	Explain that acupuncture is a medical treatment that originated in ancient China.
Explanation of a process	Explain the principles on which acupuncture is based and how scientists think it works.
Factual details	Explain who uses acupuncture, on what parts of the body it is used, and under what circumstances it is applied.
Descriptive details	Explain what acupuncture needles look and feel like.
Narrative story	Relate a personal experience that illustrates the use of acupuncture.
Causes or effects	Discuss one or two theories that explain why acupuncture works. Offer reasons for its increasing popularity.
Classification	Explain types of acupuncture treatments.
Comparison and contrast	Compare acupuncture with other forms of alternative medicine, such as massage and herbal medicines. Explain how acupuncture differs from these other treatments.
Advantages and disadvantages	Describe the pros (nonsurgical, relatively painless) and cons (fear of needles) of acupuncture.
Examples	Describe situations in which acupuncture has been used successfully—by dentists, in treating alcoholism, for pain control.
Problems	Explain that acupuncture is not always practiced by medical doctors; licensing and oversight of acupuncturists may thus be lax.
Statistics	Indicate how many acupuncturists practice in the United States.
Quotations	Quote medical experts who attest to the effectiveness of acupuncture as well as those who question its value.

Collecting Evidence to Support Your Thesis

Learning Style Options

Prewriting may help you collect evidence for your thesis. Try a different prewriting strategy from the one you used previously to arrive at a working thesis statement. Depending on your learning style, select one or more of the following suggestions to generate evidence that supports your thesis:

1. Complete the worksheet shown in Figure 6.2. For one or more types of evidence listed in the left column of the worksheet, give examples that support your thesis in the right column. Collect evidence only for those types that are appropriate for your thesis.
2. Visualize yourself speaking to your audience. What would you say to convince your audience of your thesis? Jot down ideas as they come to you.

For more on outlining, see Chapter 7, pp. 148–150.

3. On a sheet of paper or in a computer file, develop a skeletal outline of major headings. Leave plenty of blank space under each heading. Fill in ideas about each heading as they come to you.

See p. 60 in Chapter 3 for instructions on drawing a graphic organizer. For samples of graphic organizers for each pattern of development, see Parts 3 and 4. To draw detailed graphic organizers using a computer, visit www.bedfordstmartins .com/successfulcollege.

4. Draw a graphic organizer of your essay, filling in supporting evidence as you think of it.
5. Discuss your thesis statement with a classmate; try to explain why he or she should accept your thesis as valid.

Essay in Progress 3

Using the preceding list of suggestions for collecting evidence to support a thesis, generate at least three different types of evidence to support the working thesis statement you wrote in Essay in Progress 2.

Choosing the Best Evidence

Learning Style Options

In collecting evidence in support of a thesis, you will probably generate more than you need. Consequently, you will need to identify the evidence that best supports your thesis and that suits your purpose and audience. Your learning style can also influence the way you select evidence and the kinds of evidence you favor. If you are a creative or an abstract learner, for example, you may tend to focus on large ideas and overlook the need for supporting detail. However, if you are a pragmatic or concrete learner, you may tend to include too many details or fail to organize them logically.

The following guidelines will help you select the types of evidence that will best support your thesis:

1. **Make sure the evidence is relevant.** All of your evidence must clearly and directly support your thesis. Irrelevant evidence will distract your readers and cause them to question the validity of your thesis. If your thesis is that acupuncture is useful for controlling pain, you would not need to describe other, less popular alternative therapies.
2. **Provide specific evidence.** Avoid general statements that will neither engage your readers nor help you make a convincing case for your thesis. For instance, to support the thesis that acupuncture is becoming more widely accepted by patients in the United States, it would be most convincing to cite statistics that demonstrate

FIGURE 6.2 A Worksheet for Collecting Evidence

Purpose: _____

Audience: _____

Point of View: _____

Thesis Statement: _____

_____

Type of Evidence	Actual Evidence
Definitions	
Historical background	
Explanation of a process	
Factual details	
Descriptive details	
Narrative story	
Causes or effects	
Classification	
Comparison and contrast	
Advantages and disadvantages	
Examples	

(continued on next page)

FIGURE 6.2 *(continued)*

Type of Evidence	Actual Evidence
Problems	
Statistics	
Quotations	

an increase in the number of practicing acupuncturists in the United States over the past five years.

To locate detailed, specific evidence, return to your prewriting or use a different prewriting strategy to generate concrete evidence. You may also need to conduct research to find evidence for your thesis.

For more on conducting research, see Chapters 21–23.

3. **Offer a variety of evidence.** Using diverse kinds of evidence increases the likelihood that your evidence will convince your readers. If you provide only four examples of people who have found acupuncture helpful, for example, many of your readers may conclude that these few isolated examples are not convincing. If you provide statistics and quotations from experts along with an example or two, however, more readers will be likely to accept your thesis. Using different types of evidence also shows readers that you are knowledgeable and informed about your topic, thus enhancing your own credibility.

4. **Provide a sufficient amount of evidence.** The amount of evidence you need will vary according to your audience and your topic. To discover whether you have provided enough evidence, ask a classmate to read your essay and tell you whether he or she is convinced. If your reader is not convinced, ask him or her what additional evidence is needed.

5. **Provide representative evidence.** Be sure the evidence you supply is typical and usual. Do not choose unusual, rare, or exceptional situations as evidence. Suppose your thesis is that acupuncture is widely used for various types of surgery. An example of one person who underwent painless heart surgery using only acupuncture without anesthesia will not support your thesis unless the use of acupuncture in heart surgery is routine. Including such an example would mislead your reader and could bring your credibility into question.

For more on choosing reliable sources, see Chapter 21, pp. 584–85.

6. **Provide accurate evidence.** Gather your information from reliable sources. Do not guess at statistics or make estimates. If you are not certain of the accuracy of a fact or statistic, verify it through research. For example, do not estimate the number of medical doctors who are licensed to practice acupuncture in the United States. Instead, find out exactly how many U.S. physicians are licensed to practice.

Choosing Evidence for Academic Writing

For most kinds of academic writing, certain types of evidence are preferred over others. In general, your personal experiences and opinions are not considered as useful as more objective evidence such as facts, statistics, historical background, and research evidence. Suppose you are writing an academic paper on the effects of global warming. Your own observations about climate changes in your city would not be considered adequate or appropriate evidence to support the idea of climatic change as an effect of global warming. Instead, you would need to provide facts, statistics, and research evidence on climatic change in a wide range of geographic areas and demonstrate their relationship to global warming.

Essay in Progress 4
Evaluate the evidence you generated in Essay in Progress 3. Select from it the evidence that you could use to support your thesis in a two- to four-page essay.

Using Sources to Support Your Thesis

For many topics, you will need to research library or Internet sources or interview an expert on your topic to collect enough supporting evidence for your thesis. Chapter 22 provides a thorough guide to locating sources in the library and on the Internet, and it also includes tips for conducting interviews (pp. 615–16). Chapter 23 provides guidelines for integrating and documenting sources. Also see "Using Sources to Add Details to an Essay" on page 577 of Chapter 21.

Essay in Progress 5
Locate and consult at least two sources to find evidence that supports the working thesis statement you wrote in Essay in Progress 2.

Students Write

In the Students Write section of Chapter 5, you saw how student writer Christine Lee narrowed her topic and generated ideas for her essay on a contemporary trend or fad. You also saw how she decided to focus on reality TV.

After reviewing her responses to questions about her topic and her freewriting, Lee decided that reality TV had become less tasteful and less interesting. She then wrote the following working thesis statement.

> As the trend in competition reality TV wears on, shows are becoming both less interesting and less tasteful.

To generate more details to support her thesis, Lee did more freewriting and brainstorming to help her recall details from shows. Here's an excerpt from what she wrote:

- Early shows: *Cops* and *Candid Camera*
- MTV's *Real World* was first recent reality show to become popular.

- The original *Survivor* was smart and interesting.
- *Big Brother* just locked people up together and forced us to watch them bicker.
- The *Survivor* series continues to be popular, while copycats like *Fear Factor* get more graphic and unwatchable.
- People will tire of *Fear Factor* quickly because there is no plot to follow from one episode to the next and watching people eat worms and hold their breath underwater gets boring.
- Reality TV was popular because it was something different, but now there are dozens of these shows each season and few worth watching.
- Shows such as *American Idol, America's Got Talent,* and *America's Top Model* are a revival of earlier types of TV shows--the talent show and the beauty contest.
- Shows like *Top Chef* and *Project Runway* focused on special interests.
- Celebrity reality shows focusing on real people in weird situations were the next wave.

Working with Text

READING

Internet Addiction
Greg Beato

The following essay by Greg Beato was first published in 2010 in *Reason*, a magazine that offers updates on current developments in politics and culture from a libertarian perspective. Beato, a contributing editor for *Reason*, supports the essay's thesis with a variety of evidence. As you read, highlight the thesis statement and notice the types of evidence used to support it.

In 1995, in an effort to parody the way the American Psychiatric Association's hugely influential *Diagnostic and Statistical Manual of Mental Disorders* medicalizes every excessive behavior, psychiatrist Ivan Goldberg introduced on his website the concept of "Internet Addiction Disorder." Last summer Ben Alexander, a 19-year-old college student obsessed with the online multiplayer game *World of Warcraft*, was profiled by CBS News, NPR, the Associated Press, and countless other media outlets because of his status as client No. 1 at reSTART, the first residential treatment center in America for individuals trying to get themselves clean from Azeroth, iPhones, and all the other digital narcotics of our age.   1

At reSTART's five-acre haven in the woods near Seattle, clients pay big bucks to detox from pathological computer use by building chicken coops, cooking hamburgers, and engaging in daily therapy sessions with the program's two founders, psychologist Hilarie Cash and clinical social worker and life coach Cosette Rae. With room for just six addicts at a time and a $14,500 program fee, reSTART isn't designed for the masses, and so far it seems to have attracted more reporters than paying clients. When I spoke with Rae in May, she said "10 to 15" people had participated in the 45-day program to date.   2

Still, the fact that reSTART exists at all shows how far we've progressed in taking   3
Dr. Goldberg's spoof seriously. You may have been too busy monitoring Kim Kardashian's every passing thought-like thing on Twitter to notice, but Digital Detox Week took place in April, and Video Game Addiction Awareness Week followed on its heels in June. Internet addiction disorder has yet to claim a Tiger Woods of its own, but the sad, silly evidence of our worldwide cyber-bingeing mounts on a daily basis. A councilman in the Bulgarian city of Plovdiv is ousted from his position for playing *Farmville* during budget meetings. There are now at least three apps that use the iPhone's

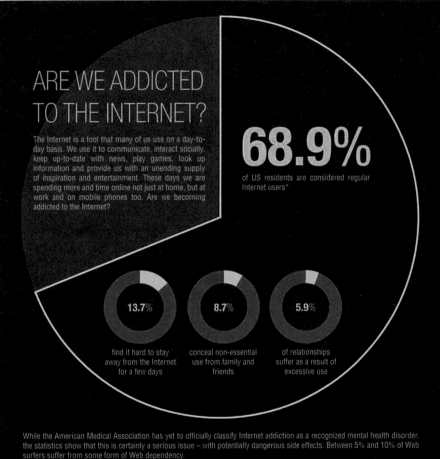

ARE WE ADDICTED TO THE INTERNET?

The Internet is a tool that many of us use on a day-to-day basis. We use it to communicate, interact socially, keep up-to-date with news, play games, look up information and provide us with an unending supply of inspiration and entertainment. These days we are spending more and time online not just at home, but at work and on mobile phones too. Are we becoming addicted to the Internet?

68.9%

of US residents are considered regular Internet users*

13.7%

find it hard to stay away from the Internet for a few days

8.7%

conceal non-essential use from family and friends

5.9%

of relationships suffer as a result of excessive use

While the American Medical Association has yet to officially classify Internet addiction as a recognized mental health disorder, the statistics show that this is certainly a serious issue – with potentially dangerous side effects. Between 5% and 10% of Web surfers suffer from some form of Web dependency.

1 in 8 individuals show signs of problematic use

camera to show the world right in front of you so you can keep texting while walking down the street, confident in your ability to avoid sinkholes, telephone poles, and traffic. Earlier this year, 200 students taking a class in media literacy at the University of Maryland went on a 24-hour media fast for a group study, then described how "jittery," "anxious," "miserable," and "crazy" they felt without Twitter, Facebook, iPods, and laptops. "I clearly am addicted," one student concluded, "and the dependency is sickening."

In the early days of the Web, dirty talk was exchanged at the excruciatingly slow rate 4 of 14.4 bits per second, connectivity charges accrued by the hour instead of the month, and the only stuff for sale online was some overpriced hot sauce from a tiny store in Pasadena. It took the patience of a Buddhist monk, thousands of dollars, and really bad TV reception to overuse the Web in a self-destructive manner. Yet even then, many people felt Ivan Goldberg's notes on Internet addiction worked better as psychiatry than comedy. A year before Goldberg posted his spoof, Kimberly Young, a psychologist at the University of Pittsburgh, had already begun conducting formal research into online addiction. By 1996 the Harvard-affiliated McLean Hospital had established a computer addiction clinic, a professor at the University of Maryland had created an Internet addiction support group, and *The New York Times* was running op-eds about the divorce epidemic that Internet addiction was about to unleash.

Fifteen years down the line, you'd think we'd all be introverted philanderers by now, 5 isolating ourselves in the virtual Snuggie of *World of Warcraft* by day and stepping out at night to destroy our marriages with our latest hook-ups from AshleyMadison.com. But the introduction of flat monthly fees, online gaming, widespread pornography, MySpace, YouTube, Facebook, WiFi, iPhones, netbooks, and free return shipping on designer shoes with substantial markdowns does not seem to have made the Internet any more addictive than it was a decade ago.

In 1998 Young told the Riverside *Press-Enterprise* that "5 to 10 percent of the 52 mil- 6 lion Internet users [were] addicted or 'potentially addicted.' " Doctors today use similar numbers when estimating the number of online junkies. In 2009 David Greenfield, a psychiatrist at the University of Connecticut, told the *San Francisco Chronicle* that studies have shown 3 percent to 6 percent of Internet users "have a problem." Is it possible that the ability to keep extremely close tabs on Ashton Kutcher actually has reduced the Internet's addictive power?

Granted, 3 percent is an awful lot of people. Argue all you like that a real addic- 7 tion should require needles, or spending time in seedy bars with people who drink vodka through their eyeballs, or at least the overwhelming and nihilistic urge to invest thousands of dollars in a broken public school system through the purchase of lottery tickets. Those working on the front lines of technology overuse have plenty of casualties to point to. In our brief conversation, Cosette Rae tells me about a Harvard student who lost a scholarship because he spent too much time playing games, a guy who spent so many sedentary hours at his computer that he developed blood clots in his leg and had to have it amputated, and an 18-year-old who chose homelessness over gamelessness when his parents told him he either had to quit playing computer games or move out.

A few minutes on Google yields even more lurid anecdotes. In 2007 an Ohio teen- 8
ager shot his parents, killing his mother and wounding his father, after they took away
his Xbox. This year a South Korean couple let their real baby starve to death because
they were spending so much time caring for their virtual baby in a role-playing game
called *Prius Online*.

On a pound-for-pound basis, the average *World of Warcraft* junkie undoubtedly rep- 9
resents a much less destructive social force than the average meth head. But it's not
extreme anecdotes that make the specter of Internet addiction so threatening; it's the
fact that Internet overuse has the potential to scale in a way that few other addictions
do. Even if Steve Jobs designed a really cool-looking syringe and started distributing
free heroin on street corners, not everyone would try it. But who among us doesn't
already check his email more often than necessary? As the Internet weaves itself more
and more tightly into our lives, only the Amish are completely safe.

As early as 1996, Kimberly Young was promoting the idea that the American Psychi- 10
atric Association (APA) should add Internet addiction disorder to the *Diagnostic and
Statistical Manual of Mental Disorders* (*DSM*). In February, the APA announced that its
coming edition of the *DSM*, the first major revision since 1994, will for the first time
classify a behavior-related condition—pathological gambling—as an "addiction" rather
than an "impulse control disorder." Internet addiction disorder is not being included
in this new category of "behavioral addictions," but the APA said it will consider it as a
"potential addition . . . as research data accumulate."

If the APA does add excessive Internet use to the *DSM*, the consequences will be 11
wide-ranging. Health insurance companies will start offering at least partial coverage
for treatment programs such as reSTART. People who suffer from Internet addiction disorder will receive protection under the Americans With Disabilities Act if their impair-
ment "substantially limits one or more major life activities." Criminal lawyers will use
their clients' online habits to fashion diminished capacity defenses.

Which means that what started as a parody in 1995 could eventually turn more 12
darkly comic than ever imagined. Picture a world where the health care system goes
bankrupt because insurers have to pay for millions of people determined to kick
their Twitter addictions once and for all. Where employees who view porn at work
are legally protected from termination. Where killing elves in cyberspace could help
absolve you for killing people in real life. Is it too late to revert to our older, healthier,
more balanced ways of living and just spend all our leisure hours watching *Love Boat*
reruns?

Examining the Reading

1. Define the term *Internet addiction.*
2. What are some examples of dangerous behavior caused by Internet addiction?
3. Why does adding Internet addiction to the *DSM* have important social
   consequences?
4. Define each of the following words as they are used in the essay: *parody* (para. 1),
   pathological (2), *nihilistic* (7), *lurid* (8), and *specter* (9).

Analyzing the Writer's Technique

1. State the author's thesis in your own words. Then, using the guidelines on pages 126–27, evaluate the effectiveness of the thesis.
2. To what audience does Beato address this essay? What purpose does the essay fulfill? How do you think the audience and purpose affect the author's choice of evidence?
3. Cite one paragraph from the essay in which you think the author provides detailed, specific information. Explain why you chose it. Does it support the thesis? Why or why not?

Visualizing the Reading

In the chart below, supply an example of each type of evidence the author has used in the reading. The first one has been done for you.

Type of Evidence	Example
Historical background	Web site parody of the *DSM* in 1995 included Internet addiction and 1996 McLean Hospital program for Internet addiction
Descriptive details	
Statistics	
Examples	
Comparison and contrast	
Quotations	

Thinking Critically about the Reading

1. Evaluate the sources that Beato uses to support his thesis. Are they trustworthy and reliable?
2. Describe the author's tone. How does it affect your response to the reading?
3. Identify at least one statement of opinion in paragraph 9. Does the author offer evidence to support the opinion?
4. What is the connotation of the word *junkies* in paragraph 6? Identify at least five other words in the selection with strong positive or negative connotations.
5. How useful are the anecdotes in paragraphs 7 and 8 as evidence?

Interpreting a Graphic

1. The large pie chart at the top of the graphic on page 135 reports that "68.9% of US residents are considered regular Internet users." What does *regular* mean here? How could the author of the graph have clarified this term?

2. One of the small circle graphs in the graphic says that 13.7% of U.S. residents "find it hard to stay away from the Internet for a few days," and the pictogram says that "1 in 8 individuals show signs of problematic use," which is 12.5% of the population. The text in between says that "between 5% and 10% of Web surfers suffer from some form of dependency." What is the difference between "find[ing] it hard to stay away," "dependency," and "problematic use"? Why might the first two statistics differ so much from the third one?

3. This graphic appeared on a blog sponsored by Flowtown, which calls itself "a social media marketing platform that helps businesses transform email contacts into engaged customers." How does this information affect how you think about the information in the graphic?

Reacting to the Reading

1. How do you think this essay would change if the author wrote it for *Parents* magazine?

2. Why do you think the number of people addicted to the Internet has actually lessened since 1998?

3. What might it mean that the American Psychological Association is not ready to include Internet addiction in the *DSM*? What does this say about the disorder?

4. In your journal, write about ways you use the Internet that may not be healthy. How does it negatively affect your life? Do you feel it has more positive than negative effects on your life? Explain.

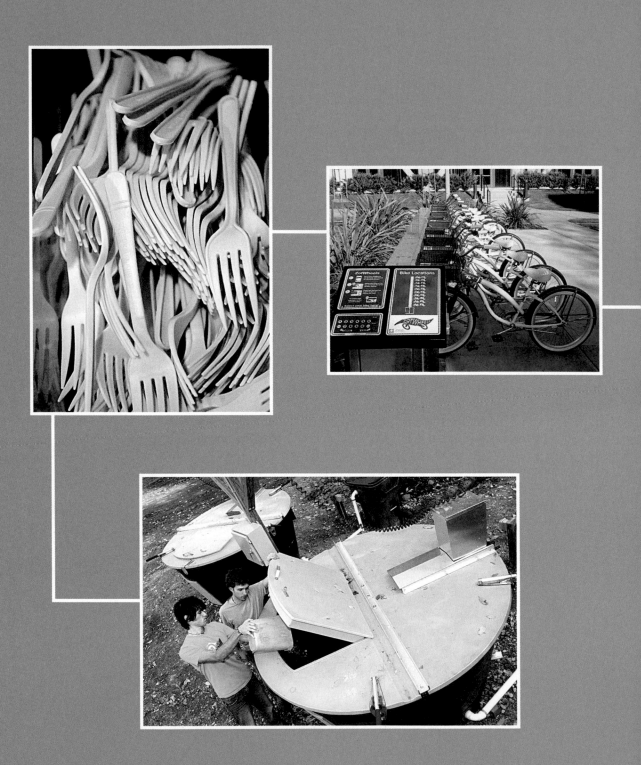

CHAPTER 7

Drafting an Essay

The photographs on the opposite page show a few examples of "green initiatives" at colleges around the country. Study these images, which show biodegradable forks, a bicycle share program, and a compost bin.

Working alone or with two or three classmates, write a sentence that states your opinion on how important (or not) these initiatives are and how likely they are to be successful. Then support this opinion with a list of details (evidence) from the three photographs and from your own knowledge of "green initiatives," either at colleges or elsewhere. Number your best evidence 1, your second-best evidence 2, and so on. Cross out any details that do not support your opinion, or adjust the sentence if the evidence you gathered disagrees with it. Finally, write a paragraph that begins with the sentence you wrote and includes your evidence in order of importance.

The paragraph you have just written could be part of an essay on the topic of how colleges are making campuses environmentally sustainable. To write an essay you would need to do additional prewriting and research to learn more about this topic. Then you would write a thesis statement, develop supporting paragraphs, write an effective introduction and conclusion, and choose a good title. This chapter will guide you through the process of developing an essay in support of a thesis statement, as part of the writing process shown in Figure 7.1.

The Structure of an Essay

Think of an essay as a complete piece of writing, much as a textbook chapter is. For example, a textbook chapter might have the title "Human Rights in Developing Countries," which gives you a clear idea of the chapter's subject. The first few paragraphs of the chapter would probably introduce and define the concept of human rights. The chapter might then assert that human rights is a controversial global issue of growing importance. The rest of the chapter might explain the issue by tracing its history, examining why it is a world issue, and discussing its current status. The chapter would conclude with a summary.

Similarly, as you can see in Figure 7.2, an essay has a title and an introduction. It also makes an assertion (the thesis statement) that is explained and sup-

FIGURE 7.1 An Overview of the Writing Process

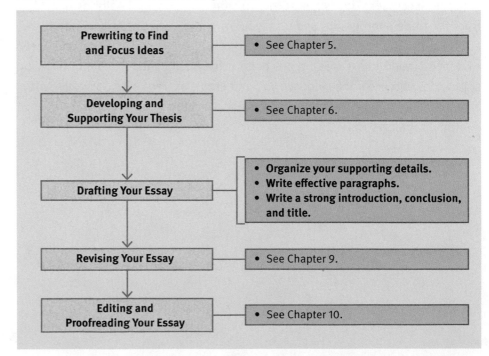

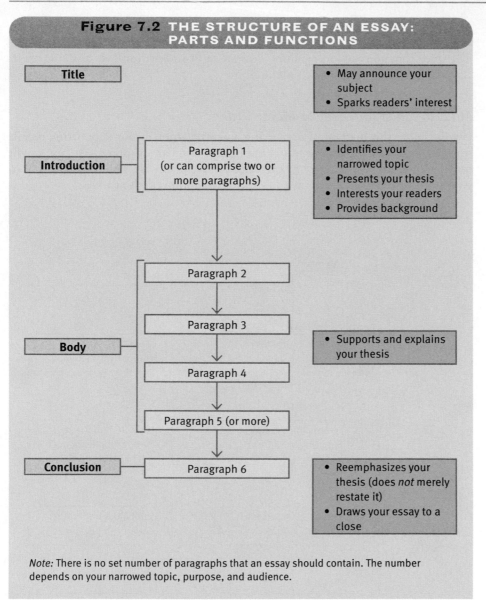

Figure 7.2 THE STRUCTURE OF AN ESSAY: PARTS AND FUNCTIONS

Note: There is no set number of paragraphs that an essay should contain. The number depends on your narrowed topic, purpose, and audience.

ported throughout the body of the essay. The essay ends with a final statement, its conclusion.

Organizing Your Supporting Details

The body of your essay contains the paragraphs that support your thesis. Before you begin writing these body paragraphs, decide on the supporting evidence you will use and the order in which you will present your evidence.

For more on developing a thesis and selecting evidence to support it, see Chapter 6.

Selecting a Method of Organization

The three common ways to organize ideas are most-to-least (or least-to-most) order, chronological order, and spatial order.

Most-to-Least (or Least-to-Most) Order

If you choose this method of organizing an essay, arrange your supporting details from most to least (or least to most) important, familiar, or interesting. You might begin with your most convincing evidence or save it for last, building gradually to your strongest point. You can visualize these two options as shown here.

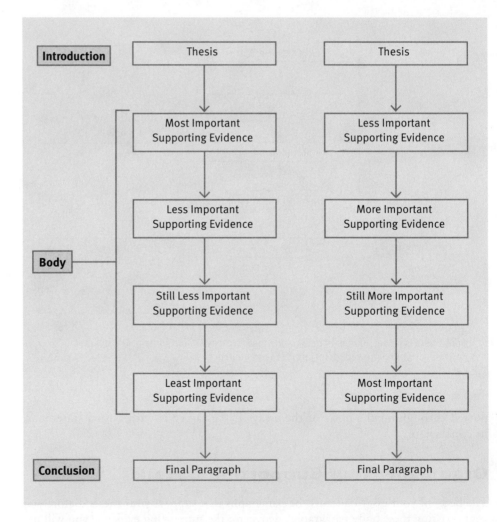

A student, Robin Ferguson, was working on the thesis statement "Working as a literacy volunteer taught me more about learning and friendship than I ever expected" and identified four primary benefits related to her thesis.

BENEFITS

- I learned about the learning process.
- I developed a permanent friendship with my student, Marie.
- Marie built self-confidence.
- I discovered the importance of reading.

Ferguson then chose to arrange these benefits from least to most important and decided that the friendship was the most important benefit. Here is how she organized her supporting evidence.

WORKING THESIS

Working as a literacy volunteer taught me more about learning and friendship than I ever expected.

LEAST	Supporting paragraph 1:	Learned about the learning process
TO	Supporting paragraph 2:	Discovered the importance of reading for Marie
MOST	Supporting paragraph 3:	Marie increased her self-confidence
IMPORTANT	Supporting paragraph 4:	Developed a permanent friendship

Exercise 7.1

For each of the following narrowed topics, identify several qualities or characteristics that you could use to organize details in most-to-least or least-to-most order:

1. Three stores in which you shop
2. Three friends
3. Three members of a sports team
4. Three fast-food restaurants
5. Three television shows you watched this week

Chronological Order

When you arrange your supporting details in **chronological order**, you put them in the order in which they happened. For this method of organization, begin the body of your essay with the first event, and progress through the others as they occurred.

Depending on the subject of your essay, the events could be minutes, days, or years apart. Chronological order is commonly used in narrative essays and process analyses. You can visualize this order as follows.

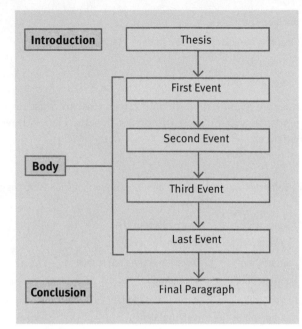

As an example, let's suppose that Robin Ferguson, writing about her experiences as a literacy volunteer, decides to demonstrate her thesis by relating the events of a typical tutoring session. In this case, she might organize her essay by narrating the events in the order in which they usually occur, using each detail about the session to demonstrate what tutoring taught her about learning and friendship.

Exercise 7.2

Working alone or with a classmate, identify at least one thesis statement from those listed below that could be supported by chronological paragraphs. Write a few sentences explaining how you would use chronological order to support this thesis.

1. European mealtimes differ from those of many American visitors, much to the visitors' surprise and discomfort.

2. Despite the many pitfalls that await those who shop at auctions, people can find bargains if they prepare in advance.

3. My first day of kindergarten was the most traumatic experience of my childhood, one that permanently shaped my view of education.

4. Learning how to drive a car increases a teenager's freedom and responsibility.

Spatial Order

When you use **spatial order**, you organize details about your subject according to its location or position in space. Consider, for example, how you might use spatial order to support the thesis that modern movie theaters are designed to shut out the outside world and create a separate reality within. You could begin by describing the ticket booth, then the lobby, and finally the individual theaters. Similarly, you might describe a basketball court from right to left or a person from head to toe. Robin Ferguson, writing about her experiences as a literacy volunteer, could describe her classroom or meeting area from front to back or left to right. Spatial organization is commonly used in descriptive essays as well as in classification and division essays.

You can best visualize spatial organization by picturing your subject in your mind or by sketching it on paper. "Look" at your subject systematically—from top to bottom, inside to outside, front to back. Cut it into imaginary sections or pieces and describe each piece. Here are two possible options for visualizing an essay that uses spatial order.

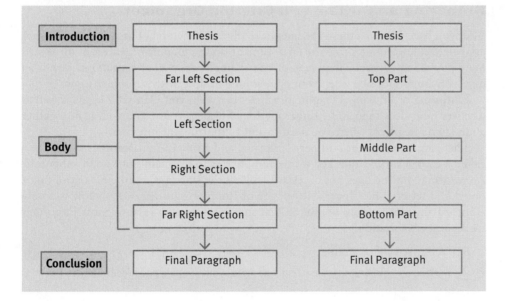

Exercise 7.3

Working alone or with a classmate, identify one thesis statement listed below that could be supported by means of spatial organization. Write a few sentences explaining how you would use spatial order to support this thesis.

1. Our family's yearly vacation at a cabin in Maine provides us with a much needed opportunity to renew family ties.
2. The Civic Theatre of Allentown's set for Tennessee Williams's play *A Streetcar Named Desire* was simple, yet striking and effective.
3. Although a pond in winter may seem frozen and lifeless, this appearance is deceptive.
4. A clear study space can cut down on time-wasting distractions.

Essay in Progress 1

Choose one of the following activities.

1. Using the thesis statement and evidence you gathered for the Essay in Progress activities in Chapter 6, choose a method for organizing your essay. Then explain briefly how you will use that method of organization.
2. Choose one of the following narrowed topics. Then, using the steps in Figure 7.1, An Overview of the Writing Process (p. 142), prewrite to produce ideas, develop a thesis, and generate evidence to support the thesis. Next, choose a method for organizing your essay. Explain briefly how you will use that method of organization.
   a. Positive or negative experiences with computers
   b. Stricter (or more lenient) regulations for teenage drivers
   c. Factors that account for the popularity of action films
   d. Discipline in public elementary schools
   e. Advantages or disadvantages of instant messaging

Preparing an Outline or a Graphic Organizer

After you have written a thesis statement and chosen a method of organization for your essay, take a few minutes to write an outline or draw a graphic organizer of the essay's main points in the order you plan to discuss them. Making an organizational plan is an especially important step when your essay is long or deals with a complex topic.

Outlining or drawing a graphic organizer can help you plan your essay as well as discover new ideas to include. Either method will help you see how ideas fit together and may reveal places where you need to add supporting information.

There are two types of outlines—informal and formal. An **informal outline**, also called a *scratch outline,* uses key words and phrases to list main points and subpoints. An informal outline does not necessarily follow the standard outline format of numbered and lettered headings. The outline of Robin Ferguson's essay below is an example of an informal outline. Recall that she chose to use a least-to-most-important method of organization.

SAMPLE INFORMAL OUTLINE

Thesis: Working as a literacy volunteer taught me more about learning and friendship than I ever expected.

Paragraph 1: Learned about the learning process
- Went through staff training program
- Learned about words "in context"

Paragraph 2: Discovered the importance of reading for Marie
- Couldn't take bus, walked to grocery store
- Couldn't buy certain products
- Couldn't write out grocery lists

Paragraph 3: Marie increased her self-confidence
- Made rapid progress

- Began taking bus
- Helped son with reading

Paragraph 4: Developed a permanent friendship

- Saw each other often
- Both single parents
- Helped each other baby-sit

Conclusion: I benefited more than Marie did.

Formal outlines use Roman numerals (I, II), capital letters (A, B), arabic numbers (1, 2), and lowercase letters (a, b) to designate levels of importance. Formal outlines fall into two categories: *Sentence outlines* use complete sentences, and *topic outlines* use only key words and phrases. In a topic or sentence outline, less important entries are indented, as in the sample formal outline below. Each topic or sentence begins with a capital letter.

FORMAT FOR A FORMAL OUTLINE

I. First main topic
    A. First subtopic of I
    B. Second subtopic of I
        1. First detail about I.B
        2. Second detail about I.B
    C. Third subtopic of I
        1. First detail about I.C
            a. First detail or example about I.C.1
            b. Second detail or example about I.C.1
        2. Second detail about I.C
II. Second main topic

Here is a sample outline that a student wrote for an essay for her interpersonal communication class:

SAMPLE FORMAL OUTLINE

I. Types of listening
    A. Participatory
        1. Involves the listener responding to the speaker
        2. Has expressive quality
            a. Maintain eye contact
            b. Express feelings using facial expressions
    B. Nonparticipatory
        1. Involves the listener listening without talking or responding
        2. Allows speaker to develop his or her thoughts without interruption
    C. Critical listening
        1. Involves the listener analyzing and evaluating the message
        2. Is especially important in college classes
            a. Listen for instructors' biases
            b. Evaluate evidence in support of opinions expressed

For more on parallel structure, see Chapter 10, p. 212.

Remember that all items labeled with the same designation (capital letters, for example) should be at the same level of importance, and each must explain or support the topic or subtopic under which it is placed. Also, all items at the same level should be grammatically parallel.

NOT PARALLEL	I. Dietary Problems 　　A. Consuming too much fat 　　B. High refined-sugar consumption
PARALLEL	I. Dietary Problems 　　A. Consuming too much fat 　　B. Consuming too much refined sugar

If your instructor allows, you can use both phrases and sentences within an outline, as long as you do so consistently. You might write all subtopics (designated by capital letters A, B, and so on) as sentences and all supporting details (designated by 1, 2, and so on) as phrases, for instance.

Learning Style Options

For more about graphic organizers, see Chapter 3, p. 60.

If you have a pragmatic learning style or a verbal learning style or both, preparing an outline will probably appeal to you. If you are a creative or spatial learner, however, you may prefer to draw a graphic organizer. Whichever method you find most appealing, begin by putting your working thesis statement at the top of a piece of paper or word-processing document. Then list your main points below your thesis. Be sure to leave plenty of space between main points. While you are filling in the details that support one main point, you will often think of details or examples to use in support of a different one. As these details or examples occur to you, jot them down under or next to the appropriate main point of your outline or graphic organizer.

The graphic organizer shown in Figure 7.3 was done for Ferguson's essay. Notice that it follows the least-to-most-important method of organization, as did her informal outline on page 148.

> **Essay in Progress 2**
> For the topic you chose in Essay in Progress 1, write a brief outline or draw a graphic organizer to show the organizational plan of your essay.

Using Transitions and Repetition to Connect Your Ideas

To show how your ideas are related, be sure to use transitions between sentences and paragraphs as well as repetition of key words and the synonyms and pronouns that refer to them. Use transitions and repetition both within your paragraphs (see Chapter 8, pp. 175–76) and between paragraphs.

Coherent Essays Use Transitional Expressions to Connect Ideas

A **transitional expression**—which can be a word, phrase, clause, or sentence—shows the reader how a new sentence or paragraph is connected to the one that precedes it. It may also remind the reader of an idea discussed earlier in the essay.

Figure 7.3 SAMPLE GRAPHIC ORGANIZER

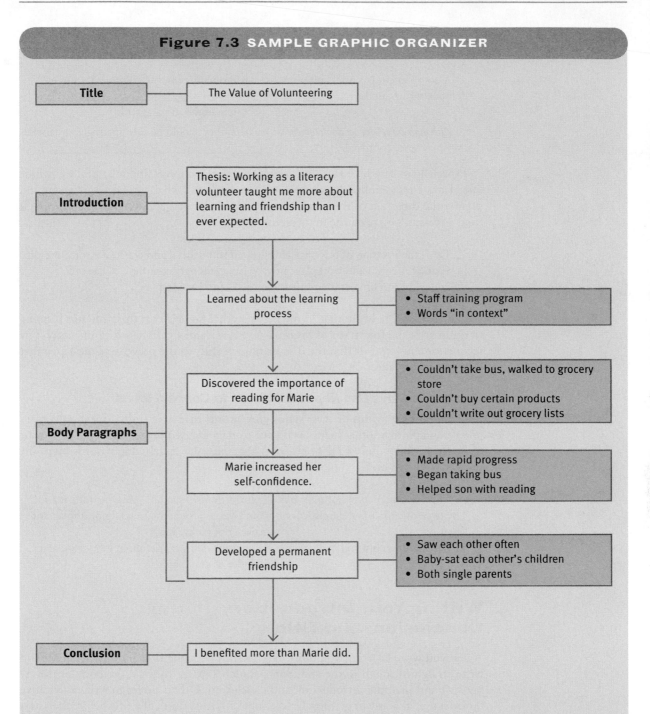

In the example that follows, the italicized transitional clause connects the two paragraphs by reminding the reader of the main point of the first.

> A compliment is a brief and pleasant way of opening lines of communication and demonstrating goodwill. _____
> [remainder of paragraph]
> *Although compliments do demonstrate goodwill,* they should be used sparingly; otherwise they may seem contrived. _____

Especially in lengthy essays (five pages or longer), you may find it helpful to include one or more transitional clauses or sentences that recap what you have said so far and suggest the direction of the essay from that point forward. The following example is from a student's essay on the invasion of privacy.

> Thus, the invasion of privacy is not limited to financial and consumer information; invasion of medical and workplace privacy is increasingly common. What can individuals do to protect their privacy in each of these areas?

The *Thus* at the beginning of the first sentence signals that this sentence is going to summarize the four types of invasion of privacy already discussed in the essay. The second sentence signals that the discussion will shift to the preventive measures that individuals can take.

Coherent Essays Use Repeated Words to Connect Ideas

Repetition of key words or their **synonyms** (words that have similar meanings) from one paragraph to another helps keep your readers focused on the main point of your essay. In the following two abbreviated paragraphs, the italicized key words focus the readers' attention on the topic of liars and lying.

> There are many types of *liars,* but all put forth *dishonest* or *misleading* information. The occasional *liar* is the most common and *lies* to avoid embarrassing or unpleasant situations.   [remainder of paragraph]
> Less common but still dangerous is the habitual *liar,* who *lies* about everyday events.   [remainder of paragraph]

Writing Your Introduction, Conclusion, and Title

When you write an essay, you don't have to start with the title and introduction and write straight through to the end. Some students prefer to write the body of the essay first and then the introduction and conclusion. Others prefer to write a tentative introduction as a way of getting started. Some students think of a title before they start writing; others find it easier to add a title when the essay is nearly finished. Regardless of when you write them, the introduction, conclusion, and title are important components of a well-written essay.

Writing a Strong Introduction

Your introduction creates a first, and often lasting, impression. It focuses your readers on your topic and establishes the tone of your essay—how you "sound" to your readers and what attitude you take toward them. Based on your introduction, your readers will form an expectation of what the essay will be about and the approach it will take. Because the introduction is crucial, take the time to get it right.

For more on tone, see Chapter 10, pp. 215–17.

Two sample introductions to student essays follow. Although they are written on the same topic, notice how each creates an entirely different impression and set of expectations.

INTRODUCTION 1

Sexual harassment has received a great deal of attention in recent years. From the highest offices of government to factories in small towns, sexual harassment cases have been tried in court and publicized on national television for all Americans to witness. This focus on sexual harassment has been, in and of itself, a good and necessary thing. However, when a first-grade boy makes national headlines because he kissed a little girl of the same age and is accused of "sexual harassment," the American public needs to take a serious look at the definition of sexual harassment.

INTRODUCTION 2

Sexual harassment in the workplace seems to happen with alarming frequency. As a woman who works part time in a male-dominated office, I have witnessed at least six incidents of sexual harassment aimed at me and my female colleagues on various occasions during the past three months alone. For example, in one incident, a male coworker repeatedly made kissing sounds whenever I passed his desk, even after I explained that his actions made me uncomfortable. A female coworker was invited to dinner several times by her male supervisor; each time she refused. The last time she refused, he made a veiled threat, "You obviously aren't happy working with me. Perhaps a transfer is in order." These incidents were not isolated, did not happen to only one woman, and were initiated by more than one man. My colleagues and I are not the only victims. Sexual harassment is on the rise and will continue to increase unless women speak out against it loudly and to a receptive audience.

In introduction 1, the writer focuses on the definition of sexual harassment. Introduction 2 has an entirely different emphasis—the frequency of incidents of sexual harassment. Each introductory paragraph reveals a different tone as well. Introduction 1 suggests a sense of mild disbelief, whereas introduction 2 suggests anger and outrage. From introduction 1, you expect the writer to examine definitions of sexual harassment and, perhaps, suggest his or her own definition. From introduction 2, you expect the writer to present additional cases of sexual harassment and suggest ways women can speak out against it.

In addition to establishing a focus and tone, your introduction should

- present your thesis statement
- interest your reader
- provide any background information your reader may need

Introductions are often difficult to write. If you have trouble, write a tentative introductory paragraph and return to it later. Once you have written the body of your essay, you may find it easier to complete the introduction. In fact, as you work out your ideas in the body of the essay, you may think of a better way to introduce them in the opening.

Tips for Writing a Strong Introduction

The following suggestions for writing a strong introduction will help you capture your readers' interest:

1. **Ask a provocative or disturbing question.** Also consider posing a series of short, related questions that will direct your readers' attention to the key points in your essay.

    Should health insurance companies pay for more than one stay in a drug rehabilitation center? Should insurance continue to pay for rehab services when patients consistently put themselves back into danger by using drugs again?

2. **Begin with a story or anecdote.** Choose one that will appeal to your audience and is relevant to your thesis.

    I used to believe that it was possible to stop smoking by simply quitting cold turkey. When I tried this approach, I soon realized that quitting was not so simple. When I did not smoke for even a short period of time, I became so uncomfortable that I started again just to alleviate the discomfort. I realized then that I would need a practical solution that would overcome my cravings.

3. **Offer a quotation.** The quotation should illustrate or emphasize your thesis.

    As Indira Gandhi once said, "You cannot shake hands with a clenched fist." This truism is important to remember whenever people communicate with one another but particularly when they are attempting to resolve a conflict. Both parties need to agree that there is a problem and then agree to listen to each other with an open mind. Shaking hands is a productive way to begin working toward a resolution.

4. **Cite a little-known or shocking fact or statistic.**

    Recent research has shown that the color pink has a calming effect on people. In fact, a prison detention center in western New York was recently painted pink to make prisoners more controllable in the days following their arrest.

    In a recent study on college student plagiarism, researchers found that 7 out of 42 students were caught plagiarizing their *entire* papers, purchasing them from term paper mills.

5. **Move from general to specific. Begin with the category or general subject area to which your topic belongs, and narrow it to arrive at your thesis.**

    The First Amendment is the basis for several cherished rights in the United States, and free speech is among them. Therefore, it would seem unlawful—even anti-American—for a disc jockey to be fired for expressing his or her views on the radio, regardless of whether those views are unpopular or offensive.

6. **State a commonly held misconception or a position that you oppose.** Your thesis would then correct the misconception or state your position on the issue.

> Many people have the mistaken notion that only homosexuals and drug users are in danger of contracting AIDS. In fact, many heterosexuals also suffer from this debilitating disease. Furthermore, the number of heterosexuals who test HIV-positive has increased substantially over the past decade. It is time the American public became better informed about the prevention and treatment of AIDS.

7. **Describe a hypothetical situation.**

> Suppose you were in a serious car accident and became unconscious. Suppose further that you slipped into a coma, with little hope for recovery. Unless you had a prewritten health-care proxy that designated someone familiar with your wishes to act on your behalf, your fate would be left in the hands of medical doctors who knew nothing about you or your preferences for treatment.

8. **Begin with a striking example.**

> The penal system sometimes protects the rights of the criminal instead of those of the victim. For example, during a rape trial, the victim can be questioned about his or her sexual history by the defense attorney, but the prosecuting attorney is forbidden by law to mention that the defendant was charged with rape in a previous trial. In fact, if the prosecution even hints at the defendant's sexual history, the defense can request a mistrial.

9. **Make a comparison. Compare your topic with one that is familiar or of special interest to your readers.**

> The process a researcher uses to locate a specific piece of information in the library is similar to the process an investigator follows in tracking a criminal; both use a series of questions and follow clues to accomplish their task.

Mistakes to Avoid

The following advice will help you avoid the most common mistakes students make in writing introductions:

1. **Do not make an announcement.** Avoid opening comments such as "I am writing to explain . . ." or "This essay will discuss . . ."
2. **Keep your introduction short.** An introduction that goes beyond two paragraphs will probably sound long-winded and make your readers impatient.
3. **Avoid statements that may discourage your readers from continuing.** Statements such as "This process may seem complicated, but . . ." may make your readers apprehensive.
4. **Avoid a casual, overly familiar, or chatty tone.** Openings such as "Whoa, did it surprise me when . . ." or "You'll never in a million years believe what happened . . ." are not appropriate.

5. **Be sure your topic is clear or explained adequately for your readers.** Do not begin an essay by stating, for example, "I oppose Proposition 413 and urge you to vote against it." Before stating your position on your topic, you need to explain to readers what that legislation is and what it proposes.

Writing an Effective Conclusion

Your essay should not end abruptly with your last supporting paragraph. Instead, it should end with a conclusion—a separate paragraph that reiterates (without directly restating) the importance of your thesis and that brings your essay to a satisfying close.

Tips for Writing a Solid Conclusion

For most essays, your conclusion should summarize your main points and reaffirm your thesis. For many essays, however, you might supplement this information and make your conclusion more memorable and forceful by using one of the following suggestions:

1. **Look ahead.** Take your readers beyond the scope and time frame of your essay.

> For now, then, the present system for policing the Internet appears to be working. In the future, though, it may be necessary to put a more formal, structured procedure in place.

2. **Remind readers of the relevance of the issue.** Suggest why your thesis is important.

> As stated earlier, research has shown that implementing the seat-belt law has saved thousands of lives. These lives would almost certainly have been lost had this law not been enacted.

3. **Offer a recommendation or make a call to action.** Urge your readers to take specific steps that follow logically from your thesis.

> To convince the local cable company to eliminate pornographic material, concerned citizens should organize, contact their local cable station, and threaten to cancel their subscriptions.

4. **Discuss broader implications.** Point to larger issues not fully addressed in the essay, but do not introduce a completely new issue.

> When fair-minded people consider whether the FBI should be allowed to tap private phone lines, the issue inevitably leads them to the larger issue of First Amendment rights.

5. **Conclude with a fact, a quotation, an anecdote, or an example that emphasizes your thesis.** These endings will bring a sense of closure and realism to your essay.

> The next time you are tempted to send a strongly worded email, consider this fact: Your friends and your enemies can forward those messages, with unforeseen consequences.

Mistakes to Avoid

The following advice will help you avoid common mistakes writers make in their conclusions:

1. **Avoid a direct restatement of your thesis.** An exact repetition of your thesis will make your essay seem dull and mechanical.
2. **Avoid standard phrases.** Don't use phrases such as "To sum up," "In conclusion," or "It can be seen, then." They are routine and tiresome.

3. **Avoid introducing new points in your conclusion.** Major points belong in the body of your essay.

4. **Avoid apologizing for yourself, your work, or your ideas.** Do not say, for example, "Although I am only twenty-one, it seems to me . . ."

5. **Avoid weakening your stance in the conclusion.** If, for instance, your essay has criticized someone's behavior, do not back down by saying "After all, she's only human."

Writing a Good Title

The title of your essay should suggest your topic and spark your readers' interest. Depending on the purpose, intended audience, and tone of your essay, your title may be direct and informative, witty, or intriguing. The following suggestions will help you write effective titles:

1. **Write straightforward, descriptive titles for most academic essays.**

   Lotteries: A Game Players Can Little Afford

2. **Ask a question that your essay answers.**

   Who Plays the Lottery?

3. **Use alliteration.** Repeating initial sounds (called *alliteration*) often produces a catchy title.

   Lotteries: Dreaming about Dollars

4. **Consider using a play on words or a catchy or humorous expression.** This technique may work well for less formal essays.

   If You Win, You Lose

5. **Avoid broad, vague titles that sound like labels.** Titles such as "Baseball Fans" or "Gun Control" provide your reader with too little information.

Exercise 7.4

For each of the following essays, suggest a title. Try to use each of the above suggestions at least once.

1. An essay explaining the legal rights of tenants
2. An essay opposing human cloning
3. An essay on causes and effects of road rage
4. An essay comparing fitness routines
5. An essay explaining how to choose a primary care physician

Essay in Progress 3
Using the outline or graphic organizer you created in Essay in Progress 2, write a first draft of your essay.

Students Write

In her first draft the writer concentrated on expressing her ideas. Consequently, it contains errors that she later corrects. See Chapter 9, p. 196, and Chapter 10, p. 222, for later versions of this essay.

The first draft of a narrative essay by Christine Lee follows. Lee used her freewriting (see Chapter 5) and her working thesis (see Chapter 6) as the basis for her draft, adding details that she came up with by doing additional brainstorming (see Chapter 6). Because she was writing a first draft, Lee did not worry about correcting the errors in grammar, punctuation, and mechanics. (You will see her revised draft in Chapter 9 and an excerpt that shows Lee's final editing and proofreading in Chapter 10.)

FIRST DRAFT

The Reality of Real TV

Do you remember life before reality TV? One look at a *TV Guide* today shows an overload of reality-based programming, even with the guaranteed failure of most of these shows. Before reality TV there was mostly situational comedies and serial dramas. When *Survivor* caught every viewer's attention, every network in American believed they must also become "real" to keep up its ratings. Shows that followed it were less interesting and less tasteful in the hopes of finding a show as original, inventive, and engaging as the first *Survivor*. [1]

When *Survivor* began in the summer of 2000, there was nothing else like it on TV. *Survivor* had real people in a contest in an exotic location. It had different kinds of players. There was a certain fascination in watching these players struggle week after week for food and shelter but the million dollar prize kept viewers tuning in week after week. Viewers wanted to find out who was going to win and who was getting "voted off the island." The last contestant on the island wins. Players developed a sense of teamwork and camaraderie, as they schemed and plotted. And we as an audience were allowed to watch every minute of it. [2]

Reality shows that followed Survivor didn't have the interesting elements that it had. *Big Brother* started as the first of the reality TV spin-offs but audiences didn't have the same things to respond to. It has never been a success because they took the basic concept of *Survivor* and added nothing new or interesting to it. *Big Brother* locked a bunch of people up together in a house and forced the audience to watch them bicker over nothing. Viewers were forced to watch bored contestants bicker and fight, locked up in a house with nothing else to do. It didn't seem the kind of competition that *Survivor* was, even though there was a cash prize on the line. The cash prize wasn't large enough anyways. We didn't choose favorites because the players weren't up against anything, except fighting off weeks of boredom. *Big Brother* introduced audience participation with the television audience voting off members, which actually only gave the house members less to do and less motive to scheme and plot their allegiances like the castaways on *Survivor*. Voting members off was an arbitrary and meaningless process. But *Big Brother* had the prize component, and it took away the housemates' access to the outside world. [3]

Although nothing seems to capture ratings like the original *Survivor*, networks have continued to use sensational gimmicks to appeal to the audience's basic instincts. Nothing good [4] was carried over from *Survivor*, and the new shows just had extreme situations. *Fear Factor* had contestants commit all sorts of gross and terrifying things like eating worms. Most viewers are disgusted by this.

When this gimmicks did not retain viewers, they turned back to two traditional types of   5
reality TV and put modern twists on them: the talent show and the beauty contest. So were born shows like *American Idol, America's Got Talent* and *America's Top Model*. Again, there was no built in drama like in *Survivor* so they tried to create drama with the colorful judges and supportive fans. At first, the shows were exciting with the singing and the beauty, but after a while, audiences lost interest. Even showing the long lines that contestants had to wait in, and footage of those who did not make the cut did not help to keep viewers hooked on these types of reality shows. Viewers could only stomach so much loud singing and mascara.

The next round of shows had to do with special interests like cooking and shows like *Hell's*   6
Kitchen and *Top Chef*. There were also dance shows like *So You Think You Can Dance* and *Danc-ing with the Stars*. *The Biggest Loser* was a weight loss competition. *Project Runway* was a fash-ion designer competition. *The Apprentice* was about business and *Shear Genius* was about hair stylists. These shows appealed to only small numbers of people and had manufactured and contrived situations for the contestants to act in.

Recently reality shows are about everyday lives or celebrities. *The Real World* was the first   7
kind, following young adults as they drank and slept around. *The Simple Life* was a celebrity show with Paris Hilton and Nicole Ritchie. Soon it seemed every celebrity had a reality show—Ozzy Osbourne, Paula Abdul, Tori Spelling, Bret Michaels and more. The next wave of shows was people in weird situations like *Jon & Kate Plus Eight*. These programs showed people at their worst. Networks had to try hard to find new and different scenarios to show since these shows are getting more tasteless.

Since *Survivor*, reality shows have gone from terror and violence to talent and beauty to   8
special interest shows and last to shows following real people. It's the viewers who decide what is popular. Reality shows continue to be popular even though they're getting more taste-less and contrived-looking. I hope viewers get tired of all these cheap gimmicks and call for more entertaining programming.

Analyzing the First Draft

1. Evaluate Lee's title and introduction.
2. Evaluate Lee's thesis statement.
3. Does Lee provide adequate details for her essay? If not, what additional information might she include?
4. How does Lee organize her ideas?
5. Evaluate her supporting paragraphs. Which paragraphs need more detail?
6. Evaluate the conclusion.

Working with Text

Black Men and Public Space
Brent Staples

Brent Staples is a journalist who has written numerous articles and editorials as well as a memoir, *Parallel Time: Growing Up in Black and White* (1994). Staples holds a Ph.D. in psychology and is currently an editor at the *New York Times*. This essay, first published in *Harper's* magazine in 1986, is a good model of a well-structured essay. As you read the selection, highlight or underline the author's thesis.

My first victim was a woman—white, well dressed, probably in her early twenties. I came upon her late one evening on a deserted street in Hyde Park, a relatively affluent neighborhood in an otherwise mean, impoverished section of Chicago. As I swung onto the avenue behind her, there seemed to be a discreet, uninflammatory distance between us. Not so. She cast back a worried glance. To her, the youngish black man—a broad six feet two inches with a beard and billowing hair, both hands shoved into the pockets of a bulky military jacket—seemed menacingly close. After a few more quick glimpses, she picked up her pace and was soon running in earnest. Within seconds she disappeared into a cross street. 1

That was more than a decade ago. I was twenty-two years old, a graduate student newly arrived at the University of Chicago. It was in the echo of that terrified woman's footfalls that I first began to know the unwieldy inheritance I'd come into—the ability to alter public space in ugly ways. It was clear that she thought herself the quarry of a mugger, a rapist, or worse. Suffering a bout of insomnia, however, I was stalking sleep, not defenseless wayfarers. As a softy who is scarcely able to take a knife to a raw chicken—let alone hold one to a person's throat—I was surprised, embarrassed, and dismayed all at once. Her flight made me feel like an accomplice in tyranny. It also made it clear that I was indistinguishable from the muggers who occasionally seeped into the area from the surrounding ghetto. That first encounter, and those that followed, signified that a vast, unnerving gulf lay between nighttime pedestrians— particularly women—and me. And I soon gathered that being perceived as dangerous is a hazard in itself. I only needed to turn a corner into a dicey situation, or crowd some frightened, armed person in a foyer somewhere, or make an errant move after being pulled over by a policeman. Where fear and weapons meet—and they often do in ur- ban America—there is always the possibility of death. 2

In that first year, my first away from my hometown, I was to become thoroughly familiar with the language of fear. At dark, shadowy intersections, I could cross in front of a car stopped at a traffic light and elicit the *thunk, thunk, thunk, thunk* of the driver—black, white, male, or female—hammering down the door locks. On less traveled streets after dark, I grew accustomed to but never comfortable with people crossing to the other side of the street rather than pass me. Then there were the standard unpleasantries with policemen, doormen, bouncers, cabdrivers, and others whose busi- ness it is to screen out troublesome individuals *before* there is any nastiness. 3

I moved to New York nearly two years ago and I have remained an avid night walker. In central Manhattan, the near-constant crowd cover minimizes tense one-on-one 4 street encounters. Elsewhere—in SoHo, for example, where sidewalks are narrow and tightly spaced buildings shut out the sky—things can get very taut indeed.

After dark, on the warrenlike streets of Brooklyn where I live, I often see women who   5
fear the worst from me. They seem to have set their faces on neutral, and with their purse straps strung across their chests bandolier-style, they forge ahead as though bracing themselves against being tackled. I understand, of course, that the danger they perceive is not a hallucination. Women are particularly vulnerable to street violence, and young black males are drastically overrepresented among the perpetrators of that violence. Yet these truths are no solace against the kind of alienation that comes of being ever the suspect, a fearsome entity with whom pedestrians avoid making eye contact.

It is not altogether clear to me how I reached the ripe old age of twenty-two without   6
being conscious of the lethality nighttime pedestrians attributed to me. Perhaps it was because in Chester, Pennsylvania, the small, angry industrial town where I came of age in the 1960s, I was scarcely noticeable against a backdrop of gang warfare, street knif- ings, and murders. I grew up one of the good boys, had perhaps a half-dozen fistfights. In retrospect, my shyness of combat has clear sources.

As a boy, I saw countless tough guys locked away; I have since buried several,   7
too. They were babies, really—a teenage cousin, a brother of twenty-two, a childhood friend in his mid-twenties—all gone down in episodes of bravado played out in the streets. I came to doubt the virtues of intimidation early on. I chose, perhaps uncon- sciously, to remain a shadow—timid, but a survivor.

The fearsomeness mistakenly attributed to me in public places often has a perilous   8
flavor. The most frightening of these confusions occurred in the late 1970s and early 1980s, when I worked as a journalist in Chicago. One day, rushing into the office of a magazine I was writing for with a deadline story in hand, I was mistaken for a burglar. The office manager called security and, with an ad hoc posse, pursued me through the labyrinthine halls, nearly to my editor's door. I had no way of proving who I was. I could only move briskly toward the company of someone who knew me.

Another time I was on assignment for a local paper and killing time before an interview.   9
I entered a jewelry store on the city's affluent Near North Side. The proprietor excused her- self and returned with an enormous red Doberman pinscher straining at the end of a leash. She stood, the dog extended toward me, silent to my questions, her eyes bulging nearly out of her head. I took a cursory look around, nodded, and bade her good night.

Relatively speaking, however, I never fared as badly as another black male journalist.   10
He went to nearby Waukegan, Illinois, a couple of summers ago to work on a story about a murderer who was born there. Mistaking the reporter for the killer, police officers hauled him from his car at gunpoint and but for his press credentials would probably have tried to book him. Such episodes are not uncommon. Black men trade tales like this all the time.

Over the years, I learned to smother the rage I felt at so often being taken for a crim-   11
inal. Not to do so would surely have led to madness. I now take precautions to make myself less threatening. I move about with care, particularly late in the evening. I give a wide berth to nervous people on subway platforms during the wee hours, particularly when I have exchanged business clothes for jeans. If I happen to be entering a building behind some people who appear skittish, I may walk by, letting them clear the lobby before I return, so as not to seem to be following them. I have been calm and extremely congenial on those rare occasions when I've been pulled over by the police.

And on late-evening constitutionals I employ what has proved to be an excellent   12
tension-reducing measure: I whistle melodies from Beethoven and Vivaldi and the
more popular classical composers. Even steely New Yorkers hunching toward nighttime
destinations seem to relax, and occasionally they even join in the tune. Virtually everybody seems to sense that a mugger wouldn't be warbling bright sunny selections from
Vivaldi's *Four Seasons*. It is my equivalent of the cowbell that hikers wear when they
know they are in bear country.

Examining the Reading

1. Explain what Staples means by "the ability to alter public space" (para. 2).
2. Staples considers himself a "survivor" (para. 7). To what does he attribute his survival?
3. What does Staples do to make himself seem less threatening to others?
4. Explain the meaning of each of the following words as it is used in the reading: *uninflammatory* (para. 1), *unwieldy* (2), *vulnerable* (5), *retrospect* (6), and *constitutionals* (12).

Analyzing the Writer's Technique

1. Evaluate Staples's opening paragraph. Does it spark your interest? Why or why not?
2. Identify Staples's thesis statement. How does the author support his thesis? What types of information does he include?
3. Cite several examples of places in the essay where Staples uses specific supporting details and transitions effectively. Explain your choices.
4. Evaluate Staples's conclusion. Does it leave you satisfied? Why or why not?
5. What is Staples's method of organization in this essay? What other method of organization could he have used?

Thinking Critically about the Reading

1. Why did Staples choose the word *victim* in paragraph 1? What connotations does it have? What images does he create through its use?
2. Highlight the facts about what Staples sees during his night walks, and underline his opinions about what he sees. Evaluate the evidence for his interpretations and opinions and consider the following question: Is he also prejudging people?
3. What other kinds of sources might Staples have considered in formulating his views? How would including such sources have changed his essay?
4. Describe the tone of the essay. What effect does the tone have on you as a reader? How effective do you find it?
5. What information has Staples omitted that would help you further understand his thesis, if any?

Visualizing the Reading

Review the reading and supply the missing information in the graphic organizer on the next page.

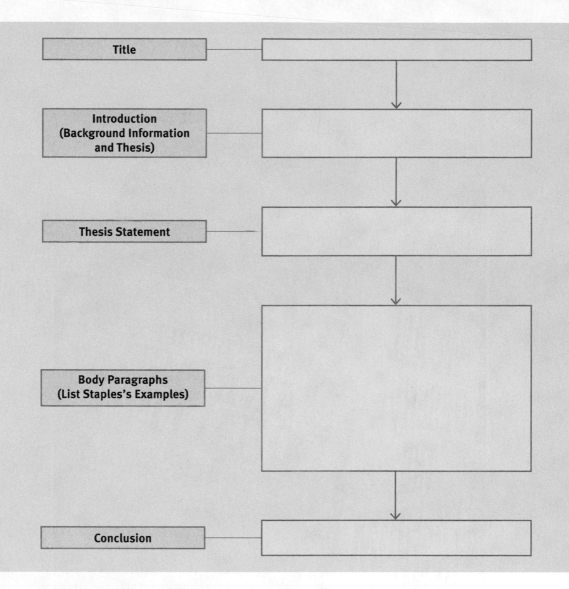

Title	
Introduction (Background Information and Thesis)	
Thesis Statement	
Body Paragraphs (List Staples's Examples)	
Conclusion	

Reacting to the Reading

1. Why is Staples's whistling of classical music similar to hikers wearing cowbells in bear country?
2. In what other ways can an individual "alter public space"?
3. Do you think Staples should alter his behavior in public to accommodate the reactions of others? Write a journal entry explaining whether you agree or disagree with Staples's actions.
4. **Essay assignment.** Staples describes himself as a "survivor" (para. 7) of the streets he grew up on. In a sense, everyone is a survivor of certain decisions or circumstances that, if played out differently, might have resulted in misfortune. Write an essay that explains how and why you or someone you know is a survivor.

CHAPTER 8

Writing Effective Paragraphs

Study the photograph on the opposite page. At what kind of event does it seem to have been taken?

Write a sentence that states the main point of the photograph. Then write several more sentences explaining what is happening in the photograph. Describe what details in the photo enabled you to identify the event.

In much the same way as a photograph does, a paragraph makes an overall impression, or main point, and includes details that support this main point. The first sentence, or topic sentence, states the main idea, and the remainder of the sentences provide the details that support it.

The Structure of a Paragraph

A paragraph is a group of connected sentences that develop an idea about a topic. Each paragraph in your essay should support your thesis and contribute to the overall meaning and effectiveness of your essay. A well-developed paragraph contains

- a well-focused topic sentence
- unified, specific supporting details (definitions, examples, explanations, or other evidence)
- transitions and repetition that show how the ideas are related

Here is a sample paragraph with its parts labeled.

Topic sentence

Audiences gather with varying degrees of willingness to hear a speaker. Some are anxious to hear the speaker, and may even have paid a substantial admission price. The "lecture circuit," for example, is a most lucrative aspect of public life. But whereas some audiences are willing to pay to hear a speaker, others don't seem to care one way or the other. Other audiences need to be persuaded to listen (or at least to sit in the audience). Still other audiences gather because they have to. For example, negotiations on a union contract may require members to attend meetings where officers give speeches.

Details and transitions

DeVito, The Essential Elements of Public Speaking

Notice also how the writer repeats the words *audience(s)* and *speaker,* along with the synonyms *lecture* and *speeches,* to help tie the paragraph to the idea in the topic sentence.

To visualize the structure of a well-developed paragraph, see Figure 8.1.

FIGURE 8.1 The Structure of a Paragraph

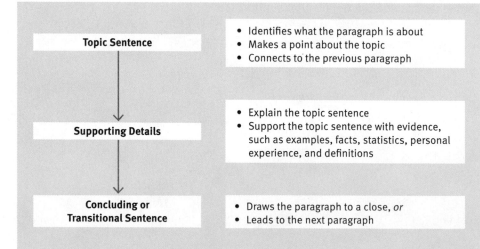

For a paragraph to develop a single idea, it needs to have unity. A unified paragraph stays focused on one idea, without switching or wandering from topic to topic. A paragraph also should be of a reasonable length, neither too short nor too long. Short paragraphs look skimpy and are often underdeveloped; long paragraphs are difficult for your reader to follow.

Writing a Topic Sentence

A topic sentence is to a paragraph what a thesis statement is to an essay. Just as a thesis announces the main point of an essay, a topic sentence states the main point of a paragraph. In addition, each paragraph's topic sentence must support the thesis of the essay. A topic sentence has several specific functions.

A Topic Sentence Should Be Focused

A topic sentence should make clear what the paragraph is about (its topic) and express a view or make a point about the topic.

- Shocking behavior by fans, including rudeness and violent language, has become
  topic

  point about the topic
  common at many sporting events.

The topic sentence should tell readers what the paragraph is about in specific and detailed language. Avoid vague or general statements. Compare these examples of unfocused and focused topic sentences.

UNFOCUSED	Some members of minority groups do not approve of affirmative action.
FOCUSED	Some members of minority groups disapprove of affirmative action because it implies that they are not capable of obtaining employment based on their own accomplishments.
UNFOCUSED	Many students believe that hate groups shouldn't be allowed on campus.
FOCUSED	The neo-Nazis, a group that promotes hate crimes, should not be permitted to speak in our local community college because most students find its members' views objectionable.

If you have trouble focusing your topic sentences, review the guidelines for writing an effective thesis statement in Chapter 6 (pp. 126–27), many of which also apply to writing effective topic sentences.

A Topic Sentence May Preview the Organization of the Paragraph

A topic sentence may suggest the order in which details are discussed in the paragraph, thereby helping readers know what to expect.

- Teaching employees how to handle conflicts through <u>anger management</u> *(first detail)* and <u>mediation</u> *(second detail)* is essential in high-stress jobs.

Readers can expect anger management to be discussed first, followed by a discussion of mediation.

Exercise 8.1

Revise each topic sentence to make it focused and specific. At least two of your revised topic sentences should also preview the organization of the paragraph.

1. In society today, there is always a new fad or fashion in clothing.
2. People watch television talk shows because they find them irresistible.
3. Body piercing is a popular trend.
4. Procrastinating can have a negative effect on your success in college.
5. In our state, the lottery is a big issue.

A Topic Sentence Should Support Your Thesis

Each topic sentence must in some way explain the thesis or show why the thesis is believable or correct. This sample thesis, for example, could be supported by the topic sentences that follow it.

THESIS   **Adoption files should not be made available to adult children who are seeking their biological parents.**

TOPIC SENTENCES

Research has shown that not all biological parents want to meet with the sons or daughters they gave up many years before.

If a woman gives up a child for adoption, it is probable that she does not ever intend to have a relationship with that child.

Adult children who try to contact their biological parents often meet resistance and even hostility, which can cause them to feel hurt and rejected.

A woman who gave up her biological child because she became pregnant as a result of rape or incest should not have to live in fear that her child will one day confront her.

All of these topic sentences support the thesis because they offer valid reasons for keeping adoption files closed.

Exercise 8.2

For each of the following thesis statements, identify the topic sentence in the list below that does not support the thesis:

1. To make a marriage work, a couple must build trust, communication, and understanding.

   a. Knowing why a spouse behaves as he or she does can improve a relationship.

   b. People get married for reasons other than love.

   c. The ability to talk about feelings, problems, likes, and dislikes should grow as a marriage develops.

   d. Marital partners must rely on each other to make sensible decisions that benefit both of them.

2. Internet sales are capturing a larger market share relative to in-store sales.

   a. Internet retailers that target a specific audience tend to be most successful.

   b. The convenience of ordering any time of day or night accounts, in part, for increased Internet sales.

   c. Many customers use Paypal for online purchases.

   d. Web sites that locate and compare prices for a specified item make comparison shopping easier on the Internet than in retail stores.

A Topic Sentence Should Be Strategically Placed

Where you place the topic sentence will determine the order and structure of the rest of the paragraph. The topic sentence also may have different effects, depending on its placement.

Topic Sentence First

The most common and often best position for a topic sentence is at the beginning of the paragraph. A paragraph that opens with the topic sentence should follow a logical sequence: You state your main point, and then you explain it. The topic sentence tells readers what to expect in the rest of the paragraph, making it clear and easy for them to follow.

> Advertising is first and foremost based on the principle of visibility—the customer must notice the product. Manufacturers often package products in glitzy, even garish, containers to grab the consumer's attention. For example, one candy company always packages its candy in reflective wrappers. When the hurried and hungry consumer glances at the candy counter, the reflective wrappers are easy to spot. It is only natural for the impatient customer to grab the candy and go.

Topic sentence

Explanatory details

Topic Sentence Early in the Paragraph

When one or two sentences at the beginning of a paragraph are needed to smooth the transition from one paragraph to the next, the topic sentence may follow these transitional sentences.

Transitional sentence

Topic sentence

However, visibility is not the only principle in advertising; it is simply the first. A second and perhaps more subtle principle is identity: The manufacturer attempts to lure the consumer into buying a product by linking it to a concept with which the consumer can identify. For instance, Boundaries perfume is advertised on television as the choice of "independent" women. Since independent women are admired in our culture, women identify with the concept and therefore are attracted to the perfume. Once the consumer identifies with the product, a sale is more likely to occur.

Topic Sentence Last

The topic sentence can also appear last in a paragraph. You first present the supporting details and then end the paragraph with the topic sentence, which usually states the conclusion that can be drawn from the details. Common in argumentative writing, this arrangement allows you to present convincing evidence before stating your point about the issue.

Evidence

Topic sentence

The saying "Guns don't kill people; people kill people" always makes me even more certain of my own position on gun control. That statement is deceptive in the same way that the statement "Heroin doesn't kill people; people kill themselves" is deceptive. Naturally, people need to pull the trigger of a gun to make the gun kill other people, just as it is necessary for a person to ingest heroin for it to kill him or her. However, these facts do not excuse us from the responsibility of keeping guns (or heroin) out of people's hands as much as possible. People cannot shoot people unless they have a gun. This fact alone should persuade the government to institute stiff gun control laws.

Essay in Progress 1

For the first draft you wrote in Essay in Progress 3 in Chapter 7, page 157, evaluate each of your topic sentences for content and placement. Revise to make each more effective, as needed.

Including Supporting Details

In addition to including well-focused topic sentences, effective paragraphs are unified and well developed, and provide concrete details that work together to support the main point.

Effective Paragraphs Have Unity

In a unified paragraph, all of the sentences directly support the topic sentence. Including details that are not relevant to the topic sentence makes your paragraph unclear and distracts your reader from the point you are making. To identify irrelevant details, evaluate each sentence by asking the following questions:

1. Does this sentence directly explain the topic sentence? What new information does it add?
2. Would any essential information be lost if this sentence were deleted? (If not, delete it.)
3. Is this information distracting or unimportant? (If so, delete it.)

The following sample paragraph lacks unity. As you read it, try to pick out the sentences that do not support the topic sentence.

PARAGRAPH LACKING UNITY

(1) Much of the violence we see in the world today may be caused by the emphasis on violence in the media. (2) More often than not, the front page of the local newspaper contains stories involving violence. (3) In fact, one recent issue of my local newspaper contained seven references to violent acts. (4) There is also violence in public school systems. (5) Television reporters frequently hasten to crime and accident scenes and film every grim, violent detail. (6) The other day, there was a drive-by shooting downtown. (7) If the media were a little more careful about the ways in which they glamorize violence, there might be less violence in the world today and children would be less influenced by it.

Topic sentence

Although sentences 4 and 6 deal with the broad topic of violence, neither is directly related to the idea of the media promoting violence—the main point stated in the topic sentence. Both should be deleted.

Exercise 8.3

Working alone or in a group of two or three students, read each paragraph and identify the sentences that do not support the topic sentence. In each paragraph, the topic sentence is underlined.

1. (a) Today many options and services for the elderly are available that did not exist years ago. (b) My grandmother is eighty-five years old now. (c) Adult care for the elderly is now provided in many parts of the country. (d) Similar to day care, adult care provides places where the elderly can go for meals and social activities. (e) Retirement homes for the elderly, where they can live fairly independently with minimal supervision, are another option. (f) My grandfather is also among the elderly at eighty-two. (g) Even many nursing homes have changed so that residents are afforded some level of privacy and independence while their needs are being met.

2. (a) Just as history repeats itself, fashions have a tendency to do the same. (b) In the late 1960s, for example, women wore miniskirts that came several inches above the knee; some forty years later, the fashion magazines are featuring this same type of dress, and many teenagers are wearing them. (c) The miniskirt has always been flattering on slender women. (d) I wonder if the fashion industry deliberately recycles fashions. (e) Men wore their hair long in the hippie period of the late 1960s and 1970s. (f) Today, some men are again letting their hair grow. (g) Beards, considered "in" during the 1970s, have once again made an appearance.

Effective Paragraphs Are Well Developed

A unified paragraph provides adequate and convincing evidence to explain the topic sentence. Include enough supporting details to demonstrate that your topic sentence is accurate and believable. Evidence can include explanations, examples, or other kinds of information that help the reader understand and believe the assertion in the topic sentence. The following example shows an underdeveloped paragraph that is revised into a well-developed paragraph.

UNDERDEVELOPED PARAGRAPH

Email and instant messaging (IM) are important technological advances, but they have hidden limitations, even dangers. It is too easy to avoid talking to people face to face. Using email can be addictive, too. Plus, they encourage ordinary people to ignore others while typing on a keyboard.

DEVELOPED PARAGRAPH

Email and instant messaging (IM) are important technological advances, but they have hidden limitations, even dangers. While email and instant messaging allow fast and efficient communication and exchange of information, they provide a different quality of human interaction. It is too easy to avoid talking to people. It is easier to click on a chat list and check to see if someone wants to meet for dinner than it would be to look up her number and actually talk to her. Online you can post a "be right back" message, avoiding an intrusion into your life. In fact, using these services can become addictive. For example, some students on campus are obsessed with checking their email several times throughout the day. They spend their free time talking to email acquaintances across the country, while ignoring interesting people right in the same room. Because computer interaction is not face to face, email and instant messenger addicts are shortchanging themselves of real human contact. There is something to be said for responding not only to a person's words but to his or her expressions, gestures, and tone of voice.

These two versions of the paragraph differ in the degree to which the ideas are developed. The first paragraph has skeletal ideas that support the topic sentence, but those ideas are not explained. For example, the first paragraph does not explain why email and instant messaging are important or provide any evidence of how or why email can be addictive. Notice that the second paragraph explains how email and instant messaging allow for fast and efficient communication and gives further information about the addictive qualities of email. The second paragraph also explains the qualities of face-to-face interaction that are absent from online communication.

To discover if your paragraphs are well developed, begin by considering your audience. Have you given them enough information to make your ideas understandable and believable? Try reading your essay aloud, or ask a friend to do so. Listen for places where you jump quickly from one idea to another without explaining the first idea. To find supporting evidence for a topic sentence, use a prewriting strategy from Chapter 4. Also, the same types of evidence shown in Table 6.1 on page 129 to support a thesis can be used to develop a paragraph. You may need to do some research to find this evidence.

Exercise 8.4

Use Table 6.1 (p. 129) to suggest the type or types of evidence that might be used to develop a paragraph based on each of the following topic sentences:

1. Many people have fallen prey to fad diets, risking their health and jeopardizing their mental well-being.

2. One can distinguish experienced soccer players from rookies by obvious signs.

3. To begin a jogging routine, take a relaxed but deliberate approach.

4. The interlibrary loan system is a fast and convenient method for obtaining print materials from libraries affiliated with the campus library.

5. Southwest Florida's rapid population growth poses a serious threat to its freshwater supply.

Exercise 8.5

Create a well-developed paragraph by adding details to the following paragraph.

Although it is convenient, online shopping is a different experience than shopping in an actual store. You don't get the same opportunity to see and feel objects. Also, you can miss out on other important information. There is much that you miss. If you enjoy shopping, turn off your computer and support your local merchants.

Effective Paragraphs Provide Specific Supporting Details

The evidence you provide to support your topic sentences should be concrete and specific. Specific details interest your readers and make your meaning clear and forceful. Compare the following two examples.

VAGUE

Many people are confused about the difference between a psychologist and a psychiatrist. Both have a license, but a psychiatrist has more education than a psychologist. Also, a psychiatrist can prescribe medication.

General statements that do not completely explain the topic sentence

CONCRETE AND SPECIFIC

Many people are confused about the difference between psychiatrists and psychologists. Both are licensed by the state to practice psychotherapy. However, a psychiatrist has earned a degree from medical school and can also practice medicine. Additionally, a psychiatrist can prescribe psychotropic medications. A psychologist, on the other hand, usually has earned a Ph.D. but has not attended medical school and therefore cannot prescribe medication of any type.

Concrete details make clear the distinction between the two terms

To make your paragraphs concrete and specific, use the following guidelines:

1. **Focus on *who, what, when, where, how,* and *why* questions.** Ask yourself these questions about your supporting details, and use the answers to expand and revise your paragraph.

   VAGUE   Some animals hibernate for part of the year.
                (What animals? When do they hibernate?)

   SPECIFIC   Some bears hibernate for three to four months each winter.

2. **Name names.** Include the names of people, places, brands, and objects.

   VAGUE   When my sixty-three-year-old aunt was refused a job, she became an
                angry victim of age discrimination.

   SPECIFIC   When my sixty-three-year-old Aunt Angela was refused a job at
                Vicki's Nail Salon, she became an angry victim of age discrimination.

3. **Use action verbs.** Select strong verbs that will help your readers visualize the action.

   VAGUE   When Silina came on stage, the audience became excited.

   SPECIFIC   When Silina burst onto the stage, the audience screamed, cheered,
                and chanted "Silina, Silina!"

4. **Use descriptive language that appeals to the senses (smell, touch, taste, sound, sight).** Words that appeal to the senses enable your readers to feel as if they are observing or participating in the experience you are describing.

   VAGUE   It's relaxing to walk on the beach.

   SPECIFIC   I walked in the sand next to the ocean, breathing in the smell of the
                salt water and listening to the rhythmic sound of the waves.

5. **Use adjectives and adverbs.** Including carefully chosen adjectives and adverbs in your description of a person, a place, or an experience can make your writing more concrete.

   VAGUE   As I weeded my garden, I let my eyes wander over the meadow sweets
                and hydrangeas, all the while listening to the chirping of a cardinal.

   SPECIFIC   As I slowly weeded my perennial garden, I let my eyes wander over
                the pink meadow sweets and blue hydrangeas, all the while listening
                absent-mindedly to the chirping of a bright red cardinal.

Exercise 8.6

Working alone or in a group of two or three students, revise and expand each sentence in the following paragraph to make it specific and concrete. Feel free to add new information and new sentences.

I saw a great concert the other night in Dallas. Two groups were performing. The music was great, and there was a large crowd. In fact, the crowd was so enthusiastic that the second group performed one hour longer than scheduled.

Details Are Arranged Logically

The details in a paragraph should follow a logical order to make them easier to follow. You might arrange the details from most to least (or least to most) important, in chronological order, or in spatial order. Refer to Chapter 7, pages 144–47, for more information on each of these arrangements.

> **Essay in Progress 2**
> For the draft you worked with in Essay in Progress 1 on page 170, evaluate the supporting details you used in each paragraph. Revise to make each paragraph unified, coherent, and logically organized. Make sure you have provided concrete, specific details.

Using Transitions and Repetition

All of the details in a paragraph must fit together and function as a connected unit of information. When a paragraph has **coherence**, its ideas flow smoothly, allowing readers to follow its progression with ease. Using one of the methods of organization discussed earlier in this chapter can help you show the connections among details and ideas. Two other useful devices for linking details are transitions between sentences and repetition of key terms.

Transitions are words, phrases, or clauses that lead your reader from one idea to another. Think of transitional expressions as guideposts, or signals, of what is coming next in a paragraph. Some commonly used transitions are shown in the box on the next page. They are grouped according to the type of connections they show.

In the two examples that follow, notice that the first paragraph is disjointed and choppy because it lacks transitions, whereas the revised version is easier to follow.

WITHOUT TRANSITIONS

Most films are structured much like a short story. The film begins with an opening scene that captures the audience's attention. The writers build up tension, preparing for the climax of the story. They complicate the situation by revealing other elements of the plot, perhaps by introducing a surprise or additional characters. They introduce a problem. It will be solved either for the betterment or to the detriment of the characters and the situation. A resolution brings the film to a close.

WITH TRANSITIONS

Most films are structured much like a short story. The film begins with an opening scene that captures the audience's attention. Gradually, the writers build up tension, preparing for the climax of the story. Soon after the first scene, they complicate the situation by revealing other elements of the plot, perhaps by introducing a surprise or additional characters. Next, they introduce a problem. Eventually, the problem will be solved either for the betterment or to the detriment of the characters and the situation. Finally, a resolution brings the film to a close.

Notice that the repetition of key terms, or pronouns that stand in for the key terms, also lends coherence to the paragraph. For example, "they" (which stands in for *writers*) appears twice, and the word *film* appears three times.

COMMONLY USED TRANSITIONAL EXPRESSIONS

Type of Connection	*Transitions*
Logical Connections	
Items in a series	then, first, second, next, another, furthermore, finally, as well as
Illustration	for instance, for example, namely, that is
Result or cause	consequently, therefore, so, hence, thus, then, as a result
Restatement	in other words, that is, in simpler terms
Summary or conclusion	finally, in conclusion, to sum up, all in all, evidently, actually
Similarity/agreement	similarly, likewise, in the same way
Difference/opposition	but, however, on the contrary, nevertheless, neither, nor, on the one/other hand, still, yet
Spatial Connections	
Direction	inside/outside, along, above/below, up/down, across, to the right/left, in front of/behind
Nearness	next to, near, nearby, facing, adjacent to
Distance	beyond, in the distance, away, over there
Time Connections	
Frequency	often, frequently, now and then, gradually, week by week, occasionally, daily, rarely
Duration	during, briefly, hour by hour
Reference to a particular time	at two o'clock, on April 27, in 2010, last Thanksgiving, three days ago
Beginning	before then, at the beginning, at first
Middle	meanwhile, simultaneously, next, then, at that time
End	finally, at last, eventually, later, at the end, subsequently, afterward

Essay in Progress 3

For the draft you worked with in Essay in Progress 2 on page 175, evaluate your use of transitions within each paragraph, adding them where needed to make the relationship among your ideas clearer.

Exercise 8.7

The following student essay by Robin Ferguson on volunteering in a literacy program was written using the graphic organizer shown in Chapter 7, page 151. Read the essay and answer the questions that follow.

READING

The Value of Volunteering

Robin Ferguson

I began working as a literacy volunteer as part of a community service course I was taking last   1
semester. The course required a community service project, and I chose literacy volunteers simply
as a means of fulfilling a course requirement. Now I realize that working as a literacy volunteer
taught me more about learning and friendship than I ever expected.

When I first went through the training program to become a literacy volunteer, I learned about   2
the process of learning--that is, the way in which people learn new words most effectively. To illustrate this concept, the person who trained me wrote a brief list of simple words on the left side of
a chalkboard and wrote phrases using the same words on the right side of the chalkboard. She in-
structed us to read the words and then asked which words we would be most likely to remember. We
all said the words on the right because they made more sense. In other words, we could remember
the words in the phrases more easily because they made more sense in context. The trainer showed
us several more examples of words in context so we could get a grasp of how people learn new information by connecting it to what they already know.

The training I received, though excellent, was no substitute for working with a real student,   3
however. When I began to discover what other people's lives are like because they cannot read, I realized the true importance of reading. For example, when I had my first tutoring session with my client,
Marie, a forty-four-year-old single mother of three, I found out she walked two miles to the nearest
grocery store twice a week because she didn't know which bus to take. When I told her I would get her
a bus schedule, she confided to me that it would not help because she could not read it and therefore
wouldn't know which bus to take. She also said she had difficulty once she got to the grocery store
because she couldn't always remember what she needed. Since she did not know words, she could not
write out a grocery list. Also, she identified items by sight, so if the manufacturer changed a label, she
could not recognize it as the product she wanted.

As we worked together, learning how to read built Marie's self-confidence, which gave her   4
an incentive to continue in her studies. She began to make rapid progress and was even able to
take the bus to the grocery store. After this successful trip, she reported how self-assured she felt.
Eventually, she began helping her youngest son, Mark, a shy first grader, with his reading. She sat
with him before he went to sleep, and together they would read bedtime stories. When his eyes
became wide with excitement as she read, her pride swelled, and she began to see how her own

hard work in learning to read paid off. As she described this experience, I swelled with pride as well. I found that helping Marie to build her self-confidence was more rewarding than anything I had ever done before.

As time went by, Marie and I developed a friendship that became permanent. Because we saw   5
each other several times a week, we spent a lot of time getting to know each other, and we discovered we had certain things in common. For instance, I'm also a single parent. So we began to share
our similar experiences with each other. In fact, we have even baby-sat for each other's children.
I would drop my children off at her house while I taught an evening adult class, and in return, I
watched her children while she worked on Saturday mornings.

As a literacy volunteer, I learned a great deal about learning, teaching, and helping others. I   6
also established what I hope will be a lifelong friendship. In fact, I may have benefited more from
the experience than Marie did.

1. Highlight each of the topic sentences in the body of the essay (between the introduction and the conclusion). Evaluate how well each supports the thesis.
2. What type(s) of evidence does Ferguson use to support each topic sentence?
3. What method(s) does Ferguson use to arrange her details logically within paragraphs?
4. Highlight transitions that Ferguson uses to connect her ideas, both within and
   between paragraphs.

Students Write

Chapters 5 to 7 show Christine Lee's progress in planning and drafting an essay on reality television. Below you can see her first-draft paragraph (also included in Chapter 7 as part of her first draft essay, p. 158) and her revision to strengthen the paragraph.

FIRST-DRAFT PARAGRAPH

Reality shows that followed *Survivor* didn't have the interesting elements that it had. *Big Brother* started as the first of the reality TV spin-offs, but audiences didn't have the same things to respond to. It has never been a success because they took the basic concept of *Survivor* and added nothing new or interesting to it. *Big Brother* locked up a bunch of people in a house and forced the audience to watch them bicker over nothing. Viewers were forced to watch bored contestants bicker and fight, locked up in a house with nothing else to do. It didn't seem the kind of competition that *Survivor* was, even though there was a cash prize on the line. The cash prize wasn't large enough anyways. We didn't choose favorites because the players weren't up against anything, except fighting off weeks of boredom. *Big Brother* introduced audience participation with the television audience voting off members, which gave the house members less to do and less motive to scheme and plot their allegiances like the castaways on *Survivor*. Voting members off was an arbitrary and meaningless process. But *Big Brother* had the prize component, and it took away the housemates' access to the outside world.

REVISED PARAGRAPH

Reality TV shows that followed *Survivor* had none of the interesting elements that it had. *Big Brother* was the first spin-off reality TV show to try to repeat the success of *Survivor*, but it did not offer the drama that *Survivor* did. In *Big Brother*, contestants were locked in a house without any outside contact for weeks. As in *Survivor*, there was a cash prize on the line, but in *Big Brother* there were not any competitions or struggles. Contestants were expelled by a viewer phone poll, so the poll gave them no motive to scheme and plot allegiances the way *Survivor* contestants did. In fact, the contestants had little to do except bicker and fight. Viewers lost interest in players who were not up against any challenge except weeks of boredom. In the end, *Big Brother* was simply not interesting.

Analyzing the Writer's Technique

1. How did Lee strengthen her topic sentence?
2. What irrelevant details did she delete?
3. What transitions did she add to provide coherence?
4. What words are repeated that contribute to coherence?
5. What further revisions do you recommend?

Working with Text

In Chapter 7, you read the essay "Black Men and Public Space" by Brent Staples (pp. 160–62). Return to this essay now and examine Staples's use and placement of topic sentences. As you read, highlight each topic sentence and study how each is supported with concrete, specific details.

CHAPTER 9

Revising Content and Organization

Looking at the photograph on the opposite page from left to right, list everything that is happening in the picture.

Examine your list, looking for ways to make it more understandable to someone who has not seen the photo. Write a few sentences summarizing what you think is going on in the photo, and then add details to your original list to describe the photo more fully. After you make these changes, will it be easier for a reader who has not seen the photo to understand what is happening in it?

Now, exchange papers with a classmate and examine how your classmate organized ideas. Look for parts that you find confusing and that need more detail. Write down your comments for your classmate. Finally, using your own comments and those of your classmate, make changes to improve your own description of the photograph.

When you changed your list, did you include more details from the photo? Leave some unimportant details out? Change the content of any details? Whatever changes you made improved the content of your writing. In other words, you have *revised* the description of the photo.

Revising an essay works in much the same way. **Revision** is a process of making changes to improve both what your essay says and how it is said. This chapter offers several approaches to revising an essay. It lists some general suggestions, describes how to use a graphic organizer for revision, offers specific questions to guide your revision, and discusses the implications of learning style for the revision process. You will notice in Figure 9.1 that revision is an essential part of the writing process.

Why Revise?

A thorough, thoughtful revision can change a C paper to an A paper! Revising can make a significant difference in how well your paper achieves your purpose and how effectively it expresses your ideas to your intended audience. Although revision takes time and hard work, it pays off and produces results.

FIGURE 9.1 An Overview of the Writing Process

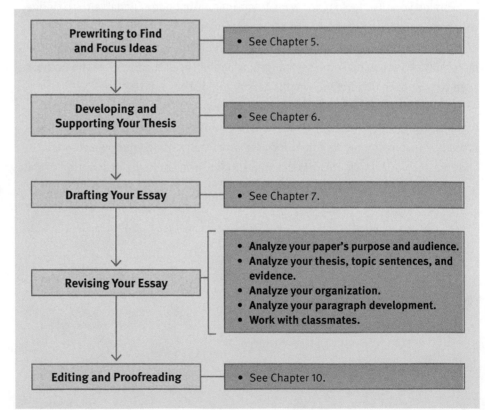

Most professional writers revise frequently and thoroughly, as do successful student writers. Revision is a process of looking again at your *ideas* to make them clearer and easier to understand. It is not merely a process of correcting surface errors. It may mean adding, eliminating, or reorganizing key elements within the essay. It may even mean revising your thesis statement and refocusing the entire essay.

The amount of revision you need to do depends, in part, on how you approach the task of writing. Some writers spend more time planning; others spend more time revising. For example, students who tend to be pragmatic learners take a highly structured approach to writing. They plan in detail what they will say before they draft. More creative learners, however, may dash off a draft as ideas come to mind. A well-planned draft usually requires less revision than one that was spontaneously written. However, regardless of how carefully planned an essay may be, any first draft will require at least some revision.

Learning Style Options

Useful Techniques for Revision

The following techniques will help you get the most benefit from the time you spend revising your essays:

- **Allow time between drafting and revising.** Once you have finished writing, set your draft aside for a while, overnight if possible. When you return to your draft, you will be able to approach it from a fresh perspective.
- **Read your draft aloud.** Hearing what you have written will help you discover main points that are unclear or that lack adequate support. You will notice confusing paragraphs, awkward wording, and vague or overused expressions.
- **Ask a friend to read your draft aloud to you.** When your reader hesitates, slows down, misreads, or sounds confused, it could be a signal that your message is not as clear as it should be. Keep a copy of your draft in front of you as you listen, and mark places where your reader falters or seems baffled.
- **Seek the opinions of classmates.** Ask a classmate to read and comment on your paper. This process, called **peer review**, is discussed in detail later in this chapter (see p. 188).
- **Look for consistent problem areas.** After they write and revise several essays, many students discover consistent problem areas, such as organization or a lack of concrete details to support main points.
- **Use a typed and printed copy.** Even if you prefer to handwrite your draft, be sure to type and print it before you revise. Because computer-generated, typed copy seems less personal, you will be able to analyze and evaluate it more impartially. You will also be able to see a full page at a time on a printed copy, instead of only a paragraph at a time on a computer screen. Finally, on a printed copy you can write marginal annotations, circle troublesome words or sentences, and draw arrows to connect details.

One of the best ways to reexamine your essay is to draw a graphic organizer—a visual display of your thesis statement and supporting paragraphs. A graphic organizer allows you to see how your thesis and topic sentences relate to one another. It also can help you evaluate both the content and the organization of your essay.

For instructions on creating a graphic organizer, see Chapter 3, pages 59–61. If you are working on an assignment in Chapters 11 to 18 or Chapter 20, each of those chapters includes a model graphic organizer for the type of writing covered in the chapter. As you are drawing your graphic organizer, if you spot a detail or an example that does not support a topic sentence or discover any other kind of problem, write notes to the right of your organizer, as shown in Figure 9.2.

Another option, instead of drawing a graphic organizer, is to write an outline of your draft. For more information on outlining, see Chapter 7, pages 148–50.

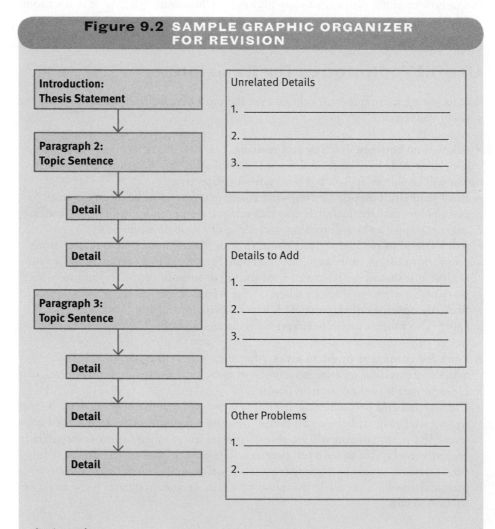

Figure 9.2 SAMPLE GRAPHIC ORGANIZER FOR REVISION

Key Questions for Revision

The five key questions listed below will help you make changes when you revise. Use the questions to identify broad areas of weakness in your essay.

- **Does your essay clearly convey a purpose, address an appropriate audience, and state a thesis?**
- **Do you have enough reasons and evidence to support your thesis?**
- **Do the ideas in your essay fit together?**
- **Is each paragraph well developed?**
- **Does your essay have a strong introduction and conclusion?**

After reading your draft or after discussing it with a classmate, answer each of these five questions to pinpoint areas that need improvement. Then refer to the self-help flowcharts in the following sections. In addition to the revision suggestions and flowcharts in this chapter, the chapters in Part 3, Chapter 20 in Part 4, and Chapters 22 and 23 in Part 5 provide revision flowcharts tailored to the specific assignments in those chapters.

Analyzing Your Purpose and Audience

First drafts are often unfocused and may go off in several directions rather than have a clear purpose. For instance, one section of an essay on divorce may inform readers of its causes, and another section may argue that it harms children. A first draft may contain sections that appeal to different audiences. For instance, one section of an essay on counseling teenagers about drug abuse might seem to be written for parents; other sections might be more appropriate for teenagers.

To find out if your paper has a clear focus, write a sentence stating what your paper is supposed to accomplish. If you cannot write such a sentence, your essay probably lacks a clear purpose. To find a purpose, do some additional thinking or brainstorming, listing as many possible purposes as you can think of.

To find out if your essay is directed to a specific audience, write a sentence or two describing your intended readers. Describe their knowledge, beliefs, and experience with your topic. If you are unable to do so, try to zero in on a particular audience and revise your essay with them in mind.

For more information about purpose and audience, see Chapter 5, pp. 106–9. For more on developing a thesis, see Chapter 6, pp. 125–27.

> **Essay in Progress 1**
> Evaluate the purpose and audience of the draft essay you wrote in Essay in Progress 3 in Chapter 7, page 157, or of any essay that you have written. Make notes on your graphic organizer or annotate your outline.

Analyzing Your Thesis, Topic Sentences, and Evidence

Once your paper is focused on a specific purpose and audience, your next step is to evaluate your thesis statement and your support for that thesis. Use Figure 9.3 to examine your thesis statement, topic sentences, and evidence.

Figure 9.3 Flowchart for Evaluating Your Thesis Statement, Topic Sentences, and Evidence

QUESTIONS

REVISION STRATEGIES

1. Does your essay have a thesis statement that identifies your topic and states your position or suggests your slant on the topic? (To find out, state your thesis aloud without looking at your essay; then highlight the sentence in your draft essay that matches or is close to what you have just said. If you cannot find such a sentence, you have probably not written a well-focused thesis statement.)

- Reread your essay and answer this question: What one main point is most of this essay concerned with?
- Write a thesis statement that expresses that main point.
- Revise your paper to focus on that main point.
- Delete parts of the essay that do not support your thesis statement.

 YES

2. Have you given your readers all the background information they need to understand your thesis? (To find out, ask someone unfamiliar with your topic to read your essay, asking questions as he or she reads.)

NO

- Answer *who*, *what*, *when*, *where*, *why*, and *how* questions to discover more background information.

 YES

3. Have you presented enough convincing evidence to support your thesis? (To find out, place checkmarks ✓ beside the evidence in your essay, and compare the evidence against the thesis. Ask yourself this question: Would I accept the thesis, or does it need more evidence to be convincing?)

NO

- Use prewriting strategies or do additional research to discover more supporting evidence.
- Evaluate this new evidence and add the most convincing evidence to your essay.

 YES

QUESTIONS		REVISION STRATEGIES
4. Does each topic sentence logically connect to and support the thesis? (To find out, <u>underline</u> each topic sentence. Read the thesis, and then read each topic sentence. When the connection between them is not obvious, revision is needed.)	**NO**	• Rewrite the topic sentence so that it clearly supports the thesis. • If necessary, broaden your thesis so that it encompasses all your supporting points.

 YES

QUESTIONS		REVISION STRATEGIES
5. Is your evidence specific and detailed? (To find out, go through your draft, and reread where you placed checkmarks ✓. Does each checkmarked item answer one of these questions: *Who? What? When? Where? Why? How?* If you have not placed a checkmark in a particular paragraph or have placed a checkmark by only one sentence or part of a sentence, you need to add more detailed evidence to that paragraph.)	**NO**	• Name names, give dates, specify places. • Use action verbs and descriptive language, including carefully chosen adjectives and adverbs. • Answer *who, what, when, where, why,* and *how* questions to discover more detailed evidence.

Essay in Progress 2

Using Figure 9.3, evaluate the thesis statement, topic sentences, and evidence of your essay in progress in Chapter 7, page 157. Make notes on your graphic organizer or annotate your outline.

Analyzing Your Organization

Your readers will not be able to follow your ideas if your essay does not hold together as a unified piece of writing. To be sure that it does, examine your essay's organization. The graphic organizer or outline of your draft (see p. 183) that you completed will help you analyze the draft's organization and discover any flaws.

To determine if the organization of your draft is clear and effective, you can also ask a classmate to read your draft and explain to you how your essay is organized. If your classmate cannot describe your essay's organization, it probably needs further work. Use one of the methods in Chapter 7 (pp. 144–147) or one of the patterns of development described in Parts 3 and 4 to reorganize your ideas.

Analyzing Your Introduction, Conclusion, and Title

Once you are satisfied with the draft's organization, evaluate your introduction, conclusion, and title. Use the following questions as guidelines:

1. **Does your introduction interest your reader and provide needed background information?** If your essay jumps into the topic without preparing readers for it, your introduction needs to be revised. Use the suggestions in Chapter 7 (pp. 154–56) to create interest. Ask the *W* questions—*who, what, when, where, why,* and *how*—to determine the background information that you need.
2. **Does your conclusion draw your essay to a satisfactory close and reinforce your thesis statement?** Does the conclusion follow logically from the introduction? If not, use the suggestions for writing conclusions in Chapter 7 (pp. 156–57). Also try imagining yourself explaining the significance or importance of your essay to a friend. Use this explanation to rewrite your conclusion.
3. **Does your title accurately reflect the content of your essay?** To improve your title, write a few words that "label" your essay. Also, reread your thesis statement, looking for a few key words that can serve as part of your title. Finally, use the suggestions in Chapter 7 (p. 157) to help you choose a title.

> **Essay in Progress 3**
> Evaluate the organization of your essay in progress. Make notes on your draft copy.

Analyzing Your Paragraph Development

See Chapter 8 for more on paragraph development.

Each paragraph in your essay must fully develop a single idea that supports your thesis. (Narrative essays are an exception to this rule. As you will see in Chapter 11, in a narrative essay, each paragraph focuses on a separate part of the action.)

In a typical first draft, paragraphs are often weak or loosely structured. They may contain irrelevant information or lack a clearly focused topic sentence. To evaluate your paragraph development, study each paragraph separately in conjunction with your thesis statement. You may need to delete or combine some paragraphs, rework or reorganize others, or move paragraphs to a more appropriate part of the essay. If you need to supply additional information to support your thesis, you may need to add paragraphs to the draft. Use Figure 9.4 to help you analyze and revise your paragraphs.

> **Essay in Progress 4**
> Using Figure 9.4, examine each paragraph of your essay in progress. Make notes on the draft copy of your essay.

Working with Classmates to Revise Your Essay

Increasingly, instructors in writing and other academic disciplines use **peer review**, a process in which two or more students read and comment on each other's papers. Students might work together in class, outside of class, via email, or via a classroom

Figure 9.4 Flowchart for Evaluating Your Paragraphs

QUESTIONS

REVISION STRATEGIES

1. Does each paragraph have a clear topic sentence that expresses the main point of the paragraph? (To find out, underline the topic sentence in each paragraph. Then evaluate whether the topic sentence makes a statement that the rest of the paragraph supports.)

— NO →

- Revise a sentence within the paragraph so that it clearly states the main point.
- Write a new sentence that states the one main point of the paragraph.

 YES

2. Do all sentences in each paragraph support the topic sentence? (To find out, read the topic sentence, and then read each supporting sentence in turn.)

— NO →

- Revise supporting sentences to make their connection to the topic sentence clear.
- Delete any sentences that do not support the topic sentence.

 YES

3. Does the paragraph offer adequate explanation and supporting details? (To find out, place checkmarks ✓ beside supporting details. Then ask yourself: Is there other information readers will want or need to know?)

— NO →

- Add more details if your paragraph seems skimpy.
- Use either the *who, what, when, where, why,* and *how* questions or the prewriting strategies in Chapter 5 to generate the details you need.

 YES

4. Will it be clear to your reader how each sentence and each paragraph connects to those before and after it? (To find out, read your paper aloud to see if it flows smoothly or sounds choppy.)

— NO →

- Add transitions where they are needed. Refer to the list of common transitions on page 176.

computer network. Working with classmates is an excellent way to get ideas for improving your essays. You'll also have the opportunity to discover how other students view and approach the writing process. The following suggestions will help both the writer and the reviewer get the most out of peer review.

How to Find a Good Reviewer

Selecting a good reviewer is key to getting good suggestions for revision. Your instructor may pair you with another class member or let you find your own reviewer, either a classmate or someone outside of class. Class members make good reviewers, since they are familiar with the assignment and with what you have learned so far in the course. If you need to find someone outside of class, try to choose a person who has already taken the writing course you are taking, preferably someone who has done well. Close friends are not necessarily the best reviewers; they may be reluctant to offer criticism, or they may be too critical. Instead, choose someone who is serious, skillful, and willing to spend the time needed to provide useful comments. If your college has a writing center, you might ask a tutor in the center to read and comment on your draft. Consider using more than one reviewer so you can get several perspectives.

Suggestions for the Writer

To get the greatest benefit from having another student review your paper, use the following suggestions:

1. **Be sure to provide readable copy.** A typed, double-spaced draft is preferred.
2. **Do some revision yourself first.** If your essay is not very far along, think it through a little more, and try to fix some obvious problems. The more developed your draft is, the more helpful the reviewer's comments will be.
3. **Offer specific questions or guidelines to your reviewer.** A sample set of Questions for Reviewers is provided below. Give your reviewer a copy of these questions, adding others that you need answered. You might also give your reviewer questions from one of the revision flowcharts in this chapter. If you have

QUESTIONS FOR REVIEWERS

1. What is the purpose of the paper?
2. Who is the intended audience?
3. Is the introduction fully developed?
4. What is the main point or thesis? Is it easy to identify?
5. Does the essay offer evidence to support each important point? Where is more evidence needed? (Be sure to indicate specific paragraphs.)
6. Is each paragraph clear and well organized?
7. Are transitions used to connect ideas within and between paragraphs?
8. Is the organization easy to follow? Where might it be improved, and how?
9. Does the conclusion draw the essay to a satisfying close?
10. What do you like about the draft?
11. What are its weaknesses, and how could they be eliminated? Underline or highlight sentences that are unclear or confusing.

written an essay in response to an assignment in a later chapter, consider giving your reviewer the revision flowchart for that assignment.

4. **Be open to criticism and new ideas.** As much as possible, try not to be defensive; instead, look at your essay objectively, seeing it as your reviewer sees it.

5. **Don't feel obligated to accept all of the advice you are given.** A reviewer might suggest a change that will not work well in your paper or wrongly identify something as an error. If you are uncertain about a suggestion, discuss it with your instructor.

Suggestions for the Reviewer

Be honest but tactful. Criticism is never easy to accept, so keep your reader's feelings in mind. The following tips will help you provide useful comments:

1. **Read the draft through completely before making any judgments or comments.** You will need to read it at least twice to evaluate it.

2. **Concentrate on content; pay attention to what the paper says.** Evaluate the writer's train of thought; focus on the main points and how clearly they are expressed. If you notice a misspelling or a grammatical error, you can circle it, but correcting errors is not your primary task.

3. **Offer some positive comments.** It will help the writer to know what is good as well as what needs improvement.

4. **Be specific.** For instance, instead of saying that more examples are needed, tell the writer which ideas in which paragraphs are unclear without examples, and suggest what kind of example would be most useful in each case.

5. **Use the Questions for Reviewers on page 190 as well as any additional questions that the writer provides to guide your review.** If the essay was written in response to an assignment in one of the chapters in Parts 3 or 4, you might use the revision flowchart in that chapter.

6. **Write notes and comments directly on the draft. At the end, write a note that summarizes your overall reaction, pointing out both strengths and weaknesses.** Here is a sample final note written by a reviewer.

> Overall, I think your paper has great ideas, and I found that it held my interest. The example about the judge did prove your point. I think you should organize it better. The last three paragraphs do not seem connected to the rest of the essay. Maybe better transitions would help, too. Also work on the conclusion. It just says the same thing as your thesis statement.

7. **If you are reviewing a draft on a computer, type your comments in brackets following the appropriate passage, or highlight them in some other way.** The writer can easily delete your comments after reading them. Some word-processing programs have features for adding comments.

8. **Do not rewrite paragraphs or sections of the paper.** Instead, suggest how the writer might revise them.

Essay in Progress 5

Give your essay in progress to a classmate to read and review. Ask your reviewer to respond to the Questions for Reviewers (p. 190). Revise your essay using your revision outline, your responses to Figures 9.3 and 9.4, and your reviewer's suggestions.

Using Your Instructor's Comments

Another resource to use in revising your essays is the commentary your instructor provides. These comments can be used not only to submit a revised version of a particular essay but also to improve your writing throughout the course.

Revising an Essay Using Your Instructor's Comments

Your instructor may want to review a draft of your essay and suggest revisions you can make for the final version. Some instructors allow students to revise and resubmit a paper and then give the students an average of the two grades. Either way, your instructor's comments can provide a road map for you to begin your revision. Review the comments on your essays carefully, looking for problems that recur, so that you can focus on these elements in your future writing.

Different instructors may use different terminology when they mark up writing assignments, but most like to point out several common problems. The marks on your essay will often address spelling and grammar errors, and problems with organization and with the clarity or development of ideas.

Figure 9.5 shows a first draft of an essay by a student, Kate Atkinson, that has been read and marked up by her instructor. The assignment was to write an essay defining a specialized term, and the student chose "guerrilla street art" as her subject. Note that the instructor has commented on a range of elements in the essay, including effectiveness of the introduction, paragraph unity and development, word choice, and source citations. Grammar, spelling, and punctuation errors have not been marked. Atkinson read the comments carefully and used them to revise her essay. Her final draft appears in Chapter 17 (pp. 461–63).

FIGURE 9.5 Using Your Instructor's Comments to Revise Your Essay

Guerilla Street Art: Definition Essay Rough Draft

Comment [KM1]: Good opening sentence. It gives readers a reason for wanting to know more about it and challenges them to look for it.

Comment [KM2]: This term is not yet defined. I know it is defined later, but readers will wonder what it is now. Perhaps chose a different example here?

Comment [KM3]: This is your thesis, but it is not very detailed. What about combining it with the following sentence to create a stronger thesis?

Guerrilla street art is everywhere, if you look for it. There are countless examples in the   1
small college town where I grew up, where the dense population of college students and artists breeds creativity. Just around the corner from my school there are stickers littering sign posts, colorful graffiti tags on exposed brick walls, homemade posters advertising local bands at the bus stop, and a cheerful Dr. Seuss character stencilled on the sidewalk. These small works of art can go easily unnoticed, but they bring an unexpected vibrancy to the city that is unique. Guerrilla street art is any unauthorized art in a public space. By taking art out of the traditional context, guerilla street artists create controversy and intrigue by making art free and accessible to a broad audience.

Graffiti is unauthorized writing or drawing on a public surface . It dates back centuries and artists have been know to use chalk, markers, paint, and even carving tools to inscribe their messages on public property. Common techniques used by street artists today include graffiti, stenciling, poster art, sticker art, and wheat pasting. Graffiti is so common that it is difficult to travel far in most urban settings without coming across a word or image scrawled in spray paint on a public surface. Stenciling is a form of graffitti in which artists use pre-cut stencils to guide their work, and pre-made stickers and posters are popular because they can be quickly appled and are easy to mass produce. "Wheat pasting " refers to the use of a vegetable-based adhesive to adhere posters to walls. Using a less common technique called "yarn bombing," crafty artists knit colorful sheaths of wool and acrylic and wrap them around telephone poles and park benches. The finished pieces are eye-catching and unusual, but not permanent or damaging to public property.

> **Comment [KM4]:** This sentence defining graffiti is almost the same definition as your definition of guerrilla street art in para. 1.

> **Comment [KM5]:** The paragraph is about graffiti-writing or drawing. Do wheat pasting and yarn bombing fall into this category? If so, can you expand the definition to fit them? Or are they other forms of guerrilla street art? If so, I'd put them in a separate paragraph. Right now you only mention one form of guerrilla art—graffiti—yet your title suggests the essay is about street art. Are there other forms you haven't mentioned?

The various motives behind guerilla street art are as diverse as the artwork itself and range from social and political activism to self-promotion of the artist . Artist embellish telephone poles with colorful yarn or train carriges with ornate murals as a way to reclaim and beautify public space. Others use public space as a billboard for *to advocate for a* cause. An example of street art as propaganda is artist Shepard Fairey's iconic image of Barack Obama . The simple design combines a striking red, white, and blue portrait of Obama with the word "Hope." With the nod of approval from Obama's campaign team, Fairey and his team dispersed and glue, stencilled, and tacked the image onto countless public surfaces across the US until it became an important facet of the campaign. The picture itself is powerful, but what made it even more effective as a campaign tool was the distribution of the image by supporters and the youth appeal that it garnered as a result.

> **Comment [KM6]:** This is a strong topic sentence.

> **Comment [KM7]:** Are all causes propaganda? You might want to chose a different word here or introduce propaganda and a separate motive first.

> **Deleted:** a

> **Comment [KM8]:** Add source citation

Street Art is also an easy way for new artists to gain notoriety withouth revealing who they really are. A tag, which is an artists signature or symbol, is the most prevalent type of graffitti. Before the Obama campaign, Shepard Fairey gained international acclaim for a sticker depicting wrestler Andre the Giant and the word "Obey." The image soon became his tag and can be found in almost all of his work, making it instantly recognizable. The anonymity of street art also gives artists the freedom to express themselves without fearing the judgement of their peers. At worst, this freedom can result in crude or offensice inscriptions on public property but at best, it can produce bold statements.

> **Comment [KM9]:** This sentence leads me to believe that the para. will be about secrecy, but midway through the topic seems to switch to reasons for street art's appeal. Maybe make this part into a separate paragraph?

Due to the illicit nature of their art, the street artist community is shrouded in secrecy . In the film "Exit through the Gift Shop," a documentary by notorious British street artist Banksy , hooded figures in ski masks are shown scaling buildings and perched precariously on ledges, armed with spray cans and buckets of industrial paste and always on the lookout for the police. Despite his celebrity, Banksy has managed to keep his identity anonymous and his face is never shown in the film. It is common for street artists to be arrested for trespassing and vandalism, and the risk and intentional disobience involved in street art adds to its appeal, especially amoung young people. Another appeal of guerrilla street art is that it is comtemporary and can be enjoyed without a visit to a museum. It is free and encourages the belief that art should be accessible and available

> **Comment [KM10]:** Add source citation

to everyone. It is also a movement that anyone can take part in and that challenges traditional standards of art.

Guerrilla street art has blossomed from and underground movement to a cultural phenomenon. 6 At the very least, it brings up the controversial questions of what constitutes art, and whether public space is an appropriate place for it. It brings beauty and intrigue to urban spaces that would otherwise go unnoticed and it is a tool for artists to exercise freedom of speech and expression.

> **Comment [KM11]:** I am glad you raised this question. I kept wondering about it all along as I read the essay. Can you raise it earlier? And should you try to answer this knotty question of "What is art"? Maybe just recognize that the question exists?

Exercise 9.1

Working either alone or in small groups, compare the first draft of Kate Atkinson's essay with the final version on pages 461–63. Make a list of the changes Atkinson made to her essay in response to her instructor's comments. Also, put a checkmark next to any problems that recur throughout the first draft of the essay.

Exercise 9.2

If your instructor has returned a marked-up first draft to you, read the comments carefully. Then draw a line down the middle of a blank piece of paper. On the left, write the instructor's comments; on the right, jot down ways you might revise the essay in response to each. Put a checkmark next to any problems that recur throughout your essay; these are areas you will want to pay particular attention to in your future writing.

Using Your Instructor's Comments to Improve Future Essays

When you receive a graded essay back from an instructor, it is tempting to note the grade and then file away the essay. To improve your writing, however, take time to study each comment. Use the following suggestions:

- **Reread your essay more than once.** Read it once to note grammatical corrections, and then read it again to study comments about organization or content. Processing numerous comments on a wide range of topics takes more than one reading.
- **For grammar errors, make sure you understand the error.** Check a grammar handbook or ask a classmate; if the error is still unclear, check with your instructor.
- **Record grammar errors in your error log (see Chapter 10, pp. 221–22).** When you proofread your next essay, be sure to look carefully for each of these errors.
- **If you did not get a high grade, try to determine why.** Was the essay weak in content, organization, or development?
- **Using Figures 9.3 (p. 186) and 9.4 (p. 189), highlight or mark weaknesses that your instructor identified.** When writing your next essay, refer back to these flowcharts. Pay special attention to these areas as you evaluate your next paper.
- **If any of your instructor's comments are unclear, first ask a classmate if he or she understands them.** If not, then ask your instructor, who will be pleased that you are taking time to study the comments.

Considering Your Learning Style

Depending on your learning style, you may need to address specific kinds of problems in your drafts. For example, a pragmatic learner tends to write tightly organized drafts, but they may lack interest, originality, or sufficient content. A creative learner may write drafts that lack organization. Following are some revision tips for other aspects of your learning style:

Learning Style Options

- *Independent* learners, who often need extra time for reflection, should be sure to allow sufficient time between drafting and revising. *Social* learners often find discussing revision plans with classmates particularly helpful.
- *Verbal* learners may prefer to use outlining to check the organization of their drafts, while *spatial* learners may find it more helpful to draw a graphic organizer.
- *Rational* learners should be sure their drafts do not seem dull or impersonal, adding vivid descriptions and personal examples where appropriate. *Emotional* learners, whose writing may tend to be overly personal, should state their ideas directly, without hedging or showing undue concern for those who may disagree.
- *Concrete* learners, who tend to focus on specifics, should check that their thesis and topic sentences are clearly stated. *Abstract* learners, who tend to focus on general ideas, should be sure they have enough supporting details.

Students Write

After writing her first draft, which appears in Chapter 7 (pp. 158–59), Christine Lee used the guidelines and revision flowcharts in this chapter to help her decide what to revise. For example, she decided that she needed to add more details about what happened on the TV show *Survivor*. She also decided that she should emphasize the uninteresting details of the examples of some other reality TV shows.

Lee asked a classmate named Sam to review her essay. A portion of Sam's comments is shown below.

Reviewer's Comments

The trend that you have chosen to write about is well-known and interesting. Beginning your introduction with a question piques the reader's interest, and your thesis is clear: Reality TV shows are becoming less interesting and tasteful. You mention why people enjoyed *Survivor* and why they didn't enjoy the other shows. You should also emphasize why television viewers watched *Survivor*. Once that point is clear, many of your ideas might fit better.

I think some specific details about the reality TV shows you mention would help readers who are not familiar with the shows. It would also help prove your point: These shows are getting worse. The title and conclusion could better help make this point too. The title doesn't indicate what the reality of reality TV is, and the conclusion could look ahead to what you think the fate of reality TV will be.

Using her own analysis and her classmate's suggestions, Lee created a graphic organizer (Figure 9.6) to help her decide how to revise her draft, using the format for an illustration essay provided in Chapter 13 (on p. 313).

Figure 9.6 GRAPHIC ORGANIZER FOR CHRISTINE LEE'S REVISION PLANS

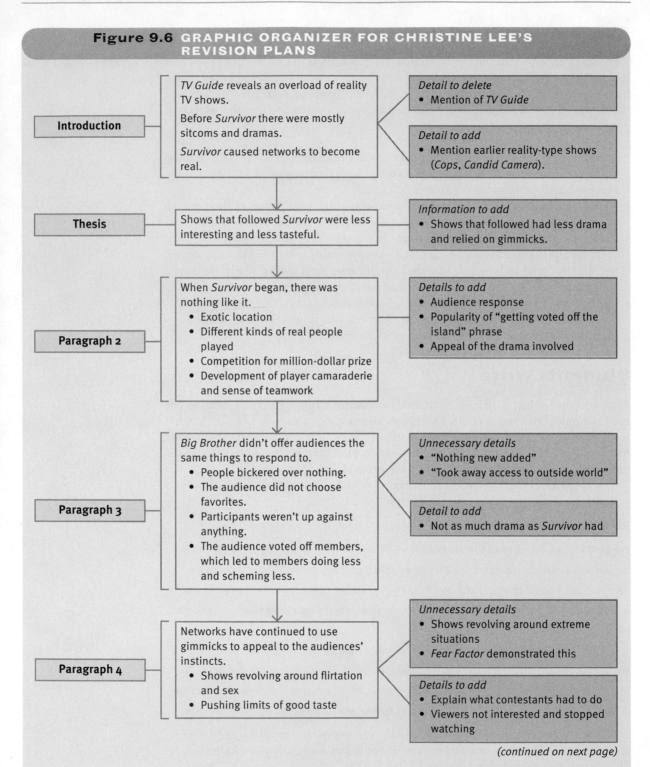

Introduction

TV Guide reveals an overload of reality TV shows.

Before Survivor there were mostly sitcoms and dramas.

Survivor caused networks to become real.

Detail to delete
- Mention of TV Guide

Detail to add
- Mention earlier reality-type shows (Cops, Candid Camera).

Thesis

Shows that followed Survivor were less interesting and less tasteful.

Information to add
- Shows that followed had less drama and relied on gimmicks.

Paragraph 2

When Survivor began, there was nothing like it.
- Exotic location
- Different kinds of real people played
- Competition for million-dollar prize
- Development of player camaraderie and sense of teamwork

Details to add
- Audience response
- Popularity of "getting voted off the island" phrase
- Appeal of the drama involved

Paragraph 3

Big Brother didn't offer audiences the same things to respond to.
- People bickered over nothing.
- The audience did not choose favorites.
- Participants weren't up against anything.
- The audience voted off members, which led to members doing less and scheming less.

Unnecessary details
- "Nothing new added"
- "Took away access to outside world"

Detail to add
- Not as much drama as Survivor had

Paragraph 4

Networks have continued to use gimmicks to appeal to the audiences' instincts.
- Shows revolving around flirtation and sex
- Pushing limits of good taste

Unnecessary details
- Shows revolving around extreme situations
- Fear Factor demonstrated this

Details to add
- Explain what contestants had to do
- Viewers not interested and stopped watching

(continued on next page)

Figure 9.6 *(continued)*

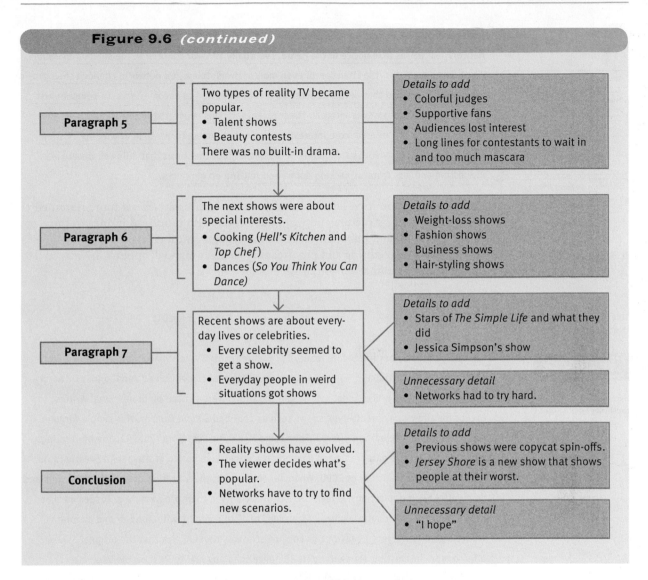

After creating the graphic organizer, Lee revised her first draft. A portion of her revised draft, with her revisions indicated using the Track Changes function, follows.

REVISED DRAFT

A Trend Taken Too Far: The Reality of Real TV

Do you remember life before the reality TV craze? <u>Before reality TV, television viewers seemed interested only in</u> situational comedies and serial dramas. <u>Characters were played by professional actors, and the shows were written by professional writers. Except for a few early reality-type shows, such as *Cops* and *Candid Camera*, this simple formula was what network television offered.</u>

> **Deleted:** One look at a *TV Guide* today shows an overload of reality-based programming, even with the guaranteed failure of most of these shows. Before reality TV there was mostly

Then came MTV's *The Real World* in 1992. The high ratings that this cable show garnered made network executives take notice of the genre. Eventually *Survivor* debuted in the summer of 2000. When *Survivor* caught ~~the~~ attention of even more viewers, television networks changed their programming. It seemed that networks acted as though they had to become "real" to compete with *Survivor* and maintain viewer interest. The problem with this copycat strategy, though, was that the original *Survivor* offered more interesting elements to its audience than any reality TV show modeled after it. *Survivor* was engaging and dramatic, but the shows that followed it were less interesting and less tasteful, lacking drama and relying on gimmicks.

Deleted: every viewer's

Deleted: every network in American believed they must also

Deleted: keep up its ratings

Deleted: Shows

Deleted: in the hopes of finding a show as original, inventive, and engaging as the first *Survivor*.

Before Lee submitted her final draft, she read her essay several more times, editing it for sentence structure and word choice. She also proofread it once to catch errors in grammar and punctuation as well as typographical errors. (A portion of Lee's revised essay, with editing and proofreading changes marked, appears in Chapter 10, pp. 222–23.) The final version of Lee's essay follows.

FINAL DRAFT

Title: a play on words catches the reader's attention

READING

Background information on shows leading up to reality TV

A Trend Taken Too Far: The Reality of Real TV

Christine Lee

Do you remember life before reality TV? Before reality TV, television viewers seemed interested only in the fictional lives of characters in situational comedies and serial dramas. Characters were played by professional actors, and the shows were written by professional writers. Except for a few early reality-type shows such as *Cops* and *Candid Camera*, this simple formula was what network television offered. Then came MTV's *The Real World* in 1992. The high ratings that this cable show garnered made network executives take notice of the genre. Eventually *Survivor* debuted in the summer of 2000. When *Survivor* caught the attention of even more viewers and dominated television ratings, television networks changed their programming. It seemed that networks acted as though they had to become "real" to compete with *Survivor* and maintain viewer interest. The problem with this copycat strategy, though, was that the original *Survivor* offered more interesting elements to its audience than any reality TV show modeled after it. *Survivor* was engaging and dramatic, but the shows that followed it were less interesting and less tasteful, lacking drama and relying on gimmicks.

The thesis statement is focused and detailed.

The topic sentence supports part of thesis: "*Survivor* was engaging and dramatic."

Survivor captured the interest of a wide viewing audience because it was fresh and entertaining. The show introduced real participants in a contest where they competed against each other in an exotic location. The participants on *Survivor* were ethnically and socially diverse and represented a variety of ages including young, middle aged, and older adults. The location was fascinating; a South Pacific island was more interesting than any house full of people on a sitcom. However, the most unique feature of *Survivor* was to make the participants compete for a million-dollar prize. Contestants were divided into two camps that had to compete to win everyday sup-

Details offer reasons that support the topic sentence.

1

2

plies, like food and shelter. At the end of each episode, players voted, and one of them was kicked off the show and lost his or her chance for the million dollars. The last contestant on the island won. To win the game, contestants created alliances and manipulated other contestants. All of these unique elements drew television viewers back each week.

The television audience responded favorably to the dramatic elements of *Survivor*. The competition gave viewers something to speculate about as the show progressed. Viewers' allegiance to one team over another or one player over another developed from episode to episode. Viewers were fascinated watching these players struggle in primitive situations, compete in tasks of strength and skill, and decide on how to cast their votes. The phrase "getting voted off the island" became a recognizable saying across America. Although players displayed positive human traits like teamwork, compassion, and camaraderie, they also schemed and plotted to win the allegiance of their fellow players. This situation made *Survivor* dramatic, and the viewers were attracted to the drama. Reality TV shows that followed *Survivor* had none of its interesting elements.

Big Brother was the first spin-off reality TV show to try to repeat the success of *Survivor*, but it did not offer the drama that *Survivor* did. In *Big Brother*, contestants were locked in a house without any outside contact for weeks. As in *Survivor*, there was a cash prize on the line, but in *Big Brother* there were not any competitions or struggles. Contestants were expelled by a viewer phone poll, but the poll gave them no motive to scheme and plot allegiances the way the *Survivor* contestants did. In fact, the contestants had little to do except bicker and fight. Viewers were not interested in players who were not up against any challenge except weeks of boredom. In the end, *Big Brother* was simply not interesting.

The next wave of reality TV shows tried to use graphic displays of terror and violence to attract viewers. *Fear Factor*, the most successful of these shows, has its contestants commit all manner of gross and terrifying acts, like eating worms or being immersed in a container of live rats. Some viewers may be interested in watching how far the contestants will go, but the majority of viewers regard these acts with disgust. Viewers might tune in once or twice but, disgusted, will not be interested in the long run.

When this gimmick did not retain viewers, two traditional types of reality TV were revived with modern twists added—the talent show and the beauty contest. So shows like *American Idol*, *America's Got Talent*, and *America's Next Top Model* were born. Again, there was no built-in drama as in *Survivor*, so the shows tried to create drama using colorful judges and supportive fans. At first, these twists provided enough spectacle to engage viewers, but after a while, audiences lost interest. Even footage showing the long lines that contestants had to wait in and the despair of those who did not make the cut did not keep viewers hooked on these types of reality shows. Viewers could only tolerate so much loud singing and mascara.

---

3   The topic sentence continues to support the thesis by explaining engaging aspects of *Survivor*.

Specific details about dramatic elements support the topic sentence.

4   The topic sentence supports the thesis that later shows were "less interesting."

Concrete details about *Big Brother* contestants

5   The topic sentence supports thesis that later shows relied on gimmicks

6   The topic sentence identifies other new gimmicks.

Details about talent shows and beauty contests

The topic sentence identifies a new focus on special interests.

The next incarnation of reality shows focused on special interests such as cooking, with shows like *Top Chef* and *Hell's Kitchen*, or dance, with shows such as *Dancing with the Stars* and *So You Think You Can Dance*. The net was spread wider with *The Biggest Loser*, a weight-loss competition; *Project Runway*, where fashion designers are pitted against each other; *The Apprentice*, a business competition; and *Shear Genius*, which offered competition among hair stylists. The problems with these shows were that they each appealed to only a very small segment of the population and offered manufactured and increasingly contrived situations for the contestants to act within.   7

Details about special-interest shows

The topic sentence identifies the latest focus of reality shows.

More recently, reality-show programming has turned increasingly to examining the everyday lives of groups of people and showcasing celebrities. *The Real World* was an early example of the first category, simply following the lives of a group of young adults as they drank and slept around. *The Simple Life* was one of the earliest celebrity reality shows, following Paris Hilton and sidekick Nicole Ritchie in ridiculously contrived situations. Soon it seemed every B-list celebrity had a reality show—Jessica Simpson, Ozzy Osbourne, Paula Abdul, Tori Spelling, Bret Michaels, and more. The next wave of shows featured ordinary people in interesting, strange, or controversial situations, such as *Jon & Kate Plus 8*, *Dog the Bounty Hunter*, *The Real Housewives*, *The Little Couple*, *Cake Boss*, *Choppers*, and more. These programs often showed people at their worst. as seen with a recent hit, *The Jersey Shore*, in which a cast of unknowns became famous for carousing and becoming caricatures of themselves. Networks have had to stretch to find new and different scenarios to offer to viewers as these shows have become increasingly tasteless.   8

Details about shows focused on ordinary people and celebrities

Examples continue to support thesis of "less tasteful."

The conclusion returns to the thesis and calls for more entertaining programming.

In the decade following the advent of *Survivor*, reality shows have evolved from copycat spin-offs to programs featuring terror and violence, talent and beauty contests, special-interest competitions, and finally to shows following real people's lives. In the end, the viewers determine what gets shown on television. Reality shows continue to be popular, despite becoming steadily more contrived and tasteless. One can hope that viewers will tire of all of these cheap gimmicks and call for more entertaining programming, If there were fewer reality shows, viewers could then return to more entertaining situational comedies and serial dramas or perhaps to another form of engaging program that may evolve.   9

Analyzing the Revision

1. Identify the major revisions that Lee made from the earlier draft in Chapter 7 (pp. 158–59). How did she carry out the plan indicated in her graphic organizer?
2. Choose one major revision that Lee made, and explain why you think it improved her essay.
3. Evaluate Lee's introduction and conclusion. In what ways are they more effective than the introduction and conclusion in her first draft? What additional improvements could she make?
4. Choose one paragraph, and compare the details provided in it with those in the corresponding paragraph of the first draft. Which added details are particularly effective, and why?

CHAPTER 10

Editing Sentences and Words

The cartoons on the facing page take a humorous view of language; however, each makes a point about writing as well.

Write a few sentences describing what you think the cartoons suggest about writing and about the focus of this chapter—editing sentences and words.

FIGURE 10.1 An Overview of the Writing Process

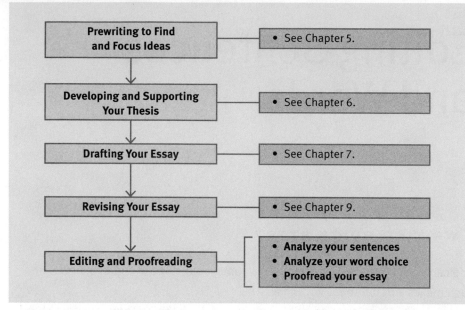

After you have revised an essay for content and organization, as discussed in Chapter 9, you are ready to edit and proofread the essay. Your task is to examine individual sentences and words with care to be sure that each conveys your meaning accurately, concisely, and in an interesting way. Even an essay with good ideas will be ineffective if its sentences are vague and wordy or if its words convey an inappropriate tone and level of diction. A good essay can be more effective, too, if you think critically about what you have said and how you have expressed it, using the strategies suggested in "Strategies for Critical Thinking and Reading" in Chapter 4 (pp. 68–77). This chapter will help you sharpen your sentences and refine your word choice.

As shown in Figure 10.1, editing and proofreading are the final steps in the writing process. Because you are almost finished with your assignment, you may be tempted to hurry through these steps or to skip them altogether. Careful editing and proofreading will always pay off in the end, however, because an error-free essay makes a good impression on the reader.

Analyzing Your Sentences

Effective sentences have four important characteristics:

- **They should be clear and concise.**
- **They should be varied.**
- **They should use parallel structure for similar ideas.**
- **They should contain strong, active verbs.**

Use the questions in the next four sections to analyze your sentences, and use the suggestions in each section to create more effective sentences.

Are Your Sentences Concise?

Sentences that are concise convey their meaning in as few words as possible. Use the following suggestions to make your sentences concise:

1. Avoid wordy expressions. Search your essay for sentences with empty phrases that contribute little or no meaning. If the sentence is clear without a particular phrase or if the phrase can be replaced by a more direct word or phrase, take it out or replace it. Here are a few examples.

- ~~In the near future,~~ another revolution in computer technology is bound to occur~~.~~ *soon.*

- ~~In light of the fact that~~ computer technology changes ~~every month or so,~~ software *Since* *monthly* upgrades are~~ what everybody has to do~~. *necessary*

2. Eliminate redundancy. Look for places where you may have repeated an idea unnecessarily by using the same words or different words that have the same meaning. Here are some examples.

- ~~My decision to choose~~ accounting as my major will lead to steady, rewarding employment. *Choosing*

- Teenagers use slang to establish ~~who they are and what~~ their identity ~~is~~.

3. Eliminate unnecessary sentence openings. When you first write down an idea, you may express it indirectly or tentatively. As you revise, look for and edit sentence openings that sound indirect or tentative. Consider these examples.

- ~~It is my opinion that~~ fast-food restaurants should post nutritional information for each menu item. *F*

- ~~Many people would agree that~~ selecting nutritious snacks is a priority for health-conscious people. *S*

4. Eliminate unnecessary adverbs. Using too many **adverbs** can weaken your writing. Adverbs such as *extremely*, *really*, and *very*, known as intensifiers, add nothing and can weaken the word they modify. Notice that the following sentence is stronger without the adverb.

> An **adverb** modifies a verb, an adjective, or another adverb.

- The journalist was ~~very~~ elated when he learned that he had won a Pulitzer Prize.

Other adverbs, such as *somewhat*, *rather*, and *quite*, also add little or no meaning and are often unnecessary.

- The college president was ~~quite~~ disturbed by the findings of the Presidential Panel on Sex Equity.

A **prepositional phrase** is a group of words that begins with a preposition and includes the object or objects of the preposition and all their modifiers: *above the low wooden table.*

5. Eliminate unnecessary phrases and clauses. Wordy phrases and clauses can make it difficult for readers to find and understand the main point of your sentence. This problem often occurs when you use too many **prepositional phrases** and clauses that begin with *who, which,* or *that.*

- The complaints ~~of students in the college~~ encouraged the dean to create additional parking spaces. *(students')*

- The ~~teenagers who were~~ mall walkers disagreed with the editorial ~~in the newspaper that supported the~~ shopping mall regulations. *(teenage)* *(newspaper)* *(supporting)*

6. Avoid weak verb-noun combinations. Weak verb-noun combinations such as *wrote a draft* instead of *drafted* or *made a change* instead of *changed* tend to make sentences wordy.

- The attorney ~~made an assessment of~~ the company's liability in the accident. *(assessed)*

- The professor ~~gave a lecture~~ on Asian American relations. *(lectured)*

Exercise 10.1

Edit the following sentences to make them concise:

1. Due to the fact that Professor Wu assigned twenty-five math problems for tomorrow, I am forced to make the decision to miss this evening's lecture to be given by the vice president of the United States.

2. In many cases, workers are forced to use old equipment that needs replacing despite the fact that equipment malfunctions cost the company more than the price of new machines.

3. Lindsay Lohan is one of the best examples of an entertainment celebrity being given too much publicity.

4. The president of Warehouse Industries has the ability and power to decide who should and who should not be hired and who should and who should not be fired.

5. The soccer league's sponsor, as a matter of fact, purchased league jerseys for the purpose of advertisement and publicity.

Are Your Sentences Varied?

Sentences that are varied will help hold your reader's interest and make your writing flow more smoothly. Vary the type, length, and pattern of your sentences.

How to Vary Sentence Type

There are four basic types of sentences—*simple, compound, complex,* and *compound-complex.* Each type consists of one or more clauses. A **clause** is a group of words with both a subject and a verb. There are two types of clauses. An **independent clause** can stand alone as a complete sentence. A **dependent clause** cannot stand alone as a complete sentence. It begins with a subordinating conjunction (for example, *because* or *although*) or a relative pronoun (for example, *when*, *which*, or *that*).

Here is a brief summary of each sentence type and its clauses.

Sentence Type	*Clauses*	*Example*
Simple	One independent clause and no dependent clauses	Credit-card fraud is increasing in the United States.
Compound	Two or more independent clauses and no dependent clauses	Credit-card fraud is increasing in the United States; it is a violation of financial privacy.
Complex	One or more dependent clauses and one independent clause	Because credit-card fraud is increasing in America, consumers must become more cautious.
Compound-Complex	One or more dependent clauses and two or more independent clauses	Because credit-card fraud is increasing in America, consumers must be cautious, and retailers must take steps to protect consumers.

Use the following suggestions to vary your sentence types:

1. Use simple sentences for emphasis and clarity. A **simple sentence** contains only one independent clause, but it is not necessarily short. It can have more than one subject, more than one verb, and several modifiers.

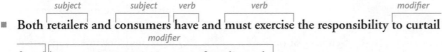

■ Both retailers and consumers have and must exercise the responsibility to curtail

fraud by reporting suspicious use of credit cards.

A short, simple sentence can be used to emphasize an important point or to make a dramatic statement.

■ **Credit-card fraud is rampant.**

If you use too many simple sentences, however, your writing will sound choppy and disjointed.

■ **It was a cold, drizzly spring morning. I was driving to school. A teenage hitchhiker stood alongside the road. He seemed distraught.**

2. Use compound sentences to show relationships between equally important ideas. A **compound sentence** consists of two or more independent clauses joined in one of the following ways:

Coordinating conjunctions
(*and, but, or, nor, for, so, yet*)
connect sentence elements that
are of equal importance.

A **conjunctive adverb** is a word
(such as *also, however,* or *still*)
that links two independent
clauses.

A **correlative conjunction** is a
word pair (such as *not only . . . but
also*) that works together to join
elements within a sentence.

- With a comma and **coordinating conjunction** (*and, but, or, nor, for, so, yet*):

  - Leon asked a question, *and* the whole class was surprised.

- With a semicolon:

  - Graffiti had been scrawled on the subway walls; passersby ignored it.

- With a semicolon and a **conjunctive adverb**:

  - Each year thousands of children are adopted; *consequently*, adoption service agencies have increased in number.

- With a **correlative conjunction**:

  - *Either* the jury will reach a verdict tonight, *or* it will recess until Monday morning.

Notice that in each example, both clauses are equally important and receive equal emphasis.

You can also use compound sentences to explain *how* equally important ideas are related. You can, for example, suggest each of the following relationships, depending on the coordinating conjunction you choose:

Coordinating Conjunction	Relationship	Example
and	additional information	The three teenage vandals were apprehended, *and* their parents were required to pay damages.
but, yet	contrast or opposites	No one wants to pay more taxes, *yet* taxes are necessary to support vital public services.
for, so	causes or effects	Telephone calls can interrupt a busy worker constantly, *so* answering machines are a necessity.
or, nor	choices or options	Quebec may become a separate country, *or* it may settle its differences with the Canadian government.

3. Use complex sentences to show that one or more ideas are less important than (or subordinate to) another idea. A **complex sentence** consists of one independent clause and at least one dependent clause; either type of clause may come first. When the dependent clause appears first, it is usually followed by a comma. When the independent clause comes first, a comma is usually not used.

- Because the dam broke, the village flooded.
- The village flooded because the dam broke.

In the preceding sentences, the main point is that the village flooded. The dependent clause explains *why* the flood happened. A dependent clause often begins with a *subordinating conjunction* that indicates how the less important (dependent) idea is related to the more important (independent) idea. Here is a list of some subordinating conjunctions and the relationships they suggest.

Subordinating Conjunction	*Relationship*	*Example*
as, as far as, as soon as, as if, as though, although, even though, even if, in order to	circumstance	*Even though* cable television has expanded, it is still unavailable in some rural areas.
because, since, so that	causes or effects	*Because* the movie industry has changed, the way theaters are built has changed.
before, after, while, until, when	time	*When* prices rise, demand falls.
whether, if, unless, even if	condition	More people will purchase hybrid cars *if* they become less expensive.

Dependent clauses can also begin with a relative pronoun (*that, who, which*).

- **Many medical doctors** *who are affiliated with a teaching hospital use interns in their practices.*

To see how complex sentences can improve your writing, study the following two paragraphs. The first paragraph consists primarily of simple and compound sentences. The revised paragraph uses complex sentences that show relationships.

ORIGINAL

Are you one of the many people who has tried to quit smoking? Well, don't give up trying. Help is here in the form of a nonprescription drug. A new nicotine patch has been developed. This patch will help you quit gradually. That way, you will experience less severe withdrawal symptoms. Quitting will be easier than ever before, but you need to be psychologically ready to quit smoking. Otherwise, you may not be successful.

REVISED

If you are one of the many people who has tried to quit smoking, don't give up trying. Help is now here in the form of a nonprescription nicotine patch, which has been developed to help you quit gradually. Because you experience less severe withdrawal symptoms, quitting is easier than ever before. However, for this patch to be successful, you need to be psychologically ready to quit.

4. Use compound-complex sentences occasionally to express complicated relationships. A compound-complex sentence contains one or more dependent clauses and two or more independent clauses.

- **If you expect to study medicine, you must take courses in biology and chemistry, and you must prepare for four more years of study after college.**

Use compound-complex sentences sparingly; when overused, they make your writing hard to follow.

> **Exercise 10.2**

Combine each of the following sentence pairs into a single compound or complex sentence.

1. A day-care center may look respectable.
   Parents assume a day-care center is safe and run well.

2. In some states, the training required to become a day-care worker is minimal.
   On-the-job supervision and evaluation of day-care workers are infrequent.

3. Restaurants are often fined or shut down for minor hygiene violations.
   Day-care centers are rarely fined or closed down for hygiene violations.

4. More and more mothers have entered the workforce.
   The need for quality day care has increased dramatically.

5. Naturally, day-care workers provide emotional support for children. Few day-care workers are trained to provide intellectual stimulation.

How to Vary Sentence Length

Usually, if you vary sentence type, you will automatically vary sentence length as well. Simple sentences tend to be short, whereas compound and complex sentences tend to be longer. Compound-complex sentences tend to be the longest. You can, however, use sentence length for specific effect. Short sentences tend to be sharp and emphatic; they move ideas along quickly, creating a fast-paced essay. In the following example, a series of short sentences creates a dramatic pace.

- **The jurors had little to debate. The incriminating evidence was clear and incontrovertible. The jury announced its verdict with astonishing speed.**

Longer sentences, in contrast, move the reader more slowly through the essay. Notice that the lengthy sentence in this example suggests a leisurely, unhurried pace.

- **While standing in line, impatient to ride the antique steam-powered train, the child begins to imagine how the train will crawl deliberately, endlessly, along the tracks, slowly gathering speed as it spews grayish steam and emits hissing noises.**

How to Vary Sentence Pattern

A sentence is usually made up of one or more subjects, verbs, and modifiers. **Modifiers** are words (adjectives or adverbs), phrases, or clauses that describe or limit another part of the sentence (a noun, pronoun, verb, phrase, or clause). Here are some examples of modifiers in sentences.

WORDS AS MODIFIERS	The *empty* classroom was unlocked. [adjective]
	The office runs *smoothly*. [adverb]
PHRASES AS MODIFIERS	The student *in the back* raised his hand.
	Schools should not have the right *to mandate community service*.
CLAUSES AS MODIFIERS	The baseball *that flew into the stands* was caught by a fan.
	When the exam was over, I knew I had earned an A.

As you can see, the placement of modifiers may vary, depending on the pattern of the sentence.

1. Modifier last: subject-verb-modifier. In this sentence pattern, the main message (expressed in the subject and verb) comes first, followed by information that clarifies or explains the message.

- The instructor walked into the room.

    subject   *verb*   *modifier*

In some cases, a string of modifiers follows the subject and verb.

- The salesperson demonstrated the word-processing software, creating and deleting files, moving text, creating directories, and formatting tables.

    subject   *verb*   *modifiers*

2. Modifier first: modifier-subject-verb. Sentences that follow this pattern are called **periodic sentences**. Notice that information in the modifier precedes the main message, elaborating the main message but slowing the overall pace. The emphasis is on the main message at the end of the sentence.

- Tired and depressed from hours of work, the divers left the scene of the accident.

    modifier   *subject*   *verb*

Use this sentence pattern sparingly. Too many periodic sentences will make your writing sound stiff and unnatural.

3. Modifier in the middle: subject-modifier-verb. In sentences that follow this pattern, the modifier or modifiers appear between the subject and the verb. The modifier thus interrupts the main message and tends to slow the pace of the sentence. The emphasis is on the subject because it comes first in the sentence.

- The paramedic, trained and experienced in water rescue, was first on the scene of the boating accident.

    subject   *modifier*   *verb*

Avoid placing too many modifiers between the subject and verb in a sentence. Doing so may cause your reader to miss the sentence's key idea.

4. Modifiers used throughout. In this pattern, modifiers are used throughout a sentence.

- Because human organs are in short supply, awarding an organ transplant, especially hearts and kidneys, to patients has become a controversial issue, requiring difficult medical and ethical decisions.

    modifier   *subject*   *modifier*   *verb*   *modifier*

By varying the order of subjects, verbs, and modifiers, you can give emphasis where it is needed as well as vary sentence patterns as shown in the paragraphs that follow.

ORIGINAL

Theme parks are growing in number and popularity. Theme parks have a single purpose—to provide family entertainment centered around high-action activities. The most famous theme parks are Disney World and Disneyland. They serve as models for other, smaller parks. Theme parks always have amusement rides. Theme parks can offer other activities such as swimming. Theme parks will probably continue to be popular.

monotonous use of same subject-verb-modifier pattern

REVISED

Theme parks are growing in number and popularity. Offering high-action activities, theme parks fulfill a single purpose—to provide family entertainment. The most famous parks, Disney World and Disneyland, serve as models for other, smaller parks. Parks always offer amusement rides, which appeal to both children and adults. Added attractions such as swimming, water slides, and boat rides provide thrills and recreation. Because of their family focus, theme parks are likely to grow in popularity.

ideas come alive through use of varied sentence patterns

> ### Exercise 10.3
>
> *Add modifiers to the following sentences to create varied sentence patterns:*
>
> 1. The divers jumped into the chilly waters.
> 2. The beach was closed because of pollution.
> 3. Coffee-flavored drinks are becoming popular.
> 4. The dorm was crowded and noisy.
> 5. The exam was more challenging than we expected.

Are Your Sentences Parallel in Structure?

Parallelism means that similar ideas in a sentence are expressed in similar grammatical form. It means balancing words with words, phrases with phrases, and clauses with clauses. Use parallelism to make your sentences flow smoothly and your thoughts easy to follow. Study the following pairs of sentences. Which sentence in each pair is easier to read?

- The horse was large, had a bony frame, and it was friendly.
- The horse was large, bony, and friendly.

- Maria enjoys swimming and sailboats.
- Maria enjoys swimming and sailing.

In each pair, the second sentence sounds better because it is balanced grammatically. *Large*, *bony*, and *friendly* are all adjectives. *Swimming* and *sailing* are nouns ending in *-ing*.

The following sentence elements should be parallel in structure:

1. **Nouns in a series should be parallel.**

    > ◾ A thesis statement ~~that is clear~~ *clear*, strong supporting paragraphs, and ~~a~~ conclusion ~~that should be interesting~~ *an interesting* are all elements of a well-written essay.

2. **Adjectives in a series should be parallel.**

    > ◾ The concertgoers were rowdy and ~~making a great deal of noise~~ *noisy.*

3. **Verbs in a series should be parallel.**

    > ◾ The sports fans jumped and ~~were applauding~~ *applauded.*

4. **Phrases and clauses within a sentence should be parallel.**

    > ◾ The parents who supervised the new playground were pleased ~~about~~ *that* the pre-schoolers ~~playing~~ *played* congenially and that everyone enjoyed the sandbox.

5. **Items being compared should be parallel.** When items within a sentence are compared or contrasted, use the same grammatical form for each item.

    > ◾ It is usually better to study for an exam over a period of time than ~~cramming~~ *to cram* the night before.

Exercise 10.4

Edit the following sentences to eliminate problems with parallelism:

1. The biology student spent Saturday morning reviewing his weekly textbook assignments, writing a research report, and with lab reports.
2. The career counselor advised Althea to take several math courses and that she should also register for at least one computer course.
3. Three reasons for the popularity of fast-food restaurants are that they are efficient, offer reasonable prices, and most people like the food they serve.
4. Driving to Boston is as expensive as it is to take the train.
5. While at a stop sign, it is important first to look both ways and then proceeding with caution is wise.

Do Your Sentences Have Strong, Active Verbs?

Strong, active verbs make your writing lively and vivid. By contrast, *to be* verbs (*is, was, were, has been*, and so on) and other **linking verbs** (*feels, became, seems, appears*)—which connect a noun or pronoun to words that describe it—can make your writing sound dull. Often, these verbs contribute little meaning to a sentence. Whenever possible, use stronger, more active verbs.

"TO BE" VERB	The puppy *was* afraid of thunder.
ACTION VERBS	The puppy *whimpered* and *quivered* during the thunderstorm.
LINKING VERB	The child *looked* frightened as she boarded the bus for her first day of kindergarten.
ACTION VERBS	The child *trembled* and *clung* to her sister as she boarded the bus for her first day of kindergarten.

To strengthen your writing, try to use active verbs rather than passive verbs as much as possible. A **passive verb** is a form of the verb *to be* combined with a past participle (*killed, chosen, elected*). In a sentence with a passive verb, the subject does not perform the action of the verb but instead receives the action. By contrast, in a sentence with an **active verb**, the subject performs the action.

| PASSIVE | It *was claimed* by the cyclist that the motorist failed to yield the right of way. |
| ACTIVE | The cyclist *claimed* that the motorist failed to yield the right of way. |

Notice that the first sentence emphasizes the action of claiming, not the person who made the claim. In the second sentence, the person who made the claim is the subject.

For more about possible problems with using passive voice, see p. 76.

Unless you decide deliberately to deemphasize the subject, try to avoid using passive verbs. On occasion, you may need to use passive verbs, however, to emphasize the object or person receiving the action.

■ The Johnsons' house *was destroyed* by the flood.

Passive verbs may also be appropriate if you do not know or choose not to reveal who performed an action. Journalists often use passive verbs for this reason.

■ It *was confirmed* late Tuesday that Senator Kraemer is resigning.

Exercise 10.5

Edit the following sentences by changing passive verbs to active ones, adding a subject when necessary:

1. Songs about peace were composed by folk singers in the 1960s.
2. The exam was thought to be difficult because it covered thirteen chapters.
3. For water conservation, it is recommended that low-water-consumption dishwashers be purchased.
4. The new satellite center was opened by the university so that students could attend classes nearer their homes.
5. In aggressive telemarketing sales calls, the consumer is urged by the caller to make an immediate decision before prices change.

Essay in Progress 1

For your essay in progress (the one you worked on in Chapters 7–9) or any essay you are working on, evaluate and edit your sentences.

Analyzing Your Word Choice

Each word you select contributes to the meaning of your essay. Consequently, when you are revising, be sure to analyze your word choice, or **diction**. The words you choose should suit your purpose, audience, and tone. This section describes four aspects of word choice to consider as you evaluate and revise your essay.

- Tone and level of diction
- Word connotations
- Concrete and specific language
- Figures of speech

Are Your Tone and Level of Diction Appropriate?

Imagine that as a technician at a computer software company you discover a time-saving shortcut for installing the company's best-selling software program. Your supervisor asks you to write two memos describing your discovery and how it works—one for your fellow technicians at the company and the other for customers who might purchase the program. Would both memos say the same thing in the same way? Definitely not. The two memos would differ not only in content but also in tone and level of diction. The memo addressed to the other technicians would be technical and concise, explaining how to use the shortcut and why it works. The memo directed to customers would praise the discovery, mention the time customers will save, and explain in nontechnical terms how to use the shortcut.

Tone refers to how you sound to your readers. Your word choice should be consistent with your tone. Your memo to the technicians would have a direct, matter-of-fact tone. Your memo to the customers would be enthusiastic.

For more about tone, see pp. 74–75.

Formal Diction

There are three common **levels of diction**—formal, popular, and informal. The **formal** level of diction is serious and dignified. Think of it as the kind of language that judges use in interpreting laws, presidents employ when greeting foreign dignitaries, or speakers choose for commencement addresses. Formal diction is often written in the third person, tends to include long sentences and multisyllabic words, and contains no slang or contractions. It has a slow, rhythmic flow and an authoritative, distant, and impersonal tone. Here is an example taken from *The Federalist, No. 51*, a political tract written by James Madison in 1788 to explain constitutional theory.

> It is of great importance in a republic, not only to guard the society against the oppression of its rulers, but to guard one part of the society against the injustice of the other part. Different interests necessarily exist in different classes of citizens. If a majority be united by a common interest, the rights of the minority will be insecure.

Formal diction is also used in scholarly publications, in operation manuals, and in most academic fields. Notice in the following excerpt from a chemistry textbook that the language is concise, exact, and marked by specialized terms, called *jargon*, used within the particular field of study. The examples of jargon are in italics.

A *catalyst* is classified as *homogeneous* if it is present in the same *phase* as that of the *reactants*. For reactants that are *gases*, a *homogeneous catalyst* is also a *gas*.

Atkins and Perkins, *Chemistry: Molecules, Matter, and Change*

Popular Diction

Popular, or casual, diction is common in magazines and newspapers. It sounds more conversational and personal than formal diction. Contractions may be used, and sentences tend to be shorter and less varied than in formal diction. The first person (*I, me, mine, we*) or second person (*you, your*) may be used. Consider this example taken from a popular arts magazine, *Paste Magazine*.

"Concert for George" pays tribute to not only one of the greatest musicians in history, but one of the freakin' Beatles. The performance took place in honor of the first anniversary of George Harrison's death, with Eric Clapton and Jeff Lynne serving as musical directors.

Wyndham Wyeth, "The 11 Best Concert Films."

In this excerpt, the writer conveys a light, conversational tone.

Informal Diction

Informal diction, also known as *colloquial language*, is the language of everyday speech and conversation. It is friendly and casual. Contractions (*wasn't, I'll*), slang expressions (*cops, chill out, What up?*), sentence fragments, and first-person and second-person pronouns are all common in informal diction. This level of diction should not be used in essays and academic writing, except when it is part of a quotation or a block of dialogue. Here is an example of informal diction.

This guy in my history class is a psycho. He doesn't let anybody talk but him. I mean, this guy interrupts all the time. Never raises his hand. He drives us nuts—what a loser.

Notice the use of the first person, slang expressions, and a loose sentence structure.

Also inappropriate for essays and academic writing is the use of language shortcuts typically used in email and texting. These include abbreviations (*u* for *you*, *r* for *are*) and emoticons (☺).

Diction in Academic Writing

When you write academic papers, essays, and exams, you should use formal diction and avoid flowery or wordy language. Here are some guidelines that can point you in the right direction.

- Use the third person (*he, she, it*) rather than the first person (*I, we*), unless you are expressing a personal opinion.
- Use standard vocabulary, not slang or a regional or an ethnic dialect.
- Use correct grammar, spelling, and punctuation.
- Aim for a clear, direct, and forthright tone.

One of the biggest mistakes students make in academic writing is trying too hard to sound "academic." Be sure to avoid writing stiff, overly formal sentences; using big words just for the sake of it; and expressing ideas indirectly.

INAPPROPRIATE DICTION

Who among us would be so bold as to venture to deny that inequities are rampant in our ailing health- and medical-care system? People of multiethnic composition overwhelmingly receive health care that is not only beneath the standard one would expect, but even in some cases threatening to their very lives. An abundance of research studies and clinical trials prove beyond a doubt that a person of non-European descent residing in the United States of America cannot rely on doctors, nurses, physician assistants, nurse practitioners, and other health-care workers to provide treatment free of invidious discrimination.

REVISED DICTION

Who can deny that inequities are common in our ailing medical care system? Racial and ethnic minorities receive health care that is substandard and in some cases life-threatening. Many research studies and clinical trials demonstrate that minorities in the United States cannot rely on doctors, nurses, physician assistants, nurse practitioners, and other health-care workers to provide unbiased treatment.

> ### Exercise 10.6
>
> *Revise the following informal statement by giving it a more formal level of diction.*
>
> It hadn't occurred to me that I might be exercising wrong, though I suppose the signs were there. I would drag myself to the gym semi-regularly and go through the motions of walking (sometimes jogging) on the treadmill and doing light weight training. But I rarely broke a sweat. I just didn't have the energy. "Just doing it" wasn't cutting it. My body wasn't improving. In fact, certain areas were getting bigger, overly muscular. I needed someone to kick my butt—and reduce it too.
>
> Wendy Schmid, "Roped In," *Vogue*

Do You Use Words with Appropriate Connotations?

Many words have two levels of meaning—a denotative meaning and a connotative meaning. A word's **denotation** is its precise dictionary definition. For example, the denotative meaning of the word *mother* is "female parent." A word's **connotation** is the collection of feelings and attitudes the word evokes—its emotional colorings or shades of meaning. A word's connotation may vary from one person to another. One common connotation of *mother* is a warm, caring person. Some people, however, may think of a mother as someone with strong authoritarian control. Similarly, the phrase *horror films* may conjure up memories of scary but fun-filled evenings for some people and terrifying experiences for others.

Since the connotations of words can elicit a wide range of responses, be sure the words you choose convey only the meanings you intend. In each pair of words that follows, notice that the two words have a similar denotation but different connotations:

For more about analyzing connotative meanings, see p. 71.

artificial/fake
firm/stubborn
lasting/endless

> ### Exercise 10.7
>
> *Describe the different connotations of the three words in each group of words.*
> 1. crowd/mob/gathering
> 2. proverb/motto/saying
> 3. prudent/penny-pinching/frugal
> 4. token/gift/keepsake
> 5. display/show/expose

Do You Use Concrete Language?

Specific words convey much more information than general words. The following examples show how you might move from general to specific word choices:

General	Less General	More Specific	Specific
store	department store	Sears	Sears at the Galleria Mall
music	popular music	country and western music	Taylor Swift's "Love Story"

Concrete words add life and meaning to your writing. In each of the following sentence pairs, notice how the underlined words in the first sentence provide little information, whereas those in the second sentence provide interesting details.

GENERAL   Our <u>vacation</u> was <u>great fun</u>.

CONCRETE   Our <u>rafting trip</u> was filled with <u>adventure</u>.

GENERAL   The <u>red flowers</u> were blooming in our yard.

CONCRETE   <u>Crimson and white petunias</u> were blooming in our yard.

Suppose you are writing about a shopping mall that has outlived its usefulness. Instead of saying "a number of stores were unoccupied, and those that were still in business were shabby," you could describe the mall in concrete, specific terms that would enable your readers to visualize it.

> The vacant storefronts with "For Rent" signs plastered across the glass, the half-empty racks in the stores that were still open, and the empty corridors suggested that the mall was soon to close.

> ### Exercise 10.8
>
> *Revise the following sentences by adding concrete, specific details:*
> 1. The book I took on vacation was exciting reading.
> 2. The students watched as the instructor entered the lecture hall.
> 3. The vase in the museum was an antique.
> 4. At the crime scene, the reporter questioned the witnesses.
> 5. Although the shop was closed, we expected someone to return at any moment.

Do You Use Fresh, Appropriate Figures of Speech?

A **figure of speech** is a comparison between two things that makes sense imaginatively or creatively but not literally. For example, if you say "the movie was *a roller coaster ride,*" you do not mean the movie was an actual ride. Rather, you mean it was thrilling, just like a ride on a roller coaster. This figure of speech, like all others, compares two seemingly unlike objects or situations by finding one point of similarity.

Fresh and imaginative figures of speech can help you create vivid images for your readers. However, overused figures of speech can detract from your essay. Be sure to avoid **clichés** (trite or overused expressions) such as *blind as a bat, green with envy, bite the bullet,* or *sick as a dog.*

Although there are many kinds of figures of speech, the most useful types are simile, metaphor, and personification. In a **simile**, the word *like* or *as* is used to make a direct comparison of two unlike things.

> The child acts *like a tiger*.

> The noise in a crowded high school cafeteria is as deafening *as a caucus of crows*.

A **metaphor** also compares unlike things but does not use *like* or *as*. Instead, the comparison is implied.

> That child is a tiger.

> If you're born in America with black skin, you're born in prison.
>
> Malcolm X, "Interview"

Personification describes an idea or object by giving it human qualities.

> A sailboat devours money.

In this example, the ability to eat is ascribed to an inanimate object, the sailboat.

When you edit an essay, look for and eliminate overused figures of speech, replacing them with creative, fresh images. If you have not used any figures of speech, look for descriptions that could be improved by using a simile, a metaphor, or personification.

For more on figures of speech, see Chapter 12, pp. 273–74.

Exercise 10.9

Invent fresh figures of speech for two items in the following list:

1. Parents of a newborn baby
2. A lengthy supermarket line or a traffic jam
3. A relative's old refrigerator
4. A man and woman obviously in love
5. Your team's star quarterback or important player

Evaluating Your Word Choice

Use Figure 10.2 to help you evaluate your word choice. If you have difficulty identifying which words to revise, ask a classmate or friend to read and evaluate your essay by using the flowchart as a guide and marking any words that may need revision.

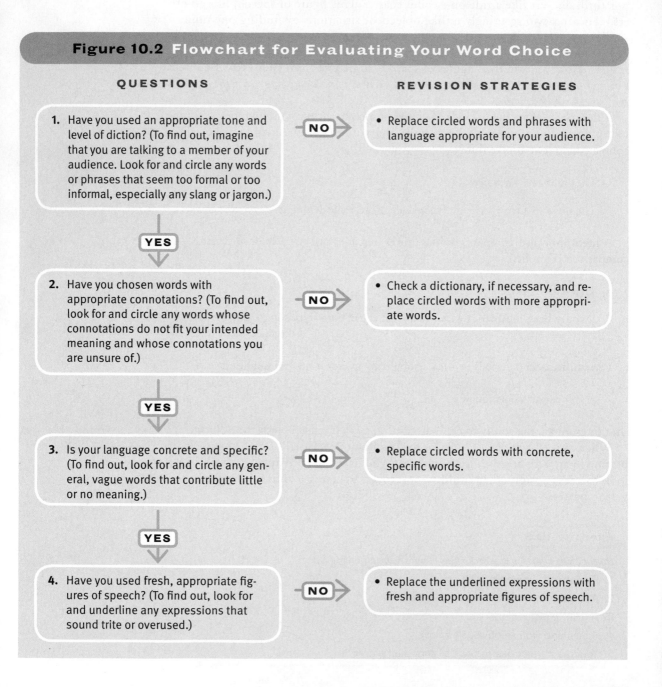

Figure 10.2 Flowchart for Evaluating Your Word Choice

QUESTIONS

REVISION STRATEGIES

1. Have you used an appropriate tone and level of diction? (To find out, imagine that you are talking to a member of your audience. Look for and circle any words or phrases that seem too formal or too informal, especially any slang or jargon.)

   NO → • Replace circled words and phrases with language appropriate for your audience.

   YES ↓

2. Have you chosen words with appropriate connotations? (To find out, look for and circle any words whose connotations do not fit your intended meaning and whose connotations you are unsure of.)

   NO → • Check a dictionary, if necessary, and replace circled words with more appropriate words.

   YES ↓

3. Is your language concrete and specific? (To find out, look for and circle any general, vague words that contribute little or no meaning.)

   NO → • Replace circled words with concrete, specific words.

   YES ↓

4. Have you used fresh, appropriate figures of speech? (To find out, look for and underline any expressions that sound trite or overused.)

   NO → • Replace the underlined expressions with fresh and appropriate figures of speech.

> **Essay in Progress 2**
> For the essay you worked on in Essay in Progress 1, use Figure 10.2 to evaluate and edit your word choice.

Suggestions for Proofreading

When you are satisfied with your words, sentences, and edited essay, you are ready for the final step of the writing process—*proofreading*. In this step, you make sure your essay is error-free and is presented in acceptable manuscript format. Your goals are to catch and correct surface errors — such as errors in grammar, punctuation, spelling, and mechanics—as well as keyboarding or typographical errors. An essay that is free of surface errors gives readers a favorable impression—of the essay and of you as its writer. Careless proofreading is a sign of a careless writer, and if you are writing for a class, careless mistakes will cause your instructor to lower your grade. The guidelines in this section will help you become a careful proofreader.

For information on manuscript format, see Chapter 23, p. 637.

If you are using a computer, print out a clean copy of your essay for proofreading. Do not attempt to work with a previously marked-up copy or on a computer screen. Spotting errors in grammar, spelling, punctuation, and mechanics is easier when you work with a clean printed copy. Be sure to double-space the copy to allow room to mark corrections between lines.

Use the following suggestions to produce an error-free essay:

1. **Review your paper once for each type of error.** Because it is difficult to spot all types of surface errors simultaneously during a single proofreading, you should read your essay several times, each time focusing on *one* error type—errors in spelling, punctuation, grammar, mechanics, and so on.
2. **Read your essay backwards, from the last sentence to the first.** Reading in this way will help you spot errors without being distracted by the flow of ideas.
3. **Use the spell-check and grammar-check functions cautiously.** The spell-check function can help you spot some—but not all—spelling and keyboarding errors. For example, it cannot detect the difference in meaning between *there* and *their* or *to* and *too*. Similarly, the grammar-check function can identify only certain kinds of errors and is not a reliable substitute for a careful proofreading.
4. **Read your essay aloud.** By reading aloud slowly, you can catch certain errors that sound awkward, such as missing words, errors in verb tense, and errors in the singular or plural forms of nouns.
5. **Ask a classmate to proofread your paper.** Another reader may spot errors you have overlooked.

Keeping an Error Log

You may find it helpful to keep an error log as part of your writing journal. Start by recording errors from several graded or peer-reviewed papers in the log. Then look for patterns in the types of errors you tend to make. Once you identify these types of errors, you can proofread your essays specifically for them.

FIGURE 10.3 Sample Error Log

Type of Error	Assignment 1	Assignment 2	Assignment 3
Subject-verb agreement	X	XX	XX
Spelling	XXXX	XXX	XXX
Verb tense	XX	XX	XXX
Word choice	X		X
Parallelism			X

In the sample error log in Figure 10.3, notice that the student kept track of five types of errors in three writing assignments. By doing so, she discovered that most of her errors fell into the categories of subject-verb agreement, spelling, and verb tense. She was then able to proofread for those errors specifically. The error log also allowed the student to keep track of her progress in avoiding these types of errors over time.

> **Essay in Progress 3**
> For the essay you edited in Essay in Progress 2, use one or more of the proofreading tips on page 221 to catch and correct errors in spelling, punctuation, grammar, and mechanics.

Students Write

Recall that Christine Lee's essay, "A Trend Taken Too Far: The Reality of Real TV," was developed, drafted, and revised in the Students Write sections of Chapters 6 to 9. Printed here are the first two paragraphs of Lee's essay with Lee's final editing and proofreading changes. Each revision has been numbered. The list following the excerpt explains the reason for each change. The final draft of Lee's essay, with these changes incorporated into it, appears in Chapter 9, on pages 198–200.

A Trend Taken Too Far: The Reality of Real TV

Do you remember life before reality TV? Before reality TV, television viewers seemed interested only in the fictional lives of characters in situational comedies and serial dramas. Characters were played by professional actors, and the shows were written by professional writers. Except for a few early reality-type shows such as *Cops* and *Candid Camera*, this simple formula was what network television offered. Then came MTV's *The Real World* in 1992. The high ratings that this cable show garnered made network executives take notice of the genre. Eventually *Survivor* debuted in the summer of 2000. When *Survivor* caught the attention of even more

(3)
(4) television
viewers' and dominated television ratings. ~~Television~~ networks changed their programming. It
seemed that networks acted as though they had to become "real" to compete with *Survivor* and
maintain viewer interest. The problem with this copycat strategy, though, was that the original
Survivor offered more interesting elements to its audience than any reality TV show modeled after it. *Survivor* was engaging and dramatic, but the shows that followed it were less interesting
and less tasteful, lacking drama and relying on gimmicks.

(5) entertaining
   Survivor captured the interest of a wide viewing audience because it was fresh and ~~provocative~~.
(6) The show introduced   (7) in   (8) they
~~Survivor~~ had real participants. ~~There was~~ a contest where ~~contestants~~ competed against each
other in an exotic location. The participants on *Survivor* were ethnically and socially diverse
and represented a variety of ages including young, middle aged, and older adults. The location
                  (9) a
for *Survivor* was fascinating: ~~A~~ South Pacific island was more interesting than any house full of
people on a sitcom. However, the most unique feature of *Survivor* was to make the participants
compete for a million-dollar prize. Contestants were divided into two camps that had to compete
to win everyday supplies, like food and shelter. At the end of each episode, players voted, and
                  (10) and lost his or her chance for
one of them was kicked off the show, ~~losing~~ the million dollars. The last contestant on the island
                  (11) manipulated
won. To win the game, contestants created alliances and ~~messed with~~ other contestants. All of
        (12) drew television viewers back each week.
these unique elements ~~kept viewers glued to their sets.~~

   Notice that in editing and proofreading these paragraphs, Lee improved the clarity
and variety of her sentences; chose clearer, more specific words; and corrected errors in
punctuation.

1. A comma was needed to separate the opening phrase from the rest of the sentence.
2. A comma was needed between two independent clauses joined by *and.*
3. *Viewers* is a plural noun but is not possessive. The apostrophe was deleted.
4. The word "television" is a common noun and is not capitalized unless it begins a
   new sentence.
5. The word *provocative* suggests something that arouses or stimulates. This
   connotation was neither intended nor supported in the paragraph, so Lee
   changed the word to *entertaining.* (For more on connotation of words,
   see page 71.)
6. To avoid repetition, Lee replaced *Survivor* with *the show.* Lee replaced the verb
   had with *introduced* because the latter is more descriptive. (For more on using
   descriptive verbs, see pages 213–14.)
7. Lee combined two sentences to connect the ideas more closely and to eliminate
   There was, a wordy expression. (For more on eliminating wordiness, see page 205.)

8. A *contest* with *contestants* is redundant, so Lee eliminated the redundancy. (For more on redundancy, see page 205.)

9. Lee combined the two sentences to tie the two ideas more closely together and to indicate that the second idea more fully explains the first. (For more on varying sentence patterns, see pages 206–12.)

10. Lee clarified that the contestant lost the *chance* to win the million dollars.

11. Lee replaced the slang term *messed with* with more formal language. (For more on slang, see pages 215–17.)

12. Lee eliminated the cliché *glued to their sets* and replaced it with a fresher expression. (For more on clichés and figures of speech, see page 219.)

PART 3

Patterns of Development

CHAPTER 11

Narration: Recounting Events

The photograph on the opposite page shows a tragic scene. Imagine what series of events led up to this tragedy. Who died? What events led up to the person's death? Who are the mourners? How are they related to the deceased? What seems to be happening in the photograph?

Working by yourself or with a classmate, construct a series of events leading up to this tragedy, culminating with the scene shown in the photograph. Write a brief summary of the events you imagined.

WRITING A NARRATIVE

As you imagined the events that led up to the tragic scene, you constructed the beginnings of a narrative. You began to describe a series of events or turning points, and you probably wrote them in the order in which they occurred. In this chapter, you will learn how to write narrative essays as well as how to use narratives in essays that rely on one or more other patterns of development.

What Is Narration?

A narrative relates a series of events, real or imaginary, in an organized sequence. It is a story, but it is *a story that makes a point.* You probably exchange family stories, tell jokes, read biographies or novels, and watch television situation comedies or dramas—all of which are examples of the narrative form. In addition, narratives are an important part of the writing you will do in college and in your career, as the examples in the accompanying box illustrate.

Narratives provide human interest and entertainment, spark our curiosity, and draw us close to the storyteller. In addition, narratives can create a sense of shared history, linking people together, and provide instruction in proper behavior or moral conduct.

The following narrative relates the author's experience with racial profiling. As you read, notice how the narrative makes a point by presenting a series of events that build to a climax.

SCENES FROM COLLEGE AND THE WORKPLACE

- Each student in your *business law course* must attend a court trial and complete the following written assignment: Describe what happened and what the proceedings illustrated about the judicial process.

- In a *sociology* course, your class is scheduled to discuss the nature and types of authority figures in U.S. society. Your instructor begins by asking class members to describe situations in which they found themselves in conflict with an authority figure.

- Your job in *sales* involves frequent business travel, and your company requires you to submit a report for each trip. You are expected to recount the meetings you attended, your contacts with current clients, and new sales leads.

Right Place, Wrong Face
Alton Fitzgerald White

This narrative was first published in the *Nation* in October 1999. Alton Fitzgerald White is an actor, singer, and dancer and has appeared in several Broadway shows. He is the author of *Uncovering the Heart Light* (1999), a collection of poems and short stories.

As the youngest of five girls and two boys growing up in Cincinnati, I was raised to believe that if I worked hard, was a good person, and always told the truth, the world would be my oyster. I was raised to be a gentleman and learned that these qualities would bring me respect.   1   *oyster*

While one has to earn respect, consideration is something owed to every human being. On Friday, June 16, 1999, when I was wrongfully arrested at my Harlem apartment building, my perception of everything I had learned as a young man was forever changed—not only because I wasn't given even a second to use the manners my parents taught me, but mostly because the police, whom I'd always naively thought were supposed to serve and protect me, were actually hunting me.   2

I had planned a pleasant day. The night before was a payday, plus I had received a standing ovation after portraying the starring role of Coalhouse Walker Jr. in the Broadway musical *Ragtime*. It is a role that requires not only talent but also an honest emotional investment of the morals and lessons I learned as a child.   3

Coalhouse Walker Jr. is a victim (an often misused word, but in this case true) of overt racism. His story is every black man's nightmare. He is hardworking, successful, talented, charismatic, friendly, and polite. Perfect prey for someone with authority and not even a fraction of those qualities. On that Friday afternoon, I became a real-life Coalhouse Walker. Nothing could have prepared me for it. Not even stories told to me by other black men who had suffered similar injustices.   4

Friday for me usually means a trip to the bank, errands, the gym, dinner, and then off to the theater. On this particular day, I decided to break my pattern of getting up and running right out of the house. Instead, I took my time, slowed my pace, and splurged by making strawberry pancakes. Before I knew it, it was 2:45; my bank closes at 3:30, leaving me less than 45 minutes to get to midtown Manhattan on the train. I was pressed for time but in a relaxed, blessed state of mind. When I walked through the lobby of my building, I noticed two light-skinned Hispanic men I'd never seen before. Not thinking much of it, I continued on to the vestibule, which is separated from the lobby by a locked door.   5

As I approached the exit, I saw people in uniforms rushing toward the door. I sped up to open it for them. I thought they might be paramedics, since many of the building's occupants are elderly. It wasn't until I had opened the door and greeted them that I recognized that they were police officers. Within seconds, I was told to "hold it"; they had received a call about young Hispanics with guns. I was told to get against the wall. I was searched, stripped of my backpack, put on my knees, handcuffed, and told to be quiet when I tried to ask questions.   6

With me were three other innocent black men who had been on their way to their 7
U-Haul. They were moving into the apartment beneath mine, and I had just bragged
to them about how safe the building was. One of these gentlemen got off his knees,
still handcuffed, and unlocked the door for the officers to get into the lobby where
the two strangers were standing. Instead of thanking or even acknowledging us, they
led us out the door past our neighbors, who were all but begging the police in our
defense.

The four of us were put into cars with the two strangers and taken to the precinct 8
station at 165th and Amsterdam. The police automatically linked us, with no questions
and no regard for our character or our lives. No consideration was given to where we
were going or why. Suppose an ailing relative was waiting upstairs, while I ran out for
her medication? Or young children, who'd been told that Daddy was running to the corner store for milk and would be right back? My new neighbors weren't even allowed to
lock their apartment or check on the U-Haul.

After we were lined up in the station, the younger of the two Hispanic men was 9
identified as an experienced criminal, and drug residue was found in a pocket of the
other. I now realize how naive I was to think that the police would then uncuff me,
apologize for their mistake, and let me go. Instead, they continued to search my backpack, questioned me, and put me in jail with the criminals.

The rest of the nearly five-hour ordeal was like a horrible dream. I was handcuffed, 10
strip-searched, taken in and out for questioning. The officers told me that they knew
exactly who I was, knew I was in *Ragtime,* and that in fact they already had the men
they wanted.

How then could they keep me there, or have brought me there in the first place? 11
I was told it was standard procedure. As if the average law-abiding citizen knows
what that is and can dispute it. From what I now know, "standard procedure" is
something that every citizen, black and white, needs to learn, and fast.

I felt completely powerless. Why, do you think? Here I was, young, pleasant, and 12
successful, in good physical shape, dressed in clean athletic attire. I was carrying a
backpack containing a substantial paycheck and a deposit slip, on my way to the bank.
Yet after hours and hours I was sitting at a desk with two officers who not only couldn't
tell me why I was there but seemed determined to find something on me, to the point
of making me miss my performance.

It was because I am a black man! 13

I sat in that cell crying silent tears of disappointment and injustice with the realiza- 14
tion of how many innocent black men are convicted for no reason. When I was handcuffed, my first instinct had been to pull away out of pure insult and violation as a
human being. Thank God I was calm enough to do what they said. When I was thrown
in jail with the criminals and strip-searched, I somehow knew to put my pride aside,
be quiet, and do exactly what I was told, hating it but coming to terms with the fact
that in this situation I was a victim. They had guns!

Before I was finally let go, exhausted, humiliated, embarrassed, and still in shock, 15
I was led to a room and given a pseudo-apology. I was told that I was at the wrong
place at the wrong time. My reply? "I was where I live."

Everything I learned growing up in Cincinnati has been shattered. Life will never be 16
the same.

Characteristics of a Narrative

As you can see from "Right Place, Wrong Face," a narrative does not merely report events; a narrative is *not* a transcript of a conversation or a news report. Instead, it is a story that conveys a particular meaning. It presents actions and details that build toward a climax, the point at which the conflict of the narrative is resolved. Most narratives use dialogue to present portions of conversations that move the story along.

Narratives Make a Point

A narrative makes a point or supports a thesis by telling readers about an event or a series of events. The point may be to describe the significance of the event or events, make an observation, or present new information. Often a writer will state the point directly, using an explicit thesis statement. Other times a writer may leave the main point unstated, using an implied thesis. Either way, the point should always be clear to your readers. The point also determines the details the writer selects and the way they are presented.

The following excerpt from a brief narrative written by a student is based on a photo of a homeless family on a street corner. After imagining the series of events that might have brought the family to homelessness, the student wrote this final paragraph.

> Jack and Melissa are kind, patient people who want nothing more than to live in a house or an apartment instead of camping out on a street curb. Unfortunately, their un-happy story and circumstances are not uncommon. Thousands of Americans, through no fault of their own, share their hopeless plight. The homeless can be found on street corners, in parks, and under bridges in the coldest months of winter. Too often, passersby shun them and their need for a helping hand. They either look away, repulsed by the conditions in which the homeless live, and assume they live this way out of choice rather than necessity, or they gaze at them with disapproving looks, walk away, and wonder why such people do not want to work.

Notice that the writer makes a point about the homeless and about people's attitudes toward them directly. Note, too, how the details support the writer's point.

Narratives Convey Action and Detail

A narrative presents a *detailed* account of an event or a series of events. In other words, a narrative is like a camera lens that zooms in and makes readers feel as if they can see the details and experience the action.

Writers of narratives can involve readers in several ways—through *dialogue,* with *physical description,* and by *recounting action.* In "Right Place, Wrong Face," both physical description and the recounting of events help build suspense and make the story come alive. Readers can easily visualize the scene at White's apartment building and the scene at the police station.

For more on descriptive writing, see Chapter 12.

Narratives Present a Conflict and Create Tension

An effective narrative presents a **conflict**—such as a struggle, question, or problem—and works toward its resolution. The conflict can be between participants or between a participant and some external force, such as a law, value, tradition, or act of nature. **Tension** is the suspense created as the story unfolds and as the reader wonders how the conflict will be resolved. In "Right Place, Wrong Face," for example, tension is first suggested in the third paragraph with "I had planned a pleasant day," suggesting that what was planned did not materialize. The tension becomes evident in paragraphs 7 to 14, and the conflict is resolved in paragraph 15, when White is released. The point just before the conflict is resolved is called the **climax**. The main point of the story—how White's life is changed by the incident of racial profiling—concludes the narrative.

> **Exercise 11.1**
>
> *Working alone or with a classmate, complete each of the following statements by setting up a conflict. Then for one of the completed statements, write three to four sentences that build tension through action or dialogue (or both).*
>
> **1.** You are ready to leave the house when . . .
>
> **2.** You have just turned in your math exam when you realize that . . .
>
> **3.** You recently moved to a new town when your spouse suddenly becomes seriously ill . . .
>
> **4.** Your child just told you that . . .
>
> **5.** Your best friend phones you in the middle of the night to tell you . . .

Narratives Sequence Events

The events in a narrative must be arranged in an order that is easy for readers to follow. A narrative often presents events in chronological order—the order in which they happened. "Right Place, Wrong Face," for example, uses this straightforward sequence. At other times writers may use the techniques of flashback and foreshadowing to make their point more effectively. A **flashback** returns the reader to events that took place in the past, whereas **foreshadowing** hints at events in the future. Both of these techniques are used frequently in drama, fiction, and film. A soap opera, for instance, might open with a scene showing a woman lying in a hospital bed, flash back to a scene showing the accident that put her there, and then return to the scene in the hospital. When used sparingly, flashback and foreshadowing can build interest and add variety to a narrative, especially a lengthy chronological account.

Narratives Use Dialogue

Just as people reveal much about themselves by what they say and how they say it, dialogue can reveal much about the characters in a narrative. Dialogue is often used to dramatize the action, emphasize the conflict, and reveal the personalities or motives of the key participants in a narrative. Keep in mind that dialogue should resemble everyday speech; it should sound natural, not forced or formal. Consider these examples.

TOO FORMAL   Maria confided to her grandfather, "I enjoy talking with you. I especially like hearing you tell of your life in Mexico long ago. I wish I could visit there with you."

NATURAL   Maria confided to her grandfather, "Your stories about Mexico when you were a kid are great. I'd like to go there with you."

Exercise 11.2

For one of the following situations, imagine what the person might say and how he or she would say it. Then write five or six sentences of natural-sounding dialogue. If your dialogue sounds forced or too formal, try saying it out loud into a tape recorder.

1. An assistant manager is trying to explain to a supervisor that an employee offends customers.

2. A man or a woman has just discovered that he or she and a best friend are dating the same person.

3. A babysitter is disciplining an eight-year-old girl for pouring chocolate syrup on her brother's head.

Narratives Are Told from a Particular Point of View

Many narratives use the first-person point of view, in which the key participant speaks directly to the reader ("*I* first realized the problem when . . ."). Other narratives use the third-person point of view, in which an unknown storyteller describes what happens to the key participants ("The problem began when Saul Overtone . . ."). The first person is used in "Right Place, Wrong Face."

Both the first person and the third person offer distinct advantages. The first person allows you to assume a personal tone and to speak directly to your audience. You can easily express your attitudes and feelings and offer your interpretation and commentary. When you narrate an event that occurred in your own life, for example, the first person is probably your best choice. In "Right Place, Wrong Face" the first person allows White to express his anger, humiliation, and outrage directly.

One drawback to using the first person, however, is that you cannot easily convey the inner thoughts of other participants unless they are shared with you. The third person gives the narrator more distance from the action and often provides a broader, more objective perspective.

Exercise 11.3

For each of the following situations, decide which point of view would work best. Discuss with your classmates the advantages and disadvantages of using the first- and third-person points of view for each example.

1. The day you and several friends played a practical joke on another friend

2. An incident of sexual or racial discrimination that happened to you or someone you know

3. An incident at work that a coworker told you about

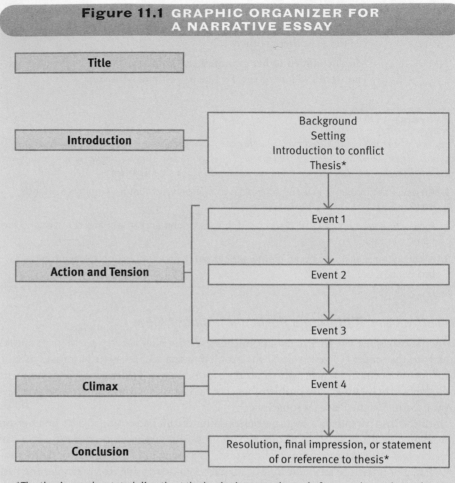

Figure 11.1 GRAPHIC ORGANIZER FOR A NARRATIVE ESSAY

Title

Introduction — Background / Setting / Introduction to conflict / Thesis*

Action and Tension — Event 1 → Event 2 → Event 3

Climax — Event 4

Conclusion — Resolution, final impression, or statement of or reference to thesis*

*The thesis may be stated directly at the beginning or at the end of a narrative, or it may be implied.

Visualizing a Narrative: A Graphic Organizer

Whether or not you are a spatial learner, it is often helpful to see the content and organization of an essay in simplified, visual form. The graphic organizer shown in Figure 11.1 is a visual diagram of the basic structure of a narrative. A graphic organizer can help you structure your writing, analyze a reading, and recall key events as you generate ideas for an essay.

For more on graphic organizers, see Chapter 3, p. 60.

Use Figure 11.1 as a basic model, but keep in mind that narrative essays vary in organization and may lack one or more of the elements included in the model.

The following selection, "The Lady in Red," is an example of a narrative. Read it first, and then study the graphic organizer for it in Figure 11.2 (on p. 238).

The Lady in Red

Richard LeMieux

Richard LeMieux was a successful businessman who operated his own publishing company and lived a life of comfort and even luxury. After his business failed, however, he was evicted from his home and became homeless, living out of his car with his dog, Willow. LeMieux details his experiences in a book titled *Breakfast at Sally's: One Homeless Man's Inspirational Journey* (2009), from which this excerpt is taken.

It went back to last Thanksgiving Day, 2002. That was the day I learned to beg. 1

I was up in Poulsbo. I had used the last of my change to buy Willow a hamburger at 2 the McDonald's drive-thru. My gas tank was almost empty, and my stomach was growling. Desperate for money just to keep moving and get something to eat, I began to consider the only option I seemed to have left: begging.

My whole life I had been a people person. As a sportswriter for the *Springfield* 3 *Sun*, I had seen Woody Hayes motivate players at Ohio State and Sparky Anderson put the spark into Pete Rose. As a sales rep, I had sold hundreds of thousands of dollars of advertising, convincing people they needed to invest in the product I was publishing. I wore the right suits and ties and kept my cordovans shined and did the corporate dance for twenty years. But this, this *begging*, was far more difficult.

I had given to others on the street. They had all types of stories: "I need to buy a 4 bus ticket to Spokane so I can go visit my dying mother." "I lost my wallet this morning, and I need five dollars for gas." I had always given, knowing all along that their tales were suspect. So I decided to just straight-up ask for money. No made-up stories. No sick grandmas waiting for my arrival. No lost wallets.

I started at the store I had shopped at for many years—Central Market. It was a 5 glitzy, upscale place with its own Starbucks, $120 bottles of wine, fresh crab, line-caught salmon, and oysters Rockefeller to go. It was a little bit of Palm Springs dropped into Poulsbo. The parking lot was full of high-priced cars: two Cadillac Escalades, three Lincoln Navigators, and a bright yellow Hummer. I had spent at least $200 a week there ($800 a month, $9,600 a year, $192,000 in twenty years), so I rationalized that I could beg there for *one* day—Thanksgiving Day at that.

I was wrong. 6

After watching forty people walk by, I finally asked a lady for help. "Ma'am, I'm 7 down on my luck. Could you help me with a couple of dollars?" I blurted out.

"Sorry," she said. "All I have is a credit card," and she moved on. 8

A man in a red Porsche pulled in. I watched him get out of his car, lock the doors 9 from his key-chain remote, and head for the store. "Sir, I hate to bother you. This is the first time I have ever done this, and I'm not very good at it. But I am down on my luck and need help. Could you—"

"Get a Goddamned job, you bum!" he interrupted and kept walking. 10

Stung, I wanted to run to the van and leave, but I knew I couldn't go far; I barely had 11 enough gas to leave the parking lot.

I spent the next twenty minutes trying to recover from the verbal blast I had received 12 and could not approach anyone else. But the exclamation point had not yet been slapped in place on my failure at begging. The young manager of the store, maybe twenty-five years old, came out to do the honors. "Sir, sir," he called out to me as he approached. "We have a . . ." He halted mid-sentence. "Don't I know you?" he asked instead.

"Probably," I replied. "I've been shopping here for twenty years." 13

"I thought I'd seen you in the store," he said. "Well," he sighed heavily, "a man 14 complained about you begging in front of the store. You're going to have to move on."

I could tell he didn't want to hear about the $192,000 I had spent in his store. 15 He just wanted to hear what I was going to spend today. So I said, "Okay." He didn't offer me a sandwich, a loaf of bread, a soy latte, or even a plain old cup of coffee.

I had no choice. I had to keep trying. I decided to go across the street to Albert- 16 sons. As I walked back to the van, tears filled my eyes. I remembered Thanksgivings of the past. By now, I would be pouring wine for our family and friends, rushing to the door to welcome guests, and taking their coats to be hung in the hall closet. My home would be filled with the smells of turkey and sage dressing. At least twenty people would be there. Children would be jumping on the sofa and racing up and down the hallways and stairs. The football game between the Cowboys and the Pack- ers would be blaring in the background. There would be a buzz. A younger, friskier Willow would stay close to the kitchen, hoping for the first bites of the bird from the oven.

But that was yesterday. Today, I drove across the highway to the "down-market" 17 store, nestled in the strip mall between the drugstore and the card shop. I stepped out of the van to try my luck again. It was getting late, and the shoppers were rushing to get home to their festivities. I had little time to succeed.

I saw an old friend of mine pull into the parking lot and get out of her car. She 18 headed for the grocery store. I turned my back to her and hid behind a pillar. I waited for her to enter the store, and then I approached a man as he walked toward the en- trance. "Sir, I'm down on my luck. Could you help me with a little money for food?" I asked.

He walked away muttering, "Jesus Christ, now we've got worthless beggars on the 19 streets of *Poulsbo*."

I closed my eyes for a moment against the failure and fatigue, and then I felt a tap 20 on my shoulder. "Sir," a lady was saying. As I opened my eyes and turned around, a lady in a red hat and an old red coat with a big brooch of an angel pinned to her lapel was standing there. She was digging through her purse as she talked.

"I overheard your conversation with that man. I hope you don't mind. I—well, I can 21 help you a little bit," she said, holding out some rolled-up bills. Her presence and the offered gift surprised me. I stood there a moment, looking into her eyes. "Here," she said, reaching her hand out again. "Take it."

I reached out my hand and took the money from her. "Thank you so much," I said 22 softly. "This is very kind of you."

"Thank you. I know what . . ." she began, and then her sentence was interrupted by 23 a cough. She clutched her purse to her chest with one hand and did her best to cover her mouth with the other. She stiffened and then bent her head toward the pavement as the cough from deep in her chest consumed her. She moved her hand from her mouth to her bosom and just held it there. When the cough subsided, she took a deep breath. She looked up at me with watery eyes. "I've had this darned hacking cough for a month or more now," she said after she recovered. "I can't seem to shake this cold. It's going to be the death of me," she added with a smile. "I'm going back to the doctor after the holiday."

"I hope you get better soon," I said.   24

The lady then moved her purse from her chest and opened it again. "Wait," she   25
said, looking inside her bag and then reaching in. "I might have some change in here too." She dug to the bottom of her purse. She took out a handful of change and handed it to me. I put my hands together and held them out, and she poured the coins into them. "I hope this helps you," she said, gently placing her hand on mine. "Remember me. I'll see you in heaven. Happy Thanksgiving!" She turned and walked away.

I watched her disappear into her car before I counted the money she had given   26
me. It was sixty-four dollars and fifty cents. I was stunned! I walked back to the van, counted the money again, and then counted my blessings.

I sat there in the drizzle, contemplating what had just happened. A sporadic church-   27
goer my entire life, I had spent recent months asking God to send his angels to me. But no angels came. Maybe *I* had to go looking for *them*.

With the glimmer of faith I still had left on that Thanksgiving Day, I said a prayer,   28
thanking God for the visit from the Lady in Red.

And now, in the church parking lot, it was time to sleep. I closed the doors of my   29
mind, one by one, and snuggled with Willow.

(MAKING (CONNECTIONS)

Harsh Treatment of Outcasts

Both "The Lady in Red" (pp. 235–37) and "Right Place, Wrong Face" (pp. 229–30) describe the harsh treatment of someone who was seen as an outcast—a person who did not deserve respect or courtesy.

Analyzing the Readings

1. Compare the situations that each man found himself in and the ways that others responded to him. Then consider how each man responded to those who treated him harshly.
2. Compare the social issues that each author addresses in the narrative of his experience.

Essay Idea

Write an essay describing a situation in which you feel you were treated as an outcast. Describe the background to the situation, the treatment you received, and your response.

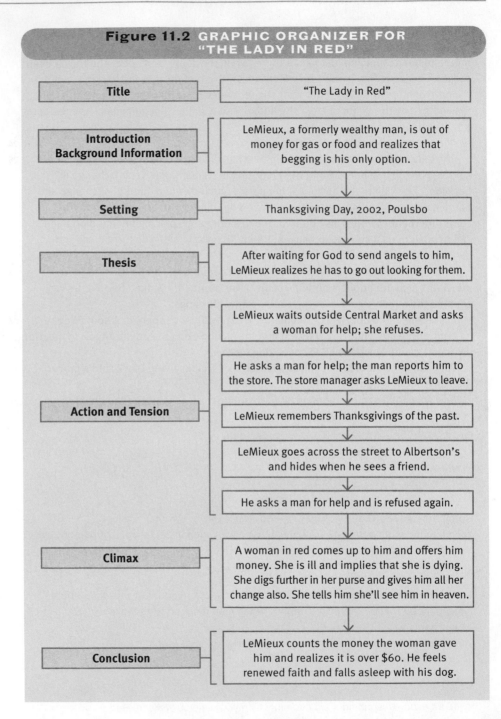

Figure 11.2 GRAPHIC ORGANIZER FOR "THE LADY IN RED"

| Title | "The Lady in Red" |

| Introduction Background Information | LeMieux, a formerly wealthy man, is out of money for gas or food and realizes that begging is his only option. |

| Setting | Thanksgiving Day, 2002, Poulsbo |

| Thesis | After waiting for God to send angels to him, LeMieux realizes he has to go out looking for them. |

Action and Tension	LeMieux waits outside Central Market and asks a woman for help; she refuses.
	He asks a man for help; the man reports him to the store. The store manager asks LeMieux to leave.
	LeMieux remembers Thanksgivings of the past.
	LeMieux goes across the street to Albertson's and hides when he sees a friend.
	He asks a man for help and is refused again.

| Climax | A woman in red comes up to him and offers him money. She is ill and implies that she is dying. She digs further in her purse and gives him all her change also. She tells him she'll see him in heaven. |

| Conclusion | LeMieux counts the money the woman gave him and realizes it is over $60. He feels renewed faith and falls asleep with his dog. |

To draw detailed graphic organizers using a computer, visit www.bedfordstmartins.com/successfulcollege.

Exercise 11.4

Using the graphic organizers in Figures 11.1 and 11.2 as models, draw a graphic organizer for "Right Place, Wrong Face" (pp. 229–30).

Integrating a Narrative into an Essay

In many of your essays, you will want to use both a narrative and one or more other patterns of development to support your thesis. In the writing you encounter in newspapers, magazines, and textbooks, the patterns of development often mix and overlap. Similarly, although "Right Place, Wrong Face" is primarily a narrative, it also uses cause and effect to explain why White was detained despite evidence that he was a respectable, law-abiding citizen. "The Lady in Red" is a narrative that contains descriptions of people's reactions to a begging man.

Although most of your college essays will not be primarily narrative, you can use stories — to illustrate a point, clarify an idea, support an argument, or capture readers' interest — in essays that rely on another pattern of development or on several patterns. Here are a few suggestions for using narration effectively in the essays you write:

For more on description and cause and effect, see Chapters 12 and 18.

1. **Be sure that your story illustrates your point accurately and well.** Don't include a story just because it's funny or interesting. It must support your thesis.
2. **Keep the narrative short.** Include only relevant details — facts that are necessary to help your reader understand the events you are describing.
3. **Introduce the story with a transitional sentence or clause that indicates you are about to shift to a narrative.** Otherwise, your readers may wonder, "What's this story doing here?" Your transition should also make clear the connection between the story and the point it illustrates.
4. **Use descriptive language, dialogue, and action.** These elements make narratives vivid, lively, and interesting in any essay.

In "Alien World: How Treacherous Border Crossing Became a Theme Park" on pages 258–63, Alexander Zaitchik uses description, illustration, and argument as well as narration to develop his ideas.

A GUIDED WRITING ASSIGNMENT

The following guide will lead you through the process of writing a narrative essay. Although your essay will be primarily a narrative, you may choose to use one or more other patterns of development as well. Depending on your learning style, you might decide to start at various points and move back and forth within the process. If you are a spatial learner, for example, you might begin by visualizing and sketching the details of your narrative. If you are a social learner, you might prefer to start out by evaluating your audience.

Learning Style Options

The Assignment

Write a narrative essay about an experience in your life that had a significant effect on you or that changed your views in some important way. Choose your own topic or use one from the list below:

1. An experience that caused you to learn something about yourself
2. An incident that revealed the true character of someone you knew
3. An experience that helped you discover a principle to live by
4. An experience that explains the personal significance of a particular object
5. An incident that has become a family legend, perhaps one that reveals the character of a family member or illustrates a clash of generations or cultures
6. An incident that has allowed you to develop an appreciation or awareness of your ethnic identity

The readers of your campus newspaper are your audience.

For more on description and comparison and contrast, see Chapters 12 and 15.

As you develop your narrative essay, be sure to consider using one or more of the other patterns of development. You might use description to present details about a family member's appearance, for example, or comparison and contrast to compare your attitudes or ideas with those of a parent or child.

Generating Ideas

Use the following steps to help you choose a topic and generate ideas about the experience or incident you decide to write about.

Choosing an Experience or Incident That Leads to a Working Thesis

Be sure that the experience you write about is memorable and vivid and that you are comfortable writing about it. When a draft is nearly complete, no student wants to discover that he or she cannot remember important details about the experience or that it does not fulfill the requirements of the assignment.

For more on formulating a working thesis, see Chapter 6, pp. 125–26.

The following suggestions will help you choose an experience:

1. You can probably eliminate one or more broad topic choices right away. List those that remain across the top of a piece of paper or on your computer screen—for

QUESTIONS

REVISION STRATEGIES

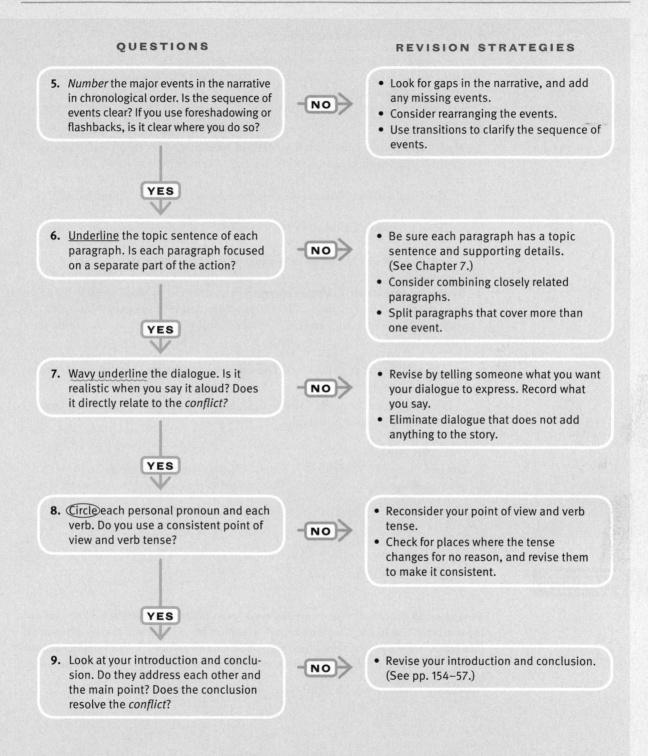

5. *Number* the major events in the narrative in chronological order. Is the sequence of events clear? If you use foreshadowing or flashbacks, is it clear where you do so?

NO

- Look for gaps in the narrative, and add any missing events.
- Consider rearranging the events.
- Use transitions to clarify the sequence of events.

YES

6. Underline the topic sentence of each paragraph. Is each paragraph focused on a separate part of the action?

NO

- Be sure each paragraph has a topic sentence and supporting details. (See Chapter 7.)
- Consider combining closely related paragraphs.
- Split paragraphs that cover more than one event.

YES

7. Wavy underline the dialogue. Is it realistic when you say it aloud? Does it directly relate to the *conflict?*

NO

- Revise by telling someone what you want your dialogue to express. Record what you say.
- Eliminate dialogue that does not add anything to the story.

YES

8. Circle each personal pronoun and each verb. Do you use a consistent point of view and verb tense?

NO

- Reconsider your point of view and verb tense.
- Check for places where the tense changes for no reason, and revise them to make it consistent.

YES

9. Look at your introduction and conclusion. Do they address each other and the main point? Does the conclusion resolve the *conflict?*

NO

- Revise your introduction and conclusion. (See pp. 154–57.)

Editing and Proofreading

For more on keeping an error log, see Chapter 10, pp. 221–22.

The last step is to check your revised narrative essay for errors in grammar, spelling, punctuation, and mechanics. Be sure to look for the types of errors that you tend to make. (Refer to your error log.)

For narrative essays, pay particular attention to the following kinds of sentence problems.

For more on varying sentence structure, see Chapter 10, pp. 206–12.

1. **Make certain that your sentences vary in structure.** A string of sentences that are similar in length and structure is tedious to read.

   ■ The Ding Darling National Wildlife Preserve, is located on Sanibel Island,

      Florida, It was established in 1945 as the Sanibel Refuge. Its name

      was changed in 1967 to honor the man who helped found it.

2. **Be sure to punctuate dialogue correctly.** Use commas to separate each quotation from the phrase that introduces it, unless the quotation is integrated into your sentence. If your sentence ends with a quotation, the period should be inside the quotation marks.

   ■ The wildlife refuge guide noted, "American crocodiles are an endangered species and must be protected."
   ■ The wildlife refuge guide noted that, "American crocodiles are an endangered species and must be protected."

> **Essay in Progress 8**
> Edit and proofread your narrative essay, remembering to vary sentence patterns and punctuate dialogue correctly. Don't forget to look for the types of errors you tend to make.

(READING)

Students Write

Mina Raine, an education major, wrote this essay for an assignment given by her first-year writing instructor. She had to describe a situation in which her involvement made a difference or affected others. As you read the essay, notice how Raine's narrative creates conflict and tension and builds to a climax and resolution. Highlight the sections where you think the tension is particularly intense.

Taking Back Control

Mina Raine

Introduction:
Raine gives background about her relationship with Beth.

   My friend Beth is soft spoken but strong in faith and character. She is one of those rare people   1

who can light up a room with her smile or make you feel at ease just by simply being near you. We met freshman year at a gathering of mutual friends in the largest dorm on campus. Since then, we've spent our time together among a close-knit circle of friends. Beth has always seemed, to me, so mature and composed and so in control of herself and her life, so giving, so caring, so nurturing in all her relationships, which is why I was deeply concerned and very much surprised when I began to notice a drastic change in her.

Thesis statement: Raine gives a rationale for her concern.

First I noticed that Beth was making a habit out of eating her dinner from a small cereal bowl instead of a plate. I didn't think much of that, at first. Maybe the dining hall had temporarily run out of plates and a bowl was all she could find. Or maybe it was just one of those funny little habits we all find ourselves adopting, eventually. (Later I would learn that the small bowl is a way to monitor and control the amount of food she eats; you can only fit so much food into the shallow dish.)

2

Transitions help sequence events. Exact details help readers imagine the scene.

A few weeks later, my friends and I noticed a dramatic change in Beth's appearance— sunken, tired eyes void of their usual sparkle, a smile that seemed forced, and the clothes that once hugged her lovely curves in a subtle and conservative way now hanging off her fragile frame. This coupled with her strange cereal bowl habit was finally enough to make us realize something was definitely wrong. Of course, we weren't sure yet if Beth really was struggling with an eating disorder, but it was certainly evident that she was not herself, and from her somewhat depressed and rather distracted demeanor, she seemed to be seriously struggling with something.

3

Tension begins to build.

Then, on one particular evening in the dining hall, my friends and I overheard Beth discussing her new workout regimen with her boyfriend, Steve. She had recently started fitting in evening running sessions between all of her studies and extracurricular activities. Steve had been running on the treadmill daily and carefully monitoring what he ate in an effort to lose the "freshman fifteen" (or twenty) he had gained. Unfortunately, it seemed his new efforts to live a healthy lifestyle had rubbed off on Beth, in an unhealthy way. My friend, who had been at a perfect weight and had been eating properly, was now eating less and exercising more. It was a sure recipe for disaster. I heard Steve talking to Beth about how many miles they had run that evening and how many more they would run the next day. He had her on the same workout schedule he was on, but she wasn't the one who was overweight. As I sat there listening to him influence her in this way, I felt myself getting angry. I didn't know for sure what was wrong with Beth at that point (though I had a pretty good idea), but it was obvious something was wrong. How could he not see that? The dark circles under Beth's eyes showed her obvious lack of sleep, and her low energy and lack of focus showed that her body wasn't getting the nutrition it needed.

4

After listening to the unsettling conversation between Beth and Steve about their strict workout routine, my friends and I began discussing the matter among ourselves and deciding on the best way to address the issue with Beth. I spent a few days wondering how best to approach her or if I even should. What if I upset her and she stopped talking to me? What if we were wrong and Beth was fine? Or worse, what if we were right and she pulled away from us? Then, Beth solved this dilemma for me: *she* came to *me*.

5

Dialogue leads to a climax.

Three weeks after my friend's struggle with food and weight became glaringly obvious, she   6
knocked on my door. "I need to talk to you," she said, "and I think you already know what it's
about." I felt unprepared for this moment. Beth responded in a calm, serious tone to my anxious
silence: "First, I feel I owe you an apology for making you worry about me. You're a good friend and
I'm sorry." Here she broke down, and it was my turn to try to be stoic.

Climax

"It's OK. It's nothing you have to apologize for. But are you OK?"   7

"Not really," Beth answered in an unsteady voice. "I have an eating disorder."   8

What do you say to that? You know it happens, but you never think it will be you or someone   9
close to you who will be plagued by a nagging, evil voice in the back of her head telling her she's
had enough to eat today (even though she's still very hungry) or that despite the fact that she is a
size 5 she really shouldn't enjoy a piece of cake for dessert. "Is it bulimia?" I asked Beth. She had
regained her composure now, and spoke matter-of-factly.

"No, I don't make myself sick. It's not really anorexia either because I do eat. I just don't eat   10
much. It's more of a control thing. When I eat my meals out of a cereal bowl, I can control the portion size, keep it small, and I'm aware of exactly how much I am eating."

"When did this start?" I asked, expecting her to say only a few weeks, maybe a few   11
months ago.

"I've struggled with it most of my life, but I had it mostly under control until around a   12
year ago."

A year! She had been fighting this ugly thing for a year, and we, I, had only just noticed in the   13
past few weeks? How could that be? Beth later told me that her now ex-boyfriend had made a trivial
but insensitive comment about her weight around a year ago. That was what had triggered the disorder to resurface. I was furious with myself and at a loss for words. All I could do was hug her, tell
her that I have absolute faith in her and her ability to fight this thing, this disgusting thing that
has taken over her body and her life, and cry into the comfort of my hands when she was finally
too far down the hall to hear me.

When I checked in with Beth a couple days after her disconcerting but unsurprising revelation,   14
she broke down and gave me an intimate glimpse into the complicated and disturbing battle being
fought within her head. She seemed so defeated but aware of this feeling of defeat, which only
made her angry at herself. I did my best to console her with the reassuring fact that her awareness
of the problem and the need to make some serious changes in her life was already a giant step toward her recovery. I also told her that while I would always be there for her, to support and encourage her, I'm not qualified to truly help her deal with her disorder.

"I know," she said, a few silent tears sliding down her pale cheeks, "I've made an appointment   15
with the counseling office on campus."

"I'm so proud of you," I responded as I embraced her.   16

"I'm hoping you'll come with me, at least for the first visit."   17

"Of course," I answered. "You're strong and smart. You will beat this. You'll get better. And 18 I'm always here if you need to talk or just need a hug. Just please promise me you'll stop working out until you get back to more normal eating habits. That means no more cereal bowls. Unless, of course, you're eating cereal."

Beth laughed a little at this last comment, which is what I had been hoping for. Even if only 19 for a moment, the Beth I knew shone through in that brief smile and soft chuckle. I knew then that though she'll probably have to work on it every day, Beth will regain control of her body and her life.

Conclusion: Raine returns to the idea in her thesis statement—her knowledge of Beth as someone in control of her life.

Analyzing the Writer's Technique

1. Evaluate the strength of Raine's thesis. How clear and specific is it?
2. What ideas in the essay, if any, do you think should be discussed more fully? Where did you feel more details were needed? Which details—if any—are unnecessary?
3. How does Raine establish conflict and create tension?
4. Where does Raine use foreshadowing? How effective is it?
5. Evaluate the title, introduction, and conclusion of the essay.

Thinking Critically about Narration

1. Describe Raine's tone. Does it change in the course of the essay? If so, how? Does it seem appropriate for the topic?
2. What connotation does the phrase "freshman fifteen" (para. 4) have?
3. Is the last sentence of the essay fact or opinion? How do you know?

Reacting to the Essay

1. Why didn't Raine speak up about the strange behaviors she noticed? Do you think you would have done the same thing?
2. Beth's illness was about her need for control. What other behaviors can you think of that are influenced by this need?
3. Write a journal entry about a friend who suffered through something difficult, describing how you reacted to it.
4. Raine felt helpless in the face of her friend's illness. Write an essay about a time when you felt helpless to solve someone else's problem.

READING A NARRATIVE

The following section provides advice for reading narratives. Two model essays illustrate the characteristics of narrative writing covered in this chapter and provide opportunities to examine, analyze, and react to the writer's ideas. The second essay uses narration as well as description, illustration, and argument.

For more on description, illustration, and argument, see Chapters 12, 13, 19, and 20.

Working with Text: Reading Narratives

For more on previewing an essay and other reading strategies, see Chapter 3.

It is usually a good idea to read a narrative essay several times before you attempt to discuss or write about it. Preview the essay first to get an overview of its content and organization. Then read it through to familiarize yourself with the events and action, noting also who did what, when, where, and how. Finally, reread the narrative, this time concentrating on its meaning.

What to Look For, Highlight, and Annotate

1. Narrative elements. When reading a narrative, it is easy to become immersed in the story and to overlook its importance or significance. Therefore, as you read, look for the answers to the following questions:

- What is the writer's thesis? Is it stated directly or implied?
- What is the role of each participant in the story?
- What does the dialogue reveal about or contribute to the main point?
- What is the conflict?
- How does the writer create tension?
- What is the climax?
- How is the conflict resolved?

Highlight those sections of the essay that reveal or suggest the answers.

2. Sequence of events. Especially for lengthy or complex narratives and for those that flash back and forward among events, it is helpful to draw a graphic organizer or number the sequence of events in the margins. Doing so will help you establish the sequence of key events.

3. Keys to meaning. The following questions will help you evaluate the reading and discover its main point:

- What is the author's purpose in writing this narrative?
- For what audience is it intended?
- What is the lasting value or merit of this essay? What does it tell me about life, people, jobs, or friendships, for example?
- What techniques does the writer use to try to achieve his or her purpose? Is the writer successful?

4. Reactions. As you read, write down your reactions to and feelings about the events, participants, and outcome of the narrative. Include both positive and negative reactions; do not hesitate to challenge participants, their actions, and their motives.

How to Find Ideas to Write About

For more about discovering ideas for a response paper, see Chapter 5.

Since you may be asked to write a response to a narrative, keep an eye out for ideas to write about *as you read*. Pay attention to the issue, struggle, or dilemma at hand. Try to discover what broader issue the essay is concerned with. For example, in a story about children who dislike eating vegetables, the larger issue might be food preferences, nutrition, or parental control. Once you've identified the larger issue, you can develop your own ideas about it by relating it to your own experience.

Thinking Critically about Narration

A nonfiction narrative is often one writer's highly personal, subjective account of an event or a series of events. Unless you have reason to believe otherwise, assume that the writer is honest—that he or she does not lie about the experiences or incidents presented in the essay. You should also assume, however, that the writer chooses details selectively—to advance his or her narrative point. Use the questions below to think critically about the narratives you read.

How Objective Is the Writer?

Because a narrative is often highly personal, a critical reader must recognize that the information it contains is probably influenced by the author's values, beliefs, and attitudes. In "Right Place, Wrong Face," for example, the police officers are presented as uncaring and insensitive, but imagine how the officers would describe the same incident. Two writers, then, may present two very different versions of a single incident.

What Is the Author's Tone?

Tone refers to how the author sounds to his or her readers or how he or she feels about the topic. Writers establish tone through word choice, sentence structure, and formality or informality. An author's tone can reflect many emotions—such as anger, joy, or fear. The tone of an essay narrating an event in the American war in Iraq might be serious, frightening, or sad, whereas an essay narrating the activities of a procrastinating, well-meaning friend or relative might be light or humorous. The author's tone affects the reader's attitude toward the topic.

What Does the Author Leave Unspoken or Unreported?

An author usually cannot report all conversations and events related to the narrative; however, the author should report all those that are relevant. Pay attention to what is said and reported but also to what might be left unsaid and unreported. In "Taking Back Control," for example, we might wonder exactly what Raine and her friends said as they discussed Beth's problem.

NARRATIVE ESSAY

As you read the following essay by Barbara Ehrenreich, consider how the writer uses the elements of narrative discussed in this chapter.

Selling in Minnesota
Barbara Ehrenreich

Barbara Ehrenreich is an award-winning political essayist, columnist, and social critic whose works have appeared in such publications as *Time*, the *Nation*, *Harper's*, and the *Atlantic*. She is the author of numerous books, including *Blood Rites: Origins and History of the Passions of War* (1997), *Bait and Switch: The (Futile) Pursuit of the American Dream* (2005), and *Bright-Sided: How the Relentless Promotion of Positive Thinking Has Undermined America* (2009). For *Nickel and Dimed: On (Not) Getting by in America* (2001), from which this selection is adapted, Ehrenreich spent a year doing minimum-wage work to discover the working conditions of low-paying jobs in the United States. As you read it, highlight or annotate each narrative element in the essay.

In my second week [of working at Wal-Mart], two things change. My shift changes from 10:00–6:00 to 2:00–11:00, the so-called closing shift, although the store remains open 24/7. No one tells me this; I find it out by studying the schedules that are posted, under glass, on the wall outside the break room. Now I have nine hours instead of eight, and my two fifteen-minute breaks, which seemed almost superfluous on the 10:00–6:00 shift, now become a matter of urgent calculation. Do I take both before dinner, which is usually about 7:30, leaving an unbroken two-and-a-half-hour stretch when I'm weariest, between 8:30 and 11:00? Or do I try to go two and a half hours without a break in the afternoon, followed by a nearly three-hour marathon before I can get away for dinner? Then there's the question of how to make the best use of a fifteen-minute break when you have three or more urgent, simultaneous needs—to pee, to drink something, to get outside the neon and into the natural light, and most of all, to sit down. I save about a minute by engaging in a little time theft and stopping at the rest room before I punch out for the break. From the time clock it's a seventy-five second walk to the store exit; if I stop at the Radio Grill, I could end up wasting a full four minutes waiting in line, not to mention the fifty-nine cents for a small-sized iced tea. So if I treat myself to an outing in the tiny fenced-off area beside the store, I get about nine minutes off my feet. 1

The other thing that happens is that the post–Memorial Day weekend lull definitely comes to an end. Now there are always a dozen or more shoppers rooting around in ladies'. New tasks arise, such as bunching up the carts left behind by customers and steering them to their place in the front of the store every half hour or so. Now I am picking up not only dropped clothes but all the odd items customers carry off from foreign departments and decide to leave with us in ladies'—pillows, upholstery hooks, Pokémon cards, earrings, sunglasses, stuffed animals, even a package of cinnamon 2 buns. And always there are the returns, augmented now by the huge volume of items that have been tossed on the floor or carried fecklessly to inappropriate sites. If I pick up misplaced items as quickly as I replace the returns, my cart never empties and things back up dangerously at the fitting room, where Rhoda or her nighttime replacement is likely to hiss: "You've got three carts waiting, Barb. What's the *problem*?"

Still, for the first half of my shift, I am the very picture of good-natured helpfulness. 3 Amazingly, I get praised by Isabelle, the thin little seventyish lady who seems to be Ellie's adjutant: I am doing "wonderfully," she tells me, and—even better—am "great to work with." But then, somewhere around 6:00 or 7:00, when the desire to sit down becomes a serious craving, a Dr. Jekyll/Mr. Hyde transformation sets in. I cannot ignore the fact that it's the customers' sloppiness and idle whims that make me bend and crouch and run. They are the shoppers, I am the antishopper, whose goal is to make it look as if they'd never been in the store. At this point, "aggressive hospitality" gives way to aggressive hostility. Their carts bang into mine, their children run amok.

It's the clothes I relate to, not the customers. And now a funny thing happens to me 4 here on my new shift: I start thinking they're mine, not mine to take home and wear, because I have no such designs on them, just mine to organize and rule over. Same with ladies' wear as a whole. I patrol the perimeter with my cart, darting in to pick up misplaced and fallen items, making everything look spiffy from the outside. I don't fondle the clothes, the way customers do; I slap them into place, commanding them to hang straight, at attention, or lie subdued on the shelves in perfect order. In this frame of mind, the last thing I want to see is a customer riffling around, disturbing the place. In fact, I hate the idea of things being sold—uprooted from their natural homes, whisked off to some closet that's in God-knows-what state of disorder. I want ladies' wear sealed off in a plastic bubble and trucked away to some place of safety, some museum of retail history.

One night I come back bone-tired from my last break and am distressed to find a 5 new person folding T-shirts in the [turtlenecks] area, *my* [turtlenecks] area. It's already been a vexing evening. Earlier, when I'd returned from dinner, the evening fitting room lady upbraided me for being late—which I actually wasn't—and said that if Howard knew, he probably wouldn't yell at me this time because I'm still pretty new, but if it happened again. . . . And I'd snapped back that I could care less if Howard yelled at me. So I'm a little wary with this intruder in [turtlenecks], and, sure enough, after our minimal introductions, she turns on me.

"Did you put anything away here today?" she demands. 6

"Well, yes, sure." In fact I've put something away everywhere today, as I do on every 7 other day.

"Because this is not in the right place. See the fabric—it's different," and she 8 thrusts the errant item up toward my chest.

True, I can see that this olive-green shirt is slightly ribbed while the others are 9 smooth. "You've *got* to put them in their right places," she continues. "Are you checking the UPC numbers?"

Of course I am not checking the ten or more digit UPC numbers, which lie just under 10 the bar codes—nobody does. What does she think this is, the National Academy of

Sciences? I'm not sure what kind of deference, if any, is due here: Is she my supervisor now? But I don't care, she's messing with my stuff. So I say, only without the numerals or the forbidden curse word, that (1) plenty of other people work here during the day, not to mention all the customers coming through, so why is she blaming me? (2) it's after 10:00 and I've got another cart full of returns to go, and wouldn't it make more sense if we both worked on the carts, instead of zoning the goddamn T-shirts?

To which she responds huffily, "I don't *do* returns. My job is to *fold.*"   11

I leave that night shaken by my response to the intruder. If she's a supervisor, I   12
could be written up for what I said, but even worse is what I thought. Am I turning mean here, and is that a normal response to the end of a nine-hour shift? There was another outbreak of mental wickedness that night. I'd gone back to the counter by the fitting room to pick up the next cart full of returns and found the guy who answers the phone at the counter at night, a pensive young fellow in a wheelchair, staring into space, looking even sadder than usual. And my uncensored thought was, At least you get to sit down.

This is not me, at least not any version of me I'd like to spend much time with.   13
What I have to face is that "Barb," the name on my ID tag, is not exactly the same person as Barbara. "Barb" is what I was called as a child, and still am by my siblings, and I sense that at some level I'm regressing. Take away the career and the higher education, and maybe what you're left with is this original Barb, the one who might have ended up working at Wal-Mart for real if her father hadn't managed to climb out of the mines. So it's interesting, and more than a little disturbing, to see how Barb turned out—that she's meaner and slyer than I am, more cherishing of grudges, and not quite as smart as I'd hoped.

Examining the Reading

1. Describe the working conditions at Wal-Mart as experienced by the author.
2. What sorts of tasks do the Wal-Mart employees perform? Provide details.
3. How and why does the author's attitude toward her job change as the essay progresses?
4. What details or sections of the essay identify Ehrenreich as a well-educated journalist rather than a low-wage worker?
5. Explain the meaning of each of the following words as it is used in the reading: *superfluous* (para. 1), *fecklessly* (2), *adjutant* (3), *errant* (8), and *regressing* (13). Refer to your dictionary as needed.

Analyzing the Writer's Technique

1. Identify the writer's thesis. Is it implied or directly stated?
2. The writer has to decide how to fit in her various breaks. Why does Ehrenreich include these details? What is she trying to convey about her job?
3. What other patterns of development does the author use? Provide examples of two, and explain how they contribute to the narrative.

Visualizing the Reading

Use the chart below to record several particularly effective examples of each narrative characteristic used by Ehrenreich in "Selling in Minnesota." The first one is done for you.

Narrative Characteristic	Examples (Paragraph Number)
Uses dialogue	"'You've got three carts waiting, Barb. What's the *problem*?'" (para. 2)
Includes sensory details	
Conveys action	
Suggests a sequence of events	
Builds tension	

Thinking Critically about Narration

1. Describe the tone of Ehrenreich's essay. Highlight key phrases that reveal her attitude toward working at Wal-Mart.
2. What is the connotation of "hiss" (para. 2)?
3. How are Ehrenreich's behavior and analysis affected by the fact that her job at Wal-Mart is not her permanent job? How might she behave and think differently if she relied on the job for her income? Do you think Wal-Mart workers would agree with Ehrenreich's narration?
4. Does Ehrenreich present an objective or a subjective view of a Wal-Mart worker? Explain your answer.

Reacting to the Reading

1. Compare the author's portrayal of a retail store worker with your experiences as a shopper. Are her descriptions consistent with what you have experienced or observed?
2. Discuss whether this essay will affect the way you treat retail store employees. What adjustments might you make to your behavior in light of the conditions under which they work?
3. Ehrenreich makes a distinction between her two names "Barb" and "Barbara"— suggesting two different parts to her personality. In what ways are you more than one person? Write a journal entry exploring this question.
4. Write an essay in which you narrate an on-the-job experience that reveals how you are treated by your employer or supervisor and suggests your attitude toward the workplace.

NARRATION COMBINED WITH OTHER PATTERNS

For more on reading and writing arguments, see Chapters 19 and 20.

In the following selection, Alexander Zaitchik uses narration as well as description, illustration, and argument.

READING

Alien World
How Treacherous Border Crossing Became a Theme Park
Alexander Zaitchik

Alexander Zaitchik is a freelance journalist and the author of *Glenn Beck and the Triumph of Ignorance* (2010). He has been a staff member of *the eXile*, an English-language newspaper published in Russia, and served as an investigative reporting fellow at the Southern Poverty Law Center, a U.S.-based legal organization that fights against extremist groups and supports racial and ethnic tolerance. He has published articles in the *Prague Post*, the *Prague Pill*, the *International Herald Tribune*, the *New Republic*, and *Reason*, a libertarian magazine in which this essay was originally published in 2009.

1   It's a little before 10 p.m. when I climb into the back of a pick-up truck full of crouching young Mexicans. We're in the lush Mezquital Valley just outside Ixmiquilpan, a dusty strip town cramped with car part shacks and taqueria[1] stalls a couple hours' drive north of Mexico City. The late-model GMC is scheduled to take its cargo—10 of us—north toward the Sonora-Arizona line. After the drop-off starts a treacherous pre-dawn border trek past armed U.S. patrols and the fanged, baying beasts of the desert wilds. Tonight we escape Mexico. El Norte or bust.

2   The truck is still idling when a young girl in an L.A. Dodgers jacket loses her nerve. "I'm worried about snakes and coyotes," she says in a quiet voice. "There are rattlers in the mountains. My brother said the little green ones are also poisonous." This is the first I've heard about poisonous snakes since signing up for this adventure.

3   "The clouds are no good," adds someone else. "We won't be able to see anything."

4   "Like the snakes," says the girl in the Dodgers jacket, her voice softer than before.

5   It's just possible to make out the faces of the group in the faint moonlight. These aren't the frightened, soiled migrants captured on green-lit night cams for network news investigations into "America's broken border." Not yet, anyway. These would-be migrants wear Diesel jeans and John Deere mesh caps, nose studs and gelled emo haircuts. Like me, each has paid $125 for two days of camping and a midnight "border crossing" experience in central Mexico. The staged run, 700 miles from the real U.S. border, covers a bruising adventure course that winds through the valley and is riddled with muddy riverbanks, bristly thwap-you-in-the-face brush, and jagged mountain passes.

6   The course is also flecked with gritty and realistic dramatic accents. Men in U.S. Border Patrol T-shirts bark insults in broken English through megaphones. Women and children are tossed into Border Patrol vehicles and driven off into the night. M-80s stand in for shotgun fire. Then there are the female screams in the distance, a sound-track of rape.

---

[1]taqueria: Mexican restaurant specializing in tacos.

It all adds up to the world's most elaborate simulation of the Mexican migrant experience. One much safer, and about $3,000 cheaper, than the real thing. 7

On my night as a hunted migrant, the Caminata Nocturna ("Night Hike") was celebrating its fourth sellout year under the direction of Mexico's leading purveyor of domestic meta-tourism, the Alberto Eco Park in the central Mexican highlands. The park was founded in 2004 by indigenous locals known as the Otomi in an attempt to staunch the flow of their working-age population, 90 percent of which has migrated to the United States over the last two decades. Faced with the extinction of the local community and culture, a few entrepreneurial Otomi decided to tap into the regional boom in culturally aware ecotourism. Their land is remote but nestled within a mountain range blessed with sheer cliffs and clean rivers. The Mexican government paved a road leading into the mountains, and with the help of a few small grants and sponsors, the Otomi built a campground replete with a rappelling cliff, zip lines, and a dock for canoes and kayaks. There is also a large riverside stage, upon which the Otomi perform their music in the local tribal dialect for Mexico's middle class and a smattering of European tourists. Today the camp is thriving. Among the growing list of sponsors is Corona. 8

The riverside picnics are pleasant enough on a summer's day, but it is the mock border run that is the park's primary draw and claim to fame. As America works on designs for its high-tech virtual border fence, middle-class Mexicans have been flocking to this low-tech virtual border, hungry for a taste of the danger experienced by their desperate compatriots who every year make the treacherous journey north. Tonight 130 of us pack into 12 pick-ups. Many are repeat visitors who have brought friends and relatives. "I heard about it from friends at school," says a teenage girl in my group. "They said it was fun." 9

Part of the fun, I learn, is staying in character. Sitting in the truck, I ask a kid in an Abercrombie sweatshirt why he came. 10

"Because there are no jobs in Mexico," he deadpans. "I want to find a better life, to live the American Dream." 11

The imitation of a pitiful migrant sparks a group laugh. But the chuckling is awkward and short-lived, as if everyone realizes a line has been crossed. The Otomi market the border crossing as an act of solidarity with Mexico's poor, but it can quickly start to feel a lot like what we gringos call slumming. When the truck finally starts moving, Abercrombie admits in perfect English to studying communications at Puebla University. When he visits the United States, which is about once a year, he gets a tourist visa and flies Mexicana. "I'm here for kicks," he says. 12

So is the girl in the Dodgers jacket with the fear of snakes. Her name is Daisy De Vasca, and she is from Lakewood, California, in Mexico visiting her aunt. Yet she swears tonight's snake threat is real. When she again begins describing the poisonous breeds that live in the mountains, I wave her off the subject. Better to talk about the American Dream, which can also bite you in the ass but usually lets you live to tell the tale. 13

The Otomi know about American dreams and nightmares. Most have made the trip north to work seasonally or settle in the large Otomi communities of Las Vagas and Los Angeles. Many have returned to Mexico, but the majority stay in the U.S., unable or unwilling to make the trip twice. An unknown number have disappeared or 14 died along the way, their bloated, hyperthermic corpses returned to their families in state vehicles if they were carrying ID cards, dispatched to anonymous graves if they weren't.

One of those who left and returned is Laura Basuado, a fresh-faced 27-year-old 15 park employee who crossed the border when she was 17. She says the border simulation is designed to offer well-off Mexicans a small but bitter dose of the ordeal endured by migrants. It is her hope that the experience will build solidarity between what she calls "the two Mexicos"—one middle class and thriving, one dirt poor and sinking.

"The Night Walk is not even 1 percent of what it's really like," says Basuado, whose 16 own journey to the U.S. involved a four-day march through the Sonoran desert. "I have never been so terrified in my life as when I went north. I was so sure we would die that I prayed the border police would catch us." Basuado eventually found her way to Minnesota, where she stayed four months before deciding she'd rather be poor and jobless in Mexico than poor and marginally employed in the U.S., living in constant dread of arrest and deportation.

The most painful memory for Basuado is the abuse she suffered at the rough hands 17 of her coyote, or hired guide, known more commonly in Mexico as a *pollero*. These guides are usually part of violent criminal networks and are often indifferent to the safety of their charges once money has changed hands. In recent years *polleros* have become famous villains in the Mexican migration drama. In the interest of realism, they are well represented in the Night Hike. From beginning to end, park employees impersonating *polleros* scream "*Vamos rapido!*" while pushing participants through some of the course's most dangerous terrain.

Then there are the screams that come from behind the bushes. During quiet lulls   18
in the walk, female park employees periodically issue blood-curdling cries that echo
through the mountains. It is not an overly histrionic touch. Rape has become so en-
demic to the border crossing experience that women often start taking birth control
before making the trip, expecting abuse from coyotes or the bandits that travel with
them. "Even if a woman is traveling with a brother or cousin, they are at the mercy of
the coyotes for survival," says Walt Staton, spokesperson for No More Deaths, a hu-
manitarian group that provides assistance to migrants on both sides of the border.

Nobody actually gets raped, robbed, or murdered during the Night Hike, but the   19
simulation is not for the weak of heart or the pregnant. There are full-speed runs
down steep unlit paths as sirens wail in pursuit and stretches along raging river
waters where the mire is almost knee high. In most countries participants would be
required to sign multiple waivers before getting in the back of the truck. During periodic breaks, everybody collapses in exhaustion, many tending to bloody knees and
sprained ankles.

It was during one of these pauses that screeching tires and high-pitched sirens   20
called our attention to the foot of the hill we were resting on. Down below, a truck
marked U.S. Border Patrol stopped before a group of migrants.

In one of the night's few dramatic set pieces, actors in camo and Border Patrol   21
T-shirts throw several young girls into the back of the truck. Before driving away, an officer looks up at our group and yells, "Go back to Mexico! We don't want you here!"

Watching the drama unfold, a kid next to me pulls out a Snickers bar and offers me   22
half. "Pendejos," he mutters. *Assholes*.

When Parque Eco Alberto opened in 2004, curious reporters immediately set upon   23
the camp with cameras and notepads. The Mexican media came first, followed by a
trickle of international outlets, including the BBC, which called the border crossing

simulation "Migrant Mountain." Most of the coverage was and remains positive, if sometimes bemused. "The media sees we are trying to build understanding and create jobs, and they support us," says Eduardo del Plan, a park employee who scripts much of the simulation based on his own multiple trips across the border. "We have become an example of an indigenous community standing on its own feet, trying to stop the bleeding to the north."

The loudest exception to the chorus of approval is the Spanish language television network Telemundo. The Miami-based channel has accused the Otomi of using the Night Hike as a training course for migrants, akin to the mercenary firm Blackwater's North Carolina training compound, where it prepares its employees for Iraq. When asked about this charge, del Plan laughs, saying the network purposely misrepresented the entire point of the exercise. "Telemundo is always trying to be sensational," he says. "They should stick to covering soap operas."   24

But the charge of preparing migrants for their journey mirrors one frequently leveled against Mexico City in Washington: that the Mexican government tolerates and even encourages migration north because it is one of the Mexican economy's three pillars (the others being oil and the *maquiladora*[2] factories along Mexico's northern border). Mexicans living in the U.S. send more than $25 billion in annual remittances to their relatives south of the border. After oil exports, this money constitutes the country's second largest stream of foreign revenue. "Migration used to be an economic safety valve for Mexico," says Laura Carlson, director of the Americas Policy Program, a Mexico City think tank. "Now it's an economic motor. The government has little incentive to crack down, and frankly views border security as a domestic issue for the U.S."   25

Community initiatives like the Eco Alberto Park aren't going to reverse these numbers. The income from the roughly 100 jobs created by the park is dwarfed by the regular bundles of cash sent back by Otomi working construction jobs in Las Vegas. Migrants will continue to go north as long as there is work there, no matter the mounting dangers illustrated by the border simulation. The same is true at border points around the globe where the poor live within walking or swimming distance of a better life. You can see it in Spain's African enclave of Ceuta, bordering Morocco, where would-be migrants routinely charge guarded double walls topped with razor wire or attempt to swim the 13-mile Strait of Gibraltar.   26

Ask any struggling Mexican if U.S. plans for a high-tech border fence will stop the flow, and he will tell you the idea is fanciful, that you cannot deter the desperate. "If you build a wall, they will build taller ladders or dig deeper tunnels," says del Plan. "If the entire border becomes clogged with armed guards, they will take boats, as the Cubans and Haitians do." Indeed, this shift is already happening. Coast Guard interdictions of Mexican boats off the coast of San Diego are on the rise, as are reports of fatal capsizings.   27

But none of this directly concerns the kids with whom I pretended to be a migrant. Mexico's growing middle class has more in common with its American counterpart than with people like the Otomi. Despite the Otomi talk of "one Mexico" and hopes of   28

---

[2]maquiladora: Assembly plants that receive parts from the United States and ship products back to the U.S.

building solidarity with the migrants, the two Mexicos reappear as soon as we return, exhausted and bruised, to the Eco Alberto campsite. At a fire I sip Modelos with a group of university students ruminating on the night's adventure. There is a comparison of light wounds, some laughter over the simulation's low-fi effects. The talk quickly turns to football.

Examining the Reading

1. What activity are Zaitchik and the other people in the narrative engaging in?
2. Why do people participate in the Night Hike?
3. In what ways does the Night Hike simulate real illegal border crossings?
4. What does Zaitchik think of border fences as a deterrent to illegal crossings?
5. Explain the meaning of each of the following words as it is used in the reading: *simulation* (para. 7), *hyperthermic* (14), *histrionic* (18), *mercenary* (24), and *interdictions* (27).

Analyzing the Writer's Technique

1. What is Zaitchik's thesis? Is it stated or implied?
2. Who seems to be Zaitchik's intended audience? How can you tell?
3. Explain how Zaitchik uses description to make his experience vivid and engaging. Cite several examples.
4. What argument does Zaitchik make about illegal immigration?

Thinking Critically about Text and Visuals

1. What tone does the author set in paragraph 1 with the phrase "fanged, baying beasts"?
2. What connotation do the phrases "Diesel jeans" and "gelled emo haircuts" (para. 5) have? What is the author saying about the people who are with him?
3. What evidence other than personal experiences (16 and 17) might the author have used to describe illegal border crossings?
4. In paragraph 27, is the statement by del Plan fact or opinion?
5. The photographs on pages 260 and 261 show people participating in the Night Walk. How do these photographs differ from what you might expect to see in photographs of actual illegal border crossings?
6. What additional insights do the photographs provide that the essay does not?

Reacting to the Reading

1. What do you think Zaitchik learned from the simulated border-crossing?
2. What does Zaitchik suggest is the future of illegal immigration from Mexico? Why does he believe this to be the case?
3. Write a journal entry exploring or explaining your position on immigration.

Applying Your Skills: Additional Essay Assignments

For more on locating and documenting sources, see Part 5.

Write a narrative on one of the topics listed below, using the elements and techniques of narration you learned in this chapter. Depending on the topic you choose, you may need to do library or Internet research to gather enough support for your ideas.

To Express Your Ideas

1. Write a narrative about an incident or experience that you see differently now than you did when it happened.
2. In "Right Place, Wrong Face," White says he always believed that the police "were supposed to serve and protect" him. After the incident he describes in the essay, White feels otherwise. Write a narrative describing an incident involving police officers or law enforcement agents that you may have experienced, observed, or read about. Did the incident change your attitude about police or law enforcement or confirm opinions you already held?

To Inform Your Reader

3. Write an essay informing your reader about the characteristics of a strong (or weak) relationship, the habits of successful (or unsuccessful) students, or the ways of keeping (or losing) a job. Use a narrative to support one or more of your main points.

To Persuade Your Reader

4. "Selling in Minnesota" discusses the working conditions at Wal-Mart, where the author worked in the clothing department. Have you been treated very poorly or particularly well by an employee? Do you think that store employees are polite or rude? Do you have low expectations for them given the nature of the job and the pay? Are improvements or changes needed? Write an essay taking a position on this issue. Support your position using a narrative of your experience with clerks or employees.
5. "Alien World" uses argument to further the author's position on illegal immigration. Write an essay persuading your reader to take a particular stand on an issue of your choosing. Use a narrative to support your position on the issue or tell how you arrived at it.

Cases Using Narration

6. Write a paper for a sociology course on the advantages of an urban, suburban, or rural lifestyle. Support some of your main points with events and examples from your own experiences.

7. Write a draft of the presentation you will give as the new personnel director of a nursing care facility in charge of training new employees. You plan to hold your first orientation session next week, and you want to emphasize the importance of teamwork and communication by telling related stories from your previous job experiences.

CHAPTER 12

Description: Portraying People, Places, and Things

Suppose you are moving to a large city and need to sell your car because the apartment you just rented does not include parking. You post the following advertisement on the local Craigslist:

12-year-old VW bug. $4,500 or best offer. Call 555-2298.

Two weeks after you post the ad, you have gotten only a few calls and no offers. Then a friend advises you to write a more appealing description of your unique vehicle that will make people want to contact you. Rewrite the advertisement, describing the car in a way that will convince prospective buyers to call you.

WRITING A DESCRIPTION

In rewriting the description of the car, did you describe how it looks — its funky paint job and its 1960s appeal? Perhaps you focused on its compact qualities — easy to park, high gas mileage, and uncomplicated mechanical maintenance? If you did either or both of these things, you have written a successful description. In this chapter, you will learn how to write descriptions and how to use description to support and develop your ideas.

What Is Description?

Description presents information in a way that appeals to one or more of the five senses — sight, sound, smell, taste, and touch — usually creating an overall impression or feeling. You use description every day, to describe a pair of shoes you bought, a flavor of ice cream you tasted, or a concert you recently attended.

Description is an important and useful communication skill. If you were an eyewitness to a car theft, for example, the detective investigating the crime would ask you to describe what you saw. You will also use description in many situations in college and on the job, as the examples in the accompanying box show.

Writers rely on description to present detailed information about people, places, and things and to grasp and sustain their readers' interest. When you write vivid descriptions, you not only make your writing more lively and interesting but also indicate your attitude toward the subject through your choice of words and details.

In the following lively description of a sensory experience of taste, you will feel as if you, too, are eating chilli peppers.

SCENES FROM COLLEGE AND THE WORKPLACE

- For a *chemistry* lab report, you are asked to describe the odor and appearance of a substance made by combining two chemicals.

- In an *art history* class, your instructor asks you to visit a local gallery, choose a particular painting, and describe in a two-page paper the artist's use of line or color.

- As a *nurse* at a local burn treatment center, one of your responsibilities is to record on each patient's chart the overall appearance of and change in second- and third-degree burns.

Eating Chilli Peppers
Jeremy MacClancy

READING

Jeremy MacClancy is an anthropologist and tutor at Oxford Brookes University in England who has written several scholarly works in the field of anthropology. This essay is taken from his book *Consuming Culture: Why You Eat What You Eat* (1993). As you read the selection, underline or highlight the descriptive words and phrases that convey what it's like to eat chilli peppers.

How come over half of the world's population have made a powerful chemical irritant the 1 center of their gastronomic lives? How can so many millions stomach chillies?

Biting into a tabasco pepper is like aiming a flame-thrower at your parted lips. There 2 might be little reaction at first, but then the burn starts to grow. A few seconds later the chilli mush in your mouth reaches critical mass and your palate prepares for liftoff. The message spreads. The sweat glands open, your eyes stream, your nose runs, your stomach warms up, your heart accelerates, and your lungs breathe faster. All this is normal. But bite off more than your body can take, and you will be left coughing, sneezing, and spitting. Tears stripe your cheeks, and your mouth belches fire like a dragon celebrating its return to life. Eater beware!

As a general stimulant, chilli is similar to amphetamines—only quicker, cheaper, 3 non-addictive, and beneficial to boot. Employees at the tabasco plant in Louisiana rarely complain of coughs, hay fever, or sinusitis. (Recent evidence, however, suggests that too many chillies can bring on stomach cancer.) Over the centuries, people have used hot peppers as a folk medicine to treat sore throats or inflamed gums, to relieve respiratory distress, and to ease gastritis induced by alcoholism. For aching muscles and tendons, a chilli plaster is more effective than one of mustard, with the added advantage that it does not blister the skin. But people do not eat tabasco, jalapeno, or cayenne peppers because of their pharmacological side-effects. They eat them for the taste—different varieties have different flavors—and for the fire they give off. In other words, they go for the burn.

Eating chillies makes for exciting times: the thrill of anticipation, the extremity of the 4 flames, and then the slow descent back to normality. This is a benign form of masochism, like going to a horror movie, riding a roller coaster, or stepping into a cold bath after a sauna. The body flashes danger signals, but the brain knows the threat is not too great. Aficionados, self-absorbed in their burning passion, know exactly how to pace their whole chilli eating so that the flames are maintained at a steady maximum. Wrenched out of normal routines by the continuing assault on their mouths, they concentrate on the sensation and ignore almost everything else. They play with fire and just ride the burn, like experienced surfers cresting along a wave. For them, without hot peppers, food would lose its zest and their days would seem too dull. A cheap, legal thrill, chilli is the spice of their life.

In the rural areas of Mexico, men can turn their chilli habit into a contest of strength by 5 seeing who can stomach the most hot peppers in a set time. This gastronomic test, however, is not used as a way to prove one's machismo, for women can play the game as well. In this context, chillies are a non-sexist form of acquired love for those with strong hearts and fiery passions—a steady source of hot sauce for their lives.

The enjoyable sensations of a running nose, crying eyes, and dragon-like mouth belch- 6 ing flames are clearly not for the timorous.

More tabasco, anyone? 7

Characteristics of Descriptive Writing

Successful descriptions offer readers more than just a list of sensory details or a catalog of characteristics. In a good description, the details work together to create a dominant effect or impression. Writers often use comparison to help readers experience what they are writing about.

Description Uses Sensory Details

Sensory details appeal to one or more of the five senses — sight, sound, smell, taste, and touch. For example, in the second paragraph of "Eating Chilli Peppers" (p. 269), MacClancy describes the physical sensations that chilli peppers create by using vivid language that appeals to the senses of sight and taste. By appealing to the senses in your writing, you too can help your readers experience the object, sensation, event, or person you aim to describe.

Sight. When you describe what something looks like, you help your reader create a mental picture of the subject. In the following excerpt, notice how Loren Eiseley uses visual detail to describe what he comes across in a field.

> One day as I cut across the field which at that time extended on one side of our suburban shopping center, I found a giant slug feeding from a funnel of pink ice cream in an abandoned Dixie cup. I could see his eyes telescope and protrude in a kind of dim, uncertain ecstasy as his dark body bunched and elongated in the curve of the cup.
>
> Loren Eiseley, "The Brown Wasps"

Eiseley describes shape ("funnel"), action ("bunched and elongated"), color ("pink," "dark"), and size ("giant") and includes details ("suburban shopping center," "Dixie cup") to help readers visualize the scene.

The description allows the reader to imagine the slug eating the ice cream in a way that a bare statement of the facts — "On my way to the mall, I saw a slug in a paper cup" — would not do.

Sound. Sound can also be a powerful descriptive tool. Can you "hear" the engines in the following description?

> They were one-cylinder and two-cylinder engines, and some were make-and-break and some were jump-spark, but they all made a sleepy sound across the lake. The one-lungers throbbed and fluttered, and the twin-cylinder ones purred and purred, and that was a quiet sound too. But now the campers all had outboards. In the daytime, in the hot mornings, these motors made a petulant, irritable sound; at night, in the still evening when the afterglow lit the water, they whined about one's ears like mosquitoes.
>
> E. B. White, "Once More to the Lake"

White conveys the sounds of the engines by using active verbs ("throbbed and fluttered," "purred and purred," "whined"), descriptive adjectives ("sleepy," "petulant," "irritable"), and a comparison ("like mosquitoes").

Writers of description also use *onomatopoeia*, words that approximate the sounds they describe. The words *hiss, whine, spurt,* and *sizzle* are common examples.

Smell. Smells are sometimes difficult to describe, partly because we do not have as many adjectives for smells as we do for sights and sounds. Smell can be an effective descriptive device, however, as shown here.

Driving through farm country at summer sunset provides a cavalcade of smells: manure, cut grass, honeysuckle, spearmint, wheat chaff, scallions, chicory, tar from the macadam road.

Diane Ackerman, *A Natural History of the Senses*

Notice how Ackerman lists nouns that evoke distinct odors and leaves it to the reader to imagine how they smell.

Taste. Words that evoke the sense of taste can make descriptions lively, as in "Eating Chilli Peppers." Consider also this restaurant critic's description of Vietnamese cuisine.

In addition to balancing the primary flavors — the sweet, sour, bitter, salty and peppery tastes whose sensations are, in the ancient Chinese system, directly related to physical and spiritual health — medicinal herbs were used in most dishes. . . . For instance, the orange-red annatto seed is used for its "cooling" effect as well as for the mildly tangy flavor it lends and the orange color it imparts.

Molly O'Neill, "Vietnam's Cuisine: Echoes of Empires"

Notice that O'Neill describes the variety of flavors ("sweet, sour, bitter, salty and peppery") in Vietnamese cuisine as well as the distinctive flavor ("mildly tangy") of annatto seeds.

Touch. Descriptions of texture, temperature, and weight allow a reader not only to visualize but almost to experience an object or a scene. In the excerpt that follows, Annie Dillard describes the experience of holding a Polyphemus moth cocoon.

We passed the cocoon around; it was heavy. As we held it in our hands, the creature within warmed and squirmed. We were delighted, and wrapped it tighter in our fists. The pupa began to jerk violently, in heart-stopping knocks. Who's there? I can still feel those thumps, urgent through a muffling of spun silk and leaf, urgent through the swaddling of many years, against the curve of my palm. We kept passing it around. When it came to me again it was hot as a bun; it jumped half out of my hand. The teacher intervened. She put it, still heaving and banging, in the ubiquitous Mason jar.

Annie Dillard, *Pilgrim at Tinker Creek*

Dillard describes the texture of the cocoon ("a muffling of spun silk and leaf"), its temperature ("warmed," "hot as a bun"), its weight ("heavy"), and its motion ("squirmed," "jerk violently, in heart-stopping knocks," "thumps," "jumped," "heaving and banging") to give readers an accurate sense of what it felt like to hold it.

Description Uses Active Verbs and Varied Sentences

Sensory details are often best presented through active, vivid verbs and varied sentences. Look, for instance, at the active verbs in this sentence from paragraph 2 of MacClancy's essay.

The sweat glands *open,* your eyes *stream,* your nose *runs,* your stomach *warms up,* your heart *accelerates,* and your lungs *breathe* faster.

In fact, active verbs are often more effective than adverbs in creating striking and lasting impressions, as the following example demonstrates.

ORIGINAL   The team captain *proudly* accepted the award.

REVISED   The team captain *marched* to the podium, *grasped* the trophy, and *gestured* toward his teammates.

Using varied sentences also contributes to the effective expression of sensory details. Be sure to use different types and patterns of sentences and to vary their lengths. Look again at the second paragraph in MacClancy's essay. Note how he varies his sentences to make the description interesting.

For more on varying sentence patterns and using active verbs, see Chapter 10, pp. 206–12 and 213–14.

Exercise 12.1

*Using **sensory details**, **active verbs**, and **varied sentences**, describe one of the common objects in the following list or one of your own choosing. Do not name the object in your description. Exchange papers with a classmate. Your reader should be able to guess the item you are describing from the details you provide.*

1. A piece of clothing
2. A food item
3. An appliance
4. A machine
5. A plant or animal

Description Creates a Dominant Impression

An effective description leaves the reader with a **dominant impression** — an overall attitude, mood, or feeling about the subject. The impression may be awe, inspiration, anger, or distaste, for example.

For more on thesis statements, see Chapter 6, pp. 125–28.

Let's suppose that you are writing about an old storage box you found in your parents' attic. The aspect of the box you want to emphasize (your slant) is *memories of childhood.* Given this slant, or angle, you might describe the box in several ways, each of which would convey a different dominant impression.

- "A box filled with treasures from my childhood brought back memories of long, sunny afternoons playing in our backyard."
- "Opening the box was like lifting the lid of a time machine, revealing toys and games from another era."
- "When I opened the box, I was eight years old again, fighting over my favorite doll with my twin sister, Erica."

Notice that each example provides a different impression of the contents of the storage box and would require a different type of support. That is, only selected objects from within the box would be relevant to each impression. Note, too, that in all of these examples, the dominant impression is stated directly rather than implied. Many times, however, writers rely on descriptive language to imply a dominant impression.

In "Eating Chilli Peppers," notice how all the details evoke the thrill of eating the peppers for those who love them. As MacClancy says, "they go for the burn." The first two sentences of the essay pose the questions that the remaining paragraphs answer. The answer is the dominant impression: Eating chilli peppers is thrilling. To write an effective description, you need to select details carefully, including only those that contribute to the dominant impression you are trying to create. Notice that MacClancy does not clutter his description by describing the size, shape, texture, or color of chilli peppers. Instead he focuses on their thrilling, fiery hotness and the side effects they cause.

Exercise 12.2

Read the following paragraph and cross out details that do not contribute to the dominant impression.

All morning I had had some vague sense that something untoward was about to happen. I suspected bad news was on its way. As I stepped outside, the heat of the summer sun, unusually oppressive for ten o'clock, seemed to sear right through me. In fact, now that I think about it, everything seemed slightly out of kilter that morning. The car, which had been newly painted the week before, had stalled several times. The flowers in the garden, planted for me by my husband, purchased from a nursery down the road, were drooping. It was as though they were wilting before they even had a chance to grow. Even my two cats, who look like furry puffballs, moved listlessly across the room, ignoring my invitation to play. It was then that I received the phone call from the emergency room telling me about my son's accident.

Description Uses Connotative Language Effectively

As noted in Chapter 10, most words have two levels of meaning—denotative and connotative. The *denotation* of a word is its precise dictionary meaning. For instance, the denotation of the word *flag* is "a piece of cloth used as a national emblem." Usually, however, feelings and attitudes are also associated with a word—emotional colorings or shades of meaning. These are the word's *connotations*. A common connotation of *flag* is patriotism—love and respect for one's country. As you write, be careful about the connotations of the words you choose. Select words that strengthen the dominant impression you are creating.

Description Uses Comparisons

When describing a person or an object, you can help your readers by comparing the person or object to something with which they are familiar. Several types of comparisons are used in descriptive writing—similes, metaphors, personification, and analogies. In a **simile** the comparison is direct and is introduced by *like* or *as.* MacClancy uses a number of telling similes in "Eating Chilli Peppers."

For more on similes, metaphors, and personification, see Chapter 10, p. 219.

- "Biting into a tabasco pepper is like aiming a flame-thrower at your parted lips."
- Eating chillies is "like going to a horror movie, riding a roller coaster, or stepping into a cold bath after a sauna."

A **metaphor** is indirect, implying the comparison by describing one thing as if it were another. Instead of the similes listed above, MacClancy could have used metaphors to describe the experience of eating chillies.

- Eating chilli peppers is a descent into a fiery hell.
- To eat chilli peppers is to ride the crest of a wave, waiting for the thrill.

Personification is a figure of speech in which an object is given human qualities or characteristics. "The television screen stared back at me" is an example. An **analogy** is an extended comparison in which one subject, often a more familiar one, is used to explain another. Like similes and metaphors, analogies add interest to your writing while making your ideas more real and accessible.

> ### Exercise 12.3
>
> *Write a paragraph describing a food you enjoy. Focus on one sense, as MacClancy does, or appeal to several senses. If possible, draw a comparison using a simile or a metaphor.*

Description Follows a Method of Organization

For more on these methods of organization, see Chapter 7, pp. 143–48.

Effective descriptions must follow a clear method of organization. Three common methods of organization used in descriptive writing are spatial order, chronological order, and most-to-least or least-to-most order.

- When you use spatial order, you describe a subject in terms of the physical position of its parts—for example, from top to bottom, from left to right, or from near to far away. Or you may start from a central focal point and then describe the objects that surround it. For example, if you are describing a college campus, you might start by describing a building at the center of the campus—the library, perhaps. You would then describe the buildings that are near the library and conclude by describing anything on the outskirts of the campus.

   In writing a description using spatial order, you can use either a fixed or a moving **vantage point**. With a *fixed vantage point*, you describe what you see from a particular position. With a *moving vantage point*, you describe your subject from different positions. A fixed vantage point is like a stationary camera trained on a subject from one direction. A moving vantage point is like a handheld camera that captures the subject from many directions.
- Chronological order works well when you need to describe events or changes that occur in objects or places over a period of time. You might use chronological order to describe the changes in a puppy's behavior as it grows or to relate changing patterns of light and shadow as the sun sets.
- You might use most-to-least or least-to-most order to describe the smells in a flower garden or the sounds of an orchestra tuning up for a concert.

Visualizing a Description: A Graphic Organizer

For more on graphic organizers, see Chapter 3, pp. 59–61.

The graphic organizer shown in Figure 12.1 will help you visualize the elements of a description. When you write an essay in which your primary purpose is to describe something, you'll need to follow the standard essay format—title, introduction, body, and conclusion—with slight adaptations and adjustments. In a descriptive essay, the

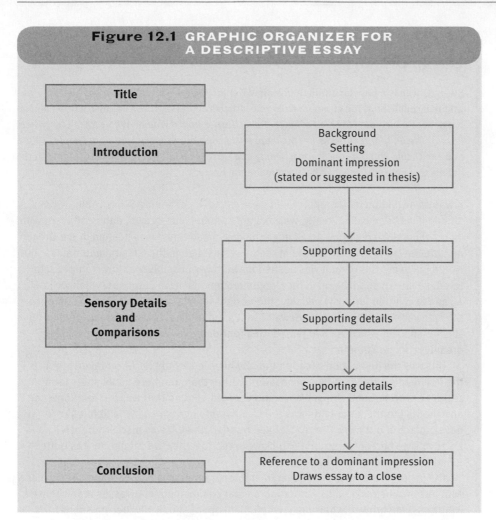

Figure 12.1 GRAPHIC ORGANIZER FOR A DESCRIPTIVE ESSAY

introduction provides a context for the description and presents the thesis statement, which states or suggests the dominant impression. The body of the essay presents sensory details that support the dominant impression. The conclusion draws the description to a close and makes a final reference to the dominant impression. It may offer a final detail or make a closing statement.

When you incorporate a description into an essay in which you also use other patterns of development, you will probably need to condense or eliminate one or more of the elements of a description essay.

The following essay, "Out of the Woods," is a good example of description. Read the essay and then study the graphic organizer for it in Figure 12.2 (p. 278).

Out of the Woods

Susan Orlean

Susan Orlean is a popular author and staff writer for *The New Yorker*, in which this essay was originally published. The author of numerous articles and essays, she has also written a number of books, including *My Kind of Place: Travel Stories from a Woman Who's Been Everywhere* (2005), *The Bullfighter Checks Her Makeup: My Encounters with Extraordinary People* (2002), and *The Orchid Thief: A True Story of Beauty and Obsession* (2000). As you read, highlight the details that help you visualize her vacation rental home.

It was an awful house. A broker would have called it a charming Swiss chalet; what it   1
should have been called, really, was a dingy A-frame, mud-brown, damp, afflicted with an air of unrelieved gloom. An ad might have claimed that it was nestled in the Oregon mountains — in fact, an ad did claim that it was nestled in the Oregon mountains — but would fail to mention that it was nestled in what was possibly the only cramped, cluttered, suburban subdivision in the Oregon mountains. It was probably when we saw a gang of children furiously pedaling their bright-orange-red Big Wheels up and down the sidewalk — Big Wheels? A sidewalk? In the mountains? — that we realized that this vacation house, which we had rented for a four-day getaway, might not be quite as dreamy as it had sounded.

This was the first actual vacation that my boyfriend and I had ever taken together —   2
the first official, grownup type of vacation, rather than our more usual short-term residences on friends' sofas. We weren't very old, and neither was our relationship, and the visit to the mountains was a watershed moment to see what it felt like to have a place of our own. The chalet had sounded ideal. It was also inexpensive, and since we had only a couple of nickels to rub together, we thought it was quite a find.

The inside of the house did seem tolerable. Granted, it was a worn-out, weary place   3
with lots of aches and pains — floorboards that complained, mattresses that wheezed, windows that shrieked when you pushed them open — but it was decent shelter. We walked around, opening cupboards and checking behind doors, taking inventory. Bedroom, fine. Bleak little kitchen, fine. Living room, fine. Bathroom, we must have missed it. We walked through the house again, opening every door a second time, then a third. There appeared to be no bathroom. Had either of us inquired when we arranged to rent the house whether it had a bathroom? Of course we hadn't — who would? It would have been like asking if the place had, say, a roof. We glanced out the kitchen window. In a mangy patch of yard, there appeared to be a heap of two-by-fours, which revealed themselves, upon investigation, to be the remains of an outhouse that must have been blown down in a storm. There was no righting it; the structure hadn't just toppled — it had exploded. So the house had once been equipped with a bathroom-type facility, although the fact that it was an outhouse seemed like something a broker might have wanted to mention.

I had been a pretty good Brownie in my day, and my boyfriend had been an avid   4
camper, so the idea of peeing in the woods was not new or discomfiting to either of us.
However, we were not in the woods. We were in a kind of Levittown, relocated to the
lovely Oregon mountains. There was no leafy glade nearby; there was no private little
thicket. Instead, there was a family just a few yards away in the house next door, with a
whale of an R.V. parked in the driveway and a swing set that gave the kiddies a good view
of our comings and goings. Furthermore, the weather was turning grim, the sky dropping
lower, the clouds starting to spit a chilly rain, all of which made our moldy mud-brown
dream-vacation home seem moldier and browner and more bathroomless by the minute.

Town was a couple of miles away. There was a Gas-N-Eat or a Stop-N-Fuel, or what-   5
ever it was called, at the end of the main drag. It had bathrooms, but it was one of
those joints where you had to go in to the cashier and ask for a key and then go back
outside to the bathroom, a cold, dimly lit concrete-block cubicle that a truck-stop pros-
titute might have found homey and familiar. We were, of course, not in a position to
fuss. We made use of the Petrol-N-Go, had dinner in town, and then stopped in again,
just to be safe. In the morning, we threw jackets on over our pajamas and made a bee-
line for the gas station. The rain, intermittent the day before, had turned apocalyptic.
We holed up in the house for the afternoon, limiting our liquids. We had counted on
the changing shifts of cashiers to keep our very frequent visits from being totted up,
but the cashiers, evidently, chatted among themselves. By the third day, racing in
at seven for our morning constitutional, wet coats akimbo over our nightclothes, we
felt — how to put this exactly? — not welcome. Even the house had turned against us,
beading up with wetness on nearly every surface, little rivulets of rain threading their
way across windowpanes and walls: so much water, and none of it running. But we
were. With one more day coming to us, we finally gave in. We packed our damp belongings, stopped in for a last visit at the gas station, and headed home.

Exercise 12.4

*After examining each part of MacClancy's "Eating Chilli Peppers" (p. 269), draw a graphic
organizer that shows how this essay is constructed.*

To draw detailed graphic
organizers using a computer,
visit www.bedfordstmartins
.com/successfulcollege.

Integrating Description into an Essay

Sometimes description alone fulfills the purpose of an essay. In most cases, however,
you will use description in other types of essays. For instance, in a narrative essay,
description helps readers experience events, reconstruct scenes, and visualize action.
Similarly, description can explain the causes or effects of a phenomenon, to compare
or contrast animal species, and to provide examples of defensive behavior in children
(illustration). Writers use description to keep their readers interested in the material.
Description, then, is essential to many types of academic and business writing.

Figure 12.2 GRAPHIC ORGANIZER FOR "OUT OF THE WOODS"

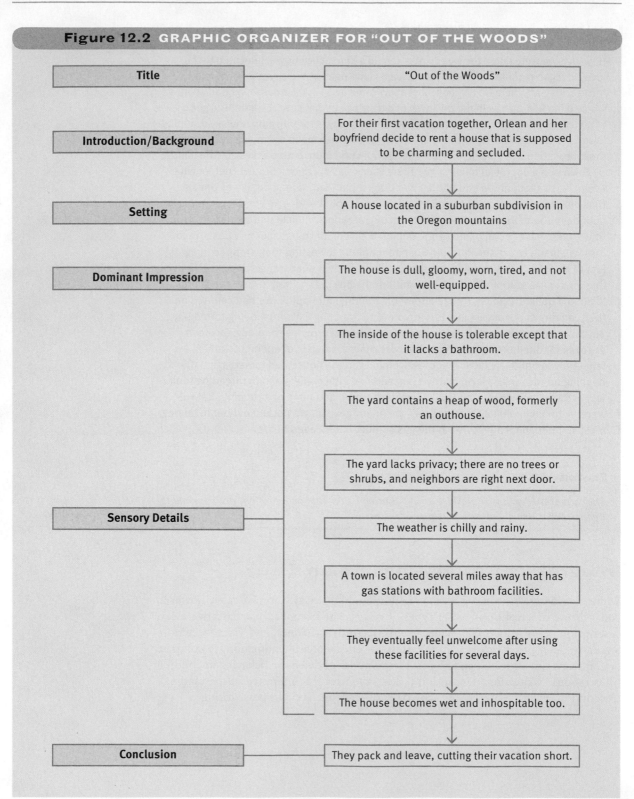

Use the following guidelines to build effective description into the essays you write:

1. **Include only relevant details.** Whether you describe an event, a person, or a scene, the sensory details you choose should enhance the reader's understanding of your subject.
2. **Keep the description focused.** Select enough details to make your essential points and dominant impression clear. Readers may become impatient if you include too many details.
3. **Make sure the description fits the essay's tone and point of view.** A personal description, for example, is not appropriate in an essay explaining a technical process.

In "Bloggers without Borders . . ." on pages 298–300, the author incorporates description into a narrative essay.

A GUIDED WRITING ASSIGNMENT

The following guide will lead you through the process of writing an essay that uses description. You may choose to write a descriptive essay or to employ description within an essay that relies on another pattern of development. Depending on your learning style, you may choose to work through this Guided Writing Assignment in various ways. If you are an abstract learner, for example, you might begin by brainstorming about the general subject. If you are a concrete learner, you might prefer to begin by freewriting specific details. If you are a pragmatic learner, you might start by thinking about how to organize your description.

Learning Style Options

The Assignment

Write a descriptive essay using one of the following topics or one that you think of on your own:

1. An adult toy, such as a camera, a DVD player, a computer, golf clubs, or a cooking gadget
2. A hobby or sport that you enjoy doing or watching others do on campus, in your neighborhood, or on television
3. An annoying or obnoxious person or a pleasant, courteous one

Your classmates are your audience.

As you develop your description, consider using other patterns of development. For example, you might compare and contrast an unfamiliar activity to one you engage in regularly, or you might narrate an incident that reveals a person's positive or negative qualities.

For more on comparison and contrast, see Chapter 15. For more on narration, see Chapter 11.

Generating Ideas and Details

Use the following steps to help you choose a topic and generate ideas.

Choosing a Topic

For more on conducting observations, see Chapter 22, pp. 617–18.

To write an effective description, you must be familiar with the subject or have the opportunity to observe the subject directly. Never try to describe the campus computer lab without visiting it or the pizza served in the snack bar without tasting it.

Use the following suggestions to choose an appropriate topic:

For more on prewriting strategies, see Chapter 5.

1. Use freewriting, mapping, group brainstorming, or another prewriting technique to generate a list of objects, activities, or people that fit the assignment.
2. Look over your list of possible topics. Identify the one or two subjects that you find most interesting and that you can describe in detail.
3. Make sure your subject is one you are familiar with or one you can readily observe. You may need to observe the object, activity, or person several times as you work through your essay.

> ### Essay in Progress 1
> Using the preceding suggestions, choose a topic to write about for the assignment option you selected on page 279.

Considering Your Purpose, Audience, and Point of View

A descriptive essay may be objective, subjective, or both, depending on the writer's purpose. In an *objective* essay, the writer's purpose is to inform—to present information or communicate ideas without obvious bias or emotion. All writers convey their feelings to some extent, but in an objective essay the writer strives to focus on giving information. For example, a geologist's description of a rock formation written for a scientific journal would be largely objective; its purpose would be to inform readers of the height of the formation, the type of rock it contains, and other characteristics of the subject. Objective essays are generally written in the third person.

For more on purpose, audience, and point of view, see Chapter 5, pp. 106–9.

In a *subjective* essay, which is often written in the first person, the writer's purpose is to create an emotional response. Whereas an objective essay describes only what the writer observes or experiences, a subjective essay describes both the observation or experience *and* the writer's feelings about it. Therefore, a rock climber's description of a rock formation would focus on the writer's impressions of and reactions to the experience of climbing it, such as the feeling of the smooth rock on a hot day and the exhilaration of reaching the top. But the rock climber's description might also include objective details about the height and composition of the rock formation to help readers see and feel what it's like to climb one.

Once you've chosen a subject and considered your purpose and point of view, think about your audience. For this assignment, your audience is your classmates. How familiar are your classmates with your subject? If they are unfamiliar with the subject, you will need to provide a more thorough introduction and a greater amount of detail than if your audience has some knowledge of it.

Choosing an Aspect of Your Subject to Emphasize

Almost any subject you choose will be made up of many more details than you could possibly include in an essay. Start by selecting several possible slants, or angles on your subject that you would like to emphasize. If your subject is a person, you might focus on a particular character trait, such as compulsiveness or sense of humor, and then generate a list of descriptive details that illustrate the trait. To describe an object, you might emphasize its usefulness, value, or beauty. Choose the one slant that seems most promising and for which you generated plenty of sensory details.

For more on narrowing a topic, see Chapter 5, pp. 104–6.

> **Essay in Progress 2**
> Using one or more prewriting techniques, come up with several possible slants on your subject and details to support them. Then choose the slant about which you can write the most effective description.

Collecting Details That Describe Your Subject

Once you've decided on a slant to emphasize, you're ready for the next step—collecting and recording additional sensory details. The following suggestions will help you generate details:

1. Brainstorm about your subject. Record any sensory details that support the slant you have chosen.
2. Try describing your subject to a friend, concentrating on the slant you have chosen. You may discover that details come quickly during conversation. Make notes on what you said and on your friend's response.
3. Draw a quick sketch of your subject and label the parts. You may find yourself recalling additional details as you draw.
4. Divide a piece of paper or a computer file into five sections. Label the sections *sight*, *sound*, *taste*, *touch*, and *smell*. Consider the following characteristics in developing sensory details.

Learning Style Options

For more on generating details, see Chapter 5, pp. 112–13.

For more on prewriting strategies, see Chapter 5.

TABLE 12.1 Characteristics to Consider in Developing Sensory Details

Sight	Sound	Smell	Taste	Touch
Color	Volume	Agreeable/ disagreeable	Pleasant/ unpleasant	Texture
Pattern	Pitch	Strength	Salty, sweet, sour, bitter	Weight
Shape	Quality			Temperature
Size				

Finding Comparisons and Choosing a Vantage Point

Try to think of appropriate comparisons — similes, metaphors, or analogies — for as many details in your list as possible. Jot down your comparisons in the margin next to the relevant details in your list. Don't expect to find a comparison for each detail. Your goal is to discover one or two strong comparisons that you can use in your essay.

Next consider whether to use a fixed or moving vantage point. Ask yourself the following questions:

1. What vantage point(s) will provide the most useful information?
2. From which vantage point(s) can I provide the most revealing or striking details?

> **Essay in Progress 3**
> Use one or more of the preceding suggestions to develop details that support the aspect of your subject that you are emphasizing. Then find comparisons and decide on a vantage point.

Evaluating Your Details

Evaluate the details you have collected to determine which ones you can use in your essay. Begin by rereading all of your notes with a critical eye. Highlight vivid, concrete details that will create pictures in your reader's mind. Eliminate vague details as well as those that do not support your slant on the subject. If you are working on a computer, highlight usable ideas by making them bold or moving them to a separate page or document for easy access when drafting.

> **Trying Out Your Ideas on Others**
>
> Working in a group of two or three students, discuss your ideas and details for this chapter's assignment. Each writer should explain his or her slant on the subject and provide a list of the details collected for the subject. Then, as a group, evaluate the writer's details and suggest improvements.

> **Essay in Progress 4**
> Use your notes and the comments of your classmates to evaluate the details you have collected so far. Omit irrelevant and vague details, and add more vivid and concrete details if they are needed.

Creating a Dominant Impression

As noted earlier, think of the dominant impression as a thesis that conveys your main point and holds the rest of your essay together. The dominant impression also creates a mood or feeling about the subject, which all other details in your essay explain or support. The dominant impression you decide on should be the one about which you feel most knowledgeable and confident. It should also appeal to your audience, offer an unusual perspective, and provide new insights on your subject.

Essay in Progress 5

Using the preceding guidelines, select the dominant impression you want to convey about your subject, and do additional prewriting, if necessary, to gather enough details to support it.

Organizing and Drafting

When you are satisfied with your dominant impression and your support for it, you are ready to organize your ideas and draft your essay.

For more on drafting an essay, see Chapter 7.

Choosing a Method of Organization

Select the method of organization that will best support your dominant impression. For example, if you have chosen to focus on a person's slovenly appearance, then a spatial (top to bottom, left to right) organization may be effective. If you are describing a scary visit to a wildlife preserve, then chronological order would be a useful method of organization. A most-to-least or least-to-most arrangement might work best for a description of the symptoms of pneumonia. Also consider organizing your details by the five senses. For instance, to describe a chocolate-chip cookie, you could give details about how it looks, how it smells, how it tastes, and how it feels in your mouth.

If you are working on a computer, cut and paste to try different methods of organization.

Regardless of which method you choose for organizing your details, be sure to connect your ideas and guide your reader with transitional words and phrases.

For a list of transitions, see Chapter 8, pp. 175–76.

Drafting the Description

As you draft your essay, remember that all of your details must support your dominant impression. Other details, no matter how interesting or important they may seem, should not be included. For example, if you are describing the way apes in a zoo imitate one another and humans, only details about how the apes mimic other apes and people should be included. Other details, such as the condition of the apes' environment and the types of animals nearby, do not belong in the essay. Be careful as well about the *number* of details you include. Too many details will tire your readers, but an insufficient number will leave your readers unconvinced of your main point. Select striking sensory details that make your point effectively; leave out details that tell the reader little or nothing.

For more on writing effective paragraphs, including introductions and conclusions, see Chapter 7.

Try also to include one or two telling metaphors or similes. If you cannot think of any, however, don't stretch to construct them. Effective comparisons usually come to mind as you examine your subject. Contrived comparisons will only lessen the impact of your essay.

As you write your description, remember that the sensory language you use should enable your readers to re-create the person, object, or scene in their minds. Keep the following three guidelines in mind as you write:

1. **Create images that appeal to the five senses.** As noted earlier, your descriptions should appeal to one or more of the senses. See pages 270–71 for examples of ways to engage each of the five senses.

2. **Avoid vague, general descriptions.** Use specific, not vague, language to describe your subject. Notice the differences between the following descriptions.

VAGUE	**The pizza was cheaply prepared.**
CONCRETE	**The supposedly "large" pizza was miniature, with a nearly imperceptible layer of sauce, a light dusting of cheese, a few paper-thin slices of pepperoni, and one or two stray mushroom slices.**

Vivid descriptions hold your readers' interest and give them a more complete picture of your subject. For example, notice how the list below becomes increasingly more concrete.

Animal → dog → golden retriever → male golden retriever → six-month-old male golden retriever puppy → Ivan, my six-month-old male golden retriever puppy

You can create a similar progression of descriptive words for any person, object, or place that you want to describe.

3. **Use figures of speech and analogies effectively.** Figures of speech (similes, metaphors) and analogies create memorable images that enliven your writing and capture your readers' attention. Here are some tips for using figurative language in your writing:

- Choose fresh, surprising images. Avoid overused clichés such as *cold as ice* and *it's a hop, skip, and a jump away.*
- Make sure the similarity between the two items being compared is apparent. If you write "Peter looked like an unpeeled tangerine," your reader will not be able to guess what characteristics Peter shares with the tangerine. "Peter's skin was as dimpled as a tangerine peel" gives the reader a clearer idea of what Peter looks like.
- Don't mix or combine figures of speech. Such expressions, called **mixed metaphors**, are confusing and often unintentionally humorous. For example, the following sentence mixes images of a hawk and a wolf.

The fighter jet was a hawk soaring into the clouds, growling as it sought its prey.

Essay in Progress 6

Draft your essay. Use the preceding suggestions to organize your details and support your dominant impression. Even if your essay is primarily descriptive, consider incorporating a narrative, an illustration, or a comparison (or another pattern of development) to strengthen the dominant impression.

Analyzing and Revising

If possible, set your draft aside for a day or two before rereading and revising it. As you reread, focus on overall effectiveness, not on grammar and mechanics. To analyze your draft, use one or more of the following strategies:

1. Reread your paper aloud, or ask a friend to do so as you listen. You may "hear" parts that seem contrived, skimpy, or do not work.

2. Ask a classmate to read your draft and describe the dominant impression, comparing his or her version to the one you intended. Note ideas that your reader overlooked or misinterpreted.

3. Write an outline or draw a graphic organizer (using the format shown on p. 275), or update the outline or graphic organizer you prepared earlier. Look for ideas that do not seem to fit or that lack supporting details and for places where your organization needs tightening.

Learning Style Options

Use Figure 12.3 to help you discover the strengths and weaknesses of your descriptive essay. You might also ask a classmate to review your essay using the questions in the flowchart. For each answer that refers you to the right column of the chart, ask your reviewer to explain why he or she answered in that way.

For more on the benefits of peer review, see Chapter 9, pp. 188–91.

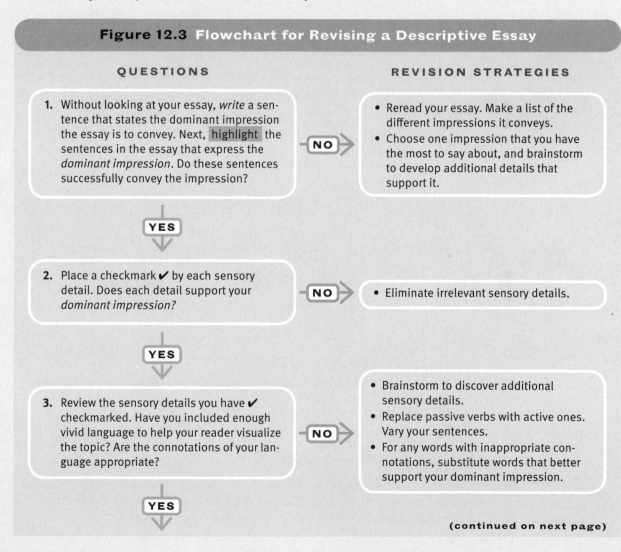

Figure 12.3 Flowchart for Revising a Descriptive Essay

QUESTIONS

REVISION STRATEGIES

1. Without looking at your essay, *write* a sentence that states the dominant impression the essay is to convey. Next, highlight the sentences in the essay that express the *dominant impression*. Do these sentences successfully convey the impression?

NO
- Reread your essay. Make a list of the different impressions it conveys.
- Choose one impression that you have the most to say about, and brainstorm to develop additional details that support it.

YES

2. Place a checkmark ✔ by each sensory detail. Does each detail support your *dominant impression?*

NO
- Eliminate irrelevant sensory details.

YES

3. Review the sensory details you have ✔ checkmarked. Have you included enough vivid language to help your reader visualize the topic? Are the connotations of your language appropriate?

NO
- Brainstorm to discover additional sensory details.
- Replace passive verbs with active ones. Vary your sentences.
- For any words with inappropriate connotations, substitute words that better support your dominant impression.

YES

(continued on next page)

(Figure 12.3 continued)

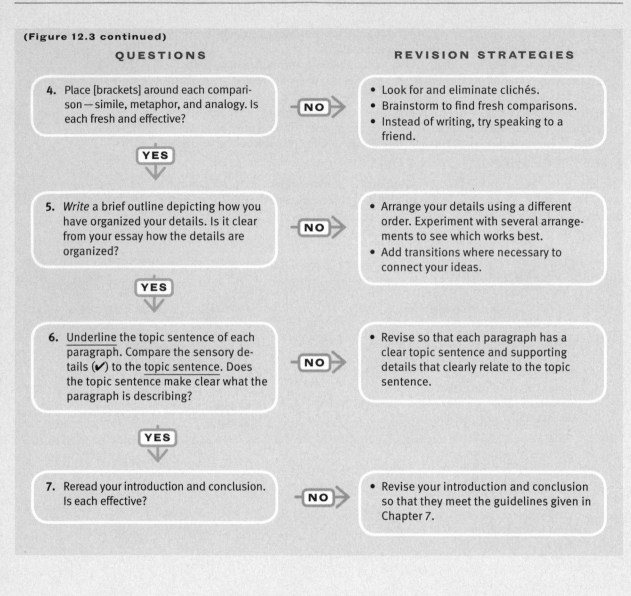

QUESTIONS

REVISION STRATEGIES

4. Place [brackets] around each comparison—simile, metaphor, and analogy. Is each fresh and effective?

–NO→

- Look for and eliminate clichés.
- Brainstorm to find fresh comparisons.
- Instead of writing, try speaking to a friend.

YES

5. *Write* a brief outline depicting how you have organized your details. Is it clear from your essay how the details are organized?

–NO→

- Arrange your details using a different order. Experiment with several arrangements to see which works best.
- Add transitions where necessary to connect your ideas.

YES

6. Underline the topic sentence of each paragraph. Compare the sensory details (✔) to the topic sentence. Does the topic sentence make clear what the paragraph is describing?

–NO→

- Revise so that each paragraph has a clear topic sentence and supporting details that clearly relate to the topic sentence.

YES

7. Reread your introduction and conclusion. Is each effective?

–NO→

- Revise your introduction and conclusion so that they meet the guidelines given in Chapter 7.

Essay in Progress 7
Using Figure 12.3 as a guide, as well as suggestions made by your classmate, revise your essay.

Editing and Proofreading

For more on keeping an error log, see Chapter 10, pp. 221–22.

The last step is to check your revised essay for errors in grammar, spelling, punctuation, and mechanics. Be sure to look for the types of errors you tend to make. (Refer to your error log.)

For descriptive writing, pay particular attention to the punctuation of adjectives. Keep the following rules in mind:

1. Use a comma between coordinate adjectives that are not joined by *and*.

■ Singh was a *confident, skilled* pianist.

Coordinate adjectives are a series of adjectives whose order can be changed (*skilled, confident pianist* or *confident, skilled pianist*).

2. Do not use commas between cumulative adjectives, whose order cannot be changed.

■ *Two frightened brown* eyes peered at us from under the sofa.

You would not write *frightened two brown eyes*.

3. Use a hyphen to connect two words that work together as an adjective before a noun unless the first word is an adverb ending in *-ly*.

■ *well-used* book
■ *foil-wrapped* pizza
■ *perfectly thrown* pass

Essay in Progress 8
Edit and proofread your essay, paying particular attention to the use and punctuation of adjectives and to the errors listed in your error log.

Students Write

Ted Sawchuck, a journalism student at the University of Maryland at College Park, wrote this essay in response to an assignment in one of his classes. He was asked to describe a workplace situation that he had experienced. As you read, study the annotations and pay particular attention to Sawchuck's use of sensory language that helps you see and feel what he has experienced.

Heatstroke with a Side of Burn Cream

Ted Sawchuck

READING

I sprinkle the last layer of cheese on top of my nachos--no time to watch the cheddar melt--and turn sideways, nearly falling face-first on grimy, spongy rubber mats. Catching my fall and the plate, I whip a towel from my belt with my free hand, open the scalding-hot oven door, and slide in the chips to toast before slapping a palm on top of the now-light-brown quesadilla on the rack below and pulling it out onto a clean part of the towel for a 180 degree turn to the counter behind. A pizza cutter makes three smooth cuts; the quesadilla is plated with three small cups

1

Introduction: Sawchuck builds toward his dominant impression by describing a hectic evening in a restaurant kitchen.

(guac, salsa, sour cream) and handed to the window. I slap the bell, bellow "Jamie! Nachos!", and spin back to my station too fast to see a gorgeous grad student scoop up the plate and scoot it out to her table.

Welcome to a restaurant kitchen during lunch or dinner rush, the time when the restaurant is packed with hungry people and the kitchen is maniacally cranking away at their orders. I'm thrashing appetizers, trying to keep up with college students' demands for fried goodies, nachos, and quesadillas. My friend A is working the grill, cooking fifteen burgers and a couple chicken breasts for sandwiches, and M, a mutual friend, is buzzing around prepping plates, flirting with waitresses, and handling salads and desserts, both of which require time away from the main preparation line.

2

The kitchen space I spend eight hours a day in is about the size of my one-room apartment, which is slightly larger than your average prison cell. Three people, and more on horribly busy days, work in that space, crammed in with four fryers, a massive grill, a griddle, an oven, a microwave, two refrigeration units with prep counters, bins of tortilla chips, a burning-hot steam table bigger than the grill, and vast tubs of bacon. If I put both arms out and rotated, I'd severely injure at least two people.

3

The most common problem for nonchefs is dealing with the heat. On one side of my work station are four fryers full of 350-degree oil. On the other, there is the steam table, so named because it boils water to keep things warm--especially deadly for forearms. Burns aren't the worst of it. You'll lose some skin, but you won't die. Overheating or dehydration can kill. When it's over 110 degrees in your workplace, fluid consumption is essential. I start gushing sweat the second I clock in and don't stop until about half an hour after clocking out. Even though we have huge buzzing exhaust fans to suck the greasy smoke away from our lungs and a warehouse-sized room fan to keep it at a low triple digits, I drink enough water to fill the steam table twice during busy times. My bandana frequently restrains ice cubes as well as rapidly tangling hair.

4

The fans add to the noise, as do the chattering servers, the head chef yelling out orders, other cooks yelling out updates, and the music. Some kitchens run on music, others don't. I like to blare NPR when it is just me and A working, but on nights with a full staff, the rap music that gives rap music a bad name is trotted out--you know the kind I mean--the mainstream, with pre-choreographed dances, predictable couplets about the joys of 'caine and loose women, and frequently more bleeped words than heard. The volume at which such music is played means I have to scream everything and never hear orders. It's like playing tennis with a ball that randomly disappears.

5

There are uncountable ways to damage yourself in a restaurant kitchen. If you didn't touch anything--just stood there--you'd still be at risk for smoke inhalation, steam burns, knife cuts from other people, spills, splatters, and being bowled over--because no one stands still in a professional

6

kitchen. Even walking in a kitchen is dangerous. The only time the kitchen floor at the to-remain-nameless restaurant at which I cook is clean is immediately after washing, a process that results in innumerable gallons of grody gray water and the inadvertent freeing of at least one mouse from his glue trap. Moving in that kitchen is a constant struggle. Because the floor is slippery red tile, we put down thick rubber mats, which make standing for eight hours much easier on the knees. Unfortunately, these mats are coated, nay permeated, with everything we've ever spilled on them. Moving is like trying to skate across a frying pan with butter strapped to your feet. Sometimes you'll need to use a skating-like sliding motion to get through without falling face-first in the awfulness. Falling is worse, because if you grab to catch something your options are a fryer (bad), the grill (worse), or your head chef (worst of all).

Working in a restaurant during rush makes journalism on deadline look like elementary basket-weaving. While reporters are expected to get everything right in every story, they're only writing at most three stories a day. At one point during the worst dinner rush I can remember, I was cooking five nachos, eight quesadillas, four sampler plates, and three orders of wings at the same time. I had to get every component of those dishes right, from the plate they were served on to the garnish, serving size, cooking temperature, and appearance--and I needed to have done it fifteen minutes ago because the customers have been waiting. They don't care that we're so stacked up there's no more room in the oven for the nachos and quesadillas that are stacking up. Did I mention sampler plates have four items each, all with different cooking times and prep methods?

Working in a restaurant kitchen is like speaking a foreign language. Once you stop thinking about it and just do it, you can keep up, sometimes. Other times, the pressure builds up. Maybe half the restaurant fills up in five minutes, or it's game night in a college town. Maybe the servers screwed up and gave you all their tables' orders at once instead of as they came in. Either way, you've got to shift into the next gear. Sometimes it means throwing on ten orders of wings in fryers only meant to hold eight, then garnishing a stack of plates for the main course guys so they can focus on getting twenty burgers of different doneness levels cooked properly. For the appetizer guy, it usually means never being allowed to make a mistake, because any delay in appetizer futzes the flow of the meal. The main course is being cooked at the same time, so if my stuff comes in late, then the properly cooked main course will either be overdone or arrive cold because no one wants the main course five minutes after receiving an appetizer.

When you're late in the restaurant world, it's called being in the weeds. The origin of the name is unclear, but friends of mine note that you hide bodies where weeds grow because it's a sign of low foot traffic. Being in the weeds is not as bad as rendition to Egypt, but everyone, servers and management included, can see you're behind. In addition to getting chewed out by the head chef (who would rather yell at you than help you), you lose any chance you had with

7

8

9

In the topic sentences of this paragraph and the next one, Sawchuck uses comparisons to try to convey the essence of restaurant kitchen work. Notice his organization for the essay: after several paragraphs presenting the concrete physical details of the job, he shifts to the more abstract issues of the mental complexity and time pressure involved.

Notice how the connotations of *futzes* support the dominant impression better than a more formal word such as *disrupts* would.

Sawchuck explains a term used in restaurant work that most readers will not know.

Conclusion: Sawchuck offers a final comment on restaurant kitchen work and makes a direct appeal to readers.

that subtle, kittenish server. Not holding your own on the line means much less fun after work. When you're in the weeds (or "weeded"), you can ask for help or suck it up. Asking for help is frowned upon; your only route is taking a breath and pulling yourself out. I spend a lot of time in the weeds, unsurprising for a kid whose only chef-like experience was making breakfast on Sundays at home and the occasional grilled cheese sandwich.

Like print journalism and the armed forces, professional cooking requires a very specific skill   10
set. If you've got it, get a good knife and get to practicing. If not, be a little nicer next time the entree doesn't come exactly when you expect it.

Analyzing the Writer's Technique

1. Describe Sawchuck's dominant impression about working in a restaurant kitchen. Is it stated explicitly or implied?
2. Which examples of sensory language did you find particularly strong and engaging? What makes them effective? Which, if any, are weak, and how can they be improved?
3. The annotations point out some of the numerous comparisons Sawchuck uses to explain his topic. Identify several others. Which ones are particularly effective? Do any seem ineffective? If so, why?
4. In addition to description, what other patterns of development does the writer use? How do these patterns make the description more effective?

Thinking Critically about Description

1. Sawchuck leaves out the name of the restaurant. What other information is omitted that might have given you a fuller understanding of Sawchuck or his job?
2. What is Sawchuck's tone? How does it affect your attitude toward the information that is contained in the essay?
3. One of the annotations (para. 8) points out the connotations of a particular word Sawchuck uses. In paragraph 4, how are the connotations of "gushing sweat" different from those of other language he could have chosen, such as "sweating profusely" or "gushing perspiration"? Do you think he made the best choice, given the dominant impression he is trying to create? Why or why not?
4. The phrase "in the weeds" (9) offers a visual metaphor. What connotations does this phrase have for you?

Reacting to the Essay

1. Sawchuck notes that falling behind on the job results in less fun after work. Have you found that job performance can affect off-the-job relationships with coworkers? If so, how?
2. Do you think Sawchuck is satisfied with his job despite the adverse working conditions? Discuss to what degree working conditions affect job performance and satisfaction.

(MAKING (CONNECTIONS)

Working Low-Paying Jobs

Both "Selling in Minnesota" (pp. 254–56) and "Heatstroke with a Side of Burn Cream" (pp. 287–90) describe the writer's work experiences. Ehrenreich works in Wal-Mart as a stock clerk, and Sawchuck works in a restaurant kitchen.

Analyzing the Readings

1. Compare how the two authors feel about their work experiences. How does each author reveal his or her attitudes? How were they the same, and how did they differ?
2. As a well-known writer who is researching low-paying jobs, Ehrenreich works "undercover," but Sawchuck is an actual worker. How do you think these differences affect the essays and the authors' reported experiences?

Essay Idea

Write an essay describing your work experiences. Choose one job you have held, describe it to create a dominant impression, and and explain whether your experiences were more similar to Ehrenreich's or Sawchuck's—or why they did not resemble those of either.

3. Is it possible to be "in the weeds" academically? Write a journal entry exploring either reasons for being in the weeds or ways to get yourself out of the weeds.
4. Sawchuck describes the time pressures he experiences. Write an essay describing the time pressures you experience in either an academic or a workplace setting.

READING A DESCRIPTION

The following section provides advice for reading descriptive essays. Two model essays illustrate the characteristics of description covered in this chapter and provide opportunities to examine, analyze, and react to the writer's ideas. The second essay uses a description as part of a narrative essay.

Working with Text: Reading Descriptive Essays

When you read descriptive essays, you are more concerned with impressions and images than you are with the logical progression of ideas. To get the full benefit of descriptive writing, you need to connect what you are reading to your own senses of sight, sound, smell, touch, and taste. Below are some guidelines for reading descriptive essays.

For more on reading strategies, see Chapter 3.

What to Look For, Highlight, and Annotate

1. Plan on reading the essay more than once. Read it the first time to get a general sense of what's going on in the essay. Then reread it, this time paying attention to sensory details and highlighting particularly striking ones.

2. Be alert for the dominant impression as you read. If it is not directly stated, ask yourself this question: How does the author want me to feel about the subject?

3. Identify the author's method of organization.

4. Analyze each paragraph and decide how it contributes to the dominant impression. In a marginal annotation, summarize your analysis.

5. Observe how the author uses language to achieve his or her effect; notice especially the use of comparisons, sentence structure, and active verbs.

6. Study the introduction and conclusion. How does the introduction engage readers? How does the conclusion bring the essay to a satisfying close?

7. Evaluate the title. What meaning does it contribute to the essay?

8. Use marginal annotations or your journal to record the thoughts and feelings the essay evokes in you. Try to answer these questions: What did I feel as I read? How did I respond? What feelings was I left with after reading the essay?

How to Find Ideas to Write About

For more on discovering ideas for a response paper, see Chapter 4.

Because you may be asked to write a response to a descriptive essay, look for ideas to write about as you read. Try to think of situations that evoked similar images and feelings in you. For example, if you are reading an essay describing the peace and serenity the author experienced at a remote lake in a forest, try to think of situations in which you felt peace and serenity or of how you felt when you visited a national park or wilderness area. Perhaps instead of pleasant feelings in this situation you had negative ones, such as anxiety about being in a remote spot. Such negative feelings may be worth exploring as well.

Thinking Critically about Description

The words a writer chooses to describe a subject can largely determine how readers view and respond to that subject. For example, suppose you want to describe a person's physical appearance. You can make the person seem attractive and appealing or ugly and repellent, depending on the details you choose and the words you select.

APPEALING   The stranger had an impish, childlike grin, a smooth complexion with high cheekbones, and strong yet gentle hands.

REPELLENT   The stranger had limp blond hair, cold vacant eyes, and teeth stained by tobacco.

Writers use details and word connotations to shape their essays and affect their readers' response. Use the following questions to think critically about the descriptions you read.

What Details Does the Writer Omit?

As you read an essay, ask yourself: What hasn't the writer told me? or What else would I like to know about the subject? As you have seen, writers often omit details because they are not relevant; they may also omit details that contradict the dominant impression they intend to convey.

To be sure you are getting a complete picture of a subject, consult more than one source of information. You have probably noticed that television news programs usually have slightly different slants on a news event, each offering different details or film footage. Once you view several versions of the same event, you eventually form your own impression of it by combining and synthesizing the various reports. Often, you must do the same thing when reading descriptions. Pull together information from several sources and form your own impression.

What Is the Writer's Attitude toward the Subject?

The sensory details writers choose often reveal their feelings and attitudes toward the subject. If a writer describes a car as "fast and sleek," the wording suggests approval, whereas if the writer describes it as "bold and glitzy," the wording suggests a less favorable attitude. As you read, pay attention to connotations; they are often used intentionally to create a particular emotional response. Get in the habit of highlighting words with strong connotations or annotating them in the margin.

Paying attention to connotations is one way to judge whether a writer is presenting a neutral, objective description or was influenced by positive or negative feelings when he or she wrote the description. For example, in thinking critically about Ted Sawchuk's "Heatstroke with a Side of Burn Cream," you might wonder how Sawchuck's friends and coworkers M and A might describe the scenes in the restaurant and the related physical and mental stresses differently than Sawchuck did.

DESCRIPTIVE ESSAY

As you read the following essay by Annie Dillard, consider how she uses the characteristics of description discussed in this chapter.

The Deer at Providencia
Annie Dillard

READING

Annie Dillard is a poet, essayist, fiction writer, and literary critic who is known for her writings about nature and humans' relation to it. Her works include *Pilgrim at Tinker Creek* (1975), for which she won a Pulitzer Prize; *The Writing Life* (1989); *The Living* (1992); *The Maytrees* (2007); and *Teaching a Stone to Talk* (1982), from which this essay was taken. As you read this descriptive essay, highlight the descriptive words and phrases that affect you most strongly.

There were four of us North Americans in the jungle, in the Ecuadorian jungle on the   1
banks of the Napo River in the Amazon watershed. The other three North Americans were

metropolitan men. We stayed in tents in one riverside village, and visited others. At the village called Providencia we saw a sight which moved us, and which shocked the men.

The first thing we saw when we climbed the riverbank to the village of Providencia was   2
the deer. It was roped to a tree on the grass clearing near the thatch shelter where we would eat lunch.

The deer was small, about the size of a whitetail fawn, but apparently full–grown. It   3
had a rope around its neck and three feet caught in the rope. Someone said that the dogs had caught it that morning and the villagers were going to cook and eat it that night.

This clearing lay at the edge of the little thatched hut village. We could see the vil-   4
lagers going about their business, scattering feed corn for hens about their houses, and wandering down paths to the river to bathe. The village headman was our host; he stood beside us as we watched the deer struggle. Several village boys were interested in the deer; they formed part of the circle we made around it in the clearing. So also did four businessmen from Quito who were attempting to guide us around the jungle. Few of the very different people standing in this circle had a common language. We watched the deer, and no one said much.

The deer lay on its side at the rope's very end, so the rope lacked slack to let it rest   5
its head in the dust. It was "pretty," delicate of bone like all deer, and thin-skinned for the tropics. Its skin looked virtually hairless, in fact, and almost translucent, like a membrane. Its neck was no thicker than my wrist; it was rubbed open on the rope, and gashed. Trying to paw itself free of the rope, the deer had scratched its own neck with its hooves. The raw underside of its neck showed red stripes and some bruises bleed-ing inside the muscles. Now three of its feet were hooked in the rope under its jaw. It could not stand, of course, on one leg, so it could not move to slacken the rope and ease the pull on its throat and enable it to rest its head.

Repeatedly the deer paused, motionless, its eyes veiled, with only its rib cage in   6
motion, and its breaths the only sound. Then, after I would think, "It has given up; now it will die," it would heave. The rope twanged; the tree leaves clattered; the deer's free foot beat the ground. We stepped back and held our breaths. It thrashed, kicking, but only one leg moved; the other three legs tightened inside the rope's loop. Its hip jerked; its spine shook. Its eyes rolled; its tongue, thick with spittle, pushed in and out. Then it would rest again. We watched this for fifteen minutes.

Once three young native boys charged in, released its trapped legs, and jumped   7
back to the circle of people. But instantly the deer scratched up its neck with its hooves and snared its forelegs in the rope again. It was easy to imagine a third and then a fourth leg soon stuck, like Brer Rabbit and the Tar Baby.

We watched the deer from the circle, and then we drifted on to lunch. Our palm-roofed   8
shelter stood on a grassy promontory from which we could see the deer tied to the tree, pigs and hens walking under village houses, and black-and-white cattle standing in the river. There was even a breeze.

Lunch, which was the second and better lunch we had that day, was hot and fried. There   9
was a big fish called *doncella*, a kind of catfish, dipped whole in corn flour and beaten egg, then deep fried. With our fingers we pulled soft fragments of it from its sides to our plates, and ate; it was delicate fish-flesh, fresh and mild. Someone found the roe, and I ate of that too — it was fat and stronger, like egg yolk, naturally enough, and warm.

There was also a stew of meat in shreds with rice and pale brown gravy. I had asked 10 what kind of deer it was tied to the tree; Pepe had answered in Spanish, "*Gama*." Now they told us this was *gama* too, stewed. I suspect the word means merely game or venison. At any rate, I heard that the village dogs had cornered another deer just yesterday, and it was this deer which we were now eating in full sight of the whole article. It was good. I was surprised at its tenderness. But it is a fact that high levels of lactic acid, which builds up in muscle tissues during exertion, tenderizes.

After the fish and meat we ate bananas fried in chunks and served on a tray; they 11 were sweet and full of flavor. I felt terrific. My shirt was wet and cool from swimming; I had had a night's sleep, two decent walks, three meals, and a swim — everything tasted good. From time to time each one of us, separately, would look beyond our shaded roof to the sunny spot where the deer was still convulsing in the dust. Our meal completed, we walked around the deer and back to the boats.

That night I learned that while we were watching the deer, the others were watching 12 me.

We four North Americans grew close in the jungle in a way that was not the usual 13 artificial intimacy of travelers. We liked each other. We stayed up all that night talking, murmuring, as though we rocked on hammocks slung above time. The others were from big cities: New York, Washington, Boston. They all said that I had no expression on my face when I was watching the deer — or at any rate, not the expression they expected.

They had looked to see how I, the only woman, and the youngest, was taking the 14 sight of the deer's struggles. I looked detached, apparently, or hard, or calm, or focused, still. I don't know. I was thinking. I remember feeling very old and energetic. I could say like Thoreau that I have traveled widely in Roanoke, Virginia. I have thought a great deal about carnivorousness; I eat meat. These things are not issues; they are mysteries.

Gentlemen of the city, what surprises you? That there is suffering here, or that I know it? 15

We lay in the tent and talked. "If it had been my wife," one man said with special 16 vigor, amazed, "she wouldn't have cared *what* was going on; she would have dropped *everything* right at that moment and gone in the village from here to there to there, she would not have *stopped* until that animal was out of its suffering one way or another. She couldn't *bear* to see a creature in agony like that."

I nodded. 17

Now I am home. When I wake I comb my hair before the mirror above my dresser. Every 18 morning for the past two years I have seen in that mirror, beside my sleep-softened face, the blackened face of a burnt man. It is a wire–service photograph clipped from a newspaper and taped to my mirror. The caption reads: "Alan McDonald in Miami hospital bed." All you can see in the photograph is a smudged triangle of face from his eyelids to his lower lip; the rest is bandages. You cannot see the expression in his eyes; the bandages shade them.

The story, headed MAN BURNED FOR SECOND TIME, begins: 19

"Why does God hate me?" Alan McDonald asked from his hospital bed.
"When the gunpowder went off, I couldn't believe it," he said. "I just couldn't believe it. I said, 'No, God couldn't do this to me again.'"

He was in a burn ward in Miami, in serious condition. I do not even know if he lived. I wrote him a letter at the time, cringing.

He had been burned before, thirteen years previously, by flaming gasoline. For years he had been having his body restored and his face remade in dozens of operations. He had been a boy, and then a burnt boy. He had already been stunned by what could happen, by how life could veer. 20

Once I read that people who survive bad burns tend to go crazy; they have a very high suicide rate. Medicine cannot ease their pain; drugs just leak away, soaking the sheets, because there is no skin to hold them in. The people just lie there and weep. Later they kill themselves. They had not known, before they were burned, that the world included such suffering, that life could permit them personally such pain. 21

This time a bowl of gunpowder has exploded on McDonald. 22

> "I didn't realize what had happened at first," he recounted. "And then I heard that sound from 13 years ago. I was burning. I rolled to put the fire out and I thought, 'Oh God, not again.'
> "If my friend hadn't been there, I would have jumped into a canal with a rock around my neck."

His wife concludes the piece, "Man, it just isn't fair."

I read the whole clipping again every morning. This is the Big Time here, every minute of it. Will someone please explain to Alan McDonald in his dignity, to the deer at Providencia in his dignity, what is going on? And mail me the carbon. 23

When we walked by the deer at Providencia for the last time, I said to Pepe, with a pitying glance at the deer, "*Pobrecito*" — "poor little thing." But I was trying out Spanish. I knew at the time it was a ridiculous thing to say. 24

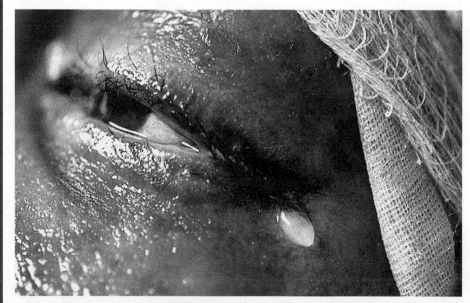

This photograph of a college student who was badly burned in a dormitory fire was awarded a Pulitzer Prize.

Examining the Reading

1. What was the author's outward reaction to the deer in distress?
2. What reaction did Dillard's fellow travelers expect her to have?
3. What is the author's attitude about eating meat?
4. Why does Alan McDonald think God is punishing him?
5. Explain the meaning of each of the following words as it is used in the reading: *thatch* (para. 2), *translucent* (5), *slacken* (5), *promontory* (8), and *carnivorousness* (14).

Analyzing the Writer's Technique

1. Express the essay's dominant impression in your own words.
2. Explain the comparison between the deer and McDonald.
3. Discuss the contrast between the author's lunch and the animal she sees. How are they different? How are they the same?
4. Evaluate the essay's conclusion. If the essay had ended with paragraph 23 instead of paragraph 24, would the conclusion have been more effective or less so? Why?

Thinking Critically about Description

1. What details are omitted from this essay that might have been included?
2. Why does the writer put the word "pretty" (para. 5) in quotations?
3. The author uses the words "tenderness" and "tenderizes" (10), which are related to each other, but have very different connotations. Discuss them and the contrast they create in the essay.
4. Discuss possible reasons that Dillard has a photograph of McDonald pasted to her mirror.

Interpreting a Photograph

What does the photograph on page 296 contribute to the reading? What aspects of it seem especially relevant to the written text? Is this photograph a better illustration for the essay than a photograph of a deer in distress would be? Why, or why not?

Reacting to the Reading

1. How would you have reacted if you were in the village on that day? Why?
2. Do you eat meat? Why or why not? Explain your reasoning and feelings about this issue in a journal entry.
3. The author chose to compare the suffering of a deer and a burn victim. What else could she have chosen to compare the deer with?
4. How do you explain suffering in the world? Write an essay exploring your feelings about this question.

DESCRIPTION COMBINED WITH OTHER PATTERNS

As you read the following essay, notice how the author uses description within an essay that traces a narrative.

Bloggers without Borders . . .
Riverbend

This selection is the final post from the blog "Baghdad Burning," written after the 2003 U.S. invasion of Iraq by a woman calling herself Riverbend. She identified herself in her first post by writing, "I'm female, Iraqi and 24. I survived the war. That's all you need to know. It's all that matters these days anyway." Between August 2003 and October 2007, she posted about her personal experiences as well as commentary on the political situation in Iraq. The blog entries, written in English, were published in book form in the United States and were translated and published in many other languages and countries as well. "Baghdad Burning" was also dramatized as a serial on BBC Radio in 2006. As you read, notice how Riverbend creates and reinforces the dominant impression of the piece.

Syria is a beautiful country — at least I think it is. I say "I think" because while I perceive it to be beautiful, I sometimes wonder if I mistake safety, security, and normalcy for 'beauty.' In so many ways, Damascus is like Baghdad before the war — bustling streets, occasional traffic jams, markets seemingly always full of shoppers . . . And in so many ways it's different. The buildings are higher, the streets are generally narrower and there's a mountain, Qasiyoun, that looms in the distance.   1

The mountain distracts me, as it does many Iraqis — especially those from Baghdad.   2 Northern Iraq is full of mountains, but the rest of Iraq is quite flat. At night, Qasiyoun blends into the black sky, and the only indication of its presence is a multitude of little, glimmering spots of light — houses and restaurants built right up there on the mountain. Every time I take a picture, I try to work Qasiyoun into it — I try to position the person so that Qasiyoun is in the background.

The first weeks here were something of a cultural shock. It has taken me these last   3 three months to work away certain habits I'd acquired in Iraq after the war. It's funny how you learn to act a certain way and don't even know you're doing strange things — like avoiding people's eyes in the street or crazily murmuring prayers to yourself when stuck in traffic. It took me at least three weeks to teach myself to walk properly again — with head lifted, not constantly looking behind me.

It is estimated that there are at least 1.5 million Iraqis in Syria today. I believe it.   4 Walking down the streets of Damascus, you can hear the Iraqi accent everywhere. There are areas like Geramana and Qudsiya that are packed full of Iraqi refugees. Syrians are few and far between in these areas. Even the public schools in the areas are full of Iraqi children. A cousin of mine is now attending a school in Qudsiya and his class is composed of twenty-six Iraqi children and five Syrian children. It's beyond belief sometimes. Most of the families have nothing to live on beyond their savings, which are quickly being depleted with rent and the costs of living.

Within a month of our being here, we began hearing talk about Syria requiring   5
visas from Iraqis, like most other countries. Apparently, our esteemed puppets in
power met with Syrian and Jordanian authorities and decided they wanted to take
away the last two safe havens remaining for Iraqis—Damascus and Amman. The talk
began in late August and was only talk until recently—early October. Iraqis entering
Syria now need a visa from the Syrian consulate or embassy in the country they are
currently in. In the case of Iraqis still in Iraq, it is said that an approval from the Ministry of Interior is also required (which kind of makes it difficult for people running away
from militias OF the Ministry of Interior . . .). Today, there's talk of a possible fifty dollar visa at the border.

Iraqis who entered Syria before the visa was implemented were getting a one-month   6
visitation visa at the border. As soon as that month was over, you could take your passport and visit the local immigration bureau. If you were lucky, they would give you an
additional month or two. When talk about visas from the Syrian embassy began, they
stopped giving an extension on the initial border visa. We, as a family, had a brilliant
idea. Before the commotion of visas began, and before we started needing a renewal,
we decided to go to one of the border crossings, cross into Iraq, and come back into
Syria—everyone was doing it. It would buy us some time—at least two months.

We chose a hot day in early September and drove the six hours to Kameshli, a   7
border town in northern Syria. My aunt and her son came with us—they also needed
an extension on their visa. There is a border crossing in Kameshli called Yaarubiya.
It's one of the simpler crossings because the Iraqi and Syrian borders are only a
matter of several meters. You walk out of Syrian territory and then walk into Iraqi
territory—simple and safe.

When we got to the Yaarubiya border patrol, it hit us that thousands of Iraqis had   8
had our brilliant idea simultaneously—the lines to the border patrol office were end-
less. Hundreds of Iraqis stood in a long line waiting to have their passports stamped
with an exit visa. We joined the line of people and waited. And waited. And waited . . .

It took four hours to leave the Syrian border, after which came the lines of the Iraqi   9
border post. Those were even longer. We joined one of the lines of weary, impatient
Iraqis. "It's looking like a gasoline line . . ." my younger cousin joked. That was the
beginning of another four hours of waiting under the sun, taking baby steps, moving
forward ever so slowly. The line kept getting longer. At one point, we could see neither
the beginning of the line, where passports were being stamped to enter Iraq, nor the
end. Running up and down the line were little boys selling glasses of water, chewing
gum and cigarettes. My aunt caught one of them by the arm as he zipped past us,
"How many people are in front of us?" He whistled and took a few steps back to assess
the situation, "A hundred! A thousand!" He was almost gleeful as he ran off to make
business.

I had such mixed feelings standing in that line. I was caught between a feeling of   10
yearning, a certain homesickness that sometimes catches me at the oddest moments,
and a heavy feeling of dread. What if they didn't agree to let us out again? It wasn't
really possible, but what if it happened? What if this was the last time I'd see the Iraqi
border? What if we were no longer allowed to enter Iraq for some reason? What if we
were never allowed to leave?

We spent the four hours standing, crouching, sitting and leaning in the line. The   11
sun beat down on everyone equally—Sunnis, Shia and Kurds alike. E. tried to convince
the aunt to faint so it would speed the process up for the family, but she just gave us a
withering look and stood straighter. People just stood there, chatting, cursing or silent.
It was yet another gathering of Iraqis—the perfect opportunity to swap sad stories and
ask about distant relations or acquaintances.

We met two families we knew while waiting for our turn. We greeted each other like   12
long lost friends and exchanged phone numbers and addresses in Damascus, promising to visit. I noticed the 23-year-old son, K., from one of the families was missing.
I beat down my curiosity and refused to ask where he was. The mother was looking
older than I remembered and the father looked constantly lost in thought, or maybe it
was grief. I didn't want to know if K. was dead or alive. I'd just have to believe he was
alive and thriving somewhere, not worrying about borders or visas. Ignorance really is
bliss sometimes. . . .

Back at the Syrian border, we waited in a large group, tired and hungry, having   13
handed over our passports for a stamp. The Syrian immigration man, sifting through
dozens of passports, called out names and looked at faces as he handed over the
passports patiently, "Stand back please—stand back." There was a general cry toward
the back of the crowded hall where we were standing as someone collapsed—as they
lifted him I recognized an old man who was there with his family being chaperoned by
his sons, leaning on a walking stick.

By the time we had reentered the Syrian border and were headed back to the cab   14
ready to take us into Kameshli, I had resigned myself to the fact that we were refugees.
I read about refugees on the Internet daily . . . in the newspapers . . . hear about them
on TV. I hear about the estimated 1.5 million plus Iraqi refugees in Syria and shake my
head, never really considering myself or my family as one of them. After all, refugees
are people who sleep in tents and have no potable water or plumbing, right? Refugees
carry their belongings in bags instead of suitcases, and they don't have cell phones
or Internet access, right? Grasping my passport in my hand like my life depended on
it, with two extra months in Syria stamped inside, it hit me how wrong I was. We were
all refugees. I was suddenly a number. No matter how wealthy or educated or comfortable, a refugee is a refugee. A refugee is someone who isn't really welcome in any
country—including their own . . . especially their own.

We live in an apartment building where two other Iraqis are renting. The people in   15
the floor above us are a Christian family from northern Iraq who got chased out of their
village by Peshmerga, and the family on our floor is a Kurdish family who lost their home
in Baghdad to militias and were waiting for immigration to Sweden or Switzerland or
some such European refugee haven.

The first evening we arrived, exhausted, dragging suitcases behind us, morale a   16
little bit bruised, the Kurdish family sent over their representative—a nine-year-old boy
missing two front teeth, holding a lopsided cake, "We're Abu Mohammed's house—
across from you—mama says if you need anything, just ask—this is our number. Abu
Dalia's family live upstairs, this is their number. We're all Iraqi too. . . . Welcome to the
building."

I cried that night because for the first time in a long time, so far away from home,   17
I felt the unity that had been stolen from us in 2003.

Examining the Reading

1. Why does Riverbend mention and describe the mountain? What is its significance?
2. Why does Riverbend object to the visa requirement?
3. What is Riverbend's attitude toward Iraqi authorities? How does she reveal it?
4. Explain Riverbend's statement "Ignorance really is bliss sometimes" (para. 12) in the context of this reading.
5. When and why does Riverbend finally feel the unity she has not experienced since 2003?
6. Explain the meaning of each of the following words or phrases as it is used in the reading: *normalcy* (1), *cultural shock* (3), *esteemed* (5), *withering look* (11), and *morale* (16). Refer to a dictionary as needed.

Analyzing the Writer's Technique

1. What dominant impression does Riverbend convey in this essay? Is it stated or implied? Explain your answers.
2. What is the significance of the essay's title?
3. How does Riverbend's descriptive language allow you to understand and picture the line at the border? What words and phrases are most descriptive in this section?
4. What patterns other than description does Riverbend use in this essay? What purposes do they serve?

Visualizing the Reading

Riverbend conveys information about her journey and surroundings by using many of the characteristics of descriptive essays. Analyze her use of these characteristics by completing the following chart. Give several examples for each type of characteristic used, including the paragraph numbers for reference. The first one has been done for you.

Descriptive Characteristic	Examples
Active verbs	1. "as he zipped past us" (para. 9) 2. "I beat down my curiosity" (12)
Sensory details (sound, smell, touch, sight, taste)	
Varied sentences	
Comparisons	
Connotative language	

Thinking Critically about Description

1. What connotation does Riverbend find in the word "refugee"?
2. Riverbend does not discuss how and why her family left Iraq, at least not in this post. How do you think this omission affects the essay?
3. What connotation does the phrase "esteemed puppets in power" (para. 5) have?
4. Is the essay objective, subjective, or a mixture of both? Explain your answer.
5. Describe Riverbend's tone in this essay. What information does her tone convey that is not directly stated?

Reacting to the Reading

1. Given the hardships of her refugee experience, how and why do you think Riverbend maintains a blog?
2. Discuss the factors that may have led to Riverbend's family's decision to leave Iraq.
3. Riverbend states that she "was suddenly a number" (para. 14). Discuss situations in which you or others have felt this way.
4. Write an essay in which you agree or disagree with Riverbend's statement that "ignorance really is bliss sometimes." Describe situations from your experience that either support or reject her view.

Applying Your Skills: Additional Essay Assignments

Using what you learned about description in this chapter, write a descriptive essay on one of the topics listed below. Depending on the topic you choose, you may need to conduct library or Internet research.

To Express Your Ideas

1. Suppose a famous person, living or dead, visited your house for dinner. Write an essay describing the person and the evening and expressing your feelings about the occasion.

For more on locating and documenting sources, see Part 5.

2. In "Eating Chilli Peppers," the author describes the love that some people have for eating peppers. Write an essay for your classmates describing a food that a family member or close friend enjoys but that you dislike.

To Inform Your Reader

3. Write an essay describing destruction or devastation you have observed as a result of a natural disaster (hurricane, flood), an accident, or a form of violence.
4. Write a report for your local newspaper on a local sporting event you recently observed or participated in.

To Persuade Your Reader

5. Write a letter to persuade your parents to loan you money. The loan may be to purchase a used car or to rent a more expensive apartment, for example. Include a description of your current car or apartment.
6. Both "Heatstroke with a Side of Burn Cream" and "The Deer at Providencia" contain descriptions of food, either its preparation or its consumption. Do you think that Americans are overly concerned with food, or is food an important social and cultural experience? Write a persuasive essay taking a position on the role of food in American culture.

Cases Using Description

7. Imagine that you are a product buyer for a cosmetics distributor, a food company, or a furniture dealership. Write a descriptive review of a product recommending to the board of directors whether or not to distribute it. Use something that you are familiar with or come up with your own product (such as an electronic gadget, an advice book on parenting, or a new cosmetic). Describe the product in a way that will help convince the company to accept your recommendation.
8. Write a brief description of your ideal internship. Then write an essay to accompany your application for your ideal summer internship. The sponsoring agency requires every applicant to submit an essay that describes the knowledge and experience the applicant can bring to the internship and the ways that the position would benefit the applicant personally and professionally.

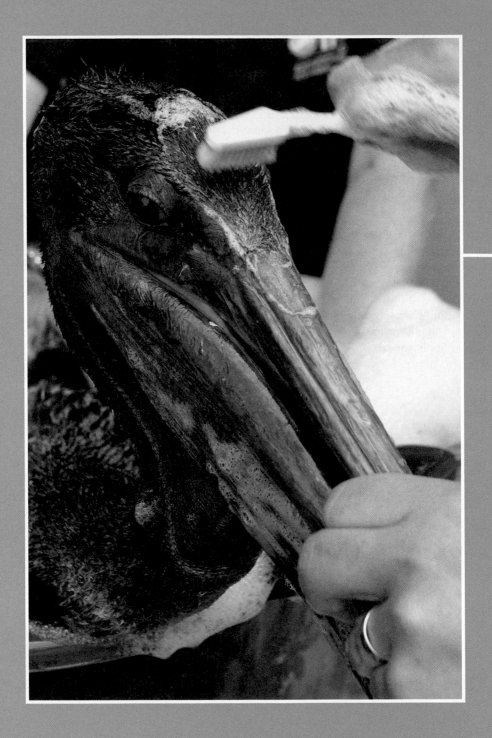

CHAPTER 13

Illustration: Explaining with Examples

In a social problems class, the instructor projects the photograph shown on the opposite page onto a screen. The instructor makes the following statement: "Environmental pollution is a growing national problem." She asks the class to think of several examples of situations similar to the one shown in the photograph that confirm this view.

Using the instructor's statement as your topic sentence, write a paragraph that supports this statement with examples of different types of environmental pollution that you have either observed or read about.

WRITING AN ILLUSTRATION ESSAY

The sentences you have just written could be part of an illustration essay. Your essay might explain situations that illustrate your thesis about pollution and the environment. When writers use illustration, they support their points with clear examples. This chapter will show you how to write an essay that uses illustration as the primary method of development, as well as how to use illustration in other types of essays.

What Is Illustration?

Illustration is a way of using examples to reveal the essential characteristics of a topic or to reinforce a thesis. By providing specific situations to make abstract ideas concrete, you can often connect them to situations within the reader's experience. Unfamiliar and complex ideas also can become clear once examples are provided. Most textbooks are filled with examples for this reason. Writers in academic and work situations commonly use illustration as well (see the accompanying box for examples).

In the following illustration essay, "Rambos of the Road," Martin Gottfried uses examples to support a thesis.

SCENES FROM COLLEGE AND THE WORKPLACE

- For a *literature class*, you are assigned to write an analysis of the poet Emily Dickinson's use of metaphor and simile. To explain your point about her use of animals in metaphors, you provide specific examples from several of her poems.

- You are studying sexual dimorphism—differences in appearance between the sexes—for a *biology* course. The following question appears on an exam: "Define sexual dimorphism, and illustrate its occurrence in several different species." In your answer, you give examples of peacocks, geese, and chickens, explaining how the males and females in each species differ in physical appearance.

- You are an *elementary school reading teacher* and have been asked by your principal to write a justification to the school board for the new computer software you have requested. You decide to give several examples of how the software will benefit particular types of students.

Rambos of the Road
Martin Gottfried

Martin Gottfried has been a drama critic for such publications as the *New York Post*, the *Saturday Review*, and *New York*. He has also written several books, including biographies of Stephen Sondheim, Arthur Miller, and Angela Lansbury. This essay was first published in *Newsweek*, the weekly newsmagazine, in 1986. As you read the selection, notice where Gottfried employs compelling examples to support his thesis and highlight those you find particularly striking.

READING

The car pulled up and its driver glared at us with such sullen intensity, such hatred, that I was truly afraid for our lives. Except for the Mohawk haircut he didn't have, he looked like Robert De Niro in *Taxi Driver,* the sort of young man who, delirious for notoriety, might kill a president.   1

He was glaring because we had passed him and for that affront he pursued us to the next stoplight so as to express his indignation and affirm his masculinity. I was with two women and, believe it, was afraid for all three of us. It was nearly midnight and we were in a small, sleeping town with no other cars on the road.   2

When the light turned green, I raced ahead, knowing it was foolish and that I was not in a movie. He didn't merely follow, he chased, and with his headlights turned off. No matter what sudden turn I took, he followed. My passengers were silent. I knew they were alarmed, and I prayed that I wouldn't be called upon to protect them. In that cheerful frame of mind, I turned off my own lights so I couldn't be followed. It was lunacy. I was responding to a crazy *as* a crazy.   3

"I'll just drive to the police station," I finally said, and as if those were the magic words, he disappeared.   4

It seems to me that there has recently been an epidemic of auto macho—a competition perceived and expressed in driving. People fight it out over parking spaces. They bully into line at the gas pump. A toll booth becomes a signal for elbowing fenders. And beetle-eyed drivers hunch over their steering wheels, squeezing the rims, glowering, preparing the excuse of not having seen you as they muscle you off the road. Approaching a highway on an entrance ramp recently, I was strong-armed by a trailer truck, so immense that its driver all but blew me away by blasting his horn. The behemoth was just inches from my hopelessly mismatched coupe when I fled for the safety of the shoulder.   5

And this is happening on city streets, too. A New York taxi driver told me that "intimidation is the name of the game. Drive as if you're deaf and blind. You don't hear the other guy's horn and you sure as hell don't see him."   6

The odd thing is that long before I was even able to drive, it seemed to me that people were at their finest and most civilized when in their cars. They seemed so orderly and considerate, so reasonable, staying in the right-hand lane unless passing, signaling all intentions. In those days you really eased into highway traffic, and the long, neat rows of cars seemed mobile testimony to the sanity of most people.   7

Perhaps memory fails, perhaps there were always testy drivers, perhaps—but everyone didn't give you the finger.

A most amazing example of driver rage occurred recently at the Manhattan end of the Lincoln Tunnel. We were four cars abreast, stopped at a traffic light. And there was no moving even when the light had changed. A bus had stopped in the cross traffic, blocking our paths: it was a normal-for-New-York-City gridlock. Perhaps impatient, perhaps late for important appointments, three of us none- theless accepted what, after all, we could not alter. One, however, would not. He would not be helpless. He would go where he was going even if he couldn't get there. A Wall Street type in suit and tie, he got out of his car and strode toward the bus, rapping smartly on its doors. When they opened, he exchanged words with the driver. The doors folded shut. He then stepped in front of the bus, took hold of one of its large windshield wipers and broke it.

The bus doors reopened and the driver appeared, apparently giving the fellow a good piece of his mind. If so, the lecture was wasted, for the man started his car and proceeded to drive directly *into the bus*. He rammed it. Even though the point at which he struck the bus, the folding doors, was its most vulnerable point, ram- ming the side of a bus with your car has to rank very high on a futility index. My first thought was that it had to be a rental car.

To tell the truth, I could not believe my eyes. The bus driver opened his doors as much as they could be opened and he stepped directly onto the hood of the attacking car, jumping up and down with both his feet. He then retreated into the bus, closing the doors behind him. Obviously a man of action, the car driver backed up and rammed the bus again. How this exercise in absurdity would have been re- solved none of us will ever know for at that point the traffic unclogged and the bus moved on. And the rest of us, we passives of the world, proceeded, our cars cross- ing a field of battle as if nothing untoward had happened.

It is tempting to blame such belligerent, uncivil and even neurotic behavior on the nuts of the world, but in our cars we all become a little crazy. How many of us speed up when a driver signals his intention of pulling in front of us? Are we resentful and anxious to pass him? How many of us try to squeeze in, or race along the shoulder of a lane merger? We may not jump on hoods, but driving the gantlet, we seethe, cursing not so silently in the safety of our steel bodies on wheels—fortresses for cowards.

What is it within us that gives birth to such antisocial behavior and why, all of a sudden, have so many drivers gone around the bend? My friend Joel Katz, a Manhat- tan psychiatrist, calls it "a Rambo pattern. People are running around thinking the American way is to take the law into your own hands when anyone does anything wrong. And what constitutes 'wrong'? Anything that cramps your style."

It seems to me that it is a new America we see on the road now. It has the men- tality of a hoodlum and the backbone of a coward. The car is its weapon and hiding place, and it is still a symbol even in this. Road Rambos no longer bespeak a self- reliant, civil people tooling around in family cruisers. In fact, there aren't families in these machines that charge headlong with their brights on in broad daylight, de- manding we get out of their way. Bullies are loners, and they have perverted our lib- erty of the open road into drivers' license. They represent an America that derides the values of decency and good manners, then roam the highways riding shotgun and shrieking freedom. By allowing this to happen, the rest of us approve.

(MAKING (CONNECTIONS)

Civility

Both "American Jerk: Be Civil, or I'll Beat You to a Pulp" (pp. 50–52) and "Rambos of the Road" (pp. 307–8) deal with bad behavior and selfishness.

Analyze the Readings

1. What types of behaviors does each reading address? Compare the authors' attitudes toward these behaviors.
2. Write a journal entry comparing the techniques that each author uses to support his thesis, especially considering the tone of each. Which is more effective? Explain your choice.

Essay Idea

Both essays discuss public selfishness and self-interest. Gottfried illustrates this concept by discussing one place that he has noticed a lack of civility (highway driving), and Schwartz discusses a variety of situations. Choose a public setting or forum in which selfish behavior and a lack of civility are evident to you. Write an essay illustrating the behavior.

Characteristics of Illustration Essays

Effective illustration essays support a generalization or explain or clarify something by providing appropriate examples that maintain readers' interest and help fulfill the author's purpose. Because an illustration essay needs to be more than a list of examples, a well-thought-out organization is essential.

Illustration Can Be Used to Support Generalizations

Examples are an effective way to support a **generalization**—a broad statement about a topic. Often the thesis of an essay contains a generalization, and the body of the essay contains examples that support it. In "Rambos of the Road," Gottfried's thesis contains a generalization about "an epidemic of auto macho" behavior.

The following statements are generalizations because they make assertions about an entire group or category:

- Most college students are energetic, ambitious, and eager to get ahead in life.
- Gestures play an important role in nonverbal communication.
- Boys are more willing to participate in class discussions than are girls.

To explain and support any one of these generalizations, you would need to provide specific examples to show how or why the statement is accurate. For instance, you could support the first generalization by describing several college students who demonstrate energy and ambition. However, other types of support would need to accompany the examples of individual students. Relevant facts, statistics, expert opinions, personal observations, or descriptions could be used to show that the generalization applies to the majority of college students.

Exercise 13.1

Using one or more prewriting strategies for generating ideas, think of at least one example that supports each general statement.

1. Television offers some programs with educational or social value.
2. Today's parents are not strict enough with their children.
3. The favorite pastime of most men is watching sports on television.

Illustration Can Be Used to Explain or Clarify

Examples are also useful when you need to explain an unfamiliar topic, a difficult concept, or an abstract term.

Unfamiliar topics. When your audience has little or no knowledge of your topic, consider using examples to help your readers understand it. In "Rambos of the Road," Gottfried uses an extended example of real-life road rage to help his readers understand the topic.

Difficult concepts. Many concepts are difficult for readers to grasp by definition alone. For instance, a reader might guess that the term *urbanization*, a key concept in sociology, has something to do with cities. Defining the concept as, say, "the process by which an area becomes part of a city" would give the reader more to go on. But examples of formerly suburban areas that have become urban would make the concept immediately understandable.

Abstract terms. Abstract terms refer to ideas, rather than to concrete things you can see and touch. Terms such as *truth* and *justice* are abstract. Because abstractions are difficult to understand, examples help clarify them.

In many cases, however, abstract terms mean different things to different people. Here you give examples to clarify what *you* mean by an abstract term. Suppose you use the term *unfair* to describe your employer's treatment of employees. Readers might have different ideas of fairness. Providing examples of the employer's unfair treatment would make your meaning clear.

Exercise 13.2

The following list contains a mix of unfamiliar topics, difficult concepts, and abstract terms. Choose three items from the list, and think of examples that illustrate their meanings.

1. Phobia
2. Conformity
3. Gender role
4. Self-fulfilling prophecy
5. Sexual harassment

Illustration Takes Purpose and Audience into Account

A successful illustration essay uses either a series of related examples or one extended example to support its thesis. The number and type of examples to include will depend on your purpose and audience. In an essay arguing that one car is a better buy than another, you would need to give a series of examples to show the various models, years, and options available to potential car buyers. But in an essay written for an audience of high school students about the consequences of dropping out of school, a single poignant example might be appropriate.

Your audience also plays a role in deciding what types of examples to include in an essay. At times, technical examples may be appropriate; at other times, more personal or everyday ones are effective. For instance, suppose you want to persuade readers that the Food and Drug Administration should approve a new cancer drug. If your audience is composed of doctors, your examples would need to include statistical studies of the drug's effectiveness. But if your audience is the general public, you would include personal anecdotes about lives being saved and nontechnical examples of the drug's safety. In addition, try to choose examples that represent different aspects of or viewpoints on your topic. In writing about the new drug, for instance, you might include expert opinion from researchers as well as the views of doctors, patients, and a representative of the company that manufactures the drug.

Exercise 13.3

For one of the following topics, suggest examples that would suit the different audiences listed.

1. Your college's policy on academic dismissal
   a. First-year students attending a college orientation session
   b. Students facing academic dismissal
   c. Parents or spouses of students who have been dismissed for academic reasons
2. A proposal recommending that drivers over age sixty-five undergo periodic assessment of their ability to operate a motor vehicle safely
   a. Senior citizens
   b. State senators
   c. Adult children of elderly drivers

Illustration Uses Carefully Selected Examples

The examples you use to explain your thesis should be carefully chosen. Select examples that are relevant, representative, accurate, and striking. *Relevant* examples have a direct and clear relationship to your thesis. If your essay advocates publicly funded and operated preschool programs, support your case with examples of successful publicly funded programs, not privately operated ones.

An example is *representative* when it shows a typical or real-life situation, not a rare or unusual one. In many cases you will need to give several representative examples. For instance, in an essay arguing that preschool programs advance children's reading skills, one example of an all-day, year-round preschool would not be representative of all or most other programs.

Be sure the examples you include are *accurate* and *specific*. Report statistics objectively, and provide readers with enough information that they can evaluate the reliability of the data. Notice how the second example below provides better detail for the reader.

EXAMPLE LACKING DETAIL	**Most students in preschool programs have better language skills than children who don't attend such programs.**
DETAILED EXAMPLE	**According to an independent evaluator, 73 percent of children who attended the Head Start program in Clearwater, after one year of attendance, had better language skills than students who did not attend the program.**

For examples that are broad general categories, you will often find it helpful to include subexamples—specific examples that help explain the general examples. Suppose you are writing an essay about the problems that new immigrants to America face and include three examples—problems with the language, with the culture, and with technology. For the broad culture example, you might give subexamples of how some immigrants do not understand certain American holidays, ways of socializing, and methods of doing business.

Finally, choose examples that are *striking and dramatic* and that will make a strong, lasting impression on your readers. In "Rambos of the Road," we can visualize Gottfried's example of a bus driver leaping out of the bus and stamping on the hood of the car. Similarly, Gottfried's opening example of being followed by an angry driver creates tension; we want to keep reading to learn the outcome.

At times it may be necessary to conduct research to find examples outside of your knowledge and experience. For the essay on preschool programs, you would need to do library or Internet research to obtain statistical information. You might also interview a preschool administrator or teacher to gather firsthand anecdotes and opinions or visit a preschool classroom to observe the program in action.

Illustration Organizes Details Effectively

When you use examples to support a thesis, you need to decide how to organize both the examples and the details that accompany them. Often one of the methods of organization discussed in Chapter 7 will be useful—most-to-least, least-to-most, chronological, or spatial order. For example, in an essay explaining why people wear unconventional dress, the examples might be arranged spatially, starting with outlandish footwear and continuing upward to headgear. In other instances you may want to organize your examples according to another pattern of development, such as comparison and contrast or cause and effect. To support the thesis that a local department store needs to improve its customer services, you might begin by contrasting the department store with several computer stores that have better services and offering examples of the services provided by each.

Visualizing an Illustration Essay: A Graphic Organizer

For more on graphic organizers, see Chapter 3, pp. 59–61.

The graphic organizer shown in Figure 13.1 will help you visualize the components of an illustration essay. As you can see, the structure is straightforward: The introduction contains background information and usually includes the thesis; the body paragraphs give one or more related examples; and the conclusion presents a final statement. For an essay using one extended example—such as a highly descriptive account of an auto

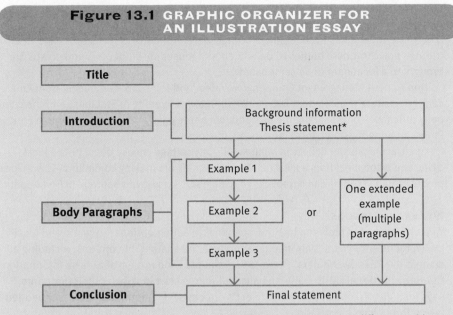

Figure 13.1 GRAPHIC ORGANIZER FOR AN ILLUSTRATION ESSAY

*In some essays, the thesis statement may be implied or may appear in a different position.

accident intended to persuade readers to wear seat belts—the body of the essay would focus on the details of that one example.

The following essay, "Sustainability on the Menu," is an illustration essay. Read the essay, and then study the graphic organizer for it in Figure 13.2 (on p. 316).

Sustainability on the Menu
Carl Pino

READING

Carl Pino is a former editorial intern of *E, The Environmental Magazine*, in which this essay was originally published. He is a former blog writer, and he worked as an editorial intern for *Econtent Magazine*. This article is a good example of an illustrative essay, but it lacks a separate conclusion. As you read, notice how the author uses examples to support his thesis statement.

Cafeterias are ground zero for "greening" a school, and the past year has seen great leaps in local and organic food purchasing: from cage-free eggs and fair-trade coffee to composting at schools nationwide. According to the Sustainable Endowments Institute's 2007 report card (which looks at environmental initiatives at the 200 colleges and universities with the largest endowment assets in the U.S. and Canada), 70 percent of schools "devote at least a portion of food budgets to buying from local farms and/or producers." Twenty-nine percent of schools on the institute's list earned an "A" in the "food and recycling" category. 1

Some schools clearly stand out. At Santa Clara University in California, 80 percent of the produce served in the dining halls comes from local farms. Carleton College in Minnesota purchases from 15 to 20 local farmers and producers, serves grass-fed meat 2 and uses 100 percent organic flour in all baking. In Massachusetts, Smith College's dining services purchase organic produce, in addition to dairy and honey, from 18 local farms. The college has even removed bottled water from one to-go location and distributes polycarbonate bottles to be refilled and reused by students. Food scraps are brought to a local farm to be composted.

Bon Appétit Management Company provides food to 17 U.S. campuses, from American University in Washington, D.C., to Washington University in St. Louis. And the company purchases only sustainable seafood, cage-free eggs and hosts the Farm to Fork Program, bringing small, local farmers big business.   3

Chefs at Macalester College in Minneapolis buy cottage cheese direct from a local dairy, and bison meat from a local rancher. "The chefs are making commitments with local producers, and farmers can improve their business," says Haven Bourque of Bon Appétit.   4

IVY LEAGUE LESSONS

Yale University has provided healthy, sustainable eating options—organic and locally grown foods—for years. Daily menus announce the sustainable options, including all-sustainable Tuesday dinners. The Yale Sustainable Food Project shares its information through nutritional cards in dining halls. "Students start looking at their footprints," says Josh Viertel, one of the Food Project's directors. "It's about the ethics embedded in you through your education."   5

Viertel and fellow director Melina Shannon-DiPietro say that Yale's local purchasing program brings more local, organic, sustainable produce to campus cafeterias. "Food tied to tradition and tied to the environment around it helps students become more aware of their impacts," Viertel says.   6

Yale also has a student-run farm, three greenhouses that serve the community and a farmer's market in the spring and summer months. Says Anastasis Curley, coordinator at the Food Project, "We try to strike a balance between food and wellness and general information about agriculture and green events going on at Yale." On a brisk December afternoon, Curley showed off garden plots where carrots, cabbage, spinach, and other cold-tolerant vegetables were growing in 30-degree weather. Students at Yale have even harvested carrots during blizzards.   7

But Robert Sullivan, assistant director of operations at Yale's dining services, says the majority of students have not fully embraced sustainability. "Some are focused on eating vegan, others on pizza," he says. "The balance is challenging." Yale's cafeterias offer grass-fed beef burgers, organic quiches and a whole assortment of locally grown produce. "We've been working with the distribution companies to ensure they buy from Connecticut and New Haven farmers," says Thomas Peterlik, executive chef at Yale.   8

A recent composting initiative at Yale was rejected after a trial period, but Sullivan says the impetus is still there. "We have a good salvage group that will contact the groups in the area to donate the food," he says.   9

Princeton University Dining Services has been working with the college's own "Greening Princeton" program. Student representative Kathryn Anderson says it started small. "The first thing we did was look at how to get organic cereal into the dining hall," she says. "We now have a large purchasing effort to make meats organic." All the chicken breast and ground beef the school serves is organic or local. Seafood purchased by dining services is raised and processed via sustainable means.   10

WASTE NOT

Princeton's excess food is packaged and distributed to local food shelters. And food   11
wastes from the dining halls are collected into bins and sent to a local pig farm for feed.

Connecticut College's proposal for a composting system lost out on MTV and GF's   12
"Ecoimagination Challenge," but an alumnus made a $25,000 contribution to fund the
initiative. "By having a composting system on campus we can reduce the distance that
the food scraps have to travel, and then we can use them to grow food locally, either
on campus or in the local area," says Misha Johnson, a student who runs the campus'
organic garden.

Pre- and post-consumer food waste generated by Connecticut College totals 8,000   13
and 9,000 pounds a week, but the compost initiatives re-direct 500 pounds of waste
daily. The college also sends food scraps to a local pig farm for feed. "By creating a
community of consciousness around good producers and consumers, the environment
can and will benefit," Johnson says. "We want students and the greater community to
realize that food is more than just what one sits down to eat at a meal." That higher
consciousness includes one all-vegetarian cafeteria on campus.

Campuses seeking sustainable waste disposal can go beyond compost piles and   14
pig feed, too. Campus Kitchens Project allows volunteers to dispense unused foods to
the elderly and homeless in local communities. Gonzaga College in Spokane, Washington, Northwestern University in Chicago, Augsburg College in Minnesota and Dillard
University in New Orleans have all signed on to the program. Environmental concerns
are tied to social ones, and initiatives like these serve not only the students, but the
local population and the planet at large.

Exercise 13.4

Draw a graphic organizer for "Rambos of the Road" (pp. 307–8).

Integrating Illustration into an Essay

Examples are an effective way to support a thesis that relies on one or more other patterns
of development. You might, for instance, use examples in the following ways:

- To *define* a particular advertising ploy
- To *compare* two types of small businesses
- To *classify* types of movies
- To *show the effects* of aerobic exercise
- To *argue* that junk food is unhealthy because of its high fat and salt content

When using examples in an essay where illustration is not the main pattern of
development, keep the following tips in mind:

1. **Be careful to choose examples that are relevant, representative, accurate, specific, and striking**, since in most cases you will include only one or two.
2. **Use clear transitions.** Be sure to use a clear transition to make it obvious that an
   example is to follow.

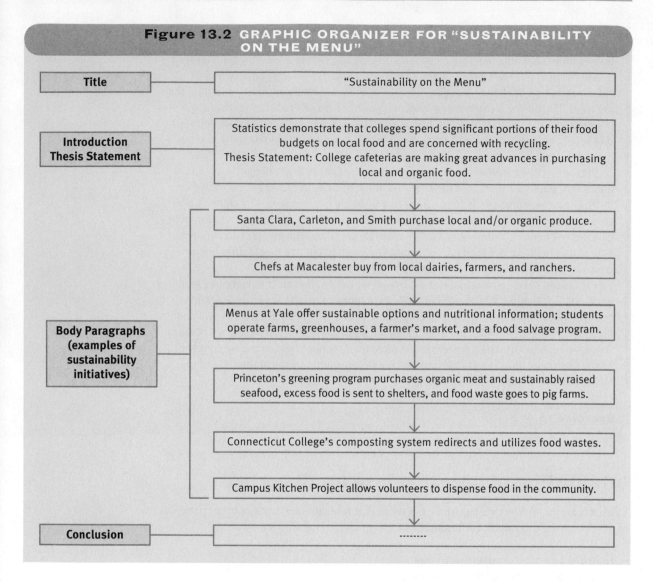

Figure 13.2 GRAPHIC ORGANIZER FOR "SUSTAINABILITY ON THE MENU"

Title — "Sustainability on the Menu"

Introduction Thesis Statement — Statistics demonstrate that colleges spend significant portions of their food budgets on local food and are concerned with recycling.
Thesis Statement: College cafeterias are making great advances in purchasing local and organic food.

Body Paragraphs (examples of sustainability initiatives)

Santa Clara, Carleton, and Smith purchase local and/or organic produce.

Chefs at Macalester buy from local dairies, farmers, and ranchers.

Menus at Yale offer sustainable options and nutritional information; students operate farms, greenhouses, a farmer's market, and a food salvage program.

Princeton's greening program purchases organic meat and sustainably raised seafood, excess food is sent to shelters, and food waste goes to pig farms.

Connecticut College's composting system redirects and utilizes food wastes.

Campus Kitchen Project allows volunteers to dispense food in the community.

Conclusion — --------

3. **Limit descriptive detail.** Provide enough details that your reader can understand how an example supports the point you want to make with it, but don't overwhelm your reader with too many details. Extended examples that are too detailed may distract your reader from the main point.

In "Hey Mom, Dad, May I Have My Room Back?" (pp. 331–33), Christina Rouvalis uses illustration along with several other patterns of development (cause-effect and definition) to make a point about the increasing number of young people who are returning to live with their parents after college.

A GUIDED WRITING ASSIGNMENT

The following guide will lead you through the process of writing an illustration essay. You will use examples to support your thesis, but you may need to use one or more of the other patterns of development to organize your examples or relate them to one another. Depending on your learning style, you may choose to work through this Guided Writing Assignment in different ways.

The Assignment

Write an illustration essay. Select one of the following topics or one that you think of on your own:

1. The connection between clothing and personality
2. The long-term benefits of a part-time job
3. The idea that you are what you eat
4. The problems of balancing school, job, and family
5. Controlling or eliminating stress
6. Decision-making techniques
7. Effective (or ineffective) parenting
8. The popularity of a particular sport, television show, or hobby

Your audience consists of readers of your campus newspaper. As you develop your essay, consider using one or more of the other patterns of development. For example, you might use narration to present an extended example that illustrates the difficulties of balancing schoolwork with a job and family. You might compare decision-making techniques and give examples of each. Or you might describe your favorite television show and give examples from particular episodes.

For more on narration, description, and comparison and contrast, see Chapters 11, 12, and 15.

Generating Ideas

Use the following guidelines to help you narrow a topic and generate ideas.

Narrowing Your Topic

When you have chosen an assignment topic, be sure to use prewriting to narrow it so that it becomes a manageable topic. Be sure your narrowed topic can be supported by one or more examples.

For more on prewriting strategies, see Chapter 5.

Considering Your Purpose and Audience

Your purpose and audience will affect the type and number of examples you include. If you are writing a persuasive essay, you may need several examples to provide sufficient evidence. However, if you are writing an informative essay in which you explain how to select educational toys, one extended example may be sufficient.

Consider your audience in deciding what kinds of examples to include. For this assignment, your audience is made up of readers of your campus newspaper. Think about

For more on thesis statements, see Chapter 6, pp. 126–27.

whether this audience is interested in and familiar with your topic. If your audience is familiar with your topic, you may want to use complex examples. However, simple, straightforward examples would be appropriate for an audience unfamiliar with your topic.

Developing Your Thesis

Your next step is to develop a working thesis about your narrowed topic. The thesis in an illustration essay is the generalization that you will support with examples.

You can develop a thesis statement in several ways, depending on your learning style. For instance, a concrete learner writing about the effects of absent fathers on families may begin by listing the problems and behaviors that children in such families exhibit, and then develop a generalization from these examples. An abstract learner, in contrast, might write the thesis first and then generate examples that support the generalization.

As you brainstorm examples, you may think of situations that illustrate a different or more interesting thesis. Don't hesitate to revise or change your thesis as you discover more about your topic. Use the suggestions that follow to generate examples:

Learning Style Options

1. Jot down all of the instances or situations you can think of that illustrate your thesis.
2. Close your eyes and visualize situations that relate to your thesis.
3. Systematically review your life—year by year, place by place, or job by job—to recall situations that illustrate your thesis.
4. Discuss your thesis with a classmate. Try to match or better each other's examples.
5. Create two columns on a piece of paper or in a computer file. In the first column, list words describing how you feel about your narrowed topic. (For example, the topic *cheating on college exams* might generate such feelings as anger, surprise, and confusion.) In the second column, elaborate on these feelings by adding details about specific situations. (For example, you might write about how surprised you were to discover your best friend had cheated on an exam.)

For more on library and Internet research, see Chapter 22.

6. Research your topic in the library or on the Internet to uncover examples outside your own experience.

Essay in Progress 1

Using the preceding guidelines, choose and narrow your topic. Then develop a working thesis statement and brainstorm examples that illustrate the thesis.

Choosing Your Examples

When you have discovered a wealth of examples, your task is to select the ones that will best support your thesis and suit your audience and purpose. Use the following criteria in choosing examples:

1. **Choose relevant examples.** The examples you choose must clearly demonstrate the point or idea you want to illustrate. To support the thesis that high schools do not provide students with the instruction and training in physical education necessary to maintain a healthy lifestyle, you would not use as an example a student who is underweight because of a recent illness. Since lack of preparation in high school is not responsible for this student's problem, the case would be irrelevant to your thesis.

2. **Choose a variety of useful examples.** If you are using more than one example, choose examples that reveal different aspects of your topic. In writing about students who lack physical education skills, you would need to provide examples of students who lack different kinds of skills—strength, agility, and so forth. You can also add variety by using expert opinion, quotations, observations, or statistics to illustrate your thesis.

3. **Choose representative examples.** Choose typical cases, not rare or unusual ones. To continue with the thesis about physical education, a high school all-star football player who lacks adequate strength or muscular control would be an exceptional case. A recent graduate who did not learn to play a sport and failed to develop a habit of regular exercise would be a more representative example.

4. **Choose striking examples.** Include examples that capture your readers' attention and make a vivid impression.

5. **Choose accurate and specific examples.** Be sure the examples you include are as precise and specific as possible. They should be neither exaggerated nor understated.

6. **Choose examples that appeal to your audience.** Some examples will appeal to one type of audience more than to another type. If you want to illustrate high school graduates' lack of training in physical education for an audience of high school seniors, examples involving actual students may be most appealing, whereas for an audience of parents, expert opinion and statistics would be appropriate.

If you are working on a computer, highlight strong examples by making them bold or moving them to a separate page or document for easy access when drafting.

Trying Out Your Ideas on Others

Working in a group of two or three students, discuss your thesis and supporting examples for this chapter's assignment. Use the list of criteria above to guide the discussion and to make suggestions for improving each student's thesis and examples.

Essay in Progress 2
Using the preceding suggestions and the feedback you received from classmates, evaluate your examples, and decide which ones you will include in your essay.

Organizing and Drafting

When you are satisfied with your thesis and the examples you have chosen to illustrate it, you are ready to organize your ideas and write your draft essay.

For more on drafting an essay, see Chapter 7.

Choosing a Method of Organization

Use the following guidelines to organize your essay:

1. **If you are using a single, extended example,** relate events in the order in which they happened. However, if the example is not made up of events, you might use most-to-least, least-to-most, or spatial organization. For instance, if you want to

For more on methods of organization, see Chapter 7, pp. 144–47.

use in-line skating as an example of the importance of protective athletic gear, you might arrange the details spatially, describing the skater's headgear first, then the elbow and wrist pads, and then the knee protection.

2. **If you are using several examples,** consider organizing the examples in terms of their importance, from most to least or from least to most important. However, other arrangements are possible. Examples of childhood memories, for instance, could follow chronological order.

3. **If you have many examples,** consider grouping the examples in categories. For instance, in an essay about the use of slang words, you might classify examples according to how they are used by teenagers, by adults, and by other groups.

For more on classification and division, see Chapter 16.

Essay in Progress 3

Using the preceding suggestions, choose a method for organizing your examples. Then draw a graphic organizer, or write an outline of your essay:

Drafting the Illustration Essay

Once you have decided on a method of organization, your next step is to write a first draft. Here are some tips for drafting an illustration essay:

1. **Use each paragraph to express one key idea; the example or examples in that paragraph should illustrate that key idea.** Develop your body paragraphs so that each one presents a single example or group of closely related examples.

2. **Use the topic sentence in each paragraph to make clear the particular idea that each example or set of examples illustrates.**

For more on description, see Chapter 12. For more on using sufficient detail, see Chapter 8, pp. 171–72.

For more on transitions, see Chapter 7, pp. 150–52.

For more on writing effective paragraphs, including introductions and conclusions, see Chapter 7.

3. **Provide sufficient detail about each example.** Explain each one using vivid descriptive language. Your goal is to make your readers feel as if they are experiencing or observing the situation.

4. **Use transitions to move your readers from one example to another.** Without transitions such as *for example* and *in particular,* your essay will seem choppy and disconnected.

5. **Begin with an effective introduction.** In most illustration essays, the thesis is stated at the outset. Your introduction should also spark readers' interest and include background information about the topic.

6. **End with an effective conclusion.** Your essay should not end with your last example but should conclude with a final statement that pulls together your ideas and reminds readers of your thesis.

Essay in Progress 4

Using the preceding guidelines, write a first draft of your illustration essay.

Analyzing and Revising

If possible, set aside your draft for a day or two before rereading and revising it. As you reread, concentrate on organization, level of detail, and overall effectiveness, not on grammar or mechanics. To evaluate and revise your draft, use the following strategies:

Learning Style Options

1. Write an outline, draw a graphic organizer, or update the outline or organizer you created earlier. Look for weaknesses in how examples are organized.

For more on the benefits of peer review, see Chapter 9, pp. 188–91.

2. Use Figure 13.3 (p. 322) to help you discover the strengths and weaknesses of your draft. You might also ask a classmate to review it using the questions in the flowchart. For each answer that refers you to the right column of the chart, ask your reviewer to explain why he or she answered in that way.

Essay in Progress 5

Revise your draft using Figure 13.3 and any comments you have received from peer reviewers.

Editing and Proofreading

The last step is to check your revised essay for errors in grammar, spelling, punctuation, and mechanics. Look for the types of errors you commonly make. (Refer to your error log.)

For more on keeping an error log, see Chapter 10, pp. 221–22.

For illustration essays, pay particular attention to the following issues:

1. **Be consistent in the verb tense that you use in your extended examples.** When using an event from the past as an example, however, always use the past tense to describe it.

   - Special events *are* an important part of children's lives. Parent visitation day at school *was* an event my daughter *talked* about for an entire week. Children *are* also excited by . . .

2. **Be consistent in using first person (*I, me, we, us*), second person (*you*), or third person (*he, she, it, him, her, they, them*).**

   - I visited my daughter's first-grade classroom during parents' week last month. Each parent was invited to read a story to the class, and ~~you~~ ^{we} were encouraged to ask the children questions afterward.

3. **Avoid sentence fragments when introducing examples.** Each sentence must have both a subject and a verb.

   - Technology has become part of teenagers' daily lives. ~~For example, high~~ ^{High} school students who carry iPhones. *are one example.*

Essay in Progress 6

Edit and proofread your illustration essay, paying particular attention to consistent use of verb tense and point of view. Don't forget to look for the types of errors you tend to make.

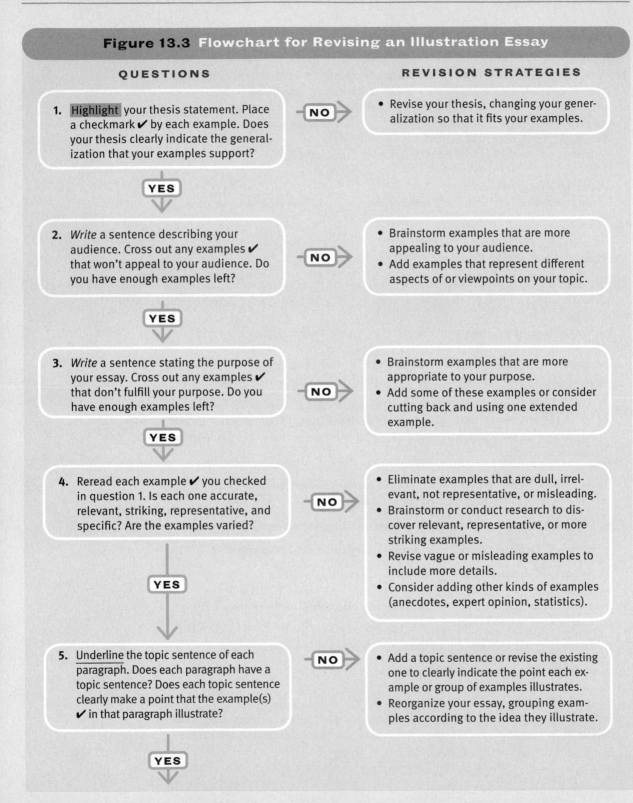

Figure 13.3 Flowchart for Revising an Illustration Essay

QUESTIONS

REVISION STRATEGIES

1. Highlight your thesis statement. Place a checkmark ✔ by each example. Does your thesis clearly indicate the generalization that your examples support?

— **NO** →
- Revise your thesis, changing your generalization so that it fits your examples.

YES

2. *Write* a sentence describing your audience. Cross out any examples ✔ that won't appeal to your audience. Do you have enough examples left?

— **NO** →
- Brainstorm examples that are more appealing to your audience.
- Add examples that represent different aspects of or viewpoints on your topic.

YES

3. *Write* a sentence stating the purpose of your essay. Cross out any examples ✔ that don't fulfill your purpose. Do you have enough examples left?

— **NO** →
- Brainstorm examples that are more appropriate to your purpose.
- Add some of these examples or consider cutting back and using one extended example.

YES

4. Reread each example ✔ you checked in question 1. Is each one accurate, relevant, striking, representative, and specific? Are the examples varied?

— **NO** →
- Eliminate examples that are dull, irrelevant, not representative, or misleading.
- Brainstorm or conduct research to discover relevant, representative, or more striking examples.
- Revise vague or misleading examples to include more details.
- Consider adding other kinds of examples (anecdotes, expert opinion, statistics).

YES

5. Underline the topic sentence of each paragraph. Does each paragraph have a topic sentence? Does each topic sentence clearly make a point that the example(s) ✔ in that paragraph illustrate?

— **NO** →
- Add a topic sentence or revise the existing one to clearly indicate the point each example or group of examples illustrates.
- Reorganize your essay, grouping examples according to the idea they illustrate.

YES

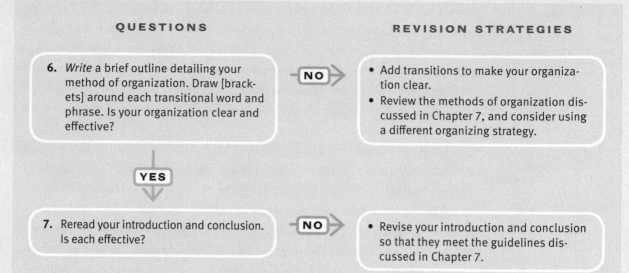

QUESTIONS

6. *Write* a brief outline detailing your method of organization. Draw [brackets] around each transitional word and phrase. Is your organization clear and effective?

NO →

REVISION STRATEGIES

- Add transitions to make your organization clear.
- Review the methods of organization discussed in Chapter 7, and consider using a different organizing strategy.

YES

7. Reread your introduction and conclusion. Is each effective?

NO →

- Revise your introduction and conclusion so that they meet the guidelines discussed in Chapter 7.

Students Write

Nick Ruggia, a student at the University of Maryland at College Park, wrote this essay in response to an assignment in which he was asked to examine an American obsession. He chose to write about Americans' obsession with physical appearance. As you read his illustration essay, notice how he supports his thesis with a variety of examples.

Conforming to Stand Out: A Look at American Beauty

Nick Ruggia

In nature, two factors largely determine survival of the species: access to resources and physical attraction (necessary for the ability to mate). Humans function under the same basic rules. In modern America, where almost everyone can acquire the basic resources to live, humans are striving harder than ever to be physically attractive. Although men are increasingly caught up in its grip, the pressure to be beautiful falls most intensely on women. The thin craze, the plastic surgery craze, and the body art craze represent some of the increasingly drastic lengths American women are being driven to in their quest for physical perfection.

Since Kate Moss's wafer-thin frame took the modeling industry by storm, skinny has driven America's aesthetics. Hollywood is a mirror for our desires, and our starlets are shrinking. Nicole Ritchie and Angelina Jolie, among others, have publicly struggled with eating disorders. Jennifer Anniston and Reese Witherspoon are rumored to be following a diet of baby food to keep weight off (Crawford A1). And the stars aren't alone. According to the United States National Institutes of Mental Health, between 0.5 and 3.7 percent of American women will suffer from

1

2

READING

Title: Ruggia identifies his topic and suggests his thesis. Introduction: Ruggia offers a biological reason for focusing on women. In his thesis statement, he makes a generalization about American women, and previews his organization by presenting his three examples in the order in which he will discuss them.

A topic sentence introduces Example 1: the thin craze. In this paragraph and the next two, Ruggia uses specific celebrities and detailed statistics to support his claims.

(continued on next page)

The statistics suggest that the celebrities are representative of Americans in general. Ruggia cites the sources for his subexamples using MLA style.

anorexia in their lifetimes, while another 1.1 to 4.2 percent will be bulimic and 2 to 5 percent will binge. These numbers exclude the disordered eaters who do not meet all the criteria necessary for diagnosis or do not accurately self-report. In a population of 300 million, these statistics represent millions of women struggling with eating disorders. Men are not immune either, accounting for 5 to 15 percent of bulimia and anorexia diagnoses and 35 percent of binge-eating cases. The skinny obsession is spiraling out of control as more people risk death to be thin through diet pills and gastric bypass surgery.

A transitional sentence leads into the topic sentence for Example 2: the plastic surgery craze.

But for every Kate Moss idolizer, there's a would-be Pamela Anderson. This ideal, fed by porn 3 and Hollywood, is plastic perfection: instead of anorexically denying their curves, many women choose to enhance their features through surgery. The American Society of Plastic Surgeons (ASPS) reports that in 2009, there were nearly 12.5 million cosmetic surgeries in the United States and an additional 5.2 million reconstructive plastic surgeries. While it must be remembered that the rule is not one surgery per person, so that the number of *patients* is lower than these figures, the scope of this practice is staggering nonetheless. Further evidence is provided by the surgically enhanced lips, stomachs, buttocks, and breasts that cover the pages of men's magazines all

Ruggia cites striking subexamples.

over the country. Strippers, porn stars like Jenna Jameson, and *Playboy* models like Anderson and the late Anna Nicole Smith flaunt enormous fake breasts. Clearly there is a disconnect between the sexless anorexic standard that so many women strive for and the bottle blonde bombshell that so many men favor. What everyone seems to agree on, though, is that plastic surgery is a response to the fear of aging. And in this way as well, men too are increasingly vulnerable to the superficial, with the ASPS reporting that they accounted for 9 percent of plastic surgeries in 2009.

A topic sentence introduces Example 3: the body art craze.

Body art, in the form of piercing and tattoos, also illustrates (literally) Americans' obsession 4 with physical appearance. The pierced and tattooed once jarred on public sensibilities, but now these body modifications have gone mainstream. Even "alternative" piercings are now accepted: Amy Winehouse, a heavily tattooed popular musician, has added to the popularity of the "Monroe" piercing, located above the lip where Marilyn Monroe had a mole. Nearly half the members of "Generation Next" have had a tattoo, piercing or "untraditional color" of hair (Pew Research Center 21). Once largely limited to sailors, criminals, and punk rockers--and to men--body art has become big business, drawing in more women as it spreads.

Conclusion: Ruggia acknowledges that attention to appearance is nothing new, but suggests that Americans today place too much emphasis on it. Ruggia lists his sources in MLA style, with the entries in alphabetical order. Notice the style for listing documents from Web sites sponsored by organizations and government agencies.

Maybe Americans have gone too far in basing their self-worth on physical appearance. Every visible 5 part of the human body has been marketed as a fixable flaw or an opportunity for more adornment. Of course, Americans have always cared about their looks and made great efforts to improve them, but once most people kept the issue in perspective. Today, appearance rules. And men increasingly are joining women in obedience to its commands. Both sexes, though, will find that basing self-esteem on physical appearance, a fleeting commodity at best, is a recipe for misery.

Works Cited

American Society of Plastic Surgeons. "2009 Quick Facts." *Plastic Surgery.org*. ASPS, 2010. Web. 25 Oct. 2010.

Crawford, Trish. "Celebrity 'Baby Food Diet' Recipe for Eating Disorder." *Toronto Star* 18 May 2010: A1. Print.

Pew Research Center for the People and the Press. *How Young People View Their Lives, Futures, and Politics: A Portrait of "Generation Next."* Washington: Pew, 2007. *Pew Research Center for the People and the Press*. Web. 25 Oct. 2010.

United States. National Institutes of Mental Health. *The Numbers Count: Mental Disorders in America*. NIMH, 7 Dec. 2007. Web. 26 Oct. 2010.

Analyzing the Writer's Technique

1. Evaluate the three main examples Ruggia provides. How well do they illustrate his thesis? What other examples could he have used?
2. Ruggia used four sources in writing the essay. What kinds of sources are they? How does his use of these sources strengthen his essay?
3. Ruggia uses celebrities and statistics as subexamples to support each of the topic sentences about his three main examples. What other types of subexamples could he have used?

Thinking Critically about Illustration

1. Do any of Ruggia's examples or subexamples create an emotional impact? If so, choose several and explain their effects.
2. What are the connotations of "bottle blond bombshell" (para. 3)?
3. What other types of sources could Ruggia have used to give alternative viewpoints?
4. Is the generalization in the last sentence of the essay well-supported and explained in the essay?

Reacting to the Essay

1. Discuss the meaning and effectiveness of Ruggia's title.
2. To what extent do you agree that piercings and tattoos are widely accepted?
3. What do you think is the reason for the "disconnect" that Ruggia mentions in paragraph 3? Is the problem that women don't understand what men want? That men don't understand what they want? Both? Something else?

4. Are Americans obsessed with appearances in other ways? Write an essay explaining another American obsession. Use examples to support your thesis.

READING AN ILLUSTRATION ESSAY

The following section provides advice for reading illustration essays. Two essays follow. The first exemplifies the characteristics of illustration covered in this chapter and provides opportunities to examine, analyze, and react to the writer's ideas. The second uses illustration along with other methods of development.

Working with Text: Reading Illustration Essays

Examples are dramatic, real, and concrete, and it is easy to pay too much attention to them. Be sure to focus on the key points the examples illustrate. Below are some suggestions for reading illustration essays with a focused eye.

What to Look For, Highlight, and Annotate

1. Read the essay more than once. Read it first to grasp its basic ideas; reread it to analyze its structure and content.
2. Begin by identifying and highlighting the thesis statement. If the thesis is not directly stated, ask yourself this question: What one major point do all of the examples illustrate?
3. Study and highlight the examples. Note in the margin the characteristics or aspects of the thesis each example illustrates.
4. Record your response to each example, either by using annotations or by writing in a journal. Try to answer these questions: How well do the examples explain or clarify the thesis? Do I feel convinced of the writer's thesis after reading the essay? Would more or different examples have been more effective?
5. Notice how the examples are organized. Are they organized in order of importance, in chronological order, in spatial order, or by some other method?
6. Note how the examples fit with any other patterns of development used in the essay.

For more on reading strategies, see Chapter 3.

How to Find Ideas to Write About

For more on discovering ideas for a response paper, see Chapter 4, pp. 89–90.

When you are asked to write a response to an illustration essay, look for ideas to write about as you read. Try to think of similar or related examples from your personal experience. While reading "Rambos of the Road," for instance, you might have thought about driving behaviors you have observed. You might have recalled other examples of drivers who exhibit road rage, who are oblivious to those around them, who are reckless, or who are careful and considerate. Each of these examples could lead you to a thesis and ideas for writing.

Thinking Critically about Illustration

When you read text that uses illustration to support generalizations, read with a critical eye. Study the examples and how they are used in the essay. Use the following questions to think critically about the examples you read.

1. What Is the Emotional Impact of the Examples?

A description of a tiger pacing in a small zoo enclosure, rubbing its body against a fence, and scratching an open sore would provide a vivid example of the behavior exhibited by some wild animals in captivity. Such an example can evoke feelings of pity, sympathy, or even outrage. Writers often choose examples to manipulate their readers' feelings, especially in persuasive writing. Although it is not necessarily wrong for a writer to use examples that evoke emotional responses, as a critical reader you should be aware of their use.

For more on emotional appeals, see Chapter 19, p. 518.

When you encounter an example that evokes an emotional response, try to set your emotions aside and look at the example objectively. In the case of the tiger, for instance, you might ask, Why are animals held in captivity? What are the benefits of zoos?

2. How Well Do the Examples Support the Generalization?

Not all writers choose examples that convey a full picture of the subject. In the example about zoos, you might ask if the animals in all zoos are confined in small enclosures. Especially when you read persuasive writing, attempt to confirm through other sources that the writer's examples are fair and representative, and try to think of examples that might contradict the writer's point. A writer who chooses dramatic but extreme examples may be attempting to make his or her case stronger than it really is. In "Rambos of the Road," Gottfried presents an extreme example of road rage when describing the incident of the bus, but he admits it is not typical by calling it "the most amazing example." If Gottfried had claimed that this incident is an everyday occurrence, he would have been misleading.

Also evaluate whether the writer provides *enough* examples and whether other types of examples, such as statistics or expert opinion, might have strengthened the essay. In the essay "Sustainability on the Menu," for instance, statistics on the amount of organic food purchased by colleges and universities in general, not just those with the largest endowments, would be relevant.

Finally, you should consider whether an example is relevant to the generalization it is illustrating. For example, Nick Ruggia's essay uses body art as an example of Americans' obsession with making themselves physically attractive. Although this may be the reason that some people get tattoos and piercings, others may desire to express their feelings or to annoy their parents.

ILLUSTRATION ESSAY

As you read the following essay by Bill Bryson, consider how the author uses the elements of illustration discussed in this chapter.

Snoopers at Work
Bill Bryson

Bill Bryson (b. 1951) grew up in the United States but lived from 1977 to 1995 in England and returned there in 2003. Originally a newspaper writer, Bryson is well known for his travel books, which include *A Walk in the Woods* (1998), *I'm a Stranger Here Myself* (1999), and *Bill Bryson's African Diary* (2002). His other works include *The Mother Tongue: English and How It Got That Way* (1990), *Made in America: An Informal History of the English Language in the United States* (1998), *The Life and Times of the Thunderbolt Kid: A Memoir* (2006), and *At Home: A Short History of Private Life* (2010).

The essays in *I'm a Stranger Here Myself* began as Sunday columns in a British newspaper, *The Mail*. In the following piece from that collection, Bryson discusses the invasion of workers' privacy by their employers. As you read, pay attention to the kinds of examples the author chooses to illustrate this disturbing trend, and notice how he uses humor to comment on the material.

Now here is something to bear in mind should you ever find yourself using a changing room in a department store or other retail establishment. It is perfectly legal—indeed, it is evidently routine—for the store to spy on you while you are trying on their clothes.   1

I know this because I have just been reading a book by Ellen Alderman and Caroline Kennedy called *The Right to Privacy*, which is full of alarming tales of ways that businesses and employers can—and enthusiastically do—intrude into what would normally be considered private affairs.   2

The business of changing-cubicle spying came to light in 1983 when a customer trying on clothes in a department store in Michigan discovered that a store employee had climbed a stepladder and was watching him through a metal vent. (Is this tacky or what?) The customer was sufficiently outraged that he sued the store for invasion of privacy. He lost. A state court held that it was reasonable for retailers to defend against shoplifting by engaging in such surveillance.   3

He shouldn't have been surprised. Nearly everyone is being spied on in some way in America these days. A combination of technological advances, employer paranoia, and commercial avarice means that many millions of Americans are having their lives delved into in ways that would have been impossible, not to say unthinkable, a dozen years ago. . . .   4

Many companies are taking advantage of technological possibilities to make their businesses more ruthlessly productive. In Maryland, according to *Time* magazine, a bank searched through the medical records of its borrowers—apparently quite legally—to find out which of them had life-threatening illnesses and used this information to cancel their loans. Other companies have focused not on customers but on their own employees—for instance, to check what prescription drugs the employees   5 are taking. One large, well-known company teamed up with a pharmaceutical firm to comb through the health records of employees to see who might benefit from a dose of antidepressants. The idea was that the company would get more serene workers; the drug company would get more customers.

According to the American Management Association two-thirds of companies in 6 the United States spy on their employees in some way. Thirty-five percent track phone calls, and 10 percent actually tape phone conversations to review at leisure later. About a quarter of companies surveyed admitted to going through their employees' computer files and reading their e-mail.

Still other companies are secretly watching their employees at work. A secretary at 7 a college in Massachusetts discovered that a hidden video camera was filming her office twenty-four hours a day. Goodness knows what the school authorities were hoping to find. What they got were images of a woman changing out of her work clothes and into a track suit each night in order to jog home from work. She is suing and will probably get a pot of money. But elsewhere courts have upheld companies' rights to spy on their workers.

There is a particular paranoia about drugs. I have a friend who got a job with a large 8 manufacturing company in Iowa a year or so ago. Across the street from the company was a tavern that was the company after-hours hangout. One night my friend was having a beer after work with his colleagues when he was approached by a fellow employee who asked if he knew where she could get some marijuana. He said he didn't use the stuff himself, but to get rid of her—for she was very persistent—he gave her the phone number of an acquaintance who sometimes sold it.

The next day he was fired. The woman, it turned out, was a company spy employed 9 solely to weed out drug use in the company. He hadn't supplied her with marijuana, you understand, hadn't encouraged her to use marijuana, and had stressed that he didn't use marijuana himself. Nonetheless he was fired for encouraging and abetting the use of an illegal substance.

Already, 91 percent of large companies—I find this almost unbelievable—now test 10 some of their workers for drugs. Scores of companies have introduced what are called TAD rules—TAD being short for "tobacco, alcohol, and drugs"—which prohibit employees from using any of these substances at any time, including at home. There are companies, if you can believe it, that forbid their employees to drink or smoke at any time—even one beer, even on a Saturday night—and enforce the rules by making their workers give urine samples.

But it gets even more sinister than that. Two leading electronics companies working 11 together have invented something called an "active badge," which tracks the movements of any worker compelled to wear one. The badge sends out an infrared signal every fifteen seconds. This signal is received by a central computer, which is thus able to keep a record of where every employee is and has been, whom they have associated with, how many times they have been to the toilet or water cooler—in short, to log every single action of their working day. If that isn't ominous, I don't know what is.

However, there is one development, I am pleased to report, that makes all of this 12 worthwhile. A company in New Jersey has patented a device for determining whether restaurant employees have washed their hands after using the lavatory. Now *that* I can go for.

Examining the Reading

1. How did it become generally known that stores watch customers in changing rooms?
2. According to Bryson, what are the reasons for today's high levels of spying?
3. What proportion of companies spy on their employees?
4. Explain what an "active badge" (para. 11) is and how it works.
5. Explain the meaning of each of the following words as it is used in the reading: *surveillance* (3), *avarice* (4), *delved* (4), *paranoia* (8), and *abetting* (9).

Analyzing the Writer's Technique

1. The essay opens with an activity that Bryson asks readers to picture themselves doing. Why is this an effective introduction?
2. "Private affairs" (para. 2) is an abstract term. How does Bryson make this term real and understandable? What is included in it, according to Bryson?
3. Bryson's humorous conclusion seems somewhat at odds with the serious tone of the rest of the essay. How effective do you find it?

Thinking Critically about Illustration

1. What generalization does Bryson make? How effectively is the generalization stated and supported in this essay? Are the examples relevant and representative? Does Bryson include enough examples? Explain your responses.
2. What is the emotional effect of Bryson's examples? What fears and insecurities do they play on? How might various readers (customers, employees, business owners) react to these examples?
3. What is the connotation of the word "tacky" (para. 3)?
4. How would the essay be different if Bryson had included examples of surveillance that caught shoplifters, employees who were stealing, or employees who were using drugs at work? What effect would such examples have had?

Reacting to the Reading

1. Imagine that the last time you tried on clothes in a store's dressing room you were watched by security workers. How does this make you feel? How might you behave differently the next time you are in a store?
2. What reasons might employers and store owners offer to defend the actions that Bryson describes? Write an essay from their point of view that defends it.
3. What other methods are used to spy on people? Write a journal entry describing some locations and activities that have video monitoring and your feelings about whether they are justified.

ILLUSTRATION COMBINED WITH OTHER PATTERNS

As you read the following essay by Christina Rouvalis, notice how she uses examples along with other patterns of development to support her main point.

Hey Mom, Dad, May I Have My Room Back?
Cristina Rouvalis

READING

Christina Rouvalis's essays and articles have appeared in magazines such as *Inc.*, *AARP Bulletin*, *Pittsburgh Quarterly*, *Carnegie Mellon Today*, and *Carnegie Magazine*. She was a feature writer for the *Pittsburgh Post-Gazette* where the following piece appeared in August 2008. As you read the selection, look for and highlight the examples Rouvalis uses to support her thesis.

Bobby Franklin Jr., confident and energetic, seemed on a trajectory to an independent 1 life—going to college, moving into an off-campus apartment and jumping into the banking industry just weeks after his last final exam. Only, the Clarion University graduate circled back home like a boomerang. Inside his parents' elegant five-bedroom house in Plum, he has settled into a roomy bedroom, with its own staircase leading outside. His return home has raised nary an eyebrow with his peers. After all, he said, most of his friends have moved home, too. "Everyone is doing it. No one says, 'Why are you still at home?'" said the 24-year-old. "I never get that. It is more like, 'Stay at home as long as you can and save.'"

Some parents who pondered the loneliness of empty-nest syndrome are facing a 2 surprising new question. When will their young adult children leave home—and this time for good? The sight of a college graduate moving into his or her childhood bedroom, filled with dusty high school trophies and curling rock-star posters, is no longer an oddity. A sour economy, big college loans and sky-high city rents have made some new graduates defer their plans to strike out on their own.

Boomerangers, as they are called, are everywhere you look. Some 14.5 million 3 children age 18 to 24 lived at home in 2007, up from 6.4 million in 1960, according to U.S. Census figures. To be sure, much of the increase simply reflects overall population growth—as the actual percentage of men living at home is up only slightly, from 52 percent in 1960 to 55 percent in 2007. The bigger change has occurred with women. Nearly half in this age range were living at home in 2007, up from 35 percent nearly a half century ago—a shift attributed in part to the delay in marriage.

Other reports suggest the number of boomerangers is even higher—and has grown 4 as a tough economy has made it harder for debt-laden college grads to find jobs. Some 77 percent of college graduates who responded to an unscientific readers survey by the online entry job site CollegeGrad.com said they were living with Mom and Dad in 2008, up from 67 percent in a 2006 survey. "We see a larger percentage of Gen-Yers or Millennials, or whatever tag we want to use, have a closer relationship to their parents and feel more comfortable relying on parental support," said Heidi Hanisko, director of client services for CollegeGrad.com. "There is less of a stigma than there was five or

Life Interrupted: % of each group who say they did the following because of the recession...

■ 18-24   ■ 25-34   □ 35+

Postponed getting married
10
21
6

Postponed having a baby
12
15
4

Moved in with a roommate
24
3
3

Moved back in with parents
6
11
1

Took in a border
2
2
2

Note: "Don't know/Refused" responses not shown.
Pew Research Center

10 years ago." "We see that as a good thing that college grads are willing to go to their parents for support, but we encourage students to stand on their own. It seems the reliance can be too much and spill over on their ability to do the job."

Others also wonder if this generation is coast- 5 ing and letting their parents do too much. But Jeffrey Jensen Arnett, author of *Emerging Adult-hood: The Winding Road from the Late Teens Through the Twenties*, is tired of hearing all the judgments against the Boomerang generation. Most of them move home for a year or two while they go through a transition and a period of self discovery—waiting for graduate school, looking for a fulfilling career option, paying down a huge loan, or saving enough so they can afford big-city rent. "People jump to the conclusion that they are lazy and irresponsible and pampered and self-indulgent," said Dr. Arnett, a research professor at Clark University in Worcester, Mass. "It is not true. Think about the ones you know. Are they lazy? Do they stand around in their un-derwear watching TV? No. They are out working their bottoms off trying to make money in these crummy jobs available to them in their 20s."

'GRANDMA'S BOY'

Mike Masilunas' old childhood bedroom—the one with photos of him fly fishing and   6
Jerome Bettis playing football—was converted into an office inside his family's Peters house. So when Mr. Masilunas, a graduate of Penn State Erie, moved home in May of 2007, he had to share a room with his older brother. In the musical bedrooms of his household, Mr. Masilunas later took over his younger sister's bedroom when she headed off to college. "We joke about the movie *Grandma's Boy*, hanging out all the time, sleeping on the coach," said Mr. Masilunas, referring to the comedy about the guy who gets evicted from his apartment and moves in with his grandmother.

The 23-year-old financial consultant said it made sense to live at home because it   7
is close to his office. Plus, there is the matter of $40,000 in student loans. "I can put $600 toward school loans instead of rent," he said. "Rather than living for right now, I am thinking about a house and retirement. I can put up with this for a few years." Most of his friends understand because they are at home too. Sometimes he catches flak. "You gotta get out of there," one friend told him recently. "The ones who give me flak are the ones spending money like idiots," he said. "They are also the same ones who complain about not having money."

And there are trade-offs to his rent-free existence. He gets along well with his par-   8
ents and pitches in with chores, but it is an adjustment to go from total freedom to being under his mother's watch. "A mother will always be a mother. They only want the best for you. They are always nagging you. I kind of zone it out. 'Do this. Do that.' The

first month it was like, 'Let's pull back the reins a little bit.'" Plus there is the culture shock of going from a college campus to a quiet residential neighborhood—something Brenna O'Shea experienced after graduating from West Virginia University and heading back to her parents' home in Mt. Lebanon.

Even though the 21-year-old Ms. O'Shea has plenty of company—most of her friends 9 from elementary school have done the same thing—she misses the energy of the campus. Her first night back in Mt. Lebanon, she caught herself yelling a little on the street. "I had to check myself," It can be a hard adjustment both ways, Dr. Arnett said. "If children regret coming home, it is not because of the stigma. They like their parents and their parents like them. But they want to make their own decisions without parental commentary. Parents aren't that crazy about it either. They like not knowing. If they don't have any idea what time their kids come home or who they are with, ignorance is bliss."

In the Franklin home, Jan and Bobby Franklin, parents of Bobby Jr., can't help but 10 worry about their son when he is out. Even so, they like having him around, especially since he follows the house rules of picking up after himself. Mrs. Franklin knows another mother who put her 30-year-old son's mattress on the porch, a not-so-subtle hint to fly on his own. "I could never do that to my son—as long as he is not causing any problems." Still mother and son have a standing joke about his boomerang back home.

"When are you going to move out?" she asks Bobby Jr. 11

Bobby, who plans to leave in a year or two, quips back, "I am not going anywhere 12 until I am at least 30."

Examining the Reading

1. Describe the type of college graduate who is most likely to return to live at home.
2. What are the most common reasons that adult children return home?
3. What are some of the disadvantages of returning home to live with one's parents?
4. What concerns do parents have about these living arrangements?
5. Explain the meaning of each of the following words as it is used in the reading: *trajectory* (para. 1), *nary* (1), *stigma* (4), *pampered* (5), and *flak* (7).

Analyzing the Writer's Technique

1. Express Rouvalis's thesis in your own words. Is it directly stated in the essay?
2. The essay opens with an example that illustrates the subject and returns to it in the final paragraph. Why is this technique effective?
3. What audience is Rouvalis addressing? How do her examples address this audience?

Visualizing the Reading

Rouvalis uses cause and effect in addition to illustration in her essay. Use the chart on page 334 to identify the causes and effects discussed in each paragraph listed. The first one has been done for you.

Paragraph Number	Cause or Effect Discussed
Paragraph 3	The increase in boomerangers may be caused by overall population growth or by delays in age at marriage.
Paragraph 4	
Paragraph 5	
Paragraph 7	

Thinking Critically about Illustration

1. What is the connotation of the term "boomerang" (para. 1)? Is it positive or negative?
2. In addition to interviewing boomerangers, Rouvalis includes statistics (from the U.S. Census and an "online entry job site") and quotations (from a representative of the site and from an academic expert on young adults). How trustworthy do you consider these sources of information?
3. Does Rouvalis provide enough examples to support her thesis? Are the examples fair and representative of the situation that college graduates face?
4. The essay focuses on examples of young people whose parents welcome them back home. How might the piece be different if Rouvalis had interviewed parents who refused to allow their kids to return or resented that they had returned?
5. Analyze the example of Mike Masilunas. Does he offer fact or opinion in his quoted statements?
6. Rouvalis's article is about recent college graduates, and the people she interviews all fit the eighteen to twenty-four age category in the graph on page 332. But the graph suggests that people age twenty-five to thirty-four have been about twice as likely as the younger group to move back in with their parents because of the recession. Those in the younger group are apparently much more likely to have moved in with a roommate instead of their parents. What might be the reasons for these patterns?
7. Consider the three living-arrangement categories in the graph on page 332. Are these categories mutually exclusive, or might they overlap with one another? What other living-arrangement categories might have been included in the survey and the graph?

Reacting to the Reading

1. What would be the strongest reason for you to live with your parents after college? How would it make you feel? How would they react?
2. What rules or agreements would make living at home after college acceptable for you? Write a journal entry describing them.

3. Mike Masilunas explains that he's willing to put up with some of the problems of living at home to get the benefits of the situation. Write an essay describing a situation in which you tolerate some disadvantages to experience the benefits associated with it.

Applying Your Skills: Additional Essay Assignments

Write an illustration essay on one of the topics below, using what you learned about illustration in this chapter. Depending on the topic you choose, you may need to conduct library or Internet research.

For more on locating and documenting sources, see Part 5.

To Express Your Ideas

1. In an article for the campus newspaper, explain what you consider to be the three most important qualities of a college instructor. Support your opinion with vivid examples from your experience.
2. Explain to a general audience the role played by grandparents within a family, citing examples from your family.

To Inform Your Reader

3. In "Rambos of the Road," Martin Gottfried explains the concept of "auto macho," also known as "road rage," using examples from his own experience. Explain the concept of *peer pressure,* using examples from your experience.
4. Describe to an audience of college students the qualities or achievements you think should be emphasized during job interviews. Give examples that show why the qualities or achievements you choose are important to potential employers.

To Persuade Your Reader

5. Argue for or against an increased emphasis on physical education in public schools. Your audience is your local school committee.
6. In a letter to the editor of a local newspaper, argue for or against the establishment of a neighborhood watch group.

Cases Using Illustration

7. Prepare the oral presentation you will give to your local town board to convince them to lower the speed limit on your street. Use examples as well as other types of evidence.
8. Write a letter to the parents of three-year-old children who will begin attending your day-care center this year, explaining how they can prepare their children for the day-care experience. Support your advice with brief but relevant examples.

CHAPTER 14

Process Analysis: Explaining How Something Works or Is Done

The screen shot on the opposite page shows people using Skype, the Internet service that offers free communication between computers allowing users both to see and to hear each other.

Write a brief paragraph describing how to get, set up, and use Skype or another Internet service or device. Your audience is other people who wish to use the service or device for the first time.

WRITING A PROCESS ANALYSIS

To describe the steps involved in using Skype, you had to explain a process. You use process analysis whenever you explain how something is done or how it works—how to make lasagna, how to change a flat tire, or how a bill becomes law. This chapter will show you how to write a well-organized, easy-to-understand process analysis essay and how to incorporate process analysis into essays that use other patterns of development.

What Is Process Analysis?

A **process analysis** explains in step-by-step fashion how something works or how something is done or made. Process analyses provide people with practical information—directions for assembling equipment, instructions for registering for classes, an explanation of how a medication works. Whatever the purpose, the information in a process analysis must be accurate, clear, and easy to follow.

Process analysis is a common type of writing in college and on the job (see the accompanying box for a few examples). Two types of writing situations call for the use of process analysis:

- To explain *how to do something* to readers *who want or need to perform the process*
- To explain *how something works* to readers *who want to understand the process but not actually perform it*

The first type, a *how-to essay,* may explain how to teach a child the alphabet, for instance. Your primary purpose in writing a how-to essay is to present the steps in the process clearly and completely so that your readers can perform the task you describe. For the second type of process analysis, a *how-it-works essay,* you might explain how a

SCENES FROM COLLEGE AND THE WORKPLACE

- For a *child development* course, your assignment is to visit a day-care center, choose one confrontation between a child and a teacher, and explain how the teacher resolved the conflict.

- As part of a *chemistry* lab report, you are asked to summarize the procedure you followed in preparing a solution or conducting an experiment.

- While working as an *engineer* at a water treatment plant, you are asked by your supervisor to write a description of how the city's drinking water is tested and treated for contamination.

popular radio talk show screens its callers. Your primary purpose in writing a how-it-works essay is to present the steps in the process clearly enough so that your readers can fully understand it. At times, you may read or write essays that contain elements of both types of process analysis. In writing about how a car alarm system works, for example, you might find it necessary to explain how to activate and deactivate the system as well as how it works.

The following essay exemplifies a how-to process analysis essay.

How to Interview
MONSTER.COM

Monster.com is one of the largest employment sites on the Internet. It offers extensive job listings and advice on job searches, résumé preparation, and salary negotiation. As you read the selection, highlight the steps in the interview process.

Today's job marketplace is hypercompetitive. There can be dozens or even hundreds of people vying for one quality position. If you want to land that dream job, you will need to know some specific tips that will keep you head and shoulders above the rest of the pack. Interviewing for a job is not most people's favorite situation. In effect, an interview is where one is evaluated by an employer. In many cases, in order to land that job, you can't crack under the pressure; you have to be strong and sell yourself. Here are some tips to remember for the next time you interview. 1

So, you are looking for a job, have sent in your résumé and finally have been called in to interview for the position. The good news is that your chances of landing the job have just gone up; the bad news is that you are not through the woods yet. While being called for an interview reduces the number of people that you are in competition with, it also raises the stakes as well. Where maybe a hundred people send in a résumé for a job, an interview usually thins the competition to about 3 to 10 applicants. If you really want to land the job, here are some things to keep in mind. 2

BE PREPARED
Being prepared cannot be emphasized enough. Preparation is essential to doing well on an interview and landing a job. You don't want to come off to your interviewer as if you just stepped in off the street. Preparation can come in many different forms; the most apparent ones are discussed below. 3

Know about the company. Interviewers want to see that you don't just want a job, but want to work for their company. 4

Be prepared to talk about yourself. Make sure you are ready to talk about yourself. This is an interview, so if you don't want to talk about your past, future goals or your skill set, don't bother showing up. 5

Be prepared to ask smart questions. Interviews are not interrogations. There should be a back and forth of communication and ideas. You should not only be answering questions, but asking intelligent questions. Before arriving for the interview, memorize or write down a few questions that interest you. 6

FIRST IMPRESSIONS

Once you are called in for an interview, you will need to sell yourself in a short period 7
of time to someone that you have never met before. Human resource recruiters are
quite skilled at arrival and judging others. There are winning candidates and candidates that are total losers. Your mission is to come off as a winner. You should show
yourself in a good light and present yourself as an excellent candidate. Here are some
tips on making a great first impression.

Show up on time. One of the worst things that you can do is show up late to an in- 8
terview. A late interviewer tells the recruiter that you don't take the job seriously, you
are not punctual and are unmotivated to find a new job. If you are running late or are
experiencing traffic or an unforeseen event, call ahead. Nine out of 10 times calling
ahead will not put any negative consequences on your chances of employment.

Dress to impress. One of the most important pieces to the puzzle of making a good 9
first impression is to dress to impress. Dressing well for an interview means that you
are wearing smart business attire and are well groomed. This shows that you care how
you look, have confidence and will be a good representative for the company if you are
hired. During the summer months, many job applicants sometimes dress down. Dressing down can only hurt your chances of landing a job. Always dress appropriately. If
you have the slightest doubts about an outfit, choose another outfit to wear.

Be confident. It is imperative that you show confidence when you show up for your 10
interview. No one is impressed by someone who is very meek or extremely shy. You
don't have to be obnoxious or act super cool, but be the best that you can be.

Greet the recruiter properly. Believe it or not, the way you greet the recruiter mat- 11
ters. A nice proper hello with a smile and a decent handshake will do the trick. Never

Which person would you hire?

frown, look down or look away when meeting someone. Also, it is good to stand up and show interest. The recruiter is a person, and it is not only what you say that matters, but also how you make the other person feel.

DURING THE INTERVIEW

Now that you are done with the meet and greet and have given the recruiter a good first 12 impression of yourself, the interview begins. Some applicants freeze up and get very self-conscious. No one likes being judged, and while the interview process is exactly this, there are ways to avoid the common pitfalls and instead shine during the interview process.

Be prepared. Make sure you have done your homework and are well prepared for 13 the interview. This means that you should have researched the company beforehand, understood its products or services and know a few interesting facts about the company. What you want to convey to the employer is that you are genuinely interested in working for this company. Anyone can find a job, but human resource recruiters want to hire people who genuinely want to work for their firm.

Answer questions clearly and completely. Obviously, the interview process involves 14 the job recruiter asking you questions. It is very important that you answer these questions clearly and be thorough with your answers. It is extremely easy to tell when someone is lying, so be honest and forthcoming. Many questions that recruiters ask are obvious questions and are quite common. You can easily prepare beforehand for many of these obvious questions. Some of the most common questions asked by recruiters are

- What are your strengths and weaknesses?
- Why do you want to work for this organization?
- Why are you leaving your current or last position?
- What would you like to achieve at your new position if hired?
- Do you work well with others or prefer to work on your own?
- What are your successes and failures?
- What kind of salary range are you looking to be in?
- What are your credentials (education, special training, etc.)
- Do you have any hobbies?

ASK QUESTIONS DURING THE INTERVIEW

Try to think of the interview as a conversation instead of an interrogation. Many job 15 applicants receive high marks by the recruiter if they ask insightful and intelligent questions. You should be very engaging in the interview. This shows the recruiter that you are genuinely interested in the position. While questions are good, make sure they are intelligent; asking questions just for sake of asking is a waste of time for both you and the recruiter. Some of the questions you might want to ask an interviewer are

- What are you looking for in an employee?
- What is the reason for the open position (is it due to growth or turnover)?
- Could you describe some of the challenges this position offers?
- Could you describe the working environment, work culture, etc.?
- Could you describe some of the benefits of working for your company?

- When will the job be available (are you looking to hire someone as soon as possible or in the next few months)?

AFTER THE INTERVIEW

Once the interview is complete, it is wise to do a couple of things. You should write the   16
recruiter a thank-you letter and follow up with the recruiter. These days, a job applicant
might have to go through 3 interviews to land a job. It is important to stay on the recruiter's radar as being a high-quality applicant. Many times, after an interview is over,
recruiters will state that if they are interested they will give you a call; other times they
will try to schedule you for a second interview.

If a recruiter doesn't give you a definite vote of confidence once the interview is   17
over, it doesn't mean that you didn't do well or you aren't a good applicant. Many
times, there are other things working in the background. Some departments wait to the
last possible moment to fill positions; other times a key executive who gives the green
light to hire might be out of the office. If you are not hired, don't consider yourself a
failure. There are plenty more jobs out in the marketplace.

Characteristics of Process Analysis Essays

A process analysis essay should include everything your reader needs to know to understand or perform the process. In addition to presenting an explicit thesis, the essay
should provide a clear, step-by-step description of the process; define key terms; give
any necessary background information; describe any equipment needed to perform
the process; supply an adequate amount of detail; and, for a how-to essay, anticipate
and offer help with potential problems.

Process Analysis Usually Includes an Explicit Thesis Statement

A process analysis usually contains a clear thesis that identifies the process to be discussed and suggests why the process is important or useful to the reader. In "How to
Interview," for instance, the writer states, "If you really want to land the job, here are
some things to keep to key in mind" (para. 2).

Here are two examples of thesis statements for how-to process analyses:

Switching to a low-fat diet, a recent nutritional trend, can improve weight control
dramatically.

By carefully preparing for a vacation in a foreign country, you can save time and prevent
hassles.

Here are two examples of thesis statements for how-it-works essays:

Although understanding the grieving process will not lessen the grief that you experience
after the death of a loved one, knowing that your experiences are normal does provide
some comfort.

Advertisers often appeal to the emotions of the audience for whom a product is targeted;
some of these appeals may be unethical.

Process Analysis Is Organized Chronologically

The steps or events in a process analysis are usually organized in chronological order—that is, the order in which the steps are normally completed. For essays that explain lengthy processes, the steps may be grouped into categories or divided into substeps to make the process easier to understand. Headings and transitional expressions and sentences are also often used to make the order of steps and substeps clear.

In "How to Interview," the writer divides the process into the stages of the interview process ("Be Prepared," "First Impressions," "During the Interview, and "After the Interview." To make the overall organization clear, the writer uses headings for these parts. To indicate movement from one stage to the next, the writer also uses transitions such as *"Once you are called for an interview," "Now that you are done with the meet and greet,"* and *"Once the interview is complete."*

On occasion, the steps of a process may not have to occur in any particular order. For example, in an essay on how to resolve a dispute between two coworkers, the order of the recommended actions may depend on the nature of the dispute. In this situation, some logical progression of recommended actions should be used, such as starting with informal or simple steps and progressing to more formal or complex ones.

Exercise 14.1

Choose one of the following processes. It should be one you are familiar with and able to explain to others. Draft a working thesis statement and a chronological list of the steps or stages of the process.

1. How to use a computer program
2. How to study for an exam
3. How to perform a task at work
4. How to operate a machine
5. How to complete an application (such as for college, a job, or a credit card)

Process Analysis Provides Background Information Helpful to Readers

In some process analysis essays, readers may need background information to understand the process. For example, in an explanation of how CPR (cardiopulmonary resuscitation) works, general readers might need information on how the heart functions to understand how pressing down on a person's breastbone propels blood into the arteries.

In some cases your audience may not be familiar with the technical terms associated with the process you are describing. If so, be sure to define such terms. In describing how CPR works, you would need to explain the meanings of such terms as *airway, sternum,* and *cardiac compression.*

For more on defining terms, see Chapter 17, p. 446–47.

When special equipment is needed to perform the process, you should describe the equipment for readers. For example, in an essay explaining how to scuba dive to unfamiliar readers, you would need to describe equipment such as dive masks, buoyancy compensators, and dive gauges. If necessary, you should also explain where to obtain the equipment.

Exercise 14.2

Choose one of the following processes that you are familiar with and are able to explain to others. For the process you choose, list the technical terms and definitions that you need to use to explain the process.

1. How to perform a task at home or at work (such as changing the oil in a car or taking notes during a court hearing)

2. How a piece of equipment or a machine works (such as a treadmill or a lawn mower)

3. How to repair an object (such as restringing a tennis racket or a violin)

Exercise 14.3

For the process you selected in Exercise 14.2 (above), consider what background information and equipment are needed to understand and perform the process.

Process Analysis Provides an Appropriate Level of Detail

In deciding what to include in a process analysis essay, you should be careful not to overwhelm your readers with too many details. An explanation of how to perform CPR written by and for physicians could be highly technical, but it should be much less so if written for a friend who is considering whether to enroll in a CPR course. In "How to Interview," the writer (although he or she is not writing about a technical topic) is careful to provide detailed information on how to be prepared and how to make a positive first impression, for example.

Keep in mind that when you write essays explaining technical or scientific processes, you can use sensory details and figures of speech to make your writing lively and interesting. Rather than giving dry technical details, try using descriptive language.

For a process involving many complex steps or highly specialized equipment, consider using a drawing or diagram to help your readers visualize the steps they need to follow or understand. For example, in an essay explaining how to detect a wiring problem in an electric stove, you might include a diagram of the stove's circuitry.

Process Analysis Anticipates Trouble Spots and Offers Solutions

Especially in a how-to essay, you need to anticipate potential trouble spots or areas of confusion and offer advice to the reader on how to avoid or resolve them. In "How to Interview," the writer cautions readers to be prepared and "not to look as if you just stepped in off the street," for example. A how-to essay should also warn readers of any difficult, complicated, or critical steps, encouraging them to pay special attention to a difficult step or to take extra care in performing a critical one. For instance, in a how-to essay on hanging wallpaper, you would warn readers about the difficulties of handling sheets of wallpaper and suggest folding the sheets to make them easier to work with.

Exercise 14.4

For one of the processes listed in Exercise 14.1 or Exercise 14.2, identify potential trouble spots in the process and describe how to avoid or resolve them.

Visualizing a Process Analysis Essay: A Graphic Organizer

The graphic organizer in Figure 14.1 shows the basic organization of a process analysis essay. When your main purpose is to explain a process, you should follow this standard format, including a title, an introduction, body paragraphs, and a conclusion. Your introduction should include any necessary background information and present your thesis statement. Your body paragraphs should explain the steps of the process in chronological order. Your conclusion should draw the essay to a satisfying close and refer to the thesis.

For more on graphic organizers, see Chapter 4, pp. 59–61.

When you incorporate process analysis into an essay using one or more other patterns of development, briefly introduce the process and then move directly to the steps involved. If the process is complex, you may want to add a brief summary of it before the transition back to the main topic of the essay.

Read the following how-it-works essay, "Inside the Engine," and then study the graphic organizer for it in Figure 14.2 (on p. 349).

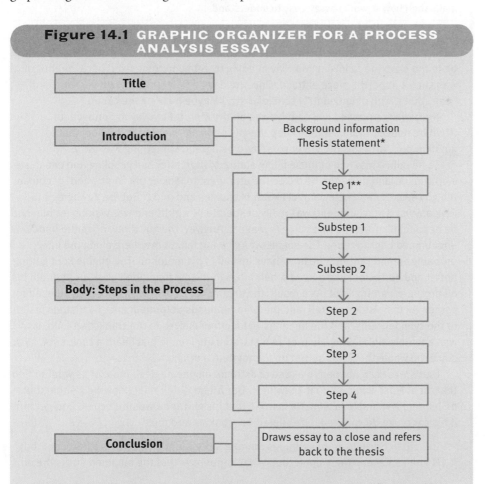

Figure 14.1 GRAPHIC ORGANIZER FOR A PROCESS ANALYSIS ESSAY

Title

Introduction — Background information / Thesis statement*

Step 1**

Substep 1

Substep 2

Body: Steps in the Process — Step 2

Step 3

Step 4

Conclusion — Draws essay to a close and refers back to the thesis

*In some essays, the thesis statement may be implied or may appear in a different position.
**In some essays, substeps may be included.

Inside the Engine
Tom and Ray Magliozzi

Tom (b. 1938) and his younger brother Ray (b. 1947) Magliozzi, better known to their listening audience as Click and Clack, the Tappet Brothers, are the award-winning hosts of *Car Talk* on National Public Radio. After graduating from MIT, the brothers opened The Good News Garage in their hometown of Cambridge, Massachusetts. In 1977 they appeared on a local radio station to talk about cars. This appearance led to *Car Talk,* a call-in radio show that is now broadcast nationally to millions of listeners every week. The show has a devoted following because the brothers mix humor with automobile repair advice and life lessons learned on the job at their auto repair shop.

This selection was taken from *Car Talk* (1991). It features some of the best advice from the brothers' radio show in its early years. The authors begin with a story about a customer. As you read, notice how effectively they explain complex terms and technology in order to make their how-it-works essay easy to understand.

1   A customer of ours had an old Thunderbird that he used to drive back and forth to New York to see a girlfriend every other weekend. And every time he made the trip he'd be in the shop the following Monday needing to get something fixed because the car was such a hopeless piece of trash. One Monday he failed to show up and Tom said, "Gee, that's kind of unusual." I said jokingly, "Maybe he blew the car up."

2   Well, what happened was that he was on the Merritt Parkway in Connecticut when he noticed that he had to keep the gas pedal all the way to the floor just to go 30 m.p.h., with this big V-8 engine,[1] and he figured something was awry.

3   So he pulled into one of those filling stations where they sell gasoline and chocolate-chip cookies and milk. And he asked the attendant to look at the engine and, of course, the guy said, "I can't help you. All I know is cookies and milk." But the guy agreed to look anyway since our friend was really desperate. His girlfriend was waiting for him and he needed to know if he was going to make it. Anyway, the guy threw open the hood and jumped back in terror. The engine was glowing red. Somewhere along the line, probably around Hartford, he must have lost all of his motor oil. The engine kept getting hotter and hotter, but like a lot of other things in the car that didn't work, neither did his oil pressure warning light. As a result, the engine got so heated up that it fused itself together. All the pistons melted, and the cylinder heads deformed, and the pistons fused to the cylinder walls, and the bearings welded themselves to the crankshaft—oh, it was a terrible sight! When he tried to restart the engine, he just heard a *click, click, click* since the whole thing was seized up tighter than a drum.

4   That's what can happen in a case of extreme engine neglect. Most of us wouldn't do that, or at least wouldn't do it knowingly. Our friend didn't do it knowingly either, but he learned a valuable lesson. He learned that his girlfriend wouldn't come and get him if his car broke down. Even if he offered her cookies and milk.

5   The oil is critical to keeping things running since it not only acts as a lubricant, but it also helps to keep the engine cool. What happens is that the oil pump sucks the oil

---

[1]V-8 engine: powerful engine so called because of its eight cylinders arranged in two rows situated at right angles to each other

out of what's called the sump (or the crankcase or the oil pan), and it pushes that oil, under pressure, up to all of the parts that need lubrication.

The way the oil works is that it acts as a cushion. The molecules of oil actually 6 separate the moving metal parts from one another so that they don't directly touch; the crankshaft *journals,* or the hard parts of the crankshaft, never touch the soft connecting-rod *bearings* because there's a film of oil between them, forced in there under pressure. From the pump.

It's pretty high pressure too. When the engine is running at highway speed, the oil, 7 at 50 or 60 pounds or more per square inch (or about 4 bars, if you're of the metric persuasion — but let's leave religion out of this), is coursing through the veins of the engine and keeping all these parts at safe, albeit microscopic, distances from each other.

But if there's a lot of dirt in the oil, the dirt particles get embedded in these metal 8 surfaces and gradually the dirt acts as an abrasive and wears away these metal surfaces. And pretty soon the engine is junk.

It's also important that the motor oil be present in sufficient quantity. In nontechni- 9 cal terms, that means there's got to be enough of it in there. If you have too little oil in your engine, there's not going to be enough of it to go around, and it will get very hot, because four quarts will be doing the work of five, and so forth. When that happens, the oil gets overheated and begins to burn up at a greater than normal rate. Pretty soon, instead of having four quarts, you have three and a half quarts, then three quarts doing the work of five. And then, next thing you know, you're down to two quarts and your engine is glowing red, just like that guy driving to New York, and it's chocolate-chip cookie time.

In order to avoid this, some cars have gauges and some have warning lights; some 10 people call them "idiot lights." Actually, we prefer to reverse it and call them "idiot gauges." I think gauges are bad. When you drive a car — maybe I'm weird about this — I think it's a good idea to look at the road most of the time. And you can't look at the road if you're busy looking at a bunch of gauges. It's the same objection we have to these stupid radios today that have so damn many buttons and slides and digital scanners and so forth that you need a copilot to change stations. Remember when you just turned a knob?

Not that gauges are bad in and of themselves. I think if you have your choice, 11 what you want is idiot lights — or what we call "genius lights" — and gauges too. It's nice to have a gauge that you can kind of keep an eye on for an overview of what's going on. For example, if you know that your engine typically runs at 215 degrees and on this particular day, which is not abnormally hot, it's running at 220 or 225, you might suspect that something is wrong and get it looked at before your radiator boils over.

On the other hand, if that gauge was the only thing you had to rely on and you 12 didn't have a light to alert you when something was going wrong, then you'd look at the thing all the time, especially if your engine had melted on you once. In that case, why don't you take the bus? Because you're not going to be a very good driver, spending most of your time looking at the gauges.

Incidentally, if that oil warning light ever comes on, shut the engine off! We don't 13 mean that you should shut it off in rush-hour traffic when you're in the passing lane. Use all necessary caution and get the thing over to the breakdown lane. But don't think you can limp to the next exit, because you can't. Spend the money to get towed and you may save the engine.

It's a little-known fact that the oil light does *not* signify whether or not you have   14
oil in the engine. The oil warning light is really monitoring the oil *pressure*. Of course, if you have no oil, you'll have no oil pressure, so the light will be on. But it's also possible to have plenty of oil and an oil pump that's not working for one reason or another. In this event, a new pump would fix the problem, but if you were to drive the car (saying, "It must be a bad light, I just checked the oil!") you'd melt the motor.

So if the oil warning light comes on, even if you just had an oil change and the oil is   15
right up to the full mark on the dipstick and is nice and clean — don't drive the car!

Here's another piece of useful info. When you turn the key to the "on" position, all   16
the little warning lights *should light up:* the temperature light, the oil light, whatever other lights you may have. Because that is the *test mode* for these lights. If those lights *don't* light up when you turn the key to the "on" position (just before you turn it all the way to start the car), does that mean you're out of oil? No. It means that something is wrong with the warning light itself. If the light doesn't work then, it's not going to work at all. Like when you need it, for example.

One more thing about oil: overfilling is just as bad as underfilling. Can you really   17
have too much of a good thing? you ask. Yes. If you're half a quart or even a quart overfilled, it's not a big deal, and I wouldn't be afraid to drive the car under those circumstances. But if you're a quart and a half or two quarts or more overfilled, you could have so much oil in the crankcase that the spinning crankshaft is going to hit the oil and turn it into suds. It's impossible for the pump to pump suds, so you'll ruin the motor. It's kind of like a front-loading washing machine that goes berserk and spills suds all over the floor when you put too much detergent in. That's what happens to your motor oil when you overfill it. . . .

The best way to protect all the other pieces that you can't get to without spend-   18
ing a lot of money is through frequent oil changes. The manufacturers recommend oil changes somewhere between seven and ten thousand miles, depending upon the car. We've always recommended that you change your oil at 3,000 miles. We realize for some people that's a bit of an inconvenience, but look at it as cheap insurance. And change the filter every time too.

And last but not least, I want to repeat this because it's important: Make sure your   19
warning lights work. The oil pressure and engine temperature warning lights are your engine's lifeline. Check them every day. You should make it as routine as checking to see if your zipper's up. You guys should do it at the same time.

What you do is, you get into the car, check to see that your zipper's up, and then   20
turn the key on and check to see if your oil pressure and temperature warning lights come on.

I don't know what women do.   21

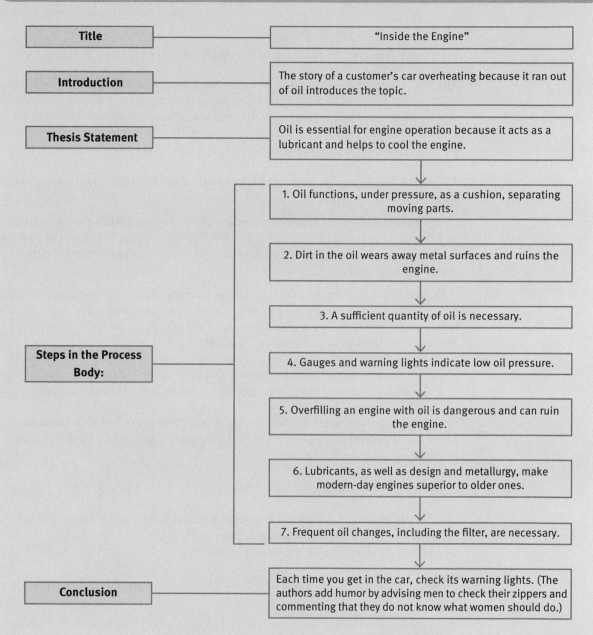

Figure 14.2 GRAPHIC ORGANIZER FOR
"INSIDE THE ENGINE"

Title	"Inside the Engine"
Introduction	The story of a customer's car overheating because it ran out of oil introduces the topic.
Thesis Statement	Oil is essential for engine operation because it acts as a lubricant and helps to cool the engine.
Steps in the Process Body:	1. Oil functions, under pressure, as a cushion, separating moving parts.
	2. Dirt in the oil wears away metal surfaces and ruins the engine.
	3. A sufficient quantity of oil is necessary.
	4. Gauges and warning lights indicate low oil pressure.
	5. Overfilling an engine with oil is dangerous and can ruin the engine.
	6. Lubricants, as well as design and metallurgy, make modern-day engines superior to older ones.
	7. Frequent oil changes, including the filter, are necessary.
Conclusion	Each time you get in the car, check its warning lights. (The authors add humor by advising men to check their zippers and commenting that they do not know what women should do.)

To draw detailed graphic organizers using a computer, visit www.bedfordstmartins .com/successfulcollege.

Exercise 14.5

Draw a graphic organizer for "How to Interview" (pp. 339–42).

Integrating Process Analysis into an Essay

Although some essays you write will focus solely on explaining a process, others will incorporate a process analysis into a discussion that relies on a different pattern of development. Suppose, for instance, that you are writing a descriptive essay about an alcohol abuse program for high school students. Although description is your primary pattern of development, you decide to include a brief process analysis of how alcohol impairs mental funtioning.

Use the following tips to incorporate process analysis into essays based on other patterns of development:

1. Provide a brief summary or overview of the process rather than a detailed step-by-step explanation. Too much detail will divert your readers from the primary focus of your essay. Consider explaining only the major steps in the process rather than every step in detail.

2. Make it clear *why* the process analysis is included. Use a transitional sentence to alert readers that a process analysis will follow and to suggest why. For example, here is how you might introduce a brief summary of the process by which AIDS is spread through HIV (human immunodeficiency virus).

> Before you explain to teenagers *how* to avoid contracting HIV, you need to let them know *what* they are avoiding. Teenagers need to know that HIV is transmitted by . . .

3. It is sometimes helpful to use the word *process* or *procedure* to let readers know that a process analysis is to follow. In the preceding example, the final sentence might be revised to read as follows.

> Teenagers need to know that HIV is transmitted by the following process.

4. When you have completed the process analysis, let readers know that you are about to return to the main topic. You might conclude the process analysis of the way HIV is transmitted with a summary statement.

> Above all, teenagers need to know that HIV is transmitted through an exchange of bodily fluids.

In "Shitty First Drafts" on pages 367–69, Anne Lamott uses process analysis along with other patterns of development to explain steps in the writing process.

A GUIDED WRITING ASSIGNMENT

The following guide will help you write a process analysis essay. It may be either a how-to or a how-it-works essay. Although you will focus on process analysis, you may need to integrate one or more other patterns of development in your essay.

The Assignment

Write a process analysis essay on one of the topics below or one of your own choosing. Be sure the process you choose is one that you know enough about to explain to others or can learn about through observation or research. Your audience consists of readers who are unfamiliar with the process, including your classmates.

How-To Essay Topics

1. How to improve _____ (your study habits, your wardrobe, your batting average)
2. How to be a successful _____ (diver, parent, gardener)
3. How to make or buy _____ (an object for personal use or enjoyment)
4. How to prepare for _____ (a test, a job interview, an oral presentation)

How-It-Works Essay Topics

1. How your college _____ (spends tuition revenues, hires professors, raises money)
2. How _____ works (an answering machine, a generator, email, a cell phone)
3. How a decision is made to _____ (accept a student at a college, add or eliminate a local or state agency)
4. How _____ is put together (a quilt, a news broadcast, a football team, a Web site)

As you develop your process analysis essay, you will probably use narrative strategies, description (for example, to describe equipment or objects), or illustration (such as to show an example of part of the process).

For more on narration, description, and illustration, see Chapters 11–13.

Generating Ideas

The following guidelines will help you select a process to write about and choose details to include. You may want to use one of the prewriting techniques discussed in Chapter 5. Consider your learning style when you select a prewriting technique. You might try questioning, group brainstorming, or sketching a diagram of a process.

Selecting a Process

Be sure to keep the following tips in mind when selecting a process:

- For a how-to essay, choose a process that you can visualize or perform as you write. Keep the equipment nearby for easy reference. In explaining how to scuba dive, for example, it may be helpful to have your scuba equipment in front of you.
- For a how-it-works essay, choose a topic about which you have background knowledge or for which you can find information. Unless you are experienced in woodworking, for example, do not try to explain how stains produce different effects on different kinds of wood.
- Choose a topic that is useful and interesting to your readers. Unless you can find a way to make an essay about how to do laundry interesting, do not write about it.

> **Essay in Progress 1**
> Using the preceding suggestions, choose a process to write about from the list of essay topics on page 351, or choose a topic of your own.

Considering Your Purpose, Audience, and Point of View

Your main aim in process analysis is to inform readers, but you may also want to persuade them that they should try the process (how-to) or that it is beneficial or should be changed (how-it-works). As you develop your essay, keep the following questions about your audience in mind:

1. What background information does my audience need or want?
2. What terms should I define?
3. What equipment should I describe?
4. How much detail does my audience need or want?
5. What trouble spots require special attention and explanation?

For more on purpose, audience, and point of view, see Chapter 5, pp. 106–9.

Writers of how-to essays commonly use the second-person point of view, addressing the reader directly as *you*. The second person is informal and draws the reader in, as in "How to Interview." For how-it-works essays, the third person (*he, she, it*) is commonly used.

> **Essay in Progress 2**
> For the process you selected in Essay in Progress 1, use the preceding guidelines to consider your purpose, the needs of your audience, and your point of view.

For more on thesis statements, see Chapter 6.

Developing Your Thesis

The thesis of a process analysis essay tells readers *why* the process is important, beneficial, or relevant to them (see p. 342). Considering your audience is especially important in developing a thesis for a process analysis, since what may be of interest or importance to one audience may be of little interest to another audience.

> **Essay in Progress 3**
> Write a working thesis statement that tells readers why the process you have chosen for your essay is important, beneficial, or relevant to them.

Gathering Details

To gather appropriate and interesting details, you may need to do additional prewriting to generate details that will help you explain the process. Use the following suggestions:

For more on prewriting strategies, see Chapter 5.

1. List the steps in the process as they occur to you, keeping these questions in mind.
   - What separate actions are involved?
   - What steps are obvious to me but may not be obvious to someone unfamiliar with the process?
   - What steps, if omitted, will lead to problems or failure?
2. Discuss your process with classmates to see what kinds of details they need to know about your topic.
3. Once you have a list of steps, generate details through additional prewriting or by doing research in the library or on the Internet. You might include sensory details about the process. (Check the five questions on page 352 to make sure you have included sufficient detail.)

For more on library and Internet research, see Chapter 22.

Essay in Progress 4
Using the preceding guidelines, brainstorm a list of the steps involved in the process. Then add details that will help you explain the steps. If necessary, interview someone knowledgeable about the process, or do library or Internet research to gather more details.

Evaluating Your Ideas and Thesis

Is the process you have chosen meaningful and relevant to your audience? Start by re-reading everything you have written with a critical eye. Highlight usable details; cross out any that seem unnecessary or repetitious. As you review your work, add steps, details, definitions, and background information where they are needed.

Trying Out Your Ideas on Others

Working in a group of two or three students, discuss your ideas and thesis for this chapter's assignment. Each writer should state his or her topic and thesis and describe the steps in the process. Then, as a group, evaluate each writer's work. Group members should answer the following questions:

1. How familiar are you with the process the writer has chosen?
2. Is the writer's explanation of the process detailed and complete?
3. What additional information do you need to understand or perform the process?
4. What unanswered questions do you have about the process?

Essay in Progress 5
Using the preceding suggestions and the feedback you have received from classmates, evaluate your thesis and your steps and decide whether you need to add details.

Organizing and Drafting

For more on drafting an essay, see Chapter 7.

Once you have gathered enough details to explain the steps in the process, developed your thesis statement, and considered the advice of peer reviewers, you are ready to organize your ideas and draft your essay.

Organizing the Steps in the Process

For a process that involves fewer than ten steps, you can usually arrange the steps chronologically, devoting one paragraph to each step. However, for a more complex process, group the steps into three or four categories (or divide the process into three or four main steps and each step into substeps) to avoid overwhelming your reader.

Try experimenting with different orders and groupings. For an essay on how to run a garage sale, the steps might be grouped in the following way:

> *Group 1:* Locating and collecting merchandise
> *Group 2:* Advertising
> *Group 3:* Pricing and setting up
> *Group 4:* Conducting the sale

You may want to devote one paragraph to each group of steps. A topic sentence introduces the group, and the rest of the paragraph explains the individual steps involved.

> **Essay in Progress 6**
> Review the list of steps you generated in Essay in Progress 5. If your process involves ten or more steps, use the preceding guidelines to group the steps into related categories. Write an outline or draw a graphic organizer to ensure that your steps are in chronological order.

Drafting the Process Analysis Essay

Use the following guidelines to draft your essay:

1. **Include reasons for the steps.** Unless the reason is obvious, explain why each step or group of steps is important and necessary. For instance, if you mention that robberies often occur during garage sales, then readers will be more likely to take the precautions you suggest, such as locking the house and wearing a waist-wallet.

2. **Consider using graphics and headings.** A drawing or diagram is sometimes necessary to make your steps easier to understand. (Remember, however, that a graphic is not a substitute for a clearly written explanation.) When using a graphic, be sure to introduce it in your essay and refer to it by its title. If you are including more than one graphic, assign a number to each one (*Figure 1*, *Figure 2*) and include the number in your text reference.

When writing about a lengthy or complicated process, consider adding headings to divide the body of your essay. Headings also call attention to your main topics and signal changes in topic.

For more on transitions, see Chapter 7, pp. 150, 152.

3. **Use transitions.** To make the process easier to follow and avoid making your analysis sound monotonous, use transitions such as *before removing the lid*, *next*, and *finally*.

4. Write an effective introduction. The introduction usually presents your thesis statement and includes necessary background information. It should also capture your readers' attention and interest. For a lengthy or complex process, consider including an overview of the steps or a brief list of them.

5. Use a tone appropriate to your audience and purpose. By the time your readers move from your introduction to the body of your essay, they should have a good idea of your tone. In some situations, a matter-of-fact tone is appropriate; other times, an emotional or humorous tone may be suitable.

6. Write a satisfying conclusion. Especially in a how-it-works essay, simply ending with the final step in the process may sound incomplete to your readers. In your conclusion, you might emphasize the value or importance of the process, describe particular situations in which it is useful, or offer a final amusing or emphatic comment or anecdote.

For more on writing effective paragraphs, including introductions and conclusions, see Chapter 7.

For more on tone, see Chapter 10, pp. 215–17.

> ### Essay in Progress 7
> Draft your process essay, using the organization you developed in Essay in Progress 6 and the preceding guidelines for drafting.

Analyzing and Revising

If possible, wait at least a day before rereading and revising your draft. As you reread, concentrate on organization and ideas, not on grammar or punctuation. Use one or more of the following suggestions to analyze your draft:

For more on the benefits of peer review, see Chapter 9, pp. 188–91.

Learning Style Options

1. Read your essay aloud to one or two friends or classmates. Ask them to interrupt you if they have questions or if a step is unclear.
2. For a how-to essay, try visualizing the steps or following them exactly. Be careful to complete only the ones actually included in your essay. Following your directions to the letter will help you discover gaps and identify sections that are unclear.
3. Update the graphic organizer or outline you prepared earlier. Look to see if the steps are sequenced correctly and if each step is covered in enough detail.

Use Figure 14.3 to guide your analysis. You might also ask a classmate to review your draft essay using the questions in the flowchart.

> ### Essay in Progress 8
> Revise your draft using Figure 14.3 (pp. 357–58) and any comments you received from peer reviewers.

Editing and Proofreading

The last step is to check your revised essay for errors in grammar, spelling, punctuation, and mechanics. As you edit and proofread your process analysis essay, watch out for two grammatical errors in particular—comma splices and shifts in verb mood.

For more on keeping an error log, see Chapter 10, p. 221.

1. Avoid comma splices. A comma splice occurs when two independent clauses are joined only by a comma. To correct a comma splice, add a coordinating conjunction (*and, but, for, nor, or, so,* or *yet*), change the comma to a semicolon, divide the sentence into two sentences, or subordinate one clause to the other.

- The first step in creating a flower arrangement is to choose an attractive
  but
  container, the container should not be the focal point of the arrangement.

- Following signs is one way to navigate a busy airport, looking for a map is another.

- To lower fat consumption in your diet, first learn to read food product labels, next
  . Next
  eliminate those products that contain trans fats or unsaturated fats.

  After you have placed
- Place the pill on the cat's tongue, hold its mouth closed, rubbing its chin until it
  swallows the pill.

2. Avoid shifts in verb mood. A verb can have three *moods*—indicative, imperative, and subjunctive. The **indicative mood** is used to express ordinary statements and to ask questions.

- The modem is built into the computer.

The **imperative mood** is used for giving orders, advice, and directions. The subject of a verb in the imperative mood is understood to be *you,* but it is not expressed.

- (You) Plant your feet firmly before swinging the club.

The **subjunctive mood** is used for making statements contrary to fact or for wishes and recommendations.

- I suggest that a new phone line be installed.

When writing a process analysis, be sure to use a consistent mood throughout your essay.

- The firefighters told the third-grade class the procedures to follow if a fire oc-

  curred in their school. They emphasized that children should leave the building
  they should
  quickly. Also, move at least 100 feet away from the building.

Essay in Progress 9
Edit and proofread your essay, paying particular attention to avoiding comma splices and shifts in verb mood.

Figure 14.3 Flowchart for Revising a Process Analysis

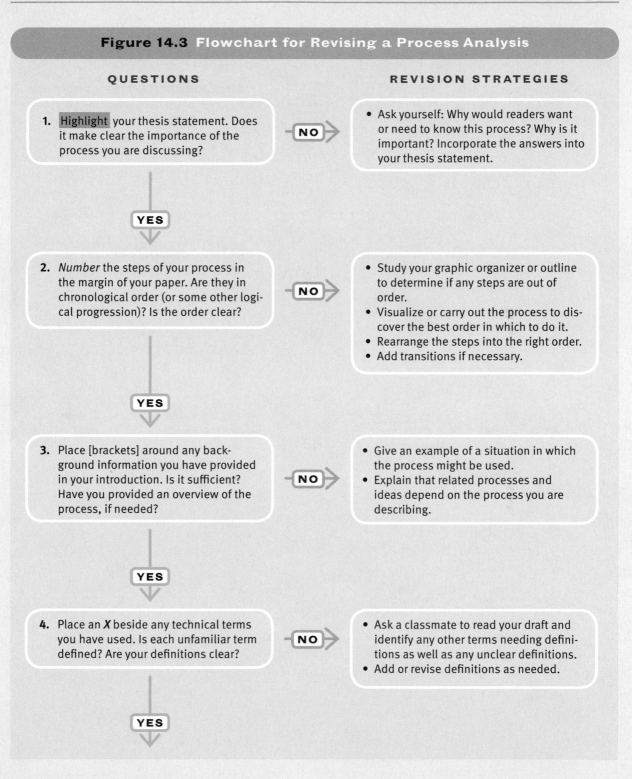

QUESTIONS

REVISION STRATEGIES

1. Highlight your thesis statement. Does it make clear the importance of the process you are discussing?

— NO →

- Ask yourself: Why would readers want or need to know this process? Why is it important? Incorporate the answers into your thesis statement.

YES

2. *Number* the steps of your process in the margin of your paper. Are they in chronological order (or some other logical progression)? Is the order clear?

— NO →

- Study your graphic organizer or outline to determine if any steps are out of order.
- Visualize or carry out the process to discover the best order in which to do it.
- Rearrange the steps into the right order.
- Add transitions if necessary.

YES

3. Place [brackets] around any background information you have provided in your introduction. Is it sufficient? Have you provided an overview of the process, if needed?

— NO →

- Give an example of a situation in which the process might be used.
- Explain that related processes and ideas depend on the process you are describing.

YES

4. Place an *X* beside any technical terms you have used. Is each unfamiliar term defined? Are your definitions clear?

— NO →

- Ask a classmate to read your draft and identify any other terms needing definitions as well as any unclear definitions.
- Add or revise definitions as needed.

YES

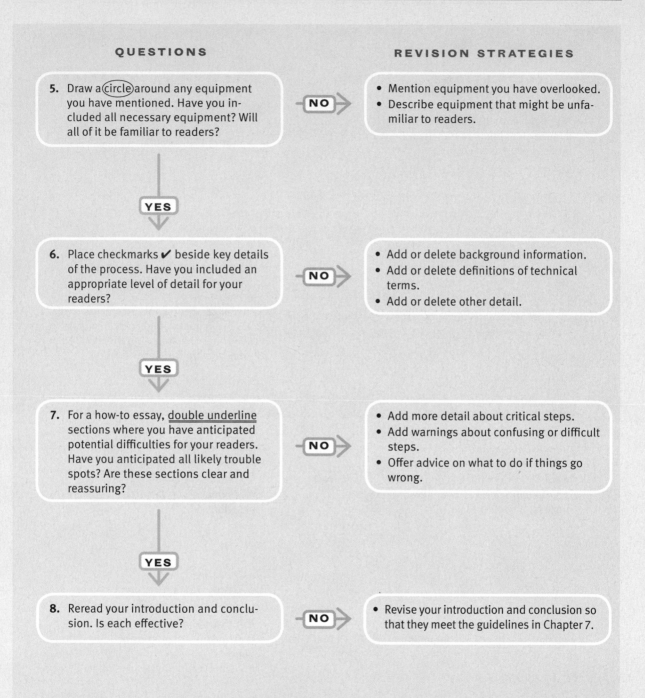

QUESTIONS

REVISION STRATEGIES

5. Draw a circle around any equipment you have mentioned. Have you included all necessary equipment? Will all of it be familiar to readers?

NO

- Mention equipment you have overlooked.
- Describe equipment that might be unfamiliar to readers.

YES

6. Place checkmarks ✔ beside key details of the process. Have you included an appropriate level of detail for your readers?

NO

- Add or delete background information.
- Add or delete definitions of technical terms.
- Add or delete other detail.

YES

7. For a how-to essay, double underline sections where you have anticipated potential difficulties for your readers. Have you anticipated all likely trouble spots? Are these sections clear and reassuring?

NO

- Add more detail about critical steps.
- Add warnings about confusing or difficult steps.
- Offer advice on what to do if things go wrong.

YES

8. Reread your introduction and conclusion. Is each effective?

NO

- Revise your introduction and conclusion so that they meet the guidelines in Chapter 7.

Students Write

Eric Michalski wrote the following essay in response to an assignment that asked him to explain a process that he had mastered. As you read the essay, consider if the steps described in the essay clearly explain the process of making chili.

Feed Your Friends . . . and Their Friends . . . and Their Friends: Chili for Fifty

Eric Michalski

Cooking up chili for a large crowd is only a tad more difficult than whipping up a fractionally smaller batch. It's quite useful being the person who can feed a full hotel floor/campsite/election office/family reunion on a trip to the grocery store and a few hours' time. If this recipe is followed accurately, it'll result in a deeply flavorful mud-brown sludge that tastes much better than it looks.

When you're feeding a crowd, though, things do get complicated. The key is following a strict sequence. It's like learning a dance--you've got to follow the steps until you know it well enough to freestyle. All ingredients require some type of processing, which has to be done at a specific time to build the right flavor and texture while preserving the integrity of the individual components. Order is important, even though "precision" and "chili" don't share too many sentences.

To start off, you'll need a huge pot with a lid. Mine's a 32-quart monstrosity you could boil a cow's head in. (Don't ask how I know.) Cooking the chili in several smaller pots results in different kinds of chili--great, but not what we're looking for here. Beg, borrow, or rent a good large pot and lid for this one. Also essential are a knife, a cutting board, a cool drink (never cook without refreshment), and something for stirring the chili. A wooden spoon works great, as does a silicone spatula. Just don't use anything that'll melt in bubbling chili. A slotted spoon is stupid because you need to be able to taste; a regular spoon will get you a hand burn before you get a taste. If you plan on moving the chili pot, which you shouldn't, potholders are useful.

This recipe can be done on a hot plate if you have a gigantic one and a separate burner for sautéing, but I tested it on a four-burner gas stove. A slow cooker would work in a pinch, but as noted below, certain ingredients need to be browned in a pan separate from the main pot. You could even do it on a propane burner if you used a wok for the protein first.

Once you've assembled your tools, cover the bottom of your pot with extra virgin olive oil and put it on medium heat. Leave it uncovered while chopping four large white or yellow onions, one head of elephant garlic and two heads (not cloves) of regular garlic. By the time you're done with the alliums, your oil is ready for you. Toss in the onions and garlic, spread until more or less even, and then cover.

Title: Michalski identifies the process to be explained.

1

Introduction: Michalski explains the value of learning to make chili. His thesis statement reveals his attitude toward the topic.

2 As he often does throughout the essay, Michalski uses a transition to keep readers on track and a topic sentence to preview a paragraph's content. Here he also uses a figure of speech to warn that following the steps in order is crucial.

3 In paragraphs 3 and 4, Michalski describes the equipment necessary to carry out the process. He also warns *against* using certain equipment or moving the pot and suggests alternatives for stirring and heating. Notice that throughout the rest of the essay, each paragraph is devoted to one step or to some other particular aspect of the process.

4

5 Another transitional phrase leads into the actual process. Michalski explains how two steps (heating oil and chopping onions and garlic) can be done simultaneously and clarifies to avoid misunderstanding.

A transitional sentence introduces the next step: cooking the sausage. Michalski uses sensory details and adds two cautionary notes at the end.

Michalski offers detailed information about the next step (preparing and cooking the cubed chuck) and anticipates the one after that (cooking the ground beef).

Michalski offers his readers alternatives for one of the ingredients.

Another transition leads to the next step: adding the vegetables and spices.

Michalski emphasizes the importance of the next-to-last step: simmering.

For the final step in the process, Michalski shares his special trick to enhance flavor.

Time for the protein! Sausage is first, three pounds of whatever kind you like. Kielbasa is great, maple breakfast sausage not so great, and Italian sausage entirely feasible. Cut the sausage into pieces of roughly equal size--dice size, like all the other protein in this recipe. Sauté the sausage in a separate pan until brown, then spread in a single layer on paper towels to drain. When cooked properly, the sausage will be brown and crisp on the outside and intensely sausagey on the inside. Unlike the chuck to be added next, this meat needs to be fully cooked before it goes in the chili pot. (But don't add any of the meat yet.) 6

Once the sausage is working and there's a little more oil in the pan, it's time to tend to the other protein. Cut up three pounds of cubed chuck and trim the fat and gristle before coating in a 50–50 mix of fine yellow cornmeal and white flour and browning in the skillet. Open your pound and a half of ground beef (or one of the alternatives mentioned below) and thaw if necessary while your chuck is getting tasty. You want it cooked about halfway--brown inside but pink inside is fine. (This chili will cook for long enough to finish it.) 7

Sauté the ground beef with cinnamon and black pepper until uniformly brown, then let sit on paper towels. (As a substitute for this part of the protein mix, bison would work fine, but I like a fattier meat because you can always drain fat, but dry meat tastes awful. Venison and even ostrich are a little lean, but can be counterbalanced with sausage or bacon. Ground turkey is fine, and shredded leftover turkey can be your reason for giving thanks when facing a fridgeful of leftovers.) 8

While the meat drains, add your veggies and spices to the mothership: one large (40.5-ounce) can dark kidney beans, one large can light kidney beans, one small (15-ounce) can mixed diced tomatoes and jalapeños, a pound of diced tomatoes (if fresh, drain them on paper towels after dicing), and a bottle of your favorite Mexican chili-garlic sauce. Let the mixture come to a boil before adding the meat. If you've followed the recipe properly to this point, you'll have a pile of disgusting soaked paper towels in your trash can. Did you really want that stuff in your chili? (Didn't think so.) 9

The best chilis become that way through their final simmer, which brings all the flavors together. Simmer for at least two hours. Skip or skimp on the simmering, and you might as well have just thrown random flavors into a pot for no reason. In fact, the truly hard-core chili cooks eschew the use of "artificial" thickeners and do the job with simmering alone. Those cooking on a more realistic time line, such as anyone making this recipe for the second time, will appreciate the way cornmeal- and flour-coated beef lends thickening mojo. 10

Long-cooked chili can also benefit from a special trick only usable with massive batches. When your chili tastes more or less how you want it to, crank the heat up on your stove and slowly stir the top of the chili only. Keep it moving, and occasionally check the bottom with your spoon. Once you've got a decent crust on the bottom, scrape it up into your chili--done with a large enough batch, this will add dense smokiness and dark nuance to your nontraditional bowla'red. 11

I hate jalapeños, but if you insist on the most overdone flavor since cheddar you can slice them and serve them on the side. When you're making chili that's going to feed this many people, chances are that some of them are turned off by high levels of spice. Tell your capsaicin-addicted friends to bring their own hot sauce. Those looking to make fiery chili need only don rubber gloves and eye protection, chop ten habañeros, and add them at the very end.

Unless you're feeding enough people to make a serious dent in the contents of the pot right away, storage can be difficult due to the sheer volume of food involved. Work out a deal with the housemate/roommates/parents to use a section of the freezer for about twelve hours. Then ladle the gloppy yumminess into zipper-lock plastic bags. Fill each of the bags halfway and flatten so they freeze as flat squares--this makes reheating very easy. Most important, make sure to freeze what's left *immediately* after you're stuffed. Chili left out for even minutes can disappear in even the most upstanding homes/dorms.

Chili's a full meal in a bowl--warm, comforting, and filling; it's like a nutritious hug. I make chili because my parents taught me, from as early as I can remember, to feed the hungry, clothe the naked, and nurse the sick. My closet is not overflowing with clothing and I have no medical training, so I cook for my friends and girlfriend and bask in their glow.

12 Michalski offers a solution to the problem of level of spice.

13 Michalski offers practical advice on storage.

Conclusion: Michalski reiterates the value of making chili, using **14** a figure of speech.

Analyzing the Writer's Technique

1. How successful is the introduction at providing a reason for learning the process?

2. Michalski uses many parentheses, dashes, slashes, and italicized words. What effect do these create?

3. Find three places in the essay where Michalski uses humor, and explain what the effect is in each place.

4. Does Michalski's conclusion bring the essay to a satisfying close? Why or why not?

5. Michalski says that he hates jalapeños. What words reveal the reasons for his opinion?

Thinking Critically about Illustration

1. How does Michalski's use of phrases such as "deeply flavorful mud-brown sludge" (para. 1) and "gloppy yumminess" (13) affect you as a reader? Do they increase or decrease the essay's effectiveness?

2. How would you describe Michalski's tone? How does it differ from the tone you might find in a cookbook or food magazine?

3. What has Michalski omitted from his process analysis, if anything? What additional information or advice might a very inexperienced cook need to prepare chili? Would you need any?

Reacting to the Essay

1. Discuss other processes in which following the steps in order is especially important.
2. Michalski regards chili as comfort food. Do you agree? What other foods fall into the same category?
3. Michalski cooks chili as an expression of friendship. Write an essay explaining something you do or have done for friends (or a particular friend) to solidify your friendship. Describe the process.

READING A PROCESS ANALYSIS

The following section provides advice for reading a process analysis. Two model essays illustrate the characteristics of process analysis covered in this chapter and provide opportunities to examine, analyze, and react to the writer's ideas. The second essay uses process analysis along with other methods of development.

Working with Text: Reading Process Analysis Essays

Process analysis is a common method of explaining; it is often used in textbooks, including this one, and in other forms of academic writing. To read a process analysis effectively, use the suggestions below.

What to Look For, Highlight, and Annotate

1. Look for and highlight the thesis statement. Try to discover why the writer believes the process is important or useful.
2. For a how-to essay, look for difficulties you might experience in the process or questions you may need to ask about it.
3. Highlight or underline each step or grouping of steps. Using a different colored highlighter or an asterisk (*), mark steps that the author warns are difficult or troublesome.
4. For a complex or especially important process (such as one you need to write about on an essay exam), outline or draw a graphic organizer of the steps. Try explaining each step in your own words without referring to the text.

For more on reading strategies, see Chapter 3.

5. For a how-to essay, imagine yourself carrying out the process as you read.
6. Highlight or use a symbol to mark new terms as they are introduced.
7. Annotate the sections that summarize complex steps.

How to Find Ideas to Write About

For more on discovering ideas for a response paper, see Chapter 4.

Look for ideas to write about *as you read.* Record your ideas and impressions as marginal annotations. Think about why *you* want or need to understand the process.

Think of situations in which you can use or apply the information. Also try to think of processes similar to the one described in the essay. If you think of metaphors or analogies, make a note of them. Consider how other processes are the same as and different from the one in the essay.

Thinking Critically about Process Analysis

Although most process analyses are straightforward and informative, you should still consider the author's motives for writing and knowledge of the topic. Use the following questions to think critically about the process analyses you read.

What Are the Writer's Motives?

As you read, ask yourself, Why does the writer want me to understand or carry out this process? What is his or her motive? At times, an author may have a hidden motive for explaining a process. For example, a writer opposed to the death penalty may use graphic details about the process of executions to shock readers and persuade them to oppose the death penalty. Even a how-to article on a noncontroversial topic can have a hidden agenda, such as one entitled "How to Lose Ten Pounds" that was written by the owner of a weight-loss clinic.

Is the Writer Knowledgeable and Experienced?

When you read process analyses, always consider whether the writer has sufficient knowledge about or experience with the process. This step is especially important if you intend to perform the task. Following the advice of someone who is not qualified to give it can be a waste of time or even dangerous. For most writers, it is possible to check credentials and determine whether the writer is considered an expert in the field. In addition to checking the writer's credentials, consider whether he or she supports assertions with outside sources, expert opinion, and quotes from authorities.

What Has the Writer Omitted?

Authors address their writing to a particular audience and make assumptions about their readers' knowledge and experience. If they assume that their readers have more knowledge than they actually have, readers may not understand or be unable to carry out the process. In "How to Interview" (pp. 339–42), the writer assumes, for example, that his or her readers are knowledgeable about how to locate research information about the company they are interviewing with. Because this essay was written for a Web site, it seems safe to assume that readers are able to conduct Web searches.

PROCESS ANALYSIS ESSAY

As you read the following essay, notice how the author uses the elements of process analysis discussed in this chapter.

Dater's Remorse
Cindy Chupack

Cindy Chupack (b. 1965) was born in Oklahoma. She trained as a journalist at Northwestern University because she wanted to make a living as a writer, but she found that journalism did not suit her. After working in advertising, Chupack contributed a personal essay to *New York Woman* magazine that attracted the attention of a television writer who encouraged her to create sitcom scripts. Ultimately, she became a writer and executive produce for the hit HBO show *Sex and the City*.

This selection below appears in a collection of Chupack's writings titled *The Between Boyfriends Book* (2003). As you read, notice the way Chupack builds her humorous analogy between shopping and dating, from her opening description of her telephone-company "suitors" to her conclusion: *Caveat emptor* — "Let the buyer beware."

I never imagined this would happen, but three men are fighting over me. They call me repeatedly. They ply me with gifts. They beg me for a commitment. Yes, they're just AT&T, MCI, and Sprint salesmen interested in being my long-distance carrier, but what I'm relishing — aside from the attention — is the sense that I am in complete control.   1

In fact, just the other day my ex (phone carrier, that is) called to find out what went wrong. Had I been unhappy? What would it take to win me back? Turns out all it took was two thousand frequent flier miles. I switched, just like that. I didn't worry about how my current carrier would feel, or how it might affect my Friends and Family. Now if only I could use that kind of healthy judgment when it comes to my love life.   2

The unfortunate truth is that while most of us are savvy shoppers, we're not sufficiently selective when looking for relationships, and that's why we often suffer from dater's remorse. Perhaps we should try to apply conventional consumer wisdom to men as well as merchandise. How satisfying love might be if we always remembered to: 3

Go with a classic, not a trend. We all know it's unwise to spend a week's salary on vinyl hip-huggers. But when it comes to men, even the most conservative among us occasionally invests in the human equivalent of a fashion fad. The furthest I ever strayed from a classic was during college. I wrote a paper about the Guardian Angels, those street toughs who unofficially patrol innercity neighborhoods, and being a very thorough student, I ended up dating one. He wore a red beret and entertained me by demonstrating martial arts moves in my dorm room. I remember telling my concerned roommate how he was *sooo* much more interesting than those boring MBA[1] types everybody else was dating. Of course, what initially seemed like a fun, impulse buy turned out to require more of an emotional investment than I was willing to make. It took me two months to break up with him — two months of getting persistent late-night calls, angry letters, and unannounced visits to my dorm room door, which I envisioned him kicking down someday. The good thing about MBAs: They're familiar with the expression "Cut your losses."   4

Beware of the phrase "Some assembly required." Anyone who has tried to follow translated-from-Swedish directions for putting together a swivel chair understands that   5

---

[1]MBA: Master of Business Administration, an advanced business degree

when you've got to assemble something yourself, the money you save isn't worth the time you spend. The same goes for men. Many women think that even though a guy is not exactly "together," we can easily straighten him out. The fact is that fixer-uppers are more likely to stay forever flawed, no matter what we do. My friend Jenny fell for a forty-one-year-old bachelor, despite the fact that he spent their first few dates detailing his dysfunctional family and boasting that he went to the same shrink as the Menendez brothers.[2] "Six weeks later, when he announced he couldn't handle a relationship, it shouldn't have surprised me," says Jenny, who now looks for men requiring a little less duct tape.

Make sure your purchase goes with the other things you own. I once fell in love 6 with a very expensive purple velvet couch, and I seriously considered buying it, even though it would mean getting my cat declawed, and I had signed an agreement when I adopted her that I would never do that. But the couch . . . the couch . . . I visited it a few more times, but I didn't buy, and not just out of sympathy for my cat. I realized that if I owned that couch, I'd have to replace all my comfy, old stuff with new furniture equal in quality and style to the purple couch. Men can be like that, too. You're drawn to them because they're attractively different, but being with them may mean changing your entire life. For example, while dating a long-distance bicyclist, my friend Janet found herself suddenly following his training regimen: bowing out of social events just as the fun began, rising at an hour at which she normally went to bed, and replacing fine dining with intensive carbo-loading. And the only bike she ever rode was the stationary one at the gym.

Check with previous owners. Once beyond age twenty-five, most men would have to 7 be classified as secondhand, and we all know how risky it is to buy used merchandise. Therefore, it's up to you to do some basic consumer research. Find out how many previous owners your selection has had. If he's such a steal, why is he still on the lot? Is it because his exterior is a bit unsightly, or because he's fundamentally a lemon? (Before becoming too critical, bear in mind that *you* are still on the lot.)

The television show *The Bachelorette* focuses on choosing the "right" mate. What traits would you focus on to decide "who's in and who's out"?

---

[2] Menendez brothers: two brothers who were convicted in 1996 of killing their parents

Caveat emptor.[3] Following these guidelines won't guarantee a great relationship,   8
but it will help you cut down on the number of times you feel dater's remorse. Obviously looking for a husband is a bit more complicated than choosing a major appliance, but since there are no lifetime guarantees or lemon laws for men, it pays to be a
savvy shopper.

[3] *Caveat emptor:* Latin phrase meaning "Let the buyer beware"

Examining the Reading

1. According to Chupack, what can happen when you date someone who is "the human equivalent of a fashion fad" (para. 4)?
2. Explain the connection between dating and buying furniture. Why does the author advise women to stay away from furniture with "some assembly required" (5)?
3. Explain Chupack's advice "to make sure your purchase goes with other things you
   own" (6).
4. Explain the meaning of each of the following words as it is used in the reading:
   relishing (1), *classic* (4), *envisioned* (4), *dysfunctional* (5), and *regimen* (6).

Analyzing the Writer's Technique

1. Chupack's thesis involves dating as well as shopping. Identify her thesis, and evaluate the effectiveness of her comparison.
2. What type of organization does Chupack use to order the steps in her process
   analysis essay? If the essay is not organized chronologically, does the author use
   any sort of logical progression such as starting with simple steps and progressing to
   more complex ones? Is her type of organization effective? Why or why not?
3. Evaluate the author's level of detail. Is it detailed enough to be of practical use?
4. Is Chupack's reference to lemon laws a satisfying conclusion? Why or why not?

Reacting to the Reading

1. Discuss some experiences you or a friend have had with dating. How difficult is it
   to find someone compatible?
2. Chupack advises readers to "go with a classic, not a trend" when choosing dating
   partners. Brainstorm a list of situations other than dating in which the same advice might apply.
3. Chupack offers advice for women seeking to date men. Discuss what advice might
   to offered to men seeking to date women.
4. Write a journal entry about a successful relationship that you have now or that you
   have had in the past. What made this relationship work out so well?

Thinking Critically about Text and Images

1. What assumption does Chupack make about her readers as revealed in the final
   paragraph?
2. Chupack makes comparisons throughout her essay between date selection and
   shopping. How legitimate do you think these comparisons are? Are there ways in

which shopping and dating differ? If so, how? Does the author address these? If so, how?

3. Is Chupack qualified to offer advice on date selection? Explain your answer.
4. What is the connotation of the terms *secondhand* and *used merchandise* (7)?
5. Chupack supports her main points primarily through the use of examples from her personal experience. What other types of supporting evidence would be useful?
6. What does the image from the Web site for the television show The Bachelorette suggest about dating? How does it relate to the reading? What does the title of the image suggest about the dating process?

(MAKING CONNECTIONS)

Interpersonal Relationships

Both "Dater's Remorse" (pp. 364–66) and "How to Interview" (pp. 339–42) discuss, in part, how to deal with others. "Dater's Remorse" discusses how to select the right men to date and "How to Interview" focuses on how to interact with an interviewer.

Analyzing the Readings

1. Evaluate the level of detail in each essay. Which author is more helpful and supportive?
2. Write a journal entry exploring how creating an online profile differs from creating an interview self-image.

Essay Idea

Think of other situations in which you need to be concerned with how to interact with others. Write a process essay explaining the steps in creating a positive interaction with others. For example, you might write about how to interact with an instructor, with the parents of your boyfriend or girlfriend, or with an elderly neighbor or relative.

PROCESS ANALYSIS COMBINED WITH OTHER PATTERNS

As you read the following essay by Anne Lamott, notice how she combines process analysis with other patterns of development.

Shitty First Drafts
Anne Lamott

READING

Anne Lamott has published several nonfiction works, including *Bird by Bird: Instructions on Writing and Life* (1995), from which this essay was taken; *All New People* (1999); *Traveling Mercies: Some Thoughts on Faith* (2000); *Operating Instructions: A Journal of My Son's First Year* (2005); and *Grace (Eventually)* (2008). She is also the author of several novels, including *Hard Laughter* (2002) and *Imperfect Birds* (2010). As you read this essay, notice how

Lamott leads you through the steps in the writing process while at the same time revealing her attitude toward the task of writing.

Now, practically even better news than that of short assignments is the idea of shitty   1
first drafts. All good writers write them. This is how they end up with good second
drafts and terrific third drafts. People tend to look at successful writers who are getting their books published and maybe even doing well financially and think that they
sit down at their desks every morning feeling like a million dollars, feeling great about
who they are and how much talent they have and what a great story they have to tell;
that they take in a few deep breaths, push back their sleeves, roll their necks a few
times to get all the cricks out, and dive in, typing fully formed passages as fast as a
court reporter. But this is just the fantasy of the uninitiated. I know some very great
writers, writers you love who write beautifully and have made a great deal of money,
and not one of them sits down routinely feeling wildly enthusiastic and confident. Not
one of them writes elegant first drafts. All right, one of them does, but we do not like
her very much. We do not think that she has a rich inner life or that God likes her or can
even stand her. (Although when I mentioned this to my priest friend Tom, he said you
can safely assume you've created God in your own image when it turns out that God
hates all the same people you do.)

Very few writers really know what they are doing until they've done it. Nor do they   2
go about their business feeling dewy and thrilled. They do not type a few stiff warm-up
sentences and then find themselves bounding along like huskies across the snow.
One writer I know tells me that he sits down every morning and says to himself nicely,
"It's not like you don't have a choice, because you do—you can either type, or kill
yourself." We all often feel like we are pulling teeth, even those writers whose prose
ends up being the most natural and fluid. The right words and sentences just do not
come pouring out like ticker tape most of the time. Now, Muriel Spark is said to have
felt that she was taking dictation from God every morning—sitting there, one sup-
poses, plugged into a Dictaphone, typing away, humming. But this is a very hostile and
aggressive position. One might hope for bad things to rain down on a person like this.

For me and most of the other writers I know, writing is not rapturous. In fact, the   3
only way I can get anything written at all is to write really, really shitty first drafts.

The first draft is the child's draft, where you let it all pour out and then let it romp   4
all over the place, knowing that no one is going to see it and that you can shape it
later. You just let this childlike part of you channel whatever voices and visions come
through and onto the page. If one of the characters wants to say, "Well, so what, Mr.
Poopy Pants?" you let her. No one is going to see it. If the kid wants to get into really
sentimental, weepy, emotional territory, you let him. Just get it all down on paper
because there may be something great in those six crazy pages that you would never
have gotten to by more rational, grown-up means. There may be something in the very
last line of the very last paragraph on page six that you just love, that is so beautiful
or wild that you now know what you're supposed to be writing about, more or less, or
in what direction you might go—but there was no way to get to this without first getting through the first five and a half pages.

I used to write food reviews for *California* magazine before it folded. (My writing   5
food reviews had nothing to do with the magazine folding, although every single review did cause a couple of canceled subscriptions. Some readers took umbrage at

my comparing mounds of vegetable puree with various ex-presidents' brains.) These reviews always took two days to write. First I'd go to a restaurant several times with a few opinionated, articulate friends in tow. I'd sit there writing down everything anyone said that was at all interesting or funny. Then on the following Monday I'd sit down at my desk with my notes and try to write the review. Even after I'd been doing this for years, panic would set in. I'd try to write a lead, but instead I'd write a couple of dreadful sentences, XX them out, try again, XX everything out, and then feel despair and worry settle on my chest like an x-ray apron. It's over, I'd think calmly. I'm not going to be able to get the magic to work this time. I'm ruined. I'm through. I'm toast. Maybe, I'd think, I can get my old job back as a clerk-typist. But probably not. I'd get up and study my teeth in the mirror for a while. Then I'd stop, remember to breathe, make a few phone calls, hit the kitchen and chow down. Eventually I'd go back and sit down at my desk, and sigh for the next ten minutes. Finally I would pick up my one-inch picture frame, stare into it as if for the answer, and every time the answer would come: all I had to do was to write a really shitty first draft of, say, the opening paragraph. And no one was going to see it.

So I'd start writing without reining myself in. It was almost just typing, just making   6
my fingers move. And the writing would be terrible. I'd write a lead paragraph that was a whole page, even though the entire review could only be three pages long, and then I'd start writing up descriptions of the food, one dish at a time, bird by bird, and the critics would be sitting on my shoulders, commenting like cartoon characters. They'd be pretending to snore, or rolling their eyes at my overwrought descriptions, no matter how hard I tried to tone those descriptions down, no matter how conscious I was of what a friend said to me gently in my early days of restaurant reviewing. "Annie," she said, "it is just a piece of *chicken*. It is just a bit of *cake*."

But because by then I had been writing for so long, I would eventually let myself trust 7
the process—sort of, more or less. I'd write a first draft that was maybe twice as long as it should be, with a self-indulgent and boring beginning, stupefying descriptions of the meal, lots of quotes from my black-humored friends that made them sound more like the Manson girls than food lovers, and no ending to speak of. The whole thing would be so long and incoherent and hideous that for the rest of the day I'd obsess about getting creamed by a car before I could write a decent second draft. I'd worry that people would read what I'd written and believe that the accident had really been a suicide, that I had panicked because my talent was waning and my mind was shot.

The next day, I'd sit down, go through it all with a colored pen, take out everything 8
I possibly could, find a new lead somewhere on the second page, figure out a kicky place to end it, and then write a second draft. It always turned out fine, sometimes even funny and weird and helpful. I'd go over it one more time and mail it in.

Then, a month later, when it was time for another review, the whole process would 9
start again, complete with the fears that people would find my first draft before I could rewrite it.

Almost all good writing begins with terrible first efforts. You need to start some- 10
where. Start by getting something—anything—down on paper. A friend of mine says that the first draft is the down draft—you just get it down. The second draft is the up draft—you fix it up. You try to say what you have to say more accurately. And the third draft is the dental draft, where you check every tooth, to see if it's loose or cramped or decayed, or even, God help us, healthy.

Examining the Reading

1. Why does Lamott believe writers must use the process she describes?
2. How does Lamott view writing? How might she describe it as a job?
3. How does Lamott's process benefit her? Why do you think she developed it?
4. According to Lamott, what is the hardest part in her process? What does she do to get through it?
5. Explain the meaning of each of the following words as it is used in the reading: *uninitiated* (para. 1), *rapturous* (3), *umbrage* (5), *overwrought* (6), and *kicky* (8).

Analyzing the Writer's Technique

1. Identify Lamott's thesis statement. What background information does she provide to support it?
2. In paragraph 1 and again in paragraph 6, Lamott begins with three short sentences followed by a much longer sentence. What effect does this sequence create?
3. Explain how Lamott's use of exaggeration supports her purpose in writing the essay.
4. Who is Lamott's audience? Does her advice apply to others outside this group?
5. What methods of development, in addition to process, does Lamott use in this essay? What does each add to your understanding of Lamott's explanation of the writing process?

Visualizing the Reading

Lamott uses examples and details to explain the steps in the process of writing. List the steps in the process and an example or detail for each. The first one has been done for you. Add additional boxes as necessary.

Step	Example or Detail
Begin writing.	Channel voices and visions; write anything and everything; cross most of it out as you go.

Thinking Critically about Process Analysis

1. How would you describe Lamott's tone? Was it supportive to you as a student of writing? How could Lamott have made the essay more user-friendly or reader-friendly?

2. How does her tone work with her message to writers? What kind of unspoken, underlying rule is she setting up for writers to follow by using this tone?
3. Lamott often uses descriptive, visual language to make her point. Identify at least two phrases that do this. Why are they effective?
4. What evidence could Lamott have included to give her essay additional weight?

Reacting to the Reading

1. Do you believe that all writers produce "shitty first drafts"? Why or why not? What evidence supports your position?
2. How does this essay make you feel about your own writing? Describe how you can use the advice in this essay the next time you need to do a writing assignment—or why you would not follow it.
3. Can you apply this advice to other tasks, projects, and obstacles in your life? Write an essay explaining how to apply this advice elsewhere.

Applying Your Skills: Additional Essay Assignments

Write a process analysis essay on one of the following topics. Depending on the topic you choose, you may need to conduct library or Internet research.

For more on locating and documenting sources, see Part 5.

To Express Your Ideas

1. How children manage their parents
2. How to relax and do nothing
3. How to find enough time for your children

To Inform Your Reader

4. How to avoid or speed up red-tape procedures
5. How a particular type of sports equipment protects an athlete
6. How to remain calm while giving a speech

To Persuade Your Reader

7. How important it is to vote in a presidential election
8. How important it is to select the right courses in order to graduate on time
9. How important it is to exercise every day

Cases Using Process Analysis

10. In your communication course, you are studying friendship development and the strategies that people use to meet others. Write an essay describing the strategies people use to meet new people and develop friendships.
11. You are employed by a toy manufacturer and have been asked to write a brochure that encourages children to use toys safely. Prepare a brochure that describes at least three steps children can follow to avoid injury.

CHAPTER 15

Comparison and Contrast: Showing Similarities and Differences

Study the photograph on the opposite page showing someone using Wii to simulate playing a game of golf. Think about how simulating the play of a sport on Wii is similar to and different from actually playing the sport.

Make two lists — ways that playing the real sport and the Wii version are similar and ways that the real and Wii versions are different. You might choose to write about golf or select a different sport. In your lists, include details about the level of physical activity, types of skills required, interaction with other players, the setting, and so on. Then write a paragraph comparing the experiences of playing the sport using Wii and playing the actual sport.

WRITING A COMPARISON OR CONTRAST ESSAY

Your paragraph about playing the actual and the Wii versions of a sport is an example of comparison-and-contrast writing. You may have written about the similarities and differences in equipment required, physical exertion involved, and so forth. In addition, you probably organized your paragraph in one of two ways: (1) by writing about playing the Wii version and then writing about playing the actual sport (or vice versa) or (2) by discussing each point of similarity or difference with examples from Wii and the actual sport. This chapter will show you how to write effective comparison or contrast essays as well as how to incorporate comparison and contrast into essays using other patterns of development.

What Are Comparison and Contrast?

Using **comparison and contrast** involves looking at both similarities and differences. Analyzing similarities and differences is a useful decision-making skill that you use daily. You make comparisons when you shop for a pair of jeans, select a sandwich in the cafeteria, or choose a television program to watch. You also compare alternatives when you make important decisions about which college to attend, which field to major in, and which person to date.

You will find many occasions to use comparison and contrast in the writing you do in college and on the job (see the accompanying box for a few examples). In most essays of this type you will use one of two primary methods of organization, as the following two readings illustrate. The first essay, "Amusing Ourselves to Depth: Is *The Onion* Our Most Intelligent Newspaper?" by Greg Beato, uses a **point-by-point organization**. The writer moves back and forth between his two subjects (*The Onion* and traditional newspapers), comparing them on the basis of several key points or characteristics. The second essay, Ian Frazier's "Dearly Disconnected," uses a **subject-by-subject organization**. Here the author describes the key points or characteristics of one subject (pay phones) before moving on to those of his other subject (cell phones).

SCENES FROM COLLEGE AND THE WORKPLACE

- For a course in *criminal justice*, your instructor asks you to participate in a panel discussion comparing organized crime in three societies—Italy, Japan, and Russia.

- For a *journalism course*, you are assigned to interview two local television news reporters and write a paper contrasting their views on journalistic responsibility.

- As a *computer technician* for a pharmaceutical firm, you are asked to compare and contrast several models of notebook computers and recommend the one the company should purchase for its salespeople.

POINT-BY-POINT ORGANIZATION

Amusing Ourselves to Depth: Is *The Onion* Our Most Intelligent Newspaper?

Greg Beato

Greg Beato is a San Francisco–based writer who has written for such publications as *Spin*, *Wired*, *Business 2.0*, and the *San Francisco Chronicle*. He created the webzine *Traffic* in 1995 and was a frequent contributor to the webzine *Suck.com* from 1996 to 2000. He also maintains a blog about media and culture, *Soundbitten*, which he started in 1997. This essay was published in *Reason*, a libertarian magazine, in 2007. As you read, notice how Beato uses comparison and contrast to make his case for the validity of "fake news."

In August 1988, college junior Tim Keck borrowed $7,000 from his mom, rented a Mac Plus, and published a twelve-page newspaper. His ambition was hardly the stuff of future journalism symposiums: He wanted to create a compelling way to deliver advertising to his fellow students. Part of the first issue's front page was devoted to a story about a monster running amok at a local lake; the rest was reserved for beer and pizza coupons. 1

Almost twenty years later, *The Onion* stands as one of the newspaper industry's few great success stories in the post-newspaper era. Currently, it prints 710,000 copies of each weekly edition, roughly 6,000 more than the *Denver Post*, the nation's ninth-largest daily. Its syndicated radio dispatches reach a weekly audience of one million, and it recently started producing video clips too. Roughly three thousand local advertisers keep *The Onion* afloat, and the paper plans to add 170 employees to its staff of 130 this year. 2

Online it attracts more than two million readers a week. Type *onion* into Google, and *The Onion* pops up first. Type *the* into Google, and *The Onion* pops up first. But type "best practices for newspapers" into Google, and *The Onion* is nowhere to be found. Maybe it should be. At a time when traditional newspapers are frantic to divest themselves of their newsy, papery legacies, *The Onion* takes a surprisingly conservative approach to innovation. As much as it has used and benefited from the Web, it owes much of its success to low-tech attributes readily available to any paper but nonetheless in short supply: candor, irreverence, and a willingness to offend. 3

While other newspapers desperately add gardening sections, ask readers to share their favorite bratwurst recipes, or throw their staffers to ravenous packs of bloggers for online question-and-answer sessions, *The Onion* has focused on reporting the news. The fake news, sure, but still the news. It doesn't ask readers to post their comments at the end of stories, allow them to rate stories on a scale of one to five, or encourage citizen-satire. It makes no effort to convince readers that it really does understand their needs and exists only to serve them. *The Onion*'s journalists concentrate on writing stories and then getting them out there in a variety of formats, and this relatively old-fashioned approach to newspapering has been tremendously successful. 4

Are there any other newspapers that can boast a 60 percent increase in their print circulation during the last three years? Yet as traditional newspapers fail to draw 5 readers, only industry mavericks like the *New York Times*' Jayson Blair and *USA Today*'s Jack Kelley have looked to *The Onion* for inspiration.

One reason *The Onion* isn't taken more seriously is that it's actually fun to read. In 6 1985 the cultural critic Neil Postman published the influential *Amusing Ourselves to Death*, which warned of the fate that would befall us if public discourse were allowed to become substantially more entertaining than, say, a Neil Postman book. Today newspapers are eager to entertain—in their Travel, Food, and Style sections, that is. But even as scope creep has made the average big-city tree killer less portable than a ten-year-old laptop, hard news invariably comes in a single flavor: Double Objectivity Sludge.

Too many high priests of journalism still see humor as the enemy of seriousness: 7 If the news goes down too easily, it can't be very good for you. But do *The Onion* and its more fact-based acolytes, *The Daily Show* and *The Colbert Report*, monitor current events and the way the news media report on them any less rigorously than, say, the *Columbia Journalism Review* or *USA Today*?

During the last few years, multiple surveys by the Pew Research Center and the 8 Annenberg Public Policy Center have found that viewers of *The Daily Show* and *The Colbert Report* are among America's most informed citizens. Now, it may be that Jon Stewart isn't making anyone smarter; perhaps America's most informed citizens simply prefer comedy over the stentorian drivel the network anchormannequins dispense. But at the very least, such surveys suggest that news sharpened with satire doesn't cause the intellectual coronaries Postman predicted. Instead, it seems to correlate with engagement.

It's easy to see why readers connect with *The Onion*, and it's not just the jokes: De- 9 spite its "fake news" purview, it's an extremely honest publication. Most dailies, especially those in monopoly or near-monopoly markets, operate as if they're focused more on not offending readers (or advertisers) than on expressing a worldview of any kind. *The Onion* takes the opposite approach. It delights in crapping on pieties and regularly publishes stories guaranteed to upset someone: "Christ Kills Two, Injures Seven, in Abortion-Clinic Attack." "Heroic PETA Commandos Kill 49, Save Rabbit." "Gay Pride Parade Sets Mainstream Acceptance of Gays Back 50 Years." There's no predictable ideology running through those headlines, just a desire to express some rude, blunt truth about the world.

One common complaint about newspapers is that they're too negative, too focused 10 on bad news, too obsessed with the most unpleasant aspects of life. *The Onion* shows how wrong this characterization is, how gingerly most newspapers dance around the unrelenting awfulness of life and refuse to acknowledge the limits of our tolerance and compassion. The perfunctory coverage that traditional newspapers give disasters in countries cursed with relatability issues is reduced to its bare, dismal essence: "15,000 Brown People Dead Somewhere." Beggars aren't grist for Pulitzers, just punch lines: "Man Can't Decide Whether to Give Sandwich to Homeless or Ducks." Triumphs of the human spirit are as rare as vegans at an NRA barbecue: "Loved Ones Recall Local Man's Cowardly Battle with Cancer."

Such headlines come with a cost, of course. Outraged readers have convinced 11 advertisers to pull ads. Ginger Rogers and Denzel Washington, among other celebrities, have objected to stories featuring their names, and former *Onion* editor Robert

Siegel once told a lecture audience that the paper was "very nearly sued out of existence" after it ran a story with the headline "Dying Boy Gets Wish: To Pork Janet Jackson." But if this irreverence is sometimes economically inconvenient, it's also a major reason for the publication's popularity. It's a refreshing antidote to the he-said/she-said balancing acts that leave so many dailies sounding mealy-mouthed. And while *The Onion* may not adhere to the facts too strictly, it would no doubt place high if the Pew Research Center ever included it in a survey ranking America's most trusted news sources.

12   During the last few years, big-city dailies have begun to introduce "commuter" papers that function as lite versions of their original fare. These publications share some of *The Onion*'s attributes: They're free, they're tabloids, and most of their stories are bite-sized. But while they may be less filling, they still taste bland. You have to wonder: Why stop at price and paper size? Why not adopt the brutal frankness, the willingness to pierce orthodoxies of all political and cultural stripes, and apply these attributes to a genuinely reported daily newspaper?

13   Today's publishers give comic strips less and less space. Editorial cartoonists and folksy syndicated humorists have been nearly eradicated. Such changes have helped make newspapers more entertaining—or at least less dull—but they're just a start. Until today's front pages can amuse our staunchest defenders of journalistic integrity to severe dyspepsia, if not death, they're not trying hard enough.

SUBJECT-BY-SUBJECT ORGANIZATION

Dearly Disconnected
Ian Frazier

READING

Ian Frazier is an American writer and humorist whose books include *Great Plains* (1989), *Family* (1996), *Travels in Siberia* (2010), and several collections of columns he wrote for *The New Yorker* magazine both as a staff writer and independently. The following essay was adapted from a column that appeared in *Mother Jones* magazine in 2000. As you read, highlight the key points Frazier makes about pay phones and cell phones and his attitude toward each.

1   Before I got married I was living by myself in an A-frame cabin in northwestern Montana. The cabin's interior was a single high-ceilinged room, and at the center of the room, mounted on the rough-hewn log that held up the ceiling beam, was a telephone. The woman I would marry was living in Sarasota, Florida, and the distance between us suggests how well we were getting along at the time. We had not been in touch for several months; she had no phone. One day she decided to call me from a pay phone. We talked for a while, and after her coins ran out I jotted the number on the wood beside my phone and called her back. A day or two later, thinking about the call, I wanted to talk to her again. The only number I had for her was the pay phone number I'd written down.

2   The pay phone was on the street some blocks from the apartment where she stayed. As it happened, though, she had just stepped out to do some errands a few

minutes before I called, and she was passing by on the sidewalk when the phone rang. She had no reason to think that a public phone ringing on a busy street would be for her. She stopped, listened to it ring again, and picked up the receiver. Love is pure luck; somehow I had known she would answer, and she had known it would be me.

Long afterwards, on a trip to Disney World in Orlando with our two kids, then aged six and two, we made a special detour to Sarasota to show them the pay phone. It didn't impress them much. It's just a nondescript Bell Atlantic pay phone on the cement wall of a building, by the vestibule. But its ordinariness and even boringness only make me like it more; ordinary places where extraordinary events have occurred are my favorite kind. On my mental map of Florida that pay phone is a landmark looming above the city it occupies, and a notable, if private, historic site.

I'm interested in pay phones in general these days, especially when I get the feeling that they are about to go away. Technology, in the form of sleek little phones in our pockets, has swept on by them and made them begin to seem antique. My lifelong entanglement with pay phones dates me; when I was young they were just there, a given, often as stubborn and uncongenial as the curbstone underfoot. They were instruments of torture sometimes. You had to feed them fistfuls of change in those pre-phone-card days, and the operator was a real person who stood maddeningly between you and whomever you were trying to call. And when the call went wrong, as communication often does, the pay phone gave you a focus for your rage. Pay phones were always getting smashed up, the receivers shattered to bits against the booth, the coin slots jammed with chewing gum, the cords yanked out and unraveled to the floor.

There was always a touch of seediness and sadness to pay phones, and a sense of transience. Drug dealers made calls from them, and shady types who did not want their whereabouts known, and otherwise respectable people planning assignations, and people too poor to have phones of their own. In the movies, any character who used a pay phone was either in trouble or contemplating a crime. Mostly, pay phones evoked the mundane: "Honey, I'm just leaving. I'll be there soon." But you could tell that a lot of undifferentiated humanity had flowed through these places, and that in the muteness of each pay phone's little space, wild emotion had howled.

The phone on the wall of the concession stand at Redwood Pool, where I used to stand dripping and call my mom to come and pick me up; the sweaty phones used almost only by men in the hallway outside the maternity ward at Lenox Hill Hospital in New York; the phone in the old wood-paneled phone booth with leaded glass windows in the drugstore in my Ohio hometown—each one is as specific as a birthmark, a point on earth unlike any other. Recently I went back to New York City after a long absence and tried to find a working pay phone. I picked up one receiver after the next without success. Meanwhile, as I scanned down the long block, I counted half a dozen or more pedestrians talking on their cell phones.

It's the cell phone, of course, that's putting the pay phone out of business. The pay phone is to the cell phone as the troubled and difficult older sibling is to the cherished newborn. You sometimes hear people yelling on their cell phones, but almost never yelling at them. Cell phones are toylike, nearly magic, and we get a huge kick out of them, as often happens with technological advances until the new wears off. When I see a cell-phone user gently push the little antenna and fit the phone back into its brushed-vinyl carrying case and tuck the case inside his jacket beside his heart, I feel sorry for the beat-up pay phone standing in the rain.

People almost always talk on cell phones while in motion—driving, walking down 8 the street, riding on a commuter train. The cell phone took the transience the pay phone implied and turned it into VIP-style mobility and speed. Even sitting in a restaurant, the person on a cell phone seems importantly busy and on the move. Cell-phone conversations seem to be unlimited by ordinary constraints of place and time, as if they represent an almost-perfect form of communication, whose perfect state would be telepathy.

And yet no matter how we factor the world away, it remains. I think this is what 9 drives me so nuts when a person sitting next to me on a bus makes a call from her cell phone. Yes, this busy and important caller is at no fixed point in space, but nevertheless I happen to be beside her. The job of providing physical context falls on me; I become her call's surroundings, as if I'm the phone booth wall. For me to lean over and comment on her cell-phone conversation would be as unseemly and unexpected as if I were in fact a wall; and yet I have no choice, as a sentient person, but to hear what my chatty fellow traveler has to say.

I don't think that pay phones will completely disappear. Probably they will survive 10 for a long while as clumsy old technology still of some use to those lagging behind, and as a backup if ever the superior systems should temporarily fail. Before pay phones became endangered I never thought of them as public spaces, which of course they are. They suggested a human average; they belonged to anybody who had a couple of coins. Now I see that, like public schools and public transportation, pay phones belong to a former commonality our culture is no longer quite so sure it needs.

I have a weakness for places—for old battlefields, car-crash sites, houses where 11 famous authors lived. Bygone passions should always have an address, it seems to me. Ideally, the world would be covered with plaques and markers listing the notable events that occurred at each particular spot. A sign on every pay phone would describe how a woman broke up with her fiancé here, how a young ballplayer learned that he had made the team. Unfortunately, the world itself is fluid, and changes out from under us. Eventually pay phones will become relics of an almost-vanished landscape, and of a time when there were fewer of us and our stories were on an earlier page. Romantics like me will have to reimagine our passions as they are—unmoored to earth, like an infinitude of cell-phone messages flying through the atmosphere.

Characteristics of Comparison or Contrast Essays

When writers use comparison and contrast, they consider subjects with characteristics in common, examining similarities, differences, or both. Whether used as the primary pattern of development or alongside another pattern, comparison and contrast can be used for various purposes to make a point about a subject.

Comparison or Contrast Has a Clear Purpose

A comparison and contrast essay usually has one of three purposes—*to express ideas, to inform,* or *to persuade.* In an essay about playing sports, Wii and actual, the purpose could be to express your ideas about playing sports, based on your experiences with Wii and actual sports. Alternatively, the purpose could be to inform readers who are going to play either form of the sport, explaining what to expect in each case. Finally, the purpose could be to persuade readers that playing the Wii form of a sport is convenient, accessible, and entertaining. In "Dearly Disconnected" (pp. 377–78), for example, the author expresses his nostalgia for the pay phone, in "Amusing Ourselves to Depth," the author tries to persuade readers that "brutal frankness" may have a place in news reporting.

Comparison or Contrast Considers Shared Characteristics

You cannot compare two things unless they have something in common. When making a comparison, a writer needs to choose a **basis of comparison**—a fairly broad common characteristic on which to base the essay. For an essay comparing baseball and football, for example, a basis of comparison might be the athletic skills required or the rules and logistics of each sport. To develop the essay, the writer examines the two subjects using **points of comparison**—characteristics relating to the basis of comparison. In an essay using athletic skills as a basis of comparison, for example, points of comparison might be height and weight requirements, running skills, and hand-eye coordination. In an essay based on rules and logistics, points of comparison might include scoring, equipment, and playing fields.

> ### Exercise 15.1
>
> *For three items in the following list, identify two possible bases of comparison you could use to compare each pair of topics:*
>
> 1. Two means of travel or transportation
> 2. Two means of communication (emails, telephone calls, postal letters, text messages)
> 3. Two pieces of equipment
> 4. Two magazines or books
> 5. Two types of television programming

A Comparison or Contrast Essay Fairly Examines Similarities, Differences, or Both

Depending on their purpose, writers using comparison and contrast may focus on similarities, differences, or both. In an essay intended to *persuade* readers that performers Beyoncé Knowles and Jennifer Lopez have much in common in terms of talent and cultural influence, the writer would focus on similarities—hit records, millions of fans, and parts in movies. However, an essay intended to *inform* readers about the singers would probably cover both similarities and differences, discussing the singers' different childhoods or singing styles.

An essay focusing on similarities often mentions a few differences, usually in the introduction, to let readers know the writer is aware of the differences. Conversely, an essay that focuses on differences might mention a few similarities.

Whether you cover similarities, differences, or both in an essay, you should strive to treat your subjects fairly. Relevant information should not be purposely omitted to show one subject in a more favorable light. In an essay about Knowles and Lopez, for instance, you should not leave out information about Lopez's charity work in an effort to make Knowles appear to be a nicer person. In "Dearly Disconnected," Frazier regrets the demise of the pay phone but admits that cell phones are "toylike, nearly magic."

Comparison or Contrast Makes a Point

Whatever the purpose of a comparison or contrast essay, its main point about its subjects should spark readers' interest rather than bore them with a mechanical listing of similarities or differences. This main point can serve as the thesis for the essay, or the thesis can be implied in the writer's choice of details. In "Amusing Ourselves to Depth," for example, the thesis statement is implied in paragraphs 3 and 13: In comparison to the brutal honesty of *The Onion*, traditional newspapers seem timid and dull.

An explicit thesis has three functions:

1. It identifies the *subjects* being compared or contrasted.
2. It suggests whether the focus is on *similarities, differences,* or *both.*
3. It states the *main point* of the comparison or contrast.

Notice how the following three sample theses meet the above criteria. Note, too, that each thesis suggests why the comparison or contrast is meaningful and worth reading about.

- ┌─────similarities─────┐ ┌────────subjects────────┐
  Similar appeals in commercials for three popular breakfast cereals reveal
  ┌───────────main point───────────┐
  America's obsession with fitness and health.

- ┌─────difference─────┐ ┌────subjects────┐ ┌────similarities────┐
  Although different in purpose, weddings and funerals each draw families
  ┌───────main point───────┐
  together and confirm family values.

- ┌────────────────subjects────────────────┐
  The two cities Niagara Falls, Ontario, and Niagara Falls, New York, demonstrate
  ┌─────differences─────┐ ┌──────────────main point──────────────┐
  two different approaches to appreciating nature and preserving the environment.

> ### Exercise 15.2
>
> *For one of the topic pairs you worked on in Exercise 15.1 (p. 380), select the basis of comparison that seems most promising. Then write a thesis statement that identifies the subjects, the focus (similarities, differences, or both), and the main point.*

Comparison or Contrast Considers a Sufficient Number of Significant Characteristics and Details

A comparison or contrast essay considers characteristics that are significant as well as relevant to the essay's purpose and thesis. In "Amusing Ourselves to Depth," for example, Beato considers such significant characteristics as circulation, type of information presented, degree of seriousness, and honesty.

Although the number of details can vary by topic, usually at least three or four significant characteristics are needed to support a thesis. Each characteristic should be fully described or explained so that readers can grasp the main point of the comparison or contrast. A writer may use sensory details, dialogue, examples, expert testimony, and other kinds of detail in a comparison or contrast essay. In "Dearly Disconnected," Frazier supports his points by using anecdotes and vivid descriptions.

Visualizing a Comparison or Contrast Essay: Two Graphic Organizers

For more on graphic organizers, see Chapter 3, pp. 59–61.

Suppose you want to compare two houses (house A and house B) built by the same architect for the purpose of evaluating how the architect's style has changed over time. After brainstorming ideas, you decide to base your essay on these points of comparison—layout, size, building materials, and landscaping. You can organize your essay in one of two ways—point by point or subject by subject.

Point-by-Point Organization

In a *point-by-point organization,* you go back and forth between the two houses, noting similarities and differences between them on each of the four points of comparison, as shown in the graphic organizer in Figure 15.1.

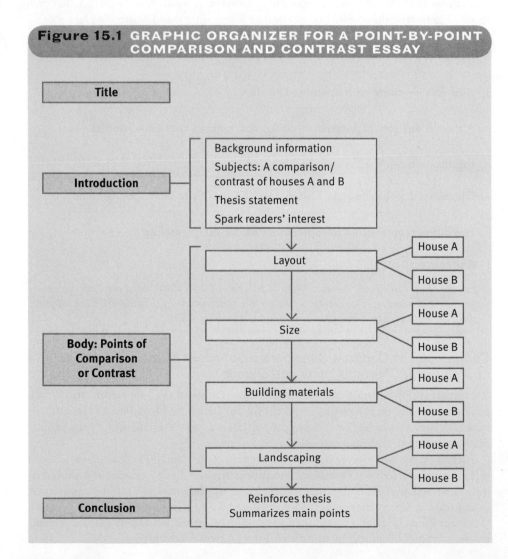

Figure 15.1 GRAPHIC ORGANIZER FOR A POINT-BY-POINT COMPARISON AND CONTRAST ESSAY

Title

Introduction
- Background information
- Subjects: A comparison/ contrast of houses A and B
- Thesis statement
- Spark readers' interest

Body: Points of Comparison or Contrast
- Layout — House A / House B
- Size — House A / House B
- Building materials — House A / House B
- Landscaping — House A / House B

Conclusion
- Reinforces thesis
- Summarizes main points

Subject-by-Subject Organization

In a *subject-by-subject organization,* you first discuss all points about house A—its layout, size, building materials, and landscaping. Then you do the same for house B. This pattern is shown in the graphic organizer in Figure 15.2.

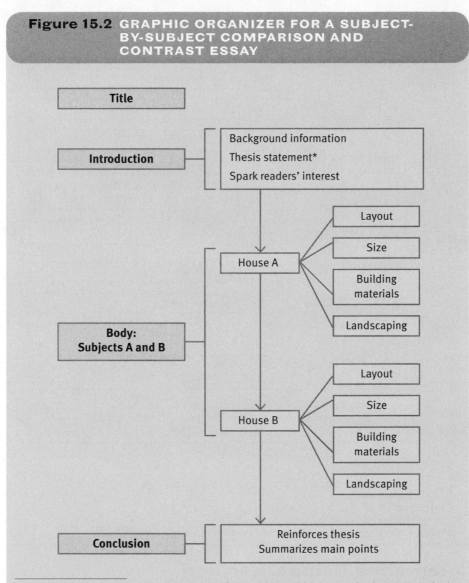

Figure 15.2 GRAPHIC ORGANIZER FOR A SUBJECT-BY-SUBJECT COMPARISON AND CONTRAST ESSAY

Title

Introduction
— Background information
— Thesis statement*
— Spark readers' interest

House A
— Layout
— Size
— Building materials
— Landscaping

Body:
Subjects A and B

House B
— Layout
— Size
— Building materials
— Landscaping

Conclusion
— Reinforces thesis
Summarizes main points

* Sometimes the thesis statement appears in the body or conclusion of the essay, or the thesis is implied rather than stated directly.

"Dearly Disconnected" uses a subject-by-subject organization. Review the essay, and then study the graphic organizer shown in Figure 15.3, on page 384.

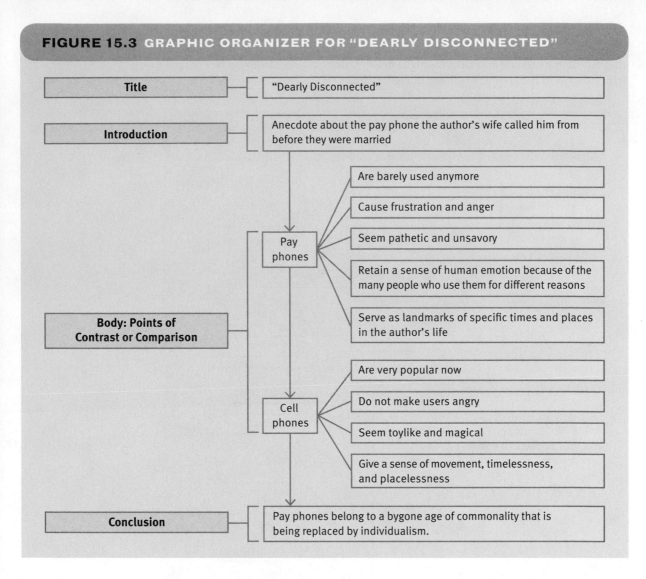

FIGURE 15.3 GRAPHIC ORGANIZER FOR "DEARLY DISCONNECTED"

| Title | "Dearly Disconnected" |

| Introduction | Anecdote about the pay phone the author's wife called him from before they were married |

Pay phones
- Are barely used anymore
- Cause frustration and anger
- Seem pathetic and unsavory
- Retain a sense of human emotion because of the many people who use them for different reasons
- Serve as landmarks of specific times and places in the author's life

Body: Points of Contrast or Comparison

Cell phones
- Are very popular now
- Do not make users angry
- Seem toylike and magical
- Give a sense of movement, timelessness, and placelessness

| Conclusion | Pay phones belong to a bygone age of commonality that is being replaced by individualism. |

To draw detailed graphic organizers using a computer, visit www .bedfordstmartins.com /successfulcollege.

Exercise 15.3

Draw a graphic organizer for "Amusing Ourselves to Depth" (pp. 375–77).

Integrating Comparison and Contrast into an Essay

Although you will write some essays using comparison and contrast as the primary pattern of development, in most cases you will integrate comparisons or contrasts into essays that rely on other patterns, such as description, process analysis, or argument. Comparisons or contrasts can be particularly effective in persuasive essays.

A special type of comparison that you may have occasion to use is an **analogy**, which helps readers understand something unfamiliar by comparing it to something familiar. For example, a writer could explain the evolution of the universe by comparing it to the stages of human life.

Use the following tips to incorporate comparison or contrast into essays based on other patterns of development:

1. **Determine the purpose of the comparison or contrast.** What will it contribute to your essay?
2. **Introduce the comparison or contrast clearly.** Tell your readers how it supports the main point of the essay. Do not leave it to them to figure out why the comparison is included.
3. **Keep the comparison or contrast short and to the point.** An extended comparison will distract readers from the overall point of your essay.
4. **Organize the points of the comparison or contrast.** Even though it is part of a larger essay, the comparison or contrast should follow a point-by-point or subject-by-subject organization.
5. **Use transitions.** Transitional words and expressions are especially important in easing the flow into the comparison or contrast and then back to the essay's primary pattern of development.

In "Defining a Doctor, with a Tear, a Shrug, and a Schedule" on pages 403–5, Abigail Zuger uses comparison and contrast along with other patterns of development.

A GUIDED WRITING ASSIGNMENT

The following guide will lead you through the process of writing a comparison or contrast essay. Although you will focus on comparing or contrasting your subjects, you may need to integrate one or more other patterns of development in your essay.

The Assignment

Write a comparison or contrast essay on one of the following topic pairs or one of your own choosing:

1. Two public figures
2. Two forms of entertainment (movies, concerts, radio, music videos) or one form of entertainment as it is used today and as it was used ten or more years ago
3. Two styles of communication, dress, or teaching
4. The right and wrong ways of doing something
5. Your views versus your parents' or grandparents' views on an issue
6. Two different cultures' approaches to a rite of passage, such as birth, puberty, marriage, or death
7. Two different cultures' views on the roles that should be played by men and women in society
8. Two products from two different eras

Depending on the topic pair you choose, you may need to use Internet or library sources to develop and support your ideas about the subjects. Your audience is your classmates. As you develop your comparison or contrast essay, consider using one or more other patterns of development. For example, you might use process analysis to explain the right and wrong ways of doing something or cause and effect to show the results of two teaching styles on learners.

For more on process analysis, see Chapter 14. For more on cause and effect, see Chapter 18.

Generating Ideas

Generating ideas involves first choosing subjects to compare and then prewriting to discover similarities, differences, and other details about the subjects.

Choosing Subjects to Compare

For more on prewriting strategies, see Chapter 5, pp. 110–18.

Learning Style Options

Take your time selecting the assignment option and identifying specific subjects for it. Use the following guidelines to get started:

1. Some of the options listed on page 385 are concrete (comparing two public figures); others are more abstract (comparing communication styles or views on an issue). Consider your learning style and choose the option with which you are most comfortable.
2. If you are a social learner, choose subjects that your classmates are familiar with so that you can discuss your subjects with them. Try group brainstorming about various possible subjects.
3. Choose subjects with which you have some firsthand experience or that you are willing to research. You might try questioning or writing assertions to help you generate ideas.
4. Choose subjects that interest you. You will have more fun writing about them, and your enthusiasm will enliven your essay. Try mapping or sketching to come up with interesting subjects.

> **Essay in Progress 1**
> Using the preceding suggestions, choose an assignment option from the list on page 385 or an option you think of on your own. Then do some prewriting to help you select two specific subjects for your comparison or contrast essay.

Choosing a Basis of Comparison and a Purpose

Suppose you want to compare or contrast two well-known football players—a quarterback and a linebacker. If you merely present the various similarities and differences between the two players, your essay will lack direction. To avoid this problem, you need to choose a basis of comparison and a purpose for writing. You could compare the players on the basis of the positions they play, using the height, weight, skills, and training needed for each position as points of comparison. Your purpose would be to *inform* readers about the two positions. Alternatively, you could base your comparison on their performances on the field; in this case, your purpose might be to *persuade* readers to accept your evaluation of both players. Other bases of comparison might be the players' media images, contributions to their teams, or service to the community.

Once you have a basis of comparison and a purpose in mind, try to state them clearly in a few sentences. Refer to these sentences as you work to keep your essay on track.

Essay in Progress 2

For the assignment option and subjects you selected in Essay in Progress 1, decide on a basis of comparison and a purpose for your essay. Describe both clearly in a few sentences. Keep in mind that you may revise your basis of comparison and purpose as your essay develops.

Considering Your Audience and Point of View

As you develop your comparison or contrast essay, keep your audience in mind. Choose points of comparison that will interest your readers. For this chapter's assignment, your audience is made up of your classmates. You also need to think about point of view, or how you should address your readers. Most comparison or contrast essays are written in the third person. However, the first person may be appropriate when you use comparison and contrast to express personal thoughts or feelings.

For more on audience and point of view, see Chapter 5, pp. 107–9.

Discovering Similarities and Differences and Generating Details

Your next step is to discover how your two subjects are similar, how they are different, or both. Depending on your learning style, you can approach this task in a number of different ways:

1. **On paper or on your computer, create a two-column list of similarities and differences.** Jot down ideas in the appropriate column.
2. **Ask a classmate to help you brainstorm aloud by mentioning only similarities; then counter each similarity with a difference.** Write notes on the brainstorming.
3. **For concrete subjects, try visualizing them.** Take notes on what you see, or draw a sketch of your subjects.
4. **Create a scenario in which your subjects interact.** For example, if your topic is automobiles of today and eighty-five years ago, imagine taking your great-grandfather, who owned a Model T Ford, for a drive in a 2012 luxury car. How would he react? What would he say?
5. **Do research on your two subjects at the library or on the Internet.**

Learning Style Options

For more on description, see Chapter 12.

For more on library and Internet research, see Chapter 22.

Your readers will need plenty of details to grasp the similarities and differences between your subjects. Use description, examples, and facts to make your subjects seem real to your readers.

Try to maintain an even balance between your two subjects; gather roughly the same amount of detail for each. This guideline is especially important if your purpose is to demonstrate that subject A is preferable to or better than subject B. Your readers will become suspicious if you provide plenty of detail for subject A and only sketchy information for subject B.

Essay in Progress 3

Use the preceding suggestions and one or more prewriting strategies to discover similarities and differences and to generate details about your two subjects.

Developing Your Thesis

For more on thesis statements, see Chapter 6.

The thesis statement for a comparison or contrast essay needs to fulfill the three criteria noted earlier: It should identify the subjects; suggest whether you will focus on similarities, differences, or both; and state your main point. In addition, your thesis should tell readers why your comparison or contrast of the two subjects is important or useful to them. Look at the following sample thesis statements:

WEAK   The books by Robert B. Parker and Sue Grafton are similar.

REVISED   The novels of Robert B. Parker and Sue Grafton are popular because readers are fascinated by the intrigues of witty, independent private detectives.

The first thesis is weak because it does not place the comparison within a context or give the reader a reason to care about it. The second thesis is more detailed and specific. It provides a basis for comparison and indicates why the similarity is worth reading about.

> **Essay in Progress 4**
> Using the preceding suggestions, write a thesis statement for this chapter's essay assignment. The thesis should identify the two subjects of your comparison; tell whether you will focus on similarities, differences, or both; and convey your main point to readers.

Evaluating Your Ideas and Thesis

With your thesis in mind, review your prewriting by underlining or highlighting ideas that pertain to your thesis and eliminating those that do not. If you are working on a computer, highlight these key ideas in bold type or move them to a separate file. Try to identify the points or characteristics by which you can best compare your subjects. For example, if your thesis is about evaluating the performance of two football players, you would probably select various facts and details about their training, the plays they make, and their records. Think of points of comparison as the main similarities or differences that support your thesis.

Take a few minutes to evaluate your ideas and thesis. Make sure you have enough points of comparison to support your thesis and enough details to develop those points. If necessary, do additional prewriting to generate sufficient support for your thesis.

> **Essay in Progress 5**
> Using the preceding suggestions and comments from your classmates, list the points of comparison you plan to use in your essay and evaluate your ideas and thesis. Refer to the list of characteristics on pages 379–81 to help you with your evaluation.

> **Trying Out Your Ideas on Others**
> Working in a group of two or three students, discuss your ideas and thesis for this chapter's assignment. Each writer should state his or her topic, thesis, and points of comparison. Then, as a group, evaluate each writer's work.

Organizing and Drafting

Once you have evaluated your thesis, points of comparison, and details, you are ready to organize your ideas and draft your essay.

For more on drafting an essay, see Chapter 7.

Choosing a Method of Organization

Before you begin writing, decide whether you will use a point-by-point or a subject-by-subject organization (review Figures 15.1 and 15.2, pp. 382–83). To select a method of organization, consider the complexity of your subjects and the length of your essay. You may also need to experiment with the two approaches to see which works better. It is a good idea to make an outline or draw a graphic organizer at this stage.

Here are a few other guidelines to consider:

1. **The subject-by-subject method tends to emphasize the larger picture, whereas the point-by-point method emphasizes details and specifics.**
2. **The point-by-point method often works better for lengthy essays because it keeps both subjects current in your reader's mind.**
3. **The point-by-point method is often preferable for complicated or technical subjects.** For example, if you compare two computer systems, it would be easier to explain the function of a memory card once and then describe the memory cards in each of the two systems.

> **Essay in Progress 6**
> Choose a method of organization—point by point or subject by subject—and organize the points of comparison you generated in Essay in Progress 5.

Drafting the Essay

Use the following guidelines when writing your first draft:

1. **If you are using point-by-point organization, keep the following suggestions in mind.**

   - Work back and forth between your two subjects, generally discussing the subjects in the same order for each point. If both subjects share a particular characteristic, then you may want to mention them together.
   - Use a separate paragraph for each point of comparison, in most cases.
   - Arrange your points of comparison carefully. You might, for example, start with the clearest, simplest points and then move on to more complex ones.

2. **If you are using a subject-by-subject organization, keep the following suggestions in mind.**

   - Be sure to cover the same points for both subjects.
   - Cover the points of comparison in the same order in both halves of your essay.
   - Write a clear statement of transition wherever you switch from one subject to the other.

3. **Use transitions.** Transitions are especially important in helping readers follow the points you make in a comparison or contrast essay. Transitions alert readers to shifts between subjects or to new points of comparison. An essay that lacks transitions sounds choppy and unconnected. Use transitional words and phrases such as *similarly, in contrast, on the one hand, on the other hand,* and *not only . . . but also.*

For more on transitions, see Chapter 7, pp. 150–52.

For more on writing effective paragraphs, including introductions and conclusions, see Chapter 7.

4. Write an effective introduction. The introduction should spark your readers' interest, present your subjects, state your thesis, and include any background information your readers may need.

5. Write a satisfying conclusion. Your conclusion should offer a final comment on your comparison or contrast, reminding readers of your thesis. For a lengthy or complex essay, you might want to summarize your main points as well.

> **Essay in Progress 7**
> Using the organization you developed in Essay in Progress 6 and the preceding guidelines for drafting, write a first draft of your comparison or contrast essay.

Analyzing and Revising

If possible, set your draft aside for a day or two before rereading and revising it. As you reread, concentrate on ideas and not on grammar or punctuation. Use one or more of the following suggestions to analyze your draft:

Learning Style Options

1. Reread your essay aloud, or ask a friend or classmate to do so as you listen.
2. Draw a graphic organizer, make an outline, or update the organizer or outline you prepared earlier. A graphic organizer or outline will indicate whether your organization contains inconsistencies or gaps.
3. Read each paragraph with this question in mind: So what? If any paragraph does not answer that question, revise or delete it.

For more on the benefits of peer review, see Chapter 9, pp. 188–91.

Use Figure 15.4 to guide your analysis of the strengths and weaknesses in your draft essay. You might also ask a classmate to review your draft essay using the questions in the flowchart. Your reviewer should consider each question listed in the flowchart, explaining each "No" answer.

> **Essay in Progress 8**
> Revise your draft using Figure 15.4 and any comments you received from peer reviewers.

Editing and Proofreading

The last step is to check your revised essay for errors in grammar, spelling, punctuation, and mechanics. Be sure to check your error log for the types of errors you tend to make.

As you edit and proofread your comparison or contrast essay, watch out for the following types of errors:

For more on keeping an error log, see Chapter 10, pp. 221–22.

1. Make sure to use the right forms of adjectives and adverbs when comparing two items (comparative) and three or more items (superlative). The following examples show how adjectives and adverbs change forms.

	Adjectives	**Adverbs**
Positive	sharp	early
Comparative	sharper	earlier
Superlative	sharpest	earliest

Figure 15.4 Flowchart for Revising a Comparison or Contrast Essay

QUESTIONS   **REVISION STRATEGIES**

1. your thesis statement. Does it identify the subjects being compared and state your main point? Does it or do nearby sentences express a clear purpose (to express ideas, inform, or persuade)?

NO →
- Revise your thesis using the suggestions on p. 388.
- Brainstorm a list of reasons for making the comparison. Make the most promising reason your purpose.

YES

2. *Write* the basis of comparison at the top of your paper. Is your basis of comparison clear? Does it clearly relate to your thesis?

NO →
- Ask a friend or classmate to help you think of a clear or new basis for comparison.

YES

3. *List* your points of comparison. Place a checkmark ✔ next to the sentences that focus on similarities between the subjects. Mark an *X* next to the sentences that focus on differences. Have you included all significant points of comparison? Do you fairly examine similarities and differences? Is each similarity or difference significant, and does each support your thesis?

NO →
- Delete any discussion of similarities or differences that are not significant or that do not support your thesis.
- Review your prewriting to see if you overlooked any significant points of comparison. If so, revise to add them.
- If you have trouble thinking of points of comparison, conduct research or ask a classmate to suggest ideas.

YES

4. the topic sentence of each paragraph. Does each paragraph have a clear topic sentence? If you are using point-by-point comparison, is each paragraph focused on a separate point or shared characteristic?

NO →
- Follow the guidelines for writing clear topic sentences (pp. 167–70).
- Consider splitting paragraphs that focus on more than one point or characteristic and combining paragraphs that focus on the same one.

YES

(continued on next page)

(Figure 15.4 continued)

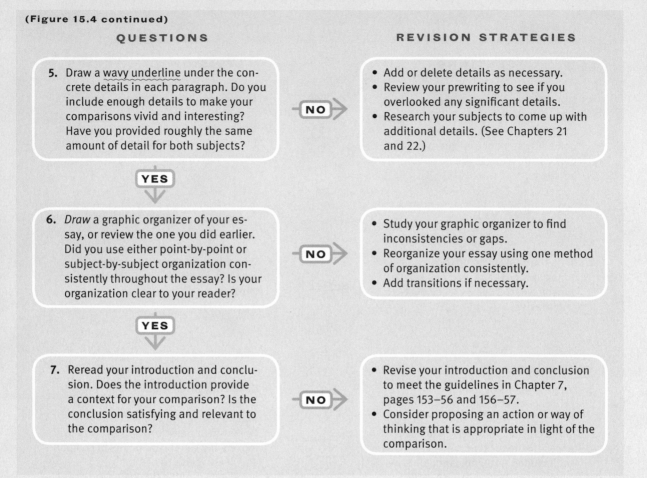

QUESTIONS

REVISION STRATEGIES

5. Draw a wavy underline under the concrete details in each paragraph. Do you include enough details to make your comparisons vivid and interesting? Have you provided roughly the same amount of detail for both subjects?

NO →

- Add or delete details as necessary.
- Review your prewriting to see if you overlooked any significant details.
- Research your subjects to come up with additional details. (See Chapters 21 and 22.)

YES

6. *Draw* a graphic organizer of your essay, or review the one you did earlier. Did you use either point-by-point or subject-by-subject organization consistently throughout the essay? Is your organization clear to your reader?

NO →

- Study your graphic organizer to find inconsistencies or gaps.
- Reorganize your essay using one method of organization consistently.
- Add transitions if necessary.

YES

7. Reread your introduction and conclusion. Does the introduction provide a context for your comparison? Is the conclusion satisfying and relevant to the comparison?

NO →

- Revise your introduction and conclusion to meet the guidelines in Chapter 7, pages 153–56 and 156–57.
- Consider proposing an action or way of thinking that is appropriate in light of the comparison.

- Both *No Country for Old Men* and *True Grit* were suspenseful, but I liked *True*

  better.
  Grit ~~best.~~

- George, Casey, and Bob are all bad at basketball, but Bob's game is *worst.* ~~worse.~~

  2. Make sure that items in a pair linked by correlative conjunctions (*either . . . or, neither . . . nor, not only . . . but also*) are in the same grammatical form.

- The Grand Canyon is not only a spectacular tourist attraction but also

  ~~scientists consider it~~ a useful geological record. *for scientists.*

Essay in Progress 9

Edit and proofread your essay, paying particular attention both to adjectives and adverbs used to compare and to items linked by correlative conjunctions.

Students Write

Heather Gianakos was a first-year student when she wrote the following comparison-and-contrast essay for her composition course. Although she has always enjoyed both styles of cooking that she discusses, she needed to do some research in the library and on the Internet to learn more about their history. As you read the essay, consider the writer's thesis and points of comparison.

Border Bites

Heather Gianakos

Chili peppers, tortillas, tacos: All these foods belong to the styles of cooking known as Mexican, Tex-Mex, and southwestern. These internationally popular styles often overlap; sometimes it can be hard to tell which style a particular dish belongs to. Two particular traditions of cooking, however, play an especially important role in the kitchens of Mexico and the American Southwest-- native-derived Mexican cooking ("Mexican"), and Anglo-influenced southwestern cooking, particularly from Texas ("southwestern"). The different traditions and geographic locations of the inhabitants of Mexico and of the Anglo American settlers in the Southwest have resulted in subtle, flavorful differences between the foods featured in Mexican and southwestern cuisine.

1

Many of the traditions of southwestern cooking grew out of difficult situations--cowboys and ranchers cooking over open fires, for example. Chili, which can contain beans, beef, tomatoes, corn, and many other ingredients, was a good dish to cook over a campfire because everything could be combined in one pot. Dry foods, such as beef jerky, were a convenient way to solve food storage problems and could be easily tucked into saddlebags. In Mexico, by contrast, fresh fruits and vegetables such as avocados and tomatoes were widely available and did not need to be dried or stored. They could be made into spicy salsa and guacamole. Mexicans living in coastal areas could also enjoy fish and lobster dishes (Jamison and Jamison 5).

2

Corn has been a staple in the American Southwest and Mexico since the time of the Aztecs, who made tortillas (flat, unleavened bread, originally made from stone-ground corn and water) similar to the ones served in Mexico today (Jamison and Jamison 5). Southwesterners, often of European descent, adopted the tortilla but often prepared it with wheat flour, which was easily available to them. Wheat-flour tortillas can now be found in both Mexican and southwestern cooking, but corn is usually the primary grain in dishes with precolonial origins. Tamales (whose name derives from a word in Nahuatl, the Aztec group of languages) are a delicious example: A hunk of cornmeal dough, sometimes combined with ground meat, is wrapped in corn husks and steamed. In southwestern cooking, corn is often used for leavened corn bread, which is made with corn flour rather than cornmeal and can be flavored with jalapeños or back bacon.

3

Introduction indicates Gianakos will examine both similarities and differences but will focus on differences. Her thesis statement gives a basis of comparison of her two subjects, Mexican and southwestern cooking: the traditions and geographic locations of the people who developed them. It also makes a point: that these differences have led to the differences in the food.

Subject A: southwestern
Subject B: Mexican

Point of comparison #1: the physical conditions in which the two styles developed. Notice that Gianakos uses point-by-point comparison, discussing both subjects in each paragraph and often using transitions between them. She also cites sources for her information.

Point of comparison #2: the use of corn and wheat

Point of comparison #3: the use of chicken

Meat of various kinds is often the centerpiece of both Mexican and southwestern tables. 4 However, although chicken, beef, and pork are staples in both traditions, they are often prepared quite differently. Fried chicken rolled in flour and dunked into sizzling oil or fat is a popular dish throughout the American Southwest. In traditional Mexican cooking, however, chicken is often cooked more slowly, in stews or baked dishes, with a variety of seasonings, including ancho chiles, garlic, and onions.

Subject A: southwestern

Subject B: Mexican

Point of comparison #4: the use of beef

Ever since cattle farming began in Texas with the early Spanish missions, beef has been 5 eaten both north and south of the border. In southwestern cooking, steak--flank, rib eye, or sirloin--grilled quickly and served rare is often a chef's crowning glory. In Mexican cooking, beef may be combined with vegetables and spices and rolled into a fajita or served ground in a taco. For a Mexican food purist, in fact, the only true fajita is made from skirt steak, although Mexican food as it is served in the United States often features chicken fajitas.

Subject A: southwestern

Subject B: Mexican

Point of comparison #5: the use of pork

In Texas and the Southwest United States, barbecued pork ribs are often prepared in bar- 6 becue cook-offs, similar to chili-cooking competitions. Such competitions have strict rules for the preparation and presentation of the food and for sanitation (Central Texas). However, while the BBQ is seen as a southwestern specialty, barbecue ribs as they are served in southwestern-themed restaurants today actually come from a Hispanic and Southwest Mexican tradition dating from the days before refrigeration: Since pork fat, unlike beef fat, has a tendency to become rancid, pork ribs were often marinated in vinegar and spices and then hung to dry. Later the ribs were basted with the same sauce and grilled (Campa 278). The resulting dish has become a favorite both north and south of the border, although in Mexican cooking, where beef is somewhat less important than in southwestern cooking, pork is equally popular in many other forms, such as chorizo sausage.

Subject A: southwestern

Subject B: Mexican

Conclusion: Gianakos returns to the idea of overlap mentioned in the introduction and makes clear her purpose—to inform readers about the differences between the two cuisines.

Cooks in San Antonio or Albuquerque would probably tell you that the food they cook is as 7 much Mexican as it is southwestern. Regional cuisines in such areas of the Southwest as New Mexico, Southern California, and Arizona feature elements of both traditions; chimichangas--deep-fried burritos--actually originated in Arizona (Jamison and Jamison 11). Food lovers who sample regional specialties, however, will note--and savor--the contrast between the spicy, fried or grilled, beef-heavy style of southwestern food and the richly seasoned, corn- and tomato-heavy style of Mexican food.

Gianakos lists her sources at the end of her paper, following MLA style.

Works Cited

Campa, Arthur L. *Hispanic Culture in the Southwest*. Norman: U of Oklahoma P, 1979. Print.

Central Texas Barbecue Association. "CTBA Rules." *Central Texas Barbecue Association*. CTBA, 16 Aug. 2004. Web. 6 May 2005.

Jamison, Cheryl Alters, and Bill Jamison. *The Border Cookbook*. Boston: Harvard Common, 1995. Print.

Analyzing the Writer's Technique

1. Evaluate Gianakos's title and introduction. Do they provide the reader with enough background on her topic?
2. Using a point-by-point organization, Gianakos presents her two subjects in the same order—first southwestern cuisine, then Mexican cuisine—for each point of comparison except in paragraph 3. Why do you think she discusses the two cuisines together in this paragraph?
3. How does Gianakos's use of sources contribute to her essay?

Thinking Critically about Comparison and Contrast

1. Reread the first sentence of the essay. What type of cooking is mentioned here and never discussed again in the essay? How does this decision by Gianakos affect your response to the first paragraph and to the essay as a whole?
2. Describe Gianakos's tone. Is it effective in this essay?
3. What do phrases such as "subtle, flavorful differences" (para. 1), "Food lovers" (7), and "richly seasoned" (7) contribute to the essay? If Gianakos had included more phrases like these, how would the essay be changed?
4. What comparisons did Gianakos not make that she could have made?

Reacting to the Essay

1. What other regional cuisines might make effective topics for a comparison and contrast essay?
2. Gianakos compares the cuisines of the American Southwest and Mexico using the traditions and geographic locations of the people who lived there as the basis of comparison. In your journal, explore several other possible bases of comparison that could be used to compare these cuisines.
3. Write an essay comparing foods of two other regional cuisines.

READING COMPARISON AND CONTRAST

The following section provides advice for reading comparison and contrast essays. Two model essays illustrate the characteristics of comparison and contrast covered in this chapter and provide opportunities to examine, analyze, and react to the writer's ideas. The second essay uses comparison and contrast along with other methods of development.

Working with Text: Reading Comparison or Contrast Essays

Reading a comparison and contrast essay is somewhat different from reading other kinds of essays. First, the essay contains two or more subjects instead of just one. Second, the subjects are being compared, contrasted, or both, so you must follow the

For more on reading strategies, see Chapter 3.

author's points of comparison between or among them. Use the guidelines below to read comparison-and-contrast essays effectively.

What to Look For, Highlight, and Annotate

For more on previewing, see Chapter 3, pp. 48–50.

1. As you preview the essay, determine whether it uses the point-by-point or subject-by-subject organization. Knowing the method of organization will help you move through the essay more easily.
2. Identify and highlight the thesis statement, if it is stated explicitly. What does it tell you about the essay's purpose, direction, and organization?
3. Read the essay once to get an overall sense of how it develops. As you read, highlight each point of comparison the writer makes.
4. Review the essay by drawing a graphic organizer (see Figures 15.1 and 15.2). Doing so will help you learn and recall the key points of the essay.

How to Find Ideas to Write About

For more on discovering ideas for a response paper, see Chapter 4, pp. 86–95.

To respond to or write about a comparison and contrast essay, consider the following strategies:

- Compare the subjects using a different basis of comparison. If, for example, an essay compares or contrasts athletes in various sports on the basis of salary, you could compare them according to the training required for each sport.
- For an essay that emphasizes differences, consider writing about similarities, and vice versa.
- To write an essay that looks at one point of comparison in more depth, you might do research or interview an expert on the topic.

Thinking Critically about Comparison and Contrast

Comparison and contrast writing can be quite straightforward when the writer's purpose is only to inform. However, when the writer's purpose is also to persuade, you need to ask the critical questions below.

1. Does the Author Treat Each Subject Fairly?

Examine whether the author gives equal and objective coverage to each subject. If one of the subjects seems to be favored or given special consideration (or if one seems not to be treated fairly, fully, or adequately), the author might be *biased*—that is, introducing his or her own values or attitudes into the comparison. The lack of balance may not be intentional, and even a biased piece of writing is not necessarily unreliable, but you should be aware that other points of view may not have been presented. In "Dearly Disconnected," Frazier devotes more coverage to pay phones than to cell phones and appears nostalgic about pay phones but somewhat annoyed by cell phones.

2. How Does the Organization Affect Meaning?

In thinking about the question of fairness, notice especially whether and how the author uses a point-by-point or subject-by-subject organization. These two organizations provide different emphases. Point by point tends to maintain a steady balance, keeping the reader focused on both subjects simultaneously, while subject by subject tends to allow in-depth consideration of each subject separately. If a writer wants to present one subject more favorably than the other, he or she may present that subject and all its characteristics first, thereby shaping the reader's attitude toward it in a positive way before the reader encounters the second subject. Alternatively, a writer may present all the faults of the less favored subject first and then leave the reader with a final impression of the more favored subject. Even in point-by-point organization, the order in which the subjects are discussed for each point may suggest the writer's preference for one or the other. As you consider the method of organization, ask yourself how the essay would be different if the other method had been used or if the order of the two subjects had been reversed.

The choice of organization may also depend on factors other than fairness or bias. In "Dearly Disconnected," if Frazier had used a point-by-point rather than subject-by-subject organization, he would have found it more difficult to include his personal reflections on the meaning of the pay phone in his life.

3. What Points of Comparison Are Omitted?

As you evaluate comparison or contrast essays, be sure to consider the other comparisons or contrasts that the author could have made. In "Amusing Ourselves to Depth," Beato could have discussed the type of audience that would be drawn to each type of publication, but he did not. "In Dearly Disconnected," Frazier could have compared the convenience of cell phones versus pay phones, but he did not.

COMPARISON AND CONTRAST ESSAY

As you read the following essay by psychologist Daniel Goleman, notice how the writer uses the elements of comparison and contrast discussed in this chapter.

His Marriage and Hers: Childhood Roots
Daniel Goleman

READING

Daniel Goleman holds a PhD in behavioral and brain sciences and has published a number of books on psychology, including, *Destructive Emotions: A Scientific Dialogue with the Dalai Lama* (2003), *Social Intelligence: The New Science of Human Relationships* (2006), and *Ecological Intelligence: How Knowing the Hidden Impacts of What We Buy Can Change Everything* (2009). Goleman reported on the brain and behavioral sciences for the *New York Times* for many years and was elected a fellow of the American Association for the Advancement of Science for his efforts to bring psychology to the public. In his book *Emotional Intelligence* (1995), from which the following selection was taken, Goleman describes the emotional skills required for daily living and explains how to develop those skills. As you read the selection, notice how the writer uses comparison and contrast to explore his subject—differences between the sexes—and highlight his key points of comparison.

As I was entering a restaurant on a recent evening, a young man stalked out the door, his face set in an expression both stony and sullen. Close on his heels a young woman came running, her fists desperately pummeling his back while she yelled, "Goddamn you! Come back here and be nice to me!" That poignant, impossibly self-contradictory plea aimed at a retreating back epitomizes the pattern most commonly seen in couples whose relationship is distressed: She seeks to engage, he withdraws. Marital therapists have long noted that by the time a couple finds their way to the therapy office, they are in this pattern of engage-withdraw, with his complaint about her "unreasonable" demands and outbursts, and her lamenting his indifference to what she is saying.   1

This marital endgame reflects the fact that there are, in effect, two emotional realities in a couple, his and hers. The roots of these emotional differences, while they may be partly biological, also can be traced back to childhood and to the separate emotional worlds boys and girls inhabit while growing up. There is a vast amount of research on these separate worlds, their barriers reinforced not just by the different games boys and girls prefer but by young children's fear of being teased for having a "girlfriend" or "boyfriend."[1] One study of children's friendships found that three-year-olds say about half their friends are of the opposite sex; for five-year-olds it's about 20 percent, and by age seven almost no boys or girls say they have a best friend of the opposite sex.[2] These separate social universes intersect little until teenagers start dating.   2

Meanwhile, boys and girls are taught very different lessons about handling emotions. Parents, in general, discuss emotions—with the exception of anger—more with their daughters than their sons.[3] Girls are exposed to more information about emotions than are boys: when parents make up stories to tell their preschool children, they use more emotion words when talking to daughters than to sons; when mothers play with their infants, they display a wider range of emotions to daughters than to sons; when mothers talk to daughters about feelings, they discuss in more detail the emotional state itself than they do with their sons—though with the sons they go into more detail about the causes and consequences of emotions like anger (probably as a cautionary tale).   3

Leslie Brody and Judith Hall, who have summarized the research on differences in emotions between the sexes, propose that because girls develop facility with language more quickly than do boys, this leads them to be more experienced at articulating their feelings and more skilled than boys at using words to explore and substitute for emotional reactions such as physical fights; in contrast, they note, "boys, for whom the verbalization of affects is de-emphasized, may become largely unconscious of their emotional states, both in themselves and others."[4]   4

At age ten, roughly the same percent of girls as boys are overtly aggressive, given to open confrontation when angered. But by age thirteen, a telling difference between the sexes emerges: Girls become more adept than boys at artful aggressive tactics like ostracism, vicious gossip, and indirect vendettas. Boys, by and large, simply continue being confrontational when angered, oblivious to these more covert strategies.[5] This is just one of many ways that boys—and later, men—are less sophisticated than the opposite sex in the byways of emotional life.   5

When girls play together, they do so in small, intimate groups, with an emphasis on minimizing hostility and maximizing cooperation, while boys' games are in larger   6 groups, with an emphasis on competition. One key difference can be seen in what happens when games boys or girls are playing get disrupted by someone getting hurt. If a boy who has gotten hurt gets upset, he is expected to get out of the way and stop crying so the game can go on. If the same happens among a group of girls who are playing, the game stops while everyone gathers around to help the girl who is crying. This difference between boys and girls at play epitomizes what Harvard's Carol Gilligan points to as

a key disparity between the sexes: boys take pride in a lone, tough-minded independence and autonomy, while girls see themselves as part of a web of connectedness.
Thus boys are threatened by anything that might challenge their independence, while
girls are more threatened by a rupture in their relationships. And, as Deborah Tannen
has pointed out in her book *You Just Don't Understand,* these differing perspectives
mean that men and women want and expect very different things out of a conversation,
with men content to talk about "things," while women seek emotional connection.

In short, these contrasts in schooling in the emotions foster very different skills, with 7
girls becoming "adept at reading both verbal and nonverbal emotional signals, at expressing and communicating their feelings," and boys becoming adept at "minimizing
emotions having to do with vulnerability, guilt, fear, and hurt."[6] Evidence for these different stances is very strong in the scientific literature. Hundreds of studies have found,
for example, that on average women are more empathic than men, at least as measured
by the ability to read someone else's unstated feelings from facial expression, tone of
voice, and other nonverbal cues. Likewise, it is generally easier to read feelings from
a woman's face than a man's; while there is no difference in facial expressiveness
among very young boys and girls, as they go through the elementary-school grades boys
become less expressive, girls more so. This may partly reflect another key difference:
women, on average, experience the entire range of emotions with greater intensity and
more volatility than men—in this sense, women are more "emotional" than men.[7]

All of this means that, in general, women come into a marriage groomed for the   8
role of emotional manager, while men arrive with much less appreciation of the importance of this task for helping a relationship survive. Indeed, the most important
element for women—but not for men—in satisfaction with their relationship reported
in a study of 264 couples was the sense that the couple has "good communication."[8]
Ted Huston, a psychologist at the University of Texas who has studied couples in
depth, observes, "For the wives, intimacy means talking things over, especially talking about the relationship itself. The men, by and large, don't understand what the
wives want from them. They say, 'I want to do things with her, and all she wants to do
is talk.' " During courtship, Huston found, men were much more willing to spend time
talking in ways that suited the wish for intimacy of their wives-to-be. But once married, as time went on the men—especially in more traditional couples—spent less
and less time talking in this way with their wives, finding a sense of closeness simply
in doing things like gardening together rather than talking things over.

This growing silence on the part of husbands may be partly due to the fact that, if 9
anything, men are a bit Pollyannaish about the state of their marriage, while their wives
are attuned to the trouble spots: in one study of marriages, men had a rosier view than
their wives of just about everything in their relationship—lovemaking, finances, ties
with in-laws, how well they listened to each other, how much their flaws mattered.[9]
Wives, in general, are more vocal about their complaints than are their husbands, particularly among unhappy couples. Combine men's rosy view of marriage with their aver-
sion to emotional confrontations, and it is clear why wives so often complain that their
husbands try to wiggle out of discussing the troubling things about their relationship.
(Of course this gender difference is a generalization and is not true in every case; a
psychiatrist friend complained that in his marriage his wife is reluctant to discuss emotional matters between them and he is the one who is left to bring them up.)

The slowness of men to bring up problems in a relationship is no doubt compounded 10
by their relative lack of skill when it comes to reading facial expressions of emotions.
Women, for example, are more sensitive to a sad expression on a man's face than are
men in detecting sadness from a woman's expression.[10] Thus a woman has to be all the
sadder for a man to notice her feelings in the first place, let alone for him to raise the
question of what is making her so sad.

Consider the implications of this emotional gender gap for how couples handle the 11
grievances and disagreements that any intimate relationship inevitably spawns. In
fact, specific issues such as how often a couple has sex, how to discipline the children,
or how much debt and savings a couple feels comfortable with are not what make or
break a marriage. Rather, it is how a couple discusses such sore points that matters
more for the fate of their marriage. Simply having reached an agreement about how
to disagree is key to marital survival; men and women have to overcome the innate
gender differences in approaching rocky emotions. Failing this, couples are vulnerable
to emotional rifts that eventually can tear their relationship apart. . . . [T]hese rifts are
far more likely to develop if one or both partners have certain deficits in emotional
intelligence.

NOTES

1. The separate worlds of boys and girls: Eleanor Maccoby and C. N. Jacklin, "Gender Segregation in Childhood," in H. Reese, ed., *Advances in Child Development and Behavior* (New York: Academic Press, 1987).

2. Same-sex playmates: John Gottman, "Same and Cross Sex Friendship in Young Children," in J. Gottman and J. Parker, eds., *Conversation of Friends* (New York: Cambridge University Press, 1986).

3. This and the following summary of sex differences in socialization of emotions are based on the excellent review in Leslie R. Brody and Judith A. Hall, "Gender and Emotion," in Michael Lewis and Jeannette Haviland, eds., *Handbook of Emotions* (New York: Guilford Press, 1993).

4. Brody and Hall, "Gender and Emotion," 456.

5. Girls and the arts of aggression: Robert B. Cairns and Beverley D. Cairns, *Lifelines and Risks* (New York: Cambridge University Press, 1994).

6. Brody and Hall, "Gender and Emotion," 454.

7. The findings about gender differences in emotion are reviewed in Brody and Hall, "Gender and Emotion."

8. The importance of good communication for women was reported in Mark H. Davis and H. Alan Oathout, "Maintenance of Satisfaction in Romantic Relationships: Empathy and Relational Competence," *Journal of Personality and Social Psychology* 53, no. 2 (1987): 397–410.

9. The study of husbands' and wives' complaints: Robert J. Sternberg, "Triangulating Love," in Robert Sternberg and Michael Barnes, eds., *The Psychology of Love* (New Haven: Yale University Press, 1988).

10. Reading sad faces: The research is by Dr. Ruben C. Gur at the University of Pennsylvania School of Medicine.

Examining the Reading

1. Summarize the differences that Goleman claims exist between men's and women's ways of expressing emotion.

2. According to Goleman, what are the root causes of the differences between how men and women express emotion?

3. How can the emotional differences between spouses cause marital difficulties, according to the writer?

4. Explain how boys and girls play differently, according to Goleman.
5. Explain the meaning of each of the following words as it is used in the reading: *epitomizes* (para. 1), *articulating* (4), *ostracism* (5), *vendettas* (5), *disparity* (6), and *empathic* (7).

Analyzing the Writer's Technique

1. What is Goleman's thesis?
2. Identify the purpose of the essay, and list the points of comparison.
3. For each point of comparison, evaluate the evidence Goleman offers to substantiate his findings. Do you find the evidence sufficient and convincing? Why or why not? What other information might the writer have included?
4. What types of details does Goleman provide to explain each point of comparison?
5. Do you think Goleman maintains an objective stance on the issue, despite his gender? Explain your answer.

Thinking Critically about Text and Visuals

1. Discuss the type of organization used by the author (point-by-point, subject-by-subject, or mixed). Does the organization seem to affect the author's fairness? Do you detect any bias? If so, explain.
2. How does the use of quotations around the word "unreasonable" (para. 1) affect its connotation?
3. How does the real-life example in paragraph 1 affect the essay and particularly its tone?
4. Do you consider the essay to be primarily fact, opinion, or informed opinion? Justify your answer.
5. What key ideas from the essay do the photographs on p. 399 illustrate?

(MAKING ◯ CONNECTIONS)

Attitudes toward Work

Both "Selling in Minnesota" (Chapter 11, pp. 254–56) and "Defining a Doctor, with a Tear, a Shrug, and a Schedule" (pp. 403–5) explore attitudes toward work.

Analyzing the Readings

1. What different attitudes toward work do the readings present?
2. Watch a television program, and then write a journal entry analyzing the attitudes toward work that the characters exhibit. How closely do the characters' attitudes match the attitudes presented in either reading?

Essay Idea

Write an essay explaining your attitude toward work and comparing or contrasting it to the attitude presented in either of the readings.

Reacting to the Reading

1. Do you think any of Goleman's generalizations about men and women are inaccurate and, if so, which one(s)? Discuss the evidence, if any, that would prove Goleman wrong.
2. In your journal, describe a situation from your experience that either confirms or contradicts one of Goleman's generalizations.
3. Make a list of the emotional differences and resulting behavioral conflicts between men and women that you have observed. Decide which differences are explained by Goleman. Write an essay reporting your findings.
4. Write an essay contrasting the emotional behaviors of a couple you know.

COMPARISON AND CONTRAST COMBINED WITH OTHER PATTERNS

In the following reading, notice how Abigail Zuger uses comparison and contrast to explain a change that is occurring in the training of doctors and in expectations for medical students' behavior.

Defining a Doctor, with a Tear, a Shrug, and a Schedule
Abigail Zuger

READING

Abigail Zuger is associate professor of clinical medicine at Columbia University College of Physicians and Surgeons and senior attending physician at St. Luke's-Roosevelt Hospital Center, both in New York City. She has been caring for HIV-infected patients in the New York area since 1981, and her experiences working in the early years of the AIDS epidemic led her to write *Strong Shadows: Scenes from an Inner City AIDS Clinic* (1995). Zuger is an associate editor of *Journal Watch*, an online medical digest, and frequently writes on medical subjects for a variety of publications. This essay was published in the *New York Times* in 2004.

I had two interns to supervise that month, and the minute they sat down for our first   1
meeting, I sensed how the month would unfold.

The man's white coat was immaculate, its pockets empty save for a sleek Palm Pilot   2
that contained his list of patients. The woman used a large loose-leaf notebook instead, every dog-eared page full of lists of things to do and check, consultants to call, questions to ask. Her pockets were stuffed, and whenever she sat down, little handbooks of drug doses, wadded phone messages, pens, highlighters, and tourniquets spilled onto the floor.

The man worked the hours legally mandated by the state, not a minute more, and   3
sometimes considerably less. He was seldom in the hospital before 8 in the morning and left by 5 unless he was on call. He ate a leisurely lunch every day and was never late for rounds. The woman got to the hospital around dawn and was on the move for the rest of the day. Sometimes she went home when she was supposed to, but sometimes, if one of her patients was particularly sick, she would sign out to the covering

intern and keep working, often talking to patients' relatives long into the night. "I am now breaking the law," she would announce cheerfully to no one in particular, then trot off to do just a few final chores.

The man had a strict definition of what it meant to be a doctor. He did not, for instance, "do nurses' work" (his phrase). When one of his patients needed a specimen sent to the lab and the nurse didn't get around to it, neither did he. No matter how important the job was, no matter how hard I pressed him, he never gave in. If I spoke sternly to him, he would turn around and speak just as sternly to the nurse. The woman did everyone's work. She would weigh her patients if necessary (nurses' work), feed them (aides' work), find salt-free pickles for them (dietitians' work), and wheel them to X-ray (transporters' work).   4

The man was cheerful, serene, and well rested. The woman was overtired, hyper-emotional, and constantly late. The man was interested in his patients, but they never kept him up at night. The woman occasionally called the hospital from home to check on hers. The man played tennis on his days off. The woman read medical articles. At least, she read the beginnings; she tended to fall asleep halfway through.   5

I felt as if I was in a medieval morality play[1] that month, living with two costumed symbols of opposing philosophies in medical education. The woman was working the way interns used to: total immersion seasoned with exhaustion and adrenaline. As far as she was concerned, her patients were her exclusive responsibility. The man was an intern of the new millennium. His hours and duties were delimited; he saw himself as part of a health-care team, and his patients' welfare as a shared responsibility.   6

This new model of medical internship got some important validation in the *New England Journal of Medicine* last week, when Harvard researchers reported the effects of reducing interns' work hours to 60 per week from 80 (now the mandated national maximum). The shorter workweek required a larger staff of interns to spell one another at more frequent intervals. With shorter hours, the interns got more sleep at home, dozed off less at work, and made considerably fewer bad mistakes in patient care.   7

Why should such an obvious finding need an elaborate controlled study to estab-lish? Why should it generate not only two long articles in the world's most prestigious medical journal but also three long, passionate editorials? Because the issue here is bigger than just scheduling and manpower.   8

The progressive shortening of residents' work hours spells nothing less than a change in the ethos of medicine itself. It means the end of Dr. Kildare, Superstar—that lone, heroic healer, omniscient, omnipotent, and ever-present. It means a revolution in the complex medical hierarchy that sustained him. Willy-nilly, medicine is becoming democratized, a team sport.   9

We can only hope the revolution will be bloodless. Everything will have to change. Doctors will have to learn to work well with others. They will have to learn to write and speak with enough clarity and precision so that the patient's story remains accurate as care passes from hand to hand. They will have to stop saying "my patient" and begin to say "our patient" instead.   10

---

[1]*morality play:* a type of play performed in the Middle Ages in which characters represent abstractions (love, death, peace, and so on); its purpose is to teach a lesson about right and wrong.

It may be, when the dust settles, that the system will be more functional, less error- 11
prone. It may be that we will simply have substituted one set of problems for another.
We may even find that nothing much has changed. Even in the Harvard data, there was
an impressive range in the hours that the interns under study worked. Some logged in
over 90 hours in their 80-hour workweek. Some put in 75 instead. Medicine has always
attracted a wide spectrum of individuals, from the lazy and disaffected to the deeply
committed. Even draconian scheduling policies may not change basic personality traits
or the kind of doctors that interns grow up to be.

My month with the intern of the past and the intern of the future certainly argues 12
for the power of the individual work ethic. Try as I might, it was not within my power
to modify the way either of them functioned. The woman cared too much. The man
cared too little. She worked too hard, and he could not be prodded into working hard
enough. They both made careless mistakes. When patients died, the man shrugged
and the woman cried. If for no other reason than that one, let us hope that the medicine of the future still has room for people like her.

Examining the Reading

1. How do the two interns differ in their approach to medicine?
2. What different philosophies of medicine do the two interns represent?
3. Describe the working conditions of interns.
4. What do we learn about the author and her philosophy of medical practice?
5. Explain the meaning of each of the following words as it is used in the reading: *de-limited* (para. 6), *ethos* (9), *omniscient* (9), *omnipotent* (9), and *draconian* (11).

Analyzing the Writer's Technique

1. Highlight Zuger's thesis and evaluate its placement.
2. Identify the points of comparison on which the essay is based.
3. What other patterns of development does the author use? Give one example and explain how it contributes to the essay.
4. Evaluate the effectiveness of the point-by-point organization. How would the essay differ if it had been written using a subject-by-subject organization?
5. Evaluate the essay's conclusion. How does it reflect the thesis and organization of the essay?

Visualizing the Reading

Analyze Zuger's use of point-by-point organization by first identifying the different points of comparison in her essay in the box on page 406. The first one has been done for you. Add additional rows to the box as needed.

Points of Comparison	The Man	The Woman
Organizational styles	Efficient (Palm Pilot)	Disorganized (overstuffed pockets and notebook)

Thinking Critically about Text

1. In her final sentence, Zuger reveals a bias toward one of the models of medical internship she is comparing. Is bias apparent anywhere else? Explain.
2. What is the connotation of "nurses' work" (para. 4)?
3. What other types of sources and information could the author have included to make this essay more comprehensive?

Reacting to the Reading

1. Discuss an experience of visiting a doctor or hospital. Within which philosophy of medical care did your treatment fall?
2. Discuss the training and education you will need for a career you are interested in pursuing. What knowledge and skills will you need to succeed in the field, and how will the training provide them?
3. Write a journal entry exploring whether medical care has become depersonalized. Give examples from your experience.
4. Write an essay comparing or contrasting males and females in another profession (teachers, police officers, nurses).

Applying Your Skills: Additional Essay Assignments

For more on locating and documenting sources, see Part 5.

Write a comparison or contrast essay on one of the topics below, using what you have learned in this chapter. Depending on the topic you choose, you may need to conduct library or Internet research.

To Express Your Ideas

1. Compare two families that you know or are part of. Include points of comparison that reveal what is valuable and important in family life.

2. Compare your values and priorities today with those you held when you were in high school.
3. Compare your lifestyle today with the lifestyle you intend to follow after you graduate from college.

To Inform Your Reader

4. Compare library resources with those available on the Internet.
5. Compare two sources of information or communication as Beato does in "Amusing Ourselves to Depth" (p. 375).

To Persuade Your Reader

6. Choose a technological change that has occurred in recent years, as Frazier does in "Dearly Disconnected" (p. 377), and argue either that it is beneficial or that its drawbacks outweigh its usefulness compared with the old technology.
7. Compare two views on a controversial issue, arguing in favor of one of them.
8. Compare two methods of doing something (such as disciplining a child or training a pet), arguing that one method is more effective than the other.

Cases Using Comparison and Contrast

9. You are taking a course in photography and have been asked to write a paper comparing and contrasting the advantages and uses of black-and-white versus color film. Your instructor is your audience.
10. You are working in the advertising department of a company that manufactures in-line skates. Your manager has asked you to evaluate two periodicals and recommend which one the company should use to run its advertisements.

CHAPTER 16

Classification and Division: Explaining Categories and Parts

The photograph on the opposite page shows fruits and vegetables on display at a farm market. Notice that they are arranged according to type of produce. Can you imagine how difficult it would be to find what you need if all produce were randomly piled onto a table or shelf, with broccoli, pears, peppers, and bananas all mixed together? Most stores and markets arrange or group their products for the convenience of their customers.

Take a few minutes to brainstorm other ways a particular store or Web site does or could group its products for customer convenience. You may propose a serious method or construct a humorous one. Then write a paragraph describing your system. Come up with a title for each group and describe what products belong in it. Include the characteristics of each product group.

WRITING A CLASSIFICATION OR DIVISION ESSAY

Whoever arranged the fruits and vegetables in the market used a process called *classification*—grouping things into categories based on specific characteristics. This chapter will show you how to write effective classification and division essays as well as how to incorporate classification and division into essays using other patterns of development.

What Are Classification and Division?

You use classification to organize things and ideas daily. Your dresser drawers are probably organized by categories, with socks and sweatshirts in different drawers. Grocery stores, phone directories, libraries, and even restaurant menus arrange items in groups according to similar characteristics.

Classification, then, is a process of sorting people, things, or ideas into groups or categories to help make them more understandable. For example, your college catalog classifies its course offerings by school, division, and department.

Division, similar to classification, begins with *one* item and breaks it down into parts. Thus, for example, the humanities department at your college may be divided into English, modern languages, and philosophy, and the modern language courses might be further divided into Spanish, French, Chinese, and Russian. Division is closely related to process analysis, which is covered in Chapter 14.

A classification or division essay explains a topic by describing types or parts. For example, a classification essay might explore types of advertising—direct mail, radio, television, newspaper, Internet, and so forth. A division essay might describe the parts of an art museum—exhibit areas, museum store, visitor services desk, and the like.

You will find many occasions to use classification and division in the writing you do in college and the workplace (see the accompanying box for a few examples). In the following essay, Jerry Newman classifies the kinds of managers he found in fast-food restaurants. An example of a division essay, "A Brush with Reality: Surprises in the Tube" by David Bodanis, appears on page 417–18.

SCENES FROM COLLEGE AND THE WORKPLACE

- For a course in *anatomy and physiology*, you are asked to study the structure and parts of the human ear by identifying the function of each part.

- As part of a *business management* report, you need to consider how debt liability differs for three types of businesses—a single proprietorship, a partnership, and a corporation.

- While working as a *facilities planner*, you are asked to conduct a feasibility study of several new sites. You begin by sorting the sites into three categories—within state, out of state, and out of country.

My Secret Life on the McJob:
Fast Food Managers
Jerry Newman

Jerry Newman is a professor of management at the State University of New York – Buffalo and coauthor of the textbook *Compensation,* tenth edition (2010). He has also worked as a business consultant at AT&T, Hewlett-Packard, RJR Nabisco, and McDonald's. This selection is from *My Secret Life on the McJob: Lessons in Leadership Guaranteed to Supersize Any Management Style* (2007), which Newman wrote after working at various fast-food restaurants to learn about their operation and management. As you read, highlight each category of manager that Newman establishes.

I thought all my fast food stores would be pretty similar. They weren't. Some stores 1 made employees wear name tags, going as far as sending people home if they repeatedly didn't wear their name tags, while other stores didn't seem to care. In some stores crews socialized after work, but in others they barely talked to each other, even during work. Even though every chain had strict rules about every facet of food production and customer interaction, how employees were treated was part of an individual store culture, and this varied from store to store. These differences could often be traced to the managers' values and practices and how consistently they were applied both by the managers and by their *sensei,*[1] much more so than any edicts from headquarters. The best-run store I worked at was [a] Burger King; the worst-run store was also a Burger King. If corporate rules had a controlling impact, shouldn't stores have been much more similar? At one McDonald's the employees were extremely friendly; at another the tension between groups was palpable. The differences, I think, can be traced to the managers. The following is a sampler of the types of managers I encountered. Only the last group, performance managers, was good at finding a *sensei* and developing consistent people practices.

THE TOXIC MANAGER
Most new employees learn through feedback. When you're first learning a job, there's 2 relatively little ego involvement in feedback; good managers seem to know this and in early days of employment are quick to point out better ways of doing a task. [Toxic] managers, though, use sarcasm or disrespectful comments to indicate when they are unhappy with your work. One of the worst offenders I ran into was the store manager at Arby's, who admitted that the main reason he was hiring me was to change the store culture. He said he was tired of employees who were vulgar and disrespectful, but it didn't take long for me to realize that the role model for their behavior was actually the manager himself—Don. His attitude and style set the tone for everyone else in his store. Almost as bad, the key individual with the necessary attributes to be a *sensei* shared Don's disregard for the feelings of others. Don, in particular, didn't confine

[1]*Sensei:* A Japanese word for "teacher" or "master." Newman uses it to mean an employee who is not a manager but who is both highly skilled at his or her job and socially influential among fellow employees.

his wrath to "bad" employees. Bill, a diligent long-timer, messed up a coupon order. A customer had an entertainment book coupon for one Value Meal free with the purchase of another. There was a labyrinth of steps to complete some of the discounts correctly. When Bill made the error, it was right before the end of Don's shift, and Don tore into him, saying loudly enough for everyone to hear, "Well, I'm leaving before Bill can make my life any more miserable." It didn't take long to infect others with this lack of respect for employees.

THE MECHANICAL MANAGER

The most common type of manager I encountered was the Mechanical Manager, who   3
was for the most part either an assistant manager or a shift manager, not a full store manager. You could spot the Mechanical Managers from across the room—they did their jobs, day after day, as if fast food was slow death. They didn't want to be there, and they were just going through the motions. They typically had gotten their jobs because they were reliable crew members and had put in enough time that some reward was needed to keep them working. A promotion has a certain finality, though—it makes you confront reality: Is this what I want out of life? Most say "No," and that's probably why I didn't see very many store managers who were mechanical. Before most store managers had reached that level (one store manager told me it was a ten-year journey), those who weren't interested in fast food as a lifetime career had moved on to other career pursuits. While looking for other opportunities, though, they did what was necessary to get by. Luis at McDonald's was the perfect example.

In my first McDonald's experience I made myself a grid showing all of the sand-   4
wiches and their ingredients. After a day of having instructions blasted at me, I needed a visual training aid to finally put things together. I shared this grid with Luis on my third day, expecting he might already have training materials like this (as was the case at Wendy's) or that he could use it to train other visual learners. As I handed Luis the Excel spreadsheet, I watched his face and saw no reaction. None. He told me he'd leave it for Kris, the store manager. Clearly he saw the value in it—he didn't toss it, after all—but a reinforcing response for my initiative required a level of involvement he didn't or couldn't muster.

THE RELATIONSHIP MANAGER

The Relationship Manager was a relatively rare breed in my experience. James was   5
the prototype. He led by building relationships and demonstrating that he cared about our destinies—hard to do when it seemed like every week someone was leaving and another person was coming on board. From the first day, James was very different from what I was used to. When I first met him for my job interview, he was fifteen minutes late because he was out picking up an employee whose car had broken down. I never saw any other manager pick up or take home a crew member who had transportation problems. In fact, at one store I watched Mary, an older worker teetering on the edge of poverty, sit in a booth out front for two hours waiting for her husband to pick her up after his shift at a Sam's Club. As I came to learn, this kindness wasn't unusual for James. And in being kind, James created a culture that was much more friendly and supportive than that in many of the other fast food places I had experienced. Even the

way James responded to my quitting was refreshing. With my back problems becoming increasingly worse, I called James to tell him that I was quitting and dreaded leaving him in the lurch. But he was amazingly kind, telling me to take care of myself and forcefully telling me to pick up my check.

THE PERFORMANCE MANAGER

It's easy to spot the Performance Manager. Here relationships are still important, but now they serve as a means to ensure performance. Through word or deed she very quickly lets you know what is expected. I like this. No ambiguity, no doubt about what it takes to make the grade. The best at this was Kris, who, it seemed to me, watched for slackers much more closely than did the managers at other fast food places. She told me during the interview that I would be watching DVDs my first day. She also mentioned that one of the new people had taken three to four bathroom breaks while watching the videos, which was an excessive number, she thought. She also commented that she might be losing some people because she thought they were slower than they should be. I got the message: She would be watching my work and looking to see if I was going to goof off. My experience in other places was that you got fired for only two things: not showing up and insubordinate behavior. Clearly she was adding a third reason—poor performance. Good for her! 6

Kris's watchful eye extended beyond bathroom breaks. I found out the hard way that taking breaks, even unpaid ones, wasn't allowed unless legally required. Apparently in New York State, you're not entitled to a break until after five hours of work. So when I asked Kris for a break before the appointed time, she answered with an emphatic "No." Kris's message was clearly that we do our jobs by the book, no exceptions. 7

Over time at this Burger King I began to notice that Kris wasn't a taskmaster all the time. Sure, during busy times she was prone to exhort the staff to work faster. And she didn't tolerate leaning (remember, "If you've got time to lean, you've got time to clean"). But this attitude relaxed a bit during slower times, and it especially relaxed for the better workers like Daniel, Eric, and Craig, three of the fastest guns on the sandwich assembly board. 8

Characteristics of Classification and Division Essays

A successful classification or division essay is meaningful to its audience. The writer uses one principle of classification or division, with exclusive categories or parts that are broad enough to include all of the members of the group.

Classification Groups and Division Divides Ideas According to One Principle

To sort items into groups, a writer needs to decide on what basis to do so. For example, birds could be classified in terms of their size, habitat, or diet. For a division essay, the writer must decide into what parts to divide the topic. A journalist writing about a new aquarium could divide the topic according to type of fish displayed, suitability for children of different ages, or quality of the exhibits.

To develop an effective set of categories or parts, a writer needs to choose one principle of classification or division and use it consistently throughout the essay or other piece of writing. In "My Secret Life on the McJob: Fast Food Managers," Newman classifies managers according to their management style.

Once a writer chooses a principle of classification or division, the next step is to identify a manageable number of categories or parts. An essay classifying birds according to diet, for example, might use five or six types of diet, not twenty.

Classification or Division Follows a Principle Determined by the Writer's Purpose and Audience

Because several different principles can be used to categorize any group, the writer's purpose and audience should determine the principle of classification. The personnel director of a college might classify professors by age in preparing a financial report for trustees that projects upcoming retirements, whereas a student writing a humor column for the campus newspaper might categorize professors by teaching style.

To develop a meaningful classification, therefore, choose a principle that will both interest your readers and fulfill your purpose. If, for instance, you want to inform parents about the types of day-care facilities in your town, you could classify day-care centers according to the services they offer because your readers would be looking for that information. A journalist writing to persuade readers of his newspaper that a new aquarium is designed for children might divide the exhibits according to their suitability for children of different ages.

Exercise 16.1

Brainstorm three different principles of classification or division you could use for each of the following topics:

1. Sports teams
2. Fast-food restaurants
3. Internet access
4. Academic subjects
5. Novels

Classification Uses Categories and Division Uses Parts That Are Exclusive and Comprehensive

The categories or parts you choose should not overlap. In other words, a particular item should fit in no more than one category. A familiar example is age: The categories *25 to 30* and *30 to 35* are not mutually exclusive since someone who is thirty would fit into both. In an essay about the nutritional value of pizza, you could divide your topic into carbohydrates, proteins, and fats, but you should not add a separate category for saturated fat, since saturated fat is already contained in the fats category.

The categories or parts you choose should also be comprehensive. In a division essay, all the major parts of an item should be included. In a classification essay, each member of the group should fit into one category or another. For example, an essay categorizing fast-food restaurants according to the type of food they serve would have to include a category for pizza.

Exercise 16.2

Choose a principle of classification or division for two of the topics listed in Exercise 16.1. Then make a list of the categories in which each item could be included or parts into which each item could be divided.

Classification or Division Fully Explains Each Category or Part

A classification or division essay contains adequate detail so that each category or part can be understood by readers. In "My Secret Life on the McJob: Fast Food Managers," Newman clearly presents the four types of managers, using personal experience, examples, and description. Details such as these enable readers to "see" the writer's categories or parts in a classification or division essay.

Classification or Division Develops a Thesis

The thesis statement in a classification or division essay identifies the topic and may reveal the principle used to classify or divide the topic. In most cases it also suggests why the classification or division is relevant or important.

Here are two examples of thesis statements:

Most people consider videos a form of entertainment; however, videos can also serve educational, commercial, and political functions.

The Grand Canyon is divided into two distinct geographical areas—the North Rim and the South Rim—each of which offers different views, facilities, and climatic conditions.

Visualizing a Classification or Division Essay: A Graphic Organizer

The graphic organizer shown in Figure 16.1 outlines the basic organization of a classification or division essay. The introduction announces the topic, gives background information, and states the thesis. The body paragraphs explain the categories or parts and their characteristics. The conclusion brings the essay to a satisfying close by reinforcing the thesis and offering a new insight on the topic.

For more on graphic organizers, see Chapter 3, pp. 59–61.

Read the division essay on page 417 and then study the graphic organizer for it in Figure 16.2 (on p. 419).

Figure 16.1 GRAPHIC ORGANIZER FOR A CLASSIFICATION OR DIVISION ESSAY

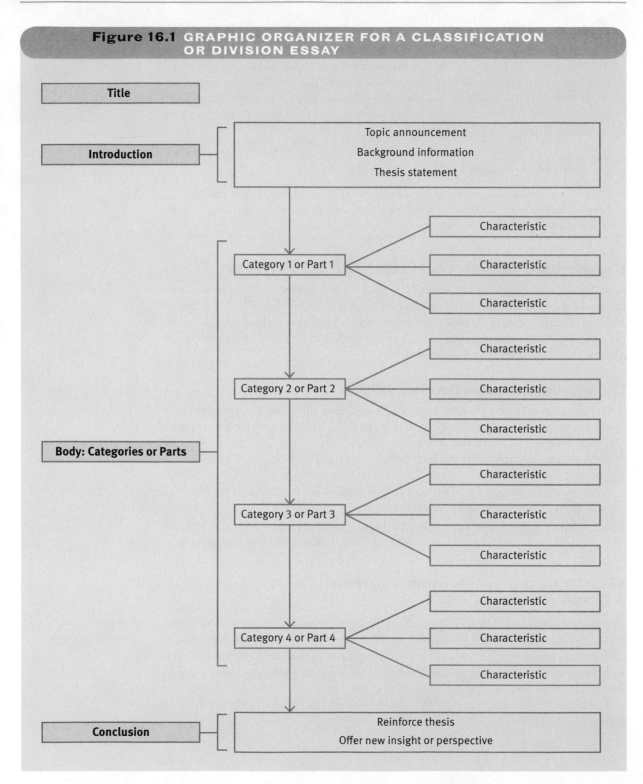

A Brush with Reality: Surprises in the Tube
David Bodanis

David Bodanis is a journalist and the author of several books, including *The Body Book* (1984), *The Secret Garden* (1992), *The Secret Family* (1997), *Electric Universe: The Shocking True Story of Electricity* (2005), and *Passionate Minds: The Great Love Affair of the Enlightenment* (2006). The following essay is from *The Secret House* (1986), a book that traces a family of five through a day, analyzing foods they eat and products they use. As you read the selection, highlight the writer's thesis and the sections where he divides his topic into parts.

1 Into the bathroom goes our male resident, and after the most pressing need is satisfied, it's time to brush the teeth. The tube of toothpaste is squeezed, its pinched metal seams are splayed, pressure waves are generated inside, and the paste begins to flow. But what's in this toothpaste, so carefully being extruded out?

2 Water mostly, 30 to 45 percent in most brands: ordinary, everyday simple tap water. It's there because people like to have a big gob of toothpaste to spread on the brush, and water is the cheapest stuff there is when it comes to making big gobs. Dripping a bit from the tap onto your brush would cost virtually nothing; whipped in with the rest of the toothpaste, the manufacturers can sell it at a neat and accountant-pleasing $2 per pound equivalent. Toothpaste manufacture is a very lucrative occupation.

3 Second to water in quantity is chalk: exactly the same material that schoolteachers use to write on blackboards. It is collected from the crushed remains of long-dead ocean creatures. In the Cretaceous seas chalk particles served as part of the wickedly sharp outer skeleton that these creatures had to wrap around themselves to keep from getting chomped by all the slightly larger other ocean creatures they met. Their massed graves are our present chalk deposits.

4 The individual chalk particles—the size of the smallest mud particles in your garden—have kept their toughness over the aeons, and now on the toothbrush they'll need it. The enamel outer coating of the tooth they'll have to face is the hardest substance in the body—tougher than skull, or bone, or nail. Only the chalk particles in toothpaste can successfully grind into the teeth during brushing, ripping off the surface layers like an abrading wheel grinding down a boulder in a quarry.

5 The craters, slashes, and channels that the chalk tears into the teeth will also remove a certain amount of built-up yellow in the carnage, and it is for that polishing function that it's there. A certain amount of unduly enlarged extra-abrasive chalk fragments tear such cavernous pits into the teeth that future decay bacteria will be able to bunker down there and thrive; the quality control people find it almost impossible to screen out these errant super-chalk pieces, and government regulations allow them to stay in.

6 In case even the gouging doesn't get all the yellow off, another substance is worked into the toothpaste cream. This is titanium dioxide. It comes in tiny spheres, and it's the stuff bobbing around in white wall paint to make it come out white. Splashed around onto your teeth during the brushing it coats much of the yellow that remains. Being water soluble it leaks off in the next few hours and is swallowed, but at least for the quick glance up in the mirror after finishing it will make the user think his teeth

are truly white. Some manufacturers add optical whitening dyes—the stuff more commonly found in washing machine bleach—to make extra sure that that glance in the mirror shows reassuring white.

These ingredients alone would not make a very attractive concoction. They would stick in the tube like a sloppy white plastic lump, hard to squeeze out as well as revolting to the touch. Few consumers would savor rubbing in a mixture of water, ground-up blackboard chalk, and the whitener from latex paint first thing in the morning. To get around that finicky distaste the manufacturers have mixed in a host of other goodies. 7

To keep the glop from drying out, a mixture including glycerine glycol—related to the most common car antifreeze ingredient—is whipped in with the chalk and water, and to give that concoction a bit of substance (all we really have so far is wet colored chalk), a large helping is added of gummy molecules from the seaweed *Chondrus crispus*. This seaweed ooze spreads in among the chalk, paint, and antifreeze, then stretches itself in all directions to hold the whole mass together. A bit of paraffin oil (the fuel that flickers in camping lamps) is pumped in with it to help the moss ooze keep the whole substance smooth. 8

With the glycol, ooze, and paraffin we're almost there. Only two major chemicals are left to make the refreshing, cleansing substance we know as toothpaste. The ingredients so far are fine for cleaning, but they wouldn't make much of the satisfying foam we have come to expect in the morning brushing. 9

To remedy that, every toothpaste on the market has a big dollop of detergent added too. You've seen the suds detergent will make in a washing machine. The same substance added here will duplicate that inside the mouth. It's not particularly necessary, but it sells. 10

The only problem is that by itself this ingredient tastes, well, too like detergent. It's horribly bitter and harsh. The chalk put in toothpaste is pretty foul-tasting too, for that matter. It's to get around that gustatory discomfort that the manufacturers put in the ingredient they tout perhaps the most of all. This is the flavoring, and it has to be strong. Double rectified peppermint oil is used—a flavorer so powerful that chemists know better than to sniff it in the raw state in the laboratory. Menthol crystals and saccharin or other sugar simulators are added to complete the camouflage operation. 11

Is that it? Chalk, water, paint, seaweed, antifreeze, paraffin oil, detergent, and peppermint? Not quite. A mix like that would be irresistible to the hundreds of thousands of individual bacteria lying on the surface of even an immaculately cleaned bathroom sink. They would get in, float in the water bubbles, ingest the ooze and paraffin, maybe even spray out enzymes to break down the chalk. The result would be an uninviting mess. The way manufacturers avoid that final obstacle is by putting something in to kill the bacteria. Something good and strong is needed, something that will zap any accidentally intrudant bacteria into oblivion. And that something is formaldehyde—the disinfectant used in anatomy labs. 12

So it's chalk, water, paint, seaweed, antifreeze, paraffin oil, detergent, peppermint, formaldehyde, and fluoride (which can go some way towards preserving children's teeth)—that's the usual mixture raised to the mouth on the toothbrush for a fresh morning's clean. If it sounds too unfortunate, take heart. Studies show that thorough brushing with just plain water will often do as good a job. 13

Figure 16.2 GRAPHIC ORGANIZER FOR "A BRUSH WITH REALITY: SURPRISES IN THE TUBE"

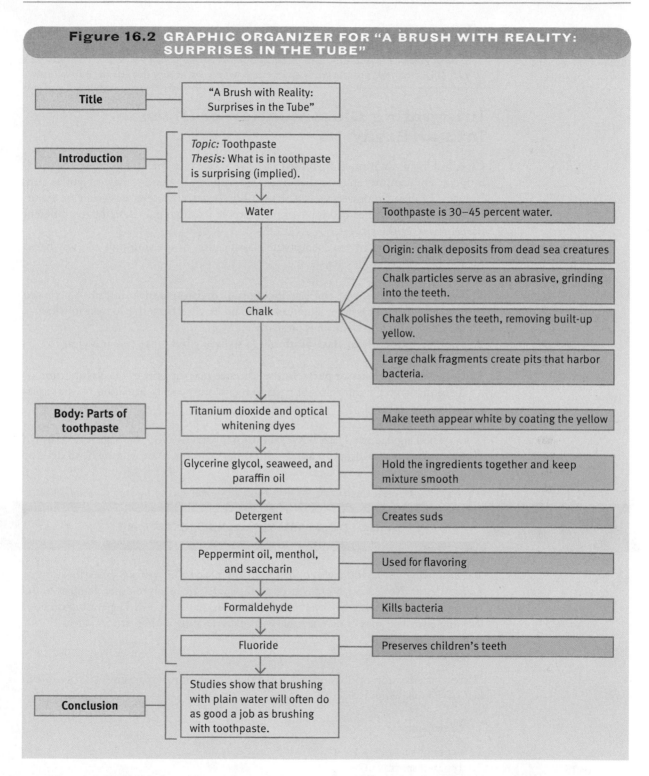

To draw detailed graphic organizers using a computer, visit www.bedfordstmartins .com/successfulcollege.

Exercise 16.3

Draw a graphic organizer for "My Secret Life on the McJob: Fast Food Managers" (pp. 411–13). Note that because this is an excerpt from a book, it does not include a conclusion.

Integrating Classification or Division into an Essay

Classification or division is often used along with one or more other patterns of development. For example, an essay that argues for stricter gun control may categorize guns in terms of their firepower, use, or availability. A narrative about a writer's frustrating experiences in a crowded international airport terminal may describe the different parts or areas of the airport.

Use the following tips to incorporate classification or division into an essay based on another pattern of development:

1. **Avoid focusing on why the classification or division is meaningful.** When used as a secondary pattern, its significance should be clear from the context in which the classification or division is presented.
2. **State the principle of classification.** Do so briefly but make sure it is clear to your readers.
3. **Name the categories or parts.** In the sentence that introduces the classification or division, name the categories or parts to focus your readers' attention on the explanation that follows.

In "The Dog Ate My Flash Drive, and Other Tales of Woe" on page 433, Carolyn Foster Segal uses classification along with other patterns of development to develop her thesis about student excuses.

A GUIDED WRITING ASSIGNMENT

The following guide will lead you through the process of writing a classification or division essay. Note that you may need to integrate one or more other patterns of development in your essay to develop your thesis or make a point. Depending on your learning style, you may choose various ways of generating and organizing ideas.

The Assignment

Write a classification or division essay on a topic of your own choosing or on a topic in one of the following lists:

Classification

1. Types of pets
2. Types of sports fans

3. Types of movies
4. Types of classmates
5. Types of shoppers
6. Types of television dramas

Division

1. Your family
2. A machine or a piece of equipment
3. An organization
4. A sports team or an extracurricular club
5. A public place (building, stadium, department store, or theme park)
6. Your college

Depending on the topic you select, you may need to use Internet or library sources to develop and support your ideas about it. You may also need to narrow the topic. Your audience consists of readers of your local newspaper.

As you develop your classification or division essay, consider using one or more other patterns of development. For example, in a classification essay, you might compare and contrast types of sports fans or give examples of types of movies. In a division essay, you might describe the parts of a theme park or another public place.

For more on description, illustration, and comparison and contrast, see Chapters 12, 13, and 15.

Generating Ideas

There are two primary methods for generating ideas and for classifying or dividing those ideas. With method 1, you first generate details and then group the details into categories or parts. With method 2, you first generate categories or parts and then generate details that support them. Here is how both methods apply to classification essays and division essays:

Classification

Method 1: First think of details that describe the group. Then use the details to categorize group members.

Method 2: First identify categories. Then think of details that describe each category.

Division

Method 1: Brainstorm details about your topic and then group the details into parts or sections.

Method 2: Think about how your topic can be divided into easy-to-understand parts. Then think of details that describe each part.

Method 1 is effective when you approach the classification or division from part to whole—identifying details and then grouping the details. Depending on your learning style and your topic, it may be easier to start by creating categories or parts and then filling in details about each one. In this case, use method 2.

For more on purpose, audience, and point of view, see Chapter 5, pp. 106–9.

Considering Your Purpose, Audience, and Point of View

Your principle of classification or division, your categories or parts, and your details must all fit your purpose and audience. If your purpose is to inform novice computer users about the components of a personal computer (PC), your parts and details must be straightforward and nontechnical. However, if your purpose is to persuade computer technicians to purchase a particular kind of PC, your parts and details would be more technical. For this Guided Writing Assignment, your audience consists of readers of your local newspaper.

As you work on your classification or division essay, ask yourself the following questions:

- Is my principle of classification or division appropriate for my purpose and audience?
- Do my categories or parts and my details advance the purpose of the essay?
- Will my readers understand the categories or parts?
- What point of view will best suit my purpose and audience—first, second, or third person? The first person (*I, we*) or second person (*you*) may be appropriate in informal writing if you or your audience have personal knowledge of or experience with the topic you are classifying or dividing. The third person (*he, she, it, they*) is appropriate in more formal writing or for topics less familiar to you or your audience.

Generating Details and Grouping Them into Categories or Parts

For more on prewriting strategies, see Chapter 5, pp. 110–18.

For more on observation, see Chapter 22, pp. 617–18.

Learning Style Options

Work through the following tasks in whatever order suits your topic and your learning style, using either method 1 or method 2 (p. 421).

Generating details.   For each category or part, you need to supply specific details that will make it clear and understandable to your readers. As you work on your essay, then, write down examples, situations, or sensory details that illustrate each category or part. Use one or more of the following strategies:

1. Visit a place where you can observe your topic or the people associated with it. For example, to generate details about pets, visit a pet store or an animal shelter. Make notes on what you see and hear. Record conversations, physical characteristics, behaviors, and so forth.
2. Discuss your topic with a classmate or friend. Focus your talk on the qualities and characteristics of your topic.
3. Brainstorm a list of all the features or characteristics of your topic that come to mind.
4. Draw a map or diagram that illustrates your topic's features and characteristics.
5. Conduct library or Internet research to discover facts, examples, and other details about your topic.

For more on library and Internet research, see Chapter 22, pp. 597–606.

Choosing a principle of classification or division.   Look for shared features or characteristics. Your principle of classification or division should be interesting, meaningful, and worthwhile to your audience. Experiment with several principles of classification or division until you find one that fits your purpose and audience.

Choosing categories or parts. Use the following suggestions to determine your categories or parts:

1. *In a classification essay*, make sure most or all members of the group fit into one of your categories. For example, in an essay about unsafe driving habits, you would include the most common bad habits. *In a division essay*, no essential parts should be left out. For example, in an essay about parts of a baseball stadium, you would not exclude the infield or bleachers.
2. *In a classification essay*, be sure the categories are exclusive; each group member should fit into one category only. In the essay about unsafe driving habits, the categories of reckless drivers and aggressive drivers would overlap, so exclusive categories should be used instead. *In a division essay*, make sure the parts do not overlap. In the essay about the parts of a baseball stadium, the parts "playing field" and "infield" would overlap, so it would be better to use three distinct parts of the field—infield, outfield, and foul-ball area.
3. Create specific categories or parts that will engage your readers. *In a classification essay*, categorizing drivers by their annoying driving habits would be more interesting than simply distinguishing between "good" and "bad" drivers. *A division essay* on players' facilities in a baseball stadium—dugout, locker room, and bullpen—might be more interesting to sports fans than an essay describing different seating sections of the stadium.
4. Choose descriptive names that emphasize the distinguishing feature of the category or part. *In a classification essay*, you might categorize highway drivers as "I-own-the-road" drivers, "I'm-in-no-hurry" drivers, and "I'm-daydreaming" drivers. *In a division essay* about the parts of a baseball stadium, you might use "home-run heaven" to name one part.

Do not hesitate to create, combine, or eliminate categories or parts, as needed.

> **Essay in Progress 1**
> Choose a topic for your classification or division essay from the list of assignment op-
> tions on pages 420–21, or choose one on your own. Then use the preceding guidelines
> for method 1 *or* method 2 to generate details about your topic, choose a principle of
> classification or division, and devise a set of categories or parts. Whatever method you
> use, list the examples, situations, or other details that you will use to describe each cat-
> egory or part. You might try drawing a graphic organizer.

Developing Your Thesis

Once you choose categories or parts and are satisfied with your details, you are ready to develop a thesis for your essay. Remember that your thesis statement should identify your topic and reveal your principle of division or classification. In most cases, it should also suggest why your classification or division is useful or important. Notice how the following weak theses have been strengthened by showing both what the categories are and why they are important.

For more on thesis statements, see Chapter 6.

WEAK	There are four types of insurance that most people can purchase.
REVISED	If you understand the four common types of insurance, you will be able to make sure that you, your family members, and your property are protected.

WEAK	Conventional stores are only one type of retailing; other types are becoming more popular.
REVISED	Although conventional stores are still where most people purchase products, three new types of shopping are becoming increasingly popular—face-to-face sales conducted in a home, sales via telephone or computer, and sales from automatic vending machines.

Draft your thesis and then check your prewriting to make sure you have enough details to support the thesis. If necessary, do some additional prewriting.

Essay in Progress 2
Using the preceding guidelines, develop a thesis for your classification or division essay.

Evaluating Your Ideas and Thesis

Take a few minutes to evaluate your ideas and thesis. Start by rereading everything you have written with a critical eye. Highlight the most useful details and delete those that are repetitious or irrelevant. If you are working on a computer, highlight useful details in bold type or move them to a separate file. As you review your work, add useful ideas that come to mind.

Trying Out Your Ideas on Others

Working in a group of two or three students, discuss your ideas and thesis for this chapter's assignment. Each writer should describe to the group his or her topic, principle of classification or division, and categories or parts. Then, as a group, evaluate each writer's work and suggest recommendations for improvement.

Essay in Progress 3
Using the preceding suggestions and comments from your classmates, evaluate your thesis, your categories or parts, and the details you plan to use in your essay. Refer to the list of characteristics on pages 413–15 to help you with your evaluation.

Organizing and Drafting

For more on drafting an essay, see Chapter 7.

Once you have evaluated your categories or parts, reviewed your thesis, and considered the advice of your classmates, you are ready to organize your ideas and draft your essay.

Choosing a Method of Organization

Choose the method of organization that best suits your purpose. One method that works well in classification essays is the least-to-most or most-to-least arrangement. You might arrange your categories in increasing order of importance or from most to least common, difficult, or frequent. Other possible sequences include chronological order (when one category occurs or is observable before another) or spatial order (when you classify physical objects).

For more on methods of organization, see Chapter 7, pp. 144–47.

Spatial order often works well in division essays, as does order of importance. In describing the parts of a baseball stadium, you might move from stands to playing field (spatial order). In writing about the parts of a hospital, you might describe the most important areas first (operating rooms and emergency department) and then move to less important facilities (waiting rooms and visitor cafeteria).

Drafting the Classification or Division Essay

Once you decide how to organize your categories or parts, your next step is to write a first draft. Use the following guidelines to draft your essay:

1. **Explain each category or part.** Begin by defining each one, taking into account the complexity of your topic and the background knowledge of your audience. Define any unfamiliar terms. Then provide details that describe each category or part, and show how each is distinct from the others. Include a wide range of details—sensory details, personal experiences, examples, and comparisons and contrasts.

2. **Provide roughly the same amount and kind of detail and description for each of your categories or parts.** For instance, if you give an example of one type of mental disorder, you should give an example for every other type discussed in the essay. Generally, allow one or more paragraphs for each category or part.

For more on transitions, see Chapter 7, pp. 150–52.

3. **Consider using headings or lists.** Presenting the parts or categories within a numbered list or in sections with headings can help make them clear and distinct. Headings or lists can be especially useful when you have a large number of categories or parts.

4. **Use transitions.** You need transitions to keep your reader on track as you move from one category or part to another. In addition, transitions help distinguish key features between and within categories or parts.

5. **Consider using a visual.** Diagrams, charts, or other visuals can make your system of classification or division clearer for your readers.

6. **Write an effective introduction.** Your introduction usually includes your thesis statement and suggests why the classification or division is useful. It also should provide background information and explain further, if needed, your principle of classification or division.

For more on writing effective paragraphs, including introductions and conclusions, see Chapter 7.

7. **Write a satisfying conclusion.** Your conclusion should bring your essay to a satisfying close, reemphasizing your thesis or offering a new insight or perspective on the topic.

If you have trouble finding an appropriate way to conclude your essay, return to your statement about why the classification or division is useful and important, and try to extend or elaborate on that statement.

> **Essay in Progress 4**
> Draft your classification or division essay, using an appropriate method of organization and the preceding guidelines for drafting.

Analyzing and Revising

As you review your draft, remember that your goal is to revise your classification or division essay to make it clearer and more effective. Focus on content and ideas and not on grammar, punctuation, or mechanics. Use one or more of the following strategies to analyze your draft:

1. **Reread your essay aloud.** You may "hear" parts that need revision.
2. **Ask a friend or classmate to read your draft** and to give you his or her impression of your categories of classification or division. Compare your reader's impressions with what you intend to convey, and revise your draft accordingly.
3. **Draw a graphic organizer, make an outline, or update the organizer or outline you drew or made earlier.** In particular, look for any categories or parts that lack sufficient details, and revise to include them.

For more on the benefits of peer review, see Chapter 9, pp. 188–91.

Use Figure 16.3 to guide your analysis of the strengths and weaknesses in your draft essay. You might also ask a classmate to review your draft using the questions in the flowchart. For each "No" response, ask your reviewer to explain his or her answer.

> **Essay in Progress 5**
> Revise your draft using Figure 16.3 and any comments you received from peer reviewers.

Editing and Proofreading

The last step is to check your revised essay for errors in grammar, spelling, punctuation, and mechanics. Watch for the types of errors you tend to make (refer to your error log).

For more on keeping an error log, see Chapter 10, pp. 221–22.

When editing a classification or division essay, pay specific attention to two particular kinds of grammatical error—choppy sentences and omitted commas following introductory elements.

For more on combining sentences and varying sentence patterns, see Chapter 10, pp. 206–12.

1. Avoid short, choppy sentences, which can make a classification or division essay sound dull and mechanical. Try combining a series of short sentences and varying sentence patterns and lengths.

- Working dogs are another one of the American Kennel Club's breed ^*, such as German shepherds and sheepherding dogs,*^ categories. ~~These include German shepherds and sheepherding dogs.~~

- *The fountain pen, one* ~~One~~ standard type of writing instrument^,^ ~~is the fountain pen. It is some-~~ times messy and inconvenient to use.

Figure 16.3 Flowchart for Revising a Classification and Division Essay

QUESTIONS   REVISION STRATEGIES

1. Highlight your thesis statement. Do it and the rest of your introduction explain your principle of classification or division and suggest why it is important?

 NO

- Revise your thesis to make your justification stronger or more apparent.
- Add explanatory information to your introduction.

 YES

2. *Write* the principle of classification you used at the top of your paper. Do you use this principle consistently throughout the essay? Does it fit your audience and purpose? Does it clearly relate to your thesis?

 NO

- Review or brainstorm other possible principles of classification of your topic, and decide if one of them better fits your audience and purpose.
- Revise your categories and parts to fit either your existing principle or a new one.
- Rewrite your thesis to reflect your principle of classification.

 YES

3. Underline the categories or parts. Do they cover all or most members of the group or all major parts of the topic? Are your categories or parts exclusive (not overlapping)?

 NO

- Brainstorm or do research to add categories or parts.
- Revise your categories or parts so that each item fits into one group only.

 YES

4. Place checkmarks ✔ beside the details that explain each category or part. Does your essay fully explain each one? (If it reads like a list, answer "No.")

 NO

- Brainstorm or do research to discover more details.
- Add examples, definitions, facts, and expert testimony to improve your explanations.

YES

(continued on next page)

(Figure 16.3 continued)

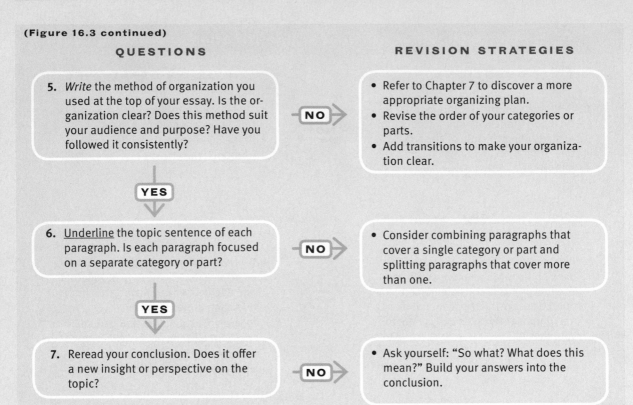

2. **Add a comma after opening phrases or clauses that are longer than four words.**

   ■ When describing types of college students, be sure to consider variations in age.

   ■ Although there are many types of cameras, most are easy to operate.

Essay in Progress 6
Edit and proofread your essay, paying particular attention to sentence variety and length as well as comma usage.

Students Write

Sunny Desai was a student at the University of Maryland at College Park when he wrote the following essay in response to an assignment for his writing course, in which he was asked to address the national debate about immigration. As you read the essay, notice how Desai uses classification as his primary method of organization.

Immigration: Legal and Illegal

Sunny Desai

The immigration debate in the United States has raged on for a number of years without much movement toward an agreement on how to deal with the issue. Some Americans believe immigration needs to be curtailed; they argue that immigrants are draining our economy and social services, and take jobs that citizens could hold. Others believe that immigration is beneficial and maintains America's identity as a melting pot of cultures. Reflecting the views of the public, lawmakers and political candidates are also sharply divided on the immigration issue. From the standpoint of legal status, there are many types and subtypes of people who are currently in the United States but not American citizens. Understanding these distinctions is the key to good policy decisions and to informed choices by voters. Most people understand that noncitizens can be classified into two major categories, legal and illegal; within each category, however, are subdivisions that are less well known.

For the millions of citizens of other countries who are in the United States legally, the most common method of entry is through a visa--a document that demonstrates a person's eligibility to enter, but with particular constraints, including purpose of visit and length of stay. The Web site of the Department of State points out that when the holder of a visa arrives at a checkpoint for entry into the United States, an immigration officer will determine whether he or she is actually allowed in. There are many types of visas; in fact, according to the Department of Homeland Security (DHS), there are over seventy types altogether *(Immigration Classifications)*. The overwhelming majority of visa holders, however, fall into four main groups. The most common one is the tourist visa, which allows a person to remain in the country only temporarily, for a variable length of time. Applicants must pass a security clearance and show that they have enough money to cover their visit.

Another major type of visa is the H1B visa, for those seeking temporary residence for work-related reasons. The visa is mostly used by outsourcing firms and technology companies. In 2007, Microsoft and Intel were among the ten highest receivers of H1B visas; the rest of the top ten were outsourcing companies, mostly based in India (Herbst 63). However, many doctors and nurses also arrive in the United States in this way. As explained on the Web site of the U.S. Citizenship and Immigration Services, a DHS agency, the H1B visa is used mostly by professional workers, since a bachelor's degree or its equivalent is often an eligibility require-ment. Even where this is not the case, unskilled laborers are often excluded because of the

1

2

3

Title: Desai identifies the subject and its two primary classifications.

Introduction: Desai describes the controversy over immigration, identifies legality as his principle of classification, and explains the importance of classifying noncitizens. In his thesis statement, he identifies the two major categories he will discuss.

Desai introduces the first category of noncitizens — people who are in the country legally, most commonly through holding visas. He cites sources for his information, as he continues to do throughout the essay.

Desai indicates that his classification is comprehensive, including all major categories, and introduces the first subcategory of the legal category: people on tourist visas.

The second subcategory: those on H1B visas. Notice that at the beginning of this paragraph and the next four, Desai uses a transition to signal the next category or subcategory.

Desai provides details to explain this type of visa.

limited number of visas available. For those who are eligible, the H1B visa is a desirable path to naturalization--the process that leads to U.S. citizenship. Typically, it is issued for three years, with the option to renew it once. However, the employer can decide to apply for fewer years *(Employment Authorization)*.

The third and fourth subcategories: holders of student and business visas

Apart from tourists and H1B workers, the other two major categories of noncitizens with temporary legal status in the United States are holders of student visas and business visas. Temporary entrance is allowed for those seeking to study in the country or having some sort of business to conduct, whether they are employees of a multinational corporation or foreign entertainers touring America. The duration of these visas varies greatly, ranging from months to years. The rules of entry also differ: Some visas allow for multiple entries whereas others only allow one entry.

The fifth subcategory: permanent legal residents

Besides these groups who are allowed to visit the United States temporarily, some people maintain permanent legal residency here but remain citizens of other nations. Permanent legal residents have identification cards generally called "green cards," also known as permanent resident cards. Most people who get green cards already live in the United States and had some sort of family relationship that helped them obtain it. According to the DHS's Office of Immigration Statistics, other factors that may enhance a person's ability to become a permanent legal resident are employment-based skills, birth in a country with a low rate of immigration to the United States, and status as a refugee or seeker of political asylum. For many, holding a green card is the first step toward becoming a citizen. Unlike a visa, it allows someone to travel abroad for up to a year without losing permanent residency status. The card is valid for ten years, after which it can be renewed (Office of Immigration Statistics).

The second category of noncitizens (those whose presence is illegal) and the first subcategory of this group (those who entered illegally)

In addition to those with green cards and valid visas, there are a large number of noncitizens living illegally in the United States. By one estimate, up to twelve million illegal immigrants were in the country as of 2006, the vast majority from Latin America ("Estimates" 2). All of these people are committing a crime under the Immigration and Nationality Act. The phrase "illegal immigrants" may conjure up images of people secretly crossing the U.S.-Mexico border, and certainly many do enter by hiding in trucks, walking through the desert, or swimming across a border river. According to the Pew Hispanic Center, more than half of illegal immigrants enter the country without a visa. Many enter for seasonal employment opportunities and return back home; however, such immigration is also deemed illegal.

The second subcategory of illegal residents: visa overstays

But people who entered the country illegally are not the only ones whose presence here is illegal. The other type of illegal "immigrants" is the visa overstays. Members of this group entered the country legally, using a visa, but have stayed beyond its expiration date. When they stay past their allotted time, they, like those who have entered without a visa, are subject to deportation.

Conclusion: Desai proposes a solution to the immigration debate.

Many immigrants, legal or illegal, are in the country because they want to work here. The temporary-work visa program is now fairly limited and restrictive, but since we already have such a

4

5

6

7

8

program in place, it would not be too difficult to add new categories to cover other kinds of "guest workers." Currently, illegal immigrants are doing mostly jobs Americans do not want to do. But if we make them leave, the economy would suffer. Therefore, creating a program that allows laborers to find seasonal work and then return home is a plausible solution to the immigration debate.

Works Cited

Herbst, Moira. "Guess Who's Getting the Most Work Visas." *Business Week* 6 Mar. 2008: 62–64. Print.

Pew Research Center. "Estimates of the Unauthorized Migrant Population for States Based on the March 2005 CPS." *Pew Hispanic Center,* 2006. Web. 16 May 2011.

United States. Dept. of Homeland Security. Office of Immigration Statistics. *U.S. Legal Permanent Residents: 2006.* U.S. Dept. of Homeland Security, 2006. Web. 16 Mar. 2011.

---.---.U.S. Citizenship and Immigration Services. *Employment Authorization.* Dept. of Homeland Security, 2008. Web. 16 Mar. 2011.

---.---.---. *Immigration Classifications and Visa Categories.* Dept. of Homeland Security, 2008. Web. 12 Mar. 2011.

---. Dept. of State. *What Is a U.S. Visa?* Dept. of State, 2008. Web. 16 Mar. 2011.

Analyzing the Writer's Technique

1. According to Desai, why is it important to understand the classification of immigrants?
2. What types of evidence does Desai use to develop his essay?
3. Evaluate Desai's introduction and conclusion. How successful are they at engaging readers' interest?

Thinking Critically about Classification and Division

1. What is the connotation of the phrase "melting pot" (para. 1)?
2. Reread the second sentence of paragraph 8. Is this fact or opinion? How can you tell?
3. Evaluate Desai's sources. What additional kinds of sources might have been useful? Why?
4. Consider Desai's tone. What kind of audience does he address?

Reacting to the Reading

1. What other reasons could Desai have used to establish the importance of his classification?
2. Discuss other principles of classification that might be used to classify noncitizens.
3. Write a journal entry describing Desai's attitude toward noncitizens.

READING A CLASSIFICATION OR DIVISION ESSAY

The following section provides advice for reading a classification or division essay as well as two model essays. The first essay illustrates the characteristics of classification covered in this chapter. The second essay uses classification along with other methods of development. Both essays provide opportunities to examine, analyze, and react to the writers' ideas.

Working with Text: Reading a Classification or Division Essay

For more on reading strategies, see Chapter 3.

A classification or division essay is usually tightly organized and relatively easy to follow. Use the suggestions below to read classification essays, division essays, or any writing that uses classification or division.

What to Look For, Highlight, and Annotate

1. Highlight the thesis statement, the principle of classification, and the name or title of each category or part.
2. Use a different color highlighter (or another marking method, such as asterisks or numbers) to identify the key details of each category.
3. Mark important definitions and vivid examples for later reference.
4. Add annotations indicating where you find a category or part confusing or where you think more detail is needed.

How to Find Ideas to Write About

For more on discovering ideas for a response paper, see Chapter 4.

To gain a different perspective on the reading, think of other ways of classifying or dividing the topic. For example, consider an essay that classifies types of exercise programs at health clubs according to the benefits they offer for cardiovascular health. Such exercise programs could also be classified according to their cost, degree of strenuousness, type of exercise, and so forth.

Thinking Critically about Classification and Division

When reading classification or division, particularly if its purpose is to persuade, focus on both the comprehensiveness and the level of detail by asking the following questions:

1. Does the Classification or Division Cover All Significant Categories or Parts?

To be fair and honest, a writer should discuss all the significant categories or parts into which a subject can be classified or divided. It would be misleading, for example, for a writer to classify unemployed workers into only two groups—those who have been laid off or downsized and those who lack skills for employment—because many people are unemployed for other reasons. This classification fails to consider those who are unable to work due to illness; those who were fired for personal reasons, such as incompetence; and those who choose not to work while they raise children or pursue an education. When reading "My Secret Life on the McJob: Fast Food Managers," you might ask whether there are other types of managers that Newman did not observe or recognize.

2. Does the Writer Provide Sufficient Detail about Each Category?

An objective and fair classification or division analysis requires that each category be treated with the same level of detail. To provide many details for some categories and just a few for others suggests a bias. For example, if a writer classifying how high school students spend their time goes into great detail about leisure activities and offers little detail on part-time jobs or volunteer work, the writer may create a false impression that students care only about having fun and make few meaningful contributions to society.

3. Is the Principle of Classification Appropriate for the Writer's Purpose?

When evaluating a classification or division essay, determine whether the subject is classified or divided in a way that fits the writer's purpose. Newman, in "My Secret Life on the McJob: Fast Food Managers," classifies managers according to management style. It would be possible, however, to compare managers according to other criteria such as productivity, experience, training, or location. Newman's purpose is to comment on relationships between employees and managers and to explore his experience as a fast-food worker, so his decision to use management style was appropriate. However, if his purpose had been to examine why some McDonald's franchises are more profitable than others, then classification of managers by financial profitability might have been a more appropriate choice.

In "A Brush with Reality: Surprises in the Tube," Bodanis devotes several paragraphs to chalk and gives far less coverage to detergent, for example. This discrepancy may be justified because chalk is, in terms of quantity, the second most important ingredient in toothpaste.

CLASSIFICATION COMBINED WITH OTHER PATTERNS

In the following essay, Carolyn Foster Segal combines classification with other patterns of development to support a thesis about student excuses.

The Dog Ate My Flash Drive, and Other Tales of Woe

Carolyn Foster Segal

Carolyn Foster Segal is professor of English at Cedar Crest College in Allentown, Pennsylvania, where she specializes in American literature, poetry, creative writing, and women's film. She has published poems in *Buffalo Spree* magazine, *Phoebe: A Journal of Feminist Scholarship, Theory, and Aesthetics*, and the *Bucks County Writer*, as well as many essays in the *Chronicle of Higher Education*, a weekly newspaper for college faculty and administrators. The following essay appeared in the *Chronicle* in 2000. With the author's permission, it has been revised slightly to update some technological references. As you read, notice how Segal's classification essay also uses description and illustration to fully explain each category she identifies.

Taped to the door of my office is a cartoon that features a cat explaining to his feline teacher, "The dog ate my homework." It is intended as a gently humorous reminder to my students that I will not accept excuses for late work, and it, like the lengthy warning on my syllabus, has had absolutely no effect. With a show of energy and creativity that would be admirable if applied to the (missing) assignments in question, my students persist, week after week, semester after semester, year after year, in offering excuses about why their work is not ready. Those reasons fall into several broad categories: the family, the best friend, the evils of dorm life, the evils of technology, and the totally bizarre.

The Family. The death of the grandfather/grandmother is, of course, the grandmother of all excuses. What heartless teacher would dare to question a student's grief or veracity? What heartless student would lie, wishing death on a revered family member, just to avoid a deadline? Creative students may win extra extensions (and days off) with a little careful planning and fuller plot development, as in the sequence of "My grandfather/grandmother is sick"; "Now my grandfather/grandmother is in the hospital"; and finally, "We could all see it coming—my grandfather/grandmother is dead."

Another favorite excuse is "the family emergency," which (always) goes like this: "There was an emergency at home, and I had to help my family." It's a lovely sentiment, one that conjures up images of Louisa May Alcott's little women rushing off with

www.CartoonStock.com

baskets of food and copies of *Pilgrim's Progress,* but I do not understand why anyone would turn to my most irresponsible students in times of trouble.

The Best Friend. This heartwarming concern for others extends beyond the family to   4
friends, as in, "My best friend was up all night and I had to (a) stay up with her in the dorm, (b) drive her to the hospital, or (c) drive to her college because (1) her boyfriend broke up with her, (2) she was throwing up blood [no one catches a cold anymore; everyone throws up blood], or (3) her grandfather/grandmother died."

At one private university where I worked as an adjunct,[1] I heard an interesting spin   5
that incorporated the motifs of both best friend and dead relative: "My best friend's mother killed herself." One has to admire the cleverness here: A mysterious woman in the prime of her life has allegedly committed suicide, and no professor can prove otherwise! And I admit I was moved, until finally I had to point out to my students that it was amazing how the simple act of my assigning a topic for a paper seemed to drive large numbers of otherwise happy and healthy middle-aged women to their deaths. I was careful to make that point during an off week, during which no deaths were reported.

The Evils of Dorm Life. These stories are usually fairly predictable; almost always fea-   6
ture the evil roommate or hallmate, with my student in the role of the innocent victim; and can be summed up as follows: My roommate, who is a horrible person, likes to party, and I, who am a good person, cannot concentrate on my work when he or she is partying. Variations include stories about the two people next door who were running around and crying loudly last night because (a) one of them had boyfriend/girlfriend problems; (b) one of them was throwing up blood; or (c) someone, somewhere, died. A friend of mine in graduate school had a student who claimed that his roommate attacked him with a hammer. That, in fact, was a true story; it came out in court when the bad roommate was tried for killing his grandfather.

The Evils of Technology. The computer age has revolutionized the student story, in-   7
spiring almost as many new excuses as it has Internet businesses. Here are just a few electronically enhanced explanations:

- The computer wouldn't let me save my work.
- The printer wouldn't print.
- The printer wouldn't print this file.
- The printer wouldn't give me time to proofread.
- The printer made a black line run through all my words, and I know you can't read this, but do you still want it, or wait, here, take my flash drive. File name? I don't know what you mean.
- I swear I attached it.
- It's my roommate's computer, and she usually helps me, but she had to go to the hospital because she was throwing up blood.
- I did write to the Listserv, but all my messages came back to me.
- I just found out that all my other Listserv messages came up under a diferent name. I just want you to know that its really me who wrote all those messages, you can tel which ones our mine because I didnt use the spelcheck! But it was yours truely :) Anyway, just in case you missed those messages or don't belief its my writting, I'll repeat what I sad: I thought the last movie we watched in clas was borring.

---

[1]*adjunct:* A part-time instructor.

The Totally Bizarre. I call the first story "The Pennsylvania Chain Saw Episode." A com-   8
muter student called to explain why she had missed my morning class. She had gotten
up early so that she would be wide awake for class. Having a bit of extra time, she walked
outside to see her neighbor, who was cutting some wood. She called out to him, and he
waved back to her with the saw. Wouldn't you know it, the safety catch wasn't on or was
broken, and the blade flew right out of the saw and across his lawn and over her fence and
across her yard and severed a tendon in her right hand. So she was calling me from the
hospital, where she was waiting for surgery. Luckily, she reassured me, she had remembered to bring her paper and a stamped envelope (in a plastic bag, to avoid bloodstains)
along with her in the ambulance, and a nurse was mailing everything to me even as we spoke.

That wasn't her first absence. In fact, this student had missed most of the class meet-   9
ings, and I had already recommended that she withdraw from the course. Now I suggested
again that it might be best if she dropped the class. I didn't harp on the absences (what if
even some of this story were true?). I did mention that she would need time to recuperate
and that making up so much missed work might be difficult. "Oh, no," she said, "I can't
drop this course. I had been planning to go on to medical school and become a surgeon,
but since I won't be able to operate because of my accident, I'll have to major in English,
and this course is more important than ever to me." She did come to the next class,
wearing—as evidence of her recent trauma—a bedraggled Ace bandage on her left hand.

You may be thinking that nothing could top that excuse, but in fact I have one more   10
story, provided by the same student, who sent me a letter to explain why her final assignment would be late. While recuperating from her surgery, she had begun corresponding
on the Internet with a man who lived in Germany. After a one-week, whirlwind Web romance, they had agreed to meet in Rome, to *rendezvous* (her phrase) at the papal Easter
Mass. Regrettably, the time of her flight made it impossible for her to attend class, but
she trusted that I—just this once—would accept late work if the pope wrote a note.

Examining the Reading

1. Identify the categories of student excuses that Segal identifies.
2. Do some student excuses turn out to be legitimate? Give an example from the
   reading.
3. What obvious mistake was made by the student who offered the chain-saw
   excuse?
4. Explain the meaning of each of the following words as it is used in the reading:
   bizarre (para. 1), *veracity* (2), *conjures* (3), *motifs* (5), and *harp* (9). Refer to your
   dictionary as needed.

Analyzing the Writer's Technique

1. Is it helpful or unnecessary for Segal to list her five categories in her thesis?
2. What is the function of the essay's title?
3. Who is Segal's audience? How can you tell?
4. What other patterns of development does Segal use in the essay?

Category	Types of Support
1. The Family	Examples (death of grandmother/grandfather) Quotations
2. The Best Friend	
3. The Evils of Dorm Life	
4. The Evils of Technology	
5. The Totally Bizarre	

Visualizing the Reading

What types of supporting information does Segal supply to make her categories seem real and believable? Review the reading and complete the chart above by filling in at least one type of support for each category. The first one has been done for you.

Thinking Critically about Text and Visuals

1. What other categories could be included in this essay?
2. What is the connotation of "an interesting spin" (para. 5)?
3. Other than students, what sources does Segal use? Explain why the essay would or would not benefit from more sources.
4. Does Segal provide sufficient detail in each category? What other kinds of details might she have included?
5. Is the classification appropriate for Segal's purpose? Why or why not?
6. Describe the tone of the essay. What does it reveal about Segal's attitude toward students?
7. What does the inclusion of the cartoon add to the essay? Why is the boy selling "Homework Done" frowning and the boy selling "Homework Eaten" smiling? What is the implied message? What other visual differences do you visual differences do you notice between the two boys?

Reacting to the Reading

1. As a student, how do you react to the essay? Have you observed these excuses being made (or perhaps even made them yourself)? Do you agree that they are overused? Or did you find the essay inaccurate, unfair, or even upsetting?
2. Write a journal entry exploring how you think instructors should handle students who make false excuses.
3. Write an essay classifying the excuses you have seen coworkers or supervisors make in the workplace to cover up or justify their poor performance, tardiness, or irresponsibility.

> ⬭ **MAKING ⬭ CONNECTIONS**
>
> ### The Workplace
>
> Both "My Secret Life on the McJob: Fast Food Managers" (pp. 411–13) and "Selling in Minnesota" (pp. 254–56) deal with employment in low-level service jobs. As you answer the following questions, keep in mind that both authors are professionals who were working under the guise of learning the habits, characteristics, and problems that everyday workers face in such jobs.
>
> #### Analyzing the Readings
>
> 1. What workplace problems did both Ehrenreich and Newman observe?
> 2. Write a journal entry exploring the differences and/or similarities that exist between working at Wal-Mart and working at fast-food restaurants.
>
> #### Essay Idea
>
> Write an essay in which you explore attitudes toward and expectations about work. You might consider its value, besides a weekly paycheck, or you might examine what type of work is rewarding.

Applying Your Skills: Additional Essay Assignments

For more on locating and documenting sources, see Part 5.

Write a classification or division essay on one of the following topics, using what you learned about classification and division in this chapter. Depending on the topic you choose, you may need to conduct library or Internet research.

To Express Your Ideas

1. Explain whether you are proud of or frustrated with your ability to budget money. For example, you might classify budget categories that are easy to master versus those that cause problems.
2. Explain why you chose your career or major. Categorize the job opportunities or benefits of your chosen field, and indicate why they are important to you.
3. Divide a store—such as a media shop, clothing store, or grocery store—into departments. Describe where you are most and least tempted to overspend.

To Inform Your Reader

4. Write an essay for the readers of your college newspaper classifying college instructors' teaching styles.
5. Explain the parts of a ceremony or an event you have attended or participated in.
6. Divide a familiar substance into its components, as Bodanis does in "A Brush with Reality: Surprises in the Tube" (pp. 417–18).

To Persuade Your Reader

7. Categorize types of television violence to develop the argument that violence on television is either harmful to children or not harmful to children.
8. In an essay that categorizes types of parenting skills and demonstrates how they are learned, develop the argument that effective parenting skills can be acquired through practice, training, or observation.

Cases Using Classification or Division

9. Write an essay for an introductory education class identifying a problem you have experienced or observed in the public education system. Divide public education into parts to better explain your problem.
10. You oversee the development of the annual catalog for a large community college, including the section describing the services offered to students. Decide how that section of the catalog should be organized, and then list the categories it should include. Finally, write a description of the services in one category.

CHAPTER 17

Definition: Explaining What You Mean

The photograph on the opposite page depicts volunteers providing food at a soup kitchen. Suppose your psychology instructor were to show this photograph to the class and ask, "What human behavior is being exhibited here?" What would be your response? You might say the volunteers are demonstrating altruism, generosity, or compassion, for example.

Write a paragraph defining the behavior of the soup kitchen volunteers. First, choose a term that describes their behavior. Then write a brief definition of the term you chose and explain the qualities or characteristics of the behavior.

WRITING A DEFINITION

In your paragraph in response to the Writing Quick Start on the previous page, you named and described the behavior illustrated in the photo, perhaps including one or more qualities or characteristics that distinguish the behavior from other behaviors. In other words, you have just written a definition. This chapter will show you how to write effective definitions, how to explore and explain a topic using an extended definition, and how to incorporate definition into essays using other patterns of development.

What Is a Definition?

A **definition** explains what a term means or which meaning is intended when a word has several different meanings. You use definitions every day in a variety of situations. If you call a friend a *nonconformist,* for example, she might ask you what you mean. If you and a friend disagree over whether you are feminists, you might need to define the term in order to resolve your dispute.

Often a definition is intended for someone who is unfamiliar with the thing or idea being defined. You might define *slicing* to someone unfamiliar with golf or explain the term *koi* to a person unfamiliar with tropical fish. Many academic and work situations require that you write or learn definitions, as the examples in the box below indicate.

The essay that follows is an example of an extended definition. The term it defines is *freegan,* a person who rejects our consumer society, culling only what he or she needs from the stuff others wastefully discard.

SCENES FROM COLLEGE AND THE WORKPLACE

- On an exam for a *health and fitness course*, the following short-answer question appears: "Define the term *wellness.*"

- Your *philosophy* instructor asks you to write a paper exploring the ethics of mercy killing; as part of the essay, you need to define the concepts *terminal illness* and *chronic condition.*

- As a *chemical engineer* responsible for your department's compliance with the company's standards for *safety* and *work efficiency*, you write a brief memo to your staff defining each term.

Freegans: They Live Off What We Throw Away

Jan Goodwin

Jan Goodwin is currently a senior fellow at Brandeis University's Schuster Center for Investigative Journalism and Senior International Editor for *Marie-Claire* magazine in which this article appeared. She has written about the threat of extremism in the Muslim world in her books *Point of Honor* (2002) and *Caught in the Crossfire* (1987) and publishes widely on issues of social justice both in the United States and overseas. As you read the essay below, highlight the different aspects of the freegan lifestyle that Goodwin describes in order to define the term.

One man's trash is another man's treasure. A group of freegans forages through bags outside a store in New York City.

It's nearly closing time on a crisp Monday night at a Midtown Manhattan supermarket,   1
when a burly crew begins tossing bulging black bags filled with the day's trash — crusty breads, salad-bar fixings, last week's fruits and vegetables — to the curb. Just then, a cadre of 15 jeans-and-sneakers-clad men and women turn the corner and quietly descend upon the heaps, gingerly opening and dissecting their contents. As they forage through the small mountains of discarded food, a 30-something woman sporting a green rain slicker calls out, "Over here, expensive Greek yogurt." Seconds later, a ponytailed guy wearing a backpack hollers, "Here's bacon and chicken for anyone who eats meat — and a perfect eggplant." Someone shouts a reminder not to tear the bags or leave litter on the ground, lest the store get fined. After less than 30 minutes, they excitedly depart the scene, each shouldering at least one tote bag filled with booty.

These urban foragers are neither homeless nor destitute. They are committed   2
freegans, radical environmentalists (typically vegan) who reject our wasteful con-

sumer culture by living almost entirely on what others throw away. Freegans rarely go hungry thanks to the colossal amount of food Americans dump every day — 38 million tons annually, according to the Environmental Protection Agency. Here's another way to look at it: The United Nations says our leftovers could satisfy every single empty stomach in Africa. Those castoffs are composed, in part, of the less-than-perfect products consumers instinctively reject: bruised apples, wilted lettuce, dented cans. Who hasn't passed on an entire carton of eggs after discovering a single slight fracture among the dozen? Supermarkets can't unload the quarts of milk tagged with yesterday's use-by date — which many of us interpret as a product's expiration but in fact refers to its period of peak flavor. Meaning, there's still plenty of life left in those quarts.

Freegans, like 24-year-old Leia MonDragon, a buxom Latina with a taste for heavy eye makeup, feast on those castoffs. "It's amazing what you can find and the good condition it's in," she exclaims, holding aloft a week's worth of produce, including watermelon, summer squash, kale, tomatoes, onions, and bananas. Though technically past their prime, they look pristine. MonDragon also scored half gallons of soy milk and lemonade, both unopened and still chilled, and bagels that only an hour earlier were for sale. "I once found 200 one-pound bags of organic fair-trade coffee beans just dumped outside a store with the trash," she brags, like a woman combing the racks at a Gucci clearance sale.   3

Aside from the $1600 a month in rent MonDragon pays for her two-bedroom Brooklyn apartment, which she shares with her boyfriend, Tate, their 1-year-old daughter, Uma, and her retired grandfather, just about everything she owns has been salvaged or handmade. She found her ivory faux-leather couch, dishes, and flatware on the street; many of Uma's clothes and toys were recovered from boxes abandoned on sidewalks and stoops, a common sight in New York, where apartment detritus — from halogen lamps to bed frames — is blithely left on the streets. MonDragon used to get around on a bicycle she and Tate cobbled together from discarded parts, but not long ago it was stolen. "So now I'm building another one," she says.   4

Though official figures are hard to come by, freegan ranks are believed to be in the thousands, with an estimated 500 practitioners living in New York City alone. Born of the extreme environmentalist and anti-globalization movements of the '90s, freeganism is a wholly modern crusade whose followers live off the grid while simultaneously exploiting it. Freegans gravitate toward cities — and their relentless mounds of garbage; Web sites keep devotees in close contact with each other so they can plan group foraging outings, recruit new members, and spread word of upcoming events, like move-out day at a college dorm, a veritable freegan Christmas. Using a discarded computer they restored, MonDragon and her boyfriend routinely scour Craigslist for freebies. (The Web connection comes from a cable package her grandfather pays for.) "The only thing I don't have yet is a skillet. But I'll find one," MonDragon declares confidently, as she ladles dinner — tofu-and-veggie stir-fry with lime zest — from a large stockpot.   5

MonDragon first embraced freeganism five years ago as a student at a Minnesota community college, where she met Tate. "We were broke, trying to find the money for   6 even a simple meal like rice and beans," she explains. "We saw a freegan flyer and hooked up with some people who showed us how to do it. And just like that, we had a source of free food. It was amazing." The more time the pair spent with entrenched freegans, the more exposure they got to the movement's renegade rhetoric. Since relocating to New York two years ago, they have become ardent practitioners, positioning their lifestyle as a boycott of "corporate greed" and an alternative to capitalism. "It's so wrong when people are losing their jobs, struggling to survive, that stores are throwing out such vast quantities of good food," MonDragon sighs, as Papo, her wiry gray mutt, nips the hem of her long black skirt. She tosses him a roasted chicken leg, retrieved from her last supermarket trash run.

MonDragon admits she was initially skeeved out by the prospect of eating garbage — 7 Dumpsters are a frequent freegan haunt — but says she was reassured by the movement's common-sense safety measures. Some freegans show up for Dumpster dives armed with rubber gloves and antibacterial lotion. Produce is washed thoroughly, withered leaves discarded; baked goods bearing even a hint of mold are tossed. Everything undergoes a basic smell test. (Tate says he once scarfed down day-old sushi, despite its funky aroma, and ended up with food poisoning.) And since stores generally separate discarded food from, say, bathroom trash bins, the ickiest finds are usually just putrid meats and dairy. MonDragon decontaminates all salvaged housewares with a mixture of vinegar, baking soda, and hydrogen peroxide and launders all of Uma's secondhand stuffed animals and clothes. Though she draws the line at pre-owned underwear, instead buying new pairs from discount stores, MonDragon makes her own reusable sanitary napkins from cloth in much the same way women did a century ago. (Think that's hard-core? Some freegans squat in abandoned buildings and jerry-rig toilets that compost their own waste matter.) "People in this country are a lot more freaked out about dirt than they need to be. We need a little dirt in our lives for our immune systems to be strong," MonDragon says.

"Freegans have been living this way for years and are very healthy," says Dr. Ruth 8 Kava, director of nutrition at the American Council on Science and Health. "In fact, a freegan's biggest risk may be falling headfirst into a Dumpster." That, or being slapped with a fine — or worse — for trespassing on private property to scavenge. It's not uncommon for store owners, mistaking freegans for homeless people or burglars, to call the police. Two years ago, a pair of freegans in Steamboat Springs, CO, were sentenced to six months in jail after jumping a fence and taking a couple of handfuls of fruit and vegetables from a grocery store's trash. For that reason, MonDragon confines her searches to whatever she finds on the street. She and Tate get by on less than $20,000 a year — he drives a taxi, and she clerks at a nonprofit during the summer. Their meager income is earmarked for inescapable expenses, like their tuition at a community college and rent. The couple qualifies for food stamps, which pay only for Uma's formula (MonDragon stopped breast-feeding once she started working).

Though she lives hand to mouth, MonDragon insists she wants for nothing. Her 9 family eats three hearty meals a day; their closets are crammed with wool coats, shoes, shirts with tags still dangling from their sleeves. She's got an active social

> life, towing Uma to playdates with other freegan moms and fielding invitations to
> watch DVDs with freegan friends. A week earlier, she and Tate uncovered a hoard of
> unopened Chinese food inside a streetside trash can, still warm in its gleaming white
> containers. They took it to a friend's house for an impromptu dinner party. "We usually
> never take more than we need," she explains, unzipping her black Patagonia shell and
> tossing it onto her bed — everything from the taupe sheets to the queen-size mattress
> were recovered from the streets of Manhattan. "We don't need to. There will be more
> trash out there tomorrow."

Characteristics of Extended Definitions

If you wanted to define the term *happiness,* you would probably have trouble coming up with a brief definition because the emotion is experienced in a variety of situations. However, you could explore the term in an essay and explain all that it means to you. Such a lengthy, detailed definition is called an **extended definition**.

Extended definitions are particularly useful in exploring a topic's various meanings and applications. In some instances, an extended definition may begin with a brief standard definition that anchors the essay's thesis statement. At other times, an extended definition may begin by introducing a new way of thinking about the term. Whatever approach is used, the remainder of the definition then clarifies the term by using one or more other patterns of development.

An Extended Definition Is Focused and Detailed

An extended definition focuses on a specific term and discusses it in detail. In "Freegans: They Live Off What We Throw Away," Goodwin concentrates on a lifestyle choice. She explains the origin of the word *freegan,* describes the freegan philosophy, explains how and where freegans forage for food, and discusses safety measures.

An Extended Definition Often Includes a Brief Explanation of the Term

In an essay that provides an extended definition of a **term**, readers often find it useful to have a brief definition to help them begin to grasp the concept. A brief or standard definition is the kind found in a dictionary and consists of three parts:

- The *term* itself
- The *class* to which the term belongs
- The *characteristics or details* that distinguish the term from all others in its class

For example, a wedding band is a piece of jewelry. "Jewelry" is the **class** or group of objects that includes wedding bands. To show how a wedding band differs from other members of that class, you would need to provide its **distinguishing characteristics**—the details that make it different from other types of jewelry: it is a ring, often made of gold, that the groom gives to the bride or the bride gives to the groom during a marriage ceremony.

Here are a few more examples of this three-part structure.

Term	Class	Distinguishing Characteristics
fork	utensil	Two or more prongs
		Used for eating or serving food
Dalmatian	breed of dog	Originated in Dalmatia
		Has short, smooth coat with black or dark brown spots

To write a standard definition, use the following guidelines:

1. **Describe the class as specifically as possible.** This will make it easier for your reader to understand the term you define. In the preceding example, notice that for *Dalmatian* the class is not *animal* or *mammal* but *breed of dog.*
2. **Do not use the term (or forms of the term) as part of your definition.** Do not write, "*Mastery* means that one has *mastered* a skill." In place of *mastered,* you could use *learned,* for example.
3. **Include enough distinguishing characteristics so that your readers will not mistake the term for something similar within the class.** If you define *answering machine* as "a machine that records phone messages," your definition would be incomplete because cell phones also record phone messages. To make the definition complete, you would need to add "land-line" before "phone messages."
4. **Do not limit the definition so much that it becomes inaccurate.** Defining *bacon* as "a smoked, salted meat from the side of a pig that is served at breakfast" would be too limited because bacon is also served at other meals. To make the definition accurate, you could either delete "that is served at breakfast" or add a qualifying expression like "usually" or "most often" before "served."

Look at the following definition of the term *bully,* taken from a magazine article on the topic. As you read it, study the highlighting and marginal notes.

Term

Three characteristics

Distinguishes this term from similar terms

Example of power difference

The term *bully* does not have a standard definition, but Dan Olweus, professor of psychology at the University of Bergen, has honed the definition to three core elements — bullying involves a pattern of *repeated aggressive behavior* with *negative intent* directed from one child to another where there is a *power difference.* Either a larger child or several children pick on one child, or one child is clearly more dominant than the others. Bullying is not the same as garden-variety aggression; although aggression may involve similar acts, it happens between two people of equal status. By definition, the bully's target has difficulty defending him- or herself, and the bully's aggressive behavior is intended to cause distress.

Hara Estroff Marano, "Big. Bad. Bully."

Exercise 17.1

Write a standard definition for two of the following terms.

1. hero
2. giraffe
3. science fiction
4. ATM
5. friendship

Exercise 17.2

For one of the terms listed in Exercise 17.1, list the distinguishing characteristics that you might use in building an extended definition.

An Extended Definition Makes a Point

The thesis of an extended definition essay tells why the term is worth reading about. In "Freegans : They Live Off What We Throw Away," Goodwin explains that a "colossal amount of food" is dumped every day (para. 2) and demonstrates how freegans salvage this waste.

The following thesis statements include a brief definition and make a point about the term.

> Produced by the body, hormones are chemicals that are important to physical as well as emotional development.

> Euthanasia, the act of ending the life of someone suffering from a terminal illness, is an issue that should not be legislated; rather, it should be a matter of personal choice.

An Extended Definition Uses Other Patterns of Development

To explain the meaning of a term, writers usually integrate one or more other patterns of development. Suppose you want to define the term *lurking* as it is used in the context of the Internet, where it usually means reading postings or comments on an online forum without directly participating in the ongoing discussion. You could develop the essay by using one or more other patterns, as noted in the following list:

Pattern of Development	*Defining the Term* Lurking
Narration (Chapter 11)	Relate a story about learning something important by lurking.
Description (Chapter 12)	Describe the experience of lurking.
Illustration (Chapter 13)	Give examples of typical situations involving lurking.
Process analysis (Chapter 14)	Explain how to lurk in an Internet chatroom.
Comparison and contrast (Chapter 15)	Compare and contrast lurking to other forms of observation.

Classification and division (Chapter 16)	Classify the reasons people lurk—for information, entertainment, and so on.
Cause and effect (Chapter 18)	Explain the benefits or outcomes of lurking.
Argument (Chapters 19 and 20)	Argue that lurking is an ethical or unethical practice.

In "Freegans : They Live Off What We Throw Away," Goodwin relies on several patterns of development. She uses *process analysis* to describe how freegans find food and other consumer goods, she uses *narrative* to tell the story of Leia MonDragon, and she uses *cause and effect* to explain why freegans have chosen their lifestyle.

Exercise 17.3

For one of the terms listed in Exercise 17.1 (p. 448), describe how you might use two or three patterns of development in an extended definition of the term.

An Extended Definition May Use Negation and Address Misconceptions

A writer may use **negation**—explaining what a term *is not* as well as what *it is*—to show how the term is different from the other terms in the same class. For example, in an essay defining *rollerblading,* you might clarify how it is unlike *roller skating,* which uses a different type of wheeled boot that allows different kinds of motions. In "Freegans: They Live Off What We Throw Away," Goodwin explains that freegans are not all strict vegetarians (1), not homeless or too poor to buy food (para. 2), and not greedy (9).

You can also use negation to clarify personal meanings. In defining what you mean by *relaxing vacation,* you might include examples of what is not relaxing—the pressure to see something new every day, long lines, crowded scenic areas, and many hours in a car each day.

In addition, an extended definition may need to address popular misconceptions about the term being defined. In an essay defining *plagiarism,* for instance, you might correct the mistaken idea that plagiarism is only passing off an entire paper written by someone else as your own, explaining that it actually also includes using excerpts from other writers' work and not giving them credit.

Exercise 17.4

For two of the following broad topics, select a narrowed term and develop a standard definition of it. Then, for each term, consider how you could address misconceptions and use negation in an extended definition of the term.

1. A type of dance
2. A play, call, or player position in a sport
3. A piece of clothing (hat, jacket, or jeans)
4. A term related to a course you are taking
5. A type of business

Visualizing an Extended Definition Essay: A Graphic Organizer

For more on graphic organizers, see Chapter 3, pp. 59–61.

The graphic organizer in Figure 17.1 shows the basic organization of an extended definition essay. The introduction announces the term, provides background information, and usually includes the thesis statement (which briefly defines the term and indicates its significance to readers). The body paragraphs, which are organized using one or more patterns of development, present the term's distinguishing characteristics along with supporting details. The conclusion refers back to the thesis and brings the essay to a satisfying close.

As you read the essay that follows, look for the elements illustrated in the basic graphic organizer for an extended definition. Then study the graphic organizer for the essay in Figure 17.2.

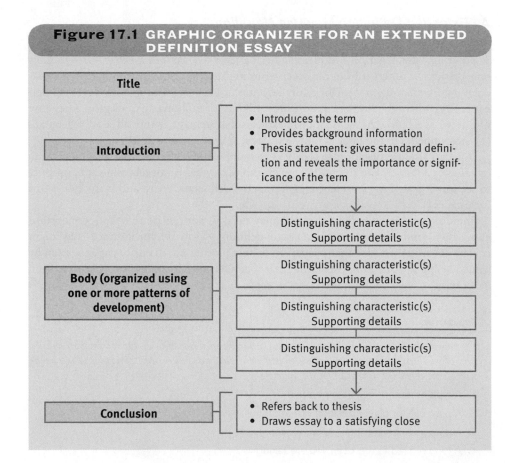

Figure 17.1 GRAPHIC ORGANIZER FOR AN EXTENDED DEFINITION ESSAY

- **Title**

- **Introduction**
  - Introduces the term
  - Provides background information
  - Thesis statement: gives standard definition and reveals the importance or significance of the term

- **Body (organized using one or more patterns of development)**
  - Distinguishing characteristic(s)
    Supporting details
  - Distinguishing characteristic(s)
    Supporting details
  - Distinguishing characteristic(s)
    Supporting details
  - Distinguishing characteristic(s)
    Supporting details

- **Conclusion**
  - Refers back to thesis
  - Draws essay to a satisfying close

Dude, Do You Know What You Just Said?
Mike Crissey

Mike Crissey is a staff writer for the Associated Press. The following article, which appeared in the *Pittsburgh Post-Gazette* on December 8, 2004, is based on research done by Scott Kiesling, a professor of linguistics at the University of Pittsburgh. Kiesling's work focuses on the relationship between language and identity, particularly in the contexts of gender, ethnicity, and class. As you read, notice how the writer uses a combination of expert testimony, anecdotal evidence, and personal observations to support his main point.

Dude, you've got to read this. A University of Pittsburgh linguist has published a scholarly 1 paper deconstructing and deciphering *dude,* the bane of parents and teachers, which has become as universal as *like* and another vulgar four-letter favorite. In his paper in the fall edition of the journal *American Speech,* Scott Kiesling says *dude* is much more than a greeting or catchall for lazy, inarticulate, and inexpressive (and mostly male) surfers, skaters, slackers, druggies, or teenagers. "Without context there is no single meaning that dude encodes and it can be used, it seems, in almost any kind of situation. But we should not confuse flexibility with meaninglessness," Kiesling said.

Originally meaning "old rags," a "dudesman" was a scarecrow. In the late 1800s, 2 a "dude" was akin to a dandy, a meticulously dressed man, especially in the western United States. *Dude* became a slang term in the 1930s and 1940s among black zoot suiters and Mexican American pachucos. The term began its rise in the teenage lexicon with the 1982 movie *Fast Times at Ridgemont High.* Around the same time, it became an exclamation as well as a noun. Pronunciation purists say it should sound like "duhd"; "dood" is an alternative, but it is considered "uncool" or old.

To decode *dude,* Kiesling listened to conversations with fraternity members he taped in 3 1993 and had undergraduate students in sociolinguistics classes in 2001 and 2002 write down the first twenty times they heard *dude* and who said it during a three-day period. He's also a lapsed *dude*-user who during his college years tried to talk like Jeff Spicoli, the slacker surfer "dude" from *Fast Times at Ridgemont High.*

According to Kiesling, *dude* has many uses: an exclamation ("Dude!" and "Whoa, 4 Dude!"); to one-up someone ("That's so lame, dude"); to disarm confrontation ("Dude, this is so boring"), or simply to agree ("Dude"). It's inclusive or exclusive, ironic or sincere.

Kiesling says *dude* derives its power from something he calls cool solidarity: an ef- 5 fortless or seemingly lazy kinship that's not too intimate; close, dude, but not that close. *Dude* "carries . . . both solidarity (camaraderie) and distance (non-intimacy) and can be deployed to create both of these kinds of stance, separately or together," Kiesling wrote. Kiesling, whose research focuses on language and masculinity, said that cool solidarity is especially important to young men — anecdotally the predominant *dude*-users — who are under social pressure to be close with other young men but not enough to be suspected as gay. "It's like *man* or *buddy.* There is often this male-male addressed term that says, 'I'm your friend but not much more than your friend,'" Kiesling said. Aside from its duality, *dude* also taps into nonconformity, despite everyone using it, and a new American image of leisurely success, he said.

The nonchalant attitude of *dude* also means that women sometimes call each other 6 *dudes*. And less frequently, men will call women *dudes* and vice versa, Kiesling said. But that comes with some rules, according to self-reporting from students in a 2002 language and gender class at the University of Pittsburgh included in his paper. "Men report that they use *dude* with women with whom they are close friends, but not with women with whom they are intimate," according to his study.

His students also reported that they were least likely to use the word with parents, 7 bosses, and professors. "It is not who they are but what your relationship is with them. With your parents, you likely have a close relationship, but unless you're Bart Simpson, you're not going to call your parent *dude*," Kiesling said. "There are a couple of young professors here in their thirties and every once in a while we use *dude*. Professors are dudes, but most of the time they are not."

And *dude* shows no signs of disappearing. "More and more our culture is becoming 8 youth centered. In southern California, youth is valued to the point that even active seniors are dressing young and talking youth," said Mary Bucholtz, an associate professor of linguistics at the University of California, Santa Barbara. "I have seen middle-aged men using *dude* with each other."

So what's the point, dude? Kiesling and linguists argue that language and how 9 we use it is important. "These things that seem frivolous are serious because we are always doing it. We need to understand language because it is what makes us human. That's my defense of studying *dude*," Kiesling said.

Exercise 17.5

Draw a graphic organizer for "Freegans: They Live Off What We Throw Away" on pages 443–46.

To draw detailed graphic organizers using a computer, visit www.bedfordstmartins .com/successfulcollege.

Integrating Definitions into an Essay

You will often need to include either standard or extended definitions in writing that is based on other patterns of development. For example, on college exams, you may need to write a definition as part of a response to an essay question. Definitions are also useful for explaining unfamiliar terms in any type of essay. Whatever the type of essay, the following kinds of terms usually require definition:

- **Define judgmental terms.** Judgmental terms mean different things to different people. If you describe a policy as "fiscally unsound," you would need to define your use of *fiscally unsound.*
- **Define technical terms**. Technical terms are used in a particular field or discipline. In the field of law, for example, such terms as *writ, deposition, hearing,* and *plea* have specific meanings. Especially when writing for an audience that is unfamiliar with your topic, be sure to define technical terms.
- **Define abstract terms**. Abstract terms refer to ideas or concepts rather than physical objects. Examples are *happiness, heroism,* and *conformity.* Because abstract terms can seem vague or, like judgmental terms, mean different things to different people, they often need explanation and definition.
- **Define controversial terms**. The definitions of terms that evoke strong emotions—such as *politically correct, affirmative action,* and *chemical warfare*—are often the subject of controversy. When writing about controversial subjects, define exactly how you use each related term in an essay.

Figure 17.2 GRAPHIC ORGANIZER FOR "DUDE, DO YOU KNOW WHAT YOU JUST SAID?"

Title	"Dude, Do You Know What You Just Said?"
Introduction	Background information on Kiesling's research on the meaning of the term *dude* Historical information on how the term has been used and what it means *Thesis:* The meaning of *dude* is flexible and depends on context.
Body	*Dude* has many uses and can be inclusive or exclusive, ironic or sincere. The word derives its power from "cool solidarity," which is important to young men. The term is used by and for both men and women but in different ways. The term is less likely to be used with parents, bosses, and professors. Use of the term shows no signs of disappearing and is even spreading to middle-aged people.
Conclusion	The study of language is important, despite those who say it is trivial, because it makes us human.

In general, if you are not sure whether a term needs a definition, you should include one. At times you may want to provide your definition in a separate sentence or section. At other times a brief definition or synonym can be incorporated into a sentence. In this case, you use commas, dashes, or parentheses to set off the definition.

Implicit memory, or the nonconscious retention of information about prior experiences, is important in eyewitness accounts of crimes.

Empathy—a shared feeling of joy for people who are happy or distress for people who are in pain—explains the success of many popular films.

In "The Appeal—and Danger—of War Porn" (p. 466), Jessica Ramirez uses definition within an essay that mixes several other methods of development.

A GUIDED WRITING ASSIGNMENT

The following guide will lead you through the process of writing an extended definition essay. Although you will focus on definition, you will need to integrate one or more other patterns of development to develop your essay.

The Assignment

Write an extended definition essay on one of the following topics or one that you choose on your own. You will need to narrow one of these general topics to a more specific term for your essay. Your audience is made up of your classmates.

1. A type of music (rock, jazz, classical)
2. Inappropriate behavior
3. A type of television show
4. Social problems
5. Leisure time
6. Athletics

For more on using examples or comparison and contrast, see Chapters 13 and 15.

As you develop your extended definition essay, consider how you can use one or more other patterns of development. For example, you might include several examples of the inappropriate behavior you choose to write about, or you might explain R & B music by comparing it to and contrasting it with rock music. For more on patterns of development, see pages 448 to 449.

Generating Ideas

The following guidelines will help you narrow your general topic and identify distinguishing characteristics.

Narrowing the General Topic to a Specific Term

For more on narrowing a topic, see Chapter 5, pp. 104–6.

For more on prewriting strategies, see Chapter 5, pp. 110–18.

Your first step is to narrow the broad topic you have selected to a more specific term. For example, *celebrity* is probably too broad a topic for a brief essay, but the topic can be narrowed to a particular type of celebrity, such as a *sports celebrity, Hollywood celebrity, local celebrity,* or *political celebrity.* You might then focus your definition on sports celebrities, using Tom Brady and Kobe Bryant as examples to illustrate the characteristics of the term.

For more on classification and division, see Chapter 16.

Use the following suggestions for finding a suitable narrowed term for your definition essay:

Learning Style Options

1. Use a branching diagram or clustering to classify the general topic into categories. Choose the category that you are especially interested in or familiar with.
2. Think of someone who might serve as an example of the general topic and consider focusing your definition essay on that person.
3. Discuss your general topic with a classmate to come up with specific terms related to it.

> **Essay in Progress 1**
> For the assignment option you chose on page 454 or on your own, narrow your general term into several specific categories of terms. Then choose one narrowed term for your extended definition essay.

Considering Your Purpose, Audience, and Point of View

Carefully consider your purpose and audience before you develop details for your essay. The purpose of a definition essay can be expressive, informative, or persuasive. You might, for example, write an essay that defines *search engines* and that expresses your frustration or success with using them to locate information on the Internet. Or you might write an informative essay on search engines in which you discuss the most popular ones. Finally, you might write a persuasive essay in which you argue that one search engine is superior to all others.

For more on purpose, audience, and point of view, see Chapter 5, pp. 106–9.

When your audience is unfamiliar with a term, you will need to present detailed background information and define all specialized terms that you use. Your audience for this Guided Writing Assignment is your classmates. As you develop your essay, keep the following questions in mind:

1. What, if anything, can I assume my audience already knows?
2. What does my audience need to know to understand or accept my definition?

In addition, consider which point of view will be most effective for your essay. Most definition essays are written in the third person, as is "Freegans: They Live Off What We Throw Away," while the first and second person are used occasionally.

Identifying Distinguishing Characteristics and Supporting Details

The following suggestions will help you identify distinguishing characteristics and supporting details for the specific term you intend to define in your essay:

Learning Style Options

1. Discuss the term with a classmate, making notes as you talk.
2. Brainstorm a list of (a) words that describe your term, (b) people and things that might serve as examples of the term, and (c) everything a person would need to know to understand the term.

   For more on observation, see Chapter 20, pp. 617–18.

3. Observe a person who is associated with the term or who performs some aspect of it. Take notes on your observations.
4. Look up the term's *etymology*, or origin, in the *Oxford English Dictionary, A Dictionary of American English,* or *A Dictionary of Americanisms,* all of which are available in the reference section of your library. Take notes; the word's etymology will give you some of its characteristics and details, and might give you ideas on how to organize your essay.
5. Think of incidents or situations that reveal the meaning of the term.
6. Think of similar and different terms with which your reader is likely to be more familiar.
7. Do a search on the Internet for the term. Visit three or four Web sites and take notes on or print out what you discover at each site.

   For more on Internet research, see Chapter 22, pp. 603–6.

> **Essay in Progress 2**
> For the narrowed term you selected in Essay in Progress 1, use the preceding
> suggestions to generate a list of distinguishing characteristics and supporting details.

Developing Your Thesis

*For more on thesis statements,
see Chapter 6.*

When you have gathered the distinguishing characteristics and supporting details for
your term, you are ready to develop your thesis. It is a good idea to include a brief
standard definition of the term within your thesis and an explanation of why your
extended definition might be useful, interesting, or important to readers.

Notice how the following weak thesis statement can be revised to reveal the writer's
main point.

WEAK	Wireless cable is a means of transmitting television signals through the air by microwave.
REVISED	The future of wireless cable, a method of transmitting television signals through the air using microwaves, is uncertain.

> **Essay in Progress 3**
> Write a working thesis statement that briefly defines your term and tells readers why un-
> derstanding it might be useful or important to them.

Evaluating Your Ideas and Thesis

Take a few minutes to evaluate your ideas and thesis. Highlight details that best help
your readers distinguish your term from other similar terms. If you are writing on a
computer, highlight key information in bold type or move it to a separate file. Also
check your prewriting to see if you have enough details—examples, facts, descriptions, expert testimony, and so forth. If you find that your characteristics or details are
skimpy, choose a different method from the list on page 455 to generate additional
material. If you find you still need more details, research the term in the library or on
the Internet.

> **Trying Out Your Ideas on Others**
> Working in a group of two or three students, discuss your ideas and thesis for this
> chapter's assignment. Each writer should state his or her term, thesis, distinguishing
> characteristics, and supporting details. Then, as a group, evaluate each writer's work
> and offer suggestions for improvement.

> **Essay in Progress 4**
> Using the preceding suggestions and comments from your classmates, evaluate your
> thesis, distinguishing characteristics, and details. Refer to the list of characteristics on
> pages 446–49 to help you with your evaluation.

Organizing and Drafting

When you have evaluated your distinguishing characteristics, supporting details, and thesis, and considered the advice of your classmates, you are ready to organize your ideas and draft your essay.

For more on drafting an essay, see Chapter 7.

Choosing Other Patterns of Development

To a considerable extent, the organization of an extended definition essay depends on the other pattern or patterns of development you decide to use. Try to choose the pattern(s) before you begin drafting your essay, using Table 5.2 on page 116 to help you. Use patterns that suit your audience and purpose as well as the term. For instance, narrating a story about lurking in online forums might capture the interest of an audience unfamiliar with such forums and thus help persuade them to explore them, whereas classifying different types of people who lurk might be of interest to an audience of forum sponsors whom you are trying to inform about ways they might encourage lurkers to participate.

With your pattern(s) firmly in mind, think about how to organize your characteristics and details. An essay incorporating several patterns of development might use a number of arrangements. At this stage, it is a good idea to make an outline or draw a graphic organizer.

> **Essay in Progress 5**
>
> For the thesis you wrote in Essay in Progress 3, decide which pattern(s) of development you will use to develop your characteristics and details. Draw a graphic organizer or write an outline to help you see how each pattern will work.

For more on organizing an essay, see Chapter 7.

Drafting an Extended Definition Essay

Use the following guidelines to draft your essay:

1. **Include enough details.** Be sure you include sufficient information to enable your reader to understand each characteristic.
2. **Consider including the history or etymology of the term.** You might include a brief history of your term in the introduction or in some other part of your essay to capture your readers' interest.
3. **Use transitions.** As you move from characteristic to characteristic, be sure to use a transitional word or phrase to signal each change and guide your readers along. The transitions *another, also,* and *in addition* are especially useful in extended definitions.

For more on transitions, see Chapter 7, pp. 150–52.

4. **Write an effective introduction and a satisfying conclusion.** Your introduction should introduce the term, provide any needed background information, and state your thesis (which often includes a standard definition as well as your main point). When introducing your term, it may be helpful to use negation, explaining what the term is and what it is not, as Goodwin does in the ninth paragraph of "Freegans: They Live Off What We Throw Away." You might also use your introduction to justify the importance of your topic, as Goodwin does in her second paragraph.

For more on drafting introductions and conclusions, see Chapter 7. For more on writing effective paragraphs, see Chapter 8.

Your conclusion should reinforce your thesis and draw the essay to a satisfying close, as Crissey's conclusion does in "Dude, Do You Know What You Just Said?"

Essay in Progress 6
Draft your extended definition essay, using the pattern(s) of development you selected in Essay in Progress 5 and the preceding guidelines for drafting.

Analyzing and Revising

If possible, set your draft aside for a day or two before rereading and revising it. As you review your draft, concentrate on your ideas and organization, not on grammar or mechanics. Use one or more of the following suggestions to analyze your draft:

Learning Style Options

1. Delete or make unreadable the title and all mentions of the term, and then ask a classmate to read your essay. Alternatively, you could read your essay aloud, substituting "Term X" each time the term occurs. Then ask your classmate to identify the term you are defining. If your reader or listener cannot come up with the term or a synonym for it, you probably need to make your distinguishing characteristics more specific or add details.

2. Test your definition by trying to think of exceptions to it as well as other terms that might be defined in the same way.
   - *Exceptions.* Try to identify exceptions to your distinguishing characteristics. Suppose, for example, you define *sports stars* as people who exemplify sportsmanlike behavior. Since most people can name current sports stars who indulge in unsportsmanlike behavior, this distinguishing characteristic needs to be modified or deleted.
   - *Other terms that fit all of your characteristics.* For example, in defining the term *bulletproof vest*, you would explain that it is a piece of clothing worn by law-enforcement officers, among others, to protect them from bullets and other life-threatening blows. Another kind of protective clothing—a helmet—would also fit your description, however. You would need to add information about *where* on the body a bulletproof vest is worn.

3. To see if your essay follows the organization you intend, draw a graphic organizer or make an outline (or update the organizer or outline you made earlier).

For more on the benefits of peer review, see Chapter 9, pp. 188–89.

Use Figure 17.3 to guide your analysis. You might also ask a classmate to review your draft using the questions in the flowchart. For each "No" answer, ask your reviewer to explain his or her answer. In addition, ask your reviewer to describe his or her impressions of your main point and distinguishing characteristics. Your reviewer's comments will help you identify the parts of your essay that need revision.

Essay in Progress 7
Revise your draft using Figure 17.3 and any comments you received from peer reviewers.

Figure 17.3 Flowchart for Revising an Extended Definition Essay

QUESTIONS

REVISION STRATEGIES

1. Highlight your thesis statement. Does it include a brief definition of the term? Does it indicate why your extended definition is useful, interesting, or important?

NO →

- Use the guidelines on pages 446–49 to identify the class and distinguishing characteristics of your term, and incorporate a standard definition into your thesis.
- Ask yourself, Why is this definition worth reading about? Add your answer to your thesis.

YES

2. Place checkmarks ✔ beside the distinguishing characteristics of your definition. Do they make your term distinct from similar terms? Is each characteristic true in all cases?

NO →

- Do additional research or prewriting to discover more characteristics and details you can add to the definition.
- Eliminate characteristics and details that limit the definition too much.

YES

3. *Write* the name of the pattern(s) of development you used in your essay. Does each clearly connect your details and help explain the distinguishing characteristics of your term?

NO →

- Review the list of patterns on pages 448–49 and consider substituting or adding one or more of them to enhance your definition.

YES

4. Draw [brackets] around sections where you use negation or address misconceptions. Does each section eliminate possible misunderstandings? Are there other places where you need to do so?

NO →

- Revise your explanation of what your term is not.
- Add facts or expert opinion to correct readers' mistaken notions about the term.

YES

(continued on next page)

(Figure 17.3 continued)

QUESTIONS   REVISION STRATEGIES

5. <u>Underline</u> the topic sentence of each paragraph. Does each paragraph have a clear topic sentence and focus on a particular characteristic? Is each paragraph well developed?

 NO

- Consider combining paragraphs that cover the same characteristic or splitting paragraphs that cover more than one.
- Add or revise topic sentences and supporting details (see Chapter 7).

 YES

6. Reread your introduction and conclusion. Does the introduction provide necessary background information? Does your conclusion bring the essay to a satisfying close?

NO

- Add background information that sets a context for the term you are defining.
- Revise your introduction and conclusion so that they meet the guidelines presented in Chapter 7 (pp. 154–56).

Editing and Proofreading

For more on keeping an error log, see Chapter 10, pp. 221–22.

The final step is to check your revised essay for errors in grammar, spelling, punctuation, and mechanics. Be sure to check your error log for the types of errors you commonly make.

As you edit and proofread your extended definition essay, watch out for the following types of errors commonly found in this type of writing:

1. Avoid the awkward expressions *is when* or *is where* in defining your term. Instead, name the class to which the term belongs.

- 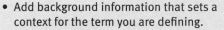 Early bird specials ~~is when~~ restaurants ~~offer reduced-price dinners~~ late in the afternoon and early in the evening.

- A rollover ~~is where~~ an employee transfers money from one retirement account to another.

2. Make sure subjects and verbs agree in number. When two subjects are joined by *and*, the verb should be plural.

- Taken together, the military and Medicare ~~costs~~ U.S. taxpayers an enormous amount of money.

When two nouns are joined by *or,* the verb should agree with the noun closest to it.

- For most birds, the markings or wing span *is* ~~are~~ easily observed with a pair of good binoculars.

When the subject and verb are separated by a prepositional phrase, the verb should agree with the subject of the sentence, not with the noun in the phrase.

- The features of a hot-air balloon *are* ~~is~~ best learned by studying the attached diagram.

Essay in Progress 8

Edit and proofread your essay, paying particular attention to avoiding *is when* or *is where* expressions and correcting errors in subject-verb agreement.

Students Write

Kate Atkinson wrote the following essay for an assignment to write an extended definition of a specialized term related to one of her interests. Atkinson decided to write about guerrilla street art. As you read, note how Atkinson uses other patterns of development—such as description and illustration—to define guerrilla street art as a nontraditional art form growing in popularity.

Guerrilla Street Art: A New Use of Public Space

Kate Atkinson

Guerrilla street art is everywhere, if you look for it. There are countless examples in the small col- 1
lege town where I grew up, where the dense population of college students and artists breeds creativity. Just around the corner from my school, stickers litter sign posts, colorful graffiti is scrawled on exposed brick walls, homemade posters advertise local bands at the bus stop, and a cheerful Dr. Seuss character is stenciled on the sidewalk. These small works of art can easily go unnoticed, but they bring an unexpected vibrancy to the city and raise the controversial question of what constitutes art. By taking art out of its traditional context, guerrilla street artists use public space to create controversy and intrigue while at the same time making art free and accessible to a broad audience.

Common forms used by street artists today include graffiti, stenciling, poster art, sticker art, 2
and yarn bombing. Graffiti, the most prevalent form of guerrilla street art, is unauthorized writing or drawing on a public surface. It dates back centuries, and artists have been known to use chalk, markers, paint, and even carving tools to inscribe their messages on public property. Graffiti is so

READING

Title: Atkinson identifies her subject and creates interest.

Introduction: Atkinson provides background information on guerrilla street art and explains by example what it is.

In her thesis statement, Atkinson offers a brief definition and suggests the value and importance of guerrilla street art. Atkinson presents the first distinguishing characteristic—use of common techniques—and describes five. Notice that the first sentence in this paragraph is the topic sentence that is supported by the rest of the paragraph — a pattern followed in each of the next three paragraphs.

common that it is difficult to travel far in most urban settings without coming across a word or image scrawled in spray paint on a public surface. Stenciling is simply a form of graffiti in which artists use precut stencils to guide their work. Posters and stickers are popular because they can be easily mass-produced and quickly applied. Posters are usually applied with a technique called "wheat pasting" -- using a vegetable-based adhesive to attach posters to walls. Artists apply the clear paste with a roller in a thin layer to both sides of the poster, making it weather-proof and durable. A less common street-art technique is "yarn bombing," in which craft artists knit colorful sheaths of wool and acrylic and wrap them around telephone poles and park benches. The finished pieces are eye-catching and unusual but not permanent or damaging to public property.

The second distinguishing characteristic: Atkinson discusses the motives of the artists and offers examples of the various motives.

The various motives behind guerrilla street art are as diverse as the artwork itself and   3
range from social and political activism to self-promotion of the artist. Artists embellish telephone poles with colorful yarn and train carriages with ornate murals as a way to reclaim and beautify public space. Others use public space as a billboard to advocate for a cause. An example of street art as political activism is artist Shepard Fairey's iconic image of Barack Obama

Atkinson uses sources to document an example of political activism, one of the motives.

(Wortham). The simple design combines a striking red, white, and blue portrait of Obama with the word "Hope." With the approval of Obama's 2008 campaign team, Fairey and his team dispersed and pasted, stenciled, or tacked the image onto countless public surfaces across the United States until it became an important facet of the campaign. The picture itself is powerful, but what made it even more effective as a campaign tool was the distribution of the image by supporters and the youth appeal that it garnered as a result.

The third distinguishing characteristic: Atkinson discusses the appeal of street art and gives examples.

Street art has many appeals. It is an easy way for new artists to gain notoriety, and any-   4
one with a spray can and a flair for creativity can partake. A tag, which is an artist's signature or symbol, is the most common type of graffiti. Before the Obama campaign, Shepard Fairey gained international acclaim for a sticker depicting wrestler Andre the Giant and the word "Obey." The image soon became his tag and can be found in almost all of his work, making it instantly recognizable. The anonymity of street art also gives artists the freedom to express themselves without fearing the judgment of their peers. At worst, this freedom can result in crude or offensive inscriptions on public property; but at best, it can produce bold, striking statements. Guerrilla street art is contemporary and can be enjoyed without a visit to a museum. It is free and encourages the belief that art should be accessible and available to everyone. It is also a movement that anyone can take part in and that challenges traditional standards of art.

The fourth distinguishing characteristic: Atkinson discusses the secrecy of the artists and uses Banksy as an example.

Due to the illicit nature of their art, the street artist community is shrouded in secrecy.   5
In the film *Exit through the Gift Shop,* a documentary by notorious British street artist Banksy, hooded figures in ski masks are shown scaling buildings and perched precariously on ledges, armed with spray cans and buckets of industrial paste and always on the lookout for the police. Despite his celebrity, Banksy has managed to keep his identity anonymous, and his face is never

shown in the film. It is common for street artists to be arrested for trespassing and vandalism, and the risk and intentional disobedience involved in street art adds to its appeal, especially among young people.

Guerrilla street art has blossomed from an underground movement to a cultural phenomenon. **6** At the very least, it brings up the question of what constitutes art and whether public space is an appropriate place for it. Although it does not adhere to all traditional standards of art, guerrilla street art provokes thought, brings beauty and intrigue to urban spaces that would otherwise go unnoticed, and is a tool for artists to exercise freedom of speech and expression.

Conclusion: Atkinson comments on the street art movement as a cultural experience, notes that it raises the question of what constitutes art, claims it is appropriate in public places, and confirms its values.

Works Cited

Exit through the Gift Shop. Dir. Banksy. Perf. Banksy and Thierry Guetta. Paranoid Pictures, 2010.
    Film.

Wortham, Jenna. "'Obey' Street Artist Churns Out 'Hope' for Obama." *Wired.com.* Condé Nast Digi-
    tal, 21 Sept. 2010. Web. 15 Nov. 2010.

Analyzing the Writer's Technique

1. How does Atkinson define *guerrilla art*?
2. Evaluate the effectiveness of the title, introduction, and conclusion.
3. Locate one of each of these in the essay—a judgment term, a technical term, an abstract term, and a controversial term.

Thinking Critically about Definition

1. Atkinson is not neutral on the subject of this essay. Explain her bias. How does this affect the essay?
2. What other types of sources could Atkinson have included to make her essay more comprehensive? What do her two sources reveal about her attitude about the topic?
3. Atkinson uses words such as "vibrancy" (para. 1) and "blossomed" (6) to describe guerrilla street art. What kind of connotation do these words have, and how do the connotations play into the overall tone of the essay?
4. Is "guerrilla street art" a euphemism? Why or why not? If so, how would the same idea be expressed in more direct language?
5. Atkinson limits her definition of guerrilla street art to items that have no commercial or financial purpose. She does not mention posters promoting businesses or paid entertainment, signs and banners used for fund-raising by organizations, and advertising flyers, even though these items also are often displayed in the same places as those she does discuss and with the same lack of legal permission. How are these items similar to and different from the kinds of items she includes in her definition?

(MAKING (CONNECTIONS)

Culture

Both "Freegans: They Live Off What We Throw Away" (pp. 443–46) and "Guerrilla Street Art" (pp. 461–63) discuss the activities of a subculture – dumpster divers and artists who create street art.

Analyzing the Readings

1. In what way does each essay demonstrate how the activities of each subgroup set it apart from the larger society?
2. Write a journal entry exploring this question: What motivates various subgroups to set themselves apart from the society as a whole, for example, through use of a specific word or phrase or through an activity?

Essay Idea

Write an essay in which you explore a subgroup of college students, such as fraternity brothers or vegans. Give examples of ways in which certain groups on campus set themselves apart through their language, their activities, or some other way.

Reacting to the Reading

1. Have you ever created any graffiti? Discuss how doing it made you feel. If you have not ever created any, discuss how doing so might make you feel.
2. Discuss the value of work like Shepard Fairey's, which takes political messages and conveys them in street art. Why is this strategy effective? How does it reach a broader audience than other methods of communication?
3. Write a journal entry discussing whether guerrilla art adds value to public space or devalues the space. How should the answer to this question be determined?

READING DEFINITIONS

The following section provides advice for reading definitions as well as a model essay. The essay uses definition along with other methods of development and provides opportunities to examine, analyze, and react to the writer's ideas.

Working with Text: Reading Definitions

For more on reading strategies, see Chapter 3.

As you encounter new fields of study throughout college, you will be asked to learn sets of terms that are specific to academic disciplines. Articles in academic journals, as well as most textbooks, contain many new terms.

If you need to learn a large number of specialized terms, try the index-card system. Using three- by five-inch cards, write a word on the front of each card, and on its back write the word's meaning, pronunciation, and any details or examples that will help you remember it. Be sure to write the definition in your own words; don't copy the author's definition. To study, test yourself by reading the front of the cards and trying to recall the definition on the back of the cards. Then reverse the process. Shuffle the pack of cards to avoid learning terms in a particular order.

What to Look For, Highlight, and Annotate

1. As you read a definition, identify the class and highlight or underline the distinguishing characteristics. Mark any that are unclear or for which you need further information.

2. Make sure you understand how the term differs from similar terms, especially those presented in the same article or chapter. If a textbook or article does not sufficiently explain how two or more terms differ, check a standard dictionary. Each academic field of study also has its own dictionaries that list terms specific to the discipline. Examples include *Music Index, Taber's Cyclopedic Medical Dictionary,* and *A Dictionary of Economics.*

3. Highlight definitions using a special color of pen or highlighter, or designate them using annotations. You might use *V* for vocabulary, *Def.* for definition, or some other annotation.

How to Find Ideas to Write About

As you read an extended definition or an article containing brief definitions, jot down any additional characteristics or examples that come to mind. When you respond to the article, you might write about how the definition could be expanded to include these. You might also try the following strategies:

For more on discovering ideas for a response paper, see Chapter 4.

- Think of other terms in the same class that you might write about.
- Try to relate the definitions to your own experience. Where or when have you observed the characteristics described? Your personal experiences might be used in an essay in which you agree with or challenge the writer's definitions.
- If the writer has not already done so, you might use negation to expand the meaning of the term, or you might explore the word's etymology.

Thinking Critically about Definition

Some definitions are more straightforward and factual than others. Standard definitions of terms such as *calendar, automobile,* or *taxes* are not likely to be disputed by most readers. At other times, however, definitions can reflect bias, hide unpleasantness, or fail to include important elements of what is being defined. Use the following questions to think critically about the definitions you read.

1. Are the Writer's Definitions Objective?

Especially in persuasive essays, definitions are sometimes expressed in subjective, emotional language that is intended to influence the reader. For example, a writer who defines a *liberal* as "someone who wants to allow criminals to run free on the streets while sacrificing the rights of innocent victims" reveals a negative bias toward liberals and intends to make the reader dislike them. When reading definitions of a term that is controversial for any reason, ask yourself the following questions:

- Do I agree with the writer's definition of this term?
- Do I think these characteristics apply to all members of this group?
- Is the writer's language meant to inflame my emotions?

2. Are the Writer's Definitions Evasive?

A **euphemism** is a word or phrase that is used in place of an unpleasant or objectionable word. For example, *irregularity* is often used in commercials as a euphemism for *constipation,* and *passed away* is often used instead of *died.* At times, a writer may offer a euphemism as a synonym. For example, in describing a military action in which innocent civilians were killed, a writer may characterize the killings as "collateral damage." Be alert to the use of euphemisms. Like persuasive definitions, they are intended to shape your thinking.

3. Is the Term Defined Completely?

As you evaluate extended definitions, determine whether the author has defined the term completely, covering all aspects or types. For example, can you think of any uses of "dude" or any aspects of its use that Crissey has not included in "Dude, Do You Know What You Just Said?"

DEFINITION COMBINED WITH OTHER PATTERNS

In the following selection, Jessica Ramirez uses definition as well as other patterns to discuss combat footage from Iraq and Afghanistan that is distributed on the Internet.

READING

The Appeal—and Danger—of War Porn
Jessica Ramirez

Jessica Ramirez is a senior reporter for *Newsweek* magazine, where this essay appeared in 2010. As you read, notice how Ramirez uses examples to make her extended definition vivid and real.

The video isn't quite clear. Three Iraqis stand in a field, unaware that a U.S. Apache helicopter is eyeing them from afar. Two of the men are handling what looks like a weapon, but there's no time to check. The Apache pilot gets an order: hit them. The 30mm bullets go clack-clack-clack. "Got [one]," says the pilot. "Good, hit the other   1 one," says a voice on the radio. Clack-clack-clack. No. 2 goes down. The third man tries to hide behind a truck as bullets slam into the vehicle. After a few seconds a figure crawls into the open. "He's wounded," says the pilot. "Hit him [again]," says the voice. Clack-clack-clack. When the dust settles, the third man is dead.

Some 7,000 miles away, Nate J. sat in front of his computer, mesmerized by these images. It was 2006, and Nate, who owns a decal company, got his first taste of what soldiers and scholars call *war porn*. Although he's never been a soldier, Nate loves all things military. But this was better than anything he'd seen on the Military Channel. "I was just like 'Wow,'" he recalls. "'I have to find more.'" 2

That was easy enough. Although the recently released footage of U.S. Apache helicopters gunning down two Reuters journalists appalled many, similar war videos are plentiful on Web sites like GotWarPorn.com and YouTube. Nate, who asked *Newsweek* not to use his last name because he's received death threats, has uploaded more than 800 to his own channel on LiveLeak.com and other sites. 3

When the Afghanistan and Iraq conflicts broke out, the military officially released some of the raw combat footage now on the Internet to build a stronger bond between the home front and the battlefield. Soldiers also took their own videos or pulled them from cameras on military systems like Predator drones. But almost as soon as these images became available, civilians and soldiers alike started splicing the clips together, often adding soundtracks and spreading them across the Web. Today there are thousands of war-porn videos, and they've been viewed millions of times. Like sexual porn, they come in degrees of violence, ranging from soft-core montages of rocket-propelled grenades blowing up buildings to snuff-film-like shots of an insurgent taking a bullet to the head. And even as the U.S. begins its march toward the end of two long conflicts, these compilations continue to attract viewers. With a videogame sensibility, they fetishize — and warp — the most brutal parts of these high-tech wars. 4

Historically, combat images have been captured and disseminated by a handful of professionals, such as the photographers Mathew Brady during the Civil War and Robert Capa during World War II. Now the immediacy of the Internet, coupled with the spread of cheap video technology, allows anyone to document war as they see it. "There's a new order," says James Der Derian, a professor at Brown University's Watson Institute for International Studies. "Unlike the photograph, the moving image creates a feeling that it more accurately depicts what it is representing, whether it does or not." 5

Academics date the origins of war porn to the scandalous images from Abu Ghraib Prison, in which Iraqi prisoners were stacked on top of each other to form naked pyramids, forced to simulate sexual acts, or otherwise abused. The snapshot of Pvt. Lynndie England holding a naked prisoner by a leash became an iconic representation of the war. The acts were born of an aimless power and a pornographic sensibility, argued the French social theorist Jean Baudrillard, who defined this form of "war porn" in a 2004 essay in the French newspaper *Libération*. 6

After Abu Ghraib the floodgates burst, with U.S. soldiers even trading war porn for real porn. Chris Wilson was running a user-generated porn site when he started getting requests for sexual material from soldiers in both war zones. But when paying via credit card proved problematic, Wilson let them swap war footage for access to the site's sexual content. The first images he received were fairly tame. But as the 7

Iraq War took a turn for the worse in late 2004, the photos and footage got bloodier and included shots of headless corpses and body parts like intestines, brains, and what appeared to be limbs. By 2005, Wilson had an estimated 30,000 U.S. military personnel as members. "It was a view of war that had never been seen," he says.

Eventually the Office of the State Attorney in Polk County, Fla., charged Wilson **8** with 300 obscenity-related misdemeanor counts and one felony count. A Pentagon investigation into the war footage on his site led to no charges against him or military members. (The Department of Defense says it is against its policy to show "recognizable photos of wounded or captured enemy." The Marines, Air Force, and Navy haven't prosecuted anyone for such posts; the Army says it has no way to track this.) Wilson did plead no contest to five of the misdemeanor charges; he served no time, but his site was shut down. He believes that decision had more to do with the war porn than the sexual content. "If you're curious, and you're an adult, and you live in a free country, there should be no reason why you can't look at this stuff," he says. "I don't think there's any harm in it."

Critics disagree. The videos, after all, depict attacks only on enemy combatants **9** and civilians — never American troops. (In many ways they're strikingly similar to jihadist propaganda.) Aside from providing a one-sided perspective of conflict, war porn soft-pedals the horrors of battle. "People watching it on their iPhone or on their home computer don't generally do it for the information; they do it because it's entertainment," says P. W. Singer, author of *Wired for War*. "That's the porn part of it. The soldiers use the word because they know there's something wrong with it."

What gets lost in the highlight reels of explosions and bodies is the moral com-   10
plexity of war, says Bryant Paul, an expert on the psychological and sexual effects of media. He points to a video of American soldiers making fun of a dog eating a dead Iraqi. "The behavior may be a coping mechanism for war, because they might have to normalize what is not normal in order to survive," he says. "But the people who watch this stuff can't know that, so they can't understand the entirety of what they're seeing."

Yet these images will perpetuate a particular version of these wars, says Paul. It   11
is a version that does not treat the enemy as human, or life as valuable. It is a version that does not recognize the pain of some of the U.S. soldiers who pull the trigger. And as realistic as these videos might seem, they do not show war for what it actually is: terrifyingly real.

Examining the Reading

1. Why does Wilson believe he was prosecuted?
2. Why does the military release combat videos?
3. What damage can these videos do, according to Ramirez?
4. Explain the meaning of each of the following words as it is used in the reading: *mesmerized* (para. 2), *montages* (4), *fetishize* (4), and *disseminated* (5).

Analyzing the Writer's Technique

1. Is it helpful or unnecessary for Ramirez to include the description of what happens in a war video?
2. Identify and evaluate Ramirez's thesis statement. How clear and specific is it?
3. Who is Ramirez's intended audience? How can you tell?

Visualizing the Reading

What other patterns of development does Ramirez use in the essay? Complete the following chart by listing the pattern and providing an example of how each pattern is used. The first one has been done for you.

Pattern of Development	Example
Narration	Para. 1 Three Iraqis being shot

Thinking Critically about Text and Images

1. What connotation does the phrase "war porn" have?
2. Describe the tone of the essay. What does it reveal about Ramirez's attitude toward the videos?
3. What is "taking a bullet in the head" (para. 4) a euphemism for?
4. What types of sources and information help to support Ramirez's thesis?
5. The photograph that Ramirez mentions and that appears on page 468 has been published around the world, both in print and online. What message did it and similar images from Abu Ghraib send about the U.S. imprisonment system in Iraq and the behavior of the guards there? Given that it was taken by one of Lynndie England's fellow guards, what would you say its purpose was?
6. What is the emotional effect of the photograph? How might its effect be different for Americans, for Iraqis, and for people in other countries?

Reacting to the Reading

1. Discuss any war footage that you have seen in the media. How did it make you feel? What type of footage was it?
2. Write a journal entry exploring how war images affect the people who view them.
3. Write an essay about real war images versus video-game war images. What are the differences? What similarities are there? Does one affect the other? How do they affect viewers?

For more on locating and documenting sources, see Chapters 22 and 23.

Applying Your Skills: Additional Essay Assignments

Write an extended definition essay on one of the following topics, using what you learned about definition in this chapter. Depending on the topic you choose, you may need to conduct library or Internet research.

To Express Your Ideas

Choose a specific audience and write an essay defining and expressing your views on one of the following terms:

1. Parenting
2. Assertiveness
3. Sexual harassment

To Inform Your Reader

4. Write an essay defining a term from a sport, hobby, or form of entertainment. Your audience is a classmate who is unfamiliar with the sport, hobby, or pastime.
5. Write an essay defining the characteristics of the "perfect job" you hope to hold after graduation. Your audience is your instructor.
6. Write an essay defining an important concept in a field of study, perhaps from one of your other courses. Your audience consists of students not enrolled in the course.

To Persuade Your Reader

"Freegans: They Live Off What We Throw Away" (pp. 443–46) addresses the issue of consumer waste and excess. Write an essay defining a term and demonstrating that the problem is either increasing or decreasing in your community. Your audience consists of readers of your local newspaper. Choose a term from the following list:

7. Racism or ethnic stereotyping
8. Sexual discrimination
9. Age discrimination

Cases Using Definition

10. You are a fifth-grade teacher working on a lesson plan entitled "What Is American Democracy?" How will you limit the term *American democracy* to define it for your audience? What characteristics and details will you include?
11. Write a press release for a new menu item as part of your job as public relations manager for a restaurant chain. First choose the new menu item, and then define the item and describe its characteristics using sensory details.

CHAPTER 18

Cause and Effect: Using Reasons and Results to Explain

Assume you are a journalist for your local newspaper reporting on a natural disaster that has occurred in a nearby town. Your immediate task is to write a story to accompany the photograph shown on the opposite page.

Write a paragraph telling your readers why the disaster occurred and what happened as a result of it. For the purpose of this activity, you should make up a plausible account of the event you see in the photograph.

WRITING A CAUSE-AND-EFFECT ESSAY

Your paragraph is an example of cause-and-effect writing. By describing why the disaster happened, you explained *causes.* By explaining what happened as a result of the disaster, you explained *effects.* This chapter will show you how to write strong causal analyses as well as how to incorporate cause and effect into essays using other patterns of development.

What Are Causes and Effects?

A **cause-and-effect essay**, also called a *causal analysis,* analyzes (1) *causes* (why an event or phenomenon happens), (2) *effects* (what happens because of the event or phenomenon), or (3) both causes and effects.

Almost everything you do has a cause and produces an effect. If you skip lunch because you need to study for a test, you feel hungry. If you drop a glass because it is slippery, it breaks. Young children attempting to discover and make sense of the world around them continually ask "Why?" Adults also think about and govern their lives in terms of causes and effects: "What would happen if I turned a paper in late?" or "Why does the wind pick up before a storm?" Many academic disciplines also focus on *why* questions: Psychologists are concerned with *why* people behave as they do; biologists study *why* the human body functions and reacts as it does; historians consider *why* historical events occurred.

Many everyday occasions require you to use causal analyses. If your child is hurt in an accident, the doctor may ask you to describe the accident and its effects on your child. You will also find many occasions to use causal analysis in the writing you do in college and on the job (see the accompanying box for examples).

In the following essay, Jurriaan Kamp examines the effects of diet on behavior.

SCENES FROM COLLEGE AND THE WORKPLACE

- For an essay exam in your *twentieth-century history* course, you are required to discuss the causes of U.S. involvement in the Korean conflict.

- For a *health and nutrition* course, you decide to write a paper on the relationship between diet and heart disease.

- For your job as an *investment analyst*, you need to explain why a certain company is going to be profitable in the next year.

Can Diet Help Stop Depression and Violence?

Jurriaan Kamp

Jurriaan Kamp is the author of *Because People Matter: Building an Economy That Works for Everyone* (2000) and *Small Change: How Fifty Dollars Can Change the World* (2006). He has worked on the staff of the European Parliament; as a freelance newspaper correspondent in India; and as chief economics editor of the *NRC Handelsblad*, a leading Dutch newspaper. In 1994, Kamp and Hélène de Puy, his wife, started the progressive monthly magazine *Ode*. As you read the following essay, published on AlterNet in 2007, highlight the results of each scientific study that Kamp uses to support the cause-and-effect relationship he proposes.

The best way to curb aggression in prisons? Longer jail terms, maybe, or stricter security measures? How about more sports and exercise? Try fish oil. How can children enhance their learning abilities at school? A well-balanced diet and safe, stimulating classrooms are essential, but fish oil can provide an important extra boost. Is there a simple, natural way to improve mood and ward off depression? Yoga and meditation are great, but—you guessed it—fish oil can also help do the trick. A diet rich in vitamins, minerals, and fatty acids like omega-3 is the basis for physical well-being. Everybody knows that. But research increasingly suggests that these same ingredients are crucial to psychological health too. And that's a fact a lot of people seem to find hard to swallow.

The relationship between nutrition and aggression is a case in point. In 2002, Bernard Gesch, a physiologist at Oxford University, investigated the effects of nutritional supplements on inmates in British prisons. Working with 231 detainees for four months, Gesch gave half the group of men, ages eighteen to twenty-one, multivitamin, mineral, and fatty-acid supplements with meals. The other half received placebos. During the study, Gesch observed that minor infractions of prison rules fell by 26 percent among men given the supplements, while rule-breaking behavior in the placebo group barely budged. The research showed more dramatic results for aggressive behavior. Incidents of violence among the group taking supplements dropped 37 percent, while the behavior of the other prisoners did not change.

Gesch's findings were recently replicated in the Netherlands, where researchers at Radboud University in Nijmegen conducted a similar study for the Dutch National Agency of Correctional Institutions. Of the 221 inmates, ages eighteen to twenty-five, who participated in the Dutch study, 116 were given daily supplements containing vitamins, minerals, and omega-3 for one to three months. The other 105 received placebos. Reports of violence and aggression declined by 34 percent among the group given supplements; at the same time, such reports among the placebo group rose 13 percent.

Gesch is quick to emphasize that nutritional supplements are not magic bullets against aggression, and that these studies are just "promising evidence" of the link between nutrition and behavior. "It is not suggested that nutrition is the only explanation of antisocial behavior," he says, "only that it might form a significant part." But Gesch is just as quick to emphasize that there is no down side to better nutrition, and in prisons in particular, the cost of an improved diet would be a fraction of the cost of other ways of addressing the problem of violence among inmates. Still, the menu in

British prisons hasn't changed in the five years since Gesch published his results, even though the former chief inspector of prisons in the United Kingdom, Lord Ramsbotham, told the British newspaper the *Guardian* last year that he is now "absolutely convinced that there is a direct link between diet and antisocial behavior, both that bad diet causes bad behavior and that good diet prevents it."

Yet the effect of nutrition on psychological health and behavior is still controversial, 5 at least in part because it is so hard to study. Our moods, emotions, and actions are influenced by so many factors: everything from our genes to our communities to our personal relationships. How can the role of diet be isolated among all these competing influences? That's exactly why Gesch conducted his study in prisons. In a prison, there are far fewer variables, since all detainees have the same routine. Do the results of the inmate trials reach beyond the prison walls? Gesch thinks so: "If it works in prisons, it should work in the community and the society at large. If it works in the United Kingdom and in the Netherlands, it should work in the rest of the world."

Another place improved nutrition seems to be working is in the city of Durham in 6 northeastern England. There, Alex Richardson, a physiologist at Oxford University, conducted a study at twelve local primary schools. The research examined 117 children ages five to twelve, all of whom were of average ability but were underachieving. In-structors suspected dyspraxia, a condition that interferes with coordination and motor skills and is thought to affect at least 5 percent of British children. Possible signs of dyspraxia *may* include having trouble tying shoelaces or maintaining balance. The condition frequently overlaps with dyslexia and attention deficit hyperactive disorder (ADHD), and is part of a range of conditions that include autistic-spectrum disorders.

Half the group of children in Richardson's study was given an omega-3 supplement 7 for three months; the other half received an olive oil placebo. The results: Children given the omega-3 supplements did substantially better at school than those in the control group. When it came to spelling, for example, the omega-3 group performed twice as well as expected, whereas the control group continued to fall behind.

Richardson came to the study of nutrition through neurology. Her interest was sparked 8 by the rapid rise of conditions like ADHD, autism, dyslexia, and dyspraxia. The incidence of these disorders has increased fourfold in the past fifteen to twenty years. "These disor-ders overlap considerably," she says, "but a real solution is rarely offered. A dyslexic child is assigned a special teacher. A kid with dyspraxia is sent to a physical therapist. One with ADHD is prescribed Ritalin. And you've got to learn to live with autism." But as Richardson writes in *They Are What You Feed Them*: "There is always something that can be done. Don't ever believe it if anyone tells you otherwise." One of the things that can be done, according to Richardson, is to boost your child's intake of omega-3.

Of course, omega-3 is not the only answer to ADHD, autism, dyslexia, dyspraxia, or 9 other psychological or behavioral disorders, which also include Alzheimer's disease. Studies like Richardson's suggest, however, that it may play an important role in stimu-lating the brain, keeping it healthy, and helping it ward off debilitating conditions.

And it looks like we need all the help we can get. Behavioral dysfunctions like ADHD 10 are currently the fastest-growing type of disorder worldwide. Twenty years ago, no one had even heard of ADHD. Today, everyone knows a kid who is taking Ritalin. The World Health Organization (WHO) estimates that the number of people with psychological disorders will double by 2020—and that around that time, depression will surpass heart and vascular disease as the No. 1 most preventable cause of death. The WHO adds that psychological disorders account for four of the ten most common causes of disability and that a quarter of the general population will be affected by them at some point in their lives.

So what's a consumer to do? Eat fish. Working with the U.S. National Institutes of   11
Health (NIH), American physician and psychiatrist Joseph Hibbeln compared data on fish consumption with figures on depression and murder in a large number of countries around the world. Fish are a rich and ready source of omega-3. In countries in which fish consumption is low, Hibbeln found that the likelihood of suffering from depression was up to fifty times greater than in countries where it is high.

Some 6.5 percent of New Zealanders suffer from severe depression; these citizens   12
also eat very little fish. In Japan, where fish consumption is high, 0.1 percent of the population suffers from depression. Manic depression (bipolar disorder) is rare in Iceland, which has the highest per capita fish consumption in the world, but is quite common in Brazil and Germany, where people don't eat as much fish. Hibbeln also found that, on average, the risk of being murdered is thirty times greater in countries where fish consumption is low compared to countries where it is high.

Cultural and other factors certainly influence these statistics, but the comparisons   13
are nevertheless illustrative. Overall, in subsequent trials, Hibbeln found that depressive and aggressive feelings diminished by about 50 percent after taking fish-oil capsules for two to four weeks. Based on this and other research, the WHO concluded in a report last year: "Certain dietary choices, including fish consumption, balanced intake of micronutrients, and a good nutritional status overall, also have been associated with reduced rates of violent behavior."

It almost sounds too good to be true, but research is beginning to confirm that vitamins,   14
minerals, and fatty acids can reduce aggression and improve psychological well-being. That could be a simple recipe for a more peaceful world.

Characteristics of Cause-and-Effect Essays

As you can see from Kamp's essay on the relation between diet and behavior, a causal analysis explains causes or effects or both. In addition, a cause-and-effect essay includes a thesis, follows a logical organizational plan, develops each cause or effect fully, and may recognize or dispel readers' assumptions about the topic.

Causal Analysis May Focus on Causes, Effects, or Both

In deciding whether to consider causes, effects, or both, it is important to distinguish the causes from the effects. Some are relatively easy to identify.

Cause	*Effect*
You get a flat tire. ———————⟶	You are late for work.
You forget to mail a loan payment. ———⟶	You receive a past-due notice.

In complex situations, however, the causes and effects are less clear, and causes may not always be clearly separable from effects. For example, some people have an obsession with dieting (*effect*) because they have a poor body image (*cause*). Yet an obsession with dieting (*cause*) can lead to a poor body image (*effect*).

To identify causes and effects, think of causes as the *reasons that something happened* and effects as the *results of the thing that happened.*

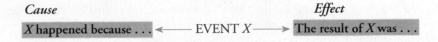

Cause

X happened because . . . ⟵ EVENT X ⟶ The result of X was . . .

Effect

Exercise 18.1

Working either alone or with a classmate, list one or more possible causes for each of the following events or phenomena.

1. You observe a peacock strutting down a city street.
2. You are notified by the airline that the flight you had planned to take tonight has been canceled.
3. Your phone frequently rings once and then stops ringing.
4. Your town decides to fund a new public park.
5. Your best friend keeps saying, "I'm too busy to get together with you."

Exercise 18.2

Working either alone or with a classmate, list one or more possible effects for each of the following events.

1. You leave your backpack containing your wallet on the bus.
2. You decide to change your major.
3. Your spouse is offered a job in a city five hundred miles away from where you live now.
4. You volunteer as a Big Brother or Big Sister.
5. A close relative becomes very ill.

Multiple causes and effects. Causal analysis can be complex when it deals with an event or phenomenon that has multiple causes, effects, or both.

1. Several causes may produce a single effect. For example, you probably chose the college you attend (*one effect*) for a number of reasons (*multiple causes*).

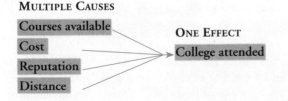

MULTIPLE CAUSES

Courses available

Cost

Reputation

Distance

ONE EFFECT

College attended

2. One cause may have several effects. For instance, your decision to quit your part-time job (*one cause*) will have several results (*multiple effects*).

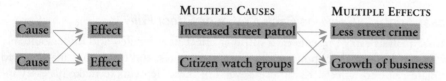

3. Related events or phenomena may have both multiple causes and multiple effects. For instance, in urban areas an increase in the number of police patrolling the street along with the formation of citizen watch groups (*multiple causes*) will result in less street crime and more small businesses (*multiple effects*).

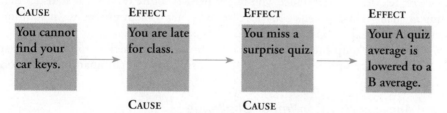

Chains of events. In some cases a series of events forms a chain in which each event is both the effect of what happened before it and the cause of the next event. In other words, a simple event can produce a chain of consequences.

CAUSE	EFFECT	EFFECT	EFFECT
You cannot find your car keys.	You are late for class.	You miss a surprise quiz.	Your A quiz average is lowered to a B average.
	CAUSE	CAUSE	

When you clearly separate causes and effects, you can decide whether to focus on causes, effects, or both.

Causal Analysis Includes a Clear Thesis Statement

Most cause-and-effect essays have a clear thesis statement that identifies the topic, makes an assertion about that topic, and suggests whether the essay focuses on causes, effects, or both. In "Can Diet Help Stop Depression and Violence?" Kamp makes it clear that his topic is diet and makes an assertion about it: A diet rich in vitamins, minerals, and fatty acids may contribute to psychological health by reducing depression and violence.

The following sample thesis statements show two other ways of approaching an essay about unsportsmanlike conduct. One emphasizes causes, the other emphasizes causes and effects, and both make assertions about the topic.

| CAUSES | The root causes of unsportsmanlike behavior lie in how society regards athletes, elevating them to positions of fame and heroism and thereby making them unaccountable for their behavior. |
| CAUSES AND EFFECTS | Unsportsmanlike behavior has numerous deep-rooted causes, and regardless of its origin, it produces negative effects on fans, other players, and the institutions they represent. |

Causal Analysis Follows a Logical Organization

A cause-and-effect essay is organized logically and systematically. It may present causes or effects in chronological order—the order in which they happened. Alternatively, a most-to-least or least-to-most order may be used to sequence the causes or effects according to their importance. An essay about increased immigration to the United States might begin with the most important causes and progress to lesser ones.

Causal Analysis Explains Each Cause or Effect Fully

A causal analysis essay presents each cause or effect in a detailed and understandable way. Examples, facts, descriptions, comparisons, statistics, and quotations may be used to explain causes or effects. Kamp uses several of these elements to make his essay interesting and understandable. He uses statistics to report the results of various research studies and includes quotations by researchers to emphasize and interpret their findings.

For most cause-and-effect essays, you will need to research your topic to locate evidence that supports your thesis. In an essay about the effects on children of viewing violence on television, for instance, you might need to locate research or statistics that document changes in children's behavior after watching violent programs. In addition to statistical data, expert opinion is often used as evidence.

For example, Kamp includes the expert opinion of physician and psychiatrist Joseph Hibbeln to emphasize the role of fish consumption in eliminating depression (para. 13).

Causal Analysis May Confirm or Challenge Readers' Assumptions

Some cause-and-effect essays affirm or question popular ideas that readers may assume to be true. An essay on the effects of capital punishment might attempt to dispel the notion that it is a deterrent to crime. Similarly, in "Can Diet Help Stop Depression and Violence?" Kamp dispels the notion that longer jail terms or stricter security measures are the best way to control aggressive behavior in prisons. Dealing with the causes or effects that readers assume to be primary is an effective strategy because it creates a sense of completeness—or the impression that nothing has been overlooked and that other viewpoints have been recognized.

Visualizing Cause-and-Effect Essays: Three Graphic Organizers

For more on graphic organizers, see Chapter 3, pp. 59–61.

The graphic organizers in Figures 18.1 through 18.3 show the basic organization of three types of causal-analysis essays. Figure 18.1 shows the organization of an essay that examines either causes *or* effects. Figure 18.2 shows the organization of an essay

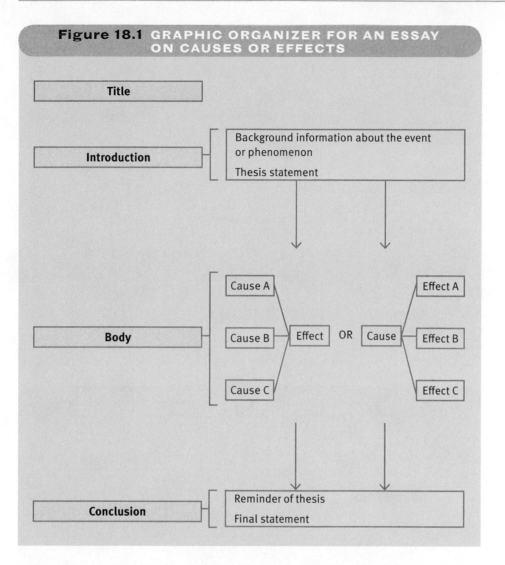

Figure 18.1 GRAPHIC ORGANIZER FOR AN ESSAY ON CAUSES OR EFFECTS

that examines a chain of causes and effects, while Figure 18.3 shows two possible arrangements for an essay that focuses on multiple causes and effects. All three types of causal analyses include an introduction (which identifies the event, provides background information, and states a thesis) as well as a conclusion. Notice in Figures 18.2 and 18.3 that causes are presented before effects. Although this is the typical arrangement, writers sometimes reverse it by discussing effects first and then causes to create a sense of drama or surprise.

When you incorporate causes, effects, or both into an essay that is not primarily a causal analysis, you can adapt one of these organizational plans to suit your purpose.

The essay on pages 483–85 —"Sprawl Is Harmful to Wildlife"—is an example of a causal analysis. Read the essay and then study the graphic organizer for it in Figure 18.4 on page 486.

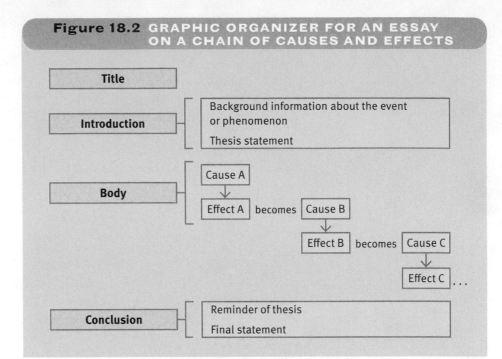

Figure 18.2 GRAPHIC ORGANIZER FOR AN ESSAY ON A CHAIN OF CAUSES AND EFFECTS

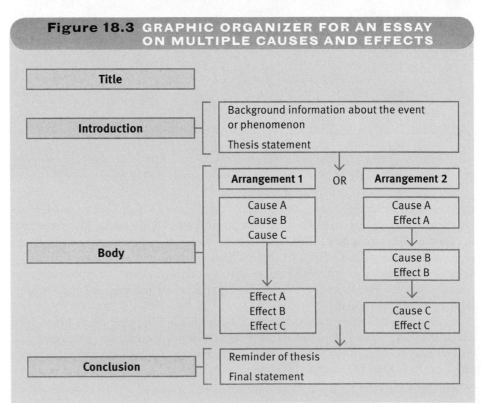

Figure 18.3 GRAPHIC ORGANIZER FOR AN ESSAY ON MULTIPLE CAUSES AND EFFECTS

Sprawl Is Harmful to Wildlife
Jutka Terris

Jutka Terris is the coauthor of *Solving Sprawl: Models of Smart Growth in Communities across America* (2001). She has worked on smart growth and transportation policy for the Natural Resources Defense Council and was previously the national field director for 20/20 Vision, a grassroots environmental and peace advocacy organization. Terris also worked on urban environmental issues during service with AmeriCorps/Neighborhood Green Corps. As you read, highlight the effects that Terris names as resulting from the cause of urban sprawl.

First there were tents, then huts, then farmhouses and fields, then towns and cities. Ever since humans set foot on this continent, permanent human settlements have been built and expanded on landscapes that were previously home to wildlife. While loss of habitat to human settlement is not new, the last few decades have seen a dramatic increase in its pace. Nearly one-sixth of the total base of land developed in our country's long history was claimed for development in just ten years, from 1982 to 1992. But this expansion was not due to an unprecedented population boom in the 1980s. Instead, urban sprawl was rapidly outpacing population growth. From 1960 to 1990, the amount of developed land in all U.S. metropolitan areas more than doubled—while population grew by less than 50 percent. Today, this rapid growth continues. Moreover, some of the fastest growth is occurring far beyond our urban areas, in still-rural communities sixty to seventy miles from metropolitan beltways. Such exurbs already account for sixty million people and one-quarter of the recent population growth of the lower forty-eight states. In the exurbs, developments are often far away from each other, connected only by a system of highways and roads. Such "leapfrog developments" exacerbate the fragmentation of wildlife habitats.

Roads and sprawling neighborhoods are replacing pristine wildlife habitats at an alarming pace, putting the survival and reproduction of plants and animals at risk. In just the last few decades, rapidly growing human settlements have consumed large amounts of land in our country, while wildlife habitats have shrunk, fragmented, or disappeared altogether. If the current land use pattern—expansion of built areas at rates much faster than population growth—continues, sprawl could become *the* problem for U.S. wildlife in the twenty-first century.

There is wildlife in all these fast-growing areas, metropolitan and rural, and species do not fare well when the natural landscapes are paved over and built on. What kind of wildlife is most at risk? Since sprawl is claiming open lands nationwide across a varied landscape, the species affected by it are also varied. One victim of sprawl, the Florida panther, is among the most endangered large mammals in the world. It is now reduced to a single population of an estimated thirty to fifty adults.

In the Southwest, where especially rapid growth is taking place, plant and animal species of the fragile desert ecosystem are at risk. For example, the silent victims of Tucson's rapid expansion into the Sonoran Desert in Arizona include the ancient ironwood, the creosote bush, and the graceful saguaro cactus. Disappearing with them are animal species such as the endangered pygmy owl—a beautiful, hand-sized, brown-and-white flecked raptor—and the Sonoran pronghorn—a graceful creature that looks like an antelope but is, in fact, the sole survivor of a distinct ancient family dating back twenty million years.

In Southern California, another booming area, the coastal sage ecosystem is   5
unraveling. Sprawling development has wiped out over 90 percent of this landscape,
identified by the U.S. Fish and Wildlife Service as "one of the most depleted habitat
types in the United States." What is left is badly fragmented, and as a result, the region
has experienced a dramatic loss of native species of birds and small mammals. Other
species in trouble include the redleg frog and the Pacific pond turtle in Sonoma Valley,
California; the piping plover, a tiny bird living and nesting on the Atlantic coast; the
dusky salamander in New York state's streams; the hawksbill sea turtle in the Gulf of
Mexico; the desert tortoise in the Mojave and Colorado deserts; and the nocturnal lynx,
with its trademark bobbed tail, in parts of the Northwest and New York State.

HABITATS ARE BEING DESTROYED

Before we can talk about change, it is important to understand the many ways that our cur-   6
rent patterns of growth hurt wildlife. Habitat loss is one of the most familiar. This concept is
perhaps easiest to grasp when a complete transformation of the natural landscape occurs.
Almost no on-site wildlife can survive the transition from a meadow to a large new factory,
or to an office complex or a "big-box" retail outlet surrounded by a vast concrete parking
lot. But can wildlife survive when the new use is a residential suburb with some grass and
trees? Or an office campus, where buildings are surrounded by green landscaping?

While a few species can adapt to such human-shaped environments, many can-   7
not. And since our suburbs and office campuses are remarkably similar all around the
country (and are thus often completely oblivious to their natural surroundings), we are
essentially cultivating the few species that do well with irrigated lawns and Norway
maples and have learned to eat from our garbage cans and bird feeders. All this is at
the expense of the many species that depend on more fragile local habitats.

This trend is called generalization of habitat, and results in the survival of hardy   8
species such as pigeons, squirrels, and raccoons. While the overall biomass may not
decline—the generalists take over where more sensitive species are disappearing—the
total number of species plummets. Standing in a suburban backyard, one may still
hear birds singing, but the choir is not nearly as diverse as it was before the subdivisions came and the mature trees were chopped down.

Another serious problem is habitat fragmentation. When roads, houses, and malls   9
break up ecosystems, large populations that were once genetically diverse are broken
up into small groups. With amphibians, for example, even a single road across their
habitat may be enough to create genetically divergent groups. A result may be a lack
of enough genetic variety within each subgroup, resulting in degenerative inbreeding.
This has been a significant factor in the decline of the Florida panther, as fragmentation of wetland and forest habitats has resulted in new generations suffering serious,
sometimes fatal, genetic flaws.

Fragmentation of habitat may also separate a species from its feeding or breed-   10
ing grounds. In some cases, not even the first generation survives. Or, a species may
survive only until the first environmental stress, such as a drought, occurs, when it is
trapped in a small and isolated area. Prior to habitat fragmentation, the thirsty wildlife
could find relief at a nearby river during droughts. After development, that river may
now be on the other side of a five-lane highway or a strip mall, impossible to reach.
The more fragmented, the more vulnerable to any stress an ecosystem is.

FURTHER EFFECTS OF SPRAWL

Habitat loss, generalization, and fragmentation are sprawl's three most damaging impacts on wildlife. But sprawl does more: it also pollutes our rivers, lakes, and air, further threatening species. It is easy to see why Michael Klemens of the Wildlife Conservation Society described sprawl as an "extremely severe problem for wildlife," and why ecologist Joseph McAuliffe calls sprawl "an environmental abomination." 11

However, not all is lost—yet. The United States still has an abundance of natural areas where wildlife thrives. The question is what we can do now to save them from the rising tide of development. Ultimately, purely defensive strategies—setting aside wildlife reserves, attempting to prevent the diminution of endangered species—are insufficient. We need to change the way we plan and manage our growth. 12

Exercise 18.3

Draw a graphic organizer for "Can Diet Help Stop Depression and Violence?" on pages 475–77. Use Figure 18.3, Arrangement 2, as a model, listing various research studies as causes and then outcomes as effects.

To draw detailed graphic organizers using a computer, visit www.bedfordstmartins .com/successfulcollege.

Integrating Cause and Effect into an Essay

Although some of your essays will focus solely on causal analysis, other essays will include cause and effect with other patterns. In an essay comparing two popular magazines that have different journalistic styles, for example, you might explain the effects of each style on readers' attitudes.

Use the following tips to integrate causal analyses into essays that rely on other patterns of development.

1. **Use transitions to announce shifts to a causal explanation.** If your readers do not expect a causal explanation, launching into one without a transition may confuse them. In writing about your college president's decision to expand the Career Planning Center, for example, you might introduce your discussion of causes by writing "Three primary factors were responsible for her decision."
2. **Keep the causal explanation direct and simple.** Since your overall purpose is not to explore causal relationships, an in-depth analysis of causes and effects will distract your readers from your main point. Therefore, focus on the most important causes and effects.
3. **Use causal analysis to emphasize why particular points or ideas are important.** For example, if you are writing an explanation of how to hold a successful yard sale, your readers are more likely to follow your advice to keep the house locked and valuables concealed if you include anecdotes and statistics that demonstrate the effect of not doing so, such as those about thefts during such sales.

To read an essay that integrates causal analysis with several other patterns of development, see "Why Class Matters in Campus Activism'" by Courtney E. Martin on pages 500–02.

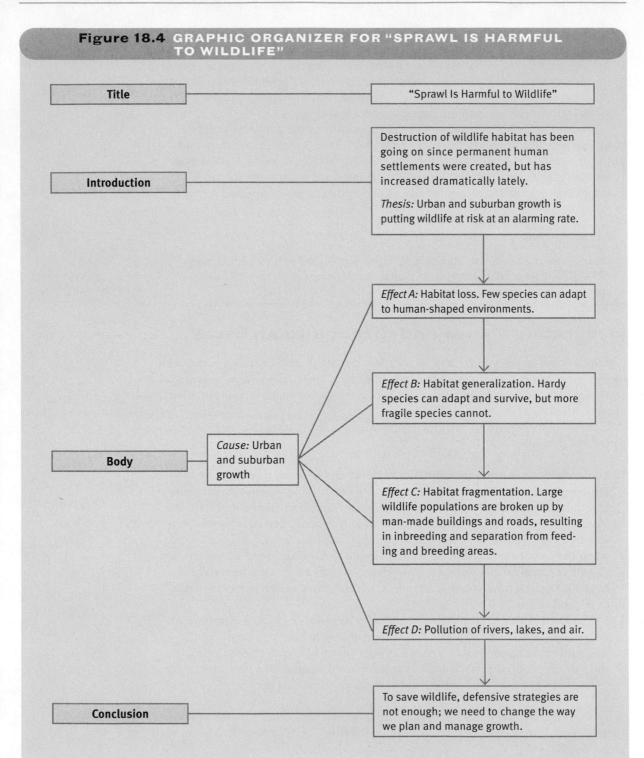

Figure 18.4 GRAPHIC ORGANIZER FOR "SPRAWL IS HARMFUL TO WILDLIFE"

Title — "Sprawl Is Harmful to Wildlife"

Introduction — Destruction of wildlife habitat has been going on since permanent human settlements were created, but has increased dramatically lately.

Thesis: Urban and suburban growth is putting wildlife at risk at an alarming rate.

Effect A: Habitat loss. Few species can adapt to human-shaped environments.

Effect B: Habitat generalization. Hardy species can adapt and survive, but more fragile species cannot.

Body — *Cause:* Urban and suburban growth

Effect C: Habitat fragmentation. Large wildlife populations are broken up by man-made buildings and roads, resulting in inbreeding and separation from feeding and breeding areas.

Effect D: Pollution of rivers, lakes, and air.

Conclusion — To save wildlife, defensive strategies are not enough; we need to change the way we plan and manage growth.

A GUIDED WRITING ASSIGNMENT

The following guide will lead you through the process of writing a cause-and-effect essay. Although you will focus primarily on causal analysis, you will probably need to integrate one or more other patterns of development into your essay. Depending on your learning style, you may work through this assignment in different ways. This Guided Writing Assignment will provide you with alternatives.

The Assignment

Write a cause-and-effect essay on one of the following topics or one that you choose on your own. Your essay may consider causes, effects, or both. Keep the length of your essay in mind as you think about this issue. It would be unrealistic, for example, to try to discuss both the causes and the effects of child abuse in a five-page paper. Your audience consists of your classmates or members of the community in which you live.

1. The popularity (or lack of popularity) of a public figure
2. Cheating on college exams
3. Rising college costs
4. A current trend or fad
5. A major change or decision in your life
6. A problem on campus or in the community
7. A major national or international event

As you develop your causal-analysis essay, consider how you can use one or more other patterns of development. For example, you might use narration to help explain the effects of a particular community problem. In an essay about the causes of a current fad, you might compare the fad to one that is obsolete. Or you might classify rising college costs in an essay covering the causes and effects of that phenomenon.

For more on narration, see Chapter 11. For more on comparison and contrast, see Chapter 15. For more on classification, see Chapter 16.

Generating Ideas

When selecting an event or phenomenon to write about, be sure to choose one that you are familiar with or that you can find information about in the library or on the Internet.

Considering Your Purpose, Audience, and Point of View

Once you choose a topic, your next step is to decide on your purpose. A cause-and-effect essay may be expressive, but more often it is informative, persuasive, or both. In an essay about the effects of the death of a close relative, for example, you would express your feelings about the person by showing how the loss affected you. An essay may examine the causes of academic cheating (informative) and propose policies that could help alleviate the problem (persuasive).

For more on purpose, audience, and point of view, see Chapter 5, pp. 106–9.

As you generate ideas, keep your audience in mind as well. For this Guided Writing Assignment, your audience consists of your classmates or members of your community.

If they are unfamiliar with the topic you are writing about or if your topic is complex, consider limiting your essay to primary causes or effects (those that are obvious and easily understood). If your audience is generally familiar with your topic, then you can deal with secondary causes or effects.

The level of technical detail you include should also be determined by your audience. Suppose you are writing to explain the climatic conditions that cause hurricanes and your audience is your classmates. For this audience, you would provide far fewer technical details than you would for an audience of environmental science majors.

The point of view you choose should suit your audience and purpose. Although academic writing usually uses the third person, the first person may be used to relate relevant personal experiences.

Discovering Causes and Effects

For more on prewriting strategies, see Chapter 5, pp. 110–18.

After considering your purpose, audience, and point of view, use the following suggestions to help you discover causes, effects, or both:

Learning Style Options

1. Write your topic in the middle of the page or at the top of your computer screen. Brainstorm all possible causes and effects, writing causes on the left and effects on the right.
2. Replay the event in your mind. Ask yourself, Why did the event happen? and What happened as a result of it? Make notes on the answers.
3. Try asking questions and writing assertions about the problem or phenomenon. Did a chain of events cause the phenomenon? What effects are not obvious?
4. Discuss your topic with a classmate or friend. Ask his or her opinion on the topic's causes, effects, or both.
5. Research your topic in the library or on the Internet. You might begin by entering a keyword about the topic into an Internet search engine. Make notes on possible causes and effects or print out copies of the relevant Web pages you discover.

For more on library and Internet research, see Chapter 22.

6. Ask a friend or classmate to interview you about your topic. Try to explain causes, effects, or both as clearly as possible.

> **Essay in Progress 1**
> For the assignment option you chose on page 487 or on your own, use the preceding suggestions to generate a list of causes, effects, or both for your topic.

Identifying Primary Causes and Effects

Once you have a list of causes or effects (or both), your next task is to sort through them and decide which causes or effects are *primary,* or most important. For example, if your topic is the possible effects of television violence on young viewers, two primary effects might be an increase in aggressive behavior and a willingness to accept violence as normal. Less important, or *secondary,* effects might include learning inappropriate or offensive words. In essays about controversial issues, primary causes or effects may differ depending on the writer.

Use the following questions to help you decide which causes and effects are most important:

Causes

What are the most obvious and immediate causes?

What cause(s), if eliminated, would drastically change the event, problem, or phenomenon?

Effects

What are the obvious effects of the event, problem, or phenomenon?

Which effects have the most serious consequences? For whom?

> **Essay in Progress 2**
> Review the list you prepared in Essay in Progress 1. Separate primary causes and primary effects from secondary ones.

Checking for Hidden Causes, Effects, and Errors in Reasoning

Once you identify primary and secondary causes and effects, examine them to be sure you have not overlooked any causes and effects and have avoided common reasoning errors.

Hidden causes and effects.   Be on the alert for the hidden causes or effects that may underlie a causal relationship. For example, if a child often reports to the nurse's office complaining of a stomachache, a parent may reason that the child has digestive problems. However, a closer study of the behavior may reveal that the stomachaches are the result of stress and anxiety. To avoid overlooking hidden causes or effects, be sure to examine a causal relationship closely. Do not assume the most obvious or simplest explanation is the only one.

Mistaking chronology for causation.   Avoid the *post hoc, ergo propter hoc* ("after this, therefore because of this") fallacy—the assumption that because event *B* followed event *A* in time, *A* caused *B* to occur. For example, suppose you decide against having a cup of coffee one morning and later the same day you score higher than ever before on a political science exam. Although one event followed the other in time, you cannot assume that reducing your coffee intake caused the high grade.

To avoid the *post hoc* fallacy, look for evidence that one event did indeed cause the other. Plausible evidence might include testimony from others who experienced the same sequence of events or documentation proving a causal relationship between the events.

Mistaking correlation for causation.   Just because two events occur at about the same time does not mean they are causally related. For example, suppose sales of snow shovels in a city increased at the same time sales of gloves and mittens increased. The fact that the two events occurred simultaneously does not mean that snow shoveling causes people to buy more mittens and gloves. Most likely, a period of cold, snowy weather caused the increased sales of these items. Again, remember that evidence is needed to verify that the two events are related and that a causal relationship exists.

For more on errors in reasoning, see Chapter 19, pp. 531–32.

Misidentifying causal relationships.   In some situations it is not clear whether one thing causes another or whether the causal relationship actually works the other way around. For example, consider the relationship between failure in school and personal problems. Does failure in school cause personal problems, or do personal problems cause failure in school? In some cases the first possibility may be true, and in others the second possibility. In still other situations a third factor, such as an inappropriate classroom environment, may be the cause of both the failure and the problems. Be sure you have evidence that a causal relationship not only exists but also works in the direction you think it does.

Gathering Evidence

A convincing cause-and-effect essay must give a complete explanation of each primary cause or effect that you include. To explain your causes and effects, you'll probably use one or more other patterns of development. For example, you may need to narrate events, present descriptive details, define important terms, explain processes unfamiliar to the reader, include examples that illustrate a cause or an effect, or make comparisons to explain unfamiliar concepts.

At this point, it is a good idea to do some additional prewriting to gather evidence to support your causes, effects, or both. You may also want to search on the Web or visit your college library to obtain more specific information. Whatever approach you take, try to discover several types of evidence, including facts, expert opinion, personal observation, quotations, and statistics.

Developing Your Thesis

For more on thesis statements, see Chapter 6.

When you are satisfied with your causes and effects and the evidence you have generated to support them, your next step is to develop a working thesis. As noted earlier, the thesis for a causal analysis identifies the topic, makes an assertion about the topic, and tells whether the essay focuses on causes, effects, or both.

Use the following tips to write a clear thesis statement:

1. State the cause-and-effect relationship. Do not leave it to your reader to figure out the causal relationship. In the following example, note that the original thesis is weak and vague, whereas the revision clearly states the causal relationship.

- Breathing paint fumes in a closed environment can be dangerous. *for people* ~~People~~ suffering from asthma and emphysema *because their lungs are especially sensitive to irritants.* ~~are particularly vulnerable.~~

The revised thesis makes the cause-and-effect connection explicit by using the word *because* and by including necessary information about the problem.

2. Avoid overly broad or absolute assertions.

- Drugs are *a major* ~~the root~~ cause of inner-city crime.

The revised thesis acknowledges drugs as one cause of crime but does not claim that drugs are the only cause.

3. Use qualifying words.

- Overemphasizing competitive sports ~~is~~ *may be* harmful to the psychological development of young children.

Changing the verb from *is* to *may be* qualifies the statement, allowing room for doubt.

4. Avoid an overly assertive or a dogmatic tone.

- *Substantial evidence suggests* ~~There is no question~~ that American youths have changed in response to the culture in which they live.

The phrase *Substantial evidence suggests* creates a less dogmatic tone than *There is no question.*

> **Essay in Progress 3**
> Using the preceding guidelines, study your list of causes, effects, or both; gather evidence; and develop a working thesis for your essay.

Evaluating Your Ideas and Thesis

Start by rereading everything you have written with a critical eye. Highlight causes, effects, and evidence that seem usable; cross out items that are unnecessary or repetitious or that don't support your thesis. If you are working on a computer, highlight useful material in bold type or move it to a separate file. If your evidence is skimpy, do additional research or prewriting to generate more information. Also think about how you can use other patterns of development (such as comparison or illustration) to further support your thesis.

> **Trying Out Your Ideas on Others**
>
> Working in a group of two or three students, discuss your ideas and thesis for this chapter's assignment. Each writer should describe his or her topic (the event, problem, or phenomenon), thesis, causes or effects (or both), and supporting evidence. Then, as a group, evaluate each writer's work and causal analysis, pointing out any errors in reasoning and suggesting additional causes, effects, or evidence.

> **Essay in Progress 4**
> Using the preceding suggestions and your classmates' comments, evaluate your thesis and the evidence you have gathered to support it. Refer to the characteristics of cause-and-effect essays discussed on pages 477–80 to help you with this step.

Organizing and Drafting

*For more on drafting an
essay, see Chapter 7.*

Once you have evaluated your cause-and-effect relationship and thesis and considered the advice of your classmates, you are ready to organize your ideas and draft your essay.

Choosing a Method of Organization

Review Figures 18.1, 18.2, and 18.3 (pp. 481–82) to find the graphic organizer that is closest to your essay's basic structure. Then choose a method of organization that will help you present your ideas effectively. Chronological order works well when there is a clear sequence of events. In explaining why an entrepreneur was successful in opening a small business, for example, you might trace the causes in the order they occurred. However, if a particular event was crucial to the entrepreneur's success (such as the decision to advertise on a local television station), you might decide to save that cause for last and lead up to it to create suspense. In this case, the causes would be arranged from least to most important. Use a word-processing program to experiment with different methods of organizing your ideas.

Drafting the Cause-and-Effect Essay

After deciding how to organize the essay, your next step is to write a first draft. Use the following guidelines to draft your essay:

*For more on transitions,
see Chapter 7, pp. 150–52.*

1. **Provide well-developed explanations.** Be sure that you provide sufficient evidence that the causal relationship exists. Choose a variety of types of evidence (examples, statistics, expert opinion, and so on), and try to develop each cause or effect into a detailed paragraph with a clear topic sentence.
2. **Use strong transitions.** Use a transition each time you move from an explanation of one cause or effect to an explanation of another. When you move from discussing causes to discussing effects (or vice versa) or when you shift to a different pattern of development, use strong transitional sentences to alert your reader to the shift. Transitional words and phrases that are useful in cause-and-effect essays include *in addition, furthermore, more important,* and *finally.*
3. **Avoid overstating causal relationships.** Words and phrases such as *it is obvious, without doubt, always,* and *never* suggest that a causal relationship is beyond question and without exception. Instead, use words and phrases that qualify, such as *it is possible, it is likely,* and *most likely.*

*For more on writing effective
paragraphs, see Chapter 8. For
more on writing introductions
and conclusions, see Chapter 7,
pp. 153–57.*

4. **Write an effective introduction.** Your introduction should identify the topic and causal relationship as well as draw your reader into the essay.
5. **Write a satisfying conclusion.** Your conclusion may remind readers of your thesis and should draw your essay to a satisfying close.

> ### Essay in Progress 5
> Draft your cause-and-effect essay, using an appropriate method of organization and the preceding guidelines for drafting.

Analyzing and Revising

As you review your draft, concentrate on how you organize and present your ideas, not on grammar, punctuation, or mechanics. Use one or more of the following suggestions to analyze your draft:

1. Reread your essay aloud or ask a friend to do so as you listen. You may "hear" sections that are unclear or that require more evidence.
2. Draw a graphic organizer or update the one you drew earlier, using Figure 18.1, 18.2, or 18.3 as a model. Then study the visual organization of your ideas. Do they proceed logically? Do you see a way to organize your ideas more effectively for your readers? As an alternative, outline your essay or update an outline you made earlier to analyze your essay's structure.

Learning Style Options

Regardless of the technique you use, look for unsupported assumptions, errors in reasoning, and primary or secondary causes or effects you may have overlooked.

Use Figure 18.5 to guide your analysis of the strengths and weaknesses of your draft. You might also ask a classmate to read your paper and then summarize the primary causes, effects, or both that your paper discusses. If he or she misses or misinterprets any causes or effects, focus your revision on strengthening your explanation of the material that confused your reader. Also ask your classmate to use Figure 18.5 to react to and critique your essay. Your reviewer should consider each question listed in the flowchart and, for each "No" response, try to explain his or her answer.

For more on the benefits of peer review, see Chapter 9, pp. 188–91.

> **Essay in Progress 6**
> Revise your draft using Figure 18.5 and any comments you received from peer reviewers.

Editing and Proofreading

The final step is to check your revised essay for errors in grammar, spelling, punctuation, and mechanics. Be sure to check your error log for the types of errors you commonly make.

For more on keeping an error log, see Chapter 10, pp. 221–22.

As you edit and proofread your causal-analysis essay, watch out for two types of errors commonly found in this type of writing—wordy sentences and mixed constructions.

1. **Revise wordy sentences.** When explaining causal relationships, writers often use complex and compound-complex sentences. These sentences can sometimes become wordy and confusing. Look for ways to eliminate empty phrases and simplify your wording.

   - ~~As you are already well aware,~~ *Certain types of computer* viruses ~~of certain types in a computer file~~ often create errors that you cannot explain ~~in documents~~ and may eventually result in lost data.

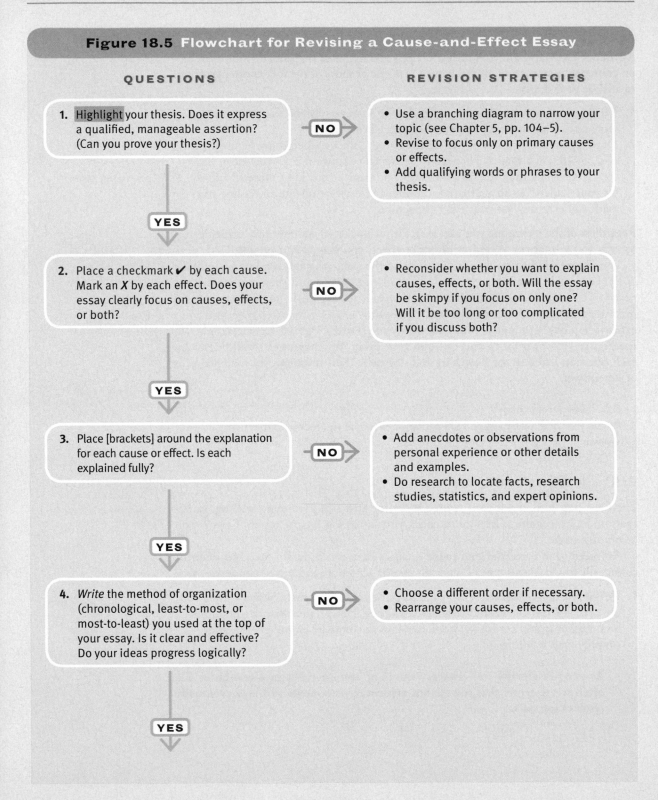

Figure 18.5 Flowchart for Revising a Cause-and-Effect Essay

QUESTIONS

REVISION STRATEGIES

1. Highlight your thesis. Does it express a qualified, manageable assertion? (Can you prove your thesis?)

NO

- Use a branching diagram to narrow your topic (see Chapter 5, pp. 104–5).
- Revise to focus only on primary causes or effects.
- Add qualifying words or phrases to your thesis.

YES

2. Place a checkmark ✔ by each cause. Mark an X by each effect. Does your essay clearly focus on causes, effects, or both?

NO

- Reconsider whether you want to explain causes, effects, or both. Will the essay be skimpy if you focus on only one? Will it be too long or too complicated if you discuss both?

YES

3. Place [brackets] around the explanation for each cause or effect. Is each explained fully?

NO

- Add anecdotes or observations from personal experience or other details and examples.
- Do research to locate facts, research studies, statistics, and expert opinions.

YES

4. *Write* the method of organization (chronological, least-to-most, or most-to-least) you used at the top of your essay. Is it clear and effective? Do your ideas progress logically?

NO

- Choose a different order if necessary.
- Rearrange your causes, effects, or both.

YES

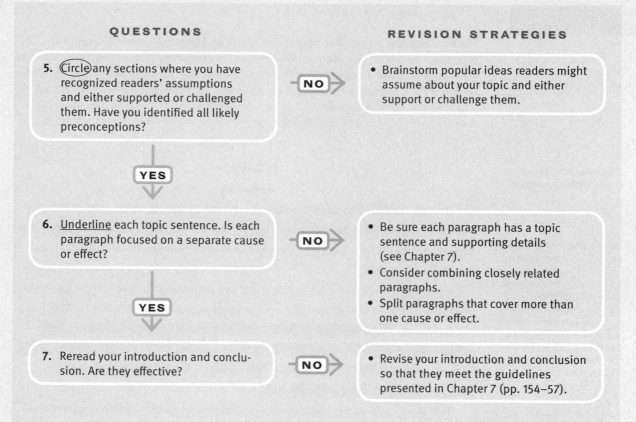

QUESTIONS

REVISION STRATEGIES

5. Circle any sections where you have recognized readers' assumptions and either supported or challenged them. Have you identified all likely preconceptions?

NO →

- Brainstorm popular ideas readers might assume about your topic and either support or challenge them.

YES ↓

6. Underline each topic sentence. Is each paragraph focused on a separate cause or effect?

NO →

- Be sure each paragraph has a topic sentence and supporting details (see Chapter 7).
- Consider combining closely related paragraphs.
- Split paragraphs that cover more than one cause or effect.

YES ↓

7. Reread your introduction and conclusion. Are they effective?

NO →

- Revise your introduction and conclusion so that they meet the guidelines presented in Chapter 7 (pp. 154–57).

2. **Revise to eliminate mixed constructions.** A mixed construction happens when a writer connects phrases, clauses, or both that do not fit together in a sentence.

> *Although*   *Samantha*
> ■ ~~Samantha,~~ although she was late for work, ~~but~~ was not reprimanded by her boss.

Using both *although* and *but* makes this a mixed sentence. To avoid mixed constructions, check words that join your phrases and clauses. Pay attention to prepositions and conjunctions. Also, check to be sure that the subjects of your sentences can perform the actions described by the verbs. If not, revise the sentence to supply the appropriate verb.

> *encourages*   *to*
> ■ The college ~~hopes~~ all students ~~will~~ take a freshman seminar.

Essay in Progress 7

Edit and proofread your essay, paying particular attention to eliminating wordiness and mixed constructions.

READING

Students Write

Harley Tong was a first-year liberal arts major at Niagara County Community College when he wrote this essay in response to an assignment for his writing class. He was asked to write a cause-and-effect essay explaining why and how he took action to correct a frustrating or unpleasant situation or resolve a problem he faced. As you read the essay, notice how Tong carefully presents the causes of his early departure from high school. Highlight the causes he cites and indicate which causes are primary.

An Early Start

Harley Tong

Title: Tong uses a descriptive title to suggest his subject.

For many students, high school is a place to enjoy the company of friends while getting an education. For some, it's a challenge to keep up with coursework while participating in clubs, organizations, and sports. For a few others, though, it seems a waste of time and a struggle to remain interested in schoolwork.

Introduction: Tong begins with general statements about his topic and then moves into his specific personal situation. In his thesis statement, he indicates that he will focus on a chain of causes and effects and gives an overview of the specific causes and effects and the order in which he will present them.

A year ago, I was a sophomore in high school and an honor roll student with an average in the nineties, but all of the courses I took seemed uninteresting. I felt that high school was not the place for me. The combination of the unchallenging coursework, hostile fellow students, mediocre faculty, and unfair school policies led me to make the decision to go directly to college after my sophomore year, a decision that in turn resulted in vocational and extracurricular benefits as well as academic and social ones.

Tong presents cause #1: lack of challenging coursework. Notice that in this paragraph and the next four, he uses a transitional word or phrase in introducing each cause and provides a full explanation of each one.

First of all, the courses I was taking in high school presented no challenge for me. Many of them were at the Regents level rather than at the higher levels like honors or advanced placement. Even though I had been moved ahead in my science and language classes, I was never placed into honors-level classes. I wanted to stay ahead and be challenged by my coursework, but there wasn't much work to do. I became bored because the classes moved so slowly and became repetitive in certain areas.

Cause #2: problems with classmates.

The way I was treated by other students also played an important part in my decision. In high school, I never seemed to fit in with anyone. A lot of students belonged to their own groups of friends. These groups discriminated against anyone who didn't fit in. They often made me feel out of place. Many students verbally assaulted me in the halls and during homeroom. Some students also started fights with me, and as a result, I was suspended frequently.

Cause #3: dissatisfaction with faculty.

In addition, I wanted to leave high school because I felt that many of my teachers and counselors were uninspiring and unsupportive. Many teachers were incapable of doing their jobs or just did them poorly. Most teachers taught by having us copy notes from the overhead projector or chalkboard, or they simply handed us our notes. I received little support from my counselor or any of the other faculty members in my attempt to leave high school early. My counselor thought that I wasn't mature enough to handle the college workload or the atmosphere. My global studies teacher, who had talked to my counselor and learned that I wanted to leave school early, told me how she felt about the idea in front of the entire class. She also told me that our principal would never approve of "such a stupid idea."

School policies were another major factor in my decision to leave high school. The administration's views on students' rights and how they should be interpreted were very unfair. Free speech was almost totally banned, and other basic rights were denied to students. Students were not allowed to voice opinions about teachers and their teaching styles or actions in class. There were no teacher evaluation forms for students to fill out. Policies concerning fighting, harassment, and skipping class could be lightly or heavily enforced depending on whether or not you were a favorite of the teachers. My suspensions resulted from the school's policy regarding fighting: Even though I was attacked and did not do anything to defend myself, I was still punished for being involved. These suspension policies, which were allegedly designed by administrators to protect students, actually prevented students from keeping up with class work and maintaining good grades.

During my sophomore year, I came up with a plan that would allow me to attend the local community college instead of taking my junior and senior years at the high school. I would take equivalent course material at the college and transfer the grades and credits back to the high school. While I took the courses required for high school graduation, I would also be completing requirements for my graduation from college. As the year drew to a close, I arranged for a meeting between the principal and my father. My father gave his permission, and the school finally agreed to my plan.

All of the things that made high school so miserable for me that year finally seemed unimportant because I was on my way to a better education. Over the summer, I held three jobs to earn money for tuition and then started to work for a local construction company, which I still work for. During my first semester, I took the maximum of eighteen credit hours and worked full time to raise money for the spring semester. I also worked at the college radio station and was given my own show for the spring semester. I worked hard over the semester and got good grades as a result.

My experiences since I left high school have been great. I have made many new friends, enjoyed all of my professors, and joined a few clubs. Everyone at college thinks my leaving high school early was an incredible opportunity, and they are all very supportive. This was probably one of the best things I have ever done, and I hope I can keep on being successful not only in school but also in other aspects of life. I have no regrets about leaving high school and hope that what I did will make it easier for students in similar situations to realize that they can live up to their potential.

6

7

8

9

Cause #4: unfair school policies.

Tong begins explaining the primary effect—his decision to leave high school for college—that resulted from the causes he has outlined. In paragraph 8, he details how this effect led to other practical effects.

Conclusion: Tong presents both the positive social and emotional effects of his decision to leave high school for college and the practical effects resulting from that decision. He ends by both dispelling an assumption readers may have had, noting that his decision did *not* cause regret, and expressing his hope that his story will have an inspiring effect on others.

Analyzing the Writer's Technique

1. Describe Tong's audience and purpose.
2. What patterns of development does the writer use to support his thesis and maintain readers' interest?
3. Evaluate the introduction and conclusion.

Thinking Critically about Cause and Effect

1. Describe the tone of Tong's essay. What words and phrases suggest his attitude toward his high school experience?
2. How might Tong's essay differ if he had included the viewpoints of his high school teachers and college professors about his academic achievements?
3. Is Tong objective in evaluating himself in this essay? Why or why not?

Reacting to the Essay

1. How does your high school experience compare with Tong's? Did you experience or observe any similar problems? Were there benefits to your high school experience that were missing from Tong's?
2. Tong mentions several grievances he had with his high school. Evaluate your high school experience. How would you grade your counselors, teachers, and peers? Be sure to support your grades with specific examples.
3. Tong devised an unconventional plan to solve a problem. Write a journal entry describing an unconventional step you either took or considered taking to solve a problem you faced.

READING CAUSE-AND-EFFECT ESSAYS

The following section provides advice for reading causal analyses. Two model essays illustrate the characteristics of causal analysis covered in this chapter and provide opportunities to examine, analyze, and react to the writer's ideas. The second essay uses causal analysis with other patterns of development.

Working with Text: Reading Causal Analyses

For more on reading strategies, see Chapter 3.

Reading cause-and-effect essays requires critical thinking and analysis as well as close attention to detail. The overall questions to keep in mind are these: What is the relationship between the events or phenomena the writer is describing and the proposed causes or effects? Has the writer perceived this relationship accurately and completely?

Use the following suggestions when reading text that deals with causes and effects.

What to Look For, Highlight, and Annotate

1. Identify the author's thesis. Look for evidence that suggests a causal relationship actually exists.
2. Make an effort to distinguish between causes and effects. Mark or highlight causes in one color and effects in another.
3. Annotate causes or effects that are unclear or that are not supported by sufficient evidence.
4. Distinguish between primary and secondary causes or effects, especially in a lengthy or complex essay. Mark primary causes *PC* and secondary causes *SC*.
5. Be alert for key words that signal a causal relationship. A writer may not always use obvious transitional words and phrases. Notice how each of the following examples suggests a cause or effect connection:

CAUSES

One *source* of confusion on the issue of gun control is . . .
A court's decision *is motivated by* . . .

EFFECTS

One *effect* of the Supreme Court decision was . . .
One *result* of a change in favored-nation status may be . . .

6. As you read, fill in a graphic organizer to map a complex causal relationship, sorting causes from effects (see Figures 18.1, 18.2, and 18.3).
7. Establish the sequence of events for an essay that is not organized chronologically. Some authors may discuss effects before presenting causes. Other authors may not mention the key events in a complex series of events in the order they occurred. Use your computer to draw a time line or write a list of the events in chronological order.

For more on discovering ideas for a response paper, see Chapter 4.

How to Find Ideas to Write About

To respond to or write about a cause-and-effect essay, consider the following strategies:

- If the essay discusses the causes of an event, a phenomenon, or a problem, consider writing about the effects or vice versa.
- Think of and write about secondary or other possible causes or effects the writer does not mention.
- For a chain-of-events essay, write about what might have happened if the chain had been broken at some point.
- Write about a cause-and-effect relationship from your own life that is similar to one in the essay.

Thinking Critically about Cause and Effect

Reading and evaluating causal relationships involves close analysis and may require that you do research to verify a writer's assertions. Use the following questions to think critically about the causal analyses you read.

What Is the Writer's Purpose?

Consider how the writer is describing certain causes or effects and how this description advances his or her purpose, such as to persuade readers to accept a particular position on an issue. A graphic description of the physical effects of an experimental drug on laboratory animals, for example, may strengthen a writer's argument against the use of animals in medical research.

Does the Writer Cover All Major Causes or Effects?

Consider whether the writer presents a fair description of all major causes or effects. For example, a writer arguing in favor of using animals for medical research might fail to mention the painful effects of testing on laboratory animals. Conversely, a writer who opposes using animals for medical research might fail to mention that several human diseases are now controllable as a result of tests performed on animals. In either case, the writer does not offer a complete, objective account.

Does the Writer Provide Sufficient Evidence for the Causal Relationship?

Look for whether the writer provides *sufficient* supporting evidence to prove the existence of a causal relationship between the events or phenomena. For example, suppose a writer makes this assertion: "Medical doctors waste the resources of health insurance companies by ordering unnecessary medical tests." For support the writer relies on one example involving a grandparent who was required to undergo twenty-two tests and procedures before being approved for minor outpatient surgery. This anecdote is relevant to the writer's assertion, but one person's experience is not enough to prove a causal relationship. Consider whether the writer might have provided the additional support (such as statistics and expert opinion) or whether adequate support could not be found for the assertion.

CAUSAL-ANALYSIS ESSAY

The following essay by Courtney E. Martin explores why American students seem less concerned than British students with college tuition increases.

READING

Why Class Matters in Campus Activism
Courtney E. Martin

Courtney Martin is a senior correspondent for *American Prospect Online*, a magazine that covers politics, culture, and public policy, where this essay first appeared in 2010. She is the author of *Do It Anyway: The New Generation of Activists* (2010) and *Perfect Girls, Starving Daughters: How the Quest for Perfection Is Harming Young Women* (2008). Her work has also appeared in the *Washington Post, Newsweek,* and the *Christian Science Monitor.* As

you read, highlight the causes for American college students' lack of concern about tuition increases.

As 50,000 students in the United Kingdom took to the streets last week in protest of pending budget cuts for school tuition, it was hard not to wonder: Where is the student movement here in the U.S.?   1

There is one, to be sure. It's fueled, in large part, by the frustration of first-generation college students who are eager to make good on their parents' and grand-parents' efforts to get the next generation to the promised land of higher education. And what a promised land it is — high school graduates are three times more likely to live in poverty than college graduates, and eight times more likely to depend on public-assistance programs.   2

Last March, a national day of college-student demonstrations against tuition hikes and program cuts brought out crowds, sometimes nearly 1,000 strong, on many campuses across the United States. Eighty students took to the streets at the University of California, Berkeley, earlier this month to protest an 8 percent tuition hike. For years there has been a small but strategic group protesting budget cuts in the City University of New York system. The budget gap has led to $2.5 million in cuts at CUNY colleges since 2009. Before long, I'd predict, the movement will also gain momentum among young veterans at community colleges, especially in California where 16,000 vets and their dependents are using their GI Bill benefits.   3

But why are the U.K. crowds almost 500 times as robust as those in the U.S.? Why does the American movement to fight tuition hikes and funding cuts remain so anemic in comparison?   4

In no small part, it's because privileged students at America's colleges and universities generally don't take the issue personally. Those who are politically active tend to set their sights on distant horizons — the poor in India, say, or the oppressed in Afghanistan. Without their privileged-kid allies, first-generation college students, immigrants, and students dependent on financial aid are going to have a hard time creating the kind of buzz that Britain has just produced.   5

Many of us from middle- and upper-income backgrounds have been socialized to believe that it is our duty to make a difference, but undertake such efforts abroad — where the "real" poor people are. We found nonprofits aimed at schooling children all over the globe while rarely acknowledging that our friend from the high school football team can't afford the same kind of opportunities we can. Or we create Third World bicycle programs while ignoring that our lab partner has to travel two hours by bus, as he is unable to get a driver's license as an undocumented immigrant. We were born lucky, so we head to the bars — oblivious to the rising tuition prices and crushing bureaucracy inside the financial aid office.   6

I know from whence I speak. As an undergraduate at Barnard College from 1998 to 2002, I felt a deep sense of commitment to "making a difference." I volunteered in a Head Start program in Harlem, protested the treatment of Amadou Diallo and Mumia Abu Jamal, had internships at the American Civil Liberties Union and the Children's Defense Fund, even studied abroad in South Africa where I taught poetry classes in a township high school. I was basically the poster child for privileged do-gooderism.   7

But I didn't once consider taking action to ease the financial struggles of my peers at school, didn't once seek out a movement in my midst that might tackle the economic disparity in my own dormitory. I regret that.

The absence of a robust, multi-class student movement in this country is a small   8
but profound manifestation of inequality writ large. In fact, the U.S. wealth gap is at its widest since 1928. A typical CEO, even in this economy, is paid more than 350 times that of the average worker. And as British public-health researchers Richard Wilkinson and Kate Pickett write in their recent book, *The Spirit Level: Why Greater Equality Makes Societies Stronger*, it's not just the poor who lose out. "Great inequality is the scourge of modern societies," they write, arguing that in 11 key areas — including educational attainment — an entire society is brought down by inequality like that which America is presently experiencing.

This is not to argue that the U.K. doesn't have its own sizable wealth gap, but British 9
students seem more motivated to act on behalf of economic rights than U.S. students, who have been encouraged from a young age to adopt the "boot strap" mentality. Privileged American college students need to see their self-interest in this movement. They need to recognize that they are inheriting an increasingly unequal society that not only contradicts fundamental American values but also threatens our collective quality of life and sense of domestic security.

Hannah Arendt wrote, "The sad truth is that most evil is done by people who never   10
make up their minds to be good or evil." I would argue that a modicum of evil is also done by those who make up their minds to be good but neglect to tackle the challenges to which they are directly linked. Let's be real: For a privileged American teenager, the Liberian child with the bloated tummy actually rests lighter on the psyche than the nanny's kid. Until we consciously prioritize fighting inequities close to home, we — the lucky, well-educated kids — will be complicit in perpetuating a culture of poverty and a country of unacceptable disparity.

Examining the Reading

1. What economic difference does Martin say that a college degree makes?
2. What kinds of causes do politically active college students tend to focus on?
3. What mentality keeps U.S. students from protesting tuition increases?
4. What kind of mental shift does Martin suggest the United States needs?

Analyzing the Writer's Technique

1. Identify Martin's thesis statement.
2. Why does the author include details about her own college activism? How do they affect your reaction to her analysis?
3. Explain the meaning of each of the following words as it is used in the reading: *strategic* (para. 3), *momentum* (3), *socialized* (6), *disparity* (7), *scourge* (8), and *complicit* (10).

Thinking Critically about Cause and Effect

1. Martin does not address the issue of who most often pays tuition in the United States (parents or students themselves) and how this varies by class. How might this information change the essay?

2. What connotation does the term "do-gooderism" (para. 7) have?
3. Is Martin's statement about "boot strap" mentality (9) fact or opinion? To whom does she seem to be applying it—U.S. students in general? Privileged students? Less privileged ones?
4. What does Martin hope to accomplish by writing this essay?
5. Evaluate the evidence Martin provides to supports her evaluation of American students. What kinds of evidence would further strengthen the essay?

Reacting to the Reading

1. Martin believes that most U.S. college students who are economically privileged are unconcerned about tuition hikes. Do you agree that this is true? Why or why not?
2. If your school raised tuition by 15% how would that affect you personally? How would it affect your friends? Write a journal entry in which you evaluate how it would affect your personal finances and how it might affect a specific friend.
3. What causes, if any, have you become involved in? Have you ever been involved in a movement to protest tuition hikes? If you were to become involved in such a movement, how do you think your message could best be sent? Write an essay explaining your proposed plan.

PATTERNS COMBINED

In the following essay, Gary M. Stern uses cause and effect as well as other patterns to support his assertion about hidden obstacles to Latinos' career advancement in U.S. workplaces.

Hitting the "Granite Wall"
Gary M. Stern

READING

Gary M. Stern is a New York–based freelance author who has written for the *Wall Street Journal*, Reuters, *Investor's Business Daily*, *Vanity Fair*, *Woman's World*, *American Way*, and *USA Weekend*. He served as ghostwriter for *Garden of Dreams*, a 2004 book about the history of Madison Square Garden; is coauthor of *Minority Rules*: *Turn Your Ethnicity into a Competitive Edge* (2006); and has written nonfiction children's books, including a biography of Andre Agassi and a book on Congress. He has profiled Eddie Murphy, Rob Reiner, Spike Lee, and Sissy Spacek. As you read, highlight the causes Stern cites for the "granite wall" Latinos face in the workplace.

Most corporations point to their finely crafted diversity mission statements, diversity councils filled with multicultural staff, and inclusion on lists of "Best Companies for Minorities" as proof of their diversity progress. Yet experts say that few companies succeed at promoting minority employees to high levels of Corporate America. Many accomplish little in diversity except window dressing, promote few Latinos to senior positions, and cause many talented Latinos and blacks to flee corporate careers. Since most employees, consultants, and even publications in search of ads don't want to

1

"burn bridges" and alienate the company endorsing their checks, rarely does anyone criticize a corporation's diversity efforts.

Yet most companies "talk the talk but don't walk the walk. When you peel back the   2 onion, there are few minorities in positions of power. There are hundreds of minorities at the junior level, but they don't advance. Many of these diversity initiatives are marketing campaigns to get consumer dollars," says Kenneth Arroyo Roldan, the CEO of Wesley, Brown, Bartle & Roldan, one of the country's largest minority executive recruiting firms, based in New York. Out of frustration with observing diversity obstacles, Roldan has decided to speak out.

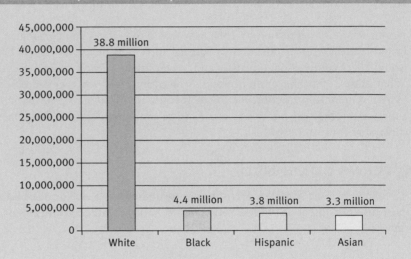

NUMBER OF PEOPLE IN MANAGEMENT POSITIONS BY RACE/ETHNICITY, 2008

Source: U.S. Census Bureau. *The 2011 Statistical Abstract. Census.gov.* U.S. Census Bureau, 2011. Web. 3 June 2011.

Many companies have done an effective job of recruiting and hiring talented minori-   3 ties and adding to their minority suppliers, he acknowledges. But many minority employees in the fifth to seventh year stagnate in their job and become frustrated, watching their white non-Hispanic colleagues advance in the corporation. "Most minorities find the glass ceiling and hit a granite wall," he says. Stuck in their jobs, "many minorities leave the corporation out of frustration and become entrepreneurial," says Roldan.

But Roldan also faults Latinos themselves for not understanding "how the dance is   4 played." Too many Latinos gravitate toward non-revenue-producing specialties such as public relations and ethnic marketing and fail to get on the fast track. "It's not your dad's Chevrolet. Many Hispanics have cultural inhibitions to jumping jobs," he says. Moreover, Latinos tend to network with each other in Hispanic organizations, which leads to "talking with each other" but not advancing their careers, he says.

Companies aren't explicitly discriminating or trying to inhibit Latino advancement.   5 "It's not intentional; it's educational. Most companies don't have the skills to advance talented minorities. They may not have the architecture in place to have certain programs or mentors," Roldan says. Corporations offer sensitivity training and minority internship programs, but until corporations open the executive suites and corporate boards to Latinos and African Americans, real progress won't happen, he says.

A study by Donna María Blancero and Robert G. Del Campo for *Hispanic MBA Maga-* 6
zine affirms Roldan's point that Latinos have been kept out of the corporate power
structure. Though Latinos account for 10 percent of the workforce, they number 4.5
percent of managers. Since serving as a CEO or senior officer is often a prerequisite for
being named to a company's influential board of directors, Hispanics are rarely named
to a board. Only 1.7 percent of board members are Hispanics.

Why do so few talented and educated Latinos advance beyond a certain plateau? 7
Blancero, an associate professor of business administration at Touro University International in Cypress, California, attributes it to a combination of factors including an
inability to identify a mentor. "Mentors only select people they think will be successful
and often that's not a racial or ethnic minority. If you're a Hispanic woman in an organization, how many senior Hispanic women can you find who will mentor you?" she asks
rhetorically. Furthermore, "most Latinos are the first ones in their family with a college
degree. We haven't learned how to play golf at a country club. We have networks that
look like ourselves," she says.

But the corporate culture often discourages Latino advancement. "Corporate culture 8
is [still] dominated by white male America," says Alfonso Martínez, the president of the
Hispanic Association on Corporate Responsibility (HACR), a Washington, D.C.–based
nonprofit that advocates for Hispanic inclusion in Corporate America and has signed
partnership agreements with twenty-seven *Fortune* 500 companies. "The formal and informal networks established by the dominant culture have not been sufficiently flexible.
People who don't fit the dominant culture are seen as different and therefore included at
lesser rates," he adds. What can companies specifically do to create actual change and
promote Latino advancement? Blancero would like to see managers held accountable for
promoting talented minorities and for their ability to create a level playing field. Training
managers to prevent them from excluding people from promotion based on stereotypes
and preconceived notions would also help. Creating a mentoring system that gives Latinos access to people in power that can groom them for future positions is critical.

The few Latinos who manage to surmount the obstacles must do more to change the 9
dominant culture, adds Martínez. He points to Jim Padilla, chief operating officer at Ford
Motor Company, who in 2003 spearheaded a Multicultural Alliance, which brings together ten divisions at Ford to collaborate on multicultural efforts. Suggestions from the
Multicultural Alliance contributed to Ford's naming Latina Kim Casiano as a member of
its board of directors, creating a Multicultural Affairs public affairs officer, and "making
everyone at Ford aware that recruiting and developing minorities is a priority," explains
Blanca Fauble, director of its Multicultural Alliance, based in Dearborn, Michigan.

Some companies are using their board of directors to make a real difference in di- 10
versity, Martínez says. For example, MGM Mirage in 2002 established a board diversity
committee, chaired by Alexis M. Herman, the former U.S. Secretary of Labor and board
member, which has the same status as the compensation and audit committees. This
sends the message that "diversity at MGM Mirage is a critical business priority," notes
Punam Mathur, its senior vice president in charge of Corporate Diversity and Community Affairs, based in Las Vegas, Nevada. Since 53 percent of its forty two thousand
employees at its ten hotel and casinos are minorities, the company is committed to
establishing a level playing field. Though 9.4 percent of its managerial staff is Latino,
the committee is trying to increase that number to reflect its 25 percent Latino staff. Accomplishments of the diversity committee include establishing a $500,000 recruitment/
scholarship at the University of Nevada–Las Vegas Hotel School to attract more minori-

ties to the school (students are 9 percent Latino and 2 percent African American) and provide paid summer internships at MGM Mirage and mentors at the hotel.

For one longtime corporate worker, finding the right mentor and taking risks were keys to his success. Carlos Linares, who was born in Cuba and immigrated to the United States at age four, started as an AT&T account executive, selling long-distance services to small businesses in San Francisco in 1984. Over an eighteen-year career, he made several job changes including a stint in human resources but then, guided by a mentor, became a sales manager for Latin America for AT&T Network Systems in Miami in 1993. He ultimately managed a staff of six thousand people, overseeing sales in the Caribbean and parts of South America.   11

How was Linares able to surmount the hurdles that thwart so many other Latinos? Art Medieros, a senior manager, mentored Linares at Lucent Technologies (a spinoff of AT&T) and "taught me a lot about being an executive and running a large, complex operation," he says. Medieros promoted Linares twice and upon his retirement recommended Linares for regional president, which helped secure the position. As regional president, Linares helped grow Lucent's business in Latin America from $185 million to $1 billion from 1997 through 1999. "I advanced because of my work ethic, results, the fact that I could lead people and work effectively in the corporation across several organizations," says Linares, who is based in Davie, Florida. In 2002, he left Lucent (which slashed two-thirds of its staff) and is now seeking a CEO position. His advice: avoid dead-end staff jobs and get involved in profit-and-loss responsibilities, where producing profits leads to promotions.   12

What will it take for Latinos to gain access to actual power at *Fortune* 500 companies? Roldan replies, "We need to develop future leaders. There's no feeder pool. Hispanics are an increasingly larger group with more buying power, but too often diversity means African Americans." Blancero adds, "There has to be an accountable culture that does not discriminate. Organizations are filled with micro-inequities. Accountable managers must be rewarded."   13

HACR's Martínez encourages Latinos to take control of their own careers, without blaming corporate culture. Hispanics have to rid themselves of feeling victimized and must "gain advanced degrees, find their own individual advocacy voice, and know that with success comes responsibility," he says.   14

Examining the Reading

1. What do corporations do to make it seem as if they are promoting diversity?
2. How does the corporate culture discourage Latino advancement?
3. According to Stern, how can Latinos move forward in the business world?
4. What can companies do to promote the advancement of Latinos?
5. Explain the meaning of each of the following words as it is used in the reading: *stagnate* (para. 3), *entrepreneurial* (3), *prerequisite* (6), *surmount* (9), and *micro-inequities* (13). Refer to your dictionary as needed.

Analyzing the Writer's Technique

1. Identify Stern's thesis statement.
2. What does Stern hope to accomplish by writing this essay?

3. Why does the author include the personal story of Carlos Linares? What causes and effects of Linares's life are relevant to the essay?
4. Evaluate Stern's comparisons of Latinos to African Americans. Why does he include these?
5. Evaluate the evidence that Stern provides to support the reasons he offers for Latinos' lack of advancement. What other kinds of evidence would strengthen the essay?

Visualizing the Reading

Stern identifies numerous causes for the lack of Latino advancement in the corporate workplace. Use the chart below to summarize these reasons. The first one is done for you.

Causes	Reasons
Cause 1	Latinos are allowed to stagnate in their jobs within 5–7 years, and they leave the company.
Cause 2	
Cause 3	
Cause 4	
Cause 5	
Cause 6	
Cause 7	

Reacting to the Reading

1. Discuss the issue of discrimination in the workplace. How widespread is it, and where do you see it?
2. Write a journal entry exploring what factors, other than those addressed by Stern, might contribute to Latinos' "hitting the granite wall."
3. Write an essay exploring the value of a mentor. What opportunities, insights, or advantages does mentorship offer?

Thinking Critically about Text and Images

1. Does Stern offer sufficient explanation and support for each of the causes he identifies? If not, what further information is needed?
2. Does Stern present an objective and fair assessment of the corporate attitude toward Latinos? Justify your answer with evidence from the reading.
3. Stern quotes and refers to several sources that he regards as authorities on the topic. Evaluate the credentials of each source used.
4. The graphic on page 504 shows the number of people in three racial or ethnic groups that held management or professional jobs in 2008. What additional information would you need to determine whether these data indicate that people of Hispanic descent are more or less likely to hold management or professional jobs than members of the other racial or ethnic groups?

> **MAKING CONNECTIONS**
>
> **Racial Discrimination**
>
> Both "Hitting the 'Granite Wall'" (pp. 503–06) and "Right Place, Wrong Face" (pp. 229–30) deal with the effects of racial discrimination.
>
> **Analyzing the Readings**
>
> 1. While both authors address racial discrimination, they use two very different approaches (one describes many incidents; the other focuses on a single incident). They also use two different points of view. Explain the advantages and disadvantages of each approach and point of view. To what type(s) of audience does each appeal?
> 2. Write a journal entry exploring whether you feel the incidents of discrimination in these two essays are typical and representative of racial discrimination in U.S. society.
>
> **Essay Idea**
>
> Write an essay in which you describe the effects of discrimination on a particular person or group with which you are familiar. Define what discrimination the group faces and propose solutions. (You need not limit yourself to racial discrimination; you might discuss age, sex, weight, or workplace discrimination, for example.)

Applying Your Skills: Additional Essay Assignments

For more on locating and documenting sources, see Chapters. 22 and 23.

Write a cause-and-effect essay on one of the following topics, using what you learned about causal analysis in this chapter. Depending on the topic you choose, you may need to conduct library or Internet research.

To Express Your Ideas

1. Write an essay explaining the causes of a "bad day" you recently experienced.
2. Suppose you or a friend or a relative won a large cash prize in a national contest. Write an essay about the effects of winning the prize.

To Inform Your Reader

3. Young children frequently ask the question *why*. Choose a *why* question you have been asked by a child or think of a *why* question you have always wondered about (Examples: Why is the sky blue? Why are sunsets red? Why do parrots learn to talk?). Write an essay answering your question. Your audience is young children.
4. Write an essay explaining how you coped with a stressful situation.
5. Write a memo to your supervisor at work explaining the causes and effects of requiring employees to work overtime.

To Persuade Your Reader

6. Write a letter to the dean of academic affairs about a problem at your school. Discuss causes, effects, or both and propose a solution to the problem.
7. Write a letter to the editor of your local newspaper explaining the possible effects of a proposed change in your community and urging citizens to take action for or against it.
8. Write a letter to the sports editor of your city's newspaper. You are a fan of a professional sports team, and you just learned that the team was sold to new owners who may move the team to a different city. In your letter, explain the effects on the city and the fans if the team moves away.

Cases Using Cause and Effect

9. Your psychology professor invites you to participate in a panel discussion on the psychology of humor. You are required to research this question: What makes a joke funny? Conduct research on the topic, and write a paper summarizing your findings for the panel discussion.
10. A controversy has arisen concerning the use of campus email. Students use the college computer system to send personal email as well as to complete course-related tasks, and some students have complained that campus email is being used to post messages on social networking sites that defame other students' character. In a letter to the student newspaper, either defend the students' right to use campus email to post such messages or call for a policy that limits such use. Be sure to give reasons in support of your position.

Reading and Writing Arguments

CHAPTER 19

Reading Arguments

The photograph on the opposite page was taken on a state university campus in California where students were demonstrating against tuition increases. Although this sign is too small to list their reasons for opposing the increases, the students might say they cannot afford to pay more for tuition, that the state is not offering them more in return for higher costs, and so forth.

Choose another issue that concerns many college students, either on your campus, statewide, or nationally. Write a paragraph that identifies the issue, takes a position on it, and offers reasons that the position should be accepted by others.

The paragraph you have just written is an example of a brief argument. An **argument** makes a claim and offers reasons and evidence in support of the claim. You evaluate arguments at home, work, and school every day. A friend may try to convince you to share an apartment, or your parents may urge you to save more money. Many arguments, including print advertisements and television commercials, require you to analyze visual as well as verbal messages. In your college courses and at work, you often need to judge the claims and weigh the evidence of arguments (see the accompanying box for a few examples).

In this chapter, you will learn how to read, analyze, and evaluate arguments. In Chapter 20, you will learn strategies for writing effective argument essays.

The Basic Parts of an Argument

In everyday conversation, an argument can be a heated exchange of ideas between two people. College roommates might argue over who should clean the sink or who left the door unlocked the previous night. Colleagues in a company might argue over policies or procedures. An effective argument is a logical, well-thought-out presentation of ideas that makes a claim about an issue and supports that claim with evidence. An ineffective argument may be an irrational, emotional release of feelings and frustrations. Many sound arguments, however, combine emotion with logic. A casual conversation can also take the form of a reasoned argument, as in the following sample dialogue.

DAMON: I've been called for jury duty. I don't want to go. They treat jurors so badly!

MARIA: Why? Everybody is supposed to do it.

SCENES FROM COLLEGE AND THE WORKPLACE

- To prepare for a class discussion in a *sociology* course, you are asked to read and evaluate an essay proposing a solution to the decline of city centers in large urban areas.

- In a *mass communication* class, your instructor assigns three articles that take different positions on the issue of whether journalists should provide graphic coverage of accidents and other human tragedies. You are asked to articulate your own opinion on this issue.

- While working as a *purchasing agent* for a carpet manufacturer, you are listening to a sales pitch by a sales representative trying to convince you to purchase a new type of plastic wrapping used for shipping carpets.

DAMON: Have you ever done it? I have. First of all, they force us to serve, whether we want to or not. And then they treat us like criminals. Two years ago I had to sit all day in a hot, crowded room with other jurors while the TV was blaring. I couldn't read, study, or even think! No wonder people will do anything to get out of it.

Damon argues that jurors are treated badly. He offers two reasons to support his claim and uses his personal experiences to support the second reason (that jurors are treated "like criminals"), which also serves as an emotional appeal.

An effective argument must clearly state an *issue*, a *claim*, and *support*. In the preceding exchange between Damon and Maria, for instance, "fairness of jury duty" is the issue, "jury duty is unfair" is the claim, and Damon's two reasons are the support. In many cases an argument also recognizes or argues against opposing viewpoints, in which case it includes a *refutation*. Although this example does not include a refutation, consider how Damon might refute the opposing claim that jury duty gives citizens the privilege of participating in the justice system. Like most types of essays, an argument should end with a *conclusion* that sums up the main points and provides a memorable closing statement or idea.

As you read the following argument essay, note the issue, the writer's claim, and the support she offers. In addition, look for places where the writer recognizes or refutes opposing views.

When Volunteerism Isn't Noble
Lynn Steirer

Lynn Steirer was a student at Northampton County Area Community College when she wrote the following essay, which was published in the *New York Times* in 1997. It appeared on the op-ed page, a forum for discussing current issues that appears opposite the editorial page.

Engraved in stone over the front entrance to my old high school is the statement, "No   1
Man Is Free Who Is Not Master of Himself." No surprise for a school named Liberty.

Some time ago, the Bethlehem school board turned its back on the principle for   2
which my school was named when it began requiring students to perform community service or other volunteer work. Students would have to show that they had done sixty hours of such service, or they would not receive their high school diploma.

That forced me to make a decision. Would I submit to the program even though I   3
thought it was involuntary servitude, or would I stand against it on principle? I chose principle and was denied a diploma.

Bethlehem is not alone in requiring students to do volunteer work to graduate.   4
Other school districts around the country have adopted such policies, and in the state of Maryland, students must do volunteer work to graduate.

Volunteerism is a national preoccupation these days. It all began when retired   5
general Colin Powell, at President Clinton's request, led a three-day gathering in
Philadelphia of political and business leaders and many others. General Powell called
for more people to volunteer. That was a noble thought.

But what President Clinton had in mind goes far beyond volunteering. He called for   6
high schools across the country to make community service mandatory for graduation.
In other words, he wanted to *force* young people to do something that should be, by its
very definition, voluntary.

That would destroy, not elevate, the American spirit of volunteerism. I saw firsthand   7
how many of my classmates treated their required service as a joke, claiming credit for
work they didn't do or exaggerating the time it actually took.

Volunteering has always been important to me. As a Meals on Wheels aide and a   8
Girl Scout, I chose to give hundreds of hours to my community, at my own initiative.

While my family and I fought the school's mandatory service requirement, I contin-   9
ued my volunteering, but I would not submit my hours for credit. Two of my classmates
joined me in this act of civil disobedience. At the same time, with the assistance of the
Institute for Justice, a Washington legal-policy group, we sued the school board.

As graduation neared, a school official pulled me aside and said it was not too late   10
to change my mind. That day, I really thought about giving in. Then he asked the question that settled it for me. "After all," he said, "what is more important, your values or
your diploma?"

I chose to give up my diploma, eventually obtaining a graduate equivalency degree   11
instead. The courts decided against us and, unfortunately, the Supreme Court declined
to hear our case. The school has continued the program.

Volunteering is important. But in a country that values its liberty, we should make   12
sure that student "service" is truly voluntary.

The Issue

An argument is concerned with an **issue**—a controversy, a problem, or an idea about
which people hold different points of view. In "When Volunteerism Isn't Noble," the
issue is mandatory community service for high school graduation.

The Claim

The **claim** is the point the writer tries to prove, usually the writer's view on the issue. Consider, for example, whether you think the death penalty is right or wrong.
You could take one of three stands—or make one of three claims—on this issue:

The death penalty is never right.
The death penalty is always right.
The death penalty is the right choice under certain circumstances.

The claim often appears as part of the thesis statement in an argument essay. In
Steirer's argument about volunteerism, the claim is that forcing students to volunteer

will "destroy, not elevate, the American spirit of volunteerism" (para. 7). In some essays, however, the claim is implied rather than stated directly.

There are three types of claims — *claims of fact, claims of value,* and *claims of policy.* A **claim of fact** can be proved or verified. A writer employing a claim of fact bases the claim on verifiable facts or data, as in the following example:

Global warming has already taken a serious toll on the environment.

A **claim of value** focuses on showing how one thing or idea is better or more desirable than other things or ideas. Issues involving questions of right versus wrong or acceptable versus unacceptable often lead to claims of value. Such claims are subjective opinions or judgments that cannot be proved. In "When Volunteerism Isn't Noble," for instance, Steirer claims that community service should be "truly voluntary" (para. 12). Here is an example of a claim of value:

Doctor-assisted suicide is a violation of the Hippocratic oath and therefore should not be legalized.

A **claim of policy** offers one or more solutions to a problem. Often the verbs *should, must,* or *ought* appear in the statement of the claim. Here is an example of a claim of policy:

The motion picture industry must accept greater responsibility for the consequences of violent films.

Exercise 19.1

Either on your own or with one or two classmates, choose two of the following issues and write two claims for each. Use different types of claims — for example, if one statement is a claim of value, the other should be a claim of policy or a claim of fact.

1. Legalization of drugs
2. Stem cell research
3. Music and the Internet
4. Protection for endangered species
5. Global warming

The Support

The support consists of the ideas and information intended to convince readers that the claim is sound or believable. Three common types of support are *reasons, evidence,* and *emotional appeals.*

Reasons

When writers make claims about issues, they have reasons for doing so. In "When Volunteerism Isn't Noble," for example, Steirer's claim — that community service should not be mandatory for high school graduation — is supported by several reasons,

For more on reasons as support in an argument, see Chapter 20, p. 549.

including her observation that students treat the mandatory community service "as a joke" (para. 7). A **reason**, then, is a general statement that backs up a claim. It explains why the writer's view on an issue is reasonable or correct. However, reasons alone are not sufficient support for an argument. Each reason must be supported by evidence and often by emotional appeals.

Evidence

In an argument, **evidence** usually consists of facts, statistics, and expert opinion. Examples and observations from personal experience can also serve as evidence. The following examples show how different types of evidence may be used to support a claim about the value of reading to children:

CLAIM	Reading aloud to preschool and kindergarten children improves their chances of success in school.
FACTS	First-grade children who were read to as preschoolers learned to read earlier than children who were not read to.
STATISTICS	A 1998 study by Robbins and Ehri demonstrated that reading aloud to children produced a 16 percent improvement in the children's ability to recognize words used in a story.
EXPERT OPINION	Dr. Maria Morealle, a child psychologist, urges parents to read two or three books to their children daily (Pearson 52).
EXAMPLES	Stories about unfamiliar places or activities increase a child's vocabulary. For example, reading a story about a farm to a child who lives in a city apartment will acquaint the child with such new terms as *barn*, *silo*, and *tractor*.
PERSONAL EXPERIENCE	When I read to my three-year-old son, I notice that he points to and tries to repeat words.

In "When Volunteerism Isn't Noble," Steirer offers several examples of how high school students treat mandatory community service "as a joke": they claim credit unfairly and exaggerate their time spent doing volunteer work. The writer also uses her personal experience at Liberty High School to support her claim.

Emotional Appeals

Emotional appeals evoke the needs or values that readers care deeply about. For instance, a writer might appeal to readers' need for safety and security when urging them to install deadbolts on their apartment doors. You would appeal to the value that a sick friend places on your friendship if you urge him to visit a medical clinic by saying, "If you won't go for your own good, then do it for me."

Appealing to needs. People have various **needs**, including physiological needs (food and drink, health, shelter, safety, sex) and psychological needs (a sense of belonging or accomplishment, self-esteem, recognition by others, self-realization). Appeals to needs are used by your friends and family, by people who write letters to the editor, and by personnel directors who write job listings. Advertisements often appeal directly or indirectly to one or more various needs.

Appealing to values. A **value** is a principle or quality that is judged to be important, worthwhile, or desirable, such as freedom, justice, loyalty, friendship, patriotism, duty, and equality. Values are difficult to define because not everyone considers the same principles or qualities important. Even when people agree on the importance of a value, they may not agree about what that value means. For example, although most people value honesty, some would say that white lies intended to protect a person's feelings are dishonest, while others would maintain that white lies are justified. Arguments often appeal to values that the writer assumes most readers will share. Steirer, in her essay on volunteerism, appeals to two widely held values — that it is worthy to stand up for one's own principles (para. 3) and that "No Man Is Free Who Is Not Master of Himself" (para. 1).

Exercise 19.2

As the director of a day-care center, you need to create a budget report for next year. The report will itemize purchases and expenses as well as justify the need for each purchase or expenditure. Choose two of the following items and write a justification (reasons) for their purchase, explaining why each item would be beneficial to the children (evidence).

1. DVD player
2. Tropical fish tank
3. Microwave
4. Read-along books with audio recordings
5. Set of Dr. Seuss books

The Refutation

The **refutation**, also called the *rebuttal*, recognizes and argues against opposing viewpoints. Suppose you want to argue that you deserve a raise at work (your claim). As support for your claim, you will remind your supervisor of the contributions and improvements you have made while you have been employed by the company, your length of employment, your conscientiousness, and your promptness. But you suspect that your supervisor may still turn you down, not because you don't deserve the raise but because other employees might demand a similar raise. By anticipating this potential objection, you can build into your argument the reasons that the objection is not valid. You may have more time invested with the company and more responsibilities than the other employees, for example. In doing so, you would be offering a refutation.

Basically, refutation involves finding a weakness in the opponent's argument, either by casting doubt on the opponent's reasons or by questioning the accuracy, relevancy, and sufficiency of the opponent's evidence.

Sometimes writers are unable to refute an opposing view or may choose not to, perhaps because the opposing view is weak. However, most writers of arguments

For more on refutation, acknowledgment, and accommodation, see Chapter 20, p. 552.

acknowledge or accommodate the opposing viewpoint in some way if they cannot refute it. They **acknowledge** an opposing view by simply stating it. By **accommodating** an opposing view, they note that the view has merit and find a way of addressing it. In an argument opposing hunting, for example, a writer might simply *acknowledge* the view that hunting bans would cause a population explosion among wild animals. The writer might *accommodate* this opposing view by stating that if a population explosion were to occur, the problem could be solved by reintroducing natural predators into the area.

General Strategies for Reading Arguments

To understand the complex relationships among the ideas presented in an argument, you'll need to read it at least two times. Read it once to get an overview of the issue, claim, and support. Then reread it to identify the structure and to evaluate the ideas and the relationships among them.

For more on reading strategies, see Chapter 3.

Because argument essays can be complex, you will find it helpful to annotate and summarize them. You may want to photocopy the essay before you begin reading so that you can mark it up in the various ways suggested in this section. The following strategies, which you should use before and while reading, will help focus your attention on what is important and make the task of writing about what you have read easier.

Before You Read

1. **Think about the title.** The title may suggest the focus of the essay in a direct statement or in a synopsis of the claim. Here are a few examples of titles:

   "In Defense of Voluntary Euthanasia"
   "The Case for Medicalizing Heroin"
   "Voting: Why Not Make It Mandatory?"

   You can tell from the titles that the first essay argues for euthanasia, the second supports the use of heroin for medical purposes, and the third argues for mandatory voting laws.

(**Exercise 19.3**)

For each of the following essay titles, predict the issue and the claim you would expect the author to make.

1. "The Drugs I Take Are None of Your Business"
2. "Watch That Leer and Stifle That Joke at the Water Cooler"
3. "Crazy in the Streets: A Call for Treatment of Street People"
4. "Penalize the Unwed Dad? Fat Chance"
5. "A Former Smoker Applauds New Laws"

2. **Check the author's name and credentials.** If you recognize the author's name, you may have some sense of what to expect or what not to expect in the essay. For example, an essay written by syndicated columnist Dave Barry, known for his humorous articles, would likely make a point through humor or sarcasm, whereas an essay by Al Gore would take an earnest, serious approach. You also want to determine whether the author is qualified to write on the issue at hand. Essays in newspapers, magazines, and academic journals often include a brief review of the author's credentials and experience related to the issue. Books include biographical notes about the author. When an article lacks an author's name, which often happens in newspapers, you need to evaluate the reliability of the publication in which the article appears.

For more on evaluating sources, see Chapter 21, pp. 583–87.

3. **Check the original source of publication.** If the essay does not appear in its original source, use the headnote, footnotes, or citations to determine where the essay was originally published. Some publications have a particular viewpoint. *Ms.* magazine, for instance, has a feminist slant. *Wired* generally favors advances in technology. If you are aware of the viewpoint that a publication advocates, you can sometimes predict the stand an essay will take on a particular issue. The publication's intended audience can also provide clues.

4. **Check the date of publication.** The date of publication provides a context for the essay and helps you evaluate it. The more recent an article is, the more likely it is to reflect current research or debate on an issue. For instance, an essay on the existence of life on other planets written in the 1980s would lack recent scientific findings that might confirm or discredit the supporting evidence. When obtaining information from the World Wide Web, you should be especially careful to check the date the article was posted or last updated.

5. **Preview the essay.** Read the opening paragraph, any headings, the first sentence of one or two paragraphs per page, and the last paragraph. Previewing may also help you determine the author's claim.

6. **Think about the issue before you read.** When you think about the subject of the argument before reading, you may be less influenced by the writer's appeals and more likely to maintain an objective, critical viewpoint. Write the issue at the top of a sheet of paper, in your journal, or in a word-processing document. Then create two columns for reasons and evidence supporting the two opposing positions on the issue, listing as many ideas as you can in each column.

While You Read

1. **Read first for an initial impression.** During your first reading, do not concentrate on specifics. Instead, read to get an overall impression of the argument and to identify the issue and the author's claim. Also try to get a general feel for the essay, the author, and the approach the author takes toward the topic. Do not judge or criticize; focus on what the author has to say.

2. **Read a second time with a pen in hand.** As you reread the essay, mark or highlight the claim, reasons, and key supporting evidence. Write annotations, noting appeals to needs and values. Jot down ideas, questions, or challenges to the writer's argument as they come to mind. Summarize reasons and key supporting evidence

as you encounter them. In an argument, one idea is often linked to the next. Consequently, readers often find it useful and necessary to reread earlier sections before moving ahead.

3. **Underline key terms or unfamiliar words.** Because an argument can depend on defining terms in a specific way, it is especially important to understand how the writer defines key terms and concepts. In arguments, precise definitions are crucial. If the author does not define terms precisely, look up their meanings in a dictionary. Jot down the definitions in the margins.

Quinne Sember was a first-year student at the State University of New York at Buffalo when she wrote the following essay for her writing class.

READING

Title: Sember clearly identifies the issue.

Introduction: Sember thoroughly defines organ donation, using a quotation from a source.

In her thesis statement, Sember makes a claim of fact.

Reason #1: Organ donation is needed to save lives. Statistics from two sources provide evidence.

Sember offers additional background information on determining brain death, again using a quotation from a source.

Organ Donation: A Life-Saving Gift
Quinne Sember

The idea of helping someone less fortunate is not a novel idea in our society. However, when people think about helping someone by giving a part of their body away, they become uncomfortable. According to Donate Life America, a Web site that promotes donation, organ donation is "the process of giving an organ or a part of an organ for the purpose of transplantation into another person" ("Understanding Donation"). In addition to organs (like the heart, liver, and eye), tissue, blood, and corneas can be donated when a person dies. It is also possible to donate parts of organs or entire organs (like a kidney) while living.

Organ, eye, and tissue donation has the potential to enhance or save the lives of many people. Surprisingly, however, most people in this country will never donate. If everyone chose to donate whatever they could during their lifetimes and after their death, a lot of grief for families could be prevented.

The most compelling argument for organ donation comes from statistics. Over 100,000 people need organ transplants right now, and someone is added to the waiting list every ten minutes ("Understanding Donation"). In 2009, a total of 7,048 patients died while waiting for an organ. This number is up from 2000, when it was only 5,000 (Delmonico). If more people were willing to donate their organs after death or even contribute while they were living, these numbers could decrease substantially.

The most common organ donor is someone who has experienced brain death. Brain death is "the death of the brain stem, and the diagnosis of brain death is made by examining the function of nerves that originate in the brain stem" (Kerridge 89). For someone to be considered as a donor after death, he or she must first be declared to be brain dead. Someone who is brain dead appears to be alive. The person continues to breathe with the help of a ventilator, and the body remains warm. Therefore, families often have a difficult time recognizing that the person is dead. The prospect of organ donation can be therapeutic to a family going through a difficult time. It is the one good thing that can come out of an unfortunate situation. The family may feel that by donating organs, their beloved did not die in vain.

Even if the person is not eligible to donate organs to someone else, he or she can donate them to research that may further medical knowledge. In 2007, researchers discovered a link between the Epstein-Barr virus and multiple sclerosis by examining the postmortem brain tissue of a donor who had MS ("Brain Tissue"). This advance in science occurred only because someone's family members decided that they wanted to try to help others with MS, even though their own family member could no longer be helped.

5

Reason #2: Organ donation may lead to advances in medical research. An example from a source. provides evidence.

I have volunteered for four years with Upstate New York Transplant Services, which works to promote organ donation awareness. I have become close to a woman who chose to work with UNYTS because of a personal experience. Her four-year-old daughter was diagnosed with a failing heart and needed a transplant as soon as possible. Every day, the girl's breathing became more labored. Finally, a heart was located. After she had the transplant, however, she began to lose blood and required a large amount of blood. Because of the generosity of a family and countless individual blood donors, this young girl now lives a healthy life. Her family is forever thankful for the gift that she received. They often hold blood drives in her name.

6

Evidence: Sember reports an example of how a life was saved through donation.

Some people dislike the prospect of organ donation, either for themselves or for their loved ones. Usually, these people have misconceptions about it. The Mayo Clinic Web site addresses some of these mistaken ideas in "Organ Donation: Don't Let These Myths Confuse You."

7

Sember acknowledges opposing views but says these are usually based on misconceptions. She introduces the source she will use to refute them.

Many people believe that if they are a registered organ donor, the hospital staff won't work as hard to save their life. This is not true. The doctor who tries to help you is not the same doctor who would be concerned with the transplantation. Your doctor's job is to save your life. In that moment, he cares about nothing else.

8

Sember refutes the opposing view that doctors don't try hard to save lives of organ donors.

Others worry that they won't actually be dead when the death certificate is signed. This is highly unlikely. According to the Mayo Clinic, "people who have agreed to organ donation are given more tests (at no charge to their families) to determine that they're truly dead than are those who haven't agreed to organ donation." These tests would be reassuring to the family, as well.

9

Sember refutes the opposing view that donors may not be dead when death certificates are signed. Note the transitions from one opposing view to another.

Another major concern that comes up is disfiguration of the body. People believe that they won't be able to have an open-casket funeral if they donate their organs. This is untrue. The body is clothed so that no signs of organ donation can be seen. For bone donation, a rod may be inserted in place of the bone. For skin donation, a small sample of skin can be taken from the back of the donor and placed where the donated skin was taken.

10

Sember refutes the opposing view that donation causes body disfigurement.

Finally, many people worry whether their religion accepts organ donation. Courtney S. Campbell addresses this issue in her article "Religion and the Body in Medical Research." She recognizes two key characteristics of organ donation—"altruistic intent" and "therapeutic expectation" (281)—that explain why most religions accept it. Altruistic intent means that the donor is giving an important gift to the recipient without expecting anything in return. Therapeutic expectation means that this gift is expected to "offer a pronounced therapeutic prospect for the recipient" (281). Basically, these concepts simply mean that because the donor is trying to help someone else save his or her life, donation is acceptable in almost any situation.

11

Sember introduces a new source to refute the opposing view that religions do not accept organ donation.

Campbell also identifies the specific beliefs that some major religions hold about organ dona- 12
tion. In Judaism, a great deal of importance is placed on the preservation of the body after death.
Campbell says, however, that "this presumption can be overridden . . . by the requirement of *pik-kuah nefesh*, the saving of human life" (281). Roman Catholicism holds much the same belief. Islam
believes organ donation to be acceptable as well, as long as the remaining parts of the body are
buried. Most Protestant denominations have no objection to organ and tissue donation.

Most people decide not to donate their organs for reasons that are untrue. If everyone do- 13
nated their organs when they died, we would make enormous advances in science as well as save
countless lives. The best way to become an organ donor is to talk to your family. If they know what
you want to happen when you pass away, they are much more likely to carry out your wishes. In
most states, you can also sign the back of your driver's license to indicate that you would like to be
an organ donor. Organ donor cards are available online, and many states have a donor registry that
you can become a part of. Become an organ donor; save a life!

Conclusion: Sember
explains ways to become
an organ donor and urges
readers to do so.

Works Cited

"Brain Tissue Donation Furthers MS Research." *Momentum* 2.3 (2009): n. pag. *MasterFILE Premier.*
    Web. 3 Oct. 2010.

Campbell, Courtney S. "Religion and the Body in Medical Research." *Kennedy Institute of Ethics
    Journal* 8.3 (1998): 275–305. *Project Muse.* Web. 3 Oct. 2010.

Delmonico, Francis L., MD, et al. "Ethical Incentives — Not Payment — for Organ Donation." *New
    England Journal of Medicine* (June 2002): n. pag. *JSTOR.* Web. 3 Oct. 2010.

Kerridge, I. H., et al. "Death, Dying and Donation: Organ Transplantation and the Diagnosis of
    Death." *Journal of Medical Ethics* 28.2 (2002): 89–94. *JSTOR.* Web. 3 Oct. 2010.

"Organ Donation: Don't Let These Myths Confuse You." *Mayo Clinic.* Mayo Foundation for Medical
    Education and Research, 3 Apr. 2010. Web. 3 Oct. 2010.

"Understanding Donation." *Donate Life America.* Donate Life America, 2010. Web. 3 Oct. 2010.

Strategies for Following the Structure of an Argument

In some ways an argument resembles a building. The writer lays a foundation and
then builds on that foundation. Reasons and evidence presented early in the essay
often support ideas introduced later on, as the lower floors in a building support the
higher ones. Once you recognize an argument's plan or overall structure, you are in a
better position to understand it and evaluate its strengths and weaknesses. This section
offers strategies for following the structure of an argument — including identifying key
elements in a graphic organizer and writing a summary — which can help you analyze
and evaluate an essay.

Using a Graphic Organizer

The graphic organizer shown in Figure 19.1 outlines the basic relationships among ideas in an argument essay. However, unlike the graphic organizers in Part 3 of this

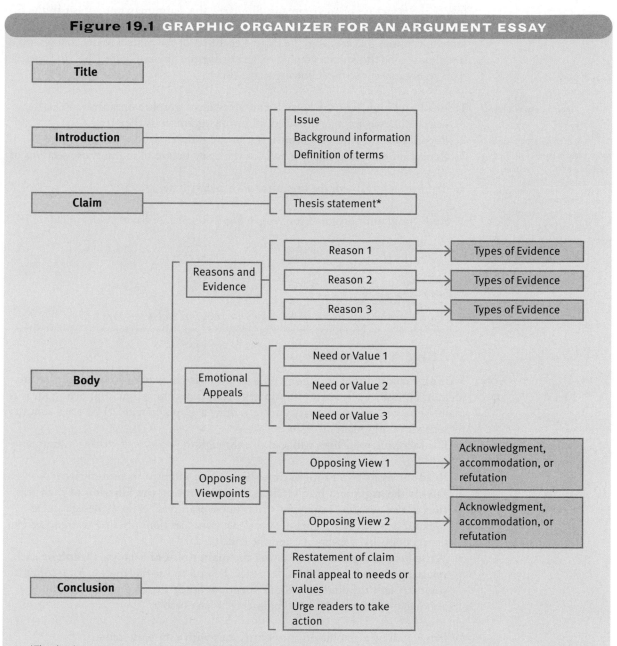

Figure 19.1 GRAPHIC ORGANIZER FOR AN ARGUMENT ESSAY

Title

Introduction — Issue / Background information / Definition of terms

Claim — Thesis statement*

Body
- Reasons and Evidence
  - Reason 1 → Types of Evidence
  - Reason 2 → Types of Evidence
  - Reason 3 → Types of Evidence
- Emotional Appeals
  - Need or Value 1
  - Need or Value 2
  - Need or Value 3
- Opposing Viewpoints
  - Opposing View 1 → Acknowledgment, accommodation, or refutation
  - Opposing View 2 → Acknowledgment, accommodation, or refutation

Conclusion — Restatement of claim / Final appeal to needs or values / Urge readers to take action

*The thesis statement may appear anywhere within the argument.

text, this organizer does not necessarily reflect the order in which the ideas are presented in an argument essay. Instead, Figure 19.1 provides a way for you, as a reader, to organize those ideas. That is, an argument does not necessarily state (or imply) the issue in the first paragraph; however; the issue is the first thing you need to identify to follow the structure of an argument. Similarly, the claim may not appear in the first paragraph (though it is often stated early in the essay), and the evidence may be presented at various places within the essay. Regardless of the order a writer follows, his or her ideas can be shown in a graphic organizer like the one in Figure 19.1. To construct such an organizer, use the following suggestions:

Learning Style Options

See Chapter 22, pp. 611–12, for suggestions on paraphrasing. For more on reading difficult material, see Chapter 3, pp. 57–61.

To draw detailed graphic organizers using a computer, visit www.bedfordstmartins .com/successfulcollege.

1. **Read and highlight the essay before drawing a graphic organizer.** Visual learners, however, may prefer to fill in the organizer as they read.
2. **Record ideas in your own words,** not in the author's words.
3. **Reread difficult or confusing parts of the essay before filling in those sections of the organizer.**
4. **Try working through the organizer with a classmate.**

Study the graphic organizer for "Organ Donation: A Life-Saving Gift" in Figure 19.2.

Exercise 19.4

Draw a graphic organizer for "When Volunteerism Isn't Noble" on page 515.

Writing a Summary

Writing a summary of an argument is another useful way to study the structure of ideas in an essay. A summary eliminates detail; only the major supporting ideas remain. You can write a summary after you draw a graphic organizer or use a summary to uncover an argument's structure.

The following guidelines will lead you through the process of writing a summary:

For more on summarizing, see Chapter 4, pp. 88–89.

1. **Read the essay two or more times before you attempt to summarize it.**
2. **Divide the argument into sections or parts, noting the function of each section in the margin.** You might write "offers examples" or "provides statistical backup," for instance. Label the issue, the claim, sections offering reasons and evidence, opposing viewpoints, and the conclusion.
3. **Write brief marginal notes stating the main point of each paragraph or each related group of paragraphs.** It may be helpful to use one margin for a content summary and the other to indicate function. Study the accompanying sample annotated portion of "When Volunteerism Isn't Noble."

(When you draw a graphic organizer first, start with summary step 4.)

4. **Develop a summary from your notes.** Depending on your learning style, you may prefer to work from parts to whole or from whole to parts. Pragmatic learners often prefer to start by putting together the pieces of the argument (individual paragraphs) to see what they produce, whereas creative learners may prefer to begin with a one-sentence restatement of the argument and then expand it to include the key points.

The following summary of "When Volunteerism Isn't Noble" shows an acceptable level of detail:

SAMPLE SUMMARY

The Bethlehem school board required sixty hours of community service for high school graduation, but the writer refused to submit her community service hours (as a volunteer for Meals on Wheels and as a Girl Scout) and was denied a diploma. Other school districts in other states have similar requirements. In addition, General Powell favored volunteerism, and President Clinton called for a mandatory graduation requirement. Nevertheless, the writer maintains that making volunteerism mandatory destroys it. She cites the following personal observation as evidence: Her classmates treated the requirement as a joke and cheated in reporting their hours. The writer feels strongly that in a free society, community service should be voluntary. She gave up her diploma because of this conviction, though she eventually received a high school equivalency degree. She also sued the school board, but the U.S. Supreme Court refused to consider the case.

Exercise 19.5

Write a summary for "Organ Donation: A Life-Saving Gift" on pages 522–24.

Thinking Critically about Argument

The graphic organizer shown in Figure 19.1 (p. 525) provides you with an easy way to lay out the ideas in an argument essay. Once you are familiar with an essay's content and organization, the next step is to analyze and evaluate the argument, including the writer's claim and support for the claim.

Review the list of reasons and evidence you wrote before reading "Organ Donation: A Life-Saving Gift" (see p. 522), noting the points covered as well as those not covered. Consider the ideas raised in the argument, and write about them in your journal. Explore your overall reaction; raise questions; talk back to the author. Compare your ideas on the issue with those of the author. You will then be ready to analyze the argument more systematically. (For a checklist covering all of these elements, see Table 19.2 on p. 533.)

For more on raising questions about an essay, see Chapter 3, pp. 52–53.

Figure 19.2 GRAPHIC ORGANIZER FOR "ORGAN DONATION"

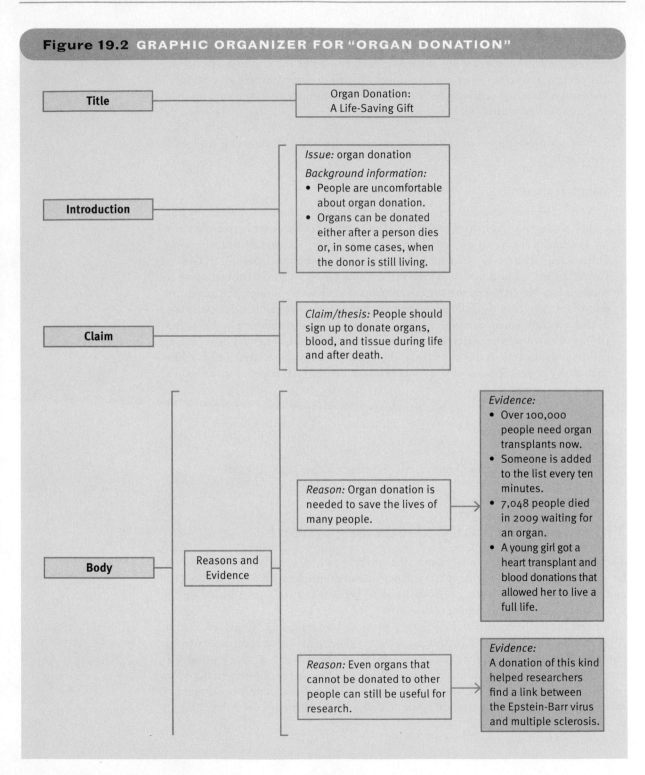

Figure 19.2 *(continued)*

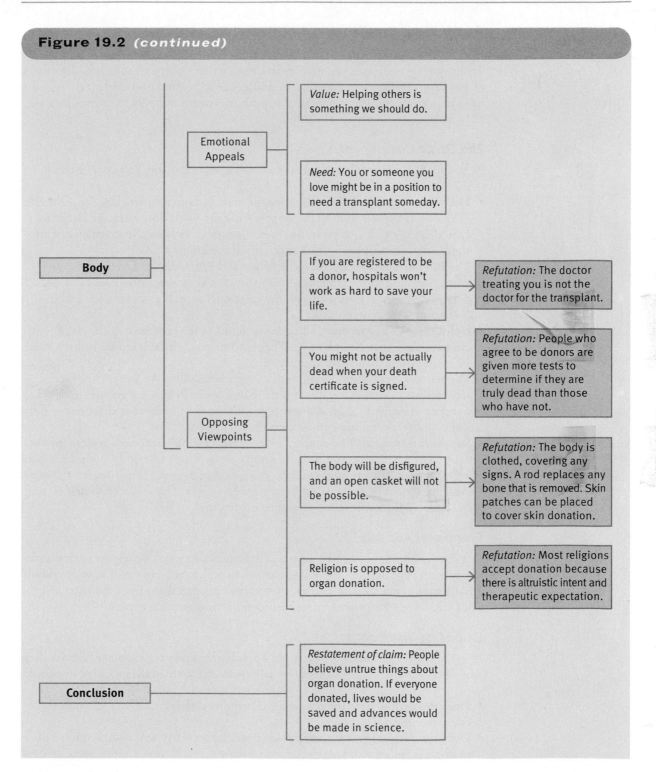

Analyzing the Elements of and Reasoning in an Argument

To analyze an argument, you need to study the writer's purpose, audience, definitions of key terms in the claim, credibility, and support (reasons and evidence). You also need to evaluate his or her emotional appeals, treatment of opposing viewpoints, possibly faulty reasoning, and conclusion.

The Basic Components

As you read an argument, consider the following aspects of any persuasive writing:

- **The writer's purpose** Try to discover the writer's motive for writing. Ask yourself: Why does the writer want to convince me of this? What does he or she stand to gain, if anything? If a writer stands to profit personally from the acceptance of an argument, be especially careful to ask critical questions.
- **The intended audience** Writers often reveal the intended audience by the language they use and the familiarity or formality of their tone. Also look at the reasons and types of evidence offered, the emotional appeals and examples, and the comparisons the writer makes.
- **Definitions of key terms** Underline any terms in the statement of the claim that can have more than one meaning. Then read through the essay to see if these terms are clearly defined and used consistently.
- **The writer's credibility** As you read an argument, judge the writer's knowledge and trustworthiness. Ask yourself if the writer seems to have a thorough understanding of the issue, acknowledges opposing views and addresses them respectfully, and establishes common ground with the reader.

For more on evaluating evidence, see Chapter 6, pp. 130–32.

- **Support: reasons and evidence** Does the writer supply sufficient reasons and evidence that are relevant to the claim and accurate? Facts offered as evidence should be accurate, complete, and taken from reputable sources. In particular, statistical evidence should be current and from reliable sources. The evidence should be typical, and any authorities cited should be experts in their field.

Emotional Appeals

As noted earlier in the chapter, writers of arguments appeal to or engage readers' emotions. Such appeals are a legitimate part of an argument. However, a writer should not attempt to manipulate readers' emotions to distract them from the issue and the evidence. Table 19.1 presents some common unfair emotional appeals.

Opposing Viewpoints

If an argument essay takes into account opposing viewpoints, you must evaluate these viewpoints and the way the writer deals with them. Ask yourself the following questions:

- **Does the author state the opposing viewpoint clearly?** Can you tell from the essay what the opposition says?
- **Does the author present the opposing viewpoint fairly and completely?** That is, does the author recognize the opposing viewpoint and treat it with respect, or does

TABLE 19.1 **Common Unfair Emotional Appeals**	
Emotional Appeal	**Example**
Name-calling: using an emotionally loaded term to create a negative response	"That reporter is an *egotistical bully*."
Ad hominem: attacking the opponent rather than his or her position on the issue	"How could anyone who didn't fight in a war criticize the president's foreign policy?"
False authority: quoting the opinions of celebrities or public figures about topics on which they are not experts	"According to singer Jennifer Hope, entitlement reform is America's most urgent economic problem."
Plain folks: urging readers to accept an idea or take an action because it is suggested by someone who is just like they are	"Vote for me. I'm just a regular guy."
Appeal to pity: arousing sympathy by telling hard-luck or excessively sentimental stories	"Latchkey children come home to an empty house or apartment, a can of soup, and a note on the refrigerator."
Bandwagon: appealing to readers' desire to conform ("Everyone's doing it, so it must be right")	"It must be okay to exceed the speed limit, since so many people speed."

he or she attempt to discredit or demean those holding the opposing view? Does the author present all the major parts of the opposing viewpoint or only those parts that he or she is able to refute?

- **Does the author clearly show why the opposing viewpoint is considered wrong or inappropriate?** Does the author apply sound logic? Are reasons and evidence provided?
- **Does the author acknowledge or accommodate points that cannot be refuted?**

As you read, jot down clues or answers to these questions in the margins of the essay.

Faulty Reasoning

In an argument essay, a writer may inadvertently or deliberately introduce **fallacies**, or errors in reasoning or thinking. Several types of fallacies can weaken an argument; undermine a writer's claim; and call into question the relevancy, believability, or consistency of supporting evidence. Following is a brief review of the most common types of faulty reasoning:

For more on reasoning, see Chapter 20, pp. 550–52.

Circular reasoning. Also called **begging the question**, *circular reasoning* occurs when a writer uses the claim (or part of it) as evidence by simply repeating the claim in different words. The statement "*Cruel* and unusual experimentation on helpless animals is *inhumane*" is an example.

Hasty generalization. A *hasty generalization* occurs when the writer draws a conclusion based on insufficient evidence or isolated examples. If you taste three chocolate cakes and conclude on the basis of that small sample that all chocolate cakes are overly sweet, you would be making a hasty generalization.

Sweeping generalization. When a writer claims that something applies to all situations and instances without exception, the claim is called a *sweeping generalization.* To claim that all computers are easy to use is a sweeping generalization because the writer is probably referring only to the models with which he or she is familiar.

False analogy. When a writer compares two situations that are not sufficiently parallel or similar, the result is a *false analogy.* Just because two items or events are alike in some ways does not mean they are alike in all ways. If you wrote, "A human body needs rest after strenuous work, and a car needs rest after a long trip," you would falsely compare the human body with an automobile engine.

Non sequitur. A *non sequitur*—which means "it does not follow"—occurs when no logical relationship exists between two or more ideas. For example, the comment "Because my sister is financially independent, she will make a good parent" is a non sequitur, as no logical relationship exists between financial independence and good parenting.

Red herring. With a *red herring,* a writer attempts to distract readers from the main issue by raising an irrelevant point. For example, suppose you are arguing that television commercials for alcoholic beverages should be banned. To mention that some parents give sips of alcohol to their children distracts readers from the issue of television commercials.

For more on the post hoc *fallacy, see Chapter 18, pp. 489–90.*

Post hoc fallacy. The *post hoc, ergo propter hoc* ("after this, therefore because of this") fallacy, or *post hoc* fallacy, occurs when a writer assumes that event A caused event B simply because B followed A. For example, the claim "Student enrollment fell dramatically this semester because of the recent appointment of the new college president" is a post hoc fallacy because other factors may have contributed to the decline in enrollment.

Either-or fallacy. An *either-or* fallacy argues that there are only two sides to an issue and that only one of them is correct. For instance, on the issue of legalizing drugs, a writer may argue that all drugs must be *either* legalized *or* banned, ignoring other positions (such as legalizing marijuana use for cancer patients undergoing chemotherapy).

> **Exercise 19.6**
>
> *Locate at least one brief argument essay or article and bring it to class. Working in a group of two or three students, analyze each argument using the preceding guidelines and the checklist in Table 19.2.*

Synthesizing Your Reading

In many academic situations, you will need to read and compare two or more sources on a given topic. This skill, called *synthesis,* involves drawing together two or more sets of ideas to discover similarities and differences and create new ideas and insights.

TABLE 19.2 Checklist for Analyzing an Argument Essay

Element	Questions
1. The issue	• What is in dispute?
2. The claim	• Is the claim stated or implied? • Is it a claim of fact, value, or policy? • Does the author give reasons for making the claim?
3. The support	• What facts, statistics, expert opinions, examples, and personal experiences are presented? • Are appeals made to needs, values, or both?
4. The writer's purpose	• Why does the author want to convince readers to accept the claim? • What if anything does the author stand to gain if the claim is accepted?
5. The intended audience	• Where is the essay published? • To whom do the reasons, evidence, emotional appeals, examples, and comparisons seem targeted?
6. Definitions of key terms	• Are key terms in the claim clearly defined, especially terms that have ambiguous meanings?
7. The writer's credibility	• Is the author qualified, fair, and knowledgeable? • Does the author establish common ground with readers?
8. The strength of the argument: reasons and evidence	• Does the author supply several reasons to back up the claim? • Is the evidence relevant, accurate, current, and typical? • Are the authorities cited reliable experts? • Are fallacies or unfair emotional appeals used?
9. Opposing viewpoints	• Does the author address opposing viewpoints clearly and completely, without using fallacies? • Does the author acknowledge, accommodate, or refute opposing viewpoints with logic and relevant evidence?

You will synthesize sources — including books, articles and essays, textbook materials, and lecture notes — in writing research papers, preparing for class discussions, and studying for tests. Synthesis is especially important when you read two or more argument essays on one issue. Because each author is trying to show that his or her point of view is the correct one, you need to consider all sides of the issue carefully to develop your own position, especially if you intend to write your own argument about the topic. Use the following questions to guide your synthesis of arguments or any other sources:

• On what points do the sources agree?
• On what points do the sources disagree?
• How do the sources differ in viewpoint, approach, purpose, and type of support?
• What did I learn about this topic from the sources?
• What can I conclude about this topic based on what I read?
• With which sources do I agree?
• How can I support my views on this topic?

The pair of essays on multitasking in this chapter provide you with two opportunities to practice your synthesizing skills.

Applying Your Skills: Additional Readings

The following essays take differing views on the issue of multitasking. Use the checklist in Table 19.2 (p. 533) and the strategies for reading arguments presented in this chapter to analyze and evaluate each essay.

How (and Why) to Stop Multitasking
Peter Bregman

Peter Bregman is a leadership consultant and CEO of Bregman Partners, Inc., a global management consulting firm. He is the author of *Point A: A Short Guide to Leading a Big Change* (2007). He blogs for *Harvard Business Review*, where this essay appeared in 2010. As you read, hightlight Bregman's claim and the reasons he gives to support it.

1   During a conference call with the executive committee of a nonprofit board on which I sit, I decided to send an email to a client. I know, I know. You'd think I'd have learned. Last week I wrote about the dangers of using a cell phone while driving. Multitasking is dangerous. And so I proposed a way to stop. But when I sent that email, I wasn't in a car. I was safe at my desk. What could go wrong?

2   Well, I sent the client the message. Then I had to send him another one, this time with the attachment I had forgotten to append. Finally, my third email to him explained why that attachment wasn't what he was expecting. When I eventually refocused on the call, I realized I hadn't heard a question the Chair of the Board had asked me.

3   I swear I wasn't smoking anything. But I might as well have been. A study showed that people distracted by incoming email and phone calls saw a 10-point fall in their IQs. What's the impact of a 10-point drop? The same as losing a night of sleep. More than twice the effect of smoking marijuana.

4   Doing several things at once is a trick we play on ourselves, thinking we're getting more done. In reality, our productivity goes down by as much as 40%. We don't actually multitask. We switch-task, rapidly shifting from one thing to another, interrupting ourselves unproductively, and losing time in the process.

5   You might think you're different, that you've done it so much you've become good at it. Practice makes perfect and all that. But you'd be wrong. Research shows that heavy multitaskers are *less competent* at doing several things at once than light multitaskers. In other words, in contrast to almost everything else in your life, the more you multitask, the worse you are at it. Practice, in this case, works against you.

I decided to do an experiment. For one week I would do no multitasking and see   6
what happened. What techniques would help? Could I sustain a focus on one thing
at a time for that long? For the most part, I succeeded. If I was on the phone, all I did
was talk or listen on the phone. In a meeting I did nothing but focus on the meeting.
Any interruptions — email, a knock on the door — I held off until I finished what I
was working on.

During the week I discovered six things: 7

- **First, it was delightful.** I noticed this most dramatically when I was with my children. I shut my cell phone off and found myself much more deeply engaged and
  present with them. I never realized how significantly a short moment of checking
  my email disengaged me from the people and things right there in front of me.
  Don't laugh, but I actually — for the first time in a while — noticed the beauty of
  leaves blowing in the wind.
- **Second, I made significant progress on challenging projects,** the kind that — like
  writing or strategizing — require thought and persistence. The kind I usually try to
  distract myself from. I stayed with each project when it got hard, and experienced
  a number of breakthroughs.
- **Third, my stress dropped dramatically.** Research shows that multitasking isn't
  just inefficient, it's stressful. And I found that to be true. It was a relief to do
  only one thing at a time. I felt liberated from the strain of keeping so many balls
  in the air at each moment. It felt reassuring to finish one thing before going to
  the next.
- **Fourth, I lost all patience for things I felt were not a good use of my time.** An
  hour-long meeting seemed interminably long. A meandering pointless conversation was excruciating. I became laser-focused on getting things done. Since I
  wasn't doing anything else, I got bored much more quickly. I had no tolerance for
  wasted time.
- **Fifth, I had tremendous patience for things I felt were useful and enjoyable.**
  When I listened to my wife Eleanor, I was in no rush. When I was brainstorming
  about a difficult problem, I stuck with it. Nothing else was competing for my attention so I was able to settle into the one thing I was doing.
- **Sixth, there was no downside.** I lost nothing by not multitasking. No projects
  were left unfinished. No one became frustrated with me for not answering a call
  or failing to return an email the second I received it.

That's why it's so surprising that multitasking is so hard to resist. If there's no   8
downside to stopping, why don't we all just stop? I think it's because our minds
move considerably faster than the outside world. You can hear far more words a
minute than someone else can speak. We have so much to do, why waste any time?
So, while you're on the phone listening to someone, why not use that *extra* brain
power to book a trip to Florence? What we neglect to realize is that we're already using that brain power to pick up nuance, think about what we're hearing, access our
creativity, and stay connected to what's happening around us. It's not really extra
brain power, and diverting it has negative consequences.

So how do we resist the temptation? First, the obvious: the best way to avoid   9
interruptions is to turn them off. Often I write at 6 a.m. when there's nothing to
distract me, I disconnect my computer from its wireless connection and turn my
phone off. In my car, I leave my phone in the trunk. Drastic? Maybe. But most of us
shouldn't trust ourselves. Second, the less obvious: Use your loss of patience to
your advantage. Create unrealistically short deadlines. Cut all meetings in half. Give
yourself a third of the time you think you need to accomplish something. There's
nothing like a deadline to keep things moving. And when things are moving fast, we
can't help but focus on them. How many people run a race while texting? If you really only have 30 minutes to finish a presentation you thought would take an hour,
are you really going to answer an interrupting call? Interestingly, because multitasking is so stressful, single-tasking to meet a tight deadline will actually reduce your
stress. In other words, giving yourself less time to do things could make you more
productive and relaxed.

Finally, it's good to remember that we're not perfect. Every once in a while it   10
might be OK to allow for a little multitasking. As I was writing this, Daniel, my
two-year-old son, walked into my office, climbed on my lap, and said "*Monsters,
Inc.* movie please." So, here we are, I'm finishing this piece on the left side of my
computer screen while Daniel is on my lap watching a movie on the right side of my
computer screen. Sometimes, it is simply impossible to resist a little multitasking.

Examining the Reading

1. Why does Bregman believe we should stop most of our multitasking?
2. Summarize the opposing views favoring multitasking that Bregman refutes.
3. What did Bregman discover after he stopped multitasking?
4. Explain the meaning of each of the following words as it is used in the
   reading: *refocused* (para. 2), *competent* (5), *disengaged* (7), *persistence* (7),
   and *meandering* (7).

Analyzing the Writer's Technique

1. What is Bregman's claim? Is it a claim of fact, value, or policy? Explain how you
   know.
2. What types of emotional appeals does Bregman make? Identify the needs and values to which he appeals.
3. What types of evidence does Bregman use to support his claim?
4. Are there any errors in reasoning? If so, explain.

Visualizing the Reading

Create a graphic organizer for the argument in this essay.

Thinking Critically about Argument

1. Describe Bregman's tone. Highlight several words or phrases that reveal this tone.
2. Bregman mentions research but fails to cite his sources. How does that affect the effectiveness of his argument?
3. What is the connotation of the word *delightful* (para. 7)?
4. What is "smoking anything" (3) a euphemism for?

Reacting to the Reading

1. Evaluate Bregman's description of his discoveries when he stopped multitasking. Are they persuasive? Could he have added anything that would make them more persuasive?
2. What do you think of Bregman's tips for how to stop multitasking? Are these things you could apply to your life? Why or why not?
3. Keep a journal for a day, and record all the times you multitask and how doing so affects you.
4. Write an essay describing your own experiences with multitasking. Offer examples of why it has or has not been useful for you.

In Defense of Multitasking
David Silverman

READING

David Silverman has worked in business and taught business writing. He is the author of *Typo: The Last American Typesetter or How I Made and Lost Four Million Dollars* (2007). He blogs for *Harvard Business Review,* where this essay appeared in 2010, ten days after the previous one by Peter Bregman. As you read, notice how Silverman attempts to refute Bregman's position.

HBR.org blogger Peter Bregman recently made some excellent points about the   1
downside of multitasking — as did Matt Richtel in his *New York Times* article on
Monday. I will not deny that single-minded devotion often produces high quality.
Nor will I attempt to join the misguided (and scientifically discredited) many who
say, "Yeah, other people can't do it, but I'm super awesome at doing 10 things at
once."

But let's remember, unitasking has a downside too — namely, what works for   2
one person slows down others. Multitasking isn't just an addiction for the short-
attention-spanned among us; it's crucial to survival in today's workplace. To see
why, take a look at computing, where the concept of multitasking came from.

Long ago, in the days of vacuum tubes and relays, computers worked in   3
"batch" mode. Jobs were loaded from punched cards, and each job waited until
the one before it was completed. This created serious problems. You didn't know
if your job had an error until it ran, which could be hours after you submitted it.

Electronic Multitasking Is on the Rise

The percentage of youngsters who multitask while using electronic media—such as checking their Facebook page on their laptops while watching TV—has increased in recent years, but the percentage who multitask while reading has changed very little.

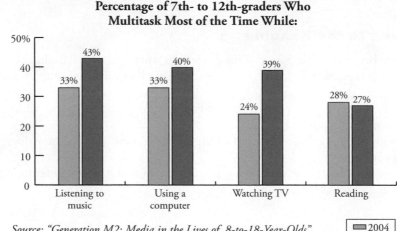

Percentage of 7th- to 12th-graders Who Multitask Most of the Time While:

Source: "Generation M2: Media in the Lives of 8-to-18-Year-Olds" (#8010), Henry J. Kaiser Family Foundation, January 2010.

☐ 2004
■ 2009

You didn't know if it would cause an infinite loop and block all the other jobs from starting. And any changes in external information that occurred during processing couldn't be accounted for.

The invention of time-sharing resolved these issues: Multiple tasks can now be 4 done concurrently, and you can interrupt a task in an emergency. Incoming missile? Stop the backup tape and send an alert to HQ. So, how does all that apply to the way people work? In several ways:

1. **Multitasking helps us get and give critical information faster.** You can get responses to questions quickly, even if the person you're asking is on another task. For example: I was at an all-day off-site (no BlackBerrys allowed) when one of my direct reports received a request from an internal customer to make a slide. Since I was unreachable by phone when he started on it, my employee worked the entire afternoon on something that, after I finally read my e-mail and called him, took us only 30 minutes to do together because I had information he didn't have.

2. **It keeps others from being held up.** If I don't allow for distractions in an attempt to be more efficient, other people may be held up waiting for me. This is the classic batch job problem. Going back to my slide example: The next day, the person who had requested the slide said he only needed a couple of bullet points. Had he been reachable earlier, and not devoted to a single task and blocking all interruptions, we wouldn't have wasted what ended up being nearly six hours of work time (my employee's and mine).

3. **It gives you something to turn to when you're stuck.** Sometimes it's good to butt your head against a task that is challenging. And sometimes it's good to walk away, do something else, and let your subconscious ponder the ponderable. When you return 25 minutes later, maybe you'll reach a better solution than you would have if you'd just stuck it out. And in the meantime, you've finished some other task, such as writing a blog post. (By the way, my 10.6 minute attempt to uncover how many minutes it takes to get back to a task after an interruption yielded a variety of answers — 11, 25, 30 — and links to a lot of dubious research, such as this University of California study of 36 workers and this study that tracked "eleven experienced Microsoft Windows users [3 female].")

4. **The higher up you are in the organization, the more important multitasking is.** The fewer things you have to do, the more you should concentrate on them. If I'm painting my house, and I'm on a ladder, I've got to keep on that one task. But if I'm the general contractor, I need to stay on top of the house painter, the carpenter, the electrician, and the guy swinging that big ball on the end of a giant chain, lest the wrong wall or an unsuspecting worker get demolished. To take this to the logical extreme: Does Barack Obama get to unitask? Can he say, "I'm not available for the rest of the day, because I'll be working on that spreadsheet I've been trying to get done on the number of my Facebook friends who aren't updating their pages with posts about their pet cats?" Or does he have to keep doing his job while handling whatever spilled milk (or, say, zillions of gallons of oil) comes his way?

What do you think? Are we comfortable pretending we really can live our lives   5
not multitasking? Or are we like my father and others who say smoking is bad but can be found on the front porch in the dead of night, a small red glow at their lips, puffing away while texting their BFFs and playing Words with Friends?

Before you answer, think about the eight *Washington Post* reporters who tried   6
to go a week without the Internet and failed miserably. The truth is, we need multitasking as much as we need air.

Examining the Reading

1. Summarize Silverman's reasons for defending multitasking.
2. Explain Silverman's analogy about computers. What is he trying to show with it?
3. What message does Silverman convey by discussing his father in the next-to-last paragraph?
4. Explain the meaning of each of the following words as it is used in the reading: *discredited* (para. 1), *unitasking* (2), *concurrently* (4), *ponderable* (4), and *lest* (4).

Analyzing the Writer's Technique

1. What type of claim does Silverman make?
2. Is Silverman's analogy about computers effective? Why or why not?
3. What additional information, evidence, or explanation would make this essay more convincing?

4. The end of the essay talks about multitasking and the presidency. Is this an effective example? How useful is it in applying the issues in this essay to regular people?
5. Who is Silverman's intended audience?

Visualizing the Reading

Create a graphic organizer for the argument in this essay.

Thinking Critically about Text and Visuals

1. To what needs and values does Silverman appeal?
2. What fallacies, if any, can you find in Silverman's essay?
3. Evaluate Silverman's use of sources in this essay. What kinds of sources could he have added?
4. How does Silverman present opposing viewpoints? Does he refute them? If so, how?
5. Discuss whether Silverman's essay is made up primarily of fact or of opinion. How does this balance affect the success of his argument?
6. What are the connotations of the word *addiction* in paragraph 2 and of the word *missile* in paragraph 4?
7. Look at the bar graph on page 538. (This graph did not appear in the original blog post.) What does the graph indicate about the rate of multitasking over time among teenagers? What do you think accounts for the fact that multitasking while watching television or listening to music has increased? Why might the percentage of teenagers who multitask while reading *not* have increased much between 2004 and 2009?

Reacting to the Reading

1. Do you agree or disagree with Silverman's assertion that multitasking is essential for survival at work? Why?
2. Keep a journal for a day to track important interruptions that you would miss if you were unitasking.
3. Write an essay describing how and why multitasking might have developed as human behavior. When would it have been a valuable skill? How would it have helped early humans?
4. Imagine you are having surgery. Explain how your surgeon might need to unitask or multitask during the procedure at different times.

Integrating the Readings

1. Which writer's argument did you find more convincing? Why?
2. Compare how each writer introduces the issue. In what context does each writer frame it?
3. Silverman and Bregman do not seem to be talking about exactly the same kinds of activities in their discussions of what people try to do simultaneously. How do you think this difference affects their opinions of multitasking?
4. What is the primary difference in the ways that Bregman and Silverman view multitasking? Do they define it differently? If so, describe how each might define it.
5. How do you think Bregman might respond to Silverman's claims?

The "I'll Just Have One More" Martini

3 oz. gin or vodka
1/2 oz. dry vermouth
3 olives
1 automobile
1 long day
1 diminishing attention span
1 too many

Combine ingredients. Drink. Repeat.
Mix with sharp turn, telephone pole.

Never underestimate 'just a few.'
Buzzed driving is drunk driving.

U.S. Department of Transportation

CHAPTER 20

Writing Arguments

WRITING QUICK START

The advertisement on the opposite page makes a simple argument, mostly in the form of a recipe. It identifies an issue — "buzzed driving" or driving after drinking just a few drinks or just one more drink. It makes the claim that buzzed driving is actually drunk driving and is dangerous, possibly fatal. It offers one reason that driving while impaired is dangerous ("diminishing attention span") and implies that impaired driving ability is another reason.

Working alone or with one or two classmates, rewrite the ad as a brief argument of one to three paragraphs. The claim is your thesis. Add support of your own to strengthen the argument — evidence, emotional appeals, and so on. Also consider why some readers might disagree with the claim and offer reasons to refute this view. Conclude your brief argument with a convincing statement.

By following the steps in the Writing Quick Start, you successfully started to build an argument. You made a claim, supported it with evidence, and refuted opposing views. This chapter will show you how to write clear, effective arguments.

What Is an Argument?

We encounter arguments daily in casual conversations, in newspapers, in classrooms, and on the job. Of the many arguments we hear and read, however, relatively few are convincing. A **sound argument** makes a claim and offers reasons and evidence in support of that claim. A sound argument also anticipates opposing viewpoints and acknowledges, accommodates, and/or refutes them.

The ability to construct and write sound arguments is an important skill in many aspects of life. Many political, social, and economic issues, for instance, are resolved through public and private debate. Knowing how to construct a sound argument is also essential to success in college and on the job (see the accompanying box for a few examples).

The essay that begins on the next page argues in favor of abolishing the U.S. penny.

SCENES FROM COLLEGE AND THE WORKPLACE

- For a *health science* course, you are part of a group working on an argument essay claiming that the results of genetic testing, which can predict a person's likelihood of contracting serious diseases, should be kept confidential.

- As a student member of the *Affirmative Action Committee* on campus, you are asked to write a letter to the editor of the campus newspaper defending the committee's recently drafted affirmative action plan for minorities and women.

- As a *lawyer* representing a client whose hand was seriously injured on the job, you must argue to a jury that your client deserves compensation for the work-related injury.

Abolish the Penny
William Safire

William Safire (1929–2009), a former speechwriter for President Richard Nixon and Vice President Spiro Agnew, was a longtime political columnist for the *New York Times*. He was also well known for "On Language," his column on grammar, usage, and etymology in the weekly *New York Times Magazine*, and he published many books, including novels, collections of his columns, and *Before the Fall: An Inside View of the Pre-Watergate White House* (2005). He won the Pulitzer Prize for commentary in 1978. As you read the following essay, published in 2004, notice how Safire gives his own reasons for abolishing the penny and anticipates possible counterarguments.

Because my staunch support of the war in Iraq has generated such overwhelming reader enthusiasm, it's time to reestablish my contrarian credentials. (Besides, I need a break.) Here's a crusade sure to infuriate the vast majority of penny-pinching traditionalists: The time has come to abolish the outdated, almost worthless, bothersome, and wasteful penny. Even President Lincoln, who distrusted the notion of paper money because he thought he would have to sign each greenback, would be ashamed to have his face on this specious specie.

That's because you can't buy anything with a penny any more. Penny candy? Not for sale at the five-and-dime (which is now a "dollar store"). Penny-ante poker? Pass the buck. Any vending machine? Put a penny in and it will sound an alarm. There is no escaping economic history: it takes nearly a dime today to buy what a penny bought back in 1950. Despite this, the U.S. Mint keeps churning out a billion pennies a month.

Where do they go? Two-thirds of them immediately drop out of circulation, into piggy banks or—as the *Times*'s John Tierney noted five years ago—behind chair cushions or at the back of sock drawers next to your old tin-foil ball. Quarters and dimes circulate; pennies disappear because they are literally more trouble than they are worth. The remaining 300 million or so—that's 10 million shiny new useless items punched out every day by government workers who could be more usefully employed tracking counterfeiters—go toward driving retailers crazy. They cost more in employee-hours—to wait for buyers to fish them out, then to count, pack up, and take them to the bank—than it would cost to toss them out. That's why you see "penny cups" next to every cash register; they save the seller time and the buyer the inconvenience of lugging around loose change that tears holes in pockets and now sets off alarms at every frisking place.

Why is the U.S. among the last of the industrialized nations to abolish the peskiest little bits of coinage? At the G-8 summit next week, the Brits and the French—even the French!—who dumped their low-denomination coins thirty years ago, will be laughing at our senseless jingling. The penny-pinching horde argues: those $9.98 price tags save the consumer 2 cents because if the penny was abolished, merchants would "round up" to the nearest dollar. That's pound-foolish: the idea behind the 98-cent (and I can't even find a cent symbol on my keyboard any more) price is to fool you into thinking that "it's less than 10 bucks." In truth, merchants would round down to $9.95, saving the consumer billions of paper dollars over the next century.

What's really behind America's clinging to the pesky penny? Nostalgia cannot be 5 the answer; if we can give up the barbershop shave with its steam towels, we can give up anything. The answer, I think, has to do with zinc, which is what pennies are mostly made of; light copper plating turns them into red cents. The powerful, outsourcing zinc lobby—financed by Canadian mines as well as Alaskan—entices front groups to whip up a frenzy of save-the-penny mail to Congress when coin reform is proposed.

But when the penny is abolished, the nickel will boom. And what is a nickel made 6 of? No, not the metallic element nickel; our 5-cent coin is mainly composed of copper. And where is most of America's copper mined? Arizona. If Senator John McCain would get off President Bush's back long enough to serve the economic interests of his Arizona constituents, we'd get some long-overdue coin reform.

What about Lincoln, who has had a century-long run on the penny? He's still hon- 7 ored on the $5 bill, and will be as long as the dollar sign remains above the 4 on keyboards. If this threatens coin reformers with the loss of Illinois votes, put Abe on the dime and bump F.D.R.[1]

What frazzled pollsters, surly op-ed[2] pages, snarling cable talkfests, and issue- 8 starved candidates for office need is a fresh source of hot-eyed national polarization. Coin reform can close the controversy gap and fill the vitriol void. Get out those bumper stickers: Abolish the penny!

---

[1] *F.D.R.:* Franklin Delano Roosevelt, U.S. president from 1933 to 1945.

[2] *op-ed:* the opinion section of the newspaper that is opposite the editorial page.

Characteristics of Argument Essays

All arguments are concerned with issues. In developing an argument essay, you need to narrow or limit the issue, make a clear and specific claim about the issue, analyze your audience, and give reasons and evidence to support the claim. In addition, you should follow a logical line of reasoning; use emotional appeals appropriately; and acknowledge, accommodate, and/or refute opposing views.

An Argument Focuses on an Arguable, Clearly Defined, and Narrowed Issue

An **issue** is a controversy, problem, or idea about which people disagree. In choosing an issue, therefore, be sure it is arguable—one that people have differing opinions on. For example, arguing that education is important in today's job market is pointless because people generally agree on that issue.

Depending on the issue you choose and the audience you write for, a clear definition of the issue may be required. Well-known issues need little definition, but for less familiar issues, readers may need background information. In an argument about the awarding of organ transplants, for example, you would give readers information about the scarcity of organ donors versus the number of people who need transplants. Notice how Safire announces and defines the issue in "Abolish the Penny," paragraph 1.

In addition, the issue you choose should be narrow enough to deal with adequately in an essay-length argument. For an essay on organ transplants, for instance, you could limit your argument to transplants of a particular organ or to one aspect of the issue, such as who does and does not receive them. When you narrow your issue, your thesis will be more precise and your evidence more specific. You can also provide more effective arguments against an opposing viewpoint.

Exercise 20.1

Working alone or in a group of two or three students, choose two of the following issues. For each issue, consider ways to limit the topic, and list the background information readers might need to understand the issue.

1. Moral implications of state-operated lotteries
2. Computer networks and the right to privacy
3. Speech codes on campus
4. Religious symbols on public property
5. Mandatory drug testing

An Argument States a Specific Claim in a Thesis

To build a convincing argument, you need to make a clear and specific **claim**, one that tells readers your position on the issue. If writing arguments is new to you, it is usually best to state your claim in a strong thesis early in the essay. Doing so will help you keep your argument on track. As you gain experience in writing arguments, you can experiment with placing your thesis later in the essay. In "Abolish the Penny," Safire makes a clear, specific claim in his opening paragraph: "The time has come to abolish the outdated, almost worthless, bothersome, and wasteful penny."

For more on types of claims, see Chapter 19, pp. 516–17.

Here are a few examples of how general claims can be narrowed into clear and specific thesis statements:

GENERAL	More standards are needed to protect children in day-care centers.
SPECIFIC	Statewide standards are needed to regulate the child-to-caregiver ratio and the qualifications of workers in day-care centers.
GENERAL	The use of animals in testing should be prohibited.
SPECIFIC	The testing of cosmetics and skin-care products on animals should be prohibited.

While all arguments make and support a claim, some also call for specific action to be taken. An essay opposing human cloning, for example, might argue for a ban on that practice as well as urge readers to voice their opinions in letters to congressional representatives. Claims of policy often include a call for action.

For more on claims of policy, see Chapter 19, p. 517.

Regardless of the argument, you need to be careful about the way you state your claim. Avoid a general or absolute statement; your claim will be more convincing if you qualify or limit it. For example, if a writer arguing in favor of single-sex education makes the claim "Single-sex educational institutions are *always* more beneficial to girls than are coeducational schools," then opponents could easily cite exceptions to the claim and thereby show weaknesses in the argument. However, if the claim is qualified—as in "Single-sex educational institutions are *often* more beneficial to girls than are coeducational schools"—then an exception would not necessarily weaken the argument.

Exercise 20.2

Choose two of the following issues. Then, for each issue, write two thesis statements—one that makes a claim and contains a qualifying term and another that makes a claim and calls for action.

1. Controlling pornography on the Internet
2. Limiting immigration
3. Limiting political campaign spending
4. Restricting testing of beauty products on animals
5. Promoting competitive sports for young children

An Argument Depends on Careful Audience Analysis

To build a convincing argument, you need to know your audience. Because an argument is intended to influence readers' thinking, begin by anticipating your readers' views. First determine how familiar your audience is with the issue. Then decide whether your audience agrees with your claim, is neutral about or wavering on the claim, or disagrees with the claim.

Agreeing audiences. When you write for an audience that agrees with your claim, the focus is usually on urging readers to take a specific action. Agreeing audiences are the easiest to write for because they already accept your claim. Instead of presenting large amounts of facts and statistics as evidence, you can concentrate on reinforcing your shared viewpoint and building emotional ties with your audience. By doing so, you encourage readers to act on their beliefs.

For more on emotional appeals, see Chapter 19, pp. 518–19.

Neutral or wavering audiences. Audiences are neutral or wavering when they have not made up their minds about or given much thought to an issue. Although they may be somewhat familiar with the issue, they may have questions about, misunderstandings about, or no interest in it. When writing for a neutral or wavering audience, emphasize the importance of the issue, and clear up misunderstandings readers may have about it. Your goals are to make readers care about the issue, establish yourself as a knowledgeable and trustworthy writer, and present solid evidence in support of your claim.

Disagreeing audiences. The most challenging type of audience is the disagreeing audience—one that holds viewpoints in opposition to yours. Such an audience may have strong feelings about the issue and may distrust you because you don't share their views on something they care deeply about.

In writing for a disagreeing audience, your goal is to persuade readers not necessarily to accept but at least to consider your views on the issue. Be sure to follow a logical line of reasoning. Rather than stating your claim early in the essay, it may be more effective to build slowly to your thesis. First establish a **common ground**—a basis of trust and goodwill—with your readers by mentioning shared interests, concerns, experiences, and points in your argument. Then when you state your claim, the audience may be more open to considering it.

In "Abolish the Penny," Safire writes for a disagreeing audience. In the opening paragraph, he recognizes that he is likely to infuriate "penny-pinching traditionalists." Safire openly acknowledges the opposing viewpoint in paragraph 4, where he summarizes the argument of the "penny-pinching horde." He establishes a common ground with his readers by mentioning shared concerns (about productivity of government workers and political lobbyists) and referring to well-respected historical figures such as Abraham Lincoln and Franklin Delano Roosevelt.

> ### Exercise 20.3
>
> *Choose one of the following claims, and discuss how you would argue in support of it for (a) an agreeing audience, (b) a neutral or wavering audience, and (c) a disagreeing audience:*
>
> 1. Public school sex education classes should be mandatory because they help students make important decisions about their lives.
>
> 2. Portraying the effects of violent crime realistically on television may help reduce the crime rate.
>
> 3. Children who spend too much time interacting with a computer may fail to learn how to interact with people.

An Argument Presents Reasons Supported by Convincing Evidence

In developing an argument, you need to have reasons for making a claim. A **reason** is a general statement that backs up a claim; it answers the question, Why do I have this opinion about the issue? You also need to support each reason with evidence. Suppose you want to argue that high school uniforms should be mandatory for three reasons: The uniforms (1) reduce clothing costs for parents, (2) help eliminate distractions in the classroom, and (3) reduce peer pressure. Each of your reasons would need to be supported by evidence, facts, statistics, examples, personal experience, or expert testimony. Carefully linking your evidence to reasons helps readers see how the evidence supports your claim.

Be sure to choose reasons and evidence that will appeal to your audience. In the argument about mandatory school uniforms, high school students would probably not be impressed by your first reason—reduced clothing costs for parents—but they might consider your second and third reasons if you cite evidence that appeals to them, such as personal anecdotes from students. For an audience of parents, facts and statistics about reduced clothing costs and improved academic performance would be appealing types of evidence. In "Abolish the Penny," Safire offers several reasons for his claim, and supports them with examples. For instance, pennies drop out of circulation, fall behind chair cushions, or hide at the back of sock drawers.

An Argument Follows a Logical Line of Reasoning

The reasons and evidence in an argument should follow a logical line of reasoning. The most common types of reasoning are induction and deduction (see the diagrams below). Whereas **inductive reasoning** begins with evidence and moves to a conclusion, **deductive reasoning** begins with a commonly accepted statement or premise and shows how a conclusion follows from it. You can use one or both types of reasoning to keep your argument on a logical path.

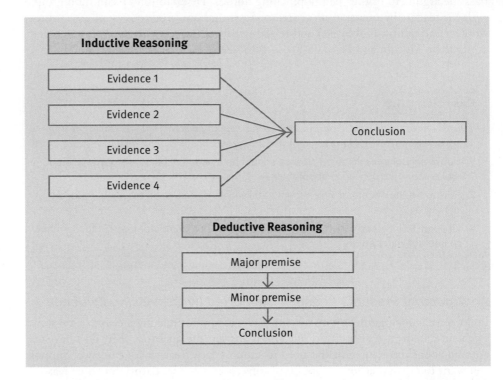

Inductive reasoning. Inductive reasoning starts with specific evidence and moves to a generalization or conclusion. For example, suppose you go shopping for a new pair of sneakers. You try on one style of Nikes. It doesn't fit, so you try a different style. It doesn't fit either. You try two more styles, neither of which fits. Finally, because of your experience, you draw the conclusion that either you need to remeasure your feet or Nike does not make a sneaker that fits your feet. Think of inductive reasoning as a process of coming to a conclusion after observing a number of examples.

When you use inductive reasoning, you make an *inference,* or guess, about the cases that you have not experienced. In doing so, you run the risk of being wrong. Perhaps some other style of Nikes would have fit.

When building an inductive argument, be sure to consider all possible explanations for the cases you observe. In the shoe store, for example, perhaps the salesperson brought you the wrong size sneakers. You also need to be sure that you have *sufficient* and *typical* evidence on which to base your conclusion. Suppose you observe one food-stamp recipient selling food stamps for cash and another using them to buy candy bars. From these observations you conclude that the food-stamp program should be abolished. Your reasoning is faulty, however, because these two cases are not typical of food-stamp recipients and not sufficient for drawing a conclusion. You must scrutinize your evidence and make sure that you have enough typical evidence to support your conclusion.

When you use inductive reasoning in an argument essay, the conclusion becomes the claim, and the specific pieces of evidence support your reasons for making the claim. For example, suppose you make a claim that Pat's Used Cars is unreliable. As support you might offer the following reasons and evidence:

REASON	Pat's Used Cars does not provide accurate information about its products.
EVIDENCE	My sister's car had its odometer reading tampered with. My best friend bought a car whose chassis had been damaged, yet the salesperson claimed the car had never been in an accident.
REASON	Pat's Used Cars doesn't honor its commitments to customers.
EVIDENCE	The dealership refused to honor the ninety-day guarantee for a car I purchased there. A local newspaper recently featured Pat's in a report on businesses that fail to honor guarantees.

Deductive reasoning. Deductive reasoning begins with **premises**, statements that are generally accepted as true. Once the premises are accepted as true, then the conclusion must also be true. The most familiar deductive argument consists of two premises and a conclusion. The first statement, called a **major premise**, is a general statement about a group. The second statement, called a **minor premise**, is a statement about an individual belonging to that group. You have probably used this three-step reasoning, called a **syllogism**, without realizing it. For example, suppose you know that any food containing dairy products makes you ill. Because frozen yogurt contains dairy products, you conclude that frozen yogurt will make you ill.

When you use deductive reasoning, putting your argument in the form of a syllogism will help you write your claim and organize and evaluate your reasons and evidence. Suppose you want to support the claim that state funding for Kids First, an early education program, should remain intact. You might use the following syllogism to build your argument:

MAJOR PREMISE	State-funded early education programs have increased the readiness of at-risk children to attend school.
MINOR PREMISE	Kids First is a popular early education program in our state.
CONCLUSION	Kids First is likely to increase the readiness of at-risk children to attend school.

Your thesis statement would be "Because early education programs are likely to increase the readiness of at-risk children to attend school, state funding for Kids First should be continued." Your evidence would be the popularity and effectiveness of Kids First.

For more on fallacies,
see Chapter 19, pp. 531–32.

As you develop a logical argument, you also need to avoid introducing **fallacies**, or errors in reasoning.

An Argument Appeals to Readers' Needs and Values

For more on emotional appeals,
see Chapter 19, pp. 518–19.

Although an effective argument relies mainly on credible evidence and logical reasoning, emotional appeals can help support and enhance a sound argument. **Emotional appeals** are directed toward readers' needs and values. **Needs** can be biological or psychological (food and drink, sex, a sense of belonging, esteem). **Values** are principles or qualities that readers consider important, worthwhile, or desirable. Examples include honesty, loyalty, privacy, and patriotism. In "Abolish the Penny," Safire appeals to the human need for efficiency to convince his readers to abolish outdated and worthless goods. Safire is also aware of the value of patriotism, as he assures readers that presidential figures will remain on currency.

An Argument Recognizes Opposing Views

Recognizing or countering opposing arguments forces you to think hard about your own claims. When you listen to readers' objections, you may find reasons to adjust your own reasoning and develop a stronger argument. In addition, readers will be more willing to consider your claim if you take their point of view into account.

There are three methods of recognizing opposing views in an argument essay: *acknowledgment, accommodation,* and *refutation.*

1. When you **acknowledge** an opposing viewpoint, you admit that it exists and show that you have considered it. For example, readers opposed to mandatory high school uniforms may argue that a uniform requirement will not eliminate peer pressure because students will use other objects to gain status—such as backpacks, iPods, hairstyles, and cell phones. You could acknowledge this viewpoint by admitting that there is no way to stop teenagers from finding ways to compete for status.

2. When you **accommodate** an opposing viewpoint, you acknowledge readers' concerns, accept some of them, and incorporate them into your own argument. In arguing for mandatory high school uniforms, you might accommodate readers' view that uniforms will not eliminate peer pressure by arguing that the uniforms will eliminate one major and expensive means of competing for status.

3. When you **refute** an opposing viewpoint, you demonstrate the weakness of the opponent's argument. Safire refutes opposing views in his essay on abolishing the penny. He acknowledges that some people fear that abolishing the penny would encourage merchants to "round up" their prices to the next dollar. He refutes this fear by reassuring readers that merchants would more likely "round down" to a lower price.

Exercise 20.4

For the three claims listed in Exercise 20.3, identify opposing viewpoints and consider how you could acknowledge, accommodate, or refute them.

Visualizing an Argument Essay: A Graphic Organizer

The graphic organizer shown in Figure 20.1 (p. 554) will help you analyze arguments as well as plan those that you write. Unlike the graphic organizers in Part 3, this organizer does not necessarily show the order in which an argument may be presented. Some arguments, for example, may begin with a claim, whereas others may start with evidence or opposing viewpoints. Whatever your argument's sequence, you can adapt this organizer to fit your essay. Note, however, that not every element will appear in every argument.

Read the following essay by Lisa M. Hamilton, and then study the graphic organizer for it in Figure 20.2 on pages 556–57.

Eating Meat for the Environment
Lisa M. Hamilton

READING

Lisa M. Hamilton is a writer and photographer who focuses on agricultural issues. She is the author of *Deeply Rooted: Unconventional Farmers in the Age of Agribusiness* (2009) and *Farming to Create Heaven on Earth* (2007). Her works have been published in *The Nation*, *Harper's*, *Geographic Traveler*, *Orion*, and *Audubon*, where this essay originally appeared. As you read, highlight Hamilton's claim, supporting evidence, and recognition or refutation of opposing viewpoints.

In fall 2008 Rajendra Pachauri, head of the United Nations Intergovernmental Panel on Climate Change, offered a simple directive for combating global warming: Eat less meat. 1

Critics pointed out that the economist and environmental scientist is a vegetarian, but the numbers back up his idea. A 2006 U.N. report found that 18 percent of the world's greenhouse gas emissions come from raising livestock for food. While Pachauri's advice is good overall, I would propose a corollary: At the same time that we begin eating less meat, we should be eating more of it. 2

More of a different kind, that is. Animals reared on organic pasture have a different climate equation from those raised in confinement on imported feed. Much of the emissions associated with livestock production come as the result of dismantling the natural farm system and replacing it with an artificial environment. For instance, in large-scale confinement systems, or CAFOs (concentrated animal feeding operations), 3

Figure 20.1 GRAPHIC ORGANIZER FOR AN ARGUMENT ESSAY

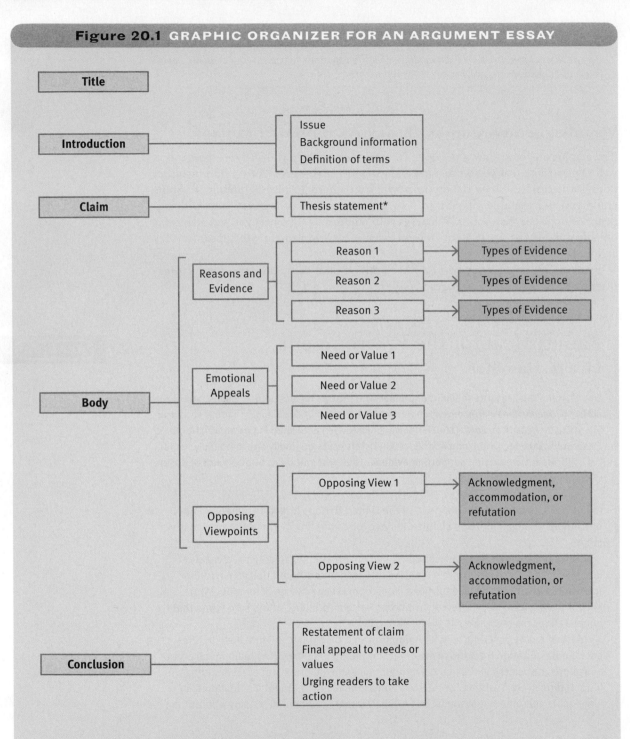

*The thesis statement may appear anywhere within the argument.

manure has nowhere to go. Managed in human-made lagoons, it produces millions of tons of methane and nitrous oxide every year through anaerobic decomposition. On pasture, that same manure is simply assimilated back into the soil with a carbon cost close to zero.

Some would argue that pasture-raised animals are just the lesser of two evils. Given 4 that livestock make for some emissions no matter where they're raised — cows, for instance, like any other ruminant, produce methane as a by-product of their digestion — wouldn't it be better to have no livestock at all? Not according to farmer Jason Mann, who grows produce and raises chickens, hogs, and cattle on pasture outside Athens, Georgia. In the age of CAFOs, many people have come to regard livestock as a problem to be solved. But on a sustainable farm system like his, animals are an essential part of the equation.

Mann likens his farm to a bank account: Every time he harvests an ear of corn or a 5 head of lettuce, he withdraws from the soil's fertility. If he doesn't redeposit that fertility, his account will hit zero. He could certainly truck in compost from 250 miles away or apply chemical fertilizers to make his vegetables grow. But by his own carbon calculation the best option is to return that fertility to the soil by using livestock, particularly cows. They do more than keep his soil rich. When cattle are managed properly, they can boost soil's ability to sequester carbon. Their manure adds organic matter to the soil, their grazing symbiotically encourages plant growth, and their heavy hooves help break down dead plant residue. Some proponents argue that highly managed, intensive grazing can shift cattle's carbon count so dramatically that the animals actually help reduce greenhouse gases. . . .

In addition to completing the farm's ecology, Mann's livestock also complement the 6 farm's economy with critical revenue for the real bank account—which keeps the operation afloat in a way that lettuce alone cannot. But that happens only when animals become meat. With the exception of laying hens, if animals stand around eating all day but never produce more than manure, they are a net loss. In order for livestock to be worthwhile in a whole farm system, they must be eaten. For Mann's farm to be sustainable, his neighbors must buy and eat his meat.

The same applies on a larger scale: In order for pasture-based livestock to become 7 a significant part of the meat industry, we need to eat more of its meat, not less. As it is, grass-fed beef accounts for less than 1 percent of U.S. beef consumption, and the numbers for chicken and pork hardly register. Even where the industry is growing, it is stunted by inadequate infrastructure. The greatest challenge is a lack of small-scale slaughterhouses, but it also suffers from a dearth of research, outreach for new producers, and investment in breeding for pasture-based systems. And those things will change only as the market grows.

So by all means follow Rajendra Pachauri's suggestion and enjoy a meatless Mon- 8 day. But on Tuesday, have a grass-fed burger—and feel good about it.

Figure 20.2 GRAPHIC ORGANIZER FOR "EATING MEAT FOR THE ENVIRONMENT"

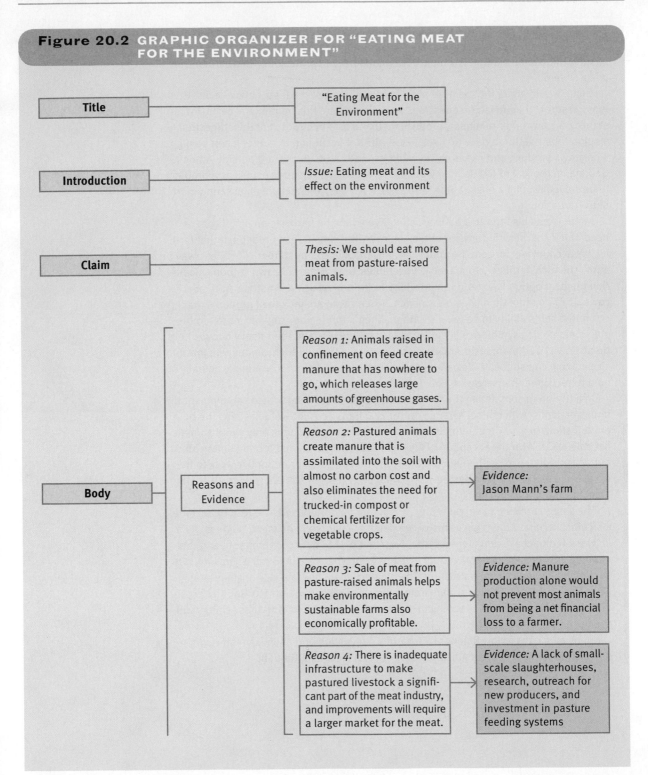

Figure 20.2 *(continued)*

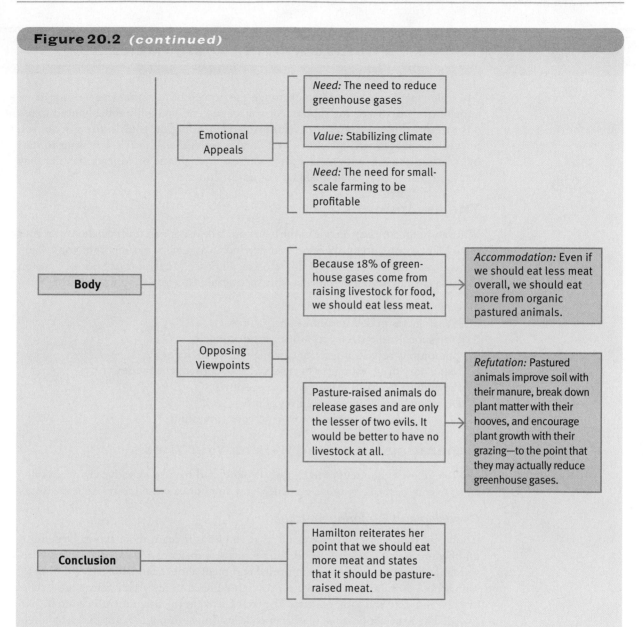

A GUIDED WRITING ASSIGNMENT

For more on the patterns of development, see Chapters 11–18.

The following guide will lead you through the process of planning and writing an argument essay. In presenting support for your argument, you will probably need to use one or more other patterns of development. Depending on your learning style, you may choose to approach the essay in different ways. A social learner may want to start by debating an issue with a classmate, whereas a pragmatic or concrete learner may want to research an issue in the library or on the Internet.

The Assignment

Write an argument essay on one of the issues listed below or one that you choose on your own. Make a claim about the issue, and develop an argument in support of your claim. For this assignment, you should also select an audience. Analyze your readers' views on the issue and target your argument to the specific audience you choose to address.

1. Buying American-made products
2. Racial quotas in college admissions policies
3. Professional athletes and celebrities as role models
4. Community service as a college graduation requirement
5. Mandatory drug testing for high school extracurricular activities
6. Providing a free college education to prisoners
7. Donating kidneys to save the lives of others
8. An environmental problem or issue in your community

Generating Ideas and Writing Your Thesis

Use the following guidelines to choose, explore, and make a tentative claim about an issue; to consider your purpose, audience, and point of view; and to research the issue.

Choosing and Exploring an Issue

Choose an issue that interests you and that you want to learn more about. Depending on how much you already know about a topic, you may need to conduct extensive research. For instance, to write an informed argument about mandatory drug testing for high school extracurricular activities, you would need to research existing laws, types of tests, and state and local policies. The issues listed in the assignment need to be narrowed. The issue about racial quotas in college admission policies, for instance, might be limited to private colleges in a particular geographic region.

For more on prewriting strategies, see Chapter 5, pp. 110–18.

If you have trouble choosing an issue, move to the next step and explore several promising issues until you can make a decision. Experiment with the following strategies to discover those that work for you and fit your learning style:

Learning Style Options

1. Brainstorm about different sides of the issue. Think of reasons and evidence that support various viewpoints.
2. Make a tentative claim, and list reasons that support the claim. Then switch sides, state an opposing claim, and brainstorm to discover reasons and corresponding supporting evidence.

3. Draw a map of the issue, connecting ideas as they come to mind. Then narrow your issue: Start with one or two key ideas you generated and draw another map.

4. Conduct a mock argument with a classmate. Choose opposing views on the issue and defend your positions. Take notes on the argument. Notice the reasons and evidence you and your opponent use to support your positions.

5. Write the issue at the top of a piece of paper or in a computer file. Then divide the list into two columns, listing pros in one column and cons in the other.

6. Examine the issue by answering these key questions:

   - What is the issue? How can I best define it?
   - Is it an arguable issue?
   - What are some related issues?
   - How can I narrow the issue for an essay-length argument?
   - What are my views on the issue? How can I state my claim?
   - What evidence supports my claim?
   - Does my argument include a call for action? What do I want readers to do, if anything, about the issue?
   - Does the issue have a compromise position?

7. Talk with others who have experience with the issue or are experts. For example, if you argue for stricter laws to prevent child abuse, a case worker for a child welfare agency may be able to help you narrow the issue, gather evidence, and address opposing viewpoints. A friend who experienced abuse as a child could provide another perspective. Keep in mind that sensitive topics should be approached tactfully and requests for confidentiality should be respected.

   For more on conducting an interview, see Chapter 22, pp. 615–16.

8. Use the Internet. Use a search engine to locate discussion forums on your topic as well as Web sites that deal with the issue.

   For more on Internet research, see Chapter 22, pp. 603–6.

Essay in Progress 1

Use the preceding suggestions to choose an issue to write about (one from the list of assignments on page 558 or one you think of on your own) and to explore and narrow the issue.

Considering Your Purpose, Audience, and Point of View

Once you choose an issue and begin to explore it, carefully consider your purpose, audience, and point of view. Think about what you want to happen as a result of your argument: Do you want your readers to change their minds? Do you want them to feel more certain of their existing beliefs? Or would you have them take some specific action?

An effective argument is tailored to its audience. The reasons and the types of evidence you offer, the needs and values to which you appeal, and the common ground you establish all depend on your audience. Remember that for this Guided Writing Assignment, you select the audience for your essay. Use the following questions to analyze your audience:

1. **What do my readers already know about the issue?** What do they need to know?

2. **How familiar are my readers with the issue?** Do they have firsthand experience with it, or is their knowledge limited to what they've heard in the media and from other people?

3. **Do my readers care about the issue?** Why or why not?
4. **Is my audience an agreeing, neutral or wavering, or disagreeing audience?** How do their beliefs or values affect their views?
5. **What shared views or concerns can I use to establish a common ground with my readers?**

For more on purpose, audience, and point of view, see Chapter 5, pp. 106–9.

In an argument essay, you can use the first-, second-, or third-person point of view, depending on the issue, your purpose for writing about it, and the reasons you offer in support of your claim. If it is important that your readers feel close to you and accept you or your experiences as part of your argument, the first person will help you achieve this closeness. If you want to establish a familiarity with your audience, the second person may be most effective. The third person creates the most distance between you and your readers and works well when you want to establish an objective, impersonal tone. Hamilton mostly uses the third-person point of view in "Eating Meat for the Environment"; she uses the first person (*we*) only in paragraph 7, where she recommends a course of action (eating more grass-fed beef) that both she and her readers should take.

Researching the Issue

Research is often an essential part of developing an argument. Reading or hearing what others have to say about an issue helps you gather background information, reliable evidence, and alternative viewpoints. Use the following guidelines to gather information on your topic:

For more on library and Internet research, see Chapter 22.

For more on note-taking and on avoiding plagiarism, see Chapter 22, pp. 613–14 & 611–12. For more on documenting sources, see Chapter 23.

1. **Skim through library sources,** such as books, magazine and newspaper articles, encyclopedia entries, and textbooks.
2. **Watch television news programs, documentaries, or talk shows on your topic.**
3. **Research the issue on the Web.**
4. **Take notes as you read your sources.** Also add ideas to your brainstormed lists, notes, or maps. As you jot down notes, take steps to avoid plagiarizing the words and ideas of other writers. Enclose direct quotations from sources in quotation marks, summarize and paraphrase information from sources carefully, and record all of the publication details you will need to cite your sources (author, title, publisher and site, publication date, page numbers, and so on).

Essay in Progress 2

Using the preceding suggestions, consider your purpose, audience, and point of view. Be sure to answer the questions listed on pages 559–60; your responses will help you tailor your argument—including your evidence and emotional appeals—to your intended audience.

Developing Your Thesis and Making a Claim

For more on thesis statements, see Chapter 6.

After doing research and reading what others have to say about the issue, your views on it may have softened, hardened, or changed in some other way. Before you develop a thesis and make a claim about the issue, consider your views on it in light of your research.

As you draft your thesis, be careful to avoid statements that are unarguable, too general, or too absolute. Note the difference between the following examples.

UNARGUABLE FACT	In recent years, U.S. consumers have experienced an increase in credit card fraud.
TOO GENERAL	Many problems that U.S. consumers complain about are mostly their own fault.
TOO ABSOLUTE	U.S. consumers have no one but themselves to blame for the recent increase in credit card fraud.
ARGUABLE/SPECIFIC/ LIMITED	Although the carelessness of merchants and electronic tampering contribute to the problem, U.S. consumers are largely to blame for the recent increase in credit card fraud.

Essay in Progress 3

Using the preceding suggestions, write a working thesis that clearly expresses your claim about the issue.

Evaluating Your Ideas, Evidence, and Claim

Once you are satisfied with your working thesis, take a few minutes to evaluate the reasons and evidence you will use to support your claim. Begin by rereading everything you have written with a critical eye. Look for ways to organize your reasons (such as in order of their strength or importance), and group your evidence for each reason. Draw a graphic organizer of your reasons and evidence, using Figure 20.1 as a model.

To draw detailed graphic organizers using a computer, visit www.bedfordstmartins .com/successfulcollege.

Trying Out Your Ideas on Others

Working in a group of two or three students, discuss your claim, reasons, and evidence. Each writer should state his or her issue, claim, reasons, and evidence for this chapter's assignment. Then, as a group, evaluate each writer's work.

Essay in Progress 4

Using the list of the characteristics of argument essays on pages 546–52 and comments from your classmates, evaluate your claim and the reasons and evidence you have gathered to support it. (You might also use the questions in Table 19.2, page 533, to help you evaluate your claim, reasons, and evidence.)

Considering Opposing Viewpoints

Once you evaluate the key elements in your argument, you are ready to consider opposing viewpoints and plan how to acknowledge, accommodate, or refute them. Your argument will be weak if you fail to at least acknowledge opposing viewpoints. Your readers may assume you did not think the issue through or that you dismissed alternative views without seriously considering them.

Create a list of reasons for and against your position, or review the one you made earlier. Then try to group the objections to form two or more points of opposition.

To acknowledge an opposing viewpoint without refuting it, you can mention the opposition in your claim, as shown in this claim about enforcing speed limits:

■ **Although speed-limit laws are intended to save lives, the conditions that apply to specific highways should be taken into account when enforcing them.**

The opposing viewpoint appears in a dependent clause attached to an independent clause that states the claim. By including the opposing viewpoint in this way, you show that you take it seriously but that you think it is outweighed by your claims.

To accommodate an opposing viewpoint, find a portion of the opposing argument that you can build into your argument. One common way to accommodate objections is to suggest alternative causes for a particular situation. For example, suppose your argument defends the competency of most high school teachers. You suspect, however, that some readers think the quality of most high school instruction is poor and attribute it to teachers' laziness or lack of skill. You can accommodate this opposing viewpoint by suggesting that the poor instruction some schools provide may be due to large class size rather than teachers' incompetence.

If you choose to argue that an opposing viewpoint is simply wrong, you must refute it by pointing out problems or flaws in your opponent's reasoning or evidence. To refute an opponent's reasoning, check to see if your opponent uses faulty reasoning or fallacies. To refute an opponent's evidence, use one or more of the following guidelines:

For more on fallacies, see Chapter 19, pp. 531–32.

1. **Give a counterexample** (one that is an exception to the opposing view). For instance, if the opponent argues that dogs are useful for protection, give an example of a situation in which a dog did not protect its owner.
2. **Question the opponent's facts.** If an opponent claims that few professors give essay exams, present statistics demonstrating that a significant percentage of professors do give essay exams.
3. **Demonstrate that an example is not representative.** If an opponent argues that professional athletes are overpaid and cites the salaries of two famous quarterbacks, cite statistics that show that these salaries are not representative of professional athletes in general.
4. **Demonstrate that the examples are insufficient.** If an opponent argues that horseback riding is a dangerous sport and offers two examples of riders who were seriously injured, point out that two examples are not sufficient proof.
5. **Question the credibility of an authority.** If an opponent quotes a television personality on reform of U.S. immigration policy, point out that the person has not studied the issue the way a sociologist or public-policy expert has.
6. **Question outdated examples, facts, or statistics.** If your opponent presents evidence that is not recent on the need for more campus parking, you can argue that the situation has changed (enrollment has declined, bus service has increased).
7. **Present the full context of a quotation or group of statistical evidence.** If an opponent quotes an authority selectively or cites incomplete statistics from a research study on ozone depletion and its effects on skin cancer, the full context may show that your opponent has "edited" the evidence to suit his or her claim.

Essay in Progress 5

Write your claim on a piece of paper or in a computer file. Below it, list all possible opposing viewpoints. Then describe one or more strategies for acknowledging, accommodating, or refuting each opposing view.

Trying Out Your Ideas on Others

Working in a group of two or three students, present your strategies for acknowledging, accommodating, or refuting opposing views. Critique each other's strategies, and suggest others that each writer might use.

Organizing and Drafting

You are now ready to organize your ideas and draft your essay. You need to decide on a line of reasoning, choose a method of organization, and develop your essay accordingly.

Choosing a Line of Reasoning and a Method of Organization

To develop a method of organizing an argument, you might use *induction, deduction,* or both. Inductive reasoning begins with specific evidence and moves to a general conclusion. Deductive reasoning starts with an observation that most people accept and shows how a certain conclusion follows from it. Whether you choose to use one or both lines of reasoning, this decision will influence how you organize your essay.

Here are four common ways to organize an argument:

Method I	**Method II**	**Method III**	**Method IV**
Claim/thesis	Claim/thesis	Reasons/evidence	Opposing viewpoints
Reasons/evidence	Opposing viewpoints	Opposing viewpoints	Reasons/evidence
Opposing viewpoints	Reasons/evidence	Claim/thesis	Claim/thesis

The method you choose depends on your audience and your issue. You also need to decide the order in which you will discuss the reasons and evidence and the opposing viewpoints. Will you arrange them from strongest to weakest? Most to least obvious? Most to least familiar? In planning your organization, try drawing a graphic organizer or making an outline. Try different ways of organizing your essay on the computer, creating a document file for each alternative.

Drafting the Argument Essay

Once you have chosen a method of organization for your argument, you are ready to write your first draft. Use the following guidelines to draft your essay:

1. **Write an effective introduction.** Your introduction should accomplish several things. It should *identify the issue* and *offer needed background information*

For more on drafting an essay, see Chapter 7.

For more on writing effective paragraphs, including introductions and conclusions, see Chapter 7.

based on your assessment of your audience's knowledge and experience. In addition, it should *define the terms* to be used in the argument. Most argument essays also include a thesis in the introduction, where you make your *claim*. Finally, the introduction should *engage readers* and *create goodwill* toward you and your argument. Several strategies can help you engage your readers right away.

- Open by relating a personal experience, ideally one with which your readers can identify. (See "Pull the Plug on Explicit Lyrics" by James Sturm, p. 568.)
- Open with an attention-getting remark. (See "Eating Meat for the Environment" by Lisa M. Hamilton, p. 553.)
- Open by recognizing counterarguments.
- Open with an engaging scene or situation. (See "Alien World: How Treacherous Border Crossing Became a Theme Park" by Alexander Zaitchik, p. 258, and "The Appeal and Danger of War Porn" by Jessica Ramirez, p. 466.)

2. **Establish an appropriate tone.** The tone you adopt should depend on the issue and the type of claim you make as well as the audience to whom you write. For an argument on a serious issue such as the death penalty, you would probably use a serious, even somber tone. For a call-to-action argument, you might use an energetic, enthusiastic tone. For a disagreeing audience, you might use a friendly, nonthreatening tone. Be sure to avoid statements that allow no room for opposing viewpoints (such as "It is obvious that . . ."). Also avoid language that may insult or alienate your reader ("Anybody who thinks differently just does not understand the issue").

3. **State your reasons clearly, and provide evidence for each one.** In an essay about mandatory high school uniforms, for example, you might use a reason (such as "Requiring high school uniforms will reduce clothing costs for parents") as a topic sentence for a paragraph. The rest of the paragraph would then consist of evidence supporting that particular reason.

For more on documenting sources, see Chapter 23.

4. **Cite the sources of your research.** As you present your evidence, be sure to include a citation for each quotation, summary, or paraphrase of ideas or information you borrow from sources. Even when you do not use an author's exact wording, you need to cite the original source.

For more on transitions, see Chapter 7, pp. 150–52.

5. **Use strong transitions.** Make sure you use transitions to move clearly from reason to reason in your argument, as in "*Also relevant* to the issue . . ." and "*Furthermore,* it is important to consider. . . ." Also be certain that you have distinguished your reasons and evidence from those of the opposition. Use a transitional sentence such as "Those opposed to the death penalty claim . . ." to indicate that you are about to introduce an opposing viewpoint. A transition such as "Contrary to what those in favor of the death penalty maintain . . ." can be used to signal a refutation.

6. **Write a satisfying conclusion.** You can end an argument essay in a number of ways. Choose the strategy that will have the strongest impact on your audience.

- Restate or make reference to your thesis. (See "In Defense of Multitasking" by David Silverman, pp. 537–39.)
- Make a final appeal to values. (See "When Volunteerism Isn't Noble" by Lynn Steirer, pp. 515–16.)

- Urge readers to take a specific action. (See "Eating Meat for the Environment" by Lisa M. Hamilton, pp. 553–55, and "Organ Donation: A Life-Saving Gift" by Quinne Sember, pp. 522–24.)
- Project into the future. (See "Schizophrenia: Definition and Treatment" by Sonia Gomez, pp. 675–80.)
- Call for further study or research.

Essay in Progress 6

Using the preceding suggestions for organizing and drafting, choose the line of reasoning your argument will follow and a method of organization; then write your first draft.

Analyzing and Revising

If possible, set your draft aside for a day or two before rereading and revising it. Then, as you review your draft, focus on discovering weak areas and strengthening your overall argument, not on grammar or mechanics. Use one or more of the following suggestions to analyze your draft:

1. Read your draft essay, put it aside, and write one sentence that summarizes your argument. Compare your summary sentence and thesis (statement of claim) to see if they agree or disagree. If they do not agree, your argument needs a stronger focus.
2. Read your essay aloud or ask a friend to do so as you listen. You may "hear" parts of your argument that do not seem to follow.
3. Make an outline or draw a graphic organizer or update one you did earlier. Look to see if the outline or graphic organizer reveals any weaknesses in your argument (for example, you don't have enough reasons to support your claim).

Learning Style Options

Use Figure 20.3 (pp. 566–67) to guide your analysis. You might also ask a classmate to review your draft essay using the questions in the flowchart. For each "No" response, ask your reviewer to explain why he or she responded in that way.

For more on the benefits of peer review, see Chapter 9, pp. 188–91.

Essay in Progress 7

Revise your draft using Figure 20.3 and any comments you received from peer reviewers.

Editing and Proofreading

The last step is to check your revised essay for errors in grammar, spelling, punctuation, and mechanics. Be sure to check your error log for the types of errors you tend to make. Look for the following two grammatical errors in particular:

For more on keeping an error log, see Chapter 10, pp. 221–22.

1. **Make sure that you use the subjunctive mood correctly.** In an argument, you often write about what would or might happen in the future. When you use the verb *be* to speculate about future conditions, use *were* in place of *was*.

   - If all animal research ~~was~~ ^{were} outlawed, progress in the control of human diseases would be slowed dramatically.

Figure 20.3 Flowchart for Revising an Argument Essay

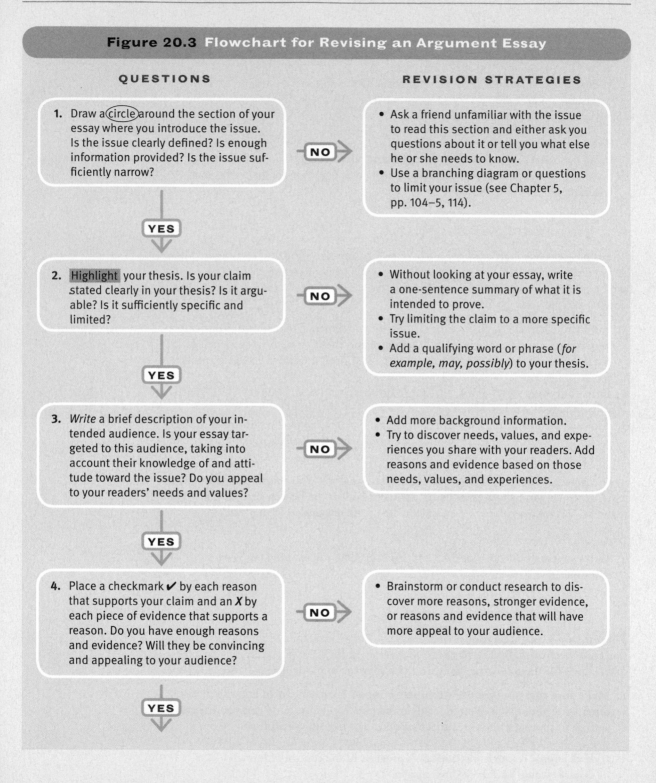

QUESTIONS

1. Draw a (circle) around the section of your essay where you introduce the issue. Is the issue clearly defined? Is enough information provided? Is the issue sufficiently narrow?

NO

2. Highlight your thesis. Is your claim stated clearly in your thesis? Is it arguable? Is it sufficiently specific and limited?

NO

3. *Write* a brief description of your intended audience. Is your essay targeted to this audience, taking into account their knowledge of and attitude toward the issue? Do you appeal to your readers' needs and values?

NO

4. Place a checkmark ✔ by each reason that supports your claim and an *X* by each piece of evidence that supports a reason. Do you have enough reasons and evidence? Will they be convincing and appealing to your audience?

NO

YES

REVISION STRATEGIES

- Ask a friend unfamiliar with the issue to read this section and either ask you questions about it or tell you what else he or she needs to know.
- Use a branching diagram or questions to limit your issue (see Chapter 5, pp. 104–5, 114).

- Without looking at your essay, write a one-sentence summary of what it is intended to prove.
- Try limiting the claim to a more specific issue.
- Add a qualifying word or phrase (*for example, may, possibly*) to your thesis.

- Add more background information.
- Try to discover needs, values, and experiences you share with your readers. Add reasons and evidence based on those needs, values, and experiences.

- Brainstorm or conduct research to discover more reasons, stronger evidence, or reasons and evidence that will have more appeal to your audience.

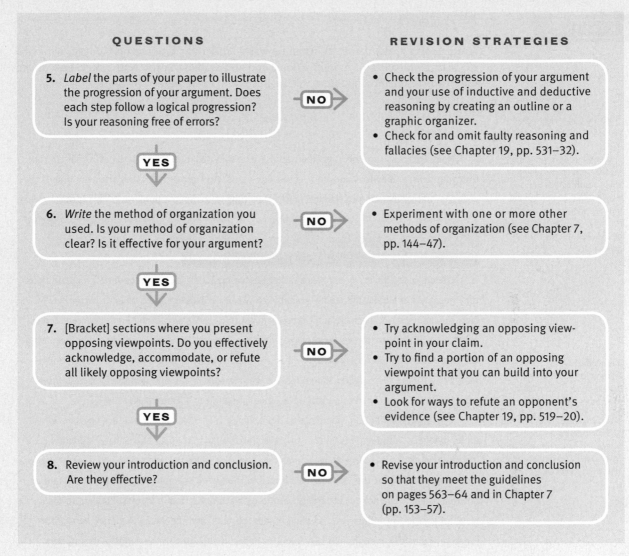

QUESTIONS		REVISION STRATEGIES
5. *Label* the parts of your paper to illustrate the progression of your argument. Does each step follow a logical progression? Is your reasoning free of errors?	**NO**	• Check the progression of your argument and your use of inductive and deductive reasoning by creating an outline or a graphic organizer. • Check for and omit faulty reasoning and fallacies (see Chapter 19, pp. 531–32).
YES		
6. *Write* the method of organization you used. Is your method of organization clear? Is it effective for your argument?	**NO**	• Experiment with one or more other methods of organization (see Chapter 7, pp. 144–47).
YES		
7. [Bracket] sections where you present opposing viewpoints. Do you effectively acknowledge, accommodate, or refute all likely opposing viewpoints?	**NO**	• Try acknowledging an opposing viewpoint in your claim. • Try to find a portion of an opposing viewpoint that you can build into your argument. • Look for ways to refute an opponent's evidence (see Chapter 19, pp. 519–20).
YES		
8. Review your introduction and conclusion. Are they effective?	**NO**	• Revise your introduction and conclusion so that they meet the guidelines on pages 563–64 and in Chapter 7 (pp. 153–57).

2. **Look for and correct ambiguous pronouns.** A pronoun must refer to another noun or pronoun, called its *antecedent*. The pronoun's antecedent should be clearly named—not just implied.

■ Children of divorced parents are often shuttled between two homes, and

    this lack of stability

  ~~that~~ can be confusing and disturbing to them.

Essay in Progress 8

Edit and proofread your essay, paying particular attention both to your use of the verb *be* in sentences that speculate about the future and to pronoun reference. Don't forget to look for errors you often make.

Students Write

James Sturm wrote this essay when he was a student at Kalamazoo College, where he graduated with a degree in international and area studies. As you read, notice how Sturm uses comparison and contrast as well as illustration to strengthen his argument.

Pull the Plug on Explicit Lyrics

James Sturm

Title: The title indicates Sturm's position on the issue of explicit lyrics.

Introduction: Sturm captures readers' interest by talking about youthful rebellion and establishes common ground with his audience by admitting his own. In his thesis statement, he clearly states his claim of policy.

Many kids pass through a rebellious phase in middle school. If the teacher asks them to stop throwing pencils, they toss one more. If the sign reads "No Trespassing," they cross the line. If they hear their father listening to classical music, they tune in to rap and punk rock. This is exactly what I did, although I now look back with regret on my actions. Having matured significantly since my middle-school days, I understand the negative effect that explicit lyrics have on youth, and I believe such music should be off-limits until the age of sixteen.   1

Currently, the government takes a rather laissez-faire attitude with regard to the music industry. Thousands of albums are readily available to young people regardless of explicit content. In fact, the main control mechanism for protecting youthful consumers from harmful content comes from the recording companies themselves. Under the Parental Advisory campaign of the Recording Industry Association of America (RIAA), it is the responsibility of artists and record labels themselves to decide if their albums should receive the infamous "Parental Advisory: Explicit Content" label. Children are allowed to purchase the albums regardless ("Parental Advisory").   2

Sturm offers background information about government regulation and record labeling, providing a source citation.

After providing a transition and accommodating an opposing viewpoint, Sturm presents his first reason and supports it with an example.

This lack of regulation would not be a problem if the music did not produce negative effects on its listeners. Although it is difficult to prove statistically that music full of hateful content fuels similar attitudes in its listeners, it requires only common sense to understand why. That is, people are influenced by what they think about. If a child thinks, for example, that he is unimportant or unloved, then he will act out in various ways to gain attention from his peers. Problem thinking is a result of a variety of influences, including friends, parents, and the media. Negative music, if listened to frequently enough, naturally implants negative thoughts in the minds of its listeners.   3

Sturm presents his second reason and supports it by establishing common ground with his audience. Here and in the next paragraph, he includes transitions between his reasons.

Furthermore, consider the unique influence of music as opposed to other forms of media. Unlike movies, video games, and magazines, music has a way of saturating one's mind. Everyone knows the feeling of having a song "stuck" in their head, repeating itself throughout the day. Unlike a movie, which is seen once, discussed among friends, and then forgotten, a song can remain lodged in one's mind for weeks on end. And if the songs are steeped in content such as violence against women, happiness found in harmful drugs, and hatred of the police, these themes will continue reverberating in the minds of the listener, slowly desensitizing them to otherwise repulsive ideas. Becoming numb to such ideas is the first step toward passively agreeing with them or even personally acting upon them.   4

Whereas adults can usually listen to such music with no behavioral ramifications, children are far more susceptible to its subtle influence. With less experience of life, a lower level of maturity, and a lack of long-term thinking, young people are prone to make impulsive decisions. Providing them with access to music that fuels negative and harmful thoughts is a dangerous decision. We live in an age where violent tragedies such as school shootings are increasingly commonplace. Although various factors contribute to such acts of violence, hatred-themed music is likely a part of the equation. Therefore, given the influential power of music and the heightened effect it can have on those still in the developmental stage of their lives, young people should have limited access to music with explicit lyrics.

5 — Sturm presents his third reason and accommodates two opposing viewpoints; he refers back to the previous paragraph to create coherence.

I propose sixteen years of age as a reasonable cut-off. Until children reach that age, they should not be allowed to purchase music with a Parental Advisory label. At sixteen, they are becoming young adults and making more and more of their own decisions. Before sixteen, they are weathering the turbulent transition from middle school to high school. This transition should not be accompanied by music that promotes rebellion as a means of coping with stress and difficulty. After reaching age sixteen, however, most young people will have obtained a driver's license, and the freedom that it allows eliminates the possibility of protecting youth from certain music. That is, those with a driver's license can seek out their own venues to hear explicit content, whether concerts or elsewhere.

6 — Sturm offers an explanation for choosing sixteen as an age cutoff.

The main critique of my position is not new. Many say that it's pointless to censor music's explicit content because, as the RIAA's Web site contends, "music is a reflection, not a cause; it doesn't create the problems our society faces, it forces us to confront them" ("Freedom of Speech"). It is true that music reflects our culture. But it is also true that music fuels the perpetuation of that culture, for better or for worse. Guarding youth from explicit music does not equate to ignoring the issues raised in the music. It merely delegates that task to adults rather than to children.

7 — In this paragraph and the next two, Sturm recognizes three opposing viewpoints and accommodates each of them. Notice that he cites a source for the first viewpoint and includes transitions between them.

Another critique says that limiting youth access to explicit music would take a financial toll on the music industry. This is true, but it would also force the music industry to adapt. We can either allow the youth of our nation to adapt to the music industry, or we can force the industry to adapt to an impressionable generation of kids.

8

A third critique is that even if explicit music were restricted to those of a certain age, younger kids would find access to it anyway. This is a legitimate concern, especially given the explosion of music-downloading software. But if not only music outlet stores but also online companies such as Amazon.com and iTunes were included in the regulations, progress would surely come.

9

Hip-hop artist Ja Rule has spoken in favor of the current Parental Advisory system, saying, "That's what we can do as musicians to try to deter the kids from getting that lyrical content." But he added, "I don't think it deters the kids—it's just another sticker on the tape right now" (Bowes). Even hip-hop artists agree that protecting the minds of our youth is a necessity. But until laws are

10 — Conclusion: Sturm quotes a hip-hop artist (and cites the source) to offer final support for his claim.

passed to restrict access to this music, the "Parental Advisory" label will just be another logo on the CD cover.

Works Cited

Bowes, Peter. "Spotlight on Explicit Lyrics Warning." *BBC News World Edition*. BBC, 27 May 2002. Web. 18 Sept. 2010.

"Freedom of Speech." *RIAA*. Recording Industry Association of America, n.d. Web. 18 Sept. 2010.

"Parental Advisory." *RIAA*. Recording Industry Association of America, n.d. Web. 18 Sept. 2010.

Analyzing the Writer's Technique

1. Analyze Sturm's thesis statement. What does it suggest about the organization of the essay? What aspect of the essay does it give no hint about?
2. What additional types of evidence could Sturm have used to support his reasons?
3. How precisely does Sturm define the term "explicit lyrics"? Does his definition need to be more precise? Why or why not?

Thinking Critically about Argument

1. What is Sturm's attitude toward explicit lyrics? Highlight words and phrases that reveal it.
2. Is Sturm relying on fact, opinion, or both to support his argument? Identify passages that support your answer.
3. Who is Sturm's main audience?
4. What is "explicit music" a euphemism for?
5. To what needs and values does Sturm appeal?

Reacting to the Reading

1. Discuss Sturm's proposal to ban the sale of "explicit music" to children. How are other media—such as books, movies, magazines, and TV shows—treated similarly or differently when it comes to children?
2. What is the benefit, if any, of having explicit lyrics in music? Why are they needed, or why should they be allowed at all?
3. Write an essay discussing the following dilemma: A middle-school student wants to listen to explicit music, but it is not legally available to her age group. Her parents do not want her to have access to such music. Is there a compromise position? What advice would you offer to each side?

Applying Your Skills: Additional Essay Assignments

To Persuade Your Reader

Write an argument essay on one of the following topics:

1. Professional sports
2. E-waste (electronic waste)
3. Alternative energy options
4. Genetic testing
5. Presidential campaigns

Narrow the topic to focus on an issue that can be debated, such as a problem that could be solved by reforms or legislation. Depending on the topic you choose, you may need to do library or Internet research. Your audience is made up of your classmates and instructor.

Cases Using Argument

1. Write an essay for a sociology course, arguing your position on the following statement: The race of a child and that of the prospective parents should be taken into consideration in making adoption decisions.
2. You have a job as a copy editor at a city newspaper. Write a proposal that explains and justifies your request to work at home one day per week. Incorporate into your argument the fact that you could use your home computer, which is connected to the newspaper's computer network.

PART 5

Writing with Sources

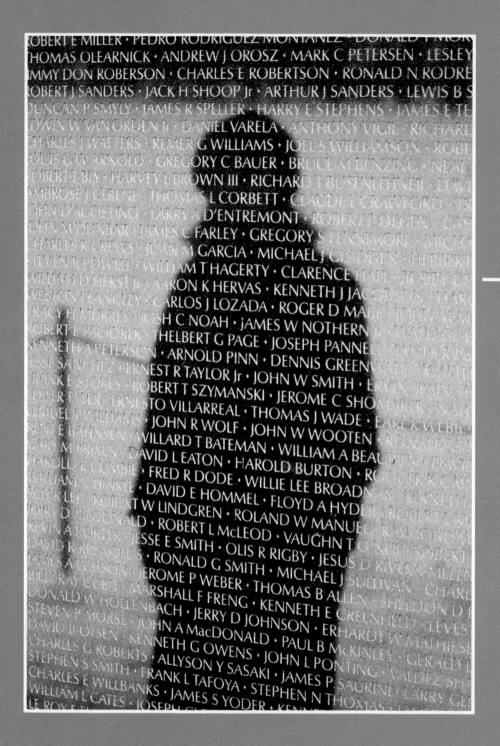

CHAPTER 21

Planning a Paper with Sources

Suppose you are enrolled in a public speaking class. Your instructor gives the class a number of photographs of significant national monuments and directs each student to choose one photograph and prepare a speech on what the history of the monument is and what it is intended to represent. You've chosen the picture of the Vietnam Veterans' Memorial Wall in Washington, D.C., shown on the opposite page.

Write a brief statement summarizing what you already know about the Vietnam Veterans' Memorial Wall and indicating what further information you would need to speak or write in detail about this monument.

Before planning a speech about the monument shown in the photograph, you would probably need to consult several sources to learn more about it. What further information would you need to support your ideas? How would you be sure the information contained in your sources is relevant and reliable? How would you detect a writer's bias? This chapter will answer these and other questions about choosing and evaluating useful sources. It will also lead you through the process of planning a paper with sources.

Sources of information come in many forms. They include materials that come in both print and electronic form (such as books, newspapers, magazines, brochures, and scholarly journals), media sources (DVDs, television, radio), and electronic sources (CD-ROMs, blogs and podcasts, email). Interviews, personal observations, and surveys are also sources of information. The various kinds of sources are discussed in more detail in Chapter 22.

You can use sources in a variety of ways. For instance, you may plan a paper that is based on your own experiences but discover that you need additional support from outside sources for aspects of the topic. At other times you may start a paper by checking several sources to narrow your topic or become more familiar with it. Finally, you may be asked to write a research paper, which requires the most extensive use of sources. See the accompanying box for a few other examples of situations that would require using sources.

When Should You Use Sources?

You should use sources whenever your topic demands more factual information than you can provide from your own personal knowledge and experience. Sources are classified as *primary* or *secondary*. **Primary sources** include historical documents (letters, diaries, speeches); literary works; autobiographies; original research reports; eyewitness accounts; and your own interviews, observations, or correspondence. For example, a report on a study of heart disease written by the researcher who conducted the study is a primary source, as is a novel by William Faulkner. In addition, what *you* say or write can be a primary source. Your own interview with a heart-attack survivor for a paper on heart disease is a primary source. **Secondary sources** report or comment on

---

SCENES FROM COLLEGE AND THE WORKPLACE

- For an *astronomy* course, you are asked to write a two-page report on black holes. Your textbook contains basic information on the subject, but you need to consult other sources to complete the assignment.

- For a *contemporary American history* assignment, you need to write a five-page research paper on a current issue (such as national health insurance), explaining the issue and reporting on current developments.

- You are a *journalist* and will interview your state governor. You need background information on the governor's position on several issues of local concern.

primary sources. A journal article that reviews several previously published research reports on heart disease is a secondary source. A book written about Faulkner by a literary critic or biographer is a secondary source.

Using Sources to Add Details to an Essay

The following suggestions will help you use sources to add details to a paper and thus provide stronger support for your thesis:

- **Make general comments more specific.** For example, instead of saying that "the crime rate in New York City has decreased over the past few years," use statistics indicating the exact percentage of the decrease.
- **Give specific examples that illustrate your main points.** If you are writing about why some companies refuse to accept orders online, for instance, locate a business that has such a policy and give details about its rationale.
- **Supply technical information.** If you are writing about a drug that lowers high blood pressure, gather information from sources about its manufacture, ingredients, effectiveness, cost, and side effects so that you can make informed, accurate comments.
- **Support opinions with evidence.** If you state that more federal assistance is needed for public education, you might provide statistics, facts, expert opinion, or other evidence to back up your statement.
- **Provide historical information.** If you are writing about space stations, for example, find out when the first one was established, what country launched it, and so forth to add background information to your paper.
- **Locate information about similar events or ideas.** For example, if you are writing about a president's intervention in a labor strike, find out if other presidents have intervened in similar strikes. You can then point out similarities and differences. You can also compare different writers' ideas on an issue. For example, in a paper about the consequences of divorce, you could use a source that deals with negative consequences and one that deals with benefits.

Using Sources to Write a Research Paper

A research paper requires you to collect and analyze information on a topic from a variety of sources. Depending on your topic, you may use primary sources, secondary sources, or both. For a research paper comparing the speeches of Abraham Lincoln with those of Franklin D. Roosevelt, you would probably read and analyze the speeches (primary sources). You might also create your own primary source by interviewing a local historian. But for a research paper comparing Lincoln's and Roosevelt's domestic policies, you would probably rely on several histories or biographies (secondary sources). Many research papers incorporate both primary and secondary sources. While researching Lincoln's and Roosevelt's domestic policies, for instance, you might consult some original documents (primary sources).

Regardless of the sources you use, your task is to organize and present your findings in a meaningful way. When you write a research paper, you don't simply "glue together" the facts, statistics, information, and quotations you find in sources. Like any other essay-length writing, a research paper has a thesis, and the thesis is supported throughout the paper. Although the information from outside sources is not your own, the interpretation you give it should be your own.

In a research paper or in any paper with sources, it is essential to acknowledge your sources fairly and correctly. To do so, include parenthetical, or in-text, citations in the body of the paper and a corresponding list of works cited or references at the end of the paper.

For more on systems for documenting sources, see Chapter 23, pp. 640–62 (MLA) and 663–81 (APA).

Whether you use sources to add details to an essay or to write a research paper, it is helpful to approach the process of locating, evaluating, and using sources in a systematic way. Figure 21.1 presents an overview of this process. The following sections of this chapter will help you plan a paper with sources and learn how to evaluate source material.

Planning Your Paper

Although starting your research in the library or on the Internet may seem like a good idea, usually the best place to begin is at your desk. There you can think about the assignment and devise a plan for completing it. This section describes several tasks that you should accomplish before you begin your research, as shown in Figure 21.2.

FIGURE 21.1 Locating and Using Sources: An Overview

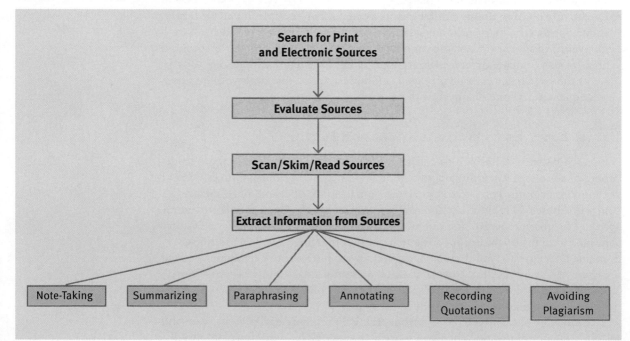

FIGURE 21.2 Writing a Paper Using Sources

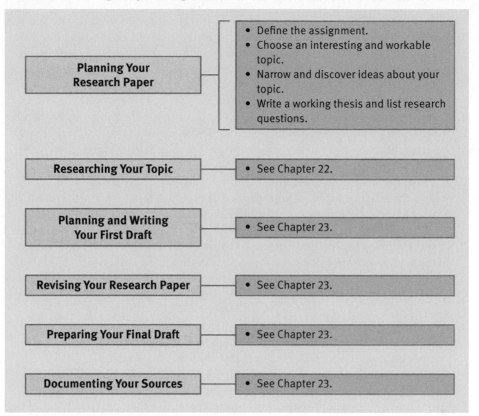

Defining the Assignment

Not all assignments have the same purpose. Many are informative, asking you to explain (for example, "Explain the treatment options for breast cancer") or to explore an issue (for example, "Examine the pros and cons of legalizing casino gambling"). Still others are persuasive, asking you to take and support a particular position (for example, "Defend or argue against your college's proposal to eliminate athletic scholarships").

Before you begin researching an assigned topic, be sure you understand what your instructor expects. If your instructor announces the assignment in class, write down what he or she says, including any examples. When you are ready to begin the research paper days or weeks later, you may find it helpful to review exactly what your instructor told you. In addition, make sure you understand any limits on the topic, any minimum or maximum length requirements, the due date (and late penalties), and any requirements about the number and kinds of sources you need to consult. Finally, be sure you know which documentation style you are expected to use.

Choosing an Interesting and Workable Topic

Most instructors allow you to choose your own topic for a research paper. You will save time in the long run if you spend enough time at the outset choosing one that is interesting and workable. Too many students waste hours researching a topic that they finally realize is too difficult, broad, or ordinary. The following tips will help you avoid such pitfalls:

1. **Choose an interesting topic.** You will enjoy the assignment and be able to write more enthusiastically if you work with a topic that captures your interest. If you have trouble choosing a topic, brainstorm with a classmate or friend. A conversation will often help you discover new angles on ordinary topics.
2. **Choose a manageable topic.** Make sure you can adequately cover the topic within the assigned length of your paper. For example, don't try to write about all kinds of family counseling programs in a five- to ten-page paper. Instead, limit your topic to one type, such as programs for adolescents.
3. **Avoid ordinary topics.** Familiar subjects that have been thoroughly explained in many sources seldom make good topics. For example, the subjects of "childhood obesity" or "the dieting craze" have been thoroughly discussed in many newspapers and magazines. If you use such a topic, be sure to come up with a different slant on it.
4. **Avoid topics that are too current.** Topics that are currently in the news or for which a new breakthrough has just been reported do not typically make good choices because in many cases little reliable information is available.
5. **Choose a practical topic.** Choose a topic for which sources are readily available—on the Internet, at your college library, or through interlibrary loan. Avoid topics that require extensive technical knowledge that you lack. Most of us, for example, should not write a paper comparing the mechanical performance of two hybrid engines or the chemical makeup of two drugs.

Narrowing and Discovering Ideas about Your Topic

The following techniques will help you narrow your topic and discover ideas about it.

Do Some Preliminary Reading

For more on library and Internet sources, see Chapter 22.

It is often a good idea to do some preliminary reading to discover the scope, depth, and breadth of your topic. Either at your library or online, you might glance through part of a general encyclopedia, such as *Encyclopaedia Britannica,* to gain a brief overview of your topic.

Be sure to consider other kinds of sources as well. A specialized encyclopedia, such as *The McGraw-Hill Encyclopedia of Science and Technology,* and your library's electronic catalog can help you identify the subtopics into which a topic can be broken. The weekly *CQ Researcher,* whose database contains thousands of articles on current topics, is another useful reference to consult for background information and to get ideas for topics. Or consider scanning a current magazine index for coverage of controversial issues. You can also ask a reference librarian for assistance.

Try Prewriting

To uncover interesting topics or to narrow a broad topic, use one or more prewriting techniques. Prewriting may also reveal an interesting idea that may eventually become your thesis. A branching diagram may be particularly helpful in narrowing a topic.

For more on prewriting, see Chapter 5, pp. 110–18.

View Your Topic from Different Perspectives

Another technique, questioning, can help you view your topic in different ways. Try asking questions about your topic from a variety of perspectives—psychological, sociological, scientific or technical, historical, political, and economic. Add other perspectives that apply to your topic. Here is how one student used questioning to analyze different perspectives on television advertising:

TOPIC: TELEVISION ADVERTISING

Perspective	*Questions*
Psychological	• How does advertising affect people?
	• Does it affect everyone the same way?
	• What emotional appeals are used?
	• How do emotional appeals work?
Sociological	• How do different groups of people respond differently to ads?
	• Is advertising targeted toward specific racial and ethnic groups?
Scientific or technical	• How are ads produced?
	• Who writes them?
	• Are the ads tested before they are broadcast?
Historical	• What is the history of advertising?
	• When and where did it begin?
Political	• What is the history of political advertising?
	• Why are negative political advertisements effective?
Economic	• How much does a television ad cost?
	• Is the cost of advertising added to the price of the product?

This list of questions yielded a wide range of interesting subtopics about advertising, including emotional appeals, targeting ads to particular racial or ethnic groups, and negative political advertising. You might try this technique with a friend or classmate, working together to devise questions.

Exercise 21.1

Working with one or two classmates, narrow each of the following topics until you reach a topic that would be manageable for a five- to ten-page research paper.

1. Job interviews

2. U.S. prison system

3. Video games

4. Terrorism

5. Extinction of animal species

Research Paper in Progress 1

Choose a broad topic for your research paper. In your paper you will state a thesis and provide evidence for your thesis. Your audience consists of your classmates. Begin by using one or more prewriting techniques to narrow and generate ideas about your topic. Then reread your work and highlight useful ideas. Choose one of the broad topics below, or come up with one on your own. Refer to Table 5.2 on page 116 for other general topic suggestions.

1. Extreme sports
2. Cross-racial child adoptions
3. Problems in the workplace
4. Internet fraud
5. Campus security and safety

If you are uncertain about the topic you have chosen, be sure to check with your instructor. Most instructors don't mind if you clear your topic with them; in fact, some encourage or even require this step. Your instructor may also suggest a way to narrow your topic, recommend a useful source, or offer to review your outline at a later stage.

Writing a Working Thesis and Listing Research Questions

Once you choose and narrow a topic, try to determine, as specifically as possible, the kinds of information you need to know about it. Begin by writing a working thesis for your paper and listing the research questions you need to answer.

One student working on the general topic of child abuse, for example, used prewriting and preliminary reading to narrow his focus to physical abuse and its causes. Since he already had a few ideas about possible causes, he used those ideas to write a working thesis. He then used his thesis to generate a list of research questions. Notice how the student's questions follow from his working thesis.

WORKING THESIS	The physical abuse of children often stems from parents' emotional instability and a family history of child abuse.
RESEARCH QUESTIONS	If a person was physically abused as a child, how likely is that person to become an abusive parent?
	What kinds of emotional problems seem to trigger the physical abuse of children?
	Which cause is more significant—a family history of abuse or emotional problems?
	Is there more physical abuse of children now than there was in the past, or is more abuse being reported?

A working thesis and a list of research questions will enable you to approach your research in a focused way. Instead of running helter-skelter from one aspect of your topic to another, you will be able to zero in on the specific information you need from sources.

Exercise 21.2

For one of the following topics, write a working thesis and four or more research questions.

1. Methods of controlling pornography on the Internet

2. The possibility that some form of life has existed on other planets

3. Reasons for the extinction of dinosaurs

4. Benefits of tracing your family's genealogy (family tree)

5. Ways that elderly family members affect family life

Research Paper in Progress 2

Review the list of ideas you generated in Research Paper in Progress 1. Underline the ideas for which you need further details or supporting evidence, and list the information you need. Then, using the preceding guidelines, write a working thesis and a list of research questions.

Choosing and Evaluating Useful Sources

Once you have a working thesis and a list of research questions, stop for a moment before you charge off to the library or your computer. Many students make the mistake of photocopying many articles, printing out dozens of Web pages, and lugging home numerous books only to find that the sources are not useful or that several contain identical information. Save yourself time by taking a few minutes to think about print and electronic sources and about which sources will be most relevant and reliable. Consider as well how to distinguish between facts and opinions, how to identify bias, and how to recognize generalizations or assumptions.

Using Online and Print Sources

Deciding when to use the Internet and when to use traditional library print sources can be complicated. In terms of convenience, it may be easier to access sources online from your dorm room or home rather than visiting the library. You may also be able to use your home computer to access many of the library's resources, including its catalog of books, indexes, and electronic databases. But even though some students find the use of print sources too cumbersome and time-consuming, online sources also have their drawbacks. First, although the Internet is a vast network of information, that information is unorganized. There is no central source that organizes or catalogs it the way a library does for print materials. Second, Internet sources are not stable—that is, a source you find one day may disappear the next, or the content may change. Finally, because almost anyone can publish on the Internet with no "screening" by publishers, editors, librarians, or experts in the subject area, you cannot be as confident as you can with print sources that a particular online source is credible and authoritative. These concerns are especially important for sources you find on your own, such as through a

Google search, rather than in an electronic database to which your library subscribes. (Use the guidelines on pp. 585–87 to evaluate Internet sources.)

Some sources are available both online and in print, including many periodicals and certain reference books, such as the *Oxford Encyclopedia of Food and Drink in America*. Some are only online, including blogs, video and audio material, and some magazines and journals. However, there are many sources that are available only in print form, including most books. Following are a few specific situations in which using a print source is often preferable to using an online source:

- **To find specific facts.** It may be easier to find a single fact, such as the date of a president's inauguration, by looking in a reference book rather than doing research on the Web.
- **To do historical or in-depth research on a topic.** Books may be essential to some types of research because they represent years of study by authorities on the subject. Some historical information and data are not available on the Internet.

Choosing Relevant Sources

A *relevant* source contains information that helps you answer one or more of your research questions. Answering the following questions will help you determine whether a source is relevant:

For more on audience, see Chapter 5, pp. 107–9.

1. **Is the source too general or too specialized for your intended audience?** Some sources may not contain the detailed information your audience requires; others may be too technical and require background knowledge that your audience does not have. For example, suppose you are researching the environmental effects of recycling cans and bottles. If your audience consists of science majors, an article in *Reader's Digest* might be too general. Conversely, an article in *Environmental Science and Technology* would be written for scientists and may be a bit too technical for your purposes.
2. **Is the source recent enough for your purposes?** In rapidly changing fields of study, outdated sources are not useful unless you need to give a historical perspective. For example, a ten-year-old article on using air bags to improve car safety will not include information on recent discoveries about the dangers that air bags pose to children riding in the front passenger seat.

Choosing Reliable Sources

A *reliable* source is honest, accurate, and credible. Answering the questions below will help you determine whether a source is reliable. (To check the reliability of an Internet source, consult pp. 585–87 as well.)

1. **Is the source scholarly?** Although scholars often disagree with one another, they make a serious attempt to present accurate information. In addition, an article that appears in a scholarly journal or textbook has been reviewed by a panel of professionals in the field prior to publication. Therefore, scholarly sources tend

to be trustworthy. For more on the differences between scholarly and popular sources, refer to Table 22.1 on page 601.

2. **Does the source have a solid reputation?** Some magazines, such as *Time* and *Newsweek,* are known for responsible reporting, whereas other periodicals have a reputation for sensationalism and should be avoided or approached skeptically. Web sites, too, may or may not be reputable.

3. **Is the author an expert in the field?** Check the author's credentials. Information about authors may be given in a headnote; at the end of an article; on a home page in a link; or in the preface, on the dust jacket, or at the beginning or end of a book. You might also check a reference book such as *Contemporary Authors* to verify an author's credentials.

4. **Does the author approach the topic fairly and objectively?** A writer who states a strong opinion is not necessarily biased. However, a writer who ignores opposing views, distorts facts, or ignores information that does not fit his or her opinion is presenting a biased and incomplete view of a topic. Although you can use a biased source to understand a particular viewpoint, you must also seek out other sources that present alternative views. For more on bias and viewpoint, see pages 589–90.

Exercise 21.3

Working in a small group, discuss why the sources listed for each topic below would or would not be considered relevant and reliable. Assume that the classmates in your writing course are your audience.

1. Topic: Caring for family members with Alzheimer's disease

    a. Introductory health and nutrition textbook

    b. Article in *Woman's Day* titled "Mother, Where Are You?"

    c. Article from a gerontology journal on caring for aging family members

2. Topic: Analyzing the effects of heroin use on teenagers

    a. Newspaper article written by a former heroin user

    b. Article from the *Journal of Neurology* on the biochemical effects of heroin on the brain

    c. Pamphlet on teenage drug use published by the National Institutes of Health

3. Topic: Implementing training programs to reduce sexual harassment in the workplace

    a. Article from the *Christian Science Monitor* titled "Removing Barriers for Working Women"

    b. Personal Web site relating an incident of harassment on the job

    c. Training manual for employees of General Motors

Evaluating Internet Sources

The Internet offers many excellent and reputable sources. Not all sites are accurate and unbiased, however, and misinformation often appears on the Web. Use the following

For more practice evaluating Web sites, visit www.bedfordstmartins .com/successfulcollege.

TABLE 21.1 Evaluating Internet Sources

Purpose	• Who sponsors or publishes the site—an organization, a corporation, a government agency, or an individual? • What are the sponsor's goals—to present information or news, opinions, products to sell, or fun?
Author	• Who wrote the information on the site? • Is the information clearly presented and well written?
Accuracy	• Are ideas supported by credible evidence? Is there a works-cited list or bibliography? • Is the information presented verifiable? • Are opinions clearly identified as such?
Timeliness	• When was the site first created? What is the date of the last revision? • Does the specific document you are using have a date? • Are the links up-to-date?

---

questions to evaluate the reliability of Internet sources. (Table 21.1 summarizes these questions.)

What Is the Site's Purpose?

Web sites have many different purposes. They may provide information or news, advocate a particular point of view, or try to sell a product. Many sites have more than one purpose. A pharmaceutical company's site, for instance, may offer health advice in addition to advertising its own drugs. Understanding the purposes of an Internet source will help you deal with its potential biases.

For more about bias, see pp. 589–90.

To determine the purpose of any site, start by identifying the sponsor of the site—the organization or person who paid to place it on the Web. The copyright usually reveals the owner of a site, and often a link labeled "About Us," "About Me," or "Mission Statement" will take you to a description of the sponsor.

What Are the Author's Credentials?

It helps to know who wrote the specific Web page you are looking at. The sponsors of many Web sites have professionals write their content. When this is the case, the writer's name and credentials are usually listed, and his or her email address may be provided. This kind of information can help you determine whether the Web page is a reliable resource. If information about an author is not available on the site or is sketchy, you might conduct a search for the author's name on the Web.

Regardless of who the author of the site is, the information should be well written and organized. If it is carelessly put together, you should be wary of it. In short, if the sponsor did not spend time presenting information correctly and clearly, the information itself may not be very accurate.

Is the Site's Information Accurate?

In addition to paying attention to how a site's material is written and organized, ask yourself the following questions:

- **Is a bibliography or a list of works cited provided?** If sources are not included, you should question the accuracy of the site.
- **Can the accuracy of the information be checked elsewhere?** In most instances you should be able to verify Internet information by checking another source, often simply by clicking on links in the original source.
- **Is the document in complete form?** If you're looking at a summary, use the site to try to find the original source. If you can't locate the original, be skeptical of the source that contains the summary. Original information generally has fewer errors and is often preferred in academic papers.

If Internet information is available in print form, it is usually a good idea to try to obtain the print version. There are several reasons for doing so. First, when an article goes on the Web, errors may creep in. In addition, since Web sites often change addresses or content, a reader of your paper may not be able to find the site or content that you used. Finally, page numbers in print sources are easier to cite than those in electronic ones (which may not include standard page numbering).

Is the Site Up-to-Date?

Even though the Web has a reputation for providing current information, not all Web sites are up-to-date. You can check the timeliness of a site by asking yourself the following questions about dates:

- **When was the site first established?**
- **If the site has been revised, what is the date of the last revision?**
- **When was the document you are looking at posted to the site?** Has it been updated?

This kind of information generally appears at the bottom of a site's home page or at the end of a particular document. If no dates are given, check some of the links. If the links are outdated and nonfunctioning, the information at the site is probably outdated as well.

Analyzing and Thinking Critically about Sources

Whether you search a library for sources—such as relevant books or journal articles—or find them on the Internet, you should first make sure that your sources are relevant and reliable. In addition, when you use sources in your paper, you will need to analyze them and think critically. As a critical reader, you need to recognize that multiple viewpoints exist and find the sources that express them. If you can sort through each writer's ideas and watch for opinions, bias, generalizations, and assumptions, you will be well on your way to locating useful research.

Separating Facts from Opinions

It is important to understand the difference between facts and opinions. **Facts** are statements that can be proven to be either true or false; evidence exists to verify facts. **Opinions**, on the other hand, are statements that reveal beliefs or feelings and are neither true nor false. For example, "The Boston Red Sox won the 2007 World Series" is a fact, whereas "The Boston Red Sox are the best team in baseball" is an opinion. For more examples of facts and opinions, see the box below on this page.

For more on fact and opinion, see Chapter 4, pp. 72–73.

Facts are considered reliable if they are taken from a reputable source or can be verified. For example, the date of President John F. Kennedy's assassination—November 22, 1963—is a fact that can be found in many reputable sources. Opinions, however, are not always based on facts and should be evaluated carefully. Before accepting someone's opinion, try to find evidence that supports it. Several opinions exist, for instance, concerning why and how President Kennedy was shot. Some of these opinions may be more reliable than others.

When authors present an opinion, they often alert their readers by using certain words and phrases, such as the following:

as I see it	possibly
in my opinion	some experts believe
in my view	supposedly
it is probable	this seems to indicate

A special type of opinion is **expert opinion**—the attitudes or beliefs expressed by authorities on the topic. Like other writers, experts often use qualifying words and phrases when they offer an opinion. An expert on government finance may write, for example, "*It seems likely* that Social Security payments will decline for future generations of Americans."

DON'T CONFUSE FACTS AND OPINIONS

FACT	The planet Earth has six times the volume of Mars.
OPINION	Humans will probably destroy the planet Earth if they don't stop polluting it.
FACT	After inventing the telephone in 1876, Alexander Graham Bell worked on dozens of other inventions, many of which aided the deaf.
OPINION	Alexander Graham Bell's invention of the telephone is considered the most important technological innovation of the nineteenth century.
FACT	Many vitamin-fortified foods are now available in supermarkets.
OPINION	Supermarkets need to carry a wider variety of organic foods.

Opinions of people who are not experts on the topic may be useful to read and consider as a means of shaping your own opinions, but they do not belong in a source-based paper. Expert opinion, however, is definitely usable. When you quote or paraphrase it, be sure to give appropriate credit to your source.

For more on documenting sources, see Chapter 23.

Exercise 21.4

Label each of the following statements as fact (F), opinion (O), or expert opinion (EO).

1. According to child psychologists Gerber and Gerber, children who watch prime-time television shows that depict crime consider the world more dangerous than those who do not watch crime shows.

2. The best symphonies are shorter than twenty minutes.

3. Most medical experts recommend that women age forty and older have a mammogram once every one to two years.

4. About half the population of Uruguay lives in Montevideo.

5. More women earned doctoral degrees in engineering in 2007 than in 1984.

6. Private companies should not be allowed to sell concessions inside our national parks.

7. The mountains of Northern Idaho contain the most scenic landscapes in the country.

8. Many business leaders agree that it is important to hire people who love their work.

Identifying Bias or Viewpoint

Many relevant and reliable sources may provide only a portion of the information you need for your essay. For example, if you are writing an essay on problems in the nursing profession, the *American Journal of Nursing* might be a reliable source, but it would probably not contain articles that are critical of nurses.

Many writers have a particular point of view and interpret information in their own way. For example, suppose you are writing an essay on home schooling for an introductory education class. You find a book titled *The Home Schooling Movement: What Children Are Missing* that was written by someone who taught high school for thirty years. While the book may offer valuable information, its title suggests that the author would probably support classroom instruction and perhaps discuss the shortcomings of home schooling in detail but downplay its advantages. This one-sided view of home schooling, then, would be biased. **Bias** refers to a publisher's or writer's own views or particular interest in a topic. A biased source is not necessarily unreliable, but you need to notice the bias and find additional sources that present other opinions.

To find bias in someone's writing, first consider the author's background. For example, the viewpoint of a father who has written a book about home schooling his five children is likely to be very different from that of a long-term high school teacher. Then look carefully at the author's descriptive and connotative language. In the father's book, for instance, does he tend to use many words with negative connotations when he is talking about traditional classroom education? Finally, consider the author's

For more information on descriptive language, connotative language, and tone, see pp. 215–18 and 270–71.

overall tone. Can you tell how the father feels about home schooling? Does he sound enthusiastic and positive?

Exercise 21.5

Examine each of the following sources and their annotations. Discuss whether the source is likely to be objective (O), somewhat biased (SB), or heavily biased (HB).

1. Roleff, Tamara L., ed. *Gun Control: Opposing Viewpoints*. Farmington Hills, MI: Greenhaven Press, 2007. Print.
   This book contains several articles that present the pros and cons of different issues relating to gun control. The articles are written by experts and give bibliographic references.
2. Malcolm X. *The Autobiography of Malcolm X*. New York: Ballantine, 1965. Print.
   Malcolm X tells his life story in this autobiography, which was published just before his death.
3. Green, Amy. "Missions Boot Camp." *Christianity Today* 52 (2008): 60. Print.
   This article describes a summer camp for young people heading off on mission trips.
4. Fink, George, ed. *Encyclopedia of Stress*. San Diego: Academic Press, 2007. Print.
   Four volumes of in-depth coverage related to the psychology and physiology of stress.

Recognizing Generalizations

A **generalization** is a statement about a large group of items based on experience with or observation of only a limited part of that group. If, for example, you often saw high school students in your town hanging out on the streets and creating disturbances, you might make the following generalization: "The high school students in this town are not well behaved." You could not be sure about your generalization, however, unless you observed every high school student in town, and doing so might well cause you to change your generalization. Look at the generalizations below. You probably won't agree with all of them.

- U.S. colleges and universities give more funding to their athletic programs than to their libraries.
- Home-schooled children do not interact socially with other children their own age.
- Banks in this country no longer provide basic customer services.
- Big companies are laying off great portions of their workforces.
- Circus animals are abused.

A writer's generalization is his or her interpretation of a particular set of facts. If generalizations are backed up by experience or sufficient evidence, they are probably trustworthy. An expert on heart disease, for example, would probably make reliable generalizations about the risks of high cholesterol. If a writer is not an expert, however, and does not provide solid support for generalizations, you would be wise to consult different sources.

Exercise 21.6

Label each of the following statements either fact (F) or generalization (G). Indicate what support or documentation would be necessary for you to evaluate its accuracy.

1. Many women want to become pilots.
2. Elephants can vocalize at frequencies below the range of human hearing.
3. In certain parts of the Red Sea, the temperature of the water can reach 138 degrees Fahrenheit.
4. Most people who live in San Diego are associated with the U.S. Navy.
5. People all over the world donated money to help the survivors of the 2010 earthquake in Haiti.

Identifying Assumptions

As you may recall from Chapter 19, assumptions are ideas or generalizations that people accept as true without questioning their validity. Writers often use an assumption at the beginning of an essay and then base the rest of the essay on that assumption. If the assumption is false or cannot be proven, however, then the ideas that flow from it may also be incorrect. For instance, the following excerpt begins with an assumption (highlighted) that the writer makes no attempt to prove or justify:

> Childbirth is a painful experience, intolerable even with appropriate medications. In response to this pain, modern women should accept the painkillers offered to them by their doctors. Why be a martyr? You have to suffer sleepless nights because of your child for the rest of your life; bring them into this world on your terms—pain free. Women should not be embarrassed or reluctant to request anesthesia during labor.

The author assumes that all women find childbirth intolerably painful and then argues that women should request anesthesia during labor. But if the writer's initial assumption is false, much of the argument that follows should be questioned.

As you read, be aware of assumptions, especially those at the start of an essay. Ask yourself how the essay would be affected if the initial assumption were untrue. If you disagree with some of the assumptions in a source, check other sources to obtain different viewpoints.

> ### Exercise 21.7
>
> *Each of the following statements contains one or more assumptions. Identify the assumption(s) made in each statement.*
>
> 1. Computer users expect Web sites to entertain them with graphics, sound, and video.
> 2. In response to the problem of ozone depletion, the U.S. Environmental Protection Agency has designed various programs to reduce harmful emissions. The EPA wants to stop the production of certain substances so that the ozone layer can repair itself over the next fifty years.
> 3. Only the routine vaccination of all children can eliminate the threat of serious disease and ensure optimum public health. These shots should be administered without hesitation. Parents must have full confidence in their doctors on this matter.
> 4. Since so many athletes and coaches approve of the use of performance-enhancing drugs, these substances should be allowed without regulation.
> 5. Because they recognize that meat consumption is environmentally damaging, environmentalists are often vegetarians.

Working with Text: Reading Sources

Reading sources involves some special skills. Unlike textbook reading, in which your purpose is to learn and recall the material, you usually read sources to extract the information you need about a topic. Therefore, you can often read sources selectively, reading only the relevant parts and skipping over the rest. Use the following strategies for reading sources: scan, skim, and then read closely.

Scanning a Source

Scanning means "looking for" the information you seek without actually reading a source from beginning to end. Just as you scan a phone directory to locate a phone number, you scan a source to extract needed information.

Use the following guidelines to scan sources effectively:

1. **Determine how the source is organized.** Is it organized chronologically or by topic? It could also be organized by chapter, subject, or author.
2. **For journal articles, check the abstract or summary; for books, scan the index and table of contents.** You can quickly determine whether the source contains the information you need and, if so, approximately where to find it.
3. **Keep key words or phrases in mind as you scan.** For example, if you are searching for information on welfare reform, key phrases might include *welfare system, entitlement programs, benefits,* and *welfare spending.*
4. **Scan systematically.** Don't scan a source randomly, hoping to see what you need. Instead, follow a pattern as you sweep your eyes across the material. For charts, tables, and indexes, use a downward sweep. For prose material, use a zigzag or Z-pattern, sweeping across several lines of print at a time.

Skimming a Source

Skimming (also called *previewing*) is a quick way to find out whether a source suits your purposes without taking the time to read it completely. Skimming also allows you to determine whether any sections deserve close reading. As you skim a source, mark or jot down sections that might be worth returning to later.

For more on previewing, see Chapter 3, pp. 48–52.

Use the guidelines on pages 49–50 to skim a source effectively; adapt them to fit each particular source.

Reading a Source Closely

Once you identify the sections within a source that contain the information you need—by scanning, skimming, or both—*read* those sections closely and carefully. To be sure you do not take information out of context, also read the paragraphs before and after the material you have chosen.

For more on strategies for close reading, see Chapter 3, pp. 52–61 and Chapter 4, pp. 68–77.

Improving Your Reading of Electronic Sources

When you read material on the Internet, you often need some different reading strategies. The following advice should help you read Web sites more productively:

For more practice reading Web sites, visit www.bedfordstmartins .com/successfulcollege.

- **When you reach a new site, explore it quickly to discover how it is organized and what information is available.** Remember that the first screen may grab your attention but rarely contains substantive information. Find out if there is a search option or a guide to the site (a site map). Doing an initial exploration is especially important on large and complex sites, where you may have a number of different choices for locating information.
- **Keep in mind that text on Web sites does not usually follow the traditional text pattern.** Instead of containing paragraphs, a Web page may show a list of topic sentences that you have to click on to get details. In addition, electronic pages are often designed to stand alone: They are brief and do not depend on other pages for meaning. In many instances, background information is not supplied.
- **Follow your own learning style in making decisions about what paths to follow.** Because Web sites have menus and links, readers create their own texts by following or ignoring different paths. This is quite different from print text, which offers readers far fewer choices. Some readers may prefer to begin with "the big picture" and then move to the details; others may prefer to do the opposite. A pragmatic learner may move through a site systematically, either clicking on or ignoring links as they appear on the screen. A spatial learner, in contrast, would probably look at the graphics first. All readers should make sure that they don't skip over important content.

Learning Style Options

- **Focus on your purpose.** Regardless of your learning style, keep in mind the information you are looking for. If you don't focus on your purpose, you may wander aimlessly through the site and waste valuable research time.

Finding Sources and Taking Notes

Suppose you are enrolled in a seminar on the environment. Your instructor gives the class a number of photographs and directs each student to choose one and write a paper about the environmental issues it reflects. You've chosen the photograph shown on the opposite page, which appeared in an article in *National Geographic* titled "High-Tech Trash: Will Your Discarded TV End Up in a Ditch in Ghana?"

Write a brief statement describing the environmental issue the photograph represents. Consider where you might go to learn more about this issue, and make a list of the sources you would consult.

What issue did you write about? What sources of information did you list? Did you include both print and Internet sources? Do you need to conduct a personal interview or do a survey? Once you find information that is useful for your paper, what procedures should you use to record information for later use? This chapter will answer these and other questions about how to locate sources and take accurate notes.

Regardless of the kind of research you are doing, it is helpful to approach the process of locating and using sources in a systematic way, as shown in Figure 22.1. If you already have a narrowed topic for a research paper, be sure to write a working thesis and research questions before you start looking for specific sources. If you have a general topic and need help narrowing it, several kinds of library or online sources—such as encyclopedias and subject directories—may be helpful. In either case, it is a good idea to consult the advice in Chapter 21 about planning a paper and evaluating sources.

You will have many opportunities to use sources in the writing you do in college and at work (see the accompanying box for a few examples).

An Overview of Library Sources

Your college library is an immense collection of print, media, and online sources on a wide variety of topics. Learning to use this library will help you locate sources effectively.

Learning Your Way around the Library

It is a good idea to become familiar with your college library *before* you need to use it. Following are a few ways to do so:

1. **Take a formal tour of the library.** Many colleges offer library tours during the first few weeks of the term. On a tour, you'll learn where everything is located and discover how to use important services, such as interlibrary loans and online database searches.

2. **Take your own tour.** Obtain a map or floor plan from the circulation desk and use it to tour the library. Inspect the popular magazine collection; see what electronic resources are available. Try to become comfortable with the library so that the first

For guided practice touring the library, visit www.bedfordstmartins .com/successfulcollege/.

SCENES FROM COLLEGE AND THE WORKPLACE

- For an *anthropology* course, you are asked to analyze the differences between the religious practices of two cultures.

- For an *art history* course, you are asked to write a biography of a famous Renaissance artist.

- As *supervisor* of a health-care facility, you decide to conduct a survey of the staff to determine employees' interest in flexible working hours.

FIGURE 22.1 Writing a Research Paper Using Sources

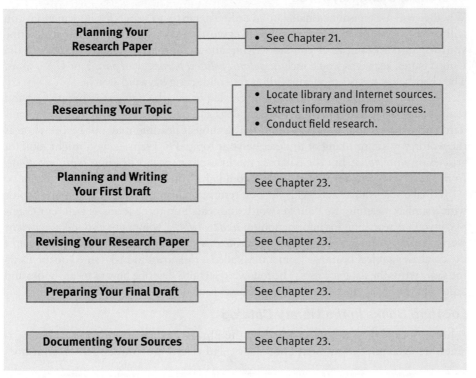

time you need to use it, you can get to work easily. Keep the floor plan in your bag or notebook for future reference.

3. **Consult reference librarians.** Librarians are usually available at the reference desk to advise you about what sources to use and where to locate them. Reference librarians can often save you time, so don't hesitate to ask them for help.

4. **Check the library's Web site.** Most libraries have a Web site created by librarians to present all the resources that are available to you. Look for a link to the library's catalog, including a way to check your library account. The online databases for journal articles will be listed on the Web site along with access instructions. Your librarians may also have posted lists of helpful Web sites that they have used with students over many semesters. Finally, library hours, services, policies, maps, and ways to contact the library staff should also appear on the site.

Locating Useful Library Sources

The sources you need will often be stored in electronic databases available through your college library or an online service. Learning how to use keyword searches and subject headings will help you locate relevant materials.

Searching Using Keywords

Whether you use an online catalog or an online database to search for information, you will need to perform keyword searches. **Keywords** are words or phrases that describe your topic. For example, if you are writing about alternative political parties in the United States, keywords would include *politics, political parties, third parties,* or *U.S. politics.* The chart below has practical suggestions for conducting keyword searches.

After you enter a keyword, the online catalog or search engine searches its files and returns a list of pertinent sources. Most catalogs and databases also search by using standard **subject headings**. Keep in mind that a subject heading may not be the same as the words you are thinking of to describe your topic. For example, you might look for articles on *drug abuse,* but the database might use the subject heading *substance abuse.* In this case, searching for *substance abuse* could give you more relevant search results.

To make sure your search yields the best results, brainstorm a list of synonyms (words with a similar meaning) for your keywords and search on those terms as well. For example, if you are searching for information on *welfare reform,* you might also include *welfare system, entitlement programs, benefits,* and *welfare spending.* Also, check your terms against the database's subject headings (sometimes called a *thesaurus*) to make sure you are using the same terms the database uses. The following sections describe how to locate books and articles in the library and in electronic databases using keywords and subject headings.

Locating Books in the Library Catalog

A library's catalog lists books owned by the library. It may also list available magazines, newspapers, government documents, and electronic sources. However, it does

---

SUGGESTIONS FOR CONDUCTING KEYWORD SEARCHES

- Place quotation marks around a phrase to limit your search. For example, **"single motherhood"** will give you topics related to *single motherhood.* Without quotation marks, a keyword search would provide all the sources that use the word *single* as well as all the sources that use the word *motherhood.*

- Use *AND* to join words that must appear in a document. For example, **psychology AND history** would provide sources that mention both *psychology* and *history.* For some searches, you may need to use a plus (+) sign instead of *AND.*

- Use *OR* to indicate synonyms when only one needs to appear in the document. For example, **job OR career** would provide more options than just *job* or just *career.*

- Place *NOT* before words that should not appear in the document. For example, **camels NOT cigarettes** would provide sources only on the animal. In some searches, you may need to use a minus (–) sign instead of *NOT.*

- Use parentheses to group together keywords and combine the group with another set of keywords. For example, **(timepiece OR watch OR clock) AND production** would provide sources on the production of any of these three items.

- Use an asterisk (*) or another symbol, such as a question mark (?) or pound sign (#), to indicate letters that may vary in spelling or words that may have variant endings. For example, a search for **"social psycholog*"** will find sources with the words *psychology, psychologist, psychologists,* and so forth.

not list individual articles included in magazines and newspapers. Before the widespread use of computers, a library's catalog was made up of three- by five-inch index cards. Now, though, almost all libraries have a computerized catalog, which allows you to search online for sources—by keyword title, author, or subject—from terminals in the library. Directions usually appear on or near the screen, and most libraries also allow access to their catalogs from outside computers—at home or in a computer lab on campus. Figure 22.2 shows a typical search page of an online library catalog.

When searching the library catalog for books on a specific topic, you may need to view two or three screens before you find information about a specific book. First you will get a list of relevant titles, then you will need to select the title that interests you. On the next screen you will get more about that item. The call number, location, and availability may be on this screen, or you might have to click once more to find specific information on obtaining that item. Figure 22.3 shows the results of an online search by subject for the topic *human-animal relationships*. Online catalogs offer many conveniences. The screen often indicates whether the book is on the shelves, whether it has been checked out, and when it is due back. Some systems allow you to reserve the book by entering your request on the computer.

For more practice using your library's catalog, visit www.bedfordstmartins.com/successfulcollege/.

FIGURE 22.2 Library Catalog Search Page

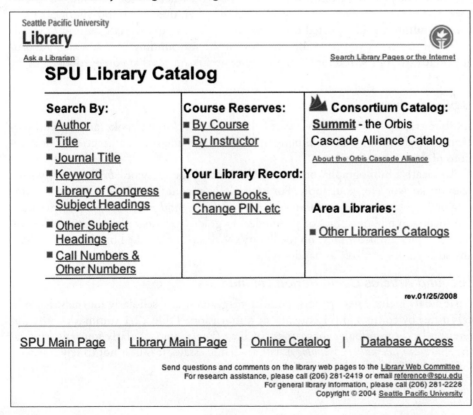

FIGURE 22.3 Library Catalog Search Results

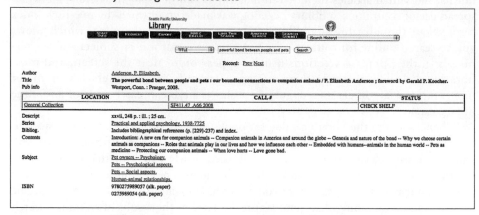

For older or special collections, some libraries still maintain card catalogs that index all the items in that particular collection. A traditional card catalog includes three types of cards: title, author, and subject. Arranged alphabetically, the three types of cards may be filed together, or there may be a separate catalog for the subject cards.

The catalog provides call numbers that tell you where to locate books on the library's shelves. Once you have a specific call number, use your library floor plan and the call-number guides posted on shelves to locate the appropriate section of the library and the book you need. Be sure to scan the surrounding books, which are usually on related topics. You may discover other useful sources that you overlooked in the catalog.

Bibliographies

A **bibliography** lists sources on a particular subject, including books, articles, and government publications. Some bibliographies also provide brief summaries or descriptions of the sources they list.

To locate a bibliography on your subject, combine the word *bibliography* with a relevant keyword for your topic. For example, you could search your library's online catalog for *human-animal communication* and *bibliography*. Also, some libraries publish their own bibliographies or pathfinders to guide students to important sources on certain topics. Look for these on the library's Web site, or ask the librarians if they have any such guides available as handouts.

Locating Articles Using Periodical Indexes

Periodicals include newspapers, popular magazines, and scholarly journals. Periodicals differ by content and frequency of publication. Table 22.1 summarizes the differences between popular magazines (such as *People*) and scholarly journals (such as the *American Journal of Psychology*). For academic essays, it is best not to rely solely on information from popular magazines.

Because periodicals are published daily, weekly, or monthly, they often contain up-to-date information about a subject. A library's catalog does not list specific articles from magazines or journals. However, it does list the periodicals, indexes, and abstracts to which the library subscribes. **Indexes** list articles by title, author, and subject. **Abstracts** provide a brief summary of each one. Most indexes and abstracts are available as computer databases.

More and more of the periodical databases provided by libraries give users access to full-text articles. Since most libraries subscribe to more than one database provider, it may be necessary to check for the full text in a database other than the one in which you found the citation or abstract. Look for an article linker that checks your library's other databases for you with one click.

Finally, when you are searching, look for options that allow you to refine your search. Many databases allow users to limit results by date and publication type. Look for a place to choose "peer reviewed" or "newspapers and magazines" if you need to locate an article

TABLE 22.1 **A Comparison of Scholarly Journals and Popular Magazines**		
	Scholarly Journal	**Popular Magazine**
Who reads it?	Researchers, professionals, students	General public
Who writes it?	Researchers, professionals	Reporters, journalists, freelance writers
Who decides what to publish in it?	Other researchers (peer review)	Editors, publishers
What does it look like?	Mostly text, some charts and graphs, little or no advertising	Many photos, many advertisements, eye-catching layout
What kind of information does it contain?	Results of research studies and experiments, statistics and analysis, in-depth evaluations of specialized topics, overviews of all the research on a subject (literature review), bibliographies and references	Articles of general interest, easy-to-understand language, news items, interviews, opinion pieces, no bibliographies (sources cited informally within the article)
Where is it available?	Sometimes by subscription only, large bookstores, large public library branches, college/university libraries, online	Newsstands, most bookstores, most public library branches, online
How often is it published?	Monthly to quarterly	Weekly to monthly
What are some examples?	*Journal of Bioethics, American Journal of Family Law, Film Quarterly*	*Newsweek, Popular Science, Psychology Today*

from a particular kind of source. Once you locate a relevant article, find out what your options are for emailing, printing, and saving it. Also, check with the librarian for inter-library loan options if you cannot locate the full text or hard copy of an article you want.

General periodical databases. General databases list articles on a wide range of subjects that have been published in popular magazines. One popular vendor is EB-SCO, whose extensive databases list articles published in thousands of magazines, journals, and newspapers. Some entries include only abstracts, but depending on the type of agreement your library has, you may have access to full-text articles as well. One EBSCO database is Academic Search Complete, which provides access to the full text of articles for more than 8,600 journals, magazines, and newspapers, as well as abstracts for another 12,500 periodicals (check with your library about getting the full text when only an abstract is provided). Academic Search Complete covers almost all subject areas and is especially geared toward college students. In fact, about 7,500 of the full-text journals are peer-reviewed.

You can search Academic Search Complete by keyword using terms that you have brainstormed for your topic. Once you find a relevant article, take a look at the sub-ject terms that Academic Search Complete has listed for that article—they may or may not match the keywords you have been using. For example, you might search for "eating habits" and discover that the database uses the term "food habits" to describe this topic. You can then click on the "food habits" link to find more articles on the topic. You can also start out by looking at a list of the database's subject terms. Click on the subject terms link on the search page and browse for applicable terms. The list of subject terms for "animal communication" appears at the bottom of this page.

Specialized periodical databases. Specialized databases reference either schol-arly and technical articles within a specific academic field of study or materials of a particular type, such as book reviews, abstracts of doctoral dissertations, and

☐ ANIMAL communication	
Scope Note	Here are entered works about any type of communication among animals; the concept includes language learning by animals. [EPC]
Broader Terms	☐ ANIMAL behavior
Narrower Terms	☐ ANIMAL sounds
	☐ HUMAN-animal communication
	☐ SOUND production by animals
Used for	ANIMAL language
	COMMUNICATION among animals
	LANGUAGE learning by animals

articles and essays published in books, rather than periodicals. A list of common specialized indexes follows. Check with your library for coverage dates and access instructions.

Applied Science and Technology Index	*Government Publications Office (GPO):*
Art Index	*First Search*
Bioline International	*Historical Abstracts*
Book Review Digest Plus	*Humanities Full Text*
Business Source Complete	*MLA (Modern Language Association)*
Congressional Quarterly Electronic	*International Bibliography*
Library	*Music Index*
Dissertation Abstracts	*Physics Abstracts*
Education Research Complete	*PsycArticles*
Engineering Index	*Science Citation Index (Web of Science)*
ERIC	*Sociological Abstracts*

Here is a sample entry on the topic of *mammals* from the *Sociological Abstracts*.

SAMPLE ENTRY FROM THE *SOCIOLOGICAL ABSTRACTS*

☐ 4. The Animal Connection and Human Evolution
Shipman, Pat
Current Anthropology, vol. 51, no. 4, pp. 519-538, Aug 2010
... characteristics distinguishes Homo sapiens from other **mammals**. Three diagnostic human behaviors played key roles in human evolution: tool making, symbolic behavior and language, and the domestication of plants and animals. I focus here on a ...
View Record | References | Check for Full Text | Check Your Library | Request via Interlibrary Loan

☐ 5. Wildlife Tourism Science and Scientists: Barriers and Opportunities
Rodger, Kate; Moore, Susan A; Newsome, David
Society and Natural Resources, vol. 23, no. 8, pp. 679-694, Aug 2010
Wildlife tourism epitomizes many of the research and management issues confronting those working at the interface of society and natural resources. Little is currently known about this interface, especially the impacts resulting from interactions ...
View Record | References | Check for Full Text | Check Your Library | Request via Interlibrary Loan

☐ 6. An ethnozoological survey of medicinal animals commercialized in the markets of Campina Grande, NE Brazil
Nobrega Alves, Romulo Romeu; das Gracas Geronimo Oliveira, Maria; Duarte Barboza, Raynner Rilke; Serramo Lopez, Luiz Carlos
Human Ecology Review, vol. 17, no. 1, pp. 11-17, summer 2010
Numbers of animal species are commercialized by herbalists in markets throughout Brazil. Nevertheless, there is a general lack of information about this type of trade in the country. This study aimed to obtain information on the trade of animals for ...
View Record | References | Check for Full Text | Check Your Library | Request via Interlibrary Loan

---

Doing Research on the World Wide Web

The Web contains millions of Web sites, most of which are not grouped together in any organized way. Therefore, you will need to use a subject directory or search engine to locate the information you need.

Subject directories. A **subject directory** uses various categories and subcategories to classify Web resources. Some subject directories also include reviews or evaluations of sites. A subject directory can be especially helpful when you have decided on a general topic for an essay but need to narrow it further. Some subject directories are part of a search engine, whereas others are stand-alone sites.

Search engines. A **search engine** is an application that can help you find information on a particular topic by typing a keyword, phrase, or question into a search box. Eight commonly used search engines and their URLs follow.

USEFUL SEARCH ENGINES

Search Engine	*URL*
Ask	www.ask.com
Bing	www.bing.com
Go.com	www.go.com
Google	www.google.com
Google Scholar	http://scholar.google.com
Yahoo!	www.yahoo.com

For more practice selecting and evaluating a search engine, visit www.bedfordstmartins .com/successfulcollege/.

If a keyword or phrase is too general, a search could turn up hundreds or perhaps thousands of sites, most of which will not be helpful to you. Your searches will be more productive if you use the guidelines for keyword searches on page 598.

Since different search engines usually generate different results, it is a good idea to use more than one search engine when you are researching a given topic. For a general search, you might start with a search engine such as Google. After you've narrowed your topic, however, you might want to use a more specialized search engine, such as one that is geared to a particular discipline or specialty. For example, if your topic involves the Democratic Party, Google might point you to a site named Political Science Resources on the Web, which has its own search engine.

Locating Useful Internet Sources

For more on evaluating Internet sources, see Chapter 21, pp. 585–87.

As noted earlier, although the Internet offers vast amounts of information, it does have one major drawback: Its information is often less reliable than information in print sources because anyone can post on the Internet. To be certain that your information from online sources is reliable, you will want to evaluate it, and you might want to maintain a list of reliable Web sites that provide accurate and thorough information.

Once you identify usable sources, be sure to keep track of their URLs so that you can find the sites again easily and cite them in your paper. You can save Web addresses on your own computer as bookmarks or favorites (depending on the Web browser you use), which allows you to return to a site by clicking on its name. You can also organize your bookmarks or favorites into folders—such as *career, library information,* or *news sites*—so that you can easily find your sources.

Following are some generally useful and reliable Web sites that you should remember.

News sites. Newspapers, television networks, and popular magazines have companion Web sites that provide current information and late-breaking news stories. Useful sites include the following:

BBC	www.bbc.co.uk
CNN Interactive	www.cnn.com
MSNBC	www.msnbc.com
The New York Times	www.nytimes.com
The Washington Post	www.washingtonpost.com

General reference sites. The following sites offer reliable general reference information:

Britannica Online   www.eb.com/
Columbia Encyclopedia   http://education.yahoo.com/reference/encyclopedia/
Encyclopedia.com   www.encyclopedia.com/
Encyclopedia Smithsonian www.si.edu/encyclopedia_si/
Merriam-Webster Online   www.merriam-webster.com/

Table 22.2 lists some good places to begin research in academic disciplines.

TABLE 22.2 Web Sources for Academic Research

Academic Discipline	Site Title and Affiliation	Site URL
Humanities	Voice of the Shuttle (University of California, Santa Barbara)	http://vos.ucsb.edu
	Edsitement (National Endowment for the Humanities)	http://edsitement.neh.gov/websites_all.asp
Literature	LitLinks (Bedford/St. Martin's)	http://www.bedfordstmartins.com/litlinks/
	Representative Poetry Online (University of Toronto)	http://rpo.library.utoronto.ca/display/index.cfm
	Literary Resources on the Net (Jack Lynch, Rutgers University)	http://andromeda.rutgers.edu/~jlynch/Lit/
History	History@Bedford/St. Martin's	http://www.bedfordstmartins.com/history/
	History Internet Resources (James Madison University Libraries)	http://www.lib.jmu.edu/history/internet.aspx
Social Sciences	Social Sciences Information Gateway (Resource Discovery Network)	http://www.intute.ac.uk/social sciences/
	Social Science Libraries and Information Services (Yale University Library)	http://www.library.yale.edu/index.php?gid=397
Science	Eurekalert (American Association for the Advancement of Science)	http://www.eurekalert.org/
	Nature.com (Nature Publishing Group)	http://www.nature.com/index.html
	SciCentral	http://www.scicentral.com/
Medicine	Health Information (National Institutes of Health)	http://health.nih.gov/
	WebMD	http://www.webmd.com/
	PubMed Central (National Institutes of Health)	http://www.ncbi.nlm.n.h.gov/pmc/
Business	Hoover's Online	http://www.hoovers.com/free/
	Bureau of Labor Statistics	http://stats.bls.gov/
	SEC Filings & Forms (EDGAR)	http://www.sec.gov/edgar.shtml

Listservs and Newsgroups

The Internet's listservs and newsgroups are discussion forums where people interested in a particular topic or field of research can communicate and share information about it. A listserv is an email discussion group; messages are sent automatically to subscribers' email accounts. Some listservs allow anyone to subscribe, whereas others require a moderator's permission. A newsgroup, in contrast, does not require membership, and messages are posted to a news server for anyone to read and respond to. A central network called *Usenet* provides access to thousands of newsgroups.

Consult the frequently asked questions (FAQs) for a listserv or newsgroup to determine if it suits your needs and, for a listserv, to see how to subscribe. Keep in mind that messages posted to listservs and newsgroups are not usually checked for accuracy and are not always reliable sources of information (though in general, listserv discussions tend to be more serious and focused than newsgroup discussions). You can use electronic discussion forums to become familiar with a topic; obtain background information; discover new issues, facets, or approaches; identify print sources of information; and build your interest in a topic. To locate discussion groups, use a Web search engine to search for the term *discussion groups* or *Usenet.*

Email

Many authors, researchers, and corporations are willing to respond to email requests for specific information, but you should first make sure the information you need is not already available through more traditional sources. To locate email addresses, consult an online directory such as Yahoo People Search (http://people.yahoo.com/) or Internet Address Finder (www.iaf.net). (Any directory may include obsolete entries.) Email search directories are also available through Yahoo! and elsewhere. While not complete, they do contain a great deal of information.

When you send an email message to someone you don't know, be sure to introduce yourself and briefly describe the purpose of your inquiry. Provide complete information about yourself, including the name of your school and how to contact you, and politely request the information you need.

Extracting Information from Sources

As you read sources, you will need to take notes to use later. The following section discusses systems for note-taking and explains how to write various types of notes—for summaries, paraphrases, and quotations. It also offers advice for avoiding plagiarism.

Gathering Necessary Citation Information

For more on works-cited lists, see Chapter 23, pp. 640–62 (MLA) and 663–81 (APA).

As you work with print sources, be sure to record complete information for each source, using a form like the one shown in Figure 22.4. Filling out an information

FIGURE 22.4 Bibliographic Information Worksheet for Print Sources

Author(s) _____

Title _____

Beginning Page _____ Ending Page _____

Title of Journal _____

Volume Number _____ Issue Number _____

Date of Issue _____

Call Number _____

Publisher _____

Place of Publication _____

Copyright Date _____

worksheet will help you locate the source again—in case you need to verify something or find additional information.

When using electronic sources, be sure to print out all the information you will need to cite the source. For Web sources, this includes the author and title of the document; the title of the site; the sponsoring organization; the date of publication or of the last update; the number of pages, paragraphs, sections, or screens, if they are numbered in the document; the access date; and the URL. For an online periodical article, be sure your printouts also include the periodical name, any volume and issue numbers, and the print publication information (periodical name, publisher, date, and so on) if the article was originally published in print.

Constructing an Annotated Bibliography

Another approach, which some instructors require, is to prepare an **annotated bibliography**—a list of all the sources you *consulted* in researching your topic and a brief summary of each source's content and focus. You will find that it is easier to write the annotations as you do your research—while each source is fresh in your mind. Although preparing an annotated bibliography is time-consuming, it can be very helpful during the drafting or revising stage. If you realize, for instance, that you need more information on a particular subtopic, your annotations can often direct you to the most useful source.

If you are putting together an annotated bibliography intended only for your own use, you might simply write your annotations at the bottom of each information worksheet. For an annotated bibliography that will be submitted to your instructor, you would need to alphabetize it and use correct bibliographic format. Here is a sample annotated bibliography for researching the use of digital textbooks and e-learning in college classrooms.

SAMPLE ANNOTATED BIBLIOGRAPHY

Garrison, D.R., and Terry Anderson. *E-learning in the Twenty-first Century: A Framework for Research and Practice*. London: Routledge, 2011. Print.

> A book that provides research-based information on how e-learning can be integrated into the college classroom in ways that make technological, practical, and educational sense

Rashid, Osman. "The Time Is Now for Digital Textbooks." *O'Reilly Radar*. O'Reilly Media, Inc., 21 Sept. 2010. Web 11 Feb. 2011.

> An online article providing opinion on the use of digital textbooks in colleges. Suggestions for implementation of e-textbooks are also provided.

Sheridan, Barret. "Textbooks' Digital Future." *Newsweek Education*. Newsweek, Inc., 12 Sept. 2010. Web. 10 Feb. 2011.

> An article from a general-interest magazine that reports on the state of digital textbooks, makes predictions about their future use, and provides information on the financial aspects of digital textbook publishing and delivery.

Woody, William Douglas, David B. Daniel, and Crystal A. Baker. "E-books or Textbooks: Students Prefer Textbooks." *Computers & Education* 55.3 (2010): 945–48. *Academic Search Complete*. Web. 12 Feb. 2011.

> An article in a scholarly journal reporting on a research study that investigated student preferences regarding print versus online textbooks

Young, Jeffrey R. "As Textbooks Go Digital, Campus Bookstores May Go Bookless." *Chronicle of Higher Education* 57.13 (2010): A10. *Academic Search Complete*. Web. 12 Feb. 2011.

> An article in a periodical for college faculty and administrators reporting on the state of campus bookstores in the face of increasing use of e-textbooks

For more on bibliographic format, see Chapter 23, pp. 640–62 (MLA) and 663–81 (APA).

Systems of Note-Taking

When you take research notes, you'll probably need to copy quotes, write paraphrases, and make summary notes. There are three ways to record your research—on note cards, on your computer, or on copies of source material.

Regardless of the system you use, be sure to designate a place to record your own ideas, such as different-colored index cards, a notepad, or a computer folder. Be careful as well not to simply record (or highlight) quotations. Writing summary notes or paraphrases helps you think about the ideas in your source, how they fit with other ideas, and how they might work in your research paper.

Note Cards

Some researchers use four- by six-inch or five- by eight-inch index cards for note-taking. If you use this system, put information from only one source or about only one subtopic on each card. At the top of the card, indicate the author of the source

FIGURE 22.5 Sample Note Card

> *Schmoke & Roques, 17-25*
>
> *Medicalization*
>
> *Medicalization is a system in which the government would control the release of narcotics to drug addicts.*
> *— would work like a prescription does now — only gov't official would write prescription*
> *— addicts would be required to get counseling and health services*
> *— would take drug control out of hands of drug traffickers (paraphrase, 18)*

and the subtopic that the note covers. Be sure to include page numbers in case you need to go back and reread the article or passage. If you copy an author's exact words, place the information in quotation marks and include the term *direct quotation* and the page number in parentheses. If you write a summary note (see pp. 610–11) or paraphrase (see pp. 611–12), write *paraphrase* or *summary* on the card and the page number of the source. When you use this system, you can rearrange your cards and experiment with different ways of organizing as you plan your paper. Figure 22.5 shows a sample note card.

Computerized Note-Taking

Another option is to type your notes into computer files and organize your files by subtopic. To do so, use a computer notebook to create small "note cards," or use a hypertext card program. As with note cards, keep track of sources by including the author's name and the page numbers for each source, and make a back-up copy of your notes. If you have access to a computer in the library, you can type in summaries, paraphrases, and direct quotations while you are doing the research, eliminating the need to type or recopy them later.

Annotated Copies of Sources

This approach is most appropriate for very short papers that do not involve numerous sources or extensive research. To use this system, photocopy or print the source material; underline or highlight useful information; and write your reactions, paraphrases, and summary notes in the margins or on attachments to the appropriate page. Annotating source material often saves time because you don't need to copy quotations or write lengthy notes. The disadvantage, in addition to the expense of photocopying, is that this system does not allow you to sort and rearrange notes by subtopic.

For more on highlighting and annotating, see Chapter 3, pp. 55–56.

When you highlight and annotate a source, be selective about what you mark or comment on, keeping the purpose of your research in mind. One student who was researching anthropomorphism annotated the following excerpt from *When Elephants*

Weep: The Emotional Lives of Animals by Jeffrey Masson and Susan McCarthy. Note how this student underlined key points related to his research. Notice also how his annotations comment on, summarize key points of, and question the text.

SAMPLE ANNOTATIONS AND UNDERLINING

*def

The greatest obstacle in science to investigating the emotions of other animals has been an inordinate desire to avoid anthropomorphism. <u>Anthropomorphism* means the ascription of human characteristics—thought, feelings, consciousness, and motivation—to the nonhuman.</u> When people claim that the elements are conspiring to ruin their picnic or that a tree is their friend, they are anthropomorphizing. Few believe that the weather is plotting against them, but anthropomorphic ideas about animals are held more widely. Outside scientific circles, it is common to speak of the thoughts and feelings of pets and wild and captive animals. Yet many scientists regard the notion that animals feel pain as the grossest sort of anthropomorphic error.

!
Wrong! If so, then why do vets use anesthesia?

<u>Cats and dogs are prime targets of anthropomorphism, both wrongly and rightly.</u> Ascribing unlikely thoughts and feelings to pets is common: "She understands every word you say." "He sings his little heart out to show how grateful he is." Some people deck reluctant pets in clothing, give them presents in which they have no interest, or assign their own opinions to the animals. Some dogs are even taught to attack people of races different from their owners'. Many dog lovers seem to enjoy believing that cats are selfish, unfeeling creatures who heartlessly use their deluded owners, compared with loving, loyal, and naive dogs. More often, however, <u>people have quite realistic views about their pets' abilities and attributes. The experience of living with an animal often provides a strong sense of its abilities and limitations</u>—although even here, as for people living intimately with people, <u>preconceptions</u> can be <u>more persuasive than lived experience</u>, and can create their own reality.

dog lovers vs. cat lovers—why?

People have preconceived notions of certain breeds of dogs as vicious.

Jeffrey Masson and Susan McCarthy,
When Elephants Weep: The Emotional Lives of Animals

Writing Summary Notes

For more on writing summaries, see Chapter 4, pp. 88–89.

Much of your note-taking will be in the form of summary notes, which condense information from sources. Take summary notes when you want to record the gist of an author's ideas but do not need the exact wording or a paraphrase. Use the guidelines below to write effective summary notes. Remember that everything you put in summary notes must be in your own words.

1. **Record only information that relates to your topic and purpose.** Do not include irrelevant information.
2. **Write notes that condense the author's ideas into your own words.** Include key terms and concepts or principles. Do not include specific examples, quotations, or anything that is not essential to the main point. Do not include your opinion, even a positive one. (You can include any comments in a separate note, as suggested earlier.)

3. **Record the ideas in the order in which they appear in the original source.**
   Reordering ideas might affect the meaning.
4. **Reread your summary to determine whether it contains sufficient information.**
   Would it be understandable to someone who has not read the original source? If
   not, revise the summary to include additional information.
5. **Jot down the publication information for the sources you summarize.** Unless
   you summarize an entire book or poem, you will need page references when you
   write your paper and prepare a works-cited list.

A sample summary is shown below. It summarizes the first four paragraphs of the
essay "Dude, Do You Know What You Just Said?" by Mike Crissey, which appears in
Chapter 17 (pp. 451–53). Read or reread the essay, and then study the summary.

SAMPLE SUMMARY

Scott Kiesling, a linguist, has studied the uses and meanings of the popularly used
word *dude*. Historically, *dude* was first used to refer to a dandy and then became a
slang term used by various social groups. For his study, Kiesling listened to tapes of
fraternity members and asked undergraduate students to record uses of the term. He
determined that it is used for a variety of purposes, including to show enthusiasm
or excitement, to one-up someone, to avoid confrontation, and to demonstrate
agreement.

Writing Paraphrases

When you paraphrase, you restate the author's ideas in your own words. You do not
condense ideas or eliminate details as you do in a summary. Instead, you use different
sentence patterns and vocabulary but keep the author's intended meaning. In most
cases, a paraphrase is approximately the same length as the original material. Compose
a paraphrase when you want to record the author's ideas and details but do not want to
use a direct quotation. Remember to paraphrase only the ideas or details you intend to
use—not an entire article.

When paraphrasing, be especially careful not to *plagiarize*—to use an author's
words or sentence structure as if they were your own (see pp. 613–14). Read the excerpt from a source below; then compare it to the acceptable paraphrase that follows
and to the example that includes plagiarism.

EXCERPT FROM ORIGINAL

Learning some items may interfere with retrieving others, especially when the
items are similar. If someone gives you a phone number to remember, you may be
able to recall it later. But if two more people give you their numbers, each successive
number will be more difficult to recall. Such proactive interference occurs when
something you learned earlier disrupts recall of something you experienced later. As
you collect more and more information, your mental attic never fills, but it certainly
gets cluttered.

David G. Myers, *Psychology*

ACCEPTABLE PARAPHRASE

When proactive interference happens, things you have already learned prevent you from remembering things you learn later. In other words, details you learn first may make it harder to recall closely related details you learn subsequently. You can think of your memory as an attic. You can always add more junk to it. However, it will become messy and disorganized. For example, you can remember one new phone number, but if you have two or more new numbers to remember, the task becomes harder.

UNACCEPTABLE PARAPHRASE — INCLUDES PLAGIARISM

When you learn some things, it may interfere with your ability to remember others. This happens when the things are similar. Suppose a person gives you a phone number to remember. You probably will be able to remember it later. Now, suppose two persons give you numbers. Each successive number will be harder to remember. Proactive interference happens when something you already learned prevents you from recalling something you experience later. As you learn more and more information, your mental attic never gets full, but it will get cluttered.

Although the preceding paraphrase does substitute some synonyms—*remember* for *retrieving,* for example—it is still an example of plagiarism. The underlined words are copied directly from the original. The shaded words show substitution of synonyms. Notice, too, that the structure of the last two sentences of the unacceptable paraphrase is nearly identical to the structure of the last two sentences of the original.

Writing paraphrases can be tricky, because simply rewording an author's ideas is not acceptable, and letting an author's language "creep in" is easy. There are also many ways to write an acceptable paraphrase of a particular passage. The following guidelines should help you write effective paraphrases:

1. **Read first; then write.** You may find it helpful to read material more than once before you try paraphrasing.
2. **If you must use any of the author's wording, enclose it in quotation marks.** If you do not use quotation marks, you may inadvertently use the same wording in your paper, which would result in plagiarism.
3. **Work sentence by sentence, restating each in your own words.** To avoid copying an author's words, read a sentence, cover it up, and then write. Be sure your version is accurate but not too similar to the original. As a rule of thumb, no more than two or three consecutive words should be the same as in the original.
4. **Choose synonyms that do not change the author's meaning or intent.** Consult a dictionary, if necessary.
5. **Use your own sentence structure.** Using an author's sentence structure can be considered plagiarism. If the original uses lengthy sentences, for example, your paraphrase of it should use shorter sentences.

Be sure to record the publication information (including page numbers) for the sources you paraphrase. You will need this information to document the sources in your paper.

Exercise 22.1

Write a paraphrase of the following excerpt from a source on animal communication.

Another vigorously debated issue is whether language is uniquely human. Animals obviously communicate. Bees, for example, communicate the location of food through an intricate dance. And several teams of psychologists have taught various species of apes, including a number of chimpanzees, to communicate with humans by signing or by pushing buttons wired to a computer. Apes have developed considerable vocabularies. They string words together to express meaning and to make and follow requests. Skeptics point out important differences between apes' and humans' facilities with language, especially in their respective abilities to order words using proper syntax. Nevertheless, these studies reveal that apes have considerable cognitive ability.

David G. Myers, *Psychology*

Recording Quotations

Sometimes it is advisable, and even necessary, to use a direct quotation—a writer's words exactly as they appear in the original source. Use quotations to record wording that is unusual or striking or to report the exact words of an expert on your topic. Such quotations, when used sparingly, can be effective in a paper. When using a direct quotation, be sure to record it precisely as it appears in the source. The author's spelling, punctuation, and capitalization must be recorded exactly. Also write down the page number on which the material being quoted appears in the original source. Be sure to indicate that you are copying a direct quotation by including the term *direct quotation* and the page number in parentheses.

You may delete a word, phrase, or sentence from a quotation as long as you do not change the meaning of the quotation. Use an ellipsis mark (three spaced periods) — . . . — to indicate that you have made a deletion.

Avoiding Plagiarism

Plagiarism is the use of someone else's ideas, wording, or organization without any acknowledgment of the source. If you take information from a source on uses of eye contact in communication and do not indicate where you got the information, you have plagiarized. If you copy the six-word phrase "Eye contact, particularly essential in negotiations" from a source without enclosing it in quotation marks, you have plagiarized.

Plagiarism is intellectually dishonest and is considered a form of cheating because you are submitting someone else's work as your own. Harsh academic penalties are applied to students found guilty of plagiarism; these often include receiving a failing grade on the paper, failing the entire course, or even being dismissed from the institution.

What Counts as Plagiarism

There are two types of plagiarism—intentional (deliberate) and unintentional (done by accident). Both are equally serious and both carry the same academic penalties. Below is a quick reference guide to determining if you have plagiarized.

For more on documentation, see Chapter 23.

To avoid plagiarism, be especially careful when taking notes from a source. Place anything you copy directly in quotation marks and record the source. Record the source for any information you paraphrase or summarize. Be sure to separate your own ideas from ideas expressed in the sources you are using. One way to do this is to use two different colors of ink or two different print sizes (if using a computer). Another way is to use different sections of a notebook or different computer files to distinguish your own ideas from those of others.

Cyberplagiarism

For more on citing Internet sources, see Chapter 23.

The term *cyberplagiarism* refers to borrowing information from the Internet without giving credit to the source posting the information. It also refers to "cut-and-paste plagiarism"—the practice of copying text directly from an Internet source and pasting it into your own essay without giving credit. Purchasing a student paper for sale on the Internet and submitting it as your own work is a third form of cyberplagiarism. Use the following suggestions to avoid unintentional plagiarism:

- Never copy and paste directly from an Internet source into your paper. Instead, cut and paste information you want to save into a separate file. Enclose the material you pasted in quotation marks to remind yourself that it is someone else's wording.
- Be sure to record all the source's information, including the name of the site, the URL, the date of access, and so on.
- When you make notes on ideas, opinions, or theories you encounter on the Internet, be sure to include complete source information for each item.

YOU HAVE PLAGIARIZED IF YOU HAVE . . .

- Directly copied information word for word without using quotation marks, whether or not you acknowledged the source.
- Reworded and reorganized (paraphrased) information from a source without acknowledging the source.
- Borrowed someone else's organization or sequence of ideas without acknowledging the source.
- Reused someone else's visual material (graphs, tables, charts, maps, diagrams) without acknowledging the source.
- Submitted another student's work as your own.

Exercise 22.2

The piece of student writing below is a paraphrase of a source on the history of advertising. Working with another student, evaluate the paraphrase and discuss whether it would be considered an example of plagiarism. If you decide the paraphrase is plagiarized, rewrite it so it is not.

ORIGINAL SOURCE

Everyone knows that advertising lies. That has been an article of faith since the Middle Ages—and a legal doctrine, too. Sixteenth-century English courts began the Age of Caveat Emptor by ruling that commercial claims—fraudulent or not—should be sorted out by the buyer, not the legal system. ("If he be tame and have ben rydden upon, then caveat emptor.") In a 1615 case, a certain Baily agreed to transport Merrell's load of wood, which Merrell claimed weighed 800 pounds. When Baily's two horses collapsed and died, he discovered that Merrell's wood actually weighed 2,000 pounds. The court ruled the problem was Baily's for not checking the weight himself; Merrell bore no blame.

Cynthia Crossen, Tainted Truth

PARAPHRASE

It is a well-known fact that advertising lies. This has been known ever since the Middle Ages. It is an article of faith as well as a legal doctrine. English courts in the sixteenth century started the Age of Caveat Emptor by finding that claims by businesses, whether legitimate or not, were the responsibility of the consumer, not the courts. For example, there was a case in which one person (Baily) used his horses to haul wood for a person named Merrell. Merrell told Baily that the wood weighed 800 pounds, but it actually weighed 2,000 pounds. Baily discovered this after his horses died. The court did not hold Merrell responsible; it stated that Baily should have weighed the wood himself instead of accepting Merrell's word.

Conducting Field Research

Depending on your research topic, you may need—or want—to do field research to collect original information. Check with your instructor before doing so. This section discusses three common types of field research—interviews, surveys, and observation—all of which generate primary source material.

Interviewing

An interview lets you obtain firsthand information from a person who is knowledgeable about your topic. For example, if the topic of your research paper is *treatment of teenage alcoholism,* it might be a good idea to interview an experienced substance abuse counselor who works with teenagers. Use the following suggestions to conduct effective interviews:

1. **Choose interview subjects carefully.** Be sure your subjects work in the field you are researching or are experts on your topic. Also try to choose subjects that may provide you with different points of view. If you are researching a corporation, for

example, try to interview someone from upper management as well as white- and blue-collar workers.

2. **Arrange your interview by letter, phone, or email well in advance.** Describe your project and purpose, explaining that you are a student working on an assignment. Indicate the amount of time you think you'll need, but don't be disappointed if the person shortens the time or denies your request altogether. You should also be somewhat flexible about whom you interview. For example, a busy vice president may refer you to an assistant or to another manager.

3. **Plan the interview.** Come to the interview with a list of questions you want to ask; your subject will appreciate the fact that you are prepared and not wasting his or her time. Try to ask open rather than closed questions, which can be answered in a word or two. "Do you think your company has a promising future?" could be answered yes or no, whereas "How do you account for your company's turnaround last year?" might spark a detailed response. Open questions usually encourage people to open up and reveal attitudes as well as facts.

4. **Take notes during the interview.** Take a notebook to write in, since you probably will not be seated at a table or desk. Write the subject's responses in note form and find out whether you may quote him or her directly. If you want to tape-record the interview, be sure to ask the subject's permission.

5. **Evaluate the interview.** As soon as possible after the interview, reread your notes and fill in information you did not have time to record. Also write down your reactions while they are still fresh in your mind. Record these in the margin or in a different color ink so that they are distinguishable from the interview notes. Try to write down your overall impression and an answer to this question: What did I learn from this interview?

Using a Survey

A survey is a set of questions designed to get information quickly from a large number of people. Surveys can be conducted face-to-face, by phone, by email, or by regular mail. Surveys are often used to assess people's attitudes or intended actions. For example, we frequently read the results of surveys that measure the popularity of political figures.

Use the following suggestions to prepare effective surveys:

1. **Clarify the purpose of the survey.** Write a detailed list of what you want to learn from the survey.

2. **Design your questions.** A survey can include closed or open questions or both, but most use closed questions in either a multiple-choice or a ranking-scale format (see box). Closed questions usually work better in surveys because their short, direct answers are easy to tally and interpret. An open question such as "What do you think of the food served in the cafeteria?" would elicit a variety of responses that would be difficult to summarize in your paper.

3. **Test your survey questions.** Try out your questions on a few classmates, family members, or friends to be sure they are clear and that they will provide the information you need.

EXAMPLES OF CLOSED QUESTIONS

Multiple Choice

How often do you purchase lunch in the campus cafeteria?

a. 1–2 days per week
b. 3–4 days per week
c. 5–6 days per week
d. Every day of the week

Ranking

On a scale of 1 to 5 (1 = poor and 5 = excellent), rate the quality of food in the campus cafeteria.

Poor   *Excellent*

1   2   3   4   5

4. **Select your respondents.** Your respondents—the people who provide answers to your survey—must be *representative* of the group you are studying and must be *chosen at random.* For example, if you are planning a survey to learn what students on your campus think about mandatory drug testing for athletes, you should choose a group of respondents—or a sample—that is similar to your school's student population. For most campuses, then, your group of respondents would contain both men and women, be racially and ethnically diverse, and represent the various ages and socioeconomic groups of students. Your sample should also be random; respondents should be unknown to you and not chosen for a specific reason. One way to draw a random sample is to give the survey to every fifth or tenth name on a list or every fifteenth person who walks by.

5. **Summarize and report your results.** Tally the results and look for patterns in the data. If the sample is fairly large, use a computer spreadsheet to tabulate results. In your paper, discuss your overall findings, not individual respondents' answers. Explain the purpose of the survey as well as how you designed it, selected a sample, and administered the survey to respondents. You may also want to include a copy of the survey and tabulations in an appendix.

Conducting Observations

The results obtained from observation—the inspection of an event, a scene, or an activity—can be an important primary source in a research paper. For instance, you might observe and report on a demonstration at a government agency or a field trial at a dog show. Firsthand observation can give you valuable insights on the job as well. You might, for example, need to observe and report on the condition of hospital patients or on the job performance of your employees.

Use the following tips to conduct observations effectively:

1. **Arrange your visit in advance.** Unless you are doing an observation in a public place, obtain permission from the company or organization in advance, and make the purpose of your visit clear when arranging your appointment.
2. **Take detailed notes on what you observe.** Write down the details you will need to describe the scene vividly in your paper. For instance, if you visit a mental health clinic, note details about patient care, security, hygiene, and the like. You might sketch the scene, especially if you are a spatial learner, or use a tape recorder or video camera if you have permission to do so. Try to gather enough information to reconstruct your visit when you draft your paper.
3. **Approach the visit with an open mind.** A closed-minded approach can defeat the purpose of observation. For example, if you observe a dog show with the preconceived notion that the dogs' owners are only interested in winning, your closed-minded view might keep you from discovering that dog shows serve other purposes (such as promoting friendship between owners).
4. **Create a dominant impression.** As soon as possible after your visit, evaluate your observations. Ask yourself about what you saw and heard. Then describe your dominant impression of what you observed and the details that support it. Details from the dog show, for example, might include the attitude and attire of owners and judges and the way the dogs were groomed.

Finding Sources for Your Own Topic

Before you begin to locate sources for your topic, you should review the information in Chapter 21, which describes how to plan a paper with sources and how to choose and evaluate useful sources, whether in the library or online. Here are a few pointers that will help you conduct your own research:

1. **Begin with a narrowed topic, a working thesis, and some research questions** (see pp. 580–82).
2. **Decide what kinds of sources will best answer your research questions—** recent journal articles, historical works, personal interviews, and so forth (see pp. 583–84).
3. **Remember to consider whether each source will be truly useful.** Is it relevant and reliable (see p. 584)? Is it biased in some way (see pp. 585–86)?
4. **Keep track of citation information for each source while you do your research** (see pp. 606–8).
5. **Decide what system of note-taking you will use**—note cards, computer files, or annotated copies (see pp. 608–10).
6. **As you take notes, paraphrase or summarize information appropriately, and copy quotations word for word** (see pp. 610–13).

Research Paper in Progress 3

For the topic you worked on in Research Papers in Progress 1 and 2, locate a minimum of six sources that answer one or more of your research questions. Your sources should include at least one book, one magazine article, one scholarly journal article, one Internet source, and two other sources of any type. On a scale of 1 to 5 (where 1 is low, 5 is high), rank the relevancy and reliability of each source you located using the guidelines provided in Chapter 21, pages 584–85. Use the following chart to structure your responses.

Source	Relevancy Rating	Reliability Rating
1.		
2.		
3.		
4.		
5.		
6.		

Research Paper in Progress 4

For the three most relevant and reliable sources you identified in Research Paper in Progress 3, use the suggestions on pages 608–10 to take notes on your sources. Your goal is to provide information and support for the ideas you developed earlier. Choose a system of note-taking, writing summary notes and paraphrases and recording quotations as needed. As you work, try to answer your research questions and keep your working thesis in mind.

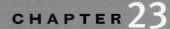

Writing a Paper Using Sources

Suppose you have been assigned to write a research paper for a mass communication course on a topic related to human communication involving more than two people. You struggle with choosing a topic for nearly a week, when suddenly, as you walk across campus, you notice many flyers tacked to a bulletin board. You decide to write about these flyers and begin to think about how to categorize them into types.

Find a bulletin board on campus, and make a list of ten organizations or activities promoted by flyers posted there. Then try to group these organizations or activities into categories.

By creating categories of organizations or activities, you took the first steps in writing a research paper—synthesizing and condensing information from sources, in this case, a primary source. In Chapter 21 you learned how to plan a paper with sources and how to choose and evaluate useful information. Chapter 22 gave you advice on finding sources and taking notes. This chapter continues the research process by showing you how to organize, draft, revise, and document a paper using sources.

You will have numerous opportunities to write research papers in your college courses. Many jobs require research skills as well. You might, for instance, need to justify a proposed change in your company's vacation policy by citing the vacation policies of other companies, or you might need to research information about a company before going on a job interview. See the box at the bottom of the page for a few other situations that would require research skills.

Think of a research paper as an opportunity to explore information about a topic, pull together ideas from sources, and present what you discover. This chapter will guide you through the process of writing a paper using sources. Figure 23.1 presents an overview of the process.

Organizing and Writing Your First Draft

After you conduct library and Internet research on your topic and take notes on your sources (as detailed in Chapter 22), you are ready to evaluate your work in preparation for writing a first draft. This stage of the research process involves evaluating your research and working thesis, developing an organizational plan, and drafting the research paper.

Evaluating Your Research and Synthesizing Information

Before you began researching your topic, you probably wrote a *working thesis*—a preliminary statement of your main point about the topic—and a list of research

---

SCENES FROM COLLEGE AND THE WORKPLACE

- For a *business* course, you are required to research a Fortune 500 company and write a report on its history and current profitability. At least two of your sources must be from the Internet.

- For a *social problems* course, you are asked to conduct your own field research (interviews or surveys) on a local or campus issue and to report your findings in a research paper.

- As *personnel director* of a publishing company, you are asked to research editorial salaries in the publishing industry and submit a report that your company will use to decide whether to change salary levels for editors.

FIGURE 23.1 Writing a Paper Using Sources

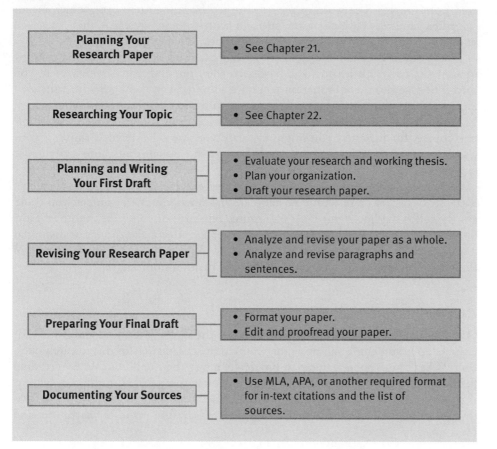

questions you hoped to answer. Then, as you researched your topic, you may have discovered new facts about your topic, statistics you were unaware of, or expert testimony that surprised you. In most cases the discoveries you make during the research process influence your thinking on the topic, requiring you to modify your working thesis. In some cases you may even need to rethink the direction of your paper.

For more on writing a working thesis and research questions, see Chapter 21, p. 582.

As you evaluate your research notes and modify your thesis, keep the following questions in mind:

1. What research questions did I begin with?
2. What answers did I find to those questions?
3. What other information did I discover about my topic?
4. What conclusions can I draw from what I've learned?
5. How does my research affect my working thesis?

To answer these questions, you'll need to **synthesize** the information you gathered from sources. The word *synthesis* is formed from the prefix *syn-,* which means "together," and *thesis,* which means "main or central point." *Synthesis,* then, means "a pulling together of information to form a new idea or point."

You synthesize information every day. For example, after you watch a preview of a movie, talk with friends who have seen the film, and read a review of it, you then pull together the information you have acquired and come up with your own idea—perhaps that you do not want to see the movie because it is too juvenile.

You often synthesize information for your college courses as well. In a biology course, for instance, you might evaluate your own lab results, those of your classmates, and the data in your textbook to reach a conclusion about a particular experiment.

As you can see, synthesis involves putting together ideas to see how they agree, disagree, or otherwise relate to one another. When working with sources, you could ask the following questions: Does one source reinforce or contradict another? How do their claims and lines of reasoning compare? Do they make similar or dissimilar assumptions and generalizations? Is their evidence alike in any way? The remainder of this section shows several ways to synthesize information from sources.

Categorizing Information

One way to arrive at a synthesis is to condense the information into categories. For example, one student found numerous sources on and answers to this research question: What causes some parents to physically abuse their children? After rereading his research notes, the student realized he could synthesize the information by putting it into three categories—lack of parenting skills, emotional instability, and family history of child abuse. He then made this two-column list of the categories and his sources.

Category	*Sources*
Lack of parenting skills	Lopez, Wexler, Thomas
Emotional instability	Wexler, Harris, Thompson, Wong
Family history of child abuse	Thompson, Harris, Lopez, Strickler, Thomas

While evaluating his research in this way, the student also realized he needed to revise both his working thesis and the scope of his paper to include lack of parenting skills as a major cause of child abuse. Notice how he modified his working thesis accordingly.

WORKING THESIS

The main reasons that children are physically abused are their parents' emotional instability and family history of child abuse.

REVISED THESIS

Some children are physically abused because of their parents' emotional instability, family history of child abuse, and lack of parenting skills.

As you work on synthesizing information from sources, keep in mind that you can categorize many kinds of events or phenomena, such as types of life insurance, effects of education level on salary, and views on environmental problems.

Exercise 23.1

Imagine that you have done research on one of the following topics; write a list of some of the information you have found. Then, working with one or two classmates, discuss how you might categorize the information. Write a thesis statement that reflects your research.

1. The health hazards of children's toys
2. The fairness of college entrance exams
3. The advantages of college athletic programs

Drawing an Organizer for Multiple Sources

Using a graphic organizer is another way to synthesize information from sources. Your organizer may reveal patterns and show similarities and differences. It will also show you how main ideas and supporting details connect with each other.

Suppose you are writing an essay on voluntary simplicity—the idea that minimizing personal possessions and commitments leads to a happier, more manageable lifestyle. You have located three reliable and relevant sources that define voluntary simplicity, but each develops the idea somewhat differently. Source 1 (Walker) is a practical how-to article that includes some personal examples. Source 2 (Parachin) is a theoretical look at statistics about workloads and complicated lifestyles and the reasons that voluntary simplicity is appealing. Source 3 (Remy) also presents strategies for simplifying but emphasizes the values of a simplified lifestyle. Figure 23.2 (on the next page) presents a sample organizer for information from these three sources.

Depending on your sources and the type of information they contain, you can use a variety of organizer formats. If all your sources compare and contrast the same things, such as the functioning and effectiveness of two presidents, you could adapt one of the graphic organizers for comparison and contrast shown in Chapter 15, pages 382 to 383. If most of your sources focus on effects, such as the effects of a recession on retail sales and employment, you could adapt one of the cause-and-effect graphic organizers shown in Chapter 18, pages 481 to 482. Whatever style of organizer you use, be sure to keep track of the sources for each idea and to use them in your organizer (as shown in Figure 23.2).

Using a Pro-and-Con List to Synthesize Confirming and Conflicting Sources

As you research a topic, especially if it is controversial, you are likely to find sources from many sides of the issue. For example, some sources may favor gun control legislation, others may oppose it, and still others may present both viewpoints. Even sources that agree or disagree, however, often do so for different reasons. On the issue of gun control legislation, one source may favor it for national-security reasons: Gun control makes it harder for terrorists to acquire guns. Another source

Figure 23.2 GRAPHIC ORGANIZER FOR THREE SOURCES ON VOLUNTARY SIMPLICITY

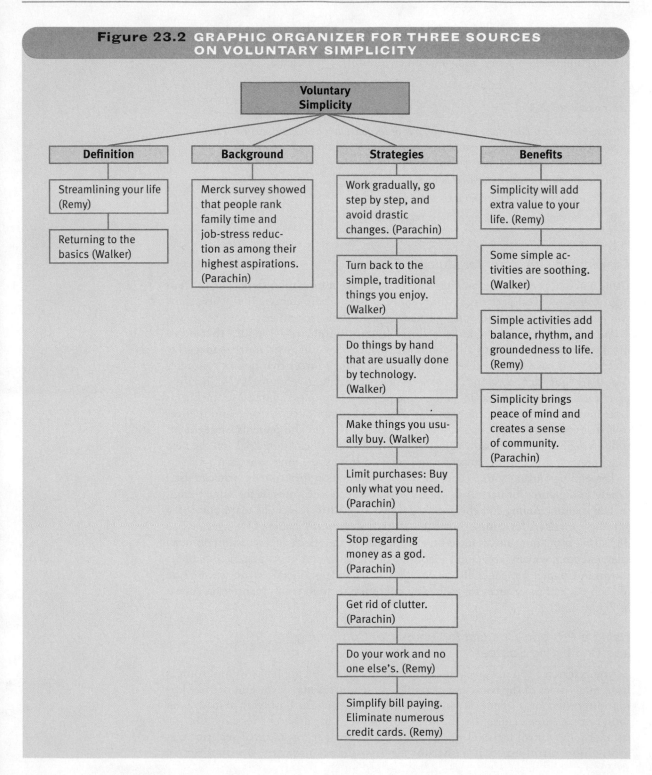

may favor legislation for a statistical reason: Statistics prove that owning a gun does not prevent crime.

As you encounter varying opinions in sources, a pro-and-con list may help you organize and synthesize your information. For the issue of gun control, you might create a two-column list such as the one shown in the box on page 628. Be sure to include the source of each entry.

Planning Your Organization

Your next step involves developing an organizational plan for your paper—deciding both what you'll say and the order in which you will say it. Think about whether you want to use chronological order, spatial order, most-to-least or least-to-most order, or one of the patterns of development discussed in Parts 3 and 4 of this text. Below are some guidelines for organizing your research paper.

Arranging Your Information

If you used note cards, begin by sorting them into piles by subtopic or category. (You may already have developed categories when you evaluated your research and thesis and worked on synthesizing source information.) For example, note cards for the thesis "Prekindergarten programs provide children with long-lasting educational advantages" might be sorted by type of educational advantage, such as reading readiness, social skills, and positive self-image.

If you took notes on a computer, you may have arranged your research information by category as you went along. If not, this is the time to do it. As you move information within or among computer files, be careful to keep track of which material belongs to which source.

If you used photocopies of sources, attach self-stick notes to indicate the various subtopics each source covers.

Once your note cards, computer files, or photocopies are organized, you are ready to develop your outline or graphic organizer.

Developing an Outline or Graphic Organizer

Use an outline or a graphic organizer to show the divisions and subdivisions you intend for your paper. Preparing such a plan is especially important for a research paper because you are working with a substantial amount of information. Without something to follow, it is easy to get lost and write an unfocused paper.

For more on outlines and graphic organizers, see Chapter 7, pp. 148–50.

Pragmatic learners tend to prefer organizing in detail before beginning to write. If this is your tendency, make sure that you are open to change and new ideas as you write your draft. Creative learners, on the other hand, may prefer to start writing and try to structure the paper as they work. Most students should not take this approach, however; those who do should allow extra time for reorganizing and making extensive revisions.

Learning Style Options

Whatever your learning style, writing an outline or graphic organizer will help you reorganize material easily and test several different organizations. Be sure to save your

PRO-AND-CON VIEWS ON GUN CONTROL LEGISLATION

Pro

Stronger federal regulations are necessary to increase homeland security following the September 11, 2001, terrorist attacks on the United States. (Melissa Robinson)

The crackdown on terrorism must close the loophole that allows many people to buy weapons at gun shows without background checks. (Fox Butterfield)

By 2000 violent crime had fallen for six consecutive years, due, in part, to mandating background checks, banning types of assault weapons, and limiting access for kids and criminals. (Brady Campaign)

A study by the Justice Department shows that background checks by the FBI and by state and local agencies have barred criminals from acquiring weapons hundreds of thousands of times. (*New York Times* editorial)

In the five years after the Brady Bill was passed (1994), background checks blocked 536,000 convicted felons and other illegal buyers from getting a gun. (Americans for Gun Safety)

Con

Stricter gun control creates vulnerable targets for enemies of a free society. (Phyllis Schlafly)

Gun control laws do not remove guns from the hands of criminals; they disarm victims. (Jack Duggan)

We should enforce the laws we have before creating new ones that may or may not provide any benefits. (Warren Ockrassa)

It is unrealistic to pass gun laws that prevent Americans from protecting themselves and their families. (Libertarian Party)

Existing laws preventing illegal purchase have proven to be effective in catching suspected terrorists, so new laws that target gun shows are not needed. (National Rifle Association)

original outline or graphic organizer and any revised versions as separate files in case you need to return to earlier versions.

Research Paper in Progress 5

Using the research notes you developed for Research Paper in Progress 4 (p. 619), sort your source notes and information into several categories and evaluate your working thesis. Then prepare an outline or a graphic organizer for your paper.

Drafting Your Research Paper

The following guidelines will help you write the first draft of a research paper:

1. **Follow the introduction, body, and conclusion format.** A straightforward organization is usually the best choice for a research paper.

For more on organization, see Chapter 7, pp. 142–50.

2. **Take a serious, academic tone, and avoid using the first or second person.** The third person (*he, she, it*) sounds more impersonal and may lend credibility to your ideas.

3. **For most research papers, place your thesis in the introduction.** However, for papers analyzing a problem or proposing a solution, try placing your thesis near the end. For example, if you were writing an essay proposing stricter traffic laws on campus, you might begin by documenting the problem—describing accidents that have occurred and detailing their frequency. You might conclude your essay by suggesting that your college lower the speed limit on campus and install two new stop signs.

4. **Keep your audience in mind.** Although you now know a great deal about your topic, your readers may not. When appropriate, be sure to provide background information, explain concepts and processes, and define terms for your readers. For example, if you were writing a paper on recycling plastics for a chemistry class, your audience might already understand some of the technical terms and concepts in your paper. You wouldn't need to explain everything. But if you were writing on the same topic for a composition class, you would need to provide thorough explanations and use more nontechnical terms.

5. **Follow your outline or graphic organizer but feel free to make changes as you work.** You may discover a better organization, think of new ideas about your topic, or realize that a subtopic belongs in a different section. Don't feel compelled to follow your outline to the letter, but be sure to address the topics you list.

6. **Determine the purpose and main point of each paragraph.** State the main point of each body paragraph in a topic sentence. Then use your sources to substantiate, explain, or provide detail in support of that main point.

7. **Use strong transitions.** Because a research paper may be lengthy or complex, strong transitions are needed to hold the paper together. In addition, transitions help your readers understand how you have divided the topic and how one point relates to another.

For more on using transitions, see Chapter 7, pp. 150–52.

8. **Support your key points with evidence.** Be sure to identify your major points first and to support each major point with evidence from several sources. Keep in mind that relying on only one or two sources weakens your thesis, suggesting to readers that you did insufficient research. Bring together facts, statistics, details, expert testimony, and other types of evidence from a variety of sources to strengthen your position.

9. **Include source material only for a specific purpose.** Just because you discovered an interesting statistic or a fascinating quote, don't feel that you must use it. Information that doesn't support your thesis will distract your reader and weaken your paper.

10. **Refer to your source notes frequently as you write.** If you do so, you will be less likely to overlook an important piece of evidence. If you suspect that a note is inaccurate in some way, check the original source.

11. **Do not overuse sources.** Make sure your paper is not just a series of facts, quotations, and so forth taken from sources. Your research paper should not merely summarize what others have written about the topic; the basis of the paper should be your ideas and thesis.

12. **Use source information in a way that does not mislead your readers.** Even though you are presenting only a portion of someone's ideas, make sure you are not using information in a way that is contrary to the writer's original intentions.

13. **Incorporate in-text citations for your sources.** Whenever you paraphrase, summarize, or quote a source, be sure to include an in-text citation. (See pp. 630–33.)

Integrating Information from Sources

After you have decided what source information to use, you will need to build that information into your essay. The three methods for extracting information—paraphrasing, summarizing, and quoting—have been discussed in Chapter 22 (pp. 610–13). In general, try to paraphrase or summarize information rather than quote it directly. Use a quotation only if the wording is unusual or unique or if you want to provide the actual statement of an expert on the topic. Regardless of how you integrate sources, be sure to acknowledge and document all direct quotations as well as the paraphrased or summarized ideas of others. You must make it clear to your readers that you have borrowed ideas or information by citing the source, whether it is a book, a Web page, a journal article, a drawing, a DVD, or another type of source. The following section provides advice on what does and does not need to be documented as well as guidelines for writing in-text citations and using quotations appropriately.

Deciding What to Document

For more on what constitutes plagiarism, see Chapter 22, pp. 613–14.

You can use another person's material in your paper as long as you give that person credit. **Plagiarism** occurs when you present the ideas of others as your own. Whether intentional or not, plagiarism is a serious error that must be avoided. The accompanying box identifies the types of material that *do* and *do not* require documentation. If you are unsure about whether to document something, ask your instructor or a reference librarian.

In the last few years, plagiarism has become widespread because it is easy to cut and paste information from online sources. To combat this problem, many instructors use Internet tracking resources like Turnitin.com to check for plagiarized material. Be sure that you have used quotation marks, paraphrased completely, and cited all source material accurately. You do not want to plagiarize anyone's ideas, even inadvertently.

Writing In-Text Citations

Many academic disciplines have their own preferred format or style for documenting sources within the text of a paper. For example, in English and the humanities, the preferred documentation format is that of the Modern Language Association

WHAT DOES AND DOES NOT REQUIRE DOCUMENTATION

Documentation Required

Summaries, paraphrases, and quotations

Obscure or recently discovered facts (such as a little-known fact about Mark Twain or a recent discovery about Mars)

Others' opinions

Others' field research (results of opinion polls, case studies, statistics)

Quotations or paraphrases from interviews you conduct

Others' visuals (photographs, charts, maps, Web images)

Information from others that you use to create visuals (statistics or other data that you use to construct a table, graph, or other visual)

Documentation Not Required

Common knowledge (George Washington was the first U.S. president, the Earth revolves around the sun)

Facts that can be found in numerous sources (winners of Olympic competitions, names of Supreme Court justices)

Standard definitions of academic terms

Your own ideas or conclusions

Your own field research (surveys or observations)

Your own visuals (such as photographs you take)

and is known as *MLA style*. In the social sciences, the guidelines of the American Psychological Association, commonly called *APA style*, are often used. Many scientists follow a format used by the Council of Science Editors (CSE). The two most widely used formats—MLA and APA—are discussed in detail later in this chapter. (See pp. 640–62 for MLA style; see pp. 663–81 for APA style.)

When you paraphrase, summarize, or quote from a source, you must provide a brief reference to the source in your paper and a complete citation in a list of sources at the end of the paper. The list is headed *Works Cited* in MLA style and *References* in APA style. This list includes only the sources you cite in your paper, not all the sources you consulted while conducting research.

What Should I Include in an MLA-style In-Text Citation?

In MLA style, an in-text citation usually includes the author's name and the page numbers of the source information. Many writers put the author's name in an introductory phrase, called an **attribution** or **signal phrase,** and the page number(s) in parentheses at the end of the sentence.

As Jo-Ellan Dimitrius observes, big spenders often suffer from low self-esteem (143).

Often, providing some background information about the source the first time you mention it is useful to readers, especially if the source is not commonly known.

> Jo-Ellan Dimitrius, a jury-selection consultant whose book *Reading People* discusses methods of predicting behavior, observes that big spenders often suffer from low self-esteem (143).

Such information helps readers understand that the source is relevant and credible. When merely citing facts or when a source author has already been identified, a parenthetical citation that includes the author's last name and the page number may be sufficient.

> Some behavioral experts claim that big spenders often suffer from low self-esteem (Dimitrius 143).

Without an attribution before and a page number after, however, readers may not be able to tell whether an idea is yours or the source's.

How Can I Integrate Sources Most Effectively?

Using an attribution such as "As Markham argues" or "Bernstein observes that" will help you integrate information from sources smoothly into your paper. Most summaries and paraphrases and *all* quotations need such an introduction. Compare the paragraphs below:

QUOTATION NOT INTEGRATED

Anecdotes indicate that animals experience emotions, but they are not considered scientifically valid. "Experimental evidence is given almost exclusive credibility over personal experience to a degree that seems almost religious" (Masson and McCarthy 3).

QUOTATION INTEGRATED

Anecdotes indicate that animals experience emotions, but they are not considered scientifically valid. Masson and McCarthy, who have done extensive field observation, comment, "Experimental evidence is given almost exclusive credibility over personal experience to a degree that seems almost religious" (3).

In the first example paragraph above, the quotation is merely dropped in. In the second, the background of the source authors is mentioned.

When writing attributions, vary the verbs you use. The following verbs are useful for introducing many kinds of source material:

advocates	contends	insists	proposes
argues	demonstrates	maintains	shows
asserts	denies	mentions	speculates
believes	emphasizes	notes	states
claims	explains	points out	suggests

In most cases, a neutral verb such as *states, explains,* or *maintains* will be most appropriate. Sometimes, however, a verb such as *denies* or *speculates* may more accurately reflect the source author's attitude. Varying the placement of the attribution will also make your paper more interesting to read.

For more practice integrating quotations into your writing, visit www.bedfordstmartins .com/successfulcollege/.

Using Quotations Appropriately

Although quotations can lend interest to your paper and support for your ideas, they need to be used appropriately. The following section answers some common questions about the use of quotations. The in-text citations in this section follow MLA style, as do the rules about changing quotations. (See p. 663 for creating in-text citations in APA style.)

When Should I Use Quotations?

1. **Use quotations sparingly.** Do not use quotations to reveal ordinary facts and opinions. Look carefully at what you intend to quote. If a quotation does not achieve one of the following purposes, use a paraphrase instead:

   • Quote when the author's wording is unusual, noteworthy, or striking. The quotation "Injustice anywhere is a threat to justice everywhere" from Martin Luther King Jr.'s "Letter from Birmingham Jail" is probably more effective than any paraphrase.

   • Quote when the original words express the exact point you want to make and a paraphrase might alter or distort the statement's meaning.

   • Quote when the statement is a strong, opinionated, exaggerated, or disputed idea that you want to make clear is not your own.

2. **Use quotations to support your ideas.** Never use a quotation as the topic sentence of a paragraph. The topic sentence should state in your own words the idea you are about to explain or prove.

3. **Follow quotations with an explanatory sentence.** Add a sentence or more to make clear to readers the purpose the quotation serves.

What Format Do I Follow for Long Quotations?

In MLA style, lengthy quotations (more than three lines of poetry or more than four typed lines of prose) are indented in a block, one inch from the left margin. In APA style, quotations of more than forty words are indented as a block half an inch from the left margin. In both styles, quotation marks are omitted, and quotations are double spaced.

Like a shorter quotation in the main text, a block quotation should always be introduced by an attribution. Use a colon at the end of the attribution if it appears in a complete sentence.

> In her book *Through a Window,* which elaborates on her thirty years of experience studying and living among the chimps in Gombe, Tanzania, Jane Goodall gives the following account of Flint's experience with grief:
>
>> Flint became increasingly lethargic, refused most food and, with his immune system thus weakened, fell sick. The last time I saw him alive, he was hollow-eyed, gaunt and utterly depressed, huddled in the vegetation close to where Flo had died. . . .

> The last short journey he made, pausing to rest every few feet, was to the very place where Flo's body had lain. There he stayed for several hours, sometimes staring and staring into the water. He struggled on a little further, then curled up—and never moved again. (196–97)

Unlike a shorter quotation in the main text, the page numbers in parentheses appear *after* the final sentence period. (For a short quotation within the text, the page numbers within parentheses precede the period.)

How Do I Punctuate Quotations?

There are specific rules and conventions for punctuating quotations. The most important rules follow:

1. **Use single quotation marks to enclose a quotation within a quotation.**

   Coleman and Cressey argue that "concern for the 'decaying family' is nothing new" (147).

2. **Use a comma after a verb that introduces a quotation.** Begin the first word of the quotation with a capital letter (enclosed in brackets if it is not capitalized in the source).

   As Thompson and Hickey report, "There are three major kinds of 'taste cultures' in complex industrial societies: high culture, folk culture, and popular culture" (76).

3. **When a quotation is not introduced by a verb, it is not necessary to use a comma or capitalize the first word.**

   Buck reports that "pets play a significant part in both physical and psychological therapy" (4).

4. **Use a colon to introduce a quotation preceded by a complete sentence.**

   The definition is clear: "Countercultures reject the conventional wisdom and standards of the dominant culture and provide alternatives to mainstream culture" (Thompson and Hickey 76).

5. **For a paraphrase or quotation integrated into the text, punctuation *follows* the parenthetical citation; for a block quotation, the punctuation *precedes* the parenthetical citation.**

   Scientists who favor a related scientific theory called *mutual altruism* believe that animals help each other because when they themselves need help, they would like to be able to count on reciprocal assistance (Hemelrijk 479–81).

   Franklin observed the following scene:

   > Her unhappy spouse moved around her incessantly, his attention and tender cares redoubled. . . . At length his companion breathed her last; from that moment he pined away, and died in the course of a few weeks. (qtd. in Barber 116)

6. **Place periods and commas inside quotation marks.**

   "The most valuable old cars," notes antique car collector Michael Patterson, "are the rarest ones."

7. **Place colons and semicolons outside quotation marks.**

"Petting a dog increases mobility of a limb or hand"; petting a dog, then, can be a form of physical therapy (Buck 4).

8. **Place question marks and exclamation points inside quotation marks when they are part of the original quotation. No period is needed if the quotation ends the sentence.**

The instructor asked, "Does the text's description of alternative lifestyles agree with your experience?"

9. **Place question marks and exclamation points that belong to your own sentence outside quotation marks.**

Is the following definition accurate: "Sociolinguistics is the study of the relationship between language and society"?

How Can I Change Quotations?

1. When you use a quotation, the spelling, punctuation, and capitalization must be copied exactly as they appear in the original source, even if they are in error. (See item 5 on p. 636 for the only exception.) If a source contains an error, copy it with the error and add the word *sic* (Latin for "thus") in brackets immediately following the error.

According to Bernstein, "The family has undergone rapid decentralization since Word [sic] War II" (39).

2. You can emphasize words by underlining or italicizing them, but you must add the notation *emphasis added* in parentheses at the end of the sentence to indicate the change.

"In *unprecedented* and *increasing* numbers, patients are consulting practitioners of every type of complementary medicine" (emphasis added) (Buckman and Sabbagh 73).

3. You can omit part of a quotation, but you must add ellipsis points — three spaced periods (. . .) — to indicate that material has been deleted. You may delete words, sentences, paragraphs, or entire pages, as long as you do not distort the author's meaning by doing so.

According to Buckman and Sabbagh, "Acupuncture . . . has been rigorously tested and proven to be effective and valid" (188).

When an omission falls at the end of a quoted sentence, use the three spaced periods in addition to the sentence period.

Thompson maintains that "marketers need to establish ethical standards for personal selling. . . . They must stress fairness and honesty in dealing with customers" (298).

If you are quoting only a word or phrase from a source, do not use ellipsis points before or after it because it will be obvious that you have omitted part of the original sentence. If you omit the beginning of a quoted sentence, you need not use ellipsis points unless what you are quoting still begins with a capitalized word and appears to be a complete sentence.

4. You can add words or phrases in brackets to make a quotation clearer or to make it fit grammatically into your sentence; be sure that in doing so you do not change the original sense.

> Masson and McCarthy note that the well-known animal researcher Jane Goodall finds that "the scientific reluctance to accept anecdotal evidence [of emotional experience is] a serious problem, one that colors all of science" (3).

5. You can change the first word of a quotation to a capital or lowercase letter to fit into your sentence. If you change it, enclose it in brackets.

> As Aaron Smith said, "The . . ." (32).
>
> Aaron Smith said that "[t]he . . ." (32).

> **Research Paper in Progress 6**
> Using your research notes, your revised thesis, and the organizational plan you developed for your research paper, write a first draft. Be sure to integrate sources carefully and to include in-text citations. (See pp. 640–44 for MLA style guidelines for in-text citations; see pp. 663–66 for APA style.)

Revising Your Research Paper

For more on revision, see Chapter 9.

Revise a research paper in two stages. First focus on the paper as a whole; then consider individual paragraphs and sentences for effectiveness and correctness. If time allows, wait at least a day before rereading your research paper.

Analyzing and Revising Your Paper as a Whole

Begin by evaluating your paper as a unified piece of writing. Focus on general issues, overall organization, and the key points that support your thesis. Use the flowchart in Figure 23.3 (pp. 638–39) to help you discover the strengths and weaknesses of your research paper as a whole. You might also ask a classmate to review your draft paper by using the questions in the flowchart.

Analyzing and Revising Paragraphs and Sentences

After evaluating your paper as a whole, check each paragraph to be sure that it supports your thesis and integrates sources appropriately. Then check your sentences for correct structure, transitions, and in-text citation format. Use your earlier work with Figure 23.3 to guide your analysis.

> **Research Paper in Progress 7**
> Using the questions in Figure 23.3, revise the first draft of your research paper.

Preparing Your Final Draft

After you have revised your paper and compiled a list of references or works cited, you are ready to prepare the final draft. Following are some guidelines to help you format, edit, and proofread your final paper. For an example of an essay in MLA style, see "Do Animals Have Emotions?" by Nicholas Destino on pages 656–62. For an example of an essay in APA style, see "Schizophrenia: Definition and Treatment" by Sonia Gomez on pages 675–81.

Formatting Your Paper

Academic papers should follow a standard manuscript format whether or not they use sources. The following guidelines are recommended by the Modern Language Association (MLA). If your instructor suggests or requires a different format, be sure to follow it. If your instructor does not recommend a format, these guidelines would probably be acceptable.

1. **Paper.** Use 8½- by 11-inch white paper. Use a paper clip; do not staple or use a binder.
2. **Your name and course information.** Do not use a title page unless your instructor requests one. Instead, position your name at the left margin one inch from the top of the page. Underneath it, list your instructor's name, your course name and number, and the date. Use separate lines for each, and double-space between the lines.
3. **Title.** Place the title two lines below the date. Center the title on the page. Capitalize the first word and all other important words (all except articles, co-ordinating conjunctions, and prepositions). Double-space after the title and type your first paragraph. Do not underline or italicize your title or put quotation marks around it.
4. **Margins, spacing, and indentation.** Use one-inch margins. Double-space between all lines of your paper (including block quotations and works-cited entries). Indent first line of each paragraph half an inch.
5. **Numbering of pages.** Number all pages using arabic numerals (1, 2, 3) in the upper-right corner. Place the numbers one-half inch below the top of the paper. (If your instructor requests a title page, do not number it and do not count it in your numbering.) Precede each with your last name, leaving a space between your name and the number.
6. **Headings.** The MLA does not provide any guidelines for using headings. However, the system recommended by the American Psychological Association (APA) should work for most papers. Main headings should be centered, and the first letter of key words should be capitalized. Subheadings should begin at the left margin, with important words capitalized.
7. **Visuals.** You may include tables and figures (graphs, charts, maps, photographs, and drawings) in your paper. Label each table or figure with an arabic numeral (*Table 1, Table 2; Fig. 1, Fig. 2*) and give it a title. Place the table number and title on separate lines above the table. Give each figure a number and title and place the figure number and title below the figure.

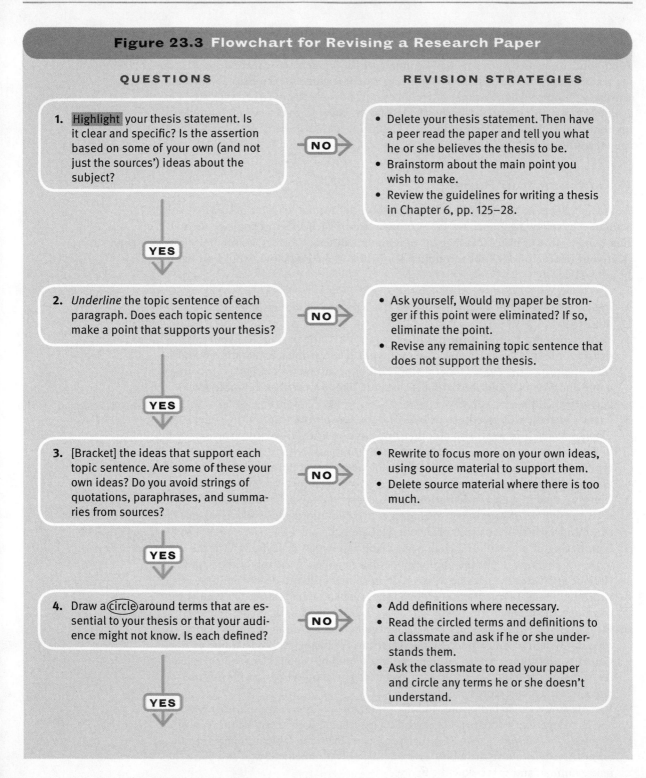

Figure 23.3 Flowchart for Revising a Research Paper

QUESTIONS

REVISION STRATEGIES

1. Highlight your thesis statement. Is it clear and specific? Is the assertion based on some of your own (and not just the sources') ideas about the subject?

   NO

   - Delete your thesis statement. Then have a peer read the paper and tell you what he or she believes the thesis to be.
   - Brainstorm about the main point you wish to make.
   - Review the guidelines for writing a thesis in Chapter 6, pp. 125–28.

   YES

2. *Underline* the topic sentence of each paragraph. Does each topic sentence make a point that supports your thesis?

   NO

   - Ask yourself, Would my paper be stronger if this point were eliminated? If so, eliminate the point.
   - Revise any remaining topic sentence that does not support the thesis.

   YES

3. [Bracket] the ideas that support each topic sentence. Are some of these your own ideas? Do you avoid strings of quotations, paraphrases, and summaries from sources?

   NO

   - Rewrite to focus more on your own ideas, using source material to support them.
   - Delete source material where there is too much.

   YES

4. Draw a circle around terms that are essential to your thesis or that your audience might not know. Is each defined?

   NO

   - Add definitions where necessary.
   - Read the circled terms and definitions to a classmate and ask if he or she understands them.
   - Ask the classmate to read your paper and circle any terms he or she doesn't understand.

   YES

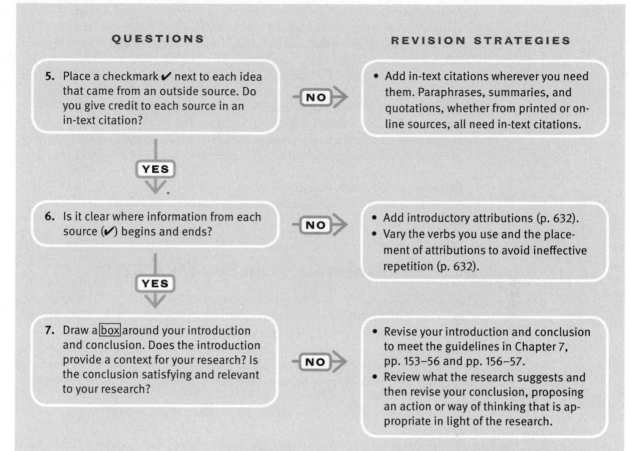

Editing and Proofreading Your Paper

As a final step, edit and proofread your revised paper for errors in grammar, spelling, punctuation, mechanics, and documentation style. In addition, be sure to check your error log for the types of errors you commonly make.

For more on editing and proofreading, see Chapter 10.

As you edit and proofread, watch out for the following common problems:

1. Does your paper contain any long, cumbersome sentences? If so, try splitting them into two separate sentences.
2. Do you use a consistent verb tense throughout your paper? Avoid shifting from present to past to future tense unless there is a good reason to do so.
3. Do you punctuate and style in-text citations correctly? Make sure that they conform to MLA style or that of another system of documentation.

4. Do you reproduce direct quotations exactly as they appear in the original source? In addition to checking the accuracy of individual words, be sure to check your use of quotation marks, capital letters, commas, and ellipses within quotations.

5. Do you avoid plagiarism by carefully quoting, paraphrasing, and summarizing the ideas of others?

6. Is your paper typed and spaced according to the format you need to follow? Be sure that block quotations are also typed appropriately.

7. Is your list of works cited or references complete? Make sure all sources cited in your paper are included in the list in the right order and are formatted correctly.

> **Research Paper in Progress 8**
> Edit and proofread your paper, paying particular attention to the questions in the preceding list.

Documenting Your Sources: MLA Style

The system described in this section is recommended by the Modern Language Association (MLA). MLA style is commonly used in English and the humanities. If you are unsure whether to use MLA style, check with your instructor.

MLA style uses in-text citations to identify sources within the text of a research paper and a list of works cited at the end of the paper to document them. For additional examples of in-text citations or works-cited entries, consult the following source:

MLA Handbook for Writers of Research Papers, 7th ed. New York: MLA, 2009. Print.

The first student paper that appears later in this chapter (see pp. 656–62) uses MLA style, as do all student papers in Chapters 7 to 16.

MLA Style for In-Text Citations

Your paper must include in-text citations for all material you paraphrase, summarize, or quote from sources. There are two basic ways to write an in-text citation:

For more on attributions (signal phrases), see p. 632.

1. **Use an attribution (or signal phrase).** Mention the author's name early in the sentence or paragraph and include only the page number(s) in parentheses at the end of the borrowed passage. Use the author's full name the first time you mention the author. Give only the author's last name in subsequent citations to the same source.

2. **Use a parenthetical citation.** Include both the author's last name and the page number(s) in parentheses at the end of the borrowed sentence or paragraph. Do not separate the name and page number(s) with a comma.

Many instructors prefer that you use attributions rather than only parenthetical citations because attributions allow you to put sources in context.

For either type of citation, use the following rules:

- Omit the word *page* or the abbreviation *p.* or *pp.*
- Place the sentence period after the closing parenthesis unless the citation follows a block quotation. (See p. 634.)
- If a quotation ends the sentence, insert the closing quotation marks before the parentheses enclosing the page reference.

Examples showing in-text citations in MLA style follow.

List of MLA in-text citation models

One author

According to Vance Packard . . . (58).

. . . (Packard 58).

Two or three authors. Include all authors' names, in either an attribution or a parenthetical citation.

Marquez and Allison assert . . . (74).

. . . (Marquez and Allison 74).

Four or more authors. You may use all of the authors' last names or the first author's last name followed by either a phrase referring to the other authors (in an attribution) or *et al.,* Latin for "and others" (in a parenthetical citation). Whichever option you choose, apply it consistently within your paper.

Hong and colleagues maintain . . . (198).

. . . (Hong et al. 198).

Two or more works by the same author. When citing two or more sources by the same author or group of authors in your paper, include the full or abbreviated title in the citation to indicate the proper work.

FIRST WORK

In *For God, Country, and Coca-Cola,* Pendergrast describes . . . (96).

Pendergrast describes . . . (*For God* 96).

. . . (Pendergrast, *For God* 96).

SECOND WORK

In *Uncommon Grounds*, Pendergrast maintains . . . (42).

Pendergrast maintains . . . (*Uncommon* 42).

. . . (Pendergrast, *Uncommon* 42).

Corporate or organizational author. When the author of the source is given as a corporation, an organization, or a government office, reference the organization's name as the author name. Use abbreviations such as *Natl.* and *Cong.* in parenthetical references.

According to the National Institute of Mental Health . . . (2).

. . . (Natl. Institute of Mental Health 2).

Unknown author. If the author is unknown, use the full title in an attribution or a shortened form in parentheses.

According to the article "Medical Mysteries and Surgical Surprises," . . . (79).

. . . ("Medical Mysteries" 79).

Authors with the same last name. Include the first initial of these authors in all parenthetical citations. Use the complete first name if both authors have the same first initial.

John Dillon proposes . . . (974).

. . . (J. Dillon 974).

Two or more sources in the same citation. When citing two or more sources of one idea in parentheses, separate the citations with a semicolon.

. . . (Breakwater 33; Holden 198).

Entire work. To refer to an entire work, such as a Web page, a film, or a book, use the author's name, preferably within the text rather than in a parenthetical reference; do not include page numbers. The title is optional.

In *For God, Country, and Coca-Cola*, Pendergrast presents an unauthorized history of Coca-Cola, the soft drink and the company that produces it.

Chapter in an edited book or work in an anthology. An *anthology* is a collection of writings (articles, stories, poems) by different authors. In the in-text citation, name the author who wrote the work (not the editor of the anthology) and include the page number(s) from the anthology. The corresponding entry in the list of works cited begins with the author's last name; it also names the editor of the anthology.

IN-TEXT CITATION

According to Ina Ferris . . . (239).

. . . (Ferris 239).

WORKS-CITED ENTRY

Ferris, Ina. "The Irish Novel 1800–1829." *Cambridge Companion to Fiction in the Romantic Period*. Ed. Richard Maxwell and Katie Trumpener. Cambridge: Cambridge UP, 2008. 235–49. Print.

Multivolume work. When citing two or more volumes of a multivolume work, indicate the volume number, followed by a colon and the page number.

Terman indicates . . . (2: 261).

. . . (Terman 2: 261).

Indirect source. When quoting an indirect source (someone whose ideas came to you through another source, such as a magazine article or book), make this clear by adding, in parentheses, the last name and page number of the source in which the quote or information appeared, preceded by the abbreviation *qtd. in.*

According to Ephron (qtd. in Thomas 33), . . .

Personal interview, letter, email, conversation. Give the name of the person in your text.

In an interview with Professor Lopez, . . .

Literature and poetry. Include information that will help readers locate the material in any edition of the literary work. Include page numbers from the edition you use.

- *For novels:* Cite page and chapter numbers.

  (109; ch. 5)

- *For poems:* Cite line numbers instead of page numbers; use the word *line* or *lines* in the first reference only.

  FIRST REFERENCE   (lines 12–15)

  LATER REFERENCES   (16–18)

- *For plays:* Give the act, scene, and line numbers in arabic numerals, separated by periods.

  (*Macbeth* 2.1.32–37)

Include complete publication information for the edition you use in the list of works cited.

Internet sources. In general, Internet sources are cited like their printed counterparts. Give enough information in the citation so that readers can locate the source in your list of works cited. If the electronic source provides page numbers, you should provide them too. If the source uses another ordering system, such as paragraphs (*par.*

or *pars.*), sections (*sec.*), or screens (*screen*), provide the abbreviation with the appropriate number.

> Brian Beckman argues that "centrifugal force is a fiction" (par. 6).
>
> . . . (Beckman, par. 6).

If the source does not have paragraphs or page numbers, which is often the case, then cite the work by author, title of the document or site, or sponsor of the site, whichever begins your entry in the list of works cited.

AUTHOR

Teresa Schmidt discusses . . .

. . . (Schmidt).

TITLE

The "Band of Brothers" section of the History Channel site . . .

. . . ("Band").

SPONSOR

According to a Web page posted by the Council for Indigenous Arts and Culture, . . .

. . . (Council).

MLA Style for the List of Works Cited

For more practice using the MLA style of documentation, visit www.bedfordstmartins .com/successfulcollege/.

Follow these general guidelines for preparing the list:

1. **List only the sources you cite in your paper.** If you consulted a source but did not cite it in your paper, do not include it in the list of works cited.
2. **Put the list on a separate page at the end of your paper.** The heading *Works Cited* should be centered an inch below the top of the page. Do not use quotation marks, underlining, or bold type for the heading.
3. **Alphabetize the list by authors' last names.** For works with multiple authors, invert only the first author's name. If no author is listed, begin the entry with the title.

> Trask, R. L., and Robert M. C. Millar. *Why Do Languages Change?* Cambridge: Cambridge UP, 2010. Print.

4. **Capitalize the first word and all other words in a title except *a, an, the, to,* coordinating conjunctions, and prepositions.**
5. **Italicize or underline titles of books and names of periodicals.**
6. **Give inclusive page numbers of articles in periodicals.** Do not use the word *page* or the abbreviation *p.* or *pp.*
7. **Indent the second and all subsequent lines half an inch or five spaces.** This is known as the *hanging indent* style.
8. **Double-space the entire list.**

The following sections describe how to format works-cited entries for books, periodicals, Internet sources, and other sources.

List of MLA works-cited entries

Books

General guidelines and sample entries for books follow. Include the elements listed below, which you will find on the book's title page and copyright page. See Figure 23.4 on page 646 for an example.

1. *Author.* Begin with the author's last name, followed by the first name.

2. *Title.* Provide the full title of the book, including the subtitle. It should be capitalized and italicized.

3. *Place of publication.* Do not abbreviate city names (use *Los Angeles,* not *LA*). It is not necessary to include an abbreviation for the state or country.

4. *Publisher.* Use a shortened form of the publisher's name; usually one word is sufficient (*Houghton Mifflin* is listed as *Houghton*). For university presses, use the abbreviations *U* for *University* and *P* for *Press* with no periods.

5. *Date.* Use the most recent publication date listed on the book's copyright page.

6. *Medium.* For printed books, the medium of publication is *Print.*

FIGURE 23.4 Where to Find Documentation Information for a Book

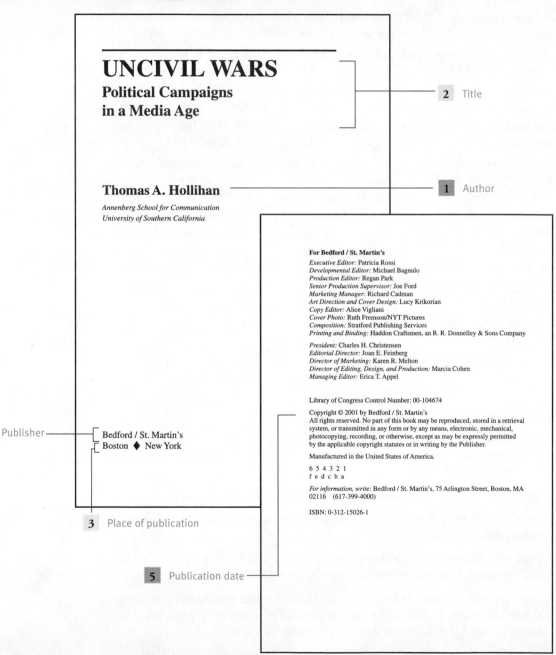

UNCIVIL WARS
**Political Campaigns
in a Media Age**

2 Title

Thomas A. Hollihan

1 Author

*Annenberg School for Communication
University of Southern California*

For Bedford / St. Martin's
Executive Editor: Patricia Rossi
Developmental Editor: Michael Bagnulo
Production Editor: Regan Park
Senior Production Supervisor: Joe Ford
Marketing Manager: Richard Cadman
Art Direction and Cover Design: Lucy Krikorian
Copy Editor: Alice Vigliani
Cover Photo: Ruth Fremson/NYT Pictures
Composition: Stratford Publishing Services
Printing and Binding: Haddon Craftsmen, an R. R. Donnelley & Sons Company

President: Charles H. Christensen
Editorial Director: Joan E. Feinberg
Director of Marketing: Karen R. Melton
Director of Editing, Design, and Production: Marcia Cohen
Managing Editor: Erica T. Appel

Library of Congress Control Number: 00-104674

Copyright © 2001 by Bedford / St. Martin's
All rights reserved. No part of this book may be reproduced, stored in a retrieval
system, or transmitted in any form or by any means, electronic, mechanical,
photocopying, recording, or otherwise, except as may be expressly permitted
by the applicable copyright statutes or in writing by the Publisher.

Manufactured in the United States of America.

6 5 4 3 2 1
f e d c b a

For information, write: Bedford / St. Martin's, 75 Arlington Street, Boston, MA
02116   (617-399-4000)

ISBN: 0-312-15026-1

4 Publisher

Bedford / St. Martin's
Boston ◆ New York

3 Place of publication

5 Publication date

MLA FORMAT FOR CITING A BOOK

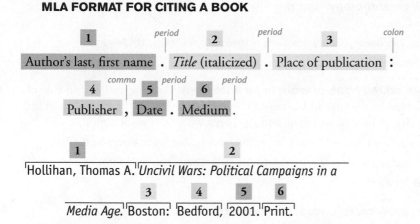

If applicable, also include the original publication date, editor, translator, edition, and volumes used; these should be placed immediately after the title of the work.

Book with one author

Rybczynski, Witold. *Makeshift Metropolis: Ideas about Cities*. New York: Scribner, 2010. Print.

Book with two or more authors. List the names in the order they appear on the title page of the book, and separate the names with commas. The second and subsequent authors' names are *not* reversed. For books with four or more authors, you can either list all names or list only the first author's name followed by *et al.*

TWO OR THREE AUTHORS

Postel, Sandra, and Brian Richter. *Rivers for Life: Managing Water for People and Nature*.
    Washington: Island, 2003. Print.

FOUR OR MORE AUTHORS

Lewin, Benjamin, Jocelyn E. Krebs, Stephen T. Kilpatrick, Elliott S. Goldstein, and
    Benjamin Lewin. *Lewin's Genes X*. Sudbury: Jones, 2011. Print.

Lewin, Benjamin, et al. *Lewin's Genes X*. Sudbury: Jones, 2011. Print.

Book with no named author. Put the title first and alphabetize the entry by title. (Do not consider the words *A, An,* and *The* when alphabetizing.)

The New Interpreter's Dictionary of the Bible. Nashville: Abingdon Press, 2006. Print.

Book by a corporation or organization. List the organization or corporation as the author, omitting any initial article (*A, An, The*).

American Red Cross. *First Aid and Safety for Babies and Children*. Yardley: StayWell, 2009. Print.

Government publication. If there is no author, list the government followed by the department and agency of the government. Use abbreviations such as *Dept.* and *Natl.* if the meaning is clear.

United States. Office of Management and Budget. *A New Era of Responsibility: Renewing
    America's Promise*. Washington: GPO, 2009. Print.

Edited book or anthology. List the editor's name followed by a comma and the abbreviation *ed.* or *eds.*

> Szeman, Imre, and Timothy Kaposy, eds. *Cultural Theory: An Anthology*. Chichester:
>> Wiley-Blackwell, 2011. Print.

Chapter in an edited book or work in an anthology. List the author and title of the work, followed by the title and editor of the anthology (*Ed.* is the abbreviation for "Edited by"); city, publisher, and date; and the pages where the work appears.

> Tillman, Barrett. "Pearl Harbor." *Today's Best Military Writing: The Finest Articles on the Past,*
>> *Present, and Future of the U.S. Military*. Ed. Walter J. Boyne. New York: Forge, 2004.
>> 311–20. Print.

Introduction, preface, foreword, or afterword

> Aaron, Hank. Foreword. *We Are the Ship: The Story of Negro League Baseball*. By Kadir
>> Nelson. New York: Jump at the Sun, 2008.

Translated book. After the title, include the abbreviation *Trans.* followed by the first and last names of the translator.

> Kawakami, Hiromi. *Manazuru*. Trans. Michael Emmerich. Berkeley: Counterpoint, 2010. Print.

Two or more works by the same author(s). Use the author's name for only the first entry. For subsequent entries, use three hyphens followed by a period. List the entries in alphabetical order by title. List works for which the person is the only author before those for which he or she is the first coauthor.

> Adams, Ryan. *Hellosunshine*. New York: Akashic, 2009. Print.
> ---. *Infinity Blues*. New York: Akashic, 2009. Print.
> Myers, Walter D. *Lockdown*. New York: Amistad, 2010. Print.
> Myers, Walter D., and Christopher Myers. *Jazz*. New York: Holiday, 2006. Print.

Edition other than the first. Indicate the number of the edition following the title.

> Barker, Ellen M. *Neuroscience Nursing*. 3rd ed. St. Louis: Mosby-Elsevier, 2008. Print.

Multivolume work. Give the number of volumes after the title.

> Price, Emmett G. *Encyclopedia of African American Music*. 3 vols. Santa Barbara: ABC-CLIO, 2011.
>> Print.

One volume of a multivolume work. Give the volume number after the title.

> Price, Emmett G. *Encyclopedia of African American Music*. Vol. 1. Santa Barbara: ABC-CLIO, 2011.
>> Print.

Encyclopedia or dictionary entry. Note that when citing well-known reference books, you do not need to give the full publication information, just the edition and year.

> Teixeira, Robert. "Suffrage Movement." *Encyclopedia of Gender and Society*. Ed. Jodi O'Brien.
>> Los Angeles: Sage, 2009. Print.

If more than one of these rules applies to a source, cite the necessary information in the order given in the preceding examples. For instance, to cite a reading from this textbook, treat it as a **work in an anthology (p. 648)** in an **edition other than the first (p. 648)**:

> Zaitchik, Alexander. "Alien World: How Treacherous Border Crossing Became a Theme Park." *Successful College Writing: Skills, Strategies, Learning Styles*. Ed. Kathleen T. McWhorter. 5th ed. Boston: Bedford, 2012. 258–63. Print.

Articles in Periodicals

A periodical is a publication that appears at regular intervals: newspapers generally appear daily, magazines weekly or monthly, and scholarly journals quarterly. General guidelines and sample entries for various types of periodical articles follow. Include the elements listed below, most of which you should find on the first page of the article. See Figure 23.5 (p. 650) for an example.

1. *Author.* Use the same format for listing authors' names as for books (see p. 647). If no author is listed, begin the entry with the article title and alphabetize the entry by its title (ignore *The, An,* or *A*).

2. *Article title.* The title should appear in double quotation marks; a period falls inside the ending quotation mark.

3. *Periodical title.* Italicize or underline the title of the periodical. Do *not* include the word *A, An,* or *The* at the beginning: *Journal of the American Medical Association, New York Times.*

4. *Date or volume/issue (year).* For magazines and newspapers, list the date in the following order: day, month, year; abbreviate the names of months except for *May, June,* and *July.* For scholarly journals, give the volume and issue numbers and year in parentheses: 72.2 (2005).

5. *Page(s).* If an article begins in one place, such as on pages 19 to 21, and is continued elsewhere, such as on pages 79 to 80, write *19+* for the page numbers (*not* 19–80). Otherwise, include the first and last page number separated by a hyphen (39–43).

6. *Medium.* For printed periodicals, the medium of publication is *Print.*

   The basic format for citing a periodical article is as follows.

MLA FORMAT FOR CITING AN ARTICLE IN A PERIODICAL

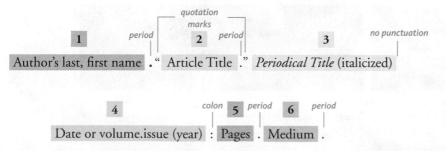

Article in a magazine

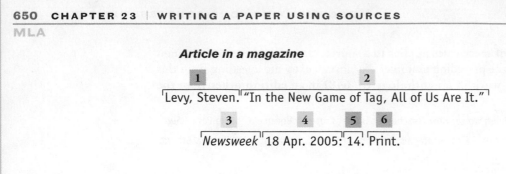

1 2
Levy, Steven. "In the New Game of Tag, All of Us Are It."

3 4 5 6
Newsweek 18 Apr. 2005: 14. Print.

FIGURE 23.5 Where to Find Documentation Information for an Article

1 Author

2 Article title

5 Page 3 Periodical title 4 Date

Article in a newspaper.

Pham, Alex. "Pandora Online Radio Service IPO." *Los Angeles Times*
12 Feb 2011: B2. Print.

Article in a scholarly journal

Prose, Francine. "Genocide without Apology." *American Scholar*
72.2 (2005): 39–43. Print.

Article in a monthly magazine

Killingsworth, Jason. "The Unbearable Lightness of Being Jonsi." *Paste Magazine* May 2010:
49–53. Print.

Article in an edition of a newspaper. If an edition name (*natl.ed*) appears on the newspaper's first page, include it after the date.

Urbina, Ian. "Gas Wells Recycle Water, but Toxic Risks Persist." *New York Times* 2 Mar.
2011, late ed., A1+. Print.

Editorial or letter to the editor. Cite the article or letter beginning with the author's name (if provided), and add the word *Editorial* or *Letter* followed by a period after the title. Often, editorials are unsigned and letters to the editor omit titles.

"The Search for Livable Worlds." Editorial. *New York Times* 8 Sept. 2004: A22. Print.

Wolansky, Taras. Letter. *Wired* May 2004: 25. Print.

Book or film review. List the reviewer's name and title of the review. After the title, add *Rev. of* and give the title and author of the book. For a film review, replace *by* with *dir*. Include publication information for the review itself, not for the material reviewed.

Gabler, Neal. "Ephemera: The Rise and Rise of Celebrity Journalism." Rev. of *The Untold Story: My*
Twenty Years Running the National Enquirer, by Iain Calder, and *The Importance of*
Being Famous: Behind the Scenes of the Celebrity Industrial Complex, by Maureen
Orth. *Columbia Journalism Review* 42.3 (2004): 48–51. Print.

Internet Sources

Citations for Internet sources should include enough information to enable readers to locate the sources. Since URLs are long and subject to change, the MLA suggests including them only when the information listed below is unlikely to be enough to enable readers to find the source.

Citing Internet sources may not be as straightforward as citing print sources because Web sites differ in how much information they provide and where and how they provide it. As a general rule, give as many of the following elements as possible, and list them in the order shown:

1. *Author.* Include the name of the person or organization if it is available.

2. *Title of the work.* Enclose titles of Web pages in quotation marks; italicize the titles of Web sites and other longer works.

3. *Print publication information.* If the material was originally published in print, tell where and when it was originally published. Include volume and issue numbers, names of periodicals, names of publishers, dates, and so forth.

4. *Electronic publication information.* The information here will differ depending on the type of source.
    a. To cite an entire Web site or a document on a Web site, provide as many of the following as are available: title of site (italicized), the sponsoring organization, and date of publication or last update.
    b. To cite an article in an online periodical, give the periodical title (italicized), the sponsoring organization or publisher, and the volume/issue or date. Also include the name of any database (italicized) through which you accessed the article.
    c. To cite an e-book, give all the information you would give for a print book.

5. *Medium.* For Internet sources, the medium of publication is *Web*. For e-books, include the file format (PDF file, Kindle e-book file) as the medium.

6. *Access date.* Include the date you accessed the document (day, month, year).

Some sample citations for different kinds of Internet sources are given below.

MLA FORMAT FOR CITING INTERNET SOURCES

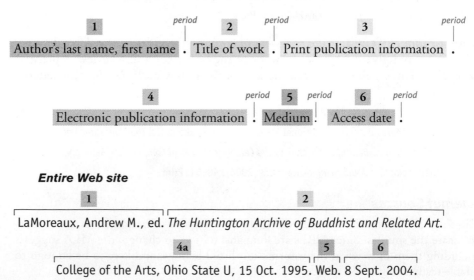

1 Author's last name, first name **.** **2** Title of work **.** **3** Print publication information **.**

4 Electronic publication information **.** **5** Medium **.** **6** Access date **.**

Entire Web site

1 LaMoreaux, Andrew M., ed. **2** *The Huntington Archive of Buddhist and Related Art.*

4a College of the Arts, Ohio State U, 15 Oct. 1995. **5** Web. **6** 8 Sept. 2004.

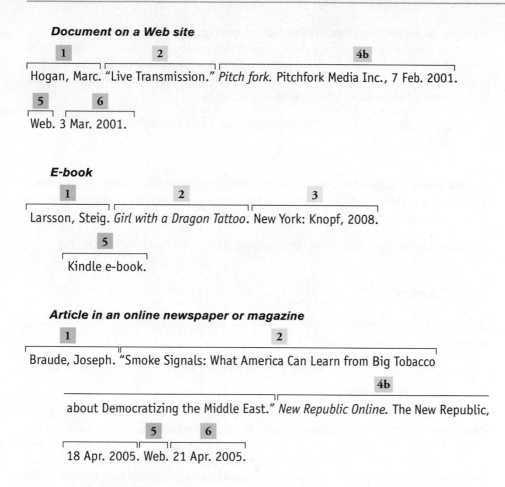

Document on a Web site

[1] [2] [4b]

Hogan, Marc. "Live Transmission." *Pitch fork*. Pitchfork Media Inc., 7 Feb. 2001.

[5] [6]

Web. 3 Mar. 2001.

E-book

[1] [2] [3]

Larsson, Steig. *Girl with a Dragon Tattoo*. New York: Knopf, 2008.

[5]

Kindle e-book.

Article in an online newspaper or magazine

[1] [2]

Braude, Joseph. "Smoke Signals: What America Can Learn from Big Tobacco

[4b]

about Democratizing the Middle East." *New Republic Online*. The New Republic,

[5] [6]

18 Apr. 2005. Web. 21 Apr. 2005.

Article from an online journal

Edmonson, Cole. "Moral Courage and the Nurse Leader." *Online Journal of Issues in Nursing* 15.3 (2010): n. pag. Web. 14 Feb. 2011.

Article from an online library database

Williams, D. M., A. Fraser, and D. A. Lawlor. "Associations of Vitamin D, Parathyroid Hormone and Calcium with Cardiovascular Risk Factors in US Adolescents." *Heart* 97.4 (2011): 315–20. *CINAHL Plus*. Web. 15 Feb. 2011.

Online government document

United States. Office of the Dir. of Natl. Intelligence. Natl. Intelligence Council. *The Terrorist Threat to the U.S. Homeland. National Intelligence Council*. Office of the Dir. of Natl. Intelligence, July 2007. Web. 3 Mar. 2011.

Posting to an online discussion list or newsgroup. For a discussion group, include the author's name, the title or subject line enclosed in quotation marks, the name of the Web site on which the group is found, the sponsor of the site, the date of posting, the medium, and the date of access. If possible, cite an archived version. If the posting has no title, label it *Online posting*.

> Jones, John. "The End of Species." *ILovePhilosophy.com*. I Love Philosophy Forum, 12 Feb. 2011. Web. 15 Feb. 2011.

Online book. Include the author's name; title (italicized); the name of any editor, translator, or compiler; original publication information (if available); the name of the Web site on which the online book appears; the medium; and date of access.

> Dickens, Charles. *Great Expectations*. Boston: Estes, 1881. *Google Books*. Web. 14 Feb. 2011.

Other Sources

DVD-ROM or CD-ROM. Include the title, the version (if specified), the publication information, and the medium.

> Poulter, Patricia A., and Anne Griffin Perry. *Mosby's Nursing Skills 2.0. Student Version*. St Louis: Mosby, 2006. CD-ROM.

Personal communication (interview, letter, email). Indicate the name of the person, followed by the type of communication and the date. For interviews you conducted, indicate the type of interview (telephone, personal, email, and so forth). For a letter, include the designation *MS* for a manuscript (a letter written by hand) or *TS* for a typescript (a letter composed on a machine). For emails, include the subject line (if available) in quotation marks.

> Burrow, Alby. Telephone interview. 28 Jan. 2011.
>
> Gomez, Pedro. Letter to the author. 19 May 2010. TS.
>
> Adams, Alex. "Pet Care Advice." Message to Rudy Simmons. 19 Feb. 2011. E-mail.

Published interview. List the person interviewed, and then list the title of the interview (if available) in quotation marks. If the interview has no title, label it *Interview*. Give the publication details for the source in which the interview was found.

> Richards, Eric. "Observation and Memory: An Interview with Eric Richards." *American Music* 27.2 (2009): 180–203.

Published letter. Cite a published letter as you would a selection in a book, but include the letter's date and number (if one has been assigned).

> Lewis, C. S. "To His Father." 4 Sept. 1907. Letter LPIII: 82 of *The Collected Letters of C. S. Lewis*.
>
> Ed. Walter Hooper. Vol. 1. San Francisco: Harper, 2004. 5. Print.

Film, video, or DVD. Begin with the title, followed by the director and key performer(s), unless you are focusing on the work of the director or another contributor. Include the name of the distributor, the release date, and the medium (*Film*). For a film on DVD, add the original release date (if relevant) before the distributor, and change the medium to DVD.

> *The Lady Eve*. Dir. Preston Sturges. Perf. Barbara Stanwyck and Henry Fonda. 1941. Criterion,
>
> 2001. DVD.

Television or radio program. Unless you are focusing on the work of a contributor (the director, screenwriter, or actor), list the title of the episode, if any (in quotation marks), and the title of the program (italicized) first. Then give key names (narrator, producer, director, actors) as necessary. Identify the network, local station and city of broadcast (if available), and broadcast date before the medium.

> "Mugged." *Flight of the Conchords*. Perf. Jermain Clement. HBO. 1 July 2008. Television.

Music recording. Begin with a contributor or title of the work, depending on the focus of your research project. Include the composer (*Comp.*) or performer (*Perf.*), and the title of the recording or composition as well as the production company, the date, and the medium (CD, audiocassette, LP, audiotape). Titles of recordings should be italicized, but titles of compositions identified by form (for example, Symphony No. 5) should not.

> Wilco. *Yankee Hotel Foxtrot*. Perf. Jeff Tweedy, John Stirratt, and Nels Cline. Nonesuch Records,
>
> 2002. CD.

> **Research Paper in Progress 9**
> For the final paper you prepared in Research Paper in Progress 8, prepare a list of works cited in MLA style.

Students Write

The following research paper was written by Nicholas Destino for his first-year writing course while he was a student at Niagara County Community College. Destino used MLA style for formatting his paper and documenting his sources. Notice how he uses in-text citations and quotations to provide evidence that supports this thesis.

Destino 1

Nicholas Destino

Professor Thomas

English 101

11 Mar. 2011

Do Animals Have Emotions?

Somewhere in the savannas of Africa a mother elephant is dying in the company of many other pachyderms. Some of them are part of her family; some are fellow members of her herd. The dying elephant tips from side to side and seems to be balancing on a thin thread in order to sustain her life. Many of the other elephants surround her as she struggles to regain her balance. They also try to help by feeding and caressing her. After many attempts by the herd to save her life, they seem to realize that there is simply nothing more that can be done. She finally collapses to the ground in the presence of her companions. Most of the other elephants move away from the scene. There are, however, two elephants who remain behind with the dead elephant--another mother and her calf. The mother turns her back to the body and taps it with one foot. Soon the other elephants call for them to follow and eventually they do (Masson and McCarthy, *When Elephants Weep* 95). These movements, which are slow and ritualistic, suggest that elephants may be capable of interpreting and responding to the notion of death.

The topic of animal emotions is one that, until recently, has rarely been discussed or studied by scientists. However, since the now-famous comprehensive field studies of chimpanzees by the internationally renowned primatologist Jane Goodall, those who study animal behavior have begun to look more closely at the notion that animals feel emotions. As a result of their observations of various species of animals, a number of these researchers have come to the conclusion that animals do exhibit a wide range of emotions, such as grief, sympathy, and joy.

One of the major reasons that research into animal emotions was traditionally avoided is that scientists fear being accused of *anthropomorphism*--the act

---

Side annotations:

Double-spaced identification: Writer's name, instructor's name, course title, and date

Double-spaced throughout
Title centered

In-text citation of a work with two authors; short title included because another work by these authors is cited later in the essay

of attributing human qualities to animals. To do so is perceived as unscientific (Masson and McCarthy, "Hope and Joy" xviii). Frans de Waal, of the Yerkes Regional Primate Research Center in Atlanta, believes that if people are not open to the possibility of animals having emotions, they may be overlooking important information about both animals and humans. He explains his position in his article "Are We in Anthropodenial?" The term *anthropodenial*, which he coined, refers to "a blindness to the humanlike characteristics of other animals, or the animal-like characteristics of ourselves" (52). De Waal proposes that because humans and animals are so closely related, it would be impossible for one not to have some characteristics of the other. He contends, "If two closely related species act in the same manner, their underlying mental processes are probably the same, too" (53). If de Waal is correct, then humans can presume that animals do have emotions because of the many similarities between human and animal behavior.

Grief has been observed in many different species. In many instances, their behaviors (and presumably, therefore, their emotions) are uncannily similar to the behaviors of humans. Birds, which mate for life, have been observed showing obvious signs of grief when their mates die. In *The Human Nature of Birds*, Theodore Barber includes a report from one Dr. Franklin, who witnessed a male parrot caring for his mate by feeding her and trying to help her raise herself when she was dying. Franklin observed the following scene:

> Her unhappy spouse moved around her incessantly, his attention and tender cares redoubled. He even tried to open her beak to give her some nourishment. . . . At intervals, he uttered the most plaintive cries, then with his eyes fixed on her, kept a mournful silence. At length his companion breathed her last; from that moment he pined away, and died in the course of a few weeks. (qtd. in Barber 116)

Veterinarian Susan Wynn, discussing the physiological symptoms brought on by emotional trauma in animals, notes that "[a]nimals definitely exhibit grief when they lose an owner or another companion animal. . . . Signs of grief vary widely, including lethargy, loss of appetite, hiding . . ." (5). This observation re-

Header: Student's name and page number

Attribution of summaries and quotations within text

Page numbers follow quotations

Attributions of paraphrase and quotation

Quotation longer than four lines indented one inch and not enclosed in quotation marks; period precedes citation

Citation for an indirect source

First letter of a quotation changed to lowercase to fit into sentence; ellipsis marks used to indicate omitted material

Destino 3

inforces de Waal's position that animals experience some of the same emotions as humans.

Perhaps the most extreme case of grief experienced by an animal is exemplified by the true story of Flint, a chimp, when Flo, his mother, died. In her book *Through a Window*, which elaborates on her thirty years of experience studying and living among the chimps in Gombe, Tanzania, Jane Goodall gives the following account of Flint's experience with grief.

> Flint became increasingly lethargic, refused most food and, with his immune system thus weakened, fell sick. The last time I saw him alive, he was hollow-eyed, gaunt and utterly depressed, huddled in the vegetation close to where Flo had died. . . . The last short journey he made, pausing to rest every few feet, was to the very place where Flo's body had lain. There he stayed for several hours, sometimes staring and staring into the water. He struggled on a little further, then curled up--and never moved again. (196–97)

Of course, animal emotions are not limited to despair, sadness, and grief. Indeed, substantial evidence indicates that animals experience other, more uplifting emotions, such as sympathy, altruism, and joy.

Many scientists who study animal behavior have found that several species demonstrate sympathy for one another. In other words, they act as if they care about one another in much the same way as humans do. It is probably safe to assume that no animal is more sympathetic, or at least displays more behaviors associated with the emotion of sympathy, than chimpanzees. Those who have studied apes in the wild, including de Waal, have observed that animals who had been fighting make up with one another by kissing and hugging. Although other primates also engage in similar behaviors, chimps even go so far as to embrace and attempt to console the defeated animal ("Going Ape"). Another striking example of one animal showing sympathy for another is the account cited by Barber of a parrot comforting its sick mate. It is not, however, the only example of this type of behavior, especially among birds. Barber cites several other instances as well. According to Barber, documented records show that responsible observers have seen robins trying to keep each other

---

Margin notes:

Source's credentials included within the text

Information from a source paraphrased

Title used in citation since source does not indicate author; page number not given since the article is on only one page in the journal

Destino 4

alive. Also, terns have been known to lift a handicapped tern by its wing and transport it to safety. Likewise, a jay has been known to successfully seek human help when a newborn bird of a different species falls out of its nest. What makes this latter example particularly noteworthy is that the newborn wasn't a jay but an altogether different type of bird.

     Had the jay been helping another jay, it would be easy to assume that the act of caring was the result of what scientists call *genetic altruism*--the sociobiological theory that animals help each other to keep their own genes alive so that they can reproduce and not become extinct. Simply put, scientists who believe in genetic altruism assume that when animals of the same species help each other out, they do so because there is something in it for them--namely, the assurance that their species will continue. This theory certainly provides an adequate, unbiased scientific explanation for why animals such as birds might be-have in a caring manner. However, if animals really help each other out only when doing so will perpetuate their species, then the jay would have had no genetic reason to help the newborn bird.

     There is another popular explanation for why a bird of one species might help a bird of another species, however. Scientists who favor a related scientific theory called *mutual altruism* believe that animals will help each other because some day they themselves may need help, and then they will be able to count on reciprocal help (Hemelrijk 479–81). This theory is a plausible, nonanthropo-morphic explanation for why animals show sympathy, regardless of whether they actually feel sympathy. This point is crucial because after all, humans can't actu-ally observe how an animal feels; we can only observe how it behaves. It is then up to the observer to draw some logical conclusion about why animals behave in the ways they do. The mutual altruism theory, however, also can be disputed. In many cases, animals have helped others even when the receiver of the help would probably never be in a position to return the favor. For example, there are many accounts of dolphins helping drowning or otherwise endangered swimmers. Phil Mercer, on the BBC Web site, reported that dolphins stopped a shark from attacking swimmers off the coast of New Zealand. The animals surrounded the

Information from a source summarized

Information in this paragraph can be found in many sources so does not need to be documented

Citation of Internet source includes only au-thor's name and site's sponsor; no page num-bers available

swimmers for about forty minutes while the great white shark circled. When the swimmers reached the shore, they remarked that they were sure that the dolphins acted deliberately to save them. Marathon swimmer Martin Strel also believes that he was deliberately helped by pink dolphins during his 2007 swim of the entire Amazon River, even believing that he heard them communicating (Butler).

Not only do animals show sympathy, but they are also clearly able to express joy. For example, on many occasions primate experts have heard apes laugh while in the presence of other apes. These experts are sure that the noise they heard was laughter because of the clarity and tone of the sound. In their book, *Visions of Caliban*, Dale Peterson and Jane Goodall describe this laughter in detail:

> I'm not referring to a sort of pinched vocalization that might be roughly compared with human laughter, as in the "laughter" of a hyena. I'm referring to real laughter, fully recognizable laughter, the kind where you lie down on the ground and shake in a paroxysm of clear amusement and simple pleasure. (181)

Although Peterson and Goodall felt that only four species (chimpanzees, gorillas, bonobos, and orangutans), in addition to humans, have the capacity to be amused and to show their amusement by laughing, Elizabeth Walter reports that researchers have found that dogs and rats are also capable of laughter.

Even the actions of animals who are not able to laugh uproariously indicate that they feel joy. Many animals engage in playful behavior that can emanate only from a sense of joy. In "Hope and Joy among the Animals," Masson and McCarthy tell an amusing, yet true, story about an elephant named Norma.

> A traveling circus once pitched its tents next to a schoolyard with a set of swings. The older elephants were chained, but Norma, a young elephant, was left loose. When Norma saw children swinging, she was greatly intrigued. Before long, she went over, waved the children away with her trunk, backed up to a swing, and attempted to sit on it. She was notably unsuccessful, even using her tail to hold the swing in place. (45)

Geese, according to experts, have an "emotional body language which can be read: goose posture, gestures, and sounds can indicate feelings such as uncertain, tense, glad,

Entire title of article included in attribution because two works by Masson and McCarthy are cited

Destino 6

victorious, sad, alert, relaxed or threatening." Additionally, birds can sometimes be seen moving their wings back and forth while listening to sounds they find pleasant (McHugh).

In short, animals exhibit a large number of behaviors that indicate that they possess not only the capacity to feel but the capacity to express those feelings in some overt way, often through body language. If these are not proof enough that animals have emotions, people need look no further than their own beloved cat or dog. Pets are so frequently the cause of joy, humor, love, sympathy, empathy, and even grief that it is difficult to imagine that animals could elicit such emotions in humans without actually having these emotions themselves. The question, then, is not, Do animals have emotions? but, Which emotions do animals have, and to what degree do they feel them?

Destino presents his own conclusion about animal emotions.

The works cited list appears on a new page; the heading is centered.

Double-spaced throughout

Entries are alphabetized by authors' last names.

First line of each entry is flush with the left margin; subsequent lines indented half an inch.

Destino 7

Works Cited

Barber, Theodore Xenophone. *The Human Nature of Birds: A Scientific Discovery with Startling Implications*. New York: St. Martin's, 1993. Print.

Butler, Rhett A. "Marathon Swimmer: An Interview with the First Man to Swim the Length of the Amazon." *Mongabay.com*. Mongabay.com, 23 Jan. 2011. Web. 14 Feb. 2011.

de Waal, Frans. "Are We in Anthropodenial?" *Discover* July 1997: 50–53. Print.

"Going Ape." *Economist* 17 Feb. 1997: 78. Print.

Goodall, Jane. *Through a Window*. Boston: Houghton, 1990. Print.

Hemelrijk, Charlotte K. "Support for Being Groomed in Long-Tailed Macaques, Macaca Fascicularis." *Animal Behaviour* 48 (1994): 479–81. Print.

Masson, Jeffrey Moussaieff, and Susan McCarthy. "Hope and Joy among the Animals." *Utne Reader* July–Aug. 1995: 44–46. Print.

--. *When Elephants Weep: The Emotional Lives of Animals*. New York: Delacorte, 1995. Print.

McHugh, Mary. "The Emotional Lives of Animals." *Global:Ideas:Bank*. Global Ideas Bank, 1998. Web. 5 Mar. 2011.

Mercer, Phil. "Dolphins Prevent NZ Shark Attack." *BBC News*. BBC, 23 Nov. 2004. Web. 6 Mar. 2011.

Peterson, Dale, and Jane Goodall. *Visions of Caliban: On Chimpanzees and People*. New York: Houghton, 1993. Print.

Walter, Elizabeth. "Tickled Pink: Why Scientists Want to Make Rats Laugh." *Greater Good*. Greater Good Science Center, Summer 2008. Web. 14 Feb. 2011.

Wynn, Susan G. "The Treatment of Trauma in Pet Animals: What Constitutes Trauma?" *Homeopathy Online* 5 (1998): n. pag. Web. 9 Mar. 2011.

Documenting Your Sources: APA Style

APA style, recommended by the American Psychological Association, is commonly used in the social sciences. Both in-text citations and a list of references are used to document sources, as the following models show. For more information on citing print and other nonelectronic sources, consult the following reference work.

American Psychological Association. *Publication Manual of the American Psychological Association.* 6th ed. Washington, DC: APA, 2010.

The student paper that appears at the end of this chapter uses APA style.

APA Style for In-Text Citations

Your paper must include in-text citations for all material you borrow or quote from sources. There are two basic ways to write an in-text citation:

1. **Use an attribution and a parenthetical citation.** Mention the author's name in a phrase or sentence introducing the material, and include the year of publication in parentheses immediately following the author's name. For quotations and paraphrases, include a page number at the end of the cited material.
2. **Use only a parenthetical citation.** Include the author's last name, the year of publication, and a page number (for quotations and paraphrases) in parentheses at the end of the sentence. Separate the name, year, and page number (if any) with commas.

Many instructors prefer that you use attributions rather than only parenthetical citations because attributions allow you to put your sources in context.

For either type of citation, use the following rules:

- Place the sentence period after the closing parenthesis. When a quotation ends the sentence, insert the closing quotation mark before the opening parenthesis. Block quotations are an exception to these rules; see pages 633–34.
- For direct quotations and paraphrases, include the page number after the year, separating it from the year with a comma. Use the abbreviation *p.* or *pp.* followed by a space and the page number.

ATTRIBUTION

Avery and Ehrlich (2008) say "nasal sounds are made with air passing through the nose" (p. 21).

PARENTHETICAL CITATION

Nasal sounds are created "with air passing through the nose" (Avery & Ehrlich, 2008, p. 21).

The following section provides guidelines for formatting in-text citations in APA style.

One author

> According to Adams (2009), . . .

> . . . (Adams, 2009).

Two authors. Include both authors' last names and the year in an attribution or parenthetical citation. In the latter case, use an ampersand (&) in place of the word *and*.

> Avery and Ehrlich (2008) assert . . .

> . . . (Avery & Ehrlich, 2008).

Three to five authors. Include all authors' last names the first time the source is mentioned. In subsequent references to the same source, use the first author's last name followed by *et al.* (Latin for "and others").

FIRST REFERENCE

Lewin, Krebs, Kilpatrick, and Goldstein (2011) have found . . .

. . . (Lewin, Krebs, Kilpatrick, & Goldstein, 2011).

LATER REFERENCES

Lewin et al. (2011) discovered . . .

. . . (Lewin et al., 2011).

Six or more authors. Use the first author's last name followed by *et al.* in all in-text citations.

Two or more works by the same author(s). Cite the works chronologically, in order of publication.

> Gaerlan (2001, 2011) believes that . . .

> . . . (Gaerlan, 2001, 2011).

Two or more works by the same author in the same year. Add the lowercase letter *a* after the publication year for the first source as it appears alphabetically by title in your reference list. Add the letter *b* to the publication year for the source that appears next, and so forth. Include the years with the corresponding lowercase letters in your in-text citations. (See p. 669 for the corresponding reference entries.)

> Adams (2009a) believes that . . .

> . . . (Adams, 2009a).

Authors with the same last name. Use the first authors' initials with his or her name.

> Research by V. M. Hoselton (2001) exemplified . . .

> According to I. Hoselton (2010), . . .

Unknown author. Use the first few words of the title and the year in the attribution or parenthetical citation. Italicize a book title; put the title of a journal article in quotation marks. Unlike the entry in the list of references, use standard capitalization in the in-text citation. (See p. 672.)

> As noted in "Gluten Free Recipes" (2009), . . .

> . . . ("Gluten Free Recipes," 2009).

Two or more sources in the same citation. When citing two or more sources in parentheses, put a semicolon between them and list them in alphabetical order.

> (Hoffman, 2011; Murphy, 2009)

Specific part of a work. When quoting, paraphrasing, or summarizing a passage, include the page number on which the passage appears. If the work does not have page numbers, use paragraph numbers, if available (with the abbreviation *para.*), or the heading of the section in which the material appears.

> Pinker (2007) offers an explanation for why swearing occurs across cultures: Obscenities "may tap into deep and ancient parts of the emotional brain" (p. 331).

> If obscenities "tap into deep and ancient parts of the emotional brain" (Pinker, 2007, p. 331), then it makes sense that swearing occurs across cultures.

Chapter in an edited book or work in an anthology. An *anthology* is a collection of writings by different authors. In the in-text citation, name the author who wrote the work (*not* the editor of the anthology) and give the year. The corresponding entry in the list of references begins with the author's last name; it also names the editor of the anthology.

IN-TEXT CITATION

As Pedelty (2010) notes . . .

. . . (Pedelty, 2010).

REFERENCES ENTRY

Pedelty, M. (2010). Musical news: Popular music in political movements. In S .E. Bird (Ed.), *The anthropology of news and journalism: Global perspectives* (pp. 215–240). Bloomington: Indiana University Press.

Multivolume work. When you cite one volume of a multivolume work, include the year of publication for that volume.

Terman (2008) indicates . . .

. . . (Terman, 2008).

When you cite two or more volumes of a multivolume work, give inclusive years for the volumes.

Terman (2008–2011) indicates . . .

Indirect sources. When you quote a source indirectly (rather than from the original source), include the works *cited in* along with the information for the source in which you found the quote.

According to Ephron, . . . (cited in Thomas, 2009, p. 33).

Personal interviews, letters, emails, and conversations. Give the last name and initial of the person, the source of the communication, and the exact date. Do not include these sources in the list of references.

Lopez (personal communication, October 30, 2011) asserts that . . .

Internet sources. For direct quotations, give the author, year, and page (if available) in the attribution or parenthetical citation. If paragraph numbers are available, cite them with the abbreviation *para*.

Stevens (2011) maintains . . .

. . . (Stevens, 2011).

APA Style for the List of References

For more practice using the APA style of documentation, visit www.bedfordstmartins .com/successfulcollege/.

Follow these general guidelines for preparing the list of references:

1. **List only the sources you cite in your paper.** If you consulted a source but did not cite it in your paper, do not include it in the list of references.
2. **Put the list on a separate page at the end of your paper.** The heading *References* should be centered an inch below the top of the page. Do not use quotation marks, underlining, or bold type for the heading.

3. **Alphabetize the list by authors' last names.** Give the last name first, followed by a comma and an initial or initials. Do not spell out authors' first names; use a space between initials: *Myers, D. G.* For works with multiple authors, list all authors' names in inverted order.

Avery, P., & Ehlrich, S. (2008). *Teaching American English pronunciation*. New York, NY: Oxford

University Press.

4. **Put the publication date in parentheses after the author's name.**
5. **Capitalize the first word of the titles of books and articles, the first word following a colon, and any proper nouns.** All other words are lowercase.
6. **Include the word *A, An,* or *The* at the beginning of titles.**
7. **Italicize titles of books and names of journals, newspapers, and magazines.** Do not italicize, underline, or use quotation marks with article titles.
8. **For magazine and journal articles, italicize the volume number.** Capitalize all important words in the names of periodicals.
9. **Indent the second and all subsequent lines half an inch.** This is the hanging indent style.
10. **Double-space the entire list.**

The following sections describe how to format reference list entries for books, articles in periodicals, Internet sources, and other sources.

List of APA reference entries

Books

The basic format for a book is as follows:

1 *Author.* Give the author's last name and initial(s). Do not spell out authors' first names; include a space between initials: *Myers, D. G.*

2 *Year.* Include the year of publication in parentheses following the author's name. Use the most recent copyright year if more than one is given.

3 *Title.* Italicize the title of the book. Capitalize only the first word of the title and subtitle (if any) and any proper nouns or adjectives, such as *Lincoln* or *American.*

4 *Place of publication.* Give the city of publication followed by the postal abbreviation for the state and a colon (*Hillsdale, NJ:*). For cities outside the United States, add the country after the city.

5 *Publisher.* Include the name of the publisher followed by a period. Use a shortened form of the publisher's name: *Alfred A. Knopf* would be listed as *Knopf,* for example. Omit words such as *Publishers* and abbreviations such as *Inc.,* but do not omit the word *Books* or *Press* if it is part of the publisher's name: *Academic Press, Basic Books.*

APA FORMAT FOR CITING A BOOK

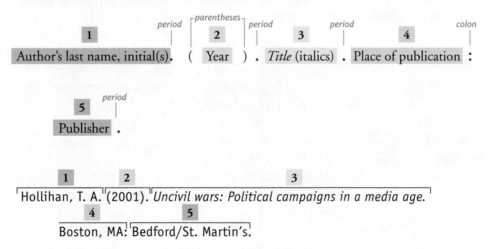

Book with one author

Olson, Z. (2010). *The constant giraffe: Stretchmarks of a lost generation.* Charleston, SC: CreateSpace.

Book with two to seven authors. List all authors' names in the order they appear on the book's title page. Use inverted order (*last name, initial*) for all authors' names. Separate the names with commas and use an ampersand (&) in place of the word *and.* Do not use *et al.* in the reference list unless the book has eight or more authors.

Myers, W. D., & Myers, C. (2006). *Jazz.* New York, NY: Holiday House.

Book with no named author. Give the full title first, and alphabetize the entry by title. (Do not consider the words *A, An,* or *The* when alphabetizing.)

The new interpreter's dictionary of the Bible. (2006). Nashville, TN: Abingdon Press.

Book by an agency or a corporation. List the agency as the author. If the publisher is the same as the author, write *Author* for the name of the publisher.

Ford Foundation. (2003). *Celebrating Indonesia: Fifty years with the Ford Foundation,*

1953–2003. Jakarta, Indonesia: Author, 2003.

Government publication. List the agency as the author, followed by the date. Include the document or publication number if available.

U.S. Office of Management and Budget. (2009). *A new era of responsibility: Renewing America's*

promise. Washington, DC: Government Printing Office.

Edited book or anthology. List the editor's or editors' names, followed by the abbreviation *Ed.* or *Eds.* in parentheses and a period.

Penzler, O., & Cook, T. H. (Eds.). (2004). *The best American crime writing.* New York, NY:

Vintage.

Chapter in an edited book or work in an anthology. List the author of the work first and then the date the work was published in the anthology. The title of the work follows. Then name the editor of the anthology (not in inverted order), give the title of the anthology (italicized), and include the inclusive page numbers in parentheses for the work (preceded by *pp.*). The publication information follows in normal order.

Dachyshyn, D. (2006). Refugee families with preschool children: Adjustment to

life in Canada. In L. Adams (Ed.), *Global migration and education: Schools,*

children and families (pp. 251–262). London, England: Lawrence Erlbaum Associates.

Translated book. After the title, include the initial(s) and last name of the translator followed by a comma and *Trans.*

Kawakami, H. (2010). *Manazuru* (M. Emmerich, Trans.). Berkeley, CA: Counterpoint.

Two or more works by the same author(s). Begin each entry with the author's name. Arrange the entries in chronological order of publication.

Pollan, M. (2006). *The omnivore's dilemma: A natural history of four meals.* New York, NY:

Penguin.

Pollan, M. (2008). *In defense of food: An eater's manifesto.* New York, NY: Penguin.

Two or more works by the same author in the same year. Arrange the works alphabetically by title; then assign a lowercase letter (*a, b, c*) to the year of publication for each source. (See p. 665 for the corresponding in-text citation.)

Adams, R. (2009a). *Hellosunshine.* New York, NY: Akashic Books.

Adams, R. (2009b). *Infinity blues.* New York, NY: Akashic Books.

Edition other than the first

Myers, D. G. (2002). *Exploring psychology* (5th ed.). New York, NY: Worth.

Multivolume work. Give the volume numbers in parentheses after the title. If all volumes were not published in the same year, the publication date should include the range of years.

McAuliffe, J. D. (Ed.). (2001–2006). *Encyclopedia of the Qur'an* (Vols. 1–5). Leiden, The Netherlands: Brill.

Article in a multivolume work. Include the author and title of the article, as well as the title, volume number, and publication information for the work.

Meerdink, J. E. (2006). Sleep. In *Encyclopedia of human development* (Vol. 3, pp. 1180–1181). Thousand Oaks, CA: Sage.

If more than one of these rules applies to a source, cite the necessary information in the order given in the preceding examples. For instance, to cite a reading from this textbook, treat it as a **work in an anthology (p. 669) in an edition other than the first (above)**. To do this, list the author of the reading, the date the reading was published in the anthology, the title of the reading, the editor and the title of this book, the edition number, the pages where the reading appears, and all other publication information.

Le Mieux, Richard. (2009). The lady in red. In K. T. McWhorter (Ed.), *Successful college writing: Skills, strategies, learning styles* (5th ed., pp. 235–37). Boston, MA: Bedford/St. Martin's.

Articles in Periodicals

General guidelines and sample entries for various types of periodical articles follow:

1 *Author.* Follow the basic format for listing authors' names (see p. 668). If no author is listed, begin with the article title and alphabetize the entry by its title (ignoring the words *A*, *An*, and *The*).

2 *Date.* For articles in journals, the year of publication appears in parentheses following the author's name. For articles in newspapers and magazines, the issue month and day, if relevant, follow the year.

3 *Article title.* Do not enclose article titles in quotation marks. Capitalize only the first word of the article title, along with any proper nouns or proper adjectives (*American*) and the first word following a colon.

4 *Periodical title.* Italicize the name of the periodical. Use standard capitalization for the titles of periodicals.

5 *Volume/issue.* For scholarly journals only, give the volume number in italics; if each issue is paginated separately, starting with page one, give the issue number in parentheses and roman type.

6 *Pages.* The abbreviation *p.* or *pp.* is used only in entries for newspaper articles.

7 *DOI.* Include the digital object identifier (DOI), a code assigned to articles in scholarly journals, when it is available.

APA FORMAT FOR CITING A PERIODICAL ARTICLE

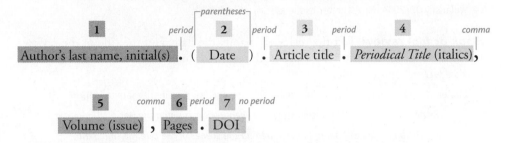

Article in a scholarly journal. If issues in each volume are numbered continuously (issue 1 ends on page 159 and issue 2 begins on page 160, for example), then omit the issue number. If the journal article has been assigned a DOI (digital object identifier), add it at the end of the citaion.

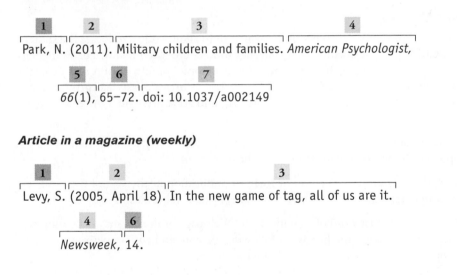

Article in a magazine (weekly)

```
    1           2                      3
Levy, S. (2005, April 18). In the new game of tag, all of us are it.
    4      6
Newsweek, 14.
```

Article in a magazine (monthly). Include the month of publication after the year.

Bethell, T. (2003, November). Democracy: A little goes a long way. *American Spectator*, 42–43.

Article in a newspaper. Include the year, month, and day in parentheses following the author's name. Page numbers for newspaper articles should be preceded by a *p.* or *pp.*

Norris, F. (2001, September 13). A symbol was destroyed, not America's financial system.
The New York Times, p. C1.

Editorial or letter to the editor. Cite the editorial or letter beginning with the author's name (if available). Include *Editorial* or *Letter to the editor* in brackets following the title (if any). If the author's name is not available, begin with the title.

> Editorial: The search for livable worlds [Editorial]. (2004, September 8). *The New York Times*, p. A22.

> Wolansky, T. (2004, May) [Letter to the editor]. *Wired*, 25.

Book or film review. List the reviewer's name, the date, and the title of the review. In brackets, give a description of the work reviewed, including the medium (*book* or *motion picture*) and the title.

> Gabler, N. (2004, July–August). Ephemera: The rise and fall of celebrity journalism.
>> [Review of the books *The untold story: My twenty years running the* National Enquirer
>> and *The importance of being famous: Behind the scenes of the celebrity-industrial*
>> *complex*]. *Columbia Journalism Review*, 48–51.

Article with no author. Use the full title as the author.

> The *Business Week* fifty. (2006, April 3). *Business Week, 2010*(3978), 82.

Internet Sources

For Internet sources, include enough information to allow readers to locate the sources online. Guidelines for documenting Internet sources are listed below. For more help with formatting entries for Internet and other electronic sources in APA style, consult the American Psychological Association's Web site at http://apastyle.org/index.aspx, the APA Style Blog at http://blog.apastyle.org, and APA Style on Twitter at http://twitter.com/APA_Style.

1. Give the author's name, if available. If not, begin the entry with the name of the sponsor of the site or with the title of the document.

2. Include in parentheses the year of Internet publication or the year of the most recent update, if available. If there is no date, use the abbreviation *n.d.*

3. Capitalize the first word of the title of the Web page or document or the subject line of the message, the first word following a colon, and any proper nouns or proper adjectives. The other words are lowercase.

4. Capitalize all important words of the Web site's title and italicize it.

5. End with the digital object identifier (DOI), a permanent code associated with specific online articles or books, or, if there is no DOI, insert the URL of the homepage for the journal or publishing company that published the source or give the URL for the source, preceded by the words *Retrieved from,* if the source will be difficult to find from the homepage. If necessary, break URLs before punctuation marks, such as dots (.) and question marks (?). DOIs and URLs are not followed by periods.

The basic APA format for an Internet source is as follows:

APA FORMAT FOR CITING INTERNET SOURCES

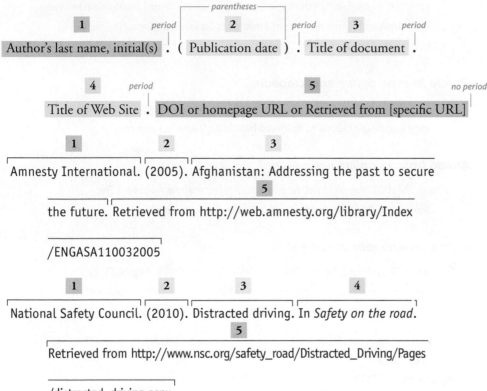

Document posted on an organization's Web site. If the document is not dated or the content could change, include a retrieval date.

The American Society for the Prevention of Cruelty to Animals. (2009). ASPCA Milestones. Retrieved February 15, 2011, from http://www.aspca.org/pressroom/~/media/files/pressroom/press-kit/aspca-milestones-2009.pdf

Article from an online journal. Provide page numbers if available. Include the digital object identifier (DOI), if one has been assigned. Look for the DOI in the database where you get the name and author of the article.

Schubert, C. (2008). The need to consider the impact of previous stressors on current stress parameter measurements. *Stress: The International Journal on the Biology of Stress*, *11*(2), 85–87. doi:10.1080/10253890801895811

For articles with no DOI, give the URL for the journal's home page. Use the article's URL if your source will be difficult to locate from the journal's homepage.

Treharne, G. J., Lyons, A. C., & Tupling, R. E. (2001, December 17). The effects of optimism, pessimism, social support, and mood on the lagged relationship between daily stress and symptoms. *Current Research in Social Psychology, 7*(5). Retrieved from http://www.uiowa.edu/~grpproc/crisp/crisp.7.5.htm

Article from an online encyclopedia

Calef, S. (2008). Dualism and mind. In J. Fieser & B. Dowden (Eds.), *The Internet encyclopedia of philosophy*. Retrieved from http://www.iep.utm.edu/

Article from an online newspaper

Sullivan, P. (2008, May 6). Quiet Va. wife ended interracial marriage ban. *The Washington Post*. Retrived from http://www.washingtonpost.com

Online government document

U.S. Justice Department, Federal Bureau of Investigation. (2011, August 2). *Byte out of history: Communist agent tells all*. Retrieved from http://www.fbi.gov/news/stories/august/communist_080211/communist_080211

Other Sources

Film, video, or DVD

Greenfield, L. (Director). (2006). *Thin* [Motion picture]. New York, NY: Home Box Office.

Television program

Murphy, R. (Writer) & Buecker, B. (Director). (2011). Comeback [Television series episode]. In I. Brennan, R. Murphy, & B. Falchuk (Creators), *Glee*. New York, NY: Fox Broadcasting.

Computer software

Mitterer, J. (1993). Dynamic concepts in psychology [Computer software]. Orlando, FL: Harcourt.

RESEARCH PAPER IN PROGRESS 10

For the final paper you prepared in Research Paper in Progress 8, prepare a list of references in APA style.

Students Write

The following research paper was written by Sonia Gomez for her introductory psychology course. She used APA style for formatting her paper and documenting her sources. Notice her use of in-text citations and paraphrases and summaries of sources to provide evidence in support of her thesis.

SCHIZOPHRENIA   1

Schizophrenia: Definition and Treatment

Sonia Gomez

Psychology 101

Professor McCombs

March 30, 2010

> **Shortened title** at top left of each page
>
> **Page number** at top right of each page
>
> Double-space **identification** on title page: Writer's name, instructor's name, course title, and date

---

SCHIZOPHRENIA   2

Abstract

Schizophrenia is a mental/brain disorder that affects about 1% of the population. The five types of schizophrenia include paranoid, disorganized, catatonic, undifferentiated, and residual. There are three categories of symptoms—positive, disorganized or cognitive, and negative. The causes of schizophrenia are not well known, but there is likely a genetic component and an environmental component. The structure of the brain of schizophrenics is also unusual. Treatments include drug therapy with typical and atypical anti-psychotics and psychosocial and cognitive-behavioral therapies.

> **Abstract:** A brief summary of the report; heading centered, not bold
>
> Double-space; one-inch margins on all sides

Full title repeated just before text of paper begins; title centered, not bold

Introduction: Presentation of the topic researched by Gomez

Citation: Authors named in sentence; ampersand (&), not the word *and*, between names

First level heading: Centered, bold

Citation: No individual author named, so Web site sponsor listed as author

Second-level heading: At left margin, bold

Schizophrenia: Definition and Treatment

The disorder schizophrenia comes with an ugly cultural stigma. There is a common belief that all schizophrenics are violent. In fact, they are more a danger to themselves than to others because they often commit suicide. Many of the movies, books, and TV shows in our culture do not help to diminish this stigma. The movie A Beautiful Mind, for example, features a paranoid schizophrenic who comes close to harming his family and others around him because of his hallucinations and delusions. He believes that the government is out to get him (Grazer & Howard, 2001). Many people are afraid of schizophrenics and believe their permanent home should be in a mental hospital or psychiatric ward. This paper helps to dispel misperceptions of the disorder by providing facts about and treatments of the disorder.

What Is Schizophrenia?

Schizophrenia is a mental/brain disorder that affects about 1% of the population or 2.2 million Americans (National Institutes of Mental Health, 2010). This disease can be very disruptive in people's lives. It causes problems with communication and maintaining jobs. It is a widely misunderstood disease; many people believe schizophrenics to be dangerous. There is no cure for schizophrenia, but it can often be successfully treated (National Institutes of Mental Health, 2010). Schizophrenia does not seem to favor a specific gender or ethnic group. The disease rarely occurs in children. Hallucinations and delusions usually begin between ages sixteen and thirty (National Alliance on Mental Illness, 2007).

Types of Schizophrenia

There are five types of schizophrenia—paranoid, disorganized, catatonic, undifferentiated, and residual. People with paranoid schizophrenia are illogically paranoid about the world around them. They often hold false beliefs about being persecuted. People with disorganized schizophrenia are confused and incoherent and jumble their speech. People with disorganized schizophrenia often show symptoms of schizophasia—creating their own words and using them in a word salad, a jumbling of coherent and noncoherent words. People with catatonic schizophrenia are usually immobile and unresponsive to everything around

SCHIZOPHRENIA   4

them. Undifferentiated schizophrenia is diagnosed when the patient does not fit into the other three categories. Residual schizophrenia occurs when schizophrenic symptoms have decreased but still exist (WebMD, 2010).

Symptoms of Schizophrenia

The symptoms of schizophrenia are separated into three categories—positive, disorganized or cognitive, and negative. Positive symptoms include hallucinations and delusions (WebMD, 2010). According to Barch (2003), disorganized or cognitive symptoms cause the person to be unable to think clearly. Disorganized or cognitive symptoms include difficulty communicating, use of nonsense words, inability to focus on one thought, slow movement, inability to make decisions, forgetfulness and losing of things, repetitive movements, inability to make sense of everyday senses, and problems with memory. Negative symptoms are an absence of normal behavior (WebMD, 2010). They include a lack of emotion or inappropriate emotions, isolation, lack of energy and motivation, loss of interest or pleasure in life, problems functioning in everyday life (such as bad hygiene), rapid mood changes, and catatonia (remaining in the same position for a long time) (WebMD, 2010).

The diagnosis of schizophrenia is often difficult because it can be confused with a number of other mental disorders including bipolar disorder. The process of diagnosis begins with an interview by a psychiatrist. The patient is usually tested for other physical illnesses using various blood tests. If the symptoms last for at least six months and there is seemingly no other cause of the problem, the person is considered to have schizophrenia (National Alliance on Mental Illness, 2007).

Causes of Schizophrenia

No one is completely sure of the causes of schizophrenia. Most scientists believe that genetics are involved, and it seems that there is either a genetic mutation in DNA or a gene that can be activated by a number of situations. Scientists are coming very close to determining the exact chromosome where the gene for schizophrenia might be located (Conklin & Iacono,

Citation: Author named in attribution; date follows in parentheses

2002). The circumstances surrounding birth may have a great effect on whether the child's schizophrenic gene becomes activated or not. For example, if a fetus is exposed to viruses or malnourished before birth or if there are complications during birth, the gene may be activated. Conklin and Iacono (2002) report a link between schizophrenia and complications during birth that result in lack of oxygen (hypoxia). Also, Bower (2008) observes that poor children or children who deal with highly stressful situations may be more likely to develop the disorder.

Besides all of these factors, the brains of schizophrenics seem to be different from other people's. People with schizophrenia have an imbalance of dopamine and glutamate in their brains. The ventricles at the center of the brain seem to be larger, and there appears to be a loss of brain tissue in comparison with a normal brain (Figure 1).

> **Citation:** Authors named in attribution, *and*, not ampersand (&), used between names

> The figure is referred to in the text.

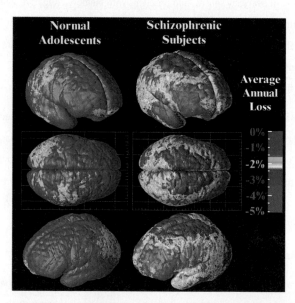

Figure 1. Brain-tissue loss. The image shows a loss of brain tissue (the areas in red) for the teens with schizophrenia. (Internet Mental Health Initiative, 2001, image by Thompson, Vidal, Rapoport, & Toga, *UCLA Laboratory of Neuro Imaging*).

> Professional publications in psychology require authors to place figures on a separate page at the end of the paper, but your instructor may prefer that you integrate your figures.

Also, some areas of the brain seem to have more or less activity than normal brains do. According to Conklin and Iacono (2002), these abnormalities in the brain appear to be pre-existing rather than caused by the disease. Schizophrenia tends to appear during puberty because of hormonal interactions occurring in the brain (WebMD, 2010).

Treatment

There is a wide variety of treatments for schizophrenia. Typical antipsychotic drugs, such as chlorpromazine and perphenazine, are an obvious choice, especially for people with hallucinations and delusions. They can help to clear up thinking problems. However, many of these drugs cause unpleasant side effects such as nausea and anxiety. Because of this, the schizophrenic may stop taking or refuse to take their medication. Many of these antipsychotic drugs have not changed since the 1950s. In the 1990s, a new set of drugs—atypical antipsychotics—was developed. Clozapine was one of these drugs, and it was deemed very effective. However, it can cause agranulocytosis, a loss of white blood cells. Between the constant testing for agranulocytosis and the cost of clozapine, many schizophrenics did not particularly like the drug (National Institutes of Mental Health, 2010).

Other treatments do not rely on medication. Psychosocial and cognitive-behavioral therapies are often used. People with schizophrenia can learn illness-management skills. They can go to rehabilitation, and their families can be educated about how to care for them. Self-help groups are also common. However, if the disease becomes unmanageable, the person with schizophrenia may end up in the hospital. Electroconvulsive therapy, in which seizures are induced, is one of the more extreme treatments for schizophrenia. It is often used to treat catatonia. If the schizophrenia is still unmanageable, a lobotomy may be performed. A lobotomy is surgery in which the connections to and from the prefrontal cortex are cut. Lobotomies cause severe personality changes; they were used much more often in the 1950s than they are today (National Alliance on Mental Illness, 2007).

People with schizophrenia are very susceptible to substance abuse. Many schizophrenics have severe drinking problems, and tobacco addiction is also common. It is harder for

SCHIZOPHRENIA   7

them than most people to break this addiction. If they combine substance abuse treatment with the other treatments for their disease, they get much more beneficial results (WebMD, 2010).

Conclusion

As scientists begin to understand schizophrenia, better treatments are becoming available. There is starting to be a better outlook for schizophrenics, and because of this, the public might develop a more sympathetic view of schizophrenics.

Conclusion indicated by heading (bold and centered)

Gomez references her introduction in her conclusion.

SCHIZOPHRENIA 8

References

Barch, D. (2003). Cognition in schizophrenia: Does working memory work? *Current Directions in Psychological Science, 12*(4), 146–150. doi:10.1111/1467-8721.01251

Bower, B. (2008). Rare mutations tied to schizophrenia. *Science News, 173*(14), 222.

Conklin, H., & Iacono, W. (2002). Schizophrenia: A neurodevelopmental perspective. *Current Directions in Psychological Science, 11*(1), 33–37.

Grazer, B. (Producer), & Howard, R. (Director). (2001). *A beautiful mind* [Motion Picture]. Los Angeles, CA: Universal Pictures.

Internet Mental Health Initiative. (2001). UCLA maps how schizophrenia engulfs teen brains. Retrieved from http://www.schizophrenia.com/research/schiz.brain.htm

National Alliance on Mental Illness. (2007). Schizophrenia. In *Mental illnesses*. Retrieved from http://www.nami.org/Template.cfm? Section=By_Illness &Template=/TaggedPage/TaggedPageDisplay.cfm&TPLID=54&ContentID =23036

National Institutes of Mental Health. (2010). Schizophrenia. In *Health topics*. Retrieved from http://www.nimh.nih.gov/health/topics/schizophrenia/index .shtml

WebMD. (2010). Schizophrenia guide. In *Mental health center*. Retrieved from http://www.webmd.com/schizophrenia/guide/default.htm

Heading centered, not bold

The DOI is provided when available for printed and online works.

Double-spaced throughout

References list appears on a new page.

Entries are alphabetized by author's last name or name of sponsor.

Only the first word and proper nouns/adjectives are capitalized in titles of shorter works (such as articles in a periodical, or Web pages on a Web site).

First, last, and all key words are capitalized in titles of longer, stand-alone works (such as books, periodicals, films, Web sites).

The URL is provided for Web sites and Web pages.

PART 6

Academic and Business Applications

The Bean Eaters
Gwendolyn Brooks

They eat beans mostly, this old yellow pair.
Dinner is a casual affair.
Plain chipware on a plain and creaking wood,
Tin flatware.

Two who are Mostly Good.   5
Two who have lived their day,
But keep on putting on their clothes
And putting things away.

And remembering . . .
Remembering, with twinklings and twinges,   10
As they lean over the beans in their rented back room that
   is full of beads and receipts and dolls and cloths,
      tobacco crumbs, vases and fringes.

CHAPTER 24

Reading and Writing about Literature

Suppose your American literature instructor asks you to read carefully the poem by Gwendolyn Brooks (1917–2000), a major American writer of poetry as well as fiction and nonfiction prose. Brooks was the first African American woman to win a Pulitzer Prize for poetry (for *Annie Allen*, 1949). "The Bean Eaters" was originally published in a collection of poems, *The Bean Eaters*, in 1960.

After reading Brooks's "The Bean Eaters," how can you describe the life of the elderly couple shown in the photo? Note that the elderly couple in the photo is not the couple described in the poem. Using information about the elderly lifestyle presented in "The Bean Eaters" as well as your own experience with elderly people, write a paragraph describing in your own words what you think the couple's relationship might be like.

Both Brooks's poem and the paragraph you just wrote paint a picture of an elderly couple. Through carefully selected details, the poem tells about the couple's daily activities, memories of the past, and current economic situation (for example, "They eat beans mostly," "Plain chipware," and "rented back room" reveal that the couple is poor). Brooks also suggests that routine is important to the couple ("But keep on putting on their clothes / And putting things away") and that their memories of the past are both good ("twinklings") and bad ("twinges").

Now think of an elderly couple you know, such as your grandparents or neighbors. Do some of the characteristics of Brooks's couple apply to the couple you know? How does Brooks's picture of one elderly couple help you understand other elderly people like the ones in the photo?

"The Bean Eaters" suggests an answer to the question many students ask: "Why should I read or write about literature?" This poem, like all literature, is about the experiences people share. Literature often deals with large issues: What is worthwhile in life? What is moral? What is beautiful? When you read and write about literature, you gain new insights into many aspects of human experience and thereby enrich your own life.

Understanding literature has practical purposes as well (see the accompanying box for a few examples). You may be asked to write about literature in many college courses—not only in English classes. Even in work situations, a knowledge of literature will make some tasks easier or more meaningful.

This chapter will help you read and respond to works of literature. The first half of the chapter offers a general approach to reading and understanding literature, including discussions of the language and other elements of short stories and poetry. The second half of the chapter focuses on the characteristics of literary analysis and helps you through the process of writing one in a Guided Writing Assignment. Although literature can take many forms—including poetry, short stories, biography, autobiography, drama, essays, and novels—this chapter concentrates on two literary genres: short stories and poetry.

SCENES FROM COLLEGE AND THE WORKPLACE

- Your *art history* professor asks you to read Ernest Hemingway's *For Whom the Bell Tolls* (a novel set in the time of the Spanish Civil War) and to write a paper discussing its meaning in conjunction with Picasso's *Guernica,* a painting that vividly portrays a scene from that war.

- In a *film* class, you watch the film *Romeo and Juliet,* directed by Franco Zeffirelli. Your instructor then asks you to read excerpts from Shakespeare's *Romeo and Juliet* and write a paper evaluating how successfully Juliet is portrayed in the film.

- You work for a *children's book store.* Your supervisor has asked you to read several children's books that she is considering featuring during story hour and to write an evaluation of each.

A General Approach to Reading Literature

Textbooks focus primarily on presenting factual information, but literature does not. Instead, *works of literature* are concerned with interpreting ideas, experiences, and events. They employ facts, description, and detail to convey larger meanings.

Use the following general guidelines to read a literary work effectively:

1. **Read with an open mind.** Be ready to respond to the work; don't make up your mind about it before you start reading.
2. **Preview the work before reading it.** Read background information about the author and the work and study the title. For a short story, read the first few and last few paragraphs and quickly skim through the pages in between, noticing the setting, the names of the characters, the amount of dialogue, and so forth. For a poem, read it through once to get an initial impression. *For more on previewing, see Chapter 3, pp. 48–50.*
3. **Read slowly and carefully.** Works of literature use language in unique and creative ways, requiring you to read them slowly and carefully with a pen in hand. Mark interesting uses of language, such as striking phrases or descriptions, as well as sections that hint at the theme of the work.
4. **Note that literature often "bends the rules" of grammar and usage.** Writers of literature may use sentence fragments, ungrammatical dialogue, or unusual punctuation to create a particular *effect* in a short story or poem. When you see such instances in literature, remember that the writers bend the rules for a purpose.
5. **Establish the literal meaning first.** During the first reading of a work, try to establish its literal meaning. Who is doing what, when, and where? Identify the general subject, specific topic, and main character. What is happening? Describe the basic plot, action, or sequence of events. Establish where and during what time period the action occurs.
6. **Reread the work to focus on your interpretation.** To analyze a literary work, you will need to reread parts of the work or the entire work several times.
7. **Anticipate a gradual understanding.** Literary works are complex; you should not expect to understand a poem or short story immediately after reading it. As you reread and think about the work, its meanings will often come to mind gradually. Consider why the writer wrote the work and what message the writer is trying to communicate. Then ask, So what? to discover deeper meanings. Try to determine the work's view of, comment on, or lesson about the human experience.
8. **Interact with the work.** Jot down your reactions to it in the margins as you read. Include hunches, insights, and feelings as well as questions about the work. Highlight or underline key words, phrases, or actions that seem important or that you want to reconsider later.
9. **Identify themes and patterns.** Study your annotations to discover how the ideas in the work link together to suggest a theme. **Themes** are large or universal topics that are important to nearly everyone. For example, the theme of a poem or short story might be that death is inescapable or that aging involves a loss of the innocence of youth. Think of the theme as the main point a poem or short story makes. (Themes are discussed in greater detail later in the chapter.)

The Language of Literature

Many writers, especially writers of literary works, use figures of speech to describe people, places, or objects and to communicate ideas. In general, **figures of speech** are comparisons that make sense imaginatively or creatively but not literally. Three common types of figurative language are *similes, metaphors,* and *personification.* Writers often use another literary device, *symbols,* to suggest larger themes. Finally, writers use *irony* to convey the incongruities of life.

Similes, Metaphors, and Personification

For more on figures of speech, see Chapter 10, p. 219, and Chapter 12, p. 284.

Similes and metaphors are comparisons between two unlike things that have one common trait. A **simile** uses the word *like* or *as* to make a comparison, whereas a **metaphor** states or implies that one thing is another thing. If you say, "My father's mustache is a housepainter's brush," your metaphor compares two dissimilar things—a mustache and a paintbrush—that share one common trait: straight bristles. Such comparisons appeal to the reader's imagination. If you say, "Martha's hair looks like she just walked through a wind tunnel," your simile creates a more vivid image of Martha's hair than if you simply stated, "Martha's hair is messy." Here are examples from literary works:

SIMILE

My soul has grown deep like the rivers.

Langston Hughes, "The Negro Speaks of Rivers"

METAPHOR

Time is but the stream I go a-fishing in.

Henry David Thoreau, *Walden*

When writers use **personification**, they attribute human characteristics to objects or ideas. A well-known example of personification is found in an Emily Dickinson poem in which she likens death and immortality to passengers in a carriage: "Because I could not stop for Death— / He kindly stopped for me— / The carriage held but just Ourselves— / and Immortality." Like similes and metaphors, personification often creates a strong visual image.

Symbols

A **symbol** suggests more than its literal meaning. A flag, for instance, suggests patriotism; the color white often suggests innocence and purity. Because the abstract idea that a symbol represents is not stated but is left for the reader to infer, a symbol may suggest more than one meaning. A white handkerchief, for example, might symbolize retreat in one context but good manners in another. Some literary critics believe the white whale in Herman Melville's novel *Moby Dick* symbolizes evil, whereas others see the whale as representing the forces of nature.

To recognize symbols in a literary work, look for objects that are given a particular or unusual emphasis. The object may be mentioned often, may be suggested in the title, or may appear at the beginning or end of the work. Also be on the lookout for familiar symbols, such as flowers, doves, and colors.

Irony

Irony is literary language or a literary style in which actions, events, or words are the opposite of what readers expect. For example, a prizefighter cowering at the sight of a spider is an ironic action, a fire station burning down is an ironic event, and a student saying that she is glad she failed an important exam is making an ironic statement.

> **Exercise 24.1**
>
> *Working with another student, make a list of common metaphors and similes; examples of personification; and symbols you have heard or seen in everyday life, in films or television programs, or in works of literature.*

Analyzing Short Stories

A **short story** is a brief fictional narrative. It contains five key elements—setting, characters, point of view, plot, and theme. Short stories are shorter than novels, and their scope is much more limited. A short story, for example, may focus on one event in a person's life, whereas a novel may chronicle the events in the lives of an entire family. Like a novel, however, a short story makes a point about some aspect of the human experience.

Read the following short story, "The Secret Lion," before continuing with this section of the chapter. Then, as you continue with the chapter, you will discover how each of the key short-story elements works in "The Secret Lion."

The Secret Lion
Alberto Ríos

READING

Alberto Ríos (b. 1952), the son of a Guatemalan father and an English mother, was raised in Nogales, Arizona, near the Mexican border. His work has appeared in numerous national and international literature anthologies. In addition to fellowships from the Guggenheim Foundation and the National Endowment for the Arts, Ríos has won several awards: the Walt Whitman Award from the Academy of American Poets, the Arizona Governor's Arts Award, the PEN Beyond Margins Award, and the Western States Book Award for *The Iguana Killer: Twelve Stories of the Heart* (1984)—a collection of stories that includes the one reprinted here. Ríos is currently a Regents Professor of English at Arizona State University.

I was twelve and in junior high school and something happened that we didn't have   1
a name for, but it was there nonetheless like a lion, and roaring, roaring that way
the biggest things do. Everything changed. Just that. Like the rug, the one that gets
pulled—or better, like the tablecloth those magicians pull where the stuff on the
table stays the same but the gasp! from the audience makes the staying-the-same
part not matter. Like that.

What happened was there were teachers now, not just one teacher, teach-erz, and   2
we felt personally abandoned somehow. When a person had all these teachers now,
he didn't get taken care of the same way, even though six was more than one. Arith-
metic went out the door when we walked in. And we saw girls now, but they weren't
the same girls we used to know because we couldn't talk to them anymore, not the
same way we used to, certainly not to Sandy, even though she was my neighbor, too.
Not even to her. She just played the piano all the time. And there were words, oh there
were words in junior high school, and we wanted to know what they were, and how
a person did them—that's what school was supposed to be for. Only, in junior high
school, school wasn't school, everything was backward-like. If you went up to a teacher
and said the word to try and find out what it meant you got in trouble for saying it. So
we didn't. And we figured it must have been that way about other stuff, too, so we
never said anything about anything—we weren't stupid.

But my friend Sergio and I, we solved junior high school. We would come home   3
from school on the bus, put our books away, change shoes, and go across the highway
to the arroyo.[1] It was the one place we were not supposed to go. So we did. This was,
after all, what junior high had at least shown us. It was our river, though, our personal
Mississippi, our friend from long back, and it was full of stories and all the branch
forts we had built in it when we were still the Vikings of America, with our own symbol,
which we had carved everywhere, even in the sand, which let the water take it. That
was good, we had decided; whoever was at the end of this river would know about us.

At the very very top of our growing lungs, what we would do down there was shout   4
every dirty word we could think of, in every combination we could come up with, and
we would yell about girls, and all the things we wanted to do with them, as loud as we
could—we didn't know what we wanted to do with them, just things—and we would
yell about teachers, and how we loved some of them, like Miss Crevelone, and how we
wanted to dissect some of them, making signs of the cross, like priests, and we would
yell this stuff over and over because it felt good, we couldn't explain why, it just felt good
and for the first time in our lives there was nobody to tell us we couldn't. So we did.

One Thursday we were walking along shouting this way, and the railroad, the   5
Southern Pacific, which ran above and along the far side of the arroyo, had dropped
a grinding ball down there, which was, we found out later, a cannonball thing used
in mining. A bunch of them were put in a big vat which turned around and crushed
the ore. One had been dropped, or thrown—what do caboose men do when they get
bored—but it got down there regardless and as we were walking along yelling about
one girl or another, a particular Claudia, we found it, one of these things, looked at
it, picked it up, and got very very excited, and held it and passed it back and forth,
and we were saying "Guythisis, this is, geeGuythis . . .": we had this perception
about nature then, that nature is imperfect and that round things are perfect: we
said "GuyGodthis is perfect, thisisthis is perfect, it's round, round and heavy, it'sit's
the best thing we'veeverseen. Whatisit?" We didn't know. We just knew it was great.
We just, whatever, we played with it, held it some more.

And then we had to decide what to do with it. We knew, because of a lot of things,   6
that if we were going to take this and show it to anybody, this discovery, this best

---

[1]*arroyo:* A creek or stream in a dry part of the country.

thing, was going to be taken away from us. That's the way it works with little kids, like all the polished quartz, the tons of it we had collected piece by piece over the years. Junior high kids too. If we took it home, my mother, we knew, was going to look at it and say "throw that dirty thing in the, get rid of it." Simple like, like that. "But ma it's the best thing I" "Getridofit." Simple.

So we didn't. Take it home. Instead, we came up with the answer. We dug a hole   7
and buried it. And we marked it secretly. Lots of secret signs. And came back the next week to dig it up and, we didn't know, pass it around some more or something, but we didn't find it. We dug up that whole bank, and we never found it again. We tried.

Sergio and I talked about that ball or whatever it was when we couldn't find it. All   8
we used were small words, neat, good. Kid words. What we were really saying, but didn't know the words, was how much that ball was like that place, that whole arroyo: couldn't tell anybody about it, didn't understand what it was, didn't have a name for it. It just felt good. It was just perfect in the way it was that place, that whole going to that place, that whole junior high school lion. It was just iron-heavy, it had no name, it felt good or not, we couldn't take it home to show our mothers, and once we buried it, it was gone forever.

The ball was gone, like the first reasons we had come to that arroyo years earlier,   9
like the first time we had seen the arroyo, it was gone like everything else that had been taken away. This was not our first lesson. We stopped going to the arroyo after not finding the thing, the same way we had stopped going there years earlier and headed for the mountains. Nature seemed to keep pushing us around one way or another, teaching us the same thing every place we ended up. Nature's gang was tough that way, teaching us stuff.

When we were young we moved away from town, me and my family. Sergio's was   10
already out there. Out in the wilds. Or at least the new place seemed like the wilds since everything looks bigger the smaller a man is. I was five, I guess, and we had moved three miles north of Nogales where we had lived, three miles north of the Mexican border. We looked across the highway in one direction and there was the arroyo; hills stood up in the other direction. Mountains, for a small man.

When the first summer came the very first place we went to was of course the one   11
place we weren't supposed to go, the arroyo. We went down in there and found water running, summer rain water mostly, and we went swimming. But every third or fourth or fifth day, the sewage treatment plant that was, we found out, upstream, would release whatever it was that it released, and we would never know exactly what day that was, and a person really couldn't tell right off by looking at the water, not every time, not so a person could get out in time. So, we went swimming that summer and some days we had a lot of fun. Some days we didn't. We found a thousand ways to explain what happened on those other days, constructing elaborate stories about the neighborhood dogs, and hadn't she, my mother, miscalculated her step before, too? But she knew something was up because we'd come running into the house those days, wanting to take a shower, even—if this can be imagined—in the middle of the day.

That was the first time we stopped going to the arroyo. It taught us to look the   12
other way. We decided, as the second side of summer came, we wanted to go into the mountains. They were still mountains then. We went running in one summer Thursday morning, my friend Sergio and I, into my mother's kitchen, and said, well,

what'zin, what'zin those hills over there—we used her word so she'd understand us—and she said nothingdon'tworryaboutit. So we went out, and we weren't dumb, we thought with our eyes to each other, ohhoshe'stryingtokeepsomethingfromus. We knew adults.

We had read the books, after all; we knew about bridges and castles and wild-treacherousraging alligatormouth rivers. We wanted them. So we were going to go out and get them. We went back that morning into that kitchen and we said, "We're going out there, we're going into the hills, we're going away for three days, don't worry." She said, "All right." 13

"You know," I said to Sergio, "if we're going to go away for three days, well, we ought to at least pack a lunch." 14

But we were two young boys with no patience for what we thought at the time was mom-stuff: making sa-and-wiches. My mother didn't offer. So we got out little kid knapsacks that my mother had sewn for us, and into them we put the jar of mustard. A loaf of bread. Knivesforksplates, bottles of Coke, a can opener. This was lunch for the two of us. And we were weighed down, humped over to be strong enough to carry this stuff. But we started walking anyway, into the hills. We were going to eat berries and stuff otherwise. "Goodbye." My mom said that. 15

After the first hill we were dead. But we walked. My mother could still see us. And we kept walking. We walked until we got to where the sun is straight overhead, noon. That place. Where that is doesn't matter; it's time to eat. The truth is we weren't anywhere close to that place. We just agreed that the sun was overhead and that it was time to eat, and by tilting our heads a little we could make that the truth. 16

"We really ought to start looking for a place to eat." 17

"Yeah. Let's look for a good place to eat." We went back and forth saying that for fifteen minutes, making it lunchtime because that's what we always said back and forth before lunchtimes at home. "Yeah, I'm hungry all right." I nodded my head. "Yeah, I'm hungry all right too. I'm hungry." He nodded his head. I nodded my head back. After a good deal more nodding, we were ready, just as we came over a little hill. We hadn't found the mountains yet. This was a little hill. 18

And on the other side of this hill we found heaven. 19

It was just what we thought it would be. 20

Perfect. Heaven was green, like nothing else in Arizona. And it wasn't a cemetery or like that because we had seen cemeteries and they had gravestones and stuff and this didn't. This was perfect, had trees, lots of trees, had birds, like we had never seen before. It was like *The Wizard of Oz*, like when they got to Oz and everything was so green, so emerald, they had to wear those glasses, and we ran just like them, laughing, laughing that way we did that moment, and we went running down to this clearing in it all, hitting each other that good way we did. 21

We got down there, we kept laughing, we kept hitting each other, we unpacked our stuff, and we started acting "rich." We knew all about how to do that, like blowing on our nails, then rubbing them on our chests for the shine. We made our sandwiches, opened our Cokes, got out the rest of the stuff, the salt and pepper shakers. I found this particular hole and I put my Coke right into it, a perfect fit, and I called it my Coke-holder. I got down next to it on my back, because everyone knows that rich people eat lying down, and I got my sandwich in one hand and put my other arm around the Coke 22 in its holder. When I wanted a drink, I lifted my neck a little, put out my lips, and tipped my Coke a little with the crook of my elbow. Ah.

We were there, lying down, eating our sandwiches, laughing, throwing bread at 23 each other and out for the birds. This was heaven. We were laughing and we couldn't believe it. My mother was keeping something from us, ah ha, but we had found her out. We even found water over at the side of the clearing to wash our plates with—we had brought plates. Sergio started washing his plates when he was done, and I was being rich with my Coke, and this day in summer was right.

When suddenly these two men came, from around a corner of trees and the tallest 24 grass we had ever seen. They had bags on their backs, leather bags, bags and sticks.

We didn't know what clubs were, but I learned later, like I learned about the grind- 25 ing balls. The two men yelled at us. Most specifically, one wanted me to take my Coke out of my Coke-holder so he could sink his golf ball into it.

Something got taken away from us that moment. Heaven. We grew up a little bit, 26 and couldn't go backward. We learned. No one had ever told us about golf. They had told us about heaven. And it went away. We got golf in exchange.

We went back to the arroyo for the rest of that summer, and tried to have fun the 27 best we could. We learned to be ready for finding the grinding ball. We loved it, and when we buried it we knew what would happen. The truth is, we didn't look so hard for it. We were two boys and twelve summers then, and not stupid. Things get taken away.

We buried it because it was perfect. We didn't tell my mother, but together it was 28 all we talked about, till we forgot. It was the lion.

Setting

The **setting** of a short story is the time, place, and circumstance in which the story occurs. The setting provides the framework and atmosphere in which the plot develops and characters interact. For example, Charles Dickens's "A Christmas Carol" is set in nineteenth-century London. The setting of "The Secret Lion" is between the arroyo and the mountains just outside of Nogales, Arizona. The action occurs near the arroyo and on the golf course.

Characters

The **characters** are the actors in the story. They are revealed through their dialogue, actions, appearance, thoughts, and feelings. The **narrator**, the person who tells the story, may also comment on or reveal information about the characters. The narrator is not necessarily the author of the story. The narrator can be one of the characters in the story or an onlooker who observes but does not participate in the action. Therefore, you need to think critically about what the narrator reveals about the personalities, needs, and motives of the characters and whether the narrator's opinions may be colored by his or her perceptions and biases. "The Secret Lion" involves two principal characters: the narrator and his childhood friend, Sergio. Both twelve-year-old boys are playful, spirited, and inquisitive. They explore, disobey, and test ideas. The narrator's mother is a secondary character in the story.

Point of View

The **point of view** is the perspective from which the story is told. There are two common points of view: first person and third person. In the first-person (*I*) point of view, the narrator tells the story as he or she sees or experiences it ("*I* saw the crowd gather at the cemetery"). A first-person narrator may be one of the characters or someone observing but not participating in the story. In the third-person (*they*) point of view, the narrator tells the story as if someone else is experiencing it ("*Laura* saw the crowd gather at the cemetery"). A third-person narrator may be able to report only the actions that can be observed from the outside or may be able to enter the minds of one or more characters and tell about their thoughts and motives. An *omniscient*, or all-knowing, third-person narrator is aware of the thoughts and actions of all characters in the story.

To identify the point of view of a story, then, consider who is narrating and what the narrator knows about the characters' actions, thoughts, and motives. "The Secret Lion" is told by a first-person narrator who both participates in the action and looks back on the events to interpret them. For example, he says of their preparations for their trip to the mountains, "But we were two young boys with no patience for what we thought at the time was mom-stuff" (para. 15). He also uses a fast-talking narrative style characteristic of twelve-year-old boys, intentionally bending rules of spelling and grammar to achieve this effect. For example, he uses sentence fragments—"Lots of secret signs" (7), "Out in the wilds" (10)—and runs words together or emphasizes syllables to show how they are pronounced—"wild-treacherousraging alligatormouth rivers" (13), "sa-and-wiches" (15). He also uses slang words—"neat" (8)—and contractions to create an informal tone.

Plot

The **plot** is the basic story line—that is, the sequence of events and actions through which the story's meaning is expressed. The plot is often centered on a **conflict**—a problem or clash between opposing forces—and the resolution of the conflict. Once the scene is set and the characters are introduced, a problem or conflict arises. Suspense builds as the conflict unfolds and the characters wrestle with the problem. Near the end of the story, the events come to a **climax**—the point at which the conflict is resolved. The story ends with a conclusion.

In "The Secret Lion," two childhood friends, while playing near an arroyo, discover a grinding ball. They bury the ball but are unable to find it when they return. The narrator recollects an earlier time, when they had planned a trip to the mountains and stopped to have lunch on what they soon discovered was a golf course. The conflict, illustrated by several events, is between the boys' imaginations and adult realities.

Theme

The **theme** of a story is its central or dominant idea, the main point the author makes about the human experience. Readers do not always agree about a story's theme. Therefore, in a literary analysis of a short story, you must give evidence to support your interpretation of the theme. The following suggestions will help you uncover clues:

1. **Study the title.** What meanings does it suggest?
2. **Analyze the main characters.** Do the characters change? If so, how, and in response to what?
3. **Look for broad statements about the conflict.** What do the characters and narrator say about the conflict or their lives?
4. **Analyze important elements.** Look for symbols, figures of speech, and meaningful names (Young Goodman Brown, for example).

Once you uncover a theme, try expressing it in sentence form rather than as a single word or brief phrase. For example, to say the theme is "dishonesty" or "parent-child relationships" does not reveal the meaning of a story. When expressed as a sentence, however, a story's theme becomes clear: "Dishonesty sometimes pays" or "Parent-child relationships are often struggles for power and control."

One possible theme of "The Secret Lion" is that change is inevitable, that nothing remains the same. After the boys discover that they can't find the buried grinding ball, the narrator hints at this theme: "The ball was gone . . . like everything else that had been taken away" (para. 9). When the boys encounter the two men on the golf course, the narrator again comments on the theme of change: "Something got taken away from us that moment. Heaven. We grew up a little bit, and couldn't go backward" (26).

Another possible theme of Ríos's story is that perfection is unattainable. The boys are attracted to the ball because it is perfect: "GuyGodthis is perfect, thisisthis is perfect . . . it'sit's the best thing we'veeverseen" (5). But once the "perfect" ball is buried, it can never be found again. In much the same way, the boys cannot return to the "heaven" they once knew at the golf course.

Exercise 24.2

Working in groups of two or three, choose a television situation comedy and watch one episode, either together, if possible, or separately. After viewing the program, identify each of the following elements: setting, characters, point of view, and plot. Then consider whether you think the episode has a theme.

Use the questions in the box on the next page to guide your analysis of short stories. As you read the story that follows, "The Story of an Hour" by Kate Chopin (pp. 696–98), keep these questions in mind. You may choose to write an analysis of this story in response to the Guided Writing Assignment on pages 704–12.

QUESTIONS FOR ANALYZING SHORT STORIES

Setting: Time
1. In what general time period (century or decade) does the story take place?
2. What major events (wars, revolutions, famines, political or cultural movements) occurred during that time, and what bearing might they have on the story?

Setting: Place
1. In what geographic area does the story take place? (Try to identify the country and the city or town, as well as whether the area is an urban or rural one.)
2. Where does the action occur? (For example, does it occur on a battlefield, in a living room, or on a city street?)
3. Why is the place important? (Why couldn't the story occur elsewhere?)

Characters
1. Who are the main characters in the story?
2. What are the distinguishing qualities and characteristics of each character?
3. Why do you like or dislike each character?
4. How and why do characters change (or not change) as the story progresses?

Point of View
1. Is the narrator a character in the story or strictly an observer?
2. Is the narrator knowledgeable about the motives, feelings, and behavior of any or all of the characters?
3. Does the narrator affect what happens in the story? If so, how? What role does the narrator play?

Plot
1. What series of events occurs? Summarize the action.
2. What is the conflict? Why does it occur? How does it build to a climax?
3. How is the conflict resolved?
4. Is the outcome satisfying? Why or why not?

Theme
1. What is the theme? What broad statement about life or the human experience does the story suggest?
2. What evidence from the story supports your interpretation of the theme?

READING

The Story of an Hour
Kate Chopin

Kate Chopin (1851–1904), a nineteenth-century American writer, is best known for her novel *The Awakening* (1899), which outraged early literary critics with its portrayal of a woman in search of sexual and professional independence. As you read the following short story, originally published in *Vogue* magazine in 1894, look for, highlight, and annotate the five primary elements of short stories discussed in this chapter.

Knowing that Mrs. Mallard was afflicted with a heart trouble, great care was taken to break to her as gently as possible the news of her husband's death.   1

It was her sister Josephine who told her, in broken sentences, veiled hints that revealed in half concealing. Her husband's friend Richards was there, too, near her.   2

It was he who had been in the newspaper office when intelligence of the railroad disaster was received, with Brently Mallard's name leading the list of "killed." He had only taken the time to assure himself of its truth by a second telegram, and had hastened to forestall any less careful, less tender friend in bearing the sad message.

She did not hear the story as many women have heard the same, with a paralyzed inability to accept its significance. She wept at once, with sudden, wild abandonment, in her sister's arms. When the storm of grief had spent itself she went away to her room alone. She would have no one follow her.

There stood, facing the open window, a comfortable, roomy armchair. Into this she sank, pressed down by a physical exhaustion that haunted her body and seemed to reach into her soul.

She could see in the open square before her house the tops of trees that were all aquiver with the new spring life. The delicious breath of rain was in the air. In the street below a peddler was crying his wares. The notes of a distant song which someone was singing reached her faintly, and countless sparrows were twittering in the eaves.

There were patches of blue sky showing here and there through the clouds that had met and piled one above the other in the west facing her window.

She sat with her head thrown back upon the cushion of the chair, quite motionless, except when a sob came up into her throat and shook her, as a child who has cried itself to sleep continues to sob in its dreams.

She was young, with a fair, calm face, whose lines bespoke repression and even a certain strength. But now there was a dull stare in her eyes, whose gaze was fixed away off yonder on one of those patches of blue sky. It was not a glance of reflection, but rather indicated a suspension of intelligent thought.

There was something coming to her and she was waiting for it, fearfully. What was it? She did not know, it was too subtle and elusive to name. But she felt it, creeping out of the sky, reaching toward her through the sounds, the scents, the color that filled the air.

Now her bosom rose and fell tumultuously. She was beginning to recognize this thing that was approaching to possess her, and she was striving to beat it back with her will—as powerless as her two white slender hands would have been.

When she abandoned herself a little whispered word escaped her slightly parted lips. She said it over and over under her breath: "Free, free, free!" The vacant stare and the look of terror that had followed it went from her eyes. They stayed keen and bright. Her pulses beat fast, and the coursing blood warmed and relaxed every inch of her body.

She did not stop to ask if it were not a monstrous joy that held her. A clear and exalted perception enabled her to dismiss the suggestion as trivial.

She knew that she would weep again when she saw the kind, tender hands folded in death; the face that had never looked save with love upon her, fixed and gray and dead. But she saw beyond that bitter moment a long procession of years to come that would belong to her absolutely. And she opened and spread her arms out to them in welcome.

There would be no one to live for during those coming years; she would live for herself. There would be no powerful will bending her in that blind persistence with which men and women believe they have a right to impose a private will upon a fellow creature. A kind intention or a cruel intention made the act seem no less a crime as she looked upon it in that brief moment of illumination.

And yet she had loved him—sometimes. Often she had not. What did it matter! What could love, the unsolved mystery, count for in face of this possession of self-assertion which she suddenly recognized as the strongest impulse of her being.

"Free! Body and soul free!" she kept whispering. 16

Josephine was kneeling before the closed door with her lips to the keyhole, imploring for admission. "Louise, open the door! I beg; open the door—you will make yourself ill. What are you doing, Louise? For heaven's sake open the door." 17

"Go away. I am not making myself ill." No; she was drinking in a very elixir of life through that open window. 18

Her fancy was running riot along those days ahead of her. Spring days, and summer days, and all sorts of days that would be her own. She breathed a quick prayer that life might be long. It was only yesterday she had thought with a shudder that life might be long. 19

She arose at length and opened the door to her sister's importunities. There was a feverish triumph in her eyes, and she carried herself unwittingly like a goddess of Victory. She clasped her sister's waist, and together they descended the stairs. Richards stood waiting for them at the bottom. 20

Some one was opening the front door with a latchkey. It was Brently Mallard who entered, a little travel-stained, composedly carrying his gripsack and umbrella. He had been far from the scene of accident, and did not even know there had been one. He stood amazed at Josephine's piercing cry; at Richards' quick motion to screen him from the view of his wife. 21

But Richards was too late. 22

When the doctors came they said she had died of heart disease—of joy that kills. 23

Analyzing Poetry

Poetry is written in lines and stanzas instead of in paragraphs. Because of poetry's unique format, ideas in poems are often expressed in compact and concise language, and reading and analyzing a poem may take as much time and effort as analyzing an essay or a short story. To grasp the meaning of a poem, it is important to pay attention to the sound and meaning of individual words and to consider how the words in the poem work together to convey meaning.

Use the following general guidelines to read and analyze poetry effectively:

1. **Read the poem through once**, without any defined purpose. Read with an open mind; try to get a general sense of what the poem is about. If you come across an unfamiliar word or a confusing reference, keep reading.
2. **Use punctuation to guide your comprehension.** Although poetry is written in lines, each line may not make sense by itself. Meaning often flows from line to line, and a single sentence can be composed of several lines. Use the poem's punctuation to guide you. If there is no punctuation at the end of a line, read it with a slight pause at the end and with an emphasis on the last word. Think about how the poet breaks lines to achieve a certain effect.
3. **Visualize as you read.** Especially if you tend to be a spatial or an abstract learner, try to visualize or see what the poem is about.
4. **Read the poem several more times.** The meaning of the poem will become clearer with each successive reading. At first you may understand some parts but not others. If you tend to be a pragmatic or rational learner, you will probably want to work through the poem line by line, from beginning to end. With poetry, however, that approach does not always work. Instead you may need to use later stanzas to help

you understand earlier ones. If you find certain sections difficult or confusing, read these sections aloud several times. You might try copying them, word for word, on a piece of paper. Look up the meanings of any unfamiliar words in a dictionary.

5. **Check unfamiliar references.** A poet may make **allusions**—references to people, objects, or events outside of the poem. Understanding an allusion is often essential to understanding the overall meaning of a poem. If you see Oedipus mentioned in a poem, for example, you may need to use a dictionary or encyclopedia to learn that he was a figure in Greek mythology who unwittingly killed his father and unknowingly married his mother. Your knowledge of Oedipus would then help you interpret the poem.

6. **Identify the speaker and tone.** Poems often refer to an unidentified *I* or *we*. Try to describe the speaker's viewpoint or feelings to figure out who he or she is. Also consider the speaker's tone: Is it serious, challenging, sad, frustrated, or joyful? To help determine the tone, read the poem aloud. Your emphasis of certain words or the rise and fall of your voice may provide clues to the tone; that is, you may "hear" the poet's anger, despondency, or elation.

7. **Identify to whom the poem is addressed.** Is it written to a person, to the reader, to an object? Consider the possibility that the poet may be writing to work out a personal problem or to express strong emotions.

8. **Analyze the language of the poem.** Consider the *connotations,* or shades of meaning, of words in the poem. Study the poem's use of descriptive language, similes, metaphors, personification, and symbols (see pp. 688–89).

For more on connotations, see Chapter 10, p. 217; for more on descriptive language, see Chapter 12, pp. 270–71.

9. **Analyze the poem's theme.** Does its overall meaning involve a feeling, a person, a memory, or an argument? Paraphrase the poem; express it in your own words, and connect it to your own experience. Then link your ideas together to discover the poem's overall meaning. Ask yourself, What is the poet trying to tell me? and What is the theme?

Use the questions in the accompanying box to guide your analysis of poetry. As you read the following poem by Robert Frost, "Two Look at Two," keep these questions in mind.

QUESTIONS FOR ANALYZING POETRY

1. How does the poem make you feel—shocked, saddened, angered, annoyed, happy? Write a sentence or two describing your reaction.
2. Who is the speaker? What do you know about him or her? What tone does the speaker use? To whom is he or she speaking?
3. What is the poem's setting? If it is unclear, why does the poet not provide a setting?
4. What emotional atmosphere or mood does the poet create? Do you sense, for example, a mood of foreboding, excitement, or contentment?
5. How does the poet use language to create an effect? Does the poet use similes, metaphors, personification, or symbols?
6. Does the poem tell a story? If so, what is its point?
7. Does the poem express emotion? If so, for what purpose?
8. Does the poem rhyme? If so, does the rhyme affect the meaning? (For example, does the poet use rhyme to emphasize key words or phrases?)
9. What is the meaning of the poem's title?
10. What is the theme of the poem?

Two Look at Two
Robert Frost

Robert Frost (1874–1963) is a major American poet whose work often focuses on familiar objects, natural scenes, and the character of New England. In his early life Frost was a farmer and teacher; later he became a poet in residence at Amherst College and taught at Dartmouth, Yale, and Harvard. Frost was awarded Pulitzer Prizes for four collections of poems: *New Hampshire* (1923), from which "Two Look at Two" is taken; *Collected Poems* (1930); *A Further Range* (1936); and *A Witness Tree* (1942). As you read the selection, use the questions in the box on page 699 to think critically about the poem.

Love and forgetting might have carried them
A little further up the mountain side
With night so near, but not much further up.
They must have halted soon in any case
With thoughts of the path back, how rough it was   5
With rock and washout, and unsafe in darkness;
When they were halted by a tumbled wall
With barbed-wire binding. They stood facing this,
Spending what onward impulse they still had
In one last look the way they must not go,   10
On up the failing path, where, if a stone
Or earthslide moved at night, it moved itself;
No footstep moved it. "This is all," they sighed,
"Good-night to woods." But not so; there was more.
A doe from round a spruce stood looking at them   15
Across the wall, as near the wall as they.
She saw them in their field, they her in hers.
The difficulty of seeing what stood still,
Like some up-ended boulder split in two,
Was in her clouded eyes: they saw no fear there.   20
She seemed to think that two thus they were safe.
Then, as if they were something that, though strange,
She could not trouble her mind with too long,
She sighed and passed unscared along the wall.
"*This,* then, is all. What more is there to ask?"   25

But no, not yet. A snort to bid them wait.

A buck from round the spruce stood looking at them

Across the wall, as near the wall as they.

This was an antlered buck of lusty nostril,

Not the same doe come back into her place.   30

He viewed them quizzically with jerks of head,

As if to ask, "Why don't you make some motion?

Or give some sign of life? Because you can't.

I doubt if you're as living as you look."

Thus till he had them almost feeling dared   35

To stretch a proffering hand—and a spell-breaking.

Then he too passed unscared along the wall.

Two had seen two, whichever side you spoke from.

"This *must* be all." It was all. Still they stood,

A great wave from it going over them,   40

As if the earth in one unlooked-for favor

Had made them certain earth returned their love.

The poem takes place on a mountainside path, near dusk. A couple walking the path finds a tumbled wall. Looking beyond the wall, the couple first encounters a doe and then a buck. The doe and buck stare at the human couple and vice versa; hence the title "Two Look at Two." Neither the animals nor the humans are frightened; both couples observe each other and continue with their lives. The action is described by a third-person narrator who can read the thoughts of the humans. The speaker creates an objective tone by reporting events as they occur.

In "Two Look at Two," Frost considers the important relationship between humans and nature. The wall is symbolic of the separation between them. Beyond the wall the couple looks at "the way they must not go" (line 10). Although humans and nature are separate, they are also equal and in balance. These qualities are suggested by the title as well as by the actions of both couples as they observe each other in a nonthreatening way. The third-person point of view contributes to this balance in that the story is narrated by an outside observer rather than a participant. One possible theme of the poem, therefore, is the balance and equality between humans and nature.

As you read the following poem, "Filling Station," by Elizabeth Bishop, use the guidelines on pages 698 to 699 and the questions in the box on page 699 to help you analyze its elements and discover its meaning. You may choose to write an analysis of this poem in response to the Guided Writing Assignment on pages 704–12.

Filling Station
Elizabeth Bishop

Elizabeth Bishop (1911–1979) is an American poet who traveled most of her life. Much of her poetry recounts the places she visited and the intimate details of everyday things. She published several collections of poems, including *North and South* (1946); *Poems: North and South—A Cold Spring* (1956), for which she was awarded a Pulitzer Prize; *Questions of Travel* (1965); *The Complete Poems* (1969), for which she received the National Book Award; and *Geography III* (1976). The following poem was originally published in *Questions of Travel*. As you read, respond to the poem by making notes in the margin.

Oh, but it is dirty!
— this little filling station,
oil-soaked, oil-permeated
to a disturbing, over-all
black translucency,   5
Be careful with that match!

Father wears a dirty,
oil-soaked monkey suit
that cuts him under the arms,
and several quick and saucy   10
and greasy sons assist him
(it's a family filling station),
all quite thoroughly dirty.

Do they live in the station?
It has a cement porch   15
behind the pumps, and on it
a set of crushed and grease-
impregnated wickerwork;
on the wicker sofa
a dirty dog, quite comfy.   20
Some comic books provide
the only note of color—
of certain color. They lie
upon a big dim doily
draping a taboret*   25

taboret: low cylindrical stool

(part of the set), beside
a big hirsute begonia.

Why the extraneous plant?
Why the taboret?
Why, oh why, the doily?   30
(Embroidered in daisy stitch
with marguerites, I think,
and heavy with gray crochet.)

Somebody embroidered the doily.
Somebody waters the plant,   35
or oils it, maybe. Somebody
arranges the rows of cans
so that they softly say:
ESSO**—SO—SO—SO

to high-strung automobiles.   40
Somebody loves us all.

**ESSO:* The mid-twentieth-century name for a petroleum products company that began in the late nineteenth century as Standard Oil Trust and continues today as ExxonMobil.

Now that you have a better understanding of the elements of poetry and short stories, you are ready to write about a literary work. In English and humanities courses, you will often be asked to read and analyze works of literature and then write literary analyses. The following sections will discuss this type of essay and take you step by step through a Guided Writing Assignment.

What Is Literary Analysis?

A **literary analysis** essay, sometimes called *literary criticism* or a *critique,* analyzes and interprets one or more aspects of a literary work. As with other types of essays, writing a literary analysis involves generating ideas through prewriting, developing a thesis, collecting supporting evidence, organizing and drafting, analyzing and revising, and editing and proofreading.

Keep in mind that a literary analysis does *not* merely summarize the work; rather, it focuses on *analysis* and *interpretation* of the work. Therefore, in a literary analysis, you take a position on some aspect of the work and support your position with evidence. In other words, you assume the role of a critic, in much the same way that a film critic argues for his or her judgment of a film rather than simply reporting its plot. For this chapter's assignment, your literary analysis should focus on *one* element of the work, even though some literary analyses cover multiple elements or more than one work.

A literary analysis has the following characteristics:

- It makes a point about one or more elements of a literary work.
- It includes and accurately documents evidence from the work. (It may also include evidence from outside sources.)
- It assumes that the audience is somewhat familiar with the work but not as familiar as the writer of the analysis.
- It has a serious tone and is written in the present tense.

A GUIDED WRITING ASSIGNMENT

The following guide will help you write a literary analysis of a poem or short story. Depending on your learning style, you may find some of the suggested strategies more suitable than others. Social or verbal learners, for instance, may prefer to generate ideas about the poem or short story through discussion with classmates. Spatial or creative learners may decide to draw a character map. Independent or concrete learners may choose to draw a time line or write a summary. This Guided Writing Assignment will provide you with alternatives.

The Assignment

Write a literary analysis of a poem or short story. Choose one of the works reprinted in this chapter, a work you select on your own, or a work assigned by your instructor. Your classmates are your audience.

1. Gwendolyn Brooks, "The Bean Eaters" (p. 684)
2. Alberto Ríos, "The Secret Lion" (pp. 689–93)
3. Kate Chopin, "The Story of an Hour" (pp. 696–98)
4. Robert Frost, "Two Look at Two" (pp. 700–01)
5. Elizabeth Bishop, "Filling Station" (pp. 702–3)

For more on illustration, comparison and contrast, and cause and effect, see Chapters 13, 15, and 18.

As you develop your literary-analysis essay, you will probably use one or more patterns of development. You will use illustration, for instance, to cite examples from the poem or short story that support your analysis of it. In addition, you might compare or contrast two main characters or analyze a plot by discussing causes and effects.

Generating Ideas

The following guidelines will help you explore the short story or poem you have selected and generate ideas for writing about it:

1. **Highlight and annotate as you read.** Record your initial impressions and responses to the work in marginal annotations as you read. For recording lengthy comments, use a separate sheet of paper. Look for and highlight figures of speech, symbols, revealing character descriptions, striking dialogue, and the like. Here is a sample annotated portion of Frost's "Two Look at Two."

Learning Style Options

For more on annotating, see Chapter 3, p. 56.

SAMPLE ANNOTATED PASSAGE

Love and forgetting might have carried them

A little further up the mountain side

With night so near, but not much further up. ◄——————— *limitations of humans*

They must have halted soon in any case

With thoughts of the path back, how rough it was ◄——— *road of life?*
difficulty of life

With rock and washout, and unsafe in darkness;

When they were halted by a tumbled wall ◄——————— *separates man and*
nature—Why is it
tumbled?

With barbed-wire binding. They stood facing this, ◄———

Spending what onward impulse they still had *sharp, penetrating*

In one last look the way they must not go, ◄——————— *prohibited from*
crossing

Robert Frost, "Two Look at Two"

2. **Discuss the literary work with classmates.** Discussing the short story or poem with others will help you generate ideas about it. Plan your discussion, moving from the general meaning of the work to a more specific paragraph-by-paragraph or line-by-line examination. Then consider your interpretation of the work's theme.

3. **Write a summary.** Especially when you draw a blank about a work, try writing a summary of it in your own words. You may find yourself raising and answering questions about the work as you summarize it. Jot down ideas as they occur to you, either on your summary page or on a separate sheet of paper.

For more on writing a summary, see Chapter 4, pp. 88–89, and Chapter 22, pp. 610–11.

4. **Draw a time line.** For a short story, especially one with a complex plot that flashes back or forward in time, draw a time line of the action in chronological sequence on paper or on a computer. Here is a sample time line for Ríos's "The Secret Lion."

Sample Time Line: "The Secret Lion"

Age 5 ⟶ Main character moves three miles north of Nogales.

First half of summer ⟶ He visits the arroyo with Sergio; goes swimming, mother suspects.

Second half of summer ⟶ Boys visit mountains; think they have found heaven but learn it is a golf course.

⟶ They return to the arroyo; try to have fun.

Age 12 (junior high school) ⟶ They visit the arroyo.

⟶ They shout dirty words and yell about girls.

One Thursday ⟶ They find grinding ball.

⟶ They bury grinding ball.

⟶ They can't find the buried ball; stop going to the arroyo.

5. **Draw a character map.** To explore the connections and interactions among the characters in a story, draw a character map. In the center of a blank piece of paper, put a main character's name inside a circle. Then add other characters' names, connecting them with lines to the main character. On the connecting lines, briefly describe the relationships between characters and the events or other factors (such as emotions) that affect their relationship. You might use a drawing or symbol to represent some aspect of a character or relationship (for instance, *$* for "wealthy" or a smiley face for "happy"). Here is a sample character map for Ríos's "The Secret Lion":

Sample Character Map: "The Secret Lion"

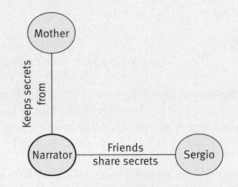

For more on finding sources, see Chapter 22.

6. **Investigate the background of the work and the author.** Research the historical context of the work as well as biographical information about the author. Look for connections among the work; the author's life; and the social, economic, and political events of the time. Investigating the background of a work and its author can give you valuable insights into the writer's meaning (or theme) and purpose. For example, an interpretation of Charles Dickens's "A Christmas Carol" might be more meaningful if you understood how the author's difficult childhood and the conditions of the poor in nineteenth-century England contributed to his portrayal of the Cratchit family.

7. **Use a two-column response journal.** Divide several pages of your journal into two vertical columns. Label the left column *Text* and the right column *Response*. In the left column, record five to ten quotations from the poem or short story. Choose only quotations that convey a main point or opinion, reveal a character's motives, or say something important about the plot or theme. In the right column, describe your reaction to each quotation. You might interpret, disagree with, or question the quotation. Try to comment on the language of the quotation and to relate it to other quotations or elements in the work. Here is a sample two-column journal response to Frost's "Two Look at Two."

For more on journal writing, see Chapter 2, pp. 32–33, and Chapter 4, pp. 91–92.

Sample Two-Column Response to "Two Look at Two"

Text	Response
"With thoughts of the path back, how rough it was" (line 5)	The couple's past has been difficult; returning to daily life may be difficult, too. Nature is rough and challenging.
" 'This is all,' they sighed, / 'Good-night to woods.' " (lines 13–14)	The couple will soon come to the end -- of their relationship or their lives.

8. **Discover parallel works or situations.** You can often evoke a response to a work by comparing it to other literary works, another narrative form (such as a film or television show), or a familiar situation. For example, after reading the poem "On His Blindness" by John Milton, one student connected it to the movie *Scent of a Woman*, in which one central character is blind. By comparing the literary work to the more familiar film, the student was better able to analyze the meaning of the poem.

9. **Use prewriting.** Prewriting helps you generate ideas for all types of essays, including a literary analysis. Try freewriting, brainstorming, sketching, questioning, or any of the other prewriting strategies discussed in Chapter 5.

> **Essay in Progress 1**
> Use one or more of the preceding techniques to generate ideas about the short story or poem you have chosen for your analysis.

Evaluating Your Ideas

Once you generate sufficient ideas about the work, begin your evaluation by reviewing your notes and prewriting. Look for a perspective or position that reflects your understanding of some aspect of the work. Here are several possible approaches you might take in a literary analysis:

1. **Evaluate symbolism.** Discuss how the author's use of images and symbols creates a particular mood and contributes to the overall meaning of the work.

2. **Analyze conflicts.** Focus on their causes, effects, or both.

3. **Evaluate characterization.** Discuss how characters are presented, whether a particular character's actions are realistic or predictable, or what the author reveals or hides about a character.
4. **Interpret characters or relationships among them.** Analyze how the true nature of a character is revealed or how a character changes in response to circumstances.
5. **Explore themes.** Discover the important point or theme the work conveys, and back up your ideas with examples from the work.

Developing Your Thesis

After evaluating your ideas and choosing an aspect of the work to focus on, it is time to write a thesis statement. Your thesis should indicate the element of the work you will analyze (its theme, characters, or use of symbols, for example) and state the main point you will make about that element, as in the following sample thesis statements:

- Flannery O'Connor's short story "A Good Man Is Hard to Find" uses color to depict various moods throughout the story.
- In Susan Glaspell's play *Trifles,* the female characters are treated condescendingly by the males, and yet the women's interest in so-called trivial matters leads them to interpret the "trivial" pieces of evidence that solve the murder mystery.

For more on thesis statements, see Chapter 6, pp. 125–33.

Be sure your thesis statement focuses on your interpretation of one specific aspect of the work. As in other types of essays, the thesis for a literary analysis should identify your narrowed topic.

Essay in Progress 2

Using the preceding guidelines, write a working thesis for your literary-analysis essay. Then review the poem or short story and your notes to make sure you have enough evidence to support your thesis. In the body paragraphs of your essay, you will need to cite examples from the work that show why your thesis is valid. You might, for example, include relevant descriptions of characters or events, snippets of dialogue, examples of imagery and figures of speech, or any other details from the work that confirm or explain your thesis.

As you review the work and your notes about it, try to meet with one or two classmates who are working on the same poem or short story. They may have noticed evidence that you have overlooked or offer insights into the work that enrich your own reading of it. No two readers will have the same interpretation of a literary work, however, so don't be alarmed if their ideas differ from yours.

Trying Out Your Ideas on Others

Working in a group of two or three students, discuss each other's thesis and supporting evidence for this chapter's assignment. Encourage your peers to ask questions about your work and suggest improvements.

> **Essay in Progress 3**
>
> Use your own analysis and the feedback you received from peer reviewers to evaluate your thesis and supporting evidence. Gather additional examples from the work if necessary, and delete any examples that do not support your thesis.

Organizing and Drafting

Use the following guidelines to organize and draft your literary analysis:

1. **Choose a method of organization.** See Chapter 7 for more detailed suggestions about organizing an essay.
2. **Focus your essay on ideas and not on events.** Remember that your literary analysis should not merely summarize the work or the plot but focus on your ideas and interpretations.
3. **Write in the present tense.** Treat the events in the work as if they are happening now rather than in the past. For example, write "Brooks describes an elderly couple . . . ," not "Brooks described . . ."
4. **Include sufficient examples from the work and cite them correctly.** Use enough examples to support your thesis but not so many that your essay becomes one long string of examples with no clear main point. In addition, provide in-text citations (including paragraph or page numbers for a short story, or line numbers for a poem) in parentheses immediately after any quotations from the work. Include a works-cited entry at the end of your paper indicating the edition of the work you used.

For help with citing examples from a literary work, see Chapter 23, p. 643.

5. **Write an effective introduction.** The introduction for a literary analysis should engage readers, name the author and title of the work, present your thesis, and suggest why your analysis of the work is useful or important. For example, to engage your readers' interest, you might include a meaningful quotation from the work, comment on the universality of a character or theme, or briefly state your response to the work.
6. **Write a satisfying conclusion.** To conclude your essay, you can use techniques similar to those just described for introductions. Your purposes are to give the essay a sense of closure as well as to reaffirm your thesis. You may want to tie your conclusion directly to your introduction, offering a final word or comment on your main point.

For more on writing effective introductions and conclusions, see Chapter 7, pp. 153–57.

> **Essay in Progress 4**
>
> Using the preceding guidelines for organizing and drafting along with the thesis you developed in Essay in Progress 2 (p. 708), draft your literary-analysis essay.

Analyzing and Revising

If possible, set aside your draft for a day or two before rereading and revising it. Then, as you reread your draft, concentrate on your ideas and organization, not on grammar or mechanics. Use Figure 24.1 (p. 710) to guide your evaluation. You might also ask a classmate to review your draft by using the questions in the flowchart.

For more on the benefits of peer review, see Chapter 9, pp. 188–91.

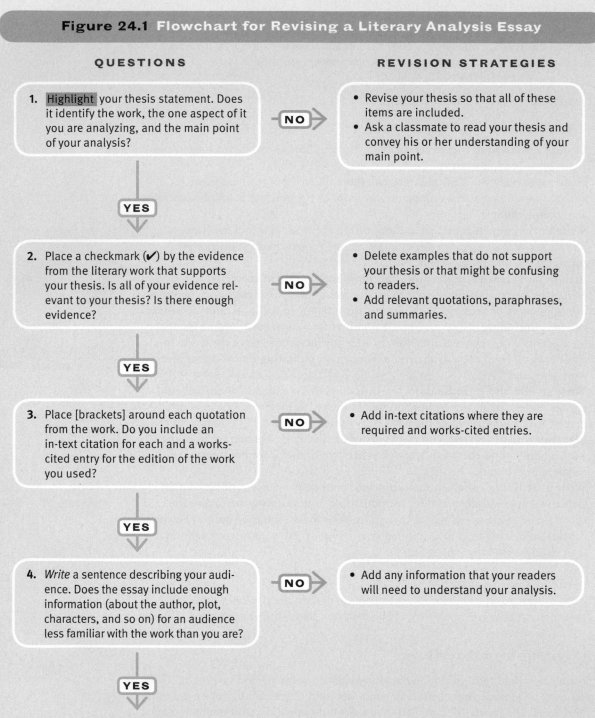

Figure 24.1 Flowchart for Revising a Literary Analysis Essay

QUESTIONS

REVISION STRATEGIES

1. Highlight your thesis statement. Does it identify the work, the one aspect of it you are analyzing, and the main point of your analysis? — NO →
   - Revise your thesis so that all of these items are included.
   - Ask a classmate to read your thesis and convey his or her understanding of your main point.

YES

2. Place a checkmark (✔) by the evidence from the literary work that supports your thesis. Is all of your evidence relevant to your thesis? Is there enough evidence? — NO →
   - Delete examples that do not support your thesis or that might be confusing to readers.
   - Add relevant quotations, paraphrases, and summaries.

YES

3. Place [brackets] around each quotation from the work. Do you include an in-text citation for each and a works-cited entry for the edition of the work you used? — NO →
   - Add in-text citations where they are required and works-cited entries.

YES

4. *Write* a sentence describing your audience. Does the essay include enough information (about the author, plot, characters, and so on) for an audience less familiar with the work than you are? — NO →
   - Add any information that your readers will need to understand your analysis.

YES

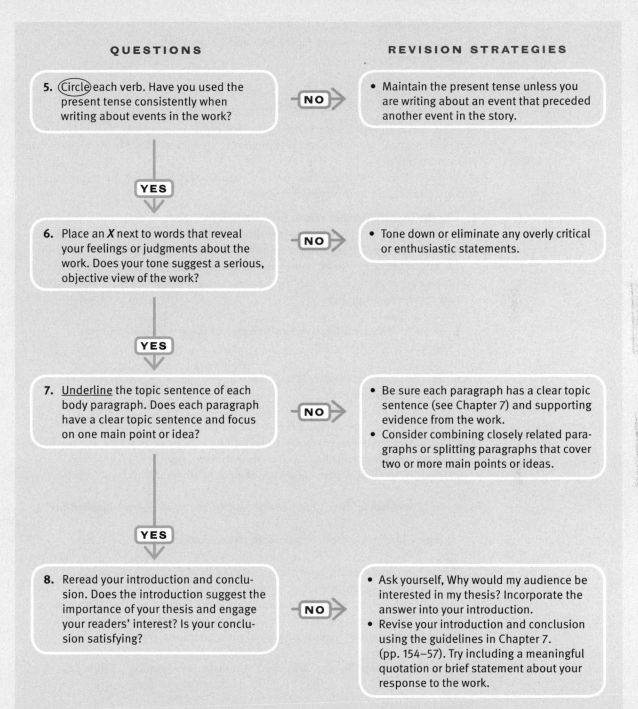

QUESTIONS

REVISION STRATEGIES

5. Circle each verb. Have you used the present tense consistently when writing about events in the work?

NO

- Maintain the present tense unless you are writing about an event that preceded another event in the story.

YES

6. Place an *X* next to words that reveal your feelings or judgments about the work. Does your tone suggest a serious, objective view of the work?

NO

- Tone down or eliminate any overly critical or enthusiastic statements.

YES

7. Underline the topic sentence of each body paragraph. Does each paragraph have a clear topic sentence and focus on one main point or idea?

NO

- Be sure each paragraph has a clear topic sentence (see Chapter 7) and supporting evidence from the work.
- Consider combining closely related paragraphs or splitting paragraphs that cover two or more main points or ideas.

YES

8. Reread your introduction and conclusion. Does the introduction suggest the importance of your thesis and engage your readers' interest? Is your conclusion satisfying?

NO

- Ask yourself, Why would my audience be interested in my thesis? Incorporate the answer into your introduction.
- Revise your introduction and conclusion using the guidelines in Chapter 7. (pp. 154–57). Try including a meaningful quotation or brief statement about your response to the work.

> **Essay in Progress 5**
> Revise your draft essay using Figure 24.1 and the comments you received from peer reviewers.

Editing and Proofreading

For more on keeping an error log, see Chapter 10, pp. 221–22.

The last step is to check your revised essay for errors in grammar, spelling, punctuation, and mechanics. In addition, be sure to check your error log for the types of errors you tend to make.

As you edit and proofread your literary analysis, watch out for the following errors that are often found in this type of writing:

1. **Use the literary present tense.** Even though the poem or short story was written in the past, as a general rule you should write about the events in it and the author's writing of it as if they were happening in the present. This is called the *literary present tense.* An exception to this rule occurs when you are referring to a time earlier than that in which the narrator speaks, in which case a switch to the past tense is appropriate.

   - Keats in "Ode on a Grecian Urn" *refers* ~~referred~~ to the urn as a "silent form" (line 44).

   - In "Two Look at Two," it is not clear why the couple *decided* to walk up the mountainside path.

   The couple made the decision before the action in the poem began.

2. **Punctuate quotations correctly.** Direct quotations from a literary work, whether spoken or written, must be placed in quotation marks. Omitted material is marked by an ellipsis mark. The lines of a poem are separated by a slash (/).

   - In "Two Look at Two," Frost concludes " that the earth in one unlooked-for

     favor / Had made them certain earth returned their love " (lines 41–42).

   Periods and commas appear within quotation marks. Question marks and exclamation points go within or outside of quotation marks, depending on the meaning of the sentence. Here the question mark goes inside the closing quotation marks because it is part of Frost's poem (line 32). Notice, too, that double and single quotation marks are required for a quotation within a quotation.

   - The buck seems "to ask, 'Why don't you make some motion ' "? (line 32).

> **Essay in Progress 6**
> Edit and proofread your literary analysis essay, paying particular attention to verb tense and punctuation of quotations.

Students Write

Andrew Decker was a student at Niagara County Community College when he wrote the following literary analysis of Ríos's "The Secret Lion" in response to an assignment in his first-year writing class. As you read the essay, notice the one aspect of the literary work that Decker focuses on, his thesis, and the evidence he uses to support it.

The Keeping of "The Secret Lion"

Andrew Decker

Alberto Ríos's "The Secret Lion" charts the initiation of a young boy into adolescence. During this climactic period of growth, the narrator experiences several shifts in perception that change him from a child to an adolescent by teaching him the value of secrets.

Within the first paragraph, the author introduces the reader to the new and perplexing feelings of the main character during his junior high years. His impression of what happened during those years remains nameless, "but it was there nonetheless like a lion, and roaring, roaring that way the biggest things do. Everything changed. Just that" (paragraph 1). It is as if the boy is being swept away by a great swell, the wave of anticipation traditionally associated with the child's entry into adolescence.

He finds that these changes are confusing and yet enticing. Evident within the context of the first page is the boy's newfound curiosity about and fascination with the opposite sex. He is also bewildered by the use of profanity and delights in the opportunity to verbally (and very loudly) explore his own feelings with respect to the use of such words.

Although adults scold him when he questions them about the meaning of these words, their dismay does not discourage him from saying the words privately. He and his friend Sergio like to hide away from such authoritarian voices, and so they cross the highway to the arroyo where they are not supposed to play. In the arroyo, they "shout every dirty word we could think of, in every combination we could come up with, and we would yell about girls, and all the things we wanted to do with them, as loud as we could" (4). Of course, they take great pleasure in this youthful audacity for "it just felt good and for the first time in our lives there was nobody to tell us we couldn't" (4). All is new. All is fresh. Opportunity abounds, and possibilities remain infinite, for time has not yet become an enemy.

One day when the two boys are playing and cussing in the arroyo, they find a perfectly round iron ball. It is heavy and smooth, and to them it is the perfect object. In the eyes of the two children, the world is formless and pure, as is the ball. Similarly, they consider the arroyo to be the perfect place--their perfect place. When faced with deciding what to do with the ball, they choose to bury it so that nobody can take it away--if only in a less literal sense.

1

2

3

4

5

Introduction: Decker gives a one-sentence synopsis, assuming his audience is familiar with the work. In his thesis statement, he indicates that he will focus on a specific aspect of it.

Decker gives background for the essay, quoting the "secret lion" passage and associating it with adolescence. He identifies quotations with paragraph numbers. Clear topic sentences identify main point of each body paragraph.

Note Decker's use of present tense and transitions.

Quotations as supporting evidence

Decker discusses the iron ball as a symbol of the purity of childhood. Note that he organizes his essay by presenting events from the work in chronological order, since his thesis focuses on changes in perception over time.

Their minds are still free of the narrow vision of an adult. They are free to roam and roar and echo the spirit of the lion, which is for Sergio and the narrator the spirit of that time. In their own words, when they talk of that ball, they speak of "how much that ball was like that place, that whole arroyo: couldn't tell anybody about it, didn't understand what it was, didn't have a name for it. It just felt good. It was just perfect in the way it was that place, that whole going to that place, that whole junior high school lion" (8). They know that once they bury the grinding ball (they only learn later what it is), it will be gone forever and yet thereby preserved.

The two boys are applying a lesson they have already learned. They understand that an experience can be stolen or changed by a shift in perception so that the original feeling, the original reality, ceases to exist in its more pure and innocent form. The boys had experienced disillusion before; when they were very young, they had also played in the arroyo and gone swimming in the stream. It was a time of naiveté, but their naiveté had been challenged when they learned that the water was at times filled with the waste flushed downstream by a local sewage plant.

Another shift in perception happened later that same summer, when the boys think **they have found a new haven beyond some small hills near their houses.** On the other side of a hill they find a green clearing, and they declare its lush beauty their "heaven." They learn, **however,** that this heaven is merely a product of their unworldly imagination; the boys have youthfully glorified a simple golf course, in which they were unwelcome visitors.

These events and others teach the boys to protect a new experience, to keep new feelings safe and virginal so as not to lose them to the ravages of time and change. **When they return to the arroyo several years later,** when they are twelve and experiencing the exuberance and excitement of adolescence, they know enough not to share or expose their experiences. The grinding ball is a symbol of that age, that sense of newness, and as they say, "when we buried it we knew what would happen" (27). Burying the ball is an attempt on their part to crystallize a certain time, a certain perception, "because it was perfect" (28). "It was the lion" (28), and the lion was the "roaring" of both that time and that place, and they bury it so that it might never truly be lost.

6

7

8

9

Decker uses more transitional phrases to move to the final events in the story and to the conclusion of his essay.

Conclusion: Decker offers a final interpretation of the work by making reference to its title and reflecting the introduction of the essay.

Work Cited

Ríos, Alberto. "The Secret Lion." *The Iguana Killer: Twelve Stories of the Heart*. Lewiston: Blue Moon, 1984.

Edition of "The Secret Lion" that Decker used

Analyzing the Writer's Technique

1. Does Decker provide sufficient evidence to support his thesis? Choose one example Decker offers and evaluate its effectiveness.
2. Evaluate Decker's introduction and conclusion. In what ways could they be improved?
3. Which paragraphs are particularly well developed? Which, if any, need further development?

Reacting to the Essay

1. How does Decker's interpretation of "The Secret Lion" compare with yours?
2. Evaluate Decker's perception of childhood and adolescence. Write a journal entry comparing his perception with your own.

CHAPTER 25

Essay Examinations and Portfolios

WRITING QUICK START

The cartoon on the opposite page humorously comments on the process of taking tests. No doubt you've been taking tests throughout school, and they are an important part of college classes as well.

Assume you are taking a short timed writing test. You have been asked to write about your experience taking tests. You might write about how you prepare for exams or share test-taking tips, for example. You have fifteen minutes to complete the writing test.

In completing the timed writing test, did you feel pressured by the fifteen-minute limit? How did you decide which assignment to complete? Did you have as much time as you would have liked to organize, plan, develop, and revise your ideas? Probably not.

Many college instructors use timed writings, essay exams, and portfolios to assess students' knowledge and skills. As you progress through college, you will take many essay exams, especially in advanced courses. In some courses you may be asked to collect and present samples of your work in a portfolio. See the accompanying box for two examples.

You may wonder why instructors give essay exams and other kinds of timed writing assignments. In many college courses, essay exams allow instructors to determine how well students have grasped important concepts and whether they can organize and integrate key concepts with other material. In addition, instructors realize that an essay exam requires students to use different and more advanced thinking skills than they use when taking a more objective type of exam, such as a multiple-choice test. For instance, an essay exam for a history course would require you to pull ideas together and focus on larger issues, perhaps analyzing historical trends or comparing two political figures. Timed writing assignments serve a similar purpose in a composition course. When you are given forty-five minutes to write a brief process analysis of something you know how to do, a short comparison of two television shows, or a description of someone you admire, your instructor wants to make sure you are learning how to write various types of essays and can do so quickly and efficiently. Finally, some colleges require students to demonstrate their writing expertise in a competency test given shortly after admission to the college, at the end of a writing course, or at the completion of a program of study.

This chapter will help you prepare for the timed essay writings you will encounter in college and in your career. Developing good study skills is a key to success on such exams. You will learn how to anticipate the types of questions instructors ask, how to organize your ideas quickly and efficiently, and how to work within the time constraints of essay exams. Although the chapter focuses on essay exams, the skills you learn here also apply to other kinds of timed writing assignments.

SCENES FROM COLLEGE AND THE WORKPLACE

- For a *business communication* class, you are asked to assemble a portfolio that illustrates your mastery of the six course objectives.

- For the midterm exam in your *philosophy of religion* course, you have one hour to complete the following essay: "Contrast the beliefs of Islam with those of either Judaism or Christianity."

Preparing for Essay Exams

Because essay exams require you to produce a written response, the best way to prepare for them is by organizing and writing. The following guidelines will help you prepare for such exams:

Write Study Sheets That Synthesize Information

Most essay exams require you to *synthesize*, or pull together, information. To prepare for this task, try to identify the key topics in a course, and write a study sheet for each main topic. Study sheets help you organize and consolidate complex or detailed information and give you brief topic outlines to study. To prepare a study sheet, draw on information from your textbook as well as from your class notes, in-class handouts, papers (note key topics), previous exams (look for emphasized topics), and assigned readings.

For more on synthesizing information, see Chapter 23, pp. 624–27.

You can organize a study sheet in a variety of ways. For example, you might draw a graphic organizer to create a visual study sheet, create a time line to connect historical events, write an outline to organize information, or construct a comparison-and-contrast chart to see relationships between different topics. Whatever method of organization you use for your study sheet, be sure to include key information about topics—definitions, facts, principles, theories, events, research studies, and the like.

Here is part of one student's study sheet for a speech communication course on the topic *audience analysis:*

SAMPLE STUDY SHEET

Topic: Audience Analysis

1. Demographic characteristics
   — Age and gender
   — Educational background (type and level of education)
   — Group membership (people who share similar interests or goals)
   — Social activities
   — Religious activities
   — Hobbies and sports
2. Psychological characteristics
   — Beliefs (about what is true or false, right or wrong)
   — Attitudes (positive or negative)
   — Values (standards for judging worth of thoughts and actions)

> **Exercise 25.1**
>
> *Use the preceding guidelines to prepare a study sheet on a general topic that you expect will be covered on an upcoming exam in one of your courses.*

Predict Essay Exam Questions

Once you prepare study sheets for a particular course, the next step is to predict questions that might be asked on an essay exam. Although essay exam questions usually focus on general topics, themes, or patterns, you will probably need to supply details in your response. For example, an essay question on an economics exam might ask you to compare and contrast the James-Lange and Cannon-Bard theories of motivation. Your answer would focus on the similarities and differences between these key theories, incorporating relevant details where necessary.

Use the following strategies to help you predict the types of questions you might be asked on an essay exam:

1. **Group topics into categories.** Review your textbook, class notes, and study sheets. Look to see how you can group topics into general subject areas or categories. For example, if you find several chapters that deal with kinship in your anthropology textbook, a question on kinship is likely to appear on one or more essay exams for the course.
2. **Study your course syllabus and objectives.** These documents contain important clues about what your instructor expects you to know at various points during the course.
3. **Study previous exams.** Notice which key ideas are emphasized in previous exams. If you had to explain the historical significance of the Boston Tea Party on your first American history exam, you can predict that you will be asked to explain the historical significance of other events on subsequent exams.
4. **Listen to your instructor's comments.** When your instructor announces or reviews material for an upcoming essay exam, pay close attention to what is said. He or she may reveal key topics or suggest areas that will be emphasized on the test.
5. **Draft some possible essay questions.** Use Table 25.1 (on p. 725) to help you draft possible essay questions using key verbs. The verb in a question affects the way you answer it. It takes time to learn how to predict exam questions, so don't get discouraged if at first you predict only one question correctly. Even if you predict none of the questions, the attempt to do so will help you learn the material.

> **Exercise 25.2**
>
> *Suppose your business marketing textbook includes a chapter with the following headings. Using the preceding guidelines for predicting essay exam questions and the key verbs in*

Table 25.1 (p. 725), write three possible questions that the course instructor might ask about the chapter material.

Textbook: *Marketing*, by William G. Nickels and Marian Burk Wood
Chapter: "Consumer Buying Behavior"
Headings:
   Marketing, Relationships, and Consumer Behavior
      Real People, Real Individuals
      Consumers as Moving Targets
   How Consumers Buy
      The Need-Recognition Stage
      The Information-Seeking Stage
      The Evaluation Stage
      The Purchase Stage
      The Postpurchase Evaluation Stage
      Involvement and the Purchase-Decision Process
   External Influences on Consumer Behavior
      Family and Household Influences
      Opinion Leaders and Word of Mouth
      Reference Groups
      Social Class
      Culture, Subculture, and Core Values
      Situational Influences
   Internal Influences on Consumer Behavior
      Perception
      Motivation
      Attitudes

Essay in Progress 1

For an upcoming essay exam in one of your courses, predict and write at least three possible questions your instructor might ask about the course material.

Draft Answers in Outline Form

After you predict several possible essay exam questions, the next step is to write a brief, rough outline of the information that answers each question. Be sure each outline responds to the *wording* of the question—that is, it should *explain, compare, describe*, or do whatever else the question asks (see Table 25.1 on p. 725). Writing a rough outline will strengthen your recall of the material. It will also save you time during the actual exam because you will have already spent some time thinking about, organizing, and writing about the material.

Here is a sample essay question and an informal outline written in response to it:

ESSAY QUESTION

Explain the ways in which material passes in and out of cells by crossing plasma membranes.

INFORMAL OUTLINE

Types of Transport

1. Passive—no use of cellular energy; random movement of molecules
   a. Diffusion—movement of molecules from areas of high concentration to areas of low concentration (example: open bottle of perfume, aroma spreads)
   b. Facilitated diffusion—similar to simple diffusion; differs in that some kinds of molecules are moved more easily than others (helped by carrier proteins in cell membrane)
   c. Osmosis—diffusion of water across membranes from area of lower to area of higher solute concentration

2. Active—requires cellular energy; usually movement against the concentration gradient
   a. Facilitated active transport—carrier molecules move ions across a membrane
   b. Endocytosis—material is surrounded by a plasma membrane and pinched off into a vacuole
   c. Exocytosis—cells expel materials

Essay in Progress 2

For one of the questions you predicted in Essay in Progress 1, prepare a brief informal outline in response to the question.

Reduce Informal Outlines to Key-Word Outlines

To help you recall your outline answer at the time of the exam, reduce it to a brief key-word outline or list of key topics. Here is a sample key-word outline for the essay question about cells:

KEY-WORD OUTLINE

Types of Transport

1. Passive
   — Diffusion
   — Facilitated diffusion
   — Osmosis

2. Active
   — Facilitated active transport
   — Endocytosis
   — Exocytosis

Essay in Progress 3
Reduce the outline answer you wrote in Essay in Progress 2 to a key-word outline.

Taking Essay Exams

Once you have done some preparation, you should be more confident about taking an essay exam. Although the time limit for an essay exam may make you feel somewhat pressured, remember that your classmates are working under the same conditions.

Some General Guidelines

Keep the following general guidelines in mind when you take essay exams:

1. **Arrive at the room where the exam is to be given a few minutes early.** You can use this time to collect your thoughts and get organized.
2. **Sit in the front of the room.** You will be less distracted and better able to see and hear the instructor as last-minute directions or corrections are announced.
3. **Read the directions carefully.** For example, some exams may direct you to answer only one of three questions, whereas other exams may ask you to answer all questions.
4. **Preview the exam and plan your time carefully.** Get a complete picture of the task at hand and then plan how you will complete the exam within the allotted time. For example, if you are given fifty minutes to complete an essay exam, spend roughly ten minutes planning, thirty minutes writing, and ten minutes editing, proofreading, and making last-minute changes. If an exam contains both objective and essay questions, do the objective questions first so that you have the remaining time to concentrate on the essay questions.
5. **Notice the point value of each question.** If your instructor assigns points to each question, use the point values to plan your time. For example, you would spend more time answering a thirty-point question than a ten-point question.
6. **Choose topics or questions carefully.** Often you will be given little or no choice of topic or question. If you do have a choice, choose the topics or answer the questions that you know the most about. If you are given a broad topic, such as a current social issue, narrow the topic to one you can write about in the specified amount of time.
7. **Answer the easiest question first.** Answering the easiest question first will boost your confidence and allow you to spend the remaining time working on the more difficult questions.
8. **Consider your audience and purpose.** For most essay exams, your instructor is your audience. Since your instructor is already knowledgeable about the topic, your purpose is to demonstrate what *you know* about the topic. Therefore, you should write thorough and complete answers, pretending that your instructor knows only what you tell him or her.

9. **Remember that your first draft is your final draft.** Plan on writing your first draft carefully and correctly so that it can serve as your final copy. You can always make minor changes and additions as you write or while you edit and proofread.

10. **Plan and organize your answer.** Because time is limited, your first response may be to start writing immediately. However, planning and organizing are especially important first steps because you will not have the opportunity to revise your essay. (If you usually write whatever comes to mind and then spend a great deal of time revising, you will need to modify your approach for essay exams.) Begin by writing a brief thesis statement. Then jot down the key supporting points and number them in the order you will present them. Leave space under each supporting point for your details. If the question is one you predicted earlier, write down your key-word outline. If an idea for an interesting introduction or an effective conclusion comes to mind, jot it down as well. As you write your answers, be sure to reserve enough time to reread your essay and correct surface errors.

Analyzing Essay Exam Questions

Essay exam questions are often concise, but if you read them closely, you will find that they *do* specifically tell you what to write about. Consider the following sample essay question from a sociology exam:

Choose a particular institution, define it, and identify its primary characteristics.

The question tells you exactly what to write about—*a particular institution*. In addition, the key verbs *define* and *identify* tell you how to approach the subject. For this essay question, then, you would give an accurate definition of an institution and discuss its primary characteristics.

Table 25.1 lists key verbs commonly used in essay exam questions along with sample questions and tips for answering them. As you study the list, notice that many of the verbs suggest a particular pattern of development. For example, *trace* suggests using a narrative sequence, and *justify* suggests using argumentation. For a more vague key verb such as *explain* or *discuss,* you might use a combination of patterns.

Writing Essay Answers

Since your first-draft essay exam is also your final draft, be sure to write in complete and grammatically correct sentences, to supply sufficient detail, and to follow a logical organization. For essay exams, instructors do not expect your writing to be as polished as it might be for an essay or research paper assignment. It is acceptable to cross out words or sentences neatly and to indicate corrections in spelling or grammar. If you

TABLE 25.1 Responding to Key Verbs in Essay Exam Questions

Key Verb	Sample Essay Question	Tips for Answering Questions
Compare	Compare the poetry of Judith Ortiz Cofer to that of Julia Alvarez.	Show how the poems are similar as well as different; use details and examples.
Contrast	Contrast classical and operant conditioning.	Show how they are different; use details and examples.
Define	Define *biofeedback* and describe its uses.	Give an accurate explanation of the term with enough detail to demonstrate that you understand it.
Discuss	Discuss the halo effect and give examples of its use.	Consider important characteristics and main points; include examples.
Evaluate	Evaluate the accomplishments of the feminist movement over the past fifty years.	Assess its merits, strengths, weaknesses, advantages, or limitations.
Explain	Explain the functions of amino acids.	Use facts and details to make the topic or concept clear and understandable.
Illustrate	Illustrate with examples from your experience how culture shapes human behavior.	Use examples that demonstrate a point or clarify an idea.
Justify	Justify laws outlawing smoking in federal buildings.	Give reasons and evidence that support an action, decision, or policy.
List	List the advantages and disadvantages of sales promotions.	List or discuss one by one; use most-to-least or least-to-most organization.
Summarize	Summarize Maslow's hierarchy of needs.	Briefly review all the major points.
Trace	Trace the life cycle of a typical household product.	Describe its development or progress in chronological order.

think of an idea to add, write the sentence at the top of your paper and draw an arrow to indicate where it should be inserted.

Essay exam answers tend to have brief introductions and conclusions. The introduction, for instance, may include only a thesis statement. If possible, include any necessary background information on the topic and write a conclusion only if the question seems to require a final evaluative statement.

If you run out of time on an essay exam, jot the unfinished portion of your outline at the end of the essay. Your instructor may give you partial credit for your ideas.

Writing Your Thesis Statement

For more on thesis statements, see Chapter 6, pp. 125–33.

Your thesis statement should be clear and direct, identify your subject, and suggest your approach to the topic. Often the thesis rephrases or answers the essay exam question. Consider the following examples:

Essay Exam Question	*Thesis Statement*
Explain how tides are produced in the earth's oceans. Account for seasonal variations.	The earth's gravitational forces are responsible for producing tides in the earth's oceans.
Distinguish between bureaucratic agencies and other government decision-making bodies.	Bureaucratic agencies are distinct from other government decision-making bodies because of their hierarchical organization, character and culture, and professionalism.

For some essay exam questions, your thesis should also suggest the organization of your essay. For example, if you are asked to explain the differences between primary and secondary groups, your thesis might be stated as follows: "Primary groups differ from secondary groups in their membership, purpose, level of interaction, and level of intimacy." Your essay, then, would be organized accordingly, discussing membership first, then purpose, and so forth.

Exercise 25.3

Write thesis statements for two of the following essay exam questions.

1. Define and illustrate the meaning of the term *freedom of the press.*
2. Distinguish between the medical care provided by private physicians and that provided by medical clinics.
3. Choose a recent television advertisement and describe its rational and emotional appeals.
4. Evaluate a current news program in terms of its breadth and depth of coverage, objectivity, and political and social viewpoints.

Developing Supporting Details

For more on topic sentences, see Chapter 8, pp. 167–70.

Write a separate paragraph for each of your key points. In an essay answer distinguishing primary from secondary groups, for example, you would devote one paragraph to each distinguishing feature—membership, purpose, level of interaction, and level of intimacy. The topic sentence for each paragraph should identify and briefly explain a key point. For example, a topic sentence for the first main point about groups might read like this: "Membership, or who belongs, is one factor that distinguishes primary from secondary groups." The rest of the paragraph would explain membership: what constitutes membership, what criteria are used to decide who belongs, and who decides. Whenever possible, supply examples to make it clear that you can apply the information you have learned. Keep in mind that on an essay exam your goal is to demonstrate your knowledge and understanding of the material.

Rereading and Proofreading Your Answer

Be sure to leave enough time to reread and proofread your essay answer. Begin by rereading the question to make sure you have answered all parts of it. Then reread your answer, checking it first for content. Add missing information, correct vague or unclear sentences, and add facts or details. Next, proofread for errors in spelling, punctuation, and grammar. Before taking an essay exam, check your error log and then evaluate your answer with those errors in mind. A neat, nearly error-free essay makes a positive impression on your instructor and identifies you as a serious, conscientious student. An error-free essay may also improve your grade.

For more on proofreading and on keeping an error log, see Chapter 10, pp. 121–22.

Essay in Progress 4
For the essay question you worked on in Essay in Progress 3, use the preceding guidelines to write a complete essay answer.

Students Write

The model essay exam response below was written by Ronald Robinson for his sociology course. As you read Ronald's essay, note that it has been annotated to identify key elements of its organization and content.

Essay Exam Response

ESSAY EXAM QUESTION
Distinguish between fads and fashions, explaining the characteristics of each type of group behavior and describing the phases each usually goes through.

Fashions and fads, types of collective group behavior, are distinct from one another in terms of their duration, their predictability, and the number of people involved. Each type follows a five-stage process of development.

Thesis statement

A fashion is a temporary trend in behavior or appearance that is followed by a relatively large number of people. Although the word *fashion* often refers to a style of dress, there are fashions in music, art, and literature as well. Trends in clothing fashions are often engineered by clothing designers, advertisers, and the media to create a particular "look." The hip-hop look is an example of a heavily promoted fashion. Fashions are more universally subscribed to than fads. Wearing athletic shoes as casual attire is a good example of a universal fashion.

Definition and characteristics of *fashion*

Definition and characteristics
of *fad*

A fad is a more temporary adoption of a particular behavior or look. Fads are in-group behaviors that often serve as identity markers for a group. Fads also tend to be adopted by smaller groups, often made up of people who want to appear different or unconventional. Unlike fashions, fads tend to be shorter-lived, less predictable, and less influenced by people outside the group. Examples of recent fads are bald heads, tattoos, and tongue piercings. Fads are usually harmless and have no long-range effects.

Description of 5-phase
process

Fashions and fads each follow a five-phase process of development. In the first phase, latency, the trend exists in the minds of a few people but shows little evidence of spreading. In the second phase, the trend spreads rapidly and reaches its peak. After that, the trend begins a slow decline (phase three). In the fourth phase, its newness is over and many users drop or abandon the trend. In its final phase, quiescence, nearly everyone has dropped the trend, and it is followed by only a few people.

Thinking Critically about Essay Exams

Read essay exam questions critically, approaching them from the viewpoint of the instructor. Try to discover the knowledge or skill that your instructor is attempting to assess by asking the question. Then, as you write your answer, make sure your response clearly demonstrates your knowledge or skill. For example, in posing the question "Discuss the issue of sexual behavior from the three major sociological perspectives," the instructor is assessing two things—how well you *understand* the three sociological perspectives and how successfully you can *apply* them to a particular issue (sexual behavior). First you would need to give a clear, complete, but brief definition of each perspective. Then you would explain how each of the three sociological perspectives approaches the issue of sexual behavior.

PORTFOLIOS

Creating a Writing Portfolio

A portfolio is a collection of materials that is representative of a person's work. It often demonstrates or exemplifies skill, talent, or proficiency. Architects create portfolios that contain drawings and photographs of buildings they have designed. Sculptors' portfolios may include photographs of their work, as well as copies of reviews, awards, or articles about their work. Similarly, your writing instructor may ask you to create a portfolio that represents your skill and proficiency as a writer. Think of your portfolio as a picture of your development as a writer over time.

Purposes of a Writing Portfolio

Usually a writing portfolio is assigned by your writing instructor to achieve one or more purposes. One purpose is assessment. Your instructor may use your collection of writing to evaluate your mastery of the objectives outlined in the course syllabus. That evaluation will become a part of your final grade in the course.

The second purpose is learning and self-assessment. Building a portfolio makes you think about yourself as a learner and as a writer. By building a writing portfolio, you can learn a great deal about the writing process, assess your strengths and weaknesses as a writer, and observe your own progress as you build writing proficiency. Think of building your writing portfolio as an opportunity to present yourself in the best possible way—highlighting the work you are proud of and demonstrating the skills you have mastered. It is also an opportunity, as you track your progress, to realize that your hard work in the course has paid off.

Deciding What to Include

Instructors often specify what their students' portfolios should include. If you are uncertain about what to include, be sure to ask your instructor for clarification. You might ask to see a sample of a portfolio that meets your instructor's expectations. Be sure you can answer each of the following questions:

- How many pieces of writing should I include? Are there limits?
- Should all writing done in the course be included, or am I allowed to choose what to include?
- What version(s) should be included—drafts, outlines, and revisions or just the final essay?
- What types of writing should be included? Should essays be based on personal experience, library or Internet research, or field research?
- Is the portfolio limited to essays, or can research notes, downloaded Web pages, or completed class exercises be included?
- Can writing from other courses or pieces of writing for nonacademic audiences (email, work-related correspondence, or service learning projects, for example) be included?
- How should the portfolio be organized?
- What type of introductory letter or essay is required? What length and format are appropriate?
- How much does the portfolio count in my grade?
- What is the due date, or is the portfolio to be submitted at various intervals throughout the term?
- How will it be graded? That is, is the grade based on improvement or only on the quality of the work included?

Using Your Course Syllabus as a Guide

Your course syllabus is an important guide that can help you decide what to include in your portfolio—especially if your instructor has given you choices in structuring and organizing it. Your course syllabus contains objectives. These are statements of what your instructor expects you to learn from the course. You can use several or all

For a sample syllabus, see Chapter 2, pp. 28–29.

of these to structure your portfolio. Suppose one objective states, "Students will develop prewriting strategies that accommodate their learning style." In your portfolio, then, you might include a copy of the results of the Learning Style Inventory (p. 35) and then show examples of your use of two or more prewriting strategies. If another objective states, "Students will demonstrate control over errors in sentence structure, spelling, and punctuation," you would want to include examples of essays in which you identified and corrected these types of errors. You might also include a copy of your error log and a list of exercises you completed using Exercise Central or other online resources.

Organizing Your Portfolio

Begin collecting materials for your portfolio as soon as you know it is required. If you wait until the due date to assemble what you need, you may have discarded or misplaced important prewriting, revision materials, or drafts of essays.

Begin by deciding whether you will keep track of materials for your portfolio using printed copies or electronic copies. If you are using printed copies, use a file folder or accordion folder divided into sections to separate your work. Keep everything associated with each writing assignment you complete. This includes the original assignment, prewriting, outlines, graphic organizers, and all drafts. If you are using sources, keep your notes, photocopies, or printouts of sources. Be sure to keep peer-review comments as well as papers with your instructor's comments.

If you are using an electronic system to collect materials for your portfolio, create a file system that will make it easy for you to locate all of your work. Be sure to make backup copies of your files on a CD. Keep a paper file for hard copies of materials such as research notes or peer-review comments that are not on your computer.

Your portfolio represents you. Be sure it is neat, complete, and carefully assembled. Use the following suggestions to present a well-organized portfolio that demonstrates that you have taken care in its preparation:

- Include a cover or title page that gives your name, course number, instructor's name, and date.
- Include a table of contents that identifies the elements in the portfolio and the page number on which each piece begins. Number the portfolio consecutively from beginning to end. Since your essays may already have page numbers, put the new page numbers in a different position or use a different color of ink.
- Attach earlier drafts of papers behind the final draft, clearly labeling each draft.
- Be sure each piece is dated so that your instructor can identify its place within your growth process.
- Label each piece, indicating what it is intended to demonstrate. For example, if an essay demonstrates your ability to use narration, be sure to label it as such.
- Plan the sequence of your portfolio. If your instructor has not expressed a preference, choose a method of organization that presents your work and skill development in the best possible way. If you are including two essays to demonstrate your effective use of narration, for example, you might present the better one first, thereby making the strongest possible first impression. If, on the other hand,

you are trying to show the growth in your ability to use narration, you might present the weaker one first.

Choosing Pieces to Include

One key to creating a successful portfolio is choosing the *right* pieces to include, assuming that you have a choice. The right pieces depend on what your portfolio is intended to demonstrate. If you are supposed to demonstrate growth, it is a mistake to include only your best papers. If you are supposed to demonstrate your ability to write for a variety of purposes and audiences, it would be a mistake to include only argumentative essays. If the length is unlimited, do not include everything; be selective and choose pieces that illustrate what your instructor wants you to evaluate. Use Table 25.2 to guide your selection.

TABLE 25.2 **Guidelines for Building a Writing Portfolio**	
If You Are Asked to . . .	What to Include
Demonstrate your growth as a writer	• Include weak papers from early in the semester and conclude with your best papers written toward the end of the semester. • You might also include an essay that demonstrates major changes from first to final draft.
Demonstrate your ability to approach writing as a process	• For several essays, include work you did for topic selection, generating ideas, drafting, revising, and proofreading. • Choose pieces that show your essay gradually developing and evolving as you worked; they should also show major changes in revised drafts. • Avoid pieces that were well developed in your early stages of writing and that required only final polishing.
Feature your best work of the semester	• Choose essays that solidly exemplify the method of organization you are using. • Use the revision flowcharts and the Evaluating Your Progress boxes in Chapters 10–17 and 19 to guide your selection.
Demonstrate your ability to write for a variety of audiences and purposes	• Review the section on audience and purpose in Chapter 5, p. 107. • Select pieces that are widely different. • Include non-course-related and nonacademic pieces, if allowed.
Demonstrate your ability to use library and Internet sources	• Review the appropriate sections of Chapters 21–23. • Choose an essay that uses both library and Internet sources rather than one or the other.

Writing the Introductory Letter or Essay

Most instructors expect you to include an essay or a letter that introduces your portfolio. It is often called a *reflective essay* or *letter* because in it you reflect on your development as a writer. This letter or essay is crucial to an effective portfolio, and you should spend a good amount of time composing it. In fact, you might begin thinking and making notes about it long before the portfolio is due, observing trends, problems, and patterns in your writing.

This essay is the key to the portfolio, since it reflects on and explains its contents. It should explain how your portfolio is organized and give an overview of what it includes. It also should explain *how* various items that you have placed in the portfolio demonstrate what you intend them to demonstrate. For example, if you have included two essays to illustrate your ability to write for a variety of audiences and purposes, then explain for whom and for what purpose each essay was written.

Your reflective letter may also include some or all of the following:

- An appraisal of what you have learned in the course, referring to specific materials included in the portfolio as evidence.
- A discussion of your strengths and weaknesses as a writer, again referring to portfolio materials that illustrate and explain your points.
- A discussion of your progress or development as a writer. Explain how you have changed, giving examples of new strategies you have learned. Point out examples of them in the portfolio.

Here are a few things to avoid when building your portfolio. Make sure you write about what you learned about *your* writing, not about writing in general. That is, do not repeat points from the book about the writing process. Instead, explain how you have used that information to become a better writer. Also, do not exaggerate your progress or try to say what you think the instructor wants to hear. Instead, be honest and forthright in assessing your progress. Finally, avoid flattery or praise of the instructor or the course. Most instructors will give you a separate opportunity to evaluate them and the courses they teach.

Here is a sample reflective essay written by Bryan Scott, a nursing student and former Marine, for his first-year writing course.

Students Write

The Portfolio Assignment

For your final assignment you will submit a portfolio containing the following:

- A table of contents listing the titles and page numbers of all included writing pieces
- A reflective essay that introduces your portfolio
- One series of writing pieces (prewriting, outlines, drafts) that demonstrates your ability to move successfully through the steps in the writing process

- At least two pieces of writing that demonstrate your growth as a writer
- One piece of writing done this term for another class
- Essays that demonstrate your ability to use various methods of organization
- A limited number of materials of your own choice

In your reflective essay, you are expected to include answers to the following questions:

1. What are your current strengths and weaknesses as a writer?
2. What specific writing skills have you developed?
3. How have you changed as a writer?
4. In what ways has your awareness of learning style improved your ability to write?
5. What critical reading and thinking skills have you learned, *or* in what ways have you strengthened your critical reading and thinking skills?

Sample Reflective Essay

TABLE OF CONTENTS

Bryan Scott

May 5, 2011

Final Portfolio

English 109

From the Marines to the Writing Classroom

    I enrolled in this course because it was a required course in my nursing curriculum, but I   1
can now say that I am glad that it was required. As a former Marine, I had little experience with
writing, other than writing letters home to my wife and parents. Now, as I prepare for a career
as a nurse, I realize that writing is an important communication skill. Writing reports about
patients, such as "Nursing Care Plan: Patient 4," requires me to present clear, precise, and ac-

curate information about patients and their care. Through this course I have learned to do so. Although I improved in almost every area of writing, my greatest improvements were in approaching writing as a process, moving from personal to informative writing, and developing an awareness of audience.

Through this course I have learned to view writing as a process rather than a "write-it-once-and–I–am–done" activity. As shown in the packet of writing for "The Wall at Sunset," I have discovered the value of prewriting as a way of coming up with ideas. Before I started writing this essay, I knew that visiting the Vietnam Veterans Memorial had been an emotional experience for me, but I found that mapping helped me define and organize my feelings. Since I am a spatial learner, I could visualize the wall and map my responses to seeing the names of other soldiers. My first draft in the packet demonstrates my ability to begin with a thesis statement and build ideas around it. My second draft shows how I added detail and arranged my impressions into an organized essay. My final draft shows my ability to catch most errors in spelling, grammar, and punctuation.

Moving from personal writing to informative writing was a valuable learning experience that is essential for my career. My first essay, "The Wall at Sunset," was a very personal account of my visit to the Vietnam Veterans Memorial, as was the essay "How the Marines Changed My Life," a personal account of life in the U.S. Marine Corps. While I had a lot to say about my own experiences, I found it difficult to write about topics that did not directly involve me. I found that learning to use sources, especially Internet sources, helped me get started with informative writing. By visiting news Web sites, doing Internet research, and reading blogs, I learned to move outside of myself and begin to think about and become interested in what other people were saying and thinking. My essay "Miracle in the Operating Room" demonstrates my ability to use sources, both print and Internet, to learn how kidney transplants are done.

As I moved from personal to informative writing, I found that the patterns of development provided a framework for developing and organizing informative writing. Process seemed to be an effective way to present information for the essay "Miracle in the Operating Room." My essay "Emotional Styles of Athletes" initially contained a lot of my own personal impressions (see the first draft that I have included), but by using classification, I was able to focus on characteristics of athletes rather than on my opinions of them.

Before I took this course, I had no idea that I should write differently for different audiences. My essay "How the Marines Changed My Life" was written for my classmates, many of whom had no military experience. I found I had to explain things about chain of command, regimentation, and living conditions--all things that I and other Marines are familiar with. In my case report for my nursing class, "Nursing Care Plan: Patient 4," my audience was other nurses and medical staff, even doctors. Because I was writing for a specialized audience, I could mention medical terms, procedures, and medications freely without defining them. However, in "Miracle in the Operating Room," I was writing for a general, nonspecialized audience, so I realized it was necessary to explain terms such as *dialysis*, *laparoscopy*, and *nephrectomy*. This essay and my nursing case report demonstrate my ability to write in a clear, direct, and concise manner in my chosen field for different audiences.

While I developed many strengths as a writer, I am still aware of many weaknesses. I have difficulty with descriptive writing; I just cannot come up with words to paint a visual picture as effectively as I would like. Fortunately, nursing will not require much creative description. I also have difficulty choosing a topic. Although I found the suggestions in our textbook helpful, I still feel as if I am overlooking important or useful topics. Finally, I have not benefited from peer review as much as others have. I still find myself uncomfortable when accepting criticism and revision ideas from other students. Perhaps my military training to look to authority for direction is still getting in the way.   6

As I developed strengths as a writer, I also became a more critical reader and thinker. I am enclosing my annotations for the professional essay "Bad Conduct, by the Numbers." These annotations demonstrate my ability to ask questions and challenge the author. I also found enlightening discussions in the text on connotative language, bias, and fact and opinion. These are things I had never thought much about, and now I find myself being aware of these things as I read.   7

Overall, by taking this course, I have become a more serious and aware writer and have come to regard writing as a rewarding challenge.   8

Note that Bryan organized his reflective essay using the principles of good writing he learned in the course. Within this organization, he was able to identify his strengths and weaknesses as a writer, discuss learning styles, and analyze his essays. Notice that Bryan identifies his strengths and weaknesses as a writer throughout the essay.

CHAPTER 26

Oral Presentations and Business Writing

WRITING QUICK START

The cartoon on the opposite page illustrates a common concern that many college students have about oral presentations — stage fright. This kind of nervousness disturbs many who are unpracticed in making speeches.

Write a paragraph exploring your attitudes about and experiences with making a speech or presentation. What are your concerns? What do you see as your strengths and weaknesses? What techniques have helped you overcome your own stage fright?

Many college professors use oral presentations to assess their students' abilities to understand and respond to a topic or issue. One professor has said, "If they can talk about it, I know they understand it." Others feel that the ability to make effective oral presentations is an important and marketable skill in all career fields. Still others find that students can learn effectively from one another and use oral presentations to enhance classroom instruction. Regardless of your instructor's reasons for assigning an oral presentation, learning to make an effective presentation is a valuable experience that will make you a more confident student and a more valued employee. In this chapter, you will learn to plan, organize, draft, rehearse, and deliver your presentation. You will also learn some basic points about how to use PowerPoint slides and prepare a Web-based presentation.

This chapter also offers an overview of writing for business. Regardless of your chosen major, your future jobs will probably involve written communication with others—clients, patients, supervisors, coworkers, vendors, financial institutions, and so forth. Success on the job depends largely on your ability to communicate clearly, correctly, and concisely. This chapter will show you how to prepare a résumé and write job application letters and memos. You will also learn how to use electronic media in business writing.

ORAL PRESENTATIONS

Giving Oral Presentations

Oral presentations are an important part of many college classes. In an ecology class, you may be asked to report on a local environmental problem. In a sociology class, you may have to summarize your findings from a survey about a campus issue. Presentations vary in type: You may express your own ideas, inform, or persuade. These purposes are similar to those you have learned for writing essays.

Effective presentations are important in academic situations and also in many jobs and careers. By learning to speak before groups, you will gain self-confidence and become a more effective communicator. As you work through this section, you will see that the steps you take in giving an oral presentation parallel the steps required in writing an essay—planning, organizing and drafting, rehearsing (similar to revising), and delivering (similar to the final submission of your essay).

SCENES FROM COLLEGE AND THE WORKPLACE

- For a *sociology class,* you are asked to conduct field research on college students' attitudes about a particular sociological trend and to report your findings to the class.

- As a *sales representative* for a Web site design company, you are required to create and give an oral presentation to a group of owners of restaurant chains to demonstrate how a Web site for a chain can increase its visibility and profitability.

Planning Your Presentation

The more carefully you plan your presentation, the more comfortable you will be in delivering it. Use the following steps.

Select Your Topic

Choosing a topic is as important for making a presentation as it is for writing an essay. The topic you choose should depend on the assignment. Make sure you understand the assignment and the type of speech you are to give. Is it to be informative or persuasive? Are visual aids permitted, encouraged, or required? Are you allowed to speak from an outline or note cards? What is the time limit? Also consider your audience, as you do when writing essays. What topics are important to your listeners and will sustain their interest? Here are a few suggestions for choosing a topic:

- **Choose a topic that is appropriate for your audience.** You might be interested in choosing a day-care center, but if your audience is mostly young college students, you may have difficulty sustaining their interest with a speech titled "How to Choose the Best Day-Care Center."
- **Choose a topic of value.** Your topic should be worthwhile or meaningful to your audience. Trivial topics such as how to create a particular hairstyle or a report about characters on a soap opera may not have sufficient merit for college classrooms.
- **Choose a narrow topic.** As in writing, if you choose a topic that is too broad, you will have too much to say in the allotted time or may resort to generalities that lack supporting evidence.
- **Choose a topic that you find interesting or know something about.** You will find it easier to exude and generate enthusiasm if you are speaking about a topic that is familiar and that you enjoy.

Identify Your Purpose

As when you are writing, first determine if your purpose is to inform or persuade. Then more carefully define your purpose. For an informative speech, what information do you want to convey? If your topic is wrestling, do you want to explain its popularity, demonstrate several wrestling holds, or discuss it as a collegiate sport? If your purpose is to persuade, do you want to argue values, encourage action, or change your audience members' thinking or beliefs?

Research Your Topic

As you would for an essay, unless your presentation is to be based on your personal knowledge or experience, you will need to research your topic. As you give your speech, be sure to mention your sources. You might mention the author, the work, or both—whatever is meaningful and adds credibility to your presentation. If you use quotations, avoid tedious expressions such as "I quote here" or "I want to quote an example." Instead, integrate your quotations into your speech as you would quotations into an essay.

For more information on researching, see Chapters 21 and 22.

For more information on integrating quotations, see Chapter 23, pp. 632–33.

Organizing and Drafting Your Presentation

Develop a Thesis and Identify Supporting Ideas

Once you have read about your topic, you are ready to draft a thesis statement and collect information that supports it. Again, these processes parallel those you have been using to write an essay. Be sure to include a variety of evidence, considering the types that would appeal to your audience. When you write an essay, your readers can reread if they miss a point. When you give an oral presentation, your listeners do not have that option, so reiterate your thesis frequently to make your presentation easier to follow.

Organize Your Speech

Using a method of organization will make your speech easier to follow and easier for you to present. By grouping your ideas together, you will be able to remember them better. If you are using classification to organize a speech titled "Types of Procrastinators," you can remember that you have four main categories, with descriptive details to explain each. Be sure to use plenty of transitions that signal your organization to ensure that your listeners don't get lost.

Use Appropriate Visuals

Visuals add interest to your presentation and can be used to reinforce your message and make your ideas clear and concrete. You may also find that using a visual aid builds your confidence and lessens apprehension. Presentation aids seem to relax speakers and distract them from thinking about themselves and how they look. A wide range of presentation aids are available, including charts, maps, photographs, tapes, CDs, videotapes, flip charts, and Microsoft PowerPoint presentations. Ask your instructor what is permissible and what media are available for classroom use.

Plan Your Introduction and Conclusion

For more information on introductions, see Chapter 7, pp. 153–56.

Your introduction should grab your audience's attention, introduce your topic, and establish a relationship between you and your audience. You can capture your reader's interest and introduce your topic in many of the same ways you do when you write essays. To build a relationship with your audience, try to make connections with them. You might mention others who are present; refer to a shared situation (a previous class or another student's speech); or establish common ground by referring to a well-known event, personality, or campus issue.

Your conclusion is a crucial part of your presentation because it is your last opportunity to leave a strong impression on your audience. Your conclusion should summarize your speech and let the audience know your presentation is ending, but it should also remind listeners of the importance of your topic. Consider closing your presentation with a powerful quotation or anecdote that reinforces your main point.

Using PowerPoint and Other Visual Aids

Visual aids add interest to your presentation, reinforce your message, and make your ideas clear and concrete. You may also find that using visual aids builds your confidence and lessens feelings of apprehension by distracting you from thinking about yourself and how you feel. Ask your instructor what is permissible and what media are available for classroom use. Below are some ideas for enhancing your presentation.

Objects and Media

Visual aids can include photographs, tapes, CDs, and even objects. Photographs can be used to call to mind a familiar object or a work of art. Tapes and CDs can allow your audience to hear a portion of an interview or a song you have been discussing. Related objects can make a discussion more real. (For example, if you were giving a speech about in-line skating, you might bring your skates.)

PowerPoint

PowerPoint, a popular presentation software, allows you to create and present slides to accompany your presentation. PowerPoint slides can remind your audience about your main points. You can also use PowerPoint to present multimedia evidence in support of your claims by embedding audio, video, and image files in your slides. The following tips will help you use PowerPoint effectively:

- **Use PowerPoint to aid understanding.** Use slides to emphasize key words or concepts or to provide an outline so your audience can follow your main points. The slides should help the audience remember key ideas, not distract them from what you are saying.
- **Use slides to display visuals and graphics.** Photos, cartoons, graphics, and embedded videos can convey your message in a memorable way. They also keep your audience interested and alert. Remember to keep graphics simple so the audience can take them in at a glance and to use images only when they are relevant to the point you are making.
- **Format your slides effectively.** Use a large font (usually 24-point font or greater) so text can be read easily by everyone in the audience. Too much content is difficult to read and will cause people to focus more on the slides than on what you are saying. A good rule of thumb is to use no more than six bullet points per slide, with no more than six words per bullet point.
- **Keep slides simple.** Complex effects and a variety of colors can make slides distracting and difficult to read. A light background with dark text and just a few animation schemes (how text enters and leaves a slide) usually work best.
- **Edit your slides.** Check for spelling, grammar, formatting, and typos. Be sure to run the entire slide show for yourself before presenting it.

Below are two sample PowerPoint slides prepared by a sales representative for a Web design company to accompany oral presentations to clients. He shows the slide on the left when he discusses how to design a Web site that can be located easily by search engines. He uses the slide on the right to emphasize two key features of Web site design.

Rehearsing Your Presentation

Practicing your speech is the key to comfortable and effective delivery. After you have drafted and organized your ideas, prepare an outline or note cards that you can use to guide your presentation. Use the following rehearsal tips:

- **Practice giving the entire speech, not just parts.** Rehearse at least three or four times. Try to improve your speech during each rehearsal.
- **Time yourself.** If you are over or seriously under the time limit, make necessary cuts or additions.
- **If possible, rehearse the speech in the room in which you will give it.**
- **Rehearse in front of an audience of a few friends or classmates.** Ask them for constructive criticism. Some students videotape their presentations to build their confidence and look for areas that need improvement.

Overcoming Apprehension

Many students are nervous about making oral presentations to their classmates. Often called "stage fright," this apprehension is normal and natural but also easily overcome. The first step to overcoming apprehension is to understand its causes.

Some speakers are apprehensive because they feel conspicuous—at the center of attention. Others feel they are competing with other, better speakers in the class. Still others are apprehensive because the task is new and they have never done it before. You can often overcome these feelings using the following suggestions:

- If you feel conspicuous, try to imagine that you are talking to one friend or one friendly and supportive classmate.
- To reduce the newness of the task, be sure to practice your speech. (See the previous section on rehearsal.)
- Preparation—knowing you have put together a solid, interesting presentation—can build your self-confidence and lessen your sense of competition.

Use Visualization to Enhance Your Performance

Many athletes, actors, and musicians use the technique of visualization to enhance their performances. Performance visualization involves imagining yourself successfully completing a task. For an oral presentation, visualize yourself successfully making the presentation. Create a mental videotape. It should begin with your arrival at the classroom and take you through each step—confidently walking to the front of the room, beginning your speech, engaging your audience, handling your notes, and so on. Be sure to visualize the presentation positively; avoid negative thoughts. Now you have the image of yourself as a successful speaker. You know what it looks and feels like to give an effective presentation. Review your visualized performance often, especially on the day of your presentation. As you give your presentation, try to model the look and feel of your visualization.

Use Desensitization

Desensitization is a method of overcoming fears by gradually building up your tolerance of the feared situation or object. If someone is afraid of snakes, for example, a desensitization therapist might begin by showing the person a photograph, then a videotape, then a small snake at a distance, and so forth, gradually building up the person's exposure time and tolerance. You can do the same thing to overcome your apprehension of oral presentations by gradually building up to making presentations. Begin by asking a question in class. When you are comfortable with that, move to answering questions in class. Then you might move toward speaking in front of small groups (practicing your speech on a group of friends, for example). Each step you take makes the next one easier. Eventually you will become more comfortable with public speaking and ready to make a presentation to the class.

Delivering an Effective Presentation

The delivery of your presentation ultimately determines its effectiveness. Use the suggestions below, as well as Table 26.1, to improve the delivery of your presentation.

- **Avoid using too many notes or a detailed outline.** Instead, construct a key-word outline that will remind you of major points in the order you wish to present them.
- **Make eye contact with your audience.** Make them part of your presentation.
- **Move around a little rather than standing stiffly.** Use gestures to add an expressive quality to your presentation.
- **Speak slowly.** It is a common mistake to speak too fast. Your audience may miss your main points and lose interest in your presentation.

Preparing a Web-Based Presentation

At some point in your education or career, you may use an online meeting application, such as GoToMeeting or Glance, which allows you to have virtual meetings with instructors, colleagues, clients, and vendors. These applications allow others to view what you have on your computer screen, so you can pull up Word documents, spreadsheets, PowerPoint presentations, and anything else for everyone to look at together in

TABLE 26.1 Frequently Asked Questions for Making Presentations

Question	Suggested Solutions
What should I do if I go blank?	• Refer to your notes or index cards. • Ask if there are any questions. Even if no one asks any, the pause will give you time to regroup your ideas.
What should I do if classmates are restless, uninterested, or even rude?	• Make eye contact with as many members of the class as possible as you speak. • For a particularly troublesome person, you might lengthen your eye contact. • Change the tone or pitch of your voice. • Try to make your speech more engaging by asking questions or using personal examples.
What should I do if I skip over or forget to include an important part of the presentation?	• Go back and add it in. Say something like, "I neglected to mention . . . " and present the portion you skipped.
What if I realize that my speech will be too short or too long?	• If you realize it will be too short, try to add examples, anecdotes, or more detailed information. • If you realize it will be too long, cut out examples or summarize instead of fully explaining sections that are less important.

real time. You may communicate by phone, by Skype, or via an online instant messenger system through the application.

In addition to the tips above about giving an effective presentation and using PowerPoint, the following tips will help you give an effective Web-based presentation:

- **Become familiar with the technology before your presentation.** Your audience may become restless if you cannot resolve technical difficulties.
- **Review all documents and materials prior to the meeting.** Be sure you know where to find the documents you need so you can display them with ease.
- **Prepare thoroughly, but be ready to adjust your presentation in response to questions from the audience.** You should know the content well enough to respond to a question or comment that draws you away from your prepared remarks.
- **Turn off all notifications and programs that are running on your computer.** It would be unprofessional if an instant message from a friend popped up on your screen while you were making your presentation.

Business Writing

Business writing will be an important part of your life after college. Good business writing is concise and correct. It is often more direct and to the point than some forms of academic or personal writing. The most important thing to keep in mind when writing business documents is that you will be judged based on them, so prepare materials that will present you and your accomplishments in the best light possible.

Preparing a Résumé and Job Application Letter

A résumé is a complete listing of all of your education, training, and work experience, written in an easy-to-read format. A job application (or cover) letter summarizes your qualifications and experience and convinces the employer that you are an excellent candidate for the opening. Together, the résumé and job application letter will determine whether an employer will interview you, so tailor them to the job you are applying for. Make sure they sell your credentials and experience effectively by being accurate, clear, and concise and by avoiding errors of grammar, punctuation, mechanics, and spelling.

Follow these tips when preparing your résumé:

For an example of a résumé, see p. 748.

- **Use a simple, easy-to-read design.** Simple is best. Print your résumé on unlined, white, 8½- × 11-inch paper, and leave one-inch margins on all sides. Do not include graphics, colors, multiple columns, or elaborate underlining and formatting. For résumés submitted online, avoid formatting with columns or tabs, and avoid special characters that may become corrupted.
- **Display your name, address, and contact information at the top of the page.** Make sure to check that your contact information is correct. (A computer's spellcheck function will not identify most mistakes.)
- **Fit your résumé onto a single page whenever possible.** Use only one side of an 8½- × 11-inch sheet of paper. Write clearly and concisely, and use categories (such as "Education," "Experience," and "Skills") so that potential employers can scan your résumé quickly.
- **Use key words.** Résumés may be scanned electronically for key words, so always use nouns ("supervisor" instead of "supervised other employees") to help employers match your skills and experience with their job database.
- **Include information about your education, job experience, awards, and any special skills you have.** Include dates you attended school or received a degree. Be sure to list your education and experience in reverse chronological order (most recent first).
- **Specify how the employer can obtain your references.** This is usually done by stating "References are available on request."

Follow these tips when writing a job application letter:

For a sample job application letter, see p. 749.

- **Use unlined, white, 8½- × 11-inch paper.** Avoid colored paper or paper with a design.
- **Use letterhead or list your address at the top of the page.** The date should appear below your address, and the address of the person to whom you are writing should appear below the date.

- **Use standard business formats.** Block style business letters have one-inch margins on all sides and are single-spaced, with an extra line space between paragraphs. All type is aligned at the left edge of the page. (The sample job application letter on page 749 is in block style.)
- **Begin the letter with a salutation ("Dear").** Follow this with "Mr." or "Ms." and then the person's last name. If you do not know to whom you should send your résumé, call the company to find out.
- **Identify the job you are applying for in the opening paragraph.** You may indicate where you learned about the position or where it was posted or listed.
- **Write the body of the letter in paragraph format.** Your letter should not repeat all the information in your résumé. Instead, use the letter to explain what you can bring to the job, describing the particular aspects of your education, job experience, or skills that make you specially qualified. You will need to revise your letter for different jobs, depending on what the requirements, responsibilities, and job duties are.
- **Make yourself available for an interview.** Indicate that you are available at the employer's convenience, or specify when you are available. Be sure to include email and telephone contact information so you are easy to reach.
- **End with a closing.** The most common are "Yours truly" or "Sincerely." Leave a few blank lines for your signature, and then type your name (first and last names).

If you are applying for a job via email, follow the email guidelines described on page 747. As with a job application letter, your email should begin with "Dear Mr. _____:" or "Dear Ms. ____:" and conclude with "Sincerely" or "Yours truly" and your name. Include your résumé as an attachment.

Writing a Memo

For a sample memo, see p. 750.

A memorandum (memo) is a piece of correspondence written to others within your organization. Memos ask or answer a question, provide information, offer some kind of evaluation, or provide a summary of a discussion or meeting. Email messages have taken the place of most formal memos, but some organizations still use them. Follow these suggestions when creating memos:

- **Begin the memo by listing on separate lines the recipient, the sender, the date, and the subject of the memo.** Be sure the subject line (often indicated by "Re:") accurately reflects the main point of the memo.
- **State the purpose of the memo in the first line.** Use the first paragraph to explain your answer to the question or issue at hand. Use the rest of the memo to explain your reasoning or to offer evidence for your position.
- **Use headings or bulleted or numbered lists, and keep the memo short and concise.** Brevity is important. A memo is not the place for lengthy discussion or analysis. Summarize information when including it in the memo. Use headings or lists so readers can scan the memo for pertinent information.
- **Close the memo by listing who has been copied on it.** As with an email message, copy only those who need to be kept apprised.

Using Electronic Media for Business Writing

Business writing is no longer limited to résumés, job application letters, and memos. In your career, you will likely use other electronic media for communication, including email, Facebook, Twitter, text messages, instant messages, and interoffice information management systems. The material below will introduce you to effective strategies for writing in all these electronic media.

Business Email

Email is the most common way to communicate with other employees within a company as well as with customers and vendors. You will likely use email every day in your career, so it is essential that you learn how to use it professionally and clearly. The rules governing writing an effective memo (p. 746) apply to email messages as well. In addition, remember these tips when writing email:

For a sample business email message, see p. 751.

- **Email is real business correspondence and should be written in complete words and sentences and with a formal tone.** Avoid online slang (such as *LoL* and *OMG*) and emoticons (such as the smiley face), avoid writing in all capital or all lowercase letters, and always reread email messages to be sure the tone is cordial and professional.
- **Email communications can easily be passed on to others.** Do not say something in an email that you would not say to your entire company and all your clients.
- **Use a specific and relevant subject line.** Using a specific and relevant subject line is important in memos, but it is even more important when writing emails, where hitting "Reply" can leave you with an irrelevant subject line. An email can easily be lost in an inbox if the subject line does not clearly reference a client, case number, file name, or other specific identifier.
- **Copy only those people who need to be informed about the topic of the email.** Do not automatically carbon copy (cc) your boss or everyone in your company on every email, and avoid "Reply all" unless the content of your reply is truly relevant to "all."
- **Remember to attach relevant files to the email.** It makes more work for everyone else if an attachment is forgotten.
- **Use an automatic signature file in each email.** An automatic signature should include your name, title, company address, and telephone and fax numbers so that people can contact you easily.

Other Electronic Media for Business

Many of the rules for writing memos and emails apply to writing in other electronic media as well. Communicate concisely and professionally, and proofread your messages before sending. It is acceptable to use abbreviations in this kind of communication, but do so only if your recipient will understand them. Most important, remember at all times that you are representing your employer and serving as the voice of your company. Do not say anything in a message that you would be embarrassed to have repeated to other colleagues or clients.

Students Write

The following résumé, job application letter, memo, and business email provide useful models for the kinds of writing you will do as you move from college to your chosen profession. As you read these models, study the annotations to identify the key characteristics of each type of writing.

Sample Résumé

Contact information is displayed at the top of the page.

Micah Jackson

3912 Elm Street

Des Moines, IA 42156

555-666-7777

mjackson@gmail.com

Boldfaced headings are used to make the résumé easy to read.

Position Desired

Full-time legal assistant

Reverse chronological order is used for information under the Education and Experience headings, so most recent items are listed first.

Education

2010–2012: Eastern Iowa Community College, Legal Assistant A.A.S. degree, May 2012. Coursework: legal research, legal writing, business communication, word processing, legal office billing, transcription

2007–2010: Regents diploma, Kennedy Central High School

Key words (nouns) are used so that skills and experience match words in the employer's electronic job database.

Employment History

2011–present: Photographer's Assistant, Jane G. Matthews Photography
Responsibilities include billing, customer service, selling packages, answering phones, packaging orders, and assisting with shoots.

2009–2011: Associate, Walmart
Responsibilities included cashing and stocking shelves.

Résumé was proofread carefully to correct errors of spelling, punctuation, and capitalization.

Special Skills

Fluent in Spanish

Excellent customer service skills

References

Available on request

Sample Job Application Letter

31 Maple Drive
Stony, NY 13331

June 19, 2011

Juanita Alvarez
Northtown Animal Hospital
5513 Main St.
San Diego, CA 34561

Dear Ms. Alvarez:

In response to your ad on Monster.com, I am applying for the position of full-time veterinary assistant at Northtown Animal Hospital.

I recently completed my Veterinary Technician A.A.S. degree at Copper Mountain Community College and obtained my state certification. My coursework included animal anatomy, animal nutrition, veterinary office management, medical mathematics, animal reproduction, animal grooming, and diagnostic imaging.

In addition, I have been a volunteer at the Copper Mountain SPCA for three years, where I assist with feeding, grooming, cleaning, and visitor management. I also work part-time at Jonelle's Dog Salon as a shampoo specialist.

My coursework in animal grooming and experience at the SPCA and at a dog salon allow me to perform normal veterinary technician work and also to perform grooming services for your clients.

As my enclosed résumé indicates, my education and experience working with animals have prepared me well for the opening you have.

I am available for an interview at your convenience and will gladly supply additional references as needed. Please call me at 555-121-1212 or email me at BHuan715@gmail.com.

Sincerely,

Blake Huan

Blake Huan

Standard block style is used (double line space between paragraphs, type aligned at left edge).

The return address appears at the top of the page.

The inside address follows the date.

The letter begins with a salutation ("Dear Ms. Alvarez:").

The opening paragraph identifies the position being applied for.

The second, third, and fourth paragraphs mention specific aspects of Blake's education and experience, not everything in the résumé.

The last paragraph provides contact information and indicates the availability of references.

The letter ends with a standard closing: "Sincerely."

The signature follows the closing, and the name is typed below.

Sample Memo

Classic Carpet Company

TO: Clarice Brown, Director of Sales

FROM: Rajat Dmeeni, District 5

DATE: September 2, 2012

RE: Reasons for the Failure of the Three Room Promotion

Since its introduction in 2011, the Three Room Promotion has been unsuccessful in District 5 and has not improved the sales of our Classic Carpet. Discussions with customers suggest three reasons for the failure of this program:

1. The Three Room Promotion has not been effectively advertised. Most customers who come into the store have not heard of it and have already made up their minds about how much carpeting they need to buy. The signs in the storefront windows are too small for people to read from the street. Radio advertising has been sporadic and not at peak listening times.

2. Although the Three Room Promotion is competitively priced, the limitations on color and style mean that it is not appealing to all customers. I have had several customers come in and select carpet only to be surprised to learn their selection was not included in the promotion.

3. The Three Room Promotion offers a competitive price for the carpet itself but does not include the cost of carpet padding and installation, which are major concerns to our customers. Some competitors offer free installation and free padding with their specials.

Copies: J. Westin, Director of Marketing

              M. Ngige, Customer Service Manager

Recipient, sender, date, and subject ("Re") are identified.

The subject line accurately reflects the memo's main point.

The purpose of the memo is stated in the first paragraph.

Standard block style is used (double line space between paragraphs, type aligned at left edge).

A numbered list is used to help readers scan for information.

The names of people receiving copies are listed at the end of the memo.

Sample Business Email

```
Klenk File - Message                                    _  □  X

File   Edit   View   Insert   Format   Tools   Table   Window   Help        ×

Send                              Options...  ▼  HTML        ▼

To...       Ryan Thompson

Cc...

Subject:    Klenk File

Attach...   Klenk billing_corrected.doc (24 KB)        Attachment Options...

Calibri              ▼  10  ▼  A  ▼  B  I  U

Attached please find the corrected billing for this client. My research indicated
that we overbilled the project for lumber. I have included the correct numbers.
Let me know if you need anything else on this matter.


Kaitlyn Botano, Office Assistant
Thompson Builders
345 West End Avenue
Pittsburgh, PA 12231
Phone: 555-212-2121
Fax: 555-212-2122
```

The subject line accurately reflects the memo's main point.

The file mentioned in the email message is attached.

The writer uses correct grammar, spelling, and punctuation and writes formally, as is appropriate in business correspondence.

An automatic signature file—including the sender's complete name, title, company, address, and telephone and fax numbers—is included.

PART 7

Handbook

Writing Problems and How to Correct Them

HANDBOOK CONTENTS

1 Parts of Speech

Each word in a sentence acts as one of eight parts of speech: *nouns, pronouns, verbs, adjectives, adverbs, conjunctions, prepositions,* and *interjections.* These are the building blocks of our language. Often, to revise your writing or to correct sentence errors, you need to understand how a word or phrase functions in a particular sentence.

1a Nouns

A **noun** names a person (*waiter, girlfriend*), a place (*classroom, beach*), a thing (*textbook, computer*), or an idea (*excitement, beauty*). **Proper nouns** name specific people (*Professor Wainwright*), places (*Texas*), things (*Game Boy*), or ideas (*Marxism*) and are always capitalized.

- *James* drove to *Williamsville* in a *Toyota* in *March.*

Common nouns name one or more of a general class or type of person, place, thing, or idea and are not capitalized.

- A *holiday* is a *celebration* of an *event.*

Collective nouns name groups: *class, jury, team.* **Concrete nouns** name tangible things that can be tasted, seen, touched, smelled, or heard: *instructor, exam, desk.* **Abstract nouns** name ideas, qualities, beliefs, and conditions: *love, faith, trust.*

Most nouns express **number** and can be singular or plural: *one test, two tests; one pen, five pens.* **Count nouns** name items that can be counted. Count nouns can be made plural, usually by adding *-s* or *-es: one telephone, three telephones; one speech, ten speeches.* Some count nouns form their plurals in an irregular way: *mouse, mice; goose, geese.* **Noncount nouns**—such as *water, anger, courage,* and *knowledge*—name ideas or entities that cannot be counted. Most noncount nouns do not have a plural form. (See Section 26 of this Handbook for more on count and noncount nouns.)

For exercises on nouns, refer to the Parts of Speech section of Exercise Central at www.bedfordstmartins .com/successfulcollege.

1b Pronouns

Pronouns are words that take the place of nouns. The noun or pronoun to which a pronoun refers is called the pronoun's **antecedent**.

- Because the *researcher* developed a new drug, *she* became famous.
  The noun *researcher* is the antecedent of the pronoun *she.*

Personal pronouns name specific people, places, or things. Personal pronouns come in three cases that describe a pronoun's function in a sentence. The **subjective case** indicates that a pronoun is a subject—a doer of an action (*I, you, he, she, it, we, they*).

■ *She* asked questions about the job.

The **objective case** indicates that a pronoun is an object—a receiver of an action (*me, you, him, her, it, us, them*).

■ The career counselor has been advising *her*.

The **possessive case** indicates ownership or belonging (*my, mine, your, yours, his, her, hers, its, our, ours, your, yours, their, theirs*).

■ *His* enthusiasm for the company does not match *theirs*.

Personal pronouns also indicate **person**, to distinguish among the speaker (first person: *I, we*), the person spoken to (second person: *you*), and the person or thing spoken about (third person: *he, she, it, they*). The **gender** of personal pronouns identifies them as masculine (*he, him*), feminine (*she, her*), or neuter (*it*). Personal pronouns also show **number**: singular (one person or thing: *I, you, he, she, it*) or plural (more than one person or thing: *we, you, they*).

Demonstrative pronouns point out a particular person or thing: *this, that, these*, and *those*. A demonstrative pronoun can be used as an adjective to describe a noun.

■ *These* research procedures are questionable.

Reflexive pronouns indicate that a subject performs actions to, for, or on itself. Reflexive pronouns end in *-self* or *-selves*.

	Singular	*Plural*
First person	myself	ourselves
Second person	yourself	yourselves
Third person	himself	themselves
	herself	
	itself	

■ We allowed *ourselves* two hours to complete the experiment.

Intensive pronouns have the same forms as reflexive pronouns and are used to emphasize their antecedents.

■ Not even the computer programmer *herself* could correct the error.

Reflexive and intensive pronouns cannot be used as the subject of a sentence, and their antecedents must appear in the same sentence as the pronoun.

INCORRECT	*Myself* disagreed with the speaker's proposal, despite my sympathy with the movement.
CORRECT	*I myself* disagreed with the speaker's proposal, despite my sympathy with the movement.

Interrogative pronouns introduce or ask a question.

REFER TO PEOPLE	who, whoever, whom, whomever, whose
REFER TO THINGS	what, which

■ *Who* will pay the bill?

Relative pronouns introduce **dependent clauses** that function as adjectives. Relative pronouns refer back to a noun or pronoun that the clause modifies.

> A **dependent clause** contains a subject and a verb but does not express a complete thought.

REFER TO PEOPLE	who, whoever, whom, whomever, whose
REFER TO THINGS	that, what, whatever, which, whose

■ The research *that* caused the literacy-test controversy was outdated.

■ Sylvia Plath was married to Ted Hughes, *who* later became poet laureate of England.

Indefinite pronouns do not refer to specific nouns; they refer to people, places, or things in general (*everyone, anywhere, everything*). Commonly used indefinite pronouns include the following:

Singular

another	either	nobody	somebody
anybody	enough	none	someone
anyone	everybody	no one	something
anything	everyone	nothing	
anywhere	everything	one	
each	neither	other	

Plural

both	many	several
few	others	

■ Hardly *anyone* had heard of the Sapir-Wharf hypothesis.

■ Although a number of psychologists have researched brain dominance, *few* have related it to learning style.

Several indefinite pronouns, such as *all*, *any*, *more*, *most*, *some*, and *none*, can be either singular or plural, depending on their antecedent (see 5e).

The **reciprocal pronouns** *each other* and *one another* indicate an interchange of information or physical objects between two or more parties.

For exercises on pronouns, refer to the Parts of Speech section of Exercise Central at www.bedfordstmartins .com/successfulcollege.

- **The debate semifinalists congratulated each other on their scores.**

See Section 7 of the Handbook for more on pronoun usage.

1c Verbs

Verbs show action (*read*, *study*), occurrence (*become*, *happen*), or a state of being (*be*, *feel*). There are three types of verbs: action verbs, linking verbs, and helping verbs (also called auxiliary verbs).

Action verbs express physical or mental activities.

- My hair *grew* longer and longer.
- Amelia *thought* her answer was correct.

Action verbs may be either transitive or intransitive. A **transitive verb** (TV) has a **direct object** (DO) that receives the action and completes the meaning of the sentence. (In the examples, S stands for *subject*.)

- Juan *wrote* lyrics for songs.

An **intransitive verb** (IV) does not need a direct object to complete the meaning of the sentence.

- The lights *flickered*.

Some verbs can be either transitive or intransitive, depending on how they are used in a sentence.

| INTRANSITIVE | The student *wrote* quickly. |
| TRANSITIVE | The student *wrote* a paper on hypnotism. |

Linking verbs show existence, explaining what something is, was, or will become. A linking verb connects a word to words that describe it.

- Dr. Lopez *is* the new college president.
- Their answers *were* evasive.

The forms of the verb *be* (*am, is, are, was, were, be, being, been*) are linking verbs. Some action verbs can also function as linking verbs. These include *appear, become, feel, grow, look, prove, remain, seem, smell, sound, stay,* and *taste.*

■ The sky *grew* dark.

■ Something in the kitchen *smells* delicious.

Helping verbs, also called **auxiliary verbs**, are used along with action or linking verbs to indicate tense, mood, or voice or to add further information. A **verb phrase** is a combination of one or more helping verbs and a main verb.

SIMPLE VERB	The newspaper *reports* the incident.
SIMPLE VERB + HELPING VERB	The newspaper *should report* the incident.

Helping verbs include the different forms of *do, be,* and *have* (which can also serve as main verbs in a sentence) along with *can, could, may, might, must, shall, should, will,* and *would.*

Verb Forms

All verbs except *be* have five forms: the base form, the past tense, the past participle, the present participle, and the *-s* form for the present tense when the subject is singular and in the third person.

The first three forms are called the verb's principal parts. The base form is the form of the verb as it appears in the dictionary: *review, study, prepare.* For regular verbs, the past tense and past participle are formed by adding *-d* or *-ed* to the base form. For regular verbs ending in *y*, the *y* is changed to *i: rely, relied.* For one-syllable regular verbs ending in a vowel plus a consonant, the consonant is doubled: *plan, planned* (see 25c).

	Regular	*Irregular*
Base form	walk	run
Past tense	walked	ran
Past participle	walked	run
Present participle	walking	running
-s form	walks	runs

Irregular verbs follow no set pattern to form their past tense and past participle.

Forms of Common Irregular Verbs

Base Form	*Past Tense*	*Past Participle*
be	was/were	been
become	became	become

FORMS OF COMMON IRREGULAR VERBS *(continued)*

Base Form	*Past Tense*	*Past Participle*
begin	began	begun
bite	bit	bitten, bit
blow	blew	blown
build	built	built
burst	burst	burst
catch	caught	caught
choose	chose	chosen
come	came	come
dive	dived, dove	dived
do	did	done
draw	drew	drawn
drive	drove	driven
eat	ate	eaten
fall	fell	fallen
feel	felt	felt
fight	fought	fought
find	found	found
fling	flung	flung
fly	flew	flown
get	got	gotten, got
give	gave	given
go	went	gone
grow	grew	grown
have	had	had
know	knew	known
lay	laid	laid
lead	led	led
leave	left	left
lie	lay	lain
lose	lost	lost
make	made	made
prove	proved	proved, proven
ride	rode	ridden

(continued on next page)

FORMS OF COMMON IRREGULAR VERBS *(continued)*

Base Form	Past Tense	Past Participle
ring	rang	rung
rise	rose	risen
run	ran	run
say	said	said
set	set	set
sit	sat	sat
speak	spoke	spoken
swear	swore	sworn
swim	swam	swum
take	took	taken
tear	tore	torn
tell	told	told
think	thought	thought
throw	threw	thrown
wear	wore	worn
win	won	won
write	wrote	written

If you are unsure of a verb's principal parts, check your dictionary. See Section 6 of the Handbook for more about verb forms.

Verb Tense

The **tenses** of a verb express time. They convey whether an action, a state of being, or an occurrence takes place in the present, past, or future. There are six basic tenses: present, past, future, present perfect, past perfect, and future perfect. There are also three groups of tenses: simple, perfect, and progressive.

Simple tenses indicate whether an action occurs in the present, past, or future.

- He *loves* Kabuki theater.
- I *downloaded* their new release immediately.
- Oprah's reputation *will grow*.

Perfect tenses indicate that the action was or will be finished by the time of some other action.

- By now, Rosa *has taken* the exam.
- Dave Matthews *had* already *performed* when they arrived.
- The centennial celebration *will have begun* before he completes the sculpture.

Progressive tenses indicate that the action does, did, or will continue.

- She *is going* to kindergarten.
- When the ambulance arrived, he *was sweating* profusely.
- During spring break, we *will be basking* on a sunny beach.

A SUMMARY OF VERB TENSES

Present Tense

Simple present: happening now or occurring regularly

- He *performs* his own stunts.

Present progressive: happening now; going on (in progress) now

- The governor *is considering* a Senate campaign.

Present perfect: began in the past and was completed in the past or is continuing now

- The children's benefactor *has followed* their progress closely.

Present perfect progressive: began in the past and is continuing now

- She *has been singing* in nightclubs for thirty years.

Past Tense

Simple past: began and ended in the past

- The doctor *treated* him with experimental drugs.

Past progressive: began and continued in the past

- They *were* not *expecting* any visitors.

Past perfect: occurred before a certain time in the past or was completed before another action was begun

- The birds *had eaten* all the berries before we knew they were ripe.

Past perfect progressive: was taking place until a second action occurred

- He *had been seeing* a psychiatrist before his collapse.

Future Tense

Simple future: will take place in the future

- The play *will begin* on time.

Future progressive: will both begin and end in the future

- After we get on the plane, we *will be sitting* for hours.

(continued on next page)

Future perfect: will be completed by a certain time in the future or before another action will begin

- By next month, the new apprentice *will have become* an expert.

Future perfect progressive: will continue until a certain time in the future

- By the time she earns her Ph.D., she *will have been studying* history for twelve years.

Most of the time you will not need to think about verb tense; you will use the correct tense automatically. There are, however, a few situations in which you need to pay special attention to verb tense.

- Use the present tense to make a generalization or to state a principle or fact.

  - Thanksgiving *falls* on the fourth Thursday of November each year.
  - Walking *is* excellent exercise.

- Use the present tense to indicate an action that occurs regularly or habitually.

  - My sister *takes* frequent trips to Dallas.

- Use the present tense when referring to literary works and artwork, even though the work was written or created in the past.

  - *Hamlet is* set in Denmark.

- Use the present tense to refer to authors no longer living when you are discussing their works.

  - Borges frequently *employs* magical realism in his fiction.

Voice

A verb is in the **active voice** when the subject of the clause or sentence performs the action of the verb.

- The diplomats *have arrived.*
- He *plays* soccer professionally.

A verb is in the **passive voice** when the subject of a clause or sentence is the receiver of the action that the verb describes. Passive verbs are formed using a form of *be* and the past participle of a verb.

- The child *was* badly *bitten* by mosquitoes.
- Her car *was stolen.*

Since the passive voice may make it difficult for your readers to understand who is performing the action of a sentence, in most writing situations, use the active voice. If you do not know who performed an action, however, or if you want to emphasize the receiver of the action, consider using the passive voice.

PASSIVE VOICE   The evidence had been carefully removed by the defendant.

ACTIVE VOICE   The defendant had carefully removed the evidence.

Mood

The **mood** of a verb indicates whether it states a fact or asks a question (**indicative**); gives a command or direction (**imperative**); or expresses a condition, wish, or suggestion (**subjunctive**). The subjunctive mood is also used for hypothetical situations or impossible or unlikely events.

INDICATIVE   Redwood trees can pull moisture from the air.

IMPERATIVE   Read the play and write an analysis of it.

SUBJUNCTIVE   It would be nice to win the lottery.

The subjunctive mood, often used in clauses that begin with *if* or *that*, expresses a wish, suggestion, or condition contrary to fact. Use the base form of the verb for the present subjunctive. For the verb *be*, the past tense subjunctive is *were*, not *was*.

For exercises on verbs, refer to the Parts of Speech section of Exercise Central at www.bedfordstmartins .com/successfulcollege.

- I suggested that she *walk* to the station.
- The new student in class wished that he *were* more outgoing.

1d Adjectives

Adjectives modify a noun or pronoun by describing it, limiting it, or giving more information about it. They answer the following questions.

WHICH ONE?   The *cutest* puppy belongs to the neighbors.

WHAT KIND?   Use only *academic* sources for the paper.

HOW MANY?   *Several hundred* protesters gathered at City Hall.

There are three types of adjectives: descriptive, limiting, and proper. **Descriptive adjectives** name a quality of the person, place, thing, or idea that they describe.

yellow backpack   *pretty* face   *disturbing* event

Limiting adjectives narrow the scope of the person, place, or thing they describe.

my laptop   *second* building   *that* notebook

Proper adjectives are derived from proper nouns. They are always capitalized.

    Japanese culture   *Elizabethan* England   *Scandinavian* mythology

The articles *a*, *an*, and *the* appear immediately before nouns and are considered adjectives. *The* refers to a specific item, while *a* and *an* do not. *A* is used before words that begin with consonant sounds. *An* is used before words that begin with vowel sounds.

- ■ *The* person behind us laughed.
  The refers to a specific person.

- ■ *An* answer will be forthcoming.
  Some answer will be provided.

The can also be used to refer to a group or class of items.

- ■ *The* cat is *a* playful animal.

For more on the use of adjectives, see Section 9 of the Handbook. For more on articles, see Section 26 of the Handbook.

For exercises on adjectives, refer to the Parts of Speech and Adjectives and Adverbs sections of Exercise Central at www.bedfordstmartins .com/successfulcollege.

1e Adverbs

Adverbs modify verbs, adjectives, other adverbs, entire sentences, or clauses by describing, qualifying, or limiting the meaning of the words they modify. They answer the following questions.

HOW?	Andrea Bocelli performed *brilliantly*.
WHEN?	*Later*, they met to discuss the proposal.
WHERE?	The taxi driver headed *downtown*.
HOW OFTEN?	The bobcat is *rarely* seen in the wild.
TO WHAT EXTENT?	He agreed to cooperate *fully* with the investigation.

Most adverbs end in *-ly:*

    particular*ly*   beautiful*ly*   secret*ly*

Note that not all words ending in *-ly* are adverbs; some are adjectives (*scholarly, unfriendly*). Common adverbs that do not end in *-ly* include *almost, never, quite, soon, then, there, too,* and *very.* Some words can function as either adjectives or adverbs depending on their use in the sentence.

ADJECTIVE	The flu victims were finally *well*.
ADVERB	His paper was *well* written.

Adverbs that modify adjectives or other adverbs appear next to the word they modify.

- Tired sloths move *especially* slowly.

- A pregnant woman may feel *extremely* tired.

Adverbs that modify verbs can appear in several different positions, however.

- He *carefully* put the toys together.
- He put the toys together *carefully*.

For more on the use of adverbs, see Section 9 of the Handbook.

For exercises on adverbs, refer to the Parts of Speech and Adjective and Adverb sections of Exercise Central at www.bedfordstmartins.com/ successfulcollege.

1f Conjunctions

Conjunctions connect words, phrases, or clauses. **Coordinating conjunctions** connect words or word groups of equal importance. There are seven coordinating conjunctions: *and*, *but*, *for*, *nor*, *or*, *so*, and *yet*.

- He attended the inauguration *but* looked unhappy.

Coordinating conjunctions must connect words, phrases, or clauses of the same kind. For example, *and* may connect two nouns, but it cannot connect a noun and a clause.

NOUNS	Books by *Russell Simmons* and *Glenn Beck* appeared on the best-seller list.
PHRASES	We searched *in the closets* and *under the beds*.
CLAUSES	*Custer graduated last in his West Point class*, but *he distinguished himself in the Civil War*.

Conjunctions that are used in pairs are called **correlative conjunctions**: *as . . . as*, *both . . . and*, *either . . . or*, *just as . . . so*, *neither . . . nor*, *not . . . but*, *not only . . . but also*, and *whether . . . or*.

- *Neither* the strikers *nor* the management was satisfied with the compromise.

Subordinating conjunctions connect **dependent clauses** to **independent clauses**. They connect ideas of unequal importance. Often used at the beginning of a dependent clause, subordinating conjunctions indicate how a less important idea (expressed in a dependent clause) relates to a more important idea (expressed in an independent clause). Here is a list of common subordinating conjunctions and the relationships they express.

A **dependent clause** contains a subject and a verb but does not express a complete thought.

An **independent clause** contains a subject and a verb and can stand alone as a sentence.

Subordinating Conjunctions

Time	after, before, until, when, while

- *While* the sky was still dark, the army prepared for battle.

Cause or effect	because, since, so that

- *Since* he doesn't like math, he should avoid calculus.

Condition	even if, if, unless, whether

- We don't do volunteer work *unless* it is for a good cause.

Circumstance	as, as far as, as if, as soon as, as though, even if, even though, in order to

- In-line skating is a popular sport, *even though* it is somewhat dangerous.

Conjunctive adverbs link sentence parts that are of equal importance; they also serve as modifiers. Conjunctive adverbs show the following relationships between the elements they connect.

Conjunctive Adverbs

Time	afterward, finally, later, meanwhile, next, subsequently, then

- The candidates campaigned for months; *finally*, a primary election was held.

Example	for example, for instance, to illustrate

- Some members of the party—*for example*, the governor—supported another candidate.

Continuation or addition	also, furthermore, in addition, in the first place, moreover

- He is poorly organized; *in addition*, his arguments are not logical.

Cause or effect	accordingly, as a result, consequently, hence, therefore, thus, unfortunately

- *As a result*, he may convince few voters.

Differences or contrast	however, nevertheless, on the contrary, on the other hand, otherwise

- *Nevertheless*, he has support from some groups.

Emphasis	in fact, in other words, that is, undoubtedly

- *In fact*, some politicians are tired of constantly needing to raise money for campaigns.

Similarities or comparison	conversely, in contrast, likewise, similarly

- *In contrast*, their opponents have received many large donations.

For exercises on conjunctions, refer to the Parts of Speech sections of Exercise Central at www.bedfordstmartins.com/ successfulcollege.

1g Prepositions

A **preposition** is a word or phrase that links and relates a noun or a pronoun (the object of the preposition) to the rest of the sentence. A **prepositional phrase** includes the preposition along with its object and modifiers. Prepositions often show relationships of time, place, direction, or manner.

- Steve Prefontaine could run *despite* excruciating pain.
- The continental shelf lies *beneath* the ocean.

Common Prepositions

about	below	except	outside	under
against	beneath	for	over	underneath
along	beside	from	past	unlike
among	between	in	since	until
around	beyond	near	through	up
as	by	off	throughout	upon
at	despite	on	till	with
before	down	onto	to	within
behind	during	out	toward	without

Compound prepositions consist of more than one word.

- *According to* historical records, the town is three hundred years old.
- The department gained its reputation *by means of* its diversity.

Common Compound Prepositions

according to	because of	in place of	out of
along with	by means of	in regard to	up to
aside from	except for	in spite of	with regard to
as of	in addition to	instead of	with respect to
as well as	in front of	on account of	

For exercises on prepositions, refer to the Parts of Speech section of Exercise Central at www.bedfordstmartins.com/successfulcollege.

1h Interjections

Interjections are words that express surprise or some other strong feeling. An exclamation point or a period often follows an interjection; a comma may precede or follow an interjection if it is a mild one.

- *Oh,* it wasn't important.
- *Ouch!*
- There were no fires reported last month, *by the way.*

2   Sentence Structure

2a Sentence parts

A **sentence** is a group of words that expresses a complete thought about something or someone. Every sentence must contain two basic parts: a subject and a predicate.

Subjects

The **subject** of a sentence names a person, place, or thing and tells whom or what the sentence is about. It identifies the performer or receiver of the action expressed in the predicate.

- *Lady Gaga,* the flamboyant performer, has made savvy decisions about her career.
- The *clock* on the mantel was given to her by her grandmother.

The noun or pronoun that names what the sentence is about is called the **simple subject**.

- *Mozart* began composing at the age of four.
- The postal *worker* was bitten by a dog.

The simple subject of an imperative sentence is understood as *you,* but *you* is not stated directly.

- Be quiet.
  The sentence is understood as *[You] be quiet.*

The **complete subject** is the simple subject plus its modifiers—words that describe, identify, qualify, or limit the meaning of a noun or pronoun.

- ┌─── complete subject ───┐
  A series of very bad *decisions* doomed the project.
- ┌─── complete subject ───┐
  There are too many *books* to fit on the shelves.

A sentence with a **compound subject** contains two or more simple subjects joined by a coordinating conjunction (*and, but, for, nor, or, so,* or *yet*).

- *Joel <u>and</u> Ethan Coen* produce and direct their films.
- *A doctor <u>or</u> a physician's assistant* will explain the results.

Predicates

The **predicate** of a sentence indicates what the subject does, what happens to the subject, or what is said about the subject. The predicate, then, can indicate an action or a state of being.

ACTION	Plant respiration *produces* oxygen.
STATE OF BEING	Stonehenge *has existed* for many centuries.

A **helping verb** (also called an **auxiliary verb**) combines with a main verb to indicate tense, mood, or voice or to add further information.

A **complement** is a word or group of words that describes or renames a subject or an object.

The **simple predicate** is the main verb along with its helping verbs.

- Reporters *should call* the subjects of their stories for comment.
- A snow bicycle for Antarctic workers *has been developed*.

The **complete predicate** consists of the simple predicate plus its modifiers and any objects or complements. (See below for more about complements.)

- The growth of Los Angeles *depended* to a large extent on finding a way to get water to the desert.

complete predicate

- Watching fishing boats *is* a relaxing and pleasant way to spend an afternoon.

complete predicate

A **compound predicate** contains two or more predicates that have the same subject and that are joined by *and, but, or, nor,* or another conjunction (see 1f).

- AIDS drugs *can save many lives <u>but</u> are seldom available in poor countries that need them desperately.*
- President Johnson *<u>neither</u> wanted to run for a second term <u>nor</u> planned to serve if elected.*

For exercises on subjects and predicates, refer to the Sentence Structure section of Exercise Central at www.bedfordstmartins .com/successfulcollege.

Objects

A **direct object** is a noun or pronoun that receives the action of a verb. A direct object answers the question What? or Whom?

- The Scottish fiddler played a lively *reel.*
  The noun *reel* answers the question, What did he play?

- The crowd in the stadium jeered the *quarterback.*
  The noun *quarterback* answers the question, Whom did they jeer?

An **indirect object** is a noun or pronoun that names the person or thing to whom or for whom something is done.

- Habitat for Humanity gave *him* an award for his work.
- A woman on a bench tossed the *pigeons* some crumbs.

Complements

A **complement** is a word or group of words that describes a subject or object and completes the meaning of the sentence. There are two kinds of complements: subject complements and object complements.

A **linking verb** (such as *be, become, feel, seem,* or *taste*) connects the subject of a sentence to a **subject complement**, a noun, a noun phrase, or an adjective that renames or describes the subject.

- Michael Jackson was a *much-loved performer.*
- She was *too disorganized to finish her science project.*

An **object complement** is a noun, a noun phrase, or an adjective that modifies or renames the **direct object**. Object complements appear with transitive verbs (such as *name, find, make, think, elect, appoint, choose,* and *consider*), which express action directed toward something or someone.

- The council appointed him *its new vice president.*
- The undercooked meat made several children *sick.*

A **direct object** receives the action of the verb: *He drove me home.*

For exercises on objects and complements, refer to the Sentence Structure section of Exercise Central at www.bedfordstmartins .com/successfulcollege.

2b Phrases

A **phrase** is a group of related words that lacks a subject, a predicate, or both. A phrase cannot stand alone as a sentence. Phrases can appear at the beginning, middle, or end of a sentence and can help make your writing more detailed and interesting.

WITHOUT PHRASES	The burglars escaped.
	Bus travel is an inexpensive choice.
WITH PHRASES	Startled by the alarm, the burglars escaped without getting any money.
	For adventurers on a budget, bus travel, while not luxurious, is an inexpensive choice.

There are four common types of phrases: prepositional phrases, verbal phrases, appositive phrases, and absolute phrases.

Prepositional Phrases

A **prepositional phrase** consists of a preposition (*in, above, with, at, behind*), the object of the preposition (a noun or pronoun), and any modifiers of the object. Prepositional phrases usually function as adjectives or adverbs to tell more about people, places, objects, or actions. They can also function as nouns. A prepositional phrase generally adds information about time, place, direction, or manner.

ADJECTIVE PHRASE   The plants *on the edge of the field* are weeds.
On the edge and *of the field* tell *where.*

ADVERB PHRASE   New Orleans is very crowded *during Mardi Gras.*
During Mardi Gras tells *when.*

NOUN PHRASE   *Down the hill* is the shortest way to town.
Down the hill acts as the subject of the sentence.

Each of the following sentences has been edited to include a prepositional phrase or phrases that expand the meaning of the sentence by adding detail.

- He fell. *on the icy sidewalk.*
- The ship suddenly appeared. *through the mist near the shore.*

Verbal Phrases

A **verbal** is a verb form used as a noun (the *barking* of the dog), an adjective (a *barking* dog), or an adverb (continued *to bark*). It cannot be used alone as the verb of a sentence, however. The three kinds of verbals are participles, gerunds, and infinitives. A **verbal phrase** consists of a verbal and its modifiers.

Participles and participial phrases. All verbs have two participles: present and past. The **present participle** is the *-ing* form of a verb (*being, hoping, studying*). The **past participle** of most verbs ends in *-d* or *-ed* (*hoped, consisted*). The past participle of irregular verbs has no set pattern (*been, ridden*). Both the present participle and the past participle can function as adjectives modifying nouns and pronouns.

- The planes flew over the foggy airport in a *holding* pattern.

- The pot was made of *molded* clay.

A **participial phrase**, which consists of a participle and its modifiers, can also function as an adjective in a sentence.

- The suspect, *wanted for questioning* on robbery charges, had vanished.

Gerunds and gerund phrases. A **gerund** is the present participle, or *-ing* form, of a verb that functions as a noun in a sentence.

- *Driving* can be a frustrating activity.
- The government has not done enough to build *housing*.

A **gerund phrase** consists of a gerund and its modifiers. Like a gerund, a gerund phrase is used as a noun and can therefore function in a sentence as a subject, a direct object, an indirect object, an object of a preposition, or a subject complement.

SUBJECT	*Catching the flu* is unpleasant.
DIRECT OBJECT	All the new recruits practiced *marching*.
INDIRECT OBJECT	One director gave his *acting* a chance.
OBJECT OF A PREPOSITION	An ambitious employee may rise by *impressing* her boss.
SUBJECT COMPLEMENT	The biggest thrill was the *skydiving*.

Infinitives and infinitive phrases. An **infinitive** is the base form of a verb preceded by *to*: *to study, to sleep*. An **infinitive phrase** consists of the infinitive plus any modifiers or objects. An infinitive phrase can function as a noun, an adjective, or an adverb.

SUBJECT	*To become* an actor is my greatest ambition.
ADJECTIVE	She had a job *to do*.
ADVERB	The weary travelers were eager *to sleep*.

Sometimes the *to* in an infinitive phrase is understood but not written.

■ Her demonstration helped me learn the software.

Note: Be sure to distinguish between infinitive phrases and prepositional phrases beginning with the preposition *to*. In an infinitive phrase, *to* is followed by a verb (*to paint*); in a prepositional phrase, *to* is followed by a noun or pronoun (*to a movie*).

Appositive Phrases

An **appositive** is a word that explains, restates, or adds new information about a noun. An **appositive phrase** consists of an appositive and its modifiers.

■ George Clooney, *a famous actor,* is very active in trying to secure peace in Africa.
   The appositive phrase adds information about the noun *George Clooney*.

Absolute Phrases

An **absolute phrase** consists of a noun or pronoun and any modifiers, usually followed by a participle. An absolute phrase modifies an entire sentence, not any particular word or words within the sentence. It can appear anywhere in a sentence and is set off from the rest of the sentence with commas.

■ *Their shift completed*, the night workers walked out at sunrise.

■ *An unsuspecting insect clamped in its mandible*, the praying mantis, *its legs folded piously*, appears serenely uninvolved.

For exercises on phrases, refer to the Sentence Structure section of Exercise Central at www.bedfordstmartins.com/ successfulcollege.

2c Clauses

A **clause** is a group of words that contains a subject and a predicate. A clause is either independent (also called *main*) or dependent (also called *subordinate*). An **independent clause** can stand alone as a grammatically complete sentence.

■ Einstein was a clerk at the Swiss Patent Office.

■ Ethnic disputes followed the disintegration of Yugoslavia.

A **dependent clause** has a subject and a predicate, but it cannot stand alone as a grammatically complete sentence because it does not express a complete thought. A dependent clause usually begins with either a subordinating conjunction or a relative pronoun that connects it to an independent clause.

Common Subordinating Conjunctions

after	in as much as	that
although	in case that	though
as	in order that	unless
as far as	in so far as	until
as if	in that	when
as soon as	now that	whenever
as though	once	where
because	provided that	wherever
before	rather than	whether
even if	since	while
even though	so that	why
how	supposing that	
if	than	

Relative Pronouns

that	whatever	who (whose, whom)
what	which	whoever (whomever)

┌─────*dependent clause*─────┐
- *When the puppies were born*, the breeder examined them carefully.

dependent clause
- Van Gogh's paintings began to command high prices *after he died.*

┌─────*dependent clause*─────┐
- Isadora Duncan, *who personified modern dance*, died in a bizarre accident.

When joined to independent clauses, dependent clauses can function as adjectives, adverbs, or nouns and are known as **adjective clauses** (also called **relative clauses**), **adverb clauses**, or **noun clauses**. A noun clause can function as a subject, an object, or a complement.

adjective clause
- Graphic novels, *which were once considered "kid stuff,"* are now taken seriously.

adverb clause
- The whistle blew *as the train approached the crossing.*

┌─────*noun clause*─────┐
- The starving artist ate *whatever he could get.*

Relative pronouns are generally the subject or object in their clauses. *Who* and *whoever* change to *whom* and *whomever* when they function as objects. Sometimes the relative pronoun or subordinating conjunction is implied or understood rather than stated.

- **African rituals are among the subjects [that] the essay discusses.**
  That is the understood relative pronoun in the subordinate clause.

A dependent clause may contain an implied predicate. When a dependent clause is missing an element that can be inferred from the context of the sentence, it is called an **elliptical clause**.

- **The shooting of Congresswoman Gabrielle Giffords disturbed Americans**
  ┌──── *elliptical clause* ────┐
  more than gang shootings.
  The predicate *disturbed them* is implied.

For exercises on clauses, refer to the Sentence Structure section of Exercise Central at www.bedfordstmartins.com/ successfulcollege.

2d Types of sentences

A sentence can be classified as one of four basic types: simple, compound, complex, or compound-complex.

Simple Sentences

A **simple sentence** has one main or **independent clause** and no subordinate or **dependent clauses**. A simple sentence contains at least one subject and one predicate. It may have a compound subject, a compound predicate, and various phrases, but it has only one clause.

- **She sprints.**
- **She and her teammates sprint.**
- **She and her teammates sprint and run laps.**
- **She and her teammates in the track-and-field events sprint and run laps to achieve their goal of winning medals.**

An **independent clause** contains a subject and a verb and can stand alone as a sentence.

A **dependent clause** contains a subject and a verb but does not express a complete thought.

Compound Sentences

A **compound sentence** consists of two or more independent clauses and no dependent clauses. The two independent clauses are usually joined with a comma and a coordinating conjunction (*and, but, for, nor, or, so,* or *yet*).

- **She runs laps, but her teammates practice throwing the javelin.**

Sometimes the two clauses are joined with a semicolon and no coordinating conjunction.

- **She runs laps; her teammates practice throwing the javelin.**

Or they may be joined with a semicolon and a conjunctive adverb (such as *nonetheless* or *still*), followed by a comma.

- **She runs laps; however, her teammates practice throwing the javelin.**

Complex Sentences

A **complex sentence** has one independent clause and one or more dependent clauses. The dependent clauses usually begin with a subordinating conjunction or a relative pronoun (see 2c for a list).

- **They are training** *while he recovers from a sprained ankle.*
- **Runners** *who win their event at more than one local track meet* **will be eligible for the district trials.**

Compound-Complex Sentences

A **compound-complex sentence** contains two or more independent clauses and one or more dependent clauses.

- **She and her teammates won the meet, and as they were celebrating, a reporter approached for an interview.**
- **A reporter approached while they were celebrating their victory, and after they doused him with champagne, they answered his questions.**

For exercises on sentences, refer to the Sentence Structure section of Exercise Central at www.bedfordstmartins.com/ successfulcollege.

WRITING CORRECT SENTENCES

3   Sentence Fragments

A **sentence fragment** is a group of words that cannot stand alone as a complete **sentence**. A fragment is often missing a subject, a complete verb, or both.

FRAGMENT   **Are hatched in sand.**
This group of words does not tell *who* or *what* are hatched in sand. It lacks a subject.

FRAGMENT   **Especially his rebounding ability.**
This group of words has a subject, *his rebounding ability,* but lacks a verb.

FRAGMENT   **To notice a friendly smile.**
This group of words lacks both a subject and a verb. *To notice* is not a complete verb. It is an infinitive.

> A **sentence** is a group of words that must include at least one independent clause (a subject and a verb that express a complete thought).

A group of words can have both a subject and a verb but still be a fragment because it does not express a complete thought.

                               subject   *verb*
FRAGMENT   **Because the *number* of voters *has* declined.**
This group of words does not tell what happened as a result of the voter decline. Its meaning is incomplete.

Notice that the preceding fragment begins with the subordinating conjunction *because*. A clause that begins with a subordinating conjunction cannot stand alone as a complete sentence. (For a list of common subordinating conjunctions, see 2c.)

     Word groups that begin with a relative pronoun (*that, which, who*) are also not complete sentences.

                            subject   *verb*
FRAGMENT   **Which *scientists studied* for many years.**
The group of words does not tell *what* the scientists studied.

Finally, when a word group begins with a transitional word or phrase (*for example, also*), make sure that it includes both a subject and a verb.

                                 subject
FRAGMENT   **For example, *the Gulf Coast of Florida.***

     Use the accompanying flowchart to help you decide whether a particular word group is a complete sentence or a sentence fragment. Also try reading your essays backwards from the end to the beginning, sentence by sentence, to check for fragments. This method allows you to evaluate each sentence in isolation, without being

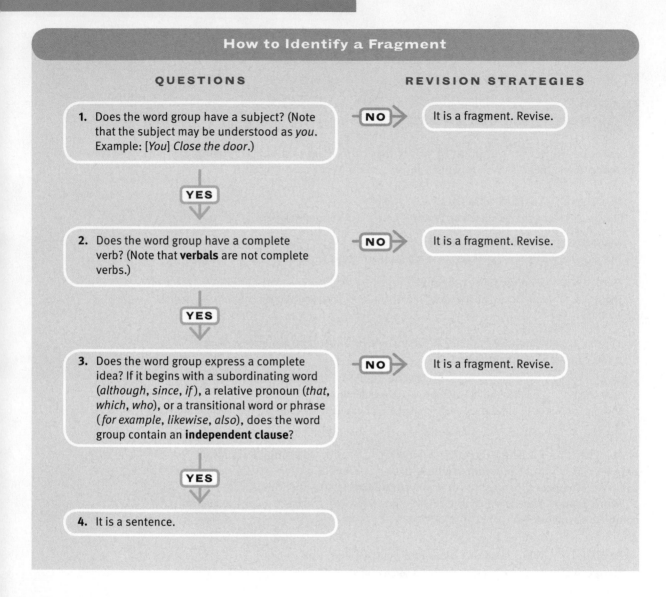

How to Identify a Fragment

QUESTIONS

REVISION STRATEGIES

1. Does the word group have a subject? (Note that the subject may be understood as *you*. Example: [*You*] *Close the door*.) — **NO** → It is a fragment. Revise.

YES ↓

2. Does the word group have a complete verb? (Note that **verbals** are not complete verbs.) — **NO** → It is a fragment. Revise.

YES ↓

3. Does the word group express a complete idea? If it begins with a subordinating word (*although*, *since*, *if*), a relative pronoun (*that*, *which*, *who*), or a transitional word or phrase (*for example*, *likewise*, *also*), does the word group contain an **independent clause**? — **NO** → It is a fragment. Revise.

YES ↓

4. It is a sentence.

A **verbal** is a verb form used as a noun (*the barking of the dog*), an adjective (*a barking dog*), or an adverb (*continued to bark*).

An **independent clause** contains a subject and a verb and can stand alone as a sentence.

distracted by the flow of ideas throughout the essay. You might also try turning each sentence into a *yes* or *no* question by adding a helping verb, such as *do*, *does*, or *did*. A complete sentence can be turned into a *yes* or *no* question, but a fragment cannot.

SENTENCE	Sociology has wide applications.
YES/NO QUESTION	Does sociology have wide applications?
FRAGMENT	While sociology has wide applications.
YES/NO QUESTION	[Cannot be formed]

A sentence fragment can be revised in two general ways: (1) by attaching it to a nearby sentence or (2) by rewriting the fragment as a complete sentence. The method you choose depends on the element the fragment lacks as well as your intended meaning.

- *Certain turtle eggs are*
  ~~Are~~ hatched in sand.

- Jamal is a basketball player of many talents./ ~~E~~specially his rebounding ability.

- *Sam was too busy to*
  ~~To~~ notice a friendly smile.

- *The*
  ~~Because~~ the number of voters has declined.

3a Join a fragment lacking a subject to another sentence or rewrite it as a complete sentence.

Attach a fragment lacking a subject to a neighboring sentence if the two are about the same person, place, or thing.

- *and*
  Jessica speaks Spanish fluently./ ~~And~~ reads French well.

As an alternative, you can add a subject to turn the fragment into a complete sentence.

- *She also*
  Jessica speaks Spanish fluently. ~~And~~ reads French well.

3b Add a helping verb to a fragment lacking a complete verb.

Make sure that every sentence you write contains a *complete* verb. For example, verb forms ending in *-ing* need helping verbs to make them complete. Helping verbs include forms of *do, be,* and *have* as well as such words as *will, can, could, shall, should, may, might,* and *must.* When you use an *-ing* verb form in a sentence without a helping verb, you create a fragment. To correct the fragment, add the helping verb.

- *is*
  The college installing a furnace to heat the library.

3c Join a fragment that lacks both a subject and a verb to another sentence, or add the missing subject and verb.

Often, fragments lacking a subject and verb begin with an **infinitive** such as *to hope, to walk,* and *to play,* which are not complete verbs, or they begin with an *-ed* or *-ing* form of a verb. Revise a fragment that begins with an infinitive or an *-ed* or *-ing* verb form by combining it with a previous sentence.

An **infinitive** is a verb form made up of *to* plus the base form (*to run, to see*).

- I plan to transfer next semester. _{to} ~~To~~ live closer to home.

- Robert E. Lee and Ulysses S. Grant met on April 9, 1865. _{bringing} ~~Bringing~~ an end to the Civil War.

You can also revise a fragment beginning with an infinitive or an *-ed* or *-ing* verb form by adding both a subject and a verb to make it a complete sentence.

- Linda was reluctant to go out alone at night. _{She was unwilling to} ~~To~~ walk across campus from the library.

- Kyle was determined to do well on his math exam. _{He studied} ~~Studied~~ during every available hour.

Watch out for fragments that begin with a transitional word or phrase. They can usually be corrected by joining them to a previous sentence.

- Annie has always wanted to become an orthopedist. _{— that} ~~That~~ is, a bone specialist.

3d Join a fragment beginning with a subordinating word to another sentence, or drop the subordinating word.

You can correct a fragment beginning with a subordinating word by joining it to the sentence before or after it.

- The students stared spellbound. _{while} ~~While~~ the professor lectured.

- Until Dr. Jonas Salk invented a vaccine. _{polio} ~~Polio~~ was a serious threat to public health.

As an alternative, you can revise this type of fragment by dropping the subordinating word.

- _{The} ~~Because the~~ 800 area code for toll-free dialing is overused. New codes—888 and 877—have been added.

3e Join a fragment beginning with a relative pronoun such as *who* or *whom* to another sentence, or rewrite it as a complete sentence.

Another common type of sentence fragment begins with a relative pronoun. **Relative pronouns** include *who, whom, whose, whoever, whomever, what, whatever, which,* and *that.*

■ My contemporary fiction instructor assigned a novel by Stephen King. ~~Whose~~ *whose* work I admire.

■ The dodo is an extinct bird. ~~That~~ *It* disappeared in the seventeenth century.

Professional writers sometimes use sentence fragments intentionally to achieve special effects, particularly in works of fiction or articles written for popular magazines. An *intentional* fragment may be used to emphasize a point, answer a question, re-create a conversation, or make an exclamation. However, you should avoid using intentional fragments in academic writing. Instructors and other readers may find the fragments distracting or too informal, or they may assume you used a fragment in error.

Exercise 3.1

Correct any fragments in the following sentences. Some groups of sentences may be correct as written.

■ More people are going to college every year. ~~Especially~~ *, especially* young women.

1. In the past, higher education was only accessible to a small number of people. However, access to higher education has expanded over the last 200 years.

2. In the United States, for example. Colleges and universities provide education to Americans of all classes and backgrounds.

3. At first, state universities were publicly funded schools. That trained students in fields such as engineering, education, and agriculture.

4. During the nineteenth and early twentieth centuries. Graduates of state universities played a key role in America's development as an industrial and economic power.

5. The number of students in college. Increased greatly in the years after World War II.

6. Because federal funding from the 1944 GI Bill made it possible. Millions of returning veterans attended colleges.

7. Many people credit this program with helping to create a strong middle class. In the United States during the 1950s and 1960s.

8. Now, about two-thirds of high school graduates will attend college. Because those with bachelor's degrees earn $20,000 more a year on average than do people with only high school diplomas.

9. Most people agree that America needs an educated workforce to compete globally.

10. However, as education costs continue to rise. Some wonder whether a traditional four-year college is always worth the expense.

For more exercises on sentence fragments, refer to the Sentence Fragments section of Exercise Central at www.bedfordstmartins.com/successfulcollege.

For more exercises on sentence fragments, refer to the Sentence Fragments section of Exercise Central at www.bedfordstmartins .com/successfulcollege.

Exercise 3.2

Rewrite the following passage as needed to eliminate sentence fragments.

■ How much and what kind of intervention should be undertaken./On behalf of
endangered species?

Gila trout are endangered in some stretches of water. That are managed as designated wilderness. A hands-off policy would be their doom. Because exotic trout species now swim in the same streams. Gila trout can survive the competition and the temptation to interbreed only if they swim in isolated tributaries. In which a waterfall blocks the upstream movement of other fish. Two decades ago, one such tributary was fortified. With a small concrete dam. In other words, a dam deliberately built in the wilderness. It is often difficult to choose the right way. To manage a wilderness area. A scientific grasp of the way the ecosystem works is essential. Yet not always available.

4 Run-On Sentences and Comma Splices

A **run-on sentence** occurs when two or more independent clauses are joined without a punctuation mark or a coordinating conjunction. Run-on sentences are also known as **fused sentences**.

RUN-ON
SENTENCE
A television addict is dependent on television I have suffered this
addiction for years.

A **comma splice** occurs when two or more independent clauses are joined with a comma but without a coordinating conjunction (such as *and, or,* or *but*).

COMMA
SPLICE
A typical magic act includes tricks and illusions, both depend
on deception.

Notice that only a comma separates the two independent clauses, causing the comma splice.

Another type of comma splice occurs when a word other than a coordinating conjunction is used with a comma to join two or more independent clauses.

COMMA
SPLICE
A typical magic act includes tricks and illusions, however,
both depend on deception.

In the preceding sentence, *however* is a conjunctive adverb, not a coordinating conjunction. There are only seven coordinating conjunctions: *and, but, for, nor, or, so,* and *yet.*

Recognizing Run-On Sentences and Comma Splices

Many students have difficulty spotting run-on sentences and comma splices in their own writing. Use the accompanying flowchart to help you identify these types of errors in your sentences.

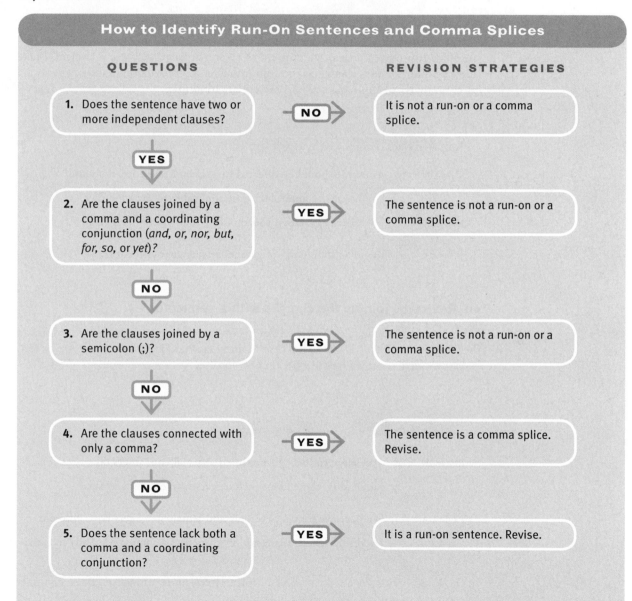

How to Identify Run-On Sentences and Comma Splices

QUESTIONS

REVISION STRATEGIES

1. Does the sentence have two or more independent clauses?
— **NO** → It is not a run-on or a comma splice.

YES

2. Are the clauses joined by a comma and a coordinating conjunction (*and, or, nor, but, for, so,* or *yet*)?
— **YES** → The sentence is not a run-on or a comma splice.

NO

3. Are the clauses joined by a semicolon (;)?
— **YES** → The sentence is not a run-on or a comma splice.

NO

4. Are the clauses connected with only a comma?
— **YES** → The sentence is a comma splice. Revise.

NO

5. Does the sentence lack both a comma and a coordinating conjunction?
— **YES** → It is a run-on sentence. Revise.

Correcting Run-On Sentences and Comma Splices

There are four basic ways to correct a run-on sentence or comma splice. Choose the method that best fits your sentence or intended meaning.

4a Revise by creating two separate sentences.

Correct a run-on sentence or comma splice by creating two separate sentences. Make sure each independent clause has the appropriate end punctuation mark—a period, a question mark, or (on rare occasions) an exclamation mark.

period   *period*

Independent clause . *Independent clause* .

RUN-ON SENTENCE	A résumé should be directed to a specific audience. ^It^ it should emphasize the applicant's potential value to the company.
COMMA SPLICE	To evaluate a charity, you should start by examining its goals/. ^T^ then you should investigate its management practices.

4b Revise by joining the clauses with a semicolon (;).

When the independent clauses are closely connected in meaning, consider joining them with a semicolon. Note that a coordinating conjunction (such as *and, or,* or *but*) is *not* included when you revise with a semicolon (see 4c).

semicolon

Independent clause ; *Independent clause* .

RUN-ON SENTENCE	Specialty products are unique items that consumers take time purchasing; these items include cars, parachutes, and skis.
COMMA SPLICE	Studies have shown that male and female managers have different leadership styles/; as a result, workers may respond differently to each.

In the second example, the semicolon joins the two clauses connected by the conjunctive adverb *as a result.* When two independent clauses are joined by a conjunctive adverb, a semicolon is needed.

4c Revise by joining the clauses with a comma and a coordinating conjunction.

Two independent clauses can be joined by using *both* a comma and a coordinating conjunction (*and, but, for, nor, or, so,* or *yet*). The coordinating conjunction indicates how the two clauses are related.

comma + coordinating conjunction

Independent clause , and independent clause .

RUN-ON SENTENCE	Closed-minded people often refuse to recognize opposing *and* views, they reject ideas without evaluating them.
COMMA SPLICE	Some educators support home schooling, *but* others oppose it vehemently.

4d Revise by making one clause dependent or by turning one clause into a phrase.

A **dependent clause** contains a subject and a verb but does not express a complete thought. It must always be linked to an independent clause. You can correct a run-on sentence or a comma splice by adding a **subordinating conjunction** (such as *because* or *although*) to one of the independent clauses, thereby making it a dependent clause. The subordinating conjunction makes the thought incomplete and dependent on the independent clause.

subordinating conjunction

Because dependent clause , independent clause .

or   *subordinating conjunction*

Independent clause because dependent clause .

RUN-ON SENTENCE	Facial expressions are very revealing they are an important communication tool.
INDEPENDENT CLAUSE	Facial expressions are very revealing.
DEPENDENT CLAUSE	*Because* facial expressions are very revealing
JOINED TO INDEPENDENT CLAUSE	Because facial expressions are very revealing, they are an important communication tool.

You can also correct a run-on sentence or a comma splice by changing one of the independent clauses to a phrase.

Phrase , *independent clause* .

or

Independent clause , *phrase* .

or

Beginning of independent clause , *phrase* , *end of independent clause* .

COMMA SPLICE	Medieval peasants in Europe ate a simple, hearty diet, they relied almost totally on agriculture.
INDEPENDENT CLAUSE	Medieval peasants in Europe ate a simple, hearty diet.
CLAUSE REDUCED TO PHRASE	having a simple, hearty diet
EMBEDDED IN INDEPENDENT CLAUSE	Medieval peasants in Europe—having a simple, hearty diet— relied almost totally on agriculture.

Note: A comma or commas may or may not be needed to separate a phrase from the rest of the sentence, depending on how the phrase affects the meaning of the sentence (see 12e). Here are two more examples that show how to revise run-on sentences and comma splices using subordination.

RUN-ON SENTENCE	Distributors open big-budget movies late in the week, ~~they hope~~ ^{hoping} moviegoers will flock to theaters over the weekend.
COMMA SPLICE	^{Although the} ~~The~~ remote fishing lodge has no heat or electricity, ~~nevertheless~~ it is a popular vacation spot.

(**Exercise 4.1**)

For more exercises on run-on sentences and comma splices, refer to the Run-On Sentences and Comma Splices section of Exercise Central at www.bedfordstmartins .com/successfulcollege.

Correct any run-ons or comma splices in the following sentences.

■ A deadly nerve poison is found on the skin of some Amazon tree frogs; native

tribes use the poison on the tips of their arrows when they hunt.

1. Nearly every American child dreams of going to Disney World, it has become one of the most popular family vacation destinations.
2. Shopping through online bookstores is convenient, some people miss the atmosphere of a traditional bookstore.

3. Openness is one way to build trust in a relationship another is to demonstrate tolerance and patience.

4. In the 1960s some Americans treated Vietnam veterans disrespectfully this situation has changed dramatically since that time.

5. William Faulkner wrote classic novels about life in the U.S. South, Eudora Welty has also written vividly about southern life.

6. With large bodies and tiny wings, bumblebees have long been a puzzle, how do they fly?

7. The Taj Mahal is aptly called the Pearl Mosque it glows in the moonlight with unearthly beauty.

8. The Supreme Court often makes controversial decisions, the justices must decide how to interpret the Constitution.

9. Although the clouds were threatening, the storm had not yet struck, however, most boats turned toward shore.

10. Restoring a painting is, indeed, delicate work too much enthusiasm can be dangerous.

(**Exercise 4.2**)

Correct any run-on sentences and comma splices in the following paragraph. Some sentences may be correct as written.

For more exercises on run-on sentences and comma splices, refer to the Run-On Sentences and Comma Splices section of Exercise Central at www.bedfordstmartins .com/successfulcollege.

- **Some people believe dreams are revealing, _{but} others think the brain is simply unloading excess information.**

  Throughout recorded history, people have been fascinated by dreams, they have wondered what meaning dreams hold. Whether the dreams are ominous or beautiful, people have always wanted to understand them. There are many ancient stories about dream interpretation one of these is the biblical story of Daniel. Daniel is able to interpret a ruler's dream, this power to interpret convinces the ruler that Daniel is a prophet. Other early writers considered the topic of dream interpretation, to Latin writers, some dreams were meaningful and some were not. Meaningful dreams could reveal the future, these writers argued, but other dreams were simply the result of eating or drinking too much. Sigmund Freud, the founder of psychoanalysis, dramatically changed the field of dream interpretation he believed that dreams come from the subconscious. According to Freud, ideas too frightening for the waking mind often appear in dreams, patients in Freudian therapy often discuss dream images. Today, not everyone agrees with Freud, scientists trying to understand the brain still pay attention to dreams. They are certain that dreams reflect modern life more and more people today dream about computers.

5 Subject-Verb Agreement

Subjects and verbs must agree in person and number. **Person** refers to the forms *I* or *we* (first person), *you* (second person), and *he, she, it,* and *they* (third person). **Number** shows whether a word refers to one thing (singular) or more than one thing (plural). In a sentence, subjects and verbs need to be consistent in person and number: *I drive, you drive, she drives.*

Subject-verb agreement errors often occur in complicated sentences, in sentences with compound subjects, or in sentences where the subject and verb are separated by other words or phrases. The following sections will help you look for and revise common errors in subject-verb agreement.

5a Make sure the verb agrees with the subject, not with words that come between the subject and verb.

■ The *number* of farm workers *has* remained constant over several decades.

  The subject *number* is singular and requires a singular verb, even though the words *of farm workers* appear between the subject and verb.

5b Use a plural verb when two or more subjects are joined by *and*.

■ A dot and a dash represents the letter *A* in Morse code.

■ Basketball star Shaquille O'Neal, comedian D. L. Hughley, and actor Tom Arnold

  were

  ~~was~~ all born on March 6.

5c Revise to make the verb agree with the subject closest to it when two or more subjects are joined by *or, either…or,* or *neither…nor*.

When two or more singular subjects are joined by *or, either…or,* or *neither…nor,* use a singular verb.

■ *Math* or *accounting appears* to be a suitable major for you.

■ Either the *waiter* or the *customer has* misplaced the bill.

■ Neither the *doctor* nor the *patient is* pessimistic about the prognosis.

When one singular and one plural subject are joined by *or, either…or,* or *neither…nor,* the verb should agree in number with the subject nearest to it.

■ Neither the *sailors* nor the *boat was* harmed by the storm.

■ Neither the *boat* nor the *sailors were* harmed by the storm.

■ Either my daughters or my wife water*s* that plant daily.

5d Use a singular verb with most collective nouns, such as *family, couple,* and *class*.

When a **collective noun** refers to a group as one unit acting together, use a singular verb. When the members of the group are acting as individuals, use a plural verb.

To make their meaning clearer and avoid awkwardness, writers often add *members* or a similar noun.

- The school *committee has* voted to increase teachers' salaries.
  The committee is acting as a unit.

- The family ~~are~~ *is* living in a cramped apartment.

- The *team members are* traveling by train, bus, and bike.
  The team members are acting individually.

- The members of the jury ~~is~~ *are* divided and unable to reach consensus.

5e Use a singular verb with most indefinite pronouns, such as *anyone*, *everyone*, *each*, *every*, *no one*, and *something*.

Indefinite pronouns do not refer to a specific person, place, or object. They refer to people, places, or things in general. Singular indefinite pronouns include the following: *each, either, neither, anyone, anybody, anything, everyone, everybody, everything, one, no one, nobody, nothing, someone, somebody, something.*

- *Everyone* in this room *is* welcome to express an opinion.

- Neither of the candidates ~~have~~ *has* run for office before.

Other indefinite pronouns, such as *several, both, many,* and *few,* take a plural verb.

- Every year *many succeed* in starting new small businesses.

- Several of you jogs at least three miles a day.

Some indefinite pronouns, such as *all, any, more, most, some,* and *none,* take either a singular or a plural verb depending on the noun they refer to. To decide which verb to use, follow this rule: Treat the indefinite pronoun as singular if it refers to something that cannot be counted and as plural if it refers to more than one of something that can be counted.

- Most of the water go*es* into this kettle.
  You cannot count water.

- Some of the children in the study chooses immediate rather than delayed rewards.
  You can count children.

An **antecedent** is the noun or pronoun to which a pronoun refers.

A **relative pronoun** introduces a dependent clause that functions as an adjective: *the patient who injured her leg.*

5f Revise to make verbs agree with the antecedents of *who, which,* and *that*.

When a **relative pronoun** (*who, which, that*) refers to a singular noun, use a singular verb. When it refers to a plural noun, use a plural verb.

- *Toni Morrison, who enjoys* unique success as both a popular and a literary author, won the Nobel Prize in literature in 1993.

  Who refers to Toni Morrison, and because *Toni Morrison* is singular, the verb *enjoys* is singular.

- Look for *stores that display* this sign.

  That refers to *stores,* a plural noun.

Using *one of the* often leads to errors in subject-verb agreement. The phrase *one of the* plus a noun is plural.

- A pigeon is *one of the two birds that drink* by suction.

  That refers to *birds,* and since *birds* is plural, the verb *drink* is plural.

However, *only one of the* plus a noun is singular: *The cheetah is the only one of the big cats that has nonretractable claws.*

5g Revise to make the verb agree with a subject that follows it.

A **prepositional phrase** is a group of words that begins with a preposition and includes the object or objects of the preposition and all their modifiers: *above the low wooden table.*

When a sentence begins with either *here* or *there* (which cannot function as a subject) or with a **prepositional phrase**, the subject often follows the verb. Look for the subject after the verb and make sure the subject and verb agree.

- There *is* a false *panel* somewhere in this room.

- Under the stairs *lurks* a solitary *spider.*

5h Make sure a linking verb agrees with its subject, not a word or phrase that renames the subject.

Linking verbs, such as forms of *be* and *feel, look,* and *taste,* connect a subject with a word or phrase that renames or describes it. In sentences with linking verbs, the verb should agree with the subject.

- The *bluebell is* any of several plants in the lily family.

- The *issue* discussed at the meeting *was* the low wages earned by factory workers.

5i Use a singular verb when the subject is a title.

■ *Gulliver's Travels* ~~are~~ a satire by the eighteenth-century British writer Jonathan Swift.

(is inserted above "are")

5j Use singular verbs with singular nouns that end in *-s*, such as *physics* and *news*.

■ *Linguistics deals* with the study of human speech.

Exercise 5.1

Correct any subject-verb agreement errors in the following sentences. Some sentences may be correct as written.

■ Most of the people in the world believes that learning a second language is important.

1. Many members of the international business community communicates by speaking English, the international language of business.

2. A student in most non-English-speaking industrialized nations expect to spend six or more years studying English.

3. The United States are different.

4. Working for laws that requires all Americans to speak English is a fairly common U.S. political tactic.

5. In American schools, often neither a teaching staff nor enough money have been available for good foreign-language programs.

6. Some linguists joke that a person who speaks two languages are called bilingual, while a person who speaks one language is called American.

7. Some states around the country has begun to change this situation.

8. If a class is given lessons in a foreign language, the students feel that they will be better prepared for the new global economy.

9. In a Spanish or French class, children of immigrants for whom English was a second language learns a new language and perhaps gains a new appreciation of their parents' accomplishments.

10. Everyone who study a foreign language are likely to benefit.

For more exercises on subject-verb agreement, refer to the Subject-Verb Agreement section of Exercise Central at www.bedfordstmartins .com/successfulcollege.

Exercise 5.2

Correct any sentences with subject-verb agreement errors in the following paragraph. Some sentences may be correct as written.

Everyone in the colder climates want to know whether the next winter will be severe. The National Weather Service, however, usually predict the weather only a short time in advance. Another method of making weather predictions are popular with many Americans. According to

For more exercises on subject-verb agreement, refer to the Subject-Verb Agreement section of Exercise Central at www.bedfordstmartins .com/successfulcollege.

folklore, there is a number of signs to alert people to a hard winter ahead. Among these signs are the brown stripe on a woolly bear caterpillar. If the brown stripe between the caterpillar's two black stripes are wide, some people believe the winter will be a short one. Another of the signs that indicate a hard winter is a large apple harvest. And, of course, almost everyone in the United States have seen news stories on February 2 about groundhogs predicting the end of winter. Folk beliefs, which are not based on science, seems silly to many people. Neither the National Weather Service nor folklore are always able to forecast the weather accurately, however.

6　Verb Forms

Except for *be,* all English verbs have five forms.

Base Form	*Past Tense*	*Past Participle*	*Present Participle*	-s *Form*
move	moved	moved	moving	moves

- Many designers *visit* Milan for fashion shows each year.
- Sarah *visited* her best friend in Thailand.
- Students have *visited* the state capital every spring for decades.
- His cousin from Iowa is *visiting* this week.
- Maria *visits* her grandmother in Puerto Rico as often as possible.

6a Use -s or -es endings for present tense verbs that have third-person singular subjects.

The *-s* form is made up of the verb's base form plus *-s* or *-es.*

- Mr. King *teaches* English.

A third-person singular subject can consist of a singular noun, a singular pronoun (*he, she,* and *it*), or a singular indefinite pronoun (such as *everyone*).

SINGULAR NOUN	The flower opens.
SINGULAR PRONOUN	He opens the door.
SINGULAR INDEFINITE PRONOUN	Everybody knows the truth.

- She ~~want~~ to be a veterinarian. *wants*
- None of the townspeople ~~understand~~ him. *understands*

6b Do not omit *-ed* endings on verbs.

For regular verbs, both the past tense and the past participle are formed by adding *-ed* or *-d* to the base form of the verb. (For more on verb tense, see 1c and 27a.)

- She *claimed* to be the czar's daughter, Anastasia.

- The defendant *faced* his accusers.

Some speakers do not fully pronounce the *-ed* endings of verbs (*asked, fixed, supposed to, used to*). As a result, they may unintentionally omit these endings in their writing.

- He ~~talk~~ ^{talked} to the safety inspectors about plant security.

- They ~~use~~ ^{used} to order lattes every morning.

6c Use the correct form of irregular verbs such as *lay* and *lie*.

The verb pairs *lay* and *lie* and *sit* and *set* have similar forms and are often confused. Each verb has its own meaning: *lie* means to recline or rest on a surface, and *lay* means to put or place something; *sit* means to be seated, as in a chair, and *set* means to place something on a surface.

- Our dog likes to ~~lay~~ ^{lie} on the couch all afternoon.

- Let me ~~set~~ ^{sit} in this chair for a while.

For more on irregular verbs, see 1c.

6d Use the active and passive voice appropriately.

When a verb is in the **active voice**, the subject performs the action.

ACTIVE VOICE   The Mississippi River flows into the Gulf of Mexico.

When a verb is in the **passive voice**, the subject receives the action.

PASSIVE VOICE   The computer file was deleted.

Notice that the sentence in the passive voice does not tell *who* deleted the file.

The active voice expresses ideas more vividly and emphatically than does the passive voice. Whenever possible, use the active voice in your sentences.

- ~~Tea was thrown~~ ^{The colonists threw tea} into Boston Harbor. ~~by the colonists.~~

No one is allowed to sell illegal

■ ~~Illegal drugs~~ ~~are not allowed to be sold~~.
   ^   ^

Sentences in the passive voice may seem indirect, as if the writer is purposely withholding information. In general, use the passive voice sparingly. There are two situations in which it is the better choice, however.

1. When you do not know or do not want to reveal who performed the action of the verb:

PASSIVE   **Several historic buildings had been torn down.**

2. When you want to emphasize the object of the action rather than the person who causes the action:

PASSIVE   **The poem "My Last Duchess" by Robert Browning was discussed in class.**
In this sentence, the title of the poem is more important than the people who discussed it.

6e Use the present tense when writing about literary works, even though they were written in the past.

depicts

■ Chaucer's *Canterbury Tales* ~~depicted~~ a tremendously varied group of travelers.
                              ^

6f Be sure to distinguish between the immediate past and the less immediate past.

Use the past perfect form of the verb, formed by adding *had* to the past participle, to indicate an action that was completed before another action or a specified time.

UNCLEAR   **Roberto finished three research papers when the semester ended.**
Roberto did not finish all three right at the end of the semester.

REVISED   **Roberto had finished three research papers when the semester ended.**

For more on verb tense, see 1c and 27a.

(**Exercise 6.1**)

For more exercises on verb forms, refer to the Verb Forms section of Exercise Central at www.bedfordstmartins .com/successfulcollege.

Correct the errors in verb form in the following sentences. Some sentences may be correct as written.

United States entered the

■ The Spanish-American War ~~was entered by the United States~~ in 1898.
   ^

1. When the nineteenth century change into the twentieth, many people in the United States became eager to expel Spain from the Americas.

2. Cuba, an island that lays ninety miles off the Florida coast, provided them with an excuse to do so.

3. Cuban rebels were trying to free themselves from Spain, and many Americans wanted to help them.

4. In addition, many people in the United States wanted to take over Spain's territories for a long time.

5. The United States won the war very quickly and assume control of Cuba, the Philippines, Guam, and Puerto Rico.

6. Cuba was allow to take control of its own affairs right away.

7. Puerto Rico became a commonwealth in 1952, a position that place it between statehood and independence.

8. In a 1998 election, the people of Puerto Rico were offered the option of full statehood.

9. It was rejected by them.

10. Many Puerto Ricans are worried that statehood would destroy the native culture of their island, and none of them want that to happen.

(**Exercise 6.2**)

Correct the errors in verb form in the following paragraph. Some sentences may be correct as written.

For more exercises on verb forms, refer to the Verb Forms section of Exercise Central at www.bedfordstmartins.com/ successfulcollege.

                          contains

▪ **Walt Whitman's** *Leaves of Grass* ~~contain~~ **long, informally structured poems.**

   Walt Whitman was usually considered one of the greatest American poets. He spent almost his whole life in Brooklyn, New York, but he like to write about all of America. He was fired from several jobs for laziness and admitted that he liked to lay in bed until noon. But he had a vision: He wanted to create an entirely new kind of poetry. Rhyme was considered unimportant by him, and he did not think new American poetry needed formal structure. Unfortunately for Whitman, his great masterpiece, *Leaves of Grass,* was not an overnight success. Ralph Waldo Emerson admire it, but Whitman sold very few copies. He revise it continuously until his death. Today, people admires *Leaves of Grass* for its optimism, its beautiful language, its very modern appreciation of the diversity of America, and its astonishing openness about sexuality. Whitman's body of work still move and surprise readers.

---

7 Pronoun Problems

Pronouns are words used in place of nouns. They provide a quick, convenient way to refer to a word that has already been named. Common problems in using pronouns include problems with pronoun reference, agreement, and case.

Pronoun Reference

A pronoun should refer clearly to its **antecedent**, the noun or pronoun for which it substitutes.

If an antecedent is missing or unclear, the meaning of the sentence is also unclear. Use the following guidelines to make certain your pronoun references are clear and correct.

7a Make sure each pronoun refers clearly to one antecedent.

■ The hip-hop radio station battled the alternative rock station for the highest ratings.

the alternative rock station
Eventually, ~~it~~ won.

The revised sentence makes it clear which station won: the alternative rock station.

7b Be sure to check for vague uses of *they*, *it*, and *you*.

They, it, and *you* often refer vaguely to antecedents in preceding sentences or to no antecedent at all.

OMITTED   On the Internet, they claimed that an asteroid would collide
ANTECEDENT   with the earth.

On the Internet does not explain what *they* refers to.

CLEAR   On the Internet, a blog claimed that an asteroid would collide with
the earth.

Adding the noun *a blog* clears up the mystery.

■ When political scientists study early political cartoons, *they gain* ~~it provides~~ insight into historical events.

people often talk
■ In Florida, ~~you often hear~~ about hurricane threats of previous years.

7c Make sure pronouns do not refer to adjectives or possessives.

Pronouns must refer to nouns or other pronouns. Adjectives and possessives cannot serve as antecedents, although they may seem to suggest a noun the pronoun *could* refer to.

he was
■ He became so depressed that ~~it made him~~ unable to get out of bed.

The pronoun *it* seems to refer to the adjective *depressed,* which suggests the noun *depression.* This noun is not in the sentence, however.

stocks
■ The stock market's rapid rise made ~~it~~ appear to be an attractive investment.

The pronoun *it* seems to refer to *stock market's,* which is a possessive, not a noun.

7d Make sure the pronouns *who*, *whom*, *which*, and *that* refer to clear, specific nouns.

■ Lake-effect storms hit cities along the Great Lakes. ~~That makes~~ winter travel treacherous.

These storms make

Exercise 7.1

Correct any errors in pronoun reference in the following sentences.

■ Innovative codes are important because ~~it means that~~ they will be hard to break.

are

For more exercises on pronoun reference, refer to the Pronoun Problems section of Exercise Central at www.bedfordstmartins .com/successfulcollege.

1. A country at war must be able to convey information to military personnel. That is always a challenge.
2. The information's importance often requires it to be transmitted secretly.
3. Military strategists use codes for these transmissions because they baffle the enemy.
4. They say that "invisible ink," which cannot be seen until the paper is heated, was once a popular way to communicate secretly.
5. Lemon juice and vinegar are good choices for invisible ink because you can't see them unless they are burned.
6. During World War II, U.S. government code specialists hired Navajo Indians because it is a difficult and little-studied language.
7. In early code writing, it involved substituting letters throughout the message.
8. These cryptograms are no longer used to transmit messages because they are too simple.
9. The Nazis' Enigma code was extremely difficult to crack. This was an enormous problem for the Allied forces.
10. Alan Turing's mathematical genius saved the day. He was a British civil servant who finally solved the Enigma code.

Pronoun-Antecedent Agreement

An **antecedent** is the noun or pronoun to which a pronoun refers.

Person indicates whether the subject is speaking (first person: *I, we*), is being spoken to (second person: *you*), or is being spoken about (third person: *he, she, it, they*).

Number is a term that classifies pronouns as singular (*I, you, he, she, it*) or plural (*we, you, they*).

Pronouns and **antecedents** must agree in **person**, **number**, and **gender**. The most common agreement error occurs when pronouns and antecedents do not agree in number. If the antecedent is singular, use a singular pronoun. If the antecedent is plural, use a plural pronoun.

In most situations you will instinctively choose the correct pronoun and antecedent. Here are a few guidelines to follow for those times when you are unsure of which pronoun or antecedent to use.

Gender is a way of classifying pronouns as masculine (*he, him*), feminine (*she, her*), or neuter (*it, its*).

An **indefinite pronoun** does not refer to a specific person, place, or object. It refers to people, places, or things in general (*anywhere, everyone, everything*).

7e Use singular pronouns to refer to indefinite pronouns that are singular in meaning.

Singular indefinite pronouns include the following:

another	anywhere	everyone	none	other
anybody	each	everything	no one	somebody
anyone	either	neither	nothing	someone
anything	everybody	nobody	one	something

■ *Each* of the experiments produced *its* desired result.

■ If *anyone* wants me, give *him or her* my email address.

■ *Everyone* in America should exercise *his or her* right to vote so *his or her* voice can be heard.

If the pronoun and antecedent do not agree, change either the pronoun or the indefinite pronoun to which it refers. If you need to use a singular pronoun, use *he or she* or *him or her* to avoid sexism.

■ ~~Everyone~~ People should check their credit card statements monthly.

■ Everyone should check ~~their~~ *his or her* credit card statement monthly.

An alternative is to eliminate the pronoun or pronouns entirely.

■ No one should lose ~~their~~ *a* job because of family responsibilities.

Note: Overuse of *him or her* and *his or her* can create awkward sentences. To avoid this problem, you can revise your sentences in one of two ways: by using a plural antecedent and a plural pronoun or by omitting the pronouns altogether.

The indefinite pronouns *all, any, more, most,* and *some* can be either singular or plural, depending on how they are used in sentences. When an indefinite pronoun refers to something that can be counted, use a plural pronoun to refer to it. When an indefinite pronoun refers to something that cannot be counted, use a singular pronoun to refer to it.

■ Of the tropical plants studied, *some* have proven *their* usefulness in fighting disease.
Because the word *plants* is a plural, countable noun, the pronoun *some* is plural in this sentence.

■ The water was warm, and *most* of *it* was murky.
The word *water* is not countable, so *most* is singular.

7f Use a plural pronoun to refer to a compound antecedent joined by *and*.

- The *walrus __and__ the carpenter* ate *their* oysters greedily.

Exception: When the singular antecedents joined by *and* refer to the same person, place, or thing, use a singular pronoun.

- As *a father and a husband, he* is a success.

Exception: When *each* or *every* comes before the antecedent, use a singular pronoun.

- *Every nut and bolt* was in *its* place for the inspection.

When a compound antecedent is joined by *or* or *nor,* the pronoun should agree with the noun closer to the verb.

- Either the panda or the sea otters should have ~~its~~ new habitat soon.

  their

7g Use a singular or plural pronoun to refer to a collective noun, depending on the meaning.

A **collective noun** names a group of people or things acting together or individually (*herd, class, team*) and may be referred to by a singular or plural pronoun depending on your intended meaning. When you refer to a group acting together as a unit, use a singular pronoun.

- The *wolf pack* surrounds *its* quarry.
  The pack is acting as a unit.

When you refer to the members of the group as acting individually, use a plural pronoun.

- After the false alarm, *members* of the bomb squad returned to *their* homes.
  The members of the squad acted individually.

⟨ **Exercise 7.2** ⟩

Correct any errors in pronoun-antecedent agreement in the following sentences. Some sentences may be correct as written.

- Every scientist has ~~their~~ own idea about the state of the environment.

  his or her

For more exercises on pronoun-antecedent agreement, refer to the Pronoun Problems section of Exercise Central at www.bedfordstmartins.com/successfulcollege.

1. Neither the many species of dinosaurs nor the flightless dodo bird could prevent their own extinction.
2. A team of researchers might disagree on its conclusions about the disappearance of the dinosaur.
3. However, most believe that their findings indicate the dodo died out because of competition from other species.
4. In one way, animals resemble plants: Some are "weeds" because it has the ability to thrive under many conditions.
5. Any species that cannot withstand their competitors may be doomed to extinction.
6. When a "weed" and a delicate native species compete for its survival, the native species usually loses.
7. If the snail darter and the spotted owl lose their fight to survive, should humans care?
8. Everyone should be more concerned about the extinction of plants and animals than they seem to be.
9. Every extinction has their effect on other species.
10. The earth has experienced several mass extinctions in its history, but another would take their toll on the quality of human life.

Pronoun Case

Most of the time you will automatically know which form, or *case,* of a pronoun to use: the **subjective**, **objective**, or **possessive** case. A pronoun's case indicates its function in a sentence. When a pronoun functions as a subject in a sentence, the subjective case (*I*) is used. When a pronoun functions as a **direct object**, an **indirect object**, or an **object of a preposition**, the objective case (*me*) is used. When a pronoun indicates ownership, the possessive case (*mine*) is used.

A **direct object** receives the action of the verb: *He drove me home.*

An **indirect object** indicates to or for whom an action is performed: *I gave her the keys.*

An **object of a preposition** is a word or phrase that follows a preposition: *with him, above the table.*

Subjective Case	Objective Case	Possessive Case
I	me	my, mine
we	us	our, ours
you	you	your, yours
he, she, it	him, her, it	his, her, hers, its
they	them	their, theirs
who	whom	whose

Use the following guidelines to correct errors in pronoun case.

7h Read the sentence aloud without the noun and the word *and* to decide which pronoun to use in a compound construction (*Yolanda and I, Yolanda and me*).

INCORRECT   Yolanda and me graduated from high school last year.

If you mentally delete *Yolanda and,* the sentence sounds wrong: *Me graduated from high school last year.*

REVISED   Yolanda and I graduated from high school last year.

If you mentally delete *Yolanda and,* the sentence sounds correct: *I graduated from high school last year.*

INCORRECT   The mayor presented the citizenship award to Mrs. Alvarez and I.

If you delete *Mrs. Alvarez and,* the sentence sounds wrong: *The mayor presented the citizenship award to I.*

REVISED   The mayor presented the citizenship award to Mrs. Alvarez and me.

If you delete *Mrs. Alvarez and,* the sentence sounds correct: *The mayor presented the citizenship award to me.*

7i Read the sentence aloud with the pronoun as the subject when a pronoun follows a form of the verb *be* (*is, are, was, were*).

INCORRECT   The leader is him.

If you substitute *him* for *the leader,* the sentence sounds wrong: *Him is the leader.*

REVISED   The leader is he.

If you substitute *he* for *the leader,* the sentence sounds correct: *He is the leader.*

■ The best singer in the group is ~~her.~~ *she.*

7j Read the sentence aloud without the noun to determine whether *we* or *us* should come before a noun.

■ If we hikers frighten them, the bears may attack.

  If you mentally delete *hikers,* the sentence sounds correct: *If we frighten them, the bears may attack.*

■ The older children never paid attention to us kindergartners.

  If you mentally delete *kindergartners,* the sentence sounds correct: *The older children never paid attention to us.*

7k Choose the correct pronoun form for a comparison using *than* or *as* by mentally adding the verb that is implied.

■ Diedre is a better athlete than I [am].

■ The coach likes her better than [he likes] me.

An **object** is the target or recipient of the action described by the verb: *I gave her the keys.*

7l Use *who* or *whoever* when the pronoun functions as the subject of a sentence. Use *whom* or *whomever* when the pronoun functions as the object of a verb or preposition.

An **object of a preposition** is a word or phrase that follows a preposition: *with him, above the table.*

To decide whether to use *who* or *whom* in a question, answer the question yourself by using the words *he* or *him* or *she* or *her*. If you use *he* or *she* in the answer, you should use *who* in the question. If you use *him* or *her* in the answer, use *whom* in the question.

QUESTION	(*Who, Whom*) photocopied the article?
ANSWER	*She* photocopied the article.
CORRECT PRONOUN	*Who* photocopied the article?

QUESTION	To (*who, whom*) is that question addressed?
ANSWER	It is addressed to *him*.
CORRECT PRONOUN	To *whom* is that question addressed?

A **dependent clause** contains a subject and a verb but does not express a complete thought.

Similarly, to decide whether to use *who* or *whom* in a **dependent clause**, turn the dependent clause into a question. The pronoun you use to answer that question will tell you whether *who* or *whom* should appear in the clause.

■ Aphra Behn's *Oronooko* dramatizes the life of a slave ~~whom~~ came from African royalty.
 who

    If you ask the question (*Who, whom*) *came from African royalty?* the answer, *He came from African royalty*, indicates that the correct pronoun is *who*.

■ The leader ~~who~~ we seek must unite the community.
 whom

    If you ask the question (*Who, whom*) *do we seek?* the answer, *We seek him*, indicates that the correct pronoun is *whom*.

A **gerund** is an *-ing* form of a verb that functions as a noun (*complaining, jogging*).

7m Use a possessive pronoun to modify a gerund.

A **participle** is an *-ing* or *-ed* form of a verb that is used as an adjective (*the terrifying monster*) or with a helping verb to indicate tense (*he was running away*). Pronouns used with participles should be in the objective case; pronouns used with gerunds should be in the possessive case.

■ *His moralizing* has never been welcome.

    The possessive pronoun *his* modifies the gerund *moralizing*.

Gerunds are often confused with **participles** because both end in *-ing*.

PARTICIPLE	Teenagers across the United States watched *her singing* on *American Idol*.

The teenagers watched her, not the singing.

GERUND   The professor discovered *their cheating* on the final exam.
The cheating was discovered, not the students doing the cheating.

(**Exercise 7.3**)

Correct any errors in pronoun case in the following sentences. Some sentences may be correct as written.

For more exercises on pronoun case, refer to the Pronoun Problems section of Exercise Central at www.bedfordstmartins .com/successfulcollege.

■ Cave explorers, ~~whom~~ _{who} are called spelunkers, sometimes find underground rooms no one has seen before.

1. Whomever discovers a large cave is usually able to attract tourists.
2. Much of Kentucky's Mammoth Cave was explored in the 1830s by Stephen Bishop, a slave who worked as a cave guide.
3. Few spelunkers today are better known than he.
4. Following the success of Mammoth Cave, many Kentucky cavers hoped to make a fortune from them spelunking.
5. Floyd Collins was one Kentucky native whom searched his property for caves.
6. In January 1925, a falling rock trapped Collins, whom was spelunking in a narrow passage in Sand Cave.
7. When his brothers found him, Collins and them worked unsuccessfully to free his trapped leg.
8. For several days, the most famous man in Kentucky was him.
9. The plea to rescue Floyd Collins was answered by whoever could travel to rural Kentucky.
10. Them failing to save Collins was a terrible tragedy for his family and the rescuers.

(**Exercise 7.4**)

Correct any errors in pronoun reference, agreement, and case in the following paragraph. Some sentences may be correct as written.

For more exercises on pronoun reference, agreement, and case, refer to the Pronoun Problems section of Exercise Central at www.bedfordstmartins .com/successfulcollege.

■ ~~Her~~ _{She} and her husband married for love, which was unusual at the time.

Lady Mary Wortley Montagu, whom was a wealthy aristocrat, was one of the eighteenth century's most interesting characters. Few women then were as well educated as her. Every parent wanted their daughter to be charming, not intellectual, so Lady Mary secretly taught herself Latin. When her husband was appointed ambassador to Turkey, she and he traveled there together. Her letters to friends in London, which were later published, were filled with detail. She described a Turkish bath's atmosphere so vividly that it became a popular setting for paintings and literature. She also learned that smallpox was rare in Turkey. Of the Turkish people she met, most had gotten his or her immunity to smallpox from a kind of inoculation. This had an effect on Lady Mary herself. Lady Mary's children were among the first British citizens who were inoculated against it.

8 Shifts and Mixed Constructions

A **shift** is a sudden, unexpected change in point of view, verb tense, voice, mood, or level of diction that may confuse your readers. Shifting from a direct to an indirect question or quotation can also confuse readers. A **mixed construction** is a sentence containing parts that do not sensibly fit together. This chapter will help you identify and correct shifts and mixed constructions in your sentences.

Shifts

8a Refer to yourself, your audience, and the people you are writing about in a consistent way.

Person shows the writer's point of view. Personal pronouns indicate whether the subject is the speaker (first person: *I, we*), the person spoken to (second person: *you*), or the person or thing spoken about (third person: *he, she, it, they, one*). (For more on person, see 1b and Chapter 5, p. 109.)

> INCONSISTENT   *I* discovered that *you* could touch some of the museum exhibits.
> Notice that the writer shifts from first-person *I* to the second-person *you*.

> CONSISTENT   *I* discovered that *I* could touch some of the museum exhibits.
> The writer uses the first-person *I* consistently within the sentence.

■ When people study a foreign language, ~~you~~ *they* also learn about another culture.

8b Maintain consistency in verb tense throughout a paragraph or an essay unless the meaning requires you to change tenses.

> INCONSISTENT   The virus *mutated* so quickly that it *develops* a resistance to most vaccines.
> The sentence shifts from past to present.

> REVISED   The virus *mutates* so quickly that it *develops* a resistance to most vaccines.

Shifts between the present and past tense are among the most common shifts writers make.

■ The city's crime rate continues to drop, but experts ~~disagreed~~ on the reasons.

8c Change verb tense when you want to indicate an actual time change.

Use the present tense for events that occur in the present; use the past tense for events that occurred in the past. When the time changes, be sure to change the tense. Notice the intentional shifts in the following passage (the verbs are in italics).

> Every spring migratory birds *return* to cooler climates to raise their young. This year a pair of bluejays *is occupying* a nest in my yard, and I *spy* on them. The hatchlings *are growing* larger and *developing* feathers. Last spring, robins *built* the nest that the jays now *call* home, and I *watched* them every morning until the young birds *left* home for the last time.

As the events switch from this year (present) to the previous year (past), the writer changes from the present tense (*is occupying*) to the past tense (*built*). (For more on verb tense, see 1c and 27a.)

8d Use a consistent voice.

Needless shifts between the **active voice** and the **passive voice** can disorient readers and create wordy sentences.

In the **active voice**, the subject of the sentence performs the action.

In the **passive voice**, the subject receives the action.

- *The researchers gave one*
  ~~One~~ group of volunteers ~~was given~~ a placebo, and ~~the researchers~~ *they* treated another group with the new drug.

- Drought and windstorms made farming impossible, and many families ~~were forced~~ to leave Oklahoma. ~~by the specter of starvation.~~ *the specter of starvation forced*

To change a sentence from the passive voice to the active voice, make the performer of the action the subject of the sentence. The original subject of the sentence becomes the direct object. Delete the form of the verb *be*.

| PASSIVE | The restraining order was signed by the judge. |
| ACTIVE | The judge signed the restraining order. |

For more on voice, see 1c and 6d.

8e Avoid sudden shifts from indirect to direct questions or quotations.

An indirect question tells what a question is or was.

| INDIRECT QUESTION | The defense attorney asked where I was on the evening of May 10. |
| DIRECT QUESTION | "Where were you on the evening of May 10?" |

Avoid shifting from direct to indirect questions.

■ Sal asked what could ~~I~~ ^{he} do to solve the problem.

8f Use a consistent mood throughout a paragraph or an essay.

Mood indicates whether the sentence states a fact or asks a question (**indicative mood**); gives a command or direction (**imperative mood**); or expresses a condition contrary to fact, a wish, or a suggestion (**subjunctive mood**). The subjunctive mood is also used for hypothetical situations or impossible or unlikely events. (For more on mood, see 1c.)

INCONSISTENT

You shouldn't expect to learn ballroom dancing immediately, and remember that even Fred Astaire had to start somewhere. First, find a qualified instructor. Then, you should not be embarrassed even if everyone else seems more graceful than you are. Finally, keep your goal in mind, and you need to practice, practice, practice.

This paragraph contains shifts between the indicative and imperative moods.

CONSISTENT

Don't expect to learn ballroom dancing immediately, and remember that even Fred Astaire had to start somewhere. First, find a qualified instructor. Then, don't be embarrassed if everyone else seems more graceful than you are. Finally, keep your goal in mind, and practice, practice, practice.

This revised paragraph uses the imperative mood consistently.

8g Use a consistent level of diction.

Your level of diction can range from formal to informal. The level you choose should be appropriate for your audience, your subject matter, and your purpose for writing. As you revise your essays, look for inappropriate shifts in diction, such as from a formal to an informal tone or vice versa.

William H. Whyte's studies of human behavior in public space yielded a number of surprises. Perhaps most unexpected was the revelation that people seem to be drawn toward, rather than driven from, crowded spaces. They tend to congregate near the entrances of stores or on street corners. Plazas and shopping districts crowded with pedestrians attract more pedestrians. For some reason, people seem to ~~get a charge out of hanging out where lots of other folks are hanging out, too.~~ ^{enjoy gathering together in public spaces.}

For academic writing, including class assignments and research papers, use formal language. (For more on levels of diction, see Chapter 10, pp. 215–17.)

(Exercise 8.1)

Correct the shifts in person, verb tense, voice, mood, and level of diction in the following sentences.

For more exercises on shifts in person, verb tense, voice, mood, and level of diction, refer to the Shifts and Mixed Constructions section of Exercise Central at www.bedfordstmartins .com/successfulcollege.

■ Experts continue to break new ground in child psychology, and their research. ~~has been studied by many parents.~~

many parents have studied

1. A new idea about the development of children's personalities had surprised many American psychologists because it challenges widely accepted theories.

2. We wondered whether our professor knew of the new theory and did she agree with it.

3. Personality is believed by some experts to be the result of parental care, but other specialists feel that biology influences personality more strongly.

4. Most parents think you have a major influence on your child's behavior.

5. The new theory suggests that children's peers are a heck of a lot more influential than parents.

6. Peer acceptance is strongly desired by children, and they want to be different from adults.

7. If adults were to think about their childhood experiences, they realize that this idea has merit.

8. Most adults recall that in childhood, your friends' opinions were extremely important to you.

9. The way people behave with family members is often different from the way we act with our friends.

10. Jittery moms and dads would be really, really relieved if this hypothesis were proven.

(Exercise 8.2)

Correct the shifts in person, verb tense, voice, mood, and level of diction in the following paragraph.

For more exercises on shifts in person, verb tense, voice, mood, and level of diction, refer to the Shifts and Mixed Constructions section of Exercise Central at www.bedfordstmartins.com/ successfulcollege.

■ Some artists long ago used techniques that still ~~surprised~~ modern students of their work.

surprise

Museum visitors can see paintings by the seventeenth-century Dutch artist Jan Vermeer, but you cannot see how he achieved his remarkable effects. Most of his paintings showed simply furnished household rooms. The people and objects in these rooms seem so real that the paintings resembled photographs. Vermeer's use of perspective and light would also contribute to the paintings' realism. Some art historians believe he used a gizmo called a *camera obscura*. This machine projected an image onto a flat surface so you could draw it. For most experts, Vermeer's possible use of technological aids does not make his totally fabulous results less impressive. It is agreed by art historians that the paintings are masterpieces. Vermeer's paintings are admired even more now than they are in his own lifetime.

Mixed Constructions

8h Make sure clauses and phrases fit together logically.

A **mixed construction** contains phrases or clauses that do not work together logically and that cause confusion in meaning.

MIXED   The fact that the marathon is twenty-six miles, a length that explains why I have never finished it.

The sentence starts with a subject (*The fact*) followed by a dependent clause (*that the marathon is twenty-six miles*). The sentence needs a predicate to complete the independent clause; instead it includes a noun (*a length*) and another dependent clause (*that explains why I have never finished it*). The independent clause that begins with *The fact* is never completed.

REVISED   The marathon is twenty-six miles long, which is why I have never finished it.

In the revision, the parts of the sentence work together.

To avoid mixed constructions in your writing, it often helps to check the words that connect clauses and phrases, especially prepositions and conjunctions.

8i Make subjects and predicates consistent.

Faulty predication occurs when a subject does not work grammatically with its predicate.

FAULTY   The most valued trait in an employee is a person who is loyal.

A person is not a trait.

REVISED   The most valued trait in an employee is loyalty.

■ Rising health-care costs decrease health insurance. ^*the number of people who can afford*^ ~~for many people.~~

Costs do not decrease health insurance.

8j Avoid the constructions *is when* or *is where* or *reason...is because.*

FAULTY   Indigestion is when you cannot digest food.

REVISED   Indigestion is the inability to digest food.

■ Gravitation is ^*the attraction of*^ ~~where~~ one body ~~is being attracted by~~ ^*for*^ another.

■ ~~The reason~~ I enjoy jogging ~~is~~ because it provides outdoor exercise.

For more exercises on mixed constructions, refer to the Shifts and Mixed Constructions section of Exercise Central at www.bedfordstmartins.com/ successfulcollege.

Exercise 8.3

Correct the mixed constructions in the following sentences.

- The reason ~~internships are valuable is because~~ they give students real-world experience.

1. Many interns earn college credit for their work, but they also gain practical experience and important contacts.

2. Surveys showing that college graduates who intern receive higher salary offers than their classmates who do not.

3. The fact that students must be careful, as all internships are not created equal.

4. The most important qualities are an intern with curiosity and a good work ethic.

5. A good internship is when the intern gains knowledge and skills in a professional environment.

6. Some companies provide little guidance that interns do not learn much from the experience.

7. Other companies may use unpaid interns that is free labor instead of hiring full-time employees.

8. The U.S. Department of Labor has strict guidelines that apply to unpaid internships.

9. Companies do not meet these federal requirements, because they must pay minimum wage or face lawsuits.

10. By having these strict federal standards, some worry that companies will eliminate internship programs rather than risk any legal problems.

9 Adjectives and Adverbs

Adjectives and adverbs are powerful. Used appropriately, they can add precision and force to your writing, as the following excerpt demonstrates.

> Seated cross-legged on a brocade pillow, wrapped in burgundy robes, was a short, rotund man with a shiny pate. He looked very old and very tired. Chhongba bowed reverently, spoke briefly to him in the Sherpa tongue, and indicated for us to come forward.
>
> Jon Krakauer, *Into Thin Air*

Adjectives modify nouns or pronouns and indicate which one, what kind, or how many. **Adverbs** modify verbs, adjectives, other adverbs, clauses, or entire sentences and indicate how, when, where, how often, or to what extent. (See also 1d and 1e.)

The two most common errors involving adjectives and adverbs occur when writers use (1) an adjective instead of an adverb (or vice versa) and (2) the wrong form of an adjective or adverb in a comparison. Use the following guidelines to identify and correct these and other common errors in your writing.

9a Use adverbs, not adjectives, to modify verbs, adjectives, or other adverbs.

Although in conversation you may often use adjectives in place of adverbs, you should be careful in your writing to use adverbs to modify verbs, adjectives, or other adverbs.

- Those pants are ~~awful~~ *awfully* expensive.

- The headlights shone ~~bright.~~ *brightly.*

9b Use adjectives, not adverbs, after linking verbs.

Linking verbs, often forms of *be* and other verbs such as *feel, look, make,* and *seem,* express a state of being. A linking verb takes a **subject complement**—a word group that completes or renames the subject of the sentence. Verbs such as *feel* and *look* can also be action verbs. When they function as action verbs in a sentence, they may be modified by an adverb.

If you are not sure whether a word should be an adjective or adverb, determine how it is used in the sentence. If the word modifies a noun, it should be an adjective.

ADJECTIVE   Our *waiter* looked *slow*.

Slow modifies the word *waiter,* a noun. In this sentence, *looked* is a linking verb.

ADVERB   Our waiter *looked slowly* for some menus.

In this sentence, *looked* is expressing an action and is not a linking verb; *slowly* modifies *looked*.

9c Use *good* and *bad* as adjectives; use *well* and *badly* as adverbs.

- Einstein was not a *good student*.
  The adjective *good* modifies the noun *student*.

- Einstein did not *perform well* in school.
  The adverb *well* modifies the verb *perform*.

- He did ~~bad~~ *badly* in the leading role.
  The adverb *badly* modifies the verb *did*.

When you are describing someone's health, *well* can also function as an adjective.

- The disease was in remission, but the *patients* were not yet *well*.

9d Be careful not to use adjectives such as *real* and *sure* to modify adverbs or other adjectives.

- The produce was crisp and ~~real~~ fresh.
  > *really*

  The adverb *really* modifies the adjective *fresh*.

9e Avoid double negatives.

A sentence with two negative words or phrases contains a **double negative**, which conveys a positive meaning. Do not use two negatives in a sentence unless you want to express a positive meaning (for example, *not uncommon* means "common").

- The company is not doing ~~nothing~~ to promote its incentive plan.
  > *anything*

- No one under eighteen ~~can't~~ vote in the presidential election.
  > *can*

  POSITIVE MEANING INTENDED

  Athletic sportswear is not uncommon as casual attire.

9f Use the comparative form of adjectives and adverbs to compare two things; use the superlative form to compare three or more things.

Adjectives and adverbs can be used to compare two or more persons, objects, actions, or ideas. The **comparative** form of an adjective or adverb compares two items. The **superlative** form compares three or more items. Use the list below to check the comparative and superlative forms of most regular adjectives and adverbs in your sentences.

	Comparatives	*Superlatives*
One-syllable adjectives and adverbs	Add *-er: colder, faster*	Add *-est: coldest, fastest*
Two-syllable adjectives	Add *-er: greasier**	Add *-est: greasiest**
Adjectives with three or more syllables or adverbs ending in *-ly*	Add *more* in front of the word: *more beautiful, more quickly*	Add *most* in front of the word: *most beautiful, most quickly*

*To form the comparative and superlative forms of adjectives ending in *-y,* change the *y* to *i* and add *-er* or *-est.*

Irregular adjectives and adverbs form their comparative and superlative forms in unpredictable ways, as the following list illustrates.

	Comparative	*Superlative*
Adjectives		
good	better	best
bad	worse	worst
little	less	least
Adverbs		
well	better	best
badly	worse	worst
Words That Function as Adjectives and Adverbs		
many	more	most
some	more	most
much	more	most

Do not use comparative or superlative forms with absolute concepts, such as *unique* and *perfect*. Something cannot be more or less unique, for example; it is either unique or not unique.

- This is ~~the most~~ unique solution to the pollution problem. ^a

9g Check your comparisons to be sure they are complete when using comparative and superlative forms.

An incomplete comparison can leave your reader confused about what is being compared.

INCOMPLETE	The Internet works more efficiently.
REVISED	For sending correspondence and documents, the Internet works more efficiently than the postal service.
INCOMPLETE	The catcher sustained the most crippling knee injury.
REVISED	The catcher sustained the most crippling knee injury of his career.

9h Do not use *more* or *most* with the -er or -est form of an adjective or adverb.

- The hypothesis must be ~~more~~ clearer.

For more exercises on adjectives and adverbs, refer to the Parts of Speech and Adjectives and Adverbs sections of Exercise Central at www.bedfordstmartins.com/ successfulcollege.

Exercise 9.1

Correct any errors involving adjectives and adverbs in the following sentences.

- *Wikipedia* is probably ~~a more~~ popular reference source in the world. ^the most

1. The site is an open source, online encyclopedia where anyone can contribute, even if he or she writes bad or inaccurate.

2. *Wikipedia* has many advantages that reflect good upon it as a source.

3. There is not nothing more convenient for getting information real quick.

4. In a way, encyclopedias are more unique because Web sites can grow to include any subject that anyone finds interesting.

5. *Wikipedia* relies heavy on the knowledge and interests of millions of people, rather than on the choices of a small group of experts.

6. The site has some really downsides, too.

7. Some of the information on *Wikipedia* can be awful inaccurate.

8. Many teachers and professors don't allow no students to use *Wikipedia* for research.

9. When students rely entire on the site, their papers usually don't get good grades.

10. If they choose to use the site, students should make it more clearer to their professors that they have researched their subjects thorough.

Exercise 9.2

Correct any errors involving adjectives and adverbs in the following paragraph. Some sentences may be correct as written.

For more exercises on adjectives and adverbs, refer to the Parts of Speech and Adjectives and Adverbs sections of Exercise Central at www.bedfordstmartins.com/ successfulcollege.

■ **Originating in China, *feng shui* is a traditionally art of balancing elements to achieve harmony.**

   Feng shui is taken very serious in many Asian societies. Some Hong Kong business executives, for example, will not feel comfortably working in an office until it has been approved by a *feng shui* master. Other people are more interested in *feng shui* for its elegance. A room designed with this idea in mind looks tranquilly. The name *feng shui* means "wind and water," and balancing elements is the more important aspect of the art. Some people believe that this balance brings good luck. Others will admit only that surroundings can have a psychological effect. It is easier to feel comfortable in a room designed according to *feng shui* principles. The placement of doors, windows, and furnishings contributes to the peaceful effect. Whether *feng shui* is magic or simple great interior design, something about it seems to work.

---

10   Misplaced and Dangling Modifiers

A **modifier** is a word or group of words that describes, changes, qualifies, or limits the meaning of another word or group of words in a sentence.

■ **The contestant *smiled delightedly*.**
   The adverb *delightedly* modifies the verb *smiled*.

■ ***Pretending to be surprised, he* greeted the guests.**
   The adjective phrase *Pretending to be surprised* modifies the pronoun *he*.

Modifiers that are carefully placed in sentences give your readers a clear picture of the details you want to convey. However, when a sentence contains a **misplaced modifier**, it is hard for the reader to tell which word or group of words the modifier is supposed to be describing.

10a Place modifiers close to the words they describe.

MISPLACED The mayor *chided* the pedestrians for jaywalking *angrily*.

The adverb *angrily* should be closer to the verb it modifies, *chided*. Here, the adverb appears to be modifying *jaywalking*, so the sentence is confusing.

REVISED The mayor *angrily chided* the pedestrians for jaywalking.

MISPLACED The press *reacted* to the story leaked from the Pentagon *with horror*.

The adverb phrase *with horror* should explain how the press reacted, not how the story was leaked, so the modifier should be closer to the verb *reacted*.

REVISED The press *reacted with horror* to the story leaked from the Pentagon.

10b Make sure each modifier clearly modifies only one word or phrase in a sentence.

When a modifier is placed near or next to the word or phrase it modifies, it may also be near another word it could conceivably modify. When a modifier's placement may cause such ambiguity, rewrite the sentence, placing the modifier so that it clearly refers to the word or phrase it is supposed to modify.

UNCLEAR The film's attempt to portray war accurately depicts a survivor's anguish.

Does the film attempt to portray war accurately, or does it accurately depict a survivor's anguish? The following revisions eliminate the uncertainty.

REVISED ~~The film's~~ *In its* attempt to portray war accurately *, the film* depicts a survivor's anguish.

REVISED The ~~film's attempt to portray war~~ *film* accurately depicts a survivor's anguish *in its attempt to portray war realistically.*

10c Revise a dangling modifier by rewriting the sentence.

A **dangling modifier** is a word or phrase that does not modify or refer to anything in a sentence. Instead, it seems to modify something that has been left out of the sentence.

A dangling modifier can make the meaning of a sentence unclear, inaccurate, or even comical. Most dangling modifiers appear at the beginning or end of sentences.

DANGLING **After singing a thrilling ballad, the crowd surged toward the stage.**
This sentence suggests that the crowd sang the ballad.

DANGLING **Laying an average of ten eggs a day, the neighboring farmer is proud of his henhouse.**
This sentence suggests that the farmer lays eggs.

To revise a sentence with a dangling modifier, follow these steps.

1. Identify the word or words that the modifier is supposed to modify.

2. Revise the sentence to correct the confusion either by changing the modifier into a clause with its own subject and verb or by rewriting the sentence so that the word being modified becomes the subject.

Kelly sang
■ **After ~~singing~~ a thrilling ballad, the crowd surged toward the stage.**
                ^

                                    his prize chickens give   *reason to be*
■ **Laying an average of ten eggs a day, the neighboring farmer ~~is~~ proud of his henhouse.**
                                        ^   ^

Exercise 10.1

Correct any misplaced or dangling modifiers in the following sentences.

scientists have built
■ **Hoping to get a message from outer space, a huge telescope. ~~has been built.~~**
                                            ^   ^

1. Solar systems exist throughout the galaxy like our own.

2. So far, no proof on other planets of the existence of life forms has been found.

3. A tremendously powerful telescope searches distant stars for signs of life in the Caribbean.

4. Astronomers monitor signals coming from other parts of the solar system carefully.

5. Wondering whether humans are alone in the universe, the telescope may provide answers.

6. Most of the signals have been caused by cell phone and satellite interference received so far.

7. While trying to intercept signals from other planets, a signal has also been sent from earth.

8. The message is on its way to other parts of our galaxy, containing information about earth.

9. The message will take twenty thousand years to reach its destination or more.

10. A signal sent to earth similarly would take a long time to reach us.

For more exercises on misplaced and dangling modifiers, refer to the Misplaced and Dangling Modifiers section of Exercise Central at www.bedfordstmartins.com/successfulcollege.

Exercise 10.2

For more exercises on misplaced
and dangling modifiers, refer
to the Misplaced and Dangling
Modifiers section of Exercise
Central at www.bedfordstmartins
.com/successfulcollege.

Correct any misplaced or dangling modifiers in the following paragraph. Some sentences may be correct as written.

■ The measurement is now based on atomic vibrations of one second.

<small>of one second</small>

Making sure standard weights and measures are the same all over the world is an important task. To trade internationally, a kilogram in Mexico must weigh the same as a kilogram in Japan. In the past, countries set standards for weighing and measuring individually. One English king declared a yard to be the distance from his nose to his thumb egotistically. Weight was once measured in barleycorns, so unethical merchants soaked barleycorns to make them heavier in water. Today, the metric system is the worldwide standard, and the weight of the U.S. pound is based even on the standard kilogram. In France, a cylinder is the world standard kilogram made of platinum. Securely, this official kilogram is kept in an airtight container. Nevertheless, losing a few billionths of a gram of weight each year, world standards might eventually be affected. Hoping to find a permanent solution, scientists want to base the kilogram measurement on an unchanging natural phenomenon.

USING PUNCTUATION CORRECTLY

11 End Punctuation

The end of a sentence can be marked with a period (.), a question mark (?), or an exclamation point (!).

11a Use a period to mark the end of a sentence that makes a statement, gives an instruction, or includes an indirect question; use periods with most abbreviations.

An indirect question is a statement that reports what was asked or is being asked: *He asked where the classroom was.*

Writers seldom omit the period at the end of a sentence that makes a statement or gives directions.

STATEMENT	**Amnesty International investigates human-rights violations.**
INSTRUCTION	**Use as little water as possible during the drought.**

Writers sometimes mistake an indirect question for a direct one, however.

■ **Most visitors want to know where the dinosaur bones were found?.**
   This sentence states what question was asked; it does not ask the question directly.

Many abbreviations use periods (*Mass., Co., St.,*). If you are not sure whether an abbreviation should include periods, check a dictionary.

When an abbreviation that uses periods ends a sentence, an additional period is not needed.

■ **My brother works for Apple Computer, Inc./**

Note, however, that the Modern Language Association (MLA) recommends omitting periods in abbreviations that consist of capital letters (*IBM, USIA, BC*) but including periods in abbreviations that consist of lowercase letters (*a.m.*).

11b Use a question mark to end a sentence that asks a direct question.

DIRECT QUESTION   **Why was the flight delayed?**

When a question is also a quotation, the question mark is placed within the quotation marks (see also 15d).

■ **"What did she want?"? Marcia asked.**

11c Use an exclamation point to end a sentence that expresses a strong emotion or a forceful command.

■ Altering experimental results to make them conform to a hypothesis is never ethical!

Use exclamation points sparingly; they lose their impact when used too frequently.

■ Government officials immediately suspected terrorism!

For more exercises on the use of end punctuation marks, refer to the End Punctuation section of Exercise Central at www.bedfordstmartins .com/successfulcollege.

Exercise 11.1

Correct any errors in the use of end punctuation marks in the following sentences. Some sentences may be correct as written.

■ Is it possible that hemophilia in the Russian czar's family contributed to the Russian Revolution?

1. When the daughters of Queen Victoria of England, who carried the gene for hemophilia, married royalty in Germany and Russia, those royal families inherited hemophilia as well?
2. The Russian czar's only son and heir to the throne suffered from hemophilia.
3. You might ask if internal bleeding can occur when a hemophiliac receives a bruise?
4. Czar Nicholas and his wife Alexandra often saw their little boy in terrible pain!
5. A phony monk named Rasputin eased the child's pain, but was he a gifted healer or just a con man.

12 Commas

A **comma** (,) is used to separate parts of a sentence from one another. Commas, when used correctly, make your sentences clear and help readers understand your meaning.

12a Use a comma before a coordinating word (*and, but, for, nor, or, so, yet*) that joins two independent clauses.

An **independent clause** contains a subject and verb and can stand alone as a sentence.

■ The ball flew past the goalie, but the score did not count.

■ Her dog was enormous, so many people found it threatening.

12b Use a comma to separate three or more items in a series.

A **series** is a list of three or more items—words, phrases, or clauses.

■ Dancing, singing, and acting are just a few of her talents.

■ Sunflowers grew on the hillsides, along the roads, and in the middle of every pasture.

Some writers omit the comma before the coordinating conjunction (such as *and, or*) in a brief series when using a casual or journalistic style. Occasionally this omission can create confusion, so it is better to include the final comma.

> CONFUSING   She insured her valuable heirlooms, watches and jewelry.
>
> Do her heirlooms consist entirely of watches and jewelry, or did she insure three kinds of items?
>
> CLEAR   She insured her valuable heirlooms, watches, and jewelry.

A comma is not used after the last item in a series.

■ Aphids, slugs, and beetles/ can severely damage a crop.

(See also 13c on when to use semicolons to separate items in a series.)

12c Use a comma to separate two or more adjectives that modify the same noun when they are not joined by a coordinating word.

■ Rescue workers found the frightened, hungry child.

To be sure a comma is needed, try reversing the two adjectives. If the phrase still sounds correct when the adjectives are reversed, a comma is needed. If the phrase sounds wrong, a comma is not needed.

■ The airy, open atrium makes visitors feel at home.

The phrase *open, airy atrium* sounds right, so a comma is needed.

■ Local businesses donated the bright red uniforms.

The phrase *red, bright uniforms* sounds wrong because *bright* modifies *red uniforms* in the original sentence. A comma is not needed.

12d Use a comma to separate introductory words, phrases, and clauses from the rest of a sentence.

INTRODUCTORY WORD	Above, the sky was a mass of clouds.

Without the comma, this sentence would be confusing.

INTRODUCTORY PHRASE	At the start of the project, the researchers were optimistic.
INTRODUCTORY CLAUSE	When alcohol was outlawed, many solid citizens broke the law.

Exception: A comma is not needed after a single word or short phrase or clause when there is no possibility of confusion.

■ **Then a rainbow appeared.**

12e Use a comma to set off a nonrestrictive word group from the rest of the sentence.

A **nonrestrictive word group** describes or modifies a word or phrase in a sentence, but it does not change the meaning of the word or phrase. To decide whether a comma is needed, read the sentence without the word group. If the basic meaning is unchanged, a comma is needed.

■ **Most people either love or hate fruitcake,** *which is a traditional holiday dessert.*
　The meaning of *fruitcake* is not changed by the relative clause *which is a traditional holiday dessert,* so the word group is **nonrestrictive** and a comma is needed.

■ **The child** *wearing a tutu* **delights in ballet lessons.**
　The phrase *wearing a tutu* identifies which child delights in ballet lessons, so the word group is **restrictive**—necessary to explain what the word it modifies means—and a comma is not needed.

12f Use a comma to set off parenthetical expressions.

A **parenthetical expression** provides extra information. It can also be a transitional word or phrase (*however, for example, at the beginning*) that is not essential to the meaning of the sentence.

■ *Furthermore,* **his essay had not been proofread.**

■ **Islamic countries were,** *in fact,* **responsible for preserving much classical scientific knowledge.**

12g Use commas with dates, addresses, titles, and numbers.

■ **She graduated on June 8, 2011.**

When you give only a month and year, a comma is not needed.

■ **She graduated in June 2011.**

Place a comma after the date when it appears before the end of the sentence.

■ **The 2010 winter Olympics began on February 12, 2010, in Vancouver.**

When you give an address within a sentence, do not place a comma between the state and the ZIP code.

- Send the package to PO Box 100, McPherson, Kansas 67460.

Separate a name from a title with a comma.

- The featured speaker was Kate Silverstein, Ph.D.

Use commas in numbers that have more than four digits.

- Estimates of the number of protesters ranged from 250,000 to 700,000.

In a number with four digits, the comma is optional: *1500* or *1,500*.

12h Use a comma to separate a direct quotation from the words that explain it.

A direct quotation gives a person's *exact* words, either spoken or written, set off by quotation marks.

- She asked, "What's the score?"

Place the comma before the closing quotation mark.

- "Wait and see," was his infuriating response.
    ^

(See also 15b and 15e.)

12i Use commas to set off the name of someone directly addressed, to set off an echo question, and with a "not" phrase.

DIRECT ADDRESS	"James, answer the question concisely." "Bail has not been granted, your honor."
ECHO QUESTION	More development will require a more expensive infrastructure, won't it?
"NOT" PHRASE	Labor Day, not the autumnal equinox, marks the end of summer for most Americans.

12j Omit unnecessary commas.

As you edit and proofread your papers, watch out for the following common errors in comma usage.

OMIT A COMMA BETWEEN A SUBJECT AND VERB.

<u>subject</u>   <u>verb</u>
- The poet Wilfred Owen, was killed a week before World War I ended.

A **complement** is a word or group of words that describes or renames a subject or object.

OMIT A COMMA BETWEEN A VERB AND COMPLEMENT.

verb   *complement*

- The school referendum is considered, very likely to pass.

OMIT A COMMA BETWEEN AN ADJECTIVE AND THE WORD IT MODIFIES.

adjective *noun modified*

- A growing family needs a large, house.

OMIT A COMMA BETWEEN TWO VERBS IN A COMPOUND PREDICATE.

compound predicate

- We sat, and waited for our punishment.

OMIT A COMMA BETWEEN TWO NOUNS OR PRONOUNS IN A COMPOUND SUBJECT.

compound subject

- Harold Johnson, and Margaret Simpson led the expedition.

OMIT A COMMA BEFORE A COORDINATING WORD JOINING TWO DEPENDENT CLAUSES.

dependent clause   *dependent clause*

- The band began to play before we arrived, but after the rain stopped.

OMIT A COMMA AFTER *THAN* IN A COMPARISON.

- The Homestead Act made the cost of land to pioneers less than, the price the government had paid.

OMIT A COMMA AFTER *LIKE* OR *SUCH AS*.

- Direct marketing techniques such as, mass mailings and telephone solicitations can be effective.

OMIT COMMAS APPEARING NEXT TO A QUESTION MARK, AN EXCLAMATION POINT, OR A DASH, OR BEFORE AN OPENING PARENTHESIS.

- "Where have you been?," she would always ask.

- "Stop!," the guard shouted.

- Keep spending to a minimum, —our resources are limited—and throw nothing away.

- Fast food, (which is usually high in fat), is growing in popularity all over the world.

OMIT COMMAS AROUND WORDS THAT RENAME AND RESTRICT ANOTHER WORD BEFORE THEM.

If the words are **restrictive**—necessary to explain what the word they modify means—do not enclose them with commas.

- The man, who brought his car in for transmission work, is a lawyer.

Exercise 12.1

Correct any errors in the use of commas in the following sentences. Some sentences may be correct as written.

For more exercises on the use of commas, refer to the Commas section of Exercise Central at www.bedfordstmartins.com/ successfulcollege.

■ After slavery was abolished in New York in 1827, several black settlements were established in what is now New York City.
                                              ^

1. Seneca Village a crowded shantytown on the Upper West Side was the home of many poorer black New Yorkers.
2. The city of New York, bought the land where the Seneca villagers lived.
3. The land became part of Central Park and everyone, who lived there, had to leave in the 1850s.
4. Household items from Seneca Village still turn up in Central Park today and a museum exhibit was recently devoted to life in the long-gone settlement.
5. In present-day Brooklyn, there was once a middle-class black settlement, called Weeksville.
6. James Weeks, an early resident owned much of the land.
7. Another, early, landholder, Sylvanus Smith, was a trustee of the African Free Schools of Brooklyn.
8. His daughter, Susan Smith McKinney-Steward, was born in Weeksville, and was the valedictorian of New York Medical College in 1870.
9. McKinney-Steward became the first, female, African American physician in New York, and the third in the United States.
10. Weeksville was a success story, for some of the houses survived into the twentieth century and have been preserved as historical monuments.

Exercise 12.2

Correct any errors in the use of commas in the following paragraph. Some sentences may be correct as written.

For more exercises on the use of commas, refer to the Commas section of Exercise Central at www.bedfordstmartins.com/ successfulcollege.

■ In June, 1998, fifty years after Korczak Ziolkowski began sculpting the Crazy Horse monument, the face of Crazy Horse was unveiled.

   A monument to the Lakota Sioux warrior, Crazy Horse, is under construction in the Black Hills of South Dakota. Korczak Ziolkowski a sculptor, who also worked on Mount Rushmore, began the project in 1948. Ziolkowski was born on September 6, 1908, – thirty-one years to the day after Crazy Horse died. A Sioux chief asked Ziolkowski, if he would create a monument to honor Crazy Horse, and other Indian heroes. Ziolkowski designed a sculpture of Crazy Horse on horseback that, when it is completed, will be the largest statue in the world. The sculpture is being shaped from Thunderhead Mountain a six-hundred-foot granite rock. Tons of rock have been blasted, from the mountain. The sculptor died in 1982 but his widow, children, and grandchildren have carried on the work.

There has been no government funding so, they have paid for the work entirely with donations and admission fees. By the middle of the twenty-first century the statue should be finished, and will depict the great Sioux hero pointing at the hills he loved.

13 Semicolons

A **semicolon** (;) indicates a stronger pause than a comma but not as strong a pause as a period.

13a Use a semicolon to join two closely related independent clauses.

Use a semicolon to join two closely related independent clauses not connected by a coordinating word (*and, but, for, nor, or, so,* or *yet*).

> An **independent clause** contains a subject and a verb and can stand alone as a sentence.

- In January and February, sunny days are rare and very short in northern countries; winter depression is common in the north.

For advice on other ways to join two independent clauses, see Section 4 of the Handbook.

13b Use a semicolon to join two independent clauses linked by a conjunctive adverb or transitional expression.

> A **conjunctive adverb** is a word (such as *also, however,* or *still*) that links two independent clauses.

- The stunt pilot had to eject from the cockpit; nevertheless, he was not injured.

- Mass transit is good for the environment; for example, as many people can fit in a bus as in fifteen cars.

13c Use semicolons to separate items in a series if commas are used within the items.

Semicolons help prevent confusion in a sentence that contains a series of items with one or more commas within the items.

- Fairy tales inspire children by depicting magical events, which appeal to their imaginations; clever boys and girls, who encourage young readers' problem-solving skills; evil creatures, who provide thrills; and good, heroic adults, who make the childhood world seem safer.

Also use a semicolon to separate a series of independent clauses that contain commas.

- He is stubborn, selfish, and conservative; she is stubborn, combative, and liberal; and no one is surprised that they do not get along.

(See also 12b on when to use commas to separate items in a series.)

13d Do not use a semicolon to introduce a list or to separate a phrase or dependent clause from the rest of the sentence.

■ A growing number of companies employ prison inmates for certain jobs; selling magazines, conducting surveys, reserving airplane tickets, and taking telephone orders.

(For more on introducing lists, see 14a.)

■ On the other hand; taking risks can bring impressive results.

■ I'll always wonder; if things could have been different.

For more exercises on the use of semicolons, refer to the Semicolons section of Exercise Central at www.bedfordstmartins.com/ successfulcollege.

Exercise 13.1

Correct any errors in the use of semicolons in the following sentences. Some sentences may be correct as written.

■ Myths and stories about vampires have been around for centuries; however, Bram Stoker's 1897 novel *Dracula* is probably the most famous fictional account of these monsters.

1. In the years since Stoker's novel, vampires have become a movie fixture; in America and throughout the world.

2. Silent versions of the vampire tale include *Les Vampires* (1915), a French film, *Nosferatu* (1921), a German film, and *London After Midnight* (1927), an American film.

3. Actor Bela Lugosi played Count Dracula as more of a romantic figure than a monster in the 1931 film *Dracula*; this depiction provided the standard image of the vampire as a sexy fiend.

4. The vampire tale has several standard traits; yet it remains remarkably versatile.

5. The vampire tale was adapted to the American movie western; for example, in *Billy the Kid vs. Dracula* in 1966.

6. The popular *Blacula* (1972); which recast the vampire as an African prince in 1970s Los Angeles; inspired a series of black-themed "blaxploitation" horror movies.

7. In the 1980s and 1990s, filmmakers used the vampire theme in teen films like *Fright Night* (1985); *The Lost Boys* (1987); and *Buffy the Vampire Slayer* (1992).

8. In the late 1990s, *Buffy the Vampire Slayer* was revived as a popular TV series; starring Sarah Michelle Gellar.

9. Now, the *Twilight* books and films have introduced vampires to a whole new generation of readers and movie goers; who remain fascinated by this ancient character.

10. Perhaps vampires do live forever; if only in books and on screen.

*For more exercises on the use of
semicolons, refer to the Semicolons
section of Exercise Central at
www.bedfordstmartins.com/
successfulcollege.*

Exercise 13.2

*Correct any errors in the use of semicolons in the following paragraph. Some sentences may
be correct as written.*

■ The word *placebo* is Latin for "I will please,"; placebos have long been used in
medical experiments.

In medicine, a placebo is a substance; often a sugar pill, that has no medicinal use. Placebos
alone cannot cure any medical problem, nevertheless, many patients improve when taking them.
Because patients who receive placebos do not know that the pills are useless, they think they are
getting help for their condition; and they get better. This strange but true fact—recognized by doctors; pharmacists; and other professionals—is called the placebo effect. Chemically, a placebo does
nothing, theoretically, the patient should not respond, but somehow this trick works on many people.
The placebo effect is often seen in patients; but it is not widely understood. Since the Middle Ages,
people have considered the mind and the body as separate; the placebo effect indicates that this
separation may not really exist. The mind can play tricks on the body, for example, the brain produces
phantom-limb pain in amputees. Doctors wonder; if the mind can also help to heal the body. If the
answer is "yes," then the advances in medical knowledge could be enormous.

14 Colons

You can use a **colon** (:) to introduce a list, an explanation, an example, or a further
thought within a sentence. The information following the colon should clarify or offer
specifics about the information that comes before it.

14a Use a colon to introduce a list or a series.

When you use a **colon** to introduce a list, make sure the list is preceded by a complete
sentence.

■ The archaeologists uncovered several items: pieces of pottery, seeds, animal bones,
and household tools.

                                                    common childhood illnesses
■ All students must be immunized against: measles, mumps, and rubella.

14b Use a colon to introduce an explanation, an example, or a summary.

■ In many ways Hollywood is very predictable: Action movies arrive in the summer,
dramas in the fall.

■ One tree is particularly famous for its spectacular autumn colors: the sugar maple.

- Disaster relief efforts began all over the country: Volunteers raised forty million dollars.

Note: If the group of words following a colon is a complete sentence, the first word can begin with either a capital or a lowercase letter. Whichever option you choose, be consistent throughout your paper.

14c Use a colon to introduce a word or phrase that renames another noun.

- A hushed group of tourists stared at the most famous statue in Florence: Michelangelo's *David.*

14d Use a colon to introduce a lengthy or heavily punctuated quotation.

A quotation that is more than one or two lines long or that contains two or more commas can be introduced by a colon.

- Without pausing for breath, his campaign manager intoned the introduction: "Ladies and gentlemen, today it is my very great privilege to introduce to you the person on whose behalf you have all worked so tirelessly and with such impressive results, the man who is the reason we are all here today—the next president of the United States."

- The instructions were confusing: "After adjusting toggles A, B, and C, connect bracket A to post A, bracket B to post B, and bracket C to post C, securing with clamps A, B, and C, as illustrated in figure 1."

14e Use a colon to separate hours and minutes, in salutations for business letters, between titles and subtitles, and in ratios.

HOURS AND MINUTES	9:15 a.m.
SALUTATIONS	Dear Professor Sung:
TITLES AND SUBTITLES	*American Sphinx: The Character of Thomas Jefferson*
RATIOS	7:1

14f Use a colon only at the end of an independent clause.

A colon should always follow an independent clause, which could stand on its own as a complete sentence. Do not use a colon between a verb and its object, between a preposition and its object, or before a list introduced by such words as *for example, including, is,* and *such as.*

An independent clause contains a subject and a verb and can stand alone as a sentence.

- A medieval map is hard to read: The top of the map points to the east, not the north.
  A medieval map is hard to read is an independent clause.

- Even a small garden can produce; beans, squash, tomatoes, and corn.

- My cat had hidden a ball of twine under; the sofa.

- Bird-watchers are thrilled to spy birds of prey such as; peregrine falcons, red-tailed hawks, and owls.

For more exercises on the use of colons, refer to the Colons section of Exercise Central at www.bedfordstmartins.com/ successfulcollege.

Exercise 14.1

Correct any errors in the use of colons in the following sentences. Some sentences may be correct as written.

- Young, impeccably dressed couples participated in the latest craze; swing dancing.
  ^

1. The shuttle launch is scheduled for precisely 10.00 a.m.

2. The proposed zoning change was defeated by a margin of 2/1.

3. On early rap records, listeners heard percussion from unusual sources such as: turntables, microphones, and synthesizers.

4. To find out whether a film is historically accurate, consult *Past Imperfect: History According to the Movies.*

5. He believes that the most American of all sports is: baseball.

6. As the entourage rushed past, the star's press agent snapped her orders: "No questions, no photos, no comment, no kidding!"

7. Travel advisories are in effect for the following areas, the northern Rocky Mountains and the upper Great Plains.

8. The neon lights gleamed: above stores and in diner windows.

9. We were not hungry, we had just eaten lunch an hour earlier.

10. Some music historians claim that the American songwriting tradition reached its peak in: the 1930s.

15 Quotation Marks

A **direct quotation** gives a person's *exact* words, either spoken or written, set off by quotation marks

Quotation marks (" ") are used to indicate **direct quotations** or to mark words used as words in your sentences. Quotation marks are always used in pairs. The opening quotation mark (") appears at the beginning of a word or quoted passage, and the closing mark (") appears at the end.

15a Place quotation marks around direct statements from other speakers or writers.

Be careful to include the *exact* words of the speaker or writer within the quotation marks.

- Lincoln recalled that the United States was "dedicated to the proposition that all men are created equal."

  Because *dedicated to the proposition that all men are created equal* repeats Lincoln's exact words, quotation marks are required.

- Lincoln recalled that the United States was "dedicated to the ~~idea~~ that all men are created equal." *(proposition)*

  Words in quotation marks must be quoted *exactly* as they appear in the original source.

In dialogue, place quotation marks around each speaker's words. Every time a different person speaks, begin a new paragraph.

> He said, "Sit down."
> "No, thank you," I replied.

With longer passages, indent prose quotations of more than four lines and verse quotations of more than three lines if you are following MLA style; do not use quotation marks. Indent the quotation ten spaces or one inch from the left margin. When you quote a poem, follow the line breaks exactly.

In "A Letter to Her Husband, Absent upon Public Employment," Ann Bradstreet poignantly longs for him to return:

> My chilled limbs now numbed lie forlorn;
> Return, return, sweet Sol, from Capricorn;
> In this dead time, alas, what can I more
> Than view those fruits which through thy heat I bore?
> Which sweet contentment yield me for a space,
> True living pictures of their father's face. (11–16)

Note: If you are following APA style, indent quotations of forty or more words five spaces from the left margin. For more on the MLA and APA styles of documentation, see Chapter 23, (pages 640–81).

15b Place a comma or period that follows a direct quotation *within* the quotation marks.

- "Play it, Sam," Rick tells the piano player in *Casablanca*.
- Willie Sutton robbed banks because "that's where the money is."

15c Place colons and semicolons *outside* of quotation marks.

■ The marching band played "Seventy-Six Trombones;": the drum major's favorite song.

■ A new national anthem should replace "The Star-Spangled Banner;"; no one can sing that song.

15d Place question marks and exclamation points according to the meaning of the sentence.

If the quotation is a question or exclamation, place the question mark or exclamation point *within* the closing quotation mark. If the punctuation mark comes at the end of a sentence, no other end punctuation is needed.

■ "How does the bridge stand up?" the child wondered.

■ Poe's insane narrator confesses, "It is the beating of his hideous heart!"

If the entire sentence, of which the quotation is part, is a question or exclamation, the question mark or exclamation point goes *outside* the closing quotation marks at the end of the sentence.

■ Was Scarlett O'Hara serious when she said, "Tomorrow is another day"?

15e Use a comma to separate a short quotation from an introductory or identifying phrase such as *he replied* or *she said*.

■ "Video games improve eye-hand coordination," he replied.

■ "The homeless population," she reported, "grew steadily throughout the 1980s."

15f Use single quotation marks (' ') to indicate a quotation or a title within a quotation.

■ The mysterious caller repeatedly insists, "Play 'Misty' for me."

15g Place quotation marks around the titles of short works.

SECTION OF A BOOK	Chapter 1, "Ozzie and Harriet in Spanish Harlem"
POEM	"Ode on a Grecian Urn"
SHORT STORY	"The Yellow Wallpaper"
ESSAY OR ARTICLE	"Their Malcolm, My Problem"
SONG	"Bad Romana"
EPISODE OF A TELEVISION PROGRAM	"Larry's Last Goodbye"

15h Do not use quotation marks to call unnecessary attention to words or phrases.

■ The manager who was originally in charge of the project "jumped ship" before the deadline.

Quotation marks can be used to mark words used as words (as an alternative to italics).

■ The word "receive" is often misspelled.

Exercise 15.1

Correct any errors in the use of quotation marks in the following sentences. Some sentences may be correct as written.

For more exercises on the use of quotation marks, refer to the Quotation Marks section of Exercise Central at www.bedfordstmartins .com/successfulcollege.

■ The hotel has an excellent restaurant specializing in "fresh" fish.

1. Her essay was entitled, " "To Be or Not to Be": Shakespeare and Existentialism."
2. Why did the professor assign "To an Athlete Dying Young?"
3. A movie line many teenagers imitated was "Hasta la vista, baby".
4. After September 11, 2001, President Bush said he was going to "fight terror".
5. "I have a dream," Martin Luther King Jr. told the civil rights marchers.
6. Come live with me and be my love, pleads the speaker in Marlowe's poem.
7. The grand jury was not "completely" convinced of the need for a trial.
8. It turned out that the pianist could play only Chopsticks.
9. O'Brien originally published the chapter called "Speaking of Courage" as a short story.
10. Our waitress announced, "The special is prime rib;" unfortunately, we are vegetarians.

---

16 Ellipsis Marks

An ellipsis mark (. . .) is written as three equally spaced periods. It is used within a direct quotation to indicate where you have left out part of the original quotation. You use an **ellipsis mark** to shorten a quotation so that it includes just the parts you want or need to quote.

ORIGINAL QUOTATION	"The prison, a high percentage of whose inmates are serving life sentences, looked surprisingly ordinary."
SHORTENED	"The prison...looked surprisingly ordinary."

Notice that the two commas were also omitted when the quotation was shortened.

However, when you shorten a quotation, be careful not to change the meaning of the original passage. Do not omit any parts that will alter or misrepresent the writer's intended meaning.

ORIGINAL   "Magicians create illusions, but sometimes audience members want to believe that magic is real."

MEANING ALTERED   "Magicians . . . want to believe that magic is real."

When you omit the last part of a quoted sentence, add a sentence period, for a total of four periods (a period plus the ellipsis mark).

ORIGINAL QUOTATION   "In the sphere of psychology, details are also the thing. God preserve us from commonplaces. Best of all is to avoid depicting the hero's state of mind; you ought to try to make it clear from the hero's actions. It is not necessary to portray many characters. The center of gravity should be in two persons: him and her."

Anton Chekhov, Letter to Alexander P. Chekhov

SHORTENED   "God preserve us from commonplaces. Best of all is to avoid depicting the hero's state of mind. . . . It is not necessary to portray many characters. The center of gravity should be in two persons: him and her."

An ellipsis mark is not needed to indicate that the quoted passage continues after the sentence ends.

■ He is modest about his contributions to the abolitionist cause: "I could do but little; but what I could, I did with a joyful heart⌢." (Douglass 54).

Do not use an ellipsis mark at the beginning of a quotation, even though there is material in the original that comes before it.

ORIGINAL QUOTATION   "As was the case after the recent cleaning of the Sistine Chapel, the makeover of the starry ceiling in Grand Central Station has revealed surprisingly brilliant color."

SHORTENED   "[T]he makeover of the starry ceiling in Grand Central Station has revealed surprisingly brilliant color."

Note: The first word of a quoted sentence should be capitalized. If you change from a lowercase to a capital letter, enclose the letter in brackets (see 18d).

(For more on MLA style for ellipsis marks, see Chapter 23, pp. 635–36.)

Exercise 16.1

Shorten each of the following quotations by omitting the underlined portion and adding an ellipsis mark where appropriate.

For more exercises on the use of ellipsis marks, refer to the Ellipsis Marks section of Exercise Central at www.bedfordstmartins.com/ successfulcollege.

■ "Some people who call themselves vegetarians still eat ~~less cuddly creatures such as~~ chicken and fish."

1. "The structure of DNA, as Watson and Crick discovered, is a double helix."
2. "Although African Americans had won Academy Awards before, Halle Berry was the first African American woman to win the Academy Award for Best Actress."
3. Hamlet muses, "To be or not to be, that is the question."
4. "Many Americans do not realize that people of all classes receive financial help from the government."
5. "Cole Porter cultivated a suave, sophisticated urban persona even though he came from a small town in Indiana."
6. "From an anthropological perspective, Zora Neale Hurston's collections of folklore proved to be valuable."
7. "We take modern conveniences for granted today, but two hundred years ago households even had to make their own soap."
8. "Folic acid, doctors now believe, can help prevent certain birth defects."
9. "Although saltwater aquariums are beautiful, they are difficult and expensive to maintain."
10. "She wrote rather doubtful grammar sometimes, and in her verses took all sorts of liberties with the metre" (Thackeray 136–37).

17 Apostrophes

An **apostrophe** (') has three functions: to show ownership or possession, to indicate omitted letters in contractions, and to form some plurals.

17a Use an apostrophe to indicate possession or ownership.

Add -'s to make a singular noun possessive, including nouns that end with *s* or the sound of *s* and **indefinite pronouns** (*anyone, nobody*).

An **indefinite pronoun** does not refer to a specific person, place, or object. It refers to people, places, or things in general (*anywhere, everyone, everything*).

■ The *fox's* prey led it across the field.

■ Whether she can win the nomination is *anybody's* guess.

Note that the possessive forms of personal pronouns do not take apostrophes: *mine, yours, his, hers, ours, theirs, its.*

■ Each bee has it's function in the hive.

The possessive form of *who* is *whose* (not *who's*).

- Marie Curie, *whose* work in chemistry made history, discovered radium.

Add an apostrophe to a plural noun to make it possessive, or add *-'s* if the plural noun does not end in *s*.

- Both *farms'* crops were lost in the flood.
- Our *children's* children will reap the benefits of our efforts to preserve the environment today.

To show individual possession by two or more people or groups, add an apostrophe or *-'s* to each noun.

- Sam is equipment manager for both the *boys'* and the *girls'* basketball teams.
  Sam works for two different teams.

To show joint possession by two people or groups, add an apostrophe or *-'s* to the last noun.

- The *coaches and players'* dream came true at the end of the season.

Add *-'s* to the last word of a compound noun to show possession.

- My *father-in-law's* boat needs a new engine.
- We were ushered into the *chairman of the department's* office.

17b Use an apostrophe to indicate the omitted letter or letters in a contraction.

- *I've* [I have] seen the answers.
- Jason *didn't* [did not] arrive last night.

17c Use an apostrophe to form the plural of a number, letter, symbol, abbreviation, or word treated as a word.

- There are three *5*'s on the license plate.
- She spells her name with two *C*'s.
- The *?*'s stand for unknown quantities.
- Using two *etc.*'s is unnecessary.
- Replace all *can*'s in the contract with *cannot*'s.

In the sentences above, note that numbers, letters, and words used as themselves are in italics. The *-s* ending should not be italicized, however. (For more on italics and underlining, see Section 23.)

When referring to the years in a decade, no apostrophe is used.

- The fashions of the 1970s returned in the 1990s.

Apostrophes are used to signal the omission of the numerals that indicate the century.

the class of '03   music of the '90s

17d Avoid using apostrophes to form plurals and to form possessives for personal pronouns.

- The trapper̸s came to town to trade.
- She paid for my lunch as well as her̸s.

For more exercises on the use of apostrophes, refer to the Apostrophes section of Exercise Central at www.bedfordstmartins .com/successfulcollege.

> ### Exercise 17.1
>
> *Correct the errors in the use of apostrophes in the following sentences. Some sentences may be correct as written.*
>
> - As newer forms of communication like Twitter, Facebook, and text messaging take over our lives, we should ask whether we're becoming more connected or less connected with other people.
>
> 1. Our's is a society almost too willing to share.
> 2. We probably know more about the day-to-day lives of other's than ever before, as the details of our many friend's days are recorded in online status report's.
> 3. Its unclear, however, whether anyone is truly benefiting from all this sharing of private information, even as the various social networking sites privacy settings reveal more and more about user's.
> 4. Todays parents' can find out about their sons and daughters personal live's online, but they have less face-to face contact with their children.
> 5. Of course, theyll have to figure out the meaning of all the LOLs', BTWs, and other shorthand slang in their kids online and text messages.

---

18 Parentheses and Brackets

Parentheses

Parentheses—( )—are used to separate nonessential information from the rest of a sentence or paragraph.

18a Use parentheses to add words, phrases, or sentences that expand on, clarify, or explain material that precedes or follows.

- The EPA (Environmental Protection Agency) is responsible for developing water-pollution standards.

- The application fee for the four-day workshop (a total of $500, including the registration fee) is due Friday.

Be sure to use parentheses sparingly; they can clutter your writing.

18b Use parentheses to insert dates or abbreviations.

- Elizabeth Cady Stanton (1815–1902) helped organize the first American women's rights convention.

- Guidelines for documenting research papers in the humanities are published by the Modern Language Association (MLA).

18c Check the placement of other punctuation used with parentheses.

Parenthetical information that appears at the end of a sentence should be inserted before the period that ends the sentence.

- Ballroom dancing has become popular in the United States (probably because of the success of *Dancing with the Stars*).

When parenthetical information appears after a word that would be followed by a comma, the comma is always placed after the closing parenthesis.

- He called when his plane landed (or so he said), but no one answered.

When a complete sentence appears within parentheses, punctuate the sentence as you would normally.

- Timber companies propose various uses for national forests. (Public land can be leased for commercial purposes.)

Exception: If the material within the parentheses is a question, it should end with a question mark.

- A few innocent-looking plants (have you heard of the Venus's-flytrap?) capture and eat insects and animals.

Brackets

Brackets ([   ]) are used within quotations and within parentheses.

18d Use brackets to add information or indicate changes you have made to a quotation.

- Whitman's preface argued, "Here [the United States] is not merely a nation but a teeming nation of nations."
  The explanation tells where *here* is.

- "Along came a spider and sat down beside [Miss Muffett]," who apparently suffered from a phobia.

  The bracketed name replaces *her* in the original.

Use brackets to enclose the word *sic* when signaling an error in original quoted material.

- The incumbent's letter to the editor announced, "My opponant's [sic] claims regarding my record are simply not true."

The Latin word *sic* lets your readers know that the misspelled word or other error in the quoted material is the original author's error, not yours.

18e Use brackets to enclose parenthetical material in a group of words already enclosed in parentheses.

- The demonstrators (including members of the National Rifle Association [NRA]) crowded around the candidate.

Exercise 18.1

Correct the errors in the use of parentheses or brackets in the following sentences. Some sentences may be correct as written.

- Typhoid Mary would probably not have infected so many victims if she had stopped working (she was a cook.).

1. Nathan Hale regretted that he had "but one life to give for (his) country."
2. The Committee for Scientific Investigation of Claims of the Paranormal (CSICOP) tests claims of supernatural abilities.
3. Malcolm X [1925–1965] was an American political figure assassinated in the 1960s.
4. The invention of anesthesia made possible many advances in medicine (including lengthy surgery.)
5. Children believe what they see on television, (at least most of it) and therefore parents should monitor their children's viewing.

For more exercises on the use of parentheses and brackets, refer to the Parentheses and Brackets section of Exercise Central at www.bedfordstmartins.com/ successfulcollege.

---

19 Dashes

Use a **dash** (—) to separate parts of a sentence. A dash suggests a stronger separation than a comma, colon, or semicolon does. To type a dash, hit the hyphen key twice (--), with no spaces before, between, or after the hyphens. Some word-processing programs automatically convert the two hyphens to a dash (—).

19a Use a dash or dashes to emphasize a sudden shift or break in thought or mood.

■ Computers have given the world instant communication—and electronic junk mail.

19b Use a dash or dashes to introduce an explanation, an example, or items in a series.

■ The tattoo artist had completed a large body of work—Fred's!

■ The tattoo artist had seen everything—a full-size bear claw on a back, bleeding heart on a bicep, even an Irish cross on the tip of a nose.

When the added thought appears in the middle of a sentence, use two dashes to set it off..

■ The tattoo artist—who would prefer to remain nameless—thinks tattoos are a waste of money.

19c Use dashes sparingly.

Dashes are emphatic. Do not overuse them, or they will lose their effectiveness. Also be careful not to use a dash as a substitute for a **conjunction** or transition.

*A **conjunction** is a word or words used to connect clauses, phrases, or individual words.*

■ Einstein's job in Switzerland was dull, —it offered him plenty of time to think; —
   but   *while working there*
   he came up with the theory of relativity.

For more exercises on the use of dashes, refer to the Dashes section of Exercise Central at www.bedfordstmartins.com/ successfulcollege.

⟨ **Exercise 19.1** ⟩

Add a dash or pair of dashes where they might be effective, and correct any errors in the use of dashes in the following sentences.

■ Food, who eats what and why?, is now a subject studied by academics.

1. One issue particularly concerns scholars of food; why are certain foods acceptable in some cultures but not in others?

2. Some foods were once popular, but today—hardly anyone has heard of them.

3. In the 1990s, people in Great Britain were alerted to a new danger, mad cow disease.

4. In the 1960s, frozen foods—icy blocks of corn, peas, and string beans—were popular—and convenient—alternatives to fresh produce.

5. Today fresh fruits and vegetables are valued once again, unless a busy cook has no time for peeling and chopping.

MANAGING MECHANICS AND SPELLING

20 Capitalization

Capitalize the first word of a sentence, **proper nouns**, and the pronoun *I*.

A **proper noun** names a particular person, place, thing, or group.

20a Capitalize the first word in a sentence and in a direct quotation.

- *R*
  revision is important.

Capitalize the first word in a direct quotation unless it is incorporated into your own sentence or it continues an earlier quotation.

- The union representative said, "*T* that meeting did not take place."

- Sam Verdon complained that "*n* No one takes college athletes seriously."

- "I prefer not to interpret my paintings," replied the famous watercolorist, "*b* Because they should speak for themselves."

20b Capitalize proper nouns, including the names of specific people, places, things, and groups.

PEOPLE AND ANIMALS	Franklin Roosevelt, his dog Fala
CITIES, STATES, NATIONS	St. Paul, Minnesota, the United States
WELL-ESTABLISHED GEOGRAPHIC REGIONS	the Gulf Coast, the U.S. Southwest
GOVERNMENT AND OTHER PUBLIC OFFICES, DEPARTMENTS, AND BUILDINGS	the Pentagon, the Supreme Court, the Puck Building
SOCIAL, POLITICAL, BUSINESS, SPORTING, AND CULTURAL ORGANIZATIONS	League of Women Voters, National Basketball Association

MONTHS, DAYS OF THE WEEK, AND HOLIDAYS	February, Thursday, Labor Day
CHAPTER OR SECTION TITLES IN BOOKS	"Why America Has Changed"
NATIONALITIES AND LANGUAGES	Ethiopian, Dutch
RELIGIONS, RELIGIOUS FIGURES, AND SACRED BOOKS	Judaism, the Pope, the Koran
TRADE NAMES	Coca-Cola, Brillo
HISTORIC EVENTS	the Treaty of Versailles, Reconstruction
SPECIFIC COURSE TITLES	Organic Chemistry 101

20c Do not capitalize common nouns.

FAMILY MEMBERS	my uncle, his father
GENERAL AREAS OF THE COUNTRY	southwestern United States
SUBJECTS	my chemistry class
CENTURIES	seventeenth-century England
GEOGRAPHICAL AREAS	the lake in the park

20d Capitalize the titles of literary and other works, such as books, articles, poems, plays, songs, films, and paintings.

Capitalize the first and last words of the title, the first word following a colon, and all other words except **articles**, **coordinating conjunctions**, and **prepositions**.

Articles are the words *a, an,* and *the.*

Coordinating conjunctions (*and, but, for, nor, or, so, yet*) connect sentence elements that are of equal importance.

Prepositions (such as *before, on,* and *to*) are used before a noun or pronoun to indicate time, place, space, direction, position, or some other relationship.

BOOK	*Confusion Is Next: The Sonic Youth Story*
ARTICLE	"Making History at Madison Park"
POEM	"My Last Duchess"
PLAY	*A Raisin in the Sun*
SONG	"Yellow Rose of Texas"
FILM	*Gone with the Wind*
PAINTING	*The Starry Night*

20e Capitalize a personal title only when it directly precedes a person's name.

- Vice President Maria Washington briefed the stockholders.
- Maria Washington was hired from a rival company to be the new vice president.

It is acceptable to capitalize the titles of certain high government officials regardless of whether they precede a name: *the President of the United States.*

Exercise 20.1

Correct the capitalization errors in the following paragraph.

> *U   N*
- The ŭnited ńations meets at its headquarters in New York City.
     ^   ^

During world war II, the governments of twenty-six countries pledged their willingness to continue fighting on behalf of the Allies. United States president Franklin Roosevelt came up with a name for the group: the united nations. The "Declaration By United Nations" promised the support of those twenty-six governments for the war effort. The Nations signed this document on New Year's day of 1942. By 1945, the number of countries involved in the united nations had grown to fifty-one. From April through June of that year, fifty Representatives attended the united nations Conference on International Organization in San Francisco. There, the Nations debated the contents of a charter. Although the War was nearing an end, the governments foresaw a need to continue international cooperation. The charter was ratified on October 24, 1945, by China, France, The Soviet Union, The United Kingdom, The United States, and a majority of the other Nations. Every year since then, October 24 has been known as united nations day.

For more exercises on capitalization, refer to the Capitalization section of Exercise Central at www.bedfordstmartins .com/successfulcollege.

21 Abbreviations

Abbreviations are shortened forms of words and phrases. It is acceptable to use abbreviations for some personal titles, names of organizations, time references, and Latin expressions. Most abbreviations use periods, but those composed of all capital letters often do not.

21a Abbreviate titles before and after a person's name.

Ms. Susan Orlean	Arthur Rodriguez, M.D.
St. Mary	Bill Cosby, Ph.D.
Dr. Gregory House	Martin Luther King Jr.

21b Abbreviate names of familiar organizations, corporations, and countries.

Use common abbreviations such as *PBS, CIA,* and *HIV* when you are certain that your readers will recognize them.

ABC	FBI	NATO
UNICEF	USA	VCR

21c Abbreviate time references that precede or follow a number.

■ The meeting will begin at 10:15 a.m. and end at 12 p.m.

■ The statues were carved in about 300 BCE.

The letters *BCE* stand for "before the common era." An alternative is *BC* ("before Christ").

■ Alfred became king in AD 871.

The letters *AD* stand for the Latin term *anno Domini* and precede the date. The alternative *CE* ("common era") follows the date.

21d Use common abbreviations for Latin terms in parentheses, footnotes, or references.

It is acceptable to use abbreviations for Latin terms in parenthetical comments as well as in source notes or citations. Avoid using these abbreviations outside of parentheses in the text of your essay; use the English equivalent instead.

e.g.	for example
et al.	and others
etc.	and so forth
i.e.	that is
vs. *or* v.	versus

        such items as   *and*

■ Edison invented the lightbulb, the motion picture camera, sound recording

devices, ~~etc.~~

21e Do not abbreviate certain words and phrases when they are used in sentences.

Some abbreviations that are acceptable in scientific or technical writing should be spelled out in most other kinds of writing.

UNITS OF MEASUREMENT	ten inches [*not* ten in.]
GEOGRAPHICAL OR PLACE NAMES	I live in New York City [*not* N.Y.C.]. (*Exceptions: Washington, D.C.; U.S.* when it is used as an adjective, as in *U.S. Senate*)
PARTS OF WRITTEN WORKS	chapter 6 [*not* ch. 6]
DAYS, MONTHS, AND HOLIDAYS	Thursday [*not* Thurs.]
NAMES OF SUBJECT AREAS	biology [*not* bio]
PERSONAL TITLES USED WITHOUT A PROPER NAME	doctor [*not* Dr.]

Exercise 21.1

Correct the misused abbreviations in the following sentences.

political science
- Students of ~~poli sci~~ know that public opinion often moves in cycles.

1. According to Washington Irving's story, Rip van Winkle fell asleep in the Catskill Mts. for twenty years.
2. The average American woman is five ft. four in. tall.
3. Since it is only ninety pp. long, the text is really a novella, not a novel.
4. The Great Depression began with the stock-market crash on Black Mon.
5. The Coen brothers have a reputation for creating unorthodox films: e.g., *Fargo* and *O Brother, Where Art Thou?*

For more exercises on abbreviations, refer to the Abbreviations section of Exercise Central at *www.bedfordstmartins .com/successfulcollege/*.

22 Numbers

As a general rule, use numbers according to the rules of your field of study. Be sure to represent numbers as numerals or as words consistently.

22a Spell out numbers that begin sentences.

Two hundred ten
- ~~210~~ students attended the lecture.

22b Spell out numbers that can be written in one or two words.

twenty-six checks	two hundred women
sixty students	one thousand pretzels

Use numerals for numbers that cannot be spelled out in one or two words.

375
- There are ~~three hundred seventy-five~~ students enrolled this fall.

Use numerals for all numbers in a sentence if one of the numbers needs to be written in numerals.

28
- Of the 420 students in my school, only ~~twenty-eight~~ have a driver's license.

When two numbers appear in succession, spell out one and use numerals for the other.

3
- Each counselor is in charge of nine ~~three~~-year-olds.

22c Use numerals according to convention.

DATES	August 10, 2008; the 1990s
DECIMALS, PERCENTAGES, FRACTIONS	56.7, 50% *or* 50 percent, 1¾ cups
EXACT TIMES	9:27 a.m.
PAGES, CHAPTERS, VOLUMES	page 27, chapter 12, volume 4
ADDRESSES	122 Peach Street
EXACT AMOUNTS OF MONEY	$5.60, $1.3 million
SCORES AND STATISTICS	23–6 victory, a factor of 12

For more exercises on the use of numbers in sentences, refer to the Numbers section of Exercise Central at www.bedfordstmartins.com/successfulcollege.

Exercise 22.1

Correct the errors in the use of numbers in the following sentences. Some sentences may be correct as written.

■ The quotation you're looking for is on page ~~seventy-seven~~. (77)

1. 77% of those responding to the poll favored increased taxes on cigarettes.
2. The estimated cost was too low by eighty-seven dollars and fourteen cents.
3. Each window is composed of 100s of small pieces of colored glass.
4. All traffic stopped as a 90-car train went slowly past.
5. February twenty-two is George Washington's birthday, but Presidents' Day is always celebrated on a Monday.

23   Italics and Underlining

Italic or *slanted type* is used for emphasizing particular words or phrases. It is also used to set off titles of longer works, names of vehicles, non-English words, and words deserving special emphasis.

When writing by hand or using a typewriter, use <u>underlining</u> to indicate italics. Most word-processing programs provide italic type, and most style guides used for college writing, such as the *MLA Handbook for Writers of Research Papers* and the *Publication Manual of the American Psychological Association* (APA), require it.

23a Italicize or underline titles of works published separately.

BOOKS	*Great Expectations*
PLAYS AND MUSICALS	*Rent*
LONG POEMS	*The Iliad*
MAGAZINES AND JOURNALS	*Entertainment Weekly;* the *New York Review of Books*
NEWSPAPERS	the *Columbus Dispatch*
MOVIES AND DVDS	*The Twilight Saga: Eclipse*
LONG MUSICAL WORKS, RECORDINGS	*Exile on Main St.*
TELEVISION AND RADIO SERIES	*Jersey Shore*
VISUAL WORKS OF ART (PAINTINGS, SCULPTURES)	*Birth of Venus*

The titles of shorter works, such as the titles of articles, short stories, and songs, should be enclosed in quotation marks (see 15g).

23b Italicize or underline the names of ships, trains, aircraft, and spacecraft.

Titanic	*Spirit of St. Louis*
Orient Express	space shuttle *Challenger*

23c Italicize or underline non-English words not in everyday use.

Words from other languages should be italicized unless they have become a part of the English language, such as "chic" or "burrito." If you are unsure, check an English dictionary. If the word is not listed, it should be italicized.

- Our instructor lectured on the technique of *Verstehen.*

- Tacos are now as much a part of American cuisine as pizza.

23d Italicize or underline numbers, letters, words, or phrases called out for special emphasis.

Use italics for numbers, letters, or words used as terms.

- Every bottle has *33* on the label.

- Hester Prynne is forced to wear a scarlet *A*.

- Today, *ain't* is listed in most dictionaries.

Italicize a word or phrase that is being defined or emphasized.

- *Alliteration*—the same sounds repeated at the beginning of each word in a group—can be an effective literary device.

Use italics for emphasis sparingly. When you italicize too many words in a sentence or paragraph, the emphasis is lost.

- The U.S. National Park system is *extremely important* (no italics) because it protects some of the most *beautiful* (no italics) and *unusual* (no italics) parts of this country.

Exercise 23.1

Correct the errors in the use of italics in the following sentences. Some sentences may be correct as written.

- <u>Oedipus</u>, written by Sophocles in the fifth century BC, is possibly the most famous play of the classical period.

1. The exchange student greeted everyone with a hearty *"Bonjour!"*
2. His professor insisted that Soap Opera Digest was not an acceptable research source.
3. Cartoons like The Simpsons have become surprisingly popular with adult audiences.
4. The first European settlers at Plymouth arrived on the Mayflower.
5. His book is discussed in depth in the article *Africa: The Hidden History*.

For more exercises on the use of italics in sentences, refer to the Italics and Underlining section of Exercise Central at www.bedfordstmartins .com/successfulcollege.

---

24   Hyphens

A **hyphen** (-) is used to join compound words, to connect parts of words, and to split words at the end of typewritten lines of text.

24a   Use a hyphen to join words that function as a unit.

Some compound nouns and verbs are spelled as one word (*download*), some are spelled as two words (*washing machine*), and some are spelled using hyphens (*foul-up*). Check a dictionary when you are unsure; if you do not find the compound listed in your dictionary, spell it as two words.

Use a hyphen to join words that together modify a noun.

■ An *icy-fingered* hand tapped her shoulder.

However, when the first word of the compound ends in *-ly* or when the compound adjective follows the noun it modifies, no hyphen is used.

■ The guard found a *clumsily hidden* duplicate key.

■ Her voice was *well trained.*

24b Use a hyphen with some prefixes (*all-, ex-, great-, self-*) and suffixes (*-elect*).

■ Most Americans' parents, grandparents, or *great-grandparents* came from another country.

■ The *governor-elect* made a stirring victory speech.

Use a hyphen for clarity to prevent confusion with certain combinations of prefixes and base words.

■ She wants the taxpayers to approve the funding for her ~~recreation~~ of the demolished
   re-creation
town hall.
   Recreation has a different meaning from *re-creation.*

24c Use a hyphen when spelling out fractions and the numbers *twenty-one* to *ninety-nine,* in word-number combinations, and to indicate inclusive numbers.

two-thirds finished   *twenty-two* sources

■ The *675-yard* path winds through a landscaped garden.

■ Pages *99-102* cover the military campaigns.

24d Use a hyphen between syllables to split a word at the end of a typewritten or handwritten line.

Although most word-processing programs automatically break the line before a long word and move the word to the next line, in typewritten or handwritten text, you should use a hyphen to divide any words that fall at the end of a line. Divide words between syllables; never break a one-syllable word. Divide a compound word between its parts. Words can also be divided between a prefix and root or between a root and suffix. Check your dictionary if you are uncertain about where to break a word.

> Viking invaders failed to conquer Ireland because the country was gov-
> erned by a number of petty kings rather than by a central authority that
> could be effectively overthrown; however, by the tenth century this situ-
> ation began to change.

For more exercises on hyphen use, refer to the Hyphens section of Exercise Central at www.bedfordstmartins .com/successfulcollege.

Exercise 24.1

Correct the errors in the use of hyphens in the following sentences. If you are not sure about a word, check your dictionary. Some sentences may be correct as written.

-         *teenager*
  Does any ~~teen-ager~~ really need liposuction?

1. Adolescents today who are unhappy with their looks can turn to the increasingly-popular option of plastic surgery.

2. For many selfconscious teens and young adults, surgery seems to be the perfect solution.

3. Until recently, very few sixteen year olds considered making permanent surgical changes.

4. But as more adults pay for nose-jobs and tummy tucks, more teens are expressing interest.

5. Are images of people with apparently perfect bodies and faces unduly influencing less-than-perfect young Americans?

25   Spelling

Misspelled words are among the most common errors for many student writers. Be sure to pay attention to spelling as you edit and proofread your papers, and keep a dictionary close at hand. Misspellings can make your paper appear carelessly written. Use the tips in the accompanying box and the basic spelling rules that follow to help improve your spelling.

25a   Remember to put *i* before *e* except after *c* or when pronounced as an *a*, as in *neighbor* and *weigh*.

> *i* before *e*: ach*ie*ve, th*ie*f
>
> **except after** *c*: conc*ei*ve, rec*ei*ve
>
> **or when pronounced as an** *a*: fr*ei*ght, th*ei*r

Memorize the exceptions, such as *either, foreign, height, leisure, neither, seize,* and *weird.*

- **Purchase a collegiate dictionary and take the time to look up the correct spellings of unfamiliar words.**

- **Use your word processor's spell-checker function.** Be sure to take advantage of the spell-checker as you edit and proofread your drafts. However, keep in mind that this function will not catch all spelling errors; for example, it cannot detect the incorrect use of *it's* versus *its* or of homonyms such as *there* versus *their* and *weather* versus *whether*. (See 25d for a list of homonyms.)

- **Proofread your drafts for spelling errors.** To avoid being distracted by the flow of ideas in your essays, proofread them backwards, from the last word to the first, looking only for misspellings. For words that sound alike but have different spellings (*to/too/two*, *their/there*), stop to check their use in the sentence and determine whether you have used the correct word.

- **Keep a list of words you commonly misspell.** Whenever you catch spelling errors in a draft or see misspellings marked by your instructor in papers returned to you, add the words to your list. Use your dictionary to locate the correct spelling and pronunciation of each word in the list. Review your list of words periodically, and practice pronouncing and writing the words until you master their correct spellings and usage.

- **Develop a spelling awareness.** As you read and write, pay attention to words and how they are spelled. When you encounter a new word, pronounce it slowly and carefully while taking note of its spelling. Try to create a mental image of each word, especially words with silent letters or unusual spellings.

25b Add *-s* or *-es* to form the plural of most nouns.

Singular common nouns ending in *-s, -ch, -sh,* or *-x* form the plural by adding *-es.* Nouns ending in *-o* usually form the plural by adding *-s* when the *-o* follows a vowel or *-es* when the *-o* follows a consonant.

Add *-s:*	professor, professor*s*	zoo, zoo*s*
Add *-es:*	sandwich, sandwich*es*	hero, hero*es*

To form the plural of common nouns ending in *-y,* change the *y* to *i* and add *-es* when the *y* is preceded by a consonant. Add only *-s* when the *y* is preceded by a vowel.

story	stor*ies*	day	day*s*
baby	bab*ies*	key	key*s*

Compound nouns form the plural by adding *-s* or *-es* to the most important word or, when all the words are equally important, to the last word of the compound.

mother-in-law	mothers-in-law
passerby	passersby
stand-in	stand-ins

Proper nouns form the plural by adding *-s* or *-es* without changing the noun's ending.

A **proper noun** names a particular person, place, thing, or group.

Thursday	Thursdays
Mr. and Mrs. Jones	the Joneses

■ The Gunderson's met us for dinner last night.

25c Drop, keep, change, or double the final letter when adding endings to some words.

Drop the silent *e* when adding an ending that begins with a vowel (*a, e, i, o, u*). Keep the silent *e* when adding an ending that begins with a consonant.

hope	hop*ing*	care	care*ful*
force	forc*ing*	encourage	encourage*ment*
advise	advis*able*	love	love*ly*

For words that end in *y*, change the final *y* to *i* before adding an ending when the *y* follows a consonant. Keep the final *y* when the *y* follows a vowel, when the ending is *-ing*, or when *y* ends a proper name.

study	stud*ies*	buy	buy*er*
marry	marr*ied*	marry	marry*ing*
		Fahey	Fahey*s*

Exception: Drop the final *y* whenever you add *-ize*.

memory	memor*ize*
category	categor*ize*

When adding an ending to one-syllable words, double the final consonant if the ending starts with a vowel and the final consonant follows a single vowel. Do *not* double the consonant when two vowels or a vowel and another consonant precede it.

hop	hop*ped*	pair	pair*ed*
trek	trek*ked*	rent	rent*ed*

When adding an ending to words with two or more syllables, double the final consonant if a single vowel precedes it and the stress falls on the last syllable.

transmit	transmit*ted*
refer	refer*ral*

Do *not* double the final consonant when two vowels or a vowel and another consonant precede it.

react	react*ed*
redeem	redeem*ing*

Do *not* double the final consonant if the ending starts with a consonant.

commit	commit*ment*
regret	regret*fully*

25d Watch out for homonyms, groups of words that sound the same but are spelled differently.

The following list includes some commonly confused groups of words.

Homonyms	*Examples of Usage*
accept (to take or receive)	Most stores *accept* credit cards.
except (other than)	Everyone has arrived *except* Harry.
affect (to influence)	The new law will *affect* us.
effect (the result, outcome)	The *effect* of the storm was frightening.
allusion (a reference to)	The poem contained an *allusion* to Greek mythology.
illusion (a fantasy)	Josette is under the *illusion* that she is famous.
already (by now)	Marguerite is *already* in class.
all ready (fully prepared)	Geoffrey is *all ready.*
cite (to refer to)	Be sure to *cite* your sources.
sight (vision, or a tourist attraction)	Her *sight* is failing.
site (a place)	We visited the *site* of the accident.
complement (to complete, a counterpart)	The side dishes *complement* the main course.
compliment (praise)	Allison received numerous *compliments.*
elicit (to bring out)	The film *elicits* an emotional response.
illicit (illegal)	The sale of *illicit* drugs is prohibited on campus.
its (possessive of *it*)	The show has found *its* audience.
it's (contraction of *it is*)	*It's* too late to go back.

(continued on next page)

(continued)

Homonyms	*Examples of Usage*
lead (verb: to guide or direct)	Professor Hong will *lead* the discussion group.
led (past tense of verb *lead*)	Professor Hong *led* the discussion group.
lead (noun: a heavy metal)	*Lead* poisoning is dangerous.
loose (not securely attached)	The button was *loose*.
lose (to fail to keep)	I often *lose* my keys.
principal (most important, or a head of a school)	The citizens' *principal* concern is educational costs.
principle (a basic rule or truth)	This *principle* should govern all of your actions.
their (possessive of *they*)	The students brought *their* books to class.
there (in that place, opposite of *here*)	*There* is the bus.
they're (contraction of *they are*)	*They're* early.
to (toward)	Please move *to* the front of the class.
too (also, or excessively)	Sal is coming *too*.
two (following *one*)	The *two* speeches were similar.
who's (contraction of *who is*)	*Who's* taking a cab?
whose (possessive of *who*)	*Whose* book is this?
your (possessive of *you*)	*Your* experiment is well designed.
you're (contraction of *you are*)	*You're* passing the course.

25e Watch out for commonly misspelled words.

absence	analysis	believe	column
accept	analyze	benefited	committee
accessible	apologize	boundary	conceive
accidentally	apparent	Britain	conscience
accommodate	appearance	bureaucracy	conscious
accuracy	argument	business	convenience
achievement	ascend	calendar	criticism
acquaintance	athlete	cemetery	criticize
acquire	attendance	changeable	curiosity
amateur	beginning	characteristic	deceive

decision	intelligence	prevalent	truly
definitely	interest	privilege	unanimous
descendant	irresistible	probably	usually
disappearance	judgment	proceed	vacuum
disappoint	knowledge	professor	vengeance
disastrous	laboratory	pronunciation	villain
discipline	leisure	psychology	weird
efficiency	length	quantity	writing
efficient	library	quiet	
eighth	license	receive	
eligible	lightning	recognize	
embarrass	loneliness	recommend	
emphasize	maintenance	reference	
environment	maneuver	referred	
especially	marriage	relieve	
exaggerate	mathematics	repetition	
excellence	miniature	restaurant	
exercise	mischievous	rhythm	
existence	necessary	ridiculous	
experience	niece	roommate	
explanation	ninety	sacrifice	
familiar	noticeable	schedule	
fascinate	occasionally	secretary	
February	occurrence	seize	
foreign	omission	separate	
forty	originally	sergeant	
fulfill *or* fulfil	parallel	several	
government	particularly	similar	
grammar	permissible	sincerely	
guarantee	physical	sophomore	
harass	picnicking	succeed	
height	pleasant	successful	
humorous	possible	summary	
hypocrisy	practically	surprise	
imagination	precede	tendency	
immediately	preference	thorough	
incredible	prejudice	through	
inevitable	preparation	tragedy	

25f Be alert for words that are formed from the same root (they may have different spellings) and for words with silent letters.

heir   heredity
aisle
pneumonia

For more exercises on catching spelling errors, refer to the Spelling section of Exercise Central at www.bedfordstmartins.com/successfulcollege.

⟨ **Exercise 25.1** ⟩

Correct the spelling errors in the following paragraph. If you are not sure about a word, check the list of commonly misspelled words on pages 852–53 or your dictionary. Some sentences may be correct as written.

■ After two ~~centurys~~ of isolation, Japan modernized very quickly.
　　　　　　　　centuries

　　In 1542, the first European visiters arrived in Japan. Traders and missionarys from the West brought firarms, tobacco, and Christianity to the island nation, which was suffring from internal strife. Japanese rulers welcomed Christianity at first, seing it as a way to reunify the country. However, after large numbers of Japanese converted, some official intolerance toward Christianity appeared. Finally, the rebellion of a Catholic Japanese community ensured that the government would act to prevent Western missionaries and merchants from joining forces with Japanese dissidents. In 1640, a policy of isolation took affect. No foreiners were aloud to enter Japan, and no Japanese were permited to travel abroad. This policy was finaly relaxed in 1853, and a new era began in 1868, with the arrival of a new imperial government. The new leaders were youthful and visionary, and they wanted to bring their country up to date. Although some Japanese who had enjoied privileges in the old society lost them during modernization, most people where delighted with the country's new direction.

ESL TROUBLESPOTS

26 Nouns and Articles

The two primary types of nouns in English are proper nouns and common nouns. A **proper noun** names a specific, unique person, place, thing, calendar item, or idea and is always capitalized.

Sarah Palin	Lake Erie	Toyota	Tuesday	Marxism

A **common noun** refers to a person, place, thing, or idea in general and is not capitalized.

writer	lake	car	day	ideology

Common nouns are classified as either count nouns or noncount nouns. A **count noun** names items that can be counted.

artists	books	towns

Count nouns have both singular and plural forms.

Singular Form	*Plural Form*
one artist	three artist*s*
every book	most book*s*
each town	all town*s*

A **noncount noun** names items that cannot be easily counted.

rain	traffic	mail

Most noncount nouns do not have a plural form.

Incorrect	*Correct*
advices	advice
informations	information
vocabularies	vocabulary

This chapter will help you use these categories—proper noun versus common noun, count noun versus noncount noun—to avoid errors in your writing, especially in your use of articles (*a*, *an*, and *the*).

26a Keep the following guidelines in mind for recognizing and using noncount nouns.

Nouns in the following categories are likely to be noncount nouns.

ABSTRACTIONS	advice, courage, grief, information, knowledge, love, satisfaction, wealth
FIELDS OF STUDY OR RESEARCH	chemistry, law, medicine, pollution, sociology, weather
SPORTS AND GAMES	chess, football, soccer, tennis
LIQUIDS	milk, water
THINGS THAT CANNOT BE EASILY COUNTED	rice, sand, snow

■ He offered some good advices.

Do not use numbers or plural quantity words before noncount nouns.

■ ~~Many rains~~ hit the windowpane.

Do not use the article *a* or *an* with noncount nouns.

■ The horses were covered with ~~a~~ mud.

Noncount nouns are used with singular verbs.

■ The milk ~~were~~ *was* sour.

Some nouns can be noncount or count, depending on whether they refer to something considered as a whole.

NONCOUNT	*Bread* is a staple in almost every cuisine. [*Bread* considered as a kind of food]
COUNT	Some *breads* are made without yeast. [Particular types of bread, such as rye or whole wheat]

26b Use an article or a demonstrative pronoun (*this, that, these, those*) with a count noun.

■ Her client sent her *a* fax.

- I found *this* fax on my chair.
  ^

26c Use *a* or *an* before a singular count noun that does not refer to a specific person, place, object, or concept.

- *A* laptop is *a* useful tool.

- She was excited to order *an* electric car.

When using the articles *a* and *an,* remember that *a* is used before words beginning with a consonant sound and *an* is used before words beginning with a vowel sound.

a baby	an eagle
a city	an hour
a fish	an island
a hope	an orange
a unicycle	an outrage

26d Use *the* before a noun that refers to something specific.

- Mohammad pointed out *the* planets in *the* evening sky.

- *The* lamp on my desk is an antique.

Be sure not to omit the article.

- He was awake before *the* alarm rang.
  ^

26e Use *a, an,* or *the* with most singular count nouns considered as general examples; no article is necessary for plural count nouns considered as general examples.

- *A* bird feeder is an entertaining addition to any yard.

- *The* cat is among the most agile creatures on earth.

- *Plants* add a cheery note to any room.

26f Use *the* with plural proper nouns (*the United States, the Joneses, the Koreans*) and certain types of singular proper nouns.

Some singular proper nouns use *the.*

PROPER NOUNS THAT CONSIST OF *THE*, A COMMON NOUN, AND *OF*	*the* Arch of Triumph, *the* state of Vermont, *the* University of Florida
NAMES OF BUILDINGS	*the* Eiffel Tower, *the* White House
COUNTRIES NAMED WITH A PHRASE	*the* Dominican Republic, *the* United Kingdom
NAMES OF HIGHWAYS	*the* Kensington Expressway
NAMES OF HOTELS AND MUSEUMS	*the* Hilton Hotel, *the* Guggenheim Museum
PARTS OF THE GLOBE	*the* Equator, *the* Northwest, *the* South Pole
HISTORICAL PERIODS AND EVENTS	*the* Renaissance, *the* Industrial Revolution
NAMES OF SEAS, OCEANS, GULFS, RIVERS, AND DESERTS	*the* Red Sea, *the* Atlantic Ocean, *the* Gulf of Mexico, *the* Missouri River, *the* Sahara
GROUPS OF ISLANDS	*the* Hawaiian Islands
MOUNTAIN RANGES	*the* Alps

26g Do not use an article with most other singular proper nouns.

■ The houses are beautiful on ~~the~~ Maple Street.

For more exercises on articles, refer to the Nouns and Articles section of Exercise Central at www.bedfordstmartins .com/successfulcollege.

Exercise 26.1

For each of the following sentences, choose the correct article. Note that X = no article.

■ For many Americans, (a/the) civil rights movement began when (X/the) Rosa Parks refused to give up her seat on a bus to a white man.

1. Rosa Parks, (an/the) African American woman living in Montgomery, Alabama, was riding (a/the) bus with sections reserved for white passengers.

2. (X/The) back of the bus, where African Americans were supposed to sit, was crowded.

3. Parks sat in (X/the) front of the bus, which took tremendous courage.

4. (A/The) bus driver forced her to get off (a/the) bus, but (X/the) incident set off the Montgomery bus boycott.

5. (X/The) people all over the United States heard (a/the) story of Rosa Parks, and the civil rights movement had its first hero.

27 Verbs

A **verb** shows an action, an occurrence, or a state of being. ESL writers need to pay special attention to their use of verb tenses, helping or modal verbs (also called auxiliary verbs), and verbs followed by an infinitive or a gerund.

27a Use the appropriate verb tense to express time accurately.

Verb tenses express time. They indicate when an action occurs, occurred, or will occur. The following sections will help you understand and form the simple, perfect, and progressive tenses.

The Simple Tenses

The simple tenses are used to show clear and simple time relationships. The accompanying box summarizes how each of the simple tenses is formed and used.

The Simple Tenses

Tense	How It Is Formed	Examples
Simple present		
Expresses an action or condition occurring at the time of speaking or writing, a statement of fact, or a habitual action	First- and second-person singular and plural, third-person plural: **base form** Third-person singular: base form + *-s* or *-es*	I *cook* for five people. They *cook* many unusual dishes. He *cooks* for a family of five.
Simple past		
Indicates that an action occurred in the past and was completed in the past	Regular verbs: base form + *-d* or *-ed* Irregular verbs: Forms vary; check the list on pages 759–61 or a dictionary.	We *played* roller hockey yesterday. He *became* agitated when the doctor approached.
Simple future		
Indicates that an action will take place in the future	*will* or form of *be* + *going to* + base form	His doctor *will try* a new approach. Ron *is going to find* a way out.

The **base form** is the form of a verb as it appears in the dictionary.

> ### The Perfect Tenses
>
> | Tense | How It Is Formed | Examples |
> |---|---|---|
> | *Present perfect* | | |
> | Indicates that a past action took place at an unspecified time or is continuing to the present | *has* or *have* + past participle | The landlord *has offered* to repair the damage.

I *have worked* in this office for two years. |
> | *Past perfect* | | |
> | Indicates that an action was completed in the past before some other past action | *had* + past participle | Rafika *had offered* to babysit, but she got sick. |
> | *Future perfect* | | |
> | Indicates that an action will take place before some specified time in the future | *will* + *have* + past participle | By Monday, the team *will have offered* him a new contract. |

The Perfect Tenses

The perfect tenses are also used to show time relationships. A verb in one of the perfect tenses indicates an action that was or will be completed by or before some specified time. The perfect tenses are constructed by using a form of *have* along with the verb's **past participle**.

The past participle of regular verbs is formed by adding *-d, -ed,* or *-en* to the verb's base form. It can be used as an adjective.

The box above summarizes how each of the perfect tenses is formed and used.

The Progressive Tenses

The simple progressive tenses describe actions in progress, indicating that an action did, does, or will continue. They are formed by using a form of *be* along with the **present participle**.

The present participle is the *-ing* form of a verb; it shows an action that is in progress or ongoing. It can be used as an adjective.

The perfect progressive tenses are used to describe actions that continue to the present or until another action takes place. They are often used to emphasize the length of time involved.

The box on the next page summarizes how the progressive and perfect progressive tenses are formed and used.

The Progressive and Perfect Progressive Tenses

Tense	How It Is Formed	Examples
Present progressive		
Indicates that an action began in the past, is happening now, and will end sometime in the future	form of *be* + present participle	Consultants *are changing* the workforce.
Past progressive		
Indicates that an action was in progress at a specified time in the past	*was* or *were* + present participle	He *was changing* a lightbulb when the ladder collapsed.
		They *were driving* to the beach when their car stalled.
Future progressive		
Indicates that an action will begin and continue in the future. The time is often specified.	*will be* + present participle, or present tense of *be* + *going to be* + present participle	New parents *will be changing* diapers for at least two years.
		Exams *are going to be changing* under the new principal.
Present perfect progressive		
Emphasizes the ongoing nature of an action that began in the past and continues into the present	*has* or *have been* + present participle	Her secretary *has been running* errands all morning.
		They *have been planning* this party for several weeks.
Past perfect progressive		
Emphasizes the duration of an action that began and continued in the past and was completed before some other past action	*had been* + present participle	He *had been running* two miles a day until he broke his toe.
Future perfect progressive		
Emphasizes the duration of an action that will continue in the future for a specified amount of time before another future action	*will have been* + present participle	When she takes over, her family *will have been running* the company for four generations.

For more exercises on verb tense, refer to the Verbs section of Exercise Central at www.bedfordstmartins .com/successfulcollege.

Exercise 27.1

Choose the correct verb tense in the sentences below.

■ Throughout most of American history, women (have had/will have) relatively few career opportunities.

1. Over the last several decades, however, women (had been/have been) making great strides in education and the workplace.

2. Now, for every two men who (were receiving/receive) a college degree, three women (earn/have been earning) the same academic credential.

3. Many manufacturing jobs that (have been relying/relied) on the physical strength of men have disappeared over the last several years.

4. As of 2010, women (become/have become) a majority of the United States work force for the first time in history.

5. These gains have led some to predict that soon women (will surpass/will be surpassing) men in economic and social power.

27b Use helping verbs to form tenses and express your meaning precisely.

Helping verbs are used before main verbs to form certain tenses. Some helping verbs—*have, do,* and *be*—change form to indicate tense (see 27a). The helping verb *do* indicates tense in questions, inverted phrases, and negative sentences. *Do you know her? Little did I realize what would happen. She does not like him.* It is also used for emphasis: *The sentence does need a comma.* The forms of these helping verbs are as follows.

> have, has, had
> be, am, is, are, was, were, being, been
> do, does, did

Other helping verbs, called **modals**, do not change form. Modals include *can, could, may, might, must, shall, should, will,* and *would.* They are used to express ability, necessity, permission, intention, and so forth. The box below summarizes the common uses of modals.

How to Use Modals		
Meaning	**Present or Future Time**	**Past Time**
Ability	*can*	*could* + *have* + past participle
	Most five-year-olds *can* tie their own shoes.	Jim *could have registered* early if he wanted to.
Necessity	*must* or *have to*	*had to*
	International travelers *must* carry passports.	The governor *had to* work with other officials.
		(continued on next page)

How to Use Modals (*continued*)

Meaning	Present or Future Time	Past Time
Necessity (*continued*)	*must* or *have to* Students *have to* read critically.	*had to*
Permission	*may*, *can* Anyone with a ticket *may* see the film. You *can* come in now.	*might* + *have* + past participle *could* + *have* + past participle You *might have waited* inside, out of the rain. We *could have gone* to the movies.
Intention	*will* He *will* encourage real estate development.	*would* + *have* + past participle I *would have hiked* last weekend, but it rained.
Advisability	*should*, *had better* Everyone *should* get an education. She *had better* buy a ticket.	*should* + *have* + past participle The trainee *should have read* the manual.
Possibility	*may*, *might* An accountant *may* work long hours during tax season.	*may* or *might* + *have* + past participle *could* + *have* + past participle The burglar *might have entered* through the window. They *could have lost* their keys.
Speculation	*would* He *would* like her.	*would* + *have* + past participle No one *would have recognized* him without his moustache.

Exercise 27.2

In each sentence, fill in the blank with a modal from the list. In most cases, more than one modal will work in the sentence. Use each modal only once.

For more exercises on modals, refer to the Verbs section of Exercise Central at www.bedfordstmartins .com/successfulcollege.

can	may	should	would
could have	might	will	would have

■ Busy professionals who are looking for a husband or wife <u>*can*</u> try online dating.

1. Other people feel that they _____ meet their potential mate in person.
2. Speed dating _____ be another way to find romance.
3. In the past, few _____ imagined such uses for technology.
4. Now people fear that technology _____ soon make many human activities obsolete, including matchmaking.
5. Human matchmakers _____ become obsolete if online dating remains popular.

27c Use gerunds or infinitives following verbs according to convention.

Often, you will need to use an **infinitive** or a **gerund** as the object of a verb in a sentence, as in the following examples.

An **infinitive** is a verb form made up of *to* plus the base form (*to run, to see*).

A **gerund** is an *-ing* form of a verb that functions as a noun (*complaining, jogging*).

■ Mustafa needs *to find* his lecture notes.

■ Lara avoids *studying* in her dormitory.

When you use an infinitive or a gerund as an object, you need to remember that some verbs are followed by infinitives, some verbs are followed by gerunds, and some can be followed by either form without a change in meaning. The following guidelines will help you determine which form to use.

Verbs Followed by Infinitives

Some verbs, including the verbs listed here, are usually followed by an infinitive in English.

agree	claim	manage	promise
ask	decide	need	refuse
beg	expect	offer	venture
bother	fail	plan	want
choose	hope	pretend	wish

In general, use these verbs with an infinitive, not a gerund.

■ Kristen managed ~~finishing~~ the project.
   to finish

Some verbs are followed by a noun or a pronoun and then by an infinitive. These verbs include *allow, cause, convince, hire, instruct, order, remind, tell,* and *warn*.

■ The bank *reminded your office to send* proof of employment.

When using a negative word (such as *no* or *not*) in a sentence containing a verb followed by an infinitive, place the word carefully; its position in the sentence often affects meaning.

■ Bella did *not* claim to know.
  She never mentioned it.

■ Bella claimed *not* to know.
  She said she did not know.

The causative verbs *have*, *let*, and *make* are followed by a noun or a pronoun and the base form of the verb (without the word *to*).

■ The noise made her *lose* her concentration.

■ The hotel lets visitors *bring* pets.

■ Have your assistant *type* those letters.

Verbs Followed by Gerunds

The following verbs are often followed by a gerund.

admit	dislike	postpone
appreciate	enjoy	practice
avoid	finish	recall
consider	imagine	resist
delay	keep	risk
deny	mention	suggest
discuss	miss	tolerate

Use these verbs with a gerund, not an infinitive.

                approving
■ The zoning committee considered ~~to approve~~ the proposal.

In a sentence containing a gerund, place a negative word (such as *no* or *not*) between the verb and the *-ing* form.

■ Some vacationers consider *not* returning to work.

Verbs Followed by Infinitives or Gerunds

Some verbs (such as *begin*, *continue*, *like*, and *prefer*) can be followed by an infinitive or a gerund with little or no change in meaning.

| INFINITIVE | Anita likes to jog. |
| GERUND | Anita likes jogging. |

Other verbs (such as *forget, remember, stop,* and *try*) can be followed by either an infinitive or a gerund, but the meaning of the sentence changes.

| INFINITIVE | Dien remembered to answer the letter. |

He remembered that he had an obligation to do something.

| GERUND | Dien remembered answering the letter. |

He remembered (the action of) doing something.

For more exercises on gerunds and infinitives, refer to the Verbs section of Exercise Central at www.bedfordstmartins .com/successfulcollege.

Exercise 27.3

Correct the errors in the use of gerunds and infinitives in the following sentences. Some sentences may be correct as written.

■ Archaeologists hope ~~discovering~~ ^{to discover} when the first Americans arrived.

1. Many archaeologists have considered to change the date they estimate that humans arrived in the Americas.

2. Until recently, scientists didn't expect finding evidence of human inhabitants older than 11,000 years, the age of stone tools found in Clovis, New Mexico, in the 1930s.

3. Recently, however, after discovering older evidence in Monte Verde, Chile, and other sites, some scientists have suggested to change this date.

4. Archaeologists began to reexamine their assumptions after it was established that Monte Verde was older than the Clovis site.

5. One site in Virginia may be over 15,000 years old, and archaeologists who keep to dig deeper may find even older evidence.

28 The Prepositions *in, on,* and *at*

These three common prepositions are used before nouns or pronouns to indicate time or location.

Time

Use *in* with
  Months: *in* April
  Years: *in* 2011
  Seasons: *in* the winter
  Certain parts of the day: *in* the morning, *in* the afternoon

Use *on* with
  Days of the week: *on* Tuesday
  Dates: *on* June 20, 2011

Use *at* with
> **Specific times:** *at* 8 p.m., *at* noon
> **Other parts of the day:** *at* night, *at* dawn, *at* dusk

Location

Use *in* with
> **Geographic places:** *in* San Francisco, *in* rural areas
> **Enclosed areas:** *in* the stadium

Use *on* with
> **A surface:** *on* a shelf
> **Forms of public transportation:** *on* the bus
> **Street names:** *on* Main Street
> **Floors of buildings:** *on* the fourth floor
> **Some areas of the country:** *on* the Gulf Coast

Use *at* with
> **Specific addresses (number and street):** *at* 130 Washington Street
> **Named locations:** *at* Juanita's house
> **General locations:** *at* the college
> **Locations with specific functions:** *at* the library

For more on prepositions, see 1g.

(**Exercise 28.1**)

In the following sentences, fill in the blank with in, on, *or* at:

- Every year __*in*__ the spring, filmmakers gather in Hollywood for the Academy Awards ceremony.

1. The Academy Awards ceremony was first televised _____ 1953.
2. The participants gathered in the RKO Pantages Theater _____ Hollywood, California.
3. In 2002, the ceremony moved from its previous location _____ the Dorothy Chandler Pavilion _____ Los Angeles to its new location _____ the Kodak Theatre _____ Hollywood.
4. The participants have to arrive _____ the middle of the afternoon because the show is timed for evening _____ the East Coast.
5. The ceremony appears on television around the world, and many members of the audience watch it very late _____ night or early _____ the morning.

For more exercises on the prepositions in, on, *or* at, *refer to the Prepositions* in, on, *and* at *section of Exercise Central at www.bedfordstmartins .com/successfulcollege.*

---

29   Adjectives

When using **adjectives**, ESL writers need to pay special attention to how adjectives are arranged when they modify the same noun and how adjectives are combined with prepositions. (For more on adjectives, see 1d and Section 9 of the Handbook.)

An **adjective** modifies a noun or pronoun.

29a Follow the conventional order when two or more adjectives modify the same noun.

Possessives come before numbers.

- *Anita's three* papers were accepted.

Ordinal numbers (*first, second*) come before cardinal numbers (*one, two*).

- James's *first three* requests were denied.

Descriptive adjectives should appear in the following order.

1. Article or possessive noun: *an, Dr. Green's, these*
2. Opinion: *favorite, hideous, lovely*
3. Size: *big, enormous, tiny*
4. Shape: *circular, rectangular, round*
5. Age: *elderly, teenaged, three-year-old*
6. Color: *black, blue, maroon*
7. National origin: *English, Nigerian, Vietnamese*
8. Religion: *Christian, Jewish, Muslim*
9. Matter or substance: *crystal, onyx, tweed*
10. Noun used as an adjective: *book* (as in *book jacket*), *picture* (as in *picture frame*), *record* (as in *record producer*)

   - *beautiful large white* horse
   - *Juan's old* coat
   - *a valuable new red British* car
   - *small oval* table

29b Combine adjectives with specific prepositions to express your meaning precisely.

Keep a list of adjective-**preposition** combinations that you hear in conversation or notice in your reading. Consult an ESL dictionary when you are not sure whether a particular combination expresses the meaning you intend. Here are some common adjective-preposition combinations.

Prepositions (such as *before, on,* and *to*) are used before a noun or pronoun to indicate time, place, space, direction, position, or some other relationship.

afraid of	grateful to (person)
ashamed of	interested in
full of	proud of
grateful for (thing)	responsible for (thing or action)

responsible to (person)   suspicious of
satisfied with   tired of
sorry for

Exercise 29.1

Correct the errors in the order of adjectives and in adjective-preposition combinations in the following sentences.

For more exercises on avoiding misplaced adjectives, refer to the Adjectives section of Exercise Central at www.bedfordstmartins .com/successfulcollege.

■ The ~~emperor Roman insane~~ Caligula succeeded his uncle, the emperor Tiberius.
   insane Roman emperor

1. Caligula made favorite his horse a Roman senator.
2. He was also responsible to declaring war on the sea god Neptune.
3. Brief Caligula's violent reign made many Roman citizens afraid for their emperor.
4. The emperor's notorious temper led to the deaths of unfortunate those Romans who angered him.
5. Upstanding many citizens were relieved when assassins left Caligula dead.

---

30 Common Sentence Problems

As you edit and proofread your writing, watch out for the following problems involving word order, relative pronouns, and negatives.

30a Place sentence elements in the correct order.

Place words and phrases that indicate time or place at the beginning or at the end of a clause. Do not place them between the verb and its direct object (DO).

INCORRECT   We did this afternoon our homework.

CORRECT   We did our homework this afternoon.

Place the indirect object (IO) after the verb and before the direct object (DO).

■ Ramon bought his sister a videotape.

■ Ramon bought her a videotape.

Exception: When a prepositional phrase takes the place of an indirect object, the phrase should follow the direct object.

$$\overbrace{\text{verb}}\quad\overbrace{\text{DO}}\quad\overbrace{\text{prep. phrase}}$$

- Ramon bought a videotape for his sister.

Some verbs (such as *describe, explain, illustrate, mention, open,* and *say*) cannot be followed by an indirect object.

INCORRECT	Lu described us the figurine.
CORRECT	Lu described the figurine to us.

For more exercises on common sentence problems, refer to the Common Sentence Problems section of Exercise Central at www.bedfordstmartins .com/successfulcollege.

Exercise 30.1

Correct the errors involving the placement of sentence elements in the following sentences. Some sentences may be correct as written.

- A park ranger explained ~~the visitors~~ the habits of the cave's bats to the visitors.

1. Every evening at sunset, thousands of bats hunt from the entrance of Carlsbad Caverns in New Mexico mosquitoes.
2. Bat experts tell people that bats are actually helpful to humans.
3. One bat can eat in a single night a huge number of insect pests.
4. At the cave entrance at dusk, the bats provide to curious onlookers a spectacular show.
5. They give the crowds who come to see them when they fly out of the cave a thrilling experience.

30b Do not omit a relative pronoun when it is the subject of a relative clause or the object of a verb or preposition within a relative clause.

A **relative pronoun** is a noun substitute that relates groups of words to nouns or other pronouns: *the patient who injured her leg.*

A **dependent clause** contains a subject and a verb but does not express a complete thought.

A **relative clause** is a **dependent clause** that begins with a **relative pronoun** (such as *that, which, who, whom,* or *whose*) and modifies a noun or pronoun. Sometimes a relative clause begins with a preposition followed by a relative pronoun (the reason *for which* I am writing).

INCORRECT	The firefighter rescued the child was given a hero's welcome.
REVISED	The firefighter *who* rescued the child was given a hero's welcome.
INCORRECT	Juanita found the book for she had been searching all morning.
REVISED	Juanita found the book for *which* she had been searching all morning.

Exception: The relative pronoun and the verb *be* are often omitted in relative clauses when the clause is restrictive (essential to the meaning of the word or phrase it modifies); they should usually be included in a nonrestrictive clause (not essential to the meaning of the word or phrase it modifies). For more on nonrestrictive word groups, see 12e.

RESTRICTIVE   **Michael grabbed the newspapers [that were] on the table.**
That were is optional because the clause is restrictive; it tells which newspapers are meant.

NONRESTRICTIVE   **Michael tripped over the stack of day-old newspapers, which were ready to be recycled.**
The clause supplies additional but nonessential information about the newspapers. It is nonrestrictive, so *which were* should be included.

Use the relative pronoun *whose* to show possession with a relative clause.

INCORRECT   **The committee sat at a table that its surface was scratched.**

REVISED   **The committee sat at a table *whose* surface was scratched.**

Use relative pronouns, not personal pronouns, to introduce relative clauses.

INCORRECT   **Computer terminals, they are scarce at certain times of the day, are an obsession for many students.**

REVISED   **Computer terminals, *which* are scarce at certain times of the day, are an obsession for many students.**

Exercise 30.2

Correct the errors in the use of relative pronouns in the following sentences. Some sentences may be correct as written.

■ The United States is a nation ^that^ was founded by settlers from other lands.

1. Immigration in the United States is a controversial subject that its implications have been debated for years.
2. Early laws, they were sometimes discriminatory, restricted immigrants from certain countries.
3. Both legal and undocumented immigrants who come to the United States often seek employment.
4. Some Americans want to limit immigration fear that new arrivals will compete for scarce jobs.
5. New immigrants, their dreams and wishes resemble those of many previous generations of Americans, continue to arrive.

For more exercises on common sentence problems, refer to the Common Sentence Problems section of Exercise Central at www.bedfordstmartins .com/successfulcollege.

30c Make a sentence negative by adding *not* or a negative adverb such as *never* or *seldom*.

Place *not* after the first helping verb.

- The speech will *not* begin on time.

In questions, the helping verb should be followed by *not* or the contraction for *not* (*-n't*). Place the helping verb and *not* before the subject and the main verb.

- *Didn't* I read that story in the newspaper yesterday?

Place negative adverbs before the main verb. In a sentence with a helping verb, place the negative adverb after the first helping verb.

- Arthur *seldom forgets* an assignment.
- Eva *may never play* the violin again.

If a negative adverb is used at the beginning of a clause, the helping verb *do* is needed.

- *Rarely* does one see a bald eagle.

For more exercises on common ESL problems, refer to the ESL section of Exercise Central at www.bedfordstmartins.com/ successfulcollege.

Exercise 30.3

Correct the errors in the use of negatives in the following sentences. Some sentences may be correct as written.

- Most reports of UFO sightings and aliens ~~not~~ are ^{not} believed.

1. Reputable scientists have confirmed never a UFO sighting.
2. A simple explanation for a sighting is difficult seldom to find.
3. People who believe aliens have contacted them offer convincing proof almost never.
4. Isn't it possible that many people simply want to convince themselves that humans are not alone?
5. Aliens may exist, but they not have arrived on earth yet.

Summary Exercise for Sections 26–30

Review Sections 26–30, and then correct the errors in standard English usage in the following paragraph.

■ Many people ~~am~~ ^{are} worried about obesity in America.

Between the 1980 and the 2008, the obesity rate among Americans to increase from 15 percent to 34 percent. According to studies recent, over 30 percent of childrens in United States are now either overweight or obese. These studies also suggest that most overweight teenagers will overweight adults become. All these excess weight will cause harms to their healths, including a increased risk of cancer and heart disease. While most people agree that obesity am a real problem, they are disagreeing about its causes. Some claiming that Americans make food choices bad, eat too much, and exercise too little Those with point of view want overweight people take more responsibility for their own healths. On the same time, others see obesity as an economic, social, and cultural problem. They point to popularity of fast-food restaurants, junk food, and sugary soft drinks, especially among younger people. In fact, companies that sell unhealthy products appeal to that children in their advertisings. People with this view also argue that healthy foods are often more expensive than unhealthy foods. Whatever its causes, widespread obesity having enormous social and financial effects. According to a study by Cornell University, the annual cost of treating obesity and obesity-related illnesses is $168 billion. Clearly, Americans not should ignore this problem.

Section 3
Exercise 3.1 page 781
Possible Revisions

2. In the United States, for example, colleges and universities provide education to Americans of all classes and backgrounds.
4. During the nineteenth and early twentieth centuries, graduates of state universities played a key role in America's development as an industrial and economic power.
6. Federal funding from the 1944 GI Bill made it possible for millions of returning veterans to attend college.
8. Now, about two-thirds of high school graduates will attend college because those with bachelor's degrees earn $20,000 more a year on average than do people with only high school diplomas.
10. However, as education costs continue to rise, some wonder whether a traditional four-year college is always worth the expense.

Section 4
Exercise 4.1 page 786
Possible Revisions

2. Shopping through online bookstores is convenient, but some people miss the atmosphere of a traditional bookstore.
4. In the 1960s some Americans treated Vietnam veterans disrespectfully, a situation that has changed dramatically since that time.
6. With large bodies and tiny wings, bumblebees have long been a puzzle. How do they fly?
8. The Supreme Court often makes controversial decisions because the justices must decide how to interpret the Constitution.
10. Restoring a painting is, indeed, delicate work, and too much enthusiasm can be dangerous.

Section 5
Exercise 5.1 page 791
Answers

2. A student in most non-English-speaking industrialized nations expects to spend six or more years studying English.

4. Working for laws that require all Americans to speak English is a fairly common U.S. political tactic.
6. Some linguists joke that a person who speaks two languages is called "bilingual," while a person who speaks one language is called "American."
8. Correct
10. Everyone who studies a foreign language is likely to benefit.

Section 6
Exercise 6.1 page 794
Answers

2. Cuba, an island that lies ninety miles off the Florida coast, provided them with an excuse to do so.
4. In addition, many people in the United States had wanted to take over Spain's territories for a long time.
6. Cuba was allowed to take control of its own affairs right away.
8. Correct
10. Many Puerto Ricans are worried that statehood would destroy the native culture of their island, and none of them wants that to happen.

Section 7
Exercise 7.1 page 797
Possible Revisions

2. Because of the importance of the information, it often must be transmitted secretly.
4. "Invisible ink," which cannot be seen until the paper is heated, was once a popular way to communicate secretly.
6. During World War II, U.S. government code specialists hired Navajo Indians because Navajo is a difficult and little-studied language.
8. Because these cryptograms are so simple, they are no longer used to transmit messages.
10. Alan Turing, a British civil servant and mathematical genius, finally solved the Enigma code.

Exercise 7.2   page 799

Answers

2. A team of researchers might disagree on their conclusions about the disappearance of the dinosaur.
4. In one way, animals resemble plants: Some are "weeds" because they have the ability to thrive under many conditions.
6. When a "weed" and a delicate native species compete for their survival, the native species usually loses.
8. People should be more concerned about the extinction of plants and animals than they seem to be.
10. The earth has experienced several mass extinctions in its history, but another would take its toll on the quality of human life.

Exercise 7.3   page 803

Answers

2. Correct
4. Following the success of Mammoth Cave, many Kentucky cavers hoped to make a fortune from their spelunking.
6. In January of 1925, a falling rock trapped Collins, who was spelunking in a narrow passage in Sand Cave.
8. For several days, the most famous man in Kentucky was he. [*Or:* For several days, he was the most famous man in Kentucky.]
10. Their failing to save Collins was a terrible tragedy for his family and the rescuers.

Section 8

Exercise 8.1   page 807

Possible Revisions

2. We wondered whether our professor knew of the new theory and whether she agreed with it.
4. Most parents think they have a major influence on their children's behavior.
6. Children strongly desire peer acceptance, and they want to be different from adults.
8. Most adults recall that, in childhood, their friends' opinions were extremely important to them.
10. Anxious parents would be greatly relieved if this hypothesis were proven.

Exercise 8.3   page 809

Possible Revisions

2. Surveys show that college graduates who intern receive higher salary offers than their classmates who do not.
4. The most important qualities are curiosity and a good work ethic.
6. Some companies provide little guidance so interns do not learn much from the experience.
8. Correct
10. Some worry that strict federal guidelines will cause companies to eliminate internship programs rather than risk any legal problems.

Section 9

Exercise 9.1   page 812

Answers

2. *Wikipedia* has many advantages that reflect well upon it as a source.
4. In a way, encyclopedias are unique because Web sites can grow to include any subject that anyone finds interesting.
6. The site has some real downsides, too.
8. Many teachers and professors don't allow students to use Wikipedia for research.
10. If they choose to use the site, students should make it clear to their professors that they have researched their subjects thoroughly.

Section 10

Exercise 10.1   page 815

Possible Revisions

2. So far, no proof of the existence of life forms on other planets has been found.
4. Astronomers carefully monitor signals coming from other parts of the solar system.
6. Most of the signals received so far have been caused by cell phone and satellite interference.
8. The message, containing information about earth, is on its way to other parts of our galaxy.
10. A signal sent to earth would take a similarly long time to reach us.

Section 11

Exercise 11.1   page 818

Answers

2. Correct
4. Czar Nicholas and his wife Alexandra often saw their little boy in terrible pain.

Section 12

Exercise 12.1   page 823

Answers

2. The city of New York bought the land where the Seneca villagers lived.
4. Household items from Seneca Village still turn up in Central Park today, and a museum exhibit was recently devoted to life in the long-gone settlement.
6. James Weeks, an early resident, owned much of the land.
8. His daughter, Susan Smith McKinney-Steward, was born in Weeksville and was the valedictorian of New York Medical College in 1870.
10. Correct

Section 13

Exercise 13.1   page 825

Answers

2. Silent versions of the vampire tale include *Les Vampires* (1915), a French film; *Nosferatu* (1921), a German film; and *London After Midnight* (1927), an American film.
4. The vampire tale has several standard traits, yet it remains remarkably versatile.
6. The popular *Blacula* (1972), which recast the vampire as an African prince in 1970s Los Angeles, inspired a series of black-themed "blaxploitation" horror movies.
8. In the late 1990s, *Buffy the Vampire Slayer* was revived as a popular TV series starring Sarah Michelle Gellar.
10. Perhaps vampires do live forever if only in books and on screen.

Section 14

Exercise 14.1   page 828

Answers

2. The proposed zoning change was defeated by a margin of 2:1.
4. Correct
6. Correct
8. The neon lights gleamed above stores and in diner windows.
10. Some music historians claim that the American songwriting tradition reached its peak in the 1930s.

Section 15

Exercise 15.1   page 831

Answers

2. Why did the professor assign "To an Athlete Dying Young"?
4. After September 11, 2001, President Bush said he was going to "fight terror."
6. "Come live with me and be my love," pleads the speaker in Marlowe's poem.
8. It turned out that the pianist could play only "Chopsticks."
10. Our waitress announced, "The special is prime rib"; unfortunately, we are vegetarians.

Section 16

Exercise 16.1   page 833

Answers

2. "Halle Berry was the first African American woman to win the Academy Award for Best Actress."
4. "[P]eople of all classes receive financial help from the government."
6. "Zora Neale Hurston's collections of folklore proved to be very valuable."
8. "Folic acid . . . can help prevent certain birth defects."
10. "She wrote rather doubtful grammar sometimes, and in her verses took . . . liberties with the metre" (Thackeray 136–37).

Section 17
Exercise 17.1   page 835
Answers

2. We probably know more about the day-to-day lives of others than ever before, as the details of our many friends' days are recorded in online status reports.
4. Today's parents can find out about their sons and daughters' personal lives online, but they have less face-to-face contact with their children.

Section 18
Exercise 18.1   page 837
Answers

2. Correct
4. The invention of anesthesia made possible many advances in medicine (including lengthy surgery).

Section 19
Exercise 19.1   page 838
Answers

2. Some foods were once popular, but today hardly anyone has heard of them.
4. In the 1960s, frozen foods — icy blocks of corn, peas, and string beans — were popular and convenient alternatives to fresh produce.

Section 21
Exercise 21.1   page 843
Answers

2. The average American woman is five feet four inches tall.
4. The Great Depression began with the stock-market crash on Black Monday.

Section 22
Exercise 22.1   page 844
Answers

2. The estimated cost was too low by $87.14.
4. All traffic stopped as a ninety-car train went slowly past.

Section 23
Exercise 23.1   page 846
Answers

2. His professor insisted that *TV Guide* was not an acceptable research source.

4. The first European settlers at Plymouth arrived on the *Mayflower.*

Section 24
Exercise 24.1   page 848
Answers

2. For many self-conscious teens and young adults, surgery seems to be the perfect solution.
4. But as more adults pay for nose jobs and tummy tucks, more teens are expressing interest.

Section 26
Exercise 26.1   page 858
Answers

2. The
4. The; the; the

Section 27
Exercise 27.1   page 862
Answers

2. Now, for every two men who receive a college degree, three women earn the same academic credential.
4. As of 2010, women have become a majority of the U.S. work force for the first time in history.

Exercise 27.2   page 863
Answers

2. may *or* might
4. will, may, *or* might

Exercise 27.3   page 866
Answers

2. Until recently, scientists didn't expect to find evidence of human inhabitants older than 11,000 years, the age of stone tools found in Clovis, New Mexico, in the 1930s.
4. Correct

Section 28
Exercise 28.1   page 867
Answers

2. in
4. in; on

Section 29

Exercise 29.1 page 869

Answers

2. He was also responsible for declaring war on the sea god Neptune.
4. The emperor's notorious temper led to the deaths of those unfortunate Romans who angered him.

Section 30

Exercise 30.1 page 870

Answers

2. Correct
4. At the cave entrance at dusk, the bats provide a spectacular show to curious onlookers. [*Or:* At the cave entrance at dusk, the bats provide curious onlookers with a spectacular show.]

Exercise 30.2 page 871

Answers

2. Early laws, which were sometimes discriminatory, restricted immigrants from certain countries.
4. Some Americans who want to limit immigration fear that new arrivals will compete for scarce jobs.

Exercise 30.3 page 872

Answers

2. A simple explanation for a sighting is seldom difficult to find.
4. Correct

Beato, Greg. "Amusing Ourselves to Depth: Is *The Onion* Our Most Intelligent Newspaper?" from *Reason* (November 2007). Copyright © 2007 by Greg Beato. Reprinted with the permission from Reason magazine and Reason.com.

Beato, Greg. "Internet Addiction." Greg Beato is a columnist for *Reason* magazine and Reason.com, where this column first appeared in the July 2010 issue. Reprinted by permission from Reason magazine and Reason.com.

Bishop, Elizabeth. "Filling Station" from *The Complete Poems 1927–1979* By Elizabeth Bishop. Copyright © 1979, 1983 by Alice Helen Methfessel. Reprinted by permission of Farrar, Straus & Giroux, LLC.

Bodanis, David. "A Brush with Reality: Surprises in the Tube" from *The Secret House*. Copyright © 1986 by David Bodanis. Reprinted with the permission of the Carol Mann Agency.

Bregman, Peter. "How (and Why) to Stop Multitasking." *HBR* blog, May 20, 2010.

Brooks, Gwendolyn. "The Bean Eaters" from *Blacks*. Copyright © 1991 by Gwendolyn Brooks. Reprinted by consent of Brooks Permissions.

Bryson, Bill. "Snoopers at Work," from *I Am a Stranger Here Myself: Notes on Returning to America after 20 Years Away*. © 2000 by Bill Bryson. Reprinted by permission of Broadway Books, a division of Random House, Inc., and Random House Canada.

Chupack, Cindy. "Dater's Remorse" from *The Between Boyfriends Book*. Copyright © 2003. By Cindy Chupack. Reprinted by permission of St. Martin's Press, LLC.

Crissey, Mike. "Dude, Do You Know What You Just Said?" *Associated Press* (December 8, 2004). Copyright © 2004 by Associated Press. All rights reserved.

Dillard, Annie. "The Deer at Providencia" (pp. 60–66) from *Teaching a Stone to Talk: Expeditions and Encounters*. Copyright © 1982 by Annie Dillard. Reprinted by permission of HarperCollins Publishers.

Ehrenreich, Barbara. Excerpt from "Selling in Minnesota" from *Nickel and Dimed: On (Not) Getting By in America*. Copyright © 2001 by Barbara Ehrenreich. Reprinted with the permission of Henry Holt and Company, LLC.

Frazier, Ian. "Dearly Disconnected" from *Mother Jones Wire* (January/February 2000). Copyright © 2000 by the Foundation for National Progress. Reprinted with permission.

Frost, Robert. "Two Look at Two" from *The Poetry of Robert Frost,* edited by Edward Connery Lathem. Copyright 1951 by Robert Frost. Copyright 1923, © 1969 by Henry Holt and Company, LLC. Reprinted with the permission of Henry Holt and Company, LLC.

Goleman, Daniel. "His Marriage and Hers: Childhood Roots" from *Emotional Intelligence*. Copyright © 1995 by Daniel Goleman. Reprinted with the permission of Bantam Books, a division of Random House, Inc.

Goodwin, Jan. "Freegans: They Live Off What We Throw Away" (editor's title; originally titled "She Lives Off What We Throw Away"). From *Marie Claire*, March 11, 2009. Reprinted by permission of the author.

Gottfried, Martin. "Rambos of the Road" from *Newsweek* (September 8, 1986). Copyright © 1986 by Martin Gottfried. Reprinted with the permission of the author.

Hamilton, Lisa. "Eating Meat for the Environment" (editor's title; originally titled "Let Them Eat Meat"). *Audubon* magazine blog, June 25, 2009. Reprinted by permission of the author.

Junger, Sebastian. "Combat High." *Newsweek*, May 10, 2010.

Kamp, Jurriaan. "Can Diet Help Stop Depression and Violence?" from *Ode Magazine* (September 2007). Reprinted with the permission of the author and *Ode Magazine*.

Lamott, Anne. "Shitty First Drafts," from *Bird by Bird* by Anne Lamont, copyright © 1995 by Anne Lamott. Used by permission of Pantheon Books, a division of Random House, Inc.

LeMieux, Richard. "The Lady in Red." Reprinted from *Breakfast at Sally's* by special arrangement with Skyhorse Publishing.

MacClancy, Jeremy. "Eating Chilli Peppers" from *Consuming Culture: Why You Eat What You Eat*. Copyright © 1992 by Jeremy MacClancy. Reprinted with the permission of A. M. Heath & Company, Ltd.

Magliozzi, Tom and Ray. "Inside the Engine." From *Car Talk*. Copyright © 1991 by Tom and Ray Magliozzi. Used by permission of Dell Publishing, a division of Random House, Inc., and the authors.

Martin, Courtney E. "Why Class Matters in Campus Activism." *The American Prospect* December 6, 2010. Reprinted by permission.

Monster.com. "How to Interview." Reprinted by permission.

Newman, Jerry. "My Secret Life on the McJob: Fast Food Managers." Excerpt from *My Secret Life on the McJob: Lessons from behind the Counter Guaranteed to Supersize Any Management Style*. Copyright © 2007 by Jerry Newman. Reprinted with the permission of McGraw-Hill, Inc.

Orlean, Susan. "Out of the Woods." *The New Yorker*, June 14, 2004. © 2004 Susan Orlean. Reprinted by permission.

Pino, Carl. "Sustainability on the Menu: College Cafeterias Are Buying Local and Going Organic," *E Magazine*, March/April 2008, Vol 19, No. 2, pp. 30–31. Reprinted by permission.

Ramirez, Jessica. "The Appeal—and Danger—of War Porn." *Newsweek.com*. April 30, 2010. © 2010 Newsweek, Inc. Reprinted by permission.

Ríos, Alberto Alvaro. "The Secret Lion" from *The Iguana Killer: Twelve Stories of the Heart*. Copyright © 1984 by Alberto Alvaro Ríos. Reprinted with the permission of the author and Confluence Press, Lewiston, Idaho.

Riverbend. "Bloggers without Borders…" from *Baghdad Burning*. Riverbend blog, Monday, October 22, 2007. Reprinted by permission.

Rouvalis, Cristina. "Hey, Mom, Dad, May I Have My Room Back?" *Pittsburgh Post-Gazette*, August 31, 2008. Reprinted by permission.

Safire, William. "Abolish the Penny" from *The New York Times*, June 2, 2004. Copyright © 2004 by The New York Times Company. Reprinted with permission.

Schwartz, Todd. "American Jerk: Be Civil, or I'll Beat You to a Pulp." Excerpted from *Oregon Humanities* (Fall–Winter 2008), www.oregonhum.org.

Segal, Carolyn Foster. "The Dog Ate My Flash Drive, and Other Tales of Woe" (editor's title; originally titled "The Dog Ate My Disk . . .") from *The Chronicle of Higher Education* (August 11, 2000). Copyright © 2000 by Carolyn Foster Segal. Reprinted with the permission of the author.

Silverman, David. "In Defense of Multitasking." *HBR* blog, June 9, 2010.

Staples, Brent. "Black Men and Public Space" from *Harpers* (1987). Copyright © 1987 by Brent Staples. Reprinted with the permission of the author.

Steirer, Lynn. "When Volunteerism Isn't Noble" from *The New York Times,* April 22, 1997. Copyright © 1997 by The New York Times Company. Reprinted with permission.

Stern, Gary M. "Hitting the 'Granite Wall'" from *Hispanic* (December 2004). Copyright © 2004 by Gary M. Stern. Reprinted with the permission of the author.

Terris, Jutka. "Sprawl Is Harmful to Wildlife" (editor's title, originally titled "Unwelcome (Human) Neighbors: The Impacts of Sprawl on Wildlife") from *Natural Resources Defense Council, www.nrdc.org*, August 1999. Copyright © 2003 by the Natural Resources Council, Inc. Reproduced by permission.

White, Alton Fitzgerald. "Right Place, Wrong Face" from the *Nation* (October 11, 1999). Originally titled "Ragtime, My Time." Reprinted with permission. For subscription information, call 1-800-333-8536. Portions of each week's *Nation* magazine can be accessed at http://www.thenation.com.

Zaitchik, Alexander. "Alien World." Alexander Zaitchik is a columnist for *Reason* magazine and Reason .com, where this column first appeared in the February 2009 issue. Reprinted by permission from Reason magazine and Reason.com.

Zuger, Abigail. "Defining a Doctor, with a Tear, a Shrug, and a Schedule" from *The New York Times* (November 2, 2004). Copyright © 2004 by The New York Times Company. Reprinted with permission.

Pictures

2: Bill Vance/Corbis; **22:** (top) Phil Boorman/Getty Images, (middle) Getty Images, (bottom) Martin Shields/Photo Researchers Inc.; **31:** By permission. From Merriam-Webster Online©2011 by Merriam-Webster, Incorporated (www.merriam-webster.com); **44:** Dinodia Photos/Alamy; **51:** Jesse Kuhn/ rawtoastdesign.com; **63:** Tim A. Hetherington/Panos Pictures; **64:** Tim A. Hetherington/Panos Pictures; **66:** Richard Levine/Alamy; **79:** WWF Public Service Announcement; **80:** Hola/Superstock; **81:** Photo by Ethan Miller/Getty Images for Silverton Casino Lodge; **84:** From Peter Katel; Caring for Veterans, April 23, 2010 (Vol. 20, No. 16) CQ Researcher Copyright © 2010 CQ Press, a division of SAGE Publications, Inc.; **100:** Elaine Sulle/Image Bank/Getty Images; **122:** www.CartoonStock.com; **135:** Are we addicted to the Internet? Graphic created by Flowtown http://www.flowtown.com/blog/are-we-addicted-to-the-internet; **140:** (top left) ©Syracuse Newspapers/S Cannerelli/The Image Works, (top right) Lynn Harris, University of California, Irvine, (bottom) Photo by Bob Handelman. Courtesy of Connecticut College; **164:** AP/Wide World Photos; **180:** AP/Wide World Photos; **202:** (top) © 2005 Leo Cullum from cartoonbank.com. All rights reserved, (bottom) © The New Yorker Collection 1987 Michael Maslin from cartoonbank.com; **226:** RICK WILKING/Reuters/Landov; **260:** Jacobo Braun; **261:** Jacobo Braun; **266:** Jeff Greenberg/PhotoEdit, Inc.; **296:** Star-Ledger Photographs/Matt Rainey © 2000. The Star-Ledger, Newark, NJ; **304:** Getty Images; **332:** Life Interrupted Graph © 2009 Pew Research Center, Social & Demographic Trends Project. *Home for the Holidays...and Every Other Day.* http://pewsocialtrendsorg/2009/11/4/home-for-the-holidays-and-every-other-day/; **336:** Image courtesy of Skype Limited; **340:** Dana White/PhotoEdit Inc.; **372:** AP/Wide World Photos; **399:** (top) © Sally and Richard Greenhill/Alamy, (bottom) David Young-Wolff/PhotoEdit, Inc.; **408:** Images Etc Ltd/Alamy; **434:** www.CartoonStock.com; **440:** © Jim West/Alamy; **443:** Stan Honda/Getty Images; **468:** AP/Wide World Photos; **472:** Nigel Cook/Daytona Beach News-Journal; **512:** Mark Ralston/Getty Images; **538:** Electronic Multitasking Is On The Rise, CQ Researcher, vol 20, no. 33, p. 776. Copyright © 2010 CQ Press, a division of SAGE Publications **542:** Department of Transportation and The Ad Council; **574:** Craig Lovell/Corbis; **594:** Peter Essick/Aurora Photos; **599:** Seattle Pacific University Library; **600:** Seattle Pacific University Library; **603:** Screenshot from Sociological Abstracts The screen shots and their contents are published with permission of ProQuest LLC. Further reproduction is prohibited without permission; **620:** Anderson Ross/Getty Images; **678:** Brain scan courtesy of Dr. Paul Thompson, Laboratory of Neuro Imaging at UCLA, published in the *Atlantic*. Distributed by Tribune Media Services; **684:** John and Yva Momatiuk/The Image Works; **716:** www.CartoonStock.com; **736:** www.CartoonStock.com.

The numbers and letters refer to chapters and sections in the Handbook. Page numbers are provided for references to sections outside of the Handbook.

abbr	Faulty abbreviation **21**		no ⌃	No comma **12j**
ad	Misuse of adjective or adverb **1d, 1e, 9, 29**		;	Semicolon **13**
agr	Faulty agreement **5, 7e, 7f, 7g**		:	Colon **14**
appr	Inappropriate language *pp. 215–20*		⌄	Apostrophe **17**
art	Article **26**		" "	Quotation mark **15**
awk	Awkward **7, 8, 10**		. ? !	End punctuation **11**
cap	Capital letter **20**		—	Dash **19**
case	Error in pronoun case **7h–7m**		( )	Parentheses **18a, 18b, 18c**
cliché	Cliché *p. 219*		[ ]	Brackets **18d, 18e**
coh	Coherence *pp. 175–76*		. . .	Ellipsis mark **16**
cs	Comma splice **4**		ref	Reference, pronoun **7a–7d**
coord	Coordination *pp. 207–8,* **1f**		run-on	Run-on sentence **4**
dm	Dangling modifier **10c**		sexist	Sexist language **7e**
ESL	ESL problem **26–30**		shift	Shift **8a–g**
exact	Inexact word *p. 217*		sl	Slang *pp. 215–17*
frag	Fragment **3**		sp	Spelling **25**
fs	Fused sentence **4**		sub	Subordination *pp. 208–9,* **1f, 2c, 2d**
hyph	Error in use of hyphen **24**		t	Error in verb tense **1c, 6e, 6f, 27a**
irreg	Error in irregular verb **1c**		trans	Transition *pp. 175–76*
ital	Italics **23**		v	Voice **1c, 6d**
lc	Lowercase letter **20**		var	Sentence variety *pp. 206–12*
mix	Mixed construction **8h, 8i, 8j**		vb	Verb error **6, 27**
mm	Misplaced modifier **10a, 10b**		wrdy	Wordiness *pp. 205–6*
num	Number **22**		//	Faulty parallelism *pp. 212–13*
para, ¶	New paragraph *pp. 166–67*		⌒	Close up
pass	Ineffective passive *pp. 213–14,* **6d**		^	Insert
p	Punctuation **11–19**		X	Obvious error
⌃	Comma **12**			